Masterplots

Fourth Edition

Masterplots

Fourth Edition

Volume 8
'night, Mother—Poetics

Editor

Laurence W. Mazzeno
Alvernia College

SALEM PRESS
Pasadena, California   Hackensack, New Jersey

Editor in Chief: Dawn P. Dawson

Editorial Director: Christina J. Moose	*Editorial Assistant:* Brett S. Weisberg
Development Editor: Tracy Irons-Georges	*Research Supervisor:* Jeffry Jensen
Project Editor: Desiree Dreeuws	*Research Assistant:* Keli Trousdale
Manuscript Editors: Constance Pollock, Judy Selhorst, Andy Perry	*Production Editor:* Joyce I. Buchea
	Design and Graphics: James Hutson
Acquisitions Editor: Mark Rehn	*Layout:* William Zimmerman

Cover photo: Molière (The Granger Collection, New York)

Library of Congress Cataloging-in-Publication Data

Masterplots / editor, Laurence W. Mazzeno. — 4th ed.
     v.   cm.
    Includes bibliographical references and indexes.
    ISBN 978-1-58765-568-5 (set : alk. paper) — ISBN 978-1-58765-576-0 (v. 8 : alk. paper)
  1. Literature—Stories, plots, etc. 2. Literature—History and criticism. I. Mazzeno, Laurence W.
    PN44.M33 2010
    809—dc22

                                                                                    2010033931

Fourth Edition
First Printing

Contents

Contents

Complete List of Titles

Volume 1

Volume 2

Contents lvii

Volume 3

Contents xcv

Complete List of Titles xcix

Volume 4

Volume 5

Contents clxxi

Complete List of Titles clxxv

Volume 6

Volume 7

Volume 8

Volume 9

Contents cccxxiii

Complete List of Titles cccxxvii

Volume 10

Contents ccclxi

Complete List of Titles ccclxv

Volume 11

Contents. cccxcix
Complete List of Titles. . . . . cdiii

Volume 12

Contents . . . . cdxxxvii
Complete List of Titles . . . . cdxxxix

Masterplots

Fourth Edition

'night, Mother

Author: Marsha Norman (1947-   )
First produced: 1982; first published, 1983
Type of work: Drama
Type of plot: Psychological realism
Time of plot: Late twentieth century
Locale: Rural United States

Principal characters:
MAMA (THELMA CATES), the main character
JESSIE CATES, her daughter

The Story:

On Saturday night, while Mama hunts for her sweets, Jessie rummages for towels and garbage bags and searches the attic for her father's gun. Jessie tells Mama that she wants the gun for protection. Mama, convinced that there are no criminals near the out-of-the-way country house where they live, thinks Jessie is foolish. Jessie eventually tells Mama of her plan to commit suicide. At first Mama thinks that Jessie, an epileptic, is ill, but Jessie feels fine physically. Then Mama says that the gun is broken, but Jessie proves that it is in good condition. She had gotten bullets by tricking her brother Dawson into believing that she was watching out for prowlers. Desperate, Mama threatens to call Dawson, but Jessie still would shoot herself before he arrived. Mama suggests calling for the ambulance driver, whom Jessie likes. Jessie insists that she wants the night alone with Mama.

Mama tries to convince Jessie that normal people do not commit suicide, but Jessie wants to die and escape to a place of quiet nothingness. Unable to convince Jessie that suicide is immoral, Mama tries to gain control by insisting that Jessie cannot commit suicide in Mama's house. Trying another tactic, Mama asks Jessie if she wants to stay around to see what she would get for her birthday. The presents turn out to be predictable and not what Jessie wants.

Jessie plans the whole evening and makes a list of things she wants to do. Mama thinks that Jessie might be trying to escape her family, but Jessie is not committing suicide simply to get away from Dawson, her meddlesome brother, or Ricky, her delinquent son with whom she is unable to communicate. Jessie admits that she does not like her life with Mama and that going to live with Mama after Cecil (Jessie's husband) left her was a mistake that both Mama and Jessie made. Jessie now feels hurt and used. Her life had come to a dead end. She had been contemplating suicide for about ten years but had started to plan it around Christmas, when she realized how empty her life was.

Mama grasps for reasons for Jessie to continue living. She suggests getting a dog, planting a garden, shopping at the A&P, and taking up crocheting. These activities are unsuit-

able to Jessie, who sees her life as a meaningless bus ride that she wants to end now. Mama then accuses Jessie of acting like a spoiled brat and blames Jessie as the cause of her own misery. Jessie retorts that it is time Mama does something about her own miserable life.

Mama continues in vain to urge Jessie to find ways to make herself happy, by buying dishes, moving furniture, or getting a driver's license. Mama even suggests that Jessie get a job, but Jessie had failed at two jobs. She could not sell over the phone, and she made people nervous when she worked at a hospital gift shop. Besides, she could not be around people. Jessie could not make her life better, so she was going to control her destiny and end her life.

After moments of tension, Mama and Jessie settle down to have some cocoa. Jessie wants a night of truth and sharing. Mama admits that she never loved Daddy because he had resented marrying a plain country woman. He never spoke to Mama, but Jessie loves him. Mama then accuses Jessie of being angry that Daddy died and left Jessie with Mama.

When Jessie tries to show Mama where all the pots are, Mama gets angry, takes the pots out of the cabinet, and then throws them, saying she will live on sweets. After things settle down, the two women discuss the breakup of Jessie's marriage. Mama had played matchmaker and brought Cecil and Jessie together, but Cecil was the wrong man for Jessie. Cecil was a positive thinker and wanted Jessie to live an active life. She tried to stay outdoors and to get more exercise, but she could not meet his expectations. Cecil felt guilty about the time that Jessie was horseback riding and took a fall that supposedly caused her epilepsy. Jessie also realized that she had taught her son that life was unfair and not to trust anyone.

Mama reveals that Jessie did not get epilepsy from a fall but inherited it from her father. Mama then blames herself for Jessie's problems. She feels that she has failed to convince Jessie not to commit suicide. Jessie tries to show Mama that suicide is a positive solution, a way of saying "No" to everything and everyone. Jessie is tired of waiting around to become the person she is never going to be.

Outraged, Mama says that people will feel sorry for her, not for Jessie. Jessie helps Mama make funeral plans and instructs Mama in what to do after the suicide. Then Jessie gives gifts for her family, asks Mama to let her go, goes into her room, and shoots herself. Mama realizes that she only thought that she had a right to Jessie's life. Doing what Jessie told her, Mama washes the pan and calls Dawson.

Critical Evaluation:

Written in 1981, *'night, Mother* was produced by Robert Brustein at the American Repertory Theatre in Cambridge, Massachusetts, in 1982. The play later moved to the John Golden Theatre on Broadway, where it ran for ten months to mostly favorable reviews. In 1983, the play won a Pulitzer Prize and Marsha Norman was awarded the Susan Smith Blackburn Prize, given annually to a female playwright from an English-speaking country. The drama has appeared widely in college anthologies of drama.

'night, Mother is a tightly crafted drama. Although it has the veneer of realism, there is a classical idealism about it. Norman wants to create real people, yet she divorces them from any set milieu. The house where the drama takes place should not show any character traits. It is neither messy nor quaint. The town is not to be associated with any regional locale or accent. The play holds to the classical unities. There are only two characters, fixed in one location. Narrative time is synchronized to performance time so that all the clocks on stage start at 8:15 P.M., or curtain time, and run throughout the performance. There are no breaks or intermissions. The drama, which moves swiftly and inevitably toward the climax, is based on the unraveling of past events.

Like Norman's other plays, *'night, Mother* treats the frustrations and trials of ordinary women who try to share their lives with each other. From one critical perspective, it is debatable how strong a feminist message the play embodies. The play depicts women's lives as hopeless and futile. The two women in the drama undergo an emotional revelation, but little is done to change their lives. Much of what they do emphasizes the deadly routine of women's lives, but little is done to effect a revolution. Many of the women's problems surround their relations with absent men—fathers, husbands, and brothers. Suicide becomes a tragic gesture but leaves little option for social change.

On the other hand, the play is a powerful one about two women who have endured suffering and try desperately to communicate their pain to each other. Jessie is dependent on her mother even though she is her mother's caretaker. Together the two women undergo an emotional sharing of their lives. In many ways, Jessie has relived her mother's life. Both women married men who accepted them at first, then rejected them for not being someone else. Daddy married a plain country woman, then resented Mama for being one. Cecil wanted to change Jessie into an active, outgoing person. Both men escape from their wives. Daddy pretended to go fishing, and Cecil went to the shed with another woman. Neither woman could get her husband to communicate with her. Daddy died without speaking to Mama. Cecil simply left, and Jessie had to write his goodbye note. At the end, Jessie wants to share her life with her mother, but she wants her mother to let her go. Mama tries, but she has difficulty letting go.

'night, Mother is a powerful and gripping story of a mother and a daughter trying to communicate the pain in their lives, but it is more than a drama about mothers and daughters—it is a play about family that focuses on the psychological return of the daughter to her father through death. Jessie is her father's daughter. She has inherited not only his epilepsy but also his solitude. Jessie makes a point of using her father's gun to shoot herself. When she plans her funeral, she wants it to be like her father's. Death to Jessie is quiet and peaceful, an escape to the protected world of the father.

Jessie, who has lost control over the events of her life, consciously seeks to control her destiny by ending her life. By reasserting her power to end her life, Jessie feels that she has found a permanent solution to her alienation and loss of identity. In suicide, she will not only choose what happens to her but will also courageously be able to say no to life and to the false promise that Mama holds out to her for a better future. All of Mama's solutions are ways of getting through life and of passing time. Shopping, rearranging furniture, and learning to drive do not appeal to Jessie, who wants to take a determined action and make a positive statement with her death. Suicide and the right to commit suicide pose a powerful theme in the play. Despite Jessie's protest, suicide is not so much a powerful existential choice, a way to say no to life, as much as it is an escape to a romantic womblike existence in which no more harm or hurt can come to her.

Paul Rosefeldt

Further Reading

Browder, Sally. "'I Thought You Were Mine': Marsha Norman's *'night, Mother.*" In *Mother Puzzles: Daughters and Mothers in Contemporary American Literature*, edited by Mickey Pearlman. New York: Greenwood Press, 1989. Looks at Jessie's reliance on her mother, Thelma's reliance on her daughter, and the impact these relationships have on the self-concept of each woman.

Brown, Linda Ginter, ed. *Marsha Norman: A Casebook.*

New York: Garland, 1996. Includes three essays on *'night, Mother*, including discussions of the mother-daughter relationship and comparisons of the play to dramas by Samuel Beckett and Lillian Hellman.

Burkman, Katherine H. "The Demeter Myth and Doubling in Marsha Norman's *'night, Mother.*" In *Modern American Drama: The Female Canon*, edited by June Schlueter. Rutherford, N.J.: Fairleigh Dickinson University Press, 1990. A psychological exploration of the relationship between mother and daughter that traces *'night, Mother* to the ancient Greek myth of Demeter and Kore.

Craig, Carolyn Casey. "Marsha Norman: Getting out the Truth About Family and Self." In *Women Pulitzer Playwrights: Biographical Profiles and Analyses of the Plays*. Jefferson, N.C.: McFarland, 2004. Analyzes the play within the context of the 1980's feminist backlash.

Demastes, William W. "Jessie and Thelma Revisited: Marsha Norman's Conceptual Challenge in *'night, Mother.*" *Modern Drama* 36, no. 1 (1993): 109-120. Demastes suggests that, although it is a realistic social drama, the play attacks the established order and denies understanding.

Kane, Leslie. "The Way Out, the Way In: Paths to Self in the Plays of Marsha Norman." In *Feminine Focus: The New Women Playwrights*, edited by Enoch Brater. New York: Oxford University Press, 1989. Compares the mother-child relationships and the development of self in *'night, Mother* to similar concepts in Norman's other plays.

Paige, Linda Rohrer. "'Off the Porch and into the Scene': Southern Women Playwrights Beth Henley, Marsha Norman, Rebecca Gilman, and Jane Martin." In *A Companion to Twentieth-Century American Drama*, edited by David Krasner. Malden, Mass.: Blackwell, 2005. Includes a discussion of *'night, Mother*, and two other plays by Norman.

Smith, Raynette Halvorsen. "*'night, Mother* and *True West*: Mirror Images of Violence and Gender." In *Violence in Drama*, edited by James Redmond. New York: Cambridge University Press, 1991. Smith compares Norman's and Sam Shepard's treatment of violence in relationship to gender.

Spencer, Jenny S. "Marsha Norman's She Tragedies." In *Making a Spectacle: Feminist Essays on Contemporary Women's Theatre*, edited by Lynda Hart. Ann Arbor: Michigan University Press, 1989. A feminist reading of Norman's plays in which *'night, Mother* is seen as a drama of feminine passivity.

_____. "Norman's *'night, Mother*: Psycho-Drama of Female Identity." *Modern Drama* 30, no. 3 (1987): 364-375. Takes a psychological approach in comparing the audience response of men to the play with the audience response of women.

The Night of the Iguana

Author: Tennessee Williams (1911-1983)
First produced: 1961; first published, 1961
Type of work: Drama
Type of plot: Psychological realism
Time of plot: Late summer, 1940
Locale: Puerto Barrio, Mexico

Principal characters:
MAXINE FAULK, a newly widowed hotel keeper
T. LAWRENCE "LARRY" SHANNON, a defrocked minister, now a tour guide
HANNAH JELKES, an artist
JONATHAN "NONNO" COFFIN, a ninety-seven-year-old poet, Hannah's grandfather
MISS FELLOWES, a lesbian voice teacher and tourist
CHARLOTTE, a teenage girl whom Shannon seduces
JAKE LATTA, the tour guide sent to replace Larry

The Story:

Maxine has been a widow for less than a month. Her husband, Fred, snagged himself with a fishhook and died of blood poisoning. Maxine has no real option but to continue running Costa Verde, a small hotel that they owned and managed, perched high above the Pacific near the remote Mexican village of Puerto Barrio. The play is set in the period shortly before the United States entered World War II. The Costa Verde has Nazi guests who cheer at the bombing of London and other German victories.

On the scene comes T. Lawrence Shannon, always called

Larry, a defrocked minister whose options are running out. He is a tour guide for Blake Tours and, in this instance, is shepherding a group of female Texans through Mexico. Miss Fellowes, seemingly the organizer and mother hen of this group, is agitated because Shannon refuses to take them to the hotel for which they had contracted. She also is disturbed by Shannon's attentions to seventeen-year-old Charlotte, the youngest person in the tour group. Fellowes is indignant that Shannon made a play for Charlotte, but the subtext suggests that she is jealous because she herself has designs on the girl.

Larry comes into the hotel to see his old friend, Maxine. It soon becomes evident that Maxine lusts after him and, with her husband recently dead, she hopes for some sort of alliance with him: marriage, or the best she could get short of marriage. Her not insubstantial physical needs are being fulfilled through purely physical acts with her bellboys, a situation that makes her fear that she is losing their respect.

On this emotionally charged scene strides Hannah Jelkes, a New England woman slightly under forty years old, who is wheeling her poet-grandfather, Jonathan Coffin, whom she always calls Nonno, around the tropics. Nonno is ninety-seven years old. The two of them are as bereft of any real future as are Larry and Maxine. They have no money and had been turned away from every hotel in town. The Costa Verde is their last hope.

Maxine assures them that she has room for them and asks for payment in advance. Hannah informs her that they have no money but that they could earn their keep, Nonno by reciting his poetry to the other guests, Hannah by doing sketches of them and possibly by selling one of her watercolors. Maxine, unimpressed, agrees to let them stay, but for only one night. Meanwhile, a native boy delivers an iguana that is tied up and left to fatten beneath the veranda. When it reaches an appropriate weight, Maxine will cook it for dinner.

It becomes increasingly clear that Larry Shannon has no reasonable future to which to look forward. He speaks of rejoining the church, but the circumstances of his leaving it were such that he would not likely be welcomed back enthusiastically. His days as a tour guide for Blake Tours are definitely numbered and, when Blake Tours replaces Larry with Jake Latta, tempers run so high that it seems reasonable that Larry will be blackballed as a tour guide anywhere.

Larry's problems began when his mother discovered him masturbating when he was an adolescent. She spanked him and told him that God deplored such self-abuse. Resentful of both his mother and God, Larry become an ordained minister who preached atheistic sermons and scandalized his congregations (his vengeance on God) and a lecher who sought out only girls below the age of majority (his vengeance on his

mother). Now, with his options narrowing, he considers going back to preach in the church or swimming the Pacific to China, his way of threatening suicide.

Meanwhile, Hannah and Nonno are ensconced in the hotel. Hannah fears that Nonno suffered a slight stroke as they came through the Sierra. The old man is dying. Hannah says that she tried to persuade her grandfather to return to Nantucket, from which they originally came, but it is clear that she did not have the wherewithal even to get them as far as Laredo. Maxine makes arrangements for Hannah and Nonno to go to another hotel in town, one that would extend them credit. It is clear that Maxine does not appreciate Hannah's presence because she senses a growing chemistry between Hannah and Larry. Larry has a confrontation with Charlotte during which it becomes evident that he had seduced her the previous night.

In this exchange, Larry is emotionally bankrupt. He tells Charlotte he loves her, but once he has his way with her, he turns mean and rejects any suggestion that the two of them might have more than the few hours of love they had recently experienced. Miss Fellowes, overhearing Charlotte's encounter with Larry, immediately calls the authorities in Texas and gets them to issue a warrant for his arrest; Larry faces arrest if he crosses the border. One more option thus is closed to him.

Shortly after this encounter, Larry tells Hannah the story of how he seduced a young girl in his congregation in Pleasant Valley, Virginia. Hannah remains nonjudgmental, ever trying to see the good in people rather than dwelling on the bad. Larry is becoming intrigued by Hannah because, unlike his mother, she does not judge.

Maxine, sensing this, explodes at Hannah, but she soon realizes that jealousy is the reason for her outburst. A storm erupts, with a somewhat cleansing effect on the scene. Then Larry runs to the beach vowing to swim to China. Maxine dispatches her bellboys to drag him back. For his own protection, she has him tied up in a hammock. He has obviously lost his mind. She threatens to admit him to the Casa de Locos the following day.

Hannah comes in to comfort Larry and to try to soothe him with tea. He begs her to undo his bonds, but she refuses. When Nonno calls Hannah away for a moment, however, Larry wiggles loose. When Hannah returns, she hears the iguana struggling to break free, at the end of his rope, as many of the play's characters figuratively are at the ends of theirs. Hannah pleads with Larry to cut the iguana's rope.

Shortly after that, Nonno calls Hannah, telling her that he finally finished his poem, which he dictates to her. As the play ends, Maxine urges Larry to stay with her to help manage the hotel, making it clear that their relationship could only be professional, not sexual. Larry tells Hannah that he had cut the iguana's rope. She thanks him. She then turns to put a shawl around her grandfather's shoulders and discovers that the old man is dead.

Critical Evaluation:

In most of Tennessee Williams's major plays, the fear of dispossession looms before the major characters. Even in the affluent setting of *Cat on a Hot Tin Roof* (1955), Brick and Maggie are threatened with disinheritance. In *The Night of the Iguana*, the themes of dispossession and homelessness run high and are sustained throughout the play. Larry Shannon, Hannah Jelkes, and Nonno are all wanderers, wandering without means. One can hardly envision a more hopeless situation than that of Hannah: Penniless, she spends her life pushing a ninety-seven-year-old man, a fourth- or fifth-rate poet, around Mexico in his wheelchair.

Despite this, Hannah emerges as a unique female character in the Williams canon. She is almost a reverse image of Blanche DuBois in *A Streetcar Named Desire* (1947), although she faces similar problems. Whereas Blanche lives in the shadow of a checkered past, Hannah has always lived within the established moral boundaries of her society.

Hannah's celibacy does not make her judgmental of those who do not practice her restraint. In the two romantic episodes of her life that she reveals to Larry Shannon in the play, she has sympathy for the men who tried to have their way with her, the first a youth who pursued her in the balcony of a darkened movie theater, the second, years later, a man who took her out on a sampan one evening when she was in Singapore and, requesting one article of her clothing, used it as his fetish while he masturbated. Hannah averted her eyes and was not disgusted by the encounter because, as she says, nothing human disgusts her.

In *A Streetcar Named Desire*, Blanche's impending homelessness leads her to the desperate state of having to depend upon her sister or public charity. She is a victim of her circumstances. Hannah, on the other hand, is at peace with herself and deplores neither her life nor the circumstances that have caused it to be as it is. When Shannon questions her situation and reminds her that birds build nests because they want at least relative permanence, Hannah replies without rancor that she is a human being, not a bird, and that she is building her nests in her heart.

This bit of dialogue shows not only the reconciliation that Hannah has reached with her lot but also something about Shannon's values: Permanence means more to him than it does to Hannah. When Maxine offers him the opportunity to

stay at Costa Verde and help her manage the hotel, hope glimmers that he eventually will find with Maxine the kind of life that will lay his "spooks," as he called them, to rest.

Maxine is a good person, one capable of genuine love. She probably is in love with Shannon, but she realizes that she cannot force him into a situation in which he will feel as trapped as the iguana beneath her veranda. The implication with which Williams leaves his audiences in *The Night of the Iguana* is that things will likely work out for all the principals in the play, a first for a playwright whose previous endings were usually darkly pessimistic.

R. Baird Shuman

Further Reading

Arnott, Catherine M., comp. *File on Tennessee Williams*. New York: Methuen, 1987. A brief overview aimed at secondary school students and others who may be unfamiliar with Williams's work.

Bauer-Briski, Senata Karolina. *The Role of Sexuality in the Major Plays of Tennessee Williams*. New York: Peter Lang, 2002. Analyzes how sexuality is a dominant element in eight plays, including *The Night of the Iguana*. Examines how the characters' behavior and relations with other characters are affected by their decisions to either express or repress their sexual inclinations.

Bigsby, C. W. *Tennessee Williams, Arthur Miller, Edward Albee*. Vol. 2 in *A Critical Introduction to Twentieth-Century American Drama*. New York: Cambridge University Press, 1985. One of the best-informed critics of modern drama offers insights into Williams's career and his standing among midcentury American dramatists.

Falk, Signi. *Tennessee Williams*. 2d ed. New York: Twayne, 1978. This revision of Falk's earlier Twayne volume on Williams is very accessible, offering a sound overview of Williams's career and excellent interpretations of his individual plays. Useful chronological table.

Paller, Michael. *Gentlemen Callers: Tennessee Williams, Homosexuality, and Mid-Twentieth-Century Broadway Drama*. New York: Palgrave Macmillan, 2005. Charts the evolution of America's acknowledgment and acceptance of homosexuality by examining Williams's life and the plays he wrote from the 1940's through the 1970's. Describes how critics initially ignored his gay characters and how gay activists in the 1970's reviled his work.

Roudané, Matthew, ed. *The Cambridge Companion to Tennessee Williams*. New York: Cambridge University Press, 1997. Collection of essays providing general discussions of Williams's plays, including examinations of European and American influences on his dramas, Williams and his Broadway critics, and romantic textures in his plays and short stories. "Before the Fall—and After: *Summer and Smoke* and *The Night of the Iguana*" by Thomas P. Adler analyzes these two plays.

Spoto, Donald. *The Kindness of Strangers: The Life of Tennessee Williams*. Boston: Little, Brown, 1985. Spoto's excellent biography deals with Williams, his background, his demons, and his individual plays and stories.

Thompson, Judith J. *Tennessee Williams' Plays: Memory, Myth, and Symbol*. Rev. ed. New York: Peter Lang, 2002. Traces a pattern of mythic recollection in several of

Williams's plays, including *The Night of the Iguana*.

Tischler, Nancy M. *Student Companion to Tennessee Williams*. Westport, Conn.: Greenwood Press, 2000. Critical study of Williams's life, career, and work. Analyzes several plays, including *The Night of the Iguana*, discussing their styles, themes, and Williams's influences from poetry, film, religion, mythology, and personal experience.

Williams, Tennessee. *Conversations with Tennessee Williams*. Edited by Albert J. Devlin. Oxford: University Press of Mississippi, 1986. Collection of conversations and interviews between Williams and a number of interviewers.

Night Rider

Author: Robert Penn Warren (1905-1989)
First published: 1939
Type of work: Novel
Type of plot: Social morality
Time of plot: 1904-1905
Locale: Kentucky

Principal characters:
PERCY MUNN, a young Kentucky lawyer and farmer
MAY MUNN, his wife
MR. CHRISTIAN, Percy's neighbor and friend
LUCILLE CHRISTIAN, his daughter
SENATOR TOLLIVER, a leader in local affairs
CAPTAIN TODD, a Civil War veteran
BENTON TODD, his son
PROFESSOR BALL and DR. MACDONALD, the leaders in the association
BUNK TREVELYAN, a poor tobacco farmer

The Story:

In the summer of 1904, Percy Munn attends a rally of the Association of Growers of Dark Fired Tobacco in Bardsville, Kentucky. After an impromptu speech pleading for the defense of an "idea," he joins the association's board of directors, having been impressed by the leadership of such men as the smooth-talking Senator Tolliver and Captain Todd, a courageous former Confederate officer. He, however, has small success in gaining support for the association.

Curtailing his association activities to defend Bunk Trevelyan, accused of murdering a neighbor, Mr. Munn commits the first of a series of lawless deeds in which he convinces himself that an end justifies the means to attain it. Trusting Bunk's protestations of innocence, Munn leads an illegal search of the home of an African American in the area to find a knife like the one belonging to Bunk, which had been found at the murder scene. When a knife is found and the African American owner tells an unlikely story of how he got it, Bunk is released and the innocent man dies for the crime.

Two rises in prices paid by the tobacco companies and an association decision to continue holding out brings a public denunciation of the association by Tolliver and a suit to recover his crop. Bitter over Tolliver's betrayal, Munn joins an activist organization, the secret Ku Klux Klan-like Free Farmers' Brotherhood of Protection and Control, whose bands of night riders scrape the tobacco beds of farmers who refuse to join the association. Captain Todd, a man of both courage and probity, disapproves of the new group within the old, and withdraws from the association. Munn inwardly defends his own action because he believes the raids will finally bring "justice" to the farmers. He learns, though, that lawlessness begets lawlessness: Bunk Trevelyan attempts to blackmail a Brotherhood member, and Munn becomes by lot the leader of a group that shoots Bunk after he refuses Munn's offer to let him escape. Again Munn defends his deed: Bunk was the killer, he tells himself, of the man for whose death an innocent man died; thus Bunk deserves death. However, Munn is nauseated at the part he had played, and, returning home, he rapes his wife, May, as if to blot out one violent deed with another. Deserted by May as a result, he soon begins a loveless liaison with Lucille Christian, at whose father's home he frequently spends his nights.

Since the companies are still buying tobacco at the prices they set, the Brotherhood members dynamite the company warehouses in Bardsville. Pursuit of the raiders leads to the death of young Benton Todd. Troops move into the area the next day to restore order. New violence, however, develops outside the Brotherhood, with the burning of the homes of planters who use African American laborers instead of white workers. Senator Tolliver's home is burned, and then Mr. Munn's. Munn is roused from bed by Mr. Christian with news of the burning. After Munn's departure, Christian finds Lucille hiding in Munn's room and suffers a stroke that leaves him speechless.

Now homeless and rejected by both his wife and Lucille, Munn moves into the Ball home where, not long afterward, he witnesses the arrest of Dr. Macdonald on a charge of arson. At Macdonald's trial only Al Turpin, a former association member, is in a position to identify Macdonald. When Turpin is killed by a shot fired from Munn's rifle through his law office window, Munn is forced to flee. He later divines that Ball killed Turpin to win an acquittal for Macdonald.

Hiding out at the farm home of Willie Proudfit, one of Macdonald's friends, Munn is visited by Lucille with news of her father's death and the suggestion that flight and marriage would solve their problems. Learning of advances that Senator Tolliver had made to Lucille, however, Munn rejects her offer and determines instead to kill Tolliver, whom he obsessively identifies as the source of the downfall of the association and of himself. For this, Tolliver has to die. When he confronts Tolliver, however, he finds he cannot shoot, and, learning that troops, informed by a relative of Proudfit's, are coming to arrest him, he flees and is shot down in the dark.

Critical Evaluation:

Among the dominant themes in the novels of Robert Penn Warren are the search for self-identity, the isolation of the individual in society, and the opposition of violence and order in the development of modern America. All three themes appear in Warren's first published novel, *Night Rider*. The principal action of *Night Rider* is based on events that occurred in Kentucky between the years 1905 and 1908. The growers of dark tobacco in Kentucky and Tennessee formed a protective association to combat the tobacco companies and to try to force them to pay higher prices for tobacco. When the companies countered with small increases offered to all who would sell to

them, some planters turned to violent action executed by bands of "night riders." This included the destruction of the plant beds of those who refused to join the fight against the companies and finally led to the dynamiting of company warehouses in Hopkinsville, Kentucky. The action of the lawless bands was finally stopped by sending troops into the area.

Though most of the events in *Night Rider* are related to the battle of the tobacco planters against the companies and the farmers who refused to join or cooperate with the protective association, the book is not, as Warren warns the reader in a prefatory note, a historical novel. The tobacco war provides the framework for the story of a young lawyer, Percy Munn (Mr. Munn), and his degeneration from a man of principle to a man of violence. It is a story of self-realization that comes too late to a man who, though intelligent, lacks the will, moral strength, or clarity of vision to make the right decisions when faced by crises in his life. From one wrong action, he seems to move inevitably to the next, troubled and brooding yet unable to stop the movement toward his certain doom.

Though *Night Rider* is a novel with extensive action and a large cast of characters, Warren has unified the work by using Munn as what Henry James called a "central consciousness." People and events are seen primarily through one mind. Introspective Munn seeks cause, meaning, and value in what is done by himself and by others. Munn's ambivalence is seen in his alternate revulsion of people and in his desire to be a part of a group or to wield power over them. This appears in the opening scene when Munn resents the crowd on the train and then experiences a moment of near exaltation when he imagines himself being greeted by the even larger crowd at the station. Throughout the novel, he examines his own paradoxes and confusions, his basic coldness opposed to momentary heated involvement in talk and action, and his sense of isolation not only when alone but also with others.

Stylistically, *Night Rider* is marked by recurrent imagery of light and dark. As in the fiction of Nathaniel Hawthorne, Joseph Conrad, and others, this opposition is symbolic. The story opens in brilliant sunshine and ends in the dark. Munn's acts, which show his progress from light into darkness, all occur in the dark: the illegal search of homes, the initiation into the Brotherhood, the night raids, the killing of Bunk, the sexual assault on May, the lust with Lucille, the dynamiting of the warehouses, the death of Benton Todd (the result of Munn's error in judgment), the final confrontation with Tolliver, and Munn's death. The opposed light and dark are sometimes shown as mirroring each other as if one contained the other, and Munn's divided self is often symbolically portrayed, as in the scene in which he reads the account in the morning news of a raid in which he participated and finds it difficult to see himself as a part of it. Such symbolic imagery serves, like the strong focus on Munn's point of view, to unify *Night Rider* and emphasize Warren's intent of writing a novel of moral as well as physical violence, of ethical more than historical significance. *Night Rider* is an important first novel that introduces the themes, style, and structure Warren employs in his later work.

Further Reading

Burt, John. "Social Realism and Romance: *Night Rider*." In *Robert Penn Warren and American Idealism*. New Haven, Conn.: Yale University Press, 1988. Analysis of Munn as a character caught in the dilemma of "social naturalism": the intellectual acceptance of naturalistic philosophy and the antithetical "desire to discover some seat of human integrity and to articulate self-knowledge."

Grimshaw, James A., Jr. *Understanding Robert Penn Warren*. Columbia: University of South Carolina Press, 2001. Comprehensive introduction to Warren's work, analyzing his fiction, poetry, and drama. Discusses the nature of his protagonists and common themes, such as history, time, truth, responsibility, and love. The references to *Night Rider* are listed in the index.

Guttenberg, Barnett. "*Night Rider*." In *Web of Being: The Novels of Robert Penn Warren*. Nashville, Tenn.: Vanderbilt University Press, 1975. Discusssion of Munn as an existential hero attempting to combine quests for personal identity and ideal justice.

Hendricks, Randy. *Lonelier than God: Robert Penn Warren and the Southern Exile*. Athens: University of Georgia Press, 2000. Focuses on the theme of exile in Warren's work and how that theme relates to his ideas about regionalism, race, and language.

Justus, James H. "*Night Rider*: An Adequate Definition of Terror." In *The Achievement of Robert Penn Warren*. Baton Rouge: Louisiana State University Press, 1981. Discussion of the novel's historical roots, themes, and techniques, especially the use of symbolic actions and of the protagonist as the governing point of view.

Law, Richard. "*Night Rider* and the Issue of Naturalism: The 'Nightmare' of Our Age." In *Robert Penn Warren: Critical Perspectives*, edited by Neil Nakadate. Lexington: University Press of Kentucky, 1981. Analysis of *Night Rider* as a philosophical novel portraying the conflict between human will and scientific determinism. Sees the focus upon Munn's consciousness as Warren's technique for demonstrating its limitations.

Madden, David, ed. *The Legacy of Robert Penn Warren*. Baton Rouge: Louisiana State University Press, 2000. Collection of essays interpreting Warren's work, including discussions of Warren as a mentor and a moral philosopher, Warren and Thomas Jefferson, and the function of geography as fate in his writings.

Ryan, Alvin S. "Robert Penn Warren's *Night Rider*: The Nihilism of the Isolated Temperament." In *Robert Penn Warren: A Collection of Critical Essays*, edited by John Lewis Longley, Jr., 1965. Reprint. Westport, Conn.: Greenwood Press, 1979. Interpretation of Munn as attempting to move from isolation to communion but failing because he lacks self-knowledge and, thus, the means to act.

Nightmare Abbey

Author: Thomas Love Peacock (1785-1866)
First published: 1818
Type of work: Novel
Type of plot: Fiction of manners
Time of plot: Early nineteenth century
Locale: England

Principal characters:
CHRISTOPHER GLOWRY, the master of Nightmare Abbey
SCYTHROP, his son
MR. FLOSKY, a visitor
MARIONETTA, Glowry's niece
MR. TOOBAD, Glowry's friend
CELINDA, his daughter
LISTLESS, a dandy

The Story:

Refused by one young lady in his youth, Christopher Glowry immediately marries another. His wife is cold and gloomy, and Nightmare Abbey is a fitting name for her house. Glowry finds relief from his unhappy life in food and drink, and when his lady dies, he is easily consoled by increasing his consumption of food and wine. She left one son, Scythrop, who is gloomy enough to suit his father and Nightmare Abbey. A university education has so stripped Scythrop of his thin veneer of social graces that he is rapidly becoming a country boor like his father.

While his father is away in London attending to an important lawsuit, Scythrop amuses himself by constructing miniature dungeons, trapdoors, and secret panels. One day, he discovers by chance an apartment in the main wing of the abbey that has no entrance or exit; through an error in construction, the apartment had remained hidden for many years. He imports a carpenter, and together they construct a cunning secret panel through which one could step from the library into the hidden apartment. Scythrop now has a private refuge for his gloomy meditations.

Miss Emily Girouette declines to marry Scythrop. In consequence, when his cousin Marionetta visits, she rapidly conquers the heart of the sad young man. Marionetta, however, has no fortune, and Glowry refuses to hear of the marriage, but Scythrop grows more enamored daily of his coquettish cousin.

Glowry views the increasing attachment of Scythrop and Marionetta with great concern. Finally, he tells Scythrop that the girl has to leave. Furious, Scythrop rushes to his tower and fills a human skull with Madeira wine. Confronting his father and holding high the skull, he declares in ringing tones that if Marionetta ever leaves Nightmare Abbey except of her own free will, he will drink the potion. Convinced that the skull contains poison, his father consents to have Marionetta stay on as a guest. Scythrop drinks the wine with gusto.

Glowry confides his troubles to his friend, Toobad, who agrees that marriage with Marionetta is unsuitable in every way. He proposes his own daughter, Celinda, a young woman then studying abroad, as a good match for Scythrop. With Glowry's hearty approval, Toobad goes to London to meet his daughter and return with her to Nightmare Abbey. Celinda, however, refuses to have a husband chosen for her and flees from her domineering father. Toobad appears at the abbey and leaves again, vowing to all that he will find his unruly daughter.

The house party at Nightmare Abbey grows larger. Mr. Flosky, a poet of the supernatural, spreads confusion with his metaphysical paradoxes. Listless, a bored dandy, arrives with Fatout, his French valet, who is the guardian of his mind and body. Another addition to the party is Mr. Asterias the ichthyologist, who engages in tracing down rumors of mermaids in the vicinity of the abbey. It is not clear what a mermaid would do in the fens around the abbey, but Mr. Asterias has faith. This faith is rewarded one night when Mr. Asterias dimly perceives the form of a woman clad in black. As he rushes across the moat, the mysterious figure disappears.

Scythrop takes as much delight as he can in Marionetta's company; but Listless is the merriest person in the room when Marionetta is present. As far as his languid airs permit, he follows her about with great eagerness.

Watching Scythrop's affection for Marionetta, Glowry decides that he has been too harsh with his son, and he suddenly announces his approval of their betrothal. To his father's surprise, Scythrop stammers that he does not want to be too precipitate. So the generosity of the father goes unrewarded.

There is some mystery about Scythrop. For some time, he had been more distraught than usual; now he practically refuses marriage with his beloved. More than that, every time Glowry goes to his son's room, he finds the door locked and Scythrop slow in answering his knock. A strange, heavy thud always sounds in the room before the door opens.

One evening, while the whole company is sitting in the drawing room, a tall and stately figure wearing a bloody turban suddenly appears. Listless rolls under the sofa. Glowry roars his alarm in Toobad's ear, and Toobad tries to run away. He mistakes a window for a door and falls into the moat below. Mr. Asterias, still looking for a mermaid, fishes him out with a landing net.

These mysteries go back to the night Mr. Asterias thought he saw the mermaid. Scythrop is sitting alone in his library when the door opens softly and in steps a beautiful, stately woman. She looks at Scythrop carefully, and reassured by what she sees, she sits down confidently. The bewildered man can only sit and stare. The mysterious stranger gently asks him if he is the illustrious author of the pamphlet, "Philosophical Gas." Flattered, Scythrop acknowledges his authorship of that profound work, only seven copies of which had been sold. Then the girl asks his protection from a marriage that would make her the slave of her sex. Already smitten, Scythrop agrees to hide her in his secret apartment.

Then Scythrop begins his dual romance. The serious girl, who calls herself Stella, talks night after night of the German metaphysicians and quotes German tragedy. Marionetta, however, is always merry and lively. Scythrop does not know whom to choose.

One night, his father demands entry into his room while Stella is there. Stella decides to show herself, regardless of consequences. Toobad recognizes his long-lost daughter Celinda. Scythrop now has to choose either Celinda or Marionetta; but he hesitates to make a choice, feeling that he cannot relinquish either. The next day, however, the decision is made for him. Marionetta has accepted Listless and Celinda will soon be Mrs. Flosky. Stoically, Glowry reminds his son that there are other maidens. Scythrop agrees and orders the Madeira.

Critical Evaluation:

Thomas Love Peacock, a satirical novelist, never had a wide audience. His ambition was not fame or fortune but merely to please himself. His concerns were not those of most writers within the Romantic movement. Still, the author gained the respect of Percy Bysshe Shelley and Lord Byron in his own times. Peacock's novels are generally set in idyllic country homes in which drinking and flirting seem to be the major activity of the day. Reading between the lines, however, especially in the case of the satirical *Nightmare Abbey*, reveals serious discussions of moral, political, economic, scientific, and aesthetic concerns.

As with most satire, critical evaluations of the writer's work tend to be somewhat negative. Satiric plots, as is true of Peacock's, tend to be insignificant if not implausible. He sketches characters rather than writing rounded characters. Those characters who are more well rounded tend to be polemic in their opinions rather than deep, as they should be in a novel, in their emotions. What Peacock's writing lacks in plot and character he makes up for in wit and epigrams. A classicist at heart, Peacock uses his fine understanding of the contemporary ideas he attacks to show opinion, not ill humor.

Scythrop Glowry, the son of Christopher Glowry, a Lincolnshire landed gentleman of gloomy disposition who presides over the family castle, Nightmare Abbey, is the hero of Peacock's satire, a witty spoof of gothic fiction and of Romantic attitudes. The reader soon learns that Scythrop was named for an ancestor who committed suicide and whose skull is being used as a punchbowl. A student of Immanuel Kant, Scythrop falls madly in love with Marionetta Celestina O'Carroll, who more or less loves him too. The elder Glowry, however, has in mind a better match: Celinda Toobad, who has been educated abroad and is the heir to a considerable fortune. Scythrop banishes himself to the tower room of Nightmare Abbey and reads gothic fiction and dreams of "venerable eleutherarchs"—chiefs of a secret society called The Eleutheri—"and ghastly confederates holding midnight conventions in subterranean caves." The novel ends with a scene that burlesques Johann Wolfgang von Goethe's *Die Leiden des jungen Werthers* (1774; *The Sorrows of Young Werther*, 1779): Scythrop, armed with a pistol and an ample supply of Madeira, waits for the fatal hour he has appointed for his death. Before the novel comes to an end, however, a "ghost" and Scythrop yield to reason.

Peacock's targets for his satire are the exalted attitude of the prose and poetry of the Romantic movement (with a special emphasis on Byron) and the coincidences and confusion that are endemic to gothic fiction. *Nightmare Abbey* is the most literary of Peacock's satires. It targets the gloom affecting contemporary literature, such as Samuel Taylor Coleridge's German transcendentalism, Byron's self-dramatizing, and Shelley's esotericism. The book opens in imitation of William Godwin's novel *Mandeville: A Tale of the Seventeenth Century in England* (1817). Nightmare Abbey is staffed by servants with long, skull-like faces and names like Diggory Deathshead. The senior Glowry gives a party attended by the millenarian pessimist Mr. Toobad; by Mr. Flosky, who is based on Coleridge; by Mr. Cypress, who is based on Byron; and by Mr. Listless, drawn to represent the common reader. The Younger Scythrop, a writer, is based on Shelley because he cannot decide which hand to take in marriage: that of Marionetta, his frivolous cousin, or that of Stella/Celinda, Mr. Toobad's sibylline daughter. Other guests include the uncommonly cheerful Mr. Asterias, a scientist, and Mr. Hilary, whose literary tastes come from the Greeks. "Peacock seems to have intended to present, in amusing contemporary terms, the dilemma facing the young Milton in 'L'Allegro' and 'Il Penseroso.'" The novel ends with the unfinished Werther-style suicide in a comic denouement.

Nightmare Abbey targets both gothicism and Romanticism, specifically the Byronic hero. Mr. Flosky, Peacock's portrait of Coleridge, observes the change: "the ghosts . . . have been laid . . . and now the delight of our spirits is to dwell on all the vices and blackest passions of our nature, tricked out in a masquerade dress of heroism and disappointed benevolence." Coleridge is depicted as a philosopher of transcendentalism and as a self-appointed leader of the counterculture. As represented by Mr. Flosky, Coleridge, according to Peacock, claims rights to divining the taste of the reading public.

The dramatic appearance of Byron (in the guise of Mr. Cypress) in the second half of *Nightmare Abbey* is a tour de force; Peacock uses quotations from *Childe Harold's Pilgrimage* (1812) and mixes them with parody of the fourth canto. When Mr. Cypress departs the abbey, he veers from misanthropic generalization to navel-peering self-observation in a speech about quarreling with his wife, which absolves him of any duty to his country.

The self-destructive Scythrop, caught between two women, is based on Shelley and his elopement with Mary Godwin. Scythrop's esotericism (only seven copies of his pamphlet, "Philosophical Gas," were sold) sheds light on the gap between literary exponents of liberty and the reading public at large. Scythrop's self-immersion in his private dilemma, likely to be judged by the public-at-large as merely scandalous, adds depth to the critique of solipsism, which underlies this literary parody. As the novel comes to an end, Scythrop cannot bring himself to dispose of either lady: "I am doomed to be the victim of eternal disappointment and I have no resource but a pistol." The ladies, however, will have none of this nonsense and reject Scythrop. His disappointment validated and his misanthropy confirmed by both women, Scythrop decides against suicide. His story ends not with a gunshot, but with a cry more familiar in Peacock's world: "Bring some Madeira." With *Nightmare Abbey* as his vehicle, Peacock acts as an active, liberating force, sounding the death knell of self-indulgent Romanticism with his *Nightmare Abbey*.

"Critical Evaluation" by Thomas D. Petitjean, Jr.

Further Reading

Butler, Marilyn. *Peacock Displayed: A Satirist in His Context*. London: Routledge & Kegan Paul, 1979. Makes *Nightmare Abbey* a focal point, maintaining that as finely drawn as the gentlemen characters are, the novel is actually the story of two women, Marionetta and Celinda/Stella.

Cavaliero, Glen. "Feasts of Reason: Thomas Love Peacock." In *The Alchemy of Laughter: Comedy in English Fiction*. New York: St. Martin's Press, 2000. Peacock's novels are included in this examination of comedy in English fiction, in which Cavaliero discusses how parody, irony, satire, and other types of humor are evident in these works.

Cunningham, Mark. "'Fatout! Who Am I?' A Model for the Honourable Mr. Listless in Thomas Love Peacock's *Nightmare Abbey*." *English Language Notes* 30, no. 1 (September, 1992): 43-45. Discusses the possibility of who may have been the model for the character of Mr. Listless, who spends whole days on a sofa in perfected ennui.

Schwank, Klaus. "From Satire to Indeterminacy: Thomas Love Peacock's *Nightmare Abbey*." In *Beyond the Suburbs of the Mind: Exploring English Romanticism*, edited by Michael Gassenmeier and Norbert H. Platz. Essen, Germany: Blaue Eule, 1987. Discusses the effectiveness of Peacock's satire, placing *Nightmare Abbey* novel in a category of works that defy satire.

Vidal, Gore. "Thomas Love Peacock: The Novel of Ideas." In *The Essential Gore Vidal*, edited by Fred Kaplan. New York: Random House, 1999. This collection of fiction, essays, and reviews includes Vidal's appraisals of the work of several writers, including an examination of Peacock's novels. Includes chronology and bibliography.

Wolf, Leonard. "Nightmare Abbey." *Horror: A Connoisseur's Guide to Literature and Film*. New York: Facts On File, 1989. Compares Peacock's satirical verse as a precursor to Oscar Wilde's similar style.

Wright, Julia M. "Peacock's Early Parody of Thomas Moore in *Nightmare Abbey*." *English Language Notes* 30, no. 4 (June, 1993): 31-38. Discusses Peacock's use of Thomas Moore as, possibly, a template for a character in *Nightmare Abbey*.

Nightwood

Author: Djuna Barnes (1892-1982)
First published: 1936
Type of work: Novel
Type of plot: Psychological surrealism
Time of plot: 1920's
Locale: Paris and Vienna

Principal characters:
FELIX VOLKBEIN, a spurious baron
DR. MATTHEW O'CONNOR, an aging medical student
NORA FLOOD, a publicist with a circus
ROBIN VOTE, Felix's wife and Nora's paramour
JENNY PETHERBRIDGE, a wealthy multiple widow
GUIDO VOLKBEIN, Felix and Robin's son

The Story:

Felix Volkbein is no sooner born in Vienna in 1880 than his mother, Hedvig, dies. His father, Guido, a descendant of Italian Jews who had tried to overcome the burden of what he took to be an ignoble past by pretending to be of noble birth, died six months earlier. The orphaned Felix is left with a rather substantial upper-middle-class household and the fictitious title of Baron Volkbein.

About thirty years later, Felix, a nominal Christian, owns little more than his spurious title and two "family portraits" that are in fact paintings of long-forgotten actors procured by Guido in his effort to create an aristocratic past for his family line. By 1920, Felix is making a living in international banking in Paris. Here he indulges in his real obsession, the nobility, aristocracy, and royalty of Old Europe. Without legitimate claims to noble blood, he envies the nobility from a discreet distance. To exercise his propensity for make-believe, he becomes a habitué of the night world of the circus and theater. Among these "night people," many of whom are also "titled," Felix meets Dr. Matthew O'Connor, an Irishman from San Francisco, and Nora Flood, an American who is in Europe as a publicist for a circus.

O'Connor is a lively and talkative eccentric with an opinion or observation to make on everything and everyone. He and Felix meet again in Paris a few weeks later. The doctor is called to assist a young woman who had fainted, and Felix is on hand when O'Connor brings her around. She is Robin Vote, mistress of this world of the night, and in her half-awakened state a beast turning human.

It is in that half-awakened state that she agrees to marry Felix when, in rather short order, he proposes to her to produce an heir to continue the Volkbein line. Felix moves Robin to Vienna, where she sleepwalks through her pregnancy, coming to, as it were, upon the birth of the child. She abandons Felix and the boy, a sickly baby, and ends up in the company of Nora Flood.

Robin is with a circus in New York in 1923 when she first meets Nora, and the two become constant companions. Although Robin is incapable of forming lasting attachments, Nora falls tragically under her spell, rearranging her life to suit Robin's needs and eventually returning with Robin to Europe, where they settle in an apartment in Paris. By 1927, however, the acquisitive Jenny Petherbridge comes into their lives and, much to Nora's mental and emotional pain, steals Robin away from her.

Jenny is a collector of everyone else's lost dreams and possessions. For a while she makes the most of her new catch, but then she too succumbs to the insane jealousy that Robin's insouciant promiscuity and casual animal magnetism inspire in others. During a mad, late-night carriage ride through the streets of Paris, while O'Connor talks about the pains of love, Jenny is distracted by the fear that a young Englishwoman might find Robin attractive, or vice versa. A short time later, Jenny and Robin leave Paris for America. For consolation, the heartbroken Nora ventures to O'Connor's apartment at 3 A.M. to find him in bed in a woman's wig, makeup, and nightgown. Nevertheless, she stays to hear his monologue about the night that is our darkness, our degradation, and our death.

The baron, meanwhile, had been raising his and Robin's son, Guido. By 1931, the boy is grown into a religious "idiot" of sorts, though O'Connor sees hope in his desire to become a Catholic, whereby he will escape the history that imprisons Felix. Felix despairs of that possibility but makes plans nevertheless to move with the boy to Vienna, where he might be among his own people.

Jenny shows up at his Paris apartment one day, ostensibly to buy a painting but really in search of information about Robin, suggesting that, like Felix and Nora before her, Jenny too had lost Robin to someone else. O'Connor pays another visit to Nora, during which they again discuss, largely through his monologues, the pain of degradation and loss that humans are born for, which for Nora and other characters in the novel is embodied in Robin. Although his ability to articulate the absurd is a source of strength to others, O'Connor is driven to despair when Nora tells him the details of her relationship with Robin. O'Connor ends up a broken man, damning all those who come to him to learn of degradation and the night.

Jenny and Robin return to New York. Robin, who had become Catholic during her marriage to Felix, still frequents churches, and her devotion, real or feigned, is yet another source of jealousy for Jenny. Robin ends up wandering northward toward Nora's country home. Nora arrives at a chapel near her home in the middle of the night with her dog to find Robin carrying on a quasi-religious ritual, as if to lure her to the spot. Then, in front of the stunned and confused Nora, Robin has sex with the dog, simultaneously fulfilling the animal nature she embodies and inflicting further emotional pain on both herself and one of her lovers. The cycle of degradation that flourishes at night promises to continue, nurtured by these kinds of symbiotic relationships between the spirit that is the human and the beast that is also the human.

Critical Evaluation:

If ever a story depended more on its telling than on the tale, Djuna Barnes's *Nightwood* is that story. The plot of *Nightwood* contains traditional elements such as an array of interesting characterizations, narrative twists that are suspenseful if no doubt also puzzling, and a not inconsiderable measure of humor and insight into the human condition. Yet those elements seem to be present only in the most elliptical manner, as if the author's real aim is not to be telling a story at all.

Barnes is, by most definitions of the term, a modernist writer essaying modernist themes and issues. Like other avant-garde literature of the period, *Nightwood* includes confrontations of cultural values; breakdowns in the social order as traditional class structures decay; daring sexual-psychological interpretations of human character and motivation; and a keen, almost morbid attention to eccentric and morally outrageous behavior. Even *Nightwood*'s surrealism, as in O'Connor's monologues, is in keeping with contemporary literary trends and techniques.

Yet *Nightwood* is a rare creation even for an epoch of experimentation in fiction. The novel nags the reader with the suggestion of a meaning that is, like that of the more traditional novel, inherent in the characters and in the way they work out their moral dilemmas. It is possible that *Nightwood*'s real achievement is the almost perfect blending of form and content, so that the story and its telling are inseparable and all enveloping, while at the same time, the vigor of the language belies the paucity of moral imperatives.

Language—both the language of the author's narrative line and the language within that narrative in which the characters communicate their feelings, values, and ideas (and misgivings, confusions, and desires)—is so much a theme of the novel that it is almost a character. It is by and through language that the night, an age-old metaphor for mystery and terror, is given human shape and made a human habitation.

The novel's two ethical poles are Matthew O'Connor, the closet insomniac who cannot stop talking, and Robin Vote, the sleepwalker who hardly seems to be alive except in the most amorally mindless, animalistic way. The other characters are located somewhere between those two extremes and are as surely caught up in this "nightwood" as anyone else. The players can penetrate that darkness to illuminate it momentarily for others, but no one can dissipate or overcome it.

The power to select one's victimhood is all each person has. That is what Felix accepts almost by virtue of circumstance, and it is certainly what O'Connor preaches in his efforts to overcome the darkness. Those in the novel who, either through a stubborn willfulness or a blind disregard, cannot accept this precept, such as Nora Flood and Jenny Petherbridge, become its victim. Robin, meanwhile, the antiprotagonist, appropriately embodies night's mindless power to victimize.

The novel ends with Robin selecting her own victimhood by becoming, in imitation of a dog, the amoral beast nature had made her. She has, however, at least made the moral choice to break free of Jenny, the possessive opportunist, and return to Nora, who is devoted to her. Such an ambiguity of action seems to be the most the reader can expect from the rich maelstrom of words and ideas that swirl through the pages of *Nightwood*.

Russell Elliott Murphy

Further Reading

Broe, Mary Lynn, ed. *Silence and Power: A Reevaluation of Djuna Barnes*. Carbondale: Southern Illinois University Press, 1991. An invaluable collection of essays on Barnes and her work, many of which are written from a feminist perspective. Includes many reproductions of Barnes's artwork. A bibliography and extensive notes are included.

Eliot, T. S. "Introduction" to *Nightwood*, by Djuna Barnes. New York: Harcourt Brace Jovanovich, 1936. Eliot's encomium in his introduction to the first edition of *Nightwood* secured the novel the recognition it deserved but might otherwise never have attained. Brief and to the point, Eliot singles out that one feature of Barnes's prose style—its poetry—that continues to make the novel a classic of modernist technique.

Field, Andrew. *Djuna: The Formidable Miss Barnes*. Austin: University of Texas Press, 1985. A corrected and revised edition of the biography that first appeared in 1983, frustrating in its lack of notes but highly inventive in form and approach—an ideal match of biographer and subject. Provides extensive information on the composition and background of *Nightwood*. Includes illustrations, including some reproductions of Barnes's artwork, and an extensive list of sources.

Frank, Joseph. *The Widening Gyre: Crisis and Mastery in Modern Literature*. New Brunswick, N.J.: Rutgers University Press, 1963. Contains Frank's influential essay "Spatial Form in Modern Literature," which originally appeared in 1945 and which discusses *Nightwood* along with works by Gustave Flaubert, Marcel Proust, and James Joyce.

Kannenstine, Louis F. *The Art of Djuna Barnes: Duality and Damnation*. New York: New York University Press, 1977. This scholarly and critically ambitious work on Barnes concludes that Barnes is a transitional writer, difficult to classify and therefore missing the attention her art and work deserve. Defines *Nightwood*, her masterpiece, as a study of mixed being and of the estrangement that results from confused identity.

Kennedy, J. Gerald. *Imagining Paris: Exile, Writing, and American Identity*. New Haven, Conn.: Yale University Press, 1993. Examines the importance of expatriation in twentieth century American literature—a highly important theme in Barnes's writing. Kennedy discusses *Nightwood* and F. Scott Fitzgerald's novel *Tender Is the Night* in the chapter "Modernism as Exile: Fitzgerald, Barnes, and the Unreal City."

Parsons, Deborah L. *Djuna Barnes*. Tavistock, England: Northcote House/British Council, 2003. *Nightwood* and Barnes's other writings are analyzed in this study of the psychological and stylistic aspects of her work. Parsons places Barnes's work within the social and cultural context of the modernist period.

Plumb, Cheryl J. *Fancy's Craft: Art and Identity in the Early Works of Djuna Barnes*. Selinsgrove, Pa.: Susquehanna University Press, 1986. Points out that Barnes deliberately rebelled against naturalist techniques in her writing, borrowing instead from methods of narrative exposition developed out of symbolist poetry. *Nightwood*, her greatest achievement, presents difficulties for scholars and readers alike precisely because it is the purest realization of these goals.

Rupprecht, Caroline. *Subject to Delusions: Narcissism, Modernism, Gender.* Evanston, Ill.: Northwestern University Press, 2006. Rupprecht describes narcissism as a relation between the self and the other that is mediated by a mirror or by reflection. She analyzes how this definition of narcissism is an important component in understanding the "other" in *Nightwood*.

Scott, James B. *Djuna Barnes*. Boston: Twayne, 1976. A good introduction to Barnes. Points out that the writer as she matured sought to mix and then fuse genres and styles. *Nightwood*, Barnes's one attempt at a "popular" novel, succeeds by fusing elements of a lurid realism with an engagingly poetic style.

Warren, Diane. *Djuna Barnes' Consuming Fictions*. Burlington, Vt.: Ashgate, 2008. Warren demonstrates how Barnes's concepts of gender and aesthetics were significant in her time and remain relevant in the early twenty-first century. She defines *Nightwood* as a "pivotal" text that raises questions about an individual's ability to subvert cultural boundaries.

Nineteen Eighty-Four

Author: George Orwell (1903-1950)
First published: 1949
Type of work: Novel
Type of plot: Science fiction
Time of plot: 1984
Locale: London

Principal characters:
WINSTON SMITH, a Party functionary
JULIA, a rebellious girl
O'BRIEN, a member of the Inner Party
MR. CHARRINGTON, one of the thought police

The Story:

Externally, Winston Smith appears well adjusted to his world. He drinks the bitter victory gin and smokes the vile victory cigarettes. In the morning, he does his exercises in front of the telescreen, and when the instructor speaks to him over the two-way television, he bends with renewed vigor to touch the floor. His apartment is dingy and rickety, but at thirty-nine years old, he is scarcely old enough to remember a time when housing had been better. He has a decent job at the Ministry of Truth because he has a good mind and the ability to write newspeak, the official language. He is a member of the outer ring of the Party.

One afternoon, after giving up his lunch at the ministry, Winston has a little free time to himself. He goes to an alcove out of reach of the telescreen and furtively takes out his journal. It is a noble book with paper of fine quality, unobtainable at present. It is an antique, bought on an illicit trip to a secondhand store run by old Mr. Charrington. Although it is not illegal to keep a diary—there are no laws in Oceania—it makes him suspect. He writes ploddingly about a film he had seen about the valiant Oceania forces strafing shipwrecked refugees in the Mediterranean.

Musing over his writing, Winston finds to his horror that he had written a slogan against Big Brother several times. He knows this act is a crime, even if the writing is due to his drinking gin. Even to think of such a slogan is a crime. Everywhere he looks, on stair landings and on storefronts, are posters showing Big Brother's all-seeing face. Citizens are reminded a hundred times a day that Big Brother is watching their every move.

At the Ministry of Truth, Winston plunges into his routine. He has the job of rewriting records. If the Party makes an inaccurate prediction about the progress of the war, or if some aspect of production does not accord with the published goals of the ninth three-year plan, Winston corrects the record. All published material is constantly changed so that all history accords with the wishes and aims of the Party.

There is a break in the day's routine for a two-minute hate period. The face of Goldstein, the enemy of the Party, appears on the big telescreen, and a government speaker works up the feelings of the viewers; Goldstein is accused of heading a great conspiracy against Oceania. Winston loudly and dutifully drums his heels as he takes part in the group orgasm of hate.

A bold, dark-haired girl, wearing a red chastity belt, often seems to be near Winston in the workrooms and in the commissary. Winston is afraid she might be a member of the thought police. Seeing her outside the ministry, he decides she is following him. For a time, he plays with the idea of killing her. One day, she slips a little note to him, confessing that she loves him.

Winston is troubled. He is married, but his wife belongs to the Anti-Sex League. For her, procreation is a Party duty. Because the couple produced no children, they split up; Winston's wife left him. Now this girl at work—her name is Julia—speaks of love. Winston has a few private words with her in the lunchroom, being careful to make their conversation look like a chance meeting. Julia quickly names a place in the country for a rendezvous. Winston meets her in the woods and, far from a telescreen, they make love. Julia boasts that she had been the mistress of several Party members and that she has no patience with the Anti-Sex League, although she works diligently for the group. She also buys sweets on the black market.

Winston again visits Mr. Charrington's antique shop, and the proprietor shows Winston an upstairs bedroom preserved as it had been before the Revolution. Although it is madness to do so, Winston rents the room and, thereafter, he and Julia have a comfortable bed for their brief meetings. Winston feels happy in the old room, which has no telescreen to spy on them.

At work, Winston sometimes sees O'Brien, a kindly looking member of the Inner Party. Winston deduces from a chance remark that O'Brien is not in sympathy with all the aims of the Party. When they can, Winston and Julia go to O'Brien's apartment. He assures them that Goldstein is really the head of a conspiracy that eventually will overthrow the Party. Julia tells of her sins against Party discipline, and Winston recounts his evidence that the Party distorts facts in public trials and purges. O'Brien then enrolls them in the conspiracy and gives them Goldstein's book to read.

After an exhausting hate week directed against another enemy, Eurasia, Winston reads aloud to the dozing Julia, both comfortably lying in bed, from Goldstein's treatise. Suddenly, a voice rings out and orders them to stand in the middle of the room. Winston grows sick when he realizes that a hidden telescreen has recorded the actions at O'Brien's apartment. Soon the room is filled with truncheon-wielding police officers. Mr. Charrington comes in, no longer a kindly member of the simple proletariat, but a keen, determined man and a member of the thought police. One of the guards hits Julia in the stomach, and the others hurry Winston off to jail.

Winston is tortured for days—beaten, kicked, and clubbed until he confesses his crimes. He willingly admits to years of conspiracy with the rulers of Eurasia and tells everything he knows of Julia. In the later phases of his torture, O'Brien is at his side constantly. O'Brien keeps him on a rack with a doctor in attendance to keep him alive. He tells Winston that Goldstein's book is a Party production, written in part by O'Brien himself.

Through it all, the tortured Winston has one small triumph: He still loves Julia. O'Brien knows about Winston's fear of rats and brings in a large cage filled with rodents; he fastens it around Winston's head. In his unreasoning terror, Winston begs him to let the rats eat Julia instead. Winston still hates Big Brother, then says so. O'Brien patiently explains that the Party wants no martyrs—they strengthen opposition—nor do the leaders want only groveling subjection. Winston must think right. The proletariat, happy in its ignorance, must never have a rousing leader. All Party members must think and feel as Big Brother directs.

Winston is finally released, now bald and without teeth. Because he had been purged and because his crime had not been serious, he is given a small job on a subcommittee. Most of the time, he sits solitary in taverns and drinks victory gin. He even sees Julia once. Her figure has coarsened and her face is scarred. The two have little to say to one another.

One day, a big celebration takes place in the tavern. Oceania has achieved an important victory in Africa. Suddenly, the doddering Winston feels himself purged—he now believes. Now he can be shot with a pure soul, for at last he loves Big Brother.

Critical Evaluation:

Nineteen Eighty-Four is one of the keenest pieces of satire to be written in the twentieth century. It was George Orwell's last novel, written between 1946 and 1949 and published less than one year before his death. If took him more than two years to write, considerably more time than he spent on any of his other novels. Orwell was seriously ill with tuberculosis during the writing of this novel. He said that his sickness might have crept into the work and added to the novel's dark and disturbing nature. Indeed, the protagonist, Winston Smith, suffers from horrible coughing fits that sometimes leave him paralyzed.

This novel's deepest impact lies in the many Orwellian words and concepts that have become a part of English vocabulary, especially the political vocabulary. The terms "newspeak," "doublethink," and "Big Brother" were all coined by Orwell. Political commentators often draw from these words when they need a negative phrase to describe a government.

Nineteen Eighty-Four is part of a small group of important futuristic novels that use the structure of science fiction to contain political satire. These have been called anti-Utopia novels. *Nineteen Eighty-Four* and Aldous Huxley's *Brave New World* (1932) are the best known in English, but both of these draw from an earlier novel, *We* (1924), written by the little-known Russian novelist Yevgeny Zamyatin.

The central theme of *Nineteen Eighty-Four* is the state's imposition of will upon thought and truth. Winston wants to keep the few cubic centimeters inside his skull to himself. He wants to be ruler of his own thoughts, but the state is powerful enough to rule even those. He wants the freedom to believe that two plus two equals four, that the past is fixed, and that love is private.

Orwell saw privacy as one of the most necessary elements in a human's life. The world of *Nineteen Eighty-Four* does not allow privacy for the individual and does not allow the individual to have a personal identity. Everyone must think in the collective way, exactly as everyone else thinks. Thought control is executed through the falsification of history. Winston's job is to falsify history, often rewriting the same event many times, making something different happen each time. Oceania was at war with Eastasia, then Eurasia, and then Eastasia again, and history had to change every time to show that Oceania had always been at war with the present enemy. People learned not to trust their own memories and learned, through doublethink, not to have memories at all, beyond what was told to them.

This depiction of thought control may be Orwell's notice on the concept of history. Different people might recount the same experience in different ways. School books of one country, for example, may reconstruct events differently from history books of another country, each set presenting its country in a positive light.

Another theme came from the propaganda that circulated during the world wars. Enemies were depicted as less than human. This mind manipulation by governments helped their own populations to believe that fighting and killing the enemy was not immoral in any way, because the enemy was a scourge of the planet and should be annihilated. Here again, the futuristic disguise of *Nineteen Eighty-Four* is only a device to magnify a situation that Orwell had witnessed throughout his life, the flagrant deception by governments of their peoples on a regular basis. Orwell gives exemplary cases in mind control, showing how easily a government can divert the attention of its populace by creating an enemy for everyone to hate together.

The severe brutality of *Nineteen Eighty-Four* is a direct link from the post-World War II era to a fierce exaggeration of the possible future. After living through the atrocities of Adolf Hitler and Joseph Stalin, and knowing of concentration camps and of mental and physical tortures, Orwell painted a picture of what the year 1984 could be like if the principles of achieving and retaining power were extended in the same vein as in the past.

The setting for *Nineteen Eighty-Four* is not a contrived high-technology world but instead a World War II-era rotting London with dilapidated nineteenth century buildings, their windows broken and covered with cardboard, insufficient heat, and strictly rationed food. Living conditions are miserable for everyone but the elite. The reason is the war, which does not progress or decrease but continues forever. Because most industry is working toward the war effort, the citizens of Oceania receive few benefits from their work. The proletariat is occupied but is never able to gain even the simplest of luxuries. Citizens are utterly dependent on the small scraps the Party gives them. The "proles" are always wanting, and they are successfully held in a position of servitude and powerlessness.

Orwell did not write *Nineteen Eighty-Four* as a prophecy of that date. It was a warning and an effort to attract people's attention to the atrocities of their own governmental bodies, and the title date was chosen as a partial inversion of 1948, during which he was writing the novel. Orwell knew that most of the people who would read his book would still be alive in 1984. The ideas in this book are overwhelming and incredibly powerful. Although it may not deserve its acclaim as being a masterwork in literature, the novel is a creative effort in leading people to question the power structures and motives behind their governments, war, and economic class distinctions.

"Critical Evaluation" by Beaird Glover

Further Reading

Bloom, Harold, ed. *George Orwell's "1984."* Updated ed. New York: Chelsea House, 2007. Collection of essays providing numerous interpretations of the novel, including discussions of "Newspeak," the demonic world of Oceania, and the novel's depiction of totalitarianism.

Bowker, Gordon. *Inside George Orwell*. New York: Palgrave Macmillan, 2003. Presents the "human face" of Orwell, describing his inner emotional life and its relationship to his political activities and ideas. One of the better books about Orwell to be published in the centenary year of his birth.

Gardner, Averil. *George Orwell*. Boston: Twayne, 1987. Examines Orwell's novels, his longer nonfiction, and his essays for theme, recurrent motifs, and critical response. Includes a chronology, an extended bibliography, and an index.

Hitchens, Christopher. *Why Orwell Matters*. New York: Basic Books, 2002. Hitchens emphasizes Orwell's criticism of Nazism and Stalinism—philosophies he never softened his view of to sell books. Hitchens says Orwell's analysis of those two governmental systems continues to apply in the early twenty-first century.

Hynes, Samuel, ed. *Twentieth Century Interpretations of "1984": A Collection of Critical Essays*. Englewood Cliffs, N.J.: Prentice-Hall, 1971. Offers both favorable and negative criticism and various interpretations from many different critics. Includes reviews, essays, and viewpoints, as well as a letter from Aldous Huxley to Orwell.

Lee, Robert A. *Orwell's Fiction*. Notre Dame, Ind.: University of Notre Dame Press, 1969. A chronicle of the development of Orwell's career as a novelist. Themed sections include Orwell's look at poverty and the stricken individual, social strife, and his apocalyptic vision as expressed in *Nineteen Eighty-Four*.

Meyers, Jeffrey. *Orwell: Wintry Conscience of a Generation*. New York: W. W. Norton, 2000. A well-researched biography that provides a balanced look at Orwell's life and work. Meyers vividly describes the contrast between Orwell the writer and Orwell the man.

Rodden, John, ed. *The Cambridge Companion to George Orwell*. New York: Cambridge University Press, 2007. Collection of essays providing an overview to Orwell's works and literary influence. Bernard Crick's piece, "*Nineteen Eighty-Four*: Context and Controversy," analyzes this novel.

Saunders, Loraine. *The Unsung Artistry of George Orwell: The Novels from "Burmese Days" to "Nineteen Eighty-Four."* Burlington, Vt.: Ashgate, 2008. Saunders reappraises all of Orwell's novels, arguing that novels published in the 1930's deserve as much credit as the subsequent *Animal House* and *Nineteen Eighty-Four*. Analyzes the influences of writer George Gissing and of 1930's politics on Orwell's work and examines his depiction of women.

Williams, Raymond, ed. *George Orwell: A Collection of Critical Essays*. Englewood Cliffs, N.J.: Prentice-Hall, 1974. A chronological arrangement of essays on the development of Orwell's writing. A study not only of Orwell's development over time but also the impact of his work over time, with essays from writers of three generations.

Ninety-two in the Shade

Author: Thomas McGuane (1939-   )
First published: 1973
Type of work: Novel
Type of plot: Comic realism
Time of plot: Late 1960's
Locale: Key West, Florida

Principal characters:
THOMAS SKELTON, who wants to become a skiff guide in Key West
NICHOL DANCE, a rival skiff guide who threatens to kill Skelton
GOLDSBORO SKELTON, Skelton's eccentric grandfather
MIRANDA COLE, Skelton's girlfriend
FARON CARTER, another guide, Dance's occasional partner
SKELTON'S MOTHER
SKELTON'S FATHER

The Story:

Thomas Skelton, having quit college, wants to become a skiff guide at home in Key West, Florida. Upset by the decadence of American culture, Skelton has fallen back on a life of drugs and promiscuity. He has arrived at his ideal occupation only after realizing that there is nothing else he would like to do. Sportfishing, suddenly, is the only job that makes sense to him in an America that prizes excess and waste.

Skelton, however, unexpectedly develops a rivalry with Nichol Dance, another skiff guide from Key Marathon. Dance is upset by Skelton's decision to be a guide, and he warns the young man to steer clear of his territory. Dance feels that Skelton has no business as a fishing guide, but Skelton feels that becoming a guide is his only chance at sanity and a somewhat normal life.

Dance goes to prison for attacking a man and "gives" Skelton his business. He sends his clients, the Rudleighs, out with Skelton. Dance is released from prison because the man he attacked did not die. While Skelton and the Rudleighs are out on their expedition, Dance finds them. He plays a practical joke on Skelton, taking the Rudleighs away as if they have been kidnapped. The joke is also meant to serve as a warning to Skelton not to compete with Dance now that he is free to reclaim his business.

The rivalry between the two men escalates. Skelton burns Dance's boat, and Dance threatens to kill Skelton. Despite knowing that Dance is capable of making good on his threat, Skelton refuses to retreat. He knows that being a skiff guide is the last chance he has of keeping his sanity, and he decides to continue. His girlfriend, father, and grandfather all try to talk Skelton out of competing with Dance. Meanwhile, Dance considers his options: If he kills Skelton, he will go to jail for life. If he does not follow through on his threat and he allows Skelton to guide, his credibility will be lost and he will be left with nothing.

Skelton takes Olie Slatt out fishing, and Dance trails them. Dance boards Skelton's boat, gun in hand. He asks Skelton where he would like to be shot. Calmly and courageously, Skelton—having previously imagined himself in this situation—tells him where to shoot. Dance shoots him in the heart, and Skelton achieves, finally, a weird sense of peace. Dance gives the gun to Slatt and sits down next to Skelton. Slatt beats Dance over the head with the gun until he feels his head turn to jelly. Then, he takes the skiff back in, Skelton and Dance crumpled at his feet.

Critical Evaluation:

Following *The Sporting Club* (1969) and *The Bushwacked Piano* (1971), *Ninety-two in the Shade* catapulted Thomas McGuane to literary stardom and announced his arrival on the larger American cultural scene. Concerned with the themes that McGuane would continue to explore in his fiction, *Ninety-two in the Shade* was especially memorable for its virtuoso language-play and its noirish vision of life in Key West. McGuane wrote and directed a film version of the novel in 1975, marking a departure point in his career. While many of his later books were well received (and, some have argued, he went on to mature as a writer), many critics consider *The Bushwacked Piano* and *Ninety-two in the Shade* to be his finest moments, full of energy and a sense of experimentation.

At times, McGuane channels Ernest Hemingway, the only other writer to write so passionately about Key West. The connection between the two authors does not end there, as McGuane is clearly influenced by Hemingway's style (though he departs from it) and by his deep sense of values.

Hemingway's *To Have and Have Not* (1937), one of his most underappreciated and neglected works, is one of the sources for McGuane's feverish vision of life at the bottom of the continental United States. *Ninety-two in the Shade*, like *To Have and Have Not*, is a study of American decay. The protagonist of *To Have and Have Not*, Harry Morgan, is an outlaw-hero who overcomes material poverty by demonstrating a wealth of spirit through his resourcefulness, self-reliance, self-command, and endurance. Thomas Skelton is, in a way, an updated version of Harry Morgan that better reflects his era, the late 1960's.

While Morgan was resourceful and self-reliant, Skelton's malaise represents a culture that has not learned its lesson. America has wallowed in the glories of excess, and Skelton's spiritual emptiness signifies the death of the human being who lives by a code. Having wallowed in excess himself, having wandered around in search of his true calling, Skelton understands that a return to routine and ritual is his only chance at sanity. He wants to leave behind the hollowness of the promiscuous life he has been leading and return to the brutal reality of "real" life.

Like Hemingway, McGuane is deeply concerned with relationships between fathers and sons. *Ninety-two in the Shade* finds three generations of Skelton men in various states of disarray and decrepitude. Like Richard Gordon in *To Have and Have Not*, Goldsboro Skelton, Thomas's grandfather, comes to represent despotism and blind thirst for power. Like his son, Skelton's father has rejected Goldsboro and the rest of the world, but he has only been able to cope by remaining bedridden behind mosquito netting, watching television and playing the violin. He has instilled in his son a sense of failure, a sense that the only thing to do is to fade quietly away as the world unravels.

Skelton may come off as a frivolous slacker, but he understands that he must ignore the deterioration and decay that he witnesses daily if he is to keep sane. He also, like the lowliest of Hemingway heroes, has a careful code that does not involve kowtowing to swank yuppies such as the Rudleighs. All around him, Skelton sees excess. Tourists gorge themselves. Banks squash working people. What once must have been a peaceful island is destroyed by the shattering presence of military and civilian aircraft. Skelton is disgusted. If McGuane is deeply influenced by Hemingway, he also has quite a bit in common with Hunter S. Thompson, a documenter of American greed and excess. In *Fear and Loathing in Las Vegas: A Savage Journey to the Heart of the American Dream* (1972), Thompson relies on the same sort of sensitivity to the dark realities of depraved America.

At the center of *Ninety-two in the Shade* is a deep sense

that competition is to blame for America's decadence and depravity. A generation that has been raised to believe that in order to win one must compete has reacted strongly against "healthy competition" as a birthright. Skelton's father, for instance, is considered a failure and a lunatic for refusing to compete in a country that he believes has lost its way. Similarly, Raoul Duke, the protagonist of *Fear and Loathing in Las Vegas*, is hell-bent on exposing the cracks in the façade of competition.

Skelton, trying to keep his sanity in a different way than Duke, cannot avoid competition and so generates the bloody conflict that serves as the novel's backbone. Nichol Dance challenges Skelton every step of the way. The novel, at times, resembles a thriller far removed from convention. Competition is the only source of suspense. As such, competition signifies the inability to find a free and peaceful space in the modern world. Skelton, like Duke, realizes that he is living in a ruined world where there will always be someone to challenge him.

The novel is, above all, a satire of American popular culture. In the late 1950's and early 1960's, there was an explosion of advertising, promiscuity, franchises and chain stores, and a twisted sense of business and survival. Along with the fear of being annihilated by a nuclear bomb came the mentality that humanity's time on earth was limited. Decadence has always existed, but nuclear threats and changing values ushered in a generation of spenders and wasters, gorgers and solipsists. McGuane's vision of American greed and excess, like Hunter S. Thompson's, is not compassionate. Stunted vision has done irreparable damage to the human consciousness and to the earth, McGuane seems to be saying repeatedly in different ways. He criticizes superficiality and phoniness, reminding readers always of the dark desire that humans have to compete and succeed at all costs. When Dance shoots Skelton at the end of the book, it is the first moment of true peace for Skelton. He has finally found a way to thwart the world, to escape, and to be free.

William Boyle

Further Reading

Carter, Albert Howard, III. "McGuane's First Three Novels: Games, Fun, Nemesis." *Critique: Studies in Contemporary Fiction* 17, no. 1 (Summer, 1975): 91-104. Reviews *The Sporting Club*, *The Bushwhacked Piano*, and *Ninety-two in the Shade*, focusing on McGuane's utilization of the comedy and sadness inherent in competition.

Grant, J. Kerry. "Apocryphal America: Thomas McGuane's Troubled Republic." *Critique: Studies in Contemporary Fiction* 48, no. 1 (Fall, 2006): 103-111. Argues that McGuane reveals, over the course of nine novels, a deep understanding of America's "sickness." While McGuane's protagonists seek to distance themselves from mainstream American life, Grant says, they cannot fully escape being guided by cultural norms of excess and decadence.

Ingram, David. "Thomas McGuane: Nature, Environmentalism, and the American West." *Journal of American Studies* 29, no. 3 (December, 1995): 423-439. Claims that the most important thing to McGuane—an ardent naturalist and conservationist—is the desire for pristine nature. McGuane's deep concern with the frontier and the American West reveals an interest in the power of nature to separate the wheat from the chaff. Notes that McGuane also recognizes the allure of urban life.

McClintock, James I. "'Unextended Selves and Unformed Visions': Roman Catholicism in Thomas McGuane's Novels." *Renascence: Essays on Values in Literature* 49, no. 2 (Winter, 1997): 139-152. Analyzes the influence of Roman Catholicism in McGuane's work. Argues that McGuane's protagonists are often in the midst of a crisis of faith and in deep need of spiritual redemption. Connects McGuane and Walker Percy, another writer whose Roman Catholic vision informed his portrayal of a spiritually sick America in the latter half of the twentieth century.

Morris, Gregory L. "How Ambivalence Won the West: Thomas McGuane and the Fiction of the New West." *Critique: Studies in Contemporary Fiction* 32, no. 3 (Spring, 1991): 180-189. Examines McGuane's representation of the "new West." Talks about the deep spirit of the American West that informs McGuane's fiction, redefining the sense of space and place.

Wallace, Jon. "The Language Plot in Thomas McGuane's *Ninety-two in the Shade*." *Critique: Studies in Contemporary Fiction* 29, no. 2 (Winter, 1988): 111-120. Examines McGuane's use of language in *Ninety-two in the Shade*, paying particular attention to shifts in point of view from third person to second person to first person and how these shifts reflect the spiritual malaise of American life.

Westrum, Dexter. *Thomas McGuane*. Boston: Twayne, 1991. Brief biographical study of McGuane's life and career, followed by several critical essays on his most important work. Includes bibliographical references and an index.

No Exit

Author: Jean-Paul Sartre (1905-1980)
First produced: Huis clos, 1944; first published, 1945 (English translation, 1946)
Type of work: Drama
Type of plot: Existentialism
Time of plot: Twentieth century
Locale: Hell

Principal characters:
VALET, escort for new guests
JOSEPH GARCIN, a newspaper reporter
ESTELLE, a young, attractive socialite
INEZ, a post office clerk

The Story:

Joseph Garcin, a South American newspaper reporter, is ushered into a drawing room by a mysterious Valet. The drawing room itself is decorated with ponderous nineteenth century furniture, and on the mantle stands a massive bronze statue. There are three couches in the room, one blue, one green, and one burgundy. The Valet, who shows him into the room, answers Garcin's many questions cryptically.

It soon becomes evident that both Garcin and the Valet know that they are in a place far removed from the ordinary world. The room is in Hell. Garcin is dead and has recently arrived in the netherworld. The former reporter tells the amused Valet that Hell is nothing like it is supposed to be. There are no hot fires nor instruments of torture. There is only this boring room, with its heavy furnishings and huge bronze sculpture. There are no windows, no mirrors, and no switch to turn off the bright lights or the relentless heat.

Garcin notices how the Valet never blinks. Garcin surmises that in Hell eyes never close and no one ever sleeps. Garcin tries to move the sculpture on the mantle, but fails. He notices a button to press for calling the Valet, but is told that the bell works only some of the time. He asks the Valet the reason why there is a paper knife (the kind used to open envelopes or to separate pages in a book) but receives only a shrug in reply. Finally, bored by the servant's taunting indifference, he lets the Valet leave, but then, nervously, tries the call button. Although Garcin cannot hear it ring, the Valet abruptly returns. With him comes another person, a rather drably dressed, plain woman named Inez. The Valet once more departs.

Inez immediately assumes that Garcin must be her torturer. He reassures her that he is no such person and tries to make polite conversation, but Inez replies testily that she does not believe in good manners. Although they take separate positions in the room, Garcin's facial expressions begin to bother Inez. They sit in silence, he on the blue sofa, she on the burgundy one, until once again the door opens.

Now the Valet leads in a third guest: Estelle, a pretty, young, well-dressed socialite. Estelle hides her eyes with her hands, afraid that Garcin is someone she knows from her time on Earth—someone whose face had somehow been destroyed. When Garcin assures her that he is someone other than this faceless man, she uncovers her eyes and observes how much the room reminds her of her old Aunt Mary's ugly home. Estelle is wearing a pale blue dress, so she begs Garcin to let her sit on the blue sofa instead of the remaining green one. Inez offers hers and flatteringly tells Estelle that she wishes she might have been able to welcome her with a bouquet of flowers, but Estelle takes Garcin's blue couch, and Garcin moves to the green.

The Valet leaves. Garcin tries to remove his coat, but Estelle is appalled at such informality, asking Inez if she approves of men in shirtsleeves. Inez replies that she does not care much for men one way or the other. The three begin to speculate as to why they were placed together in this room and speak of the possible reasons each had been sent to Hell. Estelle said that although she had been married she had run off with another man. Garcin said he, during wartime, had worked for a pacifist newspaper. Inez mocks Estelle's excuses about infidelity and Garcin's story about his unpopularity. She says she now understands that they have been placed together because they will torture one another simply by being there.

To prevent this, Garcin decides they should stay on their separate couches and just sit there, in silence—this way, no one can hurt the others. Still, after a time, Inez cannot help singing to herself, and Estelle, upset that her handbag mirror has been taken from her, complains that she cannot put on her makeup. Garcin remains quiet, but Estelle and Inez talk; Inez convinces Estelle to come over to her sofa, where she will act as Estelle's mirror. Now Estelle, with Inez's guidance, puts on her lipstick. Then Inez admits that she is attracted to Estelle, who is shocked and returns to her own sofa. Estelle tells Inez that she would have preferred Garcin to notice her.

Garcin hears their conversation but resists speaking. Now Inez exhorts him to talk, adding that it is better to choose one's own hell than to try to avoid the inevitable. Exasperated, he joins Estelle and begins to kiss her, but he is haunted by images of his wife who, still alive, had suffered from Garcin's mean behavior. Inez recognizes that his cruelty to his wife had brought him here, just as her betrayal of her cousin, whose wife she had slept with, had landed her in Hell. The two confront Estelle, who unwillingly confesses that she had not only deceived her husband but also murdered the illegitimate child she had with her lover. As they reveal their horrific acts, the images of the real world begin to disappear. They are now really dead—forgotten by the living, alone in a room.

Finally the combined irritation, guilt, and anger in the room make each character unleash the wild rage within. The characters' bitterness and hatred make it impossible for them to find any peace. Inez's scornful and scorned presence makes it impossible for Estelle and Garcin to make love. Garcin's masculine presence makes it impossible for Inez to find happiness with Estelle. Estelle's presence will forever drive a wedge between Inez and Garcin. Garcin vainly tries to open the locked door to the room. Then, suddenly, the door opens and the three face the possibility of leaving. However, they do not leave—the heat and the uncertainty of what lay beyond the part of Hell they know frightens them more than the room. They close the door.

The three attempt yet again to make their time in Hell more reasonable, but the frustration of each having the other two there becomes more than they can bear. When Garcin pushes Estelle away from him because he cannot stand letting Inez watch them together, Estelle takes the paper knife and tries to stab Inez. Inez does not die. She merely laughs uproariously because, she reminds them, they are already dead. There is never any chance of leaving their awful, eternal agony. They discover that Hell is other people.

Critical Evaluation:

Jean-Paul Sartre, professor, philosopher, and author, was internationally known as an existential writer and thinker. His many works explore how the individual is free to act and how such freedom of choice, in an otherwise meaningless universe, can be overwhelming and frightening. In France, Sartre was a leading novelist, having written *La Nausée* (1938; *Nausea*, 1949) and *L'Âge de raison* (1945; *The Age of Reason*, 1947), and a playwright, with such credits as *Les Mouches* (pr., pb. 1943; *The Flies*, 1946) and *La Putain respecteuse* (pr., pb. 1946; *The Respectful Prostitute*, 1947). He also wrote a number of philosophical works devoted to existentialism; his most famous book on the subject, *L'Être et le néant* (1943; *Being and Nothingness*, 1956), was published one year before *No Exit* made its stage debut. In 1964,

Sartre's scorn for elitism led him to refuse a Nobel Prize in Literature.

No Exit was written and first produced late in World War II, when France was occupied by Germany. The play therefore had to pass the Nazi censors, who read all scripts that were performed in the private theaters of Paris during the Occupation. Although there is nothing in the play that explicitly challenges German rule, audiences in 1944 regarded *No Exit* as subtly subversive.

For example, Garcin makes references to prewar pacifists, who at the time would have been thought of as collaborators. The three condemned souls repeatedly speak of whoever is in charge of Hell using the pronoun "they," which the French used to refer to the Germans. Moreover, life in Paris during the Occupation, like life in Sartre's drawing-room Hell, was at a standstill. Beyond these, there are perhaps other minor, less conscious references that audiences, rather than the playwright, discovered. Philosopher-writer Simone de Beauvoir recounted that in the novel, when the Valet ushers Garcin into the room, he tells the new arrival that they have all the electricity and heat they want; this passage made wartime audiences, faced with all kinds of shortages, laugh loudly. *No Exit*, like its author, was identified with the anti-German Resistance and was so successful that after Paris was liberated, the play continued running through the next season.

In part because its author was associated with the Resistance, *No Exit* initially received mixed reviews. Theater critics who collaborated or sympathized with the Germans complained that it was an immoral piece of writing. The crimes committed by Garcin, Inez, and Estelle are serious. During the Occupation, many were outraged by Sartre's frank depiction of such criminal acts. Moreover, Inez's lesbian identity was extremely controversial. Although many collaborationist critics condemned *No Exit* and called for its removal from the stage, some reviewers who disagreed with Sartre's political views could not help but praise the brilliance of his concept.

The play has also been viewed as a dramatization of Sartre's existentialist views. Hell for these three people is not a place where torture is assigned them; rather, it is embodied in their inability to alter their lives through choice. As the name of the play implies, there is no exit from the claustrophobic world in which they have been entombed. Nothing will ever change for them, and nothing they can do can ever make things better. This utter lack of freedom, Sartre implies, is for human beings the ultimate dead end—an existential Hell.

Kenneth Krauss

Further Reading

Bradby, David. *Modern French Drama, 1940-1990*. 2d ed. New York: Cambridge University Press, 1991. Looks at Sartre's career and locates *No Exit* as part of Sartre's early period. Presents a significant view of how the dramatist came to regard his own work later in his life.

Champigny, Robert. *Sartre and Drama*. Birmingham, Ala.: French Literature Publications, 1982. An evaluation of Sartre's role as a dramatist that takes the beginnings and end of his career into account. An interesting and comprehensive discussion that features an expansive examination of *No Exit*.

Cohn, Ruby. *From Desire to Godot: Pocket Theater of Postwar Paris*. Berkeley: University of California Press, 1987. An illuminating look at the original production of *No Exit* and how critics and audiences during the German occupation of France responded. A lively, fascinating interpretation emerges, complete with important details of subsequent productions.

McCall, Dorothy. *The Theatre of Jean-Paul Sartre*. New York: Columbia University Press, 1969. Although somewhat dated, this analysis of how the playwright's works relate to his views on theater still makes for highly informative reading.

O'Donohoe, Benedict. "Myth-Making: *Bariona: Ou, Le Fils du tonnerre, Les Mouches, Huis clos*." In *Sartre's Theatre: Acts for Life*. New York: Peter Lang, 2005. Reappraises Sartre's plays, including *No Exit*, drawing on his writings about philosophy, literature, and criticism. Situates each play in relation to Sartre's intellectual evolution and its broader historical context. Provides a survey of the journalistic and academic reception for each play.

Rowley, Hazel. *Tête-à-Tête: Simone de Beauvoir and Jean-Paul Sartre*. New York: HarperCollins, 2005. Rowley chronicles the relationship between the two French writers, discussing their writing, their politics, their philosophical legacy, and their commitment to each other. Includes bibliography and index.

Sartre, Jean-Paul. *Sartre on Theater*. Edited by Michel Contat and Michel Rybalka. Translated by Frank Jellinek. New York: Pantheon Books, 1976. In this collection of the playwright's own writings on his plays, the editors compile some pieces that deal directly with *No Exit* and several others that discuss Sartre's views on drama and theater during the time the play was written and performed.

Solomon, Robert C. "No Way Out There: Sartre's *No Exit* and 'Being-for-Others.'" In *Dark Feelings, Grim Thoughts: Experience and Reflection in Camus and Sartre*. New York: Oxford University Press, 2006. Examines Sartre's pre-1950 works, including *No Exit*, to highlight what is especially interesting and valuable in his philosophy and to compare it with the philosophy of Albert Camus. Concludes that both men were fundamentally moralists and one must understand their political commitments in order to understand their philosophies.

No-No Boy

Author: John Okada (1923-1971)
First published: 1957
Type of work: Novel
Type of plot: Historical realism
Time of plot: Shortly after World War II
Locale: Seattle, Washington

Principal characters:
ICHIRO YAMADA, a Japanese American "no-no boy"
KENJI, his friend and a World War II veteran
MRS. YAMADA, his mother
MR. YAMADA, his father
TARO, his brother

The Story:

Ichiro Yamada, a twenty-five-year-old Japanese American, is a "no-no boy" during World War II: That is, he refuses to serve in the U.S. armed forces if drafted and to swear unqualified allegiance to the United States. As a result, he spends two years in federal prison. After being released from prison, he returns home to Seattle to live with his mother and father. Like all Japanese immigrants and Japanese American citizens, the Yamadas had been forced to spend the war years in American internment camps; only those who were drafted into or joined the armed services were spared the relocation camps. Ichiro's refusal to fight for his country was his protest against this unjust treatment of Japanese Americans. His mother, who speaks very little English and who considers herself Japanese, even though she has lived in the United

States for thirty-five years, is proud of Ichiro for going to prison. However, Taro, Ichiro's younger brother, detests him for not serving. Ichiro himself has conflicted feelings about his decision.

After Ichiro returns to Seattle, he meets a former friend, Eto, who had fought in the war. When he learns that Ichiro was a no-no boy, Eto spits on him. Ichiro visits the University of Washington, where he had been an engineering student before the war. He wants to return to school, but he feels that he has forfeited the right to do so. Ichiro then meets Kenji Kanno, his good friend from his university days. Though he shares Ichiro's anger about the internment camps, Kenji had chosen to fight in the war. He is a hero and had lost a leg in battle; his wound has not completely healed and his health is deteriorating. Ichiro envies Kenji and wishes he could change places with him. Kenji respects Ichiro for having followed his conscience and gone to prison.

Bull, a Japanese American friend of Kenji, insults Ichiro; later, two of Taro's friends assault Ichiro. Kenji takes Ichiro to meet his girlfriend, Emi. She is married to one of Kenji's Japanese American friends in the U.S. Army, but he has left her. Ichiro and Emi have a brief affair, with Kenji's knowledge; she knows that Kenji is dying. She encourages Ichiro to put his past behind him and not feel despondent.

Ichiro observes many examples of racial prejudice among all ethnic groups. Hatred and bigotry are everywhere, but there also are many good people, among them Mr. Carrick. He is a white man who has many Japanese American friends and is ashamed of his country for its mistreatment of Japanese American citizens during the war. He offers Ichiro a job, but Ichiro decides not to accept it. Mr. Carrick's kindness gives Ichiro reason to hope that he might be able to resume a normal life.

Kenji's condition grows worse, and he is hospitalized. When Ichiro visits him, Kenji is angry and depressed. He argues that the "melting pot" does not exist; ethnic strife dominates American life. He urges Ichiro to forget that he is Japanese American and to leave Seattle. Kenji dies in the hospital and is buried in a section of the community graveyard set aside for Japanese Americans. Ichiro returns from the funeral to find that his mother has committed suicide. He feels pity for her, but he still blames her for having tried to make him a Japanese rather than an American. Ichiro finds his weak-willed father in an alcoholic stupor.

Ichiro meets up with Freddie, a fellow no-no boy with a hot temper. Ichiro visits Emi again, who informs him that she is getting a divorce. They go dancing. Ichiro begins to feel less depressed and more hopeful about the future. A Mr. Morris offers him a job at the Christian Rehabilitation Cen-

ter, and Ichiro considers taking it. Another no-no boy, Gary, who works there, relates that he had been harassed by Japanese American veterans at a former job; an African American friend had often defended him against the taunters. Gary eventually is able to make peace with himself, and he starts a new life as an artist. The conversation with Gary gives Ichiro further hope that he can renew his life.

Freddie remains filled with self-hatred and is unpredictable. When he and Ichiro go to a bar, they run into Bull again. Bull and Freddie get into a fight, and Ichiro tries to break it up. Bull chases Freddie to his car, and Freddie wildly speeds off; he loses control and dies in the crash. Ichiro is upset by the tragic incident, but his experiences with caring people such as Kenji, Emi, Mr. Carrick, and Gary allow him to face the future with hope for himself and his country.

Critical Evaluation:

A second-generation, or Nisei, Japanese American, John Okada was born and raised in Seattle, where he attended the University of Washington. Shortly after the Japanese bombed Pearl Harbor, President Franklin D. Roosevelt signed Executive Order 9066, which required that all Japanese noncitizen immigrants and Japanese American citizens be relocated to internment camps, where they were forced to remain for the duration of the war. Despite being imprisoned in their own country, Japanese American men also were subject to the military draft. Thousands of young Japanese Americans enlisted or were drafted into the U.S. armed forces, and many gave their lives defending the country that had unjustly imprisoned their relatives and friends. Outraged by the great injustice perpetrated against them, some Japanese Americans refused to serve in the armed forces and to swear allegiance to the United States; they were labeled "no-no boys."

First published in 1957, Okada's first novel, *No-No Boy*, was virtually ignored. A second novel, about the Issei, or first-generation Japanese Americans, remained unfinished at his death in 1971. Because no one seemed interested in Okada's fiction at the time, his wife burned the manuscript. However, there was indeed growing interest in Okada's work. During the 1960's and early 1970's, Asian Americans, like members of other American racial and ethnic minority groups, became increasingly interested in their ethnic heritage and in the literary works that reflected and preserved that heritage. As a result of this increasing interest, *No-No Boy* was reissued by the University of Washington Press in 1976. Since then it has been widely read and is now generally regarded as a classic of Japanese American literature.

No-No Boy is based on fact, but it is not an autobiographical novel. Okada himself was not a no-no boy; he served in the Army in World War II as an interpreter in the Pacific theater. As Okada explains in the preface to the novel, Ichiro is modeled on a friend of Okada who refused to enter the Army unless the government would release his parents from an internment camp. Like the character Kenji, Okada understood and respected his no-no boy friend for making his hard decision, a decision that, as is emphasized throughout *No-No Boy*, could bring scorn and even violence from intolerant individuals both inside and outside the Japanese American community. Instead of writing about his personal experiences serving in the war, Okada chose to document the moral issues and turbulent emotions related to the no-no boy experience, which had never before been explored in literature.

Okada does not dwell on life in the internment camps or in prison, however. The action of the novel begins after Ichiro has been released from incarceration. There are backward glances at camp and prison life, but the bulk of the narrative centers on Ichiro's attempts to resolve his conflicted feelings about his refusal to serve in the Army and about his cultural identity.

The great African American writer W. E. B. Du Bois once stated that African Americans always feel their "twoness," knowing they are both African and American. These two culturally different identities, Du Bois asserted, were ever at war in the individual. Du Bois's observations apply as well to the protagonists of many American ethnic novels, including Ichiro. Ichiro's two selves—his Japanese and American cultural identities—are at war with each other at the start of the narrative. His strong-willed mother never assimilated into American society, and she does not want her sons to assimilate either. Ichiro was born in the United States, however, and was educated in its schools; he therefore feels little connection with traditional Japanese culture. After the Japanese attack on Pearl Harbor, the U.S. government and many "white" Americans treated all Japanese Americans as if they were aliens. It is this that causes the deep psychological conflict in Ichiro: He feels American but his country considers him Japanese. He therefore exists in a cultural no-man's-land at the beginning of the novel.

By the end of the novel, Ichiro's "twoness" is resolved when he reaffirms his faith in America and forgives his country for the great injustice it dealt to Japanese Americans. Ichiro's renewed faith in America is not absolute, however; he has witnessed too much bigotry and injustice to have a naïve view of American race relations. However, the many good people whom he meets during his journey to self-knowledge—Kenji, Emi, Carrick, and others—save him from sliding into pessimism and despair. He comes to believe that America is like a bruised apple: "Not rotten in the center where it counts, but rotten in spots underneath the skin."

No-No Boy has been criticized for rejecting the Japanese half of Japanese American identity. The novel contains few positive images of Japanese culture or traditions. Ichiro's mother, the primary representative of Japanese culture, is portrayed as an oppressive force from which Ichiro must liberate himself. Thus, where many ethnic writers celebrate the traditional culture and resolve the "twoness" problem by fusing the ethnic with the American identity, Okada seems to endorse cultural assimilation. Okada's depreciation of Japanese culture, however, must be examined in historical context. *No-No Boy* was written in the 1950's, before the "ethnic revival" of the 1960's. Moreover, though Japan was officially an ally of the United States, anti-Japanese feelings still ran high in the 1950's; and the Korean War (1950-1955) fueled anti-Asian feeling in general. It is therefore not surprising that Okada would emphasize the "Americanness" of Japanese Americans.

Technically, *No-No Boy* is quite conventional. The novel is constructed of a series of scenes and dialogues in which Ichiro is exposed to different ideas and points of view, each of which leads him to new insights and self-awareness. Okada seemed primarily interested in dramatizing the moral dilemma and psychological conflicts that Japanese Americans experienced during and after World War II. Increasing numbers of readers testify that he succeeded in his aim.

Lawrence J. Oliver

Further Reading

Chen, Fu-jen. "The Cultural Mirroring In-Between Two Symbolics: A Lacanian Reading of John Okada's *No-No Boy*." In *On the Road to Baghdad: Or, Traveling Biculturalism, Theorizing a Bicultural Approach to Contemporary World Fiction*, edited by Gönül Pultar. Washington, D.C.: New Academia, 2005. Uses the theories of psychiatrist and literary critic Jacques Lacan to examine how Okada's novel depicts the biculturalism of its Japanese Americans characters.

Chu, Patricia P. "America in the Heart: Political Desire in Younghill Kang, Carlos Bulosan, Milton Murayama, and John Okada." In *Assimilating Asians: Gendered Strategies of Authorship in Asian America*. Durham, N.C.: Duke University Press, 2000. Examines how Okada in *No-No Boy* and three other Asian American writers adapted the Anglo-American bildungsroman to examine issues of Asian American identity.

Cutter, Martha J. "Finding a 'Home' in Translation: John

Okada's *No-No Boy* and Cynthia Kadohata's *The Floating World*." In *Lost and Found in Translation: Contemporary Ethnic American Writing and the Politics of Language Diversity*. Chapel Hill: University of North Carolina Press, 2005. Examines how both novels depict the rupture between Japanese Americans and other Americans that resulted from the Japanese American internment during World War II.

Kim, Elaine H. *Asian American Literature: An Introduction to the Writings and Their Social Context*. Philadelphia: Temple University Press, 1982. An excellent study of Asian American literature, which contains a sound analysis of *No-No Boy* that emphasizes the disintegrating influence of racism on the Japanese American community and psyche.

Ling, Jinqi. "*No-No Boy* by John Okada." In *A Resource Guide to Asian American Literature*, edited by Sau-ling Cynthia Wong and Stephen H. Sumida. New York: Mod-

ern Language Association of America, 2001. Provides a biographical sketch of Okada and discussion of the novel's major themes, critical issues, and historical context, as well as bibliographies of primary and secondary works.

Sato, Gayle K. Fujita. "Momotaro's Exile: John Okada's *No-No Boy*." In *Reading the Literatures of Asian America*, edited by Shirley Geok-lin Lim and Amy Ling. Philadelphia: Temple University Press, 1992. Draws on the Japanese mythic tale "Momotaro" in arguing that *No-No Boy* affirms Japanese American identity by rejecting everything Japanese. Concludes that Japanese culture is portrayed almost entirely in negative terms.

Yeh, William. "To Belong or Not to Belong: The Liminality of John Okada's *No-No-Boy*." *Amerasia Journal* 19, no. 1 (1993): 121-134. Argues that both the novel's central character and historical context represent a state of "betweenness."

No Trifling with Love

Author: Alfred de Musset (1810-1857)
First produced: On ne badine pac avec l'amour, 1861; first published, 1834 (English translation, 1890)
Type of work: Drama
Type of plot: Tragicomedy
Time of plot: Nineteenth century
Locale: France

Principal characters:
THE BARON, a French nobleman
PERDICAN, his son
CAMILLE, his niece
ROSETTE, Camille's foster sister
MAÎTRE BLAZIUS, Perdican's tutor
MAÎTRE BRIDAINE, a village priest

The Story:

Maître Blazius, with his three chins and round stomach, is proudly awaiting the arrival of Perdican, whom he tutored. Perdican recently received a doctorate at Paris, and Maître Blazius feels that the credit is due to his tutoring. Gulping a huge bowl of wine presented by the chorus of listening peasants, he announces that Camille, niece of the Baron, is also expected home from the convent. The Baron is anxious to see his son Perdican married to Camille; he knows they have been in love since childhood.

Dame Pluche, Camille's chaperon, arrives out of breath. After drinking some vinegar and water, she announces that Camille is on her way. She tells of Camille's education in the best convent in France and of the inheritance she is to get that day from her mother's estate. She does not mention the projected marriage.

The Baron brings Maître Bridaine to the house. Since he expects the marriage to take place that day, he wants the priest to perform the ceremony. To impress Camille, he arranges with Maître Bridaine to speak some Latin to Perdican at dinner; no matter if neither one understands it. Maître Bridaine is agreeable to the plan, but he is hostile at once to Maître Blazius, for he smells wine on his breath.

When Perdican and Camille meet, something seems amiss. Perdican wants to embrace his pretty cousin, but Camille speaks formally to her childhood sweetheart and refuses a kiss. She is chiefly interested in looking at a portrait of her great-aunt, who was a nun. At dinner, the two priests, Maître Bridaine and Maître Blazius, vie jealously with each other. Both are gourmets as well as gourmands, and they are apprehensive that there is no place for two priests in the luxurious household. After dinner, Camille again refuses a friendly talk with Perdican and even excuses herself from walking in the garden. The Baron, upset at her coldness, grows even more indignant when Dame Pluche upholds Camille in her refusals. Perdican, with relief, renews his acquaintance with Rosette, a pretty peasant who was Camille's foster sister.

Maître Blazius, attempting to discredit his rival, tells the Baron that Maître Bridaine drank three bottles of wine at dinner and is now walking about on unsteady feet. The Baron can scarcely listen because Maître Blazius's breath is so strong. Maître Bridaine hurries up to tell the Baron that Perdican is walking with Rosette on his arm and throwing pebbles about wildly.

Perdican is puzzled by Camille's coldness toward him. When Maître Blazius reminds him that the marriage is a project dear to the Baron's heart, the young man is willing to try again, but Camille is resolute. She will not let him hold her hand and refuses to talk to him about their childhood. She came back only to receive her inheritance; the next day, she will return to the convent. After Perdican leaves her, Camille asks the scandalized Dame Pluche to take a note to him.

Maître Bridaine is very unhappy. His rival is seated next to the Baron at mealtime, and Maître Blazius takes all the choice morsels before he passes on the serving plate. In despair, Maître Bridaine feels that he will be forced to give up his frequent visits; although the prospect is repugnant, he will devote his time to parish work. On a friendly walk, Rosette complains to Perdican that women are kissed on the forehead or the cheek by their male relatives and on the lips by their lovers; everyone kisses her on the cheek. Perdican is happy to give her a lover's kiss.

Dame Pluche is angry, but she takes the note to Perdican. On the way, she is spied on by Maître Blazius, who reports to the Baron that Camille undoubtedly has a secret correspondent. Since Perdican now is romancing a woman who watches the turkeys, surely Camille is looking for a more satisfactory husband.

Invited to meet Camille at the fountain, Perdican finds his cousin changed. She willingly kisses him and promises to remain a good friend. Then she frankly asks Perdican if he has mistresses. Embarrassed, he admits that he does. When she wants to know where his latest is, Perdican had to admit he does not know. Camille, acquainted with no men except Perdican, loved him until recently, when an older nun at the convent changed her inclinations.

The nun was rich and beautiful and much in love with her husband. After he took a mistress, she took a lover. At last, she retired to a convent. Her experience convinces Camille that men are always unfaithful. She forces Perdican to admit

that if they were married both of them might be expected to take other lovers. Perdican valiantly defends earthly love, saying that it is worth all the trouble it causes, and that most of the two hundred nuns at the convent probably would be glad to go back to their husbands and lovers. At last, seeing the futility of his argument, he tells Camille to return to the nunnery.

Meanwhile, Maître Blazius is unhappy because the servants report that he is stealing bottles of wine. In addition, the Baron decides that he made up the story of Camille's secret correspondent. Disgusted with his second priest, the Baron dismisses him. Not knowing that Maître Bridaine has fallen from favor, too, Maître Blazius asks him to intercede with the Baron. Maître Bridaine refuses; he thinks the Baron will now reinstate him to favor.

Maître Blazius thinks he sees a chance to regain lost ground when he meets Dame Pluche carrying a letter. While he is trying to take the missive from her by force, Perdican arrives on the scene, takes the letter, and reads it out of curiosity. It is from Camille to a nun at the convent. In it, Camille says she will soon be back; Perdican is hurt and his pride wounded, just as they foresaw. Perdican thinks the letter means that the whole affair with Camille was arranged in advance at the convent, and he resolves to spite her by courting Rosette seriously.

After writing a note to Camille to arrange a rendezvous, he brings Rosette to the fountain. Camille, hiding behind a tree, hears Perdican offer his heart to Rosette. As proof of his love, he gives her a chain to wear around her neck and throws a ring Camille gave him into the water. Camille retrieves the ring and tells Rosette to hide behind a curtain while she talks with Perdican. During the interview, he confesses that he loves Camille. Camille then throws aside the curtain; Rosette faints. Perdican decides to go ahead with his marriage to the peasant.

The Baron, told of his son's intention to marry Rosette, is angry. In spite of his father's displeasure, Perdican makes arrangements for the ceremony. Camille, in despair, throws herself down before an altar and prays for help. Perdican comes in unexpectedly, and, unnerved by her distress, clasps her in his arms while they confess their love for each other. Suddenly they hear a cry behind the altar. Investigating, they find Rosette dead. Camille is the first to realize their guilt in her death. To acknowledge that guilt, she says a final good-bye to Perdican.

Critical Evaluation:

Alfred de Musset did not write his plays for the stage; he used the dramatic form rather as a vehicle for lyric expression. *No Trifling with Love*, reflecting the writer's love affair with George Sand, is a romantic defense of love; considered only as stage drama, it has serious weaknesses. The chorus of peasants is a cumbersome device and extraordinary characters are mingled helter-skelter. The two priests are buffoons, Camille is very stubborn, and Rosette dies in an unconvincing manner.

This piece was classified by Musset as a comedy, but it may better be called a tragicomedy. Earlier examples of the genre include William Shakespeare's *The Merchant of Venice* (pr. c. 1596-1597, pb. 1600). A tragicomedy often includes events associated with tragedy, such as a death of a central character or a grievous situation that is not resolved at the end. The comedic elements of a tragicomedy include jokes and humor, an ending that resolves most or all of the bad situations, and a sense of providence rather than fate. Musset's approach is to dramatize the tragic overtones with comic action: He develops a comedy and resolves it with tragedy.

Most of the action of *No Trifling with Love* is time-honored material for sentimental, romantic, or even cynical comedy. A charming hero and a beautiful heroine, both high-born, go through the dramatic motions of alternately reaching toward and then rejecting each other, while their pride, vanity, and wit entertain the audience through various intrigues and counterintrigues. In the process of Musset's play, however, the pawn and plaything of their intrigues, a common and impressionable woman, kills herself. Perdican offers a pathetic justification to God: "We are two senseless children, but our hearts are pure." For Musset and for the audience, this is not sufficient: Love is not to be so trifled with. Camille, at least, has the moral fortitude to accept her responsibility for the catastrophe and to renounce the glib Perdican.

What is most interesting about this play is Musset's subtly drawn examination of love. In the first act, his theme appears to be a commonplace one—love is complex and unpredictable. It is not subject to the precise expectations and course of development calculated in advance by the Baron, a man so orderly that he knows to the minute how old his son and niece are and manages to stage their return, after ten years of absence, at the exact same moment from opposite doors. When things subsequently do not go as he expects, his whole world turns upside down, and he is utterly unable to account for the discrepancy between his planning and human behavior.

In the second act, the theme deepens as Musset turns to an examination of the value of love itself. Camille, who will accept nothing less than an ideal and eternal love, wants desperately to love, but she does not want to suffer. Love always causes suffering and misery, her nuns have assured her; since

it involves so much deceit, capriciousness, and betrayal, is it not better to avoid the problem entirely by withdrawing from the world into a cloister, where the maimed and disabled from the battlefields of love can minister to one another? Contrasted to this is Perdican's more realistic view that love—fickle, temporary, cruel, and imperfect as it is—is nevertheless a part of life and, as such, must be faced and experienced, not avoided.

One is reminded of John Milton, who could not "praise a fugitive and cloistered virtue, unexercised and unbreathed that never sallies out and sees her adversary, but slinks out of the race." One must not slink out of the race by becoming a nun, Musset suggests; choosing to run the race, one should run it honestly, without pride or intrigue, and, above all, not at the expense of other people.

Further Reading

Affron, Charles. *A Stage for Poets: Studies in the Theater of Hugo and Musset*. Princeton, N.J.: Princeton University Press, 1971. Extensive analysis of *No Trifling with Love* is included in a volume of essays examining the works of two important French dramatists. Discusses the diction of the play and Musset's handling of the problem of time.

Beus, Yifen Tsau. "Alfred de Musset's Romantic Irony." *Nineteenth Century French Studies* 31, no. 3 (Spring/Summer, 2003): 197-209. Focuses on the irony in Musset's dramatic works, discussing their depictions of love and their juxtaposition of comic and sarcastic attitudes.

Brookner, Anita. "Alfred de Musset: Enfant du siècle." In *Romanticism and Its Discontents*. New York: Farrar, Straus and Giroux, 2000. Examines the works of Musset and other French Romantic writers and artists. Argues that the Romantics created an imaginary world in order to attain fulfillment in the aftermath of the French Revolution and Napoleon I's defeat at Waterloo.

Gochberg, Herbert S. *Stage of Dreams: The Dramatic Art of Alfred de Musset (1828-1834)*. Geneva: Librairie Droz, 1967. Devotes a chapter to analysis of the play considered to be Musset's "last theatrical forum for his obsession with dream and reality." Discusses the playwright's handling of the question of love.

Rees, Margaret A. *Alfred de Musset*. New York: Twayne, 1971. Concentrates on the characterization of heroes and heroines in *No Trifling with Love*, noting how the playwright contrasts the complex Camille with the admirable but befuddled Perdican to achieve his sober ending.

Sices, David. *Theater of Solitude: The Drama of Alfred de Musset*. Hanover, N.H.: University Press of New England, 1974. One chapter examines the weaknesses of *No*

Trifling with Love, but concludes it is a successful endeavor. Sices maintains that this play best demonstrates "the author's obsession with time and its treachery."

Tilley, Arthur. *Three French Dramatists: Racine, Marivaux, Musset*. New York: Russell & Russell, 1967. Discusses the influence of Pierre Carlet de Chamblain de Marivaux and William Shakespeare on *No Trifling with Love* and some of Musset's other plays. Comments on Musset's handling of the element of the fantastic.

Wakefield, David. *The French Romantics: Literature and the Visual Arts, 1800-1840*. London: Chaucer, 2007. Wakefield's study of the French Romantic movement devotes a chapter to Musset, discussing his ideas about literature and art and his influence on painting.

The Normal Heart

Author: Larry Kramer (1935-   )
First produced: 1985; first published, 1985
Type of work: Drama
Type of plot: Problem play
Time of plot: Early 1980's
Locale: New York City

Principal characters:
NED WEEKS, an AIDS activist
BRUCE NILES, Ned's friend and rival
BEN WEEKS, Ned's brother
FELIX TURNER, Ned's lover
DR. EMMA BROOKNER, a physician
THE EXAMINING DOCTOR, Emma's enemy
HIRAM KEEBLER, the mayor's assistant
TOMMY BOATWRIGHT and MICKEY MARCUS, volunteers

The Story:

Ned Weeks visits Dr. Emma Brookner's office because he is interested in writing a journalistic story about a strange, new disease called acquired immunodeficiency syndrome, or AIDS. This disease is responsible for the symptoms experienced by two of Ned's gay associates. While Ned has a physical exam, Emma tells him what she knows about the disease: It has already killed some of her patients, it seems to strike gay men, and the press has not paid much attention to it. She tells Ned that he should get the word out and urge gay men to stop having sex; she thinks the disease might be transmitted though sex.

Ned visits Felix Turner's desk at *The New York Times* because he wants him to inform the public about the disease by writing about it. The request makes Felix uncomfortable; he is gay, but is not open about his sexual orientation. Ned also visits his brother, Ben, hoping that Ben's law firm will support an organization Ned had helped to start, an organization intended to raise money and provide information about AIDS.

Felix and Ned have their first date at Ned's apartment, where Ned compares the press's lack of interest in AIDS to its lack of interest in Adolf Hitler's extermination of the Jews during World War II. Felix and Ned become lovers.

Several members of Ned's AIDS organization meet. Bruce Niles is appointed president of the organization, although Ned is clearly interested in the office. When the members learn about Felix, Ned's new boyfriend, Tommy Boatwright is disappointed because he is romantically interested in Ned; Bruce Niles is relieved because Ned had made unwanted advances toward him.

Ned visits his brother's law office again. This time he wants to see if Ben would serve on the organization's board of directors. Ben declines, and the brothers part angrily.

Ned discusses his frustrations about the AIDS organization with Felix. The organization's board of directors thinks Ned is creating a panic about the disease and using the disease to make himself into a celebrity. Felix reveals to Ned that he has a purple lesion, one of the symptoms of AIDS, on his foot. Ned meets with Emma, who once again tells him that gay men must be told to stop having sex—to stop the spread of AIDS. Ned tells her that Felix is sick and she agrees to see him the next day.

Although New York City government officials agree to meet with officials of Ned's AIDS organization, the mayor's assistant, Hiram Keebler, is two hours late in keeping the appointment. The mayor of New York refuses to help give the organization office space, press the national government to fund research on the disease, or insist that *The New York Times* cover the disease. Ned becomes angry about the city's slow response to AIDS and verbally attacks Hiram, while

Bruce tries to be diplomatic. Ned criticizes Bruce for being such a weak leader.

Emma tells Felix that he has an early case of AIDS, and she explains to him how she will care for him. She cannot answer Felix's questions about whether or not the disease could infect Ned.

Volunteers of the organization are busy answering hotline phones. The list of gay men who have died from AIDS has grown, yet Mickey Marcus and others are angry with Ned's argument that gays should stop having sex. Mickey becomes worried that he might lose his job at the City Department of Health because the gay men's organization has been putting pressure on the mayor's office. Exhausted and angry, he attacks what he considers to be Ned's regressive ideas about gay men's sexuality. Bruce tells Ned that Bruce's lover, Albert, has died of AIDS.

Emma becomes angry with the Examining Doctor after learning that the federal government has allotted only five million dollars for AIDS research, a small sum compared to what the government is capable of funding, and that her own funding for research has been denied.

Ned pickets the mayor's office and hears that the mayor finally will meet with members of the organization. Then Bruce reads Ned a letter stating that the board of directors wants Ned to quit the organization he had cofounded. Wishing to remain in the organization, Ned delivers a passionate speech about how gay culture must be recognized for something besides sex.

Felix is very ill and depressed; he refuses to eat. Ned, who had been trying to reason with and care for Felix, finally gets angry with his lover. He throws food on the floor. After fighting, the two embrace.

Felix and Ben meet for the first time. Ben helps Felix make out a will leaving everything, including a piece of land, to Ned. With Ben present, Emma marries Ned and Felix before Felix dies. Ned and Ben are reconciled.

Critical Evaluation:

The Normal Heart was one of the first stage productions to deal with AIDS. After publishing the novel *Faggots* (1978), which many critics considered an offensive account of the promiscuous sex lives of gay men, Larry Kramer's timely and angry play *The Normal Heart*, which urged gay men to stop having sex, earned critical approval and a number of awards. As much a period piece documenting the rampant spread of AIDS in the early 1980's as it is a dramatic work of high artistic merit, *The Normal Heart* is partially autobiographical. In 1981, Kramer, like his character Ned Weeks, cofounded an organization to raise money and care for men

with AIDS, the Gay Men's Health Crisis. In 1983, Kramer, like his character, was ousted after a meeting with New York City's mayor, Ed Koch. Although critics take umbrage with what they have described as the play's banal script, melodramatic action, and overuse of facts and statistics, *The Normal Heart* is important as an educational tool capable of spurring people to action.

Besides candidly presenting the early outbreak of AIDS and the slow response of the government, media, and the medical establishment, the play also depicts the gay community, and it does so without relying on stereotypes. Although Kramer acknowledges that some gays do frequent bath houses some of the time and that some gays behave as flamboyantly and sexually as does the character Tommy Boatwright, he also depicts relationships between gay men that are based on commitment and caring. "The only way we'll have real pride," Ned says, "is when we demand recognition of a culture that isn't just sexual." One of the themes of the play, in fact, focuses on love, not just sex, between gay men. As the play's epigraph, stanzas from a poem by W. H. Auden, suggests, everyone wants "Not universal love/ But to be loved alone." This is a normal desire felt by those bearers of "the normal heart," heterosexuals and homosexuals alike.

The Normal Heart is not a subtle play. Kramer's frustration and anger about the disease killing off a whole community comes through loud and clear. His characters are angry, especially Ned, who screams, literally, at almost everyone with whom he comes in contact. Ned is rude and overbearing. The play is also notable for its graphic depiction of AIDS symptoms—the purple lesions on one character's face and another's foot, the convulsions experienced by another patient—and for its descriptions of incontinence, cancers, and general weakness. Kramer was interested in publicizing the epidemic that had been hidden for too long.

This is Ned's play, written from his point of view. He dominates all of the scenes except the three in which he does not appear. Of these, two focus on Felix, Ned's lover. The first portrays Felix when he is told by a doctor that he has AIDS; in this scene, Emma is unable to answer his questions about contagion and possible treatments. In the second scene, Felix puts his legal affairs in order before his death. Both scenes are matter-of-fact and unemotional, brief sketches of the medical and legal details thousands of persons with AIDS must negotiate each day.

The third scene in which Ned does not appear portrays Emma and the Examining Doctor, a character who personifies the medical establishment. Like Ned, Emma not only understands the horror of AIDS but also knows that to fight the epidemic she must get angry at those who have power, even if it means losing her temper, as she does in this scene. Her hurling of folders and papers into space is echoed two scenes later by Ned when he throws food on the floor.

The play ends with Ben Weeks embracing his brother, Ned. Ned and Ben finally reconcile their differences after Felix's death. Not only does this embrace unite feuding family members and suggest that Ben now accepts Ned as a healthy equal; it also depicts heterosexuals embracing gays.

Cassandra Kircher

Further Reading

Gilbey, Liz. "Being What We Are." *Plays International* 9, no. 2 (October, 1993): 14-15. Discusses *The Destiny of Me* (1992), Kramer's sequel to *The Normal Heart*. In *The Destiny of Me*, Ned Weeks, also the main character in *The Normal Heart*, reflects on his life and family.

Kramer, Larry. "AIDS Movies: A Swelling Chorus." Interview by Maria Maggenti. *Interview* 23, no. 4 (April, 1993): 112. A brief but pointed interview with Kramer in which he talks about the problems he had getting *The Normal Heart* produced. For an early review of *The Normal Heart*, see *The New York Times Book Review*, January 4, 1979.

_____. "An Interview with Larry Kramer." Interview by L. A. Winokur. *The Progressive*, June, 1994. An interview with Kramer in which he criticizes coverage of AIDS by *The New York Times* and speaks about Barbara Streisand's film version of *The Normal Heart*.

_____. "Kramer vs. Kramer." Interview by Michael Shnayerson. *Vanity Fair*, October, 1992. A portrait of Kramer and his work. Discusses Kramer's relationship to his family and friends and to the organizations that he helped to found—Gay Men's Health Crisis and AIDS Coalition to Unleash Power, or ACT UP.

_____. "Larry Kramer." Interview by Victor Zonana. *The Advocate*, December 1, 1992. Extensive magazine interview with Kramer about cultural, political, and medical establishments in the United States. Mentions both *The Normal Heart* and its sequel, *The Destiny of Me*. The second part of the interview, focusing more on personal issues in Kramer's life, such as his own health since being diagnosed as HIV-positive, was published in the December 15, 1992, issue of *The Advocate*.

Long, Thomas L. "Larry Kramer and the American Jeremiad." In *AIDS and American Apocalypticism: The Cultural Semiotics of an Epidemic*. Albany: State University of New York Press, 2005. Christian fundamentalists and others characterized the epidemic of acquired immunodeficiency syndrome (AIDS) as an apocalyptic plague, punishment for gay people's sins and a sign of the end of the world. Long describes how Kramer and other AIDS activists appropriated this apocalyptic imagery to spread awareness of AIDS and gain public support to treat the disease.

Mass, Lawrence D., et al., eds. *We Must Love One Another or Die: The Life and Legacies of Larry Kramer*. New York: St. Martin's Press, 1997. Collection of essays about Kramer, including "Larry Versus Larry: The Making of a Writer" by Mass, and discussions of Kramer and gay theater, his theatrical voices and audiences, and "The Abnormal Talent: Larry Kramer's Electro-Shock Treatment for the World Theater" by David Willinger.

North and South

Author: Elizabeth Bishop (1911-1979)
First published: 1946
Type of work: Poetry

North and South, Elizabeth Bishop's first book of poems, is full of waking up and the sea. There are poems set in Paris, others in rural Florida. Some characters are human, some animals, still others are surreal. Poems like "The Man-Moth," "Roosters," and "The Fish" stand powerfully on their own, displaying the mastery that elevated Bishop to the status of a major American poet of the twentieth century. *North and* *South* as a whole expresses the young Bishop's effort to attune her craft to the world she was encountering.

Although Bishop, unlike other poets of her time, did not use her poems to confess her personal life, the longing and sorrow in them is formidable. Loss characterized her earliest years. Eight months after her birth, her father died suddenly. Five years later, after several breakdowns, Bishop's mother became permanently insane, and Bishop never saw her again. The child lived alternately with family in Massachusetts and Nova Scotia. Illness, especially asthma, kept her from attending school regularly, but she entered Vassar in 1930 and graduated in 1934, the year that the well-known poet Marianne Moore befriended her and the year Bishop's mother died. During the decade that Bishop worked on the poems that constitute *North and South*, she lived in New York City and traveled in France and other European countries, and after 1937 (in the hope of relieving her asthma) wintered in Florida.

The first third of *North and South* conveys a sense of starting out and tentativeness. The speaker in the initial poem, "The Map," contemplates much of the Northern Hemisphere and at first playfully considers whether the land "lean[s] down to lift the sea from under." A cautious note sounds when place names run across nearby features, reminding the poet that sometimes "emotion too far exceeds its cause." "The Imaginary Iceberg" emphasizes longing for the fantastical—a condition in which one can feel "artlessly rhetorical" and "rise on finest ropes/ that airy twists of snow provide." "The Gentleman of Shalott" portrays a character content to be incomplete, even indefinite.

One element of Bishop's uncertainty is artistic. She organizes several of her poems around conceits—witty, extended metaphors. She demonstrates in "Wading at Wellfleet" that a single image—in this case, the flashing chariot wheels that depict the awesome movement of the sea—can be inadequate. In the final lines, the immensity of the water makes "the wheels/ give way; they will not bear the weight." Another element is emotional. Anxiety pervades "Chemin de Fer" from the "pounding heart" of the second line to the hermit's shotgun blast and the challenge he screams, "Love should be put into action!" A similar intimidation underlies "From the Country to the City," as the speaker is drawn irresistibly toward a city consisting of mocking images.

Of the three poems that follow, all making city life fearful, "The Man-Moth" has been most appreciated. Inspired by a newspaper misprint of "mammoth," Bishop created a surreal character—half human, half insect—who, ironically, surpasses his human counterpart. "Man" stands passive in the moonlight like an "inverted pin" and seems unable—or unwilling—to comprehend. The Man-Moth, on the other hand, while fearful, "must investigate as high as he can climb." The explanation "what the Man-Moth fears most he must do" characterizes the plight of a number of Bishop's characters. The poem contrasts characters (the first time Bishop does so in *North and South*), but there is no hero to admire. Instead, after the first stanza introduces Man, the next four stanzas

emphasize the Man-Moth's uneasiness. Mistaking the moon for a "small hole at the top of the sky," the Man-Moth scales buildings "fearfully," "his shadow dragging like a photographer's cloth behind him." When he returns underground and boards a subway train, he sits "facing the wrong way" and "travels backward." The ride seems endless. In fact, his life is a nightmare; death rides constantly beside him, and he must resist the temptation of suicide. The oppressiveness of the city, nevertheless, allows for hope. In the final stanza, the reader ("you") has the chance to break the Man-Moth's isolation and share his sorrow. Although the tear that slips from Man-Moth's eye is associated with "the bee's sting," empathy permits one to recognize it as "cool" and "pure enough to drink."

Before Bishop goes to new locales, leaving the city, "The Weed," "The Unbeliever," and "The Monument" reiterate the importance of empathy and provide a symbol of the artistic endeavor. "The Weed" dramatizes the invigorating influence of life upon a "cold heart" prone to isolation. The weed eventually splits the heart, releasing "a flood of water." The spillage into the speaker's eyes permits sight; each drop seems to contain "a small, illuminated scene," suggesting that the river has retained "all/ the scenes that it had once reflected." As jolting as the weed's intrusion has seemed, the possibility of insight seems preferable to the self-protective sleep depicted in "The Unbeliever." Understanding this distinction qualifies one to respond in the affirmative to the question that begins the third poem—"Now can you see the monument?" It turns out to be hard even to describe, and Bishop allows for a mocking response ("It's like a stage-set; it is all so flat!"). She defends the contraption: The very carelessness of its appearance "gives it away as having life, and wishing." Such is the "beginning" of art.

After this assertion of the importance of the artistic impulse, one may expect an outward movement, aesthetically speaking. Bishop's postgraduation trip to Europe in 1935 yielded several poems set in Paris, but there is little sense of expansiveness. An automobile accident cost her friend Margaret Miller the lower part of the arm with which she painted, and the poems have an intensely melancholy air. However, there is also a technical—and perhaps temperamental—advance evident in "Quai d'Orleans." Rather than impose her ideas, for the first time Bishop lets place and occasion suggest her discovery.

A larger change occurred, as the title *North and South* implies, when Bishop experienced Florida. Exotic tropical details expanded the possibilities for her art, just as they had the poetry of her modernist predecessor Wallace Stevens. The final ten poems in *North and South* contain various voices and embrace much more of physical place. In "Florida," for example, Bishop assembles detail after vivid detail—in the way that her mentor Marianne Moore had—to suggest the emotion that holds the poems together. In Florida, Bishop took great interest in the lives of Cubans and blacks. While living in Key West in the house she bought with her lover, Marjorie Stevens, she also observed signs of American industry preparing for World War II. One finds imagery of warfare and battling in several poems in the latter half of *North and South*, but "Roosters" is Bishop's greatest poetic response to militarism. Like so many poems in the book, this one begins at dawn. The clamorous crowing and the repeated use of "gun-metal blue" prepare the reader for the appearance of the birds who gloat "Deep from protruding chests/ in green-gold medals dressed,/ planned to command and terrorize the rest." The birds fight to the death, "with raging heroism defying/ even the sensation of dying." The three-line stanzas and insistent rhymes mock the martial subject but do not reduce the menace.

Such balancing characterizes not only the tone of the poem but also the commentary in the second section. Bishop recalls the rooster's role in Peter's denial of Christ and suggests that one might find hope in the forgiveness that followed. The serene portrayal of the new morning at the end of the poem perhaps confirms that hope. It is perhaps naïve, however, to miss the sarcasm in the question, "How could the night have come to grief?" Part of the greatness of "Roosters" is that, instead of deciding for the reader, it involves the reader in the emotional turmoil brought on by violence. The poem makes the reader part of the violence he or she may claim to abhor.

The other animal poem in *North and South*, "The Fish," has been, as Bishop herself came to resent, often anthologized. Her encounter with the "tremendous fish" may remind one of the shocking effect of the weed liberating the "cold heart"; the hooks and lines "Like medals with their ribbons" hanging from the fish's mouth suggest that the fish is another victim of human violence. In this fine poem, the fisher is moved to empathize with the fish to a degree unusual in Bishop's early work. As in "Florida," Bishop adds image to image to narrate the incident. Many of the details are similes that dramatize the struggle to comprehend the unforgettable fish. The description of his eyes indicates some of the difficulty—and challenge in doing so: "The irises seem backed and packed/ with tarnished tinfoil/ seen through the lenses/ of old scratched isinglass." In addition, they do not "return my stare." This is no romantic bonding with nature. The fish remains "other" and the poet continues to study hard. After she allows that the hardware in the mouth may be a "beard

of wisdom," she is overwhelmed by "victory." Partly, it is her own, having comprehended the immensity of the unlike being; but, in his dignity and survival, the fish shares the triumph.

"Anaphora," the concluding poem, harkens back not only to the many poems that recount awaking and the day's beginning but also to the euphoria of setting out in "The Map." In rhetoric, anaphora refers to figures of repetition and renewal. It can also denote the moment in Christian worship that the Eucharistic elements are offered as an oblation. "Anaphora" describes—commemorates and celebrates are better words— the passage of the days, and Bishop skillfully repeats sounds and words and extends repetition to the structure of the poem—two fourteen-line stanzas—their rhymes and thought-patterns reminding one of shrunken sonnets. Morning's "wonder" becomes "mortal/ mortal fatigue," but the poem ends hopefully, the beggar's fire providing "endless/ endless assent."

The publication of *North and South* in 1946 finally assured Bishop that she was a poet, that years of preparation, hard work, and doubt had not been wasted. That the book— nominated by Marianne Moore—had triumphed over eight hundred other entries for the Houghton Mifflin Prize alerted the literary world of an important new presence. Bishop's next book would win a Pulitzer Prize. Poet Robert Lowell's admiring response would begin Bishop's second close friendship with a writer of her own stature. Within five years, she interrupted her voyage around South America. Ill from an allergic reaction, she stopped in Brazil and remained there almost two decades with her lover, architect-designer Lota de Macedo Soares, and continuing the enlargement of her poetry's embrace of the world around her.

Jay Paul

Further Reading

Ellis, Jonathan. *Art and Memory in the Work of Elizabeth Bishop.* Burlington, Vt.: Ashgate, 2006. Ellis argues that scholars should more closely scrutinize the relationship between Bishop's art and life. His analysis of her work demonstrates how she used the events of her life to create her poetry.

Fountain, Gary, and Peter Brazeau. *Remembering Elizabeth Bishop: An Oral Biography.* Amherst: University of Massachusetts Press, 1994. Bishop's life is told through interviews with more than 120 relatives, friends, colleagues, and students and through information based on extensive research in her published and unpublished writings.

Harrison, Victoria. *Elizabeth Bishop's Poetics of Intimacy.*

New York: Cambridge University Press, 1993. Harrison studies the evolution of Bishop's poems as vehicles for expression. Chapter 2 discusses intimacy and romance; chapter 3 emphasizes the effect of events, particularly World War II, on Bishop's imagination. Includes extensive notes, bibliography, and index.

Kalstone, David. *Becoming a Poet: Elizabeth Bishop with Marianne Moore and Robert Lowell*. New York: Farrar, Straus & Giroux, 1989. Reprint. Ann Arbor: University of Michigan Press, 2001. A probing study of Bishop's complex friendship with Marianne Moore, which coincided with the making of the poems of *North and South*. Includes notes and index.

Lombardi, Marilyn May, ed. *Elizabeth Bishop: The Geography of Gender*. Charlottesville: University Press of Virginia, 1993. Collection of essays focusing on Bishop's sexual politics and her representation of gender.

Parker, Robert Dale. *The Unbeliever: The Poetry of Elizabeth Bishop*. Champaign: University of Illinois Press, 1988. Studies the wishful nature of *North and South*—the anxiousness behind Bishop's poems, as well as her readiness to look outside herself for subjects. Includes notes and index.

Stevenson, Anne. *Elizabeth Bishop*. Boston: Twayne, 1966. One of the best starting points for studying Bishop's life and work. Outlines the period relevant to *North and South* and examines several poems. Contains helpful primary and secondary bibliographies, notes, and index.

Travisano, Thomas. *Elizabeth Bishop: Her Artistic Development*. Charlottesville: University Press of Virginia, 1988. Relates *North and South* to two phases in Bishop's work—"enclosure" and "history." Provides detailed but understandable interpretations of many poems. Offers an illuminating explanation of Bishop's interest in Surrealism and the Baroque. Includes notes, primary and secondary bibliographies, and index.

Walker, Cheryl. *God and Elizabeth Bishop: Meditations on Religion and Poetry*. New York: Palgrave Macmillan, 2005. Walker examines Bishop's poetry to understand the poet's relationship with God and religion.

North and South

Author: Elizabeth Gaskell (1810-1865)
First published: 1854-1855
Type of work: Novel
Type of plot: Social realism
Time of plot: Mid-nineteenth century
Locale: England

Principal characters:
MARGARET HALE
THE REVEREND RICHARD HALE, her father
MARIA HALE, her mother
FREDERICK HALE, her brother, a sailor in exile
DIXON, the Hales's family servant
JOHN THORNTON, an industrialist
MRS. THORNTON, his mother
FANNY THORNTON, his sister
EDITH SHAW LENNOX, Margaret's cousin, a London socialite
HENRY LENNOX, her brother-in-law, a suitor to Margaret
NICHOLAS HIGGINS, a factory worker
BESSIE HIGGINS, his daughter
MR. BELL, a property owner, Oxford tutor, and godfather to Frederick

The Story:

Margaret Hale is living with her aunt Shaw and her cousin, Edith, in London. The Shaws move in upper-class society, as does Captain Lennox, Edith's fiancé, and Henry Lennox, his brother, an attorney. After Edith's wedding, Margaret returns to her parents' sheltered home, the vicarage of Helstone, a small village in the south of England. She is surprised by two events: the visit of Henry Lennox to propose marriage and the resignation of her father from the Church of England because of theological doubts. She refuses Lennox, however good his prospects, because she hardly knows him. The resignation means the family will have to move. Mr. Hale was offered a tutoring job in Milton Northern by Mr. Bell, his former Oxford professor, who owns property there. They have never lived in the north of England, let alone in an industrial city. Mr. Hale asks Margaret to break the news to her mother, who is distraught.

With the family servant, Dixon, they move to a rented house and meet John Thornton, a factory owner and leaseholder of Mr. Bell. Thornton is to be one of Margaret's father's students. She is offended by his brusque manner and cannot understand why a self-made industrialist should want to study classical languages. Margaret manages to adapt to a city life very different from that of London, as does Dixon. Her mother, however, withdraws into herself, finally suffering a breakdown. Margaret gets to know Bessie Higgins, a factory worker, and through her Nicholas Higgins, her father. She visits their home and tries to support Bessie, ill with an industrial disease of the lungs. Bessie is fearful her father either will become an alcoholic or get overinvolved in trade union agitation. Margaret introduces Nicholas to her father and the two men discuss both industrial and religious matters, coming to like each other.

Margaret is also introduced to the Thornton household, an austere family ruled over by Mrs. Thornton. Her weak daughter, Fanny, stands in great contrast to John, whose tough-minded dealings with his workers bring him into conflict with Margaret. Mr. Hale, as an outsider, could see both sides in the impending industrial dispute. When this dispute breaks out, Margaret finds herself physically between the two parties, protecting John Thornton when strikers threaten him. John feels she compromised her honor in doing this and so believes he ought to propose marriage. Margaret angrily rejects him; the feelings of both to each other are very ambivalent at this stage, ranging from admiration to bitterness. Mrs. Thornton is angry over Margaret's rejection.

Both Bessie and Maria Hale die soon after. Margaret is persuaded to send for her brother, Frederick, who had previously fled to Spain after a naval mutiny. He manages to return secretly just before his mother dies, but in escaping Milton Northern, he is spotted with Margaret by a railway worker. A scuffle ensues in which the worker is accidentally killed. John Thornton, as local magistrate, investigates the death. When asking Margaret for evidence, he is met with less than the truth. He believes Margaret has a lover and yet finds it difficult to credit her with such dishonorable behavior, even though his mother does not. Margaret becomes deeply ashamed of her behavior, and the rift between Margaret and John is now at its widest.

Margaret continues to visit Higgins and also the Bou-chers, an indigent worker's family now left fatherless by his suicide. Her father visits Mr. Bell at Oxford and suddenly dies there. Margaret, in mourning, is persuaded to return to London to nurse Edith, expecting her first child. While there she pursues the possibility of obtaining a pardon for Frederick, but this proves impossible. Mr. Bell suggests she visit him in Oxford. While on the way, she revisits Helstone, but after Milton Northern it seems very backward and uninviting. Mr. Bell gives her news about Thornton: A recession is hitting him hard. Margaret is stirred deeply by talk of him. Shortly after her return to London, Mr. Bell dies, too, and Margaret becomes the beneficiary of his property—she is now, in fact, Thornton's landlord. He comes to financial ruin through the strike and overinvesting at a time of recession. Tables are now turned.

Margaret is completely unable to settle back to the fashionable life of London, and is much happier when engaged in social action, visiting the poorer parts of the city, although this is much frowned on. Through Henry Lennox's legal work she meets Thornton again and discovers he had had a change of heart over the way his workers should be treated. He, too, discovers his misunderstanding over Frederick. Margaret now offers to refinance him. Both at last admit to themselves they love one another. Thornton proposes marriage once again.

Critical Evaluation:

North and South belongs to a group of novels written in the mid-nineteenth century often called the Condition of England novels, or more generally, industrial novels. Society as a whole was trying to come to terms with the rapid industrialization and urbanization of Great Britain, the first country to experience such development. Elizabeth Gaskell belongs to a group of novelists committed to exposing the social conditions brought about by the Industrial Revolution, and to suggesting ways to go forward and to oppose wrong values and policies. Other novelists of this group include Charles Dickens, Benjamin Disraeli, and Charles Kingsley.

Gaskell lived much of her life in Manchester, married to a Unitarian minister. She therefore experienced at first hand the living and working conditions of both rich and poor, workers and masters, and had seen the dire results of economic slumps and industrial disputes. She described these conditions in an earlier novel, *Mary Barton* (1848), which is very sympathetic to the working classes, especially her proletarian heroine, Mary. At times, however, it is melodramatic. In *North and South*, Gaskell takes a more balanced view and explores the strengths and weaknesses of both sides, allows a good deal more dialogue, and introduces intelligent outsiders (the Hales) who can be relatively impartial. The novel goes at a slower pace, therefore, but its credibility is strengthened, except for such incidents as those involving Frederick.

At a more general level, the novel may also be placed in the category of the provincial novel. This category includes novels that do not take London (or any capital city) as the cultural norm and that explore regional ways of life, speech, values and beliefs in a serious way. Gaskell is a provincial novelist through and through.

The title harkens back to Disraeli's metaphor of the two nations. He saw Britain divided sharply between rich and poor. His politics sought ways of reconstituting a single nation. Gaskell suggests the gap between the north and the south is equally wide, but avoids seeking a solution in politics. Instead, she points toward mutual understanding and intermingling through personal relationships. The marriage of the dynamic, self-made industrialist, Thornton, to Margaret, who stems from the rural home counties and fashionable London, symbolizes this. At the end of the novel, a circle leading back to London is completed to show how much Margaret has changed. She has embraced northern ways of openness and energy, and rejected the artificiality of the capital.

Part of this openness-artificiality dialectic is conveyed through the Victorian theme of what constitutes a gentleman. Thornton is stung by Margaret's accusation at one point that he has not acted as a gentleman. Gaskell wished to redefine the concept of the gentleman in terms of inner qualities of sympathy. Industrialists must move away from their own self-images as masters, self-images that are reinforced by the workers. Thornton manages to make the transition. In addition, ironically, Thornton fails financially through trying to do the right thing (invest in a new plant and improve conditions of work). Margaret's wealth is unearned. Gaskell's plot demonstrates that men need women, and that women can have and should have responsible financial power to invest in a better society. Women have a readier sympathy to face the suffering and plight of the workers and their families, and for them, this is part of the remaking of society. Men concentrate too much on profit and power alone.

Margaret Hale, however, is more than a symbol for Gaskell's wider purposes. She is developed as a complex heroine, expanding traditional gender roles. She has to take over much of the financial decision making from her father. She moves independently into the masculine Milton society, becoming involved in upper-class as well as working-class homes and in a strike. She is contrasted to the effete Edith and Fanny, and stands between the domineering Mrs. Thornton

and the helpless Mrs. Hale as the ideal Victorian woman for Gaskell.

Gaskell's style, however, does not allow for careful psychological portrayal. Her descriptions, dialogue, and narrative are realistic, but without show. They do not draw attention to themselves, and avoid not only the melodramatic but also the symbolic. She can embrace, realistically, a wide variety of speech and locale and can tackle the affairs of the day. An analysis of her style demonstrates real depth, careful arrangement of detail, and subtle insights into observed human behavior.

Gaskell refuses both high-flown rhetoric and agendas. Her beliefs, born out by her style, lie in quiet, low-key acts of reconciliation and sympathy that bring human beings together in creative relationships for the good of society as a whole.

David Barratt

Further Reading

Craik, W. A. *Elizabeth Gaskell and the English Provincial Novel*. New York: Harper & Row, 1975. A major rehabilitation of Gaskell as an important novelist, this study sets five of her novels within the provincial novel tradition. Demonstrates how she expanded the possibilities and universality of the tradition.

Duthie, Enid. *The Themes of Elizabeth Gaskell*. New York: Macmillan, 1980. Despite contrasting settings and plots, Duthie argues that there is a unity of thematic material in all of Gaskell's fiction. Draws upon Gaskell's letters to reconstruct her imaginative world and the themes central to it.

Foster, Shirley. *Elizabeth Gaskell: A Literary Life*. New York: Palgrave, 2002. This accessible introduction to the author relies on the best available biographies. It offers interesting comparisons of Gaskell's novels with others of the period and emphasizes women's issues as addressed by Gaskell.

Gerin, Winifred. *Elizabeth Gaskell*. New York: Oxford University Press, 1976. The first biography to make use of the publication in 1966 of Gaskell's letters. Although there have been a number of later biographies, this remains one of the best, particularly from the point of view of relating fictional material to its background.

Hughes, Linda K., and Michael Lund. *Victorian Publishing and Mrs. Gaskell's Work*. Charlottesville: University Press of Virginia, 1999. Places Gaskell's writing in the context of the Victorian era, describing how she negotiated her way through the publishing world by producing work that defied the conventions of her times but was also commercially successful. *North and South* is discussed in chapter 4.

Nash, Julie. *Servants and Paternalism in the Works of Maria Edgeworth and Elizabeth Gaskell.* Burlington, Vt.: Ashgate, 2007. Examines the servant characters in Gaskell's stories and novels, including *North and South,* to show how her nostalgia for a traditional ruling class conflicted with her interest in radical new ideas about social equality.

Stoneman, Patsy. *Elizabeth Gaskell.* 2d ed. New York: Manchester University Press, 2006. This feminist reading claims that previous accounts of Gaskell have seriously misread her, and that the interaction of class and gender must be made central. A condensed but provocative reading of *North and South* is included.

Uglow, Jenny. *Elizabeth Gaskell: A Habit of Stories.* Winchester, Mass.: Faber & Faber, 1993. The chapter on *North and South* expounds the novel fully. A full listing of Mrs. Gaskell's works and an index.

North of Boston

Author: Robert Frost (1874-1963)
First published: 1914
Type of work: Poetry

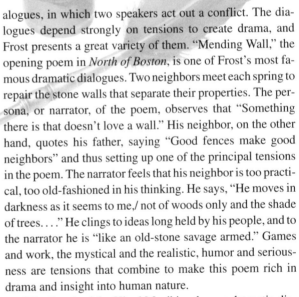

Like his first book, *A Boy's Will* (1913), Robert Frost's second, *North of Boston,* was first published in England. Despite that irony, it was, and remains, the book that connects the name Robert Frost with America's New England.

Frost began writing poetry in the 1890's while running a small farm in Derry, New Hampshire, but he found few publications that would accept his work. By the time he took his family to England in 1912, he had published a handful of poems in magazines and newspapers. He was a virtually unknown poet approaching the age of forty.

Frost was, and still is, seen as a poet on the fringe of the modernist movement from the 1910's through the 1930's. While others experimented with free verse, jazz rhythms, fragmentation, and other nontraditional methods, Frost chose to stick with conventions such as rhyme and meter. His own experiments had to do with the nuances of human speech organized along a poetic line. Frost theorized that it was possible to understand a sentence's "sound of sense" even if the listener-reader could not make out the individual words spoken. Consequently, his poems sound like talk one might hear between two people—that is, everyday conversation—but talk of uncommon wit and intelligence. Some of the finest examples of that talk appear in the poems of *North of Boston. A Boy's Will* presented a speaker who had moved away from the world of people and was observing from a distance. *North of Boston,* however, is Frost's "book of people."

Most of the poems in this volume are dramatic monologues, in which one speaker narrates a story, or dramatic dialogues, in which two speakers act out a conflict. The dialogues depend strongly on tensions to create drama, and Frost presents a great variety of them. "Mending Wall," the opening poem in *North of Boston,* is one of Frost's most famous dramatic dialogues. Two neighbors meet each spring to repair the stone walls that separate their properties. The persona, or narrator, of the poem, observes that "Something there is that doesn't love a wall." His neighbor, on the other hand, quotes his father, saying "Good fences make good neighbors" and thus setting up one of the principal tensions in the poem. The narrator feels that his neighbor is too practical, too old-fashioned in his thinking. He says, "He moves in darkness as it seems to me,/ not of woods only and the shade of trees. . . ." He clings to ideas long held by his people, and to the narrator he is "like an old-stone savage armed." Games and work, the mystical and the realistic, humor and seriousness are tensions that combine to make this poem rich in drama and insight into human nature.

"The Death of the Hired Man" is a longer dramatic dialogue that introduces the reader to a husband and wife, Warren and Mary, who have a problem to solve, and two opposing points of view. Silas, a hired hand, has returned to Warren and Mary's farm after having abandoned them to work for someone else at harvest time. Silas is dying. Mary argues for making his last days comfortable and letting bygones be bygones. Warren knows Silas to have a rich brother in a town nearby and wants to send him there.

There is very little action in the story, although the speakers summon up many scenes while talking about the past. Two opposing images form, and the reader is left to choose a side. The use of specific and general language is another source of tension in the poem, as are contrasts of darkness and light, of softness and hardness, and of inside (where Silas sleeps and dies) and outside (where Warren and Mary talk). Each concept is associated with one or the other of the principal characters, but all resolve into a kind of grayness after Silas dies.

Blank verse is Frost's favorite form in *North of Boston*. Blank verse is defined as unrhymed lines of iambic pentameter. (An iamb is a metrical foot of two syllables in which an unstressed syllable is followed by a stressed syllable—for example, the words "about" and "against"; pentameter means there are five feet in the line.) The line "And gave/ him tea/ and tried/ to make/ him smoke" from "The Death of the Hired Man" is regular blank verse. Obviously, not all the lines of a poem are equally regular. Frost was a master at substituting other metrical feet to give his lines variety. Blank verse has been used in English since the sixteenth century, but Frost was influential in establishing it as a twentieth century form.

The poet was also very fond of play in all of its forms, especially word play, which is important for understanding his poems. Metaphors and similes involving games appear often in his poems, as well as in his letters and lectures. "The Mountain" gives good examples of pun, double entendre, contradiction, and other forms of word play. The poem itself provides a clue in the often ignored line "But all the fun's in how you say a thing." From the moment Frost gives the name of the town—Lunenburg, or crazy town—until describing a brook that is "cold in summer, warm in winter," the poem is a runaway ride through a verbal landscape that is the equal of Geoffrey Chaucer and William Shakespeare. Verbal tensions are one element that keeps Frost's poems fresh, for new forms of play and meaning can be found even after many readings.

"Home Burial" is a powerful and moving dialogue between a husband and wife who represent the universal conflict between men and women. Like the previous dialogues, this one too presents limited action, and the poem progresses almost entirely through conversation. The wife, Amy, feels that her unnamed husband is cold and unfeeling because his mourning for the death of their child has ended and his thoughts have returned to everyday things. The husband, who feels that Amy is protracting her anguish, says, "What was it brought you up to think it the thing/ To take your mother-loss of a first child/ So inconsolably—in the face of love." At a time in history when infant mortality is very low,

this might seem harsh and unfeeling. Well into the early years of the twentieth century, however, infant death was a fact of life, and the husband's attitude may be understood to represent the norm, with Amy's grief indeed aberrant for the time. Unlike the situation between Warren and Mary, there seems to be no resolution to the conflict for this couple.

Although Frost's poems can be read as little dramas played out in rural New England, that would be to limit them severely. Nearly all of Frost's characters, settings, and situations can be recognized to be universally true. Names and places and times are merely ways to localize what is ubiquitous and timeless.

For years, critics interpreted the madness and decay in Frost's poems as his comment on the disintegration of the New England society he knew. He was making no such comment; rather, he was being simply honest about the characters he portrayed. If there is madness, he seems to say, it is universal.

In the monologue "A Servant to Servants," the speaker is a woman taking time out from her endless domestic duties to talk to people camping on her land. Her talk begins with local matters but quickly turns to other concerns, specifically her own mental health and a history of insanity in her family. It is a dark, distinctly human story.

> My father's brother, he went mad quite young.
> Some thought he had been bitten by a dog,
> . . . .
> But it's more likely he was crossed in love,
> . . . .
> Anyway all he talked about was love.

In the hands of a less skilled poet, much of the material might have turned sentimental. Frost's speaker, however, is poignant, not pitiable. She has a clear notion of who she is despite her failing sanity. She is noble and dignified, as Frost's characters tend to be in the hardscrabble world he witnessed and re-created.

"After Apple Picking" breaks the unrelenting sorrow built by "A Servant to Servants." It is a meditation on work. Unlike the other poems so far discussed, this one is not in blank verse, employing instead lines of varying length that rhyme irregularly. The persona of this poem is exhausted after days, perhaps weeks, of work. Read on this level, the work offers images and insights that are completely satisfying. However, the speaker gives a clue early on that the poem also seeks to universalize the experience. The first two lines read "My long two-pointed ladder's sticking through a tree/ toward heaven still." That the speaker says, "heaven," not sky, is significant. This is a clue that the speaker does not carry the memory—"the pressure of a ladder round"—in his feet from just this harvest but that he is growing old and tired from a long life of harvests. The poem mentions "sleep" or "dreaming" six times (sleep can be read, as it often is in literature, as death). The speaker is worn out by a lifetime of work and looks forward to his well-deserved rest. This is one of Frost's several masterpieces.

"The Code," too, is about work, but this poem examines the unwritten code of conduct between farmers and their hired hands. In a story within the story, a farmer is nearly killed for driving his men too hard. Readers learn that "The hand that knows his business won't be told/ to do work better or faster—those two things."

The penultimate poem in *North of Boston* is "The Wood Pile," a complex poem that appears on the surface, as do many of Frost's poems, to be terribly simple. It is, however, full of tensions between humans and nature, growth and decay, clarity and confusion. The wood pile deep in the woods seems to have been "Cut and split/ and piled" for no reason, but for Frost labor is its own reward. He finds it curious that someone would go to the trouble of cutting wood and piling it neatly only to abandon it, but he also knows the satisfaction of a job well done. The wood pile may appear not to benefit anyone but it benefited the woodsman who did the work. In Frost's world, that is enough.

Frost's reputation continues to grow as critics leave aside the public person he became in his later years to concentrate on the work. In *North of Boston*, Frost presents his narrative voice. This, with his lyrical voice, demonstrates his unusual balance of vision and ear. Both voices broadened and deepened in the course of the succeeding collections of poetry, to meld finally into one note of exquisite clarity.

H. A. Maxson

Further Reading

Brower, Reuben A. *The Poetry of Robert Frost: Constellations of Intentions*. New York: Oxford University Press, 1963. Compares Frost's poems with those of Ralph Waldo Emerson and William Wordsworth. Examines his prosody and themes.

Calder, Alex. "Robert Frost: *North of Boston*." In *A Companion to Twentieth-Century Poetry*, edited by Neil Roberts. Malden, Mass.: Blackwell, 2001. Calder's analysis of the poems in *North of Boston* is included in a collection of essays about twentieth century poetry.

Cramer, Jeffrey S. *Robert Frost Among His Poems: A Literary Companion to the Poet's Own Biographical Contexts and Associations*. Jefferson, N.C.: McFarland, 1996. Cramer places the poems in *North of Boston* within the biographical, historical, and geographical context of Frost's life and provides annotations about other aspects of the poems.

Faggen, Robert. *The Cambridge Introduction to Robert Frost*. New York: Cambridge University Press, 2008. An introductory overview of Frost's life and work. Includes discussion of Frost's use of language, sound, metaphor, and the other elements of his poetry, as well as his interest in science, religion and politics.

_____, ed. *The Cambridge Companion to Robert Frost*. New York: Cambridge University Press, 2001. Collection of essays examining Frost's life and work, including discussions of Frost as a New England poet, his use of meter, versification, and metaphor, and his politics and the Cold War. References to "Mending Wall" and many of the other poems included in *North of Boston* are listed in the index.

Lynen, John F. *The Pastoral Art of Robert Frost*. New Haven, Conn.: Yale University Press, 1960. Important examination of Frost as an artist. Discusses his adaptations of the pastoral for use in modern poetry.

Poirier, Richard. *Robert Frost: The Work of Knowing*. New York: Oxford University Press, 1977. An ardent reexamination and reemphasis of Frost's status as a major poet. Poirier reevaluates many of Frost's standard poems and finds them lacking.

Pritchard, William H. *Frost: A Literary Life Reconsidered*. New York: Oxford University Press, 1984. Examines the life through the poems, providing a balanced, fair appraisal. Shows how inseparable the man and his work were.

Stanlis, Peter J. *Robert Frost: The Poet as Philosopher*. Wilmington, Del.: ISI Books, 2007. Stanlis maintains that Frost believed in a dualism of spirit and matter, and he demonstrates how this philosophy is expressed in the poetry.

Tharpe, Jac, ed. *Frost: Centennial Essays*. 3 vols. Jackson: University Press of Mississippi, 1974-1978. Seventy-six essays on various topics, from analysis and explication to biography.

Northanger Abbey

Author: Jane Austen (1775-1817)
First published: 1818
Type of work: Novel
Type of plot: Domestic realism
Time of plot: Early nineteenth century
Locale: England

Principal characters:
CATHERINE MORLAND, an imaginative reader of gothic
  romances
MRS. ALLEN, her benefactor
ISABELLA THORPE, her friend
JOHN THORPE, Isabella's brother
JAMES MORLAND, Catherine's brother
HENRY TILNEY, a young man whom Catherine admires
GENERAL TILNEY, his father
CAPTAIN TILNEY, his brother
ELEANOR TILNEY, his sister

The Story:

Although a plain girl, Catherine Morland believes she is destined to become a heroine like those in her favorite gothic novels. She might, however, have spent her entire life in Fullerton, the small village in which she was born, had not Mrs. Allen, the wife of a wealthy neighbor, invited her to go to Bath. There a whole new world was opened to Catherine, who was delighted with the social life of the colony. At Bath, she meets Isabella Thorpe, who is more worldly than Catherine and takes it upon herself to instruct Catherine in the ways of society. Isabella also introduces Catherine to her brother, John Thorpe. He and Catherine's brother, James Morland, are friends, and the four young people spend many enjoyable hours together.

Catherine meets Henry Tilney, a young clergyman, and his sister Eleanor, with whom she is anxious to become better acquainted. John thwarts her in this desire, and Isabella and James aide him in deceptions aimed at keeping her away from Henry and Eleanor. After Isabella and James are engaged, Isabella doubles her efforts to interest Catherine in her beloved brother. Although Catherine loves her friend dearly, she cannot extend this love to John, whom she knows in her heart to be an indolent, undesirable young man.

While James is at home arranging for an allowance so that he and Isabella can be married, Henry Tilney's brother, Captain Tilney, appears on the scene. He is as worldly as Isabella and, even more important to her, extremely wealthy. Catherine is a little disturbed by the manner in which Isabella conducts herself with Captain Tilney, but she is too loyal to her friend to suspect her of being unfaithful to James.

Shortly after Captain Tilney arrives in Bath, Catherine is invited by Eleanor Tilney and her father, General Tilney, to visit them at Northanger Abbey, their old country home. Catherine is delighted; she always wanted to visit a real ab-

bey. She quickly writes for and receives a letter of permission from her parents. Henry arouses her imagination with stories of dark passageways and mysterious chests and closets.

When the party arrives at Northanger Abbey, Catherine is surprised and a little frightened to find that the Tilney's descriptions had been so exact. When she hears that Mrs. Tilney died suddenly several years previously, Catherine begins to suspect that the general murdered her. At the first opportunity, she attempts to enter the dead woman's chambers. Henry finds her there and assures her that his mother died a natural death. Catherine is almost disappointed, for this news destroys many of her romantic imaginings about Northanger Abbey.

For more than a week after this event, Catherine worries because she receives no letter from Isabella. When a letter arrives from her brother, James, she learns the reason for Isabella's silence. He wrote that Isabella was engaged to Captain Tilney. Catherine almost becomes ill when she reads the news, and Henry and Eleanor Tilney are as disturbed as she. They know that only greed and ambition drew Isabella from James to their wealthier brother, and they fear for his happiness. They believe, however, that the captain is more experienced with such women and will fare better than had James.

Shortly afterward, Catherine receives a letter from Isabella telling the story in an entirely different light. She pretends that she and James had just had a misunderstanding and begs Catherine to write to James in her behalf. Catherine is not taken in. She wastes no time in sympathy for her onetime friend and believes her brother fortunate to be rid of such a schemer.

A short time later, the general goes to London on business, and Eleanor and Catherine are alone at the abbey. Henry's clerical duties compel him to spend some time in his nearby parish. One night, soon after the general's departure, Eleanor goes to Catherine's room. In a state of great embarrassment and agitation, she tells Catherine that the general returned suddenly from London and ordered Catherine to leave the abbey early the next morning. Because she loves Catherine and does not want to hurt her, Eleanor gives no reason for the order. In great distress, Catherine departs and returns to her home for the first time in many weeks. She and her family try to forget the insult to her, but they cannot help thinking of it constantly. Most of Catherine's thoughts are of Henry, whom she fears she might never see again.

Soon after her return home, Henry calls on her and explains why his father turned against Catherine. When the Tilney family first meet Catherine, John Thorpe tells the general that she is the daughter of a wealthy family and that the Allen money will also be settled on her. He brags because at the time he himself hopes to marry Catherine; when Catherine rebuffs him, and after his sister Isabella is unable to win James again, John spitefully tells the general that Catherine had deceived him. Although she never implied that she is wealthy, the general gives her no chance to defend herself.

After Henry tells his story, he asks Catherine to marry him. Her parents give their consent with the understanding that the young couple must first win over the general. Henry returns home to wait. Eleanor's marriage to a wealthy peer proves an unexpected aid to the lovers. The general is so pleased at having his daughter become a viscountess that he is persuaded to forgive Catherine. When he also learns that the Morland family, though not wealthy, could give Catherine three thousand pounds, he gladly gives his consent to the marriage. In less than a year after they meet and despite many hardships and trials, Catherine Morland marries Henry Tilney with every prospect of happiness and comfort for the rest of her life.

Critical Evaluation:

In all the history of the novel, perhaps no genre can claim more popularity than the gothic novel of the late eighteenth century. The gothic fad, however, was all but over when *Northanger Abbey*, Jane Austen's parody of the gothic novel, was published in 1818, a year after her death. Her delightful mockery had actually been written when such works were at their height of popularity, about 1797-1798. The novel had been sold to a publisher in 1803 but was published posthumously.

In her early twenties at the time of the composition, the young author lived in the quiet rectory where she was born in the Hampshire village of Steventon; her circumstances resembled those of the young heroine of her novel—even to including such amusements as poring over gothic novels. Those persons who have not read Ann Radcliffe's *The Mysteries of Udolpho* (1794), which occupies so much of Catherine Morland's time and thoughts, will find other reasons to enjoy *Northanger Abbey*, but a knowledge of *The Mysteries of Udolpho* or any other gothic novel will bring special rewards.

At one level, *Northanger Abbey* is an amusing parody of gothic novels, with their mysterious castles and abbeys, gloomy villains, incredibly accomplished heroines, sublime landscapes, and supernatural claptrap. Austen's satire is not, however, pointed only at such novels; the romantic sensibility of the gothic enthusiast is also a target. *Northanger Abbey* is a comic study of the ironic discrepancies between the prosaic world in which Catherine lives and the fantastic shapes that her imagination, fed by gothic novels, gives to that world. The author holds up the contrast between the heroine's real situation and the gothic world she fantasizes.

The prevailing irony begins with the first sentence: "No one who had ever seen Catherine Morland in her infancy would have supposed her born to be a heroine." As she grows up, she develops neither the prodigious artistic and intellectual accomplishments nor the requisite beauty necessary for the role. She herself is merely pretty, but once her adventures get underway, she begins to assign stereotyped gothic roles to her new acquaintances. Detecting villainy in General Tilney's haughty demeanor merely because in *The Mysteries of Udolpho* the evil Montoni is haughty, she overlooks the general's real defects of snobbery and materialism, traits that eventually prove far more threatening to her than his hauteur.

Since the central feature of the gothic novel is the sinister, dilapidated castle or abbey, Catherine's most cherished daydreams center on Northanger Abbey and its long, damp passages. In reality, nothing is damp except an ordinary drizzling rain, nor is anything narrow or ruined, the abbey having been thoroughly renovated for modern living. Try as she will, she cannot manufacture genuine gothic horrors. Instead of dark revelations of murder and madness in the Tilney family, she faces self-revelation, her recognition that she has suffered from a delusion in her desire to be frightened.

If the ridicule of gothicism and the exposure of false sensibility compose major themes, another more inclusive theme, common to all Austen's novels, is the problem of limitation. Catherine at age seventeen is "launched into all the difficulties and dangers of six weeks residence at Bath," the fashionable resort, leaving a sheltered life in her village of Fullerton. She immediately discerns, however, a state of artificial confinement as a way of life in Bath.

Catherine began to feel something of disappointment—she was tired of being continually pressed against by people, the generality of whose faces possessed nothing to interest, and with all of whom she was so wholly unacquainted, that she could not relieve the irksomeness of imprisonment by the exchange of a syllable with any of her fellow captives . . . she felt yet more awkwardness of having no party to join, no acquaintance to claim, no gentleman to assist them.

Throughout the novel, Austen continues to develop this initial image of an empty, fashionable routine in which each day brought its regular duties. Catherine romanticizes this reality, her delusions culminating with the delightful invitation to visit the Tilneys at Northanger Abbey. Thus the gothic parody functions also as a study of a common response—escapism—to a society circumscribed by empty rituals and relationships. This theme is resolved when Catherine's visions of romance are shattered by the mundane discoveries at Northanger Abbey, which compel her to abandon her romantic notions and choose the alternative of acting in the future with common sense.

Nevertheless, in her dismissal of fantasy, she has not yet come to terms with the limitations in reality, the pressures of society that can impose imprisonment. Such experience is melodramatically represented by her expulsion from the abbey. The order is delivered without explanation, the time and manner of departure are determined by General Tilney, and Catherine is denied either friendship or common courtesy. With no alternatives, Catherine is in a situation that resists good sense, and she is reduced to a passive awareness of the reality and substance of life. When she is shut off in her room at the abbey, her mind is so occupied in the contemplation of actual and natural evil that she is numb to the loneliness of her situation. Confined in a hired carriage for the long, unfamiliar journey to Fullerton, she is conscious only of the pressing anxieties of thought. At home, her thought processes are lost in the reflection of her own change of feelings and spirit. She is the opposite of what she had been, an innocent young woman.

Catherine survives the transition from innocence to experience, proving to her mother, at least, that she can shift very well for herself. Catherine's maturity, however, is tested no further. The restoration of her happiness depends less on herself and Henry than it does on General Tilney, and she is finally received by the general on the basis not of personal merit but of money. Only when the Morlands prove to be a family of good financial standing is Catherine free to marry the man of her choice.

Concerning the rapid turn of events in her denouement, Austen wryly observed, "To begin perfect happiness at the respective ages of twenty-six and eighteen, is to do pretty well." Despite the happy ending that concludes the novel, Austen leaves Catherine on the threshold only of the reality of life that her experiences have revealed. The area of her testing has already been defined, for example, in the discrepancy between her image of Henry's parsonage and that of General Tilney. To Catherine, it is "something like Fullerton, but better: Fullerton had its faults, but Woodston probably had none."

Thus, *Northanger Abbey* is a novel of initiation; its heroine ironically discovers in the world not a new freedom, but a new set of restrictions. Once undeceived of her romantic illusions of escape, she is returned with a vengeance to the world as it is, small but decent. As an early novel, *Northanger Abbey* points the way to Austen's mature novels, in which the focus is on heroines who are constrained to deal with life within defined limitations.

"Critical Evaluation" by Catherine E. Moore

Further Reading

Austen, Jane. *Northanger Abbey: Backgrounds, Criticism.* Edited by Susan Fraiman. New York: W. W. Norton, 2004. In addition to the text, this volumes contains a lengthy introduction that analyzes the work, a chronology, bibliography, and other background materials.

Dwyer, June. *Jane Austen.* New York: Continuum, 1989. A good basic reference for the general reader. Dwyer suggests that *Northanger Abbey* is the novel that gives the best introduction to Austen's worldview and writing style. Includes a selected bibliography.

Fergus, Jan. *Jane Austen and the Didactic Novel.* London: Macmillan, 1983. Fergus differs from many critics in considering Austen's early novels to be primarily intended to instruct the readers. The chapter on *Northanger Abbey* considers the novel from this perspective.

Harris, Jocelyn. *Jane Austen's Art of Memory.* New York: Cambridge University Press, 1989. Explores the literary and intellectual influences of Austen's own reading on her novels, demonstrating how *Northanger Abbey* drew upon John Locke's *An Essay Concerning Human Understanding* (1690). Contains a bibliography and an index.

Jones, Vivien. *How to Study a Jane Austen Novel.* London: Macmillan, 1987. Designed to help students develop their own critical skills, this text offers practical advice about how to read, understand, and analyze literature. Jones uses selected passages from *Northanger Abbey* in her discussion of the power of the authorial voice.

Lambdin, Laura Cooner, and Robert Thomas Lambdin, eds. *A Companion to Jane Austen Studies*. New York: Greenwood Press, 2000. A collection of twenty-two essays interpreting Austen's works. Two of the essays deal with *Northanger Abbey*: "Rereading Jane Austen: Dialogic Feminism in *Northanger Abbey*" by Carole Gerster and "Austen's *Northanger Abbey*: A Bibliographic Study" by James R. Keller.

Lauber, John. *Jane Austen*. New York: Twayne, 1993. Discusses *Northanger Abbey* quite extensively. Especially interesting is Lauber's discussion of the connections between *Northanger Abbey* and Austen's juvenilia (works she composed between the ages of twelve and eighteen). Includes a chronology, bibliography, and index.

Monaghan, David. *Jane Austen: Structure and Social Vision*. London: Macmillan, 1980. Monaghan examines the use of and attitude toward formal social ritual in Austen's novels to reveal how Austen viewed her society. He devotes one chapter to *Northanger Abbey*.

Pinion, F. B. *A Jane Austen Companion: A Critical Survey and Reference Book*. New York: St. Martin's Press, 1973. The first part of the book includes chapters on biography, historical background, each of Austen's novels, her letters, and her literary reputation. The second part includes a list of people and places in Austen's fiction, as well as a glossary of unusual or outmoded words. Also contains a variety of maps and other illustrations, a bibliography, and an index.

Sulloway, Alison G. *Jane Austen and the Province of Womanhood*. Philadelphia: University of Pennsylvania Press, 1989. Places Austen within a female tradition of "outsider" satire, written by those rejected and devalued by society. Includes a bibliography and an index.

Thompson, James. *Between Self and World: The Novels of Jane Austen*. University Park: Pennsylvania State University Press, 1988. Examines Austen's portrayal of the disparity between individual and society within the context of its historical, social, economic, and literary circumstances. Includes an index and extensive footnotes.

Todd, Janet M. *The Cambridge Introduction to Jane Austen*. New York: Cambridge University Press, 2006. Todd, an Austen scholar and editor of the author's work, provides an overview of Austen's life, novels, context, and reception. Includes a detailed discussion about each novel and provides a good starting point for the study of her major works.

Nostromo
A Tale of the Seaboard

Author: Joseph Conrad (1857-1924)
First published: 1904
Type of work: Novel
Type of plot: Psychological realism
Time of plot: Early twentieth century
Locale: Costaguana, on the north coast of South America

Principal characters:
CHARLES GOULD, manager of the San Tomé silver mine
EMILIA GOULD, his wife
GIAN' "NOSTROMO" BATTISTA, the Italian leader of the stevedores
LINDA VIOLA, the woman to whom he proposes
GISELLE VIOLA, her sister
GIORGIO VIOLA, father of Linda and Giselle
MARTIN DECOUD, a newspaper editor
DR. MONYGHAM, the town physician and a friend of the Goulds

The Story:

The Republic of Costaguana is in a state of revolt. Under the leadership of Pedrito Montero, rebel troops have taken control of the eastern part of the country. When news of the revolt reaches Sulaco, the principal town of the western section, which is separated from the rest of the country by a mountain range, the leaders begin to lay defense plans. The chief interest of the town is the San Tomé silver mine in the nearby mountains, a mine managed by Charles Gould, an

Englishman who, although educated in England, was born in Sulaco, his father having been manager before him. Gould has made a great success of the mine. The semiannual shipment of silver has just come down from the mine to the customhouse when the telegraph operator in Esmeralda, on the eastern side of the mountains, sends word that troops have embarked on a transport under the command of General Sotillo and that the rebels plan to capture the silver ingots as well as Sulaco.

Gould decides to load the ingots onto a lighter, a barge used for loading and unloading ships' cargo, and set it afloat in the gulf pending the arrival of a ship that will take the cargo to the United States. The man to guide the lighter will be Gian' Battista, known in Sulaco as Nostromo—our man—for he is considered incorruptible. His companion will be Martin Decoud, editor of the local newspaper, who has been drawn from Paris and kept in Sulaco by the European-educated Antonia Avellanos, to whom he has just become engaged. Decoud has incurred the anger of Montero by denouncing the revolutionists in his paper; he has also conceived a plan for making the country around Sulaco an independent state, the Occidental Republic.

When Nostromo and Decoud set out in the black of night, Sotillo's ship, approaching the port without lights, bumps into their lighter. Nostromo steers the lighter to a nearby uninhabited island, the Great Isabel, where he buries the treasure. He then leaves Decoud behind and rows the lighter to the middle of the harbor, pulls a plug, and sinks it. He swims the remaining mile to the mainland.

Upon discovering that the silver has been spirited away, Sotillo takes possession of the customhouse, where he conducts an inquiry. The next day, Sulaco is seized by Montero, who considers Sotillo of little worth.

When the Europeans and highborn natives who have not fled the town discover that Nostromo is back, they take it for granted that the silver has been lost in the harbor. They ask Nostromo to take a message to Barrios, who commands the loyalist troops on the eastern side of the mountains. After a spectacular engine ride up the side of the mountain and a subsequent six-day horseback journey through the mountain passes, Nostromo succeeds in delivering the message, and Barrios sets out with his troops by boat to relieve the town of Sulaco.

Coming into the harbor with the troops, Nostromo sights a boat that he recognizes as the small craft that had been attached to the lighter that had carried him and Decoud to Great Isabel. He dives overboard and swims to the boat. Barrios goes on to Sulaco and drives the traitors out. Meanwhile, Gould has planted dynamite around the silver mine to de-

stroy it in case of defeat, for he is determined to keep the mine from the revolutionists at any cost.

Nostromo rows the little boat over to Great Isabel, where he discovers that Decoud is gone, as are four of the silver ingots. He sees a bloodstain on the edge of the boat and correctly guesses that Decoud has killed himself. Left to himself when Nostromo returned to the mainland, Decoud had grown more and more lonely with each passing day, until finally he dug up four of the ingots, tied them to himself, went out into the boat, shot himself, and fell overboard; the weight of the ingots carried him to the bottom of the harbor. Now Nostromo cannot tell Gould where the silver is, for he will be suspected of stealing the four missing ingots himself. Since everyone thinks the treasure is at the bottom of the sea, he decides to let the rumor stand; he plans to sell the ingots one by one, and so become rich slowly.

In gratitude for his many services to the country, the people provide Nostromo with a boat, which he uses to haul cargo as far north as California. Sometimes he is gone for months while he carries out his schemes for disposing of the hidden silver. One day, on returning from a voyage, he sees that a lighthouse is being built on Great Isabel. At first he is panic-stricken, but then he suggests that the lighthouse keeper should be old Giorgio Viola. Nostromo is interested in Viola's daughter Linda, and he thinks that with the Violas on the island no one will be suspicious about his frequent visits there. Linda has a younger sister, Giselle, for whom the vagabond Ramirez is desperate. Giorgio Viola keeps Giselle under close guard; he will not allow Giselle to receive Ramirez's attentions, and he will not permit Ramirez to visit the island.

To make his comings and goings on Great Isabel more secure, one day Nostromo asks Linda to be his wife. Almost as soon as he does so, however, he realizes that he is really in love with Giselle. In secret meetings, he and Giselle confess their mutual passion. Linda grows suspicious, and Giselle begs Nostromo to carry her away, but he tells her that he cannot do so for a while. He finally tells her about the silver and how he has to convert it into money before he can take her away.

Obsessed by his hatred of Ramirez, Giorgio Viola begins patrolling the island at night with his gun loaded. One night, as Nostromo is approaching Giselle's window, old Viola shoots him, thinking he is Ramirez. Hearing her father say that he has shot Ramirez, Linda rushes outside, but Giselle runs past her and reaches the wounded Nostromo first. It is she who accompanies him to the mainland.

In the hospital, Nostromo asks to speak to the kindly Emilia Gould, Charles Gould's wife. He tells Mrs. Gould that

Giselle is innocent and that he alone knows about the hidden treasure. Mrs. Gould, however, will not let him tell her where he has hidden the silver. It has caused so much sorrow that she does not want it to be brought to light again. Nostromo refuses any aid from Dr. Monygham and dies without revealing the location of the ingots.

Dr. Monygham takes the police galley out to Great Isabel, where he informs Linda of Nostromo's death. She is thoroughly moved by the news and whispers that she—and she alone—has loved Nostromo and that she will never forget him. As Linda cries out Nostromo's name in despair, Dr. Monygham observes that, triumphant as Nostromo had been in life, this love of Linda's was his greatest victory of all.

The region around Sulaco finally does become the Occidental Republic. The San Tomé mine continues to prosper under Gould's management, the population increases enormously, and the new country flourishes. Although Decoud, the country's first planner, and Nostromo, the hero of its inception, are dead, life in the new country goes on richly and fully.

Critical Evaluation:

Joseph Conrad has always been known among the mass of readers as a great teller of sea stories. He was also a pertinent, even prophetic, commentator on what he called land entanglements—particularly on the subject of political revolution. Conrad's father was an active revolutionary in the cause of Polish independence; he died as the result of prolonged imprisonment for revolutionary "crimes." Three of Conrad's best novels are studies in political behavior: *Nostromo*, *The Secret Agent* (1907), and *Under Western Eyes* (1911). *Nostromo* is by far the most ambitious and complex of these works. It has a very large international cast of characters of all shapes and sizes, and it employs the typical Conradian device of an intentionally jumbled (and sometimes confusing) chronology. As is typical of Conrad, the physical setting is handled superbly; the reader is drawn into the book through the wonderfully tactile descriptions of the land and sea. The setting in South America is also particularly appropriate to Conrad's skeptical consideration of progress achieved either through capitalism or through revolution.

Nostromo is a study in the politics of wealth in an underdeveloped country. The central force in the novel is the silver of the San Tomé mine—a potential of wealth so immense that a humane and cultured civilization can be built upon it. At least this is the view of the idealist Charles Gould, the owner and developer of the mine. There are other views. From the start, Gould is ready to maintain his power by force

if necessary. He remembers how the mine destroyed his father. The mine attracts politicians and armed revolutionaries from the interior, but Gould is willing to blow up his treasure and half of Sulaco, the central city, in order to defeat the revolution. He succeeds, but Conrad intends for the reader to regard his success as partial at best. His obsession with the mine separates him from his wife; as is true for Conrad's other heroes, the demands of public action distort and cancel out Gould's capacity for private affection.

One of the magnificent elements of the first half of *Nostromo* is the way in which Conrad shows Gould and his silver from many angles. Readers are given a truly panoramic spectrum of attitude. For old Giorgio Viola, who was once a member of Giuseppe Garibaldi's Redshirts, Gould's idealization of material interests is dangerous and wrong because it has the potential of violating a pure and disinterested love of liberty for all humanity. Viola, however, is as ineffectual as the austere and cultured leader of Sulaco's aristocracy, Don José Avellanos, whose unpublished manuscript "Thirty Years of Misrule" is used as gun wadding at the height of the revolution. Ranged against Avellanos and Viola, at the other end of the spectrum, are those sanguinary petty tyrants Bento, Montero, and Sotillo, who want to run the country entirely for their own personal advantage. Sotillo represents their rapacity and blind lust for Gould's treasure.

The most interesting characters, however, are those who occupy middle positions in the spectrum. Of these, two are central to any understanding of the novel, as between them they represent Conrad's own point of view most fully. The dilettante Parisian boulevardier Martin Decoud may be the object of some of Conrad's most scourging irony, but his skeptical pronouncements, as in his letter to his sister, accord well with the facts of Sulaco's politics as Conrad presents them in the early stages of the novel. Decoud saves the mine by arranging for a new rifle to be used in defense of Gould's material interests, but he does not share Gould's enthusiasm that the mine can act as the chief force in the process of civilizing the new republic. He views the whole business of revolution and counterrevolution as an elaborate charade, a comic opera.

The most trenchant charge against Gould is made by the other deeply skeptical character, Dr. Monygham. His judgment upon material interests is one of the most famous passages in the book:

There is no peace and rest in the development of material interests. They have their law and their justice. But it is founded on expediency, and is inhuman; it is without the continuity and the force that can be found only in a moral principle.... The time approaches when all that the Gould Concession stands for shall weigh as heavily upon the people as the barbarism, cruelty, and misrule of a few years back.

It is clear that Conrad intends for his readers to take Monygham's judgment at face value. The trouble is that the facts of Costaguana's postrevolutionary state do not agree with it. The land is temporarily at peace and is being developed in an orderly fashion by the mine as well as other material interests, and the workers seem better off as a result. Monygham is hinting at the workers' revolt against the suppression of material interests, but this revolt seems so far in the future that his judgment is robbed of much of its power. This surely accounts for part of the hollowness that some critics have found in the novel.

The last section of the novel is concerned with Gould's successful resistance to the attempts of both church and military to take over the mine and the moral degradation of the "incorruptible" man of the people, Nostromo. In this latter case, Conrad abandons the richness and density of his panoramic view of South American society and gives the reader a partly allegorical dramatization of the taint of the silver within the soul of a single character.

Nostromo's fate is clearly related to the legend of the two gringos that begins the book, for the silver that he has hidden has the same power to curse his soul as the "fatal spell" cast by the treasure on the gringos. ("Their souls cannot tear themselves away from their bodies mounting guard over the discovered treasure. They are now rich and hungry and thirsty.") The result of Conrad's absorption with Nostromo at the end of the novel is twofold. First, readers are denied a dramatization of the changing social conditions that would support Monygham's judgment. Second, and more important, the novel loses its superb richness and variety and comes dangerously close to insisting on the thesis that wealth is a universal corrupter, even that "money is the root of all evil."

For roughly two-thirds of its length, *Nostromo* gives readers one of the finest social panoramas in all fiction. The ending, however, suggests that underneath the complex texture of the whole novel lies a rather simplistic idea: that both "material interests" and revolution are doomed to failure. Although set in South America, *Nostromo* suggests a world in which systems and conditions change very little because people do not change.

"Critical Evaluation" by Benjamin Nyce

Further Reading

Bloom, Harold, ed. *Joseph Conrad's "Nostromo."* New York: Chelsea House, 1987. Collection of seven essays includes discussion of Conrad's use of irony in the novel, Conrad's philosophy of history, and different views of the hero.

Carabine, Keith, Owen Knowles, and Wiesław Krajka, eds. *Contexts for Conrad.* Boulder, Colo.: East European Monographs, 1993. Helpful for understanding *Nostromo* within the context of nineteenth century colonialism, capitalism, and frontier exploration. The essay focusing on the novel shows the relationship of *Nostromo* to nineteenth century criticism of capitalism.

Hamner, Robert D., ed. *Joseph Conrad: Third World Perspectives.* Washington, D.C.: Three Continents Press, 1990. Collection of essays gives the perspective of the colonized on colonialism. Asserts that *Nostromo* represents an early conceptualization of a postcolonial world.

Jordan, Elaine, ed. *Joseph Conrad.* New York: St. Martin's Press, 1996. Excellent collection of essays provides a good introduction to Conrad's work for students. Focuses on three novels—*Heart of Darkness, Nostromo,* and *The Secret Agent*—analyzing these works from postcolonial, feminist, Marxist, and other perspectives.

Kaplan, Carola M., Peter Mallios, and Andrea White, eds. *Conrad in the Twenty-First Century: Contemporary Approaches and Perspectives.* New York: Routledge, 2005. Collection of essays analyzes Conrad's depiction of postcolonialism, empire, imperialism, and modernism. Anthony Fothergill examines *Nostromo* in his essay "Connoisseurs of Terror and Political Aesthetics: *Nostromo* and *A Set of Six.*"

Peters, John G. *The Cambridge Introduction to Joseph Conrad.* New York: Cambridge University Press, 2006. Provides an introductory overview of Conrad, with information on his life, all of his works, and the critical reception of his fiction.

Robert, Andrew Michael. *Conrad and Masculinity.* New York: St. Martin's Press, 2000. Uses modern theories about masculinity to analyze Conrad's work and explore the relationship of masculinity to imperialism and modernity. *Nostromo* is discussed in a chapter titled "Gender and the Disciplined Body: *Nostromo.*"

Simmons, Allan H., and J. H. Stape, eds. *"Nostromo": Centennial Essays.* New York: Rodopi, 2004. Collection of eight essays examines *Nostromo* from various perspectives, including discussions of homecoming, free will, and determinism in the novel.

Stape, J. H., ed. *The Cambridge Companion to Joseph Con-*

rad. New York: Cambridge University Press, 1996. Collection of essays on Conrad's life and work includes discussions of the Conradian narrative, Conrad and imperialism, Conrad and modernism, and Conrad's literary influence. An essay by Eloise Knapp Hay focuses on *Nostromo*.

Watt, Ian. *Joseph Conrad: "Nostromo."* New York: Cambridge University Press, 1988. Discusses Conrad's sources, elucidates the novel's narrative technique, and provides notes on the characters. Supplemented with a chronology of Conrad's life, a chronology of events in *Nostromo*, and a guide to further reading.

Notes from the Underground

Author: Fyodor Dostoevski (1821-1881)
First published: Zapiski iz podpolya, 1864 (English translation, 1913)
Type of work: Novel
Type of plot: Impressionistic realism
Time of plot: Mid-nineteenth century
Locale: St. Petersburg, Russia

Principal characters:
THE NARRATOR
SIMONOV, his acquaintance from school days
ZVERKOV, a young Russian officer
LIZA, a prostitute

The Story:

The narrator, addressing an imaginary group of acquaintances, declares that after many years of life as a rude and spiteful government official, and after many years as a recluse, he is not really bitter in his heart. Something perverse in him, his acute consciousness, has led him to find pleasure in the pain of humiliating experiences. From experience, he advises against intellectual acuteness. The intellectual, he says, when faced with revenge, surrounds himself with a legion of doubts; then he crawls into his self-imposed rat's nest and tortures himself with petty spite. The direct man, in wreaking revenge, might with dispatch hit his head against a wall, but he will accept the wall. The intellectual will not accept the wall; indeed, he will feel responsibility for the presence of the wall. The narrator declares that he has always had to feign taking offense and that he has had, in the face of life's transiency, to pretend to love. Life to him is a colossal bore. He can never avenge wrongs done to him because the culprits, the culprits' motives, and the very misdeeds themselves are all subject to overanalysis in his doubting intellect.

Given another chance at life, the narrator states, he would choose a career of complete laziness, one in which he might revel among good and beautiful things. He declares that even if a man were to know absolutely what things in life are to his best advantage, he will perversely avoid these things. The narrator advances the idea that people may be destined for creativeness, and for this reason, conscious of their fate, they perversely practice destruction to individuate themselves.

Perhaps people are fearful of completion, of perfection; perhaps they find final attainment distasteful: Life consists in the attaining, not in the attainment. The narrator concludes his philosophical soliloquy by pointing out that conscious inertia is the ideal state. He provocatively insists that he does not believe a word he has written, that he has written only because the written word seems imposing and dignified. He is oppressed by memories that are evoked by the fall of snow outside.

At the age of twenty-four, the narrator has an inchoate character. He talks to no one. His intense self-consciousness causes him to be vain at one moment and self-loathing the next. He tries to look intelligent and fears any eccentricity in himself. This acute awareness of self makes him lonely, yet he feels superior to others. He becomes a recluse. He reads voraciously and begins to walk the streets at night.

One night, he sees a man thrown out the window of a billiard parlor. In envy, he goes into the billiard parlor in the hope that he, too, might be thrown out. He is humiliated when an officer shoves him aside without noticing him. He returns the next night, but, morally fearful that all the fools in the parlor will jeer at his being thrown out, he does not enter. Dedicated to revenge, for months he follows the officer who shoved him. He learns the officer's name and writes a satirical novel in which the officer is the principal character. The novel is rejected when he submits it for publication; its style is out of date.

Two years pass. He writes a letter challenging the officer to a duel, but he does not mail it. Instead, he begins to take regular walks along the river promenade, where he revels in his resentment. One Sunday on his walk he is rudely pushed aside by the officer. Maddened at his own weakness, the narrator conceives the idea of not giving way next time. He gloats over his idea. He practices pushing aside an imaginary officer. His courage fails him once, but he finally stands his ground when the officer tries again to push him aside. Actually, the officer does not notice him at all, but he is delirious with happiness in having gained back his self-respect.

The narrator begins to daydream. In his fantasies, he brings beauty and good to the world. During the fever pitch of his dream life, feeling the need of companionship, he visits his immediate superior, Anton, and sits in silence with Anton's family for hours.

He calls on an old schoolmate, Simonov, and finds Simonov planning, with two other old schoolmates, a farewell dinner for Zverkov, a fellow student of the direct, not too acutely conscious type, whom the narrator hates. Zverkov, a wealthy man, has been successful in the army. The narrator is greeted coldly by his boyhood acquaintances, but he invites himself to the dinner party. The other young men agree reluctantly; he is obviously not a favorite with them. Later the narrator detests himself for consciously having opened himself up to humiliation, but secretly he rather enjoys having discomfited his companions.

The next day, as he dresses for the dinner, he has misgivings. He wants to make a great impression; he wants to eclipse the popular Zverkov. Yet he knows that he really does not want to do this either. He arrives too early and is humiliated by his wait. During the dinner he antagonizes everyone and drinks too much. Having thoroughly degraded himself, he offers conciliation and seeks the love of his companions. When he apologizes to Zverkov for insulting him, Zverkov humiliates him by saying that someone such as he could not possibly insult him. Filled with the wild, unreasonable intention of slapping Zverkov and challenging him to a duel, the narrator follows the others to a brothel.

At the brothel, a young woman is brought to him in the parlor; he is pleased at the prospect of being repulsive to her. He sleeps off his drunkenness, awakes, and delivers a bookish, insincere sermon to Liza, the prostitute, on the hazards of her profession. He is grandstanding and he knows it, to his shame. He tells her of the importance of human love, something about which he actually knows nothing. Liza, to prove to him that she is not entirely lost, shows him a love letter that she has received from a young gentleman. The narrator gives Liza his address and leaves her. The next day, he regrets having given her his address. He hates himself for his insincerity with her, and he fears that she will come to his home, but she does not. He imagines an idyllic relationship between himself and Liza; he will be her tutor and will mold her into a perfect creature.

When Liza finally arrives, she is confused by the wretched condition of the poor narrator's rooms. She says that she has left the brothel. Alarmed, the narrator confesses his insincerity and declares that he had sought power over someone because he himself had been humiliated. Liza understands his inner turmoil and takes him in her arms. Liza's intuition soon tells her, however, that he is despicable and incapable of love. After she leaves, he runs after her to seek her forgiveness, but he never sees her again. He derives some consolation from the thought that her resentment of him will give her pleasure for the rest of her life.

Critical Evaluation:

In *Notes from the Underground*, Fyodor Dostoevski creates a character—the "underground man"—who is crucial not only to Dostoevski's own best fiction but also to the whole of nineteenth and twentieth century literature. Indeed, some critics even date the beginning of modern literature from the publication of this short novel and identify the underground man as the archetypal modern antihero. At the very least, *Notes from the Underground* can be seen as the prologue to the five great novels that climaxed Dostoevski's career: *Prestupleniye i nakazaniye* (1866; *Crime and Punishment*, 1886), *Idiot* (1868; *The Idiot*, 1887), *Besy* (1871-1872; *The Possessed*, 1913), *Podrostok* (1875; *A Raw Youth*, 1916), and *Bratya Karamazovy* (1879-1880; *The Brothers Karamazov*, 1912).

Some scholars and critics, however, have argued that *Notes from the Underground* is actually not a novel at all: The first part is too fragmentary and incoherent, the second is too short and arbitrary, and the relationship between the two is too unclear to allow the work that formal designation. In fact, the form and style of *Notes from the Underground* are as radical as its content and fuse perfectly to produce an organic, if unorthodox, work of art.

The first part (titled "Underground") presents the underground man's philosophy; the second part ("Apropos of Wet Snow") recounts a series of early experiences that explain the origins of that worldview while suggesting a possible alternative to it. Without part 2, part 1 is little more than the bitter rantings of a semihysterical social misfit; without part 1, part 2 is only the pathetic narrative of a petty, self-destructive neurotic. Together, however, the two parts combine into a powerful statement about the nature and situation of humanity in the nineteenth century and after.

In the first sentence of the book, the underground man states that he is sick, but he later defines that sickness as "acute consciousness"—a malady characteristic of the sensitive modern individual. This consciousness has made the narrator aware of the contradictions in his own behavior and the consequent impossibility of his acting forcefully and meaningfully in his society. He feels superior to his fellows, yet he knows he is incapable of dealing with them. He despises them, yet he obsessively wants their acceptance and approval. He acts spitefully toward them, yet he feels personally insulted when they ignore or berate him. He asserts his need for dignity and then forces himself into situations that can only end in his humiliation. The narrator is not the first Dostoevskian character to have such contradictory, self-defeating qualities, but he is the first to be aware of them and their sources, and so he represents a significant development in the novelist's career.

Even the underground man's attitude toward his own pain and humiliation is ambivalent. He does not actually enjoy his sufferings, and yet he takes satisfaction in them because they make him conscious of himself and give him a feeling of power over his own actions. The narrator claims to admire the man of action, who does things and has experiences unfettered by the doubts, hesitations, and defeats that plague the narrator. He sees a profound contradiction, however, in the very notion of a man of action; although such a person acts, he does so not of his own volition but as the end result of a long cause-and-effect sequence. The man of action does not think, so his ability to act is not so laudable.

The underground man's rebellion is a reaction against the deterministic, scientific view of humanity that was prevalent in the late nineteenth century. If all human activity is regulated by environmental and hereditary factors of which the individual is unconscious, then a person is reduced to the status of a piano key. The underground man denies that conception of himself, even while conceding that it is probably true. This posture explains Dostoevski's apparently ambiguous attitude toward his fictional creation. While the author obviously despises the underground man's pettiness, nastiness, cruelty, vanity, and spite, he also clearly admires the man, because the narrator possesses the one basic virtue: He asserts his freedom in the face of logic, self-interest, and nature itself; he insists on his "fatal fantastic element."

Dostoevski's real targets in writing *Notes from the Underground* are the social theorists and human engineers who would rationally create the perfect society—symbolized by the "Crystal Palace"—in which human happiness and fulfillment would be "scientifically" designed and implemented. The underground man rejects this view of human nature. He insists on using his free choice to assert his individuality, but the actions he takes to demonstrate this freedom are, he admits, meaningless. Thus the dilemma of the sensitive, insightful modern man: If he accepts a logical, well-ordered, "scientific" society, he gains happiness, but he gives up free will; if he rejects such a rational society and insists on expressing his individuality, he can do so only with impulsive, arbitrary gestures that have neither real meaning nor lasting effect. Is there any way out of this apparent impasse?

Dostoevski suggests an answer, or at least an approach to one, in part 2, although the fact that the underground man is incapable of seizing upon it underscores the difficulty of the solution. Readers also come to understand how he became the way he is. The action takes place sixteen years earlier and shows the narrator's contradictory attitudes in practice. He alienates those he would cultivate, plots revenge against "enemies" who are unaware of his existence, and creates situations that guarantee the humiliations and frustrations he fears.

After a number of minor skirmishes, he gives his theories a final test in two important human activities—friendship and love. Having forced himself on some old school acquaintances, he gets drunk and nearly provokes them to violence. Then, his attempt at friendship a failure, the underground man pursues the role of lover. He follows the others to a brothel, where he purchases the favors of a prostitute named Liza. Upon awakening the next morning, he berates her for her profession, describes her inevitable and appalling future, and urges her to change her life. She responds with contrition and deep emotion.

When she comes to him the next day, however, the underground man is in the midst of a vicious, demeaning argument with his manservant. Humiliated, he feels the need for revenge on her for witnessing his degradation. He realizes that it was a desire for power over another human being, not sincerity or compassion, that accounted for his moral strictures of the previous night. That power gone and his true pettiness revealed, he reacts brutally; she offers him love and he turns on her, rebukes her, mocks his earlier statements, and finally drives her off by paying for her services. Sensing his pain and desperation, however, she demonstrates her moral superiority in her response to his tirade. The underground man is thus denied even the satisfaction of bringing another human being down to his own level—a fact he realizes immediately after she leaves.

The underground man, therefore, is given a chance to escape from his self-imposed exile, and he rejects it, dooming himself to psychological fragmentation and social isolation. Had he been able to accept and respond to Liza's love, he might have transcended the narrow confines of his narcissistic world and become a whole, purposeful human being. This last positive possibility, however, is a very muted one.

Notes from the Underground leaves the reader with feelings of depression and frustration. Although he espouses the saving capacities of spontaneous love, Dostoevski does not explicitly tie that love to the Christian vision that was to become central in his last great works. Thus *Notes from the Underground* remains Dostoevski's great transitional work, not only for his own writing but also for Western literature in general.

"Critical Evaluation" by Keith Neilson

Further Reading

Dostoevski, Fyodor. *Notes from Underground: An Authoritative Translation, Backgrounds and Sources, Responses, Criticism.* 2d ed. Edited and translated by Michael R. Katz. New York: W. W. Norton, 2001. In addition to the text of the novel, which is supplemented by extensive annotations, this volume includes a selection of Dostoevski's letters and other writings relevant to the work, critical interpretations by nineteenth and twentieth century writers, and other responses to the novel, including a parody by Woody Allen.

Holquist, Michael. *Dostoevsky and the Novel.* 1977. Reprint. Evanston, Ill.: Northwestern University Press, 1986. Presents detailed readings of several of Dostoevski's works, including *Notes from the Underground.* Informative introduction provides background on Dostoevski's Russia.

Jones, Malcolm V. *Dostoyevsky: The Novel of Discord.* London: Elek Books Limited, 1976. Gives an overview of the complexity, chaos, and discord found in Dostoevski's works. Includes an extended section on *Notes from the Underground.*

Leatherbarrow, William J. *Fedor Dostoevsky.* Boston: Twayne, 1981. Presents commentary on *Notes from the Underground* as well as four of Dostoevski's major novels. Supplemented with a biographical sketch and a chronology of the events of Dostoevski's life.

_____, ed. *The Cambridge Companion to Dostoevskii.* New York: Cambridge University Press, 2006. Collection of essays examines the author's life and works, discussing his relationship to Russian folk heritage, money, the intelligentsia, psychology, religion, the family, and science, among other topics.

McReynolds, Susan. *Redemption and the Merchant God: Dostoevsky's Economy of Salvation and Antisemitism.* Evanston, Ill.: Northwestern University Press, 2008. Argues that readers cannot fully understand Dostoevski's writings without understanding his obsession with the Jews. Analyzes the elements of anti-Semitism in his works and also examines his views of the Crucifixion, the Resurrection, morality, and other aspects of Christian doctrine.

Paris, Bernard J. *Dostoevsky's Greatest Characters: A New Approach to "Notes from Underground," "Crime and Punishment," and "The Brothers Karamazov."* New York: Palgrave Macmillan, 2008. Approaches the characters in the novels discussed as imagined people whose personalities are expressed through their feelings, behavior, and ideas. Presents in-depth examination of the underground man, Zverkov, and Liza.

Scanlan, James P. *Dostoevsky the Thinker: A Philosophical Study.* Ithaca, N.Y.: Cornell University Press, 2002. Offers analysis of Dostoevski's novels, essays, letters, and notebooks—examining the weaknesses as well as the strengths of the author's ideas—in order to provide a comprehensive account of his philosophy. Concludes that Dostoevski's thought was shaped by anthropocentrism—a struggle to define the very essence of humanity.

Notes of a Native Son

Author: James Baldwin (1924-1987)
First published: 1955
Type of work: Essays

James Baldwin's *Notes of a Native Son* is his first collection of essays. Baldwin, generally acclaimed as twentieth century America's greatest essayist, helped cement this reputation with this collection. The book discusses many of the central occupations of Baldwin's career: the search for identity, how African Americans respond to racism, and racism in general. The book is an essential landmark in the thought of James Baldwin.

In examining *Notes of a Native Son*, the reader first should note the structure of the collection, because the essays are organized thematically. Part 1 deals primarily with Baldwin's commentaries on literature, with one essay additionally critiquing the film *Carmen Jones* (1954). Part 2 deals mainly with racial problems in the United States. In part 3, Baldwin examines questions of identity, specifically African Americans' perceptions of themselves and how they are perceived by others. Baldwin pondered these themes while he traveled in France and Switzerland.

Two of Baldwin's classic essays are contained in part 1: "Everybody's Protest Novel" and "Many Thousands Gone." "Everybody's Protest Novel" has become famous for Baldwin's criticisms of Harriet Beecher Stowe's *Uncle Tom's Cabin* (1852) and Richard Wright's *Native Son* (1940). Baldwin finds Stowe's novel to be ruined by sentimentality, which he feels is a mask for the author's fear of African Americans, especially assertive African Americans. Baldwin questions whether this novel should be thought to champion African Americans' freedom. Furthermore, Baldwin questions the validity of the praise of Wright's *Native Son* as promoting the African American cause. Baldwin believes that Wright's novel hinges on the acceptance by the main character, Bigger Thomas, of racists' view of him as subhuman. Baldwin expresses his concern that this ideology itself is, perhaps, Bigger's worst enemy, thus undermining the novel's focus on white racism. Consequently, Baldwin finds fault with two of the novels that had been made into such literary icons that they could have been deemed everybody's protest novels.

Baldwin's critique of the character of Bigger continues in "Many Thousands Gone," with Baldwin again noting Wright's emphasis on Bigger's self-hatred. However, in this essay, it is important to note that Baldwin recognizes the sociological significance of Bigger. Baldwin, for instance, claims that most blacks have an anger inside them against racism that is equivalent to Bigger's rage. Moreover, Baldwin indicts racism for producing black people such as Bigger, whose acquiescence to racism entails their own psychological and physical self-annihilation. This essay, therefore, is important in Baldwin's analysis of how racism, in its narcissistic arrogance, demands that African Americans submit their very identity and obey the demands of the dominant society.

Another intriguing aspect of part 1 of *Notes of a Native Son* is that, on the whole, it is a critique of American cultural productions that focus on representations of African Americans. In "*Carmen Jones*: The Dark is Light Enough," for example, Baldwin finds great faults in Otto Preminger's successful film. The film is an all-black production of the 1943 Broadway musical of the same name, and stars Dorothy Dandridge and Harry Belafonte. Baldwin is concerned that the film avoids anything that would convey reality in its presentation of life among African Americans, relying instead on such things as songs reworked to fit whites' ideas of black speech and presenting a hero and heroine devoid of real sensuality but who have a dull facade of sanitized sexiness more appropriate to dolls than to people. Baldwin sensed that Hollywood was afraid of presenting African Americans' sensuality because it is so often a subject of racist mythology. Hence, he argues that by divesting the storyline of *Carmen* of sensuality, the film reduces the characters to mere hollow shells. Consequently, as in the two previous essays, Baldwin finds that American cultural productions with African Americans as their subject are not only problematic but also indicative of societal problems in the presentation and treatment of blacks.

In part 2, two essays in particular stand out as major essays in Baldwin's career. "The Harlem Ghetto" and "Notes of a Native Son" examine various aspects of racism and race relations. In "The Harlem Ghetto," Baldwin analyzes a social problem that remains relevant: tensions between African Americans and Jews. He examines the economic factors at the heart of the maintenance of a racially divided society, and how these economic factors affect relations between the races. The black-Jewish rift, Baldwin feels, has its roots, in part, with the Jewish presence in Harlem as store owners, a position perceived by many blacks as exploitative. Baldwin points out that the hostility some blacks may feel toward Jews is not because Jews are Jewish but because Jews represent, for many blacks in ghettoes, a first contact with white Americans. Jews came to symbolize—rightly or wrongly—the racism of white society. Hence, Baldwin makes a perceptive point: Jews are caught in the American racial crossfire.

Baldwin's essay, "Notes of a Native Son," continues the analysis of race relations. The essay is central in showing Baldwin's own reactions to racism and his ideas on how African Americans should not react to racism. In the essay, Baldwin reminisces about his father, who hated whites and died an embittered man. Baldwin also recounts the racism he faced while working as a young man in New Jersey and how rude treatment, in particular at a racist restaurant, threatened not only to make him as bitter as his father but even to make him want to kill a white person. Baldwin, though, came to feel that this urge to violence would mean his own moral death, at the very least, and possibly his physical death, at worst. Baldwin writes of one of his central beliefs: African

Americans should never meet hatred with hatred and thus become like their enemy. This moral lesson is what Baldwin emphasizes as he writes of his father's death and of his own experiences with racism.

The final part of the book, part 3, explores another of what was to become a major topic in Baldwin's works: questions of identity as they arise in the lives of African Americans. "Encounter on the Seine: Black Meets Brown," for instance, tells of the relationships between Africans and African Americans. Baldwin states that African Americans are the product of different cultural experiences from Africans and thus cannot be expected to bond instantly with Africans, as some African Americans expect. The African American, Baldwin points out, is a "hybrid": a person of African heritage who is the product of the American experience.

"Stranger in the Village" is another essay that was inspired by Baldwin's travels abroad. A foreign setting yielded Baldwin many important insights into race relations. In "Stranger in the Village," Baldwin recounts the seeming innocence of the people of a Swiss village who looked at him in wonder, as they had never seen a black man before. This innocence prompts Baldwin to ponder the relations between white Americans and African Americans. Baldwin states his belief that white Americans do not have the same innocence as the Swiss villagers. White Americans want to claim that they do, however; it would morally be much cozier if African Americans were also visitors to America as Baldwin was to the Swiss village. Thus, Baldwin concludes that whites and blacks in America need to face how deeply entangled they have been in each others' histories. The challenge of how to live with this truth is the note upon which Baldwin concludes *Notes of a Native Son.*

After examining the thematic structure of the essays in *Notes of a Native Son,* the reader is in a good position to understand further the importance of the book. The book is significant for several reasons. Baldwin's insights into American literature and film, the racial situation in America, and the perceptions of African American identity are original and incisive. His essays give him a unique place in American literature; he is generally hailed as one of America's greatest essayists. *Notes of a Native Son,* therefore, marked the beginning of his career as a premier essayist.

Two of the essays in part 1, "Everybody's Protest Novel" and "Many Thousands Gone," are significant in American literary history because they are Baldwin's declaration of independence from Wright. During the 1940's and 1950's, both Wright and Baldwin were living in Paris and came to know each other. Wright was then considered by many, particularly literary critics, to be the elder statesman of African

American literature, and his books were sometimes held as an example to other African American writers of the sort of literature they were expected to write: bleak social protest, as in Wright's *Native Son.*

Baldwin, then a member of a younger generation of African American writers, did not want to be measured against Wright's themes and literary preoccupations. Baldwin later admitted that part of the reason for his literary attack on Wright in his essays was to separate himself from any expectations that he would emulate Wright's writings. He even recalled declaring early in their acquaintance, "The sons must slay their fathers!" Nevertheless, "Everybody's Protest Novel" and "Many Thousands Gone" raise central questions about the protest novel, including whether the genre is obsessed with portraying victims of racism to the point of failing to convey the humanity of the oppressed as anything but defeated victims. There is also the question of whether the novels under discussion, *Native Son* and *Uncle Tom's Cabin,* merely reproduce the prejudices of the society that they intend to criticize. "Everybody's Protest Novel" is an indication of Baldwin's own literary concerns and the problems he finds in two of America's foremost protest novels.

Baldwin's critique of *Uncle Tom's Cabin* is an essay that has gained more relevance over time. One reason for this relevance is that *Uncle Tom's Cabin* has been lauded by many feminist literary critics as a neglected classic, one of whose chief elements is the power of its sentimentality. In this light, Baldwin's withering attacks on Stowe's sentimentality, which he defines in part as an excessive and gaudy display of artificial emotions, are still important if one wants to debate the merit of Stowe's book. Baldwin's critiques of Stowe's and Wright's novels raise essential questions about these two literary classics that still engage the reader years after the publication of *Notes of a Native Son.*

Equally important to the criticisms of Wright and Stowe in "Everybody's Protest Novel" and "Many Thousands Gone" are the statements that convey inadvertently what were to become consuming interests of Baldwin as his career developed. For example, one of his chief attacks on *Native Son* is Wright's portrayal of Bigger's acceptance of how racists label and categorize him. In light of this criticism, it is especially revealing that one of the main themes of Baldwin's novels *Giovanni's Room* (1956) and *Another Country* (1962) is the need for people to reject their internalized prejudices and self-hatred. Furthermore, Baldwin's condemnations of the urge to categorize others and the internalization of such categorization by some people who are targets of prejudice were to be abiding interests in his fiction and later essays. Thus, "Everybody's Protest Novel" and "Many Thousands

Gone" are key to understanding Baldwin's preoccupations as a writer.

Baldwin's other abiding interests are evident in the essays in part 2, "The Harlem Ghetto," "Journey to Atlanta," and "Notes of a Native Son." The primary topics in these essays are racism and African Americans' responses to racism. Baldwin's belief in the hypocrisy of some whites who think of themselves as liberals is clear in "Journey to Atlanta," which chronicles his brothers' trip to Atlanta under the auspices of the Progressive Party. Among those self-proclaimed progressive whites of whom Baldwin writes, he notes patronizing and narcissistic attitudes, which to him were the hallmark of hypocritical liberalism. He would return to the subject of hypocritical liberalism in many essays, most notably in *The Fire Next Time* (1963). He also writes of this type of person in his drama about the Civil Rights era, *Blues for Mister Charlie* (1964). In addition, on the subject of black-white relations, in "The Harlem Ghetto," Baldwin became one of the first major African American writers to examine tensions between African Americans and Jews. His analysis of the reasons for these tensions—the economic disparity between blacks and Jews in such ghettoes as Harlem and blacks' perception of Jews' insensitivity to fellow members of the oppressed (specifically, African Americans)—are points that many subsequent writers have cited as being accurate descriptions of the black-Jewish rift. Baldwin's analysis is prophetic in that it raises many points made by contemporary analysts of black-Korean tensions in predominantly black areas. Hence, Baldwin's examination of the factors involved in racial tensions and in racism are timely and timeless.

Finally, *Notes of a Native Son* announces many of Baldwin's concerns on African Americans' reactions to racism. Reading the essays in *Notes of a Native Son*, one learns of one of Baldwin's lasting beliefs: that the state of African Americans' souls is at stake in how they respond to racism. While this concern is especially clear in "Notes of a Native Son," it is also present in "Everybody's Protest Novel" and "The Harlem Ghetto." Baldwin's main point is that blacks become hopelessly degraded if they respond to white racial hatred with their own racial hatred. He states that such mutual hostility leaves no hope for progress. He provides no easy solution to reacting to racism, as he frequently admits his own anger. However, one of his main beliefs, expressed in *Notes of a Native Son*, is that "all men are brothers." This vision is the alternative and challenge to mutual racial hostility.

Notes of a Native Son has become a classic for many reasons. The quality of the writing, for instance, shows why Baldwin was one of America's most acclaimed writers. The essays consist of complex social commentaries on important issues. For these reasons, *Notes of a Native Son* is a lasting classic of American literature.

Jane Davis

Further Reading

Baldwin, James, and Sol Stein. *Native Sons: A Friendship That Created One of the Greatest Works of the Twentieth Century*. New York: One World, 2004. A collection of letters and other documentation exchanged between Baldwin and Stein concerning the creation of *Notes of a Native Son*.

Boyd, Herb. *Baldwin's Harlem: A Biography of James Baldwin*. New York: Atria Books, 2008. Boyd's biography focuses on Baldwin's experiences in Harlem and his relationships with other residents of the New York City neighborhood, including writers Countee Cullen and Langston Hughes and civil rights activist Malcolm X.

Campbell, James. *Talking at the Gates: A Life of James Baldwin*. New York: Viking Press, 1991. This full biography, by a man who knew Baldwin personally, is especially interesting because it draws on the Federal Bureau of Investigation files kept on Baldwin. Campbell deals frankly with Baldwin's bisexuality. Included are sixteen pages of photographs.

Kinnamon, Kenneth, ed. *James Baldwin: A Collection of Critical Essays*. Englewood Cliffs, N.J.: Prentice-Hall, 1974. In this selection of twelve essays and Kinnamon's introduction are discussions of several of Baldwin's major works. Langston Hughes provides a short and pungent review of *Notes of a Native Son* that is interesting for Hughes's resistance to some of Baldwin's stinging commentary on racism. F. W. Dupee's essay looks at Baldwin's development from *Notes of a Native Son* through *The Fire Next Time*. Also included is Eldridge Cleaver's discussion of Baldwin's essays from *Soul on Ice* (1968).

McBride, Dwight A., ed. *James Baldwin Now*. New York: New York University Press, 1999. Collection of diverse essays that seek to reevaluate Baldwin's works and interpret from the perspective of modern criticism. Most of the essays provide a broad view of Baldwin's writings, but Lauren Rusk's "Selfhood and Strategy in *Notes of a Native Son*" focuses on that work.

O'Daniel, Therman B. *James Baldwin: A Critical Evaluation*. Washington, D.C.: Howard University Press, 1977. This volume contains essays on Baldwin as novelist, essayist, short-story writer, playwright, and scenarist, as well as a section on his raps and dialogues and a bibliography. Three of the essays offer perceptive interpretations of *Notes of a Native Son*: "The Divided Mind of James Baldwin" by C. W. E. Bigsby provides a lucid discussion of the major themes of some of the essays in the book, including the centrality of love and suffering and Baldwin's resistance to the protest novel. "Thematic Patterns in Baldwin's Essays" by Eugenia W. Collier is a perceptive discussion of Baldwin's concerns with freedom in American life, problems in relationships, and the growth of identity. Jarrett Hobart's "*From a Region in My Mind: The Essays of James Baldwin*" is an insightful thematic discussion of *Notes of a Native Son* in the context of Baldwin's later essays.

Porter, Horace A. *Stealing the Fire: The Art and Protest of James Baldwin*. Middletown, Conn.: Wesleyan University Press, 1989. Porter gives considerable attention to Baldwin's essays to study the development of his ideas about relating art to social protest. He devotes one chapter to Baldwin's relationship with Richard Wright.

Pratt, Louis H. *James Baldwin*. Boston: Twayne, 1978. A useful introduction to Baldwin's life and works. Chapters 1, 5, and 6 deal in various ways with Baldwin's essays, including an examination of their artistry. Pratt believes that the essays are Baldwin's major contribution to American letters.

Rusk, Lauren. *The Life Writing of Otherness: Woolf, Baldwin, Kingston, and Winterson*. New York: Routledge, 2002. Rusk's study of autobiographies written by authors who are outside the dominant cultures in which they live devotes a chapter to an analysis of *Notes of a Native Son*.

Standley, Fred L., and Nancy V. Burt, eds. *Critical Essays on James Baldwin*. Boston: G. K. Hall, 1988. The section on Baldwin's nonfiction works contains ten essays, including pieces by Langston Hughes, Stephen Spender, and Julius Lester; additional essays on Baldwin's nonfiction appear in the "general" section. The introduction surveys Baldwin's literary reputation, and the collection opens with a 1979 interview with Baldwin.

The Novice

Author: Mikhail Lermontov (1814-1841)
First published: "Mtsyri," 1840 (English translation, 1929)
Type of work: Poetry
Type of plot: Narrative
Time of plot: 1840
Locale: Georgia, Russia

Principal characters:
THE NOVICE, a novice monk
THE FATHER CONFESSOR
A GEORGIAN GIRL

The Poem:

As a boy of six, the young novice is captured by Russians in his native mountains. They want to take him to their own country, but he falls ill with a fever and is left with the monks of the monastery. At first, the boy refuses food and drink and seems likely to die. One of the monks, who is to become his father-confessor, takes him into his care and nurses him back to health. A Muslim by birth, he is baptized a Christian and becomes a novice confined within the narrow monastery walls. He finds his prisonlike existence intolerable. The memory of his free life in a mountain village constantly haunts him. One night, he escapes. After three days, he is found, starved and exhausted, by his father-confessor. On his deathbed, he offers his confession to the old man. It is an ac-

count of what happened to him the night he escaped and during the days that followed before his recapture.

The night he fled, the novice explains, there was a storm so violent that the monks prostrated themselves in fear before the altar. The novice took advantage of the distraction to escape into the surrounding countryside. Trying to reach his village, he wandered in the forest. He felt at home with the wild landscape and with the creatures that lived in it. His perception became heightened so that he clearly heard the many voices of nature. While drinking at a stream, he heard another song; it was that of a beautiful Georgian girl fetching water. Unseen, he watched her graceful and sensual movements and saw her go back to her home—an image that brought the uprooted novice much suffering. He longed to head toward her hut, but instead he took the path that led into the woods, and, as night fell, he became lost in the dense forest.

For the first time in his life, he cried. Suddenly, he saw two lights shining in the darkness: the eyes of a panther. The novice seized a tree branch as a weapon, the panther pounced, and the novice struck him, inflicting a bloody wound to the animal's head. The panther pounced once more. As they struggled, the novice mystically took on the spirit of the panther, knowing its ways instinctively and echoing its snarls. It was as if the panther's forlorn cry was born deep within him. Eventually, the panther tired and died in the embrace of his opponent.

When the novice emerged from the forest, it was day. With growing despair, he heard the clanging of the monastery bell. He came in a full circle. He recalled that, since childhood, the noise of the bell had destroyed his beautiful visions of his homeland and family. At that point, he realized that he would never see his birthplace again. He reflected that he was like a plant that was forced to grow in the dark; it cannot survive in the bright daylight but is scorched by the sun and dies. He knew that he, too, was about to die.

In his delirium, he dreamed that he was at the bottom of a deep stream, being caressed by the cooling waves that quenched his burning thirst. As he watched the fish swimming around him, a fish danced above his head and, meeting his gaze, sang a song to him. The song invited the novice to come live with the fish in the freedom of the water. Sadness would be driven away, and the centuries would pass quickly and sweetly. The fish ended its song with an affirmation of its love for the novice. He felt himself lured by the bright beauty and calm of the dreamworld.

The novice is found unconscious by his father-confessor and brought back to the monastery. He tells his father-confessor that he regrets that his body will lie in alien soil, and that his grave will awake a response in no one. He clasps the old man's hand in farewell, explaining that he does not seek release from worldly chains; on the contrary, he will willingly exchange heaven and eternity for one short hour among the rocks where he played as a child. He thus remains resolute, rebellious and defiant to the end. He asks to be buried in a sunny place in the garden, within view of his beloved Caucasus mountains.

Critical Evaluation:

In his native Russia, Mikhail Yurievich Lermontov is widely considered the greatest poet after Alexander Pushkin and Russia's only true Romantic poet; he also distinguished himself as a playwright and novelist. "The Novice" is one of the finest examples of Romantic poetry in Russian literature. It encompasses a theme that Lermontov explored in lyric poems such as "The Sail" and "The Angel" and was to reexamine in "The Demon" and the novel *Geroy nashego vremeni* (1839; *A Hero of Our Time*, 1854): the displaced soul, misunderstood and rebellious in nature, which seeks the storm as if calm could be found in storms.

"The Novice" is the impassioned story of an imprisoned soul and its bid for freedom in the form of a lyric monologue. Lermontov found the subject matter for this narrative poem while visiting a monastery in the former Georgian capital Mtskheti on his way to exile in the Caucasus. One of the monks told him how he came to live there. The story provided the substance of "The Novice," although Lermontov made a significant change in his source material. After the monk was recaptured, he lived on in the monastery in resignation, whereas Lermontov's novice dies defiant, asserting his preference for an hour among his childhood haunts over the heaven and eternity espoused by the monks.

The poem thus embodied a spirited bid for freedom at a time when the very word "freedom" was banned in Russia. Contemporaries saw the poem as a political allegory commenting on the repressive regime of Czar Nicholas I. However, it is far more than this. It is a vision of the romantic ideal of the unity of nature and the human spirit. It is this aspect of the poem that gives it a timeless significance beyond the transitory realities of politics.

The imagery of the poem reinforces the contrast between the two opposing worlds: the cold, dark, narrow confines of the monastery and the bright, vivid, and sensually stimulating natural landscape that surrounds it. The novice identifies himself with the natural world in a number of striking and even extravagant images: the novice embracing his brother the storm that helps him escape, the novice catching lightning in his hand, a snake—hiding from human eyes—with which the novice feels a kinship, the strange whisperings that fill the air and seem to reveal to the novice the secrets of the sky and the earth.

The apotheosis of his unity with nature comes in the fight with the panther. He echoes the panther's snarls, and he suddenly knows the ways of panthers and wolves as if he had spent his whole life in their company. He forgets human language, and within him is born the terrifying and forlorn call of the wounded beast. As the panther dies in his embrace, the novice cannot utter any other sound than this. Such concepts, though they defy the intellect, embody the loftiest spirit of Romanticism. The novice has become part of nature, a companion of the animals, both prey and predator.

In this highly sensual poem, the sense of sound plays a large part. The opposing worlds of cloister and nature, the novice's imprisonment versus his free childhood, are set apart as much by their sounds as by their appearances. The novice recalls the sweet sound of his sisters' singing and the sound of the stream that flowed beside their house. This recollection is echoed after his escape from the monastery when he hears the melodious song of the Georgian girl at the stream. Her voice, he says, has a freedom and an artlessness as if it were taught to speak only the names of friends. This remark emphasizes the emotionally nurturing quality of the novice's lost life. Finally, the dying novice derives comfort from another song, that of the compassionate fish of his dream who promises to drive the sadness from his eye and the darkness from his heart and offers him freedom and sweet sleep.

The novice's internalization of the wounded panther's cry and his sudden loss of human language is another example of his merging with nature. This wild sound, gained in victory over his opponent, stands in stark contrast with the mechanical sound that tells him of the futility of his bid for freedom— the dull, repetitive tolling of the monastery bell. This sound, like the panther's cry, resonates deeply within him, but it deprives him of power rather than bestowing it. He recalls that this very clanging always destroyed the beautiful visions that came to him of his lost home and family. He likens it to a hand of iron ceaselessly pounding at his heart.

A similar antithesis is drawn between light and dark. As the novice's cell is dark, so is his new world bright—even blindingly so. This world is described in an image of breathtaking beauty. The sky is so clear, says the novice, that an angel's flight can be perceived. The dream of the fish also has a brightly colored vividness that mesmerizes the novice. This very brightness, however, is too powerful a force for his frail body, weakened by years of darkness, to bear. He compares himself with a plant that grows in the dark between two slabs of stone. It is so weak that when it is transplanted to a garden it cannot survive the scorching sunlight and dies with the dawn. The novice refuses to renounce the world of light and intends to be reunited with it in death. He asks that he might be buried in a sunny spot in the garden, so that he might forever feast his eyes on the luminous, light-nourished day. The novice's final "confession" thus becomes both a profession of faith and a defiant challenge to physical and spiritual captivity.

Claire J. Robinson

Further Reading

Eikhenbaum, B. M. *Lermontov.* Translated by Ray Parrott and Harry Weber. Ann Arbor, Mich.: Ardis, 1981. A literary and historical evaluation of Lermontov's works, including "The Novice." Places Lermontov in Russian literary context and offers useful insights into his versification.

Garrard, John. *Mikhail Lermontov.* Boston: Twayne, 1982. One of the best overviews of Lermontov's life and works for the general reader. Contains a substantial section on "The Novice," examining its background, form, structure, and themes.

Golstein, Vladimir. *Lermontov's Narratives of Heroism.* Evanston, Ill.: Northwestern University Press, 1998. Focuses on the theme of heroism and the individual in Lermontov's works, including "The Novice." Citations of works are in Russian with English translation.

Kelly, Laurence. *Lermontov: Tragedy in the Caucasus.* 1977. Reprint. London: Tauris Parke, 2003. Colorfully illustrated biography covering Lermontov's childhood in the "wild" East, his education, his rise and fall in society, and his attitudes toward war as reflected in his works.

Lavrin, Janko. *Lermontov.* New York: Hillary House, 1959. A lucid and intelligent summary of Lermontov's life, major works, and recurrent themes. Includes a short section on "The Novice."

Mersereau, John, Jr. *Mikhail Lermontov.* Carbondale: Southern Illinois University Press, 1962. An extremely useful and readable critical analysis of Lermontov's works, incorporating a valuable discussion of Lermontov's Romanticism and a section on "The Novice."

Powelstock, David. *Becoming Mikhail Lermontov: The Ironies of Romantic Individualism in Nicholas I's Russia.* Evanston, Ill.: Northwestern University Press, 2005. Powelstock argues that Lermontov had a coherent worldview, which he defines as "Romantic individualism," and he demonstrates how this philosophy explains contradictions in the writer's life and works.

The Nun

Author: Denis Diderot (1713-1784)
First published: La Religieuse, 1796 (English
   translation, 1797)
Type of work: Novel
Type of plot: Narrative
Time of plot: 1760's
Locale: France

Principal characters:
SUZANNE SIMONIN, the young nun who writes the story
M. AND MME SIMONIN, Suzanne's parents
FATHER SÉRAPHIN, confessor of Suzanne and of her
   mother
MME DE MONI, mother superior at Longchamp, a mystic
SISTER SAINTE CHRISTINE, sadistic mother superior who
   replaces Madame de Moni
MME ***, lesbian mother superior at Sainte-Eutrope
THE MARQUIS DE CROISMARE, the nobleman to whom
   Suzanne writes her memoir

The Story:

Suzanne Simonin is one of the three daughters of M. and Mme Simonin; throughout her childhood and adolescence, her parents prefer her sisters although Suzanne is superior to them in every respect. When it is time for marriages to be arranged for the sisters, Suzanne is preferred by the suitors. However, when she tells her mother of the attention paid to her, she is sent off to a convent.

At first, Suzanne thinks that she is to remain in the convent just until her two sisters are married. Then, Father Séraphin visits her and explains that her parents have decided that she will become a nun. Suzanne objects but is convinced by the mother superior to begin her novitiate. During this time, Suzanne is very well treated, but on her second day she sees an apparently insane nun who has been confined in chains. Suzanne is terrified and sees the poor woman as a warning of what may happen to her. Suzanne informs the mother superior of her decision not to continue her preparation for the convent. Her parents are informed of her decision. She is locked in her cell in isolation, after which she is continuously visited by the priest and nuns, who harangue her to change her mind.

Eventually, Suzanne decides that she will become a nun. However, her reason for doing so is to give her the opportunity to refuse her vows publicly. During her profession of faith, she answers "no" to all of the priest's questions. She istaken home and locked in a room for six months. Finally, having received permission from her mother to reveal the truth, Father Séraphin tells Suzanne that she is not M. Simenon's daughter, that she is illegitimate. He insists that she must take the veil to expiate her mother's sin. He also tells her that she must not reveal the truth in public, because to do so would eliminate her right to inherit the family fortune.

Suzanne's mother agrees to speak with her. Suzanne attempts to convince her to try to find someone who will marry her without a dowry or to allow Suzanne legally to renounce her inheritance. Her mother refuses, stating that Suzanne's public refusal of her vows created such a scandal that there is no possibility of marriage for her and that children cannot disinherit themselves. Her mother then insists that the only way she can have her sins expiated and be delivered from the torment in which she lives is for Suzanne to enter the convent. Furthermore, Mme Simonin says that she cannot permit Suzanne to inherit an estate that is not rightfully hers because of her illegitimacy. If Suzanne does not take the veil, her mother says, she will have to confess her sin to her husband.

Suzanne acquiesces. Because of the scandal caused by Suzanne's public refusal to take her vows, there is some difficulty in finding a convent that will accept her. Finally, because of her talent as a musician and singer, the convent of Longchamp agrees to accept her. Although Suzanne abhors the thought of losing her freedom and being cloistered, her life at Longchamp is fairly pleasant. The mother superior Mme de Moni is a gentle-natured mystic who is very fond of Suzanne. She favors Suzanne to the point of incurring the jealousy of the other nuns. Suzanne manages to take her vows, although she later states that she has no recollection of the ceremony. The tension and emotional stress of Mme de Moni's efforts to attain a perfect communion with God cause her to slip from mysticism into insanity, and she dies. Following her death, the convent soon becomes everything Suzanne had feared it would be.

Sister Sainte Christine becomes the new mother superior. She and many of the other nuns believe that Suzanne is responsible for the chaos that has invaded the convent and the death of Mme de Moni. Sister Sainte Christine not only believes that Suzanne has destroyed the discipline of the convent but also intensely dislikes her. Suzanne becomes the victim of mistreatment that becomes increasingly sadistic as time passes. She is locked in her cell, from which all furniture and bedding are removed. Her clothes are also taken. No one speaks to her; the nuns are even forbidden to acknowledge that she exists. She is forced to walk on broken glass.

From the time she entered the convent, Suzanne has been in contact with M. Manouri, a lawyer who has been trying to enable her to free herself legally from her vows. It is at the very moment that Suzanne is about to die from the sadistic acts perpetrated against her that M. Manouri obtains her transfer to another convent. Although he has failed to win her case to renounce her vows, he has managed to have her transferred to Sainte-Eutrope.

At Sainte-Eutrope, Suzanne is once again favored by the mother superior, Mme ***. This mother superior is a lesbian, but the innocent Suzanne never realizes the meaning of her caresses. Mme *** dies in agony after falling into a state of delirium. With the aid of a profligate priest, Suzanne escapes from the convent, only to be taken to a house of prostitution. She escapes again. It is night, and she is pursued by men. She collapses in front of a candlemaker's shop, receives help, and eventually gets a job working in a laundry. As the novel ends, Suzanne is waiting for a reply from the Marquis de Croismare, a nobleman that she has contacted for help.

Critical Evaluation:

Denis Diderot's *The Nun* was originally a series of letters written as a ruse played on Marc-Antoine-Nicolas, marquis de Croismare. Diderot and a group of his friends were attempting to bring the marquis, who had gone to Normandy on a business matter, back to Paris. The novel is based on a true incident. Before leaving Paris, the marquis had been helping a woman who had been cloistered without her consent. The goal of the letters was to persuade the marquis that the woman had escaped by fleeing from the convent and needed his help. In the 1780's, Diderot expanded the letters into a memoir novel. The author snared himself in the trap set for the marquis, as Suzanne became a real person for Diderot, and he could be found shedding tears as he wrote about her.

In addition to the novel having its genesis in reality, it also has origins in Diderot's own life. His sister Angélique took vows as an Ursuline nun. She lost her sanity and died at the age of twenty-eight. Her death was attributed to exhaustion from the debilitating life of excessive work in the convent. In addition to Diderot's personal animosity for convents and the cloistering of women, he found the practice philosophically unacceptable. Thus, in his novel, Diderot depicts the convent as an oppressive institution where natural instincts are repressed and an abnormal lifestyle is forced upon its members. The convent corrupts and degrades human nature, bringing about aberrant sexual behavior. For Diderot, Madame de Moni's mystic exultation that drives her to insanity, Sister Sainte Christine's sadistic cruelty, and Mme ***'s lesbianism are all manifestations of deviant sexual behavior that result from the convent's forbidding "normal" heterosexual activity.

Diderot's novel also reflects his admiration for the sentimental novels of Samuel Richardson. Diderot was moved to tears whenever he read these novels. For him, Richardson was a master of creating emotion and pathos in the novel. Richardson's innocent and helpless young woman abandoned by her family and at the mercy of the cruel and unscrupulous is the model for Suzanne. However, Diderot's heroine is more complex. Although Diderot was given to sentimentalism, he was also a rationalist. Suzanne suffers excessively; she is innocent and rejected by her family. Suzanne is also very intelligent, however, and she never stops trying to liberate herself from the convent. She devises the ruse of refusing her vows publically in order to call attention to her plight. She manages to engage M. Manouri to seek a legal solution to her case.

In addition, Diderot was interested in the novel as a genre and in the techniques of novel-writing. In *The Nun*, he uses narrative elements found in his other novels, such as *Jacques le fataliste et son maître* (wr. c. 1771, pb. 1796; *Jacques the Fatalist and His Master*, 1797).

The character Suzanne has many qualities of an unreliable narrator. The entire novel is written from her viewpoint. Suzanne stresses her innocence, her virtue, and her naivete too much, while at the same time manipulating her narrative. She represents herself as helpless, naïve, and innocent of any subterfuge. She is concerned that the marquis will think she is trying to seduce him into helping her since she has mentioned her superior beauty. She assures the marquis that she is appealing to him in the name of her virtue. However, she emphasizes how very much she exceeds her sisters in loveliness.

Suzanne states that when her sister's suitor appeared to prefer her she informed her mother and was rewarded by being sent to the convent. Thus, she gives the impression that she was concerned with furthering the marriage match for her sister. As a reader becomes more familiar with the character, however, it begins to appear possible that Suzanne's real motivation was to have the match herself. Suzanne describes in detail the lesbian conduct of Mme *** but never reveals any understanding of what is occurring. Although Suzanne's plight elicits sympathy, readers may sense that Suzanne is orchestrating far more than she admits.

Movement and change play major roles in the novel's structure. Suzanne is taken to a convent; she is returned home; she is taken to Longchamp; she is transferred to Sainte-Eutrope; she escapes and is taken to the house of prostitution; she escapes again; she is at the laundry at the end of the novel, anticipating another move with the marquis's help. Suzanne is also an element of chaos within the convents. The usual atmosphere of the convent is quiet immobility, but Suzanne disrupts this atmosphere. While she is victimized by the convent, she also victimizes the rules of the convent. As a materialist, Diderot believed that everything was in a constant state of flux, that everything changed at every moment. With Suzanne, this materialistic reality of movement invades the staid immobilized reality of convent life.

Shawncey Webb

Further Reading

Caplan, Jay, and John Achulte. *Framed Narratives: Diderot's Genealogy of the Beholder.* Minneapolis: University of Minnesota Press, 1985. Two chapters are devoted exclusively to *The Nun*, discussing the techniques Diderot used to establish a dialogue between the characters, the author, and his readers. Good analysis of Diderot as a writer interested in how to write a novel.

Choufhury, Mita. *Convents and Nuns in Eighteenth Century French Politics and Culture.* Ithaca, N.Y.: Cornell University Press, 2004. Excellent study of the role and impor-

tance of the convent in eighteenth century France. Looks at the power structure within convents, the public's reaction to convents, and how convents affected the lives of women. Views the convent as a representation of despotism. Provides a good factual account for comparison with Diderot's convents and Suzanne's plight.

Cusset, Catherine. *No Tomorrow: The Ethics of Pleasure in the French Enlightenment.* Charlottesville: University Press of Virginia, 1999. Good for understanding the erotic aspects of the novel; examines how Diderot uses the ethic of pleasure (vanity and sensual enjoyment), a key component of the libertine novel of the century, in *The Nun.* Treats the topic in terms of Suzanne's experiences and her quest for freedom.

Edmiston, William. *Hindsight and Insight: Focalization in Four Eighteenth Century Novels.* University Park: Pennsylvania State University Press, 1991. Examines Diderot's experimentation with narrative form. Analyzes how the first-person narrator focuses the work. Also addresses manipulation of the reader and narrator reliability.

Marshall, David. *The Surprising Effects of Sympathy: Marivaux, Diderot, Rousseau, and Mary Shelley.* Chicago: University of Chicago Press, 1988. Chapter 3, "Sympathy and Seduction," discusses *The Nun* in terms of Diderot's admiration for the novels of Samuel Richardson; analyzes the interactions of sympathy with seduction both within the novel and in the reader-narrator relationship.

Mortimer, Armine Kotin. *Writing Realism: Representations in French Fiction.* Baltimore: Johns Hopkins University Press, 2000. A close reading of *The Nun* from the standpoint of realism in fiction. Discusses Diderot's role in establishing novel theory.

Nuns and Soldiers

Author: Iris Murdoch (1919-1999)
First published: 1980
Type of work: Novel
Type of plot: Psychological realism
Time of plot: 1970's
Locale: London and southern France

The Story:

Guy Openshaw, an administrator in the British Home Office, lies dying in his luxurious Ebury Street flat. A coterie of friends and relatives drops in frequently to console his wife,

Principal characters:
GUY OPENSHAW, a wealthy man dying of cancer
GERTRUDE OPENSHAW, his wife
TIM REEDE, a young, penniless artist
DAISY BARRETT, his mistress
ANNE CAVIDGE, a former nun
PETER SZCZEPANSKI, a Pole called the Count

Gertrude. One evening Gertrude receives a call from Anne Cavidge, once her best friend at Cambridge, who for fifteen years was a cloistered nun. Anne leaves the order and returns to the world. Gertrude invites Anne to stay with her at Ebury Street. Guy dies after telling Gertrude that she might consider the Count for her next husband. In her terrible grief Gertrude elicits Anne's promise to stay with her forever. The Count pays a condolence call, and the two women realize that he is in love with Gertrude.

Meanwhile, the fortunes of young Tim Reede and Daisy Barrett, longtime friends and lovers, deteriorate. Guy, who once administered a small trust for Tim, used to give him handouts occasionally. At Daisy's urging Tim goes to Gertrude to ask for money. Gertrude, trying to be helpful as Guy would wish, offers Tim a job repairing her house in France. Tim, overjoyed, accepts the offer and makes secret plans to have Daisy join him. He finds the house in a beautiful valley crossed by streams and mysterious stone formations. One day he returns from hiking to find that Gertrude has arrived to facilitate the sale of her house. Tim pursues his painting, and Gertrude tries to take care of business. They explore the countryside together and in one night Tim and Gertrude fall passionately in love. Gertrude insists they must marry, and Tim, overwhelmed by events, neglects to tell Gertrude about Daisy. A few days later, Gertrude's relatives arrive to whisk her home to London.

Tim rushes back to England and tells Daisy he is going to marry Gertrude. Daisy insists it can be only for money, and when Tim denies this, she throws him out in a rage. Gertrude rushes to Tim's shabby studio and declares they must keep the relationship secret until her mourning for Guy ends. Meanwhile, the Count receives an anonymous letter, which he shares with Anne, saying that Gertrude is having a love affair with Tim. Confronted by Anne, Gertrude admits the truth; Anne, horrified and jealous, tries to talk her out of continuing the affair.

Anne moves out of Gertrude's home and Tim moves in. Soon Gertrude, unnerved by Anne's bitter words and confused by her secret double life, tells Tim they will have to part and resume their relationship later. Terribly hurt, Tim leaves and goes to Daisy's flat, where they resume their affair. After a few days, he finds living with Daisy intolerable and moves into a hotel, where he longs for Gertrude. She resumes life with old friends and relatives but thinks obsessively of Tim. When they meet accidentally in the British Museum, they are overcome with happiness and marry soon afterward.

Anne falls in love with the Count, who visits her flat frequently to salve his wounded feelings over Gertrude's marriage. One day he arrives agitated, having heard that Tim has a mistress never mentioned to Gertrude. Worse yet, the Count hears that Tim and the mistress plot for Tim to marry wealth and continue to keep the mistress. Anne, who never

liked Tim, visits Daisy and asks her about the gossip. Angry, Daisy says it is true and throws her visitor out. Anne tells Gertrude of her discoveries, and Gertrude asks Tim about Daisy. Tim, embarrassed and confused, admits it is true but that they only joked about a rich marriage. Furious, Gertrude leaves, after ordering Tim to be gone when she returns.

Tim despairs, believing his life with Gertrude is over. He withdraws money from his and Gertrude's account and goes to Daisy's flat. As he enters, he sees Anne at the street corner spying on him. Anne moves back to Ebury Street and tries to soothe and comfort Gertrude. Gertrude lets herself be comforted but rages inwardly with pain and jealousy. Tim, suffering intense guilt, gives up hope of reconciliation and continues his tormented life with Daisy.

Gertrude, Anne, and the Count go to Gertrude's house in France for a holiday, where the Count again hopes for a chance with Gertrude. In London, Tim and Daisy come to an understanding that their dissolute lives are not good for either of them, and they part permanently. Tim is reconciled to his solitary life although he thinks constantly of Gertrude. One day a letter from a mutual friend arrives, saying that Gertrude is at her house in France and probably needs and wants him back.

Tim sets out immediately for France. He approaches the house from the valley and sees Gertrude holding hands with the Count. He flees but falls into a canal that sweeps him through a drainage pipe. He thinks he will die until he lands on a sandy shore. Battered, tired, and hungry, Tim creeps back to the house, where Gertrude welcomes him joyfully into her arms. Anne finally realizes that Gertrude's happiness depended upon him. She snatches the astonished Count off to the village, leaving husband and wife alone for a blissful reconciliation.

Tim and Gertrude return to London anticipating years of happiness. Gertrude, sorry for the Count's disappointment, declares her new life will include him, and he is comforted. Anne goes off to America.

Critical Evaluation:

Iris Murdoch was one of the most influential British postwar novelists. A professional philosopher who taught at St. Anne's College, Oxford, Murdoch also was respected as a literary theorist. Monographs, dissertations, and critical studies have been written about her, and although critics disagree about the strengths and weaknesses of her work, they agree the work is significant. *Nuns and Soldiers*, Murdoch's twentieth novel, is a sum of the techniques and philosophical underpinnings of its predecessors.

Religion is one of Murdoch's large themes. In *Nuns and Soldiers*, the opening word of the novel is "Wittgenstein," the name of the philosopher who argued that one cannot prove or disprove the existence of God. Murdoch's novels teem with failed priests, Christ figures, nuns, Greek and Roman gods, and religious symbolism. In *Nuns and Soldiers*, there are hints that Guy Openshaw is a Christ figure. He is a father to the other characters. He dies on Christmas Eve, he is revered for his wisdom, and he is half-Jewish. Anne Cavidge, the former nun, believes she has a vision of the true Christ, from whom she demands answers, solutions, and salvation, only to receive his answer that she must find them in herself. Even Tim, the most openly sinful of the characters, seems to be touched with an ability to see beyond the physical to the miraculous. He sees the sacred quality in the French countryside as well as in the smallest leaves fallen from autumn trees.

The god that drives the plot, however, is the ancient Greek god of love, Eros, striking suddenly and causing endless romantic entanglements. In a typical Murdoch plot device, Tim and Gertrude, indifferent to each other for years, fall in love in seconds. Tim sees Gertrude as a sexual being only after Gertrude swims in a pool of crystal springs, and he undergoes his own ordeal by water when he survives his hazardous journey through a drainpipe. Water is often invoked in Murdoch's work as a symbol of the amorous powers that overcome her characters, and here it is used to wonderful effect. Symmetrical pairings of lovers is another device Murdoch employs. In *Nuns and Soldiers*, six characters are paired: Gertrude with Guy, Tim with Daisy, and the Count with Anne. Although Guy dies early in the novel, he remains an important character and is often thought of and mentioned, especially by Gertrude. By the end of the novel, however, these neat pairings are turned around, and one is blessed while others are frustrated.

The "nuns" of the title refer to Anne and to Daisy Barrett, a woman of loose morals. Anne and Daisy both go off to America. Anne joins a group of religious activists and Daisy joins a female commune, a kind of women's order. America is a favorite place for Murdoch to send her characters when they are no longer needed for her intricate plots. The Count, one of the "soldiers" who has fantasies of fighting for his beloved Poland, accepts his disappointment in love and his role as family retainer in a soldierly way. Tim is a soldier who must undergo several ordeals to win his lady. After one of them, a fit of swooning in Hyde Park, Tim is filled with joy as if he is purified. Nuns and soldiers may also symbolize and contrast cloistered virtue with the embattled goodness acquired by struggling in the real world.

The friends and relatives who gather around Guy and Gertrude, called "*les cousins et les tantes*," form a kind of

Greek chorus for the central action. The members comment on and argue about the major characters and predict action to come, although often they are wrong. These minor characters also tie up certain loose threads of plot at the end; one or two step outside their role in the chorus and act in ways that move the story.

Critics have had difficulty classifying Murdoch's writing because she combines metaphysical themes and unlikely occurrences with an absolutely realistic surface created of precisely observed details. Each character is dressed in perfect accord with his or her class and station in life. Even Daisy's makeup and Anne's haircut are significant in delineating their characters. Interiors are carefully drawn and have a character of their own, creating a solid background for the drama. Gertrude's drawing room reflects seriousness in its arrangement as well as whimsy in the tiny china orchestra on her mantel. One of the triumphs of *Nuns and Soldiers* is the house and surrounding countryside in France, so carefully depicted that the reader could draw a map of it. Sensuous hills and valleys lend credence to the romance that occurs there, and the way Murdoch's characters are influenced by their surroundings gives another dimension to her work.

Sheila Golburgh Johnson

Further Reading

Bove, Cheryl Browning. *Understanding Iris Murdoch*. Columbia: University of South Carolina Press, 1993. Overviews of Murdoch's life and philosophical writings introduce brief summaries of her major works from 1954 to 1989, her plays, and her minor novels. Includes an annotated bibliography.

Conradi, Peter J. *The Saint and the Artist: A Study of the Fiction of Iris Murdoch*. New ed. London: HarperCollins, 2001. Detailed analysis of many of Murdoch's works, including *Nuns and Soldiers*. Traces literary precedents and influences on the novel.

Dipple, Elizabeth. *Iris Murdoch: Work for the Spirit*. Chicago: University of Chicago Press, 1982. Chapter 10 of this comprehensive analysis of Murdoch's novels concerns itself exclusively with *Nuns and Soldiers*. Illuminates many of the philosophical, religious, and literary references in the novel and traces Murdoch's development from her first to her twentieth book of fiction.

Hardy, Robert. "Will and Belief in *The Sovereignty of the Good, Henry and Cato*, and *Nuns and Soldiers*." In *Psychological and Religious Narratives in Iris Murdoch's Fiction*. Lewiston, N.Y.: Edwin Mellen Press, 2000. Examines how Murdoch's novels interweave religious and psychological narratives and are heavily influenced by the psychoanalytic theories of Sigmund Freud and Carl Jung.

Johnson, Deborah. *Iris Murdoch*. Bloomington: Indiana University Press, 1987. A good general overview of the novels, particularly the later ones, including *Nuns and Soldiers*. Part of the Key Women Writers series.

Mettler, Darlene D. *Sound and Sense: Musical Allusion and Imagery in the Novels of Iris Murdoch*. New York: Peter Lang, 1991. After overviews of the relationship between music and literature, eight of Murdoch's novels are discussed, including *Nuns and Soldiers*.

Ramanathan, Suguna. *Iris Murdoch: Figures of Good*. New York: St. Martin's Press, 1990. A well-written and clear explanation of Murdoch's ethical and religious ideas, focusing on figures of good in eight of her novels, including *Nuns and Soldiers*.

Rowe, Anne, ed. *Iris Murdoch: A Reassessment*. New York: Palgrave Macmillan, 2007. Collection of essays that reinterpret Murdoch's work in terms of twenty-first century debates about the aesthetic impulse, moral philosophy, gender and sexuality, literature, and authorship. Includes comparisons of Murdoch's work with works by other authors

Spear, Hilda D. *Iris Murdoch*. New York: Palgrave Macmillan, 2007. Spear provides an introduction to Murdoch's novels, tracing how she progressively used the plots of each book to address philosophical issues, such as the nature of reality, good, and evil. Chapter 6 discusses *Nuns and Soldiers* and Murdoch's other "mystic novels."

Todd, Richard. *Iris Murdoch*. New York: Methuen, 1984. A useful volume on Murdoch's life and work. Todd attempts to link the novels to Murdoch's philosophical positions, particularly to the existentialism of Jean-Paul Sartre and others.

O

O Pioneers!

Author: Willa Cather (1873-1947)
First published: 1913
Type of work: Novel
Type of plot: Regional
Time of plot: 1880-1910
Locale: Nebraska

Principal characters:
ALEXANDRA BERGSON, a homesteader
EMIL, her brother
CARL LINDSTRUM,
MARIE TOVESKY,
and FRANK SHABATA, Alexandra's neighbors
CRAZY IVAR, a hired man

The Story:

Hanover is a frontier town huddled on the windblown Nebraska prairie. One winter day, young Alexandra Bergson and her small brother Emil go into town from their new homestead. The Bergsons are Swedes. Their life in the new country is one of hardship because their father is sick and the children are too young to do all the work on their prairie acres. Alexandra goes to the village doctor's office to get some medicine for her father. The doctor tells her there is no hope for their father's recovery.

Emil, who had brought his kitten to town with him, is crying on the street because the cat had climbed to the top of the telegraph pole and would not come down. When Alexandra returns, she meets their neighbor, Carl Lindstrum, who rescues the cat. The three ride toward home together, and Carl talks of his drawing. When Alexandra and Emil arrive home, their supper is waiting, and their mother and father are anxious for their return. Shortly afterward, Bergson calls his family about him and tells them to listen to Alexandra, even though she is a girl, for she has proved her abilities to run the farm capably. Above all, they are to keep the land.

Alexandra is still a young girl when her father dies, but she immediately assumes the family's domestic and financial troubles; she guides everything the family does, and through her resourcefulness, she gains security and even a measure of wealth for her brothers and herself. Emil, the youngest brother, remains the dreamer of the family, in his mooning over Marie Tovesky, whom he had first loved as a little child. Marie had married Frank Shabata. Frank was wildly possessive and mistrusted everyone who showed the slightest kindness to Marie. Alexandra is in love with Carl

Lindstrum, whose father gave up his farm because the new, stubborn land seemed too hard to subdue. He returned to more settled country and took Carl with him to learn the engraver's trade.

Alexandra depends upon Crazy Ivar for many things. He is a hermit, living in a hole dug into the side of a riverbed. The kinder Swedes claim he had been touched by God. Those who are unsympathetic are sure he is dangerous. Actually, he is a kindhearted mystic who loves animals and birds and who lets his beard grow according to the custom of ancient prophets. Through his lack of concern for worldly matters, he loses his claim, and Alexandra gives him shelter on her own farm, much to the dismay of her brothers and their wives. They demand that she send Crazy Ivar to an institution, but she refuses. She respects Crazy Ivar as she does few other people.

In the same way, Alexandra defends Carl Lindstrum. After an absence of sixteen years, he returns to their settlement. He had studied much, but in the eyes of the thrifty Swedes, his life was a failure because he had not married and had no property. He seems willing to marry Alexandra, who is now quite wealthy. Her brothers, Oscar and Lou, tell Alexandra that she must not marry Carl, and she orders them from her house. Carl, hearing of the disagreement, sets out for the West at once.

Alexandra applies herself to new problems. She pays passage for other Swedes to come to America; she experiments with new farming methods. She becomes friendlier with Marie Shabata, whose husband is growing more jealous. She sees to it that Emil receives an education, and she lets him go off to the university despite the criticism of the other brothers. By now Emil knows he loves Marie, and he goes away to study because he feels that if he stays in the community, something terrible will happen. Even attending the university does not help him. Other girls he meets seem less attractive. His secret thoughts are always about Marie.

Frank Shabata discharges hired hands because he suspects them. He follows Marie everywhere. Even at the Catholic church he is at her heels scowling at everyone to whom she talks. His jealousy is like a disease. At the same time, he treats her coldly and insults her publicly in front of their friends. She, on her part, is headstrong and defiant. At last, Emil returns from college. His friend, Amedee, becomes ill while working in his wheat fields and dies shortly afterward. Following the funeral, Emil resolves to see Marie, to say good-bye to her before leaving the neighborhood permanently. He finds her in her orchard under the mulberry tree. There for the first time, they become lovers.

Frank returns from town slightly drunk. Finding a Bergson horse in his stable, he takes a weapon and searches for Emil. When he sees the two he fires, killing both. Frank, mad with horror, starts to run away. Crazy Ivar discovers the dead bodies and runs with the news to Alexandra. For the next few months, Alexandra seems in a daze and spends much of her time in the cemetery. She is caught there during a terrible storm, and Crazy Ivar has to go after her. She regains her old self-possession during the storm. Frank, who was captured soon after the shooting, was tried, convicted, and sentenced to prison. Alexandra determines to do what she can to secure his freedom. If she can no longer help her brother, she would help Frank.

While trying to help Frank, she hears that Carl has returned. He had never received her letter telling of the tragedy, but on his return from Alaska he read of the trial and hurried to Alexandra. His mine was a promising venture. The two decide that they can now marry and bring their long separation to an end.

Critical Evaluation:

Willa Cather's *O Pioneers!* is one story of the settlement of the American frontier. The title comes from lines written by nineteenth century poet Walt Whitman, who viewed the land as inspirational and a way to commune with God. Likewise, for Cather, the frontier was legendary, almost mythological, in American culture. Cather contributes to the legend of the American frontier in *O Pioneers!*

The frontier is portrayed in the novel as a noble but rugged place where dreams can come true if the characters work hard and believe in the land. *O Pioneers!* reflects the legend of American immigration. It shows the pains, hardships, beauty, and joy of life in the heartland of the United States. One of the novel's great strengths is its careful interplay of the legendary and the realistic.

In *O Pioneers!* the land plays a major role in motivation and plot development. Alexandra, for example, feels she is a part of the land. Through her endurance and ability to farm the land (while others, such as Carl Lindstrum, leave it), she achieves success and riches. In the novel, an American legend, in which the European immigrant comes to the New World to seek his or her fortune through land ownership, figures heavily. The immigrant turns the wilderness along the frontier into a farm or ranch and profits thereby. Alexandra Bergson, the protagonist of *O Pioneers!*, lives this American legend.

Other elements of the legendary can be seen in the work as well; it is difficult to think of unspoiled land being cultivated by isolated female and male figures without recalling the book of Genesis, and themes of innocence and its loss. To Cather's credit, these powerful themes do not overshadow the book's realism. Alexandra remains a particular woman living in a particular time and place, in spite of the weighty symbolic value that may be placed on her.

O Pioneers! combines two stories, "Alexandra" and "The White Mulberry Tree." Alexandra is what links the two stories, which are separated by sixteen years. The first story tells of a young immigrant woman who must care for a farm; it is about her courage and endurance. Alexandra is a woman who must survive in a man's world. Cather seems to have modeled her protagonist after herself; there are various parallels in the lives of the author and her character.

Alexandra's great courage and endurance also have a legendary quality. Alexandra is a female version, or revision, of the hardworking tamer of the land, a figure with origins in the Bible and in the legend of the American immigrant. In the second story, "The White Mulberry Tree," Alexandra is about forty years old, about the age of Cather at the time she published *O Pioneers!* As Alexandra matures, her relationship with the other characters changes. She initially is the proverbial damsel in distress whom Carl helps by rescuing the kitten. Later, she is the strong one who is wealthy and who eventually owns the Lindstrum farm.

In "The White Mulberry Tree," characters who were in the background emerge into the foreground. Emil Bergson and Marie Tovesky, who receive brief mention at the beginning of the book, develop into important parts of the subplot. The two ill-fated lovers are murdered under the mulberry tree by Marie's jealous husband, an act whose biblical echoes are apparent. This violent subplot counterbalances the primary story about the development of the farm and the fulfillment of the American legend of the successful immigrant.

The subplot of the failed romance and murder gives Carl a reason to return to the independent Alexandra. She appears weakened by the loss of her brother, Emil, and close friend Marie. "The White Mulberry Tree" subplot can be interpreted symbolically; murder, deceit, and adultery are the snake in the grass in Cather's pastoral ideal. Additionally, the novel may be read as the story of one woman's psychological development.

O Pioneers! contrasts the peaceful, pastoral world of Alexandra with violence and murder, though the story ends peacefully as Alexandra tries to rebuild her world. There is much evidence in the novel to support the argument that the story is a rejection of the American legend of the immigrant's creating an Edenic, even profitable, world. Alexandra's world has been shattered by the death of her beloved Emil and Marie. The novel, however, also ends on a note of hope; Alexandra and Carl may find happiness together.

"Critical Evaluation" by Mary C. Bagley

Further Reading

Bagley, M. C. *Cather's Myths*. New York: American Heritage, 1994. Discusses *O Pioneers!* in the context of the American myth of the settlement of the land and the countermyth of the rejection of the land. Emphasizes Alexandra's relationship to the land and how this symbolizes the settlement of America.

Cather, Willa. *O Pioneers! Authoritative Text, Context and Backgrounds, Criticism*. Edited by Sharon O'Brien. New York: W. W. Norton, 2008. In addition to the text, this edition contains autobiographical and biographical essays about Cather, discussions of other works by Cather and other authors that place *O Pioneers!* in its literary context, and contemporary reviews and modern critical interpretations of the novel.

De Roche, Linda. *Student Companion to Willa Cather*. Westport, Conn.: Greenwood Press, 2006. An introductory overview of Cather's life and work aimed at high school and college students and the general reader. Discusses character development, themes, and plots of six novels, with chapter 4 focusing on *O Pioneers!*

Meyering, Sheryl L. *Understanding "O Pioneers!" and "My Antonia": A Student Casebook to Issues, Sources, and Historical Documents*. Westport, Conn.: Greenwood Press, 2002. Contains analysis of the two novels, as well as excerpts from journals, letters, government reports, and other primary documents that provide historical context about life on the plains, farming, the railroad, women on the frontier, and foreign-born pioneers.

Murphy, John J., ed. *Critical Essays on Willa Cather*. Boston: G. K. Hall, 1984. This collection of essays deals with various themes and ideas, such as sexuality and childhood, contained in Cather's novels.

_____. *Willa Cather: Family, Community, and History*. Provo, Utah: Brigham Young University Press, 1990. Collection of conference papers examining recurrent motifs in Cather's novels, such as how concepts of socialization affect individual ideas about one's place in the family, community, and history.

O'Brien, Sharon. *Willa Cather: The Emerging Voice*. New York: Oxford University Press, 1987. O'Brien's biography examines Cather's life before 1915, when she was becoming more famous for her novels, and speculates on her search for both a gender identity and a personal narrative voice.

Rosowski, Susan J. "*O Pioneers!*: Willa Cather's New World Pastoral." In *The Voyage Perilous: Willa Cather's Romanticism*. Lincoln: University of Nebraska Press, 1986. Discusses how the two stories "Alexandra" and "The White Mulberry Tree" came to be written and then combined into *O Pioneers!* Rosowski maintains the novel is related to the classical tradition of the pastoral.

Slote, Bernice, and Virginia Faulkner, eds. *The Art of Willa Cather*. Lincoln: University of Nebraska Press, 1974. A collection of essays by noted Cather scholars discussing various aspects of her style of fiction.

Woodress, James. *Willa Cather: Her Life and Art*. New York: Egasus, 1970. A critical biography examines the connections between Cather's personal life and her writing.

Obasan

Author: Joy Kogawa (1935-   )
First published: 1981
Type of work: Novel
Type of plot: Historical realism
Time of plot: 1972, with flashbacks to the 1940's
Locale: British Columbia and Alberta, Canada;
  Nagasaki, Japan

Principal characters:
NAOMI NAKANE, an elementary-school teacher
ISAMU NAKANE, her uncle
AYAKO NAKANE, her aunt, whom she calls Obasan
EMILY KATO, another aunt, her mother's sister
STEPHEN NAKANE, Naomi's brother
SENSEI NAKAYAMA, spiritual leader of Naomi's extended
  family

The Story:

Naomi Nakane is in the middle of teaching her fifth- and sixth-grade class in the small town of Cecil, Alberta, when she receives word that her uncle has died in Granton, 150 miles south. Going home for his funeral means for her a sad reunion with several family members, notably the quiet widow, the "Obasan" of the book's title, and Stephen, Naomi's older brother. Obasan and Uncle Isamu had raised Naomi and her brother from the time that they were young children. Flamboyant Stephen, who essentially renounced his Japanese heritage and had been involved for a time with a French woman, developed a national reputation as a classical pianist and now lives in Montreal. Unmarried Naomi, on the other hand, had been stuck in a dead-end teaching job for the past seven years with no prospects of either romance or fame.

Emily Kato, Naomi's outspoken unmarried aunt living in Toronto, also makes the trip to Granton for the memorial service. Politically active, she had hounded Naomi for years to become more interested and involved with exposing the wrongs of the Canadian government in its internment of Japanese citizens during World War II. She had earlier sent Naomi a large box of newspaper clippings, letters, and government documents, which had been stored unread by Obasan under the kitchen table.

The trip home brings back painful memories to Naomi about growing up without her mother. Studying an old family photograph when she arrives in Granton sparks extended reminiscences: In September, 1941, Naomi's mother and Naomi's grandmother, Kato, travel to Japan to care for a relative who is ill, but neither returns. (Naomi, who was five years old at the time, has never been told what became of her mother.) She and her family and her Japanese neighbors are forced by the Canadian government to move inland to internment camps and abandon their successful boat-building business near Vancouver. The family members—Naomi, Stephen, Uncle Isamu, and Ayaka Obasan—are required to sell off their belongings and leave their comfortable home

indefinitely. They are moved to an abandoned mining settlement inland named Slocan, and are separated from Aunt Emily for twelve years.

Losing her doll on the train ride becomes symbolic for Naomi: the loss of all comfort and vestiges of domestic life. The living conditions in the camp are deplorable, with little food, heat, or sanitation, but at least the family have a small house to themselves, and the children attend school. Led by Sensei Nakayama, the adults constantly remind one another that they must bond together, help one another, and hide their emotions, for the sake of the children. There are challenges of illness and death: Naomi's grandmother, Nakane, dies, Stephen develops a bad limp and has to wear a cast on his leg, and her father contracts tuberculosis and later dies.

The family, already fractured, as were other Japanese families, is forced to relocate a second time, to Granton, near Lethbridge, Alberta, to live in a small hut that had been a chicken coop on the Barker farm. Black flies, contaminated drinking water, and bedbugs are but a few of their daily hardships. Children and adults alike are forced into long hours of backbreaking migrant labor in the blistering heat and dust of beet fields. The government distorts the reality of the harsh situation in newspaper reports that Aunt Emily keeps; one headline jocularly calls the Japanese workers "Grinning and Happy." Fifteen-year-old Stephen is given permission to play the piano in the school auditorium; he takes lessons and does well in a talent show on the Lethbridge radio station. In 1951, Naomi is a ninth-grader and Stephen is in his final year at Granton High School when the family moves from the farm into a two-bedroom house just off Main Street. Sensei Nakayama journeys to Japan to try to find out what had become of Naomi's mother and grandmother, but is unsuccessful. By 1954, Stephen has permanently left Granton, first for Toronto and later Montreal, after winning top marks in a music festival. His international success with music permanently frees him from the bonds of his Japanese heritage.

By 1972, the year of their Uncle Isamu's funeral, Naomi has not seen her brother for eight years. The Bakers visit Obasan's house to offer their condolences when Stephen, Aunt Emily, and Sensei Nakayama arrive. With the family united in sadness, love, and prayer, Sensei Nakayama reads the single document that resolves the painful mystery of what happened to Naomi's mother, knowledge that Emily and Obasan had been privy to all along but had shielded from Naomi and Stephen at their mother's request. The document is a letter written from Grandmother Kato to her niece, Aunt Emily, and reports that she and her daughter (Naomi's mother) were in Nagasaki when the atomic bomb was dropped. It describes how Naomi's mother had been horribly disfigured in the bombing and died in terrible and prolonged pain. Her last wish was that her children be spared from knowing how much she had suffered. Naomi is comforted by the fact of learning the terrible secret and finally being able to mourn her mother's death. She recognizes that her mother's silence is really borne of a deep love in wanting to spare her daughter and son the truth of her suffering.

Critical Evaluation:

In the United States, many eloquent first-person narratives by Japanese Americans, some more fictionalized than others, document the horrors of internment that Japanese citizens endured during World War II, but in Canada, Joy Kogawa's novel is by far the most significant account. Monica Sone's *Nisei Daughter* (1953) is perhaps the closest to *Obasan* in tone and purpose. Among other compelling accounts are Toshio Mori's *Yokohama, California* (1949), Mine Okubo's *Citizen 13660* (1946), and Yoshiko Uchida's *Desert Exile: The Uprooting of a Japanese-American Family* (1982).

Obasan is a complex and artfully crafted work. It is, in part, autobiography. Kogawa was six years old, one year older than the fictional Naomi Nakane, when Kogawa's family was evacuated from Vancouver to the ghost town of Slocan, in eastern British Columbia. Authentic newspaper clippings, government documents, and real letters of protest written by a Japanese Canadian activist elaborate and enhance Kogawa's story. Within the framing narrative and the flashback of personal memory, Kogawa infuses rich, deeply layered poetic language, which functions as a keening for the two particular deaths that frame the book, those of her uncle and her mother.

The actual time frame of the story is just a few days, from the phone call that alerts her to her uncle's death to the family gathering in Granton for the funeral. Special emphasis is placed on family unity throughout the novel, described in images of all members being knit together into one blanket. Thus, the migratory saga of both a single family and also an ethnic community evolves.

The first eleven chapters are more or less an exposition of Naomi's family history. The following twenty chapters convey the devastation that the family has experienced in being wrenched away from their home. One guiding principal validates the stoicism of the adults during the ordeal: the repeated Japanese phrase, "*kodo no tame*—for the sake of the children—*gaman shimasho*—let us endure." The path of the novel is a downward spiral from familial and community harmony into increasing discomfort and pain, until the most painful and intimate secret of all—the demise of Naomi's mother—is revealed.

Important symbols enhance Kogawa's provocative story of belated coming of age and assertion of identity. The dual themes of silence/stone and reporting/acting are separately embodied in the persons of Naomi's two aunts, who represent conflicting family forces, present within Naomi, that she must ultimately choose between. Naomi has been raised by the silent and reticent pair, Ayako and Isamu Nakane. In the narrative frame of the book, Naomi is constantly eating or serving or thinking about her uncle's famous stone bread. It is tough and hard, Stephen does not like it, but it is also nourishing. It symbolizes the hardships endured by the Japanese as well as the community spirit with which they band together for support. Ayako is remarkable in her stasis, constantly referring to herself as "old." Nothing ever changes in her house. Her voice is barely audible, her conversation always oblique. She is forgetful, confused, and bewildered. Vocal Emily Kato is aggressive and opinionated, characterized by vigor and urgency and transformation. She is a relentless attender of conferences and prides herself in sharing with other survivors mutual stories of pain and indignation. She insists that Naomi not only listen to the facts of her ethnic history but act on them.

It is appropriate that Isamu, who has nourished his family with his stone bread, should, by his death, be the occasion of Naomi overcoming the ignorance that has rendered her passive. It is even more appropriate that as all the horrors have been revealed and the novel ends, it is Aunt Emily's coat that Naomi pulls on for an early morning walk to clear her head. The strong implication is that Naomi is now braced with Emily's truth and identity, and will choose life and speech over death and silence.

Kogawa's saga functions on at least three levels. It shows how a woman is empowered and nurtured by her female ancestors. It shows how inner strength can deliver an oppressed people out of the bondage of racism and abuse. Finally, it is an illuminating historical chronicle of the Japanese internment in Canada, told with the facts of reportage and with the subjective evocation of poetic language, scripture, and reverie.

Jill B. Gidmark

Further Reading

Cheung, King-Kok. *Articulate Silences: Hisaye Yamamoto, Maxine Hong Kingston, Joy Kogawa*. Ithaca, N.Y.: Cornell University Press, 1993. Enhances understanding of the writing of three significant Asian American women. The forty-page chapter devoted to *Obasan* examines the negative and positive aspects of silence in the novel.

Chua, Cheng Lok. "Witnessing the Japanese Canadian Experience in World War II: Processual Structure, Symbolism, and Irony in Joy Kogawa's *Obasan*." In *Reading the Literatures of Asian America*, edited by Shirley Geok-lin Lim and Amy Ling. Philadelphia: Temple University Press, 1992. Explores the form and the symbolism in *Obasan*, concentrating on Kogawa's biblical references.

Darias-Beautell, Eva. *Graphies and Grafts: Contexts and Intertexts in the Fiction of Four Contemporary Canadian Women*. New York: Peter Lang, 2001. A critical examination of *Obasan* and novels by three other Canadian women writers, interpreting them from postcolonial, feminist, and poststructuralist perspectives.

Davidson, Arnold E. *Writing Against the Silence: Joy Kogawa's "Obasan."* Toronto, Ont.: ECW Press, 1993. A concise analysis of the novel, including discussions of its critical reception and its significance. Includes a chronology of Kogawa's life.

Jones, Manina. "The Avenues of Speech and Silence: Telling Difference in Joy Kogawa's *Obasan*." In *Theory Between the Disciplines: Authority/Vision/Politics*, edited by Martin Kreiswirth and Mark A. Cheetham. Ann Arbor: University of Michigan Press, 1993. Discusses the power of narrative and the strategies behind storytelling in the novel.

Lim, Shirley Geok-lin. "Japanese American Women's Life Stories: Maternality in Monica Sone's *Nisei Daughter* and Joy Kogawa's *Obasan*." *Feminist Studies* 16, no. 2 (Summer, 1990): 288-312. A primarily feminist reading of two novels of the Japanese internment experience, focusing on the mother-daughter relationship.

Peterson, Nancy J. "Joy Kogawa and the Peculiar 'Logic' of Internment." In *Against Amnesia: Contemporary Women Writers and the Crises of Historical Memory*. Philadelphia: University of Pennsylvania Press, 2001. Describes how Kogawa recovers memories of Japanese internment and depicts this experience in her work. Devotes more than fifteen pages of the chapter to an examination of *Obasan*.

Wong, Sau-ling Cynthia. *Reading Asian American Literature: From Necessity to Extravagance*. Princeton, N.J.: Princeton University Press, 1993. An analysis of contemporary Asian American literature, including the work of Kogawa, focusing on four common motifs: food and eating, the doppelgänger figure, mobility, and play.

Oblomov

Author: Ivan Goncharov (1812-1891)
First published: 1859 (English translation, 1915)
Type of work: Novel
Type of plot: Social realism
Time of plot: First half of the nineteenth century
Locale: Russia

Principal characters:
ILYA ILYITCH OBLOMOV, a slothful Russian landowner
ANDREY STOLZ, Oblomov's only real friend
TARANTYEV, a parasitical friend of Oblomov
OLGA ILYINSKY, the beloved of Oblomov
ZAKHAR, Oblomov's valet

The Story:

Ilya Ilyitch Oblomov is a Russian landowner brought up to do nothing. As a child he was pampered by his parents, even to the point where a valet put on and took off his shoes and stockings for him. The elder Oblomovs lived a bovine existence. Their land, maintained by three hundred serfs, provided them with plenty of money. Their days were taken up with eating and sleeping; they did nothing until an absolute necessity arose.

The chief influence on Oblomov during his childhood came from a German, a steward on a neighboring estate, who acted also as a tutor. Young Oblomov went to school at his home and there found his only boyhood friend, the German's son, Andrey Stolz. When the boys grew up, their lives seemed from the first destined to different ends. Stolz was sent off by his father with a few resources to make his way in the world, but among those resources was a great deal of practical experience. Within a few years, Stolz was able to amass considerable wealth for himself and to become a respected, vital businessman.

Oblomov, on the other hand, finished college after doing only enough work to get his diploma. He then became a clerk in a government office, one of the few positions considered an honorable post for a gentleman in Russia. Before three years elapsed he resigned from his post, ostensibly because of ill health but actually because he could not bring himself to accomplish all his duties; he felt that the work was simply too much trouble for a gentleman. Retiring from the government, he began to do nothing during the daytime. The indolence, spreading like a poison, finally made him extremely inactive.

By his thirtieth birthday Oblomov is no further along in life than he was at his twentieth; he is, in fact, much worse off than before. His rooms are filthy and unkempt, for he is unable to control his valet, Zakhar. Oblomov has no ambition whatever. He seldom leaves his rooms, so he has no social life. Even at home, he does nothing but lie around in a dressing gown and eat and sleep. How much money he gets from his estates in southern Russia he does not know, for it would be too much trouble to keep accounts. His bailiff, knowing his master will not stir out of Moscow, cheats Oblomov consistently, as does everyone else. Oblomov does not mind the cheating, so long as people do not disturb him.

At last two misfortunes, as Oblomov sees them, befall him. The bailiff reports by letter that only a few thousand rubles can be sent in the next year, and the landlord sends word that he needs Oblomov's apartment for a relative. Help, in the form of a parasitical friend, Tarantyev, seems a godsend to Oblomov, for Tarantyev promises to find another apartment and to see what can be done about a new bailiff for the estates.

On the same day Stolz comes to visit his boyhood friend and is aghast at the state in which he finds Oblomov. His horror increases when he learns that the doctors tell Oblomov he has only a few years to live unless he begins to lead a more active life. Stolz hustles about, taking Oblomov with him everywhere and forcing his friend to become once more interested in life. When Stolz leaves on a trip to Western Europe,

he makes Oblomov promise to meet him in Paris within a few more weeks.

Fate intervenes so that Oblomov never keeps his promise. Stolz introduces him to Olga Ilyinsky, a sensitive, vivacious, and vital young woman. Oblomov falls in love with Olga and she with him. Visiting and planning their life together after marriage keeps both of them busy throughout the summer, during which Oblomov is partly reclaimed from his apathy, but as winter draws on, the actual wedding is no closer than it was months before. Even for his marriage, Oblomov cannot expend a great deal of effort; the habit of sloth is too deeply ingrained in him. Tarantyev finds an apartment for him in an outlying quarter of Moscow, with a thirty-year-old widow, and Oblomov lives there in comfort. He cannot give up the apartment; he signs the contract without reading it, and he is bound to keep the apartment at an exorbitant price.

Although concerned over his estates, Oblomov is unable to find anyone to set them in order, and he refuses to make the journey home. He tells himself he is too much in love to leave Olga; actually, he is too apathetic to travel twelve hundred miles to Oblomovka. Olga finally realizes that she is still in love with the man who Oblomov can be but that he will never become more than a half-dead idler. In a pathetic scene, she tells him goodbye.

Following his dismissal by Olga, Oblomov takes to his bed with a fever. His valet, the valet's wife, and the landlady do all they can to help him, and so Oblomov slips again into the habit of doing nothing. He realizes the apathy of his mind and body and calls it shameful, giving it a name, Oblomovism. Tarantyev, the parasitical friend, and Mukhoyarov, the landlady's brother, plan to keep Oblomov in his clutches. First, they send a friend to look after Oblomov's estate, but most of the money goes into Tarantyev's pockets. Second, they try to bring together the cowlike landlady and Oblomov; this second plot is easy, since the lowborn woman is already in love with her gentlemanly tenant.

Meanwhile, Olga goes with her aunt to France. In Paris they meet Stolz, who is there on business. Stolz, observing the great change in Olga, at last learns what happened in Russia after his departure. Always in love with Olga, he soon wins her over, and they are married. Realizing that Olga is still in love with Oblomov, however, Stolz returns to Russia and tries to aid Oblomov by renting the estates and sending the money to Oblomov. Tarantyev is furious and recoups his losses by making Oblomov appear as the seducer of his landlady. The landlady gives a promissory note to Tarantyev and her brother, and they get one on her behalf from Oblomov. Thus Oblomov's income continues to pass into Tarantyev's hands, until Stolz learns of the arrangement and puts an end to it.

Years pass. Olga asks her husband to look up Oblomov to find out if he ever recovered from his terrible apathy. Stolz does so; Oblomov, he learns, married his landlady and still does nothing. As the doctors warned, he suffered a slight stroke. He does ask Stolz to take care of his son, born of the landlady, after his death. Stolz agrees, and not long afterward, he receives word that he is to go for the boy. Oblomov passed away as he lived much of his life, sleeping.

Critical Evaluation:

"Oblomov's Dream," which Ivan Goncharov called the overture to the complete novel *Oblomov*, was published in 1849. It took the writer ten years more to finish the whole book. When it appeared in 1859, three years before the emancipation of the serfs, *Oblomov* had an immediate and clamorous success. The period was one of growing political activity in feudal Russia. Progressive democratic forces preached an awakening from inertia and stagnation and expressed general hope for reforms. Although Goncharov had no political goals in mind, his realistic depiction of Russian life of about four decades of the first half of the nineteenth century opened the eyes of those who did not want to see the dangers of serfdom and the necessity of cardinal changes. Goncharov showed how and why the Russian gentry were in gradual decline and proved the necessity of strong, active leaders to rise up and to bring in a new epoch in which the laziness and stagnation would be overcome.

Ilya Ilyitch Oblomov, the main character of the novel, is a product and a victim of a disintegrated Russian culture and primitive natural economy. His life is a terrible process of spiritual and moral degradation. A curious and lively boy, he falls prey to the charms of Oblomovka, his family estate, where work and boredom are synonyms and where food and sleep are all that matter. There is no need for him to exercise any initiative, since hundreds of servants are always at his call.

By the age of thirty-two he is an inert and apathetic creature wrapped in his dressing gown and glued to his couch. He retires from the world and excuses his idleness with the pretense that he is preparing himself for life. His preparations are nothing but vain dreams in which a peaceful and happy childhood is mixed up with an unrealizable future without passions, conflicts, storms, or demands. Lazy, incompetent, clumsy, and good for nothing, Zakhar complements his master and shares his nostalgia for Oblomovka. Oblomov's caprices and way of life are not in the least abnormal for Zakhar; they evoke his respect and admiration. The master

and his valet cannot exist without each other and completely depend on each other.

Nothing and nobody can wake Oblomov up and bring him to active and normal life. His friend Andrey Stolz spares no effort to make Oblomov live up to what is best in him and to realize himself as an individual. Stolz introduces Oblomov to the beautiful and vivacious Olga Ilyinsky, who brings some freshness and purpose into Oblomov's life. Although initially carried away by love, Oblomov does not want to have the troubles of this feeling or to take any responsibility for another person. Fear of changing his life routine wins over the feeling of love and leads to separation. Love for Olga and friendship with Stolz are a test of Oblomov's ability to return to life, but Oblomov fails the test because the clutches of his sloth and melancholy are too strong. In the relations and the characters of Oblomov and Stolz, Goncharov shows the differences and collisions of the old patriarchal Russia and the new European Russia. Intelligent and practical, Stolz is one of the best representatives of the capitalist trend that Goncharov thinks that Russia can no longer avoid. Lean and muscular, Stolz is the complete opposite of the round, soft Oblomov; Stolz personifies energy, activity, business undertaking, and progress.

There are no complicated intrigues in the novel. The center of attention is the psychology of a person who gradually falls into apathy and the conditions that lead him to this kind of existence. There is not much action in the novel either. Even nature is undisturbed and quiet. The inactivity of nature blends with the inactivity and stagnation prevailing everywhere. The extremely simple plot, thematically based on inaction, develops slowly. This enables the reader to note details that otherwise might escape attention. Goncharov masterfully uses every detail, movement, gesture, and posture to thoroughly depict all characters. A true realist in his portraiture, Goncharov combines concrete physical details with biographical facts and description of the inner world of his characters. Goncharov shows a great talent for fitting every character and every scene into one fully developed, complete picture. Monologues, dialogues, and numerous comical situations bring color and lightness to the novel.

There is a close connection between Goncharov's life and his creation. Goncharov and his protagonist Oblomov spent their childhoods on a provincial estate; both studied at Moscow University; both worked in civil service, and both experienced disappointment in love. Goncharov openly sympathizes with his hero and feels sorry for him. He shows Oblomov as a decent, lovable human being weakened by forces beyond his control. Oblomov, with all his shortcomings, is an intelligent, honest, truthful, and faithful person, who can evoke love and devotion. He understands his personal decline and the reasons for it but has neither power nor courage to do anything about it. He finds a substitute for his Oblomovka in Pshenitsina's house, where he sleeps his life away under the maternal eye of Agafya Matveyevna, his landlady and later his wife. Conflicts between dream and reality, stagnation and striving, tradition and modernization, country and city, true love and sensual toleration bolster the main theme of the novel—the emptiness and inertia of the Russian gentry.

Oblomov is one of the best realistic novels of Russian literature and the height of Goncharov's literary activity. It precipitated much dispute and evoked contradictory interpretations by all major Russian literary critics. Some accused Goncharov of malicious slander on Russian gentry; others praised him for sincerity and authenticity. Nikolay Alexandrovich Dobrolyubov gave the first and most famous treatment of *Oblomov* in his article "What Is Oblomovism?" The article was published in 1859, immediately after the publication of the novel. Dobrolyubov gives a brilliant analysis of the book, demonstrating its significance as a genuine depiction of the disintegration of Russia. "Oblomovism" immediately entered the Russian language, denoting passivity, idleness, apathy, sloppiness, inertia, and lack of self-discipline.

"Critical Evaluation" by Paulina L. Bazin

Further Reading

Andrews, Larry. "The Spatial Imagery of Oblomovism." *Neophilologus* 72, no. 3 (July, 1988): 321-334. Discusses Oblomov's attitude toward himself and toward the outside world. Unfolds the layers Oblomov wraps around himself and explains his immaturity.

Diment, Galya, ed. *Goncharov's "Oblomov": A Critical Companion.* Evanston, Ill.: Northwestern University Press, American Association of Teachers of Slavic and East European Languages, 1998. Collection of essays combining older, traditional interpretations with newer analyses. Includes a Freudian reading and discussions of heroism, mistaken identities, and Western and Soviet views of infantilism in the novel.

Ehre, Milton. *Oblomov and His Creator: The Life and Art of Ivan Goncharov.* Princeton, N.J.: Princeton University Press, 1973. An excellent starting point for the study of *Oblomov*, with a lucid, comprehensive analysis of style, structure, themes, and characters. Draws multiple parallels between Goncharov and his creation.

Frank, Joseph. "Being and Laziness." *New Republic*, January 29, 2007. Frank, a professor of comparative literature and Slavic languages and literature at Stanford University, provides a detailed discussion of both Goncharov's life and *Oblomov* in response to the publication of a new translation of the novel.

Hainsworth, J. D. *"Don Quixote, Hamlet,* and 'Negative Capability': Aspects of Goncharov's *Oblomov." AUMLA: Journal of the Australasian Universities Language and Literature Association* 53 (May, 1980): 42-53. Compares the master-servant relationship of Oblomov and Zakhar with that of Don Quixote and Sancho Panza. Links Oblomov's and Hamlet's rationalizations for inactivity.

Lyngstad, Alexandra, and Sverre Lyngstad. *Ivan Goncharov.* Boston: Twayne, 1971. Focuses on Goncharov's achievement as a novelist. The chapter on *Oblomov* analyzes the novel and demonstrates Goncharov's great artistic versatility in depicting Oblomov.

Maguire, Robert A. "The City." In *The Cambridge Companion to the Classic Russian Novel*, edited by Malcolm V. Jones and Robin Feuer Miller. New York: Cambridge University Press, 1998. Maguire's essay about the theme of the city in *Oblomov* and novels by other authors places Goncharov's work within the broader context of the development of the Russian novel.

Singleton, Amy C. "Eternal Return: Goncharov's *Oblomov* as *Odyssey." In No Place Like Home: The Literary Artist and Russia's Search for Cultural Identity.* Albany: State University of New York Press, 1997. Examines how the novel reflects Russia's search for a sense of home and self.

Wigzell, Faith. "Dream and Fantasy in Goncharov's *Oblomov." In From Pushkin to Palisandriia: Essays on the Russian Novel in Honor of Richard Freeborn*, edited by Arnold McMillin. New York: St. Martin's Press, 1990. Examines dreams and daydreams of the main characters of the novel. Analyzes dream and fantasy as key elements of the novel.

The Obscene Bird of Night

Author: José Donoso (1924-1996)
First published: El obsceno pájaro de la noche, 1970
 (English translation, 1973)
Type of work: Novel
Type of plot: Magical Realism
Time of plot: Mid-twentieth century
Locale: Chile

Principal characters:
JERÓNIMO DE AZCOITÍA, the governor
INÉS DE AZCOITÍA, his wife
HUMBERTO PEÑALOZA, Jerónimo's secretary, a fledgling
 writer, and the narrator
MUDITO, a child who cannot speak, and an alter ego of
 Humberto
THE GIANT, a local ne'er-do-well
PETA PONCE, an old witchlike woman, and the alter ego of
 the Yellow Bitch
THE YELLOW BITCH, a dog, and a fabled figure
IRIS MATELUNA, a teenage orphan at Casa de Ejercicios
 Espirituales de la Encarnacíon
BOY, Jerónimo's disabled and disfigured son
MOTHER BENITA, the nun in charge of Casa de Ejercicios
 Espirituales de la Encarnacíon
FATHER AZÓCAR, a priest
DR. AZULA, a Swiss surgeon

The Story:

Humberto Peñaloza is a man of humble origins who resolves to improve his station in life and be like Jerónimo de Azcoitía—a rich, good-looking man who belongs to the aristocracy. To achieve his goal, Humberto follows his father's advice to become a lawyer and a writer. By chance, Jerónimo ends up hiring Humberto to be his secretary and to write a biography of the Azcoitía family. One of Jerónimo's main concerns is to have a son to perpetuate the Azcoitía name. To achieve this, he marries Inés, a beautiful lady from the aristocracy.

Inés has an old nursemaid named Peta Ponce, who is the incarnation of two other beings: A witch and a fabled figure called the Yellow Bitch. The Yellow Bitch is a witness to all that Inés does, in particular her sexual acts with her husband. Humberto, who is attracted to Inés, tries to sleep with her, and Peta arranges for the encounter to be in her own room. However, at the moment of the act, Humberto realizes it is not Inés but rather Peta who is in bed with him; nevertheless, he sleeps with Peta.

Inés becomes pregnant and conceives a monstrous baby who, according to doctors, will not survive. His face is totally deformed and he has a hump that disfigures his body. They name him Boy because he is not worthy of receiving a proper name. His father is faced with the dilemma of either letting him die or doing all that is possible to save him. He chooses

the latter and hires Dr. Azula, a Swiss specialist surgeon, to take care of his son.

Jerónimo, who finds his son repulsive, decides to hide him from society. He asks Humberto to supervise La Rinconada, the country estate to be set aside just for Boy and his keepers. In such an environment, Boy will appear normal and never know of the outside world. Dr. Azula manages to help Boy with special food blends and a number of surgeries to improve his face. Jerónimo and Inés come to understand that there is no chance they will be able to perpetuate the Azcoitía name. Boy receives no visits from his parents, and Humberto becomes the intermediary between Jerónimo and his son.

In an attempt to provide continuity to the Azcoitía name, Inés decides to travel to Rome to beatify a past ancestor, but she fails in her efforts. Humberto and Jerónimo's cousin Esmeralda remain in charge of La Rinconada and fall in love with each other. Ready to marry, Humberto becomes ill and has surgery with Dr. Azula. It seems that Azula had operated on other areas of Humberto's body as well, including his throat, leaving him almost voiceless. Humberto escapes and is found by the gate of Casa de los Ejercicios Espirituales de la Encarnacíon, home of the old ladies, the five orphans, and Mother Benita. They take Humberto in and take care of him as if he were a baby. At the casa he becomes his alter ego, the Mudito, or the "mute child," and the helper of Mother Benita.

Upon her failed attempt in Rome to sanctify her relative, Inés decides to move to the casa, too, because she does not want to face her husband. Although she knows Jerónimo loves her and cares for her, she chooses to stay among the old ladies to avoid the pressure to conceive a new son. In the casa is a teenage orphan named Iris Mateluna. She is the incarnation of Inés's pious cousin and, to the eyes of the old ladies, the embodiment of purity. Nevertheless, Inés has a double life.

Inés leaves the casa, assisted by Mudito, and has sex with the Giant, a masked ne'er-do-well who waits for her outside the casa. Mudito wants to have sex with her, too, so he asks Giant for his mask. A masked Mudito has sex with Iris, who becomes pregnant. Giant learns to use the mask to prostitute Iris; she apparently does not know she is having sex with different men, including Jerónimo. Mudito sees Jerónimo and Iris having sex, but he does not mind because he is certain that he is the real father of Iris's future son. The ladies in the home realize that Iris is pregnant, but they wholeheartedly believe her pregnancy is an immaculate conception.

Inés becomes just like one of the ladies after she vows austerity. Slowly she loses her beauty, as the home itself becomes rundown. Her pastime is to play a board game called dog track. She always chooses the yellow "bitch" as her token and wins all the games, stripping the other ladies of their possessions. Iris has her baby and the ladies take care of it as if it were God sent, for the baby is considered to be a miracle with special powers. The baby—the alter ego of Humberto/Mudito—knows that the old ladies will turn him into an *imbunche* by stitching him up. According to legend, *imbunche* refers to what witches do with children they have stolen (sew up their orifices).

Inés continues to play the dog-track game; one night, she wins Iris's baby. She orders the ladies to take the baby to her bed when she goes to sleep. The baby—Humberto/Mudito/*imbunche*—touches Inés's breast, which enrages her. She becomes so deranged that they have to call an ambulance to take her away. Mother Benita goes with her. In the meantime, the inhabitants of the casa become like ghosts, roaming the property for food and taking care of the baby by stitching him up in a sack, like an *imbunche*. The ladies kick Iris out of the casa so that she can prostitute herself. They try to do the same with the other four orphans to make money, but their plan fails. They hope that the stitched up baby soon will make a miracle.

A miracle greets the old ladies. Mother Benita returns with Father Azócar, a priest who had overseen the home after Jerónimo donated the property to the archbishopric. Mother Benita and Father Azócar tell the ladies that they are to be placed in a five-star nursing home in the aristocratic side of the city. After an odd delivery of five hundred huge pumpkins, the ladies are taken to the new casa. The pumpkins had been sent by Ms. Raquel, a well-off lady whose nanny, Brigida, had passed not long ago in the casa. Brigida had been affluent herself, but she chose to be a nanny by vocation. It is with Brigida's wealth that the ladies finally have an opportunity to live in a decent retirement home.

The baby/*imbunche* is left behind in an entirely stitched up sack. A ghostly old lady roams the casa, grabs the pack with the baby, and takes the infant with her. She walks under a bridge, near a lighted fire, and puts the sack down. Both the baby and the lady dissolve into the ashes of the fire.

"The Story" by Maria Eugenia Silva

Critical Evaluation:

The clue to the meaning of the novel appears in the epitaph, a passage from a letter by novelist Henry James, in which the following sentence appears: "The natural inheritance of everyone who is capable of spiritual life is an unsubdued forest where the wolf howls and the obscene bird of night chatters." The aim of José Donoso's *The Obscene Bird of Night* is to chart that human territory. In exploring the depths of the human mind, one important insight is revealed: Human beings hide from themselves the true realities of things because of their painful nature, just as the character Jerónimo de Azcoitía tries to shield his son from the reality of his ugliness.

Because *The Obscene Bird of Night* focuses on the world of the unconscious mind, Donoso deliberately chose to divest his narrative of linear sequentiality, thereby producing a flexible text in which the narrative voice darts quickly and without warning from the mind of one character to that of another. Often the reader is given the bare bones of an event and has to construct probable scenarios for what is being read. Sometimes the narrative swerves unexpectedly, as if it were a dream sequence. This is an appropriate device because, as Sigmund Freud once pointed out, dreams are the royal road to the unconscious mind.

The succession of the thoughts of Mudito ("little mute") operates as the voice verbalizing the events in the novel. Mudito is clearly the alter ego of two other characters: Humberto and the *imbunche*. The embodiment of *imbunche* is acquired by Mudito/Humberto when he ends up living in the Casa de Ejercicios Espirituales de la Encarnacíon, which is inhabited by socially abandoned old ladies who are the personifications of witches, a few orphans, and Mother Benita. Through the world of the unconscious minds of Mudito,

Humberto, and the *imbunche*, the narrative voice also traverses and becomes the rest of the characters in the novel. This type of narration, similar to that of stream of consciousness, does not permit a logical or a chronological unfolding of events. Nevertheless, the zigzagging recounting produces a story.

A number of scenes in the novel challenge the reader's comprehension and are good examples of Donoso's craftsmanship. The first narrative is the old wives' tale recounted in chapter 2 of the first part of the novel. It tells the spine-chilling tale of a young blonde girl who has nine brothers and, as a result of a bad harvest, is accused of being a witch. The father is reluctant to believe this, but he agrees to investigate. One night, he bursts into the room where his daughter is sleeping with her nursemaid and discovers the nursemaid in a strange state between life and death. The father accuses the nursemaid of being a witch, and the men take the witch's body, tie it to a log, and sail it down to the sea. The father sends his daughter away to a monastery, and she is never heard from again.

An important detail in the story concerns the description of a yellow bitch, a dog that starts baying outside the window when the men seize the nursemaid's body. The implicit suggestion is that the witch's incubus had inhabited the dog and is now unable to return to the nursemaid's body. The yellow bitch subsequently disappears without a trace. This scene has an impact, like a story within a story, on the narrative being read, because there are many references to a "yellow bitch" in the narrative proper. Though the novel never spells this out explicitly, the reader is persuaded to interpret the yellow dog as the witch's incubus. At one point of the story, when Humberto is having sex with the old woman Peta (he thinks she is Inés de Azcoitía, but he is being deceived by Peta), the noise of a dog howling is heard outside the window. Likewise, when Iris Mateluna has sex, called "yumyum" in the novel, with her clients, dogs often appear to watch. Thus, the novel works by the suggestion of association rather than by explicit metaphor.

A further demonstration of the ways Donoso adds mystery and intrigue to his novel occurs when the narrator, Humberto Peñaloza, attempts to rape Inés. In part 2, chapter 26, the reader is eavesdropping on what is assumed to be the thoughts of Humberto, who manages to get into the room where Inés is sleeping. The reader is privy to his thoughts; he is thinking about taking revenge on Jerónimo. Suddenly, the narrative changes: Inés screams and Mother Benita rushes into the room. She denies the possibility that a man had been in the room, given that nobody is there, in the room. The reader now realizes that he or she has been listening to the

thoughts of an incubus attempting to rape Inés. In this way, by not preparing the reader for what is coming, Donoso is able to shock the reader into believing that he or she has entered the mind of an incubus.

A degree of mystery is added to this story by the narrator, a diffuse, osmotic consciousness who appears to have several simultaneous identities: Mudito, Humberto, *imbunche*, and even a stain on the wall. Mudito is the mute child who lives in the casa and observes everything. Humberto is Jerónimo's secretary, and he is intensely jealous of his employer. The narrative voice switches disconcertingly between these identities.

This switching of narrative voice ultimately contributes to the most bizarre scene of the novel. In this scene, the reader is listening to the thoughts of someone being put into a sack and covered with layers and layers of jute. Every time the narrator tries to get out of the sack, some hand outside sews up the hole again. Then, suddenly, the narrative swerves and the reader is presented with the description of a female person who takes a sack out of the house and burns it. At this point, one is forced to read the previous scene again and to reinterpret it. The unnamed female person who burns the sack is actually burning the person inside the sack; this person had been expressing his thoughts only a few paragraphs previously. As to the identity of the female person (the reader only knows of her gender because the adjectives reveal it), the reader cannot know for certain, but it is likely to be Peta, the old witch woman who had grown to hate Humberto. The consciousness in the sack is again likely to be an amalgamation of the persons of the Seventh Witch, Mudito, Humberto, and the illegitimate baby of Iris Mateluna, which has now been turned into an *imbunche*.

The last image of the novel, the *imbunche*, is an ironic and inverse image of the birth of Christ, since the *imbunche* is wrapped in a material similar to the swaddling clothes in which Christ had been wrapped. Fittingly, the narrative consciousness is destroyed as the reader reaches the last page of the book. The novel thereby turns in on itself and destroys itself.

"Critical Evaluation" by Stephen M. Hart;
revised by Maria Eugenia Silva

Further Reading

Callan, Richard J. *Jung, Alchemy, and José Donoso's Novel "El obsceno pájaro de la noche."* Lewiston, N.Y.: Edwin Mellen Press, 2000. Examines *The Obscene Bird of Night* from the perspective of Carl Jung's analytical psychology. Explains how Donoso created his own literary version of Jungian psychology to focus on themes of imprisonment and disguise.

Carbajal, Brent J. *The Veracity of Disguise in Selected Works of José Donoso: Illusory Deception.* Lewiston, N.Y.: Edwin Mellen Press, 2000. Discusses the use of masks, both literal and metaphorical, in four of Donoso's novels. Chapter 1 focuses on *The Obscene Bird of Night.*

Donoso, José. "A Small Biography of *The Obscene Bird of Night.*" *Review of Contemporary Fiction* 12, no. 2 (1992): 18-31. A fascinating discussion, in which Donoso describes how the novel came into being, the various rewrites, and the people who inspired their novelistic counterparts.

Finnegan, Pamela May. *The Tension of Paradox: José Donoso's "The Obscene Bird of Night" as Spiritual Exercises.* Athens: Ohio University Press, 1992. Finnegan examines the novel as an expression of humanity's estrangement from the world. A difficult but rewarding study for advanced students. Includes a bibliography.

Friedman, Mary Lusky. *The Self in the Narratives of José Donoso: Chile, 1924-1996.* Lewiston, N.Y.: Edwin Mellen Press, 2004. A detailed examination of a major theme in Donoso's writing: the perils of establishing one's self.

Chapter 5 is devoted to a discussion *The Obscene Bird of Night.*

Magnarelli, Sharon. *Understanding José Donoso.* Columbia: University of South Carolina Press, 1993. A thorough study of Donoso's works. The first chapter, "How to Read José Donoso," offers an introduction to his work. Separate chapters analyze his novels, including *The Obscene Bird of Night.*

Mandri, Flora. *José Donoso's House of Fiction: A Dramatic Construction of Time and Place.* Detroit, Mich.: Wayne State University Press, 1995. An examination of all of Donoso's major fiction, including *The Obscene Bird of Night*, which explores his treatment of history and place. Contains detailed notes, an extensive bibliography, and an index.

Swanson, Philip. "José Donoso: *El obsceno pájaro de la noche.*" In *Landmarks in Modern Latin American Fiction.* New York: Routledge, 1990. A tightly argued essay that sets *The Obscene Bird of Night* in the context of Donoso's other novels. Concentrates on the different parallels constructed by the novel, such as those between Humberto and Mudito and between the yellow bitch and Peta Ponce.

The Octopus

Author: Frank Norris (1870-1902)
First published: 1901
Type of work: Novel
Type of plot: Naturalism
Time of plot: Late nineteenth century
Locale: San Joaquin Valley, California

Principal characters:
PRESLEY, a poet
MAGNUS DERRICK, owner of Los Muertos Rancho
HARRAN and LYMAN, his sons
ANNIXTER, owner of Quien Sabe Rancho
HILMA TREE, his wife, a milkmaid
VANAMEE, a shepherd and ploughman
DYKE, a railroad engineer and hop farmer
S. BEHRMAN, a railroad agent
CARAHER, a saloon-keeper and anarchist
CEDARQUIST, a manufacturer
GENSLINGER, an editor of the local newspaper
HOOVEN, a ranch worker

The Story:

Trouble had been brewing in the San Joaquin Valley of Central California. The Pacific & Southwestern (P&SW) Railroad and the wheat ranchers who leased the railroad's adjacent lands are heading for an economic collision. Presley, an Eastern poet visiting the ranch owned by the powerful and prosperous Magnus Derrick family, is caught amid the fierce bickering. As he cycles toward the town of Bonneville, he meets Hooven, a ranch worker who is agitated by the possibility of being fired. Riding on, Presley meets Dyke, who tells of being dismissed and blacklisted by the P&SW. Feeling uninvolved—even superior to these troubles—Presley continues his journey and encounters Annixter, an abrasive rancher who had been angered by the high-handed railroad "octopus," especially by the agent S. Behrman, who wants to gain control of the thriving wheat fields. The P&SW had, early on, leased its vacant, unproductive adjacent lands to the ranchers with options for them to buy. With rancher investment and toil, the once worthless lands had become golden. The P&SW is now looking for ways to keep the ranchers from winning the deal. Rebellion and warfare are in the air.

As Presley cycles about the properties, he meets Vanamee, a mystically inclined shepherd, and soon thereafter the poet witnesses the slaughter of a flock of sheep that had wandered innocently onto the railroad tracks. S. Behrman blames the accident on a broken Annixter fence. Presley is drawn into the intrigue and violence seething in the volatile community. Genslinger, a newspaper editor sympathetic to the P&SW, warns the ranchers against fighting the powerful railroad, because Shelgrim, its influential president, wields vast political clout. Annixter explodes against such a timid course and urges a unified rancher front, fighting fire with fire: The ranchers, too, need to enter the dark arena of bribery and corruption to survive.

Even though Presley is too deeply concerned with composing an epic poem of the West to immerse himself in these difficulties, Vanamee is too obsessed with the memory of his lost love, Angele, who had died eighteen years earlier. He seeks "The Answer," a mystical, spiritual response from ineffable forces he senses pulsating around him and within the mysterious wheat, undulating, it seems, with a psychic power. In the meantime, Annixter has ridden the same local journey as had Presley. He, too, meets Hooven and hears of the man's personal troubles. He saw freight cars routed from efficient delivery points to more profitable short-haul trips. He learns of Dyke's misfortune. Nervous and desperate, he makes the P&SW an offer for the purchase of the property he now leases. The offer is rejected. He and the others are securely in the tentacles of the octopus. Annixter, nevertheless, finishes building a new barn and inaugurates it with a dance attended by most Valley families.

That night, with everyone gathered together, they learn that the railroad intends to charge $27 for the ranchers' option on each acre, not the $2.50 expected. Enraged, the ranchers demand that the aloof, scrupulously honest Magnus Derrick join them in a course of bribery and crooked political machinations. His wife cries out in opposition, but Derrick, reluctantly carried along by mob frenzy, abdicates his principled life and pledges support, even leadership.

Lyman Derrick becomes the ranchers' choice for commissioner. His secret passion is, unbeknownst to the politicking group, to be governor. At a San Francisco meeting, he introduces his Valley constituents to Cedarquist, a manufacturer-tycoon who lectures them on the hard and cruel realities inherent in economic determinism and free-market trade, contrasting such with the superficiality of art in the function of society. Presley wonders about his own role and purpose as an artist. After the conversation ends, the group learns that the legal system has decided in favor of the railroad. Lyman has sold them out.

Dyke tries to escape the arm of the railroad by going into hop farming, but he is ruined when the P&SW quickly raises his shipping costs well beyond his profit margin. Distraught, he goes to the saloon of Caraher, a known revolutionary, and after hearing many incendiary tirades against capitalism, holds up a P&SW agency and steals a locomotive. He is chased by a posse and finally trapped. He tries to murder S. Behrman, leader of the pursuers, but his gun unaccountably misfires. In part influenced by the Caraher ambience and rhetoric, Presley at last produces a poem called "The Toilers," in which he identifies himself as a man of the people. The work becomes a huge success among radicals, with Presley hailed as a vibrant revolutionary voice. Magnus Derrick is ruined economically and morally as well, his condition exacerbated by the knowledge of his son's duplicity. Senile and weak, he deteriorates into a shell of a person. Vanamee, meanwhile, awash in romance, finds "The Answer" to his visions in the daughter of his lost Angele, very much alive.

A gory rabbit drive foreshadows the apocalyptic moment of human violence. Armed agents of the railroad and armed ranchers face off. While neither side looks for bloodshed, fate prevails. A slight movement—an accidental brushing of a horse—leads both sides to fire. Annixter is killed instantly, leaving lovely Hilma Tree a widow. Hooven, whose family lives on the streets, is also killed. Harran Derrick, the honest son of the rancher-leader, is also slain. Presley, now totally involved, is so emotionally wrought by the events that he journeys to confront Shelgrim, president of the P&SW and the ogre behind the pernicious octopus that had caused such massive suffering. Shelgrim, however, proves to be a compassionate, learned man who lectures the poet sternly on the forces of determinism, forces beyond the power of any one person. Presley is perplexed, his purpose unfulfilled, his mission a failure. He goes to a dinner at Cedarquist's and enjoys a table of lavishly expensive foods and imported wines. At the same time of this feast, the widow and child of Hooven, starving, stalk the streets of the city in search of food. At the moment the banquet ends, Mrs. Hooven is pronounced dead.

S. Behrman longs to be Master of the Wheat, whose force is not only economic but also mystical and transcendental. In his passionate desire to control all aspects of its production, transportation, and shipment abroad, Behrman inspects a boat being loaded with overseas-bound grain. He trips into an open hatch and is first tortured and finally suffocated to death by the continuous, furious avalanche of wheat swirling and tumbling rapidly into the hold. The wheat had been the most vital force in the drama of life: It had beggared, destroyed, killed, inspired, and given life. The seemingly human conflict had actually been one of forces, not of people.

Critical Evaluation:

The Octopus was composed as the first volume of a projected trilogy about wheat. *The Pit* (1903) focused on wheat speculation in Chicago, but *The Wolf*, a planned final volume on wheat distribution, was never written. The trilogy, as planned and partly executed, is of epic dimensions, the type of panoramic novel suggested to Frank Norris by the work of his literary idol, Émile Zola.

A tale of economic determinism, of social forces caught in Darwinist struggles of the capitalist-monopolist battles characterizing the post-American Civil War era, *The Octopus* dramatizes a crucial time in the United States when industry ran rampant and functioned virtually free from legislative constraint. A critical episode in the tale—the armed battle between ranchers and railroad—was based on a specific historical occurrence. The Mussel Slough Affair of 1878 was an actual bullet-flying conflict. Norris also energized his text by incorporating bizarre real-life incidents he had read about in newspapers. For example, an Oakland, California, train had plunged into and had slaughtered a flock of unattended sheep; in another story, two grain workers had fallen into a great vat of grain and had been smothered to death. Such unusual events became dramatic symbols for the mindless killing of innocents and the incontrovertible force of the wheat.

Norris had once noted that quality fiction examines "whole congeries of forces." In this novel he depicts contemporary antagonistic powers of significant magnitude: railroad and ranchers. The locomotive engine, symbolized as a cold, Cyclopean monster, omnipotent and unassailable, driven by corruption and greed (whose combined energies cannot be opposed), annihilates those who stand against it. The ranchers attempt to engage in the struggle, but they are clearly doomed. The result of their struggle is predictable, despite Norris's sympathetic treatment of their plight. Through their collective suffering, however, one must remember that the ranchers themselves sought merely to exploit the land, to pil-lage the resources of nature and then move on. Thus, Presley, whose process of education is traced throughout the novel, remains confused by the confluence of events and results. He moves from impersonal, escapist artist to committed radical. He inveighs against the untrammeled power of capitalism manifested by the P&SW, but he is finally made to realize that the railroad itself is simply a gigantic force, impersonally propelled, much like the wheat. Neither force can be controlled by human power. It is ironic, then, that while Norris orchestrates the human actions of S. Behrman, the unmitigated villain of the story, a visible embodiment of absolute evil, the oily, repressive agent can no more manipulate or divert the force of the P&SW than can its president. Nor can anyone control the power inherent in the wheat, with its mysterious, all-pervasive domination.

All of the characters on this large canvas are caught within the confluence of forces impelling their behaviors. No actions indicate complete freedom of the will. The late nineteenth century concept of social Darwinism, therefore, underscores *The Octopus*. The desire for survival dominates the interactions of forces. Norris contrasts the wealth of industrialist Cedarquist, whose guests dine at a table groaning under the weight of exotic viands, with the abject poverty of widowed, homeless Mrs. Hooven, forced to encourage her hungry child to eat a rotting banana peel. The novelist similarly counterpoints the realist Annixter, who plunges wholeheartedly into the struggle and whose life is destroyed, with Vanamee, above and apart from it all, a romantic who eschews the human destruction about him and finds eventual happiness through a meeting with a lost love's daughter. The Vanamee narrative is an apparent appendage to the text, an obvious catering to a fin de siècle reading audience that sought romance in fiction. Norris offered no solutions for the problems he presented. His intent was to provide entertaining fiction using such decisive and engaging materials as love and war, force and life.

Norris portrays many of the problems society needed, and still needs, to address. The challenge inherent in maintaining morality in an age of flawed conscience and widespread corruption was dramatized by Magnus Derrick's unhappy strategy to enlist evil in the attempted destruction of evil. The tendency of society to blame powerful individuals for exploitation and poverty was brought into question by the dramas of S. Behrman and Shelgrim. Both men were seemingly in control of the destinies of those afflicted by P&SW repression but were in truth nothing more than pawns in the large game of Force, the true engine driving civilization on all levels. Everyone is a mandatory participant in the vast game. The locomotive slaughters the sheep; the ranch hands massacre the rabbits; prodigal capitalists and poverty-degraded homeless are inevitable by-products of a predatory universe governed by rules of evolutionary Darwinism.

The capricious nature of life is illustrated in the fate of the three educated and thoughtful men who dominate the narrative. Presley discovers the social obligation of the artist, but remains philosophically confused. Vanamee flees from reality but is rewarded with happiness through the fulfillment of a dream. Annixter moves from misanthropy to love, but he leaves a grieving widow. She becomes another victim of the octopus.

Abe C. Ravitz

Further Reading

Davison, Richard A., ed. *The Merrill Studies in "The Octopus."* Columbus, Ohio: C. E. Merrill, 1969. A collection of essays on the novel. Included are contemporary reviews and Norris's personal letters relevant to the book's composition.

Graham, Don. *The Fiction of Frank Norris: The Aesthetic Context.* Columbia: University of Missouri Press, 1978. A study of the aesthetic sources and relationships energizing Norris's fiction. An insightful examination of *The Octopus* emphasizes the influence of the arts on the novel.

Hochman, Barbara. *The Art of Frank Norris: Storyteller.* Columbia: University of Missouri Press, 1988. A study of the recurrent motifs in Norris's fiction, emphasizing his literary methods. Analyzes use of word and symbol in *The Octopus.*

Hussman, Lawrence E. *Harbingers of a Century: The Novels of Frank Norris.* New York: Peter Lang, 1999. A reevaluation of Norris's novels, in which Hussman demonstrates how these books "rehearsed" many of the themes that would subsequently appear in twentieth century American fiction. Chapter 5 examines *The Octopus*, focusing on the theme of learning to love.

McElrath, Joseph R., Jr. "Beyond San Francisco: Frank Norris's Invention of Northern California." In *San Francisco in Fiction: Essays in a Regional Literature*, edited by David Fine and Paul Skenazy. Albuquerque: University of New Mexico Press, 1995. A discussion of Norris's depiction of San Francisco and other Northern California locations in *The Octopus* and other works.

_____. *Frank Norris Revisited.* New York: Twayne, 1992. Introductory overview features a chapter on the "novelist in the making," followed by subsequent chapters that discuss each of Norris's novels. Includes a chronology, notes, and an annotated bibliography.

McElrath, Joseph R., Jr., and Jessie S. Crisler. *Frank Norris: A Life.* Urbana: University of Illinois Press, 2006. Comprehensive biography providing an admiring portrait of Norris. McElrath and Crisler maintain that Norris remains relevant to and deserves to be read by twenty-first century audiences.

Pizer, Donald. *The Novels of Frank Norris.* 1966. Reprint. New York: Haskell House, 1973. A comprehensive and systematic examination of Norris's novels, with particular attention paid to the author's intellectual background and philosophical influences. Analysis and interpretations stress the idea of evolutionary theism and its appearance in various guises in his fictions.

West, Lon. *Deconstructing Frank Norris's Fiction: The Male-Female Dialectic.* New York: Peter Lang, 1998. West contradicts many previous critics by arguing that Norris was less of a naturalist and more of a Romantic. He focuses on Norris's representation of the "natural man" and of refined women characters in his fiction, finding connections between Norris's characters and Carl Jung's archetypes of the "great and terrible mother" and the "punishing superego-like father."

The Odd Couple

Author: Neil Simon (1927-   )
First produced: 1965; first published, 1966
Type of work: Drama
Type of plot: Comedy
Time of plot: Mid-1960's
Locale: New York City

Principal characters:
OSCAR MADISON, a divorced New York City newspaper
  sportswriter
FELIX UNGAR, Oscar's best friend, a television newswriter
  who is separated from his wife
SPEED,
MURRAY,
ROY, and
VINNIE, Oscar's and Felix's poker-playing buddies
GWENDOLYN PIGEON, an upstairs neighbor
CECILY PIGEON, Gwendolyn's sister and roommate

The Story:

The regular weekly poker game is under way on a hot summer night in the smoke-filled living room of the once well-kept and fashionable upper West Side apartment of divorced newspaper sports writer Oscar Madison. In the three months since his wife had divorced him, the easygoing, pleasant, but slovenly Oscar has managed to litter his New York City apartment with dirty dishes, discarded clothes, old newspapers, empty bottles, and other trash. Hosting the poker game, Oscar is serving his friends warm drinks (the refrigerator has been broken for two weeks) and green sandwiches that he declares were made from "either very new cheese or very old meat." The other poker players are Oscar's friends—Murray, Speed, Roy, and Vinnie. Felix Ungar, Oscar's best friend, is uncustomarily late for the game, and all the poker players are worried about him.

A phone call to Felix's wife reveals that Felix and his wife have just separated after twelve years of marriage and that Felix has disappeared, sending his wife a telegram threatening suicide. When Felix finally arrives at the poker game, all the players attempt to calm him by pretending that everything is normal. They steer Felix away from the twelfth-story window of the apartment and wait anxiously as Felix goes into the bathroom. Felix eventually confesses that he had swallowed a whole bottle of pills from his wife's medicine cabinet and had then vomited. After the poker players depart, Oscar consoles Felix, who reveals that he does not want a divorce and had stayed up the whole night before in a cheap Times Square hotel room considering a suicidal jump from the window. In an attempt to calm and help his friend, Oscar suggests that Felix move in with him. Felix, a fussy and compulsively neat person, agrees and immediately begins to clean up Oscar's apartment.

At the next poker game, two weeks later, the atmosphere is very different because Felix is in charge. The apartment is immaculate, and Felix is taking orders for food and drink, serving carefully made sandwiches and ice-cold beer, reminding the poker players to put their glasses on coasters so as not to leave rings on the freshly polished table. A Pure-A-Tron air freshener eliminates the cigar and cigarette smoke, and Felix has even used disinfectant on the playing cards. This fussy behavior unnerves some of the other players as much as it had Oscar during the preceding week, and the game breaks up prematurely. Oscar is irritated but feels guilty about his anger and suggests to Felix that they lack excitement in their lives. Oscar suggests that they take out to dinner two single British women, Gwendolyn and Cecily Pigeon, from an upstairs apartment. Felix is not enthusiastic about the plan because he still misses his wife and children and wants to save his marriage, but Felix finally agrees to give the idea a try if he can cook the meal himself in Oscar's apartment.

A few days later the evening comes for the dinner, and it is a disaster. Oscar is an hour late coming home from work and Felix is incensed because his carefully planned meal is jeopardized. When Gwendolyn and Cecily arrive, Felix is nervous, morose, and maudlin. Furthermore, he chills the romantic atmosphere Oscar is trying to create by tearfully sharing with the women snapshots of his wife and children. Nostalgically remembering their own spouses, Gwendolyn and Cecily join Felix in tears and decide that Felix is sensitive and sweet. Oscar is frustrated and angry that the potentially romantic evening has been ruined until the women suggest that they shift the dinner to their apartment upstairs. Oscar's spirits are lifted until Felix refuses to cooperate, citing his loyalty to his wife and children. Before going upstairs alone, Oscar angrily offers the twelfth-story window as a possible place for Felix to jump from.

The next evening Oscar is still not talking to Felix. When Oscar comes home from work, Felix is preparing for the night's poker game, cleaning up as usual, but Oscar purposely begins to make a mess. He pulls the plug on Felix's vacuum cleaner, throws things on the floor, walks on the couch, and even takes from the table the linguini that Felix has fixed himself for supper and throws it onto the walls of the kitchen. In the ensuing argument, Oscar claims that everything about living with Felix for the last three weeks has irritated him. He then grabs a suitcase and demands that Felix move out of his apartment. Felix leaves, but when the other poker players arrive for the game they join Oscar in worrying about what Felix will do on his own. Felix then arrives and reveals that he has temporarily moved in upstairs with the Pigeon sisters. He admits that Oscar has done two wonderful things for him—taking him in and throwing him out—and Oscar and Felix finally shake hands. Felix agrees to return for next week's poker game. After Felix leaves, the game resumes, with Oscar telling his friends to be a little more careful about their cigarette butts.

Critical Evaluation:

Neil Simon was one of the most successful commercial playwrights in the history of theater and likely the most recognizable of American playwrights. In creating a steady stream of Broadway hits, starting with *Come Blow Your Horn* (1961), Simon garnered numerous awards, including the Pulitzer Prize in drama in 1991. Though critics often found his work to be sentimental, predictable, and shallow, Simon was consistently popular with Broadway, regional, and community theater audiences. In his most popular period, the mid-1960's and early 1970's, Simon at times had as many as four hits running simultaneously on Broadway.

The Odd Couple is probably the best-known Simon comedy, owing not only to its strikingly comic situation and distinctive main characters but also to the commercially successful spin-offs from the play—a well-received film adaptation in 1968, an enormously popular television series that ran from 1970 to 1975, and a female-version sequel in 1985. Simon's plays, and especially his early plays, typically generate belly laughs through carefully orchestrated comic conflict, brisk pace, and extremely witty dialogue freely punctuated with comic one-liners. *The Odd Couple* has all of these.

The theme of *The Odd Couple*, if it has one, involves human incompatibility and the observation that compromise is necessary in any kind of marital-like relationship. Oscar and Felix illustrate that men who do not get along with their wives will probably be incompatible with others in precisely the same way. Regardless of the situation and genders involved, effective compromise in human relationships is rare. To some, however, this description of thematic elements in *The Odd Couple* might seem excessively academic. Do Simon's plays really exist to investigate thematic issues? Some find his plays, and especially his later plays, convincing in their treatment of serious thematic issues, while others find nearly all of his plays quite shallow. A large majority, however, simply assert that Simon's plays are just "good entertainment," and that the theme of a Simon play is not intended to be profound.

The comedy of Simon in general and of *The Odd Couple* as a particular example ultimately raises the larger and very important issue of whether craftsmanship, the quality of making a thing well, suffices for literary quality and lasting literary fame. Whatever the answer to that question, there is no doubt that in terms of comic theater, Simon is an adept craftsman. Casual as his style might seem, in *The Odd Couple*, Simon leaves nothing to chance. Within the overall architecture of the play, which is amazingly tight and efficient, nearly every word is carefully chosen for its desired effect. For example, the first act of the play, busy as it is, merely establishes what the conflict will be (the "marriage" of an "odd couple"); the second act demonstrates this conflict in action; and the final act resolves the conflict. The success of the play, of course, depends on the intensity and interest generated by the Oscar and Felix relationship, but *The Odd Couple* is theatrically effective because it creates and maintains this focus without appearing too obviously to do so.

Nearly the first third of the play features mainly the poker players, who are interesting in themselves but function primarily as a way of introducing the eccentric and conflicting personalities of Oscar and Felix. They characterize Felix before he arrives and react to both Oscar and, once he arrives, Felix. After a brief period with Oscar and Felix onstage alone, the poker players return at the beginning of the second act. Here the reaction of Speed and Roy to Felix's compulsive neatness mirrors Oscar's point of view, while Murray and Vinnie, who like the new atmosphere created by Felix, contrast with Oscar's response. Simon then uses the Pigeon sisters to advance the conflict between Oscar and Felix without reiterating the issue of Felix's obsession with cleanliness. In the scenes with Gwendolyn and Cecily, Felix's eccentricity takes the form of loyalty to his wife and family. This behavior further alienates him from Oscar but for slightly different reasons, which gives variety and texture to the conflict. In the final scenes of the play, Simon brings back the poker players and the Pigeon sisters to create a pleasing symmetry in the resolution of the conflict.

Simon's craftsmanship is even more obvious on the level

of comic dialogue, where he is the undisputed master of the witty one-liner. In act 1, for example, Roy says of Oscar's refrigerator, "I saw milk standing in there that wasn't even in the bottle." The image of milk defying gravity surprises at first, then surprise turns to laughter when the exaggeration is seen as in some way appropriate—the milk was left in the refrigerator so long that the container disintegrated and left a sour solid. Simon's skill with such verbal constructions is a testimony to his brilliance with language and to his training in the early 1950's as a gag writer for television. Unsympathetic critics have faulted Simon for his reliance on the humor of one-liners, but there is no denying that he excels at their creation.

Terry Nienhuis

Further Reading

Johnson, Robert K. *Neil Simon*. Boston: Twayne, 1983. A sophisticated book-length treatment of Simon's work. Argues that Simon in *The Odd Couple* was pushing beyond the simpler comedy of earlier plays, but the third act of this play is weaker than the first two.

Kerr, Walter. "What Simon Says." *The New York Times Magazine*, March 22, 1970. A landmark essay on *The Odd Couple* by a major New York drama critic who consistently championed Simon's work. Kerr considers Simon "to have discovered the exact amount of God's truth a light comedy can properly contain."

Konas, Gary, ed. *Neil Simon: A Casebook*. New York: Garland, 1997. Collection of essays examining Simon's life and works, including discussions of his Jewish heritage and its influence on his plays, the serious themes in his comedies, and his female and gay characters. Contains two interviews with Simon and an interview with his longtime Broadway producer, Emanuel Azenberg. References to *The Odd Couple* are indexed.

Koprince, Susan. *Understanding Neil Simon*. Columbia: University of South Carolina Press, 2002. An overview of Simon's career, with analyses of his major plays. Chapter 3 is devoted to *The Odd Couple*. Compares his work to Greek New Comedy, Jewish humor, and Anton Chekhov's combination of humor and pathos. Describes the reasons for Simon's popularity and commercial success.

McGovern, Edythe M. *Neil Simon: A Critical Study*. 2d ed. New York: Ungar, 1979. The first full-length study of Simon's work. The chapter on *The Odd Couple* asserts that Simon's comedy captures the essence of human incompatibility, irrespective of gender or marital status, and demonstrates that the missing ingredient in such relationships is the ability to compromise.

Simon, Neil. *Oscar and Felix: A New Look at "The Odd Couple."* New York: Samuel French, 2004. More than thirty-five years after *The Odd Couple* debuted on Broadway, Simon decided the play was dated and should be rewritten to reflect American society in the early twenty-first century. He revised more than 60 percent of the dialogue, inserted references to computers and cell phones, and changed the characters of the two British sisters to two Spanish sisters. The updated version premiered in Los Angeles in 2002.

Ode
Intimations of Immortality from Recollections of Early Childhood

Author: William Wordsworth (1770-1850)
First published: 1807, in *Poems in Two Volumes*
Type of work: Poetry

William Wordsworth was a prolific and controversial poet. A major figure in the English Romantic movement, he was known as the optimistic author of numerous lyrical poems, which were written in a simple language dedicated to a daffodil, a daisy, or a butterfly, symbols of the splendor of all nature (living and nonliving). The famous English poet and critic Matthew Arnold thought Wordsworth's poetry had "healing powers," educating people to feel again. Wordsworth's theory of poetry was based on passion and emotions. He believed that even the thoughts rest in feelings.

Ode treats the preexistence of human life, using the poet's personal life experience combined with a Platonic concept.

Wordsworth first mentioned the lasting importance of childhood memories of nature upon the adult mind in "Lines Composed a Few Miles Above Tintern Abbey" (1798). In addition to Plato's famous theory regarding such memories, another possible influence on the poet may have been the book *Silex Scintillans* (1650, 1655) by the Welsh-born religious poet Henry Vaughan.

The main concept of Wordsworth's *Ode* is based on the poet's belief that the "Child is Father of the Man" a sentiment taken from John Milton's *Paradise Regained* (1671) and used by Wordsworth in his short poem "My Heart Leaps Up" (*Complete Poetical Works*, 1802). In the *Ode*, he explains that birth is "a sleep and a forgetting," not the beginning of life. Thus, he believes, children still carry a glorious memory of the "imperial" heaven as their home with God. Innocent babies and children see the beauty of the terrestrial world not only with their physical eyes but also and even more through their hearts and souls, which carry a preexisting sense of the spiritual presence. With an elegiac and definitely a nostalgic timbre, the *Ode* starts with the poet's own memory of that blissful place (or state of spirit and mind).

Because of their still recent and fresh memory of the celestial glory, Wordsworth claims, children live in a dreamlike world of pure joy and fascination. Gradually, while growing, they start to forget. The bliss fades into the light of ordinary day. Their attention becomes self-absorbed, less dedicated to solitary thinking and curious questioning. They become physically and mentally involved in various activities, in attending school, and in the distractions of crowds. There are prevalent, pressuring, mundane routines to be learned daily. According to the poet's vision of that stage of life, each individual gradually becomes a "prisoner" and "imitator" of other people and of conventional ways of life. To fill the nagging feeling of innate loneliness, a youth craves to blend in, to be accepted into something larger, to belong. After losing the celestial freedom and the previously owned grandeur of peace and harmony, the individual is absorbed in a constant search for the self and the lost paradise.

The poet laments this loss, but he believes that it is not complete. His acclaimed positivity of outlook is expressed in numerous poems, especially lyrical poetry, and always with a philosophical, sometimes didactic, touch. He combines the ancient, pre-Christian Plato's view with his own Christian-based theory, adding a personal twist. Wordsworth believes there is wisdom in maturity and a different, truth-seeking joy in the acceptance of the body's imperfections, weaknesses, and ultimate mortality. After physical death, the soul goes back where it came from. Through the soul, humans live on. That is what Wordsworth sees as immortality.

In Wordsworth's view, the loss of the splendid memories of the child is compensated for in an adult. He is grateful that, through suffering and pain, his awareness of mortality brings "piety," "humanity," greater understanding, empathy, and closeness to others. As a part of nature, human life repeats itself, as do all other forms of life, including plants and animals. Love of nature in all its varieties offers a lasting joy, not only because of nature's visual beauty but even more because of the deeper meaning behind that beauty. In moments of peace, serenity, quiet meditation, and prayer, sudden intimations visit; moments of revelation surface and reveal a profound spiritual lesson. Many artists, philosophers, and great scientists have tried to express such epiphanic moments and spiritual experiences.

Uniting mind and nature, Wordsworth's poetry combines beauty with philosophical thought, as do Japanese haiku and other ancient forms. Already, in the poet's own time, numerous critics considered him one of Britain's greatest poets, after William Shakespeare and John Milton. Wordsworth's optimistic spirit affected generations, teaching simplicity, honesty, and often forgotten values. Such values come naturally to those who live close to and observe nature, the silent teacher. Wordsworth's life and work demonstrate how to find meaning and pleasure in life—in its simpler, purer forms, which may appear ephemeral in an individual life span but which are repeated and as such are everlasting in essence. Such knowledge brings peace of mind and joy to everyday existence, especially as society becomes more urbanized and industrialized, further removed from nature.

The *Ode* is a masterpiece, linguistically and stylistically unique and complex. The poet's language and style match the subject, and the rhythm and rhymes change with the mood (from the joy and ecstasy of childhood to mature disappointment, heartache, and final reconciliation). These mood changers are also conveyed through Wordsworth's masterful use of metaphors, images, and sounds, which alter in ways resembling the movements of a symphony. The *Ode* is divided into eleven stanzas of iambic lines ranging in length from two to five stressed syllables. It employs variable rhyme schemes, as rhymes are found within the same line, in alternate lines, or in couplets. It is thus an example of anisometric poetry with uneven metric length.

The lasting importance of Wordsworth lies in his introduction of the Romantic movement to English literature. He published *Lyrical Ballads* (1798) together with Samuel Taylor Coleridge (1772-1834), who was one of his most accurate and comprehensive critics. Their book became the Romantic manifesto, "cleaning" the English poetry of its artificially lofty eighteenth century diction and installing fresh, new themes, language, and style to express appreciation of common people, their everyday life, and the beauty of nature seen in modest objects.

Many of Wordsworth's conversational poems, in blank verse, have a natural flow and lyrical intensity, expressing a spiritual message of unity between nature and humanity that remains attractive. His interest in representing an individual consciousness, particularly in deploying a detailed poetic analysis of his own mind's development, was considered by some contemporary conservative critics to reveal an unusually egotistic streak. It would later be studied as a valuable document of the theory of artistic creation, of the works of the human mind that are influenced by the beauty of nature, memories from childhood, creativity, nature, and a sense of mortality and immortality. Ironically, it would also be criticized by more liberal critics as portraying a conservative model of individuality, in which the individual is formed through personal experiences rather than social forces.

Following his graduation from Oxford University in 1791, Wordsworth visited revolutionary France. The visit had a powerful impact on him, and he was influenced by the ideas of Jean-Jacques Rousseau and the leaders of the French Revolution. The Reign of Terror, however, disrupted this influence and complicated the young poet's intellectual development.

An orphan since early childhood, Wordsworth's life was filled with poverty and loneliness. His first poetic works were unnoticed by the public, and his passionate revolutionary mission ignited great hostility among rigid conservative critics. His most productive years were from 1797 to 1808. His friendship and collaboration with Coleridge—as well as his close relationship with his sister Dorothy, his "silent partner" and great supporter—stabilized his life and enhanced his works. His political views and writing gradually became more tempered and in tune with the British norms of the era. Dedication, talent, and perseverance brought him success and financial security, especially after 1820. Wordsworth enjoyed a successful marriage, children, great popularity, and veneration of the public and critics, as well as the title of poet laureate from 1843 until the end of his life. These transformed his early, struggling existence into well-deserved success.

Wordsworth's work is continuously reevaluated and found worth reading and studying in schools and colleges throughout the world. His life's story is as educational as is his varied and rich opus.

Mirjana N. Mataric

Further Reading

Abrams, M. H. "Varieties of Romantic Theory: Wordsworth and Coleridge." In *The Mirror and the Lamp: Romantic Theory and the Critical Tradition*. New York: Oxford University Press, 1953. One of the foundational texts in the study of Romantic poetry, theory, and ideology. Details the difference between Romantic models of aesthetic practice and those of earlier, realist traditions.

_____. "Wordsworth and Coleridge on Diction and Figures." In *English Institute Essays, 1952*, edited by Alan S. Downer. New York: Columbia University Press, 1954. Another analysis of the early Romantic poets by one of their most influential twentieth century critics.

Gill, Stephen, ed. *William Wordsworth's "The Prelude": A Casebook*. New York: Oxford University Press, 2006. This collection of essays on Wordsworth's greatest poem examines the poet's influences, his work, and the models of mind and experience informing all of his poetry.

Greenbie, Marjorie Lotta Barstow. *Wordsworth's Theory of Poetic Diction: A Study of the Historical and Personal Background of the "Lyrical Ballads."* New York: Russell & Russell, 1966. First published as the author's doctoral thesis in 1917, this book relates the formation of Wordsworth's poetic style to his personal experiences and the historical moment in which he wrote.

Hartman, Geoffrey. "Nature and Humanization of the Self in Wordsworth." In *English Romantic Poets: Modern Essays in Criticism*, edited by M. H. Abrams. 2d ed. New York: Oxford University Press, 1975. Another influential twentieth century critic of Romanticism, Hartman is a major proponent of the Yale School and an important thinker about Wordsworth's relationship to ideology and culture.

Heffernan, James A. W. *Wordsworth's Theory of Poetry: The Transforming Imagination*. Ithaca, N.Y.: Cornell University Press, 1969. Reads Wordsworth's poetics as revolving around the power of the poet's imagination to transform nature into something more.

Mellor, Ann K. "Writing the Self/Self Writing: William Wordsworth's *Prelude*/Dorothy Wordsworth's *Journals*." In *Romanticism and Gender*. New York: Routledge, 1993. One of the most important feminist critiques of Romanticism. Compares the masculine representation of self by William to the feminine representation of self by Dorothy.

Pottle, Frederick A. "The Eye and the Object in Wordsworth." *Yale Review* 40 (1950). Classic study of the relationship between observer and observed in Wordsworth's poetry and theory.

Ode on a Grecian Urn

Author: John Keats (1795-1821)
First published: 1820, in *Lamia, Isabella, The Eve of
   St. Agnes, and Other Poems*
Type of work: Poetry

An ode, typically a lengthy lyric poem dealing with lofty emotions, is dignified in style and serious in tone. Lyric poems, in general, explore elusive inner feelings. John Keats, a widely admired poet of the English Romantic period, composed his "Ode on a Grecian Urn" in five stanzas (sections), each containing ten lines of rhymed iambic pentameter. Keats invented his own rhyme scheme for the ode.

In stanza one, the poet speaks of a ceramic urn from ancient Greece; such urns often were used to hold the ashes of the dead and were decorated with scenes from daily life or from myth and legend. The imaginary urn of "Ode on a Grecian Urn" is a composite of several urns that Keats probably had seen at the British Museum or in books. He also might have been influenced by the Elgin Marbles, decorated portions of the Parthenon in Athens that had been brought to England, not without much controversy, in the early nineteenth century. One could thus imagine the poet either standing in front of a museum exhibit or looking at an illustration in an art book.

In describing the urn, Keats is reflecting on what he sees, engaging in an internal debate. The term "ekphrasis" means a description of or a meditation on a visual work of art; there exist examples of ekphrasis in literature from the classical to the modern. The poet is impressed with the antiquity of the urn and its pictured scenes, images that appear to affect the poet more strongly than do the poem's words—the poet, though, seems unsure of the exact legend being conveyed by the pictured scenes. The urn depicts several scenes, including a wild party in which men chase after girls, the playing of musical instruments such as pipes and timbrels (tambourine-like percussion instruments), and a sacrificial ritual. The poet is impressed by both the frenzy of action on the urn and the urn's status as a still object—an artifact quietly persisting for ages—but is frustrated by the silent urn's inability to answer questions.

In stanza two, the poet addresses particular parts of the urn's images—the pipes and their imagined melodies and a lover attempting to kiss the maiden—and comments on their eternal sameness. He notes that although the melodies being played by the pipers on the urn cannot be heard, this silence is somehow better, perhaps because the melodies dwell in a higher part of the mind, or the imagination or fancy, as this part of the mind had been termed at the time: "Heard melodies are sweet, but those unheard/ Are sweeter."

The poet also addresses the youthful lover, presumably one of the pursuing men of stanza one. Though this lover will never catch his maiden for a kiss, she can never fade nor ever become less than fair, thus implying that the imagined world on the vase is superior to the real world of experience.

In stanza three, the poet seems to envy the figures fixed on the urn, whose happiness and love will remain forever. To some readers, however, the middle of the stanza shows the poet, in his progressive reflection on the urn, not so sure of the superiority of art (the pictorial representation on the urn) to experience. The repetitive language here is perhaps indicating an ironic tone, and there is a release from a rapt contemplation of the urn.

In stanza four, the poet describes a different side of the urn, which depicts a heifer being led to a ritual slaughter while a small town is abandoned by its inhabitants—a desolate scene, an apparent change of tone from the previous stanza (unless read as ironic). To some critics the second and third stanzas are digressions; the poet returns to the urn and its meaning in this fourth stanza.

Finally, in the last stanza, the poet makes his last pronouncements to the urn, which seems to speak in the final two lines. The poet is released from his reverie, or rapt contemplation, of the urn. The pastoral scene (the word "pastoral" brings to mind rural perfection and happiness) is thought of as cold, though it is reaffirmed as lasting longer than the present generation. In the final two lines, the poet tells readers what message the urn would pronounce, if it could speak: that truth and beauty are equivalent—an idea that was current in the Romantic criticism and philosophy of Keats's time.

Critical Evaluation:

A few early critics from John Keats's own lifetime had disdained his work, considering him an unworthy "cockney" poet. Still, "Ode on a Grecian Urn" has become, along with Keats's "Ode to a Nightingale" (1819), one of the most famous and widely known poems in the English language.

Readers of his time had valued Keats's word-pictures and his evocation of the senses (especially, in "Ode on a Grecian Urn," the sense of sight) and his subtle use of poetic language.

Keats wrote "Ode on a Grecian Urn" probably in May, 1819, around the same time that he composed "Ode to a Nightingale"; the two odes share a similar structure and a theme, that is, the shortness and fleeting nature of happiness. Of Keats's eleven odes, five have received the most attention from critics: those known as the Great Odes or the Odes of Spring, which were written mostly in the spring of 1819.

Critics and readers admire the imagery of "Ode on a Grecian Urn," which focuses on the symbolism of the urn itself and represents pictorial art or art in general. The figures on the urn, the poet reminds readers, will never fade or lose their moment of wild happiness and excitement, thus contrasting with the transitory human experience of unhappiness ("woe"). However, by the end of the ode, as the poet's meditation progresses, the urn is rejected, in part, as an alternative to real life. The urn is a "friend" to humanity, a consoling factor, but not one that wants to escape the world. The general problem this poem explores, then, is the relative superiority of art, symbolized by the urn, and the reality of life.

Critics have disagreed about the meaning of the poem's final two lines: "'Beauty is truth, truth beauty/ —that is all/ Ye know on earth, and all ye need to know.'" Does the urn itself speak these lines as a message to the world, or is the poet making this statement? Disagreement arises out of the variation in punctuation found in the poem's early editions—that is, should the internal quotation marks surround only "Beauty is truth, truth beauty" to reflect a speaking urn, or should the entire aphorism be placed within quotation marks to reflect a speaking poet? Some critics believe that these final lines mar the poem because they introduce an abstraction to a work of concrete imagery.

Burt Thorp

Further Reading

Barnard, John, ed. *John Keats: The Complete Poems*. 3d ed. New York: Penguin Classics, 1988. This comprehensive collection of Keats's poetry includes an excellent short commentary to "Ode on a Grecian Urn."

Bate, Walter Jackson. *John Keats*. Cambridge, Mass.: Harvard University Press, 1963. A superb critical biography of Keats, despite its age. Bate is accurate with biographical details, subtle in his analyses of Keats's psychology and how it influenced his poetry, and always reliable when discussing the style and themes of the poems. "Ode on a Grecian Urn" is discussed in chapter 19.

Brooks, Cleanth. *The Well Wrought Urn: Studies in the Structure of Poetry*. 1947. Reprint. New York: Harcourt Brace Jovanovich, 1975. Literary scholar Brooks, in this analysis that includes discussion of Keats's famous poem, helped to inaugurate the then-new area of literary criticism called New Criticism.

Christensen, Allan C. *The Challenge of Keats: Bicentenary Essays, 1795-1995*. Atlanta: Rodopi, 2000. Contributors to this volume reexamine some of the criticisms and exaltations of Keats to find a new analysis of his achievements. Delivers an appraisal of the historical and cultural contexts of Keats's work and a detailed discussion of the influences and relationships among Keats and other poets.

Cox, Jeffrey N., ed. *Keats's Poetry and Prose: A Norton Critical Edition*. New York: Norton, 2009. In addition to notes on "Ode on a Grecian Urn," this edition of Keats's poetry and letters contains critical essays on his work. A good place to start for students new to Keats.

Motion, Andrew. *Keats*. New York: Farrar, Straus and Giroux, 1998. A biography that emphasizes Keats's politics as well as his poetry and personality. Highlighting the "tough" side of Keats's character, Motion clarifies the image of Keats as little more than a sickly dreamer.

O'Flinn, Paul. *How to Study Romantic Poetry*. New York: St. Martin's Press, 2001. A useful study guide for introductory students that includes overviews and outlines for Keats as well as Samuel Taylor Coleridge, William Wordsworth, and William Blake.

Vendler, Helen. *The Odes of John Keats*. Cambridge, Mass.: Harvard University Press, 1983. A well-known literary scholar examines "Ode on a Grecian Urn." Includes an analysis and interpretation of the poem.

Wolfson, Susan J., ed. *The Cambridge Companion to Keats*. New York: Cambridge University Press, 2001. Leading scholars discuss Keats's work in several contexts, covering topics such as Keats's life in London's intellectual, aesthetic, and literary cultures, and the relationship of his poetry to the visual arts. A comprehensive collection from a respected and trusted source.

_____. *John Keats*. New York: Longman, 2007. Gives a sense of the poet's thinking by interspersing poems, letters, and publications of reviews and contemporary works. The material is positioned alongside the author's poems in order of composition or appearance in print. Helpful in making clear his poetic style.

Ode to a Nightingale

Author: John Keats (1795-1821)
First published: 1819; collected in *Lamia, Isabella, The Eve of St. Agnes, and Other Poems*, 1820
Type of work: Poetry

John Keats's "Ode to a Nightingale" begins with no introduction: The poet describes himself in a profound state of mental torment, as if drugged into a sleep state, engrossed in an unseen nightingale's song. The setting is unspecified, but readers can imagine the poet in a garden or perhaps in the woods, during springtime, when nightingales nest. The poet addresses the bird directly, a poetic device known as apostrophe, stating his admiration for the nightingale's happiness. At this point the nightingale suggests to the reader that it embodies, at minimum, two symbolic meanings: The bird's song suggests that the bird represents art, while the poet's description of the bird as being like a Greek wood nymph suggests that the bird symbolizes nature.

In stanza two, the poet yearns for an imaginative identification with the bird, perhaps assisted by wine, by which he can escape the ordinary world and disappear into the happier world represented by the nightingale. In stanza three, the bird's world is contrasted to all the pain—such as aging, disease, and despair—that defines human experience. In line 26, Keats could be alluding to the death of his brother Tom in 1818.

In the fourth stanza, the poet rejects the escape that alcohol can provide, preferring the flight of poetry. Overall, through his desire for symbolic union with the bird, stanzas two through four outline the poet's desire to escape the human condition. The language of this stanza seems to suggest a change in the poet's mood, as he reflects on the nightingale's song. By the end of stanza four, the poet is aware of being separate from the nightingale.

In the fifth stanza, the poet experiences a failure of his senses and seems to be caught up in a an area of nature that is "lower" than that represented by the nightingale. Stanza six introduces the thought of death; the poet longs for death as a means of escape. By the final two lines of the stanza, however, the poet admits that death would mean the end of singing and, thus, the end of art and nature. In stanza seven, the poet becomes less enchanted with the bird. In some sense immortal (variously interpreted by critics), the bird represents a flight from reality, which Keats rejects.

A logical development between stanzas is hard to demonstrate, though some readers have seen such a development.

The poem has been read as a sequence of dreamlike or trancelike images, from which the poet "awakens" in the final stanza—an epilogue to the poem. In the end, the experience of the bird has been a deception, and its music vanishes.

Critical Evaluation:

John Keats, a widely admired poet of the English romantic period, composed his "Ode to a Nightingale" in eight stanzas (sections), each containing ten lines of rhymed iambic pentameter, with the exception of the eighth line of each stanza, which is short. Also, Keats invented his own rhyme scheme for the ode.

"Ode to a Nightingale" has become, along with Keats's "Ode on a Grecian Urn" (1820), one of the most famous poems in the English language. Readers are moved by his word-pictures, his evocation of the senses, and his subtle use of poetic language.

Notably, "Ode to a Nightingale" was composed in a single morning. Two facets of the poem are its original stanza form, masterfully adapted by Keats from earlier models, and its focus on a central symbol, the nightingale, whose interpretation remains elusive and thus poetically interesting. Whether the bird symbolizes the ideal type of music, art, or nature, the poet still suggests both its appeal to humanity and its contrast with human reality, a contrast between a cold immortality and the fading away that is human mortality.

The ode's ambiguous language creates room for scholarly debate and explication. Debated by many critics is the difficult line "Already with thee!" in stanza four, which in one interpretation signals that the poet has entered a trance. However, this slippery language also contributes to the poem's universal appeal, as readers have discovered many ideas and rich emotional power in its lines and images. The ode's movement from sleep or trance through dream to final awakening gives it a dramatic quality, indicated also by the internal discussion between the poet's thoughts and the nightingale's song, a discussion mediated by imagination, called fancy in line 73.

"Ode to a Nightingale" continues Keats's concerns and themes from his earlier poetry. It embodies his own perspective on the obsession of other Romantic poets with subjectivity and the nature of self-consciousness, and on the mind's independence from ordinary (often painful) reality through the power of imagination. How far Keats recommends a rejection of the escape offered by wine, by "easeful Death," by art, or by imaginative identification with wild nature, has been debated by critics.

Keats's use of the word "forlorn" in stanza eight and the phrase "deceiving elf" to describe the bird suggests his changed view of the bird, a change inspired by poetic meditation. "The fancy cannot cheat so well/ As she is famed to do" claims imagination (fancy) as a creator of illusion. A comparison of the beauty of art or of nature with painful human life makes that life less endurable; thus, in stanza eight, the poet withdraws from his reflection on the nightingale, suggesting loss. If one follows such an interpretation, then "Ode to a Nightingale" shows Keats moving beyond the enthusiastic celebration of imagination's power and value that is found in other Romantic poets.

Burt Thorp

Further Reading

Barnard, John, ed. *John Keats: The Complete Poems.* 3d ed. New York: Penguin Classics, 1988. This comprehensive collection of Keats's poetry includes an excellent short commentary to "Ode to a Nightingale."

Bate, Walter Jackson. *John Keats.* Cambridge, Mass.: Harvard University Press, 1963. A superb critical biography of Keats, despite its age. Bate is accurate with biographical details, subtle in his analyses of Keats's psychology and how it influenced his poetry, and always reliable when discussing the style and themes of the poems.

Christensen, Allan C. *The Challenge of Keats: Bicentenary Essays, 1795-1995.* Atlanta: Rodopi, 2000. Contributors

to this volume reexamine some of the criticisms and exaltations of Keats to find a new analysis of his achievements. Delivers an appraisal of the historical and cultural contexts of Keats's work and a detailed discussion of the influences and relationships among Keats and other poets.

Cox, Jeffrey N., ed. *Keats's Poetry and Prose.* New York: Norton, 2009. In addition to notes on "Ode to a Nightingale," this edition of Keats's poetry and letters contains critical essays on his work. A good place to start for students new to Keats.

Motion, Andrew. *Keats.* New York: Farrar, Straus and Giroux, 1998. A biography that emphasizes Keats's politics as well as his poetry and personality. Highlighting the "tough" side of Keats's character, Motion clarifies the image of Keats as little more than a sickly dreamer.

O'Flinn, Paul. *How to Study Romantic Poetry.* New York: St. Martin's Press, 2001. A useful study guide for introductory students that includes overviews and outlines for Keats as well as Samuel Taylor Coleridge, William Wordsworth, and William Blake.

Wolfson, Susan J., ed. *The Cambridge Companion to Keats.* New York: Cambridge University Press, 2001. Leading scholars discuss Keats's work in several contexts, covering topics such as Keats's life in London's intellectual, aesthetic, and literary cultures, and the relationship of his poetry to the visual arts. A comprehensive collection from a respected and trusted source.

_____. *John Keats.* New York: Longman, 2007. Gives a sense of the poet's thinking by interspersing poems, letters, and publications of reviews and contemporary works. The material is positioned alongside the author's poems in order of composition or appearance in print. Helpful in making clear his poetic style.

Ode to Aphrodite

Author: Sappho (c. 630 B.C.E.-c. 580 B.C.E.)
First published: Sixth century B.C.E. (English translation, 1929)
Type of work: Poetry

Sappho of Mytilene, a city on the island of Lesbos in the Aegean Sea, is universally considered the greatest female poet of ancient Greece, if not of all time. Considered the beginning of the tradition of female same-gender poetry (and

the ultimate source of the somewhat misleading label "lesbian"), Sappho's work has played a central role in feminist theories about sexuality in literature, art, culture, and history. Among many fragmentary texts and partial quotations of her work, the "Ode to Aphrodite" is the only complete poem of Sappho to have survived. Accordingly, it cannot fail to interest students both of the art of poetry and of classical Greek culture.

"Ode to Aphrodite" survives because it had been quoted in a work on literary composition, *De compositione verborum*, by the ancient critic Dionysius of Halicarnassus, as an example of Sappho's polished style. Portions of the poem also have been found on papyrus at Oxyrhynchus in Egypt. The poem consists of twenty-eight lines, arranged in seven Sapphic stanzas, each consisting of, in extreme oversimplification, three eleven-syllable lines followed by a shorter line of five syllables, according to a specific pattern. (The 1980 edition of *The Meters of Greek and Latin Poetry*, by James W. Halporn, Martin Ostwald, and Thomas G. Rosenmeyer, offers a more exact, and more complex, account of Greek metrical practice.)

The basic story of the poem is straightforward: The first stanza invokes the goddess of love, Aphrodite, and seeks her help in dealing with a recalcitrant lover. The following stanzas describes Aphrodite's earlier assistance. In the heart of the poem (the epiphany or manifestation of the goddess), Aphrodite addresses Sappho directly, calling her by name. The poem concludes, in the last stanza, with Sappho's renewed request for the goddess's intervention.

Though this outline sounds simple enough, controversy surrounds the text and its interpretation, literally from the first word on. For example, most scholars read the first words as *poikilothron*, though there is some slight textual authority for that first word to be *poikilophron*. Some Greek manuscripts include the latter, but most of them, along with the papyrus evidence, support the less interesting *poikilothron*. (The difference in Greek turns on a single letter, either a *theta* or a *phi*, with similar written forms—an oval with a line.) The term is unfortunately a *hapax legomenon* (that is, a word that occurs nowhere else in classical literature), but its uncontroversial first part is clearly derived from *poikilos*, which has a range of meanings suggesting "multiple aspects": many-colored, dappled, complex, ambiguous, subtle.

The textual dispute concerns the second part of that first word. The root *thron* suggests "seat" or "throne" (or possibly "flowers"—as discussed in D. E. Gerber, 1970). The root *phron*, however, means "mind." Most translators have offered some version of the first: "dapple-throned" (Mary Barnard, 1958), "throned in splendor" (Richmond Lattimore, 1960), "patterned throne" (C. M. Bowra, 1961), "caparisoned throne" (Paul Roche, 1966), "elaborate-throned" (Richard Jenkyns, 1982), "ornate-throned" (David A. Campbell, 1985), "coloured-throned" (Peter Levi, 1985),

"dazzling throne" (Barbara Hughes Fowler, 1992), "rich-throned" (M. L. West, 1994), "rainbow-throned" (Erica Jong, 2003). Despite limited manuscript support, classicist and poet Anne Carson opts for the alternative textual reading (as does poet Algernon Charles Swinburne), which is "of the spangled mind," arguably the poetically richer option. Among other things, this alternative phrase introduces into the prayer a double note of uncertainty, raising the question of whether the goddess will comply with the request and reminding readers of the changeableness of lovers' minds.

Jenkyns, though he opts for the conventional text, notes that *poikilothron* "sounds remarkably like *poikilophron*. . . . Whether or not Sappho's original audience sensed a double entendre, *poikilos* and its compounds are inherently ambivalent." This allows a few translations to evade the issue entirely: Jack Winkler (1981) settles for "intricate" and Stanley Lombardo (2002) offers "shimmering, iridescent." Both classicists write as if the first part of the first word applies directly to the goddess, rather than to her furniture or her thought. Perhaps there is not much difference between talking about Aphrodite and talking about her mind; if so, then such evasive translations are kindred to Carson's choice.

In addition to disputes about the text and the meaning of particular words, issues arise about the significance of larger structural elements. The poem utilizes, for example, standard features of *kletic* prayer: invoking the god, mentioning past services, and calling for current aid. Many critics recognize in this a literary allusion to the prayer Diomedes offers in Homer's *Iliad* (c. 750 B.C.E.; English translation, 1611; book 5, lines 115-120). This episode involves Aphrodite's intervention in battle to rescue her son, Aeneas, and results in her being injured. Sappho's audience would have been familiar with this episode, given the centrality of Homer in ancient Greek education. However, is Sappho merely giving a nod to a well-known precedent, or is she doing something more complex, such as offering a subtle critique of Homer or of military values or of male dominance as a whole, as some critics have suggested? Remaining is the question of what parts of the common literary background Sappho is implicitly appealing to in the "Ode to Aphrodite"

Beyond questions concerning words and literary context is the question of what the poem is saying. What sort of aid is Sappho (the persona in the poem, if not the author herself) really requesting? Does she want Aphrodite to make the unnamed woman return Sappho's love, or does she merely want her to experience the pain of rejection (from some future lover) so she will feel then what Sappho feels now? Does Sappho want relief, or revenge? Carson supports the latter interpretation, adding that Aphrodite does not say that the unnamed woman will seek Sappho, give her presents, or love her; she only guarantees that she will do these things (to or with someone). Many readers, however, find it natural to suppose that Sappho seeks divine assistance in attracting the affection of the woman she desires. Does Aphrodite really promise this to Sappho? Classicist Bruce S. Thornton's interpretation is that "Aphrodite offers Sappho the consolation of knowing that the suffering will end, even if it will be followed by a different kind of pain, the pain of getting what you want and not wanting it anymore."

The poem is full of other subtle touches that scholars have highlighted. To mention only one instance, Campbell notes that the participle meaning "unwilling" in line 24 (*kouk etheloisa*) "gives the only indication in this poem that Sappho's love is for one of her own sex." The sole complete example of Sappho's poetic genius, this lyric of 28 lines, after almost as many centuries of interpretation, continues to pose new problems and provoke fresh responses, from both critics and poets.

Edward Johnson

Further Reading

Campbell, David A. *Greek Lyric Poetry: A Selection of Early Greek Lyric, Elegiac, and Iambic Poetry.* 1967. Reprint. Bristol, England: Bristol Classical Press, 1994. Campbell's classic study of Greek lyric poetry includes the original Greek text of the "Ode to Aphrodite" and his commentary on the poem.

Carson, Anne. *Eros the Bittersweet: An Essay.* 1986. Reprint. Normal, Ill.: Dalkey Archive Press, 2003. A critical account of Sappho's work, focusing on the meanings of love, or eros, and including discussion of the importance of the word *deute* ("now again") in the "Ode to Aphrodite."

_____. *If Not, Winter: Fragments of Sappho.* New York: Alfred A. Knopf, 2002. An annotated translation of Sappho's poems, including the "Ode to Aphrodite" in Carson's distinctive version, along with her defense of her preference for the term *poikilophron* as the "right" translation of the original Greek.

Gerber, Douglas E., ed. *Euterpe: An Anthology of Early Greek Lyric, Elegiac, and Iambic Poetry.* Amsterdam: Hakkert, 1970. Presents the "Ode to Aphrodite" in its original Greek, with commentary by the editor.

Greene, Ellen, ed. *Reading Sappho: Contemporary Approaches.* Berkeley: University of California Press, 1996. A valuable collection of essays by contemporary scholars on the interpretation of Sappho's work, including "Ode to Aphrodite."

_____. *Re-Reading Sappho: Reception and Transmission.* Berkeley: University of California Press, 1996. An anthology of essays examining and discussing how Sappho has been read through the centuries.

Halporn, James W., Martin Ostwald, and Thomas G. Rosenmeyer. *The Meters of Greek and Latin Poetry.* Rev. ed. Norman: University of Oklahoma Press, 1980. An introduction to technical aspects of ancient Greek poetry, including Sappho's meters.

Jenkyns, Richard. *Three Classical Poets: Sappho, Catullus, and Juvenal.* Cambridge, Mass.: Harvard University Press, 1982. This study of classical poets includes a subtle discussion of the "Ode to Aphrodite," along with a prose translation of the poem.

Jong, Erica. *Sappho's Leap: A Novel.* New York: W. W. Norton, 2003. American poet and novelist Jong embeds her interesting translations of Sappho's poems in a fictional account of the poet's life.

Snyder, Jane McIntosh. *Lesbian Desire in the Lyrics of Sappho.* New York: Columbia University Press, 1997. Snyder's aim in this book is to read Sappho's lyrics "against a woman-centered framework in which emotional and/or erotic bonds between women take center stage."

Thornton, Bruce S. *Eros: The Myth of Ancient Greek Sexuality.* Boulder, Colo.: Westview Press, 1997. This discussion of Sappho is part of a revisionist account of sexual ideas and practices in ancient Greece.

Ode to the West Wind

Author: Percy Bysshe Shelley (1792-1822)
First published: 1820
Type of work: Poetry

In the powerful and frequently quoted "Ode to the West Wind," Percy Bysshe Shelley employs a poetic structure of five cantos with four tercets each (a tercet is three lines of verse). The third line of each tercet allows for change in the direction of the poet's thought. The end of each canto features a rhyming couplet that allows the passionate urgency of the poet's words to gain strength as his persona strives to merge his essence with that of the driving West Wind. Shelley's wild, proud, untamed wind forms his personal emblem, the perfect symbol for and the impetuous agent of radical social change.

Shelley, a poet of the second generation of English Romantics, wrote his ode shortly after the Peterloo Massacre, in which royal soldiers attacked and killed working people at a protest rally in the St. Peter's Field area of Manchester. The poem also followed shortly after some of Shelley's own most terrible personal losses. Together with other works written in 1819, such as "Sonnet: England in 1819" and "Song to the Men of England," "Ode to the West Wind" did much to shore up Shelley's reputation as radical thinker.

The first of five cantos of the ode summon the West Wind, referring to it as a kind of magician, a transformer in and of the world emanating from autumn itself, an invisible enchanter from whom ghostly dead leaves scurry. The first canto makes grief-spawned allusions to the deaths of the poet's son William and of others close to him, as well as his knowledge of and sympathy for England's poor: Shelley speaks of autumn leaves as "pestilence-stricken multitudes" that the great wind blows to their "dark wintry bed" (graves). He finds intermixed with those driven leaves, however, the "winged seeds" that, as stanza 3 has it, will soon be awakened from a death-like sleep by the West Wind's "azure sister of the Spring." This wind from the warm south will open the buds whose flowers feed on the sweet springtime air as a flock of sheep feeds on pasture grass.

In the couplet ending canto 1, the poet's persona calls out to praise the wildness of the West Wind and call it "Destroyer and preserver." He sees it as the force that must listen to his cry for the transformation of society, a cry he made more directly in poems such as "Sonnet: England in 1819." In "Ode to the West Wind," Shelley oxymoronically portrays the wind as something that at once "preserves" the world from destruction and destroys the existing order that is waging war against humanity.

Canto 2 begins with a continuation of the speaker's sense of awe concerning the wind's might; he hails the wind as the clouds' creator—a "living stream" in the sky that moves the "trees" of heaven and ocean. In stanza 2, the poet delineates a vision of angels that flow with the wind and that, in his simile, are like the "bright hair" streaming "from the head of some fierce Maenad." Inducing in his readers a sense of vertigo, Shelley takes them to the height of the skies and to the distant horizon, where they see "the locks of the approaching storm," a storm that will bring about changes on the earth.

At the end of canto 1, stanza 4, and at the beginning of the ending rhyming couplet, the term "dirge" is Shelley's descriptor of the stormy wind signaling the old year's demise. This melancholy wind will in turn create "the dome of a vast sepulcher" that will have as its ceiling vaulting a host of vapors from whose seeming solidity a rain of darkness and hail will explode as—once again—a pleading voice cries for people to heed what is foretold: "O hear!" With this cry, Shelley the prophet announces the end of an old, dehumanizing order and the beginning of a new order that will offer freedom to the oppressed.

In canto 3, the poet's persona furthers the notion of things changing instantly from sweetness to darkness and cold through the action of his ever-driving West Wind. He asks readers to envision a Mediterranean Sea suddenly being awakened from deep summer sleep "Beneath a pumice isle in Baiae's Bay," a place "All overgrown with azure moss, and flowers/ So sweet, the sense faints picturing them!" Below the sea wrack floating in great ocean depths, the realization occurs that profound change is happening in the world, and the sea's denizens "tremble and despoil themselves" out of panic. Something is indeed afoot in Europe, and it does not simply have to do with a change in weather: The palpable fear expressed by the powers of the ocean, one is led to believe, is the fear felt by earth's great and mighty, who will out of fear "grow gray" when catastrophic change finally comes.

Beginning with canto 4, the poet shifts into a more personal voice. Shelley praises, contrasts himself with, and longs like a leaf to be wafted by his beloved West Wind. His yearnings for oneness with this spirit of nature have the intensity of heartfelt prayer. The poet would choose to be a dead leaf blown about by the wind, or a flying cloud, or a wave on the sea being pushed to shore rather than stay in his present despairing condition. Hoping to share in the West Wind's power in order to be freed from the bonds of earth, he calls upon the "uncontrollable" to control him, to be for him a strong friend who would lead him just as an older, stronger adult would mentor a child, saying, "if even/ I were as in my boyhood, and could be/ The comrade of thy wanderings over heaven."

The fourth line in the fourth stanza is another prayer to the wind, and this time Shelley asks it to "lift me as a wave, a leaf, a cloud" because, as he exclaims in one of the most memorable phrases of the poem, "I fall upon the thorns of life! I bleed!" The speaker feels weighed down by time and life's circumstances, and he suffers unmercifully. He cries out for the release that his reigning West Wind can provide.

Canto 5 ends "Ode to the West Wind" with the persona's most passionate pleas, then features his commands to the invisible mover and shaker of the world. In the first stanza, he petitions the wind to be its lyre, asking that, if his own leaves are falling as those in Nature, the wind should use them to help create a melancholy tone befitting the autumn season. Then he asks the wind for the ultimate favor—to be one with it: "Be thou, Spirit fierce,/ My spirit! Be thou me, impetuous one!" He compares his thoughts to those dead leaves the wind blows, asking that those thoughts, like leaves, be whirled through the world to "quicken a new birth."

Finally, when the poet's persona prays for the wind to "Scatter, as from an unextinguish'd hearth/ Ashes and sparks, my words among mankind!" he makes clear that he now sees himself as the wind's agent, doing its bidding by prophesying through his written words. The prediction he makes is subtle and—on the surface—even pedestrian, with its common-sensical observation, "If Winter comes, can Spring be far behind?" The question becomes a profound one, however, if

winter is equated with an England hobbled by the darkness and cold of greed, tyranny, and scorn for the poor and if spring stands for the happy birth of an England of noble aspiration—as was Shelley's intent.

John Raymer

Further Reading

Abrams, M. H., ed. *English Romantic Poets: Modern Essays in Criticism.* New York: Oxford University Press, 1975. A time-tested collection, offering analysis by important Shelley authorities.

Bloom, Harold, ed. *Percy Bysshe Shelley.* New York: Chelsea House, 1985. A solid introduction to Shelley edited by one of the world's noted literary critics.

_____. *Shelley's Mythmaking.* New Haven, Conn.: Yale University Press, 1959. Here American critic and scholar Bloom portrays Shelley not simply as appropriating classical myths but also as creating a deeply personal mythology.

Morton, Timothy, ed. *The Cambridge Guide to Shelley.* New York: Cambridge University Press, 2006. An excellent compendium of essays by distinguished Shelley scholars delving into his life, times, and works; the critical reception of those works; and his literary, historical, and philosophical contexts.

Scrivener, Michael. *Radical Shelley: The Philosophical Anarchism and Utopian Thought of Percy Bysshe Shelley.* Princeton, N.J.: Princeton University Press, 1982. Concentrates upon Shelley's passionate and radical political views and the vehicles he used to express them.

Wasserman, Earl. *Shelley: A Critical Reading.* Baltimore: Johns Hopkins University Press, 1971. Shelley's moral stance is examined in this acclaimed text.

White, Newman Ivey. *Shelley.* 2 vols. New York: Alfred A. Knopf, 1940. A great biography that remains among the best books written about the poet.

Odes

Author: Pindar (c. 518-c. 438 B.C.E.)
First transcribed: Epinikia, 498-446 B.C.E. (English
    translation, 1656)
Type of work: Poetry

By a stroke of luck, Pindar's victory odes have survived almost in their entirety. This is not the case for the author's other works—including hymns, dirges, songs of praise, and processional songs—which have either been lost or are known only from short fragments. Although the victory odes, known as the *epinikia*, were Pindar's most famous and influential works, even in antiquity, they seem typical of their author's general approach and style. Shifting frequently from subject to subject, Pindar's poems have a dreamlike quality. Each line flows logically from what has preceded it but, by the end of the poem, the author often has made so many twists and turns that he sometimes seems to conclude on a radically different note from the one with which he began.

A second element that adds to Pindar's complexity of style is his highly ornate language. Pindar avoids the language of everyday speech; his secular works are modeled on Greek hymns. The religious songs that honored the Olympian gods in the fifth century B.C.E. preserved a reverent tone and exalted style that provided Pindar with a model for his own poems celebrating the glories of human achievement. The complex nature of his poetry also appears to be due to a preference among the archaic Greek poets for elaborate metaphors and difficult allusions. The appreciation of a Pindaric poem often necessitates the reader's knowing much about Greek mythology and athletics. Moreover, it requires the reader to accept each poem as simultaneously having several levels of meaning.

The *epinikia* were originally choral works, sung in celebration of athletic victories at the four Panhellenic games of antiquity: the Olympian games, held in honor of Zeus at the sacred city of Olympia; the Pythian games, held in honor of the god Apollo in his oracular city of Delphi; the Nemean games, held in honor of Zeus near the site where Heracles is said to have slain the Nemean lion; and the Isthmian games, held in honor of Poseidon near the Argive city of Corinth. The title *epinikia* suggests that these poems celebrate victory in an athletic event. The works were occasionally performed at the festival where the victory occurred; more frequently, however, they were commissioned for a later celebration in the victor's home city. The athletic events for which Pindar composed victory odes include boxing, wrestling, the pankration (a combined form of boxing and wrestling in which no holds were barred), the pentathlon (a series of five events featuring running, jumping, throwing the discus, hurling the javelin, and wrestling), running, and chariot racing. Pindar also wrote one ode, *Pythian Ode* 12, for the victor of a musical competition—Midas of Akragas in a flute contest.

The Panhellenic games were religious celebrations as well as athletic competitions; as a result, Pindar's poetry tends to mingle religious and athletic imagery. One theme of these poems is that perfecting the human body and winning an athletic victory are supreme acts of worship. The idea behind this value is that, in seeking physical perfection, people honor the perfect gods by trying to imitate them. For this reason, the athletic victory may be viewed as the winner's sacrifice to the gods. The poet's song is also represented as a religious act in the poem's celebrating the victory and making it immortal. Finally, Pindar thought that the euphoria felt after success in the Panhellenic games was as close as human beings would ever come to the bliss eternally enjoyed by the Olympian gods. Even if only for a moment, therefore, athletic victory elevates humanity to the divine level. Glorification of the victor in these poems aims at glorification of the gods.

These values were shared more frequently by the Greek aristocracy than by the common people. To a large extent, the aristocratic nature of Pindar's poetry reflects the poet's own upbringing. Pindar's family claimed ties to the royal families of Sparta, Cyrene, and Thera. Pindar inherited a priesthood and had clear aristocratic sympathies. As a result of his family's wealth, he was able to travel freely. He studied in Athens under the musicians and poets Apollodorus and Agathocles. When Pindar was a young man, the lyric poetry of Ionia was just beginning to be widely imitated in Athens. Pindar united this lyrical and highly polished style with the Doric taste in choral poems, producing a form of poetry that embodies the intricacy of lyric poetry and the majesty of the choral song. Pindar's language, too, was a mixture of Doric elements (as was nearly all Greek choral poetry), epic forms found in the authors Homer and Hesiod (both eighth century B.C.E.), and his own native dialect.

The poems included in the *epinikia* are either written in strophic form (with the same meter for each verse) or composed of three-verse units. The latter structure is slightly more common and is similar to the choral songs of Greek tragedy. Each three-verse unit consists of a strophe (a "turning," because, as these lines were being sung, the chorus would turn), an antistrophe (a "turning backwards" because the chorus would then reverse its direction), and an epode (an "end song" that brought the unit to a close and was sung by the chorus from its original position). Pindar's epinician poems consist of any number of three-verse units, depending upon the importance of the victory and the nobility of the victor.

The forty-five poems of the *epinikia* vary somewhat in structure, but they have certain organizational similarities to one another. Usually, after a brief introduction on the theme of excellence or human achievement, Pindar quickly mentions the victor, the festival at which he has won his victory, and the event. Praise for the individual's success frequently develops into praise for the victor's family, city, or patron deities. If the victor's family was particularly distinguished, Pindar may introduce legends connected with those gods whom the family claimed as ancestors. Rarely, however, does Pindar ever tell a myth in its entirety. In most cases, he makes only brief, sometimes obscure, allusions to a story that everyone in the audience could have been expected to know. There are a number of moral maxims, scattered through the typical ode; sometimes the maxims were only loosely connected to the subject at hand. On a few occasions, Pindar feels free to discuss his own life and the art of poetry that has produced his ode. In these cases, the patron's triumph may be linked directly to the immortal nature of the poet's song.

A number of themes appear repeatedly in the *epinikia*. Important is the theme dealing with the quality of human excellence. In keeping with the poet's aristocratic values, Pindar regarded excellence as an innate quality that could never be learned. For example, in *Olympian Ode* 9, lines 100-104, he says,

> That which is best by nature is best of all.
> Many men have been eager to win glory
> through skills that they have learned. But what
> God has not given is best passed over in silence.

In the *Olympian Ode* 10 (lines 20-21), Pindar speaks of the man who "is born to natural excellence" while, in *Olympian Ode* 13 (line 13), he says that "It is impossible to hide intrinsic character." Inborn excellence, the poet says in *Nemean Ode* 3 (lines 40-42), matters most of all. One who

has merely learned a skill is on uncertain ground and will never be sure of success.

To reinforce the theme of innate human excellence, Pindar introduces a variety of images associating humanity's achievement with the gleaming light of the gods. Such images as the sheen of light on rippling water, the warm glow of gold, the flash of a thunderbolt, and the burst of a volcano are introduced by Pindar to provide a visual parallel to his notion of supreme athletic accomplishment. One of the most famous of these images appears at the beginning of *Olympian Ode* 1 (lines 1-6).

> Best of all things is water. But gold, like a fire
> blazing at night, is prized among mortal wealth.
> And so, my heart, if you would sing of games,
> know that there is no star in the empty heavens
> more vibrant than the sun, nor any contest more worthy
> of your song than Olympia.

In this passage, as occurs frequently in Pindar's poetry, the subject seems to shift from line to line. However, one unifying theme—the glory of light—holds the poem together and serves to symbolize the human glory that the poet's patron has won through his victory.

A second theme that appears repeatedly in the *epinikia* is Pindar's effort to provide a true account of the gods' deeds. This true account is often set in contrast to the many false and barbaric legends that Pindar has heard. Unlike many of the Greek poets, Pindar views the gods as morally superior to human beings and incapable of the crimes and injustices that others attribute to them. In *Olympian Ode* 1 (lines 41-58), for instance, he rejects the traditional forms of the myth of Pelops, in which that hero was said to have been slaughtered by his own father and his flesh served up in a banquet to the gods. "I cannot attribute such gluttony to the blessed gods," Pindar concludes. "I am repelled." In *Olympian Ode* 9 (lines 35-49), Pindar rejects the ancient myths that depict Heracles as doing battle with the Olympian gods and says,

> Cast away, O lips, such stories from me!
> To insult the gods is mere sophistry—hateful to me!—
> and to boast beyond measure is akin to madness.
> Do not repeat such rumors. Let the gods be seen as
> free of all hostility and discord.

The central goal of a Pindaric poem is to present the true account both of the patron's victory and of the glory of the Olympian gods.

Jeffrey L. Buller

Further Reading

Boeke, Hanna. *The Value of Victory in Pindar's Odes: Gnomai, Cosmology, and the Role of the Poet.* Boston: Brill, 2007. Discusses ideas about the nature of the universe that are based on *gnomai*, or "wisdom sayings," and how these cosmological concepts influence the presentation of praise in Pindar's odes.

Burnett, Anne Pippin. *Pindar.* London: Bristol Classical Press, 2008. Focuses on the depiction of fragments of mythology in Pindar's odes to Greek athletes. Argues that these fragments were a means by which dancers could bring an experience of another world to guests attending the athletes' victory banquets.

Currie, Bruno. *Pindar and the Cult of Heroes.* New York: Oxford University Press, 2005. Study of Greek culture and religion, focusing on the hero cult in the fifth century B.C.E. Provides a close reading of five of Pindar's odes to demonstrate how they reflect the era's religious ideas about heroes.

Hubbard, Thomas Kent. *The Pindaric Mind: A Study of Logical Structure in Early Greek Poetry.* New York: Brill, 1985. Provides criticism and interpretation of the *epinicia*; broadens the discussion to explore the issue of thought and structure in archaic Greek poetry as a whole. Includes a bibliography.

Lefkowitz, Mary R. *First-Person Fictions: Pindar's Poetic "I."* New York: Oxford University Press, 1991. A rhetorical analysis of the *epinicia*, focusing upon the poet's image of self and how that image is conveyed. Includes bibliographical references and an index.

Race, William H. *Pindar.* 2 vols. Cambridge, Mass.: Harvard University Press, 1997. A good starting place for a study of Pindar's poetry. Contains a summary of all that is known about Pindar's life. Discusses Greek athletics and the legacy of Pindar. Part of the Loeb Classic Library series.

Steiner, Deborah. *The Crown of Song: Metaphor in Pindar.* London: Duckworth, 1986. Studies the imagery in Pindar's poetry. Includes an analysis of metaphors concerning plants and animals and a treatment of Pindar's use of Greek legends. Discusses the athletic metaphor in the *epinicia*.

Odyssey

Author: Homer (c. early eighth century-c. late eighth century B.C.E.)

First transcribed: c. 725 B.C.E. (English translation, 1614)

Type of work: Poetry

Type of plot: Epic

Time of plot: Years immediately following the Trojan War

Locale: Greece and Mediterranean lands

Principal characters:

ODYSSEUS, the wandering hero of the Trojan War

PENELOPE, his faithful wife

TELEMACHUS, his son

The Poem:

Of the Greek heroes who survive the Trojan War only Odysseus does not return home, because he is detained by the god of the sea, Poseidon, for an offense that he committed against that god. At a conclave of the gods on Olympus, Zeus decrees that Odysseus should at last be allowed to return to his home and family in Ithaca. The goddess Athena is sent to Ithaca where, in disguise, she tells Telemachus, Odysseus's son, that his father is alive. She advises the youth to rid his home of the great number of suitors suing for the hand of his mother, Penelope, and to go in search of his father. The suitors refuse to leave the house of Odysseus, but they give ready approval to the suggestion that Telemachus begin a quest for his father, since the venture will take him far from the shores of Ithaca.

The youth and his crew sail to Pylos, where the prince questions King Nestor concerning the whereabouts of Odysseus. Nestor, a wartime comrade of Odysseus, advises Telemachus to go to Lacedaemon, where King Menelaus can possibly give him the information he seeks. At the palace of Menelaus and Helen, for whom the Trojan War was waged, Telemachus learns that Odysseus is a prisoner of the nymph Calypso on her island of Ogygia in the Mediterranean Sea.

Zeus in the meantime sends Hermes, the messenger of the gods, to Ogygia, with orders that Calypso is to release Odysseus. When the nymph reluctantly complies, the hero constructs a boat in four days and sails away from his island prison. Poseidon, ever the enemy of Odysseus, sends great winds to destroy his boat and to wash him ashore on the coast of the Phaeacians. There he is found by Nausicaa, daughter of King Alcinoüs of the Phaeacians, when she goes down to the river mouth with her handmaidens to wash linen. When the naked Odysseus awakens and sees Nausicaa and her maidens, he asks them where he is. Frightened at first by the stranger hiding behind the shrubbery, Nausicaa soon perceives that he is no vulgar person. She tells him where he is, supplies him with clothing, and gives him food and drink. Then she conducts him to the palace of King Alcinoüs and Queen Arete. The royal pair welcome him and promise to provide him with passage to his native land. At a great feast the minstrel Demodocus sings of the Trojan War and of the hardships suffered by the returning Greeks; Alcinoüs sees that the stranger weeps during the singing. At the games that follow the banquet and songs, Odysseus is goaded by a young Phaeacian athlete into revealing his great strength. Later, at Alcinoüs's insistence, Odysseus tells the following story of his wanderings since the war's end.

When Odysseus left Ilium he was blown to Ismarus, the Cicones' city, which he and his men sacked. Then they were blown by an ill wind to the land of the Lotus-eaters, where Odysseus had difficulty in getting his men to leave a slothful life of ease. Arriving in the land of the Cyclops, the one-eyed monsters who herded giant sheep, Odysseus and twelve of his men were caught by a Cyclops, Polyphemus, who ate the men one by one, saving Odysseus until last. That wily hero tricked the giant into a drunken stupor, however, and then blinded him with a sharpened pole and fled back to his ship. On an impulse, Odysseus disclosed his name to the blinded Polyphemus as he sailed away. Polyphemus called upon his father, Poseidon, to avenge him by hindering Odysseus's return to his homeland.

Odysseus's next landfall was Aeolia, where lived Aeolus, the god of the winds. Aeolus gave Odysseus a sealed bag containing all the contrary winds, so that they could not block his homeward voyage. However, the crew, thinking that the bag contained treasure, opened it, releasing all the winds, and the ship was blown back to Aeolia. When he learned what had happened, Aeolus was very angry that Odysseus's men had defied the gods by opening the bag of winds. He ordered them to leave Aeolia at once and denied them any winds for their homeward journey. They rowed for six days and then came to the land of the Laestrigonians, half-men, half-giants, who plucked members of the crew from the ship and devoured them. Most managed to escape,

however, and came to Aeaea, the land of the enchantress Circe. Circe changed the crew members into swine, but with the aid of the herb Moly, which Hermes gave him, Odysseus withstood Circe's magic and forced her to change his crew back into men. Reconciled to the great leader, Circe told the hero that he could not get home without first consulting the shade of Teiresias, the blind Theban prophet. In the dark region of the Cimmerians Odysseus sacrificed sheep. Thereupon spirits from Hades appeared, among them the shade of Teiresias, who warned Odysseus to beware of danger in the land of the sun god.

On his homeward journey, Odysseus was forced to sail past the isle of the sirens, maidens who by their beautiful voices drew men to their death on treacherous rocks. By sealing the sailors' ears with wax and by having himself tied to the ship's mast, Odysseus passed the sirens safely. Next, he sailed into a narrow sea passage guarded by the monsters Scylla and Charybdis. Scylla's six horrible heads seized six of the crew, but the ship passed safely through the narrow channel. On the island of the sun god, Hyperion, the starving crew slaughtered some of Hyperion's sacred cows, despite a warning from their leader. The sun god thereupon caused the ship to be wrecked in a storm, all of the crew being lost but Odysseus, who was ultimately washed ashore on Ogygia, the island of Calypso.

When he concludes his story, Odysseus receives many gifts from Alcinoüs and Arete. They accompany him to a ship they provide for his voyage to Ithaca and bid him farewell, and the ship brings him at last to his own land.

Odysseus hides in a cave the vast treasure he receives from his Phaeacian hosts. The goddess Athena appears to him and counsels him on a plan by which he can avenge himself on the rapacious suitors of his wife. The goddess, after changing Odysseus into an old beggar, goes to Lacedaemon to arrange the return of Telemachus from the court of Menelaus and Helen.

Odysseus goes to the rustic cottage of his old steward, Eumaeus, who welcomes the apparent stranger and offers him hospitality. The faithful servant discloses the unpardonable behavior of Penelope's suitors and tells how Odysseus's estate was greatly reduced by their greed and love of luxury.

Meanwhile, Athena advises Telemachus to leave the ease of the Lacedaemon court and return home. On his arrival, he goes first to the hut of Eumaeus to get information from the old steward. There, Athena transforming Odysseus back to his heroic self, son and father are reunited. After pledging his son to secrecy, Odysseus describes his plan of attack. Eumaeus and Odysseus, again disguised as a beggar, go to Odysseus's house where a meal is in progress. Reviled by the suitors, who forget that hospitality to a stranger is a practice demanded by Zeus himself, Odysseus bides his time, even when arrogant Antinous throws a stool that strikes Odysseus on the shoulder.

Odysseus orders Telemachus to lock up all weapons except a few that are to be used by his own party; the women servants are to be locked in their quarters. Penelope questions Odysseus concerning his identity but Odysseus deceives her with a fantastic tale. When Eurycleia, ancient servant of the king, washes the beggar's feet and legs, she recognizes her master by a scar above the knee, but she does not disclose his identity.

Penelope plans an impossible feat of strength to free herself of her suitors. One day, showing the famous bow of Eurytus, and twelve battle-axes, she says that she will give her hand to the suitor who can shoot an arrow through all twelve ax handles. Telemachus, to prove his worth, attempts but fails to string the bow. One after another the suitors fail even to string the bow. Finally Odysseus asks if an old beggar might attempt the feat. The suitors laugh scornfully at his presumption. Then Odysseus strings the bow with ease and shoots an arrow through the twelve ax hafts. Throwing aside his disguise, he next shoots Antinous in the throat. There ensues a furious battle, in which all the suitors are killed by Odysseus and his small party. Twelve women servants who were sympathetic to the suitors are hanged in the courtyard. When Penelope, in her room, hears what the purported beggar did, husband and wife are happily reunited.

Critical Evaluation:

Odyssey is undoubtedly the most popular epic of Western culture. Its chief character, Odysseus, or Ulysses, inspired more literary works than any other legendary hero. From Homer to James Joyce, Nikos Kazantzakis, and after, Odysseus has been a central figure in European literature, and one who has undergone many sea changes. *Odyssey* has the ingredients of a perennial best seller: pathos, sexuality, violence; a strong, resourceful hero with a firm purpose braving many dangers and hardships to accomplish it; a romantic account of exploits in strange places; a more or less realistic approach to characterization; a soundly constructed plot; and an author with a gift for description. It is, in fact, one of the greatest adventure stories of all time.

Of the poet, or poets, who wrote the poem there is only conjecture. Tradition says that Homer lived in Chios or Smyrna in Ionia, a part of Asia Minor, and it is probable that he, or whoever composed this epic, did so late in the eighth century B.C.E. *Odyssey* was originally sung or recited, as is evident from its style and content, and it was based on legend,

folk tale, and free invention, forming part of a minstrel tradition similar to that of the Middle Ages.

The style of the poem is visual, explanatory, repetitive, and stately. Like *Iliad* (c. 750 B.C.E.; English translation, 1611), the work uses extended similes and repeated epithets, phrases, and sentences. Homer, whoever he was, wanted his audience to visualize and understand everything that happened. He grasped the principles of rhetoric, and he composed in a plain, direct fashion that possesses great eloquence and dignity.

Homer also mastered certain crucial problems of organization. When the audience knows the story that is going to be told, as Homer's did, it becomes necessary to introduce diversions from the main action, to delay the climax as long as possible. In this manner the leisurely development of the plot stirs anticipation and gives the climactic scene redoubled force. However, the intervening action must have interest on its own and must have a bearing on the main action. *Odyssey* shows remarkable ability on all of these counts.

If the subject of *Iliad* is the wrath of Achilles during the Trojan War, the subject of *Odyssey* is the homecoming of Odysseus ten years after the Trojan War ends. The immediate action of the poem takes place in no more than a few weeks, dramatizing the very end of Odysseus's wanderings and his restoration of order at home. Homer allows Odysseus to narrate his earlier adventures, from the sack of Troy to his confinement on Calypso's island, which extends the magnitude of the poem. Moreover, through Nestor and Menelaus, Homer places Odysseus's homecoming into the wider context of the returns of all the major heroes from Troy, most of which were disastrous. Thus the epic has a sweeping scope condensed into a very brief span of time.

The Telemachy (the first four books dealing with the travels and education of Telemachus) sets the stage for Odysseus's return. The gods make the arrangements, and then the audience is shown the terrible situation in Odysseus's palace, where the suitors are devouring Odysseus's substance, bullying his son, and growing impatient with Penelope. They intend to kill Odysseus if he should ever return, and they arrange an ambush to kill Telemachus. Their radical abuse of hospitality is contrasted with the excellent relations between guest and host when Telemachus goes to visit Nestor and then Menelaus. In an epic whose theme is travel, the auxiliary theme must be the nature of hospitality. In Odysseus's journeys, his best host is Alcinoüs and his worst is the savage Cyclops.

At first Telemachus is a disheartened young man trying to be hospitable in a house where it is impossible. Then Athena, as Mentes, puts pluck into him with the idea that his long-lost father is alive and detained. Telemachus calls an assembly to state his grievances and then undertakes a hazardous trip to learn of his father. He plainly has the makings of a hero, and he proves himself his father's true son when he helps slay the rapacious suitors, after displaying some tact and cunning of his own.

Odysseus is the model of the worldly, well-traveled, persevering man who overcomes obstacles. He has courage, stamina, and power, but his real strength lies in his brain, which is shrewd, quick-witted, diplomatic, and resourceful. He is also eloquent and persuasive. He needs all of these qualities to survive and make his way home. His mettle is tested at every turn, either by dangers or temptations to remain in a place. Calypso even offers him immortality, but he is steadfast in his desire to return home. Athena may intercede for him with Zeus and aid and advise him, yet the will to return and the valor in doing so are those of Odysseus alone. The one thing Odysseus finds truly unbearable in his travels was stasis, being stranded for seven years, even though he has an amorous nymph for company.

However, a good deal of the tale is taken up with Odysseus's preparations, once he arrives at Ithaca, for killing the suitors. The point is that the suitors are the most formidable enemy Odysseus encounters, since they number well over a hundred and only he and Telemachus are there to face them. It is here that his strategic and tactical cunning is truly needed; the previous wanderings were merely a long prologue to this climactic exploit. Coming after nine chapters in which nothing much happens, the killing of the suitors and their henchmen and maids is stunning in its exulting, deliberate violence. The house of Odysseus is at last purged of its predators, and the emotions of the audience are restored to an equilibrium.

"Critical Evaluation" by James Weigel, Jr.

Further Reading

Bloom, Harold, ed. *Homer's the "Odyssey."* Updated ed. New York: Bloom's Literary Criticism, 2007. Collection of critical essays, including discussions of transition and of ritual in Odysseus's return, male and female internal narrators in the poem, and the characterization of Penelope.

Brann, Eva. *Homeric Moments: Clues to Delight in Reading the "Odyssey" and the "Iliad."* Philadelphia: Paul Dry, 2002. A close and witty exploration of the experience of reading Homer.

Camps, W. A. *An Introduction to Homer.* New York: Oxford University Press, 1980. Excellent source for beginners. Provides an introductory essay that compares *Odyssey* with *Iliad.* Includes extensive notes and appendixes to each work.

Dalby, Andrew. *Rediscovering Homer: Inside the Origins of the Epic.* New York: W. W. Norton, 2006. Dalby explores the historical development of written poetry and examines the debate regarding the authorship of Homer's epics.

Gaunt, D. M., trans. *Surge and Thunder: Critical Reading in Homer's "Odyssey."* New York: Oxford University Press, 1971. Designed for general readers. Gaunt translates selected passages, explaining fine points of language and meaning that are lost in translation. Text includes explication, analysis, and discussion. Contains a guide to pronunciation, a list of Greek proper nouns, and an index of literary topics.

Gottschall, Jonathan. *The Rape of Troy: Evolution, Violence, and the World of Homer.* New York: Cambridge University Press, 2008. An analysis of Homer's epics from the perspective of evolutionary biology. Gottschall argues that the main conflicts in *Iliad* and *Odyssey* involve disputes over women. He explains how the shortage of available young women in ancient Greece drove men to fiercely compete for women.

Hall, Edith. *The Return of Ulysses: A Cultural History of Homer's "Odyssey."* New York: I. B. Tauris, 2008. Examines the reasons for the epic's enduring resonance. Defines fifteen key themes in the work and demonstrates how the poem has affected the cultural imagination, spurring adaptations as diverse as James Joyce's *Ulysses* and the Coen brothers' film *O Brother, Where Art Thou?*

Lamberton, Robert. *Homer the Theologian: Neoplatonist Allegorical Reading and the Growth of the Epic Tradition.* Berkeley: University of California Press, 1986. Addresses *Odyssey* as allegory, presenting a commentary and summary of the work. Supports points with material from Greek scholars. Includes a particularly interesting discussion on Homer as theologian. Well-indexed, well-documented, and scholarly.

Manguel, Alberto. *Homer's "The Iliad" and "The Odyssey": A Biography.* New York: Atlantic Monthly Press, 2007. Traces the more than two-thousand-year lineage of Homer's epic poems, providing information about their original purpose, their reception by Christians and Muslims, and their various translations and adaptations.

Taylor, Charles H., Jr. *Essays on the "Odyssey": Selected Modern Criticism.* Bloomington: Indiana University Press, 1963. Seven selected essays, arranged chronologically. Taylor contends that interest grew in the "emblematic or symbolic implications" at work in events and images in the poem. Includes extensive notes.

The Odyssey
A Modern Sequel

Author: Nikos Kazantzakis (1883-1957)
First published: Odysseia, 1938 (English translation, 1958)
Type of work: Poetry
Type of plot: Epic
Time of plot: Antiquity
Locale: Ithaca, Sparta, Crete, Egypt, Africa, and
     Antarctica

Principal character:
ODYSSEUS, king of Ithaca

The Poem:

Odysseus, king of Ithaca, subdues a revolt against him soon after his return from the Trojan War. Growing discontent with the routine obligations of lawgiver, husband, and father, he builds a ship, forms a crew of similarly individualistic characters, and begins another journey—of no return. In Sparta, Odysseus tempts Helen to abandon, once again, her life of sumptuous boredom and accompany him. The shipmates next anchor in Crete, where, outraged by the disparity of wealth between the hedonistic court elite, presided over by the indolent King Idomeneus, and the impoverished kingdom, Odysseus leads an uprising of slaves and invading barbarians. Helen becomes the lover of one of the Dorian invaders and chooses to remain in Crete, to rear her child—a symbol for Kazantzakis of the golden age of Greece yet to come—when the conquering shipmates sail on.

In contrast to the triumphant overthrow of the Cretan court, Odysseus and his crew next join forces with revolutionaries and barbarians in Egypt to fight against a much larger and stronger army, at whose hands they meet bloody defeat, barely surviving. They become prisoners in an Egyptian dungeon. Odysseus eventually manages to terrify the superstitious Pharaoh, who banishes him into the desert. Having observed the corruption and injustice of various civilizations, Odysseus determines to create a type of utopian society for the ranks of the lawless and dejected who had followed him into exile, and for his remaining crew. Enduring a slow, painful desert flight, and skirmishes with fierce African tribes, Odysseus formulates plans for an ideal city.

At the moment he concludes the exodus to the sea, Odysseus withdraws from his followers to fast and meditate, commencing an inward, spiritual journey from which he emerges with a new concept of God—the epitome of the evolutionary force present in all life. Great celebrations set to mark the foundation of the city are halted by a devastating earthquake. Odysseus's efforts to create an ideal society are laid waste and, for the first time, he is without companionship.

Repudiating his long attempts to clarify a concept of God, Odysseus substitutes the creative power of the human mind as the object of his intense religious devotion and invokes an image of death—anthropomorphized as his identical twin—for his constant companion. Odysseus presses his journey toward the southern tip of Africa, as word of Odysseus the ascetic spreads across the land.

Before leaving on a last sea voyage, Odysseus meets prominent religious figures, unique thinkers, and literary characters, such as Christ, Buddha, Faust, and Don Quixote. Odysseus spends his final moments in human company in an Eskimo village (where he is hailed as a god). Although for the humble Eskimos hope means merely clinging to the will to survive until spring, as spring arrives, it brings death and wholesale destruction. As Odysseus paddles away from the village, he watches as once again the sudden, inescapable churning of the earth decimates the society that had nurtured him.

Once alone on the frozen seas, Odysseus paddles toward the unsetting sun, and bids a mystical farewell to life. When his skiff rams an iceberg, he leaps onto its frigid surface and hangs there. As his life slips away, Odysseus thanks his five senses for the earthly aid they had provided him, and, in his final moment of life, he shapes a call to his departed comrades, who, both the living and the dead, appear to join him once again: The moment is a broad and joyful affirmation.

Critical Evaluation:

Nikos Kazantzakis's prolific career included the publication of several novels, for which he is best known; close to two dozen dramas, most of them in poetic form; and three philosophical studies, one on Friedrich Nietzsche, one on Henri Bergson, and one on his own vision of life. In addition to these, Kazantzakis published travel books on Spain, Greece, England, China, Japan, Israel, and Russia, hundreds of articles for newspapers and encyclopedias, dozens of books for the public schools of Greece, and several translations, including Homer's *Iliad* (c. 800 B.C.E.) and *Odyssey* (c. 800 B.C.E.), Dante's *La divina commedia* (c. 1320; *The Divine Comedy*, 1802), Nietzsche's *Die Geburt der Tragödie aus dem Geiste der Musik* (1872; *The Birth of Tragedy out of the Spirit of Music*, 1909), Bergson's *Le Rire: Essai sur la signification du comique* (1900; *Laughter: An Essay on the Meaning of the Comic*, 1911), and Charles Darwin's *On the Origin of Species by Means of Natural Selection* (1859). Kazantzakis also published two books of poetry. It was *The Odyssey* that Kazantzakis considered his masterpiece, or, in Morton P. Levitt's phrase, "the central document of his life."

The Odyssey is, according to Levitt, "one of the great encyclopedic works of our time," embracing the major themes of Western civilization. It consists of twenty-four books or cantos (one for every letter of the Greek alphabet), comprising 33,333 lines—almost three times the length of the original *Odyssey*. These are in an extremely unusual seventeen-syllable unrhymed iambic measure of eight beats. The poem employs a form of simplified spelling and syntax, eschews the accentual marks that have been part of the Greek language since Byzantine times, and relies upon an idiomatic diction that, at the time of its publication in December, 1938, was more familiar to the shepherds and fishermen throughout the islands and villages of Greece than to Greek scholars. Greatly influenced by the author's work on language reform as it is, *The Odyssey* is by no means an academic work. Pandelis Prevelakis, Kazantzakis's first biographer, said that if the book is "read with the attention it deserves, it is capable of changing the reader's soul."

As much as it is a journey through exotic lands and moments of intense experience, *The Odyssey* is a passionate exploration of ideas, with Odysseus threading a path through philosophies of life, adapting and discarding, by turn, sensuality, political engagement, and ascetic detachment. Each new phase provides him with a new perspective from which he can examine life, and, given new insights, re-create himself accordingly. Although each successive phase of his journey rises out of the destruction of the previous one, the whole of Odysseus's journey constitutes a continuum: a single evolutionary flight toward freedom.

Odysseus flees Ithaca to escape the harsh restrictions of a meaningless existence, going off in what Peter Bien describes as "the attempt to gain happiness through sensual gratification." Odysseus becomes an aesthete. Through successive encounters with social injustice—in Sparta, Crete, and Egypt—Odysseus gains an understanding that the aesthetic attitude can lead only to surfeit and indifference, perpetuating misery and human suffering. Recoiling from the isolation of the ego, Odysseus reaches toward an ethical theory that is responsive to a humanitarian concern for the future of the human race. This culminates in his attempt to postulate the Ideal City.

The sudden, unimaginable desolation of the Ideal City plunges Odysseus into despair, from which he emerges as an ascetic. In essence, Kazantzakis exposes the limitations of an ethical self as one dependent upon false polarities of being. In his new state, Odysseus views the inevitable destruction of every human endeavor not as a tragic fact or fate, but as an incentive toward spiritual growth. The struggle between good and evil, or life and death, becomes apparent as a form of disguised collaboration; and the specter of death becomes a tool by which Odysseus may sharpen his perception of the meaning of life—thus, paradoxically, a cause for celebration. Of Odysseus's ascetic insight, translator Kimon Friar has written, Odysseus "sees that through his mind and senses now all creative impulse flows and plunges, laughing, down the abyss: an image of a deathless flowing stream."

Already having forsaken the prison of the self, with this transformation Odysseus achieves an even greater freedom from the loneliness and human estrangement of differentiation. His fundamental mode for organizing life becomes contemplative rather than experiential: Life becomes spectacle for him.

In his conversations with other ascetics and unique thinkers—such as Prince Motherth, a type of the Buddha; Captain Sole, a type of Don Quixote; the Hermit, a type of Faust; and the black fisher-lad, a type of Christ—Odysseus reaffirms the oneness of nature, of process, of the woven unity of life, yet honors its particulars. While recognizing the unity of life, Odysseus also accepts the unenlightened aspects of his humanity that constitute part of his existence. In his dialogue with the black fisher-lad, he exclaims that, although the fisher-lad might love the human soul, he, Odysseus, loved the flesh, the stench, and even the death of the individual.

With his death on the iceberg, Odysseus recognizes and embraces his final absolute freedom—escape from the broad concept of ascetic detachment. Odysseus gains freedom from freedom itself.

Although Kazantzakis sought, through *The Odyssey*, to revolutionize the Greek language, his modern epic rose to popularity in the English translation by Kimon Friar. Having been chosen by Kazantzakis for the task, Friar left an academic career and devoted himself to the translation for four years. Although he did not complete his translation until a year after Kazantzakis's death, the poet read the entire manuscript and approved, according to Friar, "even those few sections with which he did not agree," and declared it to be "not a translation" but instead a "re-creation" of his poem. James Lea has written that one "will never be able to read this *Odyssey* without thinking also of Friar." It was Friar who completed the title of the poem, by adding *A Modern Sequel* as a subtitle to Kazantzakis simple title, *The Odyssey*.

Michael Scott Joseph

Further Reading

Bien, Peter. *Kazantzakis: Politics of Spirit*. 2 vols. Princeton, N.J.: Princeton University Press, 1989-2007. The first volume focuses on the evolution of Kazantzakis's personal philosophy from 1906 up to the publication of *The Odyssey* in 1938. Volume 2 completes this definitive biography, describing the period of Kazantzakis's life in which he wrote *Zorba the Greek* and *The Last Temptation of Christ*.

Dombrowski, Daniel A. *Kazantzakis and God*. Albany: State University of New York Press, 1997. Analyzes Kazantzakis's novels and other works to describe his religious vision, interpreting his ideas in terms of contemporary "process theology." Explains how Kazantzakis combined his ideas about God with a Darwinian belief in the evolution of all creatures—including God.

Dossor, Howard F. *The Existential Theology of Nikos Kazantzakis*. Wallingford, Pa.: Pendle Hill, 2001. Discusses Kazantzakis's religious ideas, describing how he created a personal theology based upon his existential belief that human beings are mortal and must live as if they are heading toward death.

Kazantzakis, Nikos. *The Odyssey: A Modern Sequel*. Translated by Kimon Friar. New York: Simon & Schuster, 1958. Kazantzakis considered Friar to be a collaborator more than a translator, and Friar bears a major share of the responsibility for the success of *The Odyssey: A Modern Sequel* in the English-speaking world. His introduction and synopsis are among the clearest and most meaningful available.

Lea, James F. *Kazantzakis: The Politics of Salvation*. Foreword by Helen Kazantzakis. University: University of Alabama Press, 1979. Examines Kazantzakis in the context of his age and culture, providing a general explication of the evolution of his political thought and his approach to history.

Levitt, Morton. *The Cretan Glance: The World and Art of Nikos Kazantzakis*. Columbus: Ohio State University Press, 1980. Deals with the work of the last two phases of Kazantzakis's long and varied career—the period in which he created *The Odyssey* and several novels.

Middleton, Darren J. N., and Peter Bien, eds. *God's Struggler: Religion in the Writings of Nikos Kazantzakis*. Macon, Ga.: Mercer University Press, 1996. Collection of essays exploring the theme of religion in Kazantzakis's works, including a Greek Orthodox interpretation of his religious ideas, a discussion of mysticism in his writings, and an analysis of Christology in the *Odyssey*.

Owens, Lewis. *Creative Destruction: Nikos Kazantzakis and the Literature of Responsibility*. Macon, Ga.: Mercer University Press, 2003. Detailed study of Kazantzakis's writings, describing how he was influenced by the philosophy of Henri Bergson. Lewis argues that Kazantzakis believed destruction was a necessary prerequisite for renewed creative activity.

Prevelakis, Pandelis. *Nikos Kazantzakis and His Odyssey: A Study of the Poet and the Poem*. New York: Simon & Schuster, 1961. First biographical study of Kazantzakis by his longtime friend, which integrates the motifs of *The Odyssey: A Modern Sequel* with the events of the poet's life.

Oedipus at Colonus

Author: Sophocles (c. 496-406 B.C.E.)
First produced: Oidipous epi Kolōnōi, 401 B.C.E. (English translation, 1729)
Type of work: Drama
Type of plot: Tragedy
Time of plot: Antiquity
Locale: Colonus, near Athens

Principal characters:
OEDIPUS, the former king of Thebes
ANTIGONE and ISMENE, his daughters
THESEUS, the king of Athens
CREON, the former regent of Thebes
POLYNICES, Oedipus's older son
ELDERS OF COLONUS

The Story:

Many years have passed since King Oedipus discovered to his horror that he had murdered his father and married his mother, with whom he has children. After having blinded himself and given up his royal authority in Thebes, he has been cared for by his faithful daughters, Antigone and Ismene. When internal strife breaks out in Thebes, Oedipus is believed to be the cause of the trouble because of the curse the gods had put upon his family, and he is banished from the city.

Oedipus and Antigone wander far. At last, they arrive at an olive grove in Colonus, a sacred place near Athens. A man of Colonus warns the strangers that the grove in which they have stopped is sacred to the Furies. Oedipus, having known supreme mortal suffering, replies that he knows the Furies well and that he will remain in the grove. Disturbed, the man of Colonus states that he will have to report this irregularity to Theseus, the king of Athens and overlord of Colonus. Oedipus replies that he will welcome the king, for he has important words to say to Theseus.

The old men of Colonus, who fear the Furies, are upset at Oedipus's calm in the grove. They inquire, from a discreet distance, the identity of the blind stranger and are horror-stricken to learn that he is the infamous king of Thebes whose dreadful story the whole civilized world had heard. Fearing the terrible wrath of the gods, they order him and his daughter to leave. Oedipus is able to quiet them, however, by explaining that he has suffered greatly, despite never having consciously sinned against the gods. To the mystification of the old men, he hints that he has strange powers and will bring good fortune to the land that provides a place of refuge for him.

Ismene, another daughter of Oedipus, arrives in the grove at Colonus after searching throughout Greece for her father and sister. She brings Oedipus the unhappy news that his two sons, Polynices and Eteocles, have fought for supremacy in Thebes. When Polynices was defeated, he was banished to Argos, where he is now gathering a host to return to Thebes. Ismene also informs her father that the Oracle of Delphi has prophesied that Thebes is doomed to terrible misfortune if Oedipus should be buried anywhere but in that city. With this prophecy in mind, the Thebans hope that Oedipus will return from his exile. Oedipus, however, mindful of his banishment and of the faithlessness of his sons, declares that he will remain in Colonus and that the land of Attica will be his tomb.

Informed of the arrival of Oedipus, Theseus goes to Colonus and welcomes the pitiful old man and his daughters. Oedipus offers his body to Attica and Colonus and prophe-sies that it will bring good fortune to Attica if he is buried in its soil. Theseus, who knows exile, is sympathetic; he promises to care for Oedipus and to protect the old man from seizure by any Theban.

After Theseus returns to Athens, Creon, the former regent of Thebes, comes to the grove with his followers. Deceitfully, he urges Oedipus to return with him to Thebes, but Oedipus is aware of Creon's motives and reviles him for his duplicity. Oedipus curses Thebes for the way it has disavowed him in his great suffering. Creon's men, at the command of their leader, seize Antigone and Ismene and carry them away. Blind Oedipus and the aged men of Colonus are too old and feeble to prevent their capture. By the time Creon attempts to seize Oedipus, however, the alarm has been sounded, and Theseus returns to confront Creon and to order the return of Antigone and Ismene. Asked to explain his actions, Creon weakly argues that he has come to rid Attica of the taint that Oedipus surely will place on the kingdom if its citizens offer shelter to any of the cursed progeny of Cadmus. Theseus checks Creon and rescues Oedipus's two daughters.

Polynices, Oedipus's older son, has been searching for his father. Hoping to see the prophecy of the Delphic Oracle fulfilled, but also for his own selfish ends, the young man comes to the olive grove. With professions of repentance and filial devotion he begs Oedipus to return with him to Argos. Oedipus knows that his son wishes only to ensure the success of his expedition against his brother, Eteocles, who is in authority at Thebes. He hears Polynices out in silence; then he denounces both sons as traitors. Vehemently, he prophesies that Polynices and Eteocles will die by violence. Polynices, impressed by his father's words but still ambitious and arrogant, ignores Antigone's pleas to spare their native city. He departs, convinced that he is going to certain death.

Three rolls of thunder presage the impending death of old Oedipus. Impatiently, but at the same time with a certain air of resignation, Oedipus calls for Theseus. Guiding the king and his two daughters to a nearby grotto, he predicts that as long as his burial place remains a secret known only to Theseus and his male descendants, Attica will successfully resist all invasions. After begging Theseus to protect Antigone and Ismene, he dismisses his daughters. Only Theseus is with Oedipus when he suddenly disappears. Antigone and Ismene try to return to their father's tomb, but Theseus, true to his solemn promise, prevents them. He does, however, second them in their desire to return to Thebes, that they might prevent the dreadful bloodshed that threatens their native city because of Polynices and Eteocles.

Critical Evaluation:

Written when Sophocles was about ninety years old and approaching death, *Oedipus at Colonus* is the dramatist's valedictory to the stage, to Athens, and to life. In its transcendent spiritual power it is reminiscent of William Shakespeare's last great play, *The Tempest* (pr. 1611, pb. 1623). It was probably inevitable that the great Athenian patriot Sophocles should have written a play based on the story of the legendary past of his birthplace. Indeed, two of the high points of this drama are magnificent odes in praise of Colonus and Attica. *Oedipus at Colonus* represents the culmination of Sophocles' handling of the Cadmean legend, which he had treated earlier in *Antigone* (441 B.C.E.) and *Oidipous Tyrannos* (c. 429 B.C.E.; *Oedipus Tyrannus*, 1715). It is at the same time his last, luminous affirmation of human dignity in the face of an incomprehensible universe.

The theme of the suppliants, or refugees, pleading for protection, was common in Greek tragedy. Both Aeschylus and Euripides had written patriotic dramas on this subject. The plot formula was simple: People threatened with capture sue a powerful but democratic king for aid and receive it. *Oedipus at Colonus* is remarkably similar in its patriotic content to Euripides' *The Suppliants* (423 B.C.E.). Both plays treat the Theban myth and feature an aspect of the War of Seven Against Thebes; both conform to the same plot formula; and both present Theseus and Athens in a heroic light as the defenders of the weak from tyrannical force.

When Sophocles wrote his play, Athens was in the final throes of the disastrous Peloponnesian War, which would result in Athens's defeat at the hands of Sparta. In its arrogance of power, the city had become rapacious and morally degenerate. Sophocles' purpose in writing this play, at least from a civic viewpoint, was to remind the Athenians of their legendary respect for the rights of the helpless, a respect that up to that point had kept them safe from invaders. With the Greek tragedians, civic welfare depended directly on moral rectitude. By defending Oedipus and his daughters, Theseus ensures the safety of Athens for generations. Sophocles also shows Theseus acting disinterestedly, however, out of concern for the suppliants and thus as a model ruler. The playwright wished to inspire his fellow citizens with the virtues they had cast aside: piety, courage in a good cause, and manliness.

Sophocles' patriotism went beyond state morality. In his two beautiful choral odes on Colonus and Attica there is an intense, wistful passion for the land itself, for the life it supported, and for the people's activities there. Sophocles believed that there was something holy about the place. It is not accidental that the entire action of this play takes place before a sacred grove, for he wanted his audience to feel the presence of divinity. The goddesses here were the hideous and awesome Furies, who judge and punish evildoers. As agents of divine justice they preside invisibly over all that occurs in *Oedipus at Colonus*.

The center of the play, however, is not Theseus or Athens but a frightful beggar who has suffered terribly in his long life—the blind Oedipus. Although he is reconciled to exile, beggary, and blindness, he remains proud and hot-tempered, and he cannot forgive Creon and Polynices, the two men who inflicted exile and penury on him. Oedipus has paid in full for the infamous deeds he committed in ignorance. He rightly insists upon his innocence, not of killing his father, marrying his mother, and having children by her, but of having done these things knowingly. Fate led him into that trap, and the Furies punished him for it. His nobility consists in bearing his suffering with dignity. Even if in his blindness he is the weakest and most pitiful of men, and though he must be led around by a young girl, there is true manliness in him.

By contrast, Creon lives by expediency, using force when persuasion fails but tamely submitting when Theseus gains the upper hand. In pursuing a reasonable goal, namely the defense of Thebes, he is willing to use any means, including kidnapping Oedipus's only supports, his two daughters. His ruthlessness is distasteful, but even more unpleasant is Polynices's whining plea for Oedipus's aid in attacking Thebes. It stems from selfish ambition rather than concern for his poor father. The curses Oedipus levels at Creon, Polynices, Eteocles, and Thebes are justified and apt. For dishonoring a helpless, blind man they deserve the calamity they have incurred.

In this play, Oedipus is preparing for death, as Sophocles must have been as he wrote it. Despite his hard destiny, and despite his power to curse those who have shamed him, Oedipus carries in his breast a profound blessing. In the end, the very Furies who hounded him bestow upon him a tremendous potency in death, the power to protect Athens just as Athens had protected him. The ultimate reason for his suffering remains obscure, but the manhood with which he faced it was the sole blessing he himself received, and that was all he needed. His mysterious and fearsome apotheosis amid flashes of lightning and earth tremors is the tribute the gods pay to Oedipus's supreme courage. Sophocles here offered his last and most sublime testament to a human being's ability to take unmerited pain and transform it into glory.

"Critical Evaluation" by James Weigel, Jr.

Further Reading

Beer, Josh. *Sophocles and the Tragedy of Athenian Democracy*. Westport, Conn.: Praeger, 2004. Analyzes Sophocles' plays within the context of Athenian democracy in the fifth century B.C.E., focusing on the political issues in the dramas. Examines Sophocles' dramatic techniques and how they "revolutionized the concept of dramatic space." Chapter 10 discusses *Oedipus at Colonus*.

Garvie, A. F. *The Plays of Sophocles*. Bristol, England: Bristol Classical, 2005. Concise analysis of Sophocles' plays, with a chapter devoted to *Oedipus at Colonus*. Focuses on Sophocles' tragic thinking, the concept of the Sophoclean hero, and the structure of his plays.

Kirkwood, Gordon MacDonald. *A Study of Sophoclean Drama*. 1958. Reprint. Ithaca, N.Y.: Cornell University Press, 1994. An examination and analysis of the methods and structures of dramatic composition used by Sophocles. Compares his plays to consider the characters, irony, illustrative forms, and use of diction and oracles in each. Excellent coverage of *Oedipus at Colonus*.

Markantonatos, Andreas. *"Oedipus at Colonus": Sophocles, Athens, and the World*. New York: Walter de Gruyter, 2007. A detailed interpretation of the play, discussing its underlying historical, religious, social, moral, and mythological issues. Examines the play in relation to *Antigone* and *Oedipus Tyrannus*. Surveys the literary and performance reception of the play and later scholarship.

Morwood, James. *The Tragedies of Sophocles*. Exeter, England: Bristol Phoenix Press, 2008. Analyzes each of Sophocles' seven plays, with chapter 8 devoted to *Oedipus at Colonus*. Discusses several modern productions and adaptations of the tragedies.

Ringer, Mark. *"Electra" and the Empty Urn: Metatheater and Role Playing in Sophocles*. Chapel Hill: University of North Carolina Press, 1998. Focuses on elements of metatheater, or theater within theater, and the ironic self-awareness in Sophocles' plays. Analyzes plays-within-plays, characters who are in rivalry with the playwright, and characters who assume roles to deceive one another. *Oedipus at Colonus* is discussed in chapter 5.

Scodel, Ruth. *Sophocles*. Boston: Twayne, 1984. Includes a synopsis and discussion of the plot of *Oedipus at Colonus*, as well as an analysis of Oedipus and the characters that oppose him. Provides information on Sophocles' other plays and a chronology of his life. Includes a bibliography and an index.

Seale, David. *Vision and Stagecraft in Sophocles*. Chicago: University of Chicago Press, 1982. Distinguishes Sophocles from other playwrights of his time and demonstrates his influence on later dramatists. Considers the theatrical technicalities in Sophocles' plays and contains an extended section on *Oedipus at Colonus*. Excellent study for nonspecialists, students, and classicists.

Woodard, Thomas, ed. *Sophocles: A Collection of Critical Essays*. Englewood Cliffs, N.J.: Prentice-Hall, 1966. A fine collection of essays, including writings by Friedrich Nietzsche, Sigmund Freud, and Virginia Woolf. Examines *Oedipus at Colonus* as a play from Sophocles' later years and draws connections with his other plays.

Oedipus Tyrannus

Author: Sophocles (c. 496-406 B.C.E.)
First produced: Oidipous Tyrannos, c. 429 B.C.E. (English translation, 1715)
Type of work: Drama
Type of plot: Tragedy
Time of plot: Antiquity
Locale: Thebes

Principal characters:
OEDIPUS, the king of Thebes
JOCASTA, his wife
CREON, Jocasta's brother
TEIRESIAS, a seer

The Story:

When Thebes is struck by a plague, the people ask King Oedipus to deliver them from its horrors. Creon, the brother of Jocasta, Oedipus's queen, returns from the oracle of Apollo and discloses that the plague is punishment for the murder of King Laius, Oedipus's immediate predecessor, to whom Jocasta was married. Creon further discloses that the citizens of Thebes need to discover and punish the murderer before the plague can be lifted. The people mourn their dead, and Oedipus advises them, in their own interest, to search out and apprehend the murderer of Laius.

Asked to help find the murderer, Teiresias, the ancient, blind seer of Thebes, tells Oedipus that it would be better for all if he does not tell what he knows. He says that coming events will reveal themselves. Oedipus rages at the seer's reluctance to tell the secret until he goads the old man to reveal that Oedipus is the one responsible for Thebes's afflictions because he is the murderer, and that he is living in intimacy with his nearest kin. Oedipus accuses the old man of being in league with Creon, whom he suspects of plotting against his throne, but Teiresias answers that Oedipus will be ashamed and horrified when he learns the truth about his true parentage. Oedipus defies the seer, saying he will welcome the truth as long as it frees his kingdom from the plague. Oedipus threatens Creon with death, but Jocasta and the people advise him against doing violence on the strength of rumor or momentary passion. Oedipus yields, but he banishes Creon.

Jocasta, grieved by the enmity between her brother and Oedipus, tells her husband that an oracle informed King Laius that he would be killed by his own child, the offspring of Laius and Jocasta. Jocasta assures Oedipus that this could not happen because the child was abandoned on a deserted mountainside soon after birth. When Oedipus hears further that Laius was killed by robbers at the meeting place of three roads and that the three roads met in Phocis, he is deeply disturbed and begins to suspect that he is, after all, the murderer. He hesitates to reveal his suspicion, but he becomes more and more convinced of his own guilt.

Oedipus tells Jocasta that he believed himself to be the son of Polybus of Corinth and Merope until a drunken man on one occasion announced that the young Oedipus was not really Polybus's son. Disturbed, Oedipus consulted the oracle of Apollo, who told him he would sire children by his own mother and that he would kill his own father. After he left Corinth, at a meeting place of three roads, Oedipus was offended by a man in a chariot. He killed the man and all of his servants but one. From there he went on to Thebes, where he became the new king by answering the riddle of the Sphinx. The riddle asked what went on all fours before noon, on two legs at noon, and on three legs after noon. Oedipus answered, correctly, that human beings walk on all fours as an infant, on two legs in their prime, and with the aid of a stick in their old age. With the kingship, he also won the hand of Jocasta, King Laius's queen.

Oedipus summons the servant who reported King Laius's death, but he awaits his arrival fearfully. Jocasta assures her husband that the entire matter is of no great consequence, that surely the prophecies of the oracles will not come true.

A messenger from Corinth announces that King Polybus is dead and that Oedipus is his successor. Polybus died of natural causes, so Oedipus and Jocasta are relieved for the time being. Oedipus tells the messenger he will not go to Corinth for fear of siring children by his mother, Merope.

The messenger goes on to reveal that Oedipus is not the son of Polybus and Merope but a foundling whom the messenger, at that time a shepherd, took to Polybus. The messenger relates how he received the baby from another shepherd, who was a servant of the house of King Laius. At that point Jocasta realizes the dreadful truth. She does not wish to see the old servant who was summoned, but Oedipus desires clarity regardless of the cost. He again calls for the servant. When the servant appears, the messenger recognizes him as the herdsman from whom he received the child years earlier. The old servant confesses that King Laius ordered him to destroy the boy but that out of pity he gave the infant to the Corinthian to raise as his foster son.

Oedipus, now all but mad from the realization of what he did, enters the palace and discovers that Jocasta hanged herself by her hair. He removes her golden brooches and with them puts out his eyes so that he will not be able to see the results of the horrible prophecy. Then, blind and bloody and miserable, he displays himself to the Thebans and announces himself as the murderer of their king and the defiler of his own mother's bed. He curses the herdsman who saved him from death years before.

Creon, returning, orders the attendants to lead Oedipus back into the palace. Oedipus asks Creon to have him conducted out of Thebes where no man will ever see him again. He also asks Creon to give Jocasta a proper burial and to see that the sons and daughters of the unnatural marriage should be cared for and not be allowed to live poor and unmarried because of the shame attached to their parentage. Creon leads the wretched Oedipus away to his exile of blindness and torment.

Critical Evaluation:

Aristotle considered *Oedipus Tyrannus* the supreme example of tragic drama and modeled his theory of tragedy on it. He mentions the play no fewer than eleven times in his *De poetica* (c. 334-323 B.C.E.; *Poetics*, 1705). Sigmund Freud in the twentieth century used the story to name the rivalry of male children with their fathers for the affection of their mothers, and Jean Cocteau adapted the tale to the modern stage in *La Machine infernale* (1934; *The Infernal Machine*, 1936). However, no matter what changes the Oedipus myth underwent in two and a half millennia, the finest expression of it remains this tragedy by Sophocles.

Brilliantly conceived and written, *Oedipus Tyrannus* is a drama of self-discovery. Sophocles achieves an amazing compression and force by limiting the dramatic action to the day on which Oedipus learns the true nature of his birth and his destiny. The fact that the audience knows the dark secret that Oedipus unwittingly slew his true father and married his mother does nothing to destroy the suspense. Oedipus's search for the truth has all the tautness of a detective tale, and yet because audiences already know the truth they are aware of all the ironies in which Oedipus is enmeshed. That knowledge enables them to fear the final revelation at the same time that they pity the man whose past is gradually and relentlessly uncovered to him.

The plot is thoroughly integrated with the characterization of Oedipus, for it is he who impels the action forward in his concern for Thebes, his personal rashness, and his ignorance of his past. His flaws are a hot temper and impulsiveness, but without those traits his heroic course of self-discovery would never occur.

Fate for Sophocles is not something essentially external to human beings but something at once inherent in them and transcendent. Oracles and prophets in this play may show the will of the gods and indicate future events, but it is the individual who gives substance to the prophecies. Moreover, there is an element of freedom granted to human beings, an ability to choose, where the compulsions of character and the compulsions of the gods are powerless. It is in the way individuals meet the necessities of their destiny that freedom lies. They can succumb to fate, pleading extenuating circumstances, or they can shoulder the full responsibility for what they do. In the first case they are merely pitiful, but in the second they are tragic and take on a greatness of soul that nothing can conquer.

A crucial point in the play is that Oedipus is entirely unaware that he killed his father and wedded his mother. He himself is the cause of the plague on Thebes, and in vowing to find the murderer of Laius and exile him he unconsciously pronounces judgment on himself. Oedipus, the king and the hero who saved Thebes from the Sphinx, believes in his own innocence. He is angry and incredulous when the provoked Teiresias accuses him of the crime, so he jumps to the conclusion that Teiresias and Creon are conspirators against him. As plausible as that explanation may be, Oedipus maintains it with irrational vehemence, not even bothering to investigate it before he decides to have Creon put to death. Every act of his is performed rashly: his hot-tempered killing of Laius, his investigation of the murder, his violent blinding of himself, and his insistence on being exiled. He is a man of great pride and passion who is intent on serving Thebes, but he does not have tragic stature until the evidence of his guilt begins to accumulate.

Ironically, his past is revealed to him by people who wish him well and who want to reassure him. Each time a character tries to comfort him with information, the information serves to damn him more thoroughly. Jocasta, in proving how false oracles can be, first suggests to him that he unknowingly really did kill Laius, thus corroborating the oracles. The messenger from Corinth in reassuring Oedipus about his parentage brings his true parentage into question, but he says enough to convince Jocasta that Oedipus is her son. It is at this point, when he determines to complete the search for the truth, knowing that he killed Laius and knowing that the result of his investigation may be utterly damnable, that Oedipus's true heroism starts to emerge. His rashness at this point is no longer a liability but becomes part of his integrity.

Learning the full truth of his dark destiny, his last act as king is to blind himself over the dead body of Jocasta, his wife and his mother. It is a terrible, agonizing moment, even in description, but in the depths of his pain Oedipus is magnificent. He does not submit passively to his woe or plead that he committed his foul acts in ignorance, though he could be justified in doing so. He blinds himself in a rage of penitence, accepting total responsibility for what he did and determined to take the punishment of exile as well. As piteous as he appears in the final scene with Creon, there is more public spirit and more strength in his fierce grief and his resolution of exile than in any other tragic hero in the history of the theater. Oedipus unravels his life to its utmost limits of agony and finds there an unsurpassed grandeur of soul.

"Critical Evaluation" by James Weigel, Jr.

Further Reading

Beer, Josh. *Sophocles and the Tragedy of Athenian Democracy.* Westport, Conn.: Praeger, 2004. Analyzes Sophocles' plays within the context of Athenian democracy in the fifth century B.C.E., focusing on the political issues in the dramas. Examines Sophocles' dramatic techniques and how they "revolutionized the concept of dramatic space." Chapter 7 discusses *Oedipus Rex* (another name for *Oedipus Tyrannus*).

Garvie, A. F. *The Plays of Sophocles.* Bristol, England: Bristol Classical, 2005. Concise analysis of Sophocles' plays, with a chapter devoted to *Oedipus the King* (another name for *Oedipus Tyrannus*). Focuses on Sophocles' tragic thinking, the concept of the Sophoclean hero, and the structure of his plays.

Kirkwood, Gordon MacDonald. *A Study of Sophoclean Drama.* Ithaca, N.Y.: Cornell University Press, 1958. Reprint. 1994. Examines and analyzes the structures Sophocles uses and his methods of dramatic composition. Compares his plays, considering characters, irony, illustrative forms, and the use of diction and oracles in each. Excellent coverage of *Oedipus Tyrannus.*

Morwood, James. *The Tragedies of Sophocles.* Exeter, England: Bristol Phoenix Press, 2008. Analyzes each of Sophocles' seven extant plays, with chapter 5 devoted to *Oedipus Rex.* Discusses several modern productions and adaptations of the tragedies.

Ringer, Mark. *"Electra" and the Empty Urn: Metatheater and Role Playing in Sophocles.* Chapel Hill: University of North Carolina Press, 1998. Focuses on elements of metatheater, or "theater within theater," and the ironic self-awareness in Sophocles' plays. Analyzes plays-within-plays, characters who are in rivalry with the playwright, and characters who assume roles in order to deceive one another. *Oedipus Tyrannus* is discussed in chapter 5.

Scodel, Ruth. *Sophocles.* Boston: Twayne, 1984. Provides synopses of the seven Sophoclean plays. Considers works that may have influenced Sophocles. Examines the plays' structure and the use of mythological gods and oracles. Includes a chronology of Sophocles' life, a bibliography, and an index.

Segal, Charles. *"Oedipus Tyrannus": Tragic Heroism and the Limits of Knowledge.* New York: Twayne, 1993. Provides an extensive chronology of the life of Sophocles. Gives historical and cultural background, as well as a discussion of the design and structure, for *Oedipus Tyrannus.* Refers to influences on the play and its author and discusses interpretation of the Oedipus myth.

_____. *Tragedy and Civilization: An Interpretation of Sophocles.* Cambridge, Mass.: Harvard University Press, 1981. Discusses the seven plays of Sophocles, including *Oedipus Tyrannus.* Provides extensive interpretation on the identity of Oedipus, including the implications inherent in his name. Breaks down the plot and discusses it with regard to Greek language and English translation.

Woodard, Thomas, ed. *Sophocles: A Collection of Critical Essays.* Englewood Cliffs, N.J.: Prentice-Hall, 1966. A fine collection of essays, including writings by Friedrich Nietzsche, Sigmund Freud, and Virginia Woolf. Contains a thought-provoking section on the character of Oedipus.

Of Dramatic Poesie
An Essay

Author: John Dryden (1631-1700)
First published: 1668
Type of work: Literary criticism

Principal characters:
CRITES, a sharp-tongued gentleman, a staunch classicist
EUGENIUS, a defender of the English theater of his own time
LISIDEIUS, a devotee of the French classical drama
NEANDER, representative of the author, a lover of the great Elizabethans

John Dryden's *Of Dramatic Poesie* (also known as *An Essay of Dramatic Poesy*) is an exposition of several of the major critical positions of the time, set out in a semidramatic form that gives life to the abstract theories. *Of Dramatic Poesie* not only offers a capsule summary of the status of literary criticism in the late seventeenth century; it also provides a succinct view of the tastes of cultured men and women of the period. Dryden synthesizes the best of both English and Continental (particularly French) criticism; hence, the essay is a single source for understanding neoclassical attitudes to-

ward dramatic art. Moreover, in his discussion of the ancients versus the moderns, in his defense of the use of rhyme, and in his argument concerning Aristotelian prescripts for drama, Dryden depicts and reflects upon the tastes of literate Europeans who shaped the cultural climate in France and England for a century.

Although it is clear that Dryden uses Neander as a mouthpiece for his own views about drama, he is careful to allow his other characters to present cogent arguments for the literature of the classical period, of France, and of Renaissance

England. More significantly, although he was a practitioner of the modern form of writing plays himself, Dryden does not insist that the dramatists of the past are to be faulted simply because they did not adhere to methods of composition that his own age venerated. For example, he does not adopt the views of the more strident critics whose insistence on slavish adherence to the rules derived from Aristotle had led to a narrow definition for greatness among playwrights. Instead, he pleads for commonsensical application of these prescriptions, appealing to a higher standard of judgment: the discriminating sensibility of the reader or playgoer who can recognize greatness even when the rules are not followed.

For this reason, Dryden can champion the works of William Shakespeare over those of many dramatists who were more careful in preserving the unities of time, place, and action. It may be difficult to imagine, after centuries of veneration, that at one time Shakespeare was not held in high esteem; in the late seventeenth century, critics reviled him for his disregard for decorum and his seemingly careless attitudes regarding the mixing of genres. Dryden, however, recognized the greatness of Shakespeare's productions; his support for Shakespeare's "natural genius" had a significant impact on the elevation of the Renaissance playwright to a place of preeminence among dramatists.

The period after the restoration of the Stuarts to the throne is notable in English literary history as an age in which criticism flourished, probably in no small part as a result of the emphasis on neoclassical rules of art in seventeenth century France, where many of King Charles II's courtiers and literati had passed the years of Cromwell's rule. Dryden sets his discussion in June, 1665, during a naval battle between England and the Netherlands. Four cultivated gentlemen, Eugenius, Lisideius, Crites, and Neander, have taken a barge down the River Thames to observe the combat and, as guns sound in the background, they comment on the sorry state of modern literature; this naval encounter will inspire hundreds of bad verses commending the victors or consoling the vanquished. Crites laments that his contemporaries will never equal the standard set by the Greeks and the Romans. Eugenius, more optimistic, disagrees and suggests that they pass the remainder of the day debating the relative merits of classical and modern literature. He proposes that Crites choose one literary genre for comparison and initiate the discussion.

As Crites begins his defense of the classical drama, he mentions one point that is accepted by all the others: Drama is, as Aristotle wrote, an imitation of life, and it is successful as it reflects human nature clearly. He also discusses the three unities, rules dear to both the classicist and the neoclassicist,

requiring that a play take place in one locale during one day, and that it encompass one action or plot.

Crites contends that modern playwrights are but pale shadows of Aeschylus, Sophocles, Seneca, and Terence. The classical dramatists not only followed the unities successfully; they also used language more skillfully than their successors. He calls to witness Ben Jonson, the Elizabethan dramatist most highly respected by the neoclassical critics, a writer who borrowed copiously from many of the classical authors and prided himself on being a modern Horace. Crites says

> I will use no further argument to you than his example: I will produce before you Father Ben, dressed in all the ornaments and colours of the ancients; you will need no other guide to our party, if you follow him.

Eugenius pleads the cause of the modern English dramatists, not by pointing out their virtues, but by criticizing the faults of the classical playwrights. He objects to the absence of division by acts in the works of the latter, as well as to the lack of originality in their plots. Tragedies are based on threadbare myths familiar to the whole audience; comedies revolve around hackneyed intrigues of stolen heiresses and miraculous restorations. A more serious defect is these authors' disregard of poetic justice: "Instead of punishing vice and rewarding virtue, they have often shown a prosperous wickedness, and an unhappy piety."

Pointing to scenes from several plays, Eugenius notes the lack of tenderness in classical drama. Crites grants Eugenius his preference, but he argues that each age has its own modes of behavior; Homer's heroes were "men of great appetites, lovers of beef broiled upon the coals, and good fellows," while the principal characters of modern French romances "neither eat, nor drink, nor sleep, for love."

Lisideius takes up the debate on behalf of the French theater of the early seventeenth century. The French classical dramatists, led by Pierre Corneille, were careful observers of the unities, and they did not attempt to combine tragedy and comedy, an English practice he finds absurd: "Here a course of mirth, there another of sadness and passion, and a third of honour and a duel: thus, in two hours and a half, we run through all the fits of Bedlam."

The French playwrights are so attentive to poetic justice that, when they base their plots on historical events, they alter the original situations to mete out just reward and punishment. The French dramatist "so interweaves truth with probable fiction that he puts a pleasing fallacy upon us; mends the intrigues of fate, and dispenses with the severity of history, to reward that virtue which has been rendered to us there unfortunate." Plot, as the preceding comments might suggest, is of secondary concern in these plays. The dramatist's chief aim is to express appropriate emotions; violent action always takes place offstage, and it is generally reported by a messenger.

Just as Eugenius devoted much of his discussion to refuting Crites' arguments, Neander, whose views are generally Dryden's own, contradicts Lisideius's claims for the superiority of the French drama. Stating his own preference for the works of English writers, especially of the great Elizabethans, Neander suggests that it is they who best fulfill the primary requirement of drama, that it be "an imitation of life." The beauties of the French stage are, to him, cold; they may "raise perfection higher where it is, but are not sufficient to give it where it is not." He compares these beauties to those of a statue, flawless, but without a soul. Intense human feeling is, Neander feels, an essential part of drama.

Neander argues that tragicomedy is the best form for drama, for it is the closest to life; emotions are heightened by contrast, and both mirth and sadness are more vivid when they are set side by side. He believes, too, that subplots enrich a play; he finds the French drama, with its single action, thin. Like Samuel Johnson, who defended Shakespeare's disregard of the unities, Dryden suggests that close adherence to the rules prevents dramatic depth. Human actions will be more believable if there is time for the characters' emotions to develop. Neander sees no validity in the argument that changes of place and time in plays lessen dramatic credibility; theatergoers know that they are in a world of illusion from the beginning, and they can easily accept leaps in time and place, as well as makeshift battles.

Concluding his comparison of French and English drama, Neander characterizes the best of the Elizabethan playwrights. His judgments have often been quoted for their perceptivity. He calls Shakespeare "the man who of all modern, and perhaps ancient poets, had the largest and most comprehensive soul." Francis Beaumont and John Fletcher are praised for their wit and for their language, whose smoothness and polish Dryden considers their greatest accomplishment: "I am apt to believe the English language in them arrived to its highest perfection."

Dryden commends Jonson for his learning and judgment, for his "correctness," yet he feels that Shakespeare surpassed him in "wit," by which he seems to mean something like natural ability or inspiration. This discussion ends with the familiar comparison: "Shakespeare was the Homer, or father of our dramatic poets; Jonson was the Virgil, the pattern of elaborate writing; I admire him, but I love Shakespeare."

Neander concludes his argument for the superiority of the Elizabethans with a close critical analysis of a play by Ben Jonson, which Neander believes a perfect demonstration that the English were capable of following classical rules triumphantly. Dryden's allegiance to the neoclassical tradition is clear here; Samuel Johnson could disparage the unities in his *Preface to Shakespeare* (1765), but Dryden, even as he refuses to be a slave to the rules, makes Ben Jonson's successful observance of them his decisive argument.

The essay closes with a long discussion of the value of rhyme in plays. Crites feels that blank verse, as the poetic form nearest prose, is most suitable for drama, while Neander favors rhyme, which encourages succinctness and clarity. He believes that the Restoration dramatists can make their one claim to superiority through their development of the heroic couplet. Dryden is very much of his time in this argument; the modern reader who has suffered through the often empty declamation of the Restoration hero returns with relief to the blank verse of the Elizabethans.

Dryden ends his work without a real conclusion; the barge reaches its destination, the stairs at Somerset House, and the debate is, of necessity, over. Moving with the digressions and contradictions of a real conversation, the discussion provides a clear, lively picture of many of the literary opinions of Dryden's time.

Revised by Laurence W. Mazzeno

Further Reading

Hammond, Paul, and David Hopkins, eds. *John Dryden: Tercentenary Essays*. New York: Oxford University Press, 2000. This collection, published during the tercentenary of Dryden's death, examines some of Dryden's individual works, as well as more general characteristics of his writing. Some of the essays question whether Dryden is a classicist, explore Dryden and the "staging of popular politics," and describe the dissolution evident in his later writing.

Hopkins, David. *John Dryden*. Tavistock, England: Northcote House/British Council, 2004. Concise overview of Dryden's life and work. Hopkins demonstrates that Dryden not only was of his times but also continues to have significance for twenty-first century audiences.

Kramer, David Bruce. *The Imperial Dryden: The Poetics of Appropriation in Seventeenth-Century England*. Athens: University of Georgia Press, 1994. Examines the French influence on Dryden's thinking; a section focuses on the connection between Dryden and the French critical tradition by way of some contemporary French writers.

Lewis, Jayne, and Maximillian E. Novak, eds. *Enchanted Ground: Reimagining John Dryden.* Buffalo, N.Y.: University of Toronto Press, 2004. Collection of essays that apply twenty-first century critical perspectives to Dryden's work. The first section focuses on Dryden's role as a public poet and the voice of the Stuart court during Restoration; the second explores his relationship to drama and music.

Pechter, Edward. *Dryden's Classical Theory of Literature.* New York: Cambridge University Press, 1975. A review of Dryden's classical inheritance. In a chapter discussing *Of Dramatic Poesie*, Pechter is primarily concerned with the classical structure of the argument in that work.

Rawson, Claude, and Aaron Santesso, eds. *John Dryden, 1631-1700: His Politics, His Plays, and His Poets.* Newark: University of Delaware Press, 2004. Contains papers presented at a Yale University conference held in 2000 to commemorate the tercentenary of Dryden's death. The essays focus on the politics of Dryden's plays and how his poetry was poised between ancient and modern influences.

Zwicker, Steven N., ed. *The Cambridge Companion to John Dryden.* New York: Cambridge University Press, 2004. Among these seventeen essays are discussions of Dryden and the theatrical imagination, the invention of Augustan culture and patronage, Dryden's London, and the "passion of politics" in his theater.

Of Grammatology

Author: Jacques Derrida (1930-2004)
First published: De la Grammatologie, 1967 (English translation, 1976)
Type of work: Literary criticism

Jacques Derrida's *Of Grammatology* is a fundamental work of what has come to be called deconstructionist criticism. "Grammatology" is a term borrowed from Ignace J. Gelb, a linguist and ancient historian who first used it in his *A Study of Writing: The Foundations of Grammatology* (1952). Derrida's *Of Grammatology* reexamines and aims to replace traditional Western logocentrism. By logocentrism, Derrida means the identification of the words of a text with the truth the text contains.

From the pre-Socratics to the post-Hegelians, *logos* (Greek for "word," "reason," or "spirit") has been the origin of truth, its constitutive element. Western culture, influenced by the book of Genesis, and also by Plato, has identified *logos* with the source of creation itself. The thought of God or some overriding transcendent principle is thus identifiable with *logos*, while *logos* at its essence implies creation.

Language conveys signs, and signs contain two elements: the signifier (the physical symbol) and the signified (the thought beyond the symbol). The signifier and signified are ever present, and they are always distinct from one another. They may be distinct only to a small degree, or they may have a wide separation. For example, the coldness of ice cream might make one person think of winter, another person of a summer day at the beach, and a third person of the pain from a sensitive tooth.

It is thus apparent that there is something like a logocentric hierarchy of signification. Things signified have a greater or lesser validity insofar as they approach the universal, or in more metaphysical terms, insofar as they approach a *primum signatum*—the signified that requires no signification. This first and highest signified validates all those that are lower. Furthermore, the *primum signatum* is "logologically" essential, and without it a chaos of signifiers would make a sign lose all signification.

Presence validates the signified because one cannot doubt that which clearly exists; the higher the signified, the greater its degree of presence. Cold as signifier of winter has a greater degree of presence for anyone who has experienced winter. It is likely to be more universal than cold as signifier of ice cream if one has never eaten ice cream. Concomitantly, an individual is absolutely real to that same individual. Reality thus validates presence.

The most potent signifiers are intelligible. Love as concept or idea, for example, is immediately apprehensible intellectually, though the path through which the mind apprehends it is in its relation to absolute logos. Physical reality, which is necessarily on the level of sense, traces a higher metaphysical counterpart. Physical entities thus signify intelligible ideas, and intelligible ideas have validity and reality.

Derrida privileges speech to writing. Speech has a higher signification because it eliminates the intermediary of the written word. One thinks in words—inner speech—whereas the written word, by interposing itself, simply signifies the spoken signifier. The written word is a mediator of a mediator and, thereby, imposes distance on idea and, thus, on presence. Because logocentrism seeks presence, it attempts to efface written words by implying unity between signifier and signified. Though the spoken word is closer to presence than the written word, even it can never reach the truth or pure presence that transcendent validity requires.

Logocentric linguistics itself, therefore, ultimately fails because it can never reach the universality of absolute presence and, through this, ultimate truth. Logocentric linguistics deludes a person with illusions of unity through a chain of signifiers and entities signified, but it eventually collapses in failure to signify anything. As a basic example, consider technical operational or repair manuals for such things as automobiles or computers. They proceed through a hierarchic series of comprehensible signs that initially appear to have clearly signified entities. Even so, they ultimately become babble to all but those initiated into their jargon. Even initiates and initiator, however, frequently find a welter of contradictory significations.

Because reaching the truth is impossible through logocentric linguistics, Derrida proposes a new conception of language, grammatology, which privileges writing. This results in an endless chain of signifiers and eliminates the need for the transcendent signification of logocentric linguistics. It also destroys both the concept and the logic of the sign. Every signifier inherently differs from that which it signifies and defers recognition of what it signifies. This is what Derrida calls *différance*, which he spells with the letter *a* to show simultaneously both "difference" and "deference."

Signs and hierarchic signification are nevertheless embedded in the logocentric tradition; this trace remains visible. In Derrida's grammatology, one always writes under erasure, crossing out signifiers with an *X* while allowing them to remain visible to indicate necessary reliance upon them.

Derrida, in part two, continues his analysis, looking at what he considers the concealment of language in Jean-Jacques Rousseau's *Confessions* (1781-1788). It is in Rousseau that Derrida sees the origins of the grammatology he proposes. *Confessions*, Derrida argues, describes the process by which Rousseau became a writer in terms of a calculated effacement of presence in speech. Writing thus allows Rousseau a calculated means of presenting his true self.

Of course, anyone who has read Rousseau's *Confessions*, or even Rousseau's fiction, realizes that its author is always present and always absent in what he writes. Having claimed that truth is the primary criterion of his *Confessions*, Rousseau declares that his is a type of work never before written, though he had been clearly aware of Saint Augustine's work of the same name. Rousseau writes that he intends to offer the work to his creator (though he does not believe in God; Rousseau's creator is Rousseau), and because he has written every word, he has become his own recording angel. His self-indictments become his accomplishments, and his failures become his distinctions.

For Derrida, then, Rousseau becomes a pivotal example of the failure of the logocentric epoch and the birth of the new grammatology. *Confessions* fills a lack of nature; it is a supplement and it substitutes (it is a *suppléance*). Language is the "mother" Rousseau lacks; mama is the name he gives his first mistress. Rousseau desires "to lie at the feet of an imperious mistress." The writer is the servant of language insofar as language invariably limits.

Even so, none of these elements is truly what it appears to be because signification does not truly signify. Neither language nor his first mistress and patron—Louise Eleonore de Warens—nor the imperious mistress of Rousseau's fantasies can be the mother who died giving birth to him. *Confessions* is his child and not his child. The work's primary character both is and is not the autobiographer, and its protagonist both is and is not the recording angel who submits the work to the creator in whom he does not believe (nor ever confesses he believes) exists. The signifiers chase one another almost as instruments in a musical fugue, but they never transcend themselves.

Robert J. Forman

Further Reading

Bennington, Geoffrey. *Interrupting Derrida*. New York: Routledge, 2000. A collection of essays on works by and about Derrida. Bennington argues that Derrida's work "interrupts" metaphysics by rendering it indefinite.

Boyne, Roy. *Foucault and Derrida: The Other Side of Reason*. 1990. Reprint. New York: Routledge, 2001. Michel Foucault and Derrida are in some respects at separate poles, especially on questions of epistemology and the nature of reason. Boyne examines and simplifies their ideas in this book designed for students.

Bradley, Arthur. *Derrida's "Of Grammatology."* Bloomington: Indiana University Press, 2008. A thorough explanatory study of Derrida's difficult work. Essential reading for students of contemporary philosophy, literary theory, and intellectual history. Accessible to interdisciplinary readers at all levels.

Caputo, John D., ed. *Deconstruction in a Nutshell: A Conversation with Jacques Derrida.* New York: Fordham University Press, 1998. Summary of a roundtable held at Villanova University in 1994. Features Derrida's responses to wide-ranging questions, such as the nature of justice and the role of philosophy. Includes his interpretation of the language of novelist James Joyce.

Derrida, Jacques. *Learning to Live Finally: The Last Interview.* Santa Maria, Calif.: Melville, 2007. An interview conducted by a writer with the French newsmagazine *Le Monde.* Derrida discusses his work, realistically assessing it in anticipation of his own impending death.

Hartman, Geoffrey H. *Saving the Text: Literature/Derrida/Philosophy.* 1981. Reprint. Baltimore: Johns Hopkins University Press, 1995. A careful analysis by a former colleague of Derrida at Yale University that situates Derrida as a mediator between creative literature and philosophy.

Mikics, David. *Who Was Jacques Derrida? An Intellectual Biography.* New Haven, Conn.: Yale University Press, 2009. The first intellectual biography of Derrida, examining his career, his influence, and his philosophical roots. The book also explores Derrida's role in bringing theory to the humanities.

Smith, Robert. *Derrida and Autobiography.* New York: Cambridge University Press, 1995. Places the philosophy of Derrida in the context of various theories of autobiography. For Derrida, autobiography is a condition of writing that belies the self-centered finitude of a single individual's life and death.

Wood, David, ed. *Derrida: A Critical Reader.* 1992. Reprint. Malden, Mass.: Blackwell, 1997. An intriguing series of critical essays on Derrida by outstanding scholars, including Jean-Luc Nancy, Manfred Frank, John Sallis, Robert Bernasconi, Irene Harvey, Michel Haar, Christopher Norris, Geoffrey Bennington, and John Llewelyn.

Of Human Bondage

Author: W. Somerset Maugham (1874-1965)
First published: 1915
Type of work: Novel
Type of plot: Naturalism
Time of plot: Early twentieth century
Locale: England

Principal characters:
PHILIP CAREY, an orphan boy
WILLIAM CAREY, his uncle
LOUISA CAREY, his aunt
MISS WILKINSON, Philip's first love
MILDRED ROGERS, a waitress
THORPE ATHELNEY, Philip's friend
SALLY ATHELNEY, his daughter

The Story:

Philip Carey is nine years old when his mother dies, and he is sent to live with his aunt and uncle at the vicarage of Blackstable, forty miles outside London. Uncle William Carey is a penny-pinching, smugly religious man who makes Philip's life miserable. Having been born with a clubfoot, Philip is extremely sensitive about his deformity, and he grows up bitter and rebellious. The only love he is shown is given to him by his aunt, Louisa, who has never been able to have children of her own. At school, Philip's clubfoot is a source of much ridicule, for the children are cruel. Philip is so sensitive that any reference to his foot, even a kind reference, causes him to strike out at the speaker.

When he is eighteen years old, Philip, with a small inheritance of his own, goes to Berlin to study. He takes a room in the home of Professor and Frau Erlin. There, he studies German, French, and mathematics with tutors from the University of Heidelberg. He meets several young men, among them Weeks, an American, and Hayward, a radical young Englishman. From their serious discussions on religion, Philip decides that he no longer believes in God. This decision makes him feel free; for in discarding God, he subconsciously discards his memories of his cold and bitter youth at the vicarage.

Shortly after his return to Blackstable, Philip becomes involved with a woman, Miss Emily Wilkinson, who is twice his age and a friend of Aunt Louisa. She is not attractive to him, but he thinks a man of twenty years of age should experience love. It is typical of Philip's attitude that even after they become lovers he continues to call her Miss Wilkinson. Not long after the affair, Philip goes to London to begin a career as a clerk in an accounting firm. Dissatisfied, he works only a year; then he goes to Paris to study art. Two years later, he gives up the idea of becoming an artist and returns to London for his third great start on a career. He has decided to study medicine.

In London, Philip meets Mildred Rogers, a waitress. She is really nothing more than a wanton, but Philip nevertheless loves her and desires her above all else. He gives her presents that are extravagant for his small income, and he neglects his studies to be with her. She gives him nothing in return. When he asks her to marry him—seemingly the only way he can possess her—she tells him bluntly that he does not have enough money for her and that she is marrying someone else. Philip both loves her and hates her so much that he is almost consumed by his emotions.

In his affection for another girl, he starts to forget Mildred as she returns to London. Alone and penniless, Mildred tells him that the other man had not married her and that he already had a wife and children. Mildred is pregnant, and Philip forgets the other girl and takes Mildred back. He pays her hospital bill and her lodging bills and sends her to the coast to rest. Mildred repays him by going off for a holiday with a man Philip considers his good friend. They use Philip's money to pay their expenses. Despising himself, he begs Mildred to come back to him after her trip with the other man; he cannot overcome his insane desire for her. Mildred, however, does not come back.

Philip then forces himself to study harder than ever. He meets Thorpe Athelney, a patient in the hospital where he is studying, and the two men become good friends. Philip visits the Athelney home almost every Sunday. It is a noisy house, filled with happy children, love, and kindness, and the cheerful atmosphere fills an empty place in Philip's heart. One evening, Philip sees Mildred again. She is highly painted and overdressed, and she is sauntering slowly down the street with a vulgar swing of her hips. She has become a common streetwalker. Although Philip knows then that he has lost his desire for her, out of pity he takes her and her child into his home. Mildred is to act as his housekeeper. Because Philip's funds are small, they are forced to live frugally. Mildred once again takes all that he has to offer and gives him nothing in return. Her only payment is an unknowing one, for Philip loves her child very much, and he has many hours of pleasure hold-

ing the baby girl in his arms. Mildred tries again and again to resume their old relationship, but each time, Philip repulses her. At last, she becomes insanely angry and leaves his apartment with her baby. Before she leaves, however, she completely wrecks the apartment, rips his clothing and linens with a knife, smashes furniture and dishes, and tears up his pictures.

A short time later, Philip loses what little money he had in a bad investment. The Athelney family takes him into their home, and Thorpe obtains work for him as a window dresser in the store where Thorpe himself is employed. Philip has to give up his studies at the hospital because of lack of money. Then, when he is thirty years old, his Uncle William dies and leaves him enough money to finish his medical education. When he walks down the steps with his diploma in his hand, Philip thinks that he is ready at last to begin his real life. He plans to sign on as a ship's doctor and sail around the world before he settles down to a permanent practice.

Before he accepts a position, Philip goes on a holiday trip with the Athelneys. While on the holiday, he realizes with a sudden shock that one of the Athelney girls whom he had always thought of as a child had definitely grown up. As they walk home together one night, he and Sally Athelney become lovers. Back in London a few weeks later, Sally tells him that she thinks she is pregnant. Philip immediately gives up his dreams of traveling over the world and accepts a small-salaried practice in a little fishing village, so that he and Sally can be married. Sally's fears, however, prove groundless. Free to travel and be his own master, Philip suddenly realizes that what he really wants is a home, a family, and security. He has never been normal because of his deformity, and he has never done what he wanted to do but always what he thought he should do. He has always lived in the future. Now he wants to live in the present. Therefore, he asks Sally to marry him and to go with him to that little fishing village. He offers her nothing but his love and the fruit of the lessons he has learned from hard teachers. Sally accepts his proposal. Philip feels that he is his own master after his bleak, bitter years of mortal bondage.

Critical Evaluation:

Almost all of W. Somerset Maugham's writings deal, in one way or another, with the individual's attempt to assert his (or her) freedom from "human bondage." Because it is the most direct, thorough, and personal of his works, *Of Human Bondage* is generally considered to be his masterpiece and its hero, Philip Carey, to be a thinly disguised portrait of the author. Like Carey, Maugham lost his beautiful, affectionate mother when he was quite young; was raised in an austere, financially pinched, religiously narrow environment; suffered abuse because of a physical disability (stammering); and fled to the Continent as soon as he was able. From that point on, the novel does not follow Maugham's personal life so literally, but it is clear that Philip's education follows Maugham's and that many of the characters and situations had their real-life counterparts. *Of Human Bondage* was, as Maugham himself admitted, an "autobiographical novel."

The first "bondage" that Philip must transcend—outgrow, really—is the oppressive environment of the vicarage. Deprived of his mother's love and thrust into a cold, moralistic milieu, young Philip is starved for affection and approval but finds little of it in his uncle's household. William Carey, a childless, middle-aged parson, is never able to understand or warm up to the boy, and his wife, Aunt Louisa, although well-meaning, lacks the emotional strength necessary to give the boy the needed support. These insecurities are exacerbated by his clubfoot, which makes him an object of ridicule at school. The only mitigating factor in these early years is his uncle's library. Books become his only pleasure and excitement and help him to mature; they also provide him with an escape from everyday reality and encourage his natural tendency toward daydreaming and indulging in fantasies. Therefore, his early experiences fix several important character traits: first, his thirst for love; second, his extreme self-consciousness and sensitivity, especially with regard to his clubfoot; third, his need to dominate and his envy of those who can; fourth, his distaste for social pieties and arbitrary moralities; and finally, his taste for literature and the life of the imagination.

As soon as he is physically capable of it, Philip flees to Germany. There, following closely upon his first experience of personal freedom, Philip has his initial taste of intellectual and spiritual emancipation. Two new friends, Hayward and Weeks, introduce him to the world of ideas. Hayward becomes his mentor and gives him a thorough grounding in the great books of the day, but it is Weeks who supplies him with the one volume, Ernest Renan's *The Life of Jesus* (1863), which has the most profound effect. It liberates Philip from his unconscious acceptance of Christian dogma and gives him an exultant new sense of personal freedom.

Philip's first intellectual awakening is followed shortly by his first sexual involvement. Back in Blackstable, he seduces Miss Wilkinson, an aging friend of his aunt, and quickly learns the difference between his idealized conception of sexual love and the reality he experiences with this demanding and physically unpleasant woman. She satisfies none of his emotional needs and leaves him feeling ridiculous and vulnerable. Miss Wilkinson, it turns out, introduces him to a

second crucial book, Henri Murger's *Scènes de la vie de Bohème* (1851; *The Bohemians of the Latin Quarter*, 1901). This romanticization of the lives and loves of the bohemian set stimulates Philip to attempt a career as a painter in Paris. At first, he is fascinated by the atmosphere, the activity, and the personalities, but he soon sees the reality beneath the glamorous surface. From careful observation and repeated exposures, he comes to understand the fakery, pretentiousness, and self-deception that characterizes most of this artistic activity. For the untalented, the life is brutal and destructive. He watches talentless friends like Fanny Price and Miguel Ajuria waste their lives in futile, feverish quest of the impossible. It is Fanny's suicide that finally ends his Paris pilgrimage.

Philip does not regret his Paris sojourn. He knows that he has had important experiences and has learned some valuable lessons; he is not disappointed to discover that he is without real ability. Even the truly talented artist is in bondage to his discipline and must commit himself completely if he is to realize that talent. Philip has no taste for such total dedication; he would rather live than create. Art study in Paris has taught him how to look at things in a new way, and that is, for him, a sufficient reward.

If Philip's experience with Miss Wilkinson gave him a taste of the reality of sex and love, it did not stifle his need for them. Upon his return from Paris, Philip begins one of the strangest and most intense romantic involvements in modern literature. There is nothing about Mildred Rogers that should logically attract Philip. She is physically unattractive, crude, stupid, and abrasive. Indeed, it is her very insolence that seems initially to interest him and, once attracted, he becomes obsessed with her. His knowledge of who Mildred is, and even his deliberate rejection of her, has no effect whatsoever on his passion—a fact that Philip himself clearly recognizes. Given this powerful, irrational need, her continuing arrogance and abuse only excite his desire, and the more unavailable she seems, the more intense it becomes.

Mildred is, finally, like a fever that must be endured until it runs its course. Maugham suggests that such is the nature of romantic love. Once the fever is dissipated, Philip is cured, and Mildred becomes simply an object of charity to him—at least that is Philip's belief. With the situation reversed, however, his adamant rejections of her sexuality must have at least some elements of subconscious revenge, and it is hard to believe that Philip does not, at some level, enjoy her final rage. In any event, the affair with Mildred has two lasting effects: Philip gains control of his passions and, at the same time, comes to understand the limits of rationality in the face of ungovernable emotions.

The last third of the novel has disappointed many readers. Especially disconcerting is the apparent contradiction between the sophisticated bleakness of Philip's final philosophical conclusion and the domestic felicity he expects to attain as a result of his marriage to a simple country girl. A number of events bring Philip to his final intellectual position. Following the end of his affair with Mildred, he meets Thorpe Athelney and his family, endures a short period of economic deprivation, and learns of the meaningless death of two old friends, Cronshaw and Hayward. These circumstances bring him face-to-face with the last bondage. Having emancipated himself from environmental, physical, cultural, religious, aesthetic, and emotional restraints, one final bond remains: Philip's need to understand the meaning of life. Out of his anguished rumination Philip gains a new and final insight: "suddenly the answer occurred to him. . . . Life had no meaning. . . . Life was insignificant and death without consequence."

Instead of depressing Philip, this revelation, reminiscent of his earlier conversion from Christianity, excites him: "For the first time he was utterly free . . . he was almighty because he had wrenched from chaos the secret of its nothingness." To many, such an insight looks dismal, but to Philip—and Maugham—this view is exhilarating because it frees a person to make the most of oneself and one's talents in purely human terms without needing to measure him- or herself against impossible transcendental absolutes.

It is in this context that Philip's marriage to Sally must be examined. Her father, Thorpe Athelney, is the only truly independent person whom Philip meets during his lifetime. Athelney is free of the religious, cultural, social, and economic pressures that distorted Philip's early environment. On the other hand, he has no need to play any of the false artistic or rebel roles that Philip encountered during his Paris sojourn. Athelney follows no false gods and pursues no impossible dreams. He is, in short, his own man who has lived his life completely in accordance with his own needs, instincts, and desires. The results have been personal satisfaction and happiness.

Because Philip accepts life as it is, he decides to settle for the one kind of happiness and existential meaning that he has seen demonstrated in action, not theory. Sally Athelney may not excite his passion or intellect, but he feels a "loving kindness" toward her and, to him, that promises a more satisfying life than to continue his search for nonexistent absolutes.

Therefore, the resolution of the novel is not inconsistent and can be justified on an intellectual level. These final scenes, however, remain artistically unsatisfying. Maugham himself, in his book of reminiscences, *The Summing Up* (1938), admitted that his final vision of domestic contentment was the one experience in the novel that he did not know personally. "Turning my wishes into fiction," he wrote, "I drew a picture of the marriage I should like to make. Readers on the whole have found it the least satisfactory part of my book." Maugham, who was gay, did not find personal felicity in marriage, but he did remain true to the ideas articulated in *Of Human Bondage*. In talking about the importance of the novel to his life, he stated, "It was the kind of effort that one can make once in a lifetime. I put everything into it, everything I knew, everything I experienced."

"Critical Evaluation" by Keith Neilson

Further Reading

Buckley, Jerome Hamilton. *Season of Youth: The Bildungsroman from Dickens to Golding.* 1974. Reprint. Bridgewater, N.J.: Replica Books, 2000. Praises *Of Human Bondage* for its theme and "remarkable detachment," considering that it is autobiographical. Discusses freedom realized through the "unfolding of an aesthetic sensibility."

Calder, Robert. *Willie: The Life of W. Somerset Maugham.* New York: St. Martin's Press, 1989. Organized into ten chapters, each delineating approximately one decade. *Of Human Bondage* is most fully related to Maugham's life in the first three chapters. Insightful, sympathetic treatment supported by useful illustrations.

Cordell, Richard A. *Somerset Maugham: A Writer for All Seasons—A Biographical and Critical Study.* 2d ed. Bloomington: Indiana University Press, 1969. The earliest useful critical biography. Offers a separate chapter on *Of Human Bondage* and discusses the novel throughout. Warmer and more sympathetic than Ted Morgan's *Maugham* (below).

Curtis, Anthony, and John Whitehead, eds. *W. Somerset Maugham: The Critical Heritage.* New ed. New York: Routledge, 1997. An anthology of reviews, including 150 selected items of British and American contemporary criticism, arranged chronologically within genres. Among the five reviews on *Of Human Bondage* is Theodore Dreiser's landmark "As a Realist Sees It: *Of Human Bondage*," the first serious critic to praise the novel highly.

Holden, Philip. *Orienting Masculinity, Orienting Nation: W. Somerset Maugham's Exotic Fiction.* Westport, Conn.: Greenwood Press, 1996. Examines the themes of homosexuality, gender identity, and race relations in Maugham's works. Maintains that his writing was a way for him to negotiate between two different masculine identities: the private gay man and the public writer.

Meyers, Jeffrey. *Somerset Maugham: A Life.* New York: Alfred A. Knopf, 2004. Meyers's biography emphasizes Maugham's "otherness," particularly that he was gay. Unlike other critics who have dismissed Maugham's work, Meyers defends Maugham as a great writer who influenced George Orwell, V. S. Naipaul, and others.

Morgan, Ted. *Maugham.* London: J. Cape, 1980. The standard critical biography, essential for worthwhile study. Establishes correlations between Maugham's life and his works, particularly *Of Human Bondage.* Balanced, perceptive, and carefully documented with extensive notes.

Rogal, Samuel J. *A Companion to the Characters in the Fiction and Drama of W. Somerset Maugham.* Westport, Conn.: Greenwood Press, 1996. An alphabetical listing of the characters—animal and human, unnamed and named—in Maugham's fiction and drama. Each entry identifies the work in which a character appears and the character's role in the overall work.

_____. *A William Somerset Maugham Encyclopedia.* Westport, Conn.: Greenwood Press, 1997. Alphabetically arranged entries on Maugham's writings, family members, friends, settings, and the historical, cultural, social, and political issues associated with his life and work. Includes a bibliography and an index.

Of Mice and Men

Author: John Steinbeck (1902-1968)
First published: 1937
Type of work: Novel
Type of plot: Impressionistic realism
Time of plot: Mid-twentieth century
Locale: Salinas Valley, California

Principal characters:
LENNIE SMALL, a simpleminded giant
GEORGE MILTON, his friend
CANDY, a ranch swamper
CURLEY, the ranch owner's son
SLIM, the jerkline skinner on the ranch
CROOKS, the black stable buck

The Story:

Late one hot afternoon, two men carrying blanket rolls trudge down the path that leads to the bank of the Salinas River. One man, George Milton, is small and wiry. The other man, Lennie Small, is a large, lumbering fellow whose arms hang loosely at his sides. After they drink at the sluggish water and wash their faces, George sits back with his legs drawn up. Lennie imitates him.

George and Lennie are on their way to a ranch, hired to buck barley there. Lennie had cost them their jobs at their last stop in Weed, where he was attracted by a woman's red dress. He had grabbed at her clothes. He became frightened by her screaming and then would not let go of her; George was forced to hit him over the head to make him let go. They ran away to avoid a lynching.

After George lectures his companion about letting him talk to their new employer when they are interviewed, Lennie begs for a story he has already heard many times. It is the story of the farm they would own one day. It would have chickens, rabbits, and a vegetable garden, and Lennie would

be allowed to feed the rabbits. The threat that Lennie would not be allowed to care for the rabbits if he does not obey causes him to keep still when they arrive at the ranch the next day. In spite of George's precautions, their new boss is not easy to deal with. He is puzzled because George gives Lennie no chance to talk.

While the men are waiting for the lunch gong, the owner's son, Curley, comes in, ostensibly looking for his father, but actually to examine the new men. After he leaves, Candy, the swamper who sweeps out the bunkhouse, warns them that Curley is a prizefighter who delights in picking on the men and that he is extremely jealous of any attention given to his slatternly bride.

Lennie has a foreboding of evil and wants to leave, but the two men have no money with which to continue their wanderings. By evening, however, Lennie is happy again. The dog belonging to Slim, the jerkline skinner, had pups the night before, and Slim gave one to simpleminded Lennie.

Slim is easy to talk to. While George plays solitaire that

evening, he tells his new friend of the incident in Weed. He has just finished his confidence when Lennie comes in, hiding his puppy inside his coat. George tells Lennie to take the pup back to the barn. He says that Lennie will probably spend the night there with the animal.

The bunkhouse had been deserted by all except old Candy when Lennie asks once more to hear the story of the land they would some day buy. At its conclusion, the swamper speaks up. He has $350 saved, he says, and he knows he will not be able to work many more years. He wants to join George and Lennie in their plan. George finally agrees, for with Candy's money they will soon be able to buy the farm they had in mind.

Lennie is still grinning with delighted anticipation when Curley comes to the bunkhouse in search of his wife. The men had been taunting him about her wantonness when he spies Lennie's grin. Infuriated with the thought that he was being laughed at, Curley attacks the larger man. Lennie, remembering George's warnings, does nothing to defend himself at first. Finally, he grabs Curley's hand and squeezes. When he lets go, every bone has been crushed. Curley is driven off to town for treatment, with instructions from Slim to say that he had caught his hand in a machine. Slim warns him that the humiliating truth will soon be known if he fails to tell a convincing story.

After the others start to town with Curley, Lennie leaves to talk to Crooks, the black stable buck, who has his quarters in the harness room instead of the bunkhouse. Crooks's coolness quickly melts before Lennie's innocence. While Lennie tells Crooks about the dream of the farm, Candy joins them. They are deep in discussion when Curley's wife appears, looking for her husband. The story about her husband and the machine does not deceive her, and she hints that she is pleased with Lennie for what he has done. Having put an end to the men's talk, she slips out noiselessly when she hears the others come back from town.

Lennie is in the barn petting his puppy. The other workmen pitch horseshoes outside. Lennie does not realize that the puppy is already dead from the mauling he had innocently given it. As he sits in the straw, Curley's wife comes around the corner of the stalls. He does not speak to her at first, afraid that he will not get to feed the rabbits if he does anything wrong, but the woman gradually manages to draw his attention to her and persuades him to stroke her hair. When she tries to pull her head away, Lennie holds on, growing afraid as she tries to yell. Finally, he shakes her violently and breaks her neck.

Curley's wife is lying half-buried in the hay when Candy comes into the barn in search of Lennie. Finding Lennie

gone, he calls George, and while the latter leaves to get a gun, the swamper spreads the alarm. Carrying a loaded shotgun, Curley starts off with the men, George among them. It is George who finds Lennie hiding in the bushes at the edge of a stream. Hurriedly, for the last time, he tells his companion the story of the rabbit farm, and when he finishes, Lennie begs that they leave at once to look for the farm. Knowing that Lennie cannot escape from Curley and the other men, George puts the muzzle of his gun to the back of his friend's head and pulls the trigger. Lennie is dead when the others arrive.

Critical Evaluation:

Throughout John Steinbeck's career, his affinity and compassion for the average person's struggle for autonomy surfaces as a recurrent link among his works. *Of Mice and Men*, set in California's Salinas Valley, depicts the world of the migrant worker, a world in which Steinbeck himself had lived, and the workers' search for independence. Steinbeck was critical of what he perceived as the United States' materialism, and his work echoes his convictions about the land and its people. Like the characters in his Pulitzer Prize-winning novel *The Grapes of Wrath* (1939), *Of Mice and Men*'s George and Lennie dream of a piece of land to call their own.

Published in 1937, *Of Mice and Men* was Steinbeck's first major success. Unlike later novels, *Of Mice and Men* is not a politically motivated protest novel. It does, however, reflect Steinbeck's belief in the interdependence of society, a theme he continues to explore in the body of his work. For Steinbeck's characters, the dream of land represents independence and dignity: the American Dream. George and Lennie embody the ordinary person's struggle to grasp the dream, which consists of "a little bit of land, not much. Jus' som'thin that was his." This is one of the central themes that propels the novel's characters and their actions.

As the title suggests, the best laid plans of mice and men can, and do, go awry. They are doomed from the start because of Lennie's fatal flaw—he is developmentally disabled and therefore incapable of bringing the dream to fruition—but his naïveté also allows both him and George to pursue the dream. Lennie's innocence permits George to believe that the dream might be attainable: "George said softly, 'I think I knowed we'd never do her. He usta like to hear about it so much I got to thinking maybe we would.'" Lennie is the keeper of the dream; he does not question its inevitable fulfillment, he simply believes. Without this innocence, George would be like all the other ranch hands, wasting his money on whiskey and women, drifting aimlessly from one job to the next.

George and Lennie are juxtaposed against a group of isolated misfits, to show not only that they need each other but also that humans cannot live in isolation without consequences. Steinbeck uses characters such as Candy, Crooks, and Curley's wife to illustrate the isolation of the human condition. Each of these characters is drawn to George and Lennie and their vision; they, too, want to share in the dream. Their dreams have been systematically destroyed by the insensitivity of the world; as a result, they must appropriate George and Lennie's dream. George, Crooks, Candy, and Curley's wife all have the mental capacity to attain the dream, but lack the innocent belief that is needed to make it come true. It is their experience that keeps them from attaining the dream. In the world, innocence is inevitably shattered—one must wake from the dream.

Because Lennie can never pass from his state of innocence to that of experience, he must be destroyed. Lennie represents that part in George, possibly in everyone, that remains childlike. It is important that George, himself, must destroy Lennie and that Lennie literally dies with the dream. Before his death, Lennie repeats the dream like a catechism and urges George, "Le's do it now," after which George pulls the trigger. Lennie dies with the dream.

Lennie becomes a metaphor for the death of innocence within a selfish society that cannot comprehend him or his relationship with George. To illustrate this point, Steinbeck allows the character Carlson the final word, "Now what the hell ya suppose is eatin' them two guys?" Carlson embodies an apathetic society that cannot understand a relationship based upon trust and love rather than avarice. Carlson insists upon killing Candy's dog because "He don't have no fun." Like the society he epitomizes, all of Carlson's judgments deal in the superficial. For Steinbeck, that is a world that cannot sustain innocence.

"Critical Evaluation" by Angela D. Hickey

Further Reading

Benson, Jackson J. *The True Adventures of John Steinbeck, Writer.* New York: Viking Press, 1984. Definitive biography of Steinbeck. Calls *Of Mice and Men*'s popularity the turning point between poverty and success in Steinbeck's career. Traces the novel's composition and its adaptation as a drama, also in 1937.

_____, ed. *The Short Novels of John Steinbeck: Critical Essays with a Checklist to Steinbeck Criticism.* Durham, N.C.: Duke University Press, 1990. Contains Anne Loftis's "A Historical Introduction to *Of Mice and Men*," William Goldhurst's "*Of Mice and Men*: John Steinbeck's

Parable of the Curse of Cain," and Mark Spilka's "Of George and Lennie and Curley's Wife: Sweet Violence in Steinbeck's Eden."

Bloom, Harold, ed. *John Steinbeck's "Of Mice and Men."* New York: Chelsea House, 2006. Features a biographical sketch of Steinbeck, plot summary and analysis, a list of characters, and essays interpreting the novel. Essays examine political influences on the novel, its philosophical ideas and experimental form, and the significance of George and Lennie's dream.

French, Warren. *John Steinbeck.* Boston: Twayne, 1975. Calls *Of Mice and Men* a naturalistic fable resulting from Steinbeck's fascination with Ed Ricketts's nonteleological belief "that *what* things are matters less than the fact that they *are*." Discusses Steinbeck's deliberate writing of a fiction work that could be easily revised into a play.

George, Stephen K., and Barbara A. Heavilin, eds. *John Steinbeck and His Contemporaries.* Lanham, Md.: Scarecrow Press, 2007. A collection of papers from a 2006 conference about Steinbeck and the writers who influenced or informed his work. One of the essays compares *Of Mice and Men* with Zora Neale Hurston's *Their Eyes Were Watching God*, while another provides a black writer's perspective of the character of Crooks.

Hayashi, Testsumaro, ed. *John Steinbeck: The Years of Greatness, 1936-1939.* Tuscaloosa: University of Alabama Press, 1993. Contains Charlotte Cook Hadella's "The Dialogic Tension in Steinbeck's Portrait of Curley's Wife," Thomas Fensch's "Reflections of Doc: The Persona of Ed Ricketts in *Of Mice and Men*," and Robert E. Morseberger's "Tell Again, George."

Johnson, Claudia Durst, ed. *Understanding "Of Mice and Men," "The Red Pony," and "The Pearl": A Student Casebook to Issues, Sources, and Historical Documents.* Westport, Conn.: Greenwood Press, 1997. Contains historical, sociological, and political materials offering a context for the three novels. Includes information about California and the West, land ownership, the male worker, and homelessness.

Meyer, Michael J., ed. *The Betrayal of Brotherhood in the Work of John Steinbeck.* Lewiston, N.Y.: Edwin Mellen Press, 2000. Examines how Steinbeck adapted the biblical story of Cain and Abel in many of his works. Includes two essays focusing on *Of Mice and Men*, one defining it as a "story of innocence retained," the other exploring its parable of the curse of Cain.

Owens, Louis. *John Steinbeck's Re-vision of America.* Athens: University of Georgia Press, 1985. Discusses the importance of setting to the Eden myth in terms of Lennie's dream of living "off the fatta the lan'." The novel seems pessimistic because Eden cannot be achieved, but commitment between people allows for hope.

Simmonds, Roy S. *A Biographical and Critical Introduction of John Steinbeck*. Lewiston, N.Y.: E. Mellen Press,

2000. Charts Steinbeck's evolution as a writer from 1929 through 1968, discussing the themes of his works and the concepts and philosophies that influenced his depictions of human nature and the psyche. Interweaves details about his writings with accounts of his personal life.

Of Time and the River
A Legend of Man's Hunger in His Youth

Author: Thomas Wolfe (1900-1938)
First published: 1935
Type of work: Novel
Type of plot: Impressionistic realism
Time of plot: 1920's
Locale: Cambridge, Massachusetts; New York; France

Principal characters:
EUGENE GANT, a young student and writer
BASCOM PENTLAND, his uncle
FRANCIS STARWICK, his friend
ANN and ELINOR, Starwick's friends
ROBERT WEAVER, Eugene's friend

The Story:

Eugene Gant is leaving Altamont for study at Harvard University. His mother and his sister, Helen, stand on the station platform and wait with him for the train that will take him north. Eugene feels that he is escaping from his strange, unhappy childhood, that the train will take him away from sickness and worry over money; away from his mother's boardinghouse, the Dixieland; away from memories of his gruff yet kind brother Ben; away from all ghosts of the past. While they wait, they meet Robert Weaver, who also is on his way to Harvard. Mrs. Gant says that Robert is a fine boy, but there is insanity in his family. Before the train arrives at the station, Mrs. Gant tells Eugene about family scandals of the town.

Eugene stops in Baltimore to visit his father, who is slowly dying of cancer. Old Gant spends much of his time on the sunlit hospital porch, dreaming of a former time and of his youth.

At Harvard, Eugene enrolls in Professor Hatcher's drama class. Hungry for knowledge, he browses the library, pulling books from the shelves and reading them as he stands by the open stacks. He writes plays for the drama workshop. Prowling the streets of Cambridge and Boston, he wonders about the lives of people he meets, whose names he will never know.

One day, Eugene receives a note from Francis Starwick, Professor Hatcher's assistant, asking Eugene to have dinner with him. As Eugene has made no friends at the university, he is surprised by Starwick's invitation. Starwick turns out to be

a pleasant young man who welcomes Eugene's confidences but returns none. In Boston, Eugene meets his uncle, Bascom Pentland, and his wife. Uncle Bascom had once been a preacher, but he had left the ministry and is now working in a law office.

Eugene later receives a telegram telling him that his father is dying. He has no money for a ticket home, and so he goes to see Wang, a strange, secretive Chinese student who rooms in the same house. Wang gives him money, and Eugene goes back to Altamont, but he arrives too late to see his father alive. Old Gant had died painfully and horribly. Only with his death do his wife and children realize how much this ranting, roaring old man had meant in their lives.

Back at Harvard, Eugene and Starwick become close friends. Starwick always confuses Eugene when they are together; Eugene has the feeling that everything Starwick does or says is like the surface of a shield, protecting his real thoughts or feelings underneath.

One night, Robert Weaver visits Eugene's room. He is drunk and shouts at the top of his voice. He wants Eugene to go out with him, but Eugene finally manages to get him to go to bed on a cot in Wang's room.

Eugene dreams of becoming a great playwright. After he has completed his course at Harvard, he returns to Altamont and waits to have one of his plays accepted for production on Broadway. This is a summer of unhappiness and suspense. His plays are rejected. While visiting a married sister in

South Carolina, he runs into Robert Weaver again. The two get drunk and land in jail.

In the fall, Eugene goes to New York to become an English instructor at a city university. After a time, Robert appears. He has been living at a club, but now he insists that Eugene get him a room at the apartment hotel where Eugene lives. Eugene hesitates, knowing what will happen if Weaver goes on one of his sprees. The worst does happen. Weaver smashes furniture and sets fire to his room. He also has a mistress, a woman who had married her husband because she knew he was dying and would leave her his money. One night, the husband finds his wife and Weaver together, and a scuffle ensues. The husband pulls a gun and attempts to shoot Weaver before he collapses. It looks very much as if Eliza Gant's statement about insanity in the Weaver family is true.

Eugene also renews a college friendship with Joel Pierce, the son of a wealthy family. At Joel's invitation, he visits the magnificent Pierce estate along the Hudson River. Seeing the fabulously rich close at hand for the first time, Eugene is both fascinated and disappointed.

At vacation time, Eugene goes abroad, first to England, where he lives with the strange Coulson family, and then to France. In Paris, he meets Starwick again, standing enraptured upon the steps of the Louvre. Starwick is visiting Europe with two women from Boston, Elinor and Ann. Elinor, who had left her husband, is mistakenly believed by her friends to be Starwick's mistress. Eugene goes to see the sights of Paris with them. Ann and Elinor pay all of Starwick's bills. One night, in a cabaret, Starwick gets into an argument with a Frenchman and accepts a challenge to duel. Ann, wanting to end the ridiculous affair, pays the Frenchman money to satisfy him for damages to his honor. Eugene attempts to make love to Ann, but when she resists him he realizes that she is in love with Starwick. Eugene then makes the discovery that Ann's love is wasted because Starwick is gay.

Disgusted with the three, Eugene goes to Chartres by himself. From Chartres, he goes to Orleans. There he meets an eccentric old countess who believes that Eugene is a correspondent for *The New York Times*, a journalist planning to write a book of travel impressions. She secures for him an invitation to visit the Marquise de Mornaye, who is under the mistaken impression that Eugene had known her son in the United States.

Eugene next goes to Tours. In this old town of white buildings and narrow, cobblestoned streets, memories of America suddenly come flooding back to Eugene. He remembers the square of Altamont on a summer afternoon, the smell of wood smoke in the early morning, and the whistle of a train in the mountain passes. He remembers the names of American rivers, the parade of the states that stretched from the rocky New England coastline across the flat plains and the high mountains to the thunder of the Pacific slope and the names of battles fought on American soil. He remembers his family and his own childhood. He feels that he has recaptured the lost dream of time itself. Homesick, he starts back to America. One day, he catches sight of Starwick and his two women companions in a Marseilles café, but he leaves before they see him.

Eugene sails from Cherbourg. On the tender taking passengers out to the ocean liner, he hears an American voice above the babble of the passengers grouped about him. He looks. A woman points eagerly toward the ship, her face glowing with an excitement as great as that Eugene himself feels. A woman companion calls her Esther. Watching Esther, Eugene knows that she is to be his fate.

Critical Evaluation:

Of Time and the River is the last of Thomas Wolfe's novels to be published before his early death in 1938 (*The Web and the Rock* and *You Can't Go Home Again* were published posthumously in 1939 and 1940, respectively). It also is the last work to be completed under the extensive editorial guidance of Maxwell Perkins and is appropriately read as a sequel to *Look Homeward, Angel* (1929), whose hero, Eugene Gant, is Wolfe himself.

As is the case with *Look Homeward, Angel*, the subtitle of *Of Time and the River* is a somewhat useful advertisement for its contents. Wolfe subtitled his first book *A Story of the Buried Life*, and the strain felt by a gifted youth in confined circumstances is a salient theme. Wolfe subtitled his second novel *A Legend of a Man's Hunger in His Youth*. This hunger, which is felt for somewhat more than nine hundred pages, traces Eugene's life from his departure for graduate study at Harvard University to his days at Harvard, his return home at the time of his father's death, his first experience of New York City (when he accepts a position to teach college composition there), his growing acquaintance with a more varied circle of people while living in New York, his extended trip to England and then France, and finally his preparations to return to America and resume teaching in New York. As the book concludes, he catches sight of a woman who is to be a fellow passenger on the ship home. In this novel she is called only Esther, but through the concluding paragraphs she is made to appear portentous in Eugene's future. She in fact represents Aline Bernstein, an older married woman who was to play a large role in the books published after Wolfe's death, being the great love of his life.

Wolfe toyed with more than one title for *Of Time and the River* before making his final choice. What these titles have in common is the word "river," which he saw as a suitable metaphor for his task—to drain from experience and memory the enormous variety and complexity of American life, even as a river, particularly the Mississippi, drains the vast continent of North America. All of this occurs in time, the dimension that settles events in memory before they are called up by the writer's art.

Wolfe's narratives are close to his life, so a certain amount of form is imposed on his material by virtue of circumstance. Beyond this, Wolfe had great difficulty in shaping the things he wanted to say so as to make a coherent story, however close it might be to his own experience. He labored over the manuscript of *Of Time and the River* until Perkins simply announced to the writer that the work was done and took it from him.

It seems that *Of Time and the River* improves as it goes along, as if Eugene's hunger becomes increasingly articulate as he removes himself from the familiar things of youth and engages with the larger world. For example, the train ride north, with which the novel opens, is not particularly strong but seems rather an episode wherein Wolfe, in the guise of Eugene, settles scores with people of his home town. At the conclusion of this passage Eugene visits his father in a hospital in Baltimore. Here the author tries to use material he had written earlier—W. O. Gant's recollection of the Battle of Gettysburg—which Wolfe's father did in fact experience as a boy, but again the reader may sense that the material is not presented with the brilliance of which Wolfe is sometimes capable.

Of the characters that emerge during Eugene's Harvard days, the most memorable is Uncle Bascom Pentland, modeled on an uncle of Wolfe, curiously educated, who left the ministry to convey property titles in a Boston real estate office. The portrait is memorable, but the exaggerations are improbable and not perfectly flattering (Wolfe's uncle considered a lawsuit).

When Eugene goes to New York City to teach college, three things in his condition are different from the past. First, he is no longer a schoolboy at his studies, even if advanced, but an independent young man. Second, his father has died, which may deprive him of an emotional anchor, but serves adult self-reliance all the same. Third, Eugene begins to incline toward romantic entanglements that may be necessary to complete the psyche, and perhaps the creative energy, of a young man. Eugene first feels himself drawn toward Rosiland Pierce, the daughter in the family of Hudson River gentry he knows through his friendship with Joel, the son.

Then in England, Eugene rooms with the Coulson family, whose daughter, Edith, seems attracted to Eugene, as he is later to Ann when he travels in France with her, Elinor, and his Harvard acquaintance Starwick. Finally there is the brief glimpse of Esther with which the novel concludes.

Much of the writing from the time of Eugene's New York City days seems vivid, honest, and effective, as if the writer has learned how to serve his hunger. It may be that the presence of young women renders Eugene a complete person able to encounter experience and forge from it some of the best parts of *Of Time and the River*.

"Critical Evaluation" by John Higby

Further Reading

Bloom, Harold, ed. *Thomas Wolfe*. New York: Chelsea House, 2000. A compendium of critical essays on Wolfe's oeuvre, including a general overview of his fiction, an examination of his treatment of the American South, and a look at *Of Time and the River*. Includes an introduction, a chronology, and a bibliography.

Ensign, Robert Taylor. *Lean Down Your Ear upon the Earth, and Listen: Thomas Wolfe's Greener Modernism*. Columbia: University of South Carolina Press, 2003. An ecocritical interpretation of Wolfe's work, examining his depiction of the natural world and his characters' connections with it. The references to *Of Time and the River* are listed in the index.

Holliday, Shawn. *Thomas Wolfe and the Politics of Modernism*. New York: Peter Lang, 2001. A reevaluation of Wolfe, describing how the experimental nature of his fiction and other aspects of his work and life define him as a modernist writer.

Idol, John Lane, Jr. *A Thomas Wolfe Companion*. Westport, Conn.: Greenwood Press, 1987. A reference text for the study of Wolfe. Includes useful information not readily available in other sources, such as a list of special collections of material on Wolfe, genealogies of major families in his fiction, a glossary of people and places in his work, and primary and secondary bibliographies.

Johnston, Carol Ingalls. *Of Time and the Artist: Thomas Wolfe, His Novels, and the Critics*. Columbia, S.C.: Camden House, 1996. Johnston examines the bitter relationship between Wolfe and the literary critics, and how he responds to their critiques in his fiction and letters. The section on *Of Time and the River* includes information about the initial American, English, and German reviews and reviews published from the 1940's until after the 1960's.

Kennedy, Richard S. *The Window of Memory: The Literary Career of Thomas Wolfe*. Chapel Hill: University of North Carolina Press, 1962. A major critical study of Wolfe, tracing his career from his early work to the novels published after his death. *Of Time and the River* receives extended treatment.

_____, ed. *Thomas Wolfe: A Harvard Perspective*. Athens, Ohio: Croissant, 1983. A collection of essays in two groupings, "Critical Considerations" and "Texts and Manuscripts." *Of Time and the River* is treated specifically in one essay and incidentally in another.

Wolfe, Thomas. *The Story of a Novel*. New York: Charles Scribner's Sons, 1936. This book began as a speech Wolfe gave at the University of Colorado Writer's Conference in August, 1935. It is an account of the creative effort that resulted in *Of Time and the River* and acknowledges Wolfe's debt to his editor, Maxwell Perkins.

The Old Bachelor

Author: William Congreve (1670-1729)
First produced: 1693; first published, 1693
Type of work: Drama
Type of plot: Comedy of manners
Time of plot: Seventeenth century
Locale: London

Principal characters:
HEARTWELL, an old bachelor
BELINDA, a fashionable young woman
ARAMINTA, her cousin
BELLMOUR, a young bachelor in love with Belinda
VAINLOVE, his friend, in love with Araminta
SILVIA, Vainlove's former mistress
SIR JOSEPH WITTOL, a fool
CAPTAIN BLUFFE, his parasite
FONDLEWIFE, a banker
LAETITIA, his young wife

The Story:

Sir Joseph Wittol, a foolish young country knight, returns to the spot in London where he had been attacked by footpads the night before, a fracas from which the gallant Ned Bellmour had rescued him. Bellmour had told his friend Sharper of the incident, whereupon Sharper, encountering Wittol, pretends to be the man who had rescued him. Having ingratiated himself with his false story, Sharper declares that he lost one hundred pounds in the scuffle, and Wittol promises to make good the loss. Wittol and Sharper are joined by Captain Bluffe, a spurious veteran of campaigns in the Low Countries and Wittol's mentor in the ways of the city. Bluffe's boasting and swaggering ways deeply impress the foolish young Wittol.

In her apartment, Araminta is reproved by her cousin Belinda for being devoted to love. A footman announces that Vainlove and Bellmour have arrived to pay their respects to Araminta. Belinda, who is charmed by Bellmour, declares that she will remain to keep Araminta company, even though she had been preparing to go out. The young men having been admitted, Bellmour and Belinda exchange amiable insults. Gavot, Araminta's singing-master, entertains the group with a song.

Silvia, a prostitute and Vainlove's discarded mistress, pines for him. Lucy, her maid, suggests that they write a letter filled with foolish protestations of love, sign Araminta's name to it, and send it to Vainlove. This deception, they are sure, will cool Vainlove's ardor for Araminta. Meanwhile, Heartwell, a professed woman-hater and a surly old bachelor, is against his will in front of Silvia's door. Bellmour and Vainlove see him enter.

The masked Lucy encounters Setter, Vainlove's man. When Setter uses abusive language in speaking to her, she unmasks and demands reparation from her old acquaintance in the form of information about the affair between Vainlove and Araminta. At the same time, Wittol gives Sharper a note of credit for one hundred pounds, to be collected from Fondlewife, a banker. Bluffe rebukes Wittol for his misdirected generosity. When Sharper appears with the cash and thanks Wittol, Bluffe intimates to Wittol that Sharper is a trickster. Sharper rejoins by suggesting that Bluffe is a fraud.

When he strikes Bluffe, the braggart is afraid to retaliate, and Sharper thereupon soundly trounces him and departs. Only then does Bluffe draw his sword and rant brave words.

At Silvia's house, Heartwell entertains the prostitute with hired singers and dancers. When he professes his love for her, she puts him off coyly, asserting that she must be married to a man before he can enjoy her favors. Overcome by passion and by Silvia's wiles, he at last agrees to marry her. Saying he will return in the evening, he leaves to procure a marriage license.

Fondlewife, the banker, arranges to have a Puritan minister visit his young wife, Laetitia, while he is away on business. At the last minute, however, he grows wary and decides not to leave the city. Vainlove, who had been invited to visit Laetitia during the absence of her ancient, doting husband, sends Bellmour in his place. Vainlove receives the letter, to which Silvia had signed Araminta's name. The writer pleads for an end to a slight disagreement between them. Disappointed to find the lady so eager, Vainlove announces that his interest in Araminta has waned.

Bellmour, disguised as the Puritan minister, visits Laetitia and in private reveals his true identity. He explains that he had indiscreetly opened her letter to Vainlove and, the intrigue appealing to him, came in Vainlove's stead. Laetitia, charmed by Bellmour's gallantry, entertains him in her bedroom.

Vainlove meets Araminta in St. James Park and treats her coolly. Araminta fails to understand when he tosses the letter at her feet and stalks away. A few minutes later, Wittol encounters Araminta for the first time and falls in love with her.

Fondlewife, accompanied by Wittol, who had come to get money from the banker, returns home prematurely, and Bellmour hides in the bedroom. Fondlewife goes to get cash for Wittol. On his return, a frantic Laetitia accuses Wittol of having attempted to rape her. Wittol is asked to leave the house. Laetitia and Bellmour cleverly succeed in keeping Bellmour's identity from Fondlewife until the cuckolded old gentleman discovers the Scarron novel in the parlor that Bellmour, in his disguise, had carried as a prayer book. Bellmour confesses to evil intentions, but declares that Fondlewife has returned too soon for the couple to have sinned. When Laetitia weeps and declares their innocence, Fondlewife reluctantly accepts Bellmour's story.

Bellmour, still in his disguise, passes Silvia's apartment. Lucy, believing him a parson who will marry her mistress and Heartwell, stops Bellmour. Bellmour reveals his true identity to Lucy and tells her that he will provide both her and Silvia with proper husbands if she will agree to no more than a mock marriage of Heartwell and Silvia. Bellmour, practical

joker that he is, cannot bear to see his friend Heartwell marry a prostitute. He performs the service; then, during Heartwell's momentary absence, he tells Silvia of the trick he has played.

Vainlove, meanwhile, learns from Setter that the letter signed by Araminta is probably Lucy's work, since Lucy had made inquiries about the relationship between Araminta and Vainlove. At the same time, Sharper and Setter fool Wittol into thinking that Araminta has conceived a passion for him. Wittol gives Setter gold to bring Araminta to him. Bluffe privately pays Setter a counter-bribe to convey Araminta to him.

Sharper, pretending no knowledge of Heartwell's marriage to Silvia, asks Heartwell to join him in a visit to the prostitute. Heartwell, in a predicament, tells of his marriage and warns Sharper not to go near Silvia's house. Vainlove and Bellmour bring Araminta and Belinda, both masked, to Silvia's house. Setter has taken Lucy and Silvia, both also masked, to meet Wittol and Bluffe. Finding Heartwell alone, Vainlove, Bellmour, and the young ladies tease him unmercifully about his marriage. Setter returns with Wittol, Silvia, Bluffe, and Lucy. When the ladies all unmask, the foolish knight and his roaring companion admit indulgently that they have been hoodwinked. Heartwell, learning of the mock marriage, thanks Bellmour for his salvation; he vows that if he were to marry, it would be to an old crone. Vainlove and Araminta, and Bellmour and Belinda, plan their weddings for the next day.

Critical Evaluation:

When the grand old man of Restoration theater, John Dryden, finished reading the manuscript of *The Old Bachelor*, he declared that he had never seen such a first play in his life. With several other experienced playwrights, Dryden helped William Congreve put the finishing touches on his play. With the added enhancement of music by England's leading composer, Henry Purcell, Congreve's fledgling dramatic effort propelled the young playwright to fame and fortune. The reasons are not hard to find.

The Old Bachelor is cast in the tried and tested mold of Restoration comedy, but if the bottle is old, the wine is new. Congreve's dramatic situations are varied and interesting. The plot is not too complicated to follow, the dialogue is sparkling, the characters appealing, and the obligatory Restoration cynicism tempered with just a hint of pathos.

Congreve uses such stock characters as skeptical, witty rakes and reluctant heroines, as well as the cast-off mistress, the braggart soldier, the elderly cuckold, and the old, supposedly woman-hating bachelor. The philosophical assumptions behind the drama are also common Restoration currency: Pursuing women is like pursuing game, the pleasure being in the pursuit more than in the catch (and certainly the game is not expected to pursue the hunter); there is no more ridiculous a sight in nature than the old bachelor taking a young wife; the married state, though it is the goal to which all strive, is by its very nature, an unsatisfying one; the most reprehensible faults of character are dullness, age, and taking oneself seriously.

One of the qualities that distinguishes Congreve from such earlier Restoration masters as William Wycherley and Sir George Etherege (in addition to his more consistently brilliant dialogue) is that he shows a trace of compassion, as well as scorn, for his characters. The cuckold Fondlewife, for instance, and to a greater extent, the old bachelor Heartwell, are figures of pathos as well as fun. The latter is aware of his dangerously intense feelings for Silvia, knows that he should resist them because they will only serve to make him look foolish, and yet is unable to overcome his passion with reason. "O dotage, dotage!" he moans, "that ever that noble passion, lust, should ebb to this degree." Readers cannot help but sympathize as he writhes in the toils of the old, familiar snake, especially when he is mocked by others (including Belinda) for his folly. Luckily, Bellmour, with a stroke of generosity unusual in a Restoration rake, has taken pity on the poor man: "Heartwell is my friend; and tho he is blind, I must not see him fall into the snare and unwittingly marry a whore." Neither Wycherley nor Etherege would have troubled their heads for a moment about this piece of cruelty; indeed, they would have considered it as more fodder for their comic resolutions.

At the end of the play, all of the characters, even the fools, seem reasonably content, though their hopes and expectations have in some cases been thwarted. Congreve intends that the audience arise from its comic repast remembering a good taste, though one that is spiced and sauced with the relieved Heartwell's dour conclusions on the perils of aging: "All coursers the first heat with vigour run; But 'tis with whip and spur the race is won."

Further Reading

Dobrée, Bonamy. *Restoration Comedy: 1660-1720.* 1946. Reprint. Westport, Conn.: Greenwood Press, 1981. The essays on Congreve in this collection emphasize the easy flow of language and incidents, the French connection, and the spontaneity of scenes and situations in his comedic works.

Owen, Susan J., ed. *A Companion to Restoration Drama.* Malden, Mass.: Blackwell, 2001. Essays examine the types of Restoration drama. Places these plays within the context of their society, and analyzes works by individual playwrights. Numerous references to Congreve and his plays are listed in the index. His work is also considered in Miriam Handley's essay "William Congreve and Thomas Southerne."

Peters, Julie S. *Congreve, the Drama, and the Printed Word.* Stanford, Calif.: Stanford University Press, 1990. Examines the diction, speech patterns, stage conventions, and editorial practices associated with Congreve's plays. Concludes that *The Old Bachelor* is recognized as the culmination of comic routines, philosophical assumptions, and acquired follies.

Sieber, Anita. *Character Portrayal in Congreve's Comedies "The Old Batchelour," "Love for Love," and "The Way of the World."* Lewiston, N.Y.: Edwin Mellen Press, 1996. Focuses on the numerous types of characters in the comedies, including some who are placed in opposition to each other, such as wits versus fools and fops, country characters versus city gallants and ladies, and old people versus young people. Sieber also discusses Congreve's use of historical characters and his themes of love and marriage.

Thomas, David. *William Congreve.* New York: St. Martin's Press, 1992. An overview of Congreve's career. Reinforces the critical opinion of *The Old Bachelor* as new wine in an old bottle—largely the result of Congreve's brilliant use of repartee. Asserts that the strong conclusion in act 5 reorganizes the disparate elements in acts 1 through 4, which saves the plot from disintegration.

Van Voris, W. H. *The Cultivated Stance: The Designs of Congreve's Plays.* Dublin: Dolmen Press, 1965. Analyzes *The Old Bachelor* in the thematic context of time and dialogue in Restoration drama. Examines the relationship between dramatic technique and stage conventions.

Williams, Aubrey L. *An Approach to Congreve.* New Haven, Conn.: Yale University Press, 1979. Accentuates the moralizing effect of Congreve's characterizations and argues against a determinist reading of *The Old Bachelor*. Offers an informative look at the religious background that symbolically frames the play and adds spice to every innuendo.

Young, Douglas M. *The Feminist Voices in Restoration Comedy: The Virtuous Women in the Play-Worlds of Etherege, Wycherley, and Congreve.* Lanham, Md.: University Press of America, 1997. Focuses on the female characters in Congreve's plays who demand independence from and equality with men before they commit to courtship or marriage. Devotes a chapter to *The Old Bachelor*.

The Old Curiosity Shop

Author: Charles Dickens (1812-1870)
First published: 1840-1841, serial; 1841, book
Type of work: Novel
Type of plot: Social realism
Time of plot: Early nineteenth century
Locale: England

Principal characters:
LITTLE NELL TRENT, an orphan
NELL'S GRANDFATHER, a curiosity dealer and gambler
QUILP, a misanthropic dwarf
KIT NUBBLES, Nell's friend
DICK SWIVELLER, a profligate young man and Quilp's tool
SAMPSON BRASS, an attorney and Quilp's aide in crime
SALLY BRASS, Sampson's sister and fellow criminal
THE SINGLE GENTLEMAN, Nell's granduncle

The Story:

Little Nell Trent lives alone with her aged grandfather, who runs an old curiosity shop. The grandfather, Little Nell's mother's father, has two obsessions. One is keeping Little Nell away from her brother, Fred, a drunken profligate. The other is a burning desire to gamble. Hoping to provide a fortune for the little girl, the old man gambles away every penny he can get. Not content with using the income of the curiosity shop, the old man borrows money recklessly.

One of the old man's creditors is an ugly, misshapen, cruel dwarf named Quilp. The husband of a pretty but browbeaten young woman, Quilp plots to ruin the old man and someday marry Little Nell, who is only fourteen years old. Having discovered the old man's passion for gambling by forcing his wife to spy on Little Nell, Quilp is soon able to take over the old curiosity shop by due process of law. Little Nell and her grandfather leave during the night and start an aimless journey from London to western England.

Almost penniless, the old man and the little girl find many friends on their way. For a time, they travel with a Punch-and-Judy troupe, until the girl becomes alarmed at the habits of the men connected with the show and persuades her grandfather to leave them. She and the old man are next befriended by Mrs. Jarley, owner of a waxworks, but the grandfather's passion for gambling causes them to leave their benefactor. At last a schoolmaster, on his way to fill a new post, takes them under his wing.

Under the schoolmaster's guidance, the girl and her grandfather are established in a little town as caretakers of a church. Their duties are very light because the church has a regular sexton as well. Meanwhile, the only friend Little Nell and her grandfather had left behind in London is a poor boy named Kit Nubbles. He is attempting to find them but is hampered by the enmity of Quilp and by the fact that he has to help support his widowed mother and two other children. In addition, Quilp, who has an unreasonable hatred for anyone honest, is trying to find Little Nell to wed her to one of her brother's worthless companions. This worthless companion, Dick Swiveller, is a clerk in the office of Quilp's unscrupulous lawyer, Sampson Brass.

After Little Nell and her grandfather had disappeared, a strange, Single Gentleman appeared to rent an apartment from Sampson Brass. It turns out that he also is hunting for Little Nell and her grandfather. Since he is obviously a man of wealth, no one can be certain of the stranger's motives. The Single Gentleman soon proves to Kit and Kit's honest employer that he wants to aid the two runaways, and Kit tries to help the stranger locate Little Nell and her grandfather. When they try to follow the elusive trail of the old man and the girl, they reach a dead end. Their search carries them as far as the woman who runs the waxworks. Afterward, apparently, the two had vanished from the face of the earth.

Quilp is angered that anyone might be willing to help Little Nell and prevent his plans for her marriage; he then tries to circumvent the Single Gentleman's efforts. To do so, he plots with Sampson Brass and his sister, Sally, to make it appear that Kit has stolen some money. During one of the boy's visits to the stranger's room, Brass places a five-pound note in the boy's hat. When the money is discovered a few minutes later, Kit is accused of stealing it. Despite his protestations of innocence and the belief of the Single Gentleman and Kit's employer that the boy has been unjustly accused, he is found guilty and sentenced to be transported to the colonies.

Dick Swiveller, not a complete rogue, discovers through a little girl he befriends, a girl kept virtually as a slave by the Brasses, that Kit has been falsely accused. With his aid, the Single Gentleman and Kit's employer are able to have the lad released before he is sent out of England. In addition, they discover evidence that causes Brass to be stripped of his professional status and sent to prison. Sally Brass had been just as guilty in her brother's affairs, and she disappeared. Warned by Sally Brass of the turn his plot has taken, Quilp tries to flee prosecution. He leaves his riverside retreat late at night, falls into the Thames, and drowns.

Shortly afterward, the Single Gentleman learns the whereabouts of Little Nell and her grandfather. Kit's employer's brother lives with the vicar of the church, where the girl and her grandfather are caretakers, and the employer's brother had written to tell of the new couple in the village. Accompanied by Kit and his employer, the Single Gentleman starts off at once to find Little Nell and her grandfather. During the journey, the Single Gentleman relates his reasons for being interested in the pair.

The Single Gentleman is the grandfather's younger brother. Years before, the grandfather and he had both been in love with the same woman. Unsuccessful in his suit, the younger brother had left England. After many years, he returned to learn that Nell's father and his profligate son, Nell's brother, had wasted the family fortune, leaving Nell and the old man in straitened circumstances from which her grandfather had tried desperately to rescue them. Wealthy in his own right, the Single Gentleman wishes to rescue his brother and Little Nell from the plight into which they have fallen.

The rescuers arrive in the village too late. Little Nell has just died, and she is buried the day after their arrival in the churchyard where she had found happiness and employment. Her grandfather, who feels he now has nothing to live for, dies on her tomb a few days later and is buried beside her.

Kit had been in love with Little Nell as an ideal; he now returns with Nell's granduncle to London. Through his patron's influence and with help from the same men who had judged him guilty of stealing money, only to find him honest and innocent, he finds a proper place in society and soon is married to a worthy young woman. After Sampson Brass is released from prison, the Brasses become beggars in and about London. Mrs. Quilp is released by her dwarfish husband's death, and she happily marries again. The old curiosity shop is soon destroyed to make way for a new building. Even Kit cannot tell exactly where it had stood.

Critical Evaluation:

Considered by many critics to be one of the best writers of the nineteenth century, Charles Dickens continues to attract readers. *The Old Curiosity Shop*, the author's fourth novel, drew a large audience when it first appeared. In the opening chapter, the narrator who meets Nell and her grandfather is probably Master Humphrey, a persona who was providing a framework for all of the serial's literary selections. The first-person narration later changes to a third-person narration. The third-person narrator provides insightful, ironic, and philosophical commentary.

As in most of his early novels, Dickens criticizes contemporary social, political, and industrial injustices. The ethics of Victorian society allowed the gambling that seduces Nell's grandfather into losing their livelihood and home at the hands of cardsharps. The legal system threatens to imprison Nell's aged, mentally deteriorating grandfather and thus separate him from his beloved grandchild. Economic constraints force people, including children, to work in hellish mills. Also, Dickens's Christian society disregards the immoral conditions of poverty and desperation that lead children to steal and then, as the novel illustrates, punishes a youth's petty theft by transporting him over his mother's cries of protest. From such a society, death is the only release. Despite the protests of original readers of the serial novel, Dickens therefore has Little Nell die. Her death before the Single Gentleman can rescue her may be read as Dickens's message that the novel is not intended as mere emotional escapism, but that it is intended as a serious denunciation of his society's moral failings.

Like Dickens's more critically acclaimed works, *The Old Curiosity Shop* is most successful in its characterization. Dickens's typical method is to identify a character, major or minor, with some repetitive speech and mannerism. For example, there are Dick Swiveller's fantastically imaginative diction, the Single Gentleman's abrupt actions, the tiny Marchioness's penchant for looking through keyholes, Tom Scott's standing on his head, and Quilp's shrieks of laughter, to name only a few. Although this repetition tends to flatten the character, the artistic device not only provides humor and variety, it also supports the use of characters to form a moral mosaic.

As do many of Dickens's good characters, the selfless Nell Trent inspires more loving devotion in other characters in the novel than she does in the contemporary reader. Many other thoroughly good characters, such as the Garlands, Kit Nubbles, the poor schoolmaster, and the Single Gentleman, support the romantic concept, more widely held in Dickens's time, that those who are good are naturally good. One of the few characters who manages to span the gap between the evil and the good characters is Dick Swiveller. Although originally the pawn of Frederick Trent and Quilp, Swiveller switches to the side of goodness by revealing to the police Quilp's part in framing Kit Nubbles because, as the narrator assures the reader, Swiveller is "essentially good-natured."

Quilp, the dwarf, is the figure of consummate evil who dominates the novel. Quilp possesses such vitality in his evil designs that he enlivens the scenes in which he appears. At one point, his voice interrupts a conversation criticizing him; he seems as omnipresent as the devil. Another set of evil, materialistic characters, Samuel Brass and his "dragon" of a sister, Sally, also provide examples of moral degeneration. Samuel's subservience in his avowed admiration of Quilp, regardless of that man's outrageous treatment of him, rivals Sally's determined competitiveness. Eventually the greed of these siblings is appropriately rewarded by a life of destitution. Such is the majesty of fiction. They wander through the worst slums of London scavenging for food.

One of the serious weaknesses of the novel lies in the weak connection between the two plot lines. The experiences of Nell and her grandfather as they try to escape the pursuit of Quilp is one plot line, and the events in the lives of those who remain in London is the other. Toward the end of the novel, these two strands meet, but at one point even the narrator apologizes for abandoning one set of characters for an unconscionable period of time while he deals with the other group.

The Old Curiosity Shop contains one of Dickens's favorite recurring themes: the reversal of roles of parent and child. In this novel, granddaughter Nell cares for her gambling-addict grandfather. Amy Dorrit cares for her debt-imprisoned father in *Little Dorrit* (1855-1857), and Jenny Wren supports her alcoholic father in *Our Mutual Friend* (1864-1865). This theme probably originated in Dickens's childhood experience. When his father was put in debtors' prison, the young Dickens was forced to support himself in a blacking factory until an inheritance paid off his father's debt.

Dickens expresses, through the voice of the narrator, some comic and forgiving perceptions of human nature to counterbalance the novel's satiric attacks on social justice. Some examples include the dialogue between the aged sexton and the deaf gravedigger regarding the age of the corpse they are burying. One insists she is their contemporary; the other protests she must be at least ten years their senior. The second estimate gives them ten more years before they need to consider their own deaths. In another scene, in which several friends of Mrs. Quilp come like Job's comforters to criticize her choice of a husband, she astutely observes that if she died, any one of those present would agree to marry him. Another example of the work's ironies is that the pragmatic, materialistic Sally Brass, after years of self-sufficient spinsterhood, is quite smitten with the lazy, improvident Dick Swiveller when he comes to clerk for her brother.

Dickens's observations of human inconsistency appeal to today's readers as much as they did to the readers of the nineteenth century. The title of the work suggests a central theme: Only the past contains peace and joy. Nell is looking for such peace when she leaves the curiosity shop, but at the end of her journey she finds only the ultimate peace, death.

"Critical Evaluation" by Agnes A. Shields

Further Reading

Dyson, A. E. "*The Old Curiosity Shop*: Innocence and the Grotesque." In *Dickens*, edited by A. E. Dyson. Nashville, Tenn.: Aurora, 1970. Argues that justifications of the character of Nell on artistic grounds ordinarily emphasize the ironies that attend her and deny the sentimentality.

Hardy, Barbara. *Dickens and Creativity*. London: Continuum, 2008. Focuses on the workings of Dickens's creativity and imagination, which Hardy argues is at the heart of his self-awareness, subject matter, and narrative. *The Old Curiosity Shop* is discussed in chapter 3.

Johnson, Edgar. *Charles Dickens: His Tragedy and Triumph*. 1952. Rev. ed. New York: Penguin, 1986. This definitive critical biography includes a critical essay on *The Old Curiosity Shop* that defends Dickens's sentimentality over modern cynicism.

Jordan, John O., ed. *The Cambridge Companion to Charles Dickens*. New York: Cambridge University Press, 2001. Essays examine Dickens's life and times, analyze his novels, and discuss Dickens in relation to language, gender, family, domestic ideology, the form of the novel, illustration, theater, and film.

Kincaid, James R. *Dickens and the Rhetoric of Laughter*. Oxford, England: Clarendon Press, 1971. Argues that laughter makes the pathos effective in *The Old Curiosity Shop*. Includes a bibliography.

Marcus, Steven. *Dickens, from Pickwick to Dombey*. 1965. Reprint. New York: W. W. Norton, 1985. Provides a lengthy analysis of *The Old Curiosity Shop*, ascribing the inspiration for Nell and Dickens's absorption with death in this novel to the death of Mary Hogarth, his young sister-in-law. Proposes that Nell and Quilp, polar representations of spirituality and carnality, respectively, actually represent two sides of one person.

Paroissien, David, ed. *A Companion to Charles Dickens*. Malden, Mass.: Blackwell, 2008. Collection of essays discussing Dickens as a reformer, Christian, and journalist. Also examines Dickens and the topics of gender, technology, and the United States. Includes the essay "*The Old Curiosity Shop*" by Gillian Ballinger.

Walder, Dennis. *Dickens and Religion*. 1981. Reprint. New York: Routledge, 2007. Shows how Dickens uses death as a moral gauge: Good Nell dies loved and mourned by those who knew her. Evil Quilp, trying to escape the police, drowns alone.

Old Fortunatus

Author: Thomas Dekker (c. 1572-1632)
First produced: 1599, as *The Whole History of Fortunatus*;
   first published, 1600
Type of work: Drama
Type of plot: Allegory
Time of plot: Tenth century
Locale: Cyprus, Babylon, and England

Principal characters:
FORTUNATUS, a foolish man endowed by Fortune
ANDELOCIA, his worldly younger son
AMPEDO, his virtuous older son
AGRIPYNE, daughter of the king of England
FORTUNE, a goddess
VIRTUE, a goddess
VICE, a goddess

The Story:

Fortunatus has never assiduously pursued virtue. He has been compelled, however, by his poverty to lead a life of patience and temperance. One day, after wandering for three days in a forest and sustaining himself by eating nuts, he unexpectedly encounters the goddess Fortune. This meeting is to transform his life. The goddess, who enjoys both the praises and the curses of men as tokens of her power, chooses to smile on the old man. Of her six gifts—wisdom, strength, health, beauty, long life, and riches—she offers him one. Believing that all other blessings will naturally flow from it, Fortunatus chooses wealth. To effect his wish, she gives to him a magic purse that will always contain ten pieces of gold, no matter how frequently he draws from it. This gift, she tells him, will last until he and his sons die. After reproaching him for his foolish choice, she sends him on his way home.

At home, Fortunatus finds his sons, Ampedo and Andelocia, in a despondent mood. Andelocia, the worldly son, has been lamenting his lack of food and money, while his more virtuous brother, Ampedo, has been greatly worried about their father's plight. Fortunatus, returning in rich attire, tells them they need sorrow no longer, for he is presenting them with four bags of gold and will give them more when it is gone. Then he announces his intention to travel and associate with the mighty men of the world.

Meanwhile, Fortune is joined in the forest by Virtue and Vice, goddesses who have come to Cyprus to plant trees of good and evil. Virtue's tree has withered leaves and little fruit, while Vice's flourishes. Although Virtue has experienced defeats and is forced to endure the taunts of Vice, she resolves once again to seek fertile ground for her tree. Fortune, who advances both the virtuous and the vicious, cares not whose tree flourishes, but agrees to judge the contest and declare the winner.

Fortunatus, once scorned, is now honored in every court. Among other rulers, he visits the soldan of Babylon, who has heard of the purse and wishes it for himself. The crafty

Fortunatus says that he has given away three of the purses and will make another for him. In gratitude, the soldan proposes to show the old man the wondrous sights of Babylon. He starts with his most highly valued possession, a hat that carries its wearer wherever he wishes to be. Tricking the soldan into letting him try on the hat, Fortunatus wishes himself in Cyprus and disappears.

Convinced of the supreme value of money, he returns home at the height of his triumph. His self-congratulations are interrupted, however, by a second encounter with Fortune, who, this time, decrees his death. His dying wish that his sons might have wisdom instead of wealth is denied. Bequeathing them the purse and the wishing hat, he asks that the two gifts be kept together and shared equally. No sooner had he died than Andelocia insists that they be exchanged each year.

Andelocia, in possession of the purse, follows the example of his father by going to court. His first destination is England, where he plans to test the effect of gold on the beautiful Agripyne, daughter of King Athelstane. When Athelstane observes the lavish spending of Andelocia, he advises his daughter to try to discover the source of this wealth. With ease she draws the secret from the foolish young man, then drugs him and takes the purse.

Awaking and discovering the theft, Andelocia, discouraged, determines to return home, steal from his brother the hat of Misery, and there make his home. He carries out his resolution to possess the magic hat; but, instead of seeking Misery, he returns to England, abducts Agripyne, and carries her away into the wilderness. She is able to outsmart him, this time accidentally gaining possession of the hat and wishing herself in England.

The hapless Andelocia, after having eaten an apple, discovers that he has grown horns. The goddess Vice stands before him and mocks him, for it is her apple that has caused his deformity. Virtue also stands before him, grieving and offering him apples that will remove the horns. He accepts Virtue's apples and pledges himself to be her minion.

Andelocia's resolve is short-lived, however, for his love of money is much more compelling than his promise to Virtue. He returns to England, determined to recover the purse and hat. Disguised as Irish costermongers, he and his servant peddle the apples of Vice, which he has brought with him. By falsely representing the effect of eating the apples, he sells them to Agripyne and two courtiers, Longaville and Montrose. While thus employed, he is discovered by his brother Ampedo, who had come to England to find the purse and hat and to burn those sources of grief and shame.

Longaville, Montrose, and Agripyne grow horns; and Agripyne is promptly deserted by all but one of her many suitors. After they discover that the horns grow back after being cut, they seek the help of a French physician, who is, in reality, Andelocia in another disguise. By using a medicine taken from the apples of Virtue, he removes Longaville's horns. As he turns to treat Agripyne, he spies the magic hat. Warning everyone to look the other way so that his cure will work, he grabs the hat, takes Agripyne by the hand, and wishes himself with his brother.

After he recovers the purse, Andelocia removes the horns from Agripyne and releases her. He is not destined to enjoy his possessions long. Ampedo, according to his pledge, burns the hat. Soon afterward, Longaville and Montrose find Andelocia and take the magic purse. Seeking revenge for the indignities they had suffered, they place the brothers in the stocks, where Ampedo dies of grief and Andelocia is strangled.

Longaville and Montrose then turn to quarreling between themselves over the purse, but are interrupted by the arrival of members of the court and the three goddesses. The purse is reclaimed by Fortune, and the two courtiers are condemned by Vice to spend their lives wandering with tormented consciences.

Again a quarrel breaks out between Virtue and Vice. This time Fortune turns to the audience for judgment. For her judge, Virtue singles out Queen Elizabeth. At the sight of this paragon of virtue, Vice flees. Fortune bows to this superior force, and Virtue admits that she, by comparison, is a mere counterfeit.

Critical Evaluation:

Thomas Dekker's *Old Fortunatus*, first performed before Queen Elizabeth I on December 27, 1599, is an uneasy combination of morality play and light comedy, combining a serious, allegorical message with a series of highly inventive, fantastic events that propel the characters throughout the

world known to the English of the Renaissance, from Turkey to Cyprus to England. Never entirely realistic or completely symbolic, it suffers from internal contradictions and a certain weakness of structure but offers the audience an intensely moral lesson. Moral instruction, aimed at the members of the English court, seems to have been the major intention of the play.

The plot is simple: Fortunatus is confronted by the goddess Fortune, who offers him a choice of strength, health, beauty, long life, riches, or wisdom. Unwisely, Fortunatus chooses wealth, and he is given a magical purse that always contains ten gold pieces. Later, through an equally unrealistic turn of events, he obtains the magical hat of the Turkish sultan, which allows him to transport himself from place to place merely by wishing.

Fortunatus dies, and his two sons, Andelocia, the worldly younger boy, and Ampedo, the virtuous older youth, must share the inheritance. Despite their differing ways of using Fortunatus's gifts, they are no better in making use of their legacy than their father, and in the end they, too, come to bitter ends. The theme that this world is a sum of "vanity of vanities," so familiar in Elizabethan literature, is central to *Old Fortunatus*.

The power and capriciousness of Fortune, as the ruling goddess of the world, was a familiar theme during the period. Fortune's wheel, that instrument that causes some to rise and others to fall, and that keeps turning, was a popular image in Dekker's time in poetry and the visual arts. Dekker emphasizes the irrational nature of Fortune and her ways: "This world is Fortune's ball wherewith she sports." The essence of Fortune is that she is fickle, completely devoid of moral sense, arbitrary in her judgments and without regard for the vices and virtues of individual human beings. Given Fortune's arbitrary nature, it is no surprise Old Fortunatus is first blessed, then condemned by Fortune; his sons follow suit in their fashion. Only by embracing virtue (which, at the end of the play, is identified as Queen Elizabeth, the earthly personification of the quality) can human beings rise above the fickle, transitory nature of human life.

This sense of morality—and Dekker's debt to traditional English morality plays such as *Everyman*—has a considerable impact on *Old Fortunatus*. The characters are almost stock figures, representing traditional virtues and vices, rather than complex individuals. Allegorical figures such as Fortune, who embody forces beyond human life, are most representative of this tendency; a number of critics have rightfully noted that Fortune begins as indifferent, even scornful of human beings, only to end the play by announcing her allegiance to Queen Elizabeth as the embodiment of virtue.

Again, such a discrepancy was hardly likely to have caused problems during the period when the play was written and first produced.

The source of Dekker's play almost certainly was an old German folktale known as "Old Fortunatus and His Magic Purse and Hat," published in 1509. Dekker adapted the story to fit the conventions of the English stage by emphasizing the spectacular and visual elements of the work and by providing his characters, especially Fortune, with elaborate rhetorical set pieces. It is the sometimes awkward fit between the two elements that has caused some critics to comment on the divided nature of Dekker's drama, which is part fantastic comedy and part moralizing sermon.

It is highly unlikely that Dekker's audience would have been troubled by such a division of purpose and approach. In the context of the dispute between the Puritan culture, which denigrated poetry and popular music, and Renaissance humanism, which endorsed the works of the human imagination, many of the Elizabethans believed that a major purpose of art, especially poetry and the theater, was to serve a didactic purpose. The basis of Sir Philip Sidney's *Defence of Poesie* (1595), the premier apology of poetic art as a worthwhile effort and an answer to Puritan attacks, was that poetry is better able than history or biography to provide a moral lesson to readers; *Old Fortunatus* is a drama that fits precisely into that worldview. The spectacle and romantic elements are to delight the audience, while important moral lessons are being imparted. The classical belief of rhetoric as an art that teaches, delights, and persuades is worked out in the play, and Dekker freely combines the fantastic and the moral to achieve his aim.

Such is the purpose of *Old Fortunatus*, and Dekker was eminently qualified to write such a drama. One of the most productive and popular of Elizabethan and Jacobean playwrights, he claimed an "entire hand" or "at least a major finger" in some 220 plays. He was among the best for tragedy, while the dramatist John Webster ranked Dekker along with William Shakespeare as an example of a playwright of the first order. *Old Fortunatus*, apparently Dekker's first work for the stage, provides an excellent example of what the writers and audiences of Elizabethan London saw in his work: smoothly flowing verse, a strong sense of individual character, and a lively plot that, however fantastic in its individual moments, always provides a moral lesson to courtier and commoner alike.

"Critical Evaluation" by Michael Witkoski

Further Reading

Champion, Larry S. *Thomas Dekker and the Traditions of English Drama*. New York: Peter Lang, 1985. Situates *Old Fortunatus* at the intersection of the traditions of morality plays and newer, humanist drama.

Hoy, Cyrus. Introduction to *The Dramatic Works of Thomas Dekker*, edited by Fredson Bowers. New York: Cambridge University Press, 1980. Places the drama within the context of Dekker's career and in the general literary scene of the period.

McLuskie, Kathleen. *Dekker and Heywood: Professional Dramatists*. New York: St. Martin's Press, 1994. Focuses on the performances of the two playwrights' works, examining the relationship between their plays and the cultural moment when these plays were produced.

Price, George. *Thomas Dekker*. New York: Twayne, 1969. A basic study of Dekker's life and work that is especially valuable as a starting place for students and general readers. Includes a helpful discussion of *Old Fortunatus*.

Wells, Stanley W. "Thomas Dekker and London." In *Shakespeare and Co.: Christopher Marlowe, Thomas Dekker, Ben Jonson, Thomas Middleton, John Fletcher, and the Other Players in His Story*. New York: Penguin Books, 2007. Wells examines the plays of William Shakespeare by placing them within the broader context of Elizabethan theater, discussing other playwrights of the period, the work of acting companies, and the staging of theatrical productions. The chapter on Dekker recounts his life, career, and collaborations, and describes some of his plays, including *Old Fortunatus*.

The Old Gringo

Author: Carlos Fuentes (1928-   )
First published: Gringo viejo, 1985 (English
   translation, 1985)
Type of work: Novel
Type of plot: Symbolic realism
Time of plot: c. 1914 and after
Locale: Chihuahua, Mexico; Washington, D.C.;
   Arlington, Virginia

Principal characters:
HARRIET WINSLOW, a teacher
OLD GRINGO, an old man
TOMÁS ARROYO, a general

The Story:

Harriet Winslow, at home in Washington, D.C., remembers her Mexican adventure, one that had shaped her life. She recalls the time she set off to accept a position as English teacher to the children of a wealthy landowner in Chihuahua, Mexico.

Arriving at the hacienda, as Harriet remembers, she finds revolutionary chaos. The hacienda, taken over by the revolutionaries following Pancho Villa and led by General Tomás Arroyo, is burning to the ground. Among revolutionaries and villagers is another American known to the locals as the old gringo, a name reflecting his age as well as the antagonistic Mexican attitude toward Americans. Old gringo is now buried in Harriet's father's cemetery plot, and Arroyo, his assassin, now wanders through her thoughts, more real to her than the living.

The three lives become intertwined when the old man, the young woman, and the revolutionary meet in the beautiful, private rail car owned by the Miranda family, who have all fled to France. The three express their reasons for being on the train and discuss their intentions, their impressions of each other, and their respective countries. Having fled a boring life with her solicitous mother and tepid fiancé, Harriet is now determined to stay in Mexico even though her prospective employers are gone and Arroyo has offered her safe passage home. The old gringo, having no one left in his life who cares for him and tired of his own cynicism, intends to die fighting with Villa.

Arroyo, an angry revolutionary, holds in his hands the deed to the Miranda estate, where, as illegitimate son of Miranda, he had lived as a servant. Though resentful of both Americans, he decides, at least temporarily, to tolerate their presence. The three then begin to reshape their lives and redirect the lives of each other.

The old gringo falls in love with thirty-year-old Harriet, who reminds him of his wife and daughter. His feelings for her fluctuate between the sexual and the fatherly. He recognizes fatherly feeling for Arroyo as well. Harriet and Arroyo feel antagonism for each other yet experience a sexual attraction. Though the old gringo tells Arroyo of his military credentials—he was a volunteer with a Union regiment from Indiana in the American Civil War—and proves his skill with a gun, he is not welcomed by Arroyo as one of the revolutionary forces. Nevertheless, Arroyo allows him to ride against the government troops, the *federales*. Facing the enemy and ready to die, the old gringo rides bravely alone into gun fire, returning unscathed and earning high praise from his comrades, a recognition that Arroyo resents. Arroyo challenges the old man further, demanding that he execute a prisoner. When the gringo refuses, Arroyo promises to kill him.

Harriet remains in the village while the revolutionaries fight. Though the students she was hired to teach are gone, she decides to stay and "civilize" the Mexicans. She organizes the peasants, sets up a school for the children, starts the men repairing the burned structure, and instructs the women in organizing the clothes. Looked up to as a leader, she wins the love and admiration of all the villagers for her efforts; she then inspires awe for what they consider the miraculous saving of the life of the two-year-old daughter of the prostitute who has followed the troops.

When the men return, Harriet, the old gringo, and Arroyo reconnect at a celebration in the ballroom. The old gringo and Harriet recount that they have both dreamed of each other. She has dreamed of him as a replacement for the father who abandoned her, and he has dreamed of her as idealized love. Arroyo sees them talking and becomes jealous, despite his finding happiness with a woman named La Luna. Harriet and Arroyo dance, and he persuades her to make love with him, telling her that unless she does he will kill the old gringo. In having sex with Arroyo, she gives in to the moment, enjoying the sensuality of the experience.

Angry and vengeful, the old gringo gains possession of and burns the deed so prized by Arroyo. With this provocation, Arroyo kills the gringo. Harriet vows vengeance. She construes an opportunity both to get the body of the old gringo, claiming it as her father, and to persuade Villa, who arrives in town followed by many American journalists reporting on the war, to have Arroyo killed. Villa, seeing in Arroyo a person who has placed his own interests above the cause of the revolution, shoots him to death.

Harriet, with Arroyo's lover, La Luna, leave the camp with the bodies of their men. Harriet returns to the United States to bury the old gringo in her father's cemetery plot in Arlington, Virginia, next to her mother. La Luna sets out to some indeterminate spot in the desert with the body of Arroyo. Harriet spends the rest of her time musing on these two men and living the lonely days of her life.

Critical Evaluation:

Carlos Fuentes's *The Old Gringo* demonstrates many of the writer's artistic and philosophic concerns. In this multifaceted story, Fuentes reflects his passion for language and literature and the influences of many writers and thinkers. He expands on his consideration of the nature of time; explores the contrast between reality and dreams and other psychological, often unconscious, motivations; continues to define the Mexican character; and contributes to the canon of modern, innovative literature

This novel is a story of the Mexican Revolution (1910-1920). Drawing on other Latin American writers who have explored the revolution and elaborating on the theme of time—*la edad del tiempo* ("the age of time")—around which he has organized all of his fiction, Fuentes shows in this novel, the fourth cycle of time explorations, *el tiempo revolucionario* ("the time of revolution"), the ways the revolution reveals both the ideals and betrayal of those ideals in this cause. He simultaneously shows the influence of unconscious motivation on action and the ways such motivation impacts the lives of others.

The influence of dreams, a theme inspired by Argentine writer Jorge Luis Borges, inspires the actions of the characters. The central characters often inhabit a dream world that is more real to them than is "real life." Here they fulfill their dreams imaginatively or symbolically, transforming their lives and the lives of others. The old gringo comes to Mexico planning to die as a man of action; Harriet Winslow wants to reinvent herself and find, in some way, her father who has abandoned his family while ostensibly going to fight in Cuba; Tomás Arroyo, a young Mexican revolutionary, seeks to overthrow the social order and the government and to take

revenge on his father as well. They all use each other to fulfill their own dreams.

While the gringo comes to die, he then becomes enthralled with Harriet. He sees in Arroyo both a son and a competitor. Harriet sees the gringo as a replacement for the father who left her and her mother for a Cuban woman. She finds in Arroyo a passionate lover, with whom she expresses her own passion and acts out the freedom she thinks her father felt with the Cuban woman. Arroyo hates his father and the oppressive state, both of which have left him disenfranchised. Motivated to overthrow the old order, Arroyo sees landowner Miranda, the man who denied his existence, as a representative of the old order, so he burns down the hacienda, leaving intact the ballroom full of mirrors. He is fascinated by the mirrors, as are all of the characters who use them to create alternative selves.

Utilizing symbols to extend meaning and suggest motivation, Fuentes employs the mirrors in the ballroom to effect doubling. With mirrors, characters create an alternative experience imaginatively reflected in the mirror. As the gringo and Harriet dance, he sees a daughter, and she imagines a father. When Arroyo dances with Harriet, he supplants the father figure; in the mirror he sees himself dancing with his mother, thus granting her the status she never had. When Harriet dances with Arroyo, she becomes the sensual prostitute who seduced her father. Symbolic frontiers also describe double lives. Characters cross borders, entering new physical and psychological spaces. Distance from their past is symbolized by a burning bridge.

The father-child conflict also accounts for motivation, as the younger generation attempts to overthrow the older generation. The revolution itself represents this attempt. Fuentes reinforces the theme of patricide, alluding to a story by Ambrose Bierce, in which a young Union soldier kills his Confederate father in the Civil War. Here, the old soldier, who has come to die, changes his mind. When he wants to live, he is killed by Arroyo. Arroyo, intent on vengeance, kills all representatives of the old order. Harriet symbolically kills her own father. She then persuades Pancho Villa, a father figure to Arroyo, to kill Arroyo.

Fuentes also defines in the novel the Mexican character, which includes the qualities of the peasants, the indigenous peoples, who are patient, gentle, and passionate for life. They embrace individuals. Having lived with gods and superstition, they accept the Catholic religion with its saints and celebrations, confession and redemption. Mexican people also derive from Western Europeans, the aristocrats: oppressive, powerful, and self-serving. Arroyo himself represents the mix of cultures; he is cruel and kind, sentimental and vulgar, idealistic and selfish, usurping old oppression with new violence.

Unlike the stereotypical journalists reporting for American newspapers whose attitude toward Mexico is judgmental and superior, Harriet develops a new realization, asserting that Mexico should be accepted as it is, not changed. Mexico becomes emblematic of the complexity of history and human experience. Fuentes's acceptance of Mexican culture lies at the heart of this novel of artistic innovation and psychological probing.

Bernadette Flynn Low

Further Reading

Boldy, Steven. *The Narrative of Carlos Fuentes: Family, Texts, Nation.* Durham, England: University of Durham Press, 2002. Presents analyses of ten works by Fuentes written between 1958 and 1995. Topics discussed include Mexico and memory, the Mexican national identity and history, literature and evil, the carnivalesque, violence and impunity, and intellectual traditions of Mexican national thinking.

"Carlos Fuentes." In *The Paris Review: Latin American Writers at Work*, edited by George Plimpton. New York: Modern Library, 2003. Fuentes explains his connection with Mexican and Latin American culture and writers as well as the writing intentions expressed in this novel and elsewhere.

Chrzanowski, Joseph. "Patricide and the Double in Carlos Fuentes's *Gringo Viejo.*" *International Fiction Review* 16, no. 1 (Winter, 1989): 11-16. Elucidates the theme of patricide and the technique of doubling in *The Old Gringo.*

Gyurko, Lanin A. *Lifting the Obsidian Mask: The Artistic Vision of Carlos Fuentes.* Potomac, Md.: Scripta Humanistica, 2007. A thorough examination of Fuentes's artistic vision, the motifs in his novels, and the way his work reflects his influences and concerns.

Harss, Luis, and Barbara Dohmann. *Into the Mainstream: Conversations with Latin American Writers.* New York: Harper & Row, 1967. Features an interview with Fuentes that emphasizes his particular concern with the evolution and nature of the Mexican character.

William, Raymond Leslie. "The Novels of Carlos Fuentes." In *The Modern Latin American Novel.* New York: Twayne, 1998. A comparative study of Fuentes's works. Also examines Fuentes's assertion that all of his fiction explores a preoccupation with time.

_____. *The Writings of Carlos Fuentes.* Austin: University of Texas Press, 1996. Explores Fuentes's life and writings as well as his concerns with the culture and style of what he identifies as Indo-Afro-Ibero-America.

The Old Maid

Author: Edith Wharton (1862-1937)
First published: 1924
Type of work: Novella
Type of plot: Social realism
Time of plot: 1850's
Locale: New York

Principal characters:
DELIA RALSTON, a New York matron
JAMES RALSTON, her husband
CHARLOTTE LOVELL, Delia's cousin
JOE RALSTON, James's cousin
TINA LOVELL, Delia's ward

The Story:

Among the leading families in New York in the 1850's, none is more correct or more highly regarded than the Ralstons. Their ancestors came to America not for religious freedom but for wealth. By the time Delia Lovell marries James Ralston, the Ralstons consider themselves the ruling class, and all their thoughts and actions are dictated by convention. They shun new ideas as they do strange people, and the sons and daughters of the numerous branches of the family marry only the sons and daughters of similar good families.

Delia is conventional and correct by birth as well as by marriage. Before her marriage, she was in love with Clement Spender, a penniless young painter; but since he would not give up his proposed trip to Rome and settle down to a disciplined life in New York, it was impossible for a Lovell to marry him. Against her will, Delia often imagines herself married to Clement, but the image is only momentary, for Delia has no place in her life for strong emotions or great passions. Her life with James and their two children is perfect.

She is glad, too, that her cousin, Charlotte Lovell, is going to marry James's cousin, Joe Ralston, for at one time she feared that Charlotte might never have a suitable proposal.

Charlotte is a strange girl who has become quite prudish in the years since she made her debut. At that time, she was lively and beautiful. Then a sudden illness caused her to go to Georgia for her health. Since her return, she has been colorless and drab, spending all of her time with the children of the poor. She sets up a little nursery where she cares for the children, and to this nursery comes a baby who was abandoned by a veiled woman whom no one could identify. Charlotte seems especially fond of the orphan child and favors her with better toys and clothes than those given the other children.

One day, Charlotte tells Delia that she will not marry Joe. She tells Delia that the orphaned baby in the nursery is her own, and that she went to Georgia to give birth to the child. Charlotte is ill with a racking cough that often causes a hemorrhage, but it is not her cough that causes her to worry. Joe insists that she give up her work with the children after they are married. Since her baby has no known parents, it will have to be placed in an orphanage, and Charlotte could not bear to think of her child in a charity home.

Joe, being a Ralston, would never marry Charlotte and accept her child if he knew the truth. Delia does not know what action to suggest until she learns that the baby's father is Clement. Charlotte always loved Clement, who, when he returned from Rome and found Delia married, turned to Charlotte. When he goes back to Rome, Charlotte does not tell him of the baby, for she knows that Clement still loves Delia.

Although Delia thinks she no longer cares for Clement, she, too, cannot bring herself to let his child be placed in an orphanage. She persuades her husband to provide a home for Charlotte and the baby, telling him and the rest of the family that Charlotte and Joe should not marry because of Charlotte's cough. Joe, who wants healthy children, is not hard to convince.

After Charlotte and the baby, Tina, are established in a little house, Charlotte's health improves. In fact, she becomes quite robust, and each day grows more and more into an old maid. After James is killed by a fall from a horse, Delia takes Charlotte and the little girl into her home. Tina grows up with the Ralston children and copies them in calling Delia "Mother" and Charlotte "Aunt."

Delia's children make proper marriages, and at last, she and Charlotte and Tina are left alone in the house. Charlotte often seems to resent Delia's interest in Tina and the fact that the young girl goes to Delia's room for private talks, but she dares not give any hint that Tina owes her love or affection.

When Delia learns that the sons of the good families will not marry Tina because she has no family background, she asks Charlotte to let her adopt the girl and give her the Ralston name. Both women fear that Tina might make the same mistake Charlotte made if she continues to see the young men who love her but will not marry her. Soon afterward, Delia makes Tina her legal daughter, and the girl becomes engaged to a correct young man.

Tina is delighted with her new status as Delia's daughter, for she long thought of her as a mother. The two make endless plans for Tina's wedding. On the night before the wedding, Delia wants to go up to Tina's room to tell the girl all the things a mother usually tells her daughter on the eve of her wedding, but Charlotte flies into a rage. She accuses Delia of having helped her and Tina only because she wants revenge for Charlotte's affair with Clement. She tells Delia that she knows Delia still loves Clement, that she turned to Delia in her need, years ago, because she knew that Delia would help her for Clement's sake. Charlotte has carried hatred for Delia in her heart for many years, thinking always that Delia is trying to take Tina from her real mother. Charlotte declares fiercely that on her wedding eve Tina should talk with her real mother, and she starts up to the girl's room.

When Charlotte leaves, Delia realizes that there is some truth in what Charlotte said. She chose James and the Ralston life willingly and knowingly, but she often unconsciously wishes for a life filled with love and unpredictable passions. She knows, too, that she made Tina her own child, leaving Charlotte nothing for herself.

Delia starts up to her room. She wants to see Tina, but she thinks that Charlotte deserves this one night with her daughter. Delia meets Charlotte coming downstairs. Charlotte was not with Tina, knowing that the girl would prefer her adopted mother. There is nothing an old maid aunt can say to a bride unless she were to tell her the truth, and that Charlotte can never do. Delia has her talk with Tina. She does not stay long, for she knows that Charlotte is alone and unhappy. As she kisses Tina goodnight, she asks one favor. On the morrow, for Delia's sake, Tina is to give her last good-bye kiss to her Aunt Charlotte.

Critical Evaluation:

Considered by many critics to be one of the most important American fiction writers of the twentieth century, Edith Wharton in 1921 became the first woman to be awarded the Pulitzer Prize in fiction. She was then just past the midpoint of a prolific forty-year writing career that included the publication of more than twenty novels and novellas, numerous short stories, travel books, works on interior decoration and gardening, and three volumes of poetry. In the first part of the twentieth century, critics often regarded Wharton as being solely a chronicler of the social mores of the upper classes of old New York. That reductive opinion was later corrected, as many other aspects of her career and works were fruitfully explored and analyzed from various critical angles.

The Old Maid, the second of a quartet of novellas published under the title *Old New York* in 1924, belongs to that phase of Wharton's career after World War I when she focused on the city's aristocracy in the decades prior to her birth. It was written shortly after the publication in 1920 of *The Age of Innocence*, the somewhat nostalgic novel of 1870's New York high society for which Wharton was awarded the Pulitzer Prize. *The Old Maid* is definitely not a nostalgic fictional reminiscence but represents instead a backward glance marked by a keen sense of disappointment, anguish, and loss about the shortcomings of the past. In fact, the topic of illegitimacy, around which the novella revolves, made publishers initially reluctant to accept the work for publication. Despite such prudish fears, the novella turned out to be one of Wharton's most popular and durable successes; it was adapted for the stage by Zoë Atkins and won the Pulitzer Prize in drama in 1935, and a melodramatic film version in 1939 starred Bette Davis and Miriam Hopkins.

The four novellas of *Old New York* are carefully linked and unified through such narrative strategies as chronological sequencing from the 1840's through the 1870's, recurrent family names and characters, and the gradual revelation in each novella of some crucial factors. Such a linking of four novellas under a unified title was an innovation in American literature. In fact, Wharton may have been attempting no less than to emulate a writer she much admired, Honoré de Balzac, and write a short American version of his grand series of interrelated novels of French society, the *Comédie Humaine* (1829-1848). Wharton was also indebted to the work of her friend Henry James, who wrote a set of related short stories.

Like the other tales of *Old New York*, *The Old Maid* consists of two short stories linked by the passage of time. The first short story describes how Delia Ralston helps her cousin, Charlotte Lovell, to keep her illegitimate daughter, Tina; the second, set years later, describes her legal adoption of Tina to be able to provide her with the social respectability she needs to find a husband. Both parts revolve around crucial moments in the lives of Delia and Charlotte; both culminate in conversations between Delia and Charlotte in which the two women, despite grave differences, agree to cooperate for the sake of Tina.

The novella's themes—the stifling power of convention, the dubious value of sacrifice, the conflict between passion and social order—reflect common Wharton preoccupations. Meticulously describing the conservative high society of New York of the 1850's in all its variations of stifling uniformity, Wharton explores the problem of finding fulfillment, sexual or emotional, in a society that rigorously ignores and shuts its eyes to such needs. The novella also presents one of Wharton's superb analyses of the mother-daughter relationship, here with the twist that results from the struggle between two women, both of whom claim Tina as a daughter.

The novella's title is rather ironic. On the surface, it seems to refer to Charlotte who is forced to disavow her own child and who becomes in the eyes of everyone, including her daughter, an old maid with all the accompanying stereotypical character traits. However, despite being married and having children, Delia is an old maid at heart because she never gives in to passion and remains emotionally unfulfilled and repressed. In an ironic reversion typical of Wharton, it is Charlotte who knows passion but cannot acknowledge the fact because of society's repressive rules, whereas while Delia enjoys all the social privileges of being a wife and mother, she remains unfulfilled in her yearnings for an emotionally satisfying relationship.

Delia is the novella's major character, and the entire novella is narrated from her point of view. It is difficult to assess how Charlotte or Tina actually feels, because Delia's losses—in which the reader fully participates—seem greater. Charlotte's loss—giving up her daughter, first by renouncing her relationship with Tina, then by actually consenting to have her adopted by Delia—is not diminished, but Wharton does not describe the full extent of her anguish; it can only be inferred. Through focusing on Delia, Wharton wants the reader to detect yet another loss under the seemingly imperturbable social surface: the fate of a woman who married for security, not for love, and who regrets this choice for the rest of her life. Although the social conventions of the time prevent Charlotte from openly proclaiming to be Tina's mother, Delia can, through Tina, relive her youthful fantasies about Tina's father, Clement Spender, whom she herself loved. Delia is successful in imposing her wishes and desires by manipulating most people around her, but her victory is shallow at best; only in living out her fantasies through Tina can she find satisfaction and fulfillment. Wharton's descriptions of the lives of Delia and Charlotte show what it is like, as critic Cynthia Griffin Wolff wrote, to "grow old and to be lonely—with all life's options already taken and all life's expectations harshly foreclosed."

"Critical Evaluation" by Ludger Brinker

Further Reading

Farwell, Tricia M. *Love and Death in Edith Wharton's Fiction*. New York: Peter Lang, 2006. An insightful look at Wharton's beliefs about the nature of love and the way they reflect her philosophical views, namely those of Plato and of Charles Darwin. Wharton's own shifting feelings on the role of love in life are revealed in conjunction with the shifting role that love played for her fictional characters.

Funston, Judith E. "Clocks and Mirrors, Dreams and Destinies: Edith Wharton's *The Old Maid*." In *Edith Wharton: New Critical Essays*, edited by Alfred Bendixen and Annette Zilversmit. New York: Garland, 1992. Uses the images of clocks and mirrors to raise larger questions about motherhood and the ways in which women can find their identity in a repressive society.

Lee, Hermione. *Edith Wharton*. New York: Knopf, 2007. An exhaustive study of Wharton's life, offering valuable insights and pointing out interesting analogies between her life and her fiction.

Lewis, R. W. B. *Edith Wharton: A Biography*. New York: Harper & Row, 1975. Discusses the novella in the context of Wharton's conflict with publishers who initially refused to accept the work because of its theme of illegitimacy.

Rae, Catherine. *Edith Wharton's New York Quartet*. Lanham, Md.: University Press of America, 1984. A book-length study of the four novellas that make up *Old New York*. Provides analysis and background material.

Raphael, Lev. *Edith Wharton's Prisoners of Shame: A New Perspective on Her Neglected Fiction*. New York: St. Martin's Press, 1991. Discusses shame and its devastating effect on the psyche. Analyzes the novella in the context of jealousy and shame, which distort the relationship between two women and stifle both.

Wolff, Cynthia Griffin. *A Feast of Words: The Triumph of Edith Wharton*. New York: Oxford University Press, 1977. Analyzes the novella in the context of Wharton's look backward at the New York of her youth. Maintains that the work is filled with a sense of disappointment and loss. Convincingly argues that the work depicts Wharton's own fear of growing old and lonely.

The Old Man and the Sea

Author: Ernest Hemingway (1899-1961)
First published: 1952
Type of work: Novella
Type of plot: Symbolic realism
Time of plot: Mid-twentieth century
Locale: Cuba and the Gulf Stream

Principal characters:
SANTIAGO, an old Cuban fisherman
MANOLIN, a young boy

The Story:

For eighty-four days, old Santiago has not caught a single fish. At first a young boy, Manolin, shared his bad fortune, but after the fortieth luckless day, the boy's father tells his son to go in another boat. From that time on, Santiago works alone. Each morning he rows his skiff out into the Gulf Stream, where the big fish are. Each evening he comes home empty-handed.

The boy loves the old fisherman and pities him. When Manolin has no money of his own, he begs or steals to make sure that Santiago has enough to eat and has fresh baits for his lines. The old man accepts his kindness with a humility that is like a quiet kind of pride. Over their evening meals of rice or black beans, they talk about the fish they had caught in luckier times or about American baseball and the great Joe DiMaggio. At night, alone in his shack, Santiago dreams of lions on the beaches of Africa, where he had gone on a sailing ship years before. He no longer dreams of his dead wife.

On the eighty-fifth day, Santiago rows out of the harbor in the cool dark before dawn. After leaving the smell of land behind him, he sets his lines. Two of his baits are fresh tunas the boy had given him, as well as sardines to cover his hooks. The lines sink straight down into deep dark water. As the sun rises, he sees other boats in toward shore, which is only a low green line on the sea. A hovering man-of-war bird shows him where dolphins are chasing some flying fish, but the school is moving too fast and is too far away. The bird circles again.

This time Santiago sees tuna leaping in the sunlight. A small one takes the hook on his stern line. Hauling the quivering fish aboard, the old man thinks it a good omen.

Toward noon, a marlin starts nibbling at the bait, which is one hundred fathoms down. Gently the old man plays the fish, a big one, as he knows from the weight on the line. At last, he strikes to settle the hook. The fish does not surface. Instead, it begins to tow the skiff to the northwest. The old man braces himself, the line taut across his shoulders. He is skilled and knows many tricks; he waits patiently for the fish to tire.

The old man shivers in the cold that comes after sunset. When something takes one of his remaining baits, he cuts the line with his sheath knife. The fish lurches suddenly, pulling Santiago forward on his face, cutting his cheek. By dawn, his left hand is stiff and cramped. The fish has headed northward; there is no land in sight. Another strong tug on the line slices Santiago's right hand. Hungry, he cuts strips from the tuna and chews them slowly while he waits for the sun to warm him and ease his cramped fingers.

That morning the fish jumps. Seeing it leap, Santiago knows he has hooked the biggest marlin he has ever seen. Then the fish goes under and turns toward the east. Santiago drinks sparingly from his water bottle during the hot afternoon. Once an airplane drones overhead on its way to Miami. Trying to forget his cut hand and aching back, he remembers the days when men had called him *El Campeón*, and he had wrestled with a giant man in the tavern at Cienfuegos.

Close to nightfall, a dolphin takes the small hook Santiago has rebaited. He lifts the fish aboard, careful not to jerk the line over his shoulder. After he rests, he cuts fillets from the dolphin and also keeps the two flying fish he finds in its maw. That night he sleeps. He awakes to feel the line running through his fingers as the fish jumps. Feeding line slowly, he tries to tire the marlin. After the fish slows its run, Santiago washes his cut hands in seawater and eats one of the flying fish. At sunrise, the marlin begins to circle. Faint and dizzy, he works to bring the big fish nearer with each turn. Almost exhausted, he finally draws his catch alongside and drives in the harpoon. He drinks a little water before he lashes the marlin to the bow and stern of his skiff. The fish is two feet longer than the boat. No catch like it has ever been seen in Havana harbor. It will make his fortune, Santiago thinks, as he hoists his patched sails and sets his course toward the southwest.

An hour later, Santiago sights the first shark. It is a fierce Mako, and it comes in fast to slash with raking teeth at the dead marlin. With failing might, the old man strikes the shark with his harpoon. The Mako rolls and sinks, carrying the har-

poon with it and leaving the marlin mutilated and bloody. Santiago knows the scent will spread. Watching, he sees two shovel-nosed sharks closing in. He strikes at one with his knife lashed to the end of an oar and watches the scavenger slide down into deep water. He kills the other while it tears at the flesh of the marlin. When the third appears, he thrusts at it with the knife, only to feel the blade snap as the fish rolls. The other sharks come at sunset. At first, Santiago tries to club them with the tiller from the skiff, but his hands are raw and bleeding and there are too many in the pack. In the darkness, as he steers toward the faint glow of Havana against the sky, he hears them hitting the carcass again and again. Yet the old man thinks only of his steering and his great tiredness. He has gone out too far and the sharks have beaten him. He knows they will leave him nothing but the stripped skeleton of his great catch.

All lights are out when he sails into the little harbor and beaches his skiff. In the gloom, he can just make out the white backbone and the upstanding tail of the fish. He starts up the shore with the mast and furls the sail of his boat. Once he falls under their weight and lays patiently until he can gather his strength. In the shack, he falls on his bed and goes to sleep.

There the boy finds him later that morning. Meanwhile, other fishermen, gathered about the skiff, marvel at the giant marlin, eighteen feet long from nose to tail. Manolin returns to Santiago's shack with hot coffee, and the old man wakes up. The boy, he says, can have the spear of his fish. Manolin tells him to rest, to make himself fit for the days of fishing they will have together. All that afternoon, the old man sleeps, the boy sitting by his bed. Santiago is dreaming of lions.

Critical Evaluation:

The publication of the novella *The Old Man and the Sea* near the end of Ernest Hemingway's writing career restored his flagging reputation as a writer. It came at a time when critics thought Hemingway was losing his creative powers. They had panned his previous novel, *Across the River and into the Trees* (1950). The novella earned Hemingway the 1953 Pulitzer Prize and helped him win the Nobel Prize in Literature in 1954. For about fifteen years, the work enjoyed wide critical approval and attention, although it had its detractors. By the late 1960's, critics had begun a reassessment. Only a handful of articles were written about the novella in later years.

The Old Man and the Sea works on multiple levels of theme, image, and symbol. It has been compared to Herman Melville's *Moby Dick* (1851) and to Samuel Taylor Coleridge's "The Rime of the Ancient Mariner" (1798)—great tales of sea adventure and the testing of human endurance. The story depicts a world in which the heroic and the mundane intermingle. Hemingway claimed to be writing a story about a real fisherman, the real sea, and a real fish. There is no question, however, that the effort at realism does not mask the metaphorical and symbolic dimensions of the story. The story's lean and spare style focuses readers' attention on a timeless drama nearly devoid of contemporary reference, but the modern world is a backdrop to one man's heroic struggle with nature. On one level, the story is a heroic testimony to that person's endurance and courage. This interpretation is based on a reading of the text without recognition of its many ironies. The old man puts up a fierce and superhuman effort against the great marlin, a fish so large and powerful as to remind readers of Moby Dick. In Hemingway's book, the fish is not entirely like Melville's leviathan. The marlin is not malicious or a malignant force of nature. It never attacks its pursuer the way Moby Dick does, but it does put up a fierce and noble fight for its life. The endurance of the old man, and perhaps his intelligence, proves to be superior to that of the fish. The man conquers the fish but, in the end, loses the fish to the sharks.

On one level, the novella also is a gripping account of a man in search of meaning and dignity in a world that gives little quarter. To survive in this world and to feel that life has meaning is to struggle. This struggle is not unique to Santiago but rather is typical of the Hemingway hero. The struggle and how it is conducted provide meaning in a person's life. Hemingway puts so much poetic energy into depicting this struggle that it becomes an object of beauty, much as does the perfect pass in the bullring or the swing of Joe DiMaggio. This struggle requires tenacious will, intelligence, and prowess, or, as the old man refers to it, "ability." Readers of Hemingway's greatest works are familiar with his ethos of the graceful struggle. Those who live the struggle and exhibit special prowess are Hemingway's heroes. Such people include bullfighters, soldiers, and even, for that matter, bulls. Those who do not accept that life is a struggle and fail to exhibit prowess in whatever they do are depicted as failures and weaklings.

Hemingway dramatizes this struggle in the sparest of terms. The story presents only two characters, the old man and a boy who is friend and helper. The boy may be seen as the embodiment of the promise of uncorrupted youth. The boy's many kindnesses to the old man reflect a self-effacing and generous spirit that can only be seen as examples of human virtue. Santiago resembles Christ in his sufferings: Readers may note the attention paid to the laceration of Santiago's hands and to his ascent up the hill to his hovel while he carries the mast. He falls five times, as did Christ carrying his cross, and finally lies in his bed, arms outstretched and palms turned upward. The spirit of Christ also informs the actions of the boy. Santiago suffers greatly (which is his primary similarity to Christ), but he does nothing to help anyone. He is on the receiving end of help from the boy, who makes sure Santiago has food and care. The owner of the bar also sends the old man food.

Santiago lives an impoverished life. He barely eats, owns almost nothing, reads only yesterday's newspapers, and lives in a tiny shack with a dirt floor. He owns a small fishing boat, but he has barely enough gear to outfit himself as a fisherman. His food and drink are charity.

Santiago's inner life is almost as impoverished. He holds a few memories as points of reference. He dreams of the lions on the beach in Africa that he saw as young man and of a titanic arm wrestling match with a powerful man. These dreams symbolize the power of his youth. Santiago does not speak of his strength, but he credits himself with an ability to triumph over adversity through a combination of will and intelligence. When he is awake, he refers repeatedly to DiMaggio as the epitome of prowess or ability—a model against which Santiago judges himself. His connection to DiMaggio and the world of baseball is indicative of his values. Baseball embodies the values of physical strength and ability. Santiago also refers to Jesus and Mary and seems aware of a higher spiritual realm beyond his present struggle. These symbolic dimensions add depth and complexity to the narrative and contribute the great enjoyment readers continue to derive from this simple, beautifully written tale.

"Critical Evaluation" by Richard Damashek

Further Reading

Bloom, Harold, ed. *Ernest Hemingway's "The Old Man and the Sea."* New York: Bloom's Literary Criticism, 2008. Collection of interpretive essays, including existential and Taoist readings of the novella; comparisons of the novella to works by William Faulkner, Albert Camus, and Derek Walcott; and a discussion of gender issues.

Brenner, Gerry. *"The Old Man and the Sea": Story of a Common Man.* New York: Twayne, 1991. Sets the novella's literary and historical contexts and discusses its critical reception. Considers the novella's structure, character, style, psychology, and biographical elements.

Killinger, John. *Hemingway and the Dead Gods: A Study in Existentialism.* Lexington: University Press of Kentucky, 1960. Compares Hemingway's views to those of such European existentialists as Jean Paul Sartre and Albert

Camus. Adds much to the understanding of Santiago's character.

Ott, Mark P. *A Sea of Change: Ernest Hemingway and the Gulf Stream—A Contextual Biography*. Kent, Ohio: Kent State University Press, 2008. Ott argues that Hemingway's interest in and studies of the Gulf Stream of Florida moved his fiction from 1920's Paris modernism to 1950's realism. Includes analysis of *The Old Man and The Sea*.

Sojka, Gregory S. *Ernest Hemingway: The Angler as Artist*. New York: Peter Lang, 1985. Examines fishing in Hemingway's life and works as "an important exercise in ordering and reinforcing an entire philosophy and style of life." Devotes chapter 5 to *The Old Man and the Sea*.

Trogdon, Robert W., ed. *Ernest Hemingway: A Literary Reference*. New York: Carroll & Graf, 2002. A compendium of information about Hemingway, including photographs, letters, interviews, essays, speeches, book reviews, copies of his unfinished manuscripts, and his comments about his and other writers' works.

Valenti, Patricia Dunlavy. *Understanding "The Old Man and the Sea": A Student Casebook to Issues, Sources, and Historical Documents*. Westport, Conn.: Greenwood Press, 2002. Provides a literary analysis of the novella and primary documents about baseball, fishing, and the Cuban environment and its politics, history, economic issues, and culture in the late 1940's and early 1950's.

Wagner-Martin, Linda. *Ernest Hemingway: A Literary Life*. New York: Palgrave Macmillan, 2007. Examines Hemingway's life, especially his troubled relationship with his parents. Wagner-Martin makes insightful connections between Hemingway's personal life, his emotions, and his writing.

Waldhorn, Arthur. *A Reader's Guide to Ernest Hemingway*. New York: Farrar, Straus and Giroux, 1972. Examines the terms "Hemingway hero" and "Hemingway code" and then applies these terms to Hemingway's works. Notes that Santiago's humility is an unusual quality in a Hemingway character.

Old Mortality

Author: Sir Walter Scott (1771-1832)
First published: 1816
Type of work: Novel
Type of plot: Historical
Time of plot: 1679
Locale: Scotland

Principal characters:
HENRY MORTON, the heir of Milnwood
LADY MARGARET BELLENDEN, the lady of Tillietudlem
EDITH, her granddaughter
COLONEL GRAHAME OF CLAVERHOUSE, later viscount of Dundee
LORD EVANDALE, a Royalist
JOHN BALFOUR OF BURLEY, a Covenanter
BASIL OLIFANT, a renegade Covenanter

The Story:

Henry Morton has the misfortune of being a moderate man, a man who can see both sides of a question. During the rebellion of the Covenanters against the Crown in 1679, his position became an exceedingly precarious one. His uncle and guardian is the squire of Milnwood, by faith a Covenanter and by nature a miser, and Henry's dead father had fought for the Covenanters at Marston Moor. The story of his family is frequently cause for comment among the cavalier gentry of the district, especially at the tower of Tillietudlem, the home of Lady Margaret Bellenden and Edith, her granddaughter.

Henry and Lord Evandale contest as marksmen, and

Edith Bellenden is among the spectators when Henry defeats his opponent. Declared the victor at this festival of the popinjay, Henry bows his respects to Edith Bellenden, who responds with embarrassed courtesy under the watchful eyes of her grandmother. After the shooting, Henry goes with friends to a tavern where some dragoons of Claverhouse's troop, under Sergeant Francis Bothwell, are also carousing. Bothwell, a descendant of the Stuart kings through the bar sinister line, is a man of domineering disposition. Henry and his friends drink a toast to the health of the king; Bothwell, intending to humiliate the Covenanters, resolves that they should drink also to the archbishop of St. Andrew's. A stranger in the company proposes the toast to the archbishop, ending with the hope that each prelate in Scotland will soon be in the same position as his grace.

Henry and the stranger leave the inn; soon afterward, word comes that the archbishop has been assassinated. Bothwell realizes then that the stranger must have been one of the plotters in the deed, and he orders a pursuit.

Meanwhile, Henry has learned that his companion is John Balfour of Burley, a Covenanter leader who had saved the life of Henry's father at Marston Moor. That night, Henry gives Balfour lodging at Milnwood without his uncle's knowledge and next morning shows the fugitive a safe path into the hills. Bothwell and his troops arrive shortly afterward. Henry is arrested and taken away. In company with Henry in his arrest are Mause Headrigg, a staunch Covenanter, and her son, Cuddie. The prisoners are taken to Tillietudlem Castle, where Claverhouse sentences Henry to execution. He is saved, however, by the intercession of Edith and Lord Evandale.

Lord Evandale brings information that a group of Covenanters is gathering in the hills, and Claverhouse gives orders to have his troops advance against them. At a council of war, Lord Evandale, among others, suggests a parley in which both sides can air their grievances. Claverhouse sends his nephew, Cornet Grahame, to carry a flag of truce to the Covenanters. Balfour and a small group meet Cornet Grahame, but the Covenanters refuse to meet Claverhouse's demands. To the surprise and suppressed indignation of all, Balfour shoots Cornet Grahame in cold blood after an interchange of words.

The killing of the young officer is the signal for a general fight. Bothwell and Balfour meet beard to beard, and Balfour kills Bothwell with his sword as the dragoon stands defenseless, his sword arm broken by the kick of a horse. In the fray, Henry saves the life of Lord Evandale after the young nobleman's horse had been shot from under him.

Balfour's rebels are victorious and next plan to capture Castle Tillietudlem. Claverhouse leaves a few of his men to defend the place under the command of Major Bellenden, brother-in-law of Lady Margaret. Balfour had taken Henry Morton from the troops of Claverhouse on the battlefield and now wants Henry to join with the rebels; Henry, however, still holds back. Trying to convince Henry of the righteousness of his cause, Balfour takes him to a council of war, where Henry is elected one of a council of six through Balfour's insistence.

Major Bellenden refuses to surrender the castle to the insurgents, who then decide to starve out the small garrison. Realizing that Henry wishes to remain in the vicinity of the

castle because he is concerned for Edith's safety, Balfour sends the young man to Glasgow, the objective of the main Covenanter army. Claverhouse had retreated to Glasgow and laid careful plans for the defense of the city. Henry returns to Milnwood with Cuddie to learn what is happening at Tillietudlem. Hearing that Lord Evandale had been captured during a sortie from the castle, Henry once again saves Lord Evandale's life from Balfour's rough justice. Then Henry draws up a document stating the grievances of and the conditions offered by the Covenanters and sends Lord Evandale with the paper to the castle. Edith and Lady Margaret escape from the castle, and Henry raises the flag of the Covenanters to the castle tower.

The Covenanters are finally defeated at the battle of Bothwell Bridge. In the retreat from the field, Henry is taken prisoner by a party of Covenanter fanatics, who believe him to have deserted their cause. He is sentenced to death. Cuddie Headrigg catches a horse and escapes. He rides to Claverhouse and explains Henry's predicament. Since Henry's death is decreed on a Sabbath day, his captors decide he could not be executed until after midnight. This decision gives Claverhouse and his men time to rescue Henry. With the Covenanter revolt now broken, Claverhouse agrees to put Henry on a parole of honor. Henry accepts exile from Scotland, promising to remain in banishment until the king's pleasure allows his return. Henry goes to Holland, where he lives in exile for several years, until William and Mary come to the throne.

When Henry returns to Scotland, he calls upon Cuddie, who has married Jenny Dennison, Edith's maid. He learns from Cuddie of all that has occurred during his absence. He is informed that a man named Basil Olifant, a turncoat kinsman of Lady Margaret, has seized Tillietudlem and that Lady Margaret and Edith are forced to depend upon the charity of friends. Henry also learns that Balfour is still alive and that Lord Evandale is soon to marry Edith Bellenden. Henry sets out to find Balfour and get a document from him that will place the Bellenden estates in Edith's possession once more. Balfour, however, burns the document and then threatens to fight Henry to the death; but Henry refuses to fight with the man who had saved his father's life, and he makes his escape from Balfour's fury by leaping across a ravine.

Meanwhile, Edith has refused marriage to Lord Evandale because she had caught a glimpse of Henry Morton as he passed her window. Later, at an inn, Henry overhears a plot to murder Lord Evandale; the murderers hope to obtain a substantial sum of money from Basil Olifant for so doing. Henry scribbles a note of warning to Lord Evandale and sends his message by Cuddie. Then he goes to Glasgow, intending to find Wittenbold, a Dutch commander of dragoons, and to get help from him to protect Lord Evandale. Cuddie, however, tarries too long at an alehouse and forgets that the letter is to be delivered to Lord Evandale. Instead, he asks to see Lady Margaret; when he is refused admittance, he stumbles away, bearing the letter with him. Therefore, Lord Evandale is not warned of his danger.

A party of horsemen, led by Basil Olifant, arrives to kill Lord Evandale. Cuddie knows the danger but warns him too late. Shots are exchanged, and Lord Evandale falls. Olifant orders Lord Evandale murdered in cold blood just before Henry arrives with a magistrate and a detachment of dragoons.

The troopers quickly disperse the attackers, and Olifant falls during the charge. Balfour attempts to escape but is swept to his death in a flooded stream. Henry hurries to the side of Lord Evandale, who recognizes him and makes signs that he wishes to be carried into Lady Margaret's house. There he dies, surrounded by his weeping friends. His last act is to place Edith's hand in that of Henry Morton. To the great joy of the countryside, Henry marries the young heir of Tillietudlem several months later. In the meantime, Basil Olifant dies without a will, and Lady Margaret recovers her castle and her estates.

Critical Evaluation:

Old Mortality is a representation of Robert Paterson, who lived from 1715 to 1801. Sir Walter Scott claims to have met Paterson and, according to the first chapter of *Old Mortality*, Scott's Old Mortality reportedly shared many of Scott's Covenanting memories. Readers learn nothing further of him. Old Mortality disappears from the narrative, but he remains a presence in the novel as its title character.

Old Mortality's role as title character is symbolic, given that Scott had intended, with a degree of irony, to personify human transience, the incessant change that history represents, and the futility of attempting to resist the ravages of time. The gravestones of the Covenanters will soon erode into nothingness, destroying all memory of them, their cause, and their concerns. In attempting to resuscitate them and their history in his novel, Scott knowingly becomes a kind of Old Mortality himself.

Because of the success of his earlier novels—*Guy Mannering* (1815) and *The Antiquary* (1816)—Scott invested more than he should have in a country estate he called Abbotsford. Needing additional income, he changed publishers, invented a second authorial guise for himself, and began developing a series called *Tales of My Landlord*. This series was ostensibly written by the landlord of the Wallace

Inn of Gandercleugh, a fictitious Scottish village about halfway between Edinburgh and Glasgow. There, a Jedediah Cleishbotham tutors the landlord's six children. When an inn guest, Pattieson, dies, Cleishbotham finds among his papers a parcel called "Tales of My Landlord," which Cleishbotham sells to a bookseller to pay Pattieson's funeral expenses. In an introduction to the tales, Cleishbotham insists that he is not their writer, editor, or compiler. It was Pattieson, Cleishbotham claimed, who had prepared the tales for the press and who was therefore responsible for their departures from historical accuracy.

All this detail is yarn-spinning by Scott, given that no landlord, no Pattieson, and no Cleishbotham, other than Scott himself, had existed. Why Scott thought it necessary to adopt such an elaborate disguise has been variously explained. It was common knowledge that "the author of Waverley" and *Tales of My Landlord* were written by the same person. The first of these tales was *The Black Dwarf* (1816), one of Scott's shorter and less successful efforts. The second was *Old Mortality*, which Oliver Elton was first to praise as "the swiftest, the most varied, the least alloyed, the most fully alive of all" of Scott's novels. Critics laud *Old Mortality* as by far the best constructed. With *The Heart of Midlothian* (1818), *Old Mortality* is generally regarded as Scott's finest work.

The title of the novel seems at first glance to be another of Scott's subterfuges. *Old Mortality* is ostensibly a narrative by Pattieson, as edited first by Cleisbotham and then by his publishers. The narrative begins with Pattieson's meeting an aged Cameronian sympathizer known only as Old Mortality. The old Cameronian has this name because his sole occupation is to traverse rural Scotland repairing and maintaining the graves of other Cameronians who, like their cause, would otherwise be forgotten. Cameronians were followers of Richard Cameron, who, in opposition to English efforts toward unification, upheld the covenants of 1638 and 1643, which were designed to protect the established Church of Scotland and its rites from governmental interference. The Cameronians were also known as Covenanters.

The alleged authenticity of the narrative—which Cleishbotham defends as real history rather than fiction—is compromised by its having supposedly passed through so many hands, from Old Mortality (and other sources) to the landlord to Pattieson to Cleishbotham, with some interference from the publishers after that. The most immediate effects of this fictitious transmission are apparent in the novel, and are fundamental to it. First, although Old Mortality may have provided the landlord with useful recollections of past events, they could not have been at first hand. The novel proper begins precisely on May 5, 1679, and ends ten years later. Its events, therefore, take place before Old Mortality was born.

Second, the novel's point of view is not that of the Cameronians, who are represented throughout as overly zealous biblical literalists inspired by the harsh retributive ethics of the Old Testament rather than the more accommodating forgiveness of the New Testament. For Scott, Old Mortality is the last of his kind—the sole survivor of a bygone era. Scott's understanding of the Cameronians' outdated mentality, however, is remarkable. Scott recognizes so fully that human awareness of the actual is historically conditioned and that what one generation takes as its eternal verities seems nonsensical or fanatic to later ones. The historicity of mentality is therefore fundamental to *Old Mortality* and many of Scott's other novels.

Just as thought changes through time, so must language. The oldest language in the book would properly belong to Old Mortality, but he never speaks. The Cameronians speak an older, more biblical English than other characters do; one can judge the degree of their religious extremity (and their obsolescence) by their talk. The more moderate Scots, and the English characters uniformly, sound a good deal more modern. As is usual with Scott, the narrator understands and transcribes Scots (most modern editions of the novel include a full glossary) but does not write it.

Third, the alleged origin of the novel's text cannot adequately explain the omniscient knowledge of the narrator, who is privy to the minds not only of the Covenanters but also all the characters. It is soon apparent that neither Pattieson nor any other of the narrative's supposed transmitters, alone or in combination, could have all the necessary facts at his disposal, if this were indeed true history. In actuality, the novel is not history at all but fiction, and those interested in such things have pointed out how Scott has sometimes altered fact. Scott himself points out, for example, that the Castle of Tillietudlem (with its siege and all that takes place within) is imaginary.

Old Mortality actually existed but plays no part in the real business of the novel. The several Cameronian preachers, with their highly artificial names, are constructs designed to represent a spectrum of religious fanaticism grading into mania. Monmouth and Claverhouse are both historical, although Scott had to create for each a personality. His Claverhouse has been called the most successful characterization of a historical personage in any of his novels, particularly because Claverhouse strikes readers as both complex and modern. Surprisingly modern too are Scott's low-born characters, including Cuddie Headrigg the plowman, whose ability to survive and to influence events is noteworthy. Jenny, his eventual wife, is similarly likeable and equally successful. Whereas other female characters in the novel feel bound to act in highly constrained and sometimes artificial ways, Jenny is spontaneous and natural.

Later perspectives on literary study have encouraged closer attention to the roles of women in fiction. Their importance to the society depicted in *Old Mortality* is clear not only from their high social stations but also their influence on events. Despite Scott's apparent preoccupation with Scottish history, the center of *Old Mortality* is unquestionably the triangular relationship of Edith Bellenden, Lord Evandale, and Henry Morton, in which traditional conflicts between love, friendship, and duty are resolved more by fate than by choice. These three are perhaps the most admirable characters in the novel, but readers sense (as perhaps Scott did also) that such scrupulous nobility as theirs was doomed, like the religious fanaticism of the Cameronians, to fail to survive.

"Critical Evaluation" by Dennis R. Dean

Further Reading

D'Arcy, Julian Meldon. *Subversive Scott: The Waverley Novels and Scottish Nationalism.* Reykjavík: University of Iceland Press, 2005. Demonstrates how the novels contain dissonant elements, undetected manifestations of Scottish nationalism, and criticism of the United Kingdom and its imperial policy. Chapter 5 examines *Old Mortality*.

Dickson, Beth. "Sir Walter Scott and the Limits of Toleration." *Scottish Literary Journal* 18, no. 2 (November, 1991): 46-62. Argues that although Scott struggles to understand the Cameronians, it is clear throughout that he also disapproves of them and does not regret their passing.

Fleischner, Jennifer B. "Class, Character, and Landscape in *Old Mortality*." *Scottish Literary Journal* 9, no. 2 (December, 1982): 21-36. Landscape, a prominent element in many of Scott's novels, is often overlooked by critics. Fleischner examines the Scottish landscape in relation to the social and moral standings of major characters in the novel.

Lincoln, Andrew. "Liberal Dilemmas—Scott and Covenanting Tradition: *The Tale of Old Mortality* and *The Heart of Mid-Lothian*." In *Walter Scott and Modernity*. Edinburgh: Edinburgh University Press, 2007. In his examination of Scott's novels and poems, Lincoln argues that these were not works of nostalgia; instead, Scott used the past as a means of exploring modernist moral, political, and social issues.

Rigney, Ann. *Imperfect Histories: The Elusive Past and the Legacy of Romantic Historicism.* Ithaca, N.Y.: Cornell University Press, 2001. A scholarly study of the complex and controversial intersections of historical fiction and the "facts" of history. Chapter 1, "Hybridity: The Case of Sir Walter Scott," examines Scott's combining of fact and fiction in *Old Mortality* and how the novel's hybrid nature was received by his contemporaries.

Shaw, Harry E., ed. *Critical Essays on Sir Walter Scott: The Waverley Novels.* New York: G. K. Hall, 1996. Collection of essays published between 1858 and 1996 about Scott's series of novels. Includes journalist Walter Bagehot's 1858 article about the Waverley novels and discussions of Scott's rationalism, the storytelling and subversion of the literary form in his fiction, and what his work meant to Victorian readers. Peter D. Garside's essay "*Old Mortality*'s Silent Minority" examines this novel.

Whitmore, Daniel. "Bibliolatry and the Rule of the World: A Study of Scott's *Old Mortality.*" *Philological Quarterly* 65, no. 2 (Spring, 1986): 243-262. "Bibliolatry" is excessive veneration of the Bible, a term the Cameronians would have found objectionable in its presumption. Illuminates the clash within the novel between church and state.

The Old Wives' Tale

Author: Arnold Bennett (1867-1931)
First published: 1908
Type of work: Novel
Type of plot: Naturalism
Time of plot: Nineteenth century
Locale: England and Paris

Principal characters:
CONSTANCE BAINES POVEY and SOPHIA BAINES SCALES, sisters
JOHN BAINES, their father
MRS. BAINES, their mother
SAMUEL POVEY, Constance's husband
GERALD SCALES, Sophia's husband
CYRIL POVEY, the son of Constance and Samuel

The Story:

Sixteen-year-old Constance Baines is a plump, pleasant girl with a snub nose. Sophia Baines, fifteen years old, is a handsome girl with imagination and daring. The first symptoms of her rebelliousness and strong individuality come when she announces her desire to be a teacher in 1864. Mr. and Mrs. Baines own a draper's shop, and their income is adequate. They are most respectable and are therefore horrified at their daughter's unconventional plan, for it had been taken for granted that she as well as Constance would assist in the shop.

When Sophia was four years old, John Baines, her father, had suffered a stroke of paralysis that left him disabled and his faculties greatly impaired. Prodded by his capable wife, he joins in forbidding Sophia to think of teaching, but his opposition only strengthens Sophia's resolve.

When Sophia is left alone to care for her father one day, she sees a handsome young man, a representative of a wholesale firm, enter the store. She invents an errand to take her into the shop. She learns that his name is Gerald Scales. When Sophia returns to her father's room, she finds that he had slipped off the bed and, unable to move himself, died of asphyxia. Mr. Baines's old friend, Mr. Critchlow, is called immediately; having seen Sophia in the shop with Gerald, he instantly accuses her of killing her father. Presumably as a gesture of repentance but actually because she hopes for an opportunity to see Gerald again, Sophia offers to give up her plans to teach.

Sophia was working in millinery when Constance assisted Samuel Povey, the clerk, a small quiet man without dignity and without imagination. He and Constance gradually fall in love.

After two years, Gerald Scales returns. By artful contriving, Sophia manages to meet him alone and to initiate a correspondence. Mrs. Baines recognizes Sophia's infatuation and sends her off to visit her aunt Harriet. Several weeks later, Sophia runs off with Gerald. She writes her mother that they were married and planning to live abroad. A short time later, Constance and Samuel Povey are married. Mrs. Baines turns over the house and shop to them and goes to live with her sister.

The married life of Constance holds few surprises, and the couple soon settles into a routine tradesman's existence. Nothing further is heard of Sophia except for an occasional Christmas card giving no address. After six years of marriage, the couple has a son, Cyril. Constance centers her life on the baby, more so since her own mother had died shortly after his birth. Povey also devotes much attention to his son, but he makes his wife miserable by his insistence on discipline. When, after twenty years of marriage, Povey catches pneumonia, dies, and leaves Constance a widow, she devotes herself entirely to Cyril. He is a charming, intelligent boy, but he seems indifferent to his mother's efforts to please him. When he is eighteen years old, he wins a scholarship in art and is sent to London. His mother is left alone.

Life has not dealt so quietly with Sophia. In a London hotel room, after her elopement, she suffers her first disillusionment when Gerald begins to make excuses for delaying their marriage; but after Sophia refuses to go to Paris with him except as his wife, he reluctantly agrees to the ceremony. Gerald has inherited twelve thousand pounds. He and Sophia live lavishly in Paris. Gerald's weakness, his irresponsibility, and lack of any morals or common sense soon become apparent. Realizing that Gerald has little regard for her welfare, Sophia takes two hundred pounds in bank notes from his pocket and hides them in case of an emergency. As Gerald loses more money at gambling, they live in shabbier hotels, wear mended clothes, and eat sparingly. Their funds nearly exhausted, Gerald suggests that Sophia should write to her family for help. When Sophia refuses, Gerald abandons her.

The next day, she wakes up ill and is visited by Gerald's friend, Chirac, who has come to collect money Gerald had borrowed from him. Chirac had risked his own reputation by taking money from the cash box of the newspaper where he is employed. Sophia unhesitatingly uses some of the notes she had taken from Gerald to repay Chirac. When she again becomes ill, Chirac leaves her in the care of a middle-aged courtesan, Madam Faucault, who treats Sophia kindly during her long illness.

Madame Faucault is deeply in debt. Sophia rents Madame Faucault's flat and takes roomers and boarders. At that time, France is at war with Germany, and the siege of Paris soon begins. Food is scarce. Only by hard work and the most careful management is Sophia able to feed her boarders. She grows hard and businesslike. When the siege is lifted and Paris returns to normal, Sophia buys a pension, named Frensham, at her own price. This pension is well-known for its excellence and respectability, and under Sophia's management, it prospers. She does not hear from her husband again. By the exhibition year, she has built up a modest fortune from the two hundred pounds she had taken from Gerald.

One day, Cyril Povey's young English friend stays at the pension Frensham. Sophia's beauty and dignity intrigue him, and he learns enough about her to recognize her as his friend's aunt. On his return to England, he hastily informs both Cyril and Constance of Sophia's situation. Constance immediately writes Sophia a warm, affectionate letter begging her to come to England for a visit. Meanwhile, in Paris, Sophia has suffered a slight stroke; when she is offered a large sum for the pension, she reluctantly lets it go. Soon afterward, she visits England.

Although Sophia had intended to make only a short visit, the sisters end up living together for nine years. On the surface, they seem to get along well together, but Sophia has never forgiven her sister for her refusal to move from the ugly, inconvenient old house. Constance, on her part, silently resents Sophia's domineering ways.

Their tranquil existence is interrupted by a telegram to Sophia, informing her that Gerald Scales is very ill in a neighboring town. She goes to him at once, but on her arrival, she learns that he is already dead. He died shabby, thin, and old. Sophia is greatly shocked when she sees Gerald; she is shocked, in part, by her lack of feeling for the man who had both made and ruined her life. She suffers another stroke while driving home and lives only a few hours. Cyril is left all of Sophia's money. He continues to live in London on an allowance, completely absorbed in his art, still secretive and indifferent to his mother. When Constance dies several years later, he is abroad and does not return in time for the funeral. When the servants leave for Constance's burial, only Sophia's old poodle is left in the house. She waddles into the kitchen to see if any food has been left in her dish.

Critical Evaluation:

Late nineteenth century literary naturalism insists on the determining forces of heredity and environment. Realism concentrates objectively on the social and historical conditions of experience, but it allows for a greater independence in the principal characters. Arnold Bennett's fiction is marked by a blending of these two literary movements. He cultivated detachment and technique in his writing because he felt that the English novel had neglected what he called a "scientific" eye; satire and sentiment, from Henry Fielding to Charles Dickens, had colored the English author's presentation of reality. Bennett turned to France for new models. By absorbing realism and naturalism, he became a master of the "impressions of the moment," but he retained an English sense for the uniqueness of character.

The Old Wives' Tale is his masterpiece. The title is revealing in that, instead of describing a superstitious tale, it dramatizes his objectivity by obliging readers to interpret the phrase literally. The novel is about two women who become old; their story, despite its inevitability, is far more wondrous in its simple reality than any fantastic or "superstitious" tale. What is remarkable about them is that despite their having lived entirely different lives, they emerge, at the end, remarkably similar. This is primarily because of the moral fiber woven into their characters from earliest childhood. Neither woman "has any imagination" (which was Bennett's intention), but each has the stability of a rock. Constance leads a conventional life and never leaves St. Luke's square; Sophia runs off with an attractive salesman, is deserted in Paris, and runs a successful boardinghouse during the siege of Paris and the Commune. (It is no coincidence that Bennett chose to name each symbolically for her main character trait: constancy and wisdom, respectively.) Despite the difference of circumstance in their lives, they remain the self-reliant middle-class daughters of John Baines. Bennett achieves his desired effect of parallelism amid contrast. This pattern is illustrative of what Bennett meant by technique and craftsmanship; it also reveals the interweaving of naturalist and realist techniques in fiction.

The "judicial murder" of Daniel Povey, Samuel's cousin, in the prison at Stafford parallels the public execution of the murderer Rivain, which Sophia and Gerald take in as an unusual "attraction." This and many other parallels in the plot—for example, young Cyril's theft from the till at the shop and Sophia's prudent appropriation of Gerald's two hundred pounds—are done so cleverly that they never seem forced or artificial. Life is simply like this, says Bennett, and the range and sureness of his story vindicate his method.

Bennett's respect for his ordinary characters is intense. He admires their capacity for survival and never underestimates their souls. In the middle of bourgeois contentment, Constance is never free from a strange sadness. She lacks the imaginative power of a Hamlet, but she feels a similar anguish: "The vast inherent melancholy of the universe did not exempt her." Her simple and undistinguished husband, Samuel Povey, dies of toxemia contracted from pneumonia. His death is oddly heroic, because the illness that kills him is a cruelly ironic reward for his selfless dedication to his poor cousin, Daniel. Bennett is unequivocal in his praise. He concedes that he thought Povey a "little" man easy to ridicule but that his honesty finally earns a great deal of respect. The end of his life displays a touch of greatness that all souls, insists Bennett, have in common.

It is important that readers understand that Constance's melancholy, Samuel's humility, and Sophia's passionate na-

ture are secondary to what Bennett felt was the mainstream running through all of their natures: the will to survive. Fossette, the aged poodle, is the emblem of that instinct at the close of the novel. The great enemy of all is time, and it always wins in the end. Readers may object to assigning Bennett such a cold view of life. To end on a beastly comparison between Fossette and Sophia seems out of keeping with Bennett's fondness and respect for his characters. Nevertheless, readers remember that what Bennett praises the most in Sophia is precisely her pluck, her ability to survive in a totally alien environment.

Sophia's emotional life is not a rich one, and the last glimpse of Gerald as an old man does not rekindle her feelings. Unlike Samuel's death, which was senseless but pathetic because of his selflessness, Sophia's death is the result of an unbearable knowledge; she confronts her own death in Gerald's death, which strikes her as overwhelming in its physical meaning. Once a handsome and vital young man who had excited her passions and moved her to abandon respectability, Gerald in the end appears before her as the corpse of a withered and aged man. Sophia is not concerned with his moral weakness or the grief that he caused her. All she can think of is that a young man, once proud and bold, has been reduced to a horribly decimated version of his former self. The cruelty of time, which has made a mockery of all the feelings of love and hatred they shared, shatters her self-confidence. She can no longer separate herself from the mortality around her. When the inevitability of death becomes apparent, even to someone without imagination like Sophia, the will to survive is gone. Suddenly the full weight of her life, the great struggle for survival in Paris, descends with crushing force. It is more than she can stand. Although she fears death, she begs for its deliverance. When she can take no more, she dies. Despite all the pressures and forces that shape *The Old Wives' Tale*, it does not end until the hearts of its protagonists stop beating.

"Critical Evaluation" by Peter A. Brier

Further Reading

Fromm, Gloria G. "Remythologizing Arnold Bennett." *Novel: A Forum on Fiction* 16, no. 1 (Fall, 1982): 19-34. Discusses Virginia Woolf's criticism, which had a devastating effect on Bennett's reputation. Argues that Woolf missed Bennett's assertion that there is no escaping expression of the self, no matter how skillful a writer may be.

Lucas, John. *Arnold Bennett: A Study of His Fiction*. New York: Methuen, 1974. Lucas argues that Guy de Maupassant's cynicism influenced Bennett's portrayal of Constance. Bennett considered *The Old Wives' Tale* an important demonstration of his seriousness as a writer.

Meckier, Jerome. "Distortion Versus Revaluation: Three Twentieth-Century Responses to Victorian Fiction." *Victorian Newsletter* 73 (Spring, 1988): 3-8. Suggests that *The Old Wives' Tale* is a criticism of the cynicism found in William Makepeace Thackeray's *Vanity Fair* (1847-1848, serial; 1848, book). Bennett drew more joy than Thackeray did from the secular world.

Roby, Kinley E. *A Writer at War: Arnold Bennett, 1914-1918.* Baton Rouge: Louisiana State University Press, 1972. Roby maintains that *The Old Wives' Tale*, which shows no meaning in the lives of its characters, anticipates a major theme of twentieth century British and American literature.

Squillace, Robert. *Modernism, Modernity, and Arnold Ben-* nett. Lewisburg, Pa.: Bucknell University Press, 1997. Squillace argues that Bennett saw more clearly than his contemporaries the emergence of the modern era, which transformed a male-dominated society to one open to all people regardless of class or gender. The detailed notes and a bibliography acknowledge the work of some of the best scholars.

_____. "Self-Isolation and Self-Advertisement in *The Old Wives' Tale*." In *Seeing Double: Revisioning Edwardian and Modernist Literature*, edited by Carol M. Kaplan and Anne B. Simpson. New York: St. Martin's Press, 1996. Squillace maintains that in *The Old Wives' Tale*, Bennett achieved "an analysis of secrecy and exposure, of the secret self that obsessed Edwardian novelists, as remarkable as that found in any work by [Joseph] Conrad or [Henry] James and strikingly different in form."

The Old Wives' Tale

Author: George Peele (1556-1596?)
First produced: c. 1591-1594; first published, 1595
Type of work: Drama
Type of plot: Comedy
Time of plot: Indeterminate
Locale: England

Principal characters:
ANTIC,
FROLIC, and
FANTASTIC, pages
CLUNCH, a blacksmith
MADGE, his wife
ERESTUS, an enchanted man, called Senex
LAMPRISCUS, a farmer
HUANEBANGO, a braggart
SACRAPANT, a magician
EUMENIDES, a knight
DELIA, a princess of Thessaly
CALYPHA and THELEA, her brothers
VENELIA, the betrothed of Erestus
ZANTIPPA and CELANTA, the daughters of Lampriscus

The Story:

Antic, Frolic, and Fantastic, three pages, are lost at night in an English forest. There they encounter Clunch, a blacksmith, who takes them to his cottage to spend the night in comfort and safety. When Madge, Clunch's wife, offers them food, they refuse it; Antic asks for a story instead. Oddly enough, Antic thereupon goes to sleep with old Clunch; his companions stay up to hear Madge's story.

Once upon a time, a king had a daughter of great beauty. This daughter was stolen away. The king sent men in search of her until there were no men left in the realm except her brothers. Finally they, too, went in search of their sister. It was a magician disguised as a dragon who had kidnapped her. This magician imprisoned her in a great stone castle. The magician also placed at the crossroad a young man who by enchantment appeared by day as an old man, but who by night was changed into a bear.

At this point in Madge's tale two young men appear and declare dejectedly that they have arrived in England in search of their sister, Delia. They have given alms to an old man whom they encounter at a crossroad. In return for their kindness, the old man repeats a verse for them and tells them to say to anyone who asks about the rhyme that they had learned it from the white bear of England's wood.

After the brothers leave, the old man tells aloud his own story. He had been happily married to a beautiful woman in Thessaly. Sacrapant, a sorcerer, had fallen in love with her and had enchanted the husband, Erestus, so that now, by day, he appears to be an old man and by night a bear. His beloved Venelia, under the influence of Sacrapant, becomes a lunatic. Distracted, she runs past the crossroad and is recognized by Senex, as Erestus is called in his enchanted form of an old man.

A farmer named Lampriscus, knowing a bear's fondness for sweets, gives Erestus a pot of honey. Lampriscus discloses that he is twice a widower; by his first wife he has a beautiful daughter who, in her pride and petulance, is a great burden to him; by his second wife he has another daughter who is ugly and deformed. Erestus directs Lampriscus to send his daughters to the well to drink of the water of life; there they will find their fortunes.

Huanebango, a braggart who claims that he can overpower sorcerers, and Booby, a peasant, arrive at the crossroad. Both seek to win the favor of the fair lady enchanted by Sacrapant. Huanebango refuses to give alms to Erestus; Booby, however, gives him a piece of cake. Erestus predicts that Huanebango will soon be deaf and that Booby will go blind.

In his study room, meanwhile, Sacrapant discloses that he, the son of a witch, has transformed himself into a dragon and has kidnapped Delia, the daughter of the king. Delia enters the study and sits down to a magic feast with her captor. As the pair dine, the two brothers enter. Delia and Sacrapant flee, but Sacrapant soon returns to overcome the brothers with his magic. After they are taken to a dungeon in the castle, Sacrapant triumphantly reveals aloud that he can die only by a dead man's hand.

When Eumenides, a wandering knight, arrives at the crossroad, Erestus forecasts his fortune for him in a rhymed riddle. Eumenides lays down to sleep. Before long he is awakened by an argument between two country fellows and a churchwarden; the churchwarden refuses to bury their friend, Jack, who has died a pauper. Eumenides, recalling a stipulation of the riddle, pays the churchwarden all of the money he has so that Jack will be properly buried.

Huanebango and Booby arrive at Sacrapant's stronghold. Huanebango is struck down by a flame; Booby is stricken blind and turned loose to wander. Sacrapant then changes Delia's name to Berecynthia and takes her to the fields to supervise the labors of her brothers, who are digging in the enchanted ground. Delia, ignorant of her true identity, fails to recognize her brothers.

In the meantime, Zantippa, the proud daughter of Lampriscus, and Celanta, the deformed daughter, go to the well of life. Zantippa breaks Celanta's water pot. At the same time, two Furies bring Huanebango, in a trance, to the well. As Zantippa dips her pot into the well, she beholds a head in the water. She impetuously breaks her pot on the head; thunder and lightning follow. Huanebango, deaf by enchantment, awakes from his trance. Unable to hear the strident railings of the beautiful Zantippa, he is smitten with love for her. The two leave the well together.

Eumenides, continuing his wanderings, arrives at the well, where he is joined by the ghost of Jack, for whose burial he had given all of his money. The ghost declares its intention to serve him, but Eumenides insists that the ghost should be his equal and share his worldly wealth. The ghost goes ahead to an inn to arrange supper for the destitute Eumenides. As he is eating, Eumenides looks into his purse, which he believes completely empty, and discovers that it is full of money. Having dined, Eumenides, followed by the ghost, turns his steps toward Sacrapant's castle.

At the well, Celanta, with a new pot, has returned in the company of the blinded Booby. The peasant, unable to see her deformity, falls in love with her. Celanta, who is a gentle creature, obeys the dictates of the head in the well and is thereupon rewarded with a pot of gold.

Eumenides and the ghost approach the castle. The ghost, placing wool in the knight's ears, directs him to sit quietly. When Sacrapant comes out of his cell and asks Eumenides' identity, the ghost removes Sacrapant's magic wreath and takes away his sword. Shorn of his magic powers, Sacrapant dies. At the ghost's direction, Eumenides digs into the hillside and discovers a light enclosed in glass, but he is unable to get to the light. The ghost then gives Eumenides a horn to blow. At the sound of the blast, Venelia appears, breaks the glass, and extinguishes the magic light to free everyone from the power of Sacrapant.

Eumenides and Delia pledge their troth. Eumenides sounds the horn again, and Venelia, the two brothers, and Erestus appear. Now that all are together, the ghost demands, upon the terms of equality with Eumenides, one-half of Delia. Eumenides is reluctant; but, true to his word, he prepares to cut Delia in half with his sword. Convinced of Eumenides' good faith, the ghost withholds the stroke of the sword and leaves the group. All declare their intention of returning immediately to Thessaly.

Fantastic awakes Madge, for day is breaking. The old woman moves toward the kitchen and declares that breakfast will soon be ready.

Critical Evaluation:

Although often mentioned as one of the earlier Elizabethan plays, *The Old Wives' Tale* has not had a very distinguished critical or theatrical history. It was largely ignored in the seventeenth and eighteenth centuries, while nineteenth century critics did little more than compare it contemptuously to John Milton's *Comus* (1637), for which it was probably a partial source. The twentieth century gave the play a more favorable critical reading, but theatrical revivals beyond occasional amateur performances have been lacking.

The Old Wives' Tale was a highly innovative play when first written, and the passage of more than four hundred years has made it no less uncommon. First, it is a play with a frame; the main action is a play within the play. Unlike in William Shakespeare's *The Taming of the Shrew* (pr. c. 1593-1594, pb. 1623), which also uses a frame, in George Peele's play the characters remain on stage and comment from time to time on the action. The result is an unusual intimacy, and at the same time a certain aesthetic distance from the action. A closer and more useful comparison can be made with Shakespeare's *A Midsummer Night's Dream* (pr. c. 1595-1596, pb. 1600), in which there is a play within the play, in this case with an audience that comments on the action. In Shakespeare's play, however, the audience is courtly and can only laugh at the foolish efforts of the "bumpkin" actors to dramatize the story of Pyramis and Thisbe, or at best sympathize with their good intentions. The audience sees the action largely as the court party does. In *The Old Wives' Tale*, however, the audience is drawn into the fantastic fairy-tale world of the story.

The old wife who tells the story and her husband are presented as crude rustics, but their speech is not made comic, as is usually the case with Elizabethan rustic characters, and the parental attitude they take toward the three pages the husband has found lost in the woods is accepted by the young men. The pages belong to a more educated class than their hosts, but their age acts as a bridge for the audience. They are close enough to childhood to make the audience accept their uncritical interest in a fairy story, and yet educated and adult enough that their acceptance leads the audience to accept the fantasy as well.

The frame of the play is well conceived, but the plot is rather harder to judge. Peele has taken a number of folktale plots and motifs and woven them together in a single story that retains all the atmosphere of a fairy story while being far more elaborate in structure. The several story lines, which at first seem independent of each other, all merge ultimately, and every problem and conflict is resolved. The use of multiple interwoven story lines is alien to the folktale and was likely suggested by medieval romance in general and Ludovico Ariosto's *Orlando furioso* (1516; English translation, 1591) in particular. In a play, however, especially one as short as *The Old Wives' Tale*, there is no time for the separate stories to take on a real life of their own, and the continual introduction of new story lines is likely to make the plot seem jumbled and confused. With such a structure, it is also difficult to become involved with any of the numerous characters, even as superficially as one does with the hero or heroine of a fairy tale, or even to know which characters are most worth becoming involved with.

The apparent hero, a wandering knight named Eumenides, does not appear on stage until well into the play, and when he does his importance is not immediately evident. For a hero, Eumenides shows very little initiative. The one thing that he does on his own is provide money for a pauper named Jack to be properly buried. As a result the grateful ghost directs Eumenides' actions, showing him how to destroy the enchanter and to free the princess.

There are two points of convergence in the play. The first is the crossroad presided over by an enchanted bear-man; the second is the castle of the evil sorcerer, Sacrapant. The various characters must first arrive at the crossroad and are there tested. Some then go another way, but most end at the castle. Though the chief unifying factor of the story is the search for the stolen princess, these two geographical points further bring the actions together and help make the plot more coherent than it would be otherwise.

Folktale situations and motifs are a staple of Western literature, but Peele is perhaps the first to use them on their own terms without attempting to disguise them or to transform them into "literature," for although Peele's play is not exactly a folktale it retains all the atmosphere, the sense of magic, and the sense of childhood wonder that are associated with such tales.

Even in modern times, when folk art and literature are taken more seriously than in the past, there is something revolutionary about making an adult play out of fairy-tale material without also making it somehow tongue-in-cheek. For that reason even modern critics, more sympathetic to such material than critics of the past, have tended to read the play as somehow ironic. Otherwise they tend to read it as an appealing, but mindlessly naïve work. It would seem simpler to consider it just what it appears to be—a play that makes unselfconscious and unapologetic use of the situations and motifs of folktales to tell a story that, like a dream, is impossibly strange but strangely compelling because it touches a level deeper than adult cynicism and rationality.

"Critical Evaluation" by Jack Hart

Further Reading

Ardolino, Frank. "The Protestant Context of George Peele's 'Pleasant Conceited' Old Wives Tale." *Medieval and Renaissance Drama in England* 18 (2005): 146-165. Describes how Peele uses figures of speech from folklore, romance, and religious ritual to demonstrate the conflict between Catholicism and English Protestantism in the character of Sacrapant. Examines how Peele's other plays reflect his pro-Protestant view of religion and politics.

Boas, Frederick S. *An Introduction to Tudor Drama.* 1933. Reprint. Oxford, England: Clarendon Press, 1966. A dated but still helpful introduction by a major twentieth century scholar on the beginnings of Elizabethan drama. Not much discussion of *The Old Wives' Tale*, but a good introduction to its general context.

Bruster, Douglas. "Kingly Harp and Iron Pen in the Playhouse: George Peele." In *Prologues to Shakespeare's Theatre: Performance and Liminality in Early Modern Drama.* New York: Routledge, 2004. Examines the function of the prologue in English Renaissance plays, including Peele's *The Old Wives' Tale*.

Nardo, Don. *Great Elizabethan Playwrights.* San Diego, Calif.: Lucent Books, 2003. In this biography written for younger readers, Nardo explains the origins of English theater and playwriting, including the dramatic works of Peele and William Shakespeare.

Peele, George. *The Dramatic Works of George Peele.* New Haven, Conn.: Yale University Press, 1970. The long introduction provides a good appraisal of *The Old Wives' Tale* that also attempts a rational compromise between earlier schools of thought. Part of the Life and Works of George Peele series.

_____. *The Old Wives' Tale.* Edited by Patricia Binnie. Baltimore: Johns Hopkins University Press, 1980. A carefully prepared edition with an enthusiastic, but intelligent and readable, introduction to the play.

Oldtown Folks

Author: Harriet Beecher Stowe (1811-1896)
First published: 1869
Type of work: Novel
Type of plot: Regional
Time of plot: Late eighteenth century
Locale: Massachusetts

Principal characters:
HORACE HOLYOKE, the narrator
DEACON BADGER, his grandfather
MRS. BADGER, his grandmother
MR. LOTHROP, the village minister
MRS. LOTHROP, his wife
HARRY PERCIVAL, Horace's friend
EGLANTINE (TINA) PERCIVAL, Harry's sister
MEHITABLE ROSSITER, Tina's adopted mother
ELLERY DAVENPORT, Tina's first husband
ESTHER AVERY, a minister's daughter and later, Harry's wife
SAM LAWSON, the village do-nothing

The Story:

Horace Holyoke can remember Oldtown as he had known it when he was a boy, a quiet little village beside a tranquil river in Massachusetts. Surrounded by farmhouses deep in green hollows or high on windy hilltops, Oldtown consists of one rustic street, where the chief landmarks of the community stand. Among these landmarks are the meetinghouse with its classic white spire, the schoolhouse, the academy, a tavern, and the general store, which is also the post office.

As was common in those days, when New England was changing from a Puritan theocracy of little villages to being part of a group of states under a federal government, the minister was still the leading citizen of the town. Mr. Lothrop, descended from generations of ministers, was an Arminian in his views, a sedate, sensible man whose sermons were examples of elegant Addisonian English. His wife, the daughter of an aristocratic family of Boston, had never forsaken the Church of England, and each Easter, Whitsunday, and Christmas, she traveled in her coach to Boston to attend services in Christ Church. The people of Oldtown called her, without disrespect, Lady Lothrop.

As the story goes, famous John Eliot has come to Oldtown as an apostle to the Indians. Three generations later, Horace Holyoke's father arrives in the town to teach in the local academy. There he falls in love with Susy Badger, one of the prettiest of his pupils, and marries her. With marriage comes responsibilities that dim forever his hopes of completing his education at Harvard College. Horace's father's household is a place of penny-pinching hardships. His mother's beauty fades and his father's health, weakened by his attempts to provide for his family and to continue his studies, slowly breaks. Horace is ten years old and his brother, Bill, a few years older when their father dies of consumption. Horace grieves as only a small boy can over his father's death.

Horace's chief comfort in those dark days comes from Sam Lawson, the village handyman and do-nothing. Many people call Sam shiftless. A few pity him because his wife is a scold. Of good humor and garrulous tongue, he is never too busy to take small boys on fishing or hunting trips and to tell them stories.

After the funeral, Mrs. Holyoke and her sons live with her father, Deacon Badger, a leading farmer and miller of Oldtown. He, like Mr. Lothrop, is an Arminian, and a serene, affable man. His wife is a strict Puritan Calvinist, as fond of theological dispute as she is of cleanliness. Horace overhears many arguments between the two, with scriptural texts flying thick and fast in proof of their contentions. Their unmarried daughters are named Keziah and Lois. Keziah is a romantic-minded woman with a reputation for homeliness. Lois is like a chestnut burr, prickly and rough on the outside but soft and smooth within, as her tart tongue and warmhearted nature prove.

Just as the life of the village revolves around the meeting-house, so the center of the Badger household is the spacious, white-sanded kitchen. There the friends of the family gather—Miss Mehitable Rossiter, daughter of a former minister of the town, Major Broad, Squire Jones, Sam, and others. While there, Horace listens to discussions on politics, religion, philosophy, and varied local lore, all of which will influence him throughout his lifetime. There, too, it is decided that his brother, Bill, who shows very little promise as a scholar, is to work on the farm with Jacob Badger, his mother's brother, while Horace will be allowed to continue his studies in the village school. Horace grows into a dreamy, imaginative boy. Sometimes he feels that auras suggestive of good or evil surround people whom he meets. Often he

dreams of a silent, lonely lad of about his own age. The boy begins to fade from Horace's visions, however, after he finds a friend in young Harry Percival.

Harry's father is an English officer, the younger son of a landed family, who brought his wife to America near the end of the Revolutionary War. The wife is a curate's daughter with whom the officer had eloped and married secretly. The husband proves worthless and dissipated, and at last he deserts his wife and two children when his regiment returns to England. He takes his wife's wedding certificate with him and leaves behind a letter denying the legality of their marriage. Friendless and without funds, the wife sets out to walk to Boston with Harry and his sister, Eglantine. On the way, the mother gets sick and dies in the house of miserly Caleb Smith, called by his neighbors Old Crab Smith. The farmer decides to keep the boy as a field hand. Eglantine, or Tina, as her brother calls her, is taken in by Caleb's sister, Miss Asphyxia. The children are treated so harshly, however, that at last they decide to run away. After a night spent with an old Indian woman in the woods, they find a refuge in the Dench mansion, reported to be haunted, on the outskirts of Oldtown. There, Sam and some neighbors find the children after smoke is seen coming from the chimney of the old house.

Harry and Tina are befriended by Deacon Badger and his wife. Within a few days, it is decided that Harry is to remain with the Badgers, an arrangement made even more satisfactory by Mrs. Lothrop's promise to provide for the boy's clothing and education. Miss Mehitable Rossiter, whose life had been saddened some years before by the mysterious disappearance of her young half sister, Emily, adopts Tina. From that time on, the lives of Horace, Harry, and Tina are to be closely intertwined. As a special Easter treat, Mrs. Lothrop arranges to take the children to Boston with her. They are entertained by Madame Kittery, Mrs. Lothrop's mother, and during their stay, they meet Ellery Davenport. Ellery, Mrs. Lothrop's cousin, had served in the Continental army and had held several diplomatic posts abroad. He is handsome and clever. A grandson of the great Jonathan Edwards, he had turned away from the Church; his preceptors are the French philosophers of the day. Horace hears that his wife is mad.

Madame Kittery, a kindly old woman, takes a great interest in Horace and listens sympathetically while he tells of his father's death and of his own desire to attend college. Shortly after the party returns to Oldtown, he is told that money will be provided so that he and Harry can go to Harvard together. Madame Kittery has become his benefactor. Over Thanksgiving, Ellery Davenport and Mrs. Lothrop's sister, Deborah, come to Oldtown for a visit. At a harvest dance at the Badger homestead, Ellery pays marked attention to young Tina. He also promises Miss Mehitable that on his return to France he will look for her lost sister, who is believed to have fled to that country.

Tina became more beautiful as she grew older. When the schoolmaster falls in love with her—and Miss Mehitable's cousin, Mordecai, hired as her tutor, also succumbs to her charms—it is finally decided that she, with Horace and Harry, will go to Cloudland, where Jonathan Rossiter, Miss Mehitable's half brother, is master of the academy. The boys live with Mr. Rossiter. Tina boards with the minister, Mr. Avery, whose daughter, Esther, becomes the friend and companion of the three newcomers. Esther and Harry soon fall in love.

Under Mr. Avery's influence, Harry decides to study for the ministry. Horace dreams of a career that will ensure his future with Tina, whom he has loved since childhood. When Ellery Davenport returns from England, he has important news for Harry. The boy's father is now Sir Harry Percival. Ellery has also secured possession of the stolen marriage certificate, which he gives to Mr. Lothrop for safekeeping.

Horace and Harry enter Harvard as sophomores. Tina, visiting with the Kitterys in Boston or staying with Miss Mehitable in Oldtown, writes them letters that are playful, almost mocking in tone. Horace begins to worry about Ellery Davenport's influence on the girl. A short time later, he hears that Ellery's insane wife has died. Then word comes that Harry's father has died in England. Harry is now Sir Harry Percival. The two friends return to Oldtown for the spring vacation, to learn on their arrival that Tina is engaged to marry Ellery. Horace, reflecting wryly on the contrast between his own humble position and the high estate to which his friends have been lifted, conceals with stubborn pride the deep hurt he feels.

Because Ellery is soon to return to the embassy in London, preparations for the wedding are hurried. After the ceremony, Ellery and his bride are to spend a short time, before sailing, in the reconditioned Dench mansion. When they arrive, they find a woman dressed in black waiting for them in the parlor of the old house. The caller is Emily Rossiter, whom Ellery had seduced and taken away from her family years before. Emily, spurning the settlement he had provided for her, has followed him to America. To her horror, Tina also learns that he is the father of the unfortunate woman's child.

The course Tina takes is both noble and tragic. In spite of the wrong Ellery has done, both to Emily and to his bride, Tina refuses to desert him. Instead, she uses the fortune she has inherited from her father to establish Miss Mehitable and her sister in a house near Boston. She takes the child with her

to England when she goes there with Ellery. After his graduation, Harry marries Esther Avery and leaves for England with his bride. At first, he plans to return shortly to America, but as time passes, it becomes apparent that his interests lay abroad and that he intends to make his home there. Horace feels that he has been left alone in the world.

Eight years pass before Ellery and Tina return to make their home near Boston. By that time, Tina has grown faded and worn. Horace, a successful lawyer, sees her and her husband frequently; as a sympathetic spectator, he watches the course of Ellery's reckless and unprincipled career, which, fed by his ambition, is to bring him close to madness. Ten years after his marriage, Ellery is killed in a political duel. Two more years pass before Horace and Tina are married. Their wedding journey takes them to England to see Harry and Esther. Later, as the years come and go softly, Horace and his wife often visit Oldtown, and it is there they renew the familiar associations of earlier days.

Critical Evaluation:

Harriet Beecher Stowe wrote *Oldtown Folks*, a historical novel and an early example of local-color fiction, to interpret early New England life and to understand how New England influenced its own people as well as the growing United States. To analyze and interpret the small Massachusetts community she re-creates, Stowe focuses on character rather than plot, hypothesizing through her first-person narrator Horace Holyoke that to analyze the life of any given person one must study the society and history that produced that person.

Stowe uses character description and analysis as a means to understand the history of New England, a history that, Stowe believed, profoundly influenced the United States as a whole. In this work, plot takes a lesser importance. The novel may be read as an index of how New England heritage, which forms certain characters, influences their lives. If readers understand *Oldtown Folks* to be about how culture produces character, and how characters in turn create their lives, readers can see why the book is preoccupied with childhood and child rearing. As the narrator and his friends grow up, the plot is foreshortened, until the final chapters summarize the adult outcomes experienced by the characters.

In *Oldtown Folks*, families are created out of difficult circumstances and none of the children whose stories the book tells are raised by their mother and father in a nuclear family. Horace's father dies in the opening chapters, and his mother moves back to her parental household along with her children. Horace's grandmother, Mrs. Badger, becomes his dominant motherly influence. Harry and Tina Percival are orphaned; they flee from Crab Smith and his sister, Asphyxia Smith, who attempt to rear them to be efficient workers, and happen upon Horace's grandmother's house. The Badgers take in Harry, while Tina is adopted by village spinster Mehitable Rossiter. The displacement of the children emphasizes how regional culture, rather than simply parental guidance, may play a crucial role in the formation of character.

Stowe discusses at length the theology professed and the religion practiced by the adults involved in the children's upbringing, particularly focusing on Calvinist, Arminian, and Episcopalian faiths, but also pointing out the influence of skepticism. Crab and Asphyxia reject religion altogether, and not coincidentally they lack any compassion for children and are wholly unfit to raise them. Grandmother Badger is a determined Puritan Calvinist, yet she tempers the harsh doctrines of that faith through her own generosity, charity, and love. Her husband, Deacon Badger, is Arminian, and while disagreeing with Grandmother Badger's convictions concerning Original Sin and predestination, he is in accord with her practice of Christian charity. Mehitable Rossiter has long lived in religious doubt, but her faith is renewed when Tina comes to live with her. She has trouble disciplining Tina according to child-rearing advice she reads and hears, and Tina is indulged constantly as she grows up. The children encounter Episcopalian faith, with its tolerant doctrines and aristocratic ritual, when they visit Boston. Harry gravitates toward the Episcopal Church, in which he eventually will be ordained.

Oldtown Folks avoids oversimplifying the characters who ascribe to certain church dogmas; each individual understands and practices faith in complex ways, and Stowe never suggests that personality is simply a product of religious training. Rather, she explores how various temperaments may respond in different ways to a culture whose identity was grounded in religion, and in which religious debate was characteristic of many household discussions.

The plots that the characters eventually live out demonstrate how their New England upbringing influenced them. A harsh Calvinist training unrelieved by compassion taught children that God did not love them and that they were sinful until they experienced conversion. The children raised under this faith struggle in their adult lives, as illustrated by secondary characters Ellery Davenport (the fictional grandson of Puritan theologian Jonathan Edwards) and Emily Rossiter. Ellery rejects the faith of his forefathers and becomes the clever, charming, and skeptical villain of the novel. His fall is paralleled by the story of Emily Rossiter, Mehitable's half sister, who, in revulsion from Calvinism, accepted French

philosophy and rationalized her decision to become Ellery's mistress. Tina Percival, who was first too harshly, and then too leniently, treated, is unable to see Ellery's moral weakness and marries him. She suffers through ten years of increasingly unhappy marriage, until Ellery is killed in a duel, and then marries the narrator Horace, who has always loved her. Harry's simple but strong faith helps rescue Esther Avery, a minister's daughter, from the painful self-doubts created by her Puritan upbringing, and they marry happily.

These plots are common in popular fiction: a courtship plot with deserving hero and worthy heroine, and a seduction and betrayal plot with unworthy hero and misguided heroine. Stowe's interest is not in rehashing these narratives, which she briefly summarizes in the final chapters of the novel, but in showing why some characters are more likely than others to establish harmonious domestic lives. Children raised with a balance of discipline and love are inclined to choose a happily resolving courtship plot. Children raised with an excess of either strictness or leniency are more apt to experience an unhappily resolving seduction plot or to enter an unfortunate marriage.

Oldtown Folks contributes to American literature in several ways. It explores conflicting doctrines from the perspective of someone whose life experience and deep reading informed what she wrote. It also portrays with precision and grace many New England characters, customs, and places. Therefore, it is a pioneering work within the local-color literary tradition. As a product of the post-American Civil War era, *Oldtown Folks* critiques the rapacious capitalism of Reconstruction politics and affirms some claims of the women's rights movement. Within *Oldtown Folks*, Stowe advocates equal education for women, critiques the sexual double standard, and creates a gallery of strong and independent female characters who experience richly complex internal lives.

"Critical Evaluation" by Karen Tracey

Further Reading

Adams, John R. *Harriet Beecher Stowe*. Boston: Twayne, 1989. Analyzes Stowe's novels according to conventional literary criteria. Argues that *Oldtown Folks*, although flawed by a contrived plot, is the most realistic and imaginative of Stowe's works.

Allen, William. *Rethinking Uncle Tom: The Political Philosophy of Harriet Beecher Stowe*. Lanham, Md.: Lexington Books, 2009. Examines the genesis of Stowe's political ideas by providing close readings of *Oldtown Folks* and other works by Stowe.

Ammons, Elizabeth, ed. *Critical Essays on Harriet Beecher Stowe*. Boston: G. K. Hall, 1980. Includes early reviews and later critical assessments of Stowe's fiction. Excerpts a reading of *Oldtown Folks* by Charles H. Foster, who analyzes how Stowe critiques Jonathan Edwards's influence on Puritan New England.

Crozier, Alice C. *The Novels of Harriet Beecher Stowe*. New York: Oxford University Press, 1969. Dated but still useful discussion of Stowe's novels that considers *Oldtown Folks* in the context of her other historical fiction. Argues that Stowe is at times bitingly ironic toward her religious characters.

Donovan, Josephine. *New England Local Color Literature: A Women's Tradition*. New York: Frederick Ungar, 1983. Discusses Stowe's role as a pioneer of the women's tradition of local-color realism, arguing that *Oldtown Folks* is the best of Stowe's regional novels.

Hedrick, Joan D. *Harriet Beecher Stowe: A Life*. New York: Oxford University Press, 1994. This biography discusses the inception and writing of *Oldtown Folks*. Examines whether Stowe's awareness of her readers and the changing critical climate could have influenced her writing.

Kent, Kathryn R. "'Single White Female': The Sexual Politics of Spinsterhood in Harriet Beecher Stowe's *Oldtown Folks*." In *Making Girls into Women: American Women's Writing and the Rise of Lesbian Identity*. Durham, N.C.: Duke University Press, 2003. Kent uses Stowe's "spinster" characters in *Oldtown Folks* as a point of analysis. Traces the emergence of lesbian identity, which Kent maintains is rooted in white, middle-class culture.

Robbins, Sarah. *The Cambridge Introduction to Harriet Beecher Stowe*. New York: Cambridge University Press, 2007. A concise introduction, designed to familiarize students and general readers with Stowe. Contains biographical information and analysis of Stowe's writings, and discusses her life and work within the context of nineteenth century American literature, womanhood, racial politics, religion, and class identity. Surveys critical reception of her works in both the nineteenth and twentieth centuries.

Weinstein, Cindy. *The Cambridge Companion to Harriet Beecher Stowe*. New York: Cambridge University Press, 2004. Collection of essays examining Stowe's works and literary influence. Includes discussions of race, regionalism, the law, and the American reform tradition. References to *Oldtown Folks* are listed in the index.

Oliver Twist
Or, The Parish Boy's Progress

Author: Charles Dickens (1812-1870)
First published: 1837-1839, serial; 1838, book
Type of work: Novel
Type of plot: Social realism
Time of plot: Early nineteenth century
Locale: England, especially London

Principal characters:
OLIVER TWIST, a workhouse waif
MR. BROWNLOW, Oliver's benefactor
MRS. MAYLIE, a woman who befriends Oliver
ROSE MAYLIE, her adopted daughter
FAGIN, a thief-trainer
BILL SIKES, his confederate
NANCY, Sikes's beloved
MONKS (EDWARD LEEFORD), Oliver's half brother
MR. BUMBLE, a workhouse official

The Story:

Oliver Twist is born in the lying-in room of a parochial workhouse about seventy-five miles north of London. His mother, whose name is unknown, is found later unconscious by the roadside, exhausted by a long journey on foot; she dies leaving a locket and a ring as the only tokens of her child's identity. These tokens are stolen by old Sally, a pauper present at her death.

Oliver owes his name to Mr. Bumble, the parish beadle and a bullying official of the workhouse, who always names his unknown orphans in the order of an alphabetical system he had devised. Twist is the name between Swubble and Unwin on Bumble's list. An offered reward of ten pounds fails to discover Oliver's parentage, and he is sent to a nearby poor farm, where he passes his early childhood in neglect and near starvation. At the age of nine, he is moved back to the workhouse. Always hungry, he asks one day for a second serving of porridge. The scandalized authorities put him in solitary confinement and post a bill offering five pounds to someone who will take him away from the parish.

Oliver is apprenticed to Sowerberry, a casket maker, to learn a trade. Sowerberry employs little Oliver, dressed in miniature mourning clothing, as an attendant at children's funerals. Another Sowerberry employee, Noah Claypole, often teases Oliver about his parentage. One day, goaded beyond endurance, Oliver fiercely attacks Claypole and is subsequently locked in the cellar by Mrs. Sowerberry. When Sowerberry releases Oliver one night, he bundle up his meager belongings and starts out for London.

In a London suburb, Oliver, worn out from walking and weak from hunger, meets Jack Dawkins, a sharp-witted slum gamin. Known as the Artful Dodger, Dawkins offers Oliver lodgings in the city, and Oliver soon finds himself in the middle of a gang of young thieves led by a miserly old Jew, Fagin. Oliver is trained as a pickpocket. On his first mission, he is caught and taken to the police station. There he is rescued by kindly Mr. Brownlow, the man whose pocket Oliver is accused of having picked. Mr. Brownlow, his gruff friend, Grimwig, and the old housekeeper, Mrs. Bedwin, care for the sickly Oliver, marveling at the resemblance of the boy to a portrait of a young lady in Mr. Brownlow's possession. Once he recuperates, Oliver is given some books and money to take to a bookseller. Grimwig wagers that Oliver will not return. Fagin and his gang had been on constant lookout for the boy's appearance. Oliver is intercepted by Nancy, a young street girl associated with the gang, and falls into Fagin's clutches again.

Bumble, in London on parochial business, sees Mr. Brownlow's advertisement for word leading to Oliver's recovery. Hoping to profit, Bumble hastens to Mr. Brownlow and reports that Oliver is incorrigible. Mr. Brownlow thereupon refuses to have Oliver's name mentioned in his presence.

During Oliver's absence, Fagin's gang had been studying a house in Chertsey, west of London, in preparation for breaking into it at night. When the time comes, Oliver, much to his horror, is forced to participate. He and Bill Sikes, a brutal young member of the gang, meet the housebreaker, Toby Crackit, and in the dark of early morning they pry open a small window of the house. Oliver, being the smallest, is the first to enter, but he is determined to warn the occupants. The thieves are discovered, and the trio flees; Oliver, however, is wounded by gunshot.

In fleeing, Sikes throws the wounded Oliver into a ditch

and covers him with a cape. Toby Crackit returns and reports to Fagin, who, as it turns out, is more interested than ever in Oliver after a conversation he had had with Monks. Nancy overhears them talking about Oliver's parentage and Monks expressing his wish to have the boy made a felon.

Oliver crawls feebly back to the house into which he had gone the night before, where he is taken in by the owner Mrs. Maylie and Rose, her adopted daughter. Oliver's story arouses their sympathy, and he is saved from police investigation by Dr. Losberne, a friend of the Maylies. Upon his recovery, the boy goes with the doctor to find Mr. Brownlow, but it is learned that the old gentleman, his friend, Grimwig, and Mrs. Bedwin had gone to the West Indies.

Bumble is meanwhile courting the widow Corney. During one of their conversations, Mrs. Corney had been called out to attend the death of old Sally, who had attended the death of Oliver's mother. After old Sally died, Mrs. Corney removed a pawn ticket from her hand. In Mrs. Corney's absence, Bumble appraised her property to his satisfaction, and when she returned, he proposed marriage.

The Maylies move to the country, where Oliver reads and takes long walks. During this holiday, Rose Maylie falls sick and nearly dies. Harry Maylie, Mrs. Maylie's son, who is in love with Rose, joins the group. Harry asks Rose to marry him, but Rose refuses on the grounds that she cannot marry him unless she discovers who she is and unless he mends his ways. One night, Oliver is frightened when he sees Fagin and Monks peering through the study window.

Bumble discovers that married life with the former Mrs. Corney is not all happiness, for she dominates him completely. When Monks goes to the workhouse seeking information about Oliver, he meets with Mr. and Mrs. Bumble and learns that Mrs. Bumble redeemed a locket and a wedding ring with the pawn ticket she had recovered from old Sally. Monks buys the trinkets from Mrs. Bumble and throws them into the river. Nancy overhears Monks telling Fagin that he had disposed of the proofs of Oliver's parentage. After drugging Bill Sikes, whom she had been nursing to recovery from gunshot wounds received in the ill-fated venture at Chertsey, she goes to see Rose Maylie, whose name and address she had overheard in the conversation between Fagin and Monks.

Nancy tells Rose everything she had heard concerning Oliver. Rose is unable to understand fully the various connections of the plot nor can she see Monks's connection with Oliver. She offers the miserable girl the protection of her own home, but Nancy refuses; she knows that she could never leave Bill Sikes. The two young women agree on a time and place for a later meeting. Rose and Oliver call on Mr.

Brownlow, whom Oliver had glimpsed in the street. The reunion of the boy, Mr. Brownlow, and Mrs. Bedwin is a joyous one. Even old Grimwig gruffly expresses his pleasure at seeing Oliver again. Rose tells Mr. Brownlow Nancy's story.

Noah Claypole and Charlotte, the Sowerberrys' maidservant, run away from the casket maker and arrive in London. They then go to the public house where Fagin and his gang frequently meet. Fagin flatters Noah into his employ; his job is to steal small coins from children on household errands.

At the time agreed upon for her appointment with Rose Maylie, Nancy is unable to leave the demanding Bill Sikes. Fagin notices Nancy's impatience and decides that she has tired of Sikes and has another lover. Fagin hates Sikes because of the younger man's power over the gang, and he sees this situation as an opportunity to rid himself of Sikes. Fagin sets Noah on Nancy's trail.

The following week, Nancy is freed with the aid of Fagin. She goes to Rose and Mr. Brownlow and reveals to them the haunts of all the gang except Sikes. Noah overhears all this and secretly tells Fagin, who in turn tells Sikes. In his rage, Sikes brutally murders Nancy, never knowing that the girl had been faithful to him. He flees, pursued by the vision of Nancy's staring dead eyes. Frantic with fear, he even tries to kill his dog, whose presence could betray him. The dog runs away.

Monks is apprehended and confesses to Mr. Brownlow the plot against Oliver. Oliver's father, Edward Leeford, had married a woman older than himself. Their son, Edward Leeford, is the man now known as Monks. After several years of unhappiness, the couple had separated; Monks and his mother remained on the Continent and Mr. Leeford returned to England. Later, Leeford met a retired naval officer with two daughters, one three years old, the other seventeen. Leeford fell in love with the older daughter and contracted to marry the girl, but before the marriage could be performed, he was called to Rome, where an old friend had died. On the way to Rome, he stopped at the house of Mr. Brownlow, his best friend, and left a portrait of his betrothed. He himself fell sick in Rome and died, and his first wife seized his papers. Leeford's young wife-to-be was pregnant; when she heard of Leeford's death, she ran away to hide her pregnancy. Her father died soon afterward, and the younger sister was eventually adopted by Mrs. Maylie.

Rose was consequently Oliver's aunt. Monks had gone on to live a dissolute life, going to the West Indies when his mother died. Mr. Brownlow had gone in search of him there, but by then Monks had already returned to England to track down his young half brother, whose part of his father's settlement he wishes to keep for himself. It was Monks who had offered the reward at the workhouse for information about Oliver's parentage, and it was Monks who had paid Fagin to see that the boy remained with the gang as a common thief.

After Fagin and the Artful Dodger are seized, Bill Sikes and the remainder of the gang meet on Jacob's Island in the Thames River. They intend to stay there in a deserted house until the hunt dies down. Sikes's dog, however, leads their pursuers to the hideout. Sikes hangs himself accidentally with the rope he was using as a means of escape. The other thieves are captured. Fagin is hanged publicly at Newgate after he had revealed to Oliver the location of papers concerning his heritage, which Monks had entrusted to him for safekeeping.

Harry Maylie becomes a minister and marries Rose Maylie. Mr. Brownlow adopts Oliver and takes up residence near the church of the Reverend Harry Maylie. Mr. and Mrs. Bumble lose their parochial positions and become inmates of the workhouse that once had been their domain. Monks is allowed to retain his share of his father's property, and he moves to the United States; eventually he dies in prison. Oliver's years of hardship and unhappiness are at an end.

Critical Evaluation:

When *Oliver Twist* was published, many people were shocked, and clergymen and magazine editors accused the young novelist of having written an immoral book. In later editions, Charles Dickens defended the book, explaining that one of his purposes had been to take the romance out of crime and show the underworld of London as the sordid, filthy place he knew it to be. Few of his readers ever doubted that he had succeeded in this task.

When Dickens began writing, a popular form of fiction was the Newgate novel, or the novel dealing in part with prison life and the rogues and highwaymen who ended up in prison. These heroes often resembled Macheath of John Gay's *The Beggar's Opera* (1728). Dickens took this tradition and form and turned it around, making it serve the purposes of his new realism. The subplot concerning Bill Sikes and Nancy contains melodramatic elements, but Sikes is no Macheath and Nancy no Polly Peachum.

The grim birth of the infant who was named Oliver opens the book, immediately plunging the reader into an uncomfortably unromantic world where people are starving to death, children are "accidentally" killed off by their charitable keepers, the innocent suffer, and the cruel and unscrupulous prosper. Dickens does not hesitate to lay the facts out clearly: Nancy is a prostitute, Bill is a murderer, Fagin is a fence, and the boys are pickpockets. The supporting cast includes Bumble and Thingummy and Mrs. Mann, individuals who never hesitate to deprive others of what they themselves could use. Poverty is the great leveler, the universal corruptor; in the pages of *Oliver Twist*, the results of widespread poverty are portrayed with a startling lack of sentimentality. Dickens may become sentimental when dealing with virtue but never when dealing with vice.

The petty villains and small-time corrupt officials, such as Bumble, are treated humorously, but the brutal Bill Sikes is portrayed with complete realism. Although Dickens's contemporaries thought Bill was too relentlessly evil, Dickens challenged them to deny that such men existed in London, products of the foul life forced on them from infancy. He holds up Sikes in all his nastiness, without making any attempt to find redeeming characteristics. Nancy, both immoral and kindhearted, is a more complicated character. She is sentimental because she is basically good, while Sikes is entirely practical, one who will step on anybody who gets in his way and feel no regrets.

In *Oliver Twist*, Dickens attempts a deliberate contrast to his previous work, *The Pickwick Papers* (1836-1837). While there is much humor in *Oliver Twist*, it is seldom like that of its predecessor, and it is woven into a realistic and melodramatic narrative of a particularly grim and dark kind. The readers of Mr. Pickwick's exploits must have been startled when they picked up the magazines containing this new novel by Dickens and discovered old Fagin teaching the innocent Oliver how to pick pockets and children swigging gin like practiced drunkards. Dickens had many talents, however, and in *Oliver Twist*, he exploits for the first time his abilities to invoke both pathos and horror and to combine these qualities in a gripping narrative. United with the vitality that always infuses Dickens's prose, these powers guaranteed *Oliver Twist* a wide readership.

The book was the first of Dickens's nightmare stories and the first of his social tracts. A certain amount of social protest could be read into Mr. Pickwick's time in prison, but it is a long distance from the prison depicted there to the almshouse in *Oliver Twist*. The leap from farce to melodrama and social reform is dramatically successful, and Dickens continued in the same vein for many years. Some critics called his work vulgar, but his readers loved it. He was accused of exaggeration, but, as he repeatedly emphasized, his readers had only to walk the streets of London to discover the characters and conditions of which he wrote so vividly. If his characterizations of some individuals suggest the "humours" theory of Ben Jonson rather than fully rounded psychological portraits, the total effect of the book is that of an entire society, pulsing with life and energy.

In *Oliver Twist*, Dickens displays for the first time his amazing gift of entering into the psychology of a pathological individual. He follows Sikes and Fagin closely to their respective ends, and he never flinches from revealing their true natures. The death of the unrepentant Sikes remains one of the most truly horrible scenes in English fiction. (When Dickens performed this passage to audiences in his public readings, it was common for women in the audience to scream or faint.) When Fagin is sitting in court, awaiting the verdict of his trial, Dickens describes his thoughts as roaming from one triviality to another, although the fact of his approaching death by hanging is never far away. The combination of the irrelevant and the grimly pertinent is a kind of psychological realism that was completely new in 1838.

Dickens entertained a lifelong fondness for the theater, and this interest in drama had a profound influence on his fiction. He was himself an actor, and he became famous for his readings from his books toward the end of his life. In his novels, the actor in Dickens is also discernible. At times, it is as if the author is impersonating a living individual; at other times, the plots bear the imprint of the popular stage fare of the day, including heavy doses of melodrama, romance, and coincidence. All of these aspects are seen in *Oliver Twist*, particularly the violence of the melodrama and the coincidences that shuffle Oliver in and out of Mr. Brownlow's house.

Above all and ultimately much more important, however, stands the realism that Dickens uses to unite the different elements of his story. Perhaps the greatest achievement of the author in this early novel is the giant stride he makes in the realm of realism. He had not yet perfected his skills, but he knew the direction in which he was moving, and he was taking the novel with him.

"Critical Evaluation" by Bruce D. Reeves

Further Reading

Dunn, Richard J. *"Oliver Twist": Whole Heart and Soul.* New York: Macmillan, 1993. A thorough reader's companion to the story. Dunn closely examines both the literary and historical contexts of the novel, and includes five critical readings of *Oliver Twist*. A particularly useful text for students and general readers.

Ginsburg, Michal Peled. "Truth and Persuasion: The Language of Realism and of Ideology in *Oliver Twist*." *Novel: A Forum on Fiction* 20, no. 3 (Spring, 1987): 220-226. Ginsburg discusses how Dickens created a convincing narrative voice to persuade his readers that most commoners in Victorian Britain were living difficult lives because of their low socioeconomic status. He suggests that this novel was Dickens's call for action against the industrialists.

Hardy, Barbara. *Dickens and Creativity.* London: Continuum, 2008. Focuses on Dickens's creativity and imagination, which Hardy argues is at the heart of the author's self-awareness, subject matter, and narrative. *Oliver Twist* is discussed in chapters 3 and 8.

John, Juliet, ed. *Charles Dickens's "Oliver Twist": A Sourcebook.* New York: Routledge, 2006. A supplement to the novel, with discussions of the literary, biographical, social, historical, and cultural contexts of the work and with primary source documents about Poor Laws, poverty, orphans, and other relevant subjects. Features a selection of nineteenth century criticism as well as later critical essays by, among others, G. K. Chesterton, Edmund Wilson, George Orwell, and Graham Greene. Essays also look at stage and screen adaptations of *Oliver Twist*, and analyze key passages in the novel.

Jordan, John O., ed. *The Cambridge Companion to Charles Dickens.* New York: Cambridge University Press, 2001. Essays examine Dickens's life and times, analyze his novels, and discuss Dickens in relation to language, gender, family, domestic ideology, the form of the novel, illustration, theater, and film.

McMaster, Juliet. "Diabolic Trinity in *Oliver Twist.*" *Dalhousie Review* 61 (Summer, 1981): 263-277. McMaster maintains that the characters Fagin, Sikes, and Monks constitute a depraved inversion of the holy trinity, representing knowledge, power, and love. Each of these characters takes one of the aspects of the trinity and uses it in an evil way.

Parker, David. *The Doughty Street Novels: "Pickwick Papers," "Oliver Twist," "Nicholas Nickleby," "Barnaby Rudge."* New York: AMS Press, 2002. Parker, a longtime curator of the Dickens House, traces Dickens's work on four early novels during his time living on Doughty Street in London.

Paroissien, David, ed. *A Companion to Charles Dickens.* Malden, Mass.: Blackwell, 2008. Collection of essays discussing Dickens as a reformer, Christian, and journalist. Also examines Dickens and the topics gender, technology, the United States, and the uses of history.

Omensetter's Luck

Author: William H. Gass (1924-   )
First published: 1966
Type of work: Novel
Type of plot: Symbolic realism
Time of plot: 1890's
Locale: Gilean, Ohio

Principal characters:
BRACKETT OMENSETTER, a newcomer to Gilean
HENRY PIMBER, a neighbor of Omensetter
JETHRO FURBER, the pastor
ISRABESTIS TOTT, a storyteller

The Story:

Brackett Omensetter moves his pregnant wife, Lucy, and their two daughters to Gilean, a late nineteenth century town on the Ohio River. After persuading the blacksmith to hire him as an assistant, Omensetter visits Henry Pimber to rent a house. Although the gentle Pimber responds immediately to Omensetter's charismatic ease and self-confidence, he considers Omensetter "a foolish, dirty, careless man." Nevertheless, Omensetter's "carelessness" stirs him, for it seems to him to be the basis of spiritual grace. Unlike Pimber, who is clumsy and heavy-hearted, Omensetter seems buoyant: "Shed of his guilty skin, who wouldn't dance?" Pimber asks himself.

When Pimber comes by one day to collect the rent, Omensetter takes him to see a fox that fell into the well and is now trapped at the bottom. When Omensetter refuses to intervene to save the fox or do anything to put him out of his misery, Pimber shoots several rifle shots down into the well. Besides killing the fox, Pimber also wounds himself when a bullet ricochets off a stone wall and penetrates his arm. The wound becomes badly infected and leads to lockjaw, and Dr. Truxton Orcutt, the town doctor, is unable to cure him. As Pimber's life ebbs, the Reverend Jethro Furber prays for his soul, but Omensetter prepares a beet root poultice that, to everyone's amazement, saves Pimber's life.

The townspeople in Gilean, already impressed by Omensetter's manner and curious luck, now regard him with amazement. Pimber heals slowly, his gratitude toward Omensetter deepening into adulation. Having wearied of the routine of life in Gilean and of his wife's habitual demands, Pimber feels the need to possess Omensetter's grace and fluency, his "wide and happy" relation to the natural world around him. Compared with Omensetter, the normal people of Gilean seem ghostly and unreal to Pimber.

Pimber learns that Omensetter's luck cannot be learned or his way of life be imitated. Unable to establish a meaningful relationship with Omensetter, Pimber, weakened and dispirited and swept by a wave of self-pity, hangs himself from one of the topmost branches of a remote oak tree.

Because of the isolated location of the tree Pimber had chosen, the townspeople of Gilean cannot find his body. Furber, who dislikes Omensetter with fanatical intensity—even to the point of persuading himself that Omensetter might be the devil—exploits Pimber's disappearance to turn the townspeople against the newcomer. Omensetter remains oblivious to Furber's hatred and to being ostracized, just as he had been oblivious to Pimber's love.

When Furber discovers Pimber's body in the tree, Omensetter visits Furber to ask him to convince the townspeople of his innocence. Confronted by Omensetter's directness, as well as his sheer ordinariness and vulnerability, Furber's hatred vanishes. His combativeness takes on a new purpose and meaning when he learns that Omensetter's infant son, Amos, has become seriously ill. He strives to convince Omensetter to send for Dr. Orcutt, whom Omensetter distrusts. Omensetter refuses, apparently as unable to save his son as he was unwilling to rescue the fox. When Lucy begs him to bring the doctor, Omensetter can only counsel her to trust in his "luck." Having listened to the townspeople of Gilean speak so reverently about it, Omensetter has, at last, come to believe in it, an act of self-consciousness that Furber laments as a fall from grace.

The crisis of Amos's illness coincides with the removal of Pimber's body from the tree. While Lucy despairs, several of the village men argue intensely among themselves about whether Omensetter is guilty of Pimber's death. Orcutt arrives at Omensetter's house in time to apply the force of common sense and logic to the argument, in favor of Omensetter's innocence, and thus saves his life. Nevertheless, he feels he has arrived too late to save Amos. While Orcutt reasons with the men, Furber improvises mad, pointless, and obscene limericks.

Amos's illness lifts by the following February, and the Omensetters move down river. Amos "lingered on alive, an outcome altogether outside science." Omensetter's luck remains a legend on the Ohio River for quite a while, "perhaps forever." With Omensetter and Furber gone, equilibrium and drab normalcy return to Gilean, as symbolized in the person of the well-balanced, innocuous new minister, Mr. Huffley.

Critical Evaluation:

Although Bracket Omensetter appears to be the protagonist of *Omensetter's Luck*, he functions principally as the catalyst who forces the three articulate character-narrators—Henry Pimber, Israbestis Tott, and Jethro Furber—to confront their dissatisfactions, limitations, and perceptions. In telling contrast with their human foibles, Omensetter is described in natural terms as "a wide and happy man [who] could whistle like the cardinal whistles in the deep snow, or whirr like the shy 'white rising from its cover, or be the lark a-chuckle at the sky.'" By creating in Omensetter a kind of anthropomorphic nature, William H. Gass sought to examine the painful definitions of the human condition.

Tott, who introduces the novel, looks back at the pivotal events. His impressionistic vision, somewhat blurred and unsynchronized by age, has been likened to Benjy's dreamlike impressions that introduce William Faulkner's *The Sound and the Fury* (1929). The significant details that constitute a part of Tott's miscellaneous stream of meditations serve as intimations that later give the more fully narrated events of the story a sense of familiarity and importance. In contrast to the other character-narrators, Tott remains detached from Omensetter, neither loving him, as Pimber does, nor hating him, as Furber does. Gass uses Tott's remoteness from Omensetter to delineate his social irrelevance and remoteness from life.

Pimber, whose admiration and love for Omensetter drive him to suicide, is characterized as weak, impressionable, and self-conscious. Omensetter's simple laughter at their first meeting touches Pimber profoundly. "Sweetly merciful God, Henry wondered, sweetly merciful God, what has struck me?" Thereafter, his sensitivity to Omensetter's vitality and "luck" brings home to him his own dissatisfactions and frailties. For him, the human condition signifies ceaseless ineptitude, inferiority, and humiliation, which were the primary colors of his boyhood and of his marriage to Lucy Pimber. Both his wife's physical makeup and her sexual needs repel Pimber, as do the human weaknesses and needs of the townspeople of Gilean. Like the other characters of *Omensetter's Luck*, he interprets Omensetter's power to validate his own preoccupations.

Yearning for escape, Pimber sees Omensetter as the symbol of that escape, the refuge of nature. To Pimber, Omensetter, who "always seemed inhuman as a tree," represents the chance of "losing Henry Pimber" for something larger, richer, and undefined. Yet when Pimber attempts to follow Omensetter, to join him on a remote, windswept, hillside, he cannot. The desolation of nature, which so attracted him, is inhospitable to him. Nature becomes "noise," although Omensetter shrugs happily and asks if he does not love it. Just as Pimber had met failure in his marriage and in childhood, he fails once again when he makes the even harder attempt to overcome the familiar comforts of the self, however wearisome: "No, Henry thought, I don't love the noise; the wind will wash my wits out."

Pimber's dilemma, the dilemma of all human beings, is the conflict between the irresistible need to try to avoid the confines of the human condition and the immovable resistance of the mind to the emptiness of nature. This brings Pimber to the one act open to him. In a gesture ironically combining self-denial and self-aggrandizement, Pimber hangs himself from the highest branch of the tallest oak tree, thus narcissistically exhibiting himself to all and to no one, to admire and, paradoxically, to pity.

Earlier, while meditating on Omensetter's relation to Gilean, Pimber reflects with the following words: "Everybody but the preacher stole from him. Furber merely hated." Furber, modeled on the type of hypocritical clergyman who has flourished in English literature since Geoffrey Chaucer's *Canterbury Tales* (1387-1400), hates Omensetter for reasons that partly correspond to Pimber's for loving him: Whereas Omensetter's natural grace provokes Furber's furious envy, his abundant, sensuous life undermines Furber's torturous asceticism. Unlike Pimber, however, Furber quickly retreats from Omensetter—much as he has retreated into the church, into the remote outpost of Gilean, into the confines of his own small garden, and, finally, into the tricks and traps of language. Furber's withdrawal from nature and from society relegates Omensetter to the margins of the novel, but the mercurial, cultured monologues with which he explains his withdrawal make Furber the dominant force in *Omensetter's Luck*. All subsequent narrators in Gass's fiction, including the celebrated shorter fiction of *In the Heart of the Heart of the Country* (1966) and *The Tunnel* (1995), are to some degree, reworkings of Furber.

Furber's few direct confrontations with the implacable Omensetter upset him. When, upon Furber's invitation, Omensetter attends church service, Furber is both dazzled and bewildered by his presence—a reaction that echoes that of Pimber when Omensetter arrived on his doorstep. Like Pimber, who fantasizes that Omensetter can offer him salvation, Furber grasps at the absurd notion that Omensetter rep-

resents a supernatural menace and in his charged imagination, the visitor becomes a demon who must be destroyed. In casting Omensetter as personified nature, however, Gass implies that Furber is fighting an invisible foe, a component of his own making.

Just as Furber had almost succeeded in destroying Omensetter—and, at the same time, of immuring himself within the maze of his own bizarre fictions—Omensetter arrives at his door. This final, dead-of-night confrontation is devastating for Furber, for his deviousness is no match for Omensetter's terrible and mysterious innocence. In a dialogue resonant with biblical nuances that underscore his transcendence, Omensetter compels the obstinate Furber to aid him in fending off accusations that he has murdered Pimber. Daunted by Omensetter's inscrutability, by the very intractability of the enigma he has sought both to evade and destroy, Furber meekly agrees. Ironically, although Furber's surrender constitutes intellectual defeat, perhaps even a kind of death, the fruit of his defeat sustains him and, in a final contrast to Pimber, enables him to regenerate human society. Finding himself, at the novel's end, with money Omensetter had used to pay Pimber his last rent, Furber places it in the church's offertory envelope in what Arthur Saltzman has described as "his last, and only sincere, religious gesture."

Michael Scott Joseph

Further Reading

Ammon, Theodore G., ed. *Conversations with William H. Gass*. Jackson: University Press of Mississippi, 2003. A collection of interviews with Gass, in which the author discusses his ideas about writing and the philosophical ideas that have influenced his work. Includes a debate with John Gardner, in which the two writers express their differences about the art of fiction writing.

Brans, Jo. *Listen to the Voices: Conversations with Contemporary Writers*. Dallas, Tex.: Southern Methodist University Press, 1988. Includes an interview with the author that provides interesting anecdotes about the composition of *Omensetter's Luck*.

Hix, H. L. *Understanding William H. Gass*. Columbia: University of South Carolina Press, 2002. Hix examines similarities between Gass's fiction and nonfiction works and explores the ethical, metaphysical, and psychological themes in four novels and other writings. Chapter 2 is devoted to an analysis of *Omensetter's Luck*.

Holloway, Watson. *William Gass*. Boston: Twayne, 1990. A comprehensive study of Gass that includes a chapter devoted to the major themes in *Omensetter's Luck*.

Hove, Thomas B. "William H. Gass." In *Postmodernism: The Key Figures*, edited by Hans Bertens and Joseph Natoli. Malden, Mass.: Blackwell, 2002. This examination of postmodernism not only includes authors, like Gass, but screenwriters, directors, actors, visual artists, and philosophers. The essay on Gass summarizes his work, and the book places him within a larger cultural context.

McCaffery, Larry. *The Metafictional Muse: The Works of Robert Coover, Donald Barthelme, and William H. Gass.* Pittsburgh, Pa.: University of Pittsburgh Press, 1982. Includes a chapter on Gass that examines his essays, short stories, and novels, including *Omensetter's Luck*. The au-

thor places Gass's work in the context of a "contemporary metasensibility."

Saltzman, Arthur M. *The Fiction of William Gass: The Consolation of Language.* Carbondale: Southern Illinois University Press, 1986. In the chapter on *Omensetter's Luck*, Saltzman analyzes the works of Gass with reference to the author's philosophical beliefs about the insularity of fiction.

Tanner, Tony. *Scenes of Nature, Signs of Men.* New York: Cambridge University Press, 1987. An overview of twenty-five years of American fiction. Includes a skillful summary of *Omensetter's Luck*.

Omeros

Author: Derek Walcott (1930-   )
First published: 1990
Type of work: Poetry
Type of plot: Epic
Time of plot: Seventeenth century and late twentieth century
Locale: St. Lucia, West Indies; Africa

Principal characters:
OMEROS, the Homeric narrator of the poem
ACHILLE, a poor fisherman
HECTOR, a taxicab driver and former fisherman, rival of Achille for Helen's affections
HELEN, a beautiful island woman
PHILOCTETE, a fisherman disabled by a festering leg wound
DENNIS PLUNKETT, a retired major in the British army turned St. Lucia émigré pig farmer
MAUD PLUNKETT, his Irish-born wife, who cultivates orchids commercially
MA KILMAN, a local bar owner and a healer

The Poem:

Hector has resigned his traditional fisherman's life to become a taxicab driver. This allows him to afford the small gifts he gives to Helen, the most beautiful woman on St. Lucia. Helen, in turn, reciprocates with sexual favors. This arrangement exacerbates the jealousy of Achille, a fisherman who also seeks Helen's attentions. Hector's cab races at breakneck speed through the quiet streets of the island. He specializes in driving wealthy tourists to and from the local airport, but his reckless driving will ultimately bring about his death. He risks life and limb, his own as well as those of his passengers and of anyone who happens to be in the way of his racing cab.

The life of Achille, by contrast, seems more tranquil. It is certainly more traditional, but his occupation of fisherman is in its way no less dangerous than that of Hector. Undertows, current shifts, and unexpected tides can easily carry Achille

in unexpected directions, figuratively and literally. He sets off on a journey, following the tides with no known destination, after he loses Helen. From this point on, he places his faith in his *cacique*, his hollowed-out boat. He paints "In God We Troust" on its side. When he learns of his spelling error, Achille declares that it is not an error but rather God's way of spelling "trust." Achille departs with perfect faith in God, in fate, and in the way things have eventuated. He follows the sea-swift, or hirondelle, a swallow-like bird that flies straight into a storm. As a result, Achille heads to Africa.

Meanwhile, another fisherman, Philoctete, receives a thigh wound from a rusty anchor. The wound festers, refuses to heal, and renders him unable to practice his trade effectively. Philoctete is abandoned by his fellow fishermen and awaits a cure, which is ultimately provided by Ma Kilman. Until he is healed, he poses for pictures with tourists, accepting the coins they give him with a broad smile while always suffering from his wound.

Achille reaches Africa. He meets Afolabe, whom Achille instinctively recognizes as his ancestral father. Achille seems to have regressed in time and is present when enemy warriors stage a surprise raid and capture villagers to be transported as slaves to America. His past and present have merged.

The Plunketts, a British couple, have lived in St. Lucia since economic hardship after World War II forced them to emigrate from England. Maud, a commercial orchid grower, recalls the Ireland of her childhood wistfully, knowing it is unlikely that she will ever return. Dennis, a major in the British army during the war, has adopted St. Lucia for its benign climate and inexpensive way of life. He has become a pig farmer, and his relations with the native St. Lucians are generally civil and courteous but always restrained.

Critical Evaluation:

Like many Caribbean islanders, Derek Walcott is able to see history prismatically. His European education allows him to see the daily life of his fellow St. Lucians in epic terms that resemble those of Homer's *Iliad* and *Odyssey* or the tale of Philoctetes, best known through Sophocles' play *Philoktētēs* (409 B.C.E.; *Philoctetes*, 1729). The Franco-Antillean forms "Achille" and "Philoctete" substitute for "Achilles" and "Philoctetes," but such minor accidental adjustments pale beside the timeless human realities of unobtainable love and unhealed wounds. *Omeros* moves simultaneously through several time periods and tells several stories concurrently. On the simplest level, the narrative voice of the Seven Seas (Omeros) presents portraits of the fishermen Achille, Hector, and Philoctete. As in Homer's *Iliad* (c. 750 B.C.E.; English translation, 1611), Achille and Hector contend for Helen, the island beauty. Helen's beauty is central to the poem, and the golden yellow dress she wears, a gift of Ma Kilman, makes Helen resemble a monarch butterfly.

The unhealed wound of Philoctete resembles that of Philoctetes, the Greek warrior to whom the dying Heracles willed his bow and arrows. It was because Philoctetes unknowingly brought that bow into the sacred precincts of Artemis that a serpent gave him a wound that would not heal. Philoctete's plight also resembles that of Amfortas, one of the chief knights of the arthurian quest for the Holy Grail. It is the wound of humanity itself, the wound in Jesus Christ's side. It is the wound that one cures only through an inner source such as the native medicine of Ma Kilman. Philoctete received his wound from a rusty anchor, and his fellow fishermen have left him behind on St. Lucia, just as the Greeks abandoned Philoctetes on the island of Lemnos.

One might read the Greek myth as a commentary on intolerance and expediency. The Greeks rescue Philoctetes only when they realize that they require the bow and arrows of Heracles that Philoctetes inherited. They tolerate the odor of his wound only because they have to do so to defeat the Trojans. The St. Lucians tolerate but isolate Philoctete, and his fate is to accept handouts from the tourist armies that descend upon the island.

Ma Kilman resembles the witch Circe from Homer's *Odyssey* (c. 725 B.C.E.; English translation, 1614) insofar as she uses transforming magic. Circe turns men into swine. Ma Kilman kills though the intoxicants she sells at her bar, but she also transforms Helen into a monarch butterfly through the gift of a castoff yellow dress and turns Philoctete back into a fisherman through her herbal magic. Ma is also a native mother who saves her young, yet her transformation of Helen is a fatal intoxicant for Hector. He dies just outside his city, as did his Homeric namesake.

Walcott's poem also alludes to *Maud* (1855), a poem by Alfred, Lord Tennyson. One of the subsections of Tennyson's work is titled "Come into the Garden, Maud," and orchid farming is Maud Plunkett's profession. The male narrator of *Maud* describes his emotions as they evolve through his father's death; his family's ruin as contrived by the lord of the Hall; his forbidden love for the old lord's daughter, Maud; and his successful courtship and flight abroad with her. This is, on one level, the love story of English-born Dennis Plunkett, his Irish-born wife, and their emigration to St. Lucia. Dennis is a military officer turned pig farmer, an English version of Homer's Eumaeus, while Maud is an orchid grower trying to forget her homeland, much as do the Lotus-eaters of Homer or Tennyson.

The ships that invade St. Lucia are those of American and European cruise lines, not those of the Greeks, but they bring invading armies nonetheless. Some islanders, such as Hector, the fisherman turned taxi driver, are willing to serve them.

The prevailing meter of *Omeros* resembles Dante's *terza rima*, three-line stanzas in *aba* form that Dante used in *La divina commedia* (c. 1320, 3 volumes; *The Divine Comedy*, 1802). Walcott incorporates this meter to pay tribute to the epic poet, and he modifies it to assert his own powers of innovation. *Omeros* is a vernacular Caribbean epic. Likewise, Dante's innovation was his use of vernacular Italian rather than Latin or Provençal. It was a native meter and a native tongue. Walcott combines St. Lucian patois with an innovative Italian verse form.

Robert J. Forman

Further Reading

Bloom, Harold, ed. *Derek Walcott*. New York: Chelsea House, 2003. Examines Walcott's major works through full-length critical essays by various critics. Includes a short biography of Walcott, a chronology of his life, and an introduction by Bloom.

Hamner, Robert D., ed. *Critical Perspectives on Derek Walcott*. Washington, D.C.: Three Continents Press, 1997. Collection of essays by noted critics. Chronology, essays, and selected bibliography.

Ismond, Patricia. *Abandoning Dead Metaphors: The Caribbean Phase of Derek Walcott's Poetry*. Kingston, Jamaica: University of West Indies Press, 2002. Closely examines Walcott's Caribbean poetry, particularly his use of metaphor and his relationship to the Western tradition of literature. Considers Walcott's engagement with the landscape, culture, and society of the Caribbean region.

King, Bruce. *Derek Walcott: A Caribbean Life*. New York: Oxford University Press, 2000. The first authorized literary biography of Walcott; analyzes his life through his works.

Thieme, John. *Derek Walcott*. New York: Manchester University Press, 1999. A comprehensive study of Walcott's works from their beginnings in the 1940's through the 1990's.

Walcott, Derek. *Conversations with Derek Walcott*. Edited by William Baer. Jackson: University Press of Mississippi, 1996. In these collected interviews, Walcott discusses the art of poetry, the status of contemporary poetry and drama, his founding of the Trinidad Theatre Workshop, and his perspectives on several writers.

Omoo
A Narrative of Adventures in the South Seas

Author: Herman Melville (1819-1891)
First published: 1847
Type of work: Novel
Type of plot: Adventure
Time of plot: Early 1840's
Locale: Tahiti and the South Seas

Principal characters:
HERMAN MELVILLE, an American sailor
DOCTOR LONG GHOST, his companion in his adventures
CAPTAIN BOB, a jovial Tahitian jailer

The Story:

Rescued from the island of Typee by the crew of a British whaler, Herman Melville agrees to stay on the ship as a deckhand until it reaches the next port, where he is to be placed ashore. The *Julia*, however, is not a well-managed vessel. Soon after Melville joins it, several of the men make an attempt to desert. These unfortunates are recovered quickly, however, by the timely aid of the islanders and the crew of a French man-of-war.

In the weeks of cruising that followed this adventure, Melville, relieved from duty because of a lameness in his leg, spends his time playing chess with the ship's doctor and reading the doctor's books. These are not, however, weeks of pleasure. During this time, two of the men in the forecastle die, and the entire crew lives under the most abominable conditions. The rat-infested, rotten old ship should have been condemned years before. Finally, when the captain himself falls ill, the ship changes its course to Tahiti, the nearest island.

The crew convince themselves that when the captain leaves the ship, they will no longer be bound by the agreements they had signed. They intend to leave the ship when it arrives in the harbor at Papeetee. The captain attempts to prevent their desertion by keeping the ship under way just outside the harbor while he goes ashore in a small boat. Only Doctor Long Ghost's influence prevents the men from disregarding orders and taking the vessel into the harbor to anchor it. The crew does, however, protest their treatment in a letter sent to the British consul ashore by means of the black cook. The acting consul in Papeetee and the captain of the *Julia* are old acquaintances, and the official's only action is to inform the men they will have to stay with the ship and cruise for three months under the command of the first mate. The captain himself will remain in Tahiti. After a Mauri harpooner attempts to wreck the ship, the drunken mate decides to take the whaler into the harbor, regardless of the consequences.

In Papeetee, the acting consul has the men, including Melville and Doctor Long Ghost, imprisoned on a French frigate. After five days aboard the French ship, they are removed and are once more given an opportunity to return to their ship. When they refuse, the mutineers are taken into custody by a Tahitian native called Captain Bob, who takes them to an oval-shaped thatched house, which is to be their jail.

There they are confined in stocks, two timbers about twenty feet long, serving to secure all the prisoners. Each morning, the jailer comes to free the men and supervise their baths in a neighboring stream. The islanders, in return for hard ship's biscuit from the *Julia*, feed the men baked bread-fruit and Indian turnips. Sometimes the kindly jailer leads the men to his orange grove, where they gather fruit for their meals. This fruit diet is precisely what they need to regain the health they had lost while eating sea rations of salt pork and biscuit.

The prisoners in the thatched hut are in sight of Broom Road, the island's chief thoroughfare. Since the prisoners are easily accessible, the idle, inquisitive Tahitians are constantly visiting, and the prisoners do not lack for company. Within a few days, their jailer frees the sailors from the stocks during the daytime, except when white men are in the vicinity. Once this leniency is granted, the men roam the neighborhood to take advantage of the local hospitality. Doctor Long Ghost always carries salt with him, in case he finds some food to flavor.

When the consul sends a doctor to look at the prisoners, all the sailors pretend to be sick. Shortly after the doctor has made his examinations and departs, a native boy appears with a basket of medicines. The sailors discard the powders and pills, but eagerly drink the contents of all the bottles which smell the least bit alcoholic.

British missionaries on the island take no notice of the sailors from the *Julia* other than sending them a handful of tracts. Three French priests, however, come to see the men. The natives, it seems, look upon the priests as magicians, and so they have been able to make only a few converts among the islanders. The priests are popular with the sailors because they give freshly baked wheat bread and liquor to the prisoners. Three weeks after arriving in the port of Papeetee, the captain of the *Julia* sails away with a new crew recruited from beachcombers idling about the island. After his departure, the mutineers are no longer confined to their jail but continue to live there because the building is as convenient as any other thatched dwelling in the neighborhood. They exist by foraging the surrounding country and by smuggling provisions from visiting ships with the aid of the sailors aboard.

Melville finds this life not unpleasant at first, but after a time, he grows bored. He even goes to a native church to hear the missionary preach. The theme of the sermon is that all white men except the British are bad and so are the natives, unless they begin to contribute more baskets of food to the missionary's larder. Melville does not go to the missionary church again.

Several weeks after the *Julia* had sailed, Melville meets two white men who inform him that a plantation on a neighboring island is in need of laborers. Melville and Doctor Long Ghost, introduced to the planters as Peter and Paul, are immediately hired. One moonlit night, the pair boards the boat belonging to their employers. They leave their former shipmates without ceremony, lest the authorities prevent their departure.

The planters live by themselves in an inland valley on the mosquito-infested island of Imeeo. The prospect of plying a hoe in the heat of the day amid swarms of insects does not appeal to the two sailors, and so at noon of the first day in the fields, Doctor Long Ghost pretends illness. He and Melville agree to do as little work as possible. After a few days, they give up farming for good and leave on foot to Tamai, an inland village unspoiled by missionaries or other white men. There they see a dance by native girls, a rite that has been banned as pagan by the missionaries on the island. A day or two later, while the two white men are considering settling permanently at Tamai, the natives force them to flee, for a reason they were never able to discover.

The next adventure they contemplate is an audience with the queen of Tahiti. Traveling by easy stages from one village to the next on foot or by canoe, they make their way to Partoowye, where the island queen has her residence. They meet a runaway ship's carpenter who has settled there and who keeps busy building boxes and cabinets for the natives. From him, they learn that a whaler is in the local harbor. When they talk to the crew of the vessel, however, they are told that it is not a good ship on which to sail, and they give up all thought of shipping away from the islands aboard the whaler.

After five weeks in the village, Doctor Long Ghost and Melville finally obtain admittance to the queen through the good offices of a Marquesan attendant at her court. When they come into the queen's presence, she is eating, and she waves them out of her palace in high-handed fashion, at the same time reprimanding their guide. Disappointed by their reception at court, the two travelers again decide to go to sea. They make friends with the third mate of the whaler, which is still in the harbor. The mate reassures them concerning conditions aboard the ship. The other sailors, knowing the ship cannot sail away from the pleasant islands without more men in the crew, had deliberately lied.

Having confidence in the mate, Doctor Long Ghost and Melville then approach the captain and ask to sign on as members of the crew. The captain, however, will not accept Doctor Long Ghost as a deckhand or as the ship's doctor. Reluctantly, Melville ships out alone on the voyage that will take him to the coast of Japan and, he hopes, eventually home.

Critical Evaluation:

In the language of the Marquesan islanders, *omoo* signifies a rover, one who travels from island to island among the island groups of Polynesia. These islands provide the setting for Herman Melville's first two works. In Melville's day, these islands were still fairly unknown except to missionaries and whalers, and since the latter ships tended to follow known courses through the region, it was still possible to come in contact with islands that had rarely been visited by European or American peoples.

A sequel to Melville's popular first travel novel, *Typee: A Peep at Polynesian Life* (1846), *Omoo* continues the story of Melville's experiences in the region. The question of how factual a reader should consider these experiences has been much debated since the book was first published in 1847. Reviewers objected to various aspects of Melville's first two books, declaring they must be fiction. Melville responded that he had observed "a strict adherence to facts." Research in the twentieth century showed that he had embellished his true experiences—that he had lived one month among the Typee people of Nukuheva, for instance, rather than four as he had claimed. As a result, readers must consider both of these books novels, in which Melville has felt free to alter the details of his experience to deliver a better story.

Omoo stands out among Melville's novels as his most reckless and carefree. Perhaps, for an author associated with darkness, depths of thought, and brooding about the nature of evil, it is Melville at his happiest as well. Like *Typee*, it contains some complaints about missionary activity in Tahiti, but *Omoo* is mostly a light and comical travelogue, as Melville and his shipboard companion, Doctor Long Ghost, tour and have adventures on Tahiti and neighboring islands. This free spiritedness implies a Melville who has escaped his Puritan demons, a Melville whose narrator can give himself over to pleasure without guilt and to desire without comeuppance. Unlike Melville's other books, there is no dark side to pleasure in *Omoo*, and Melville and Doctor Long Ghost laze around, a couple of beachcombers, throughout much of the novel, entertaining themselves with various escapades.

Doctor Long Ghost is, like Melville himself was, well read. In the first part of the novel the two play chess and quote poetry from memory to each other aboard their ship, the *Julia*. The two also regale each other with tales of their travels. It was this type of characterization to which British reviewers most objected at the time of *Omoo*'s publication; they argued that no common seaman would have had the breeding to be exposed to literature and the finer pleasures of life. This, Melville countered, was a demonstration of America's democratic, classless society, versus England's more rigid class system. The nineteenth century United States was still new to the world in these respects. In Melville's day, public education allowed the working class to be educated, and learning did not mean that one who had it considered physical labor demeaning.

Democracy is an issue in *Omoo*. Protesting various injustices and the questionable seaworthiness of their captain and ship, several members of the *Julia*'s crew engage in a democratic resistance. Each participant signs the declaration of rebellion, so that no leader may be singled out, with the narrator authoring the document, in effect becoming their Thomas Jefferson. The mutineers are locked up once ashore and for a moment it seems as if all the forces that would seek to restrain American-style democracy are arraigned against them: "four or five Europeans," figures of decadent authority, as well as the ancient ship's articles, "a discolored, musty, bilious affair," are pressed into service far past the age when they might have been relevant. These are more symbols of the forces that once held democracy in check than they are the forces themselves. When the men are not intimidated by them, they are simply allowed to escape by the native warden, Captain Bob.

In its illustration of the possibilities of democratic organization, then, *Omoo* stands out among Melville's work. Melville is more often obsessed with describing the dangers to democracy in his works. In *Moby Dick* (1851), Captain Ahab destroys the possibility of democratic organization among the multicultural crew of the *Pequod* by ruling them with an iron hand and subjecting the desires of all of his crew to his monomaniacal quest to hunt the white whale. Once at sea, there is nothing that can restrain the tyrannical authority of the captain, and dictatorial sea captains are seen as well in *Typee* and *Redburn: His First Voyage* (1849). A mutiny fails to achieve its desired end in *Moby Dick*'s "Town-Ho's Story," and *Billy Budd, Foretopman* (1924) illustrates the typical severity of justice at sea.

Omoo, one of Melville's most neglected works, reveals much about the young Melville and provides interesting commentaries when viewed in the context of the author's work as a whole. The book provides evidence of his commitment to the American project. Melville abandoned one ship and helped lead a mutiny on another; he was often highly critical of Western influence, in the form of missionaries and armed intrusions, in the South Seas, but he never imagined a life apart from the American ideal. Melville's critique of American abuses of democracy in later works should be viewed as expressions of patriotism, for Melville is an author who examines democracy seriously.

"Critical Evaluation" by Ted Pelton

Further Reading

Anderson, Charles Roberts. *Melville in the South Seas*. 1939. New ed. New York: Columbia University Press, 1967. A reliable account of Melville's South Seas voyages, featuring comparisons between the facts of Melville's experience and the fictions of *Moby Dick*, *Typee*, and *Omoo*.

Delbanco, Andrew. *Melville: His World and Work*. New York: Knopf, 2005. Delbanco's critically acclaimed biography places Melville in his time, with discussion about the debate over slavery and details of life in 1840's New York. Delbanco also discusses the significance of Melville's works at the time they were published and their reception into the twenty-first century.

Kelley, Wyn. "'Making Literary Use of the Story': *Typee* and *Omoo*." In *Herman Melville: An Introduction*. Malden, Mass.: Blackwell, 2008. Chronicles Melville's development as a writer, providing analyses of his works.

_____, ed. *A Companion to Herman Melville*. Malden, Mass.: Blackwell, 2006. Collection of thirty-five original essays aimed at twenty-first century readers of Melville's works. Includes discussions of Melville's travels; Melville and religion, slavery, and gender; and the Melville revival. Features the essay "The Motive for Metaphor: *Typee*, *Omoo*, and *Mardi*" by Geoffrey Sanborn.

Lawrence, D. H. *Studies in Classic American Literature*. 1923. New ed. Edited by Ezra Greenspan, Lindeth Vasey, and John Worthen. New York: Cambridge University Press, 2003. Lawrence was important for the reevaluation of Melville in the 1920's. This classic work contains essays, many revised, on American literature, including Melville's novels *Omoo* and *Typee*.

Melville, Herman. *"Omoo": A Narrative of Adventures in the South Seas*. 1968. New ed. Edited by Harrison Hayford, Hershel Parker, and G. Thomas Tanselle. Evanston, Ill.: Northwestern University Press, 1999. Updated edition of a multivolume work. Features an excellent, concise note that places the novel in the context of Melville's career.

Rogin, Michael Paul. *Subversive Genealogy: The Politics and Art of Herman Melville*. Berkeley: University of California Press, 1985. Incisive psychological and Marxist reading of Melville's life and work, arguing that he was one of the leading thinkers of his age. The book's reading of Melville's family's place in the historical context of the 1840's is unparalleled.

Rollyson, Carl E., and Lisa Paddock. *Herman Melville A to Z: The Essential Reference to His Life and Work*. New York: Checkmark Books, 2001. Comprehensive coverage of Melville's life, works, and times. The 675 detailed entries examine the characters, settings, allusions, and references in his fiction, his friends and associates, and the critics and scholars who have studied his work.

On Heroes, Hero-Worship, and the Heroic in History

Author: Thomas Carlyle (1795-1881)
First published: 1841
Type of work: Social criticism

Thomas Carlyle's *On Heroes, Hero-Worship, and the Heroic in History* remains one of the best repositories in English of the development in late Romanticism called heroic vitalism. The book, a series of six lectures that Carlyle delivered to London audiences in 1840, represents not so much soundly based ideas about the making of history as it does Carlyle's view of how the world would be if powerful and inspired people were to have the power he thought they deserved. The book thus became England's contribution to the nineteenth century cult of the "great man," a dream that was most seductively attractive to intellectuals forced to put their ideas in the marketplace with all the other merchants, but closed off from the real power that was being exercised in the newly industrialized world by economic entrepreneurs.

This work has received mixed reviews from readers and critics. Some consider it inferior; even Carlyle made disparaging remarks about it in his later years. Others, however, find in the volume a clear sense of the values that Carlyle preached consistently in his writings from his earliest sustained social analysis, *Sartor Resartus* (1833-1834), to his later historical writings on Oliver Cromwell and Frederick the Great.

Like most nineteenth century historians and philosophers, Carlyle promotes the notion that progress is good and inevitable; unlike many of his contemporaries, however, he does not believe that the passage of time in and of itself assures progress. Only when persons of heroic temperament step forward to lead the masses can true progress for society occur. The persons featured in *On Heroes, Hero-Worship, and the Heroic in History* were just such people; their actions, and their willingness to live in accordance with the vision of society that motivated them, changed history for the better. Carlyle finds no one around him acting in a way to set his own age right; given to commercialism and self-gratification, the people of nineteenth century Europe lack the will or the leadership to make something worthwhile of their lives. If his work is not totally successful in conveying a portrait of heroism good for all times, it does succeed in showing Carlyle's disenchantment with the nineteenth century and its lack of heroes.

Carlyle's basic idea is that all history is the making of great persons, gifted with supreme power of vision or action. It thus becomes one's duty to "worship Heroes."

> We all of us reverence and must ever reverence Great Men: this is, to me, the living rock amid all the rushings-down whatsoever; the one fixed point in modern revolutionary history, otherwise as if bottomless and shoreless.

In the world of onrushing liberalism and industrialism, with the memory of God ever dimming through the growth of science and skepticism, Carlyle needs a faith and develops one based on the worship of great men.

This faith, dubious enough under restrictions of law and order, not to mention the existence of great women, becomes even more dubious as handled by Carlyle. As the six lectures progress, he moves from myth to history with no clear distinction. He offers leaders of religious movements, great poets, and military conquerors as equally great or heroic. Hero worship not only should be devout; it actually was. In Carlyle's estimation, love of God is virtually identical with loyalty to a leader. Despite his scorn for business activity and its operators, Carlyle's heroes are all men of practical intelligence. He values the same kind of industriousness, resoluteness, and obvious sincerity that could serve to build economic as well as political or clerical empires.

The performance of heroism depends on the interaction of the person with the great social forces of the age; heroes cannot change the course of history alone. In this sense, Carlyle disagrees with his intellectual successor, Friedrich Nietzsche, who argues that the hero can, by sheer force of will, determine the course of events in his or her own life and in society. Carlyle also is at odds with his contemporary Karl Marx, whose view of the inevitability of the "march of history" leaves no room for individuals to alter the inexorable course of human events.

Carlyle believes that heroes must use their power in the service of others; all of his heroes are in some fashion selfless. Carlyle expands the notion of heroism to include those who not only lead but also serve. Every person is capable of being heroic; hero-worship, the act of recognizing and willingly obeying those who are given the gift to lead, can make heroes of ordinary people. Such a concept may be unacceptable to those who believe in egalitarian societies; for Carlyle, however, the balance of selfless leaders and willing followers was essential to the attainment of the good society.

Carlyle begins his historical survey with the hero as prophet. Muhammad made Islam a historical force through the sword, but history sustained his vision and rewarded him; hence, he is a hero in Carlyle's pantheon. The prophet as hero is a terrifying figure of a bygone age; more in character with the spirit of the time is the poet as hero. After discussing poetry as a romantic vision that makes the poet the spiritual kinsman of the prophet, Carlyle treats Dante's *La divina commedia* (c. 1320; *The Divine Comedy*, 1802) as the poem of an age of faith. He calls it "genuine song," but it is the Christian message that Carlyle truly values: The literary work is an allegory of the invisible idea. As Dante gave "Faith, or a soul," so William Shakespeare gave "Practice, or body." Poet-heroes are born, not made; thus, Carlyle labels Shakespeare a romantic visionary who can be adored, not analyzed. Shakespeare must have suffered heroically himself; otherwise he could not have created Hamlet or Macbeth.

The hero as priest is a spiritual captain, unlike the prophet, who was a spiritual king. Martin Luther and John Knox are Carlyle's subjects—although they were primarily reformers, they become more priestlike than the priests. As are all of Carlyle's heroes, they are visionaries who saw the truth and led their followers to battle for it. (Carlyle abounds in military metaphor, whether he writes of peace or war.) Great religious leaders battle idolatry: Idolatry is symbolic, but it is insincere symbolism and therefore must be destroyed. Carlyle notes that the significant visionary is the person who combats delusion and outworn convention. Every hero, every image breaker, comes to a new sense of reality and brings it to the world. A hero must "stand upon things, not upon the shadow of things."

Protestantism dwindled into factions in Germany, according to Carlyle, but in Scotland, with John Knox, Lutherism found its true home. (Here, and later with James Boswell and Robert Burns, the Scottish Carlyle shows a special fondness for his countrymen who found fame and success.) Some may censure Puritanism, but it is fervent faith that brought democracy to England, through Oliver Cromwell, and colonized much of America as well. Knox was intolerant and despotic, but he was a zealot and therefore a hero for Carlyle, who distinguishes between good and bad tyrannies with reasons he never discusses.

The heroes who are closest to Carlyle's audience were Samuel Johnson, Jean-Jacques Rousseau, and Burns. As the priests are less than the prophets, so the heroic men of letters are less than the poets. In Carlyle's opinion, Johann Wolfgang von Goethe is the only heroic poet of the preceding century. Johnson, Rousseau, and Burns were seekers rather than "bringers" of truth. Carlyle delivers a famous paean of praise for learning and publishing, from the Bible to the newspaper. All ideas are first books; then they become institutions and empires. The eighteenth century was a skeptical age, disbelieving, and therefore unheroic and insincere. Carlyle's three heroes in this section had to struggle against both the climate of opinion and poverty, as all real visionaries should. Boswell picked his hero well, for Johnson's gospel of moral prudence and practical sense was necessary in an age of cant.

Carlyle was more doubtful about Rousseau. Too complex and introspective to be favored by Carlyle, and French as well, Rousseau stands as an ambiguous hero whom Carlyle acclaims as a zealot but blames for the fanaticism of the French Revolution. Carlyle believes that Rousseau venerated the "savage" and thus abetted the French lapse into savagery. Burns is a much more engaging figure (and Scottish as well). Carlyle contradicts himself, however, by admitting that Burns's career was virtually ruined by the lionizing paid him by his hero worshipers in Edinburgh.

The last heroism for Carlyle is kingship—the leadership of people in war and politics. Interestingly, the leaders he specifically presents are not revolutionary heroes, but antirevolutionaries. Heroes seek order, and order, to Carlyle, is discipline and peace, even at the cost of liberty and variety.

Napoleon came to equate himself with France, and so fulfilled his ego at the cost of his nation. Carlyle respects Napoleon's practical intelligence, which enabled him to seize the salient factor in a situation and make fools of Europe's conventional generals and statesmen.

Throughout his effusive presentation, Carlyle never analyzes, but exhorts, praises, and condemns. He admires the movers and shakers of the earth; his praise of Dante and Shakespeare is perfunctory compared with his veneration of Cromwell, who could barely speak coherently, but could and did act eloquently. Anti-intellectualism, veneration of power, and love of enthusiasm as an end in itself are everywhere in this work.

Revised by Laurence W. Mazzeno

Further Reading

Goldberg, Michael K., Joel J. Brattin, and Mark Engel, eds. *On Heroes, Hero-Worship, and the Heroic in History.* Berkeley: University of California Press, 1993. Provides an extensive introduction to Carlyle's text. More than 170 pages of notes further explain and interpret the work.

LaValley, Albert J. *Carlyle and the Idea of the Modern: Studies in Carlyle's Prophetic Literature and Its Relation to Blake, Nietzsche, Marx, and Others.* New Haven, Conn.: Yale University Press, 1968. Two chapters place Carlyle's ideas relating to the hero within the historical development of the concept of the prophetic hero. Contains a useful annotated bibliography.

Morrow, John. *Thomas Carlyle.* New York: Hambledon Continuum, 2006. Chronicles Carlyle's personal life and intellectual career and discusses his works.

Ralli, Augustus. *Guide to Carlyle.* 1920. 2 vols. New York: Haskell House, 1969. Two detailed chapters in volume 1 provide a comprehensive introduction to *On Heroes, Hero-Worship, and the Heroic in History.* The first analyzes the contents of the work; the second offers a general interpretation.

Rosenberg, Philip. *The Seventh Hero: Thomas Carlyle and the Theory of Radical Activism.* Cambridge, Mass.: Harvard University Press, 1974. Focusing on the major works that culminate Carlyle's literary career, Rosenberg examines Carlyle's ideas and discusses *On Heroes, Hero-Worship, and the Heroic in History* in detail in the final chapter.

Seigel, Jules Paul, ed. *Thomas Carlyle: The Critical Heritage.* New York: Barnes & Noble, 1971. Offers a brief discussion of *On Heroes, Hero-Worship, and the Heroic in History* and some of Carlyle's other works in the context of contemporary reaction to his ideas. Reprints many essays by Carlyle's contemporaries, two of which discuss this work specifically, with one attacking, and the other defending, the work.

Trela, D. J., and Rodger L. Tarr, eds. *The Critical Response to Thomas Carlyle's Major Works*. Westport, Conn.: Greenwood Press, 1997. Collection of reviews and essays examine *On Heroes, Hero-Worship, and the Heroic in History* and Carlyle's other major works that date from the initial publication of his works until the end of the twentieth century. The introduction discusses how Carlyle responded to his critics.

On Liberty

Author: John Stuart Mill (1806-1873)
First published: 1859
Type of work: Philosophy

John Stuart Mill, the English utilitarian, concerns himself in this work with the problem of defining the limits of the power of the state to interfere with personal liberty. The result is one of the most important statements in the history of Western democracy. The essay is distinguished by its clarity and the orderly arrangement of its persuasive argument. The work reveals Mill's interest in the happiness and rights of all people and his serious concern that happiness may be threatened by governmental power unwisely used.

Mill states concisely that the purpose of his essay is to

assert one very simple principle, as entitled to govern absolutely the dealings of society with the individual in the way of compulsion and control, whether the means used be physical force in the form of legal penalties, or the moral coercion of public opinion. That principle is, that the sole end for which mankind are warranted, individually or collectively, in interfering with the liberty of action of any of their number, is self-protection. That the only purpose for which power can be rightfully exercised over any member of a civilized community, against his will, is to prevent harm to others.

Another statement of the author's intention is found in the last chapter, "Applications," in which Mill states that two maxims together form "the entire doctrine" of the essay. The first maxim is "that the individual is not accountable to society for his actions, in so far as these concern the interests of no person but himself," and the second is

that for such actions as are prejudicial to the interests of others, the individual is accountable, and may be subjected either to social or to legal punishment, if society is of the opinion that the one or the other is requisite for its protection.

It would be an error of interpretation of Mill's intention to suppose that he is explicitly objecting to all efforts of government to improve the condition of its citizens. What Mill objects to is the restriction of human liberty for the sake of human welfare; he has nothing against welfare itself. On the contrary, as a utilitarian, he believes that a right act is one that aims at the greatest happiness of the greatest number of persons; and it is precisely because the restriction of human liberty is so destructive to human happiness that he makes a plea for a judicious use of restrictive power, justifying it only when it is used to prevent harm, or unhappiness of whatever sort, to others than the person being restricted.

Restricting personal liberty for one's own good, for one's happiness, is not morally justifiable. Mill permits, even encourages, "remonstrating" and "reasoning" with a person who is determined to act against his or her own best interests, but he does not approve of using force to keep that person from such actions.

After reviewing some of the acts a person may rightfully be compelled to do—such as to give evidence in court, to bear a fair share of the common defense, and to defend the helpless—Mill asserts that society has no right to interfere when a person's acts concern, for the most part, only that person. This statement means that a person must be free in conscience, thought, and feeling, and that the person must have freedom of opinion and sentiment on all subjects. This latter freedom involves freedom of the press. In addition, people should be free to do what they like and to enjoy what they prefer—provided what they do is not harmful to others. Finally, each should be free to unite with others for any purpose—again, provided no one is harmed by this action.

This theme is pertinent, because there exists a present or possible danger of government interference in human affairs. Mill admits that his principal thesis has the "air of a truism," but he goes on to remind the reader that states have often felt justified in using their power to limit the liberty of citizens in areas that Mill regards as sacrosanct. In the context of Mill's philosophic work, *On Liberty* remains one of his most important essays.

In perhaps the most carefully articulated part of his argument, in chapter 2, "On the Liberty of Thought and Discussion," Mill considers the consequences of suppressing the expression of opinion if the suppressed opinion were true; and then, having countered a series of objections to his arguments against suppression, he continues by considering the consequences of suppressing opinion if the opinion were false.

Suppressing true opinion is wrong, particularly if the opinion is suppressed on the claim that it is false. Silencing the expression of opinion on the ground that the opinion is false is a sign of an assumption of infallibility. A moment's thought shows that the assumption may be mistaken, and that suppressing opinion may very well make discovery of error impossible.

In response to the objection that it is permissible to suppress opinion, even true opinion, because the truth always triumphs, Mill answers that the idea that truth always wins out is a "pleasant falsehood" proved false by experience. To the objection that at least in some parts of the world people no longer put others to death for expressing their opinions, Mill counters with the argument that other kinds of persecution continue to be practiced, destroying truth and moral courage.

If the opinion suppressed be false, Mill continues, the prevailing and true opinion, lacking opposition, becomes a dead dogma. When ideas are not continually met by opposing ideas they tend to become either meaningless or groundless. Beliefs that at one time had force and reasons behind them may come to be nothing but empty words.

The argument in favor of freedom of opinion and the press closes with the claim that most opinions are neither wholly true nor wholly false, but mixtures of the two, and that only in free discussion can the difference be made out. To reinforce his central contention—that it is always wrong to hinder the freedom of an individual when what the individual does is not harmful to others—Mill devotes a chapter to an argument designed to show that development of individuality is essential to one's happiness. Since there is nothing better than happiness, it follows that individuality should be fostered and

guaranteed. Mill supports Baron Wilhelm von Humboldt's injunction that every human being aim at "individuality of power and development," for which there are two prerequisites: "freedom and the variety of situations."

There is a refreshing pertinence to Mill's discussion of the value of individuality, which recalls Ralph Waldo Emerson's defense of nonconformity. Mill states, "Originality is the one thing which unoriginal minds cannot feel the use of," and "He who lets the world, or his own portion of it, choose his plan of life for him, has no need of any other faculty than the ape-like one of imitation." Mill argues that only if uncustomary acts are allowed to show their merits can anyone decide which mode of action should become customary, and, in any case, the differences among people demand that differences of conduct be allowed so that each person may realize what is best within.

In his discussion of the harm that results from a state's interference with the rights of an individual to act in ways that concern only the individual, Mill reviews some of the consequences of religious intolerance, prohibition, and other attempts to restrict liberty for the common good. In each case, he argues, the result is not only failure to achieve the goal of the prohibitive act but also some damage to the character of the state and its citizens.

Mill closes *On Liberty* by saying that "a State which dwarfs its men, in order that they may be more docile instruments in its hands even for beneficial purposes—will find that with small men no great thing can be accomplished."

Further Reading

Berger, Fred R. *Happiness, Justice, and Freedom: The Moral and Political Philosophy of John Stuart Mill.* Berkeley: University of California Press, 1984. A thorough evaluation of the moral and political contributions and implications of Mill's utilitarianism.

Berlin, Isaiah. *Liberty: Incorporating "Four Essays on Liberty."* Edited by Henry Hardy. New York: Oxford University Press, 2002. Expanded edition of Berlin's 1969 work. Essays on some of the issues raised by Mill in his *On Liberty.*

Cowling, Maurice. *Mill and Liberalism.* 2d ed. New York: Cambridge University Press, 1990. Contains extended modern criticism of Mill, who is accused of "more than a touch of something resembling moral totalitarianism." *On Liberty,* Cowling argues, is a selective defense of the individuality of the elevated.

Donner, Wendy. *The Liberal Self: John Stuart Mill's Moral and Political Philosophy.* Ithaca, N.Y.: Cornell University Press, 1991. A carefully developed interpretation of the basic themes and arguments in Mill's political philosophy and ethics.

Dworkin, Gerald, ed. *Mill's "On Liberty": Critical Essays.* Lanham, Md.: Rowman & Littlefield, 1997. Noted Mill scholars address the perspectives, problems, and prospects contained in Mill's famous study of liberty.

Gray, John. *Mill on Liberty: A Defence.* 2d ed. New York: Routledge & Kegan Paul, 1996. A spirited defense of Mill's consistency in promoting the right of liberty from a utilitarian point of view. Gray considers *On Liberty* the most important of philosophical arguments about liberty, utility, and rights.

Lyons, David. *Rights, Welfare, and Mill's Moral Theory.* New York: Oxford University Press, 1994. Interprets Mill's understanding of human rights and responsible public policy within the framework of his utilitarianism.

O'Rourke, K. C. *John Stuart Mill and Freedom of Expression: The Genesis of a Theory.* New York: Routledge, 2001. Traces the evolution of Mill's theories about freedom of thought and discussion as expressed in his *On Liberty*.

Rees, John Collwyn. *John Stuart Mill's "On Liberty."* Edited by G. L. Williams. New York: Oxford University Press, 1985. A valuable blend of historical, philosophical, and textual analysis. Deals substantially with the criticisms of Cowling (above) and Gertrude Himmelfarb's *On Liberty and Liberalism* (1974).

Reeves, Richard. *John Stuart Mill: Victorian Firebrand.* London: Atlantic Books, 2007. An authoritative and well-received biography that recounts Mill's life, philosophy, and pursuit of truth and liberty for all.

Riley, Jonathan. *Liberal Utilitarianism: Social Choice Theory and John Stuart Mill's Philosophy.* New York: Cambridge University Press, 1988. A thoughtful discussion of Mill's philosophy and its relationship to contemporary political and economic policy.

Scarre, Geoffrey. *Mill's "On Liberty": A Reader's Guide.* London: Continuum, 2007. Overview of the work, describing its context, themes, reception, and influence. Explains Mill's ideas about liberty of thought and discussion, individuality as an element of well being, and the limits of society's authority over the individual.

On Sepulchres

Author: Ugo Foscolo (1778-1827)

First published: *Dei sepolcri*, 1807 (English translation, 1835, 1971)

Type of work: Poetry

On Sepulchres, written in 1806, is also known as *Of Tombs*, *On Tombs*, or *The Sepulchres*. The poem is addressed to Ugo Foscolo's friend Ippolito Pindemonte, a wealthy, prominent traveler who had translated Homer's *Odyssey* (c. 725 B.C.E.). Pindemonte wrote a poem on tombs before Foscolo, but abandoned it to write an epistle responding to his friend's superior verse. Pindemonte inspired *On Sepulchres* by complaining about a Napoleonic government decree regarding interments, which stated that cemeteries should be set some distance away from inhabited areas, that tombstones should follow a uniform design, and that the living should be banned from visiting graves. Like Pindemonte, Foscolo found the decree unreasonable.

Foscolo explored many of the subjects in *On Sepulchres* in previous, shorter sonnets and odes, forms Foscolo found too limiting. Foscolo wrote that his "hymn" was composed in the style of the Greeks, using the rhetorical device of question and response to give the poem structure. His purpose is political, and he attempts to reach the heart rather than the mind to awaken Italian reverence for its fallen heroes. He treats his subject with a lofty, epic, heroic, and lyrical tone and a civil, moral, and educational spirit.

Throughout the poem, his theme is that the living and the dead are united in immortal love, and that tombs communicate the past to the living. Some critics claim the poem says that death is but another country after life, but Foscolo chooses the word "sepulchre" carefully, as the term "cemetery" had Christian connotations he wishes to avoid. In Catholic Italy, cemeteries are places for bodies to rest before resurrection. For Foscolo, immortality is in the memory of the living, not heaven or hell, and tombs are simply monuments to the dead.

The poem begins with a desolate tone, the dead reflecting on what they lost under the shade of cypress trees, a symbol of immortality. They remember life as having love, hope, and music now replaced by the oblivion of "melancholy harmony." The poet asks why one living should want to visit the dead and answers by saying they deserve reverence because the living, the dead, and nature are interconnected, nature inspiring serene reflection on the past.

The poet addresses the new law that would deny solace for the living and "the dead their names." He calls on Calliope, the Muse of poetry, to give grieving poets the same spirit she gave previous singers such as Homer, asking her to give him inspiration to justly memorialize past heroes. The poet describes how people mourned in the past: how graves, altars, and tombs are designed, and how the greatness of past leaders inspires him.

The second part of the poem emphasizes the importance of memory. Speaking to Pindemonte, the poet recalls the glory of Troy, Italian cities including Florence and Tuscany, and famous Italians. He praises fictional and real ancient Romans and Greeks including Plutarch, Plato, Ajax, and Hector. He describes Electra's death, and how she asked for her fame to be immortalized in song. These names, some critics claim, underline Foscolo's antiplebeian, antiegalitarian, and aristocratic point of view. This is possible, but Foscolo is primarily celebrating a pantheon of brave Italian immortals who conquered death in their fame, monuments, and literature.

The poem then prophesies the ruins of contemporary life, warning of dangers to people separated from their past glories. The dead carry secrets and glory the living must embrace and carry on. Part of the popular graveyard school of eighteenth century poetry, *On Sepulchres* is but one of Foscolo's explorations of Italian heroes, myth, and death. On the poem's publication, Foscolo's reputation was elevated into prominence, prompting quick translations into European languages. His detractors, primarily the clergy, objected to his anti-Christian stance and the womanizing in his personal life.

On Sepulchres is now generally regarded as Foscolo's masterpiece. His role as a patriotic bard of Italy's greatness adds much interest into the poem in his mother country. In 1871, the city of Florence had his bones moved to the Church of Santa Croce to be enshrined alongside heroes he elegized.

Wesley Britton

Further Reading

Brose, Margaret. "Ugo Foscolo and Giacomo Leopardi: Italy's Classical Romantics." In *A Companion to European Romanticism*, edited by Michael Ferber. Malden, Mass.: Blackwell, 2005. An analysis of the works of Foscolo and poet Leopardi, placing them within the broader context of European Romanticism.

Cambon, Glauco. *Ugo Foscolo: Poet of Exile*. Princeton, N.J.: Princeton University Press, 1980. Discusses *On Sepulchres* in passing, but provides a wealth of information on Ippolito Pindemonte's friendship with Foscolo, including a discussion of the two friends writing poems on the same subject—the decree on tombs. Also discussed is the historical setting that helped shape Foscolo's poem.

Carsaniga, Giovanni. "Foscolo." In *The Cambridge History of Italian Literature*, edited by Peter Brand and Lino Pertile. New York: Cambridge University Press, 1996. Includes discussion of *On Sepulchres* and Foscolo's other works.

Cippico, Antonio. "The Poetry of Ugo Foscolo." In *Proceedings of the British Academy, 1924-1925*. Vol. 11. London: British Academy Press, 1927. First placing the poem in historical and literary contexts, Cippico evaluates the work's religious and political nature, emphasizing and explaining in detail the poem's classical allusions.

Foscolo, Ugo. *On Sepulchres: An Ode to Ippolito Pindemonte*. Translated by Thomas C. Bergin. Bethany, Minn.: Bethany Press, 1971. Contains both Italian and English texts of the poem on facing pages. Also features historical background, explanatory notes, and comments on translating the poem into English.

Lindon, John. "Englishing Foscolo's *Sepolcri*." *Italianist* 28, no. 1 (2008): 162-176. Lindon discusses various English translations of *On Sepulchres*, arguing that these translations are not easily understandable and fail to capture the deeper meaning of the poem. He provides his own translation in the article.

Radcliff-Umstead, Douglas. *Ugo Foscolo*. New York: Twayne, 1970. This literary biography discusses Foscolo's place in the Romantic movement, comparing the poet with other authors and musicians of the era. Considers Foscolo's interest in and use of classical myth, music, and Italian history and poetic traditions. Describes Foscolo's poetic style and imagery, compares *On Sepulchres* with other Foscolo poems, and briefly evaluates Foscolo's critical reception. The explication of *On Sepulchres* is extensive and indispensable.

On the Genealogy of Morals

Author: Friedrich Nietzsche (1844-1900)
First published: Zur Genealogie der Moral, 1887
   (English translation, 1896)
Type of work: Philosophy

Friedrich Nietzsche's *On the Genealogy of Morals*, published late in his career, demonstrates the philosopher's academic roots in nineteenth century classical philology. Divided into three interrelated essays subdivided by sections, the work is a relatively compact but provocative examination of morality and ethics. Subtitled "A Polemic" in certain editions, the work undertakes a radical break with previous examinations of moral philosophy. Both for its style and its argument, many contemporary philosophers judge *On the Genealogy of Morals* to be among Nietzsche's most important works. Many notable modern English translations exist, and scholars generally regard the 1968 German-language version of *On the Genealogy of Morals* by Italian editors Giorgio Colli and Mazzino Montinari to be the standard German edition of the work.

On the Genealogy of Morals inaugurates Nietzsche's genealogical critique (which is about something other than tracing family histories). The philosophical method of genealogy, for Nietzsche, problematizes fundamental assumptions about morality and moral theories through a careful differentiation between origin and purpose. In other words, morality is viewed not as an unassailable, static set of facts or as an ideal realm of transcendental essences. Instead, the meaning and value of morality emerge from a sequence of shifting contexts that reveal and obscure a long, complicated chain of nonlinear historical developments and blurred psychological states. For Nietzsche, the most prominent "facts" about morality are its contingency and its hidden though recognizable development.

As a prejudice, morality is itself an interpretation of life, making it uniquely suited to genealogical interpretation. In other words, previous thinking on morality stopped at a crude empirical level or, conversely, posited supernatural authorization. According to Nietzsche, both these approaches distort and oversimplify a cultural hieroglyph. Through a moral genealogy, Nietzsche proposes to go behind these putative sources of moral valuation to get at something more fundamental and entirely human. Though not consistently expressed in *On the Genealogy of Morals*, clues in support of this critique can be found in etymology and in a kind of conjectural sociology of value formation, an approach partly based on allegorized history. Nietzsche seeks to describe and highlight the types of agency that create morality. He also wants to show how agency is constituted so that it manufactures guilt and enforces punishment.

Nietzsche's preface is typical of his prose. By turns conversational and aggressive, challenging and witty, he suggests that this book is the culmination of a train of thought that began in his youth and that appears in all of his writings up to this point. The value of morality, and in particular the value of pity and the creative power of *ressentiment* (a negative, reactionary mode of moral interpretation rooted in suffering and malice), came to occupy his thoughts as he considered previous theories on this subject. Apart from the seductive, expressionist quality of Nietzsche's style, his philosophical argument becomes especially interesting when he suggests that victorious "herd" moralities may constitute a grave danger to the very conditions that make morality a positive, adaptive mechanism for enhancing human flourishing.

The first essay contrasts the linguistic origins of the binary terms "good and evil" and "good and bad." Rejecting utilitarianism and its corollary, "unegoistic" acts, as taking priority in the formation of morality, Nietzsche asserts that these binary oppositions are primordial and originally conceived by ruling elites (nobles) to distinguish between and among themselves and an undifferentiated mass of people unlike themselves. A digression on word origins indicates the emergence of warrior and priestly (caste) systems of moral valuation that were momentarily aligned but eventually clashed over the value and meaning of conflict and suffering. For Nietzsche, the fundamental cause of this rift had to do with whether emphasis (and value) should be put on physiological vitality or deepening spirituality, with spirituality considered a reactive negative state, arising from *ressentiment* and weakness. Nietzsche maintains that this conflict is cross-cultural and timeless, and he cites several examples to support his contention. If noble morality is spontaneous, direct, open, and self-affirming, then herd morality, according to Nietzsche, is reactive, indirect, calculating, and vengeful.

It is worth noting, too, how polemical strategies are deployed in this essay. Nietzsche begins with a speculative hypothesis, then moves to linguistic analysis coupled with selective historical illustrations, and concludes with a catalog of existential states. In section fifteen of the first essay, he uses a striking quotation from Christian apologist and polemicist Tertullian (second and third centuries) about the suffering of sinners in the afterlife to epitomize the spirit of *ressentiment*.

The second essay, on guilt and bad conscience, opens with a discussion of memory and promise-making and the contrasting roles they play in the "sovereign individual" and as codified in legal obligations. Once again, through antithesis, Nietzsche heightens the tension and ambiguity inherent in genealogical critique. Memory has implications for moral accountability, because for Nietzsche the concept of justice originates in the particular kind of promise built into the debtor-creditor contract. This is taken to be a primordial formative experience for the development of human beings. In this account, when a contract is breached (forgotten), the creditor uses the law to indulge in cruelty and revenge with a clear conscience, recalling a now transposed characteristic of noble morality. An improbable but related claim in *On the Genealogy of Morals* is that cruelty and suffering internalized human nature and thereby gave new depth and meaning to life. Nietzsche cites as proof the odd notion that that ancient Greek epic, with all its violence and suffering, was a festival play for the gods. The second essay returns at this point to the view that law and just retribution are designed to regulate outbreaks of *ressentiment* and vengeance.

In the concluding sections of the second essay Nietzsche develops his ideas on punishment and bad conscience as signs or events in the play of forces that have shaped human nature and culture over millennia. In section twenty, he links monotheism and empire and states that modern atheism as an outgrowth of monotheism signifies liberation from the psychic guilt incurred by being perpetually in "debt" to the gods (or God), recalling his previous discussion on justice in this essay.

In the third and concluding essay, on ascetic ideals, Nietzsche finds rancor at the origin of certain aesthetic theories and particularly in the figure of the ascetic priest. The prose here is phantasmagoric, as Nietzsche plunges through psychology, autobiographical snippets, and religious history to trace the mostly negative impact of ascetic values in different cultural spheres, including modern science and historiography. Nietzsche highlights the priestly exploitation of guilt and the subsequent formation of the sinner as a mutually reinforcing feedback loop. The polemic against ascetic ideals becomes strident as Nietzsche blames it for ruining taste (by rejecting classical literature) and health (through self-

torment leading to depression and suicide). In sum, the ascetic ideal assumes terrifying power as it becomes the necessary antidote to an impoverished, intolerable reality that has been produced by the near total triumph of the ascetic ideal itself. Art, says Nietzsche, is the only power capable of resisting and overcoming ascetic ideals; his striking formulation for this conflict is "Plato versus Homer." The ascetic ideal ultimately triumphed, he says, because it gave meaning and justification to suffering and alleviated rancor.

As a conjectural examination of morality and political philosophy Nietzsche's *On the Genealogy of Morals* has few equals. Philosopher Jean-Jacques Rousseau, about whom he was ambivalent, certainly comes to mind in terms of his seductive stylistic power and psychological acumen. However, for intellectual depth, dramatic appeal, and rhetorical brilliance, only Plato among philosophers offers a comparable treatment of psychology, morality, power, and state formation.

Robert N. Matuozzi

Further Reading

Acampora, Christa Davis, ed. *Nietzsche's "On the Genealogy of Morals": Critical Essays*. Lanham, Md.: Rowman & Littlefield, 2006. Similar to Richard Schacht's book, this collection of contemporary essays examining *On the Genealogy of Morals* has sections on the idea of genealogy, analyses of specific passages, critiques of the genealogical method, and a section on politics and community.

Conway, Daniel. *Nietzsche's "On the Genealogy of Morals": A Reader's Guide*. New York: Continuum, 2008. By offering a section-by-section textual commentary with a student apparatus, including section summaries, this book is suitable for classroom use. Shows how *On the Genealogy of Morals* construes morality as constitutive of agency.

Deleuze, Giles. *Nietzsche and Philosophy*. Translated by Hugh Tomlinson. 1962. Reprint. New York: Continuum, 2006. A classic, sophisticated conceptual analysis of force and power in Nietzsche's ontology and in the book *On the Genealogy of Morals*. Argues that Nietzsche's signal philosophical insight was to conceive of values and morality as expressive of primordial existential states.

Hatab, Lawrence J. *Nietzsche's "On the Genealogy of Morality": An Introduction*. New York: Cambridge University Press, 2008. A synthetic, section-by-section analysis of the work placed in the larger context of Nietzsche's other writings and his overall political philosophy.

Kaufmann, Walter. *Nietzsche: Philosopher, Psychologist,*

Antichrist. 4th ed. Princeton, N.J.: Princeton University Press, 1974. The publication of the first edition of this book in 1950 transformed Nietzsche's reception in the English-speaking world through a careful examination of his life and the development of his philosophy. Places Nietzsche's thought in the mainstream of Western philosophy and in the tradition of perennial philosophical problems.

Ridley, Aaron. *Nietzsche's Conscience: Six Character Studies from the "Genealogy."* Ithaca, N.Y.: Cornell University Press, 1998. Persuasive study of the notional figures in Nietzsche's *On the Genealogy of Morals*: Slave, Priest, Philosopher, Artist, Scientist, and Noble. Indicates what these abstractions reveal about value and the transformative power of the will to affirm and creatively utilize suffering. Claims the genealogy to be the most important work of moral philosophy since that of Immanuel Kant.

Schacht, Richard, ed. *Nietzsche, Genealogy, Morality: Essays on Nietzsche's "Genealogy of Morals."* Berkeley: University of California Press, 1994. A collection of essays by philosophers examining *On the Genealogy of Morals* and immoralism as well as analytical philosophy, stoicism, and a variety of other topics. An indispensable collection.

On the Nature of Things

Author: Lucretius (c. 98-55 B.C.E.)
First transcribed: De rerum natura, c. 60 B.C.E.
    (English translation, 1682)
Type of work: Poetry

The staying power of *On the Nature of Things* is unquestionable. The work has been, over the centuries, both widely influential on the greatest writers and widely reviled. Quickly dubbed atheistic by early Christian fathers, the book continued to provoke negative reactions from Catholic theologians for nearly a millennium.

Rediscovered during the Renaissance, the work became an oft-quoted source of inspiration for figures as diverse as Giordano Bruno in Italy, Michel de Montaigne in France, and Edmund Spenser in England. British poets John Evelyn and John Dryden translated passages into English; Voltaire found it valuable in his attacks on the Catholic Church. The figure of Lucretius, the skeptical scientist struggling to resolve the seemingly random qualities of the natural world with humankind's insistent belief in a controlling deity, served as the source of one of Alfred, Lord Tennyson's finest dramatic monologues. In the twentieth century, the work found its devotees as well, including noted philosopher Henri Bergson.

Critics of Lucretius most often focus on three major aspects of *On the Nature of Things*: his investigation of scientific phenomena, his approach to religious issues, and his poetic skills. For the first two, the poet has been alternatively valued and vilified; for the last, however, he has been universally hailed as a master of language, technique, and vision.

At the heart of this lengthy analysis of the ways the universe works is a human message that transcends the centuries and speaks to people of all times. Lucretius displays, in his long poem about atoms and gods who are born of the fears and hopes of humans, an appreciation of both humankind and nature that reminds one of the best works of the Romantics.

Often overlooked, especially by those who read *On the Nature of Things* in translation, is Lucretius's contribution to his native Latin. The Latin of the first century B.C.E. was rough and direct (especially when compared to the more sophisticated Greek); hence, Lucretius lacked an adequate vocabulary for philosophic or scientific discussion. The self-imposed demand to transmit his ideas about religion and philosophy in verse rather than prose made his task even more difficult (many words simply would not fit into hexameters, the meter of choice for most serious Latin poetry); hence, his accomplishment is even more significant. The resultant work displays the passion of a sincerely religious man, the scientific insight of a studied practitioner, and the mastery of language characteristic of the most accomplished literary artists; many consider it the finest didactic poem in any language.

On the Nature of Things is also renowned as the greatest poetic monument of Epicurean philosophy. It is outstanding both as a scientific explanation of the poet's atomic theory and as a fine poem. Vergil was much influenced by Lucretius's verse, and he echoes passages of *On the Nature of Things* in the *Georgics* (36-29 B.C.E.), a didactic epic modeled on Lucretius's poem, and in the *Aeneid* (30-19 B.C.E.).

Lucretius, following his master Epicurus's doctrine, believed that fear of the gods and fear of death were the greatest obstacles to peace of mind, the object of Epicurean philosophy. He considers that he could dispel these unfounded terrors by explaining the workings of the universe and showing that phenomena interpreted as signs from the deities were simply natural happenings. His goal in *On the Nature of Things* is thus to explain natural events and to expound thereby on Epicurean philosophy.

Lucretius's scientific speculations are based on Democritus's atomic theory and Epicurus's interpretation of it. Lucretius outlines the fundamental laws of this system in the first book of his poem. According to Lucretius, everything is composed of small "first bodies," tiny particles made up of a few "minima" or "least parts," which cannot be separated. These first bodies, or atoms, are solid, indestructible, and of infinite number. They are mixed with void to make objects of greater hardness or softness, strength or weakness.

Lucretius calls upon the reader's reason and his or her observation of nature, pointing out absurdities that might come about if his own point were not true. For example, he substantiates his statement that nothing can be created from nothing by saying,

> For if things came to being from nothing, every kind might be born from all things, nought would need a seed. First men might arise from the sea, and from the land the race of scaly creatures, and birds burst forth from the sky.

These "proofs," which may fill fifty or one hundred lines of poetry, are often unconvincing, but they reveal the author's knowledge of nature and his imaginative gifts.

The universe is infinite in the Epicurean system. Lucretius would ask one who believes it finite the following question:

> If one were to run on to the end . . . and throw a flying dart, would you have it that that dart . . . goes on whither it is sped and flies afar, or do you think that something can check and bar its way?

Lucretius ridicules the Stoic theory that all things press toward a center, for the universe, being infinite, can have no center. Lucretius, in his proof that the universe is infinite, does not consider what it ended up taking some two millennia for another thinker to consider; one could go to the "end" of a finite universe, throw a dart from there, and have it sail on unimpeded into another part of the universe, giving the appearance that the universe has no end, if space is curved. He often contradicts what science has since proved true, but he is remarkably accurate for his time.

Book 2 opens with a poetic description of the pleasure of standing apart from the confusion and conflicts of life.

> Nothing is more gladdening than to dwell in the calm high places, firmly embattled on the heights by the teaching of the wise, whence you can look down on others, and see them wandering hither and thither.

Lucretius is providing this teaching by continuing his discussion of atoms, which he says move continuously downward like dust particles in a sunbeam. They have a form of free will and can swerve to unite with one another to form objects. Lucretius adds that if the atoms could not will motion for themselves, there would be no explanation for the ability of animals to move voluntarily.

The poet outlines other properties of atoms in the latter part of the second book: they are colorless, insensible, and of a variety of shapes that determine properties of the objects the atoms compose. Sweet honey contains round, smooth particles; bitter wormwood, hooked atoms.

While Lucretius scorns superstitious fear of the gods, he worships the creative force of nature, personified as Venus in the invocation to book 1. Nature controls the unending cycle of creation and destruction. There are gods, but they dwell in their tranquil homes in space, unconcerned for the fate of humanity. A passage in praise of Epicurus precedes book 3, the book of the soul. Lucretius says that fear of death arises from superstitions about the soul's afterlife in Hades. This fear is foolish, for the soul is, like the body, mortal. The poet describes the soul as the life force in the body, composed of very fine particles that disperse into the air when the body dies. Since the individual will neither know nor feel anything when the soul has dissolved, fear of death is unnecessary. One should not regret leaving life, even if it has been full and rich. One should die as "a guest sated with the banquet of life and with calm mind embrace . . . a rest that knows no care." If existence has been painful, then an end to it should be welcome.

The introductory lines of book 4 express Lucretius's desire to make philosophy more palatable to his readers by presenting it in poetry. His task is a new one: "I traverse the distant haunts of the Pierides (the Muses), never trodden before by the foot of man." The poet begins this book on the topic of sensation with an explanation of idols, the films of atoms that float from the surfaces of objects and make sense perception possible. People see because idols touch their eyes, and they taste the bitter salt air because idols of hooked atoms reach their tongues. Idols become blunted when they travel a long distance, causing people to see far-off square towers as round.

Lucretius blames the misconceptions arising from visual phenomena such as refraction and perspective on reason, not sense, for accuracy of sense perceptions is an important part of his theory: "Unless they are true, all reason, too, becomes false."

A second eulogy of Epicurus introduces the fifth book, for some readers the most interesting of all. In it Lucretius discusses the creation of the world and the development of human civilization. Earth was created by a chance conjunction of atoms, which squeezed out Sun, Moon, and stars as they gathered together to form land. The world, which is constantly disintegrating and being rebuilt, is still young, for human history does not go back beyond the Theban and Trojan wars. The poet gives several explanations for the motion of stars, the causes of night, and eclipses. Since proof can come only from the senses, any theory that does not contradict perception is possible.

Lucretius presents the curious idea that the first animals were born from wombs rooted in the earth. Monsters were created, but only strong animals and those useful to people could survive. What follows is a delightful picture of primitive people, hardy creatures living on nuts and berries and living in caves. Lucretius describes the process of civilization as people uniting for protection, and learning to talk, use metals, weave, and wage war. Problems began for them with the discovery of wealth and property, breeding envy and discord. It was at this point that Epicurus taught people the highest good, to free them from their cares.

The sixth book continues the explanation of the natural phenomena—thunder, lightning, clouds, rain, earthquakes—that inspired people to fear the gods. Lucretius examines many subjects, giving several explanations for many of them. He concludes the poem with a vivid description of the plague of Athens, modeled on Thucydides's account.

Further Reading

Bréhier, Émile. *The Hellenistic and Roman Age.* Translated by Wade Baskin. Chicago: University of Chicago Press, 1965. Deals with Lucretius, Epicurus, and atomistic metaphysics in the broad context of ancient Greek and Roman philosophies.

Clay, Diskin. *Lucretius and Epicurus.* Ithaca, N.Y.: Cornell University Press, 1983. A helpful comparative study of the metaphysical and ethical philosophies of two important thinkers from the ancient world.

Copleston, Frederick. *A History of Philosophy: Greece and Rome.* Garden City, N.Y.: Doubleday, 1962. Copleston provides a brief but clear discussion of Lucretius in the chapter "Epicureanism."

Dalzell, Alexander. *The Criticism of Didactic Poetry: Essays on Lucretius, Virgil, and Ovid.* Toronto, Ont.: University of Toronto Press, 1997. Explores how Lucretius used poetic forms to express his philosophical views.

Gale, Monica. *Myth and Poetry in Lucretius.* New York: Cambridge University Press, 1994. Lucretius's distinctive use of poetic imagery is analyzed in a study that sheds light on his methods and metaphysics.

_____, ed. *Lucretius.* New York: Oxford University Press, 2007. Collection of essays, several of which analyze various aspects of *On the Nature of Things.* Other essays discuss the sources of Lucretius's inspiration, Lucretius the Epicurean, and Lucretius and politics.

Guillespie, Stuart, and Philip Hardie, eds. *The Cambridge Companion to Lucretius.* New York: Cambridge University Press, 2007. Collection of essays, including discussions placing Lucretius within the context of Greek philosophy, Roman politics and history, and previous poetic traditions; other essays focus on the structure, argument, style, meter, and rhetoric of *On the Nature of Things.* Several of the contributors assess Lucretius's reception in the Middle Ages and early Renaissance, the Italian and English renaissance eras, the European Enlightenment, and Romantic and Victorian Britain.

Hadzsits, George D. *Lucretius and His Influence.* New York: Cooper Square, 1963. A solid analysis of the influence of *On the Nature of Things* from the Roman era through the Middle Ages and Renaissance to modern criticism. The fourth chapter is especially good regarding the work's place in relation to other ancient authors.

Jones, W. T. *A History of Western Philosophy: The Classical Mind.* New York: Harcourt Brace, 1969. In a chapter on ancient atomism and materialism, Jones discusses Lucretius in a clear and accessible way.

Sedley, D. N. *Lucretius and the Transformation of Greek Wisdom.* New York: Cambridge University Press, 1998. Shows how Lucretius built on and departed from Greek traditions that informed the context in which he worked.

Segal, Charles. *Lucretius on Death and Anxiety: Poetry and Philosophy in "De Rerum Natura."* Princeton, N.J.: Princeton University Press, 1990. Shows how Lucretius developed his understanding that death is not to be feared.

On the Origin of Species by Means of Natural Selection
Or, The Preservation of Favoured Races in the Struggle for Life

Author: Charles Darwin (1809-1882)
First published: 1859
Type of work: Science

Charles Darwin was not the first to come up with the concept of evolution. Many scientists, including Darwin's grandfather, had accepted that plants and animals on Earth had changed form over time. Already in 1809, Jean-Baptiste Lamarck had argued that modern animals, including humans, had descended from other species. Lamarck promoted the idea of "inheritance of acquired characteristics" as the mechanism governing this evolution. For example, Lamarck argued that the neck of a giraffe stretching for food would eventually lengthen slightly, a physical characteristic that would be passed to its offspring.

In *On the Origin of Species by Means of Natural Selection*, better known as *On the Origin of Species*, Darwin achieves two things that Lamarck does not. He gathers detailed evidence to support evolution and offers a different, and ultimately workable, mechanism to govern it. This mechanism, natural selection, has been supported by later research, whereas Lamarck's idea of inheritance of acquired characteristics has not. Natural selection is believed to be the major (but not only) force driving species evolution.

Natural selection is a simple concept. Consider animals. First, individuals of any species vary in size, coloration, behavior, and other characteristics. Second, these variations tend to be passed on to an individual's offspring. Third, more offspring are born than those surviving to reproduce. Fourth, any characteristic (such as coloration) that allows one individual to survive better than others will help that individual reproduce more. Fifth, this characteristic will increase in frequency in the species over time.

Natural selection has been observed in many species. The finches of the Galapagos Islands provide a good example. The Galapagos finches are a group of closely related bird species that helped Darwin discover natural selection. These birds differ primarily in behavior and in beak size and shape. In dry years, heavier-beaked finches survive and reproduce better because they can open bigger seeds. Average beak size can change dramatically over a single breeding season. This illustrates natural selection.

Small changes within a species represent "microevolution," although Darwin did not use this term in *On the Origin of Species*. Microevolutionary changes that continue over time can lead to new species, especially if physical barriers (such as isolation on different islands in, for example, the Galapagos) separate subgroups of the original species. This is "macroevolution," which also has been observed in the laboratory, although with relatively small changes.

On the Origin of Species is a long work, but Darwin, in the book's introduction, describes it as an "abstract." He had been working on a longer book, but decided to publish his core thoughts after Alfred Russell Wallace independently discovered natural selection in 1858. Darwin had worked on the concept since 1837 and had written an unpublished 230-page report on it by 1844. Ultimately, he produced six editions, and historians are undecided as to whether the first edition or the sixth edition should be considered definitive. The primary information is similar in all editions, but the sixth contains "An Historical Sketch," which discusses evolutionary thinking before the work was published.

On the Origin of Species is one long argument for evolution and for natural selection as the primary force behind it. Chapter 1 discusses variation among domesticated plants and animals and shows how humans have used this variation to produce specialized subvarieties. Darwin illustrates his concepts through a study of domesticated pigeons, which have been selected and bred by humans for certain desirable characteristics. Darwin calls this selected breeding artificial selection.

In chapter 2, Darwin examines the tremendous variability seen among plants and animals in nature. Even naturalists disagree on how to divide species and subspecies because of individual variability within each species. Darwin shows that common species with wide geographical ranges vary more than localized species. Chapter 3 focuses on the "struggle for existence." From reading Thomas Malthus's *An Essay on the Principle of Population as It Affects the Future Improvement of Society* (1798) and from personal observations, Darwin came to realize that far more offspring are born in a species than ever reach adulthood. This causes a ceaseless struggle for natural resources. Competition is most fierce among members of the same species.

Chapter 4 fully describes and defines natural selection. Darwin shows how the principle must act across all species and how it could explain extinction of previously living forms as well as the wide divergence of forms seen in the modern world. He also introduces the idea of sexual selection, which involves competition for mates, especially among male animals. Sexual selection favors characteristics (for example, horns) that help males defeat other males or (as in the elaborate plumage of male birds) help attract females.

In chapter 5, Darwin explores potential causes for natural variation. He admits not knowing the causes, but he argues that "use and disuse," a Lamarckian concept, could play some role. For example, he suggests that flightless birds had become flightless for failing, over time, to use their wings. From a modern perspective, this chapter can be considered relatively weak because Darwin knew nothing of genetics, which later resolved the issue of natural variation in favor of natural selection over the concept of use and disuse.

Scientists should point out potential flaws in their own theories, as Darwin does in chapters 6, 7, 8, and 9. Chapter 6 acknowledges that good transitional fossils are rare in the fossil record (although many such fossils have since been discovered). Darwin also discusses organs (such as eyes) that seem too complicated to have evolved through natural selection, and he examines the difficulties in imagining dramatic changes, such as land mammals transforming gradually into aquatic ones. However, he gives numerous examples of intermediate characteristics in living animals that could be worked on by natural selection. For example, he describes modern species with simple eyes that are still adaptive.

Chapter 7 points out that complex instincts, such as those governing honeycomb-building by bees, pose some difficulty for natural selection. However, Darwin shows that instinctive behavior varies within individuals of a species and that this variability could be acted on by natural selection. Chapter 8 deals with hybridism, the crossing of closely related species, which usually results in sterile offspring. Knowledge of genetics would have helped Darwin here.

Chapter 9 discusses the imperfection of the fossil record. From reading Sir Charles Lyell's masterwork *The Principles of Geology* (1830-1833; 3 vols.), Darwin understood the earth's vast age and how it changed over time. He understood that fossils rarely form, and that many existing ones are buried and irretrievable. Others are destroyed by upheavals of the earth or by erosion. Chapter 10 reemphasizes the imperfection of the record but argues that available fossils do support natural selection. Darwin discusses the role of extinction, and points out that recent fossils resemble still-living creatures more closely than do earlier fossils.

Chapters 11 and 12 focus on the geographical distribution of plants and animals. Darwin shows how similar species live in related geographical areas, and he shows the importance of natural barriers in creating new species. He focuses on islands, like the Galapagos, which illustrate his points. Chapter 13 discusses how humans naturally organize species by their similarities and how these similarities reflect real biological relationships. Darwin also covers anatomical similarities, embryonic similarities, and the existence of vestigial organs such as rudimentary wings in some insects. Chapter 14 summarizes and restates the work's major points.

On the Origin of Species is one of the most influential scientific books in history. It revolutionized biology and has greatly influenced modern psychology and philosophy, among other fields. Darwin's concepts of natural and sexual selection remain mainstays of evolutionary thinking, but most of his original ideas have been modified and extended by the field of genetics. Darwin's book remains controversial, but the controversy is more cultural and political than it is scientific.

Charles A. Gramlich

Further Reading

Browne, Janet. *Darwin's "Origin of Species": Books That Changed the World*. New York: Grove Press, 2008. A readable book for students that includes biographical information on Darwin and covers his development of *On the Origin of Species*, its publication, legacy, and the resulting controversy. A good, but not detailed, overview.

Darwin, Charles. *The Autobiography of Charles Darwin, 1801-1882*. Edited by Nora Barlow. New York: W. W. Norton, 1993. Darwin's autobiography, first published in 1887, was edited by his family to remove some controversial material. That material was restored in a subsequent edition and is included here. An excellent book for understanding *On the Origin of Species*. Remarkably readable. Edited by Darwin's granddaughter.

Larson, Edward J. *Evolution: The Remarkable History of a Scientific Theory*. New York: Modern Library, 2004. Provides a history of the concept of evolution. Covers, particularly in chapter 3, Darwin's development of the ideas that went into *On the Origin of Species*. Also establishes the historical context for Darwin's thinking, discusses how his theory has been applied in the modern world, and examines how it has been revised based upon new discoveries.

Reznick, David N. *The "Origin" Then and Now: An Interpretive Guide to the "Origin of Species."* Princeton, N.J.:

Princeton University Press, 2010. A section-by-section guide to Darwin's *On the Origin of Species*. Includes a helpful introduction and a concluding chapter that surveys late scholarship on the state of evolution and evolutionary theory.

Richards, Robert J., and Michael Ruse, eds. *The Cambridge Companion to the "Origin of Species."* New York: Cambridge University Press, 2008. A collection of articles that includes Michael Ruse's "The Origin of the Origin." Each article reviews an element either of Darwin's theory or of his legacy. Most sections are quite readable.

Weiner, Jonathan. *The Beak of the Finch: A Story of Evolution in Our Time.* New York: Vintage Books, 1994. A readable book discussing Darwin's thinking in *On the Origin of Species*, especially regarding his visit to the Galapagos Islands, where he studied the finches. Details modern studies of the finches, but does not require a deep understanding of scientific techniques.

On the Road

Author: Jack Kerouac (1922-1969)
First published: 1957
Type of work: Novel
Type of plot: Autobiographical
Time of plot: 1947-1950
Locale: United States

Principal characters:
SAL PARADISE, the narrator, a writer
DEAN MORIARITY, a young drifter
CARLO MARX, a poet and intellectual
OLD BULL LEE, an eccentric and a drug addict
ED DUNKEL, Dean's simple-minded disciple
GALETA DUNKEL, Ed's wife
REMI BONCOEUR, a merchant seaman
MARYLOU, Dean's first wife
CAMILLE, Dean's second wife
INEZ, Dean's third wife

The Story:

Sal Paradise is living at his aunt's house in New Jersey while working on his first novel. His "life on the road" begins when he reads letters written from reform school by Dean Moriarity. When Dean arrives in New York with his new wife, Marylou, Sal is impressed with the younger man's enthusiasm and flattered by Dean's desire to learn to write. He recognizes that Dean is a con man who is probably conning him as well, but he enjoys his company. Sal is sorry when Dean meets Carlo Marx, a poet with a "dark mind," for he cannot keep up with Dean and Carlo's wild energy.

Sal leaves New York in the spring of 1947, planning to hitchhike to Denver and continue to San Francisco, where his friend, Remi Boncoeur, has promised to get him a job on a ship. Sal spends most of his money taking a bus to Chicago. From there, he hitchhikes to Denver and finds Carlo and Dean. Dean wants to divorce Marylou and plans to marry Camille, a young woman he had just met; meanwhile, he is having relations with each of the women in separate hotel rooms. Sal observes as Carlo's and Dean's intellectual pur-

suits dissolve into drunken parties in town and in the mountains. Depressed, he wires his aunt for money and takes a bus to San Francisco.

The seafaring job falls through, but Remi lets Sal move into the shack he shares with his girlfriend, Lee Ann. Sal attempts to write a screenplay for Remi to sell in Hollywood; meanwhile, Remi gets Sal a job as a security guard. After several months, the three thoroughly resent one another, and Sal leaves. On a bus to Los Angeles he meets Terri, a Mexican woman who has abandoned her husband and son. After two weeks of drinking in Los Angeles, they hitchhike north to Terri's home town. Sal and Terri move into a tent and Sal gets a job picking cotton. Terri's relatives disapprove of Sal, and he knows he has to leave. He promises to meet Terri in New York, but both of them know she will not go there.

With money wired from his aunt, Sal takes a bus back east, where he works on his book and attends school on the GI Bill. During Christmas, 1948, he is visiting relatives in Virginia when Dean arrives in a new Hudson. Dean had married Camille and settled down to work in San Francisco, but one day he put a down payment on the Hudson and headed east with his friend, Ed Dunkel, and Ed's wife, Galeta. When Galeta ran out of money, the two men abandoned her in a hotel lobby. Dean picked up Marylou on a detour to Denver, then drove straight to Virginia.

Drawn again into Dean's orbit, Sal abandons college and a steady girlfriend to take another trip across the country after the usual three-day drunken farewell party in New York. Driving the southern route, Dean steals gas, cons a police officer, and talks like a modern mystic all the way to New Orleans. There they visit Old Bull Lee, an iconoclast and drug addict from a rich family. They all take drugs and listen to Bull expound his wild social theories. Sal had been the only person actually invited, so the group wears out its welcome quickly. Galeta has been waiting for Ed at Bull's; the couple decides to stay in New Orleans while Sal, Dean, and Marylou head for California. Sal and Marylou come to an understanding that they will be lovers when they reach the coast.

Dean abruptly leaves Sal and Marylou in San Francisco. They get a room on credit but are unable to find work. Marylou deserts Sal; Dean finds him starving and brings him to Camille's house. He and Dean tour the local jazz clubs, and Dean finds Marylou again, but the threesome quickly become disenchanted with one another. Using his next government check, Sal again returns to New York by bus.

In the spring of 1949, Sal wanders back to Denver. A rich girlfriend gives him a hundred dollars and he rushes to San Francisco to find Dean. Though Dean had fathered another child by Camille, he is still obsessed with Marylou. Furious, Camille orders him to leave the house. Sal proposes that they go first to New York, then to Italy, using the money from his soon-to-be-published book. Dean agrees, but they decide to have "two days of kicks" in San Francisco first. They visit Galeta; Ed has abandoned her again, and she and other women friends confront Dean with his irresponsibility.

Sal defends Dean, and after an all-night party they leave for the east in a travel bureau car. Dean takes over the wheel and drives at dangerous speeds to Denver. Sal and Dean quarrel in a restaurant, then make up and go on a two-day drinking binge. Dean steals several cars, but the two escape the police and zoom east at 110 miles per hour in a new travel bureau Cadillac. By the time they reach Chicago's jazz clubs, the Cadillac is wrecked. Sal and Dean take a bus to Detroit, and then another travel bureau car to New York. Five nights later, Dean meets a girl named Inez at a party and proposes marriage. He gets a job as a parking lot attendant, and the trip to Italy is canceled.

The next spring, Sal leaves Dean working in New York

and heads for Mexico. Dean buys an old car and catches up with Sal in Denver. Dean, Sal, and a young man from Denver drive through Texas to Mexico. In Gregoria, a Mexican teenager sells them marijuana and leads them to the town brothel, where they have a tremendous party with the blessings of the local police. Afterward, they continue south through the jungles and into Mexico City. They carouse until Sal gets a bad case of dysentery. Suddenly, Dean abandons him, drives back to Inez with a Mexican divorce from Camille. The night he marries Inez, he leaves her and takes a bus bound for San Francisco and Camille.

Sal returns to New York and meets Laura, the girl of his dreams. Dean writes that he will arrive in six weeks to help them move to San Francisco, but he shows up three days later, almost incoherent in his mysticism. Dean visits Inez and suggests that she move to San Francisco and live on the other side of town, but she refuses. The last Sal saw of Dean was when he and Laura left for a concert with Remi Boncoeur, who had arrived in New York from an ocean liner cruise. Remi refuses to give Dean a ride, and Dean wanders off to take the train back to San Francisco.

Critical Evaluation:

Jack Kerouac coined the term "Beat generation," and he was stereotyped—both positively and negatively—as a beatnik writer for most of his short but prolific career. Reaction to *On the Road* has been quite diverse; the novel has been called everything from incoherent blather to pure genius. The final version was not published until six years after Kerouac drafted it in one long paragraph in 1951. In 1957, the Beat poem "Howl" (by Kerouac's friend Allen Ginsberg) had achieved notoriety; the newly published *On the Road* was able to ride the wave of interest in the Beats and make Kerouac an instant celebrity.

On the Road's literary antecedents could include the "road" poetry of Walt Whitman; the mysticism of poets William Butler Yeats, Arthur Rimbaud, and Charles Baudelaire; Marcel Proust's interconnected narratives; the stream-of-consciousness techniques pioneered by James Joyce and John Dos Passos; and the lost-generation novels of F. Scott Fitzgerald. As with most of Kerouac's work, *On the Road* is largely autobiographical. Dean is based on Neal Cassady, later one of Ken Kesey's Merry Pranksters as chronicled in Tom Wolfe's *Electric Kool-Aid Acid Test* (1968). Carlo represents Ginsberg, "Old Bull Lee" is novelist William Burroughs, and numerous other real friends of Kerouac appear under pseudonyms.

On the Road has been criticized for its lack of plot, but while the narrative is episodic, characters do change. The novel can be read as another in a long line of tales in which middle-class lads are exposed to—and finally reject—a lower-class lifestyle. Far from promoting the irresponsibility that Sal chronicles, the underlying mood is restlessness, disillusion, and depression. The road trips are not so much journeys of ecstatic self-expression or even escape as they are mobile drinking binges. *Big Sur* (1962), a later novel featuring renamed versions of Sal and Dean, makes this aspect of Sal's (and Kerouac's) character very clear. Whenever they arrive anywhere, Dean and company quickly alienate their hosts; taking to the road becomes necessary for outcasts who have nowhere to go. In a telling scene after Dean and Sal's debauched trip east, they restlessly walk around the block, symbolically rejecting the fact that they can go no further, that they must change their approach to life or backtrack the tired road again. By the end of the novel, Sal is settled down and off the road, and the split with Dean—the "holy goof"—seems permanent.

Sal's unsparing critique of himself and his friends makes *On the Road* more than the simple-minded "buddy novel" some critics have labeled it. Despite his attraction, Sal is aware of Dean's sociopathic tendencies. Dean and Ed are "cads" when they abandon Galeta; he later labels Dean a "rat" for abandoning him in Mexico. Other characters also appear as less than romantic: Carlo is "prissy" and paranoid, Bull Lee maniacal. Sal is also unsparing of his own flaws. Between binges, he is usually depressed, and he leaves "the road" with pangs of nostalgia but no real regret.

The novel has survived not because of the subject matter; its real strength is Kerouac's writing: poetic yet lucid, a brilliant mix of detail and compression. Kerouac wrote his first novel, *The Town and the City* (1950), in verbose emulation of Thomas Wolfe, but with *On the Road*, he adopted a spare, rhythmic, driving prose based on the letters of Cassady. Some passages may be too self-consciously lyrical or poetic by contemporary standards, but these elements add to the depth of Sal Paradise as an interestingly unreliable narrator. Whatever one thinks of the characters and their lifestyles, *On the Road* will remain an important American novel that mirrors popular culture at the midpoint of the twentieth century.

Richard A. Hill

Further Reading

Bloom, Harold, ed. *Jack Kerouac's "On the Road."* Philadelphia: Chelsea House, 2004. Collection of critical essays providing various interpretations of the novel, including discussions of the dynamics of friendship, jazz and African American culture, and the vision of social deviance in *On the Road.*

Cassady, Carolyn. *Off the Road: My Years with Cassady, Kerouac, and Ginsberg.* New York: William Morrow, 1990. Background and chronology of *On the Road* from a woman's point of view of the Beats. Cassady's 1978 memoir *Heartbeat: My Life with Jack and Neal* is also telling.

Charters, Ann. *Kerouac: A Biography.* San Francisco: Straight Arrow Books, 1973. First book by Charters, a tireless Kerouac scholar. Discusses *On the Road*'s biographical underpinnings and connections.

French, Warren. *Jack Kerouac.* Boston: Twayne, 1986. Contains two chapters analyzing *On the Road* from biographical and critical approaches.

Grace, Nancy McCampbell. *Jack Kerouac and the Literary Imagination.* New York: Palgrave Macmillan, 2007. Analyzes *On the Road* and other works, describing how they express Kerouac's vision of American literature. Grace maintains that this vision includes Kerouac's fictional rewriting of his life, his quest for spiritual enlightenment, and his blending of popular and academic culture to create new literary forms.

Holton, Robert. *"On the Road": Kerouac's Ragged American Journey.* New York: Twayne, 1999. Examines the connection between *On the Road* and American postwar culture. Holton describes the novel's origins in the Beat movement and how the book influenced youth movements from the 1960's through the 1990's.

Kerouac, Jack. *Visions of Cody.* New York: McGraw-Hill, 1972. Contains notes, early drafts, and passages expurgated from *On the Road.*

Leland, John. *Why Kerouac Matters: The Lessons of "On the Road" (They're Not What You Think).* New York: Viking Press, 2007. Leland's examination of the novel focuses on Sal Paradise, describing how his automobile journey provides valuable lessons about work, money, love, sex, art, holiness, and their connections to manhood. These lessons, Leland argues, remain relevant in the early twenty-first century.

Theado, Matt. *Understanding Jack Kerouac.* Columbia: University of South Carolina Press, 2000. Analyzes what Theado describes as Kerouac's "unwieldy accretion of published work," devoting a chapter to *On the Road.* Outlines the common themes and literary techniques in Kerouac's writing and chronicles his development as a writer whose work has outlived its negative beatnik associations.

On the Soul

Author: Aristotle (384-322 B.C.E.)
First transcribed: Peri psychés, c. 335-323 B.C.E.
   (English translation, 1812)
Type of work: Philosophy and psychology

Aristotle's works on politics, ethics, and metaphysics have made him one of the most widely read of the Greek philosophers. The title of this book, *On the Soul,* is a signal to the reader that the topic is critical to understanding humans. Some scholars believe *On the Soul* was part of Aristotle's general lectures on biology at his institution of learning, the Lyceum, while others place the work at a later point in his life. Aristotle typically wrote and then revised many of his works, and this book likely was revised several times as well.

On the Soul is divided into three books with several chapters in each. Book 1 begins with Aristotle's assertion of the importance of his topic. Understanding the nature of the soul, he claims, is important to understanding the principle that animates all animal life. He is quick to acknowledge that the topic is a difficult one; but its importance is obvious. Equally important, he argues, is how one approaches the topic of understanding the essence of the soul, its form or true nature. Accounting for the properties that make up that essence can lead a person to understand the soul itself.

The balance of book 1 is taken up with Aristotle's effort to obtain an understanding of these properties through the works of other philosophers. While he advances his reasons for disagreeing with their wisdom, Aristotle concludes from his survey of their thinking that all are in agreement that the soul is in some way joined to the body and is therefore the origin of movement. He rejects this conclusion for several reasons, however, not the least because it would mean the soul would have to have a location or place in the body, a conclusion he doubts. In other words, Aristotle makes it clear from the beginning of *On the Soul* that he believes the essence of the soul is not a material thing.

Aristotle ends book 1 by arguing against what he considers the implausible belief that the soul is created through parts of the body or a mixture of parts of the body, corresponding to the elements of fire, water, and air (earth, he acknowledges, has no advocates on this point). Instead, he argues, the soul is unified in its essence.

After disposing of the thoughts of others on the soul, Aristotle sets out in book 2 to make a fresh start on his subject. He proposes to study the nature of the soul in all living things, arguing that the soul is the source of all movement and the essence of life. From this, he goes on to examine life in terms of growth, finding that all living things possess a nutritive soul that urges them to feed themselves and to reproduce. In this sense, he concludes, all living things, both plant and animal, are animated by this type of soul.

Animal life can be distinguished from plant life, however, by virtue of the possession of sense. All animals have senses, he observes, which plants lack; whether the sense is a potential feeling or an actual one, all animals possess them. Any object in nature is knowable to animals through the use of at least one sense, and often all senses. From this, Aristotle goes into a lengthy discussion of the senses, analyzing how each sense perceives objects in the world around it. Through this discussion, he finds that each sense involves receiving information about the form of things and uses some organ as the seat for that sense. Through these senses, the animal soul perceives things, and from the use of the senses, as well as feelings of pleasure and pain, all animals feel desire, and even a kind of memory and imagination.

With this new understanding of the soul in all living things, and the soul in animal life in particular, Aristotle begins book 3, the final book in *On the Soul,* with a discussion of the rational soul that exists only in human beings. To understand this aspect of the soul, Aristotle draws an important distinction between perception and thinking. All animals use their senses to perceive objects in the world around them, but only humans exercise their imagination and judgment to think. He makes this argument by noting that perception requires some object in the world for the senses to act upon, but thinking is different because it does not require an object; one can think of anything.

Aristotle divides this kind of thinking into two types, actual and potential. Actual knowledge and the sensation connected with it are associated with objects in the world, and potential knowledge and sensation are associated with potentialities. Potential knowledge, therefore, requires actual knowledge to trigger it. In other words, Aristotle is suggesting that each human has a collection of potential knowledge, concepts derived from experience, waiting to be triggered by actual knowledge; humans can also contemplate with this potential knowledge and combine these concepts in thoughts. However, potential knowledge is not directly connected to the senses and objects in the world around it; this side of the soul, Aristotle argues, is without material form and is able to exist without a body and its senses. Therefore, he concludes, this part of the soul is, in fact, immortal.

The movement Aristotle speaks of in book 1, therefore, is explained by both appetite and the rational mind. The first, appetite, moves all animals as they perceive the world through their senses, triggering the sense imagination. Calculative imagination, in which the rational mind deliberates on the world, is solely a human activity and, therefore, only human beings have movement triggered by the mind. In this sense, the human soul is the accumulation of all three types of souls: the nutritive soul, common to all plants and animals; the sensible (as relating to the senses) soul shared by all animals; and the rational soul, shared only by human beings.

Aristotle's analysis of the human soul, therefore, has less to do with theology (the way many talk about "soul" in religious doctrines about an eternal "afterlife" of either reward or punishment) and more to do with psychology. He gives an explanation of the source of thought and the motivation behind movement in the world.

Although Aristotle is not giving a religious accounting of the soul, theologians have made use of his description of the soul, most notably Saint Thomas Aquinas. Aquinas had attempted to reconcile Aristotle's observations about the soul with an understanding of Christian theology, which also acknowledges the idea of a soul that lacks materiality and is immortal. However, most modern discussion of *On the Soul* takes place in the field of psychology, and it is through the study of the human mind that Aristotle's ideas still have an important part to play in human ways of understanding.

David Smailes

Further Reading

Adler, Mortimer J. *Aristotle for Everybody: Difficult Thought Made Easy.* New York: Macmillan, 1978. Adler gives an excellent introduction to Aristotle's thinking for readers new to the philosopher. The book describes Aristotle's approach to philosophy and the arguments presented in his major works in clear, modern language.

Elders, Leon. "The Aristotelian Commentaries of St. Thomas Aquinas." *Review of Metaphysics* 63, no. 1 (September, 2009): 29-53. An excellent discussion of the large body of work done by Aquinas on various aspects of Aristotle's thought. Elders's section on the soul and *De anima* is particularly insightful on the relationship between the thinking of both Aristotle and Aquinas.

McKeon, Richard. "*De anima*: Psychology and Science." *Journal of Philosophy* 27, no. 25 (December 4, 1930): 673-690. Although dated, McKeon's account of the importance of *On the Soul* to psychology remains one of the best descriptions of how Aristotle's book has influenced this field of knowledge.

Nussbaum, Martha, and Amelie Oksenberg Rorty, eds. *Essays on Aristotle's "De anima."* New York: Oxford University Press, 1992. An excellent collection of essays relating to *On the Soul*, particularly for advanced readers. The chapters on Aristotle's concept of the soul and psychology are particularly useful for those studying *On the Soul*'s import to the science of the mind.

Polansky, Ronald. *Aristotle's "De anima": A Critical Commentary.* New York: Cambridge University Press, 2007. Gives an excellent summary of *On the Soul* while making a strong case that Aristotle's book follows a carefully constructed design. Requires some familiarity with Aristotle's thought.

Veatch, Henry B. *Aristotle: A Contemporary Appreciation.* Bloomington: Indiana University Press, 1974. Another accessible introduction to Aristotle's work, with a particularly excellent section covering *On the Soul*. Puts Aristotle's books into a context that makes his method clearer than most introductions.

On the Sublime

Author: Longinus (fl. first century)
First transcribed: Peri hypsous, first century C.E.
　　(English translation, 1652)
Type of work: Literary criticism

On the Sublime is one of a number of classical literary treatises that pose the often-considered problem of nature versus art, of the relative contributions of natural genius or inspiration and of acquired skill to great writing. The author of *On the Sublime*, who almost certainly was not Longinus, but instead was an anonymous Greek rhetorician of the first century, argues throughout the work that it is a writer's genius that lifts the reader out of himself (or herself), above the limitations of reason. The author also points out that it takes great skill, training, and self-discipline to know when to give free rein to one's genius and when to hold it in check.

This treatise is an interesting combination of philosophical speculation about the elevating, moving powers of poetry and oratory and of practical suggestions about the grammatical constructions and figures of speech that contribute to the effectiveness of great or sublime writing. The author, an enthusiastic critic of his literary predecessors, often quotes Homer, Demosthenes, the great Greek dramatists, and even the book of Genesis to illustrate the powers of literature, and he points out faults with examples from the works of less skilled writers and from inferior passages in the works of the masters.

The author begins *On the Sublime* with a definition of the sublime in literature as a "loftiness and excellence in language" that uplifts the reader and makes him or her react as the writer desires. Sublimity may arise from a few words that cast light on a whole subject, or it may be the result of the expansion and development of an idea; the treatise suggests that the former method is generally the more powerful.

The great danger for the writer who seeks to create a sublime passage is the possibility of lapsing into bombast, that what is intended to be majestic will be simply an empty show. Other potential traps are affectation in expression and empty emotionalism, the display of passion that is not sufficiently motivated. The search for novelty, which on occasion can create a striking effect, may also result in inappropriate imagery and diction. The elements of the truly sublime in literature are often hard to distinguish; they are known chiefly by their effect—the reader's sense of exaltation. Too, a great passage will grow in meaning and significance with each rereading.

Five sources of the sublime are outlined. Two of these are results of the natural capacities of the author: grandeur of thought and the vivid portrayal of the passions. The other three are basically rhetorical skills: the appropriate use of figures of speech, suitable diction and metaphors, and the majestic composition or structure of the whole work. An important source is the first, which rests upon the sweep of the author's mind. Although a great intellect is likely innate, it may be enlarged by association with great ideas. Reading the finest works of the past and pondering them is always valuable, although even the greatest minds can sometimes fall below their customary level. The author suggests that Homer's *Odyssey* (c. 800 B.C.E.) is on a lower plane of intensity throughout than his *Iliad* (c. 800 B.C.E.). It is the work of an aging man who dreams, but "he dreams as Zeus might dream."

One of the tormented love lyrics of Sappho, the Greek poet, is analyzed to illustrate the power of emotion to create an impression of sublimity. The tumultuous succession of feelings, burning, shivering, and fainting are described so vividly and follow one another so closely that the reader participates in the emotional crises of the poet. This technique can, however, in the hands of a lesser skilled writer than Sappho, seem contrived, even ridiculous.

The author digresses from this discussion to elaborate on his earlier consideration of the relative merits of succinctness and diffuseness in the creation of sublime literature. He suggests that quickly moving, powerful language can overcome readers or listeners, convincing them in spite of their reason, whereas the more diffuse style tends to hammer an argument in through repetition, if not through logical argument. There are appropriate occasions for the use of each technique; some writers, like Demosthenes, excel in the vehement passionate outburst, while others, including Plato and Cicero, uplift their readers with a majestic flow of language.

The mention of these great masters suggests the next major point: The aspiring writer can learn much by imitating the outstanding writers of the past, by attempting to decide how Plato, Homer, or Thucydides would have expressed the idea with which the writer now is struggling. The helpfulness of such study can be far more than stylistic, because great writing always has the power to inspire, to expand the understanding of the would-be writer.

Moving on to his third source of sublimity, the use of imagery in poetry and oratory, the author notes that the purpose of all figures of speech is to enlighten, convince, enrapture, and overcome all doubt by their emotional power. Many kinds of images can create these effects. Close examination of passages from Demosthenes and others shows how the skillful choice of verbs, the use of an oath at the proper moment, the omission of conjunctions, or rhetorical questions can make the hearer assent, almost unconsciously, to the orator's premises. Again, natural genius must play an important part, for if the figures of speech are not fused into an impressive whole, they will only be an annoyance, convincing the listener that the speaker is trying to dupe her or him.

The writer has many ways of influencing the emotional reactions of readers, and the student of composition would do well to read in full the discussion of the ways in which sentence structure can be varied, or singular and plural interchanged to produce different effects. So simple a device as shifting from the past to the present tense or from the third person to the first can bring a narrative to life.

Appropriate diction is immeasurably important in the creation of great literature. The author notes that the suitable words are not always the most beautiful or elevated ones, and he illustrates the power of commonplace expressions. A writer must depend on taste to avoid vulgarity or bombast.

In another important digression, the author considers the relative value of the writer whose work is almost always flawless, polished, and in perfect taste, but never rises to great heights, versus the one whose work has both moments of sublimity and occasional lapses in taste. It is almost impossible for these two virtues to be combined, because the mind that is dwelling on the heights may sometimes overlook details, while the one that is attentive to correctness is never free enough of trivial concerns to achieve greatness. *On the Sublime*'s author gives unqualified approval to the flawed genius, on the grounds that humans are blessed with a wide-ranging intellect that can project them beyond the bounds of individual existence. It is both a duty and a privilege to keep one's eyes focused on heavenly lights, rather than on the tiny flames lit by humans.

Turning to the fifth source of sublimity, the author comments on the power of harmony in writing, as in music, to move people. It is the fusion of thought, diction, and imagery into one harmonious whole that builds up the reader's impression of power. The rhythm of cadence of the language, too, may enhance the almost hypnotic effect of sublime writing.

The final section of *On the Sublime* deals with the lack of great writing and oratory in the age in which the treatise was written. The author argues that the benevolent despotism of the age has curtailed humans' creative spirit, but he contends that it is rather people's greed and their search for pleasure that enervate them. When humans are bound to Earth by the quest for wealth, they no longer reach out to achieve that magnitude of mind and spirit that is essential for the great writer. Human apathy and indifference to all but its own immediate interests prevent people from achieving the greatness of their predecessors. On this discouraged and discouragingly modern note, the treatise ends, as its author states his intention to begin another work, enlarging on what he has said here about the place of the passions in great writing.

Further Reading

Benediktson, D. Thomas. *Literature and the Visual Arts in Ancient Greece and Rome*. Norman: University of Oklahoma Press, 2000. Charts the development of an aesthetic theory that enabled the ancient Greeks and Romans to compare literature and the visual arts. Much of the information about Longinus is provided in chapter 5, but there are references to him throughout the book that are listed in the index.

Blamires, Harry. *A History of Literary Criticism*. New York: St. Martin's Press, 1991. Summarizes the place of *On the Sublime* in the development of critical ideas; explains relevant issues. Includes notes and bibliography.

Habib, Rafey. *A History of Literary Criticism: From Plato to the Present*. Malden, Mass.: Blackwell, 2005. Chapter 6 provides an overview of Longinus's theories of literary criticism.

Innes, Doreen, Harry Hine, and Christopher Pelling, eds. *Ethics and Rhetoric: Classical Essays for Donald Russell on His Seventy-fifth Birthday*. New York: Oxford University Press, 1995. Includes two essays about Longinus: "Longinus, Sublimity, and the Low Emotions" by Doreen Innes and "'Longinus' and the Grandeur of God" by Martin West.

Kennedy, George A., ed. *Classical Criticism*. Vol. 1 in *The Cambridge History of Literary Criticism*. New York: Cambridge University Press, 1989. The section covering *On the Sublime* summarizes its content, significance, and relevant questions. Includes notes, bibliography, and index.

Longinus. *On the Sublime*. Edited and translated by James A. Arieti and John M. Crossett. New York: Edwin Mellen Press, 1985. Gives a line-by-line commentary on the work and its critics. Includes bibliography.

Roberts, W. Rhys, ed. *Longinus: On the Sublime.* New York: AMS Press, 1979. This definitive textual, critical, and historical study by an eminent nineteenth century classical scholar forms the basis for subsequent studies of Longinus. Includes introduction, facsimiles, appendixes, notes, indices, and bibliography of seventeenth, eighteenth, and nineteenth century scholarship.

Wimsatt, William K., and Cleanth Brooks. *Classical and Neo-Classical Criticism.* Vol. 1 in *Literary Criticism: A Short History.* Chicago: University of Chicago Press, 1978. The analysis of *On the Sublime* in chapter 6 is especially useful for the student, as it distinguishes between the sublime of Longinus and the sublime of Immanuel Kant.

The Once and Future King

Author: T. H. White (1906-1964)
First published: 1958; includes *The Sword in the Stone,* 1938; *The Witch in the Wood,* 1939; *The Ill-Made Knight,* 1940; *The Candle in the Wind,* 1958; *The Book of Merlyn,* 1977
Type of work: Novel
Type of plot: Arthurian romance
Time of plot: Middle Ages
Locale: England

Principal characters:
KING ARTHUR, earlier known as WART, king of Gramarye
SIR KAY, Arthur's childhood playmate
SIR ECTOR, Arthur's guardian and the father of Sir Kay
SIR CRUMMORE GRUMMURSUM, a friend of Sir Ector
KING PELLIMORE, a gentle and absentminded knight
MERLYN, a magician and Arthur's tutor
ROBIN WOOD, a robber who lives in the forest
MORGAN LE FAY, a wicked sorceress
UTHER PENDRAGON, Arthur's father and his predecessor on the throne
QUEEN MORGAUSE, the sister of Morgan le Fay and wife of King Lot of Orkney
GAWAINE,
AGRAVAINE,
GARETH, and
GAHERIS, the sons of King Lot and Queen Morgause
ST. TOIRDEALBLACH, a Pelagian heretic from Cornwall
LANCELOT, an ugly boy who becomes Arthur's chief knight and Guenever's lover
GUENEVER, Arthur's adulterous queen
UNCLE DAP, Lancelot's tutor
ELAINE, a girl who seduces Lancelot and gives birth to his son
GALAHAD, Lancelot's son
KING PELLES, Elaine's father
MORDRED, the son of Arthur and Morgause, who hates his father
SIR MADOR DE LA PORTE, a knight who accuses Guenever of adultery
SIR MELIAGRANCE, a knight who kidnaps Guenever

The Story:

In educating the Wart, as Arthur is called, to understand the world and its moral and ethical values, Merlyn allows the boy to assume the forms of various animals so that he can view life in different social orders. When he becomes a fish and swims in the castle moat, the great pike tells him that "Might is Right," demonstrating how the most powerful fish can rule the moat. From falcons, he learns about the rigors of military life; from ants, about societies that demand total conformity; from wild geese, about heroism; and from the badger, about the potential greatness of humans. Arthur's childhood is filled with the wonders of the universe as revealed by Merlyn and with adventures of the sort all boys dream about.

Arthur receives his education with no knowledge that he is being prepared for a throne. Rather, as the mere ward of Sir Ector, he expects to see Ector's son Kay reap whatever success is to be attained. When word comes that Uther Pendragon, ruler of Gramarye, has died and that his successor is to be the person who can pull a sword out of an anvil, it is as much a surprise to Arthur as it is to Sir Ector and Sir Kay when it is he, the Wart, who accomplishes that feat and becomes king. The tone of Arthur's rule is foreshadowed by the fact that he performs the deed that puts him on the throne without knowing about how the new king is to be chosen; the boy is merely trying to find a sword for Sir Kay to use in a tournament. Arthur's subsequent reign represents the establishment of a new order. In defending his right to the throne, Arthur first has to abandon the polite forms of chivalric warfare for other tactics. Then, announcing that he will use might only to accomplish right, he establishes the Round Table.

The first test to Arthur's reign as a just king is the enmity of Queen Morgause, wife of King Lot and sister of Morgan le Fay. Morgause hates anyone who sits on the throne of Uther Pendragon because Uther murdered her father and raped her mother, but she does not realize that Arthur is the child of Uther and her mother. When she seduces Arthur in an attempt to gain power over him, she unknowingly commits incest with her half brother. She teaches the child that results from this union, Mordred, along with her other sons—Gawaine, Gareth, Gaheris, and Agravaine—to hate Arthur. Mordred becomes the embodiment of the ultimate destruction of the Round Table.

The second test of Arthur's reign comes from the love that Lancelot, despite his worship of Arthur, bears for Arthur's queen, Guenever. Lancelot fights his attraction to Guenever by spending most of his time on quests, but eventually he succumbs to temptation and is seduced by Elaine, whom he has rescued from Morgan le Fay, when she pretends to be Guenever. After this union, which produces Galahad, Lancelot gives up his resistance and begins an adulterous relationship with Guenever. Plagued by the loss of his virginity and purity, he breaks off with Guenever and is even insane for a time. His unsuccessful fight against temptation becomes a kind of microcosmic representation of Arthur's ultimately unsuccessful attempt to establish a kingdom of justice.

Arthur attempts to find ways to control and use wisely the might at his command, but his troubles increase. The "Ork-

ney faction," the sons of Morgause, stir up discontent. Arthur initiates the quest for the Holy Grail to provide a healthy outlet for the energies of the knights of the Round Table; although Galahad eventually finds the Grail, the best knights are lost in the search, and the other knights become quarrelsome and decadent. Lancelot and Guenever are twice accused of adultery, and Lancelot has to face two trials by combat, in the second of which he murders Sir Meliagrance to keep him from revealing the truth.

Faced with the spiritual and physical disintegration of his kingdom, Arthur turns to the idea of justice under law as a last resort. As he does, he sets the stage for the final blow to be struck against his dream. Mordred now has the means to turn his father's own concept of justice against him. When Mordred and Agravaine accuse Guenever of adultery and demand that she be tried in a court of law, Arthur's failure is assured because he finds that he cannot accept the burden of his principles; he indirectly warns Lancelot and Guenever of danger, and he confesses to having tried to murder Mordred as an infant in a vain attempt to escape the prophecy that his son would become his enemy.

Arthur is unable to stem the tide of forces moving irrevocably toward the destruction of his kingdom. While Arthur is away on a hunting trip, Lancelot goes to Guenever's bedroom, whereby he unknowingly gives Mordred the evidence needed to convict Guenever of adultery. When Guenever is sentenced to be burned at the stake, Arthur is unable to intervene and yet remain true to his ideal of justice. When his hope is fulfilled and Lancelot rescues Guenever, Arthur has to go to France to lay siege to Lancelot's castle. Even an appeal to the Church in the form of the pope cannot reconcile the forces of destruction. Although the pope orders Arthur to take Guenever back and Lancelot to go into exile, Arthur is forced to return to his siege of Lancelot's castle to obtain justice for the murders of Gareth and Gaheris.

In the end, Arthur is forced to fight for what is left of his once glorious kingdom. In his absence, Mordred has proclaimed himself king and announced that he will marry Guenever. Arthur thereupon prepares to go into battle against Mordred. Even when faced with the possibility of failure, however, Arthur recalls the noble ideals that Merlyn taught him. He realizes that although he has been unsuccessful in putting those ideals into action, his having been able to make the attempt bodes well for the future. At last, he can face the future with a peaceful heart.

Critical Evaluation:

At the end of book 2 of *The Once and Future King*, T. H. White states that the story of King Arthur is a tragedy in the true Aristotelian sense, according to which most tragic heroes have an inherent flaw that contributes to their "reversal of fortune." The hero's tragic flaw is not necessarily a bad quality—Arthur's flaw, in fact, is his belief in the decency and perfectibility of humanity.

Arthur's flaw is revealed as the novel moves from descriptions of his innocent childhood to the imperfect, even corrupt world of his adulthood and, finally, to the loss of his kingdom; this movement is the "reversal of fortune" that results from Arthur's tragic flaw. It is the movement that unites the four narrative strands of the novel. The stories of Gawaine (book 2), Lancelot (book 3), and Mordred (book 4), considered within the framework of Arthur's own story, illustrate the theme that while some people may be decent, there will always be those who make Arthur's dreams of a better civilization impossible.

Believing people to be basically good, Arthur establishes the Round Table to destroy the authority of those who rule through brutal force and to impose on humanity the notion of decency. Arthur remains blind, however, to reminders that his vision will fail. He willfully overlooks the affair between Lancelot and Guenever, the murderous depth of Gawaine's rage, and the evil madness of his son Mordred. If he were to acknowledge deception, rage, and evil in those closest to him, he would have to deny humanity's perfectibility. Lancelot and Gawaine do turn out to be good and honorable men, however, thus reinforcing Arthur's convictions.

By nature, Lancelot is not deceptive, but he is weak. As a medieval Christian, he knows that his sinful nature stands in the way of one of his greatest ambitions: to perform a miracle. Lured by Guenever and encouraged by Arthur's blindness, he can never resist the queen's seduction and he remains, at least in his own eyes, a weak man. Yet, as he tells Guenever, his awareness of his own flawed nature drives him to be the best knight in the world. Significantly, when he fully accepts his own imperfect nature, he is allowed to perform a miracle by healing Sir Urre of his bleeding wounds.

Gawaine, too, reinforces Arthur's belief in the goodness of humanity. Gawaine has learned rage, even hatred, from his mother, Morgause, who is consumed by hatred for Uther Pendragon, Arthur's father, who killed Cornwall, the husband of her mother Igraine. She passes her hatred for the Pendragons on to her sons, and Gawaine pledges to get revenge. Gawaine has an inclination to do good, however. Thus, once he is a knight of the Round Table, Gawaine transfers much of his loyalty to the king. Gawaine knows that Arthur is not an evil man, but he experiences tremendous conflict when Lancelot kills his two brothers while rescuing Guenever. Gawaine vows revenge but eventually overcomes his vindic-

tiveness, forgiving Lancelot and so performing an act nearly as miraculous as Lancelot's healing of Sir Urre.

The political machinations of Mordred reveal Arthur's tragic flaw clearly. An extraordinarily bright young man, Mordred is both insane and evil. His mother, Morgause, has taught him to hate Arthur, and, unlike Gawaine, Mordred never relinquishes this hatred. Knowing of Arthur's belief in the decency of humanity and realizing that his father is fond of him, Mordred easily takes the kingdom from Arthur and shatters Arthur's world. Indeed, White's point seems to be that as long as there are Mordreds, the human race will never reach perfection, or even decency, and will continue to perpetuate its greatest evil, war.

Beyond its contribution to Arthurian literature and its tragic plot structure, *The Once and Future King* is a novel about war and evil and thus deserves a place alongside Stephen Crane's *The Red Badge of Courage* (1895), Erich Maria Remarque's *Im Westen nichts Neues* (1929; *All Quiet on the Western Front*, 1929), William Golding's *Lord of the Flies* (1954), and Joseph Heller's *Catch-22* (1961). It is significant that White lived in England and, little more than a decade before the publication of the final part of *The Once and Future King*, witnessed a terrible war and terrible evil waged by humans. The novel suggests that wars are not started by the Arthurs of the world but by the Mordreds, who take advantage of the goodness of others and abuse power to maintain power. Indeed, according to White's novel, if there is hope for humanity, it lies not in its innate goodness (for humanity is neither innately good nor innately evil) but in the existence of people like Arthur, who devote their lives to decency and justice.

"Critical Evaluation" by Richard Logsdon

Further Reading

Brewer, Elisabeth. *T. H. White's "The Once and Future King."* Cambridge, England: D. S. Brewer, 1993. Examines White's tetralogy, with separate chapters on each of the four novels and another on the fifth, unfinished work, *The Book of Merlyn*. Discusses comedy in the tetralogy and places White's work within the context of other Arthurian romances, historical fiction, and fantasy literature.

Gallix, François. "T. H. White and the Legend of King Arthur: From Animal Fantasy to Political Morality." In *King Arthur: A Casebook*, edited by Edward Donald Kennedy. New York: Garland, 1996. Analysis of *The Once and Future King* is part of a volume devoted to the examination of how the legend of King Arthur has been recounted in medieval romances, nineteenth century art, and twentieth century literature.

Lacy, Norris J., and Geoffrey Ashe, with Debra N. Mancoff. *The Arthurian Handbook.* 2d ed. New York: Garland, 1997. Comprehensive volume provides a critical survey of Arthurian legend, history, literature, and the arts from the fifth century to the late twentieth century.

Lagorio, Valerie M., and Mildred Leake Day, eds. *King Arthur Through the Ages.* 2 vols. New York: Garland, 1990. Collection of essays examines contributions to Arthurian literature from the Victorian period into the twentieth century. Acknowledges *The Once and Future King* as the "most influential and enduringly popular [work] of modern Arthurian fiction."

Lupack, Alan. "*The Once and Future King*: The Book That Grows Up." In *King Arthur*, edited by Harold Bloom. Philadelphia: Chelsea House, 2004. Argues that the tetralogy is an "experiment in artistic structure" that "grows up with the characters," moving from children's story to bildungsroman and on to romance and tragedy. Describes how White intended the final, unfinished book, *The Book of Merlyn*, to be a philosophical dialogue reflecting on all of Arthur's experiences.

Matthews, Richard. "Shining Past and Future: The Persistence of Camelot (T. H. White's *The Once and Future King*)." In *Fantasy: The Liberation of Imagination.* New York: Twayne, 1997. Essay discussing the novel is part of a study of fantasy fiction that examines the genre's origins and development from antiquity to the late twentieth century through analyses of works by White and other writers.

Sprague, Kurth. *T. H. White's Troubled Heart: Women in "The Once and Future King."* Rochester, N.Y.: Boydell & Brewer, 2007. Analyzes White's depiction of women in the tetralogy. Argues that White displays misogyny in the work (despite his charming portrait of Queen Guenever) as a reaction to his own experience of living with a difficult mother.

Tanner, William E. "Tangled Web of Time in T. H. White's *The Once and Future King*." In *Arthurian Myth of Quest and Magic: A Festschrift in Honor of Lavon Fulwiler.* Dallas, Tex.: Caxton Modern Arts, 1993. Focuses on White's treatment of historical time in relation to his concern for war.

One Day in the Life of Ivan Denisovich

Author: Aleksandr Solzhenitsyn (1918-2008)
First published: Odin den Ivana Denisovicha, 1962 (English translation, 1963)
Type of work: Novel
Type of plot: Historical realism
Time of plot: 1951
Locale: Siberia, northern Soviet Union

Principal characters:
IVAN DENISOVICH SHUKHOV, a prisoner in a Soviet labor camp
TSEZAR,
ALYOSHA,
PAVLO,
FETIKOV,
SENKA,
KILGAS, and
BUINOVSKY, members of Shukov's work squad
TIURIN, Shukhov's squad leader

The Story:

Reveille begins the day for Ivan Denisovich Shukhov, a victim of the mass imprisonments that took place in the Soviet Union during the Stalin era. Ivan has been unjustly sentenced to ten years imprisonment on spurious charges of espionage while serving in the Soviet Army during World War II. He is serving his term in a labor camp in a remote corner of Siberia. It is the dead of winter, and Ivan wakes up feeling ill. He intends to report for sick call.

Ivan's plan to report for sick call is apparently thwarted when a camp guard detains him for violating a rule: not getting up at reveille. Ivan is told he will be sentenced to ten days in the guardhouse but soon discovers the prison guard only wants someone to mop the guardhouse floor. Having been thus "let off," Ivan adroitly manages to get out of the work he was assigned as punishment and returns to his barracks. The sort of adroitness he demonstrates in this incident is a necessary characteristic for survival in the brutal environment of the camp.

Ivan then begins the routine of his day. After a trip to the mess hall, he still has time to go to the infirmary and try to get on sick call. At the infirmary, he is turned down because the daily quota of two prisoners exempted from work because of sickness has already been filled. A bureaucratic culture rules the camp. In contrast to the filth of the barracks and the mess hall, the infirmary is clean, quiet, orderly, and warm. When Ivan enters, the doctors are still asleep. The orderly on duty is writing not a medical report but poetry for the doctor in charge. The orderly, one of the better-off prisoners, has an easy job and some privileges because of his education level. There is a definite hierarchy in the camp, even among the prisoners, or "zeks."

Ivan reports to his squad, which moves out to the work site. As the squad members begin their work, they start telling the stories of their lives. The prison camp is a microcosm of Soviet RussiaL Tiurin, the squad leader, has been imprisoned because his father was a kulak (a well-to-do peasant), a member of a group persecuted by Stalin. Senka is a deaf former soldier who survived the Nazi concentration camp at Buchenwald; Fetikov, a former high-ranking member of the Communist Party, was arrested in one of Stalin's purges; Captain Buinovsky is also a loyal Communist and a Soviet naval captain unjustly accused of spying; Alyosha, a Baptist, has been imprisoned for practicing his religion; Tsezar is an intellectual. These men together with other squad members, struggle through the day with Ivan, sharing the victories, harassment, tragedies, and triumphs of prison life.

After breakfast, the squad is sent to work at an outpost where a power station is being built. The disorganization, ruin, and waste seen at the building site illustrate the Soviet government's overall management of society. Ivan works as a mason on the building. As the squad continues working, the building of the wall becomes a heroic task; the dignity of work preserves Ivan's humanity.

Adroitness carries with it additional benefits. Ivan, who by camp standards is poor and does not receive money or food packets from home, is able to survive and live a bit better because of his abilities. Ample opportunities to use his skills arise through the day. He has his own trowel, which he hides in different places so it will not be confiscated by the authorities; at the noon meal, he is able to steal two extra bowls of oatmeal when a server is distracted. Such things, though small, empower the inmates of the camp and create a sense of independence that the authorities cannot crush.

After the meal, the job of building continues. One of the prisoners, an "overseer" for the camp authorities named Der, comes to the site and notices that Ivan's squad has pilfered some building material to seal windows. He threatens to report Tiurin and his squad, but the men surround him and Tiurin declares that the day Der turns in the squad will be his last day on Earth. Reduced to passivity, the overseer promises not to say anything about the pilfering. This incident is a great moral victory for Ivan's squad.

The workday ends, and the men line up to return to the prison compound. For some reason, there is a delay, and since time is a precious commodity to the prisoners, they deeply resent being kept waiting for half an hour in the freezing cold. The trouble is finally revealed to be a missing Moldavian prisoner who has fallen asleep in one of the buildings. He is charged with attempted escape, and the column finally returns to the prison compound.

Once in the compound, Ivan helps Tsezar get his food parcel from home and manages to fight his way into the mess hall afterward. Later, Tsezar shares some items from his parcel with Ivan as payment for his help. While in the mess hall, Ivan observes a legendary prisoner, an old man, eating near him. Despite decades in prison camps and many physical infirmities, the old man eats with irrepressible dignity, a symbol of the unconquerable humanity demonstrated again and again by Ivan and the other camp inmates.

As the day draws to an end, there is more harassment by the camp authorities. The men are called out for a final assembly. Captain Buinovsky is sent for ten days of solitary confinement for an infraction committed that morning. Ivan lies down for the night, thankful for the many good things that had happened that day, and utters a prayer. His prayer is overheard by Alyosha, the Baptist, and the two engage in a discussion of the reasons they are in the prison camp. Alyosha believes that he is there because God has willed it so, and thus he can fully accept his lack of freedom. Ivan, however, believes that he is suffering only because his country was unprepared for war. He wants only to return home and he cannot accept his incarceration as Alyosha does. After another assembly, Ivan is able to go to sleep. It has been, the narrator comments, an "almost happy day."

"The Story" by David W. Landrum

Critical Evaluation:

Aleksandr Solzhenitsyn is considered by many to be the greatest Russian author of the twentieth century. His writing has attracted worldwide attention, and he has been the recipient of numerous awards and honors, including the Nobel Prize in Literature in 1970.

Solzhenitsyn's own experience as a prisoner in a Siberian labor camp is the basis for *One Day in the Life of Ivan Denisovich*. Solzhenitsyn was born in 1918, received a degree in mathematics and physics in 1941, and began teaching high school. He served with distinction as an artillery officer in World War II but was arrested in 1945 for allegedly making a derogatory remark about Stalin in a letter to a friend. Sentenced to eight years' imprisonment, he was incarcerated in a camp similar to the one described in the novel. He survived and was released in 1953, but he was exiled to Central Asia until Stalin was denounced by the new Soviet premier, Nikita Khrushchev, in 1956, and restrictions upon those who had suffered during Stalin's political purges were eased.

Solzhenitsyn moved to a small Russian town near Moscow and began to teach mathematics and to render some of his experiences in fictional form. It was the anti-Stalinist mood of the day that enabled him to get his first novel published. *One Day in the Life of Ivan Denisovich* appeared in the November 20, 1962, issue of *Novy Mir* (new world), the official literary journal of the Communist Party. It was published largely because the editors of the journal thought it represented a specifically anti-Stalinist piece of literature. The work's success was immediate. The entire November run of *Novy Mir* sold out in a day, and Solzhenitsyn was catapulted to international fame.

The officials of the Soviet Communist Party soon realized they had made a mistake. *One Day in the Life of Ivan Denisovich* was not, as they had assumed, a piece of literature denouncing Stalin, but an indictment of the Soviet system as a whole, a denunciation of the repression and totalitarianism of Communist Russia. Solzhenitsyn became a symbol of freedom for the persecuted Soviet artistic community and of courage and individualism to all who read him around the world. The government soon moved against him. He was denounced, dismissed from his teaching position, and exiled from Moscow. In 1974, he was arrested, charged with treason, and imprisoned; he was exiled from the Soviet Union that same year. Solzhenitsyn resided in the United States until returning to Russia in 1993, after the collapse of communism.

Solzhenitsyn's output as a writer is tremendous. Some of his more important works of fiction include *Rakovy korpus* (1968; *Cancer Ward*, 1968), *V kruge pervom* (1968; *The First Circle*, 1968), and *Avgust chetyrnadtsatogo* (1971, expanded version 1983; *August 1914*, 1972, expanded version 1989 as *The Red Wheel*). He is also well known for his massive nonfictional chronicle of the repressive activities of the Stalin era, *Arkhipelag GULag, 1918-1956: Opyt khudozhestvennogo issledovaniya* (1973-1975; *The Gulag Archipelago, 1918-1956: An Experiment in Literary Investigation*, 1974-1978). Like *One Day in the Life of Ivan Denisovich*, these

works championed human rights and denounced the totalitarian nature of the Soviet regime. After the Soviet Union's fall, Solzhenitsyn attempted to set Russian literature back on course, seeing Socialist Realism as a hiatus that stultified Russian arts and letters during the years of Communist domination. His historical novels recall the rich Russian literary heritage of the nineteenth century, an influence that almost disappeared during the years of Soviet realism.

One Day in the Life of Ivan Denisovich is a prime example of Solzhenitsyn's art; it makes political statements but never falls to the level of a mere tract or manifesto. The story of Ivan Denisovich and his companions creates feelings of fellowship, empathy, and admiration in readers, but it does not force or impose such reactions—unlike Socialist Realism, which tends to impel readers toward approved conclusions and to demand certain reactions to politically approved storylines. Solzhenitsyn's approach is indirect, ironic, even humorous.

At times, the novel seems almost allegorical. Ivan Denisovich represents an Everyman figure, the average Russian peasant persecuted by larger forces he does not understand. The other characters in the book fill similar symbolic slots: Tsezar represents the persecuted artist; Fetikov, who is called the jackal or the scavenger, symbolizes the Communist Party opportunist who has no morals or scruples and has ironically landed at the bottom of a system he helped create; Captain Buinovsky is a loyal Communist officer imprisoned by Stalinist paranoia and completely bewildered by this turn of events; Tiurin, the squad leader, is another innocent Russian persecuted merely because his father was a kulak; Alyosha, representing all those who experienced religious persecution, has been sentenced to twenty-five years merely because of his Baptist religion. All these are "types," figures of the groups who suffered under Soviet totalitarianism.

One Day in the Life of Ivan Denisovich is labeled by Solzhenitsyn as a *povest'*, or novella, so it is short and moves quickly. Its crisp, fast-paced narrative enables the author to sketch his characters quickly and to involve readers in the thoughts of Ivan Denisovich, from whose perspective the action is often reported by means of indirect discourse. That is, the narrator speaks from Ivan's point of view, ventriloquizing his thoughts without directly quoting them. In these passages the narrator's consciousness and knowledge are limited to what Ivan is capable of observing and knowing. In addition, there is an omniscient authorial voice that employs more literary, formal language and provides information and observations that are outside Ivan's ken.

Solzhenitsyn also employs defamiliarization in the novel. That is, he describes the details of an event or phenomenon from the viewpoint of a naïve observer who lacks the sophistication to process the data. For example, when Ivan observes the medical orderly Vdovushkin writing something at his desk, the narrator takes note of the even lines, each of which begins with a capital letter, but Ivan concludes only that this activity is not official work but something "on the side." A reader may recognize this as a description of a poem, an assumption the authorial voice later confirms, but Ivan himself does not register the writing as poetry. The chronicle of the day is told in the racy slang of the camp, often profane, always colorful and rich, giving readers a further sense of participation.

Overall, readers are likely to come away from *One Day in the Life of Ivan Denisovich* with a sense of triumph. Though the conditions in the camp are brutal, though the prisoners have been stripped of all human rights and are harassed and badgered through the day, life in the concentration camp has not broken them. An implicit theme lodged strongly in the story is that the rulers of the Soviet regime that created the camp will no more succeed at stifling the spirit of freedom in the Russian people than the local camp officials have succeeded in stamping that spirit out of Ivan Denisovich and his fellow prisoners. The human spirit, which always craves freedom, will ultimately triumph.

"Critical Evaluation" by David W. Landrum;
revised by Carl Moody

Further Reading

Barker, Francis. *Solzhenitsyn: Politics and Form.* New York: Barnes & Noble, 1977. A study of Solzhenitsyn's literary works, with emphasis on their important political aspects. Discusses how his writings are shaped by political considerations.

Bloom, Harold, ed. *Aleksandr Solzhenitsyn.* Philadelphia: Chelsea House, 2001. A collection of critical essays, including comparisons of Solzhenitsyn's work with that of Leo Tolstoy and Boris Pasternak, an analysis of the representation of detention in the works of Solzhenitsyn and Fyodor Dostoevski, and a discussion of Solzhenitsyn's experiences as a creative artist in a totalitarian state. Two of the essays focus on *One Day in the Life of Ivan Denisovich*: "Humanity in Extremis: *One Day in the Life of Ivan Denisovich* and *The Love-Girl and the Innocent*," by Edward E. Ericson, Jr., and "The Subtext of Christian Asceticism in *One Day in the Life of Ivan Denisovich*," by Svitlana Kobets.

Curtis, James M. *Solzhenitsyn's Traditional Imagination.* Athens: University of Georgia Press, 1984. Examines the currents of imaginative thought in Solzhenitsyn's works and emphasizes his transformation of traditional material into new, creative forms.

Ericson, Edward E. *Solzhenitsyn and the Modern World.* Washington, D.C.: Regnery Gateway, 1993. Examines Solzhenitsyn in the light of the collapse of communism in Russia. Answers some of the common criticisms that are leveled at his writing.

_____. *Solzhenitsyn: The Moral Vision.* Grand Rapids, Mich.: Eerdmans, 1980. Excellent overview of Solzhenitsyn's works with an eye to their sources, origins, and relationship to modern political and social reality.

Ericson, Edward E., and Alexis Klimoff. *The Soul and Barbed Wire: An Introduction to Solzhenitsyn.* Wilmington, Del.: ISI Books, 2008. Two major Solzhenitsyn scholars provide a detailed biography of the writer and analyses of all of his major fiction. Includes a chapter on *One Day in the Life of Ivan Denisovich*.

Klimoff, Alexis. *"One Day in the Life of Ivan Denisovich": A Critical Companion.* Evanston, Ill.: Northwestern University Press, 1997. A guide for readers encountering Solzhenitsyn's novel for the first time, providing primary source materials, a discussion of the novel within the context of Solzhenitsyn's body of work and of Russian literary tradition, and an annotated bibliography.

Mahoney, Daniel J. *Aleksandr Solzhenitsyn: The Ascent from Ideology.* Lanham, Md.: Rowman & Littlefield, 2001. Focuses on Solzhenitsyn's political philosophy and its impact on twentieth century thinking. Analyzes Solzhenitsyn's writings to demonstrate how they represent the political condition of modern man.

Medina, Loreta, ed. *Readings on "One Day in the Life of Ivan Denisovich."* San Diego, Calif.: Greenhaven Press, 2001. Collection of critical essays designed to assist students and other readers. The essays interpret the novel from a variety of perspectives and provide biographical information about Solzhenitsyn.

Nielsen, Niels Christian. *Solzhenitsyn's Religion.* Nashville, Tenn.: Nelson, 1975. A discussion of the important religious aspect in Solzhenitsyn's writing, tracing it through all of his early works.

One Flew over the Cuckoo's Nest

Author: Ken Kesey (1935-2001)
First published: 1962
Type of work: Novel
Type of plot: Psychological realism
Time of plot: Fall, 1960
Locale: Oregon

Principal characters:
CHIEF BROMDEN, an Indian patient
RANDLE P. MCMURPHY, a new patient
NURSE RATCHED, the ward boss, also known as Big Nurse
BILLY BIBBIT and CHARLES CHESWICK, longtime patients

The Story:

Chief Bromden, thought by all to be deaf and unable to speak, hears the booming voice of a new patient, Randle Patrick McMurphy, a big, red-headed Irishman with scarred hands and a free laugh, who resists the aides' pushing him around. McMurphy came from prison, having been banished for fighting. When McMurphy shakes the Chief's hand it seems to swell and became big again, the first small step in McMurphy's rescue of the Chief from his fog.

The Chief sees the ward as a repair shop for the Combine, the nationwide conspiracy that turns people into machines run by remote control. The asylum is the repair shop populated by two kinds of broken-down machines: the chronics and the acutes. The chronics are considered hopelessly insane; the acutes are considered to have hope of recovery. Nurse Ratched seeks to make her ward a smoothly running repair shop, so when McMurphy arrives, free from the controls of the Combine, he upsets the mechanistic routine. On his first day on the ward, McMurphy urges the patients to stand up against the Big Nurse, to show their guts by voting for something. He bets that he can make her crack within a week.

That week, McMurphy is eager to see the World Series on television; to do so requires a change in ward policy. Eventually he gets the patients to vote for the change, the deciding vote coming from the Chief, but the Big Nurse vetoes the result on a technicality. At game time, McMurphy and the other acutes sit down in front of a blank television and have a party, making believe they are watching the game. When the Big Nurse cannot get them to move, she loses control of herself. McMurphy wins his bet, showing that she is beatable.

Shortly thereafter, McMurphy discovers that as a committed patient he can be held indefinitely. To prevent that, he begins to cooperate, no longer standing up for the other patients. One day Cheswick looks to McMurphy for support in an argument, but the Irishman stays silent. The next day Cheswick drowns himself. McMurphy feels responsible for Cheswick's death. The decisive blow against McMurphy's self-interested stance comes when he learns that most of the acutes are not committed but are voluntary inmates. Their

problems have more to do with how they see themselves than with clinical insanity. This realization changes McMurphy, bringing him back into the battle against the Big Nurse. First, he "accidentally" punches through her window to get his cigarettes, then, after it was replaced he does it again, apologizing profusely. After a month passes, McMurphy gets the Chief to speak again, bringing him closer to health and freedom. They talk about the Combine, how it turned the Chief's father into an alcoholic by buying out their fishing village to make a dam. When his father shriveled, the Chief did, too.

The first of three final dramatic episodes in the story is the fishing trip, on which McMurphy and his twelve friends catch several huge fish. They come to see that they can be free, that a trip outside the machinelike asylum into the world of nature can be successful. The biggest step is their laughing binge, led by McMurphy, because laughter shows people are free. All the men become stronger, except McMurphy, because he is bearing the weight of their burdens, doling out his life for the others.

The next day, when the aides bully one of the fishing crew, McMurphy goes to his defense. That starts a fight in which the Chief joins. Later both are taken to the shock shop and blasted into unconsciousness by a jolt of electricity. Unlike on previous occasions, the Chief comes quickly out of the fog of the shock treatment. Since McMurphy made him big again, he does not need to hide from the world. After giving McMurphy three more shock treatments, the Big Nurse brings him back to the ward, threatening a lobotomy. All of McMurphy's friends urge him to escape the next weekend when McMurphy's friend Candy is coming for a visit. She brings another whore with her, helping the patients have an uproarious party filled with games, drunkenness, and sex. The orgy is a victory to the Chief; it shows that even at the center of the Combine people can be free.

McMurphy is supposed to escape at dawn but oversleeps. In the morning, the Big Nurse finds Billy Bibbit in bed with Candy. In front of all the other patients, the Big Nurse shames Billy, threatening to tell his possessive mother about his sexual experience. That drives Billy to kill himself, and Nurse

Ratched blames McMurphy for it. Outraged by the accusation, McMurphy attacks the Big Nurse, tearing her dress open to expose her breasts, showing that she is really a woman, not a machine. The terror that the inmates see in her eyes forever diminishes her power over them. She finally loses the war.

Over the next few weeks, almost all the acutes leave the ward. The Chief stays, to counter the Big Nurse's final move. Her gambit is a body on a gurney, a vegetable with black eyes (indicating that a lobotomy was performed), with the name Randle P. McMurphy attached to it. The Chief decides that McMurphy would never allow such proof of the nurse's power to lie around the ward. So he smothers the vegetable. Then he lifts a huge control panel and throws it through the reinforced window screen. Escaping finally from the cuckoo's nest, he returns to his free life, ready to tell McMurphy's story.

Critical Evaluation:

The central theme of the story is how Chief Bromden becomes strong, self-confident, and sane again. This rescue and transformation succeed because McMurphy treats him as a worthwhile, intelligent, and sane individual. In addition, McMurphy gives him the example of standing up to and occasionally beating the apparently all-powerful Combine.

That machine is the central symbol of evil in the story. The Chief accurately sees that the powerful in society subtly and unsubtly coerce people into becoming cogs in the machine. The Chief imagines the ruling part of the mechanistic society as a combine, which is a huge harvesting machine. It chews up the growing plants in the field and spits them out as identical products for sale. Thus, the Combine is the machinelike conspiracy that sucks people in, turns them into robots, and spits them out to carry out the Combine's will in society. In the cuckoo's nest, the repair shop for the Combine, the same kind of oppression continues. The shop symbolizes the hidden oppression operating in the outside world. The patients are broken-down machines that the asylum seeks to adjust. The Big Nurse's basic method is to destroy the patients' self-confidence by making them admit their guilt, shame, and uselessness.

Into that repair shop McMurphy comes, a man free from the controls of the Combine because he never stays in one place long enough for the controls to be installed. He is an outsider, like the three geese flying overhead in the song: One flew east, one flew west, one flew over the cuckoo's nest. The last goose comes to rescue the singer, just as McMurphy rescues the Chief, who is the singer of this novel-length song. The Chief, the narrator of the story, provides a central source

of its power. Readers initially see the ward through the Chief's psychotic haze. His fantastic visions show his paranoia and how oppressive the asylum really is. Then as McMurphy brings him back to sanity, the picture gradually clears, the fantastic visions becoming realistic. The Chief comes to see that his slavery is due not only to the Combine but also to his own capitulation. McMurphy's refusal to give in provides the example the Chief needs to give him confidence in his own ability to live freely.

The Chief sees McMurphy not only as the goose who rescues the slaves from a cuckoo's nest but also as other popular culture heroes. He speaks of him as a superman, calling him a giant come out of the sky to rescue them. Often the Chief describes him as a cowboy hero coming into town to gun down the bad guys. In particular, one of the patients identifies McMurphy as the Lone Ranger. The allusion that the Chief uses most to place McMurphy in the pantheon of heroes is that of Jesus, the self-sacrificing savior. On the fishing trip, for example, the group is called McMurphy and His Twelve, and one patient tells them to be fishers of men. On the way back, the Chief sees McMurphy as a Man of Sorrows, doling out his life for his friends. The shock treatment takes place on a table shaped like a cross, with McMurphy referring to their anointing his head and asking if he will get a crown of thorns. A patient speaks like Pilate, saying he washes his hands of the whole affair. The ward party is a Last Supper parody. In the end the powers destroy McMurphy by lobotomy, just as Jesus was killed by the Combine of his day. After that, the Chief (a big fisherman) escapes to tell his story, just as Jesus' disciples escaped.

Though the Chief's portrait of McMurphy in some central ways alludes to Jesus, in a variety of other ways it provides a contrast. McMurphy is not simply a selfless savior; he is also the fabled western American fighter, sexual braggart, and con man, which contrasts with Jesus' nonviolence, chastity, and honesty. In particular McMurphy promotes sexual indulgence as a saving activity. In the story, however, the Chief realizes that sexual indulgence is what leads to Billy's death, thereby portraying his savior as far from perfect. That imperfection has led some critics to object to the novel as promoting immorality. Whether one considers that the novel promotes immorality or not depends on whether one takes McMurphy as a model for all that is good. The Chief does not. He sees the good and the bad in his rescuer. An even stronger criticism made of the novel is that it is misogynist. The women in the novel are either tyrannical emasculators or sweet-natured whores. The novel offers no example of an ideal woman; it offers no model men either; McMurphy's considerable weaknesses lead to his destruction.

The great value of the novel is that it provides a picture of a universal fact of human life. Oppression of the weak by the strong is a constant reality. Rebellion by the weak is occasionally successful and can appropriately be celebrated and encouraged by stories such as this. In the end, the two chief opponents, Big Nurse and McMurphy, do not provide the only two choices available to readers. Instead, the model is the Chief, for he gains his free life again and lives to tell the tale.

Peter W. Macky

Further Reading

Bloom, Harold, ed. *Ken Kesey's "One Flew over the Cuckoo's Nest."* New York: Bloom's Literary Criticism, 2008. A collection of essays examining various aspects of the novel, including discussions of Kesey and the cultural revolution, the novel's narrative, and the Western American context of the book.

Carnes, Bruce. *Ken Kesey.* Boise, Idaho: Boise State University Press, 1974. A short summary of the author's novels with emphasis on imagery.

Kesey, Ken. *One Flew over the Cuckoo's Nest: Text and Criticism.* Edited by John Clark Pratt. New York: Viking Press, 1973. Reprint. New York: Penguin Books, 1996. Contains the text of the novel, articles on the author, and literary criticism of the novel.

Leeds, Barry H. *Ken Kesey.* New York: Frederick Ungar, 1981. A discussion of Kesey and his works. Beginning with a brief biography, it continues with summaries and evaluations of each of the author's published works.

Napierski-Prancl, Michelle. "Role Traps in Ken Kesey's *One Flew over the Cuckoo's Nest.*" In *Women in Literature: Reading Through the Lens of Gender,* edited by Jerilyn Fisher and Ellen S. Silber. Westport, Conn.: Greenwood Press, 2003. This essay examining the representation of gender in Kesey's novel is included in a collection of ninety-six essays that interpret the most frequently taught literary works from the perspective of gender criticism.

Porter, M. Gilbert. *The Art of Grit: Ken Kesey's Fiction.* Columbia: University of Missouri Press, 1982. An analysis of Kesey's published works, emphasizing their affirmation of traditional American values, especially optimism and heroism. The chapter on *One Flew over the Cuckoo's Nest* also emphasizes the significance of Chief Bromden as the narrator.

Tanner, Stephen L. *Ken Kesey.* Boston: Twayne, 1983. A short introduction to the author and his works. The chapter on *One Flew over the Cuckoo's Nest* emphasizes the frontier values of self-reliance and independence.

One Hundred Years of Solitude

Author: Gabriel García Márquez (1927-   )
First published: Cien años de soledad, 1967 (English translation, 1970)
Type of work: Novel
Type of plot: Magical Realism
Time of plot: 1820's to 1920's
Locale: Macondo, a town in Latin America

Principal characters:
JOSÉ ARCADIO BUENDÍA, the Buendía family patriarch and founder of Macondo
ÚRSULA IGUARÁN, the Buendía family matriarch and wife of José
MELQUÍADES, a gypsy
COLONEL AURELIANO BUENDÍA, the younger son of José and Úrsula
JOSÉ ARCADIO BUENDÍA, the older son of José and Úrsula
AMARANTA, the daughter of José and Úrsula
REBECA, the adopted daughter of José and Úrsula
PIETRO CRESPI, suitor to both Rebeca and Amaranta
AURELIANO SEGUNDO and JOSÉ ARCADIO SEGUNDO, twin great-grandchildren of José and Úrsula
REMEDIOS THE BEAUTY, sister of the twins
AURELIANO, a sixth-generation Buendía who deciphers family history and is the father of the last Buendía
AURELIANO, the last Buendía, born with a pig's tail

The Story:

Standing before a firing squad, Colonel Aureliano Buendía remembers the day that his father, José Arcadio Buendía, had taken him to see ice for the first time. This had taken place in the early years of Macondo, the town that the elder Buendía, his wife Úrsula, and others had founded after José Arcadio and Úrsula had sought to escape the ghost of a man who José Arcadio had killed. The dead man had accused José Arcadio of impotence, when the real reason that the Buendías had avoided sex for so long after marriage was that they were afraid of producing a child with a pig's tail, something that had already happened between their two "inbred" families.

Soon after the founding of Macondo, gypsies begin to visit the town with incredible inventions, the wonder of which ignites the scientific curiosity of José Arcadio. Through these visits the Buendías meet Melquíades, a wise and magical gypsy and author of a mysterious manuscript. On one particular visit by the gypsies, right after the town learns of Melquíades's death in a far-off land, José Arcadio Buendía and his sons are introduced to ice, which the elder Buendía calls "the great invention of our time."

José Arcadio and Úrsula Buendía have two sons, Aureliano and José Arcadio, and two daughters, Amaranta and Rebeca, the latter of whom they had adopted after she had shown up on their doorstep, orphaned and with her parents' bones in a canvas sack. The two sons both father illegitimate children by Pilar Ternera, and the older son, José Arcadio, soon runs off with the gypsies. An insomnia plague attacks the town and brings with it a temporary but severe loss of memory. Melquíades, who has died "but could not bear the solitude," returns to Macondo. A conservative magistrate, the peaceful town's first, settles in shortly thereafter.

An Italian dance teacher, Pietro Crespi, arrives to tune the pianola and to teach the Buendía girls the latest steps. He begins to court Rebeca, which touches off a lifelong jealousy and bitterness in Amaranta. Meanwhile, Melquíades continues to be a presence (as would his manuscript) in the Buendía house. José Arcadio (the elder) attempts to photograph God, begins having visits from the ghost of Prudencio Aguilar (the man he killed years before), starts speaking a strange language (later identified as Latin), and is tethered to a chestnut tree in the backyard. Aureliano falls in love with and marries Remedios, the magistrate's barely pubescent daughter, who dies, pregnant with twins, just days before Rebeca's scheduled marriage to Pietro Crespi.

José Arcadio (the son) returns, enormous and tattooed, and marries his adopted sister (Rebeca), and Pietro Crespi turns his affections to Amaranta. Aureliano becomes Colonel Aureliano Buendía and leads an uprising against the conservatives. He leads thirty-two uprisings and all end in failure before an embittered Aureliano returns home to live out his days making little fish of gold, melting them down, and making them again, over and over. He also fathers seventeen illegitimate sons with seventeen different women. While Aureliano is off fighting the government, Amaranta rejects Pietro Crespi, who then commits suicide. Brother José Arcadio is killed mysteriously, his blood flowing in a stream from his house across town to the Buendía house, José Arcadio (the father) dies, initiating a rain of yellow flowers from the sky, and Arcadio (José Arcadio's illegitimate son) becomes the town dictator and is executed. This is not before, however, he and wife Santa Sofía de la Piedad have three children: twin sons Aureliano Segundo and José Arcadio Segundo (whose identities are accidentally switched), and one daughter, Remedios the Beauty.

Aureliano Segundo spends most of his time with Petra Cotes, but he marries Fernanda del Carpio, who will never quite fit in with the Buendías, and with whom Aureliano Segundo, too, has three children: José Arcadio, who is sent to seminary in Rome; Renata Remedios, or Meme, who has an illegitimate child by auto mechanic Mauricio Babilonia, who is always accompanied by a swarm of yellow butterflies; and Amaranta Úrsula, who is sent to school in Belgium. Colonel Aureliano Buendía's seventeen bastard sons suddenly show up in Macondo. One of them, Aureliano Triste, eventually brings a train to town, and with it comes inventions every bit as wondrous as those the gypsies had brought years before: electric light bulbs, moving pictures, and phonographs.

The intrusion from the outside world also brings something else: a North American banana company. Meanwhile, Remedios the Beauty, whose physical perfection drives men mad, ascends to heaven while hanging laundry on the line. Soon thereafter, sixteen of Colonel Aureliano Buendía's illegitimate sons are hunted down and killed; the seventeenth was killed later. Amaranta begins sewing her own shroud, soon after which Colonel Aureliano Buendía dies. Amaranta continues to sew her shroud with the intention of dying on the day that she finishes it, which she does. It was at this time that Meme has Mauricio Babilonia's illegitimate son (Aureliano).

Relations between the banana company and Macondo gradually worsen, and soon there is a strike. José Arcadio Segundo, now a union leader, is in a crowd of demonstrators when army soldiers fire and kill three thousand people. José Arcadio Segundo is not killed but is unable thereafter to find anyone else who will say that the massacre occurred. Officially at least, the massacre simply did not happen.

A continuous five-year rainstorm follows. Úrsula, now well over one hundred years old, dies, as does Rebeca, Aureliano Segundo, and José Arcadio Segundo. Santa Sofía soon moves out and Fernanda dies as well. Meanwhile, Aureliano (son of Meme and Mauricio Babilonia) becomes obsessed with Melquíades's mysterious manuscript. José Arcadio returns home from Rome and opens the house to children he picks up, some of whom come back later, murder him, and make off with a stash of gold.

Amaranta Úrsula returns from Belgium with her husband and soon engages in an incestuous relationship with her nephew, Aureliano. Their child is born with a pig's tail. Amaranta Úrsula dies, and the baby is eaten by an army of ants. Suddenly, Melquíades's mysterious manuscript becomes clear to Aureliano. The manuscript contains the history of Macondo and the Buendías, written before it actually happened, and that history will be complete, with Aureliano's death and the destruction of Macondo, as soon as Aureliano finishes deciphering the manuscript.

Critical Evaluation:

One Hundred Years of Solitude is considered by many critics to be the most important Latin American novel of the twentieth century and the most important and most famous Spanish-language novel since Miguel de Cervantes' *Don Quixote de la Mancha* (1605, 1615). Written during the "boom" in the Latin American novel, the period in the 1960's during which writers such as Carlos Fuentes and Mario Vargas Llosa wrote their masterpieces, Gabriel García Márquez's *One Hundred Years of Solitude* contributed greatly to the Latin American novel's placement on the world literary map.

Like many Latin American novels, and the most acclaimed ones published in the latter half of the twentieth century, *One Hundred Years of Solitude* is what is known as a New Novel. It is "new," or nontraditional (particularly when compared to the Latin American novels of the 1920's and 1930's), in many ways, including its version of reality. Macondo, with its characters who die but return as ghosts, its clairvoyant residents, its stream of blood with a mind of its own, its flowers falling from the sky, its young woman ascending to heaven, and its five-year-long rainstorm, for example, presents a reality that is anything but the one to be found in realistic fiction. The book does not slip into pure fantasy, however, but remains in the domain of Magical Realism. Instead of presenting nonrealistic elements side-by-side with realistic ones in such a way that the nonrealistic stands out as odd, the author frequently describes the normal as if it were fantastic (the description of ice in the first chapter, for example) and the fantastic as if it were normal (Remedios the

Beauty's ascension, for example). The reader's reaction is to take a new perspective on what is real versus what is not real. This technique, along with the fact that García Márquez bombards the reader with characters and events (the book is approximately four hundred pages long but contains the plot of a much longer book), pulls the reader into the world of Macondo, where the outside rules of what is real and what is not do not apply.

One Hundred Years of Solitude is a New Novel as well in that although it deals with Latin American themes, such as political strife from within (the liberals versus the conservatives) and exploitation from without (the banana company), it also deals with universal themes, most notably solitude— the solitude of power, language, envy, insanity, death, blindness, and the act of reading. The book's enormous popularity outside Latin America is vivid testament to the story's universal reach.

This enormous popularity, however, separates *One Hundred Years of Solitude* from other Latin American New Novels. While novels such as Fuentes's *La muerte de Artemio Cruz* (1962; *The Death of Artemio Cruz*, 1964) and Vargas Llosa's *La casa verde* (1966; *The Green House*, 1968), for example, clearly contributed to the Latin American novel's international reputation, works such as these remain largely the interest of the intellectual reader. *One Hundred Years of Solitude*, however, is readable; except for keeping track of the repetitive names and the numerous events, one does not have to work nearly as hard to read the work as one does for most other New Novels. It is, moreover, an entertaining, and even spellbinding story of biblical proportions (with numerous biblical parallels), and it has reached audiences of all kinds and interests. It is one of the few books appreciated by literary critics and by those simply looking for a "good read." Few books have ever been able to accomplish such a feat.

Keith H. Brower

Further Reading

Bell-Villada, Gene H. *Gabriel García Márquez: The Man and His Work*. 1990. Rev. and expanded ed. Chapel Hill: University of North Carolina Press, 2009. Definitive book-length study of García Márquez and his work aimed at North American readers. Contains a twenty-eight-page chapter about *One Hundred Years of Solitude*.

_____, ed. *Gabriel García Márquez's "One Hundred Years of Solitude": A Casebook*. New York: Oxford University Press, 2002. Includes an interview with García Márquez, an analysis of García Márquez's works by writer Carlos Fuentes, and several essays discussing numerous aspects of the novel, including its humor, the novel as a chronicle of Latin America, and a comparison of the novel with Joseph Conrad's *Nostromo*.

Bloom, Harold, ed. *Gabriel García Márquez's "One Hundred Years of Solitude."* New York: Chelsea House, 2006. Includes a biographical sketch of García Márquez, a list of characters, a plot summary, and several essays interpreting the novel. Some of the essays examine the images of women as well as humor, Magical Realism, biblical and Hellenic devices, and use of journalistic techniques. Also features an interview in which García Márquez discusses the creation of *One Hundred Years of Solitude*.

McMurray, George R. *Gabriel García Márquez*. New York: Frederick Ungar, 1984. *One Hundred Years of Solitude* is the subject of a forty-page chapter discussing diverse topics, including the story's connection to Colombian history, the use of cyclical and mythical time, humor, and the significance of the novel's final three pages.

Pelayo, Rubén. *Gabriel García Márquez: A Critical Companion*. Westport, Conn.: Greenwood Press, 2001. Designed for students, this book offers an introductory overview of García Márquez's life and analyses of his works. Chapter 6 is devoted to *One Hundred Years of Solitude*, examining the novel's historical context, characters, narrative techniques, themes, and other elements.

Vázquez Amaral, José. *The Contemporary Latin American Narrative*. New York: Las Américas, 1970. Topics covered in the chapter on *One Hundred Years of Solitude* include the novel's focus on the subject of revolution, the theme of the "solitude of the warrior" once he has attained power, and the possible influence on García Márquez of Mexican writers Elena Garro and Juan Rulfo.

Williams, Raymond L. *Gabriel García Márquez*. Boston: Twayne, 1984. A twenty-three-page chapter on *One Hundred Years of Solitude* presents an excellent overview of García Márquez's masterpiece.

One of Ours

Author: Willa Cather (1873-1947)
First published: 1922
Type of work: Novel
Type of plot: Historical
Time of plot: World War I era
Locale: Nebraska and France

Principal characters:
CLAUDE WHEELER, a farm boy who becomes a soldier
THE WHEELER FAMILY, father Nat, mother Evangeline, and brothers Bayliss and Ralph
ENID ROYCE, Claude's wife
MAHAILEY, the Wheeler family's domestic
GLADYS FARMER, a schoolteacher
THE EHRLICH FAMILY
ERNST HAVEL, a childhood friend of Claude
VICTOR MORSE, an aviator who befriends Claude
LIEUTENANT DAVID GERHARDT, a violin-playing soldier
THE JOUBERT FAMILY, a French family that provides rest for soldiers

The Story:

Claude Wheeler is a young man living on a farm near Frankfort, Nebraska. He has no confidence in any of his abilities or his physical appearance and frequently makes reference to his own deficiencies. Above all else, he wants to go away to study. Because of his family's beliefs, he first attends Temple University, a religious school in Lincoln. Eventually, he manages to enroll in special classes at Nebraska State University, also in Lincoln.

While there, he befriends a student, Julius Ehrlich, and meets the Ehrlich family, who intrigues him with their intellectual lives. Claude indulges in contrasting them with his own family and friends. Growing up on a farm, he has known primarily other farmers, most of whom were, like Ernst Havel, immigrants to the United States.

Just as Claude is doing well at the university, his studies are cut short when his father, Nat, announces that he has purchased a ranch in Colorado. Nat tells Claude that he will begin living most of the time on the ranch and will take Claude's youngest brother, Ralph, with him. Claude is told to drop out of college, manage the Nebraska farm, and care for his mother. Bayliss, Claude and Ralph's brother, is a well-known banker in Frankfort.

Claude complies with his father's orders, and he does a good job running the farm, introducing modern methods. One day, he is severely injured while driving the mule team; the mules had been frightened by a loud noise. Claude's face is cut, leading to erysipelas, a skin disorder. During convalescence, a childhood friend named Enid Royce begins visiting him. He enjoys her company. After a short courtship, the two marry. On the first night of their marriage, she asks him to sleep elsewhere.

About one year later, Enid's sister, a missionary in China, gets sick and begs for a family member to come to China to attend to her. Enid, in an unhappy and unconsummated marriage, quickly volunteers. Claude is not sad to see her go.

News of political conflicts in Europe begin to filter through to Claude and the others around Frankfort. Claude enlists in the military, feeling that he should do so not only because his wife has left him but also because the rest of his life stretches boringly in front of him.

After training, Claude is commissioned a lieutenant and sails for France on a ship named the *Anchises*. The voyage is a hardship for the twenty-five hundred soldiers on board. Twenty-five die from diseases during the voyage to France, and another eleven die shortly thereafter. Claude thrives on the trip and is given special duties as a medical assistant. He meets an aviator named Victor Morse. Morse is from Iowa but serves in the Canadian air force. He is intriguing to Claude because of his worldliness and bravery.

After arriving, Claude and the soldiers begin marching through French villages en route to the front. All of them are acutely aware of the landscape and culture of the country. Claude's colonel sends him an officer named David Gerhardt. Lieutenant Gerhardt is also a professional violinist, and he expands Claude's notions of the world and art. Gerhardt also introduces Claude to the Joubert family, whom they visit while on leave. The Jouberts have lost two sons in the war.

Claude and the soldiers continue marching. On the outskirts of one village, Claude stops to help a sick, starving woman with a little girl and a baby. He is aghast to learn that the woman's French husband has been killed and that the baby's father is German. The soldiers arrive at the first of many trenches and are shelled. They find a dead German soldier in the muddy pit they use for bathing. Claude learns that Victor had been shot down while fighting eight German planes.

Claude and the soldiers march to different trenches and take positions. They continue to encounter horrific scenes, such as the rare survivor of the so-called pal battalions, underage British school boys sent to the war with their friends. Claude barely survives a mortar blast. In the village of Beau-

fort, he sees a little girl shot to death in a village center, and he also bayonets a German officer. He does have some enjoyable encounters, though, such as the evening spent with a French family, thanks to Gerhardt's introduction. On a rare Amati violin, Gerhardt plays a poignant solo for Claude and the family.

Claude becomes more cognizant of the war's affect on him, and he considers his experiences to be positive. Claude is put in charge of an entire company. They take positions at the dangerous Boar's Head section of the Moltke trench. Under heavy fire, he sends Gerhardt back to headquarters with a message. Realizing the peril for his friend, he bargains with God to take him, not Gerhardt. The Germans are a scant fifty yards away, and both sides are firing at point-blank range. Claude feels his men are fearful, so he makes himself visible and urges them on. He is shot dead with three bullets to the chest. He never knows that Gerhardt is killed.

Critical Evaluation:

Willa Cather was awarded the Pulitzer Prize in fiction in 1923 for *One of Ours*. Nearly all of her twelve novels and her short stories and poetry are rooted in her experiences growing up in Red Cloud, Nebraska; *One of Ours* is no exception. Ultimately, the novel takes Claude Wheeler to the battlefields of France during World War I, but everything he experiences is filtered through his youth on a Nebraska farm and in a small town.

The novel is not autobiographical, but in midlife, Cather had moved to New York and also had traveled to Europe. These experiences are reflected in *One of Ours* with allusions, for example, to the Statue of Liberty and with a prosaic description of New York City seen through smog. Her detailed descriptions of the French countryside also come from first-hand knowledge.

On one level, *One of Ours* is a coming-of-age story, or bildungsroman. Claude also symbolizes a young America that was also forced to reexamine itself because of World War I. The country had to mature, become less isolated, and become more cynical. Cather complicates this genre by allowing Claude to speak or think disparagingly of himself right to the end when, after all he has accomplished, he still thinks poorly of himself. He considers himself unattractive, boring, and incapable of doing anything well.

However, others relate or demonstrate their belief in his qualities. Gladys Farmer and Julie Ehrlich both show romantic interest in him, he is made a lieutenant upon completing basic training, and he is asked to assist the ship's doctor after thriving during the difficult voyage across the Atlantic. Admirable men, such as Victor Morse and David Gerhardt, befriend him. French families enjoy his company. He is put in charge of an entire company of soldiers and, finally, in an act partly of desperation and partly of heroism, he gives his life for his men.

Rarely does Claude criticize his Nebraska family and friends, but he is hurt by them and feels strongly that something is lacking in their lives. The elusive truth Claude seeks all his life and finds in the mud of the French trenches is that there are things worth dying for. Cather does not glorify war and does not create Claude to enjoy it either. Rather, war is the vehicle that catapults him out of the narrow confines of farm life, where life is often seen through myopic eyes. It is a life of farming, gossip, conformity, and capitalism.

The truth for Claude is not revealed in the aerial battles, trench warfare, or forced marches. The truth for him is in finding and seeing beauty and culture. He discovers these truths in the simple but elegant lives of the French families, in churches, in a worldly woman named Mademoiselle de Courcy, and in Gerhardt's music.

While living in Nebraska, Claude had reason to despise religion and capitalism. Both inflicted much pain on him as a young man. His frigid and deceptive wife, Enid, marries him, but only after consulting with Preacher Weldon; in marriage, she is told, she could save his soul. His own mother is saddened but not opposed to his going to war, and his father remains committed to his business, even if it means forcing his son to give up any dreams of his own. The negatives of both religion and capitalism are combined in Claude's calculating brother Bayliss, the town banker, who ultimately joins forces with cold, pious Enid in the temperance movement.

One of the sadder parts of the story is that Claude realizes too late that he should have loved Gladys, the vivacious school teacher who is impervious to the town gossip about her. As he leaves for war, he learns she had never planned to marry Bayliss because she came to understand the constraints and soul-mutilating effects of money and greed.

Cather is at her most eloquent when describing the land. From the fields of grain in America to the timber stand where Claude frequently takes refuge to the descriptions of poppies and cornflowers in France, Cather writes of the value of the earth and its resources. Claude realizes just before he dies that the earth produces things of substance; the farmer works hard to get these things to market but, he then buys human-made items that are of no lasting value. Before the war, Claude would have been incapable of articulating these insights; after experiencing war—and French culture—he has no trouble doing so.

The novel's time line is about six years. Claude is nineteen years old at the beginning and scarcely twenty-five years old when he dies. The wisdom he gains in those six years comes from his realization of the lasting qualities of the land and of art and culture. Just as the land feeds the body, art and culture feed the soul; both are absolutely necessary for happiness. Shortly before his death, he daydreams that life is short and, therefore, must be reinforced by something that endures. He has no regrets as he mounts the trench to face the German gunfire.

Judith Steininger

Further Reading

De Roche, Linda. *Student Companion to Willa Cather*. Westport, Conn.: Greenwood Press, 2006. This companion provides an introductory overview of Cather's life and work and is aimed at high school students, college undergraduates, and general readers. Includes analysis of *One of Ours*, *O Pioneers!*, *My Ántonia*, and *Death Comes for the Archbishop*.

Gerber, Philip L., ed. *Willa Cather*. New York: Twayne, 1995. The "Novels of the Middle Years" section includes information about Cather's impetus for writing *One of Ours*: the death of her cousin G. P. Cather.

Lindermann, Marilee. *The Cambridge Companion to Willa Cather*. New York: Cambridge University Press, 2005. This collection of essays includes examinations of such topics as politics, sexuality, and modernism in Cather's works.

Murphy, John, ed. *Critical Essays on Willa Cather*. Boston: G. K. Hall, 1984. This collection includes a 1922 review of *One of Ours* by Dorothy Canfield Fisher. The review is of special interest because World War I was still fresh in the public's mind. Fisher's review is in this cultural context.

Stout, Janis P. *Willa Cather: The Writer and Her World*. Charlottesville: University Press of Virginia, 2000. Explores the biographical context of Cather's writings. Emphasis is on specific American issues, including what is now called diversity.

Trout, Steven, ed. *Cather Studies: History, Memory, and War*. Vol. 6. Lincoln: University of Nebraska Press, 2006. This volume in an ongoing multivolume series includes an essay discussing character Claude Wheeler's possible gay identity as a means for Cather to discuss her own sexuality.

Urgo, Joseph R., and Merrill Maguire Skaggs, eds. *Violence, the Arts, and Willa Cather*. Madison, N.J.: Fairleigh Dickinson University Press, 2007. Cather's writings, including *One of Ours*, contain lyrical descriptions of the land but are also punctuated with violence. This collection of essays explores this topic.

The Open Boat
And Other Tales of Adventure

Author: Stephen Crane (1871-1900)
First published: 1897
Type of work: Short fiction
Type of plot: Naturalism
Time of plot: c. 1897
Locale: Off the coast of Florida or Cuba

Principal characters:
COOK, a *Commodore* crewmember
OILER, a *Commodore* crewmember
CORRESPONDENT, a passenger on the *Commodore*
CAPTAIN, of the *Commodore*

The Story:

Four men, crewmembers and a passenger of the sunken ship *Commodore*, are floating in a lifeboat scarcely bigger than a bathtub, their eyes fixed on the ocean waves that continually threaten to overwhelm them. The cook bails water from the boat while the oiler and correspondent row. The captain of the *Commodore* is injured, consumed with despair and visions of the sinking of the ship and the faces of its crewmembers.

The struggle to keep the boat upright and free of the waves is continuous. The men know it is daytime only because the color of the sea changes. They have no cause to look at the sky; their attention is only on the menacing waves. The cook says hopefully that he knows of a house of refuge on shore with a crew that could rescue the shipwrecked men. The men begin to squabble about whether the house of refuge will indeed have a crew, but the oiler twice reminds them that they are not yet ashore.

The ocean, "probably splendid," continues tossing the boat, but the men are in such danger and hardship that they have no inclination to consider the sea's beauties. Caught between childish optimism and hopelessness, the men talk idly about whether they have a chance of making land. The captain spots a lighthouse so far away that it looks like the point of a pin. The men still cannot discern any progress through the ocean, but the cook is cheerful as he bails water. The men begin to feel an intense sense of fellowship. Even the cynical correspondent knows that this is the best experience of his life.

On the captain's suggestion, the men rig up a mast and sail. The lighthouse has been growing in size, indicating they are getting closer to it. The cook mentions, as if in passing, that he believes the life-saving station on shore had been abandoned about a year ago. The wind dies, and the men take the oars. The men had hardly slept for two days and nights before getting on the dingy, and had eaten little as well. Their efforts are so great that the correspondent wonders desperately how anyone could row a boat for pleasure.

As the land comes closer, the captain is able to make out a house on the shore; the cook and the captain anticipate men coming out to rescue them. The oiler notes that none of the other lifeboats can have made it to land, given that no rescuers have been looking for survivors. As the men approach shore, their mood lightens. The correspondent finds four dry cigars, and everyone smokes and takes a drink of water.

The house of refuge shows no signs of life. The men are puzzled; they do not realize that there are no life-saving stations for miles. The men's spirits fade. The captain says that they will have to try to get in to shore themselves, before they are too tired to make the swim. The men are filled with anger, wondering why they should endure so much if they might be drowned before they reach shore.

The waves grow so large that the boat is sure to be swamped before the men can get close enough to swim, so they take the boat farther out. They then see a man on shore, and their spirits soar. He begins to wave a coat at them. The man is joined by a second man and by something on wheels, which the shipwrecked men excitedly hope is a boat being readied for launch. Eventually, in despair, they identify the thing on wheels as only a bus (an omnibus). The man waves the coat until the sunset obscures him, while the men finally lose hope that someone on shore understands their dilemma and will launch a boat to save them. Once again, they begin to wonder why they might have been brought so close to shore if they are going to drown before reaching it.

Darkness settles in. The correspondent rows as the others sleep and sees a flash of phosphorescence like a blue flame on the sea—the fin of a shark. The correspondent repeats a lament: Why should he and the other men endure so much if they are to drown within sight of land? The thought dawns on him that nature does not feel the men are important; he responds by affirming that he thinks he is important, that he loves himself. A cold star seems to be the answer.

The correspondent remembers a verse about a dying soldier in Algiers, which never before struck him as important.

Now he imagines the dying soldier in detail and is deeply moved by the scene. Exhausted, the correspondent and the oiler, now awake, take turns rowing.

At dawn, the men see deserted cottages and a windmill on shore. The captain suggests they try a run for shore, before they are too tired to make it. They position the boat in the rough surf, and the men are swept into the icy sea. The correspondent sees the oiler, who is swimming strongly; he sees the cook from behind and the captain hanging on to the overturned dingy. The correspondent reaches a difficult current. The captain tells the cook to turn on his back and paddle with the oar, and the boat sweeps past with the captain still clinging. A wave pushes the correspondent out of the current, and the captain calls him to the boat. The effort to get to the boat is so great that the correspondent realizes that drowning would be easy and comfortable. He sees a man running along the shore, tearing off his clothes. A wave hurls the correspondent over the boat. The man on shore plunges in the water and grabs the cook, and then heads toward the captain, who directs him to the correspondent. The correspondent, from excessive casualness, says, "Thanks, old man," but the man exclaims at something: In the shallow water floats the oiler, face down.

The correspondent reaches land as if falling from a roof. A swarm of people provide blankets, clothes, and drinks. The welcome for the survivors contrasts strongly with the sinister welcome of the grave for the dead man, the oiler. At night, the survivors feel as if they can interpret the great voice of the sea.

Critical Evaluation:

"The Open Boat" is based on Stephen Crane's own experience of a shipwreck in 1897. Crane had been working as a war correspondent when he sailed for Cuba on the ship *Commodore*. He was stranded in a lifeboat with three other men for thirty hours. Three of the men made it to land, but as in the story, the fourth, an oiler, drowned while attempting to swim to shore.

Crane's depiction of the harsh forces arrayed against the shipwrecked men marks the story as an example of literary naturalism, a genre closely related to literary realism. Both schools champion realistic detail over idealized pictures of the world. Naturalism, specifically, tends to focus on the plight of humans in the face of larger forces—often society, but also the overwhelming, indifferent forces of nature.

The correspondent's sense of this indifference is one of the key developments in "The Open Boat." One thought returns to the correspondent again and again as the ordeal continues: Why should he (and the others) have to endure so much, to come within sight of land, only to drown just before reaching shore? The devastating injustice of this haunts him. This feeling might just be a temporary loss of faith in providence, but it is proven apt in the case of the oiler, who indeed drowns just on the brink of making it to shore. The story meditates on these questions further when the correspondent comes to the conviction that nature does not care about his personal fate. Nature's indifference cannot, however, take away the correspondent's own sense of his ineluctable importance: Unimportant though he may be, he loves himself.

Crane's style of realism is also distinctive and groundbreaking in the way in which it focuses on the minute-by-minute thoughts and emotions of the men, particularly of the viewpoint character, the correspondent. In this way the story resembles Crane's most famous work, the novel *The Red Badge of Courage: An Episode of the American Civil War* (1895). Like "The Open Boat," *The Red Badge of Courage* follows the reactions of a single man, a soldier, under extreme duress. In both stories, Crane traces the sometimes contradictory, sometimes unheroic inner life of a person who might outwardly appear to be resolute and unemotional.

Although Crane does not similarly enter into the minds of the other men in "The Open Boat," he allows their seemingly casual remarks to reveal their inner states. The men's conversations about the house of refuge, the likelihood of rescue, and the chances of making it to shore veer between alarm and casual certainty. After one man expresses an opinion, the others contradict him, revealing the continuing tension between the two states of mind. Near the end of the novel, the correspondent becomes so exhausted that he says that drowning would be easy and comfortable; only then can he admit to himself that throughout this ordeal he has been terrified that drowning would be agony. Crane's observations on the mental and emotional processes of men in desperate trouble are acute. The story also brings home the tragic ironies of such situations, such as the correspondent's studied casual remark on being saved, as if he is unmoved by his ordeal, only to have his casual demeanor made wholly inappropriate by the discovery of the death of the oiler. Such incisive observation and trenchant irony makes "The Open Boat" a landmark of literary naturalism.

Martha Bayless

Further Reading

Berryman, John. *Stephen Crane*. 1950. Reprint. New York: Cooper Square Press, 2001. A combined biography and analysis of Crane's works that provides an absorbing Freudian reading of Crane's life and work. Berryman, himself a major American poet, eloquently explains the patterns of family conflict that appear in Crane's fiction. Also examines Crane's influence on the development of the short story, a form that came to prominence only in the 1890's.

Blythe, Hal. "Understanding the Method of Narration in 'The Open Boat.'" *Eureka Studies in Teaching Short Fiction* 8, no. 1 (2007): 6-14. An introductory study of Crane's narration in "The Open Boat" written especially for teachers but helpful for students and general readers as well.

Dooley, Patrick K. *The Pluralistic Philosophy of Stephen Crane*. Urbana: University of Illinois Press, 1994. A study of "The Open Boat" and other fiction by Crane in the context of the thinking of his day. Discusses how Crane's writings embody his ideas about truth and reality.

Schaefer, Michael W. *A Reader's Guide to the Short Stories of Stephen Crane*. New York: G. K. Hall, 1996. An examination and analysis of Crane's many short stories, with "The Open Boat" receiving the most attention.

Sorrentino, Paul. *Student Companion to Stephen Crane.*
New York: Greenwood Press, 2005. An accessible overview of Crane's career, works, and thought, including a chapter on his own shipwreck experience with the *Commodore* and that experience's representation in "The Open Boat."

_____, ed. *Stephen Crane Remembered*. Tuscaloosa: University of Alabama Press, 2006. Brings together nearly one hundred documents from acquaintances of the writer and poet for a somewhat more revealing look at Crane than has previously been available.

Szumski, Bonnie, ed. *Readings on Stephen Crane*. San Diego, Calif.: Greenhaven, 1998. Aimed at students, this is an anthology of articles on Crane, including several on "The Open Boat." Examines the story's theme and style.

Wertheim, Stanley. *A Stephen Crane Encyclopedia*. Westport, Conn.: Greenwood Press, 1997. A thorough volume that features articles about the full range of Crane's work, his family and its influence on him, the places he lived, his employers, the literary movement with which he is associated, and his characters.

The Optimist's Daughter

Author: Eudora Welty (1909-2001)
First published: 1972
Type of work: Novel
Type of plot: Psychological realism
Time of plot: March and April, late 1950's or early 1960's
Locale: New Orleans, Louisiana; Mississippi

Principal characters:
LAUREL MCKELVA HAND, a fabric designer
CLINTON MCKELVA, her father, a retired judge
BECKY THURSTON MCKELVA, her mother
WANDA FAY MCKELVA, the judge's second wife
THE CHISOM FAMILY, Fay's family from Texas and Mississippi
DR. NATE COURTLAND, an eye specialist
ADELE COURTLAND, his sister, a first-grade teacher

The Story:

In New Orleans, Judge Clinton McKelva is diagnosed with a detached retina. As his second wife, Wanda Fay, along with his daughter Laurel and a night nurse, take shifts sitting with him in his hospital room, he gives no sign of wanting to live. He only lies still, on Dr. Nate Courtland's orders, concentrating, it seems, only on the passing of time. His double room eventually gets a new patient, Mr. Dalzell, a fellow Mississippian who has cancer. Mr. Dalzell is unaware of his surroundings and thinks the judge is his estranged son.

At night, Laurel inexplicably returns to the hospital, hours after her own shift there, to find a nurse pulling Fay out of the judge's room, irate that Fay has tried to urge the judge

from bed so they could celebrate her birthday and Mardi Gras. In the waiting room, members of the Dalzell family attempt to calm Fay, outraged at the nurse's treatment of her—typically concentrating on herself rather than on the impending death of the judge. He dies minutes after Fay's attempt to move him. The next afternoon, Laurel and Fay take the train to Mount Salus, Mississippi, with the judge's body on board.

In the evening, the judge's body is brought home; his funeral is set for the next day, and his body is viewed in the family home beforehand. Friends of the judge have organized a dinner for both days in his honor. Fay objects to people taking over her home. The Chisoms, Fay's family, arrive and prove outspoken and vulgar to most of Laurel's friends and to her parents. After the burial of the judge in the newest part of the cemetery, near the highway and not in the plot with his first wife, Becky, Fay decides to return for a few days to Texas with her family.

Laurel spends the weekend in her family home. Saturday afternoon she tends her mother's garden while four of her mother's old friends gossip mainly about Fay and her relationship with the judge. That evening, Laurel, alone, goes through her father's library, finding no trace of his life with her mother, only his books and papers and some drops of nail polish on his desk, presumably traces of his life with Fay. Laurel removes each drop. Sunday evening, Laurel spends time with her old friends, her six bridesmaids, in Mount Salus; they reminisce about Laurel's extravagant wartime wedding and about her parents.

Laurel returns home and notices that a bird, a chimney swift, is trapped in the house. She closes herself off in her parents' bedroom, now ostentatiously redecorated by Fay. The remainder of the night, with the backdrop of a storm outside and the sounds of a bird flying within, Laurel thinks of the past. She enters the sewing room, a small room off the master bedroom where Laurel slept as an infant. Her mother's desk, unlike that of the judge, is filled with papers, including personal letters—those from the judge and from her own mother in West Virginia. Laurel's mind takes her from her earliest memories of visiting West Virginia to her mother's life, marriage, and five-year illness and death. The memories soften what had seemed to be a personality ruled by practicality and restraint. Laurel cries with her head on her mother's desk. She imagines her former husband, Phil, crying out that he wants back the life that had been cut short by war. She wonders what their marriage would have been like had he lived.

On Monday morning, when she awakens, Laurel recalls her dream of traveling with Phil from Chicago to Mount Salus for their wedding. On the train they had sighted birds flying in the *V* pattern and saw the Ohio and Mississippi Rivers converging, both images symbolizing their own union.

Laurel next has to deal with the bird in the house. Mr. Cheek arrives, looking for odd jobs, but he proves useless in ridding the house of the bird. Missouri, a longtime housekeeper, first for the judge and Becky and then for the judge and Fay, arrives at the house, too. Laurel catches the bird between two baskets and frees it outside. Missouri then takes down the curtains to be cleaned; the bird had soiled them.

Laurel burns the papers and letters she found in her mother's desk, keeping only one token, a rock, carved with the judge's initials, given to Becky when they were courting. Laurel offers the keepsake to Adele Courtland, the eye doctor's sister, who presumably had loved the judge. Adele refuses it, saying Laurel must keep it.

Fay arrives home just before Laurel leaves, and what has been a cold and distant relationship between the two turns into an argument: Laurel's dislike of Fay and of her taking the place of her mother becomes clear; Fay replies that, nonetheless, the house is now hers. Laurel briefly considers taking with her a breadboard Phil had made for Becky, but decides that she needs nothing physical to hold on to the past; she needs no material reminders, as her memory and dreams have freshened her heart and provided a path forward. Adele and her first-grade students wave good-bye to Laurel as she rides by the school with her six bridesmaids on the way to the airport.

Critical Evaluation:

Eudora Welty, a literary icon of the twentieth century, had been a lifelong resident of Jackson, Mississippi. One of her many honors was bestowed May 2, 1973, when the state of Mississippi celebrated Eudora Welty Day during the Annual Mississippi Arts Festival in Jackson. Welty devoted her life to her art, publishing not only fiction but also photographs, essays, criticism, and reviews. Novelist Reynolds Price, in his foreword to *The Late Novels of Eudora Welty* (1998), noted that Welty had "fertilized and encouraged a whole new generation of Southern-born novelists." She received the Pulitzer Prize in fiction in 1973 for *The Optimist's Daughter.*

Set in the American South, *The Optimist's Daughter* confronts perennial questions about everyday life, such as family relations, the nature of time and of love, and the function of memory in helping the individual deal with mortality. These are also preoccupations of her autobiographical book, *One Writer's Beginnings* (1984), suggesting that Welty's themes, not her plots, are drawn from her life experiences. Throughout her career, Welty effectively reshaped experience into fiction.

Welty's narrative method in *The Optimist's Daughter* works perfectly to reveal her themes and her suggestion of Laurel's growth. An outside voice tells the story but always from the stance of Laurel, the protagonist. The reader only has access to what Laurel can see or feel or know, and Welty only slowly reveals Laurel's inner life. Readers get early intimations of conflicts, for example, some unexpressed issue surrounding her mother's death, but likely remain confused because the conflict is not clear. Laurel, at first, is not ready to face the conflicts, so the reader feels tentative, matching Laurel's own feelings.

Not until part 3 of the novel do readers get a prolonged view of Laurel's inner world—when she is alone in the rooms that best represent her parents, the library and the sewing room. Spending the last few weeks watching her father's stoic approach to death and her stepmother's selfish attitudes, then spending the last few days in her childhood home surrounded by the people she grew up with, Laurel seems ready to face the past and make sense of it. She reevaluates her attitude toward her parents and their relationship; her own relationship with her husband, Phil; and her attitude toward her own life away from the community. Laurel is ready to stop expecting relationships to be static and perfect and to recognize that family and marital love and life are complicated and contain much pain.

The novel moves from Laurel as an observer to her inner wrangling and to another confrontation with Fay. The movement of the novel implies that Laurel has been living without fully understanding and accepting her past, but she soon reevaluates her past and is in a better position to live with understanding.

The images of *The Optimist's Daughter* also support the themes of a reawakening. Set in spring, the novel abounds with images of birds and flowers. Becky's climbing rose defies ravaging and then blooms. The night that Laurel spends in the sewing room, thinking about her mother, is the same night she has the dream about her marriage to Phil and the night the swift is caught in the McKelva house. Still, Laurel wakes renewed, and she safely carries the bird to freedom.

Slowly, through telling details, readers come to understand that Laurel is not typical. Unlike her six bridesmaids, she has not settled to raise a family in her hometown, but instead lives independently, working as an artist in Chicago. Laurel does not want to return home to take Becky's place at the bridge table, nor does she want a life like Fay's, based on the present with no concern for what is past. *The Optimist's Daughter* paints Laurel as a woman with inner conflicts about her relationship with her parents, who seems to have buried her emotions after her short-lived marriage to Phil; the novel also paints her as a woman who faces these conflicts and chooses to move forward with memories and new knowledge. *The Optimist's Daughter* has the setting of a southern novel but the reach of the universal.

Marion Petrillo

Further Reading

Bloom, Harold, ed. *Eudora Welty.* Updated ed. New York: Chelsea House, 2007. A collection of essays analyzing Welty's work, including discussions of *The Optimist's Daughter.* Includes essays by American writer and literary critic Robert Penn Warren and British writer Elizabeth Bowen.

Gretlund, Jan Nordby, and Karl-Heinz Westarp, eds. *The Late Novels of Eudora Welty.* Columbia: University of South Carolina Press, 1998. Two introductory and two concluding essays frame four essays on *The Optimist's Daughter.* Also discusses Welty as a significant novelist.

Kreyling, Michael. *Understanding Eudora Welty.* Columbia: University of South Carolina Press, 1999. Chapter 9 links *The Optimist's Daughter* with Welty's autobiography, *One Writer's Beginnings*, suggesting that the key to Welty's art may lie in understanding mother-daughter relationships. Part of the Understanding Contemporary American Literature series, intended for students and general readers.

Marrs, Suzanne. *Eudora Welty: A Biography.* New York: Harcourt, 2005. An authorized biography, written by an academic and a friend of Welty. Concentrates on the inner life of the writer. Stresses the importance of family, friendships, and writing to her life. Includes many excerpts from Welty's letters.

_____. *One Writer's Imagination: The Fiction of Eudora Welty.* Baton Rouge: Louisiana State University Press, 2002. Discusses how Welty transforms factual material into her fiction. Chapter 9 traces the development of the protagonist in *The Optimist's Daughter* from the first published version that appeared as a story in *The New Yorker* to its final version as a novel. Also discusses how the novel treats the changing American South and race.

Prenshaw, Peggy Whitman, ed. *More Conversations with Eudora Welty.* Jackson: University Press of Mississippi, 1996. This collection features twenty-six interviews with Welty, who discusses her life and works. Contains an editor's introduction, a chronology, and an index.

Vande Kieft, Ruth M. *Eudora Welty.* Rev. ed. Boston: Twayne, 1987. Chapter 10 provides an extensive plot summary of *The Optimist's Daughter*, with an explication and many direct quotations from the novel. A significantly updated version of the original 1962 edition.

Welty, Eudora. *Welty: Stories, Essays, and Memoir.* New York: Library of America, 1998. In this collection of writings, including her memoir, *One Writer's Beginnings* (1984), Welty looks at the early influences that shaped her as a writer. Provides insight into autobiographical material that was reshaped for *The Optimist's Daughter* and into the novel's themes of creativity, memory, family relationships, love, and mortality.

Oration on the Dignity of Man

Author: Giovanni Pico della Mirandola (1463-1494)
First published: Oratio de hominis dignitate, 1496
   (English translation, 1940)
Type of work: Philosophy

Giovanni Pico della Mirandola's *Oration on the Dignity of Man* is a remarkable document, but not for the reason that is sometimes thought. Even though it is an important statement by an influential early Renaissance humanist, the *Oration on the Dignity of Man* is neither a proclamation of the worth and glory of worldly life and achievement nor an attack on the medieval worldview as such. Pico was a man of his time, and he was willing to defend the medieval theologians and philosophers from the attacks of his humanist friends. However, in his statement he does go beyond what was then the traditional view of human nature.

Pico was a scholar whose erudition included a familiarity not only with Italian, Latin, and Greek but also with Hebrew, Chaldean, and Arabic. He had read widely in several non-Christian traditions of philosophy, and he had concluded that all philosophy, whether written by Christians, Jews, or pagans, was in basic agreement.

In Rome, in December, 1486, Pico published nine hundred theses and invited all interested scholars to dispute them with him the following month. The *Oration on the Dignity of Man* was to have been the introduction to his defense. Pope Innocent VIII forbade the disputation, however, and appointed a papal commission to investigate the theses; the commission found some of them heretical. Pico tried to defend himself in a published *Apologia,* but this made matters worse, and for several years he remained in conflict with the Catholic Church. Pico had not expected this state of affairs and, being no conscious rebel, he was very much disturbed by it. As a result he became increasingly religious and finally joined the Dominican order. The *Oration on the Dignity of Man* was never published in Pico's lifetime, though part of it was used in his *Apologia* to the papal commission.

In form, the *Oration on the Dignity of Man* follows the then-standard academic, humanistic, rhetorical pattern. The piece is divided into two parts. The first part presents and deals with the philosophical basis of the speaker; the second part announces and justifies the topics to be disputed. The philosophical first part of the *Oration on the Dignity of Man* begins by praising human beings; this, as Pico points out, is a common topic. However, he immediately rejects the traditional bases for praise, that is, the medieval view that the distinction of human beings is a function of their unique place at the center of creation, in other words, that each individual is a microcosm.

Pico accepted the premise that human beings are the most wonderful of all creations, but he inquired into the reasons why this should be so. Some, he said, believed that human beings are wonderful because they can reason and are close to God, yet the same qualities, he pointed out, may be found among the angels. Pico's view was that God was ready to create human beings only after he had created the world and everything in it, which are the objects of human contemplation in the divine scheme of things. Everything, including the angels, had been given a fixed and immutable form, but human beings, created with no definite abode or form, were given both free will and the use of all of God's creatures. Pico claimed that human beings were neither heaven nor earth, mortal nor immortal, but free to choose between sinking to the level of animals or rising to the divine.

God's great gift to humankind was free choice. Individuals can be what they will to be. If they choose to be vegetables, then they will act like plants; if they choose to be sensual, they will act like animals; if they choose to be rational, they will be saintlike; if they choose to be intellectual, they will appear like angels; and if they reject the lot of all created things, they will draw into the center of their own beings and thus unite their spirits with the divine. Human beings have this capability of becoming either an animal or more than an angel, and their inconstant nature is their greatest blessing. It is, therefore, their duty to seek out the highest level they can obtain, striving to rise above the angels who, fixed in form, cannot surpass themselves and reach the godhead.

Pico's is an exalted idea of human nature. Though it is otherworldly in focus and thus resembles what is considered as the worldly view of the Renaissance, it is also Renaissance in embracing the position that human beings are limitless by their very nature. Pico sees as a great human strength that inconstancy of being that had so long been the despair of Christian dogmatists.

In the second part of his *Oration on the Dignity of Man,*

Pico points out that human beings are assisted in their attempt to achieve the highest form of existence by philosophy. This view explains Pico's own interest in philosophy and also the plan of the disputation that was to follow the *Oration on the Dignity of Man*. Pico says that he must undertake to defend so great a number of theses because he is not an adherent of any one philosopher or school of philosophy. He feels the need to argue for positions drawn from a great variety of sources. He broadly surveys his nine hundred theses, commenting on the various writers from whom they are drawn. In so doing he displays the full extent of his learning in both Christian and non-Christian writings. As he concludes this longer and more involved part of his *Oration on the Dignity of Man*, he challenges his readers to plunge joyfully into argument with him as if joining in battle to the sound of a war trumpet.

In this second part of the *Oration on the Dignity of Man*, Pico rejects the idea that any one philosopher may have a monopoly on final truth. He proclaims instead the idea of the unity of truth. He adopts this position in an attempt to solve the ancient problem of reconciling the great multiplicity and many contradictions of varying philosophical schools. Ancient thinkers as well as later ones have tended to adopt a relativistic position and to use the idea of philosophical multiplicity to prove there can be no truth or absolute. Pico, writing in the tradition of the ancient eclectics and neo-Platonists, assumes that opposing philosophical doctrines share in both error and insight into universal truth. For him, truth is a collection of true statements drawn from various sources. He recognizes some error but also some truth in all the different philosophers.

In his work, Pico hoped to winnow out error, to extract various aspects of truth, and to combine them eclectically into a unified statement of truth that would help human beings take advantage of their freedom to seek the highest form of existence. Although this is not an original position, it is humanistic and thus a justification for the typically Renaissance humanistic desire to study all ancient writings rather than just those thought to support the medieval Christian tradition of philosophy and theology.

Further Reading

Cassirer, Ernst. "Giovanni Pico della Mirandola." *Journal of the History of Ideas* 3 (1942): 123-144. The second part of this article analyzes Pico's philosophy as it is outlined specifically in the *Oration on the Dignity of Man*. Remains an important source on the work that is frequently cited in other studies.

Copenhaver, Brian P. "The Secret of Pico's *Oration*: Cabala and Renaissance Philosophy." *Midwest Studies in Philosophy* 26, no. 1 (2002): 56-81. Discusses why Pico wrote *Oration on the Dignity of Man*. Argues that the work is not about human dignity and freedom in the sense that a modern reader understands these topics; maintains instead that most of the oration deals with magic and the Kabbala.

Dougherty, M. V., ed. *Pico della Mirandola: New Essays*. New York: Cambridge University Press, 2008. Includes a detailed analysis of the genre and contents of the oration, focusing on Pico's defense of humans as unique beings in the order of creation.

Kristeller, Paul Oskar. "Introduction to *Oration on the Dignity of Man*." In *Renaissance Philosophy of Man*, edited by Ernst Cassirer et al. Chicago: University of Chicago Press, 1948. An excellent survey of the treatise, written by a preeminent scholar of Renaissance philosophy who places it within its historical and intellectual context.

Trinkaus, Charles Edward. *In Our Image and Likeness: Humanity and Divinity in Italian Humanist Thought*. 2 vols. London: Constable, 1970. Chapter 10 of this important study focuses on Pico and the *Oration on the Dignity of Man*, relating them to other Renaissance humanists' conceptions of the essence of human existence.

Vasoli, Cesare. "The Renaissance Concept of Philosophy." In *The Cambridge History of Renaissance Philosophy*, edited by Quentin Skinner and Eckhard Kessler. New York: Cambridge University Press, 1988. Places the *Oration on the Dignity of Man* in its philosophical context. Other articles in this volume provide information on the intellectual heritage upon which the *Oration on the Dignity of Man* drew.

The Orations

Author: Cicero (106-43 B.C.E.)
First transcribed: Orationes, 81-43 B.C.E. (English
translation, 1741-1743)
Type of work: Politics and rhetoric

Thoughts of the greatness of Rome, and especially of its government, are likely to bring to mind the name of Cicero. Whereas a figure such as Julius Caesar may symbolize the military greatness of imperial Rome, the figure of Cicero is a symbol of Roman justice and law, of the Roman senate and its traditions, and of landmark strides in philosophy and literature. Cicero is important in literature primarily for his orations and his many writings about oratory and rhetoric. Through his writings Cicero set a pattern in public speaking that is still alive in Western culture. Moreover, on the bases of what he wrote and said and of the viewpoints he held and defended to the point of dying for them, Cicero became historically one of the great advocates of culture and conservatism.

Cicero took ten years to prepare himself as a lawyer before he appeared on behalf of a client in public. He believed that a thorough education is necessary for success in any activity. Some exponents of oratory have averred that manner is everything; Cicero disagreed, believing that matter is as inescapably a factor in oratorical success as manner. In the *Orator* (46 B.C.E.; English translation, 1776), one of his most mature pieces of writing on the art of oratory, Cicero wrote that his own success, like that of any orator, was more to be credited to his study of the philosophers than to his study of earlier rhetoricians, and that no one can express wide views, or speak fluently on many and various subjects, without philosophy. Although Cicero tried to make a science of rhetoric and saw profit in his own attempts at its systematization, he also realized that no simple set of formulas could ever make a great orator. As he put it, an eloquent person should be able to speak "of small things in a lowly manner, of moderate things in a temperate manner, and of great things with dignity."

In Cicero's time, one prevalent style in oratory was the Asian style. In the Asian type, Cicero himself discerned two subtypes, one epigrammatic and euphuistic, dependent on artful structure rather than on importance of content, and the other characterized by a swift and passionate flow of speech in which choice of words for precise and elegant effect was a dominant factor. Cicero found both styles wanting in some degree and built his own style on an eclectic combination of the two.

Fifty-eight speeches by Cicero are still extant, although not all are complete. The number of his speeches is unknown, but more than forty are known to have been lost. Not all the speeches Cicero wrote were delivered; sometimes he wrote them for occasions that did not occur. His second *Philippic* (44-43 B.C.E.; English translation, 1868) is an example of such a speech. Marc Antony (Marcus Antonius) had been so enraged by Cicero's first speech against him after the death of Julius Caesar that Cicero's friends persuaded the orator to leave the city of Rome temporarily. While absent from Rome, living at a villa near Naples, Cicero wrote the second *Philippic*, which was not spoken in the senate or even published immediately. A copy was, however, sent to Marcus Junius Brutus and Cassius, who enjoyed its invective against their enemy.

Not all of Cicero's speeches are of equal interest to later readers. His earliest extant oration, containing relatively little of interest, was delivered in a law court on behalf of Publius Quinctius. Cicero appeared for the defense, as he usually did, and spoke against Quintus Hortensius, the greatest lawyer in Rome at the time. Cicero won his case, but it may be difficult to retain interest in a case decided more than two thousand years ago when the stuff of the argument is largely points of law. This speech, however, along with other early efforts, provided Cicero the opportunity to prove himself. He made such a reputation that he was chosen to prosecute Gaius Verres, who had been accused of tyranny and maladministration in Sicily. Once again the famous Hortensius was Cicero's legal opponent. In the second oration he made against Verres, Cicero managed to produce such overwhelming evidence against the defendant that he went voluntarily into banishment. The evidence included chicanery designed to prevent the case from coming to trial, and even Hortensius could find little to say for the defendant.

Although Cicero had no occasion to deliver five additional speeches he had written for the trial, scholars have judged that they are among Cicero's best and have found them excellent sources for material about Sicilian government, history, and art. Another of Cicero's noteworthy speeches is the one given in defense of Aulus Cluentius, who was tried and acquitted on a charge of having poisoned his father-in-law, who had in turn tried a few years earlier to poison Cluentius.

Cicero's intent was to move his hearers, and his devices to ensure victory in court were not always above reproach, as his speech in defense of Lucius Flaccus indicates. That defendant had been accused of extortion while he was an administrator in Asia, and apparently Cicero could find little to say in his client's defense beyond impugning the Jews and Greeks who were witnesses against him, members of groups not much in favor in Rome. Also of great interest is Cicero's defense of Aulus Licinius Archias, a poet of Greek descent whose status as a Roman citizen had been questioned. In this oration Cicero developed a long passage in praise of literature, saying that literature and its creators are of paramount interest to a nation because they afford excellent material for speeches, because they make great deeds immortal by preserving them in writing, and because they give readers a useful and refreshing pastime.

Not all of Cicero's speeches were intended for courtroom presentation. Some were written for delivery in the senate and some with a view to Cicero's own benefit. In 58 B.C.E., Cicero was exiled temporarily as a result of his activities in crushing the conspiracy of Catiline. When Pompey recalled him to Rome a year later, he thanked the Roman senate in one speech for his recall, in another he thanked the Roman people generally, and in a third he made a request to the senate for the return of his home, which had been taken over by Clodius for the state.

The most famous of Cicero's speeches are those he wrote against Marc Antony after the death of Julius Caesar. Cicero, a conservative, had not been favorable to the autocracy of Caesar, and he rejoiced when Caesar was assassinated. During an eight-month period in 44-43 B.C.E., when Marc Antony presumed to try to succeed Caesar, Cicero directed fourteen orations against him. These orations, passionate and sincere, are called the *Philippicae* (*Philippics*) for the famous speeches of Demosthenes against Philip, the father of Alexander the Great. In his first speech Cicero spoke with some moderation, referring only to Antony's public life and appealing to his sense of patriotism. In later speeches, especially the second *Philippic*, he made various attacks on Antony's private life, accusing him of almost every conceivable type of immorality. Eventually Antony had his revenge: When he, Lepidus, and Octavianus formed their triumvirate, Cicero was put to death.

Further Reading

Dorey, Thomas Alan, ed. *Cicero.* London: Routledge & Kegan Paul, 1965. Collection of essays is valuable for its breadth and degree of detail concerning Cicero's speeches. Topics addressed include Roman politics; Cicero's political career, speeches, poetry, philosophy, and character; and evaluation of Cicero's style and form in oration and the oratorical devices he used.

Fantham, Elaine. *The Roman World of Cicero's "De oratore."* New York: Oxford University Press, 2004. Presents analysis of Cicero's dialogue *On Oratory* (55 B.C.E.; English translation, 1742), in which he discusses his ideas about the ideal orator-statesman. Provides information about Cicero's return from exile, his response to Plato's ideas about rhetoric, and his contributions to the development of rhetoric and public education in Rome.

Martyn, John, ed. *Cicero and Virgil: Studies in Honour of Harold Hunt.* Amsterdam: Adolf M. Hakkert, 1972. Contains six informative, detailed essays on the style, techniques, influence, and philosophy of Cicero's writings and speeches. An important resource for those pursuing in-depth study of Cicero's work.

Petersson, Torsten. *Cicero: A Biography.* 1920. Reprint. New York: Biblo and Tannen, 1963. Remains one of the best general biographies of Cicero available, offering a comprehensive and detailed analysis of the orator's life, career, orations, and treatises. Includes a thorough and insightful discussion of Cicero's philosophy and speeches.

Richards, George Chatterton. *Cicero: A Study.* 1935. Reprint. Whitefish, Mont.: Kessinger, 2008. Brief work provides an accessible introduction to Cicero's orations. Includes two chapters devoted to his speeches and rhetorical treatises. Discusses the character and technique of the speeches in a concise survey.

Steel, C. E. W. *Cicero, Rhetoric, and Empire.* New York: Oxford University Press, 2001. Examination of Cicero's political oratory focuses on his ideas about empire. Places Cicero's attitudes within the context of the debate about Roman imperialism that occurred in the late Roman Republic.

_____. *Reading Cicero: Genre and Performance in Late Republican Rome.* London: Duckworth, 2005. Analyzes the relationship between Cicero's writing and his position as a major political figure, arguing that his works are best read within the context of Roman politics.

The Ordeal of Richard Feverel
A History of Father and Son

Author: George Meredith (1828-1909)
First published: 1859
Type of work: Novel
Type of plot: Tragicomedy
Time of plot: Mid-nineteenth century
Locale: England

Principal characters:
RICHARD FEVEREL, the young heir to Raynham Abbey
SIR AUSTIN FEVEREL, his father
ADRIAN HARLEY, Sir Austin's nephew
RIPTON THOMPSON, Richard's playmate and friend
BLAIZE, a neighboring farmer
LUCY DESBOROUGH, Blaize's niece
CLARE, Richard's cousin and his beloved

The Story:

Richard Feverel is the only son of Sir Austin Feverel of Raynham Abbey. After Sir Austin's wife leaves him, the baronet becomes a misogynist and determines to rear his son according to a system that, among other things, virtually excludes females from the boy's life until the boy is twenty-five years old. At that time, Sir Austin thinks, his son may marry, so long as a woman good enough for the young man can be found.

Raised within his father's system, Richard's early life is carefully controlled. The boy is kept from lakes and rivers so he will not drown, from firecrackers so he will not be burned, and from cricket fields so he will not be bruised. Adrian Harley, Sir Austin's nephew, is entrusted with Richard's education. Adrian calls his young charge the Hope of Raynham.

When he is fourteen years old, Richard becomes restless. It is decided that he needs a companion of his own age, and his father chooses young Ripton Thompson, the none-too-brilliant son of Sir Austin's lawyer. In their escapades around Raynham Abbey together, Richard leads and Ripton follows. Despite Ripton's subordinate position, however, he apparently has much to do with corrupting his companion and weakening Sir Austin's system. Soon after Ripton arrives at Raynham, the two boys decide to go shooting. A quarrel arises between them when Ripton, who is not a sportsman by nature, cries out as Richard is aiming at a bird. Richard calls his companion a fool, and a fight ensues. Richard wins because he is a scientific boxer.

The two boys soon make up their differences, but the state of harmony is short lived. The same afternoon, they trespass on the farm of a neighbor named Blaize, who finds them after they shoot a pheasant on his property. Blaize orders the boys off his land, and, when they refuse to go, he horsewhips them. Richard and Ripton are compelled to retreat. Ripton suggests that he stone the farmer, but Richard refuses to let

his companion use such ungentlemanly tactics. The two boys do, however, speculate on ways to get even with farmer Blaize.

Richard is in disgrace when he returns to Raynham because his father knows of his fight with Ripton. Sir Austin orders his son to go to bed immediately after supper; he later discovers that Richard disobeyed him and met up with Ripton instead. The boys are overheard talking mysteriously about setting something on fire. Shortly afterward, when Sir Austin discovers that farmer Blaize's hayricks are on fire, he suspects Richard. Sir Austin is chagrined, but he does not try to make his son confess. Adrian Harley suspects both Richard and Ripton, and the latter boy is soon sent home to his father.

The next day, a laborer named Tom Bakewell is arrested on suspicion of having committed arson. Tom did set fire to Blaize's property, but he was bribed by Richard to do so. Nevertheless, Tom refuses to implicate Richard. Conscience-stricken and aware that a commoner is shielding him, Richard confesses to Blaize. Blaize is not surprised by Richard's visit, for Sir Austin has already called and paid the damages resulting from the fire.

Richard is humiliated by the necessity of apologizing to a farmer. He tells Blaize that he was the one who set fire to the farmer's grain stacks; Blaize, however, implies that Richard is a liar: Blaize has a witness, a dull-witted fellow, who insists that Tom Bakewell was the arsonist. Richard maintains that he himself was responsible, and he succeeds in confusing Blaize's star witness. Afterward, Richard leaves the farm in an irritated frame of mind. He has been so distracted while there that he never notices the farmer's pretty thirteen-year-old niece, Lucy Desborough, when she lets him in and out of Blaize's house. At Tom's trial, Blaize's witness is so uncertain about the identity of the arsonist that the accused is released. Thereafter, Tom becomes Richard's devoted servant.

When Richard reaches the age of eighteen, Sir Austin sets about finding him a prospective wife, a girl who could be trained for seven years to be a fit mate for Sir Austin's perfect son. Richard, however, cannot wait seven years before beginning to show an interest in women. He is first attracted to his cousin, Clare, who adores him and dreams of marrying the handsome young man. In a single afternoon, however, Richard completely forgets Clare. While boating on the weir, he comes upon a young lady in distress and saves her boat from capsizing. In an instant, the system collapses completely. She introduces herself as farmer Blaize's niece, Lucy Desborough. Richard and Lucy are immediately attracted to each other, and they meet every day in the meadow by the weir.

Meanwhile, Sir Austin has found in London someone he thinks will be the perfect mate for his son, a young woman named Carola Grandison. Informed by Adrian and his butler that Richard is secretly meeting Lucy, Sir Austin orders his son to come to London immediately to meet Carola. At first, Richard refuses to obey his father, but Adrian tricks Richard into going to London by saying that Sir Austin has apoplexy.

Richard finds his father physically well but mentally disturbed by the young man's interest in Lucy. He tells Richard that women are the ordeal of all men, and although he hopes for a confession of Richard's affair with Lucy, he receives none. Sir Austin, however, refuses to let the young man return to Raynham. Richard meets the Grandisons, listens to his father's lectures on the folly of young men who imagine themselves in love, and mopes when, after two weeks, Lucy mysteriously stops writing.

When Sir Austin and his son finally return to Raynham Abbey, Richard finds out that Lucy has been sent away to school against her will by her uncle so that she will not interfere with Sir Austin's system. Although the farmer does not object to Richard, he refuses to have his niece brought back. After his unsuccessful attempt to have his sweetheart returned to him, Richard decides upon drastic measures. Sir Austin unwittingly aides his son's designs when he sends Richard to London to see the Grandisons. Tom Blaize, farmer Blaize's son, has been chosen by Sir Austin and her uncle to be Lucy's husband, and he travels to London by the same train.

Richard gets in touch with his old friend, Ripton Thompson, and asks him to secure lodgings for a lady. While in London, Richard runs into Adrian Harley, Clare's mother, and Clare. Richard accidentally drops a wedding ring, and Clare—unbeknown to the boy—picks it up. Tom Blaize is tricked into going to the wrong station to find Lucy, and Richard meets her instead. He sets her up with Mrs. Berry in lodgings in Kensington and marries her soon afterward. Good-hearted Mrs. Berry gives them her own wedding ring to replace the one Richard has lost.

When Adrian learns of Richard's marriage, he admits that the system has failed. Ripton breaks the news to Sir Austin, who remarks bitterly that he was mistaken to believe that any system could be based on a human being. Actually, Sir Austin objects not so much to his son's marriage as to the deception involved.

Efforts are made to reconcile Richard and his father, but they are unsuccessful. Richard is uneasy because he has not heard from his father, and Sir Austin is too proud to take the first step. While Richard and Lucy are honeymooning in the Isle of Wight, he is introduced to a fast yachting crowd, including Lord Mountfalcon, a man of doubtful reputation. Richard naïvely asks him to watch over Lucy while Richard himself goes to London to see his father and ask his forgiveness.

In London, Richard meets a Mrs. Mount, whom Lord Mountfalcon has bribed to bring about Richard's downfall. Mountfalcon plans to win Lucy for himself by convincing her of Richard's infidelity. Richard does not know that Mrs. Mount is being bribed to detain him and that, while she keeps him in London, Lord Mountfalcon is attempting to seduce Lucy.

Because he cannot bear separation from his son any longer, Sir Austin consents to see Richard. Relations between Richard and his father are still strained, however, for Sir Austin has not yet accepted Lucy. Meanwhile, since she cannot have Richard, Clare has married a man much older than herself. Shortly after her marriage, she dies and is buried with both her own wedding ring and Richard's lost one on her finger.

The death of Clare and the realization that she had loved him deeply shocks Richard. Moreover, his indiscretions with Mrs. Mount make him ashamed of himself; he thinks he is unworthy to touch Lucy's hand. He does not know that Mrs. Berry has gone to the Isle of Wight and brought Lucy back to live with her in Kensington. Richard himself goes to the Continent, traveling aimlessly, unaware that Lucy has given birth to a son.

An uncle who disbelieves in all systems returns to London. Learning of Lucy and her child, he bundles them off to Raynham Abbey and prevails on Sir Austin to receive them. Then, he goes to the Continent, finds Richard, and breaks the news that he is a father. Richard rushes back to Raynham to be with Lucy and to reconcile completely with his father.

The reunion between Lucy and Richard is brief. Richard sees his son and receives complete forgiveness for his past misdeeds from his wife. A letter from Mrs. Mount to Richard reveals Lord Mountfalcon's schemes to see Lucy and separate her from Richard. Knowing Lucy's innocence and Mountfalcon's villainy, Richard immediately travels to France, where he is slightly wounded in a duel with Lord Mountfalcon. The news of the duel, however, is fatal for Lucy. She becomes ill of brain fever and dies of shock, crying for her husband. Richard is heartbroken. Sir Austin also grieves, but his closest friend often wonders whether he ever perceived any flaws in his system.

Critical Evaluation:

The Ordeal of Richard Feverel was George Meredith's first novel, although by the time of its publication he had already published poetry, journalism, and two entertaining prose fantasies. George Eliot praised the novel, but other critics found it unconvincing and excessively intellectual. Later critics have generally agreed that it is somewhat thesis-ridden, but they find its flaws counterbalanced by wit and emotional force. It remains probably the most popular if not the most admired of Meredith's novels.

There is no denying that at times Meredith's concern for his thesis acts to the detriment of the novel. As a result, the novel serves as a kind of unintentional exemplification of this thesis: that life is too various, too rich, and too spontaneous to conform to even the most admirable system. Few readers can quite believe that Richard would remain separated from Lucy for as long as the plot requires, and the deaths of both Lucy and Clare seem to be less from natural than from authorial causes. These events are necessary to Meredith's design, but he is unable to give them the quality of inevitability that characterize other elements of the plot.

The novel nevertheless works remarkably well. Meredith may have intended to keep Sir Austin Feverel at center stage, demonstrating the fatuity of high intelligence and lofty ideals when they lack the precious leaven of humor and common sense. The message is effectively conveyed, and Meredith's comic purpose is served by a reader's last sight of Sir Austin, still blindly clinging to his theories in the shipwreck of his beloved son's life. It is, however, the romantic pathos of the love between Richard and Lucy that most fully engages readers and is most vivid at the novel's conclusion. Meredith's later revisions for a new edition suggest that he recognized what had happened to his original intention and concluded that the gain in emotional power was worth preserving. To thus value intense feeling above strict adherence to his preconceived system was a thoroughly Meredithian decision.

There is some latent Romanticism evident in Meredith's representation of his characters. Adrian, young Richard's tutor, is a sophisticated, classically educated epicurean whose detachment from emotion enables him to be present and catalystically involved in the events of the plot without being personally affected by them. Inasmuch as he could have alleviated the suffering of many of the characters, had he chosen to care enough to inform them about crucial facts of which he was in possession, his character serves as a negative comment on the sterility of classicism and its failure to bring about human happiness.

Lucy is also a Romantic figure, almost stereotypically beautiful, innocent, and natural. As such, she falls victim to the sophisticated degeneracy of the higher-born, better-educated, more urbane characters, illustrating how the rustic and intrinsically good values of the countryside can be poisoned by "civilized" behavior. Richard's natural virtue is also effectively destroyed by too much association with the machiavellian machinations of the citified and worldly Bella Mount. Sir Austin's system for raising children, consisting as it does of purely rational principles, not only destroys Richard's happiness but also alienates Lady Blandish, thereby destroying the baronet's own prospects for a redeeming domestic fulfillment as well.

Meredith seeks to demonstrate that one ignores emotion and instinct at one's peril. Inasmuch as Sir Austin's entire misogynistic system has been created in response to his wife's leaving him for another man, it is based upon the very forces it repudiates. It is thus an instrument for not only self-deception but also ruination. The characters' virtue can be measured in inverse proportion to the amount of intellectual education they have received: Simple, rustic, and untitled characters such as Mrs. Berry, Tom Bakewell, Lucy, Farmer Blaize, and Ripton Thompson provide all the goodness in the novel, while titled and educated characters such as Sir Austin and Lord Mountfalcon bring about only evil and destruction. Meredith thus suggests that one should never try to subvert nature.

Many critics have noted similarities in plot between *The Ordeal of Richard Feverel* and William Shakespeare's *Romeo and Juliet* (pr. c. 1595-1596, pb. 1597). In both works, impetuous, unspoiled, and passionate young lovers are thwarted by the machinations of their elders, with tragic results. There are also parallel characters; Mrs. Berry echos Juliet's nurse, and the witty Adrian corresponds in some ways to Mercutio. Destructive and unnecessary duels occur in both, and the duel in Meredith's novel seems a bit anachronistic in its mid-Victorian setting. Critics have also noted autobiographical features of the novel, finding parallels between Meredith's life and outlook and those of Sir Austin, the baronet, who is also an author.

The writing style employed by Meredith is heavily allusive to classical and contemporary literary works, incorporating frequent authorial comments and discursions into philosophy. This, along with the novel's length, makes for heavy going among readers accustomed to later, more transparent and direct, narrative styles. However, in relating the events of Richard and Lucy's elopement, Meredith's style becomes less ornate, enabling readers to become more caught up in the action. Some plot threads dangle and disappear, leaving readers to wonder what happened to certain characters, such as Carola Grandison. Equally puzzling are allusions to previous events about which readers have not been told. Perhaps Meredith's intention is to enhance the credibility of his story in this way—real life is not composed of self-contained, neatly tied up narratives, nor does one always know the origins of events.

Revised by Sally B. Palmer

Further Reading

Harris, Margaret. "George Meredith at the Crossways." In *A Companion to the Victorian Novel*, edited by William Baker and Kenneth Womack. Westport, Conn.: Greenwood Press, 2002. Discussion of a turning point in Meredith's literary career. Part of a collection that provides an introductory overview of the Victorian novel and discusses the historical and social context of the Victorian novel, the growth of serialization, and the different genres of Victorian fiction.

Horne, Lewis. "Sir Austin, His Devil, and the Well-Designed World." *Studies in the Novel* 24, no. 1 (Spring, 1992): 35-48. Argues that Richard Feverel's ordeal is also to a great extent that of his father, Sir Austin. Analyzes the novel's metaphors and classical references.

Jones, Mervyn. *The Amazing Victorian: A Life of George Meredith*. London: Constable, 1999. Jones's biography aims to recover Meredith from obscurity and to introduce the author to a new generation of readers. Links Meredith's life to his writing and includes a forty-page appendix recounting the plots of all of Meredith's novels.

Muendel, Renate. *George Meredith*. New York: Twayne, 1986. Good introduction to the Victorian writer and his works, with broad, insightful analyses. Includes a bibliography and a concordance to Meredith's poetry.

Roberts, Neil. *Meredith and the Novel*. New York: St. Martin's Press, 1997. Employs twentieth century literary criticism, especially the ideas of Mikhail Bakhtin, to analyze all of Meredith's novels. Includes bibliographical references and an index.

Shaheen, Mohammad. *George Meredith: A Reappraisal of the Novels*. Totowa, N.J.: Barnes & Noble, 1981. Suggests that traditional Meredith criticism has viewed his fiction too much in the light of *The Egoist: A Comedy in Narrative* (1879). Concentrates on the writer's other major works as being more representative of his truly independent mind. Specifically explores how character expresses theme in Meredith's novels.

Stevenson, Richard C. *The Experimental Impulse in George Meredith's Fiction*. Lewisburg, Pa.: Bucknell University Press, 2004. Stevenson focuses on the novels he considers most representative of Meredith's experimental fiction, including *The Ordeal of Richard Feverel*, to demonstrate that these books feature controversial contemporary themes, innovative narrative structures, depictions of human consciousness, and other unconventional elements.

Stone, James Stuart. *George Meredith's Politics: As Seen in His Life, Friendships, and Works*. Port Credit, Ont.: P. D. Meany, 1986. Attempts to expound what Stone calls Meredith's "evolutionary radicalism" and the complex and interesting ways in which it suffuses his greatest novels. Useful for beginning students.

Tague, Gregory. *Ethos and Behavior: The English Novel from Jane Austen to Henry James (including George Meredith, W. M. Thackeray, George Eliot, and Thomas Hardy)*. Bethesda, Md.: Academica Press, 2008. *The Ordeal of Richard Feverel* is among the novels Tague analyzes in his examination of English didactic literature. His study includes a discussion of the ethical aspect of the novel and the conduct of its characters.

Williams, Joan, ed. *Meredith: The Critical Heritage*. London: Routledge & Kegan Paul, 1971. A collection of reviews and essays examining the critical reception of Meredith's work from 1851 through 1911.

The Order of Things
An Archeology of the Human Sciences

Author: Michel Foucault (1926-1984)
*First published: Les Mots et les choses: Une
   Archéologie des sciences humaines*, 1966 (English
   translation, 1970)
Type of work: Philosophy and history

In his original and controversial book, *The Order of Things*, Michel Foucault asks a simple question: Where do books come from, especially those that seem definitive in one way or another? One obvious answer comes to mind: Books are the works of individual geniuses, and they reflect progress in the authors' disciplines or in their larger intellectual climates. Foucault resists the obvious, however, in his search for the answer to his simple question. He suggests, to the contrary, that books—as well as authors, disciplines, and periods—are products of the way people agree to use language, and all reflect the possibilities and limits of particular verbal systems.

Foucault's challenge to traditional notions of authorship and authority is not new. The early twentieth century had seen marked resistance to the belief that authors were heroes or "great men" who changed the world—a view championed by thinkers such as Thomas Carlyle and Ralph Waldo Emerson. In France, structuralists challenged the subjectivity behind the cult of personal genius and explored the implications of the proposition that the words of a text are "signs"— even arbitrary signs. This idea of texts as signs can be traced to the time of Aristotle, but it had been reexamined by linguist Ferdinand de Saussure, who exerted a strong influence in French thought. Following Saussure's distinction between the verbal sign and the signified object or idea, structuralist thinkers, particularly anthropologist Claude Lévi-Strauss and child psychologist Jean Piaget, tried to identify distinctions in human behavior that were as clear as those within grammatical categories such as noun cases and verb tenses.

Foucault was attracted to structuralism and its verbal "games." He attended the lectures of philosopher Louis Althusser, who had systematized Karl Marx's thought, and he tried without success to understand the writings of Jacques Lacan, who had systematized the thinking of Sigmund Freud. However, Foucault began to think that structuralism was simply another *ism* and, hence, that it did not mark a genuine step forward in human thought. If anything, structuralism helped to show that all steps forward in the human sciences are largely illusory. For Foucault, the human sciences

(*sciences humaines*) are, mainly, what Americans call the social sciences, coupled with the humanities. The French, however, do not always include the humanities as a human science.

In *The Order of Things*, Foucault is concerned primarily with three disciplines that emerged in the nineteenth century: philology, biology, and economics. He assumes that each discipline has structural principles of its own, if each is a true science, and he suspects that the human sciences themselves may have a single set of principles, or agreed-upon axioms, that no one has challenged. Lacking a French word for these axioms, he borrows the Greek word *episteme*. Foucault uses it as shorthand to describe the knowledge of an "epistemological space specific to a particular period." Finally, he thinks of this "space" as a site to be excavated, much like a site for an archeologist.

The metaphor of the historian of ideas as an archeologist begins to make sense when one reflects on the root meaning of the word "archeology," which is "ancient discourse." Archeology as a term originally was used to describe any writing about the past. When the modern discipline of archeology was organized, its practitioners took special interest in inscriptions and in other evidence of what people said in the past. Like an archeologist, Foucault treats the several *epistemes* of Western Europe since the Middle Ages as so many strata in a single archeological dig.

Existing before the modern age that gave rise to the human sciences were the Classical period, in the seventeenth and eighteenth centuries, and the Renaissance, concentrated in the sixteenth century. Foucault treats representative books from these eras as the equivalents of an archeologist's core samples. In each sample, he studies the relations of the words on the page to the things being described. Hence the title of the French original, *Les Mots et les choses* ("words and things"). He looks for the breaking points or ruptures that occur when the relations of words and things somehow change, relations that arise as a result of changes in the way people agree to represent the world on paper. Foucault tends to find rupture and discontinuity where other historians have found gradual change.

The Order of Things comprises two parts of roughly equal length. The first part discusses the Renaissance and the Classical period. The Renaissance is associated with a process of endless elaboration or "commentary" on the world as God's creation; the Classical period is associated with attempts at a more rational "criticism" of the world, criticism of the sort that draws distinctions. The second part of the book treats the modern age and, more briefly, what follows the modern. Foucault does not have a name for this age that follows the modern, though his readers have been quick to call it the postmodern.

The modern age, known for its careful systems of classification, seems to be characterized by a passage that opens the book. Foucault quotes an absurd system of classification discussed in a 1942 essay by Argentinian writer Jorge Luis Borges, "El idioma analítico de John Wilkins" ("The Analytical Language of John Wilkins," 1964). In his preface to *The Order of Things*, Foucault tells his readers that the work grew out of his amusement at such a system, which pretends to be scientific but is clearly not. Foucault's Renaissance, with its system of occult correspondences, is not quite as absurd as the system in Borges's fable, but none of the *epistemes* seem quite so rational or systematic as its representative writers may have thought.

Some critics of Foucault's work have complained that he overlooks the obvious representatives of a period or discipline—such as Wilhem Grimm, creator of the great German dictionary, and Charles Darwin and Marx in the modern age—and instead chooses more eccentric figures. Foucault responded by saying that his own choices—philologist Franz Bopp, biologist Georges Cuvier, and economist David Ricardo, for example—are more representative of their "discourse communities."

Foucault's prose is challenging because it engages the content of the books under discussion, incorporating and playing with terms used in those works. At its best, his prose is highly stimulating, as in his discussion of the Renaissance practice of describing the world as though it were written in the language of God. Sometimes, however, as in his long discussion of perspective lines in a painting by Goya, his prose is tedious and seems to say little to advance the book's argument. Beyond question, though, the range of examples not only is impressive but also is refreshing. In addition to the parable from Borges, later examples from novelist Miguel de Cervantes and poet Stéphane Mallarmé add life to the book's often abstract language.

The final chapter, on the human sciences, begins with a startling suggestion: The modern age created the human sciences by interjecting the modern notion of "man" into disciplines that were once more concerned with God or nature or abstract reason. The demise of nineteenth century positivism means, then, the death of humanity as it had been enshrined in the human sciences. Furthermore, with this death came the demise of many academic disciplines. The old triad of economics, biology, and philology has been replaced by a new alliance of sociology, psychology, and literary study. It was only a short step further to the proposition that "the author," too, was dead, replaced by a "classifying principle," as Foucault suggested in his 1969 lecture "Qu'est-ce qu'un auteur?" ("What Is an Author?"), which was translated into English in 1977.

The Order of Things received a chilly reception in France. Thinkers of the previous generation saw it as fundamentally nihilistic and as a challenge to the integrity of their own work. Other reviewers, especially in England and North America, recognized that Foucault was a clever reader of texts, well-schooled in the poetry and prose of, for example, Surrealists such as Raymond Roussel, about whom he had written a full-length study.

Foucault's methodology has been applied to other academic discourses, such as those concerned with race, class, gender, and disability. Whether these applications expose true *epistemes*, in the sense of different ways of scientific knowing, or rather doxies, in the sense of heterodox opinions, remains a matter of debate, as do the aims and values of postmodernism per se. For his part, Foucault had welcomed the opportunity to distance himself from his contemporaries, and he does so in his introduction to the English translation of *The Order of Things*.

Thomas Willard

Further Reading

Barker, Philip. *Michel Foucault: An Introduction.* Edinburgh, Scotland: Edinburgh University Press, 1998. Chapter 5 of this introduction to Foucault's life and work discusses his methodology and his challenge to structuralism.

Danaher, Geoff, Tony Schirato, and Jen Webb. *Understanding Foucault.* 2000. Reprint. Thousand Oaks, Calif.: Sage, 2007. A good general introduction to Foucault's thought written in a clear and accessible style. Part one examines *The Order of Things.* Includes a useful glossary of terms.

Flynn, Thomas. "Foucault's Mapping of History." In *The Cambridge Companion to Foucault*, edited by Gary Gutting. 2d ed. New York: Cambridge University Press, 2005. In this comprehensive companion to the life and work of Foucault, Flynn's essay notes similarities among the thinker's historical methodologies: The "archeologies" of *The Order of Things* and early work on madness is compared to the genealogy and "problematizations" of later work on sexuality.

Gutting, Gary. *Michel Foucault's Archaeology of Scientific Reason.* 1989. Reprint. New York: Cambridge University Press, 1995. An extensive treatment of the origins and applications of Foucault's methodology, with two chapters on *The Order of Things.*

May, Todd. *The Philosophy of Foucault.* Ithaca, N.Y.: McGill-Queen's University Press, 2006. Chapter 2 discusses Foucault's use of archeological methods and metaphors in forming his theses in *The Order of Things* and other early works.

Miller, James. *The Passion of Michel Foucault.* Cambridge, Mass.: Harvard University Press, 2000. The first full-length biography of Foucault, first published in 1993, treating his private life to an extent impossible in Foucault's native France. Chapter 5 discusses the genesis of *The Order of Things.*

Mills, Sara. *Discourse.* New York: Routledge, 2004. A broad analysis of the term "discourse" and its use in a range of theories. Also examines how Foucault used the term and how his understandings of the word have been applied in fields such as linguistics, social psychology, and feminist and postcolonial theories.

O'Leary, Timothy, and Christopher Falzon, eds. *Foucault and Philosophy.* Malden, Mass.: Wiley-Blackwell, 2010. This thorough collection on Foucault's ideas includes the chapter "The Death of Man: Foucault and Anti-humanism," which examines a critical aspect of Foucault's thesis in *The Order of Things.*

Sheridan, Alan. *Michel Foucault: The Will to Truth.* 1980. Reprint. New York: Routledge, 1994. A careful study of Foucault's work. Part 1 includes a fine chapter on *The Order of Things*, which Sheridan translated.

White, Hayden. *Tropics of Discourse: Essays in Cultural Criticism.* 1978. Reprint. Baltimore: Johns Hopkins University Press, 1994. Chapter 11 in this classic work "decodes" *The Order of Things* by associating a different rhetorical trope with each Foucault *episteme.*

Ordinary People

Author: Judith Guest (1936-   )
First published: 1976
Type of work: Novel
Type of plot: Psychological realism
Time of plot: 1970's
Locale: Illinois and Texas

Principal characters:
CONRAD JARRETT, a young high school student
CALVIN JARRETT, his father
BETH JARRETT, his mother
DR. BERGER, his psychiatrist

The Story:

In the upper-middle-class Chicago suburb of Lake Forest, Illinois, Conrad Jarrett is preparing for school. The seventeen-year-old joins his parents, Calvin and Beth, for breakfast, during which they exchange uncomfortable small talk. It is one month to the day since Conrad returned from a mental institution. He was institutionalized after he tried to kill himself following the accidental drowning of his older brother, Buck.

Conrad rides to school with several friends; he feels out of place in English class, and his swim coach alludes tactlessly to Conrad's experiences in the mental hospital. Conrad feels less guarded and uncomfortable only in chorus class. When Conrad comes home, he and his mother engage in a brief, strained verbal exchange.

Beth recommends to Cal that they take a Christmas trip to London, which makes Cal uncomfortable since he not only is worried about Conrad but also is grieving silently over Buck's death. As part of his recovery from clinical depression, Conrad begins psychotherapy with Dr. Berger. He reveals that his brother drowned in a boating accident, confesses his own suicide attempt using razor blades, and announces that he wants to be in better control of his emotions and his life.

Conrad meets Karen, a friend from the mental institution.

He learns that, far from experiencing his awkwardness and discomfort, she is very happily involved in her school. At a neighbor's dinner party, Cal angers Beth by drinking too much and revealing that Conrad is seeing a therapist.

When Conrad reveals to Dr. Berger his increasing disgust with being on the swim team, Berger encourages Conrad to trust and act upon his feelings. Conrad quietly quits the team, causing an unpleasant confrontation with his mother, who verbally attacks him because she found out about his decision from a friend and not from Conrad himself. Conrad angrily accuses his mother of not caring about him and accuses his father of not understanding the simmering hostility between mother and son. Dr. Berger encourages Conrad to accept his mother's emotional limitations while not blaming himself for them.

Under Dr. Berger's care, Conrad becomes increasingly strong emotionally; on Conrad's eighteenth birthday, Cal admits that he wants to see Dr. Berger himself. Cal and Dr. Berger discuss Cal's guilt at being a poor father and husband. He blames himself for failing to recognize signs that Conrad might attempt suicide, and he feels powerless to stop Beth and Conrad's increasing isolation from each other and from him. Calvin ponders Beth's coldness and need for perfection and order.

Conrad's confidence grows to the point that, when he is unable to reach Karen by phone, he asks a friend from chorus class, Jeanine, out on a mutually enjoyable date. Later, however, Conrad loses control and punches a male student for making a vulgar remark about Conrad's friendship with Jeanine. Lazenby, who was Conrad and Buck's best friend, rebukes Conrad for his sudden aggression, whereas Calvin excuses Conrad for his outward, rather than inward, expression of anger.

Conrad stays with his maternal grandparents while Cal and Beth visit Beth's brother and sister-in-law in Texas. Conrad spends a very relaxing evening with Jeanine; shortly after, however, he reads in the newspaper that his friend Karen has committed suicide. This triggers traumatic panic attacks, in which Conrad relives the horrors of the mental institution, feels again his powerlessness to save his brother during the boating accident, and remembers his own suicide attempt. Badly shaken, he meets with Dr. Berger in the middle of the night.

Through Conrad's eruption of guilt, rage, and pain, Berger helps him understand that he is not responsible for his brother's death, and that his only "crime"—a forgivable one—is that he chose to cling to the boat and live. Berger explains that guilt is nothing more than irrational and undeserved self-punishment, that depression is a counterproductive stifling of feeling, and that being fully alive requires openness to all emotions, not just to happy ones. Berger uses their mutual sadness at Karen's suicide to demonstrate that ugly things happen in life that cannot be understood or explained, but self-lacerating depression and guilt are not the answers.

In Texas, Calvin becomes increasingly enraged at Beth's refusal to deal with Buck's death and Conrad's suicide attempt. Beth's self-centeredness and need for predictability and neatness in life make her explode with paranoid rage. She even suggests that Conrad's suicide attempt was intended to hurt her.

Conrad, now at peace, warmly welcomes his parents home, although Cal and Beth interact with each other icily. As his relationship with Jeanine deepens, Conrad is shocked by his mother's sudden, unexplained return to Texas. When he blames himself, Calvin explains that people's actions—like life events—are not always governed by logical cause and effect, are not always fully understandable, and are no one's fault. Calvin and Conrad express their love for each other, and Conrad opens himself up to his old friends and to whatever life may bring his way.

Critical Evaluation:

Born in 1936 in Detroit, Michigan, Judith Guest graduated from the University of Michigan and got married in 1958. She taught briefly and began to write when her three sons were in school, turning three early short stories into her first novel. *Ordinary People* had the distinction of being the first unsolicited manuscript to be published by Viking Press in some twenty-six years; it became a best seller. Actor Robert Redford, impressed by this sensitive and realist novel, chose *Ordinary People* as the basis for his first directorial effort; the 1980 film adaptation won the Academy Award for Best Picture in 1981.

Ordinary People captures brilliantly and honestly the reality of a modern family. The character of Conrad, whose adolescent angst degenerates into self-destructive clinical depression after a tragic accident interrupts his life, is compellingly drawn. The life-giving relationship between Dr. Berger and Conrad is beautifully explored, as is Calvin's gradual metamorphosis into a deeply empathic father. Readers see Beth through the other characters' eyes rather than through her own, heightening the mystery of how she, despite being raised in a "good" home, becomes coldly obsessed with predictability.

Through the effective use of such narrative devices as flashback and interior monologue, Guest enables readers to see into the lives and minds of her major characters. The juxtaposition of present-day events with brief, focused flashback scenes elucidates and sharpens the background and context for the characters' present words and feelings. Moreover, readers are concurrently presented with characters' external conversations and their contrasting interior monologues, which often reveal the characters' true feelings.

Guest's stylistic devices underscore a primary theme in *Ordinary People*: the extreme complexity and difficulty of communication. Words are supposed to facilitate and clarify, not obstruct, communication. Of Buck's death, Guest writes that the euphemism "deceased" is "a symbol . . . without power to hurt, or to heal." At a dinner party, a country club, and family gatherings, Guest shows the ways in which ritualized cliché and small talk are attractive for Beth because they avoid truth, while they are annoying to Cal for the very same reason. "Why is this always so hard? The first time you talk to somebody," quips Jeanine after she and Conrad try to communicate over the loud television, her intrusive brother, and their own awkwardness. Guest writes, "The distance between people. In miles. In time. In thought. Staggering when you think about it . . . Communication. The bridge between the distances." Conrad's intense sessions with Dr. Berger prove that honest, uncontaminated communication is difficult yet ultimately healing and life-giving.

The importance of *Ordinary People* in literature derives in part from its portrayal of the stark reality of the modern American family. The media of the 1950's and early 1960's portrayed family life as neat, predictable, and safe, devoid of unexpected tragedy. It effaced divorce, emotional dysfunction, and substance abuse. In 1976, *Ordinary People* powerfully demonstrated that real families, far from perfect, are often composed of parents and children who do not know themselves or one another.

Calvin Jarrett's attempts to be a good father are colored by the fact that he was orphaned at age eleven. As an adult, he completes the statement, "I'm the kind of man who—" with, "hasn't the least idea what kind of man I am." He marries Beth, whom he describes as "a marvelous mystery." In response to a comment that Conrad is not his "old self," Calvin asks, "And who was that?"

Rather than learning who he really is, Conrad follows his suicide attempt by striving to recapture his former self— unknown to him—by choosing to maintain control rather than facing his emotions. Even Karen, Conrad's closest friend in the mental hospital, says, "I don't really know you, Con." Virtually emotionless and self-possessed, Beth is a compulsive perfectionist, despite the terrible damage it does to her family. Guest powerfully illustrates that with such a weak foundation, unexpected tragedy, such as an accidental death and a suicide attempt, will tear a modern family apart.

Ordinary People explores agonizing loss and the grieving process. Early on, Calvin believes that dealing with grief is "simply the stubborn mindless hanging on until it's over," yet later he realizes that grieving is an active and courageous process. "Why can't we ever talk about it?" he asks. A self-confessed "emotional cripple," Beth grieves by imploding and shutting down emotionally, whereas Conrad's active grieving, with Berger's help, leads him to accept himself, as well as life's imperfections and unpredictability.

Judith Guest's great-uncle, poet Edgar A. Guest, was known as the "peoples' poet" because he wrote for ordinary people. Everyone is an ordinary person, struggling with life's extraordinary events because they threaten the comfortable but false perception that life is ordered, neat, and predictable. Such shocking challenges must be faced directly to be seen for what they are ("Guilt is not punishment . . ." Guest writes. "Guilt is simply guilt"). Otherwise, negative eneregy will either be turned inward, destroying the self in implosion, or explode outward, inflicting pain cruelly onto others. *Ordinary People* shows its subjects surviving life's unexpected tragedies by eliminating barriers within themselves and between one another; embracing their imperfect, unpredictable lives; and choosing to live bravely, open to life's triumphs and tragedies.

Howard A. Kerner

Further Reading

Guest, Judith. "How I Wrote *Ordinary People*." *Writer* 120, no. 8 (August, 2007): 24-26. Details the genesis of the novel and Guest's work on creating Conrad and Calvin's perspectives.

_____. "Judith Guest: No Ordinary Talent." Interview by Karen Reeves. *Helicon Nine* 4 (Spring, 1981): 30-37. Usefully details the process by which Guest wrote and published her novel, the elements of her own life within it, and the experience of adapting the book for the cinema.

Lehmann-Haupt, Christopher. "Books of the Times: *Ordinary People*." *The New York Times*, July 16, 1976, p. 68. One of the first reviews of the book; praises the great sensitivity of its portrayal of Conrad and his struggle toward sanity and strength.

Moss, Joyce, and George Wilson. "Overview: *Ordinary People*." In *Civil Rights Movements to Future Times, 1960-2000*. Vol. 5 in *Literature and Its Times: Profiles of Three Hundred Notable Literary Works and the Historical Events That Influenced Them*. Detroit, Mich.: Gale, 1997. Effectively places the novel within the sociohistorical milieu of the 1970's, including the emergence of teen depression, psychotherapy, and suicide, as well as the end of the façade of the perfect American family.

Neuhaus, Ron. "Threshold Literature: A Discussion of *Ordinary People*." In *Novels for Students*, edited by Diane Telgen. Vol. 1. Detroit, Mich.: Gale, 1998. Thoughtfully suggests that students who read the novel would be drawn to Conrad's adolescent issues but could also be taught to understand Calvin's parenting concerns.

Simmons, John. "Dealing with Troubled Writers: A Literacy Teacher's Dilemma." *Journal of Adolescent and Adult*

Literacy 51, no. 1 (September, 2007): 4-8. Offers a unique teaching perspective by suggesting that student writing about the novel could reveal young people's predisposition to do violence to themselves or others.

Szabo, Victoria, and Angela D. Jones. "The Uninvited Guest: Erasure of Women in *Ordinary People*." In *Vision/Re-Vision: Adapting Contemporary American Fiction by Women to Film*, edited by Barbara Tepa Lupack. Bowling Green, Ohio: Bowling Green State University Popular Press, 1996. Feminist reading of the novel that criticizes Guest's portrayal of Beth as one-dimensional.

Oresteia

Author: Aeschylus (525/524-456/455 B.C.E.)

First produced: 458 B.C.E.; includes *Agamemnon*, *Libation Bearers*, *Eumenides* (English translation, 1777)

Type of work: Drama

Type of plot: Tragedy

Time of plot: After the fall of Troy

Locale: Argos, Delphi, and Athens

Principal characters:

CLYTEMNESTRA, queen of Argos

AGAMEMNON, king of Argos

ORESTES, their son

PYLADES, his friend

ELECTRA, his sister

CASSANDRA, the captured princess of Troy

AEGISTHUS, Agamemnon's cousin and Clytemnestra's lover

APOLLO, the god of prophesy and light, son of Zeus and Leto

ATHENE, the goddess of wisdom, war, and crafts, and the daughter of Zeus

The Story:

Agamemnon. Clytemnestra's watchman spies a beacon signaling victory for the Greek army at Troy. Hoping that Agamemnon will restore order in Argos, the watchman leaves to inform Clytemnestra.

The chorus, the old men of Argos, laments the ten-year war against Troy and questions whether or not it was justified. It was fought for Helen, Clytemnestra's sister and the wife of Agamemnon's brother, Menalaus, who was abducted by the Trojan prince Paris. Although Paris violated a guest's obligations in stealing Helen, she was unworthy of the anguish caused by the war. The brothers' attack wedded Greeks and Trojans in spilled blood, with the first sacrifice being Clytemnestra's innocent daughter, Iphigenia. When the Greek fleet was beached at Aulis, a prophet named Calacas said the goddess Artemis had demanded Iphigenia as the

price of reaching Troy. Agamemnon had complied. Now, as Clytemnestra lays offerings at her altars, the chorus, anticipating trouble, prays to Zeus for guidance.

Clytemnestra reports Agamemnon's victory, while expressing a fear that the victors, by glorying excessively, may offend the gods. The chorus, considering the suffering the brothers caused and the curses that may bring divine wrath upon them, hope the message of the beacons is false. However, a herald confirms that Troy has been destroyed, and the Greeks are celebrating their victory.

Agamemnon, accompanied by Cassandra, credits the gods with his victory. Clytemnestra claims that their son, Orestes, was sent away because, after rumors that Agamemnon had been killed, she had tried to commit suicide. She lays out crimson tapestries for him as a welcome home. Agamemnon fears that stepping on the tapestries will show too much pride in the eyes of the gods, but Clytemnestra goads him into doing so.

Left alone with Cassandra, the chorus wants to be joyous but instead sings a dirge. Returning, Clytemnestra invites Cassandra into the palace, but, foreseeing herself entangled in a net, she remains outside. She bewails her fate after Clytemnestra leaves, predicting a dreadful slaughter in Agamemnon's house.

The chorus is perplexed because, after promising Apollo her love, Cassandra had reneged, for which he had punished her with prophetic visions that cannot be understood by those to whom she attempts to communicate them. They know well that Aegisthus, whose father had been deceived by Agamemnon's father into eating his own children, has used Agamemnon's absence to seduce Clytemnestra. The prediction that the two will kill Cassandra and Agamemnon leaves them mystified. Despairing of being able to stop what is fated, Cassandra enters the palace.

Agamemnon cries out from within. Clytemnestra emerges triumphant with her husband's blood on her hands. She admits her deceptions but says they were born of necessity and expresses her delight in stabbing Agamemnon so viciously that his blood drenches her. His lust for Cassandra had been a contributory motivation, but she attributes his death to the curse on Atreus and to guilt for Iphigenia's death. Revenged, Clytemnestra says she will relinquish power.

Aegisthus, however, has grand plans. Intending to use Agamemnon's wealth to consolidate his own power, he takes credit for plotting this "justice bringing day." Clytemnestra wants to end the bloodshed, but the chorus opposes them both. Disdainful, the two enter the palace, buoyed by the apparent helplessness of their enemies.

Libation Bearers. Orestes, now grown to a young man, returns with Pylades and places a lock of hair at Agamemnon's tomb. When Electra arrives with a chorus of serving-women, the two hide. The chorus mentions Clytemnestra's nightmare, which has led her to send offerings to the tomb. Electra wonders how to supplicate the spirits of the dead. Should she ask for good omens for her mother, or spill the libations on the ground? The chorus suggests blessings for those who hated Aegisthus. Urged to ask for vengeance, Electra thinks that may be impious, but the chorus claims that violence has earned violence.

While following their advice, Electra finds Orestes' hair. They all wonder if Orestes sent it because he could not return, but Electra then finds footprints that look like hers. Thus discovered, Orestes identifies himself. Electra welcomes him with four loves: love of their father; love she wishes to bestow on Clytemnestra; love of Iphigenia; and love for him. Orestes prays for Zeus's aid. Apollo has ordered him to avenge Agamemnon. Both he and Electra would have wanted it otherwise: Orestes wishes Agamemnon had died nobly at Troy; Electra, that his murderers had been killed by their friends. The chorus invokes the law—blood for blood—but killing will place Orestes in the chain of those already murdered. Spurred on, he claims he is willing to pay with his life for vengeance, in a battle of one just cause against another. Electra sees only their side as right and prays for justice.

Both ultimately hope to kill and survive. When Orestes asks why Clytemnestra has sent offerings, Electra recounts Clytemnestra's dream—that she had given birth to a snake, gave it her breast, and, as it sucked, was bitten, spilling blood and milk into its mouth. Orestes, claiming to be that snake, lays out his plan for vengeance, and then leaves.

After the chorus has recalled treacheries of past women, Orestes returns in disguise and reports his own death to Clytemnestra. She seems saddened, averring that she relinquished Orestes to save him. They enter the palace, and Cilissa, Orestes' old nurse, seeks out Aegisthus with what is, for her, heartbreaking news: Orestes is dead. The chorus, having convinced her to have Aegisthus come to the palace alone, anticipates success.

Aegisthus, lamenting Orestes' death, enters the palace to learn whether the strangers actually have seen the body. His scream informs the chorus that the assassination is underway and, to avoid complicity, they leave.

Aegisthus's servant stumbles out, horrified by the murder of his master, to warn Clytemnestra. She attempts to arm herself, but Orestes and Pylades stop her. Clytemnestra mourns her dead lover, reinforcing Orestes' desire to kill her, but she appeals to him as the child that had suckled at her breast. Shaken and momentarily hesitant, Orestes is advised by Pylades to be loyal first to the gods. This advice carries Orestes through his mother's subsequent pleading and threats. He slays Clytemnestra in the palace, returning to claim that right is on his side.

The chorus expects trouble, however, and almost immediately Orestes feels stained by matricide. Convinced that Clytemnestra's Furies are attacking him, he rushes off to seek Apollo's aid.

Eumenides. At Delphi, Apollo's Pythian priest honors Earth, Themis, and Phoebe, who gave the gift of prophesy to Apollo, enshrined as fourth prophet by Zeus. She also honors Athene, before entering the temple, but soon rushes out again. Within, she sees Orestes, dripping blood, surrounded by Gorgon-like women, and abandons the problem to Apollo.

Inside, Apollo and Hermes protect Orestes, for Apollo

had demanded Clytemnestra's death. The shade of Clytemnestra, seeking vengeance, awakens the sleeping Furies, who accuse Apollo of stealing power from older gods, inspiring matricide, being stained with blood, and relying upon force. Apollo thinks that killing the murderer of a husband is just, but the Furies see no kindred bloodshed in Clytemnestra's deed.

Handing the case to Athene, Apollo sends Orestes as suppliant to Athens, where he claims to have been cleansed of pollution by Apollo's sacrifice of a pig. The Furies reject this: Their subterranean powers precede that of the Olympians.

When Athene arrives, she finds the Furies interesting rather than terrifying. Valuing justice, she decides to hear both sides, but, after preliminary inquiry, rules herself unqualified to adjudicate. She then empowers a jury of Athenian citizens to decide the case. The Furies see this as a threat to their order, which employs fear to ward off evil, punish misdeeds, and reward pain with wisdom. If the new order's first decision is to free a matricide, it will be useless from the start. The trial proceeds, with the Furies arguing for blood guilt and Apollo for the fulfillment of Zeus's demand that Agamemnon be avenged. Mothers are only vessels, he ultimately says; fathers alone are blood relatives of offspring.

Aware that the jury may end up divided, Athene casts an anticipatory tie-breaking vote—not guilty, because, as daughter of Zeus, who gave birth to her, she is partial to men. The jury deadlocks and her vote thus proves decisive. Orestes vows allegiance to Athene and Athens.

Athene wisely placates the outraged Furies, claiming the jury's decision was aimed at justice, not at their defeat and humiliation. As an inducement to peace, she offers them eternal honor among Athenians as the Eumenides, "kindly ones." Patiently, she convinces them and, in the end, accepting this offer of veneration, they bless Athens and embrace peace between old and new gods.

Critical Evaluation:

Aeschylus created what is now called drama, conceiving of a second actor and, thus, the possibility of dialogue between individuals on stage. *Oresteia*, his last triumph at the festival of Dionysus in Athens (he wrote more than seventy plays and won the festival thirteen times during his lifetime), is the only extant trilogy, a unit of three related plays performed on one day.

Although interested in characterization and individual motivation, Aeschylus's concerns are larger than individuals or even human character generally. He explores relationships between gods and humanity; the roles of power, hatred, and

love in the creation of human values; the transformation of divinity from a rigid threat to a generous force for good; and the creation of justice out of a chaos of sexual aggression and brute rage. *Oresteia* explores all of these issues through a sequence of events taking place in the royal house of Atreus over successive generations.

Agamemnon, the current king, inherits a family line marked by murder, cannibalism, and other acts of extreme violence. Although the setting of the drama is in the time of the Trojan War, Aeschylus's retelling of the myth is directed to an audience of Athenian citizens. The main details of the story would be well known to these viewers; it is the dramatist's particular interpretation and how he relates the themes of the myth to contemporary concerns that would be of greatest interest.

Aeschylus writes in a highly metaphorical poetic style, making frequent use of images. Many of these draw upon agricultural activity, and he is particularly fond of connecting ideas of growth and fertility with sexual intercourse, bloodshed, and sacrifice. Criminal acts sow more bad deeds, and the cycle continues as inexorably as the seasons or the passage of years. Necessity is characterized as a "harness" or a "net" in which an individual is driven along like a horse or trapped like a captured animal. The songs of the chorus are rich in allusions to myths and religious rituals, frequently offering an impressionistic interpretation of events rather than a clear vision of what is happening and why. The language of the first play, *Agamemnon*, is particularly complex, a rich tapestry of sound and imagery with relatively little dialogue; by the time of the third play, *Eumenides*, the mode of expression has become notably clearer, reflecting perhaps the trilogy's trajectory toward a resolution of the dire situation that has arisen in the royal household.

The presentation of Agamemnon in Aeschylus's version of the tale is far from positive. His disregard for the life of his daughter, Iphigenia, as well as for the emotions of her mother, are indicative of a certain harshness of character. On the other hand, his single-minded pursuit of victory over the Trojans at all costs is what would be expected of a military leader in the heroic era. The actions of Clytemnestra, by contrast, take her far beyond what is deemed appropriate for a woman, even one of distinguished royal lineage. In luring Agamemnon onto the red tapestries, she exhibits all the cunning and deceitfulness that might be expected from a sister of Helen; in planning and carrying out the murder of her husband, she comes dangerously close to appropriating a masculine role for herself. The action of the trilogy is fraught with the clash between male and female, whose root lies in the unhappy marriage of Agamemnon and Clytemnestra and, beyond that, in the adulterous relationship of Helen and Paris. The trilogy also examines the corruption of the parent-child relationship in a family scarred by abuse and mistrust.

What initially passes for justice in *Agamemnon* demands the abandonment of personal values and takes no account of the complexity of motivation. This is not suitable for life in a settled city-state like Athens. Outrage merits retribution through outrage, which just starts the cycle again. Agamemnon's sacrifice of his daughter to reach Troy had been wrong, but the Trojan Paris had been wrong, too, to violate laws of hospitality, stealing Helen from his host. Clytemnestra was right to kill her daughter's murderer but wrong to kill her husband, who was himself the murderer. Although complicated by adultery and a lust for power, the slaughter of Agamemnon falls into the primitive pattern of one crime begetting another. The chain of guilt and retribution, begetting more guilt and retribution, goes all the way back to primordial humanity and even into the brutal histories of Titans and gods—Cronos castrating his father, Uranus, to escape imprisonment; Zeus's conquest of his father, Cronos, who was consuming his own children in an effort to retain power.

Libation Bearers continues the pattern, but with a critical difference: Unlike self-motivated Clytemnestra, Orestes kills his father's murderers because, knowingly or in ignorance, he is told to do so by Apollo, who tells him the murders would be for a reason greater than blood guilt (represented by the Furies who threaten to drive Orestes mad). The issue is larger than filial or political loyalty: Orestes' history is the mythological instrumentality by which civilized justice is born. When the tragic double bind of individual motives becomes clear—he is both right and wrong; his mother was both right and wrong; so, too, his father—there can be no escape from slaughter unless governing principles change. As Aeschylus understands the problem, such fundamental changes cannot occur justly or unjustly. For him, means are not justified by ends; injustice will not lead to justice, but neither will old justice lead to change. Initially, there must be recourse to an intermediate justice, and an arbitrary severance of past practices, for change to occur.

Under the beneficent guidance of Athene, who represents wisdom and social order, the action of *Eumenides* accomplishes just that. Her capriciously determined vote of not guilty amounts to an admission that justice in the case of Orestes is impossible because both sides are right and wrong. Through her genius, the anguish of the house of Agamemnon has been ended. Blood vengeance is replaced by disinterested justice, in the form of trial by jury, in a state controlled by and devoted to the good of its citizens. The net in which Clytemnestra caught Agamemnon metaphorically invoked nets of serial injustice in which humanity and gods were caught. *Oresteia* traces a route by which humans can be set free from such nets. The system of justice established by Athene is closely connected with the Athenian legal system that was continuing to evolve in Aeschylus's day, amid tensions between older, aristocratic power structures and newer, democratic forces.

Aeschylus generally favors the reconciliation of opposing principles, such as old and new or male and female, under the all-encompassing system of order and justice established by Olympian Zeus. Rehabilitation replaces retribution. Nonetheless, Aeschylus's resolution remains tragic, and the ending has been viewed as less than fully convincing. Although some have questioned the reasoning behind Athene's partiality toward the male and her denial of a mother (she did actually have one, Metis, whom Zeus swallowed and absorbed into himself), there is a definite movement in the trilogy toward a more harmonious existence. *Oresteia* documents the creation of a legal system and an organized system of justice, without which peaceful and productive life in a settled community would be impossible. Although Zeus remains a distant and somewhat enigmatic figure throughout the action, acting mainly through his surrogates Apollo and Athene, it is his order that is shown to triumph, however incomprehensible it may appear to human eyes.

Albert Wachtel; revised by David H. J. Larmour

Further Reading

Gagarin, Michael. *Aeschylean Drama.* Berkeley: University of California Press, 1976. An accessible and worthwhile source for the nonspecialist. Clearly written and argued, with helpful notes and a bibliography. Includes two excellent chapters devoted to *Oresteia*.

Goldhill, Simon. *Aeschylus: "The Oresteia."* 2d ed. New York: Cambridge University Press, 2004. A short but informative introduction to *Oresteia*. Provides an especially good discussion of the social contexts for the plays.

Herington, John. *Aeschylus.* New Haven, Conn.: Yale University Press, 1986. Designed for the nonspecialist. Part 1 provides background for Aeschylus's plays, and part 2 discusses the seven existing plays in detail. Discusses *Oresteia* as the reconciliation of male and female principles.

Lloyd, Michael, ed. *Aeschylus.* New York: Oxford University Press, 2007. This collection of significant articles on Aeschylus published since the mid-1950's contains the following essays about *Oresteia*: "Morals and Politics in *The Oresteia*" by E. R. Dodds, "Politics and *The*

Oresteia" by Colin Macleod, and "Religion and Politics in Aeschylus' *Oresteia*" by A. M. Bowie.

Rosenmeyer, Thomas G. *The Art of Aeschylus*. Berkeley: University of California Press, 1982. Intended for the somewhat advanced student of Greek drama, but includes an excellent discussion of Aeschylus's stagecraft that is accessible to the general reader as well. Includes a useful selected bibliography.

Zak, William F. *The Polis and the Divine Order: "The Oresteia," Sophocles, and the Defense of Democracy*. Lewisburg, Pa.: Bucknell University Press, 1995. Zak contradicts the modernist view that Greek tragedy lionizes individuals who challenge social norms. He maintains that the fall of heroic characters is part of a broader concern with family, civic, and religious obligations and with the overall good of society.

Orfeo

Author: Poliziano (1454-1494)
First produced: 1480; first published, 1863 (English translation, 1879)
Type of work: Drama
Type of plot: Pastoral
Time of plot: Antiquity
Locale: Sicily

Principal characters:
ORPHEUS, a singer
EURYDICE, his beloved
ARISTAEUS,
MOPSUS, and
THYRSIS, shepherds
PLUTO
PROSERPINA
TISIPHONE, one of the Furies

The Story:

While looking for a lost calf, old Mopsus comes upon Aristaeus and his servant Thyrsis. They did not see the animal, but Aristaeus sends the young man in search of it. Meanwhile, he tells Mopsus that he saw a nymph more beautiful than Diana in the woods. Although she was accompanied by a youthful sweetheart, Aristaeus declares that either he must win her love or he will die. Mopsus tried to warn him of the desolation and unhappiness caused by love, but without success; the return of Thyrsis with word that the girl is still in the woods sends Aristaeus hurrying to find her. The shepherds are convinced that he is mad and that some evil will result from his actions.

After finding the nymph, Aristaeus tries to woo her, but she flees. A moment later another nymph appears with news that the lovely Eurydice just died of a serpent bite by the riverside. She calls on her sister dryads to join in a dirge "to set the air ringing with the sound of wailing." As they sing, they see Orpheus, her sweetheart, approaching with his lyre. The dryad takes it upon herself to break to him the sad news of Eurydice's death.

When Orpheus's song about the exploits of Hercules is interrupted by the nymph bearing "crushing tidings," the deso-

late poet calls on sky and sea to hear him lament his bitter fate. At last he vows to go to the gates of Tartarus in an attempt to win back his dead love—perhaps the magic of his lyre will move even Death to pity. The satyr Mnesillus, who is been listening, has his doubts.

In Tartarus, Orpheus's lyre of gold and his beautiful voice move "the gates immovable." In fact, Pluto acknowledges that everything stands still at his melody. Proserpina is so charmed by it that she seconds Orpheus's request that Eurydice should be returned to him. Pluto agrees on condition that the poet return to earth without looking behind. In spite of Orpheus's promise not to look back, his doubts betray him. Orpheus looks back and sees Eurydice drawing again toward Tartarus. When he tries to follow her, Tisiphone refuses to let him pass.

While he is lamenting his woes and expressing his determination never again to desire a woman's love, Orpheus is overheard by a chorus of Maenads. One of the Bacchantes, angered that a man should scorn love, exhorts the others to take revenge, and the fierce creatures tear him to pieces in their rage, so that every twig close by is soaked with his blood.

Critical Evaluation:

Orfeo by Poliziano holds several distinctions. Literary scholars consider it the first modern pastoral drama, that is, one set in the countryside; it is the first modern drama drawing on a classical, or ancient, theme and on classical authors, and also the first Italian play with a nonreligious theme. In addition, musicologists consider it the first modern opera, or at least opera's precursor, since it was intended to be accompanied by music in its public performance.

Above all, *Orfeo* is a testament to the poetic talents of its author. When he was still a relatively young man, Poliziano wrote the entire drama in the span of only two days. The drama was a part of the festivities, in 1480, celebrating a visit by the child duke of Milan, Giangaleazzo Sforza, to Mantua; the drama was commissioned by the Mantuan cardinal Franceso Gonzaga. The Sforza dukes were delighted with music, and they sponsored the Milanese choir and individual composers. Lorenzo de Médici, Poliziano's patron for most of his life, also cultivated music in his city, Florence. Poliziano's drama emerged from a historical setting that encouraged his natural poetic and musical talents.

In composing *Orfeo*, Poliziano employed his vast knowledge of classical literature to produce elegant poetry in several languages (Italian, Latin, and Greek). He adopted his theme from Greek mythology, recounting a tale that was well known to his audience. The challenge was to weave together an entertaining presentation. Although the legend of Orpheus concerns his journey to the underworld in order to retrieve his wife, Eurydice, Poliziano begins the story at an earlier point, before her untimely death. It seems that he almost shifts the traditional plot line from Orpheus's endeavors to those of Aristaeus, who first seeks to make Eurydice his lover.

Set in a pastoral scene, *Orfeo* gives freedom to the audience to enjoy all the warmth and the instinctive emotions of their earthy existence. Although the story itself is tragic (Orpheus loses Eurydice), the tone of the play is light and lyrical, a tone in which audiences can revel. Listeners can participate, cheering on Orpheus in his efforts to regain his wife. They can join in his excitement when he sings, "Eurydice is won—my life restored.... Triumph, by my skill achieved." When he, in his careless pride, however, loses her on the way back, they can just as eagerly enjoy condemning him. Poliziano succeeds in turning the classical tragedy into a Renaissance sport, as passionately entertaining as any joust. Indeed, the gaiety of the drama and of its occasion is reinforced in *Orfeo*'s ending, in which a chorus of bacchants urges everyone to "drink down the wine."

The theme may be classical and the circumstances festive, but *Orfeo* stands also in the tradition of medieval religious dramas. From the eleventh century, mystery plays—called mystery plays because they deal with the wonders of Christian history and beliefs—were presented publicly as entertainment and as tools of instruction. Audience members were already familiar with the stories, such as Noah and the flood, but they nevertheless enjoyed the performances. Poliziano succeeds in drawing upon this tradition for the basic form of his play, but he creates for it a wholly new content with *Orfeo*. The ancient legend of Orpheus was well known, but Poliziano gives it new life in this festive setting.

The structure of *Orfeo* reflects the rapidity with which Poliziano composed it. The play begins with shepherds discovering the beauty of Eurydice, and Aristaeus's desire to make her his lover. There is dramatic potential in that story portion alone for Poliziano to develop, but he does not do so. Instead, he uses the pretext of Orpheus singing to insert public praise of Cardinal Gonzaga, whom he applauds as a great patron. From there, Poliziano quickly moves to Orpheus's resolve to journey to the underworld. The audience, therefore, receives a seemingly new principal character, in place of Aristaeus. Finally, after Orpheus's unsuccessful endeavors to be reunited with Eurydice, a chorus of women overhears him complaining of the futility of loving women. In response, they decapitate him, and so the play's structure takes another, seemingly illogical turn before culminating with the call to drink. Despite these structural inconsistencies, the play's purpose is entertainment, for which such discrepancies are minor.

Orfeo serves two purposes. First, it expresses a celebration for the young duke and the cardinal and anticipation for their future leadership of their cities. Second, it serves as a harbinger of Poliziano's talents and of the presumably glorious literary achievements that he will produce for all Italians. Orpheus is so charming that his music is able to calm the savage beast and even to cause rocks to sway. By implication, Poliziano's music will surely inspire comparable responses among his human listeners.

"Critical Evaluation" by Alan Cottrell

Further Reading

Bolgar, R. R. "Imitation in the Vernaculars." In *The Classical Heritage and Its Beneficiaries*. New York: Cambridge University Press, 1977. Places *Orfeo* in its literary framework as the first contemporary drama with a classical theme drawing on classical authors.

Buller, Jeffrey L. "Looking Backwards: Baroque Opera and the Ending of the Orpheus Myth."*International Journal* of the *Classical Tradition* 1, no. 3 (Winter, 1995): 57-79. Analyzes *Orfeo* by Poliziano and other operas about Orpheus, discussing the reasons why the composers changed the ending of the Orpheus legend. Examines the relationship between these operas and Italian pastoral poetry.

Godman, Peter. *From Poliziano to Machiavelli: Florentine Humanism in the High Renaissance.* Princeton, N.J.: Princeton University Press, 1998. Focuses on Poliziano's philological and critical writings, placing the writer and his work within the context of late fifteenth and early sixteenth century Florentine humanism. In the 1490's, Florentine intellectuals were divided in their opinions about the aims of scholarship. Poliziano argued that intellectual life should be removed from worldly matters and scholarship should focus on philological and textual studies of classical texts; his opponents maintained that this philological humanism was merely enabling scholars to toy with words.

Haar, James. *Essays on Italian Poetry and Music in the Renaissance, 1350-1600.* Berkeley: University of California Press, 1986. Analyzes the relationship between poetry and music. Provides much information for those interested in the historical context of Poliziano's work.

Pirrotta, Nino. "Music and Cultural Tendencies in Fifteenth-Century Italy." *Journal of the American Musicological Society* 19 (1966): 139-146. Indicates Poliziano's interest in music.

Pirrotta, Nino, and Elena Povoledo. *Music and Theatre from Poliziano to Monteverdi.* Translated by Karen Eales. New York: Cambridge University Press, 1982. Places Poliziano's poetic work within the historical framework of Italian Renaissance musical performance.

Poliziano, Angelo. *A Translation of the Orpheus of Angelo Politian and the Aminta of Torquato Tasso.* Translated by Louis E. Lord. London: Humphrey Milford, 1931. Reprint. Westport, Conn.: Greenwood Press, 1986. Contains translations of Poliziano's original edition and of an expanded edition published in the late eighteenth century. Includes a seventy-page introduction to pastoral drama, the form that *Orfeo* takes.

Orlando
A Biography

Author: Virginia Woolf (1882-1941)
First published: 1928
Type of work: Novel
Type of plot: Phantasmagoric
Time of plot: 1588-1928
Locale: England

Principal characters:
ORLANDO, first a man, then a woman
SASHA, a Russian princess loved by Orlando
NICHOLAS GREENE, a poet pensioned by Orlando
ARCHDUCHESS HARRIET OF RUMANIA, an admirer of Orlando
MARMADUKE BONTHROP SHELMERDINE, ESQUIRE, Orlando's husband

The Story:

One day in 1588, young Orlando is slashing at the head of a Moor tied to the rafters in his ancestral castle. His forefathers had been of noble rank for centuries and had lived out their lives in action, but Orlando is inclined toward writing. Bored by his play in the attic, he goes to his room and writes for a while on his poetic drama, "Aethelbert: A Tragedy in Five Acts." Tiring of poetry before long, he runs outdoors and up a nearby hill, where he throws himself down under his favorite oak tree and lets himself fall into a contemplative reverie.

Orlando is still lying there when he hears trumpet calls announcing the arrival of Queen Elizabeth. He hurries to the castle to dress in his finest clothes and then dashes toward the banquet hall. On the way, he notices a shabbily dressed man in the servants' quarters, a man who looks like a poet, but he has no time to stop. The man's image is to haunt him the rest of his life. Reaching the banquet hall, Orlando kneels before the queen and offers a bowl of rose water for her to wash her hands after her journey. Elizabeth is so impressed with the boy that she deeds a great house to his father. Two years later, she summons Orlando to court, where in time he is made her treasurer and steward. One day, however, she sees Orlando kissing a lady of the court and becomes so angry that Orlando loses her royal favor.

Orlando has many adventures with women. He decides to marry at the time of the Great Frost in 1604. That year, the river Thames is frozen so deeply that King James has the court hold carnival on the ice. There Orlando meets and falls in love with Sasha, a Russian princess, with whom he skates far down the river. They go aboard a Russian ship to get something for Sasha, and she remains belowdecks so long that Orlando goes to investigate. He is angry when he finds her sitting on the knee of a common seaman. Sasha is able to reconcile with Orlando, however, and the two plan to elope. While waiting for her on the night of their planned elopement, Orlando begins to feel raindrops; the thaw has set in. After waiting two hours, he dashes down to the riverbank, where he sees great pieces of ice crashing down the flooded waters. Far out to sea, he sees the Russian ship sailing for home. Sasha has betrayed him.

For six months, Orlando lives in grief. One morning in June, he fails to get out of bed as usual, and he sleeps for seven days. When he awakes at last, he seems to have forgotten much of the past. He begins to think a great deal about the subject of death, and he enjoys reading from Sir Thomas Browne's *Urn Burial* (1658). He spends his time reading, thinking, and writing.

Orlando summons Mr. Nicholas Greene, a poet, to visit him. Greene talks to him almost incessantly about the poets, about life, and about literature. Orlando is so grateful to Greene that he settles a generous pension on the poet. Greene cannot, however, endure living in the quiet countryside. One morning, he returns to his beloved London.

Still pondering the meaning of life, Orlando decides to try filling his life with material achievement. First, he sets about refurbishing his house. He spends a substantial part of his fortune and travels to distant countries in his search for precious ornaments. The time is that of the Restoration; Charles II is king.

One day, while Orlando is working on a long poem, "The Oak Tree," he is interrupted by a tall, bold woman, Archduchess Harriet of Rumania. She has heard of Orlando and wants to meet him. She stays so long in his vicinity that Orlando asks King Charles to send him to Constantinople as ambassador extraordinary. Orlando's duties in the Turkish capital are formal and arid, and he becomes extremely bored; he begins to wander about the city in disguise. While he is abroad, the king of England makes him a member of the Order of the Bath and grants him a dukedom by proxy.

The next morning, Orlando cannot be awakened; for seven days, he sleeps soundly. When at last he does rouse himself, he finds that he is no longer a man. He has become a beautiful woman. In confusion, Orlando leaves Constantinople and joins a nomadic tribe. Although Orlando spends many happy days with the tribespeople, she cannot bring herself to live with them permanently. Selling some of the pearls she had brought with her from Constantinople, she pays for passage on a ship back to England.

Orlando notices a difference in people's attitudes toward her while on the ship. She who had been a man now receives courteous attention from the captain, and she sees that her new role will require new responsibilities and bring new privileges. Back in England, she learns that all of her estates are in chancery, for she is considered legally dead. At her country house, she is received courteously by her servants. Again, she is haunted by Archduchess Harriet, who now, however, has become a man, Archduke Harry; at last, however, Orlando manages to rid herself of his attentions.

Orlando goes to London to get a taste of society. The reign of Queen Anne is a brilliant one. Conversation flows freely, and dinners and receptions are entertaining affairs. Joseph Addison, John Dryden, and Alexander Pope are the great names of the age. After a time, however, Orlando becomes bored by social interaction with the great wits and goes looking for adventure. She begins to associate with women of the streets and pubs, finding their earthiness a welcome change from the formalities of the drawing room. The company of women without men, however, soon grows dull and repetitive.

At last come the darkness and doubt of the Victorian era. Orlando sees that, under Queen Victoria's influence, marriage is the career toward which most women are striving. Orlando marries a man named Marmaduke Bonthrop Shelmerdine, Esquire, who takes off immediately on a sea voyage. A wedding ring on her left hand, however, is Orlando's emblem of belonging to accepted society. Orlando's lawsuits have been settled in her favor, but they have been so expensive that she is no longer a rich woman.

Orlando visits London, where she sees her old friend Greene, now a prominent literary critic. He offers to find a publisher for her poem "The Oak Tree." It is October 11, 1928, and London has become a roaring metropolis. Orlando begins to muse over her long heritage. She recalls Sasha, the archduchess, Constantinople, the archduke, and the eighteenth and nineteenth centuries. She sees herself now as the culmination of many influences.

Orlando drives back to her country house and walks out to the great oak tree under which, more than three hundred years before, she had watched the arrival of Queen Elizabeth. The stable clock begins to strike twelve. She hears a roar in the heavens and looks up; Shelmerdine, now a sea captain of renown, is arriving home by airplane.

Critical Evaluation:

One of the most prolific and influential modernist writers, Virginia Woolf wrote *Orlando* as a radically different response to the literary genre of biography. Her father, Leslie Stephen, had begun editing the massive *Dictionary of Literary Biography* when Woolf was born; in her diaries, she wrote that his serious immersion in that work had the effect of making her more clever but less stable. In *Orlando*, her response to the traditionally serious business of writing biographies, Woolf consciously uses exaggeration and fictitious sources to create the half-serious biography of a nonexistent person.

The work is, however, based on the life of a real person. Vita Sackville-West, who came from an aristocratic family and was a writer and intellectual, was also Woolf's friend and lover. Like Woolf, she and her husband, Harold Nicolson, belonged to the Bloomsbury Group, a loose association of English artists, writers, and intellectuals in the early twentieth century that included the economist John Maynard Keynes, the artists Roger Fry and Duncan Grant, Vanessa Bell (Woolf's sister) and her husband Clive Bell, and another writer of a new kind of biography, Lytton Strachey, who wrote *Eminent Victorians* (1918). Strachey's book departed from traditional biography by painting subjective and critical portraits of four representatives of the Victorian age: Cardinal Henry Edward Manning, Florence Nightingale, Thomas Arnold, and General Charles George Gordon. Strachey did not, however, cross the line into fiction, as Woolf does in *Orlando*. By doing so, Woolf tacitly acknowledges that any biography is necessarily subjective and biased and that it includes fictional elements although pretending to be factual. Woolf's work, too, pretends to be factual while wildly violating facts of time and gender. By breaking with the traditions of biography, Woolf was also breaking with the tradition that was the basis of her father's work.

Sackville-West had grown up in the ancient castle at Knole, which had belonged to her family for many centuries. Much of Woolf's description of the young Orlando is based on what she knew of Sackville-West's early life. The pseudobiography provides many parallels to her life, but because the character lives for more than three hundred years—Orlando is a sixteen-year-old boy in 1588 during the reign of Queen Elizabeth and a woman of thirty-six in 1928—Woolf at the same time describes the fictional character's entire family heritage. In Orlando's romantic involvements with various women and men, Woolf explores the attitudes and experiences of any two people involved in a physical and spiritual relationship; through Orlando's gender-changing character, Woolf is able to examine how social roles and expectations are based on gender and in turn how these values affect personal attitudes and experiences. Orlando's romantic life, based as it is on the relationship between Woolf and Sackville-West, illustrates a romance that existed in fact yet did not conform to the prescribed gender roles of Victorian society.

The gender switch from man to woman is an important aspect of this new kind of biography. Woolf wrote a fictional work that claims to be an actual biography as part of her analysis of how gender affects a person's true biography. Woolf comments on this by showing how the character is treated differently in social and legal situations depending on his or her gender. These observations, disguised as fanciful biography, allow Woolf to deliver a social and political critique in a satirical form. While the work therefore mocks the contemporary seriousness of Victorian English literature and society, it resides firmly in the English literary tradition of satire represented by such writers as Jonathan Swift and Daniel Defoe.

Woolf also wrote serious social and political essays on gender inequality. Her most influential feminist work, *A Room of One's Own* (1929), was written at the same time she was writing *Orlando* and is therefore often considered to be a companion piece to *Orlando*. Both works examine how gender affects literature, social roles, and financial opportunities, especially for women living in the strongly patriarchal Victorian society. In both works, Woolf elaborates on the set of values accepted by men and women and believed to be universal and genderless. She suggests that the accepted social and political norms are inherently masculine and patriarchal; in her 1938 essay *Three Guineas*, she elaborates on the different ways in which women, compared with men, would handle issues such as education and war.

Woolf's portrait of her friend and lover Sackville-West has been described by Sackville-West's son, Nigel Nicolson, as the longest love letter in English literature. More important, Woolf continues in *Orlando* the rebellion against the standard forms of English literature on which she embarked in her earlier novels. She challenges female writers to create a different style, a "woman's sentence" that will capture an androgynous picture of the world rather than the prevailing masculine one. *Orlando* is both part of Woolf's long and articulate analysis of gender and a lighthearted argument in favor of androgyny, where a person, especially an artist, can be either "woman-manly" or "man-womanly." The work has been difficult for readers and critics to categorize—as biography or fiction, as social criticism or fantasy—and has therefore perhaps not been as influential as Woolf's other works. It continues, however, to challenge accepted notions of the role gender plays in literature and society, and it provides a whimsical look at gender inequality in recent English history.

"Critical Evaluation" by Bradley R. Bowers

Further Reading

Apter, T. E. *Virginia Woolf: A Study of Her Novels.* New York: New York University Press, 1979. Broad overview of Woolf's novels examines the epistemological and psychological ramifications of the author's vision, sensibility, and symbolism. Devotes a brief chapter to *Orlando.*

Barrett, Eileen, and Patricia Cramer, eds. *Virginia Woolf: Lesbian Readings.* New York: New York University Press, 1997. Part 2 of this collection of conference papers focuses on the novels, with lesbian interpretations of *Orlando* and six other books.

Booth, Alison. *Greatness Engendered: George Eliot and Virginia Woolf.* Ithaca, N.Y.: Cornell University Press, 1992. Approaches the works of the two novelists from a feminist perspective, with an emphasis on their depictions of women characters. The chapter "Trespassing in Cultural History: The Heroines of *Romola* and *Orlando*" offers insight into Orlando's changing sexuality.

Briggs, Julia. *Virginia Woolf: An Inner Life.* Orlando, Fla.: Harcourt, 2005. Biography focuses on Woolf's work and her fascination with the workings of the mind. Traces the creation of each of Woolf's books from *The Voyage Out* (1915) through *Between the Acts* (1941), combining literary analysis with details of Woolf's life.

De Gay, Jane. "Rewriting Literary History in *Orlando.*" In *Virginia Woolf's Novels and the Literary Past.* Edinburgh: Edinburgh University Press, 2006. Discussion of *Orlando* is part of a larger examination of Woolf's preoccupation with the fiction of her predecessors. Explores Woolf's allusions to and revisions of the plots and motifs of earlier fiction.

Goldman, Jane. *The Cambridge Introduction to Virginia Woolf.* New York: Cambridge University Press, 2006. Provides a wealth of information designed to help students and other readers better understand Woolf, including biographical details and discussions of her novels and other writings. One section places Woolf's life and work within historical, political, and cultural context, including information about the Bloomsbury Group; another focuses on the critical reception of her writings.

Gorsky, Susan Rubinow. *Virginia Woolf.* Rev. ed. Boston: Twayne, 1989. Competent study of Woolf's literary career includes an examination of *Orlando* that draws clear parallels between Orlando and Woolf's close friend and lover Vita Sackville-West. Recommended as a good overall guide to Woolf.

Hussey, Mark, and Vara Neverow, eds. *Virginia Woolf: Emerging Perspectives.* New York: Pace University Press, 1994. Collection of essays addresses such topics as Woolf's sexual identity, her attitude toward gender, and her writing techniques. Includes discussion of *Orlando.*

Lee, Hermione. *The Novels of Virginia Woolf.* 1977. Reprint. London: Routledge, 2009. Presents a sensible examination of Woolf, depicting her as an admirable writer but not foremost in the modernist movement. Contains an informative chapter on *Orlando.*

Woolf, Virginia. *A Room of One's Own.* 1929. Reprint. Orlando, Fla.: Harcourt, 2005. Written as an essay for students at a women's college, this nonfiction work explores the same social and political aspects of gender roles as does *Orlando.*

Orlando Furioso

Author: Ludovico Ariosto (1474-1533)

First published: 1516; second revised edition, 1521; third revised edition, 1532 (English translation, 1591)

Type of work: Poetry

Type of plot: Romance

Time of plot: Eighth century

Locale: France, Spain, and Africa

Principal characters:

CHARLEMAGNE, king of France

ORLANDO, his nephew, a paladin of France

RINALDO, his nephew, a paladin of France

BRADAMANT, Rinaldo's sister, a knight

ROGERO, a Saracen prince, in love with Bradamant

AGRAMANT, a Saracen leader

ANGELICA, princess of Cathay

RODOMONT, king of Algiers

LEO, a Greek prince

ASTOLPHO, an English knight

ATLANTES, an evil magician

ALCINA, an evil magician

The Poem:

The Saracens (Muslims) have invaded France, led by Agramant and Rodomont, the king of Algiers, and many other kings and warriors from all over the Muslim world. French king Charlemagne and the Christian forces have retreated to Paris. Meanwhile, Angelica, a princess from Cathay, has arrived in France and has turned Charlemagne's peers into rivals for her favor.

Angelica then flees on horseback into a forest, hoping to reach a seaport and take a ship back to Cathay. She meets Rinaldo, a suitor she hates, and flees from him. He pursues her, and they come upon Ferro, a Saracen knight. While the knights fight over her, she escapes from both. The knights follow on Ferro's horse, but part at a fork in the road. Rinaldo comes upon his horse, Braid, but it runs away from him.

Sacripant, king of Circassia, another Saracen, stops by a forest stream and sits lamenting his unrequited love for Angelica. Angelica, who has been sleeping nearby, approaches him and, wanting his protection, pretends to be in love with him. Sacripant, however, is quickly unhorsed by a knight in white armor, the female knight Bradamant, Rinaldo's sister. While Angelica is consoling her champion, Rinaldo arrives, and while he and Sacripant fight, Angelica flees again. She meets a hermit who is actually an evil magician. He spirits Angelica off to a remote seacoast, where he intends to rape her. He then sends a sprite to tell the combatants that Angelica has gone off to Paris with Orlando. Rinaldo finds his horse, who had actually been leading him to Angelica, and sets off in pursuit.

Meanwhile, Bradamant learns that her love, the Saracen knight Rogero, has been captured by the evil magician Atlantes by means of a hippogriff and a shield that stuns its victims

with its sunlike rays. She goes in search of him accompanied by Pinabel, a treacherous knight. Pinabel pushes her into a chasm, but she is saved by an overhanging branch. Recovering, she discovers herself in Merlin's cave. Melissa, a seer, gives her a prophecy of her many glorious descendants and tells her where she can obtain a magic ring with which she can free Rogero from his enchantment.

Leaving there and finding the castle of Atlantes, Bradamant defeats the wizard, taking the hippogriff and shield and freeing all Atlantes's prisoners, including Rogero. Rogero mounts the hippogriff, and it unexpectedly carries him off.

Rogero arrives at the island of the enchantress Alcina and remains there under her spell, forgetting Bradamant and living in sensual idleness. Melissa borrows Bradamant's magic ring, disguises herself as Atlantes, and comes to Alcina's island. She shames Rogero into action, and by use of the ring breaks the enchantment and frees Alcina's prisoners, including the peer Astolpho, who had been transformed into a laurel bush.

Meanwhile, the aged hermit/magician is about to rape Angelica. He puts her to sleep with a potion, but then cannot get an erection, and so abandons her. She is discovered by sailors looking for women to sacrifice to the orc, a sea monster. She is captured and chained naked to a rock by the sea. Arriving on a hippogriff is Rogero, just in time to rescue her. He intends to have his reward from her, but while he is eagerly tearing off his armor, she escapes by using a ring of invisibility. The hippogriff, too, flies away.

The Saracens, meanwhile, have set fire to Paris, but a God-sent rain saves the city. Orlando dreams that Angelica is in peril, and to Charlemagne's outrage, leaves the city to seek her. Among his many adventures along the way by land and sea, he too rescues a maiden from the orc.

Rogero is again taken by the sorcerer Atlantes, who loves him and wants to keep him safe, especially from the danger of being converted to Christianity.

Angelica, still hoping to reach Cathay, and seeking Orlando or Sacripant as a protector, comes to Atlantes's magic castle and enters using the ring of invisibility. She frees Orlando and many others, but decides to have none of them. She puts the ring in her mouth and once again vanishes, leaving the knights to search for her and quarrel among themselves.

Charlemagne prepares the defenses of Paris. Rinaldo arrives with reinforcements. The Saracens breach the first ditch and slaughter many Christians, but they are stopped by fire at the second ditch.

Two young Saracens, Cloridano and Medoro, make a night excursion into the Christian camp, killing many, but are discovered as they are escaping. Cloridano is killed and Medoro is badly wounded. Angelica finds him and nurses him back to health, then takes him to Cathay with her and makes him king. Orlando, who is still searching for Angelica, hears the story and goes mad, raging through the forest like a wild beast, killing men and uprooting trees with his bare hands.

Rogero is freed by Astolpho, who blows his magic horn, breaking the enchantment and making Atlantes flee. Astolpho then mounts the hippogriff and flies around the world, stopping to visit Prester John in Ethiopia and finally flying to the moon, where he is shown vials containing the senses of poets and lovers who have lost them on Earth. He returns to Earth with the vial containing Orlando's senses and restores him. He and Orlando then gather an army of Nubians and take the city of Biserta.

Rogero rejoins the Saracen army. An agreement is made to settle the war by single combat. Rinaldo is chosen by the French, Rogero by the Saracens. During the combat, the Saracens break the truce and are driven back by the Christians. Rogero becomes separated from his companions and finally ends up on a desert island. There he is converted and baptized by a holy man.

The Christian forces drive the Saracens south and out of France, while Astolpho brings another force north from Ethiopia, wiping out the whole Saracen army and killing its leaders. Orlando rescues Rogero from the island. Rinaldo promises his sister, Bradamant, to Rogero, but their parents want her to wed Leo, son of the Greek emperor. They lock her up in a castle, and Rogero goes to Greece to kill Leo. While there he joins a Bulgarian army fighting against the Greeks. He kills the son of Theodora, the sister of the emperor, and is

imprisoned by her. Leo, however, rescues him and gives him shelter.

Bradamant will only marry the one who can defeat her in combat, and so Leo makes Rogero his champion. Rogero defeats Bradamant, but nearly dies of sorrow when he learns who she is, and that by defeating her, he has lost her. However, when Leo learns that Rogero and Bradamant are lovers, he renounces his claim on her and goes with Rogero back to France, where Rogero and Bradamant are finally married. Rodomont comes to the court to accuse Rogero of apostasy, but Rogero kills him. Finally, for his aid in the war against the Greeks, the Bulgarians name Rogero their king.

Critical Evaluation:

Ludovico Ariosto was pressured by a practical-minded father into studying law before he was able to pursue his true interests, literature and classical learning. The need to support his family, however, forced him to take service under Cardinal Ippolito d'Este, and later under Alphonso, duke of Ferrara. Meanwhile, Ariosto found time to write a number of works of varying literary merit, none of them well known outside Italy except for *Orlando Furioso*. The 1521 version adds numerous revisions, and much polishing, but no major additions. The 1532 version polishes and revises further, as well as extends the poem from forty cantos to forty-six.

Orlando Furioso is not an entirely new conception; it continues and partially retells the story of Matteo Maria Boiardo's *Orlando innamorato* (1483-1495; English translation, 1823). This highly innovative romance combines Carolingian and Arthurian tradition with the classical tastes of the Italian Renaissance. The work has the feel of a classical epic, but the numerous, complexly interwoven plot lines are a feature of many medieval knightly romances. The values and worldview that lay behind the medieval romance were becoming anachronistic by the time the poem was written, and the knightly values the poem expresses are often undercut by literary distance and flashes of irony.

Ariosto follows Boiardo closely in many respects. His huge poem (38,736 lines) has an even greater variety of incidents, and an even more complex interweaving of storylines. Drama, wonder, and high adventure are seasoned everywhere with humor and irony. Ariosto even retains Boiardo's stanza form, ottava rima, a form familiar to many English readers from Lord Byron's book-length poem, *Don Juan* (1819-1824, 1826). The form is useful to both poets in that the couplet that ends each eight-line stanza is ideally suited for a witty, ironic, or humorous commentary or counterpoint.

The plot of *Orlando Furioso* cannot be called loose in that the huge number of incidents, both original and drawn from medieval or classical sources, are all elaborately connected. The story does, however, have a number of centers of interest, and Orlando's temporary madness is not an adequate frame to hold them all. The Saracen invasion of France, culminating in the siege of Paris, would seem to provide a larger frame for the action, and to a degree it does, but much of the time the story is so caught up in the loves, hates, and rivalries of individuals that this war, which could determine the whole future of human history, fades to the background. Much of the story is taken up with the rivalry between Rinaldo and Orlando, and their pursuit of the temptress, Angelica. However, the exploits, love, and final marriage of the Saracen warrior Rogero and the knight Bradamant is equally large, and perhaps is of even greater interest. This latter storyline is one the poet has good motive to stress, since his patron claims descent from Rogero and Bradamant, but he portrays the female knight with so much vividness, energy, and psychological insight that the author obviously has a greater interest in the character than a mere desire to please his patron. Bradamant is the model of Britomart, the most popular and appealing character in Edmund Spenser's *The Faerie Queene* (1590, 1596).

The question of unity in *Orlando Furioso* is not new. Renaissance critics complained that Ariosto violates Aristotle's rule for unity in the epic. Ariosto's defenders argued that the poem is a romance and, therefore, operates under different rules than the epic. Rules aside, the poem both gains and loses by its structure. Ariosto has chosen to impress with richness of texture and with variety, inventiveness, surprise, and wonder. He succeeds, but at a price. Readers are always wondering, what next? Furthermore, the countless individual scenes lose much of their sense of urgency and seriousness.

Orlando Furioso has a long history of influence and popularity, attested by Spenser's close imitation of it with *The Faerie Queene*. *Orlando Furioso*'s continued popularity in the nineteenth and early twentieth centuries are indicated by paintings, by Gustave Doré's elaborate illustrations of the story, and by retellings in children's books. More recently, however, the poem has been comparatively neglected. The reason may be the modern era's sharp distinction between popular and serious literature; *Orlando Furioso*, with its emphasis on action and adventure, has too much in common with popular literature, in spite of its polished verse and wide learning. Readers who base their literary taste on the dramatic realism of Gustave Flaubert, Leo Tolstoy, and Fyodor Dostoevski, for example, may be less satisfied with a story in which one hero rides a hippogriff to the moon and another rescues a chained and naked heroine from a sea monster, only

to have his amorous advances thwarted when she escapes him by means of a ring of invisibility, and in which people have been turned into bushes and can speak only when their twigs and branches are broken off and then bleed. There are modern works that have similar situations, but none of them are taken with high seriousness.

Another weakness of the poem is that the strange and magical elements have a rootless quality; they are neither Christian nor pagan. The medieval Charlemagne cycle was a hard and masculine tradition with strong historical roots. When the much more exotic Breton lays of King Arthur became known in French, the Charlemagne tradition had to adapt to keep up. In the Arthur stories, half-remembered fragments of Celtic myth and legend create an air of mystery and magic that still resonates. Boiardo and Ariosto have no such roots, and their incidents, consciously echoing the King Arthur stories and stories from Homer, Vergil, Ovid, and other ancient authors, have more the sense of clever invention than of inherent strangeness.

Whatever its limitations, *Orlando Furioso* belongs to the great narrative tradition. It borrows freely from Homer, Vergil, Ovid, Statius, and Dante, and in turn passes on themes, situations, and motifs to such later narrative poets as Spenser, Torquato Tasso, and John Milton. A work that has remained popular and influential for so many centuries is likely to outlive the comparative neglect of the twentieth century.

Jack Hart

Further Reading

Beecher, Donald, Massimo Ciavolella, and Roberto Fedi, eds. *Ariosto Today: Contemporary Perspectives.* Toronto, Ont.: University of Toronto Press, 2003. Several of the essays in this collection examine *Orlando Furioso*, including discussions of its genesis, history, and plot structure.

Brand, C. P. *Ludovico Ariosto: A Preface to the "Orlando Furioso."* Edinburgh: Edinburgh University Press, 1974. A general introduction to Ariosto and his work. Includes a biography, a survey of literary forms that influenced *Orlando Furioso*, a discussion of the poem's major themes, a review of important criticism, and a bibliography.

Cavallo, Jo Ann. *The Romance Epics of Boiardo, Ariosto, and Tasso: From Public Duty to Private Pleasure.* Toronto, Ont.: University of Toronto Press, 2004. Cavallo's history of the Italian Renaissance romance epic includes analysis of *Orlando Furioso*. Compares this work to epic poems by Matteo Maria Boiardo and Torquato Tasso, who, like Ariosto, were part of the Este court.

Craig, D. H. *Sir John Harington*. Boston: Twayne, 1985. Harington wrote the first important English translation of *Orlando Furioso* in the 1580's. This critical study of Harington's work, focusing especially on canto 10, sheds light on the themes and images of Ariosto's poem. Also examines Harington's illustrations, critical comments, and notes.

Giamatti, A. Bartlett. *The Earthly Paradise and the Renaissance Epic*. Princeton, N.J.: Princeton University Press, 1966. A scholarly but lively examination of images of a blessed landscape in European literature. Illuminating chapter on *Orlando Furioso* as an early Renaissance epic. Annotated bibliography.

Kisacky, Julia. *Magic in Boiardo and Ariosto*. New York: Peter Lang, 2000. Examines the function of magic in *Orlando Furioso* and Boiardo's *Orlando Innamorato*. Demonstrates how the authors associate magic with chaos and the irrational, in contrast with order and reason, and how they use magic to explore Renaissance debate about fortune versus self-determination.

Pavlock, Barbara. "Ariosto and Roman Epic Values." In *Eros, Imitation, and the Epic Tradition*. Ithaca, N.Y.: Cornell University Press, 1990. Traces the forces of love and piety as they act on the work's two protagonists. Also takes up the centuries-old question of whether *Orlando Furioso* is an epic or a romance, and finds the influence of both.

Zatti, Sergio. *The Quest for Epic: From Ariosto to Tasso*. Translated by Sally Hill and Dennis Looney. Edited by Dennis Looney. Toronto, Ont.: University of Toronto Press, 2006. Zatti, an Italian literary critic, traces the development of the epic poem in the fifteenth and sixteenth centuries. He focuses on *Orlando Furioso* and Torquato Tasso's *Jerusalem Delivered*.

Orlando Innamorato

Author: Matteo Maria Boiardo (1440/1441-1494)
First transcribed: 1483-1495 (English translation, 1823)
Type of work: Poetry
Type of plot: Romance
Time of plot: Eighth century
Locale: France, India, and Africa

Principal characters:
CHARLEMAGNE, the king of France
ORLANDO, his nephew, a paladin of France
ANGELICA, a princess of Cathay
UBERTO, in reality Argalia, her brother
RINALDO, a paladin of France
MALAGIGI, a magician, Rinaldo's brother
BRADAMANT, a maiden knight, Rinaldo's sister
ROGERO, a noble young Saracen
FERRAÙ, a Spanish knight
ASTOLPHO, an English knight
AGRAMANT, the king of Africa

The Poem:

King Charlemagne summons all his paladins and vassal barons to a court plenary meeting in Paris, an occasion to be celebrated with magnificent tournaments and great feasts. Christians and Saracens, friend and foe alike, are invited to take part. To the banquet on the opening night of this fete comes an unknown knight, a beautiful damsel, and four giants serving as bodyguards. The knight, who calls himself Uberto, offers his lovely sister, Angelica, as the prize to any man who can defeat him in the jousts to be held the next day. He, in turn, will claim as his prisoner any knight whom he unhorses.

Orlando, the greatest paladin of Charlemagne's court, immediately falls in love with the beautiful damsel. Only respect for the monarch keeps Ferraù, a Spanish knight, from snatching her up and carrying her away in his arms. Even the great Charlemagne is affected by her charms. The only person who remains unmoved is Malagigi, a magician, who senses in the visitors some purpose quite different from that which they claim.

After the damsel and her brother retire for the night, Malagigi summons a fiend who informs him that Uberto is in reality Argalia, the son of King Galaphron of Cathay, who has been sent with his sister to demoralize the Christian knights. With Angelica as his lure, protected by a magic ring that would ward off all enchantment or make him invisible if placed in the mouth, Argalia plans to overcome the Christian knights and dispatch them as prisoners to distant Cathay. Armed with this knowledge, Malagigi mounts a magic steed and flies through the air to the stair of Merlin, where Argalia and Angelica are asleep. There he casts a spell over the watchers that causes them to fall into a deep slumber. The magician approaches Angelica with the intention of killing her, for she is as false as she is fair, but he himself becomes enslaved by her beauty and clasps her in his arms. Angelica wakes with a shriek. Argalia, aroused by her scream, runs to her assistance and together they overcome Malagigi. Angelica summons fiends and orders them to carry the magician to Cathay. There, King Galaphron confines him in a dungeon beneath the sea.

Dissension has meanwhile broken out among the knights of Charlemagne's court, for all wish to try their skill against the strange knight to win such an enchanting prize. At length lots are cast to determine the order of combat. The first falls to Astolpho, the second to Ferraù, and the third to the giant Grandonio. Next in order is Berlinghier, Otho, and Charlemagne himself. Orlando, much to his indignation, is thirty-seventh on the list.

At the running of the first course, Astolpho is jolted from his saddle. Ferraù, who follows, is also unhorsed, but, contrary to the rules of the joust, he leaps to his feet and continues the fight on foot. After he has slain the giants who attempt to restrain him, he bears himself so fiercely that Argalia, even though he is protected by enchanted armor, finally calls a brief truce. When the combat is renewed, Angelica suddenly disappears, followed by Argalia. Ferraù pursues them into Arden forest but finds no trace of the knight or the damsel. Rinaldo and Orlando also set off in pursuit of the fleeing maiden. Meanwhile, Astolpho has taken up the magic spear that Argalia had left behind; with this weapon he performs great feats of valor until, carried away by the excitement of the combat, he kills friends and foes alike. Finally, Charlemagne commands that he be subdued.

Rinaldo, Ferraù, and Orlando wander through the forest in search of Angelica. Rinaldo has a rather ironic success in his quest. After drinking from a fountain that Merlin had created years before to relieve the love pangs of Tristram and Isolde, the knight's love for Angelica turns to hate. A short time later he falls asleep beside a nearby stream. Angelica, coming upon the stream, drinks from its magic waters and immediately becomes enamored of the sleeping knight. When she pulls a handful of flowers and throws them over him,

Rinaldo awakes and, in spite of her piteous pleas and avowals of love, flees from her in loathing.

Ferraù, riding through the forest, comes upon Argalia asleep beneath a tree. The two engage in fierce combat. Ferraù, finding a chink in his enemy's magic armor, strikes him to the heart. Dying, Argalia asks that his body and armor be thrown into the stream. Ferraù agrees, keeping only the helmet of his adversary. As he rides on through the woods, he comes upon Angelica and Orlando, who, having chanced upon the sleeping maiden, has thrown himself down by her side. Supposing that Orlando is her protector, Ferraù awakes the sleeping man with taunts and insults. Orlando, starting up, reveals himself, but Ferraù, although surprised, stands his ground. A duel follows, in the middle of which Angelica again flees. The combat of champions ends only when a strange maiden, Flordespina, appears with news that Gradasso, the king of Sericane, is ravaging the Spanish dominions. Ferraù, torn between love and duty, departs for Spain with Flordespina.

Gradasso, a mighty monarch who covets whatever he does not possess, has invaded Europe to obtain possession of Durindana, the famed sword of Orlando, and Bayardo, Rinaldo's horse. Charlemagne, assembling all the knights summoned to the tournament, dispatches a mighty army under Rinaldo to aid King Marsilius against the pagans. During a battle fought near Barcelona, Gradasso and Rinaldo engage in single combat. Neither prevailing, they agree to fight again on the following day; if Rinaldo is the victor, Gradasso will release all the prisoners he has taken, but if the victory goes to Gradasso, Rinaldo will surrender Bayardo to the king.

Angelica has meanwhile returned to Cathay. Deciding to use Malagigi as the mediator in her pursuit of the disdainful Rinaldo, she releases the magician and promises to give him his complete liberty if he will bring Rinaldo to her. Deceived by his own brother, Rinaldo is decoyed away from his encounter with Gradasso. His troops, left leaderless, return home, whereupon Gradasso invades France and takes Charlemagne and his knights prisoner. When Charlemagne is offered his liberty and the restoration of his lands if he surrenders Durindana and Bayardo to the conqueror, he agrees. He sends to Paris for the horse, which had been returned from Spain, but Astolpho refuses to give up the animal and challenges Gradasso to a duel. Using the enchanted lance, Astolpho overthrows the king. Gradasso, true to his promise, releases his prisoners and returns to Sericane.

Orlando, continuing his wanderings, learns that Agrican, the king of Tartary, has sought the hand of Angelica in marriage. Angered by the girl's refusal, Agrican besieges Albracca, the capital of Cathay; he had sworn to raze the city, if need be, to possess the princess. Because news of the war has spread far and wide, Orlando, Astolpho, and Rinaldo journey by different routes to the kingdom of Cathay. There, Orlando and Astolpho join the side of the defenders, while Rinaldo, still filled with loathing for Angelica, joins the forces of King Agrican. Orlando, riding to the defense of King Galaphron, meets Agrican in single combat and slays the Tartar king. Later, Orlando and Rinaldo engage in furious combat. When night falls, each withdraws in expectation of resuming the struggle on the following day; that night, however, lovesick Angelica, scheming to save Rinaldo from his kinsman's fury, sends Orlando on a quest to destroy the garden of Falerina in the kingdom of Orgagna.

Agramant, the young king of Africa, prepares to lay siege to Paris in revenge for the killing of his father. One of his advisers prophesies failure in his efforts, however, unless he can obtain the help of Rogero, a gallant young knight held prisoner by the magician Atlantes on the mountain of Carena.

After Orlando sets out on his quest, Rinaldo and several of his companions leave the camp near Albracca and start in pursuit because Rinaldo is still eager to settle the quarrel. On the way, Rinaldo encounters a ruffian with whom he fights until both plunge into a lake and disappear beneath the waves. While these events are taking place, the messenger of Agramant returns with word that he could not find Rogero. Irked by the delay, Rodomont, a vassal king, decides to embark with his forces on the invasion of France. Agramant is told that the garden of Atlantes is invisible and that the young knight can be freed only by possession of Angelica's magic ring. A dwarf, Brunello, offers to obtain the prize for his master.

Orlando, having accomplished his quest, arrives at the lake where Rinaldo has been carried under the waves. Seeing his kinsman's arms stacked by the shore, Orlando determines to avenge his former companion in arms. He and the guardian of the place fight a mighty battle in which Orlando is victorious. From the enchanted garden beneath the lake he frees all the prisoners held there by Morgana, the sorceress. All the knights except Orlando then return to France to aid in the defense of Christendom. Orlando, now reconciled with Rinaldo, turns back toward Albracca. On the way he encounters Brunello, who had in the meantime stolen Angelica's magic ring.

In possession of the ring to dispel the mists of enchantment, Agramant comes at last to the castle where Atlantes holds Rogero. At Brunello's suggestion, the king announces a tournament. Joining in the tourney, Rogero is wounded but revenges himself on his assailant. When his wounds are mi-

raculously healed and he returns to the tourney, Agramant recognizes him and makes him his knight. Rinaldo and Rodomont have meanwhile engaged in single combat in a great battle between Christians and pagans. When they are separated during the fighting, Rinaldo, in pursuit of his enemy, rides once more into the forest of Arden.

On his arrival in Albracca after his perilous quest, Angelica prevails upon Orlando to help her in her escape from the beleaguered city and to escort her into France. Orlando does not suspect that her real purpose is the pursuit of Rinaldo, and he immediately agrees. After many adventures they embark for France and at length arrive, hot and tired, in the forest of Arden. There, Angelica drinks from the waters of hate; at the same time Rinaldo drinks from the waters of love. When they meet a short time later, the circumstances of their love have become reversed. Angelica now flees from Rinaldo in disgust, while he pursues her with passionate avowals. Again, Orlando and Rinaldo fight, and in the middle of their struggle, Angelica flees. When she takes refuge in Charlemagne's camp, the king, hearing her story, gives her into the keeping of Namus, the duke of Bavaria.

Agramant, joined by Gradasso, begins the siege of Paris. In the ensuing battle, Bradamant, a maiden warrior and the sister of Rinaldo, becomes enamored of Rogero and goes over to the side of the Saracens. When she removes her helmet and allows her hair to fall down, Rogero falls in love with the valiant maiden. They are attacked from ambush and Bradamant, unhelmeted, is wounded slightly in the head, but Rogero avenges her hurt by routing their enemies. When Rogero pursues the enemy, he and Bradamant are separated, but she will later become his wife and the mother of the illustrious line of Este.

Critical Evaluation:

Matteo Maria Boiardo's *Orlando Innamorato* (Orlando in love) is a romance epic whose first part was published in the early 1480's during the Italian Renaissance. The humanist poet Ludovico Ariosto (1474-1533) composed a sequel, *Orlando furioso* (1516; English translation, 1591), which reinforced Boiardo's fame and, with *Orlando Innamorato*, influenced the composition of the famous English epic *The Faerie Queene* (1590/1596) by Edmund Spenser. Other later poets also drew on *Orlando Innamorato*, among them Miguel de Cervantes in his *Don Quixote de la Mancha* (1605, 1616; English translation, 1612-1620), and John Milton in his *Paradise Lost* (1667, 1674) and *Paradise Regained* (1671).

Boiardo lived in Ferrara, a minor but influential center of Renaissance humanistic culture under the ruling Este family. Because the Ferrarese regional dialect of the poem's verse limited the appeal of the original, the work was popularized through a version by Francesco Berni (c. 1497-1535), who recast it in the Tuscan dialect. The Renaissance's cultural center, Florence, was in the region of Tuscany, and this dialect became the dominant form of the Italian language.

Orlando Innamorato consists of sixty-nine cantos, or chapters, grouped in three books, or divisions. Even though unfinished when Boiardo died in 1494, the work contains more than four thousand ottava rima stanzas, groups of eight lines of heroic verse with a rhyme scheme of *ababbcc*. The epic relates a series of military adventures motivated principally by love, which provides the unifying element to the work. It is Orlando's infatuation for Angelica that inspires his actions, and the epic revolves around his subsequent pursuit of his love from France to distant India and back. The work's intriguing quality is found not so much in its combination of romance and militaristic glory as it is in the opposition of the values of those pursuits.

Love inspires the warrior to great deeds, motivating him to set off in quest of a lady or even causing him to risk death in defending a lady in his charge. Yet love is also capable of urging on a knight excessively and without reason, leading him to his ultimate destruction. Individual episodes in *Orlando Innamorato* hold specific allegorical lessons that contribute to the underlying moral lesson of the entire epic.

The multiple interpretations that are possible for the epic and its scenes have led to doubt as to Boiardo's purpose. The delightful tales of *Orlando Innamorato* were, to be sure, intended as entertainment for the Ferrarese courtly audience, and they continued to be enjoyed since then. The work also had didactic aims, however, for Boiardo incorporated a moral vision in the work. The goal of Renaissance humanistic education was to mold character, that is, to instruct on how to act virtuously in a way that would advance the good of society as a whole. The stories of Orlando, Rinaldo, Angelica, and the other characters all contribute to such ethical instruction for Boiardo's audience. Boiardo mocks Orlando, for example, for his inability to perceive the deeper meanings in fables that he reads, yet Boiardo implies that Orlando has the capacity to become enlightened, or educated. *Orlando Innamorato* offers insight into human character and into human motivation, and it depicts a natural hierarchy of emotions, actions, and subsequent consequences, both fortunate and punitive.

Boiardo drew on three fundamental intellectual heritages. The structure and setting of his epic reflect the twelfth century French epic *The Song of Roland*, an account of the eighth century struggle by the Christian emperor Charlemagne against the incursion of Muslim forces from the Iberian peninsula into the heart of Europe. That epic concerns the exploits of Charlemagne's ideal knight, Count Roland (Orlando), who fought for the honor of his feudal lord and the Christian god in the Battle of Roncesvalles in 778.

Boiardo also incorporated the medieval legends of the English king Arthur and the chivalric deeds of his knights of the Round Table, popularized by the northern French writer Chrétien de Troyes. Specific adventures are included in *Orlando Innamorato*, among them the appearance of Uberto and his challenge to the other knights in the beginning of the epic. Even more important was the moral ideal underlying the legendary world of Arthur.

Finally, classical Roman authors inspired elements of *Orlando Innamorato*. The influence of Ovid's *Metamorphoses* (1-8 C.E.), in particular, added the spirit of fantasy and a fairy-tale element to the epic; Ovid, too, had in his other poetic works asserted the ideal that romantic love conquers all misfortunes. Boiardo composed his epic in the cultural context of Renaissance humanism, which emphasized classical literature as its basis of learning.

An important aspect of *Orlando Innamorato* is the way in which Boiardo interlaces his episodes, many of which occur simultaneously. The narrative often jumps from one adventure to an unrelated one, creating an intricate pattern that does not unfold in a sequential manner. Also interwoven into this structure are features of Boiardo's own historical context, for he makes many references to Renaissance court life and specific individuals and events. Moreover, he uses the epic's eighth century narrative to herald the future glory of the Este family in the fifteenth century. The poem concludes with a description of the turmoil that the invasion of the French king Charles VIII had brought upon Italy shortly before Boiardo's death.

"Critical Evaluation" by Alan Cottrell

Further Reading

Boiardo, Matteo Maria. *Orlando Innamorato*. Translated by Charles Stanley Ross. Berkeley: University of California Press, 1989. The first complete modern English-verse translation, with an excellent thirty-page introduction by the translator. Also contains the Italian text for a comparison of the intricacies of the two languages.

Cavallo, Jo Ann. *Boiardo's "Orlando Innamorato": An Ethics of Desire*. Madison, N.J.: Fairleigh Dickinson University Press, 1993. Analyzes the epic in terms of Ferrara's status as a center of humanistic education. Argues that the work forms a coherent argument for classical ethics based on the traditionally moralistic interpretation of ancient texts.

_____. *The Romance Epics of Boiardo, Ariosto, and Tasso: From Public Duty to Private Pleasure.* Buffalo, N.Y.: University of Toronto Press, 2004. Cavallo's history of the Italian Renaissance romance epic includes a lengthy analysis of *Orlando Innamorato*. She compares this work to epic poems by Ludovico Ariosto and Torquato Tasso, who, like Boiardo, were part of the Este court.

Di Tommaso, Andrea. *Structure and Ideology in Boiardo's "Orlando Innamorato."* Chapel Hill: University of North Carolina Press, 1972. A brief but perceptive work. Regards *Orlando Innamorato* as an independent work rather than as an inspiration for Ariosto's sequel *Orlando Furioso*. Reveals how courtly ideology emerges in contrast to the epic's warrior features.

Kisacky, Julia. *Magic in Boiardo and Ariosto.* New York: Peter Lang, 2000. Examines the function of magic in *Orlando Innamorato* and Ariosto's *Orlando Furioso.*

Kisacky demonstrates how the authors associated magic with chaos and the irrational, in contrast to order and reason, and how they used magic to explore the Renaissance debate about fortune versus self-determination.

Looney, Dennis. *Compromising the Classics: Romance Epic Narrative in the Italian Renaissance.* Detroit, Mich.: Wayne State University Press, 1996. Looney analyzes the "radical neoclassicism" in Boiardo's *Orlando Innamorato* and in Italian Renaissance romance epics by Ariosto and Tasso. He demonstrates how these poets adapted the romance epic by imitating classic epics, as well as pastorals, satires, and other literary genres.

Marinelli, Peter V. *Ariosto and Boiardo: The Origins of "Orlando Furioso."* Columbia: University of Missouri Press, 1987. Analyzes *Orlando Innamorato* as a source of literary capital that Ariosto consciously drew upon while he manipulated and re-created it in his *Orlando Furioso.*

Orley Farm

Author: Anthony Trollope (1815-1882)
First published: 1861-1862, serial; 1862, book
Type of work: Novel
Type of plot: Domestic realism
Time of plot: Mid-nineteenth century
Locale: England

Principal characters:
LADY MASON, the mistress of Orley Farm
LUCIUS MASON, her son
JOSEPH MASON, ESQ., the owner of Groby Park
SIR PEREGRINE ORME, a gallant old gentleman
MRS. ORME, his daughter-in-law
PEREGRINE ORME, his grandson
SAMUEL DOCKWRATH, a rascally attorney
MIRIAM, his wife
MR. FURNIVAL, a London attorney
SOPHIA, his daughter, loved by Lucius
MR. CHAFFANBRASS, a celebrated lawyer
FELIX GRAHAM, a penniless young barrister
MADELINE STAVELY, Graham's beloved

The Story:

Sir Joseph Mason is nearing seventy years of age when he marries a second wife forty-five years his junior. Having been in turn merchant, alderman, mayor, and knight, he has by this time amassed a large fortune, out of which he has purchased Groby Park, a landed estate in Yorkshire. He turns over this property to the son of his first marriage, Joseph Mason, Esq., who under his father's generous provision is able to lead the life of a country gentleman with as much magnificence as his mean, grasping nature will allow. Sir Joseph himself makes his home at Orley Farm, a country resi-

dence not far from London. Joseph Mason has always been assured that the farm will go to him, as head of the family, at his father's death.

The baronet's second marriage is little more than an old man's attempt to find companionship and comfort in his declining years, and young Lady Mason, a quiet, sensible, clever woman, cheerfully accepts it as such. One son, Lucius, is born to Sir Joseph and Lady Mason. Then Sir Joseph dies suddenly, and when the time comes for the reading of his will, it is discovered that in an attached codicil he has bequeathed Orley Farm to his infant son. Joseph Mason feels that he has been deprived of property rightfully his, and he contests the codicil.

The Orley Farm Case, as it is called, has many complications. The will was drawn up by Jonathan Usbech, Sir Joseph's attorney, but it, like the codicil, is in Lady Mason's handwriting, because old Usbech had suffered from a gouty hand at the time. It was witnessed by John Kennerby, Sir Joseph's clerk, and by Bridget Bolster, a housemaid. In court, both witnesses swear that they were called to their master's bedside and there, in the presence of Usbech and Lady Mason, signed a document that all assumed was the codicil. Lady Mason readily admits that while she had asked nothing for herself, she had wanted much for her child. She also states that before Usbech and Mr. Furnival, a barrister, she had often urged her husband to leave Orley Farm to little Lucius. Old Usbech having died in the meantime, she is unable to have her statement confirmed by him, but Mr. Furnival testifies to the truth of her assertion.

Joseph Mason loses his case. The will and codicil are upheld, and Lady Mason and her son continue to live at Orley Farm and to enjoy its yearly income of eight hundred pounds. Joseph Mason retires to Groby Park to sulk. Miriam Usbech, old Jonathan's daughter, also benefits under the terms of the codicil to the extent of two thousand pounds, an inheritance she loses when she entrusts it to her husband, Samuel Dockwrath, a shady young attorney from the neighboring town of Hamworth. Relations between Usbech's daughter and the mistress of Orley Farm are always friendly. Thanks to Lady Mason, Dockwrath holds two outlying fields on the estate at low rental.

Sir Peregrine Orme of The Cleeve is among the neighbors who stood by Lady Mason during the trial. Other members of his household are his daughter-in-law, Mrs. Orme, who is Lady Mason's best friend, and his grandson, namesake, and heir. Young Peregrine Orme and Lucius Mason are the same age but have little else in common. As the boys have grown up, Peregrine, heir to a great estate, has been educated at Harrow and Oxford. A well-meaning but somewhat wild young man, Peregrine pursues two chief interests: foxhunting and rat baiting. He is also in love with Madeline Stavely, the lovely daughter of Judge Stavely of Noningsby.

After a term at a German university, Lucius Mason returns to Orley Farm with the plan of putting into practice some methods of scientific farming he learned abroad. One of his first acts is to serve notice of his intention to repossess the fields leased to Dockwrath. An unpleasant interview between Lady Mason and the angry attorney follows, and, concerned about Dockwrath's vague threats, Lady Mason then goes to Sir Peregrine for advice, as she has on many occasions during the previous twenty years. Sir Peregrine snorts with disgust over Lucius's agricultural theories and announces that he will bring the young man to his senses. Lucius dines with Sir Peregrine at The Cleeve, but the older man is unable to convince him to give up his plans. Sir Peregrine decides that the earnest young man is as conceited as he is stubborn.

In the meantime, Dockwrath has been busy. He has gone through his father-in-law's papers and has learned that on the date carried by the codicil, Sir Joseph signed a deed of separation dissolving a business partnership between him and a man named Mr. Martock. Either Sir Joseph signed two legal documents on that day, a possibility that the evidence presented in court makes unlikely, or the codicil is a forgery. Armed with this information, Dockwrath goes to Groby Park to confer with Joseph Mason. As a result of that conference, Mason decides to reopen the Orley Farm Case.

Dockwrath hopes to advance himself in his profession and begs for an opportunity to handle the case, but the squire, aware of Dockwrath's reputation, tells him to take his information to the firm of Round and Crook, reputable London lawyers who will be above suspicion. Mason, however, does promise that Dockwrath will be rewarded if Lady Mason is convicted and Orley Farm is returned to its rightful owner. The Hamworth lawyer then goes to London and offers his services to Round and Crook. They are willing to use him, but only to collect information that might prove useful.

When Miriam Dockwrath carries an account of her husband's activities to Orley Farm, Lady Mason appeals to Sir Peregrine, her good friend, and Mr. Furnival, her attorney, for advice and help. With the passing of time, Mr. Furnival has changed from a hardworking young barrister into a fashionable attorney with a weakness for port wine and lovely women. Lady Mason is still attractive, and so he comforts her more as a woman than as a client, assuring her that the Orley Farm Case, unappealed at the time, is not likely to be reviewed. The chivalrous Sir Peregrine is stirred to great indignation by what he considers the dastardly conduct of Joseph Mason, whom he has always disliked. Hearing the news, Lucius is equally indignant and tells his mother to leave the matter in his hands. Sir Peregrine and Mr. Furnival have difficulty in restraining him from acting rashly.

The outcome of the suit is more important to Lucius than he realizes. He is in love with Sophia Furnival, daughter of his mother's attorney, but the prudent young woman intends to choose her husband with discretion. Another of her suitors is Adolphus Stavely, son of the distinguished jurist. She can afford to wait for the present time.

Meanwhile, Peregrine's wooing of Madeline Stavely has fared badly, for Madeline has no interest in anyone except Felix Graham, a penniless young barrister. The judge, convinced that Graham will make his way in the world, silently approves his daughter's choice, but her mother, eager to see her daughter mistress of The Cleeve, grows impatient with her husband because of his refusal to speak up for young Orme.

There is some delay in the determination of grounds for a lawsuit. The will was upheld years before, so it is felt that a charge of forgery is impossible after such a long time. Finally, Round and Crook decide to prosecute for perjury; they charge that in the previous trial Lady Mason swore falsely to the execution of the will. When word comes that Lady Mason will have to stand trial, Mrs. Orme invites her to stay at The Cleeve. This invitation, dictated by Sir Peregrine, is intended to show to the county the Ormes's confidence in their neighbor's innocence. Sir Peregrine's chivalry, however, does not stop there. At last, he offers Lady Mason the protection of his name as well as his house, and she, almost overwhelmed by the prospect of the coming trial, promises to marry him.

Lucius and Peregrine are both opposed to the marriage, although Sir Peregrine reconciles his grandson to it in part by encouraging the young man in his own unsuccessful suit. Mr. Furnival becomes less gallant. Lady Mason's conscience, however, will not allow her to accept Sir Peregrine's offer after all. One night she goes to him and confesses that she forged the codicil in a desperate effort to keep the property for her son. Sir Peregrine is shocked by this information, but he is still determined to stand by her during the trial.

Mr. Furnival is shrewd. When he hears that his client is not going to marry Sir Peregrine after all, he is convinced that the whole story has not been told. Suspecting Lady Mason's possible guilt, he hires the famous Mr. Chaffanbrass and his associate, Mr. Solomon Aram, noted criminal lawyers, to defend Lady Mason at the trial. Felix Graham is to act as junior counsel for the defense.

The trial lasts for two days and part of another. The heckling attorneys so confuse John Kennerby that his testimony is worthless. Bridget Bolster insists, however, that she signed only one document on that particular day. Even Mr. Chaffanbrass is unable to break down her story; the most damaging admission she makes is that she likes an occasional glass of liquor. Dockwrath, however, is completely discredited, especially after Mr. Chaffanbrass forces him to admit his vengeful motives and Joseph Mason's promise to reward him for his services. At the end of the second day of the trial, Lady Mason confesses her guilt to her son. He is not in court with her the next morning when the verdict is announced: Lady Mason is acquitted.

The jury's verdict is legal but not moral, and a few days later, Mr. Furnival notifies Joseph Mason that Lucius is transferring ownership of Orley Farm to his half brother. Lucius is returning to Germany with his mother; eventually, he hopes to become a farmer in Australia. Sir Peregrine goes to London to see Lady Mason before she leaves for Germany. Their farewell is gentle and sad on his part, final on hers. Dockwrath sues Joseph Mason to collect payment for his help and is completely ruined in the suit. Sophia Furnival decides that she can never be anything but a sister to Lucius. Madeline Stavely marries her penniless barrister and lives more happily than her mother thinks she deserves. Young Peregrine Orme eases his broken heart by shooting lions and elephants in central Africa.

Critical Evaluation:

Anthony Trollope considered his lengthy novel *Orley Farm* to be one of his most ambitious undertakings. This work incorporates more central characters than do any of Trollope's previous novels, and it has a more complicated plot and offers deeper insights into social and legal hierarchies. It was met with praise from novelist George Eliot and critic G. H. Lewes. In its day *Orley Farm* was a popular work, one that Trollope considered possibly his finest.

The effect of *Orley Farm* depends largely on irony; often, characters are not as they seem to be, and the plot frequently takes unexpected turns. For example, Lady Mason seems to be a model of fragile innocence and is found innocent of the charges brought against her by Samuel Dockwrath and Joseph Mason, but she is unquestionably guilty of the crime she is accused of committing and displays incredible strength, rather than ladylike fragility, in the middle of the adversity she has brought upon herself. Although she has committed a crime by forging a codicil to her late husband's will, Trollope would have the reader consider Lady Mason to be anything but a criminal, because she forged the codicil only out of love for her son. Furthermore, although she is guilty and is acknowledged as being so by most of the attorneys involved in her trial, she is treated far more sympathetically than her accusers, Dockwrath and Joseph Mason. Although they are clearly in the right concerning the charges they bring against Lady Mason, they prove to be two of the most contemptible characters in the novel. In a final ironic twist, after she is found innocent, Lady Mason agrees with Lucius's decision that she should follow her conscience and turns Orley Farm over to its rightful heir, Joseph Mason.

The fact that the court ultimately finds for Lady Mason is

not merely an ironic defense of the woman's character; it is also an indictment of the corruption and inefficacy of the English legal system. Trollope's purpose in writing *Orley Farm* goes beyond the telling of a story of guilt and innocence. The ultimate ironic point of the novel is that the execution of justice in the English courts of the first half of the nineteenth century bore little relationship to the Christian worldview on which the laws of those courts were supposedly based.

Trollope's belief in the working out of divine justice, and in the importance of the related virtues of repentance and forgiveness, is made clear throughout the novel. For example, Mrs. Orme quickly forgives Lady Mason after she learns of her sin. Mrs. Orme remains Lady Mason's best friend during the trial and repeatedly encourages Lady Mason to repent and ask forgiveness from God. Other examples of forgiveness are provided by Mrs. Furnival, who forgives Mrs. Mason for becoming too familiar with her husband, and Sir Peregrine, who at one point asks Lady Mason to marry him and is devastated when he learns that Lady Mason is guilty of the crime of which she is accused. When the trial is over, Sir Peregrine forgives Lady Mason and makes a statement regarding the adversity Lady Mason has had to suffer that the narrator reinforces: "No lesson is truer than that which teaches us to believe that God does temper the wind to the shorn lamb." In other words, the trials that Lady Mason has had to endure have been allowed by God for the spiritual strengthening of her character and have brought her to a point at which she asks God's forgiveness and forgives those who took her to court. At this point, and even earlier in the novel, the narrator asks the reader to sympathize with—and therefore forgive—Lady Mason, comparing her to the biblical character of Rebekah, the wife of Isaac, who deceived her husband to secure a blessing for her son, Jacob.

Trollope emphasizes the importance of forgiveness again in the final scene of the novel, as Felix Graham and young Peregrine Orme nearly part from each other as enemies because Graham has won the heart of Madeline Stavely, whom Peregrine also loves. In a movement away from the animosity that has characterized many of the relationships in the novel, Peregrine overcomes his bitterness toward Graham, acknowledges his wrong, and shakes his friend's hand. The two young men then separate on a note of reconciliation.

Trollope's belief in a system of justice, in a code of ethics that transcends the dealings of the English court, is made clear through the characters of Felix Graham and Madeline Stavely. An attorney, Graham conducts his career in line with the Ten Commandments of the Bible. The point is made early in the novel that Graham, in his determination to be guided by his conscience, is not following the standards of most attorneys and therefore, monetarily at least, will not be rewarded in this world. For conducting himself during Lady Mason's trial according to the dictates of his conscience and of the Bible, for sympathizing with witnesses who suffer character assassination simply because they attempt to tell the truth about the Orley case, Graham earns only the scorn of the top criminal defense lawyer, Mr. Chaffanbrass. Graham does, however, receive a reward of sorts: He is to be married to Madeline Stavely, the woman whom the narrator extols as the most interesting of the novel. Madeline spends her spare time caring for the poor, is not at all concerned about wealth or associating with the rich and famous, and, in her relationship with Felix Graham, goes beyond the young man's rather plain surface to discern his truly noble and moral character. Part of the couple's reward is that Judge Stavely will provide his daughter and her husband with an income sufficient to support them in the lifestyle to which they are accustomed.

One should not conclude that *Orley Farm* is simply an eight-hundred-page novel about the rewards for good behavior. Trollope's vision is more complicated than this, for he makes it clear that almost no one involved in the Orley Farm Case is concerned with carrying out justice. Most of the characters—from the most base to the most seemingly noble—act primarily out of self-interest. For example, Joseph Mason agrees to proceed with the trial against his half sister not to right a wrong but chiefly to get even. Ironically, when Lucius offers him the lands of which he has been deprived, Joseph first rejects the offer and seeks legal help to sue the lawyers who represented him as well as those standing for Mrs. Mason. He simply wants to see Lady Mason—and everyone else associated with her defense—punished. The lawyer Dockwrath, initially deprived of his land when Lucius reaches legal age, is a small, mean-spirited man who derives far more enjoyment from bullying others than he does from seeing justice done. Mr. Furnival initially agrees to represent Lady Mason not because he is concerned that justice be done—indeed, he deduces that Lady Mason is guilty of the crime with which she is charged—but because he is attracted to her. To emphasize that the English courts are not at all about the carrying out of justice, Trollope introduces the characters Aram and Chaffanbrass, two criminal defense attorneys whose reputations are built on their ability to destroy witnesses and gain verdicts of not guilty for people who are unquestionably guilty.

Orley Farm is a good, possibly great, novel. Unity of design as well as shrewd and ironic conceptualization of character and plot enable Trollope to depict an English court system that protects the guilty and punishes the innocent.

Trollope emphasizes the need for change through his indictment of the English courts and his revelation of the types of characters that the courts sustain.

"Critical Evaluation" by Richard Logsdon

Further Reading

Bridgham, Elizabeth A. *Spaces of the Sacred and Profane: Dickens, Trollope, and the Victorian Cathedral Town.* New York: Routledge, 2008. Describes how Trollope and Charles Dickens use the setting of Victorian cathedral towns to critique religious attitudes, business practices, aesthetic ideas, and other aspects of nineteenth century English life.

Bury, Laurent. *Seductive Strategies in the Novels of Anthony Trollope, 1815-1882.* Lewiston, N.Y.: Edwin Mellen Press, 2004. Focuses on scenes of seduction in all of Trollope's novels, arguing that seduction was a survival skill for both men and women in the Victorian era. Examines how Trollope depicted the era's sexual politics.

King, Margaret F. "Trollope's *Orley Farm*: Chivalry Versus Commercialism." *Essays in Literature* 3, no. 2 (Fall, 1976): 181-193. Explores the novel's conflict between characters who are motivated by their pocketbooks and those who act out of a sense of honor and integrity.

Markwick, Margaret. *New Men in Trollope's Novels: Rewriting the Victorian Male.* Burlington, Vt.: Ashgate, 2007. Examines Trollope's novels, tracing the development of his ideas about masculinity. Argues that Trollope's male characters are not the conventional Victorian patriarchs and demonstrates how his works promoted a "startlingly modern model of manhood."

_____. *Trollope and Women.* London: Hambledon Press, 1997. Discusses how Trollope could simultaneously accept the conventional Victorian ideas about women while also sympathizing with women's difficult situations. Demonstrates the individuality of his female characters and addresses his depiction of both happy and unhappy marriages, male-female relationships, bigamy, and scandal.

Mullen, Richard, and James Munson. *The Penguin Companion to Trollope.* New York: Penguin Books, 1996. Comprehensive guide describes all of Trollope's novels, short stories, travel books, and other works, providing discussion of plot, characters, background, tone, allusions, and contemporary references that place the works in their historical context.

Oroonoko
Or, The Royal Slave, a True History

Author: Aphra Behn (1640-1689)
First published: 1688
Type of work: Novel
Type of plot: Didactic
Time of plot: Seventeenth century
Locale: Africa and Suriname

Principal characters:
OROONOKO, an African prince
IMOINDA, his wife
ABOAN, a friend of Oroonoko
THE KING, Oroonoko's grandfather

The Story:

In the African kingdom of Coromantien, the ruler is an old man more than one hundred years of age. His grandson, Prince Oroonoko, is the bravest, most beloved young man in all the land. When the commanding general is killed in battle, Oroonoko is chosen to take his place, even though the prince is only seventeen years old. After a great victory in battle, Prince Oroonoko presents himself at the court of his grandfather, the king. His noble and martial bearing makes him an instant favorite with lords and ladies alike.

Oroonoko also visits Imoinda, the daughter of his dead general, a girl as beautiful and modest as he is handsome and brave. The two noble young people immediately fall in love. They marry, but before the marriage can be consummated, Oroonoko makes known his plans to his grandfather the king. Although the old man already has many wives, he had heard of the loveliness of Imoinda and wants her for his own. When Oroonoko is absent one day, the king sends his veil to Imoinda, a royal command that she is to join his harem. Since it is against the law for even a king to take another man's wife, the old man makes her forswear her marriage and acknowledge him as her husband.

When Oroonoko returns and learns of the old man's treachery, he renounces all pleasures in longing for his lost wife. The lovers dare not let the king know their true feelings, for to do so means death for both of them (even though Oroonoko is of the king's own blood). While pretending not to care for his lost Imoinda, Oroonoko is again invited to the royal palace. There he learns from some of the king's women that Imoinda is still a virgin. Oroonoko plans to rescue her. With the help of his friend, Aboan, and one of the older wives of the king, Oroonoko enters the apartment of Imoinda and takes her as his true wife. Spied upon by the king's orders, Oroonoko is apprehended and forced to flee back to his army camp, leaving Imoinda to the mercies of the king. Enraged because he had been betrayed by his own blood, the old man determines to kill the girl and then punish Oroonoko. To save her life, Imoinda tells the king that Oroonoko had raped her. The king then declares that she must be punished with worse than death; he sells her into slavery.

The king gives up his intent to punish his grandson, for Oroonoko controls the soldiers and the king fears they might be turned against him. Instead, he takes Oroonoko back into his favor after telling the boy that Imoinda had been given an honorable death for her betrayal of the king. Oroonoko holds no grudge against the king and does not act against him; for a long time, however, he pines for his lost wife. At last, his grief grows less, and he once more takes his place at the royal court.

Soon afterward, an English merchant ship arrives in the port of Coromantien. When the ship's master, well known to Oroonoko, invites the prince and his friends to a party on board, Oroonoko, Aboan, and others gladly accept the invitation. Once on board, all are seized and made prisoners and later sold as slaves in Suriname on the coast of South America. The man who bought Oroonoko, seeing the nobility of his slave, immediately feels great esteem for him. Indeed, except for the fact that he has been bought, Oroonoko is not a slave at all, but rather a friend to his master. In the colony as in his own homeland, Oroonoko is loved, admired, and respected by all who see him. His name is changed to Caesar.

In a short time, Oroonoko, now known as Caesar, hears of a lovely young girl whom all the men want for their own. It is believed, however, that she pines for a lost love. When Oroonoko sees her, he sees Imoinda, whom he had thought dead. Reunited with great joy, the lovers are allowed to live together and are promised their freedom and passage to their own country as soon as the governor arrives to make the arrangements.

Oroonoko, however, begins to fear that he and his wife are never going to be set free, that the promise will not be kept. Imoinda is pregnant and they fear that they are to be kept until the child is born, another slave. When the masters are gone one day, Oroonoko tries to persuade the slaves to revolt against their bondage; he promises to lead them to his own country and there give them liberty. Although most of the slaves follow him, they quickly desert him when they are overtaken by their masters; Oroonoko is left with Imoinda and one man. The governor, who is with the pursuers, promises Oroonoko that if he surrenders, there will be no punishment. Again, Oroonoko is betrayed. Upon his surrender, he is seized, tied to a stake, and whipped until the flesh falls from his bones. Oroonoko endures his punishment with great courage, but he vows revenge on his captors even if it means his own death. His master, still his friend, had also been betrayed into believing the promises made to Oroonoko. He takes the sick and feeble man back to his own plantation and nurses him. There he refuses to let anyone near Oroonoko except his friends, and he posts a guard to see that no harm comes to the sick man.

Oroonoko is resolved to have his revenge on his tormentors, and he conceives a grim plan. Fearing that Imoinda will be raped and suffer a shameful death, he tells her that she must die at his hand so that he will be free to accomplish his revenge. Imoinda blesses her husband for his thoughtfulness; after many caresses and words of love, Oroonoko severs her head from her body. Then he lays down beside her and does not eat or drink for many days while he grieves for his beloved.

Found by the side of his dead wife by those who had come to beat him again, he takes his knife, cuts off his own flesh, and rips his own bowels, all the while vowing that he will never be whipped a second time. Again, friends take him home and care for him with love and kindness. Then the governor tricks his friends once more, and Oroonoko is tied to a stake and whipped publicly. After the beating, the executioner cuts off his arms, legs, nose, and ears. Because of his enemies' treachery, Oroonoko dies a cruel and shameful death.

Critical Evaluation:

Aphra Behn was the first woman in the history of English literature to earn her living as a writer. While earlier women had left important works in varied genres, none had achieved commercial success. Behn's primary significance to literary history lies in her prose fiction. She is an important figure in the transition between the prose romances of the Renaissance and the novel in the early eighteenth century. Her narrative art assures her place in literature, and the humanitarian themes of her works endow them with enduring relevance.

Through its narrative techniques and extensive use of specific details to promote verisimilitude, *Oroonoko*, the most significant and best known of Behn's seventeen prose romances, represents a critical work in the development of the English novel. Ostensibly narrating from the authorial point of view, Behn asserts at the outset that the story is factual and claims to have known the characters and witnessed much of the action. She injects numerous details to enhance the realism, foreshadowing the narrative techniques of Daniel Defoe and Jonathan Swift. Like her successors in prose fiction, she selects details calculated to appeal to the interest of the English in exotic places like the New World. She describes, for example, South American creatures like the armadillo and the anaconda, and her account of the indigenous peoples idealizes their primitive and simple lives. The numerous descriptive details are highly specific, though sometimes inaccurate, as when Behn describes a serpent thirty-six yards long or discusses tigers in Suriname.

The narrator persona assures the reader that the account is true, and claims periodically to have encountered Oroonoko personally at specified points in the action. Also, the narrative incorporates names of actual people known to have been officials in Suriname at the time of the plot. At one point, Behn leads the reader to assume that she was sent to gather information from the hero by colonists who feared a slave uprising. This detail is in accord with her previous work as an intelligence agent for Charles II in Holland. In 1664, she may have actually traveled to Suriname, as she claims. Other details relevant to her own experiences and life include references to her writings, especially her dramatic works. Collectively, these details support her assurances to the reader that she had been a witness to many of the episodes.

The most important parts of her book, like its themes and characters, show that she is following not a real life, but a literary convention. Measured against a hero who is larger than life in the narrative, many details must be regarded as conscious art, not truth, even though they effectively lend the narrative a strong air of authenticity.

The primary interest of the work lies in the depiction of its protagonist, who is also shaped by literary convention and contemporary taste. Oroonoko is a Restoration hero, capable of intense passions and modeled more on the protagonists of the heroic dramas of the period than on a living person. In love, he knows no half measures, for Behn embraces the assumption that great love implies a great soul. A man of natural nobility, Oroonoko embodies both the Achilles type of active hero and the Oedipus type of suffering, contemplative hero.

Though his character owes something to the literary concept of the noble savage, he is more than this. Despite his origin in tribal Africa, he is not primitive, but a well-educated, charismatic youth who has learned to read Latin and French and who speaks fluent English. An admirer of Roman virtues, he becomes known as Caesar when he arrives in Suriname because he is invincible in warfare, eloquent and inspiring in speech, and triumphant in the daunting challenges posed by nature.

Oroonoko's first obstacle in love is his own grandfather, the king of his country, who wants Oroonoko's beloved Imoinda for himself. Once he has overcome this challenge, he must confront the evils of slavery. While he will endure servitude for himself, he is unwilling to accept it for his unborn child. His struggle against institutional slavery, however, is doomed to failure. Behn depicts her hero as the epitome of honor and dignity whose happiness is destroyed by evils brought to Africa and the New World by Europeans. Ironically, he represents the ideals professed by Europeans, ideals that they themselves have disregarded.

Thematically the work touches on values typical in Behn's fiction, including the right of women to select their spouses and the paramount value of romantic love. The two dominant themes, however, are opposition to slavery and the celebration of primitivism. In terms of modern understanding, both themes must be severely qualified. The celebration of primitive tribal life is calculated to appeal to a contemporaneous audience fascinated with the New World. Although she develops the theme in both Africa and Suriname, her most extensive depiction of primitive nobility relates to the New World. The indigenous peoples of Suriname demonstrate the superiority of the primitive over the more complex European civilization. A people guided by modesty, simplicity, and innocence, they have no concept of sin, no natural sense of guilt, no words for falsehood and deception. They have no need of complex laws to govern their behavior, but are guided by a natural sense of right and wrong. Admirably adjusted to their environment, they live a life of basic virtue and do little harm. Behn cautions that European mores and religion could only harm their idyllic lives.

As for its antislavery message, the approach is less clear. Slavery is depicted as endemic in Africa, though a clear evil. Even Oroonoko and his grandfather sell their low-ranking captives into slavery, though Oroonoko attempts to protect his noble captives. Those who are enslaved think first and foremost of regaining their liberty and attempt this whenever an opportunity arises. The narrative exposes the violence done to family units under slavery. Europeans involved in the slave trade are portrayed as treacherous and evil, yet once the slaves have reached plantations, not all masters are unkind to them. The supervisor of Oroonoko's plantation, Trefrey, treats him as an equal and attempts to intercede on his behalf and to offer protection. By portraying Oroonoko as a noble savage, unjustly and treacherously enslaved, Behn contributed to the growing antislavery sentiment in England. The story of Oroonoko gained further public exposure after the dramatist Thomas Southerne used the romance as the source for his popular drama *Oroonoko* (1695).

"Critical Evaluation" by Stanley Archer

Further Reading

Altaba-Artal, Dolors. *Aphra Behn's English Feminism: Wit and Satire*. Cranbury, N.J.: Associated University Presses, 1999. Chapters examine Behn's satirical writings from a feminist perspective. Includes a bibliography and an index.

Anderson, Emily Hodgson. "Novelty in Novels: A Look at What's New in Aphra Behn's *Oroonoko*." *Studies in the Novel* 39, no. 1 (Spring, 2007): 1-16. Explores the aspects of novelty in novels through a focused reading of *Oroonoko*. Argues that the novel demonstrates a concern for didacticism and its own newness that was characteristic of many eighteenth century novels.

Chalmers, Hero. *Royalist Women Writers, 1650-1689*. New York: Oxford University Press, 2004. An examination of the work of Behn, Margaret Cavendish, and Katherine Philips. Chalmers maintains that these seventeenth century women inspired "a more assertive model of the Englishwoman as literary author" that was "enabled by their royalist affiliations."

Hughes, Derek, and Janet Todd, eds. *The Cambridge Companion to Aphra Behn*. New York: Cambridge University Press, 2004. Collection of essays about Behn's life and work, including two analyses of *Oroonoko*: "*Oroonoko*: Reception, Ideology, and Narrative Strategy" by Laura J. Rosenthal and "Others, Slaves, and Colonists in *Oroonoko*" by Joanna Lipking.

Hunter, Heidi, ed. *Rereading Aphra Behn: History, Theory, and Criticism*. Charlottesville: University Press of Virginia, 1993. A selection of essays on various aspects of Behn's works. Includes an essay by Charlotte Sussman that centers on the character Imoinda and explores women's experiences under polygamy and slavery.

Iwanisziw, Susan B., ed. *Troping "Oroonoko" from Behn to Bandele*. Burlington, Vt.: Ashgate, 2004. Behn's novel has been adapted in numerous forms since its first publication in 1688. This collection of essays considers the characters, abolitionist influences, and marketing strategies from the story's beginning in Restoration England through its modern adaptations.

Rivero, Albert J. "Aphra Behn's *Oroonoko* and the 'Blank Spaces' of Colonial Fictions." *Studies in English Literature, 1500-1900* 39, no. 3 (Summer, 1999): 443-462. Discusses Joseph Conrad's *Heart of Darkness* (1902) and Behn's *Oroonoko*. Both works feature characters who begin as "civilized" and go "spectacularly native," and both attempt to preserve hierarchies of race and class while representing the impossibility of doing so in chaotic colonial settings.

Spencer, Jane. *Aphra Behn's Afterlife*. New York: Oxford University Press, 2000. Spencer discusses Behn's reputation as a novelist, poet, and playwright, describing her influence on eighteenth century literature. Chapter 6 focuses on the critical reception of *Oroonoko*.

Sypher, Wylie. *Guinea's Captive Kings: British Anti-slavery Literature of the Eighteenth Century*. 1942. Reprint. New York: Octagon Books, 1969. Sypher places *Oroonoko* within the context of antislavery literature. His analysis shows that, by combining the antislavery theme with that of the noble savage, Behn swayed sentiment against slavery.

Todd, Janet. *The Secret Life of Aphra Behn*. 1996. Reprint. New York: Pandora, 2000. Todd's biography aims to uncover the facts about Behn's life, with all of its contradictions. Based on Todd's discovery of new material by and about Behn in the Dutch archives in the Netherlands.

Wiseman, Susan. *Aphra Behn*. 2d ed. Tavistock, England: Northcote House/British Council, 2007. Wiseman's biography examines Behn's life and work and discusses Behn's works in all genres. Includes analysis of *Oroonoko*.

Orpheus

Author: Jean Cocteau (1889-1963)
First produced: *Orphée*, 1926; first published, 1927
    (English translation, 1933)
Type of work: Drama
Type of plot: Tragicomedy
Time of plot: Early twentieth century
Locale: Thrace, Greece

Principal characters:
ORPHEUS, a poet
EURYDICE, his wife
HEURTEBISE, their guardian angel, a glazier in appearance
ALGAONICE, leader of the Bacchantes
DEATH, an elegantly dressed woman
THE COMMISSIONER OF POLICE, a bumbling bureaucrat

The Story:

Seated across from his wife, Eurydice, in their villa in Thrace, the poet Orpheus concentrates on the tapping of a white horse that is housed in a niche in the center of the room. Orpheus believes that the horse's tapping will indicate the next letter in an inspired message. Eventually, the horse taps out "hell" and, finally, "hello" (in the original French, *mer* becomes *merci*). Orpheus has submitted a previous message, "Orpheus hunts Eurydice's lost life," to the Thracian poetry competition. Eurydice's complaints of neglect, compounded by her doubts regarding these messages, begin to provoke Orpheus. In response to her warnings regarding the jealousy of the Bacchantes, a cult of women to whom Eurydice used to belong, Orpheus accuses her of disloyalty. He goes on to insist that Eurydice break a windowpane each day so that the glazier, Heurtebise, will come to their villa. To deny his jealousy, he breaks a pane himself and summons Heurtebise.

Upon Heurtebise's entrance, Orpheus departs for town to prepare for the poetry competition. In exchange for some poison-laced sugar from the Bacchante leader, Algaonice, Eurydice hands Heurtebise an incriminating letter she has had in her possession. Heurtebise also gives Eurydice an envelope from Algaonice in which to place the letter to eliminate any trace of Eurydice's involvement. Shrinking from giving the poison to the horse herself, Eurydice convinces Heurtebise to do the deed. Heurtebise, however, interrupted by Orpheus's reappearance, stands on a chair at the window, pretending to take measurements. Orpheus has returned because he forgot to take his birth certificate with him for the competition. To retrieve the document from the top of the bookcase, Orpheus grabs the chair on which Heurtebise stands, and after the chair is pulled from beneath him, Heurtebise remains suspended in the air. Orpheus, oblivious to this fact, retrieves the certificate and leaves. Eurydice, however, demands an explanation from Heurtebise, who refuses to acknowledge that anything unusual has happened. Eurydice hastily seals Algaonice's envelope with her tongue in order to give the letter to Heurtebise before dismissing

him. She remarks on its peculiar taste and then, calling Heurtebise back, reveals that she is dying; the envelope had been poisoned. She sends Heurtebise after Orpheus.

Death then enters through a mirror, followed by two attendants dressed in surgeons' uniforms. Death herself wears an evening dress and cloak, which she exchanges for a white tunic. Before beginning her "operation" on Eurydice, Death orders the horse to take the sugar Heurtebise has tossed on the table, and the horse disappears. An elaborate procedure to obtain Eurydice's soul begins. It involves calculations, measurements, mechanical devices, and a watch supplied by an audience member. Following a drumroll, a dove attached to a thread emerges from Eurydice's room; once the thread is cut, the dove—Eurydice's soul—flies off. Death and her attendants leave the way they came. Death, however, has forgotten her gloves.

Orpheus and Heurtebise enter to find Eurydice dead. Heurtebise counsels Orpheus to put on Death's gloves and return them to her for a reward. Heurtebise leads Orpheus to the mirror, revealing it to be the door through which Death has traveled. Orpheus sinks into the mirror, Eurydice's name on his lips. A postman comes to deliver a letter, which Heurtebise instructs him to slip under the door. The scene repeats, implying the arbitrariness of time. Orpheus reappears through the mirror, Eurydice behind him. As explained by Orpheus, he and Death have made a pact that Eurydice can remain with him as long as he never looks at her. Their initial bliss at reunion degenerates into bickering. Having avoided looking at Eurydice several times, Orpheus, careless in his anger, loses his balance and finds himself gazing at her. She disappears.

Orpheus insists that his look was deliberate, Eurydice having stifled his artistry. He spies the delivered letter and holds it up to the mirror to read it, as it is written backward. The letter warns Orpheus that his entry in the competition has been denounced by Algaonice as an offense. The initial letters of the sentence he submitted spell out "O Hell!" The jury considers the entry a hoax. A mob, led by the Bacchantes, is on its way for revenge. Orpheus acknowledges that the horse, as Eurydice feared, tricked him. He walks out onto the balcony to meet his fate. Following clamoring and drums, something flies through the window: Orpheus's head. It calls out to Eurydice, who comes through the mirror to take Orpheus's invisible body by the hand. Together, they sink into the mirror.

A knock on the door is heard, followed by a voice demanding entrance. Before opening the door, Heurtebise places Orpheus's head on a pedestal. The Commissioner of Police enters, with a scrivener. The Commissioner announces a reversal in public opinion in Orpheus's favor. An eclipse of the sun that day has been interpreted as a sign of anger at Orpheus's humiliation, the poet being a priest of the sun god. The Commissioner has been sent to investigate Orpheus's murder and also to obtain a bust of Orpheus for a celebration in his honor. Orpheus's head begins to speak to distract the Commissioner from Heurtebise, now the prime suspect. Heurtebise flees into the mirror. In response to the Commissioner's questions, the head gives Jean Cocteau's place of birth, name, and current address. Having noticed Heurtebise's absence, the Commissioner and scrivener exit in search of him, rushing back later for the "bust."

Orpheus, Eurydice, and Heurtebise—revealed to be the couple's guardian angel—appear together in Paradise. They smile and leisurely prepare to take lunch, prayed over by Orpheus.

Critical Evaluation:

Jean Cocteau began his career during one of the most fertile periods in French cultural and artistic history: the 1920's. His work was conspicuously avant-garde. *Orpheus* shares characteristics of the Theater of the Absurd, particularly its grim delight in the twisting of language. Attention is drawn to the fact that language is a construct—that is, a purely arbitrary system of signs and symbols. Meaning itself may therefore be unstable. The language of *Orpheus* is replete with puns and wordplay. Structurally, the course of the play is determined more by the ambiguities of language than by the twists and turns of conventional plotting. The protagonist's fate, for example, depends on the interpretation (or misinterpretation) of a phrase. Nevertheless, *Orpheus* cannot truly be categorized as absurdist theater, as its resolution lacks the rigor of absurdism.

In fact, Cocteau remained aloof from any particular "school" of dramatic thought, despite the fact that his work at times appears Dadaist, Surrealist, or Futurist in style if not in substance. Cocteau was even denounced by the Surrealists,

who judged him a "dabbler," unable to appreciate fully the movement's profound and radical intent. Indeed, the play's mockery of Orpheus's attempts to extract poetry from the tapping of a horse ridicules Surrealism's attachment to automatic writing, a system in which people attempted to ascertain meaning from words written without conscious thought. While Cocteau, like the Surrealists and Dadaists, created art to shock the public, his use of surprise was determinedly conscious. Cocteau's detailed production notes, which, unprecedentedly, he published, show the tight rein he kept on theatrical effects.

The myth of Orpheus provided a vehicle for Cocteau to explore themes relating to the creative imagination and the destiny of the artist, ideas that obsessed him throughout his career. Orpheus was the paradigmatic poet and musician; his songs charmed any creature who heard them. His gifts softened the hearts of the god of the underworld and his consort, to the point that they allowed Orpheus's dead bride to accompany him back to the world of the living. The Orphic myth had inspired numerous musical and literary works before Cocteau addressed it. Starting with the Latin poet Vergil, the love story between Orpheus and Eurydice had moved to the forefront, obscuring the myth's original focus on the transformative power of poetry and art. Cocteau's burlesquing of the marriage of Orpheus and Eurydice not only contributed to the play's collage effect of Greek tragedy, melodrama, spectacle, and music-hall magic show but also allowed him to shift the myth's thematic weight back to the eternally regenerative power of art. Cocteau saw creativity, death, and immortality as interrelated; he was convinced that true artists would be vindicated despite the persecution they suffered in their own times. Tellingly, Cocteau never used his full first name, Jean-Maurice, and later derived satisfaction from sharing the initials, *JC*, of the martyred Christian god.

Notably, the figure of Orpheus appeared in early Christian tomb paintings in Rome, indicating a link in Greek and Christian myth via the theme of resurrection. *Orpheus* itself was written when Cocteau was under the influence of the Catholic poet Jacques Maritain. A one-act play in nine scenes, it began as a five-act theatrical work about the Incarnation, featuring Mary, Joseph, and Gabriel, the angel of the Annunciation. The character of Heurtebise remains from Cocteau's original intent to explore the Christian myth. When Heurtebise first enters, he kneels and crosses his arms in the pose of Gabriel. He is forced to reveal his angelic nature when he must remain suspended in air at one point in the play. Significantly, as the couple's guardian angel, Heurtebise is the one who suggests a way for Orpheus to win over Death and also reveals to him Death's passageway to and from this world. Cocteau evidences the religious conversion he was undergoing at the time by associating the horse/medium with the devil and by ending the play with a prayer that affirms to God, "thou art poetry."

Another myth that Cocteau incorporates in *Orpheus* is that of the machine. Processes in the play operate mechanistically and with the mystique surrounding technology and its promise of precision. The horse appears to function as a kind of "poetry machine." Death's procedures are a blend of magic-show theatrics and mechanical wizardry. The machinery of the state, degenerated into bureaucracy, is personified in the Commissioner of Police. In *Orpheus*, the machine behaves like fate in modern dress. It proceeds as inescapably and as mercilessly.

The author himself claimed that the play was "half farce, half meditation upon death." Whether a pastiche or a serious attempt to dramatize the various mythologies informing twentieth century life, *Orpheus* is historically significant as one of the first in a series of modernizations of Greek myths by French playwrights. This trend also includes Jean Giraudoux's *Amphitryon 38* (pr., pb. 1929; English translation, 1938), Jean-Paul Sartre's *Les Mouches* (pr., pb. 1943; *The Flies*, 1946), and Jean Anouilh's *Antigone* (pr. 1944; English translation, 1946). Most critics agree that the dramatists used the myths as shared points of reference from which to examine Western culture in a state of crisis and doubt. Ever an intuitive artist, Cocteau appears to have grasped early the vestigial power of the myths.

Amy Spitalnick

Further Reading

Centre Georges Pompidou. *Cocteau*. Paris: Author, 2003. Retrospective catalog compiled by the Centre Pompidou and the Montreal Museum to accompany an exhibit of Cocteau's work. Presents, in addition to reproductions of the artworks, seventeen essays on Cocteau's life and work, including discussions of the Cocteau image, Orphic self-portraits, and Cocteau and Dadaism.

Crowson, Lydia. *The Esthetic of Jean Cocteau*. Hanover, N.H.: University Press of New England, 1978. Scholarly work devotes chapters to Cocteau's milieu, the nature of the real, and the roles of myth, consciousness, and power. The clarity of Crowson's writing belies an elusive thesis: On a certain level, *Orpheus* reflects Cocteau's personal conflicts regarding sex and gender.

Fowlie, Wallace. *Jean Cocteau: The History of a Poet's Age*. Bloomington: Indiana University Press, 1966. General study defines Cocteau's originality by comparing him with other French writers and film directors of his lifetime. A distinctive element of this work is an epilogue describing a meeting between Fowlie and Cocteau shortly before the latter's death.

Freeman, E. Introduction to *Orphée/Jean Cocteau*. 1976. New ed. London: Bristol Classical Press, 1992. Introduction to both the play and the film adaptation, along with notes on the play, offers a wealth of background information as well as details about the production. Presents an investigation of the work's mythological matrix that broadens the reader's understanding of the work. Includes many quotations from the play in the original French.

González, Pedro Blas. "Subjectivity and Philosophical Reflection in Jean Cocteau's Orpheus Trilogy." In *Fragments: Essays in Subjectivity, Individuality, and Autonomy*. New York: Algora, 2005. Focuses on Cocteau's three Orpheus films, but provides analysis of the themes of subjectivity and the nature of the self that pertains also to the stage play.

Knapp, Bettina Liebowitz. *Jean Cocteau*. Updated ed. Boston: Twayne, 1989. Thorough study pursues both psychological and literary views of Cocteau's work, with chapters following a chronological approach. Knapp acknowledges the paradoxes that inform her understanding of Cocteau and then attempts to analyze those paradoxes.

Oxenhandler, Neal. *Scandal and Parade: The Theatre of Jean Cocteau*. New Brunswick, N.J.: Rutgers University Press, 1957. First American study of Cocteau focuses on his work in the theater, taking a philosophical approach. Argues that Cocteau's inability to "engage" in the world around him was a kind of tragedy for the modern age.

Williams, James S. *Jean Cocteau*. London: Reaktion Books, 2008. Biography chronicles the development of Cocteau's aesthetic and his work as a novelist, poet, dramatist, filmmaker, and designer. Concludes that Cocteau's oeuvre is characterized by a continual self-questioning.

Orpheus and Eurydice

Author: Unknown
First published: Unknown
Type of work: Short fiction
Type of plot: Mythic
Time of plot: Antiquity
Locale: Thrace and the Underworld

Principal characters:
ORPHEUS, a musician
EURYDICE, his wife

The Story:

Orpheus, son of Apollo and the Muse Calliope, grows up in Thrace, a land long noted for the purity and richness of its divine gift of song. His father presents him with a lyre and teaches him to play it. So lovely are the songs of Orpheus that the wild beasts follow him when he plays, and even the trees, the rocks, and the hills gather near him. It is said his music softens the composition of stones.

Orpheus charms Eurydice with his music, but Hymen brings no happy omens to their wedding. His torch smokes so that tears come to their eyes. Passionately in love with his wife, Orpheus becomes mad with grief when Eurydice dies. Fleeing from a shepherd who desires her, she steps upon a snake and dies from its bite.

Heartbroken, Orpheus wanders over the hills composing and singing melancholy songs of memory for the lost Eurydice. Finally he descends into the Underworld and makes his way past the sentries by means of his music. Approaching the throne of Proserpine and Hades, he sings a lovely song in which he says that love brings him to the Underworld. He complains that Eurydice was taken from him before her time and if they will not release her, he will not leave Hades. Proserpine and Hades cannot resist his pleas. They agree to set Eurydice free if Orpheus will promise not to look upon her until they safely reach the Upperworld.

The music of Orpheus is so tender that even the ghosts shed tears. Tantalus forgets his search for water; Ixion's wheel stops; the vulture stops feeding on the giant's liver; the daughters of Danaus stop drawing water; and Sisyphus himself stops to listen. Tears stream from the eyes of the Furies. Eurydice then appears, limping. The two walk the long and dismal passageway to the Upperworld, and Orpheus does not look back toward Eurydice. At last, forgetting his vow, he turns, and, as they reach out their arms to embrace, Eurydice disappears.

Orpheus tries to follow her, but the stern ferryman refuses him passage across the River Styx. Declining food and drink, he sits by the River Strymon and sings his twice-felt grief. As he sings his melancholy songs, so sad that oaks move and ti-

gers grieve, a group of Thracian maidens attempt to console him, but he repulses them. One day, while they are observing the sacred rites of Bacchus, they begin to stone him. At first, the stones fall without harm when they come within the sound of the lyre. As the frenzy of the maidens increases, however, their shouting drowns out the notes of the lyre so that it no longer protects Orpheus. Soon he is covered with blood.

Then the savage women tear his limbs from his body and hurl his head and his lyre into the river. Both continue singing sad songs as they float downstream. The fragments of Orpheus's body are buried at Libethra, and it is said that nightingales sang more sweetly over his grave than in any other part of Greece. Jupiter makes his lyre a constellation of stars in the heavens. Orpheus joins Eurydice in the Underworld, and there, happy at last, they wander through the fields together.

Critical Evaluation:

The longest and most familiar version of this myth is found in Ovid's *Metamorphoses* (c. 8 C.E.; English translation, 1567), and Ovid may well have been inspired by Vergil's less florid account, carefully placed at the dramatic end of his *Georgics* (c. 37-29 B.C.E.; English translation, 1589). In Vergil's work, Eurydice is bitten by a snake as she flees the lustful rustic deity, Aristaeus. There, the Orpheus-Eurydice theme is most appropriate to Vergil's subject of rebirth and fruitfulness through sacrifice and discipline; indeed, this myth, perhaps more than any other, illustrates that humanity can never achieve victory over death without divine aid and that human immortality can be gained only through art.

Through extraordinary powers of music, Orpheus is able to perform unnatural feats, such as moving beasts, trees, and even rocks, and ultimately to obtain a rare favor from the rulers of the dead; yet his lack of discipline, that is, his inability to obey the command of Proserpine and Hades to the letter, results in his failure to achieve victory over death for Eurydice. (Even if he won, however, one must assume that death would eventually come again for them both.) Nevertheless, there is a hopeful side to the myth: Eventually the two lovers are permanently united in death.

This may be satisfying romantically, but it is less important than Orpheus's literary legacy, symbolized by his severed head continuing to sing his beloved's name, harmoniously echoed by sympathetic nature. Orpheus, therefore, achieves ultimate victory over death: His art gives him the life after death he seeks for Eurydice. This is further symbolized in his burial by the Muses near Olympus, in Apollo's petrifying his head on Lesbos (an island renowned for its poets), and finally by the transformation of Orpheus's lyre into a constellation of stars. Vergil, if not Ovid, has this victory in mind, since their versions break with the tradition in which Orpheus succeeds in rescuing Eurydice from death.

Both parts of the original myth—the retrieval of Eurydice and the death of Orpheus—probably originated in preclassical poetry, perhaps in cultic Orphism. Orpheus himself was believed to be the earliest of poets, along with Musaeus (his son), Homer, and Hesiod. He is given a place among Jason's Argonauts. His remote Thracian origins lend mystery to his myth, and no doubt this had a bearing on the relatively restricted popularity of Orphism, which seems to have been more of a philosophy than a religion. The aim of the Orphics was to lead a life of purity and purification, so that eventually the successively reincarnated soul, having purged itself of the Titanic (or earthly) element, would be pure spirit divinely born of Zeus through his son Dionysus and thus would be released from the cycle, eternally to wander the Elysian fields.

Exactly how Orpheus is connected with this cult is unclear and indeed confusing. In Ovid's version, Orpheus refuses to love any woman other than Eurydice; furthermore, he turns his attention to boys, which is why the Thracian women murder him. However, these women are bacchants, that is, Dionysian orgiasts, and, in other versions, Dionysus himself directs them to kill Orpheus because the bard, in his devotion to Apollo the sun god, prevents the wine god's acceptance in Thrace. On the other hand, the oracle established in Lesbos in honor of Orpheus is suppressed by Apollo. If Orpheus is the poet-priest-prophet of Apollo who refuses the frenzy of Dionysus, it may well be that he became the cultic model whose sacrifice ironically inspired others to accept Dionysus. Orphic mysteries seem to have resembled the orgies of Dionysus, but whereas the Dionysiac is striving for that momentary ecstatic union with the god, the Orphic is striving for eternal peace.

The descent of Orpheus into the Underworld obviously symbolizes an Orphic's death, which will be followed by a new life, repeated until the cycle is complete. Other symbolic interpretations aside, the descent and return would be frightening were they not so entertaining. Having given readers a whirlwind classic tour of the Underworld, including introductions to the king and queen, Ovid slowly leads readers back along the murky upward path until suddenly Orpheus's concern for Eurydice outstrips his easy promise. The pathos of this second separation is intensified by its swiftness and by Orpheus's inability even to regain passage across the Styx, much less to see or to hear his love again.

Few love stories from classical antiquity made such an impression on succeeding ages. This myth became the subject of the first secular drama in vernacular, *Orfeo* (1480), composed in the era of the Medici family by Angelo Poliziano. In 1600, the first Italian opera, *Euridice*, was composed. Christoph Gluck's *Orfeo ed Eurydice* (1762) is considered the first "modern" opera for its balance of music and tragic drama, although a happy ending was supplied: Amore (Love) brings Eurydice back to prevent Orfeo's suicide. Twentieth century playwrights have adapted the story to their own settings and purposes, among them, Jean Anouilh and Tennessee Williams. Composers such as Jacques Offenbach, Darius Milhaud, and Igor Stravinsky have borrowed the theme. In film, Vinicius de Moraes's Brazilian masterpiece, *Black Orpheus* (1957), takes place in Rio de Janeiro during Carnival and deftly uses the primitive color of the celebration to heighten the frenzy of Orpheus's search for his love, who vainly tries to elude her stalking killer costumed as Death.

Further Reading

Anouilh, Jean. *Eurydice and Medée*. Edited by E. Freeman. New York: Blackwell, 1984. A modern analysis of the Orpheus and Eurydice story and the story of Medea as dramatized by modern writers. Compares the two women as opposites, while exploring the loss of love as it relates to one's view of the world.

Cotterell, Arthur. *The Macmillan Illustrated Encyclopedia of Myths and Legends*. New York: Macmillan, 1989. Associates Orpheus with the doctrines of Orphism, a mystery cult derived from Orpheus's poetry to his lost love, Eurydice.

Detienne, Marcel. *The Writing of Orpheus: Greek Myth in Cultural Context*. Translated by Janet Lloyd. Baltimore: Johns Hopkins University Press, 2003. Detienne analyzes writings ascribed to Orpheus, demonstrating how these works provide an understanding of ancient Greek philosophy and of Greek and Roman mythology.

Graf, Fritz, and Sarah Iles Johnston. *Ritual Texts for the Af-*

terlife: *Orpheus and the Bacchic Gold Tablets*. New York: Routledge, 2007. In ancient Greece, initiates of the Dionysus Bacchus mysteries possessed gold tablets that offered them information about the afterlife; these tablets relied heavily on the myths ascribed to Orpheus. Graf and Johnston translate the tablets, analyze their role in the mysteries of Dionysus, and describe the Orphic myths and sacred texts about the origins of humanity.

Graves, Robert. *The Greek Myths*. New York: Penguin Books, 1960. Reprint. Combined ed. New York: Penguin Books, 1992. Graves retells the story of Orpheus, father of music, and his beloved Eurydice, who dies and is held in the Underworld. Orpheus is seen both as a hero and as one who spreads the culture of music throughout the world.

Guthrie, W. K. C. *Orpheus and Greek Religion: A Study of the Orphic Movement*. Princeton, N.J.: Princeton University Press, 1993. Analyzes Orpheus and Dionysus as the catalysts for the Orphic religion. Places emphasis on the mysteries of the cult and their attraction for women.

Warden, John, ed. *Orpheus: The Metamorphoses of a Myth*. Buffalo, N.Y.: University of Toronto Press, 1982. A good analysis of the uses to which ancient Greek, Roman, and modern Western European poets, playwrights, musicians, and composers have put the Orpheus legend. Includes a look at the songs of Orpheus compared to the songs of Christ. Since Orpheus, like Christ, was killed as a sacrifice, the mythic implications of the two stories are of major significance.

Oscar and Lucinda

Author: Peter Carey (1943-   )
First published: 1988
Type of work: Novel
Type of plot: Historical realism
Time of plot: 1850's-1866 and 1986
Locale: Devon, England; New South Wales, Australia

Principal characters:
OSCAR HOPKINS, a shy, awkward, English-born Anglican minister with a compulsion for gambling
LUCINDA LEPLASTRIER, an Australian owner of a glass factory with a similar penchant for gambling
THEOPHILUS HOPKINS, Oscar's father
IAN WARDLEY-FISH, Oscar's friend at Oxford
DENNIS HASSET, the vicar of Woollahra and Lucinda's mentor
BOB, Oscar's great-grandson, who writes his ancestor's story in 1986
HUGH STRATTON, the Anglican minister who accepts that Oscar has been called to his church
JIMMY D'ABBS, the co-owner of an accounting firm
MR. JEFFRIS, the head clerk in d'Abbs's accounting firm
PERCY SMITH, an Australian passenger on the *Leviathan*, later engaged, supposedly, as a collector of animals on the expedition
MIRIAM CHADWICK, a widow, an opportunist, and the narrator's great-grandmother

The Story:

In 1986, Bob writes about his great-grandfather, Oscar Hopkins. Bob reveals his mother's complacent sense of propriety over Hopkins, her grandfather.

In 1856, Theophilus Hopkins, a preacher for the Plymouth Brethren, does not acknowledge the festive trappings of Christmas. He is furious when a servant makes a Christmas pudding for his fifteen-year-old son Oscar to taste. Although Theophilus tells Oscar the pudding is from Satan, Oscar knows his father is wrong because the dessert is delicious. Angry because his father strikes him, Oscar calls on God to test his father's belief. When God seems to reply, Oscar devises other ways of reading the signs of the Lord. Eventually, he sorrowfully reads the signs as directing him to become the protege of the impoverished Anglican minister Hugh Stratton.

Later, Stratton sends Oscar to Oriel College, Oxford University, to read for the Anglican ministry. At Oxford, Ian Wardley-Fish befriends Oscar and introduces him to the racetrack and gambling. Oscar wins his first bet and devises an elaborate betting system, sending some money to the Strattons, keeping a meagre amount for himself, and donating the rest to the Church.

In New South Wales, Australia, on her ninth birthday, Lucinda Leplastrier takes her new doll to the creek. She plucks the gold hair from the doll and replaces it with black horsehair, imagining the doll as a native of unmapped land, much to the anger and angst of her parents, Abel and Elizabeth.

Lucinda's father is killed by a horse in 1852, and Lucinda's mother dies when Lucinda is seventeen. At eighteen, she comes into her considerable inheritance. She is forced to leave the subdivided farm for the city, determined to experience the working world. As a child, Lucinda experienced the wonder of the explosion of a glass ornament called a Prince Rupert's Drop. She is now drawn to the glassworks for sale at Darling Harbour.

In 1859, in order to purchase the glassworks, Lucinda seeks assistance from Dennis Hasset, a vicar with a fascination with glass, and Jimmy d'Abbs, an accountant. Hasset instructs her in the properties of glass; d'Abbs handles the finances. Though Hasset and Lucinda are not lovers, people begin to talk about them, as well as about Lucinda's frequent visits to d'Abbs's house to gamble.

In England, Oscar becomes a school teacher at a Notting Hill boys' school. He sees betting as a vile monster that he must, yet cannot, deny. Though he is afraid of the sea, he thinks of joining a missionary society and immigrating to Australia. He insists that Wardley-Fish toss a coin to decide whether or not he should take the journey.

On board the ship *Leviathan*, Oscar is seen off by his father, the Strattons, and Wardley-Fish. Lucinda is also a passenger. She has been in London to study glass manufacture. She watches as Oscar, blindfolded and terrified, is lowered onto the ship in one of the cattle cages. Oscar's father gives his son a caul said to save one from drowning.

During the journey, Lucinda longs to gamble and eavesdrops on the crew playing cards. When she goes in search of the game below decks, she finds herself face to face with Oscar by chance. She pretends she wants him to hear her confession. In Lucinda's stateroom, Oscar finds Lucinda's pack of cards. Forgetting everything else, the pair plays poker until early morning, when a storm terrifies Oscar as a sign from God. Oscar collapses and is carried from Lucinda's cabin on a stretcher, thus creating a scandal.

In New South Wales, Oscar lives within hearing of the Randwick racecourse. The sounds of the races torture him. He preaches to his flock against gambling, though he still gambles. Meanwhile, Lucinda finds her glassworks neglected by her foreman, d'Abbs, and Hasset. Hasset is called before the bishop of Sydney to discuss his sermons. The bishop directs that Lucinda's friend be sent to the rough town of Boat Harbour.

From her lonely house on Longnose Point, Lucinda corresponds regularly with the exiled Hasset and reads Victorian novels. In desperation, she heads toward the Chinese gambling dens on the Rocks, where she meets Oscar. Lucinda drives Oscar home to St. John's vicarage, where they play cards until the belligerent housekeeper discovers them the next morning. The scandal is made public, and Oscar is cast from the Church.

When Lucinda chances upon Oscar again, she takes him home to live with her. To make Oscar more comfortable in her house, Lucinda invents a story about her love for the absent Hasset. She finds Oscar clerical work in an office run by Mr. Jeffris, until Arthur Phelps, her glassblower, invites the pair as a couple to the glassworks. The men treat Oscar deferentially, whereas they are uncomfortable with a woman in the works. Oscar is struck with wonder, and later, when Lucinda shows him a prototype of a glass building, he thinks of it as a church. Oscar and Lucinda each bet their inheritance that a glass church can be made and delivered by Oscar to Hasset at Boat Harbour on Good Friday.

Mr. Jeffris is employed to lead the expedition for Boat Harbour, which leaves in 1866. Jeffris insists that Percy Smith administer laudanum to Oscar. Oscar is horrified by Jeffris as he kills Aboriginal people indiscriminately. He challenges Jeffris, who chases him. Oscar and Smith kill Jeffris. Together, Oscar, Smith, and others erect the church on a lighter. With Oscar inside the church, the lighter arrives by river at Boat Harbour. Oscar wins the bet.

Oscar falls ill. A widowed governess, Miriam Chadwick, is asked to care for him. She seduces Oscar, who feels compelled to marry her as a result. On Good Friday eve, Oscar drowns inside the fractured glass church on the Bellinger River as he asks for forgiveness. He does not know that Miriam is pregnant. She inherits the glassworks and the church, while Lucinda eventually becomes a well-known figure in the Australian labor movement.

Critical Evaluation:

Oscar and Lucinda, Peter Carey's third novel, won the Booker Prize in 1988 and three Australian literary prizes the following year. The novel consists of 110 chapters, and, though readers might assume it is a romance based on its title, the novel plays with audience expectations. Carey interweaves Oscar's story and Lucinda's story until they meet (briefly) in chapter 50.

Oscar and Lucinda is a parody of the Victorian novel, juxtaposing the realist conventions of that form with self-conscious narrative interruptions from Oscar's great-grandson as he narrates the Victorian-era story. Some critics have likened this metafictional novel to *The French Lieutenant's Woman* (1969) by John Fowles. Carey's method of ordering the novel promotes questions about partial truths, lies, and omissions of personal and public history. On a personal level, for instance, the narrator's mother ferociously guards the memory of her grandfather, Oscar, as a heroic pioneer minister, not the fidgety gambler who lost his parish because of scandal. The narrator also draws attention to the falsity of local stories about the naming of a wooded area above the town before beginning his own story. Throughout the novel, Carey suggests the ambivalence of any narrative—whether it be a told story, diary, historical record, newspaper report, journal of exploration, or a novel such as *Oscar and Lucinda*.

Because the novel was first published in Australia's bicentennial year, it is most often perceived as a literary revision of imperial colonization. The eccentricity and relative integrity of the two main characters, who are alienated from so-called respectable society, serves to reveal the hypocrisy, greed, and vanity of other characters. Meanwhile, the institution of Christianity and the powerful compulsion to invade, survey, map, and populate the landscape ignores the culture, sacred stories, lore, and practices of Australia's first inhabitants, whose culture is tied to that same landscape. The narrator introduces some stories told to him about Oscar's expedition, including the slaughter and rape of the indigenous Narcoo and Kumbaingiri people, as well as the dangerous nature of glass from their point of view. The story of the dangers of glass undercuts the idealism and folly of the glass church, connected as it is with the processes of colonization.

Colonization itself is represented as an ugly and pitiless process, as people are killed and land is cut, sliced, and mapped so that Mr. Jeffris can write his journals of exploration and settlers can establish farms and industries. Even a good man such as Oscar is unaware of the relevance of earlier history to his experiences, as he applies to the Missionary Society in London and as the expedition to Boat Harbour begins. Earlier in the novel, it is made clear that Lucinda's dying mother recognizes her implication in something wrong. Ghostly figures and the sound of keening accompany the memory that her husband, Abel Leplastrier, once shot a black man. This revelation is behind the fury that fills the house when Lucinda returns to it with her ruined English doll on her ninth birthday. It may also suggest why Lucinda is so willing to forfeit her inheritance.

The theme of individual alienation is relevant to the main protagonists and to many characters. Characters feel caged by their isolation, by conventional behavior and dress, by gender expectations, by mourning, by ignorance, by the glass church, and even by their own stories. The idea of chance, coincidence, or contingency operates as a narrative strategy in the text. As Oscar claims, one gambles on religion in contemplating the existence or not of an afterlife. In order for the narrator to exist, two gamblers had to meet. Lucinda comes upon Oscar by sheer chance on the *Leviathan*. Their meetings in Sydney are also chance encounters, and the narrator is not related to Lucinda. Miriam's ministrations to Oscar are opportunistic, made possible only because she chanced to see the church gliding down the river. The narrator exists because of the accident of conception.

Peter Carey is an important contemporary writer. In *Oscar and Lucinda*, his style is alternately amusing, ironic, satirical, or tragic. His characters are complex, and his subject matter is compelling.

Christine Ferrari

Further Reading

Carey, Peter. *Thirty Days in Sydney: A Wildly Distorted Account*. New York: Bloomsbury, 2001. A reflection on Sydney, Australia, that is always alert to the hidden history of colonization.

Gaile, Andreas, ed. *Fabulating Beauty: Perspectives on the Fiction of Peter Carey*. Amsterdam: Rodopi, 2005. A collection of essays on Carey's oeuvre that includes two pieces on *Oscar and Lucinda*.

Gillett, Sue. "*Oscar and Lucinda*: Shattering History's Self-Reflection." In *Representation, Discourse, and Desire: Contemporary Australian Culture and Critical Theory*, edited by Patrick Fuery. Melbourne: Longman Cheshire, 1994. Explores the processes of constructing truth in fictional and historical narratives.

Hassall, Anthony J. *Dancing on Hot Macadam: Peter Carey's Fiction*. St. Lucia: University of Queensland Press, 1994. This introduction to Carey's fiction provides a useful section on *Oscar and Lucinda*'s narrator.

Huggan, Graham. *Oxford Australian Writers: Peter Carey.* New York: Oxford University Press, 1996. Outlines Carey's writing, from his short stories to the novel *The Unusual Life of Tristan Smith* (1994).

Lamb, Karen. *Peter Carey: The Genesis of Fame.* Pymble, N.S.W.: HarperCollins, 1992. Explores Carey's evolution and reception as an author and analyzes *Oscar and Lucinda* as a parody of the Victorian novel.

Woodcock, Bruce. *Peter Carey.* 2d ed. New York: Manchester University Press, 2003. Links *Oscar and Lucinda* to Carey's earlier, metafictional approach to story and history.

Othello
The Moor of Venice

Author: William Shakespeare (1564-1616)
First produced: 1604; first published, 1622
Type of work: Drama
Type of plot: Tragedy
Time of plot: Early sixteenth century
Locale: Venice and Cyprus

Principal characters:
OTHELLO, the Moor of Venice
DESDEMONA, his wife
IAGO, a villain
CASSIO, Othello's lieutenant
EMILIA, Iago's wife

The Story:

Iago, an ensign serving under Othello, Moorish commander of the armed forces of Venice, is passed over in promotion when Othello chooses Cassio to be his chief of staff. In revenge, Iago and his follower, Roderigo, arouse from his sleep Brabantio, senator of Venice, to tell him that his daughter, Desdemona, has stolen away and married Othello. Brabantio, incensed that his daughter would marry a Moor, leads his servants to Othello's quarters.

Meanwhile, the duke of Venice has learned that armed Turkish galleys are preparing to attack the island of Cyprus, and in this emergency he has summoned Othello to the senate chambers. Brabantio and Othello meet in the streets but postpone any violence in the national interest. Othello, upon arriving at the senate, is commanded by the duke to lead the Venetian forces to Cyprus. Then, Brabantio tells the duke that Othello has beguiled his daughter into marriage without her father's consent. When Brabantio asks the duke for redress, Othello vigorously defends his honor and reputation; he is seconded by Desdemona, who appears during the proceedings. Othello, cleared of all suspicion, prepares to sail for Cyprus immediately. For the time being, he places Desdemona in the care of Iago; Iago's wife, Emilia, is to be her attendant during the voyage to Cyprus.

A great storm destroys the Turkish fleet and scatters the Venetians. One by one, the ships under Othello's command head for Cyprus until all are safely ashore and Othello and Desdemona are once again united. Still intent on revenge, Iago tells Roderigo that Desdemona is in love with Cassio.

Roderigo, himself in love with Desdemona, is promised all of his desires by Iago if he will engage Cassio, who does not know him, in a personal brawl while Cassio is officer of the guard.

Othello declares the night dedicated to celebrating the destruction of the enemy, but he cautions Cassio to keep a careful watch on Venetian troops in the city. Iago talks Cassio into drinking too much, so that when provoked by Roderigo, Cassio loses control of himself and fights with Roderigo. Cries of riot and mutiny spread through the streets. Othello, aroused by the commotion, demotes Cassio for permitting a fight to start. Cassio, his reputation all but ruined, welcomes Iago's promise to secure Desdemona's goodwill and through her have Othello restore Cassio's rank.

Cassio importunes Iago to arrange a meeting between him and Desdemona. While Cassio and Desdemona are talking, Iago entices Othello into view of the pair, and speaks vague innuendoes. Afterward, Iago from time to time asks Othello questions in such a manner as to lead Othello to think there might have been something between Cassio and Desdemona before Desdemona married him. Once Iago has sown these seeds of jealousy, Othello begins to doubt his wife.

When Othello complains to Desdemona of a headache, she offers to bind his head with the handkerchief that had been Othello's first gift to her. She drops the handkerchief inadvertently, and Emilia picks it up. Iago, seeing an opportunity to further his scheme, takes the handkerchief from his wife and hides it in Cassio's room. When Othello asks Iago for proof that Desdemona is untrue to him, threatening his life if he cannot produce any evidence, Iago says that he had slept in Cassio's room and had heard Cassio speak sweet words in his sleep to Desdemona. He reminds Othello of the handkerchief and says that he had seen Cassio wipe his beard that day with that very handkerchief. Othello, completely overcome by passion, vows revenge. He orders Iago to kill Cassio, and he appoints the ensign his new lieutenant.

Othello asks Desdemona to account for the loss of the handkerchief, but she is unable to explain its disappearance. She is mystified by Othello's shortness of speech, and his dark moods. Goaded by Iago's continuing innuendoes, the Moor succumbs to mad rages of jealousy in which he falls into fits resembling epilepsy. In the presence of an envoy from Venice, Othello strikes Desdemona, to the consternation of all. Emilia swears that her mistress is honest and true, but Othello, who in his madness can no longer believe anything good of Desdemona, reviles and insults her with harsh words.

One night, Othello orders Desdemona to dismiss her attendant and to go to bed immediately. That same night Iago persuades Roderigo to waylay Cassio. When Roderigo is wounded by Cassio, Iago, who had been standing nearby, stabs Cassio. In the scuffle Iago stabs Roderigo to death as well, so as to be rid of his dupe, who might talk. Then a strumpet friend of Cassio comes upon the scene of the killing and reveals to the assembled crowd her relationship with Cassio. Although Cassio is not dead, Iago hopes to use this woman to defame Cassio beyond all hope of regaining his former reputation. Pretending friendship, he assists the wounded Cassio back to Othello's house. They are accompanied by Venetian noblemen who had gathered after the fight.

Othello enters his wife's bedchamber and smothers her, after telling her, mistakenly, that Cassio has confessed his love for her and has been killed. Then Emilia enters the bedchamber and reports that Roderigo has been killed, but not Cassio. This information makes doubly bitter for Othello his murder of his wife. Othello tells Emilia that he learned of Desdemona's guilt from Iago. Emilia cannot believe that Iago had made such charges.

When Iago and other Venetians arrive at Othello's house, Emilia asks Iago to refute Othello's statement. Then the great wickedness of Iago comes to light, and Othello learns how the handkerchief had come into Cassio's possession. When Emilia gives further proof of her husband's villainy, Iago stabs her. Othello lunges at Iago and manages to wound him before the Venetian gentlemen could seize the Moor. Emilia dies, still protesting the innocence of Desdemona. Mad with grief, Othello plunges a dagger into his own heart. The Vene-tian envoy promises that Iago will be tortured to death at the hands of the governor general of Cyprus.

Critical Evaluation:

Although *Othello* has frequently been praised as William Shakespeare's most unified tragedy, many critics have found the central character to be the most unheroic of Shakespeare's heroes. Some have found him stupid beyond redemption; others have described him as a passionate being overwhelmed by powerful emotion; still others have found him self-pitying and insensitive to the enormity of his actions. Yet all of these denigrations pale before the excitement and sympathy generated for the noble soldier in the course of the play.

As a Moor, or black man, Othello is an exotic, a foreigner from a fascinating and mysterious land. He is passionate, but he is not devoid of sensitivity. Rather, his problem is that he is thrust into the sophisticated and highly cultivated context of Renaissance Italy, a land that in the England of Shakespeare's time had a reputation for connivance and intrigue. Shakespeare uses the racial difference to many effects: most obviously, to emphasize Othello's difference from the society in which he finds himself and to which he allies himself through marriage; more subtly and ironically to heighten his tragic stance against the white Iago, the embodiment of evil in the play. More than anything, Othello is "natural man" confronted with the machinations and contrivances of an overly civilized society. His instincts are to be loving and trusting, but he is cast into a society where these natural virtues would have made him extremely vulnerable.

The prime source of that vulnerability is personified in the figure of Iago, perhaps Shakespeare's consummate villain. Iago is so evil by nature that he does not even need any motivation for his antagonism toward Othello. He has been passed over for promotion, but that is clearly a pretext for a malignant nature whose hatred for Othello needs no specific grounds. It is Othello's candor, openness, and spontaneous, generous love that Iago finds offensive. His suggestion that Othello has seduced his own wife is an even flimsier fabrication to cover his essential corruption.

Iago sees other human beings only as victims or tools. He is the classical Renaissance atheist—intelligent, beyond moral scruple, and one who finds pleasure in the corruption of the virtuous and the abuse of the pliable. That he brings himself into danger is of no consequence, because he relies on his wit and believes that all can be duped and destroyed. There is no further purpose to his life. For such a manipulator, Othello, a good man out of his cultural element, is the perfect target.

More so than in any other Shakespeare play, one character, Iago, is the stage manager of the whole action. Once he sets out to destroy Othello, he proceeds by plot and by innuendo to achieve his goal. He tells others just what he wishes them to know, sets one character against another, and develops an elaborate web of circumstantial evidence to dupe the vulnerable Moor. Edgar Stoll has argued that the extraordinary success of Iago in convincing other characters of his fabrications is simply a matter of the conventional ability of the Renaissance villain. Yet there is more to the conflict than Iago's abilities, conventional or natural. Othello is the perfect victim because he bases his opinions and his human relationships on intuition rather than reason. His courtship of Desdemona is brief and his devotion absolute, as is his trust of his comrades, including Iago. It is not simply that Iago is universally believed. Ironically, he is able to fool everyone about everything except the subject of Desdemona's chastity. On that subject it is only Othello whom he is able to deceive. Roderigo, Cassio, and Emilia all reject Iago's allegations that Desdemona has been unfaithful. Only Othello is deceived, but that is because Iago is able to make him play a game with unfamiliar rules.

Iago entices Othello to use Venetian criteria of truth rather than the intuition on which he should rely. Iago plants doubts in Othello's mind, but his decisive success comes when he gets Othello to demand "ocular proof." Although it seems that Othello is demanding conclusive evidence before jumping to the conclusion that his wife has been unfaithful, it is more important that he has accepted Iago's idea of concrete evidence. From that point on, it is easy for Iago to falsify evidence and create appearances that will lead to erroneous judgments. Othello betrays hyperemotional behavior in his rantings and his fits, but these are the result of his acceptance of what seems indisputable proof. It takes a long time, and a lot of falsifications, before Othello finally abandons his intuitive perception of the truth of his domestic situation. As Othello himself recognizes, he is not quick to anger but, once angered, his natural passion takes over.

The crime that Othello commits is made to appear all the more heinous because of Desdemona's utter loyalty. It is not that she is naïve—indeed, her conversation reflects that she is sophisticated—but there is no question of her total fidelity to her husband. The evil represented by the murder is intensified by the audience's perception of the contrast between the victim's virtue and Othello's conviction that he is an instrument of justice. His chilling conviction reminds readers of the essential probity of a man deranged by confrontation with an evil he cannot comprehend.

Critics such as T. S. Eliot have argued that Othello never comes to an understanding of the gravity of his crime—that he realizes his error but consoles himself in his final speech with cheering reminders of his own virtue. That does not, however, seem consistent with the valiant and honest military character who has thus far been depicted. Othello may have been grossly deceived, and he may be responsible for not clinging to the truth of his mutual love with Desdemona, but, in his final speech, he does face up to his error with the same passion with which he had followed his earlier misconception. Just as he had believed that his murder of Desdemona was divine retribution, he now believes that his suicide is a just act. His passionate nature believes it is meting out justice for the earlier transgression. There is a reference to punishment for Iago, but Shakespeare dismisses the obvious villain so as to focus on Othello's final act of expiation.

Edward E. Foster

Further Reading

Bartels, Emily C. "'The Stranger Here and Everywhere': *Othello* and the Moor of Venice." In *Speaking of the Moor: From Alcazar to Othello*. Philadelphia: University of Pennsylvania Press, 2008. In the late sixteenth and early seventeenth centuries, as England expanded its influence around the globe, the Moor became a central character in *Othello* and other English plays. Bartels analyzes the depiction of Moorish characters in these plays, as well as in contemporary historical writings and the letters of Elizabeth I.

Bloom, Harold, ed. *William Shakespeare's "Othello."* New York: Chelsea House, 1987. Seven essays that explore the issues of power and the difference between male and female roles and occupations. Holds that the play is at once tragic and comic. Includes a helpful bibliography and a Shakespeare chronology.

Calderwood, James L. *The Properties of "Othello."* Amherst: University of Massachusetts Press, 1989. Takes the theme of ownership as a starting point and provides an overview of Elizabethan property lines to set the stage for argument. Stretches the term "property" to include not only material and territorial possessions but racial, social, and personal identities.

Erickson, Peter, and Maurice Hunt, eds. *Approaches to Teaching Shakespeare's "Othello."* New York: Modern Language Association of America, 2005. Provides a range of interpretations of the play that are useful to students, as well as teachers. Includes essays analyzing race and gender issues; *Othello* as an adventure play, tragedy and comedy, and antirevenge play; the character of Iago; and the play in performance.

Kolin, Philip C., ed. *"Othello": New Critical Essays.* New York: Routledge, 2002. The essays include discussions of the audience's role, images of white identity, water imagery and religious diversity, and morality, ethics, and the failure of love in *Othello*. Other essays examine Othello's Judaic ancestry and the characters of Iago, Desdemona, Emilia, and Roderigo.

Leggatt, Alexander. *"Othello*: I Took You for That Cunning Whore of Venice."* In *Shakespeare's Tragedies: Violation and Identity.* New York: Cambridge University Press, 2005. Examines how acts of violence in *Othello* and six other tragedies generate questions about the identities of the victims, the perpetrators, and the acts themselves.

Nevo, Ruth. *Tragic Form in Shakespeare.* Princeton, N.J.: Princeton University Press, 1972. The chapter on *Othello* describes the two primary ways of looking at the Moor of Venice: as a man blinded by love and as a man blinded by his tainted vision of that love. Chronicles the events leading to the protagonist's downfall.

Potter, Nick. *"Othello": Character Studies.* New York: Continuum, 2008. Uses an analysis of the play's central characters—Othello, Iago, and Desdemona—to examine the themes of "otherness," race, gender, and power. Provides an introductory overview discussing the reception history and narrative structure of *Othello*. Devotes a chapter on the minor characters.

Vaughan, Virginia Mason, and Kent Cartwright, eds. *"Othello": New Perspectives.* Rutherford: Fairleigh Dickinson University Press, 1991. Twelve essays examine different theoretical approaches to *Othello*. Goes beyond a discussion of good versus evil to reveal a variety of nuances in the play. Traces readings and misreadings from the first quarto to the early 1990's.

The Other One

Author: Colette (1873-1954)
First published: La Seconde, 1929 (English translation, 1931)
Type of work: Novel
Type of plot: Psychological
Time of plot: 1920's
Locale: Franche-Comté and Paris, France

Principal characters:
FAROU, a playwright
FANNY, his wife
JANE, their secretary-companion and Farou's mistress
JEAN FAROU, Farou's son by a former mistress

The Story:

The difference in the way Fanny and Jane wait for a letter from Farou, who is in Paris, points up the contrast between their personalities. The beautiful, heavy-set Fanny, whose dark Mediterranean beauty had long ago won Farou's devotion, sleeps on the sofa, while Jane, a thin, nervous, ash-blond woman nearly thirty years old, stands weeping quietly on the veranda. Fanny's stepson, Jean, awakes her when the letter arrives. Farou writes enthusiastically about a young lady who is obviously his new mistress. Fanny is amazed at Jane's violent reaction to this news and wonders why, despite her companion's affection and indispensability, she does not regard Jane as a close friend.

Fanny's and Jane's lives quicken with Farou's return. Jane is happy, busy taking dictation as Farou works on his play. To Fanny, Farou's roaring voice and the murmur of the bees sounds in the heat like the office of the Mass. Farou's immense presence completely absorbs them. When Fanny is alone with him, it is clear that she both depends upon him and supports him. He is her one love, and in this knowledge she is proud. Farou and his son are uneasy when together. Jean has developed an unhappy passion for Jane, and he watches her and Farou very closely. When Jane goes for a walk, he climbs into the lime tree to see where she went.

Farou's establishment dates from a time before his plays had become successful. At one point, Jean had contracted typhus, Farou's last play had failed, and the secretary had left. Then Jane arrived; she nursed Jean, worked for Farou, and established an easy relationship of affection and respect with Fanny. After the crisis passed, Jane begged to stay, and the Farous were glad to keep her on as a secretary for Farou and a companion for Fanny.

Soon afterward, the family leaves for their first summer in

the Franche-Comté, and they are now spending their second summer there. During the hot days, Fanny, whose intelligence is more an emotional awareness than an intellectual penetration, cannot consider Jean and his father objectively. The household revolves around Farou, and they all rejoice when he sells a play. Their practical dependence on Jane continues. Jean's restlessness increases, and at last he wins Farou's unwilling permission to leave France for South America after the summer.

Once, when Jean and Fanny are on the balcony and hear Jane and Farou talking in the garden, Jean leaps to the wall to watch them. Fanny joins him. Both are suddenly aware of the intimate nature of Jane's relationship with Farou. When Farou returns to the balcony, Fanny feels nothing but unaltered devotion toward him. Only later does she feel vulnerable, even indignant that she should have been pulled into one of Farou's affairs. This realization, however, does not significantly alter her feelings for Jane.

Fanny sleeps little that night. At dawn she hears Jane moving about. Fanny realizes that she is disturbed by the fact that Jane, too, suffers over Farou and that no longer does she alone, as it were, possess his unfaithfulness. The sight of Farou sleeping intensifies her emotions of hurt and tenderness and emphasizes her need for self-control.

One morning, Fanny finds Jean lying on the path leading from the village where she had been to shop. He fainted from the heat and from his agony over Jane and Farou's relationship. He is scornful of the telegram Fanny is bringing, a message that summons Farou to Paris, and he mocks its theatricality. Farou, meeting them, calls Jane to arrange their return to Paris. Fanny becomes convinced that her moral duty is to feel wounded, but instead she is afraid of the possible disruption in their lives. Jean is angered by her obvious lack of pride and emotion.

Surprisingly, Fanny is regretful when they leave the house the next day. Farou teases Jane, who immediately tells him to help Fanny. Suddenly, Fanny remembers how often Jane had done that. In the train, Jane tries to persuade Fanny to read or sleep, but Fanny declares that she is managing very well. Then she is surprised to find that what she had said is true.

In Paris, Fanny entertains the friends who gather around toward the end of rehearsals for Farou's new play. Farou is harsh and demanding with Jane. Fanny scolds him and defends Jane—terrified that their relationship will somehow be exposed. The women dine together after Farou leaves for the theater. When Jean finds them amicably reading, he taunts Jane for her endless companionship with Fanny, a relationship he despises because he thinks it hypocritical.

Farou's nervousness and Fanny's jealousy and feeling of responsibility increases as the confusions of the rehearsals continue. One day, upon returning from her dressmaker, Fanny sees Farou kiss Jane. She realizes then that she will have to face the fear of desertion within her own home, which had previously been inviolate. Hoping that they had not seen her, Fanny pretends to be ill. Jane and Farou are solicitous, but Jean, because of his own obsession with Jane, is anxious only to learn what exactly has upset Fanny. When Farou returns home exhausted from the rehearsal, Fanny pretends to be asleep instead of soothing him; her loss is at least as great as his.

By the time of the dress rehearsal, Fanny is utterly exhausted, and Jane and Jean are tense. Farou is approaching the state of boredom from which he always suffers when a new play is finally out of his hands. After the rehearsal, critics pronounce the play strong, direct, and dynamic. Fanny wonders whether Farou's reputation, if he had been small and wiry instead of being massive and having the head of a pagan god, would have been for subtlety and insight instead of force and power. On the way home, Fanny fears that the relaxation after weeks of strain might precipitate a crisis in the taxi. She dreads the prospect that this might happen before she has time to prepare herself for it or while she is not protected by the familiarities of her home.

The next day, Fanny reluctantly tells Jane that she knows that Farou is her lover. She is discomposed when Jane sees the matter as a joint problem. They keep reasonably calm. Jane appeals to her friendship, explaining that she is no longer Farou's mistress and reproaching herself because she has helped to create the situation by disregarding Farou's infidelities in the past. Farou interrupts them and, discovering the situation, wonders why Fanny has spoken at all. He reminds her that it is she who has always commanded his greatest passion and devotion. This fact makes him confident that Fanny will reorder their lives satisfactorily.

Fanny and Jane spend the rest of that evening together. As Jane prepares to leave, Fanny realizes that she could not bear to be alone, abandoned to Farou's moods, absences, and frequent inarticulateness. Gently, and with only a few words, it is arranged that Jane should stay and that in this solution will lie a measure of security for them all.

Critical Evaluation:

Colette, considered the premier French woman novelist of the early twentieth century, began her career by writing, in the Claudine novels, stories of her girlhood. She went on to produce other novels, novellas, short stories, sketches, and memoirs. Among her most famous works are *Chéri* (1920; English translation, 1929) and *Gigi* (1944; English translation, 1952), a collection of four short stories, the title story of which was made into a play and a popular film.

In *The Other One*, one of her last major novels, Colette explores a theme that appears in many of her works: the relationship between a woman and her unfaithful husband. Colette, who was fascinated with the effect of infidelity on a marriage, examines the tensions created by such situations. In a variation on the theme of jealousy, Colette focuses on the relationship between Farou's wife, Fanny, and Jane, his secretary and occasional mistress. Instead of dealing with themes of hatred or revenge, Colette shows the strength and endurance of the women, who bond together for survival.

The autobiographical nature of Colette's writing is evident in the novel. At the age of twenty, Colette had married Henri Gauthier-Villars, who wrote under the pen name Willy and remained a strong influence in her life. Like Farou, Willy, a well-known figure in literary and theatrical circles, engaged in extramarital affairs, one of which bore a resemblance to the situation in the novel. When she learned of Willy's affair with Charlotte Kinceler, Colette befriended the other woman and occasionally met with Willy and Charlotte.

The other strong influence in Colette's life was Sido, her mother. As Willy was the symbol of male sexuality, Sido became the symbol of female strength. In *The Other One*, the two women emerge as stronger than the man, implying that a woman's basic identity is found in relationships with other women.

The relationship between a wife and her husband's mistress lies at the heart of the novel. Fanny has long accepted her husband's other women, but Jane has a difficult time dealing with his infidelities. Fanny is secure in her role as wife and as the most important woman in Farou's life, but Jane plays an increasingly minor part in his life. Jane, like many of Colette's characters, exists on the fringe of society. Unlike Fanny, who is defined by her attachment to her husband, Jane is the unmarried secretary; she is replaceable, and she depends on Farou for her livelihood and on Fanny for her emotional support. Fanny looks to Jane for companionship, realizing that Farou can easily find another mistress but that she would have trouble finding a friend like Jane. Each woman depends on the other for support and friendship and for a way of filling in the empty space caused by Farou's absences and affairs.

Colette provides little in the way of descriptions of scenes or actions, relying instead on dialogue to further the plot. The story is told from the third-person point of view and develops in conversations between the two women. Dialogue between Fanny and Farou is brief, signaling their lack of communication. Conversation between Farou and Jane is even more rare, for Jane does not speak in front of Farou but only when she

and Fanny are alone. Both women speak more openly when Farou is absent.

In addition to dialogue, Colette shows the strength of the relationship through the small, ordinary gestures of everyday life. Jane performs small acts for Fanny's comfort, placing a pillow under her head, covering her with a blanket, or combing her hair. Yet early in the novel Colette shows that it is Jane who looks to Fanny for support and contact. In one scene, as Jane takes Fanny's arm, she asks why Fanny never takes her arm. Later in the story, when Farou interrupts the conversation between the two women, Jane "advanced on Farou with an aggressive movement," revealing the desire to protect her relationship with Fanny. After Farou leaves the room, Jane "let her arms fall down, along her sides" in a gesture that signaled a more relaxed atmosphere. The novel ends with a tranquil scene, one woman reading and the other sewing, each comfortable in the security of the bond between them.

The novel opens with the women discussing Farou's play, *The House Without Women*, a title that echoes themes of the novel. As Farou enters his house, he greets his women heartily with this phrase, "Aha, all my fine women! I have women in my house!" Drawing energy from the admiration of the women around him, Farou is young at the age of forty-eight, "like all men who surround themselves, in the course of life, only with women." When Fanny confronts Jane about the affair, Jane stresses the importance of her relationship with Fanny, saying, "For four years I have thought so much more of you than of Farou." She shows her admiration for Fanny who, she says, is "a much finer person" than Farou. At the end of the novel, when Farou walks in on the scene between his "fine women," his presence seems extraneous and indicates that the relationship between wife and mistress is at center stage.

The resolution of the novel is similar to the end of Charlotte Perkins Gilman's short story "Turned" (1911), in which a husband's affair with the maid leaves the girl pregnant; once she recovers from the initial shock, the wife leaves her husband, resumes her teaching career, and sets up a new household with the maid and her baby. In both stories, the women work together to create a bond that promotes healing and renewal.

Colette resolves the conflict in *The Other One* in favor of the women. The female rivals come to an understanding, deciding to share the man and continue their relationship rather than jeopardize their friendship. In doing so, they establish a refuge for each other. A relationship that begins in jealousy ends in a bond that goes beyond the women's relationship as rivals. Colette shows that the women's maturity allows them to make constructive choices during a crisis in their lives.

"Critical Evaluation" by Judith Barton Williamson

Further Reading

Flieger, Jerry Aline. *Colette and the Fantom Subject of Autobiography*. Ithaca, N.Y.: Cornell University Press, 1992. Examines resolution between rival female characters, a common theme in Colette's novels.

Francis, Claude, and Fernande Gontier. *Creating Colette*. 2 vols. South Royalton, Vt.: Steerforth Press, 1998-1999. A comprehensive biography of Colette. The first volume chronicles the first forty years of her life and stresses the importance of her African ancestry and maternal family background in understanding her work. The second volume covers the years from 1912 until 1954. Includes bibliographical references and an index.

Kristeva, Julia. *Colette*. Translated by Jane Marie Todd. New York: Columbia University Press, 2004. This scholarly biography, volume 3 of Julia Kristeva's *Female Genius: Life, Madness, Words—Hannah Arendt, Melanie Klein, Colette*, examines Colette's undervalued genius and creativity. Also explores the writer's influences, which included "entertainers, courtesans, an aristocratic Parisian lesbian subculture, and fin de siècle gay aesthetes."

McCarty, Mari. "Possessing Female Space: *The Tender Shoot*." *Women's Studies* 8 (1981): 367-374. Part of a special issue devoted to Colette's works. McCarty claims that Fanny and Jane escape from male shallowness by cultivating their own inner resources.

Marks, Elaine. *Colette*. New Brunswick, N.J.: Rutgers University Press, 1960. An examination, insofar as possible, of the relationship of Colette's works to her life. Begins from the premise that Colette's books lack analogues in philosophy and politics, asserting that her works are informed by a highly personal moral admonition, summed up in the term *regarde*—look, experience, feel.

Southworth, Helen. *The Intersecting Realities and Fictions of Virginia Woolf and Colette*. Columbus: Ohio State University Press, 2004. Argues that although the two authors lived in different countries, there were similarities in their lives, literary styles, and the themes of their works. Southworth places her two subjects within the context of a group of early twentieth century artists and writers and describes Woolf's contacts with France and Colette's connections with British and American writers.

Stewart, Joan Hinde. *Colette*. Boston: Twayne, 1983. Argues that victory and revenge, typical themes in stories of love triangles, are not the issues in *The Other One*. Colette chose instead to focus on the role and meaning of female friendships.

_____. *Colette*. Updated ed. New York: Twayne, 1996. Stewart reassesses Colette's work. Describes how Colette emerged as a writer, her apprenticeship years, the erotic nature of her novels, and her use of dialogue. Provides a chronology, notes, and an annotated bibliography.

Thurman, Judith. *Secrets of the Flesh: A Life of Colette*. New York: Alfred A. Knopf, 1999. Presents an admiring and candid account of the life and times of Colette, helping to place her work in a larger context.

Other Voices, Other Rooms

Author: Truman Capote (1924-1984)
First published: 1948
Type of work: Novel
Type of plot: Psychological realism
Time of plot: Mid-twentieth century
Locale: Mississippi

Principal characters:
JOEL KNOX, thirteen-year-old protagonist
COUSIN RANDOLPH, the antagonist
AMY SANSOM, Randolph's cousin
ZOO FEVER, the cook at the Landing
IDABEL, Joel's tomboy friend
LITTLE SUNSHINE, a hermit
ELLEN KENDALL, Joel's aunt
ED SANSOM, Joel's father

The Story:

Joel Knox is traveling to his father's at Skully's Landing. He has never met his father, and after his mother dies, he lives with his Aunt Ellen in New Orleans. She treats him kindly, but he feels abandoned. When a letter comes from his father asking Joel to live with him, he wants to go. Ellen allows it, saying she loves him and to come back if he becomes unhappy. On his eventful trip, he meets the twin adolescents Idabel and Florabel Thompkins, neighbors to his father.

Joel's father is ill, and Joel has to wait to meet him. He meets Amy, his stepmother, and Zoo, who nurtures him. Exploring the grounds, he sees a "queer lady" staring down at him from a window. At dinner with Cousin Randolph and Amy, he mentions the lady. Randolph says that to Joel she is a ghost. While Amy plays the pianola, Randolph holds Joel's hand. He finds that distasteful.

Joel writes Ellen, telling her he hates the Landing. As he puts stamp money in the mailbox with the letter, he notices Little Sunshine giving Zoo a charm. Joel, headed for the twins', asks the hermit for a protective charm. Little Sunshine tells him to come to the Cloud Hotel for one. At the twins' house, Idabel and Florabel begin brawling, and Joel leaves. Back home, the mail arrives; he assumes his letter to Ellen was delivered, though he finds his coins spilled on the ground.

Joel finally meets his partially paralyzed father who, seemingly, has lidless eyes. He begins feeding and reading to him, but feels nothing for him. By now, Joel and Idabel have become friends. One day as they fish and talk, Joel learns Idabel yearns to be male. Feeling tender, he kisses her cheek. She beats him up, but he forgives her. One day in Randolph's room, Joel notices a snapshot of Randolph, Ed, another man, and a woman. Randolph tells a sordid story about the group's relationships, which explains how he realized his homosexuality, how he happened to shoot Ed, and how his cousin, Amy, a nurse, came to help him with Ed and bring him to the Landing.

Idabel asks Joel to run away with her. She and Florabel had fought, and Idabel had broken her twin's teeth and nose. Joel agrees to go, but gets a sword Zoo had given him and says they first have to go to Little Sunshine's and get his charm. As they cross Drownin' Creek on a rotting log, Joel spies a cottonmouth staring at him, and freezes. Already, he feels stung with the snake's poison, seeing in it the adults who had betrayed him, especially Ed's staring eyes. Idabel grabs his sword, steps past him, and kills the snake. Having survived the snake, Joel refuses to go after the charm, saying he no longer needs it.

After dinner, Randolph sends Joel to his room for a bottle of wine. There, he sees a letter Randolph is writing and realizes that Randolph, not Ed, had sent for him. He tells his father good-bye, and runs off with Idabel. They plan to stop, in their flight, at the fair in town. On their way to town, Idabel and Joel see a black couple tenderly making love. Instinctively, Joel knows such a union defines "making love": It means "withness." Idabel flees, hating the sight. Joel wants to tell her he loves her, but knows not to.

At the fair, they meet Miss Wisteria, a twenty-four-old "midget" who looks like Shirley Temple. Joel watches Idabel fall in love with her. The three ride the Ferris wheel. On Joel's turn riding with Wisteria, a thunderstorm comes and rains descend. From high above, he watches as Idabel flees for cover. Lightning outlines a man whom Joel thinks is Randolph. On the ground, Joel runs, searching for Idabel. He finally falls asleep in an old house and becomes ill and delirious.

Joel awakens, in his room at the Landing, with Randolph nursing him. As he gains strength, Joel decides he likes being dependent. He feels Randolph is the only person who cares for him. Ellen, he thinks, has rejected him. He wants to stop the calendar and stay forever in Randolph's room. Then one day, Randolph rushes in saying Little Sunshine wants them, and they have to go. Joel argues, but fruitlessly.

When they reach Cloud Hotel, it is obvious Little Sunshine has not sent for them. They spend the night, and the next day walk home. When they reach home, Amy tells Randolph she had followed his instructions. She had told the people from New Orleans that he and Joel were on a hunting trip. Randolph and Amy go inside, and Joel asks Zoo about the people. She tells him a lady with a deaf girl has come. Joel says he has a deaf cousin in New Orleans. He yearns for New Orleans, wondering why Ellen has rejected him.

Joel sits a long while in the garden, finally looking toward the house. The "queer lady" is staring down at him from Randolph's window. She beckons. Joel, with a brief backward glance, goes into the house.

Critical Evaluation:

Truman Capote's first novel, *Other Voices, Other Rooms*, quickly drew literary acclaim. Its pathos and psychological realism are starkly drawn in the simple language of its thirteen-year-old protagonist. The novel's central theme is that the elemental need for "withness" drives people to any lengths to acquire it. The setting, replete with grotesques and mystical overtones, is the legendary Deep South. Capote intermingles the physical and the psychological to weave his story. That story is a boy's effort to maneuver himself, unguided—and often misguided—from childhood into adulthood. Such rites of passage stories are often the choice of beginning novelists.

Capote builds tension by weaving two plots together: Randolph manipulates events so that Joel will be driven to fulfill his elemental need through Randolph. Tension multiplies when Capote creates a Randolph who not only wants Joel at the Landing to satisfy his sexual desires, but also wants Joel to choose to satisfy and enjoy those desires, himself. By creating a Joel at the beginning of puberty as the character whose choice provides the plot's resolution, Capote compels audiences to invest abundant emotional energy in the novel. Randolph, using his knowledge of human needs, sets the action in motion. He manipulates events to get Joel to the Landing, monitors events to keep him there, takes advantage of events to make himself the boy's only dependable friend, and averts Ellen's effort to visit him. This effectively closes all other doors of fulfillment, erases all other voices of love that might speak to the boy, leaving Joel but one room and one voice to satisfy his elemental need. Joel, after visiting that room, finds he must visit others—hence the title.

Capote mirrors Randolph in Joel. For example, when Randolph holds Joel's hand, whispering, "Try to like me, will you?" the lonely Joel thinks Randolph is mocking him, "so he questioned the round innocent eyes, and saw his own boy-face focused as in double camera lenses." Randolph's definition of love mirrors the definition Joel later stumbles upon for himself. Telling Joel his story, Randolph says, "few of us learn that love is tenderness." Later, just prior to his illness, recovery, and surrender, Joel discovers this truth in the crucial scene in which he watches the black lovers and learns in a deeply personal and psychological way that love is tender. Joel would have turned to Idabel, but she wants to be a male. They meet Wisteria, and Joel watches Idabel fall in love. Capote uses Joel's stifled yearnings to foreshadow his surrender to Randolph after the fair.

At the fair, lonely Wisteria makes advances to Joel, so he hides as she searches the old house for him. His hiding fills him with self-contempt; he thinks, "What . . . terror compared with" hers? When he awakens from feverish delirium later, he is in that bed, that room, and Randolph is there.

Seeing himself as both a child to leave behind and a man to become, Joel examines his face, and the hand glass affirms his approaching manhood. This passage makes it clearer that Joel and Randolph mirror each other. Joel notes the ageless quality of his own face, clearly connecting himself with Randolph's "impeccably young," still-hairless face.

As the implication becomes clearer, Joel's decision draws nearer. Capote makes believable Joel's willingness to surrender. Joel moves beyond a victimlike dependency on Randolph (which developed, briefly, during Joel's recovery) and wonders if he should tell Randolph he loves him. Joel decides no, because he realizes Randolph is "neither man nor woman, an X, an outline to be colored in." This passage reveals that Joel is now no innocent being led to slaughter. Further evidence of lost innocence comes at Little Sunshine's, where Randolph claims they were expected. At the hotel, Joel knows Randolph lied, but he asks no questions; more significant, he does not even wonder why Randolph lied. He simply stares into the fire, drifting toward sleep, hearing the old hotel's whispers of other voices, other rooms, wondering who will love him.

Joel's answer comes when, with morning, he and Randolph, of one accord, feel it is a new day, "a slate clean for any future . . . as though an end had come." Joel is elated by this, not regretful. He asks who he is. Randolph does not answer, so Joel whoops, "I am Joel, we are the same people." Gladly, it seems, Joel identifies completely with Randolph. Later in the day, when Joel takes that last poignant look at "the boy he had left behind," and moves toward the beckoning figure, he goes unhesitatingly.

Jo Culbertson Davis

Further Reading

Bloom, Harold, ed. *Truman Capote*. Philadelphia: Chelsea House, 2003. Collection of critical essays examining Capote's works. Includes "Boundless Hearts in a Nightmare World: Queer Sentimentalism and Southern Gothicism in Truman Capote's *Other Voices, Other Rooms*" by William White Tison Pugh.

Capote, Truman. Preface to *Other Voices, Other Rooms*. New York: Random House, 1968. Capote reflects on his first novel, explaining the source of its inspiration and discussing its autobiographical nature. Reading Capote's insights into his own work enriches the reading of the novel.

_____. *Truman Capote: Conversations*. Edited by M. Thomas Inge. Jackson: University Press of Mississippi, 1987. Compilation of more than two dozen interviews, including those conducted by journalists Gloria Steinem, George Plimpton, and David Frost. Among other subjects, Capote discusses the writers who influenced him, his methods of research and writing, and his personal reverence for the craft of authorship.

Clarke, Gerald. *Capote: A Biography*. New York: Ballantine, 1989. Well documented from primary sources, including seven years of interviews with Capote. *Other Voices, Other Rooms* gets extensive coverage, from publication to theme to the novel's symbolism. Gives Capote's view on the theme of homosexuality in the novel. Includes a bibliography, notes, and an annotated index.

Long, Robert Emmet. *Truman Capote, Enfant Terrible*. New York: Continuum, 2008. Critical biography, in which Long places Capote's works within the context of the author's life and times. Demonstrates how Capote's tragic life resulted in the gothic nature of his prose. Chapter 4 is devoted to a discussion of *Other Voices, Other Rooms*.

Moates, Marianne M. *A Bridge of Childhood: Truman Capote's Southern Years*. New York: Henry Holt, 1989. A compilation of stories about Capote's childhood, giving background on Joel Knox as an autobiographical character. The pathos in Joel comes from Capote's investing his adult sense of abandonment in the child character.

Nance, William L. *The Worlds of Truman Capote*. Briarcliff Manor, N.Y.: Stein & Day, 1970. Illuminates Capote's insight on his use of imagination. Contains a full chapter on *Other Voices, Other Rooms* providing a plot summary and thorough analysis of themes in the novel.

Reed, Kenneth T. *Truman Capote*. Boston: Twayne: 1981. Gives extensive plot summary and analysis of *Other Voices, Other Rooms*. A good place to start.

Waldmeir, Joseph J., and John C. Waldmeir, eds. *The Critical Response to Truman Capote*. Westport, Conn.: Greenwood Press, 1999. Compilation of previously published reviews and essays, as well as some essays written for this collection. Includes pieces by literary critics Eric Bentley, Leslie Fiedler, Diana Trilling, and Kenneth Tynan. Also includes "*Other Voices, Other Rooms*: Oedipus Between the Covers" by Marvin E. Mengeling.

Other Women

Author: Lisa Alther (1944-   )
First published: 1984
Type of work: Novel
Type of plot: Social realism
Time of plot: Early 1980's
Locale: A city in New Hampshire

Principal characters:
CAROLINE KELLY, emergency room nurse, weaver, mother of two boys
HANNAH BURKE, psychotherapist
JASON and JACKIE, Caroline's sons
DIANA, Caroline's housemate and sometime lover
JACKSON, physician, Caroline's former husband
RICHARD DEAN, Caroline's onetime hippie lover
BRIAN STONE, physician and Caroline's suitor
ARTHUR BURKE, Hannah's husband

The Story:

Caroline Kelly is a thoroughly and helplessly divided woman. She has been married and divorced. She left her husband for a hippie and his commune only to find that she is strongly attracted to a woman with whom she shares her lover. She currently lives with another woman, Diana, in a downstairs apartment with her two sons, while Diana lives upstairs with her adolescent daughter, Sharon. The two women have been physically involved, but their relationship is under great strain; Caroline decides she must have help. She goes to Hannah Burke for therapy.

Caroline's divided nature displays itself as soon as Hannah asks her to think of words that define herself. When Caroline thinks of a positive quality, such as kindness, it is immediately negated by recollections of times when she had been cruel to someone she loved. When she comes up with generosity, she remembers occasions of parsimony in her dealings with others. Her problems are deeply personal, but she feels that to focus on them is pointless when there is so much pain and agony in the world. Her sexual nature, in

which she prefers women but also enjoys sex with men and looks to men for security, is a further manifestation of the division in her psyche. So is her choice of profession. She not only chooses to be a nurse, but she also works in situations in which human pain and misery are constantly and immediately present, although that pain hurts her deeply.

As Caroline's therapy proceeds, the stories of her life and of Hannah's are gradually revealed. Some of their experiences are similar. Hannah's mother had died when Hannah was very young and her father had taken her from Australia to England, leaving her to be raised by a grandmother. Caroline's father was gone for years during World War II, and her parents always maintained an emotional distance from her and their other children. Hannah is distinctly heterosexual, an orientation that Caroline, for a time, takes as implying a criticism of her own divided nature and less conventional lifestyle. Hannah is considerably older than her patient but like Caroline has to wrestle with depression and misery. For years after two of her four children had been killed in a freak accident, she alternated periods of rage and of despair. The equanimity that Caroline envies is hard-won.

Caroline's troubles are traceable to her childhood. Both of her parents were heavily involved in charitable work of one kind or another, and they continually reminded their children that they were much more fortunate than the subjects of the parents' charities. Having given themselves so completely to their good works, the parents had no warmth left for Caroline or her younger brother. At an early age, Caroline was charged with becoming a surrogate mother for her brother and with much of the responsibility for running the household. She also was made to feel somehow responsible for all the starving children, the victims of wars and oppression, and all the poor and downtrodden. Any attempt to claim attention for herself was met by reminders of how lucky she was to have a roof over her head and food on the table.

In the course of the novel, Caroline receives a forceful reminder of this upbringing and of the damage it has done her when she and her sons go to her parents' house for a Thanksgiving dinner. As usual, the family is joined by unhappy, poor, and half-mad acquaintances of her parents. There are too many guests for the amount of food that had been prepared and the family, including Caroline's small sons, are warned not to ask for more food than they are given. Jackie, the younger son, receives very little to eat and no dessert. When the company is gone, Jackie complains that he is hungry, only to be reminded by his grandparents how lucky he is to have been given anything. He leaves the house, and Caroline has to search for him to find him half-frozen, several blocks away. The episode creates a breakthrough in Caroline's struggle to come to terms with her strong sense of guilt.

During the course of her therapy, significant changes are taking place in Caroline's life. The relationship with Diana goes through several phases. Habituated to rivaling each other in making gifts and adjustments to the other's needs, they swear to break this pattern only to fall back into it whenever they try to renew their physical intimacy. Caroline makes one final attempt to find happiness in the financial and psychological security of a heterosexual relationship, experiencing a brief affair with Brian Stone, a doctor she met at the hospital where she is an emergency room nurse. When she recognizes how similar she is to Brian's first wife and how Brian, despite appearances, would grow to be much like Jackson, Caroline's first spouse, she breaks off the affair.

While she is guiding Caroline through a difficult process, the therapist, Hannah, is also going through a similar period of growth. The deaths of two of her children had caused her years of guilt and grief, although the accident had been in no way her fault. She emerged from her depression in part through determining to become a psychotherapist to help others who are similarly afflicted. She succeeds in part by shutting off her own emotions in her contacts with those she advises. In coming to know Caroline and her problems, Hannah is forced to respond on a more personal level to the emotions of the other woman. The experience enables Hannah to come to a fuller recognition of her own needs and a stronger sense of commitment to those she loves. In the end, the patient-therapist relationship is transformed into close friendship.

Caroline is able to confront her personal problems, including the growing pains of her children, by recognizing that she cannot be responsible for all of the world's miseries or even all of the problems that confront those she loves. She can be of service to others only if she accepts herself and those others as independent beings who must take responsibility for their own actions. She has not solved all of her problems, but she is able to face new experiences with an open mind. Hannah's experience with Caroline's therapy makes her a more effective healer and helps renew the warmth of her solid marriage.

Critical Evaluation:

Other Women is a realistic novel whose intention is to convince the reader that the two principal characters represent real people with the problems of the real world, and these characters live with other real people in real circumstances and locations. Lisa Alther is dealing with what she regards as serious problems in a serious manner, so *Other Women* lacks the satiric bite and comic dimension of her *Kinflicks* (1976) and *Original Sins* (1981). There is some humor in the novel, for example, in the jokes Caroline and Hannah tell each other when the therapeutic sessions become too intense. There is also satire in the depiction of Caroline's grotesque parents: They are so extreme in their "do-gooding" that they are nearly caricatures. Still, the tone of the novel is serious.

In *Other Women*, Alther explores the therapeutic relationship in two ways that break new ground. First, the novel is entirely sympathetic to the role of psychotherapy in assisting troubled women to face life without fear. Hannah is no Freudian, but she uses many of the techniques in general use in psychiatry and in some psychoanalysis. Second, Alther portrays the patient-therapist relationship as very much a two-way street. The therapy that Hannah supplies for Caroline is affected directly and indirectly by events, memories, and changes in Hannah's personal life. At the same time,

Caroline's experiences and the emotions she shows during sessions of therapy have their own effect on Hannah's life.

There have been critical objections to the considerable length of *Other Women*. It is a very detailed account of the lives of its characters. Caroline's experiences and her emotional and psychological changes add genuine depth to Alther's pictures of her protagonist. In a realistic novel like this one, a lack of supporting detail would be a considerable deficiency.

Other critics, comparing *Other Women* to Alther's other novels, especially to *Kinflicks*, have raised the objection that Alther loads the scales against men, too didactically favoring lesbian relationships. It is true that none of the three men with whom Caroline has had relationships is an admirable person, and that all of her heterosexual connections have turned sour. Caroline's first husband, Jackson, became so thoroughly involved in his medical practice that he totally neglected his wife and children. Richard Dean, after seemingly rescuing Caroline from a failed marriage, almost immediately was flagrantly unfaithful to her and showed little regard for her well-being. Brian Stone, as already noted, was on the road to becoming another Jackson.

It is also true, however, that Caroline's affairs with other women are neither emotionally secure nor permanent. At the end of the novel she recognizes that her life with Diana will soon end. The relationships Caroline has had with women have been warmer and more supportive than those with men, but they also have been troubled. In *Other Women* the single important relationship between two adults that persists to the satisfaction of both is the marriage of Hannah and Arthur Burke. They have provided a home for each other and their children; they have survived by supporting each other through the trauma of losing two of those children; and they have sustained a nurturing physical and emotional relationship.

Other Women lacks some of the variety and other ingratiating qualities that attracted popular attention to Alther's earlier novels. It is not only a serious novel but one in which the resolutions of its protagonists' problems are too cut-and-dried and in some senses too neatly achieved. Caroline and Hannah are, nevertheless, believable and memorable characters, and the novel makes a real contribution to the understanding of how psychotherapy can work successfully.

John M. Muste

Further Reading

Evans, Nancy. "Lives of Caroline." *The New York Times Book Review*, November 11, 1984. Evans points to a lack of humor and originality in *Other Women* but praises the characterization in the novel.

Greiner, Donald J. "Lisa Alther: *Other Women*." In *Women Without Men: Female Bonding and the American Novel of the 1980's*. Columbia: University of South Carolina Press, 1993. Greiner includes an analysis of Alther's novel in his study of how female bonding is depicted in novels written by American women.

Hart, Vada. "Woebegone Dykes: The Novels of Lisa Alther." In *Beyond Sex and Romance? The Politics of Contemporary Lesbian Fiction*, edited by Elaine Hutton. London: Women's Press, 1998. Hart analyzes the lesbian characters in Alther's novels in this collection exploring ideas of sex and romance in lesbian-themed fiction.

King, Francis. "Hannah and Caroline." *Spectator* 254 (March 9, 1985). A friendly reading of *Other Women*, pointing out the solidity of Alther's depiction of psychotherapy but lamenting the novel's lack of humor.

Oktenberg, Adrian. "Odd Couple." *New Directions for Women* 14, no. 1 (January/February, 1985): 17-20. Regards *Other Women* as the most successful of Alther's novels, praising it for its reverberations and accuracy in depicting a successful relationship between women.

Peel, Ellen. "Subject, Object, and the Alternation of First- and Third-Person Narration in Novels by Alther, Atwood, and Drabble." *Critique* 30, no. 2 (1989): 107-122. Places Alther in the company of distinguished novelists Margaret Atwood and Margaret Drabble and discusses the narrative techniques of their fiction.

Our Ancestors

Author: Italo Calvino (1923-1985)
First published: I nostri antenati, 1960 (English
   translation, 1980); includes *Il visconte dimezzato*,
   1952 (*The Cloven Viscount*, 1962); *Il barone
   rampante*, 1957 (*The Baron in the Trees*, 1959); *Il
   cavaliere inesistente*, 1959 (*The Non-existent
   Knight*, 1962)
Type of work: Novels
Type of plot: Satire
Time of plot: Middle Ages to early nineteenth century
Locale: Europe

Principal characters:
The Cloven Viscount:
VISCOUNT MEDARDO OF TERRALBA, a Christian knight
DOCTOR TRELAWNEY, his nephew's tutor
PAMELA, a goatherd

The Baron in the Trees:
COSIMO PIOVASCO DI RONDO, the son of the baron of
   Rondò
ENEA SILVIO CARREGA, his father's illegitimate brother
VIOLANTE, daughter of the marchese of Ondariva
GIAN DEI BRUGHI, a bandit
URSULA, daughter of Don Frederico Alonso Sanchez y
   Tobasco

The Non-existent Knight:
AGILULF, a nonexistent knight in the army of Charlemagne
RAIMBAUD OF ROUSILLON, a young recruit taken under
   Agilulf's wing
BRADAMANTE, a warrior maid
TORRISMUND OF CORNWALL, another knight
SOPHRONIA, the woman whose rescue from brigands
   qualifies Agilulf for knighthood

The Story:

The Cloven Viscount. The idealistic Viscount Medardo
goes to fight for Christendom against the Turks in Bohemia
and is awarded the rank of lieutenant by the Holy Roman
Emperor. In his first battle, he charges a cannon and is blown
apart; the surgeons manage to save the right half of his body
and send him home to Terralba, but he soon becomes deeply
embittered and increasingly disposed to terrible acts of cruelty. He places traps on his estate that nearly cause the deaths
of his nephew (the story's narrator) and his nephew's tutor,
the amiable Dr. Trelawney. The viscount falls in love with a
goatherding girl named Pamela, but she is understandably reluctant to marry him.

The viscount's other half, which was saved and nursed
back to health by monks, reappears in Terralba. Unlike his
counterpart, the left side of Medardo has been infused with
such sympathy for his fellow human beings that he becomes
a virtual saint. The right half will not admit him to the castle,
but he sets about undoing much of the evil his other half has
done. The left half, too, falls in love with Pamela, and the two
halves fight a duel over her. Because neither is properly
equipped for combat, they succeed only in ripping open each

other's wounds, and Dr. Trelawney takes advantage of the
opportunity to sew them up as a single individual. The resultant whole man combines the characteristics of the two
halves, but he has obtained considerable wisdom from his
disjunct experience.

The Baron in the Trees. In 1767, when he is twelve years
old, Cosimo quarrels with his father, an Italian baron in the
province of Ombrosa, at a meal over a basket of snails. After
being ordered to leave the table, he climbs a tree in the garden
and swears never to set foot on the ground again. He resists
all attempts at capture and lives for fifty-three years in the
canopy of the heavily wooded estate, which he eventually inherits, occasionally undertaking arboreal journeys much farther afield.

Cosimo is able to strike up an acquaintance with Violante
(called Viola for short), the daughter of a neighboring family.
He forms a firm friendship with the Cavalier Carrega, his father's illegitimate brother, until the latter is killed in a fight
against Muslim pirates. He also makes friends with the noto-
rious bandit Gian dei Brughi after saving him from pursuing
constables, and the two of them collaborate in educating

themselves from books until Gian is captured and executed. Cosimo continues his studies alone, constructing an arboreal library in which he accumulates all the volumes of Denis Diderot and Jean D'Alembert's *Encyclopedia* (1751-1752) and many other volumes.

On one of his expeditions, Cosimo visits Olivabassa in Spain, where he falls in love with Ursula, the daughter of a grandee exiled by the Inquisition. Ursula joins him in the trees for a while, but she is eventually reclaimed by her family members when they become reconciled with the Church. After that, Cosimo is reputed to have had many brief liaisons before being reunited with Viola; their love affair is soon broken off, however, and Cosimo goes mad for a while.

Cosimo has many adventures during the Napoleonic Wars. At one point he encounters the emperor himself and briefly exchanges words with a Russian nobleman—Prince Bolkonsky, from Leo Tolstoy's *Voyna i mir* (1865-1869; *War and Peace*, 1886). Eventually, Cosimo dies, but even then he refuses to descend to the ground. He is carried out to sea by a hot-air balloon.

The Non-existent Knight. During a roll call of his army, Charlemagne discovers that it includes a knight named Agilulf who does not exist but who, nevertheless, contrives to animate an empty suit of armor by sheer willpower and faith in the king's holy cause. Although he presents the outward appearance of the ideal knight—noble, brave, and utterly chaste—Agilulf is constantly beset by worries about the way other men see and think of him.

The legendary warrior-maid Bradamante, borrowed, along with the entire background of the story, from Ludovico Ariosto's *Orlando furioso* (1516, 1521, 1532; English translation, 1591), is disdainful of all existing men, but she passionately loves Agilulf. Agilulf's infallible memory enables him to correct the exaggerations that his fellow knights incorporate into their own accounts of their exploits. This causes such bad feelings that Torrismund of Cornwall is led to challenge the legitimacy of Agilulf's knighthood, alleging that the supposed virgin whom Agilulf saved from rape was, in fact, Torrismund's mother. Agilulf sets out to find Sophronia, the lady in question, and he eventually recovers her from the harem of a Moroccan sultan, into which she had been sold as a slave. He hides her in a cave while he fetches Charlemagne to investigate her virginity. By the time they return, Torrismund, recently returned from a grail quest, has found her and—without having any inkling of her identity—has made love to her.

The distraught Torrismund is able to confirm that Sophronia had been a virgin, but it is too late; all that remains of poor Agilulf is his scattered armor. Agilulf's armor is recovered by his protégé, Raimbaud of Rousillon, who is then fortunate enough to be mistaken for its previous owner by Bradamante. Charlemagne makes Torrismund a count, but Torrismund has difficulty exerting his authority over the serfs he had previously saved from the villainous Knights of the Holy Grail; the serfs are now beginning to absorb the lesson that they, too, are not mere nonentities.

Critical Evaluation:

In combining his three comic fantasies into an eccentric trilogy, Italo Calvino contended that they made up "a family tree for contemporary man" cast in the mold of the *contes philosophiques* of Voltaire. In his introduction to the omnibus edition of *Our Ancestors*, the author informs readers that each fantasy contains allegorical references to the period in which it was written: *The Cloven Viscount* is, in part, a commentary on the Cold War, *The Baron in the Trees* is partly about the problem of ideological commitment in a world of rapidly shifting values, and *The Non-existent Knight* includes an investigation of the psychology of fitting into large bureaucratic organizations. Calvino's observations are obviously as studiously ironic as the stories themselves.

The Cloven Viscount carries forward a long tradition of doppelgänger stories, which Calvino's introduction traces back to the German writers Adelbert von Chamisso and E. T. A. Hoffmann, although *The Cloven Viscount* is actually closest in form and spirit to Théophile Gautier's "Le Chevalier Double" (1840). Its moral is simple enough: All human beings have both good and bad in them, and a healthy person is one who can reconcile contrary impulses into a coherent whole. The book relates to the Cold War in its insistence that division and opposition inflame and exaggerate contrary tendencies to the point where conflict becomes inevitable—but the final confrontation in the story occurs because both halves of the unfortunate viscount have the same ideal in the humble but lovely Pamela.

The Baron in the Trees is a more original work, although it discovers its central motif simply by literalizing the common saying that idealistic intellectuals are not sufficiently "down to earth." Cosimo has a good heart, and his sympathies are all of the right kind—he is as whole and complete, in his own way, as the reunited Medardo—but he can never get fully involved in the affairs of his fellow human beings. He loses his close friends and both his lovers because he cannot join in their adventures. He wins the respect of great men (and the enmity of some who are not great) for his nobility of spirit, but they are the doers while he remains an observer. Although he remains true to his reckless promise to the very end, his is not an example that can or should be followed. By the time he has lived through the Enlightenment, the French Revolution, and the Napoleonic Wars, a quieter evolution of folkways has devastated the great forests that had allowed him such freedom as he had; in the final paragraph, the anonymous brother who has told Cosimo's story observes that Ombrosa itself no longer exists.

On one level, *The Baron in the Trees* is a forthright assault on the kind of idealism that refuses all material anchorage, arguing that such an attitude of mind is ultimately futile. The work is, however, a sympathetic commentary that deftly develops a great fondness for Cosimo, to the extent that his fate seems authentically tragic. What, after all, do the earthbound doers actually achieve? Their deaths are, for the most part, ignominious—Cosimo learns that Ursula eventually died in a convent. The titles of the utopian tracts that Cosimo writes in later life—but that hardly anyone reads—are pompously overblown, but so was the empire that Napoleon tried to build. When Tolstoy's borrowed hero tells Cosimo about his quest to understand the appalling phenomenon of war, and Cosimo replies that his own equally problematic devotion to trees has been "entirely good," the reader is entitled to wonder which of them has pursued the nobler cause. Such open-mindedness is typical of Calvino; the politeness of his satire is remarkable, and it is almost without parallel.

Although it is told in fewer than one hundred pages, *The Non-existent Knight* is the most complicated and the most eventful of the three tales. It is also very humorous, and it fully deserves to be ranked as one of the comedic masterpieces of world literature. Like Miguel de Cervantes' *El ingenioso hidalgo don Quixote de la Mancha* (1605, 1615; *The History of the Valorous and Wittie Knight-Errant, Don Quixote of the Mancha*, 1612-1620; better known as *Don Quixote de la Mancha*), it looks with a coolly cynical eye at the tradition of chivalric romance, taking as its primary model the greatest Italian contribution to that tradition, Ariosto's sixteenth century epic poem *Orlando Furioso*.

On a superficial level, *The Non-existent Knight* performs much the same deflationary task as Cervantes' novel, revealing the perfect knight of romance as a phantom unsustainable in confrontation with a more down-to-earth view of reality. Even though Calvino wrote three and a half centuries after Cervantes, it cannot be said that the puncturing of such illusions was no longer necessary; many of the myths of "romance" have proved astonishingly resilient, surviving into the present in degraded but nevertheless powerful versions. The story is, however, more evidently multilayered than its predecessors; the passive narrators are by no means disinterested in the events they report, but the hypothetical reporter

of this tale—a nun named Sister Theodora, who is writing it as a penance—turns out to have been much more intimately involved in it than is first apparent. This adds a further twist to an already convoluted plot.

Calvino may well have been justified in claiming a particularly timeliness for *The Non-existent Knight* because the problem of facelessness and lack of identity became particularly marked in the era of bureaucratization, but the text itself claims a much wider relevance. The unwillingness of the serfs to accept Torrismund as their appointed overlord provides a reminder that chivalric romance and real history have been equally culpable in ignoring the vast majority of the people who lived in the past, tacitly pretending that progress is the work of the few rather than of the many.

While he is correcting the self-congratulatory exaggerations of braggarts, Agilulf becomes a spokesman for all those who have been excluded from the many-stranded story of ancestors. When he uses his expertise to obtain a place in the line of battle where Raimbaud might take reprisals against the slayer of his father but, instead, succeeds only in enabling him to kill his enemy's spectacle bearer, he stands in the place of anyone who has ever seen well-laid plans go awry. His anxieties regarding his own nonexistence and his consequent problems of self-image are the anxieties of every person who feels that the social self presented to the world is not a true self at all. This is nowhere more evident than in Agilulf's amours: On one hand, Bradamante loves him only because he does not exist; on the other, the lovely Priscilla spends one unforgettable night with him only because she is under the misapprehension that he does exist.

Agilulf's adventure, however impossible and nonsensical it may be, compels readers to consider the extent and nature of their own existences and perhaps to find them tragically lacking in some intangible but vital respect. All people obtain their identities from their roles—their suits of armor—and all are in danger of seeing those roles fall apart only to be reassembled and redefined by others luckier than themselves.

Some readers may be puzzled by the order of the three stories, but they are not arranged as they are simply because that is the order in which Calvino wrote them. The cloven viscount is, indeed, the most remote ancestor, crudely separated into good and evil halves, without a great deal of philosophical sophistication residing in either. The baron in the trees is much more contemporary, possessed of an encyclopedic education that he really ought to be able to put to practical use but, somehow, cannot. The nonexistent knight may belong to a distant era (an era that never was, save in the literary imagination), but he is the closest of all to being like an actual person—a person as he was the last time he turned to look at himself with a sadly critical and contemplative eye— and he is a caricature more apt than the most carefully detailed character of any mundane novel.

Brian Stableford

Further Reading

Bolongaro, Eugenio. *Italo Calvino and the Compass of Literature*. Toronto, Ont.: University of Toronto Press, 2003. Examines five of Calvino's early works, including *Our Ancestors*, demonstrating how they meditate on the role of the intellectual and on the ethical and political dimensions of literature.

Cannon, JoAnn. *Italo Calvino: Writer and Critic*. Ravenna, Italy: Longo, 1981. Provides a brief but comprehensive survey of Calvino's work.

Carter, Albert Howard, III. *Italo Calvino: Metamorphoses of Fantasy*. Ann Arbor: University of Michigan Press, 1987. Offers masterful analysis of Calvino as a fantasist. Explores Calvino's contribution to what is possible in literature by analyzing his use of the contrafactual realms of imagination, speculation, and hypothesis.

Hume, Kathryn. *Calvino's Fictions: Cogito and Cosmos*. New York: Oxford University Press, 1992. One of the most comprehensive studies of Calvino's works includes discussion of *Our Ancestors* in the chapter "Identifying the Labyrinth."

Jeannet, Angela M. *Under the Radiant Sun and the Crescent Moon: Italo Calvino's Storytelling*. Toronto: University of Toronto Press, 2000. Examines Calvino as both a creative writer and a critical thinker. Traces the events in his life and his creative influences to shed light on their significance in his writing.

McLaughlin, Martin. *Italo Calvino*. Edinburgh: Edinburgh University Press, 1998. Detailed study of Calvino's fiction begins with his early stories and his development of a neorealistic style. Chapter 3, "From Neorealism to Fantasy," presents an analysis of *Our Ancestors*. Includes a chronology of Calvino's fictional works.

Markey, Constance. *Italo Calvino: A Journey Toward Postmodernism*. Gainesville: University Press of Florida, 1999. Examines postmodernist literature in Italy, tracing Calvino's development as a postmodernist writer. Also analyzes the connections between Calvino's work and that of Samuel Beckett, Jorge Luis Borges, Franz Kafka, Joseph Conrad, and Mark Twain.

Woodhouse, J. R. "From Italo Calvino to Tonio Cavilla: The First Twenty Years." In *Calvino Revisited*, edited by Franco Ricci. Ottawa, Ont.: Dovehouse, 1989. Provides a compact overview of the writer's earlier work, including a commentary on the trilogy.

Our House in the Last World

Author: Oscar Hijuelos (1951-   )
First published: 1983
Type of work: Novel
Type of plot: Bildungsroman
Time of plot: 1920's-1970's
Locale: Cuba and the United States

Principal characters:
ALEJO SANTINIO, an immigrant from Cuba
MERCEDES SANTINIO, his wife
HORACIO and HECTOR, their sons

The Story:

The aristocratic Sorrea family lives in Holguín, a prosperous old city in eastern Cuba. Their immense house has to be sold when the patriarch, Teodoro Sorrea, dies in 1929. Mercedes, the second of three daughters, sees the ghost of her father frequently and dreams about the happy life she has lived in the house. She marries Alejo Santinio, a well-dressed dandy from the small town of San Pedro, ten miles from Holguín. He is the youngest of two brothers and nine sisters. His family owns farmland, but he wants a more exciting life away from rural Cuba and decides to emigrate with Mercedes to the United States.

Alejo sends his wife and children to visit their relatives in Cuba. The three-year-old Hector loves Cuba, but his other brother, Horacio, is only impressed by the sight of Teodoro

Sorrea's ghost. They meet Alejo's great-grandmother, Concepción O'Connors; she had married an Irish sailor, which explains the light skin and European looks of the two brothers.

Upon their return to New York, Hector has to be hospitalized for almost a year because he contracted an infection in Cuba. The nurses ridicule him for not speaking English and make him afraid of speaking Spanish. Hector becomes sickly and obese. His brother tries to make him tougher so that other children will not treat him like a freak. Horacio is very talented and hardworking; he is a choirboy and has several jobs to help the family. Frustrated by his family and failed love relationships, he joins the U.S. Air Force.

Alejo has a heart attack because he works too much and stays out too late, and Mercedes has to get a job scrubbing floors. She has two sisters in Cuba, Rina and Luisa. The latter came to the United States with her family in the 1960's, escaping from the government of Fidel Castro. The arrival of Hector's relatives makes him remember the smells and tastes of Cuban things. Mercedes realizes that, after twenty years of life in America, her family does not have anything, while her relatives, who have recently arrived, have established themselves quickly and prospered in a short time.

Two of Alejo's sisters, Lolita and Margarita, live in the United States. Margarita has been living in New York City since 1932 with her husband, Eduardo Delgado, a Cuban tobacco exporter. They welcome the new immigrants who settle in as boarders in their apartment in Spanish Harlem. Alejo enjoys having fun with his friends while Mercedes worries about the expenses. He spends their savings on gifts, worthless business investments, and gambling. After several jobs, he becomes a cook in a hotel restaurant.

Horacio was named for his maternal great-grandfather, and Hector was named for Alejo's older brother, who had died in Cuba. Buita, Alejo's eldest sister, comes to visit from Cuba with her husband, Alberto Piñón, a musician who is the leader of a popular band. She hates Mercedes and makes life unbearable for her. Mercedes dreams about Buita coming at her with a knife. Margarita and Eduardo also have a son and move back to Cuba. When her husband dies, Margarita returns to the United States. She, her son, Buita, and Alberto settle in Miami, where many other Cubans live.

Alejo starts drinking heavily after the news of his brother's death. Influenced by Buita, he is treating Mercedes badly and responds with physical abuse when she complains about their poverty. He hits his wife and children to show them that he is the "man of the house." He spends many nights away from home; Mercedes is afraid that he will abandon her and that she will be thrown out of the country.

When Horacio comes back from military service in Europe, he criticizes his family, not wanting their life of poverty. He moves out of the house and marries. Hector does not listen to his parents, gets drunk often, and dreams of escaping to a better life; he visits his Aunt Buita and her rich husband in Miami. Hector admires the Cubans who live well, wanting to be like them. One day he suddenly hears about his father's death and has to return home.

For a few years, Alejo has been holding two jobs. While Hector is in Miami, he suffers an injury at work and dies. Mercedes becomes oblivious to everything, keeps the apartment dark, walks in circles, goes into trances, imitates the voices of the dead, and talks to herself. Hector, who has not been able to cry for his father, is afraid to see his ghost at night. He cannot sleep because of the strange noises around him; ghosts seem to inhabit the house.

Hector graduates from high school and college; he also travels throughout the country. After he moves out, he lives near his mother's apartment, helping her with shopping and household chores. At the age of twenty-five, he works a few blocks from where his father used to work. He writes thoughts down, dreaming about writing a book. He often hears the voices of his family members; by writing down his dreams and theirs, he feels closer to them.

Critical Evaluation:

Oscar Hijuelos, a native New Yorker of Cuban parentage, graduated from City College of New York. He was awarded the Rome Fellowship in Literature of the American Academy and Institute of Arts and Letters for *Our House in the Last World*. He won a Pulitzer Prize, the first given to a Latino, for his second novel, *The Mambo Kings Play Songs of Love* (1989), which became a major motion picture. He published *The Fourteen Sisters of Emilio Montez O'Brien* in 1993. The first novel illustrates the experience of immigrant life and coming of age in America.

Narrated in the third person, the novel is divided into fifteen sections, each headed by a title and, except for the last section, with years indicating the time of plot covered. The last section, "Voices from the Last World," includes the first-person memories of the dreams of the principal characters. Several literary techniques are used successfully; flashbacks, anticipation, monologues, and dialogues enliven the narrative. Familiar incidents are seen from different points of view. The use of Spanish words, with a fluid transition from that language to English, represents the sociocultural dualism of bilingual texts.

Just as their ancestors had emigrated from Spain to Cuba, Alejo and Mercedes Santinio move to the United States in search of more opportunity. They remain attached to memories of the old country while their children, born in the new country, struggle to achieve an identity within the two cultures. Horacio and Hector provide an account of the experience of growing up in an immigrant family, one in which the tension between generations allows the author to portray the cross-cultural differences between two worlds.

The nostalgia for the warm and sunny island nation Cuba clashes with the cold reality of life in a crowded inner-city neighborhood. The parents have moved from a privileged position in Cuba to become an underprivileged ethnic minority in the United States. They compensate for their feelings of powerlessness by committing violent acts against each other and their sons. Life in the urban barrio gives them all a sense of alienation, fear, and bitterness. While other Cubans prosper, they allow circumstances to destroy their self-confidence and self-respect; they feel isolated because they cannot communicate in English and do not take advantage of sound opportunities. They scream, cry, and fight, making the lives of their sons miserable.

Horacio and Hector encounter street violence and discrimination; they are called Whitey or Pinky because of their light skin and are told "Why don't you go back to where you came from." Children shout at the sickly Hector, "Look at the little queer," and make fun of his Spanish. For Hector, to be Americanized means to be fearful and lonely, and yet Spanish represents "the language of memory, of violence and sadness" which his parents use. Hector, "tired of being a Cuban cook's son," reacts by refusing to talk to his father, not wanting to be like him. He admires the Cubans who did not despair and "did not fall down."

Hector's identity crisis is revealed when the reader is told that he feels "Part 'Pop,' part Mercedes; part Cuban, part American—all wrapped tightly inside a skin in which he sometimes could not move." He questions what it is to be Cuban because he is considered American by the Cubans. He is not sure whether Cuba is a paradise, and his sense of marginality prevails. Horacio decides to leave his drunken father, his lunatic mother, and his troubled brother; he escapes from the world of ghosts.

In the novel, Cuba becomes a poetic motif. Recollections and nostalgic remembrances are the driving force for poetic creation. In the end, one listens to the voices of the protagonists relating their dreams. Horacio imagines Alejo visiting him, his wife, Marilyn, and his son, Stevie; he realizes that, after all, the father gave them the ability to love and survive. Hector imagines a house that is "memory," where he finds love, respect, and happiness. He feels transported by a light into "another world before awareness of problems" and is mesmerized by images of Cuba.

Hector understands that his parents never had the chance to get what they wanted out of life. His mother used to write poetry and was a singer but never achieved her dreams; she searched for the lost house of her father and was surrounded by ghosts in her own house. Their future was destroyed by fear, worries, and memories; they were not strong enough to face social injustice, racism, and economic suffering. Hector realizes that writing is a form of survival and that it will help him succeed in the future. Alejo's words to Mercedes in a dream will guide him: "Do not be afraid." With this message, Hijuelos's novel represents a valuable contribution to the Latino narrative that has been integrated into American mainstream fiction.

Ludmila Kapschutschenko-Schmitt

Further Reading

Augenbraum, Harold, and Ilan Stavans, eds. *Growing up Latino: Memoirs and Stories.* Boston: Houghton Mifflin, 1993. This collection of Latino fiction and nonfiction discusses the coming-of-age and memoir literary tradition, which helps to understand Hijuelos's works.

Fein, Esther B. "Oscar Hijuelos's Unease, Wordly and Otherwise." *The New York Times*, April 1, 1993. Excellent article about Hijuelos, his life and works, and his personal observations. Confirms the autobiographical nature of his first novel.

Foster, David William. *Handbook of Latin American Literature.* New York: Garland, 1992. Includes Latino writing in the United States. Discusses Hijuelos's works in the context of the cultural history and social and cultural contributions of Cuban Americans.

Kanellos, Nicolás. *Biographical Dictionary of Hispanic Literature in the United States.* Westport, Conn.: Greenwood Press, 1989. Each entry provides a biography; the literary genres, themes and analyses of works by each covered author; and a bibliography. Hijuelos's novel is discussed for its treatment of Cuban assimilation in the United States.

Pérez Firmat, Gustavo. *Life on the Hyphen: The Cuban-American Way.* Austin: University of Texas Press, 1994. Focuses on Cuban American performers and writers. Hijuelos is presented as a cultural figure whose work exemplifies a bilingual, bicultural identity in search of a collective identity.

_____. "Teaching Oscar Hijuelos' *Our House in the Last World.*" In *U.S. Latino Literature: A Critical Guide for*

Students and Teachers, edited by Harold Augenbraum and Margarite Fernández Olmos. Westport, Conn.: Greenwood Press, 2000. Provides a literary analysis of Hijuelos's novel and a brief biography of the writer. Although aimed at teachers, this book also is useful to students and general readers.

Stavans, Ilan. "Words and Music: Oscar Hijuelos." In *Conversations with Ilan Stavans*. Tucson: University of Arizona Press, 2005. Reprints literary critic Stavans's interviews with Hijuelos and other Latino/Latina writers, artists, and intellectuals.

Our Mutual Friend

Author: Charles Dickens (1812-1870)
First published: 1864-1865, serial; 1865, book
Type of work: Novel
Type of plot: Domestic realism
Time of plot: Mid-nineteenth century
Locale: London

Principal characters:
JOHN HARMON, alias JULIUS HANDFORD, alias JOHN ROKESMITH, the son of Old John Harmon
MR. BOFFIN and MRS. BOFFIN, Old John Harmon's employees and heirs
BELLA WILFER, the young woman betrothed to John Harmon
WEGG, a scheming street peddler with a wooden leg
MR. VENUS, a taxidermist and Wegg's compatriot
MORTIMER LIGHTWOOD, an indolent lawyer hired by Mr. Boffin
EUGENE WRAYBURN, his friend
GAFFER HEXAM, a man who gets his living from the river
LIZZIE HEXAM, his daughter
ROGUE RIDERHOOD, another waterfront character

The Story:

John Harmon is thought to have been murdered soon after he left the ship upon his return to England to marry Bella Wilfer in compliance with the conditions of his father's will; a body found by Gaffer Hexam is identified as Harmon's. Actually, Harmon has not died; fearing for his life and shrinking from the forced marriage, he assumes the name of Julius Handford, then that of John Rokesmith.

As Rokesmith, Harmon becomes a secretary to Mr. Boffin, who inherited the estate of Harmon's father after young John Harmon was pronounced dead. Before that, Mr. Boffin, who never learned to read, began to employ a street peddler named Wegg to read to him such books as took his fancy. Mr. and Mrs. Boffin enjoy their new wealth and leisure, but they both regret that the son and disinherited daughter of old Harmon did not live to enjoy the fortune that has come to them. They try to find a little orphan whom they can rear, hoping to provide a boy with some of the advantages little John Harmon did not have. The Boffins also bring Bella Wilfer to live with them in their grand new house, wishing to provide her with the kind of life she might have had as John Harmon's wife.

Bella, who is beautiful but mercenary, intends to make a good match. When Harmon, in his role as Rokesmith, declares his love for her, she rejects him with disdain. When, much later, Mr. Boffin hears that Rokesmith had aspired to her hand, a bitter scene ensues in which he charges Rokesmith with impudence and discharges him. By that time, however, Bella has become wiser, having seen how money and wealth have apparently changed the easygoing Mr. Boffin into an ill-tempered, avaricious miser. She refuses to stay any longer with the Boffins and returns to the modest life of her father's home.

Mr. Boffin begins to have trouble with Wegg, whom he has established in the comfortable house in which the Boffins live. Not satisfied with his good fortune, Wegg has become increasingly avaricious and spends all his time searching the house and the dustheaps in the yard for possible items of value that old Harmon might have secreted when he lived there. In his searches, Wegg finds a will dated after the will from which the Boffins have profited; in the later will, most of old Harmon's money was to go to the Crown. With the assistance of an acquaintance, a taxidermist named Venus, Wegg blackmails Mr. Boffin, telling him that unless he shares the fortune equally with them, they will make known the existence of the later will. Mr. Boffin pretends to agree.

Mr. Boffin has offered a reward to anyone giving information about the murderer of young Harmon and has placed the matter in the hands of Mortimer Lightwood, a lawyer. Lightwood's only clue comes from Handford (actually John Harmon), who was present when the body was identified as young Harmon's. For a time, Lightwood thinks that the murderer might have been Gaffer Hexam, who is known to make a living from finding corpses in the river. Hearing that Hexam's daughter is suffering under the suspicion attached to her father, Harmon, in his role as Rokesmith, secures an affidavit from Rogue Riderhood, who had informed against Hexam; in the affidavit Riderhood admits to having given false information.

When Bella Wilfer returns to her father's home, she is much improved; she has realized that she can marry only a man she loves, and she also realizes that she loves Rokesmith, who was unjustly discharged on her account. When Rokesmith, apparently penniless and without a job, comes to her, she joyfully accepts his suit. Their marriage proves a happy one, for Rokesmith tells her that he has found a job that will keep them in modest comfort. Both are happy when their child is born.

One day, Lightwood meets Rokesmith and Bella on the street by chance and immediately recognizes Rokesmith as Handford. That evening, a police officer arrests Rokesmith, who is forced to admit his real identity as John Harmon. As it turns out, the corpse identified as Harmon's was really that of his would-be murderer, who was killed by thieves. The mistake occurred because the man had changed into Harmon's clothes after drugging him. Harmon has to admit his real identity to his wife, and more besides. Mrs. Boffin had early guessed his true identity, and Mr. Boffin had only pretended to become an unpleasant miser for the purpose of showing Bella the kind of person she might become if she continued in her mercenary ways. The success of their scheme was proved when she defended Rokesmith to Mr. Boffin and returned to her father's home. Eager for Harmon to inherit his father's fortune, the Boffins turn the estate over to him; Bella thus becomes the rich woman she had at one time wished to be.

The situation with Wegg and Venus is easily settled because Mr. Boffin had only pretended when he agreed to the terms of their blackmail. Mr. Boffin actually possesses an even later will, which he has kept secret only because of its insulting language about Harmon and his dead sister. This later will, too, leaves the fortune to the Boffins, but they return it to Harmon and his family. Wegg is taken out of the house by a servant and dropped into a wagon piled high with garbage.

Critical Evaluation:

Charles Dickens's last completed novel, *Our Mutual Friend*, is among his greatest works, containing perhaps the most mature expression of his artistic abilities. The novel, which reflects many of his major concerns as a writer and social critic, is a complicated one, with an intricately constructed and elaborate plot. The first two chapters provide a stark contrast. In the first, Gaffer Hexam, the "bird of prey," is in a boat on the Thames with his daughter Lizzie, on the lookout for the drowned bodies that are the source of his livelihood; in the second, the newly rich Veneerings are giving a dinner party. The unexpected link between the two worlds is provided in the third chapter.

By revealing the real links between people and classes that would seem to have no connection at all (this culminates in the wedding of Eugene Wrayburn and Lizzie Hexam at the end), Dickens shows that different worlds, though separated from each other in thought, are physically close, each involved with the other. In holding a mirror up to the cumbersome structure of society, Dickens uses the idea of depth and surface to reflect the polite world on top and the seething, half-known world of misery and crime below. Dickens also implies that the sophisticated few are often stupid and easy to understand, while the unlettered many can be complex and intriguing.

This inversion of the expected is one of the book's dominating features. Other reversions include Betty Higden's hounding by misguided charity, the reversed parent-child relationship of Jenny Wren and her father (to some extent, though in a more benign sense, this is also true of Bella Wilfer and her father), and the unequal relationship between the morally upright Riah and the scoundrel Fledgeby. These reversals indicate something of a newfound flexibility in Dickens's treatment of moral problems. As the problems come to seem more doubtful and difficult, his literary treatment of them becomes that much more clear and intense.

Also central to the novel is the theme of the relationships among marriage, money, and societal values. This theme is worked out in the three important marriages in the novel, those between Harmon and Bella, Eugene and Lizzie, and Alfred and Sophronia Lammle. In each of these marriages, money is an important issue. Harmon, though he is or could be rich, must pretend to be poor to be certain that Bella is not marrying him for his money. Eugene must marry Lizzie in the face of pressures from his family and society that he marry a woman with money. When the Lammles marry, each is motivated solely by the delusion that the other has money.

In the novel, money destroys and corrupts in a wide variety of ways. Old Harmon was the ruined victim of his own money. His son, too, is nearly ruined by this money. Boffin pretends to be corrupted by money in order to show its corruptive force and is so harassed by his money that he can scarcely wait to get rid of it. Bella begins to be corrupted by money but is saved.

The two major symbols in *Our Mutual Friend*, the river and the dustheap, show Dickens at the height of his abilities. The river cuts across all inflated, unreal social distinctions in much the same way the epidemic cuts across these same boundaries in Dickens's *Bleak House* (1852-1853, serial; 1853, book). At times, the river—its motion, mystery, swell, and obscurity—is used quite overtly as a symbol for the passage of life itself. It is also hard to resist the idea that the river has a sacramental, baptismal character. It is a source of mystery, bringing salvation or damnation. In the course of the narrative, many of the characters fall into the river, either to drown or to emerge as new men. John Harmon emerges as John Rokesmith, a guise he can abandon only when he has been assured that Bella Wilfer loves him and not his money. Eugene Wrayburn's narrow escape from drowning comes at a time when he has at last overcome the view natural to a man of his class that someone like Lizzie is not a suitable marriage partner. For characters such as Headstone and Riderhood, however, the river is a source of death. Riderhood, a man to whom the river means nothing more than a criminal livelihood, almost drowned once before. Others expect him to change after he is rescued, but he refuses the gift of a second chance and eventually does drown, locked in the murderous grasp of the schoolmaster Headstone.

The novel's other dominant symbol is the dustheap. The image of the dustheap is, in fact, less fantastic than it may at first appear. Dust, dustheaps, and dust contractors were all common in England in Dickens's time. The dust and refuse collected from the streets was piled in huge heaps that came to have great value and were often the source of great fortunes in early Victorian times, as frequently the dustheaps contained buried treasures along with the wastes. Thus there is an obvious connection between money and dirt. Money equals dust. The dustheaps were filth, ordure, excrement— and money.

Money is also linked with dirt in the novel's tales about misers, all of whom are physically unclean and squalid. This equation of money with dirt and the quest of money with the sifting of rubbish pervades the work. The comical figure that Wegg cuts in his lantern-lit scavenging on the dustheap finds a sinister echo in Lizzie Hexam's father at his grisly occupation on the river and a refined, although equally precise, reverberation in the economic maneuvering of the Lammles and the Veneerings. At every level of society, people of all ages are shown in the act of hunting for money. The heroine herself does so in the beginning. The force of the dustheaps as a symbol resides in its absurdity, the high ironic comedy that clings to the surreptitious activity of digging through refuse to find nonexistent gold. It is as if the whole society were being not chastised but made to appear mad. Few novelists have dealt better with the fascination that money exerts on people than Dickens does in *Our Mutual Friend*.

"Critical Evaluation" by Craig A. Larson

Further Reading

Ackroyd, Peter. *Dickens*. New York: HarperCollins, 1990. Biography by a major English novelist offers exhaustive, critical coverage of Dickens's life and work.

Allen, Michelle. "A More Expansive Reach: The Geography of the Thames in *Our Mutual Friend*." In *Cleansing the City: Sanitary Geographies in Victorian London*. Athens: Ohio University Press, 2008. During the nineteenth century, reformers set out to clean and sanitize the city of London, but these efforts met with stiff resistance. Allen examines *Our Mutual Friend* and other literature from the period in which this resistance was expressed as a sense of nostalgia for the threatened urban landscape.

Cockshut, A. O. J. *The Imagination of Charles Dickens*. 1962. Reprint. New York: Routledge, 2009. Contains an insightful chapter on *Our Mutual Friend* that focuses on the symbolic meanings of the river and the dustheaps.

Cotsell, Michael. *The Companion to "Our Mutual Friend."* 1986. Reprint. New York: Routledge, 2009. Offers factual annotations on every aspect of the text as well as notes on the work's allusions to events of the time in which it was written, intellectual and social issues, and customs. An excellent accompaniment to the novel.

Hardy, Barbara. *Dickens and Creativity*. London: Continuum, 2008. Focuses on the workings of Dickens's creativity and imagination, arguing that these are at the heart of his self-awareness, subject matter, and narrative. *Our Mutual Friend* is discussed in chapter 10, "Creative Conversation in *Hard Times*, *Great Expectations*, and *Our Mutual Friend*," and in chapter 11, "Assertions of Style: Rhythm and Repetition in *A Tale of Two Cities* and *Our Mutual Friend*."

Herst, Beth F. *The Dickens Hero: Selfhood and Alienation in the Dickens World.* New York: St. Martin's Press, 1990. Informative examination of Dickens's protagonists discusses John Harmon as a person who moves "from alienation through self-discovery to a new sort of alienation."

Jordan, John O., ed. *The Cambridge Companion to Charles Dickens.* New York: Cambridge University Press, 2001. Collection of essays includes examinations of Dickens's life and times, analyses of individual novels, and discussions of Dickens's work in relation to such topics as language, gender, family, domestic ideology, and the form of the novel.

Paroissien, David, ed. *A Companion to Charles Dickens.* Malden, Mass.: Blackwell, 2008. Collection of essays discusses Dickens as a reformer, as a Christian, and as a journalist. Includes an essay on *Our Mutual Friend* by Leon Litvack.

Romano, John. *Dickens and Reality.* New York: Columbia University Press, 1978. Examines realism in Dickens's work, using *Our Mutual Friend* as one of the primary examples. Asserts that, despite the novel's realist nature, Dickens makes no effort to conform the events in the work to the "real" world, and this contributes to the novel's overall success.

Our Town

Author: Thornton Wilder (1897-1975)
First produced: 1938; first published, 1938
Type of work: Drama
Type of plot: Symbolism
Time of plot: 1901-1913
Locale: Grover's Corners, New Hampshire

Principal characters:
DR. GIBBS, a physician
MRS. GIBBS, his wife
GEORGE and REBECCA, their children
MR. WEBB, a newspaper editor
MRS. WEBB, his wife
EMILY and WALLY, their children
SIMON STIMSON, director of the choir

The Story:

Early one morning in 1901, Dr. Gibbs returns to his home in Grover's Corners, New Hampshire. He has just been across the tracks to Polish Town to deliver Mrs. Goruslowski's twins. On the street he meets Joe Crowell, the morning paperboy, and Howie Newsome, the milkman. The day's work is beginning in Grover's Corners. Mrs. Gibbs has breakfast ready when her husband arrives, and she calls the children, George and Rebecca, to the table. After breakfast the children leave for school in the company of the Webb children, Wally and Emily, who are neighbors.

After the children leave, Mrs. Gibbs steps out to feed her chickens. Seeing Mrs. Webb stringing beans in her back yard, she crosses over to talk with her. Mrs. Gibbs has been offered $350 for some antique furniture; she will sell the furniture, she decides, if she can get Dr. Gibbs to take a vacation with her. Dr. Gibbs has no wish to take a vacation, however; if he can visit the Civil War battlegrounds every other year, he is satisfied.

The warm day passes, and the children return home from school. Emily Webb walks home alone, pretending she is a great lady. George Gibbs, on his way to play baseball, stops to talk to Emily and tells her how much he admires her success at school. He cannot, he insists, imagine how anyone could spend so much time over homework as she does. Flattered, Emily promises to help George with his algebra. He says that he does not really need school work, because he is going to be a farmer as soon as he graduates from high school. When George leaves, Emily runs to her mother and asks if she is pretty enough to make boys notice her. Grudgingly, her mother admits that she is, but Mrs. Webb tries to turn Emily's mind to other subjects.

That evening, while Mrs. Webb and Mrs. Gibbs are at choir practice, George and Emily sit upstairs studying. Their windows face each other, and George calls to Emily for some advice on his algebra. Emily helps him, but she is more interested in the moonlight. When she calls George's attention to the beautiful night, he seems only mildly interested.

The ladies coming home from choir practice gossip about

their leader, Simon Stimson. He drinks most of the time, and for some reason he cannot adjust himself to small-town life. The ladies wonder how it will all end. Mr. Webb also wonders. He is the editor of the local paper; as he goes home, he meets Simon roaming the deserted streets. When Mr. Webb reaches his home, he finds Emily still gazing out of her window at the moon—and dreaming.

At the end of his junior year in high school George is elected president of his class, and Emily is elected secretary-treasurer. When George walks home with Emily after the election, she seems so cold and indifferent that George asks for an explanation. She tells him that all the girls think him conceited and stuck-up because he cares more for baseball than he does for his friends. She expects men to be perfect, like her father and his.

George says that men cannot be perfect, but that women can—like Emily. Then Emily begins to cry, insisting that she is far from perfect. George offers to buy her a soda. As they drink their sodas, they find that they really have liked each other for some time. George says he now believes he will not go away to agricultural school, after all. When he graduates from high school, he will start working on the farm.

After a time, Dr. and Mrs. Gibbs learn that George wants to marry Emily as soon as he leaves high school At first it is a shock to them, for they cannot imagine that George is anything but a child. They wonder how he could provide for a wife, and whether Emily could take care of a house. Then Dr. and Mrs. Gibbs remember their own first years of married life. They had had troubles, but now they feel that the troubles have been overshadowed by their joys. They decide that George could marry Emily if he wishes.

On the morning of the wedding day George drops in on Mr. and Mrs. Webb, and Mrs. Webb leaves the men alone so that her husband can advise George. All that Mr. Webb has to say, however, is that no one can advise anyone else on matters as personal as marriage. When George leaves, Emily comes down to her last breakfast in her parents' home. Both she and Mrs. Webb cry. Mrs. Webb had meant to give her daughter some advice on marriage, but she is unable to bring herself to it.

At the church, just before the ceremony, both Emily and George feel as if they are making a mistake; they do not want to get married. By the time the music starts, however, both of them are calm. The wedding ceremony is soon over. Grover's Corners has lost one of its best baseball players. Nine years pass; it is the summer of 1913. Up in the graveyard above the town the dead lay, resting from the cares of their lives on Earth. Now there is a new grave; Emily died in childbirth and George is left alone with their four-year-old son.

It is raining as the funeral procession winds its way up the hill to the new grave. Then Emily appears shyly before the other dead. Solemnly they welcome her to her rest—but she does not want to rest; she wants to live over again the joys of her life. It is possible to do so, but the others warn her against trying to relive a day in her mortal life.

Emily chooses to relive her twelfth birthday. At first it is exciting to be young again, but the excitement wears off quickly. The day holds no joy, now that Emily knows what is in store for the future. It is unbearably painful to realize how unaware she had been of the meaning and wonder of life while she was alive. Simon Stimson, who had killed himself, tells her that life is like that, a time of ignorance and blindness and folly. He is still bitter in death.

Emily returns to her resting place. When night has fallen, George approaches, full of grief, and throws himself on Emily's grave. She feels pity for him and for all the rest of the living. For now she knows how little they really understand of the wonderful gift that is life itself.

Critical Evaluation:

Thornton Wilder won a Pulitzer Prize in fiction in 1928 for his second novel, *The Bridge of San Luis Rey*, and then won Pulitzer Prizes for drama in 1938 and 1943 for *Our Town* and *The Skin of Our Teeth* (pr., pb. 1942), thus making him the only writer ever to win Pulitzers both for fiction and for drama. Wilder is most remembered and admired for *Our Town*, perhaps the most popular and frequently produced of all American plays, given the great number of high school and community theater productions it has generated. The popularity and simplicity of *Our Town* frequently obscure its fundamentally radical style and theme.

In a period when realism was the common style of the American theater, Wilder's dramatic style was militantly antirealistic. In *The Happy Journey to Trenton and Camden* (1931), Wilder uses a bare stage and four kitchen chairs to represent a family making a journey of seventy miles by automobile. In *Our Town*, the act 1 stage directions insist on "No curtain. No scenery. The audience, arriving, sees an empty stage in half-light." In the earliest productions of *Our Town*, many audience members were uncomfortable with the stage manager, who comments on the action, and actors who pantomime to create the illusion of set and props. In his preface to *Three Plays* (1957), Wilder asserts that by the 1930's in American theater, stage realism had undermined the audience's capacity for a full emotional and intellectual response to plays. According to Wilder, when the stage set is filled with scenery, furniture, and props designed to trick the audience into believing that the present moment is "real," the audience's imagination is also chained to the particularity of that play's time and place.

Wilder wanted to communicate general ideas that transcended the particularity of individual experience, so he created characters who were types rather than psychologically complex individuals, and he placed these characters in bare stage environments, avoiding particulars of time and place. Thus, George and Emily have little depth as characters, but as types they can represent all young people who court one another, marry, and encounter catastrophic loss. The town Emily and George live in is also not simply Grover's Corners, New Hampshire, but a little New England town that is part of "the United States of America; Continent of North America; Western Hemisphere; the Earth; the Solar System; the Universe; the Mind of God," as Rebecca Gibbs puts it in act 2. When George and Emily talk to each other from their upper-story bedroom windows, they do so from the tops of stepladders rather than from realistically represented rooms. Thus, the audience focuses on George and Emily's conversation rather than on particulars of place and time.

Thematically, Wilder asserts that a sensitivity to human sadness and failure does not have to lead to despair. Awareness of human pain can coexist with a belief in an essentially benevolent universe. In Wilder's plays, human lives are disappointingly brief and their actions seem small when measured against the cosmic scale, yet Wilder insists that humans and their lives are not insignificant. Humans may suffer profoundly or survive by the skin of their teeth, but life remains worth living. The glory of existence resides in the mundane and particular moment—in the birth of a child, the singing of a hymn, or even in the clanking of Howie Newsome's milk bottles as he delivers milk on his morning route. In act 3 of *Our Town*, Emily discovers that human beings are generally blind to the joys of life and do not "ever realize life while they live it—every, every minute." Wilder's plays exhort their audiences to rediscover their zest for life.

Our Town is most significant in the history of American drama for its innovations in dramatic style. Wilder brought to prominence in America the possibilities of non-realistic staging. These possibilities were also developed in the revolutionary modern dramas of the Italian playwright Luigi Pirandello and of the German playwright Bertolt Brecht. Wilder is also important because he confronts the pain and disappointment of human life yet maintains an optimistic vision. Measuring human lives against a cosmic scale, without the comfort of God, led many writers in the twentieth century to various forms of despair. For Wilder, however, the prevalence of human pain, frustration, and failure meant that people could rediscover the simple joys

of existence. Human beings can face life's pain and live with hope because, as the stage manager says, there is "something way down deep that's eternal about every human being."

Ironically, Wilder is perhaps more respected in Europe, especially in Germany, than he is in the United States. European dramatists as important as Brecht, Max Frisch, and Eugène Ionesco have acknowledged their debt to Wilder's stylistic innovations and profound themes.

"Critical Evaluation" by Terry Nienhuis

Further Reading

Blank, Martin, Dalma Hunyadi Brunauer, and David Garrett Izzo, eds. *Thornton Wilder: New Essays*. West Cornwall, Conn.: Locust Hill Press, 1999. Essays discuss both his novels and plays, examining his legacy and achievement, Wilder and the critics, his use of myth, and American Puritanism in his early plays and novels. Two of the essays focus on *Our Town* specifically.

Bloom, Harold, ed. *Thornton Wilder*. Philadelphia: Chelsea House, 2003. Essays assess Wilder's contributions to American theater, the unique qualities of his work, the tragic features of his vision, and other elements of his plays. Contains a plot summary, a list of characters for *Our Town*, and interpretive essays—one by playwright Arthur Miller, who examines the play's family themes, and another by writer Mary McCarthy, who examines the play's use of deceased characters. Also studies the play's expressionist influences, its depiction of time, and the function of the stage manager.

Bryer, Jackson R., ed. *Conversations with Thornton Wilder*. Jackson: University Press of Mississippi, 1992. A collection of interviews with Wilder, providing interesting perspectives on the man and his literary works. Includes an index.

Castronovo, David. "The Major Full-Length Plays: Visions of Survival." In *Thornton Wilder*. New York: Frederick Ungar, 1986. A striking, intelligent, and convincing reading of *Our Town* as "American folk art."

Corrigan, Robert W. "Thornton Wilder and the Tragic Sense of Life." In *The Theater in Search of a Fix*. New York: Delacorte Press, 1973. Finds that Wilder's plays "fall short of tragedy" but argues that "no other American dramatist more fully affirms that miracle of life" denied by much modern drama.

Haberman, Donald C. *"Our Town": An American Play*. Boston: Twayne, 1989. A thorough examination of the play and its place in literary history. Attempts "to recover the play's intellectual respectability" and to demonstrate its solidity and "revolutionary . . . stagecraft."

Konkle, Lincoln. *Thornton Wilder and the Puritan Narrative Tradition*. Columbia: University of Missouri Press, 2006. Konkle argues that Wilder, a descendent of Puritans, inherited the Puritans' worldview, particularly the Calvinist aesthetic, and drew upon it to create his novels and plays. Includes a chronology, a bibliography, and an index.

Lifton, Paul. *"Vast Encyclopedia": The Theatre of Thornton Wilder*. Westport, Conn.: Greenwood Press, 1995. A critical overview of Wilder's drama.

Out of Africa

Author: Isak Dinesen (1885-1962)
First published: Den afrikanske Farm, 1937 (English translation, 1937)
Type of work: Memoir

Principal characters:
KAREN BLIXEN, a passionate, courageous Danish woman
DENYS FINCH-HATTON, a British trader and hunter
FARAH ADEN, Karen's Somali servant
KAMANTE GATURA, a young Kikuyu boy
BERKELEY COLE and INGRID LINDSTROM, friends and neighboring landowners
BROR BLIXEN, Karen's husband

The Story:

Karen Blixen once owned a coffee farm in Africa, at the foot of the Ngong Hills. As she sits at home in Rungsted, Denmark, many years later, she remembers her seventeen years in Kenya. Captivated by the beauty of the African landscape and its people, she is struck by the feeling of having lived for a time up in the air.

When Karen and her husband, Bror, first arrive in Africa, there are no cars. Nairobi, the town closest to their farm, is twelve miles away, and Karen travels to and from the farm, Mbogani House, by mule cart. Her able overseer, Farah Aden, helps her make the adjustment to her new life. From her first weeks in Africa, she feels a great affection for the East African tribes: the Somali, the Kikuyu, and the Masai.

Karen meets Kamante Gatura when he comes to the small medical clinic she operates for the people who live and work on the farm. The nine-year-old boy looks as if he is dying. Open sores cover his legs, and he seems to face death with passionless resignation. In spite of her best efforts, Karen's treatment fails; arresting the disease is beyond her capabilities. She decides to send Kamante to the Scotch Mission hospital, where he remains for three months. He returns to the farm on Easter Sunday, his legs completely healed. He says to Karen, "I am like you," meaning that now he, too, is a Christian.

In time, Kamante is trained to be Karen's chef. A genius in the kitchen, he can pick out the plumpest hen in the poultry yard, and his whipped egg whites tower up like clouds. He rarely tastes the dishes he prepares for Karen, preferring the food of his fathers, yet he grows famous preparing meals for Karen's friends and guests, including the Prince of Wales.

Following a yearlong drought, when it seems the universe is turning away from her, Karen begins to write. When her workers ask what she is doing, she tells them that she is trying to write a book, and they view this as an attempt to save the farm. Comparing her scattered loose-leaf pages to a bound book he has pulled from her library shelves, Kamante expresses doubt that she will ever be able to write a book. He asks what she will write about, and she replies that she might write of him. He looks down at himself and asks, in a low voice, "Which part?" Many years will pass before she publishes her reflections of Africa, but when she finally does, Kamante is an important part of her story.

Karen does not understand the various African dialects, but the regal and intelligent Farah serves as interpreter throughout her sojourn in Kenya. Many of the tribes look to Karen to settle their disputes. On one occasion, when she is asked to judge who is to blame in a shooting accident, she turns to her friend Chief Kinanjui, who rules over more than one hundred thousand Kikuyu. By this time, the automobile has come to Africa, and when Chief Kinanjui arrives in his new car, he does not want to get out until she has seen him sitting in it. Finally alighting, he takes his seat next to Karen and Farah, and together they agree on fair restitution for the parties in the case: One man must give the other a cow with a heifer calf. Karen never shies away from becoming involved in such disputes. Eventually she advocates for the rights of all East Africans to each successive governor of the colony and to any wealthy or influential settlers who will listen.

After Karen and Bror divorce, the farm has many visitors, from large groups of Africans who come for the *Ngomas* (social dances) to European friends. Berkeley Cole calls Mbogani House his sylvan retreat; he brings leopard and cheetah skins to be made into fur coats and fine wines to serve with dinner. He reminds Karen of a cat, a constant source of heat and fun. His stories of the old days can make even the Masai chiefs laugh, and they are prepared to travel many miles to hear them. When Berkeley dies young, Karen feels a tremendous sense of loss.

Karen's friend Ingrid Lindstrom comes to Africa with her husband and children to operate a flax farm. Like Karen, Ingrid works passionately to save her farm during the hard times. The two women weep together at the thought of losing their land. As the years pass and one bad harvest follows another, Karen's chances of keeping her farm grow slimmer.

Denys Finch-Hatton gives Karen a powerful reason to stay in Africa, and, thanks to his love and encouragement, she fights to stay as long as she can. Although he owns land in another part of the continent, Denys makes Karen's farm his home. He lives there between safaris, returning unexpectedly after weeks or months away. His visits are like sparkling jewels. Denys teaches Karen Latin and introduces her to the Greek poets; he brings her a gramophone and records with classical music. In the evenings, he spreads cushions on the floor, and she sits on them and spins for him the long tales she has made up while he has been away.

Karen and Denys have great luck hunting lions together. One spring, two lions come to the farm and kill two of Karen's oxen. That night, Denys is determined to get the pair before they can strike again. With Karen holding a torch, they track the lions and kill them near the edge of the property.

One of Karen's greatest pleasures is flying in Denys's airplane. His moth machine, as she calls it, can land on her farm only a few minutes from the house, and the two often make short flights over the Ngong Hills at sunset. Other times, they travel farther to find huge herds of buffalo or to soar with the eagles. These happy days do not last, however, because the coffee plantation is rapidly failing. Too little rain produces poor yields, and when the price of coffee falls, Karen's investors tell her that she will have to sell.

Karen is making plans to dispose of her belongings and to find suitable land for her workers when the news comes that Denys has been killed in the crash of his plane. Heartbroken,

Karen searches in the rain to find an appropriate burial site for him. Finally she chooses a narrow, natural terrace in the hillside behind the farm. At the grave, she and Farah erect a tall white flag so that from her window she can look to the hills and see a small white star. After she leaves Africa, the Masai report to the district commissioner that many times at sunrise and sunset they have seen a lion and lioness standing on the grave.

In the dark days following Denys's funeral, Ingrid stays with Karen. They do not talk of the past or the future. They walk together on the farm, taking stock of Karen's losses, naming each item and lingering fondly at the animal pens and the beautiful flower gardens. Karen's last months in Africa take her on a beggar's journey from one government official to the next. Her goal is to find enough land for her workers to settle on together, so that they can preserve their community. Finally, the government agrees to give them a piece of the Dagoretti Forest Reserve. In the end, Farah drives Karen to the train station. She can see the Ngong Hills to the southwest, but as the train moves farther from her home, the hand of distance slowly smooths and levels the outline of the mountain.

Critical Evaluation:

Only things at a distance can be seen clearly. Although Isak Dinesen did not publish *Out of Africa* until several years after her African experience, her early formal training at the Royal Academy of Fine Arts helped form her sense of what it meant to be a writer. The notes for her book had been written in times of great weariness and anger. Distanced from those conflicts, she became essentially a modernist artist, attempting to replace the real with the ideal. Critics have said that there are no real Africans in her writing, only mythical representations of a lost era. *Out of Africa* was written for and well received by Europeans and Americans. It is Dinesen's vision of the Africans' vision of her. With this widely read book, Dinesen participated in the construction of Africa and Africans in the Western consciousness. At the same time, she constructed her own identity.

Taking a line from philosopher Friedrich Nietzsche as the epigraph for *Out of Africa*—"Equitare, arcem tendere, veritatem dicere" (To ride, to shoot with a bow, to tell the truth)—Dinesen echoes many of Nietzsche's ideas. An important theme, well illustrated by Karen Blixen's character as well as by the Africans, is Nietzsche's belief that fate, rather than guilt or sin, is the cause of suffering, and that fate should be courageously accepted. Denys Finch-Hatton, who clearly emerges as a hero in the work, represents Nietzsche's call for a new nobility, individuals who have learned to know life through action and who, therefore, have a use for history. In essence, Finch-Hatton teaches Karen Blixen how to become herself. Before knowing him, she had found her teachers in the library and become herself only in her imagination, while her false self acquiesced to society's demands. As she constructs her new life in Africa, both in the living and in the remembering, those restraints are lifted and she truly soars. Much of the book's appeal rests in its power to allow readers to find themselves through their imaginations.

Dinesen's philosophical flights are grounded, however, in very real cultural concerns: the relations between the colonizers and the oppressed; the encroachment upon Africa of modern life; and the implications of a sexist, racist, and classist society. Her writing is full of paradox. Although she sympathizes with the problems of Africans under colonization, she frequently refers to them as primitive children and sees the ideal situation as that of colonial settler and African working harmoniously side by side, as she and Farah do. Although she supports Denys's beloved safaris, she portrays the lion hunts as efforts by wealthy Europeans to play at being self-sufficient by hunting their own food. Finally, in spite of her efforts to cultivate an independent woman's life, her relationship with Denys, and indeed with the land, places her in a variation of the African mythic figure of suffering woman. The notion of a paradise lost dominates *Out of Africa*. Perhaps Dinesen's greatest gift in this work is her assurance that the most tragic losses, whether real or imagined, can be overcome.

Carol F. Bender

Further Reading

Brantly, Susan. *Understanding Isak Dinesen*. Columbia: University of South Carolina Press, 2002. Provides an informative introduction to Dinesen that aims to demonstrate the irony, allusiveness, and ambiguity in her work. Chapter 3 provides a close reading of *Out of Africa*.

Dinesen, Isak. *Letters from Africa, 1914-1931*. Translated by Anne Born, edited by Frans Lasson. Chicago: University of Chicago Press, 1981. Excellent collection of correspondence illuminates the reality of Dinesen's African experience.

Donelson, Linda. *Out of Isak Dinesen in Africa: The Untold Story*. Iowa City, Iowa: Coulsong List, 1995. Presents thoughtful analysis of Dinesen's correspondence. Donelson, a physician, gives special attention to Dinesen's persistent ill health and the myths surrounding it.

Hansen, Frantz Leander. *The Aristocratic Universe of Karen Blixen: Destiny and the Denial of Fate*. Translated by Gaye Kynoch. Portland, Oreg.: Sussex Press, 2003. Hansen, an employee of the Karen Blixen Museum in Denmark, examines Dinesen's works. He uses the word "aristocratic" to refer to Dinesen's depiction of a conduct of life that is faithful to destiny; using this definition, the world of Africa illustrates the consummate example of an "aristocratic" culture.

Horton, Susan. *Difficult Women, Artful Lives: Olive Shreiner and Isak Dinesen in and out of Africa*. Baltimore: Johns Hopkins University Press, 1995. Offers outstanding analysis of how Dinesen journeyed to Africa to discover herself.

Langbaum, Robert. *The Gayety of Vision: A Study of Isak Dinesen's Art*. New York: Random House, 1965. Contains an excellent chapter on *Out of Africa* in which its mythical nature is analyzed. Shows Dinesen's central theme to be the unfortunate decay of an old, humane social order and examines Dinesen's claim that the myth-making tradition of Africans is similar to that of Danes centuries ago.

Lewis, Simon. *White Women Writers and Their African Invention*. Gainesville: University Press of Florida, 2003. Examination of *Out of Africa* and Olive Shreiner's *The Story of an African Farm* (1883) focuses on the perspective of white female settlers in the male-dominated African culture. Argues that these socially and racially privileged writers were marginalized because they were women and that they wrote about discrimination without escaping the practice themselves.

Pelensky, Olga Anastasia. *Isak Dinesen: The Life and Imagination of a Seducer*. Athens: Ohio University Press, 1991. Biography presents previously unpublished information and includes discussion of the influence on Dinesen's imagination of her father and of the writings of Charles Darwin and Friedrich Nietzsche. A chapter on *Out of Africa* examines the book as a thematic extension of her collection of short fiction *Seven Gothic Tales* (1934).

Thurman, Judith. *Isak Dinesen: The Life of a Storyteller*. 1982. Reprint. New York: Picador, 1995. Biography focuses on Dinesen's literary career, drawing on her letters and family documents. Provides detailed descriptions of important events in Dinesen's life, such as lion hunts, that were later incorporated into *Out of Africa*. Also touches on Dinesen's religious faith.

Out of the Silent Planet

Author: C. S. Lewis (1898-1963)
First published: 1938
Type of work: Novel
Type of plot: Science fiction
Time of plot: Early twentieth century
Locale: England and the planet Mars

Principal characters:
ELWIN RANSOM, a Cambridge philologist
WESTON, a renowned physicist
DEVINE, a greedy academic
SORNS, tall, intellectual Martians
HROSSA, friendly, otterlike Martians
HYOI, a hross who befriends Ransom
HNAKRA, a ferocious water beast
PFIFLTRIGGI, dwarflike Martians
ELDILS, translucent spirit beings
OYARSA, the ruling spirit of Mars

The Story:

Elwin Ransom is on vacation, taking a walking tour alone through the English countryside. Seeking shelter from the rain and lodging for the night, he meets a farm woman, frantic that her mentally disabled son, Harry, has not yet come home from his job at a neighboring professor's home. Hoping this professor might provide lodging, he promises to find Harry.

The professor's house is dark and locked. Ransom squeezes through the hedge and finds Professor Weston and his friend, Devine, in a scuffle with young Harry. Startled, they let Harry go. Devine recognizes Ransom as an old schoolmate and then introduces him to Weston, a renowned physicist. They offer Ransom a drink, and Ransom realizes too late that he has been drugged.

Ransom regains consciousness aboard a spaceship. He overhears Weston and Devine say they are returning to Malacandra, where aliens called sorns ordered them to bring a human sacrifice. Ransom realizes he is that sacrifice.

As they travel, Ransom finds that space is not black, cold, or vacant but flooded with invigorating light. A month later, they land on Malacandra. The ground is covered by a rubbery pink vegetation, the sky is pale blue, and the distant mountains are lavender: It is a bright, pastel world. Since the gravity is so low, everything (mountains, trees, ocean waves) is thinner and taller than on Earth.

The three men set up camp. Six sorns approach, each one fourteen feet tall, pale, and spidery thin. Devine and Weston grab Ransom and pull him toward the sorns, but as they step into a lake, a large sea monster with crocodile-like jaws attacks them. As Devine and Weston shoot at it, Ransom escapes. The next day, Ransom encounters an alien that looks like a tall otter. They stare curiously at each other and try to communicate. The alien is a hross, and Ransom is eager to

learn its language. After a long, choppy boat ride and a short walk, they arrive at the hross village.

Ransom lives peacefully among the hrossa for about five weeks, studying the language and becoming close friends with Hyoi, the hross who first found him. He learns that in addition to sorns and hrossa, there is a third intelligent species on the planet called pfifltriggi, crafters who make articles from gold. The three species, or hnau, live in harmony.

Ransom is also instructed in their religion: Maleldil the Young created all things, and now lives with the Old One. A spirit called Oyarsa rules the whole planet, and lesser spirit beings named eldil frequently visit the planet and talk to its inhabitants. The hrossa insist that Ransom should go to Oyarsa. Ransom tells the hrossa about the sea monster with the crocodile jaws. They get intensely excited: The hnakra has not been seen for many years. The greatest honor in their culture is to kill the hnakra. The entire village begins to prepare their boats and spears for the great hunt. Ransom is honored by an invitation to fight alongside Hyoi and Whin. As they seek the hnakra, an eldil appears and commands Ransom to go to Oyarsa. Ransom refuses. Immediately the hnakra appears. After a furious fight, Ransom, Hyoi, and Whin kill it. As they rest on the shore, jubilant in their victory, Hyoi is suddenly shot and killed by Weston, who had been hiding in the forest. As he dies, Hyoi calls Ransom his eternal brother because they have slain the hnakra together.

Whin tells Ransom that Hyoi has died because Ransom had disobeyed the eldil. Ransom leaves immediately to seek Oyarsa. He climbs a steep mountain, where he meets Augray, a sorn. Augray gives him oxygen and food, and shows him Earth through his telescope. Augray calls Earth Thulcandra, which means "the silent planet." The next day, Ransom climbs onto Augray's shoulder, and Augray carries him to Meldilorn, an island covered with huge golden flowers and filled with eldils. While exploring the island, Ransom sees a row of stone monoliths, each one bearing an intricate relief carving of significant events. One shows the solar system, and by studying it, Ransom realizes Malacandra is Mars. A pfifltrigg named Kanakaberaka carves a likeness of Ransom, Weston, Devine, and their spaceship into a monolith.

The next morning, Ransom is awakened by an eldil who announces, "Oyarsa sends for you." Ransom walks between two long rows of hrossa, sorns, and pfifltriggi to where Oyarsa appears as a shimmer of light hovering over the water. Oyarsa says that he sent for Ransom to learn about Earth. He explains that each planet has its own Oyarsa, but that long ago the Oyarsa of Earth had rebelled against the Old One. Since then, no word has come from the silent planet. Weston and Devine also are brought before Oyarsa. They cannot see Oyarsa and suspect a trick. Weston bellows, in his broken version of the Martian language, "Everyone who no do all we say pouff! bang! we kill him." Then Weston tries to bribe them with cheap beads. They burst out laughing: Weston is making a fool of himself.

Oyarsa orders Weston to be taken away and doused with cold water, hoping to bring him to his senses. Meanwhile, the Malacandrians sing a beautiful, elaborate funeral song to honor Hyoi and the two other hrossa that Weston had murdered. Then, with blinding light, Oyarsa disintegrates the three bodies. Weston returns dripping wet, and answers Oyarsa's questions, with Ransom acting as interpreter. Weston says he wants to perpetuate the human race on other planets. He expects Oyarsa to be impressed, but instead Oyarsa becomes convinced that Weston is utterly corrupt. Oyarsa orders Weston and Devine to return to Earth. He gives them exactly ninety days' worth of air and food.

Oyarsa dismisses Weston and Devine and talks with Ransom about Earth. He gives Ransom the choice to remain on Malacandra or to return to Thulcandra. Ransom chooses to return. On the trip back, the spaceship passes dangerously close to the sun. Then the moon cuts in front of them, and they are forced to turn the ship away from Earth. Realizing they are almost out of air and food, Ransom returns to his cabin to prepare for death. He falls asleep, and when he wakes up, he hears rain. The ship has somehow landed on Earth.

Ransom emerges from the ship and walks half an hour through the English countryside. Suddenly he hears a loud noise as the ship disintegrates. He walks into a pub and orders a pint of bitter. Ransom falls ill and fears that the trip was a delusion. Then he receives a letter from Lewis asking about the word "Oyarses," found in an ancient book. Ransom tells Lewis the whole story. They agree no one would believe it, so they decide to write the novel. The postscript is a letter from Ransom to Lewis criticizing the "mistakes" in the book.

Critical Evaluation:

Out of the Silent Planet is the first of three books that tell the story of Elwin Ransom. In the second book, *Perelandra* (1943), Ransom is transported to Venus, where he prevents the king and queen of that world from falling to temptation. In the third book, *That Hideous Strength* (1945), the focus shifts to Earth, where a team of scientists threaten England. In *Out of the Silent Planet*, C. S. Lewis writes a fairly straightforward narrative. What gives the book its unusual power is its mythic quality. The complexity of the Martian cultures, the sensitivity of the description, and the themes of courage, friendship, and charity all combine to create a cosmic vision that is moving, poetic, and uniquely beautiful.

Lewis intends his space trilogy to be a criticism of typical space operas and an answer to the scientific materialism of writers such as H. G. Wells, Olaf Stapledon, and J. B. S. Haldane. Lewis mocks science-fiction conventions—such as aliens that are insects or bug-eyed monsters, the need for page after page of pseudoscientific explanation, and constant conflict and adventure. Lewis addresses each of these conventions by contrasting Ransom's expectations with the reality he finds on Malacandra. Ransom expects cold, dark space; instead, as he travels he is flooded with light, "totally immersed in a bath of pure ethereal colour and of unrelenting though unwounding brightness." Ransom expects Martians to be characterized by "twitching feelers, rasping wings, slimy coils, curling tentacles"; instead, he meets aliens who are thoughtful, not physically repulsive, and civilized. Ransom expects science to be central to advanced cultures; instead, he finds a superior culture in which art, music, and poetry are integral to survival. Ransom expects nonstop, hair-raising adventure; instead, he is most moved by his experience as part of the ordinary, decent, daily life of the hrossa.

Lewis also uses the novel as a platform to condemn the notion of progress for its own sake, progress without regard for the worth of the individual. This is seen most clearly in the discussion between Weston and Oyarsa toward the end of the book. Ransom must act as interpreter between them, and through this ingenious device, Lewis shows that Weston's high-sounding goals—more technology, human progress, greater space exploration—are motivated by selfish ambition. Oyarsa emphasizes that it is impossible to love humanity as an abstract concept; one can only love each individual person. It is clear from everything Weston has said and done that he does not know how to do that.

In his letters, Lewis also makes clear that he intended his novels to elaborate Christian truths without using typical Christian symbols. In his description of Maleldil the Younger, for example, Lewis is making reference to Jesus Christ. In discussing the rebellion of the Oyarsa of Earth, Lewis is making reference to the rebellion of Satan. The silence that has come to the planet as a result of this great rebellion has separated Earth from the other planets, and has separated Earth's people from knowledge of their creator. Throughout the novel, Lewis is arguing that the peace, charity, artistry, and productivity of the hnau of Malacandra are the direct result of their harmony with God.

Diana Pavlac Glyer

Further Reading

Dickerson, Matthew T., and David O'Hara. *Narnia and the Fields of Arbol: The Environmental Vision of C. S. Lewis.* Lexington: University Press of Kentucky, 2009. Devotes a separate chapter to *Out of the Silent Planet* and the other two books in the Ransom trilogy, examining Lewis's ecological themes and his view of humankind's relation to nature.

Downing, David C. *Planets in Peril: A Critical Study of C. S. Lewis's Ransom Trilogy.* Amherst: University of Massachusetts Press, 1992. Exceptionally insightful, helpful, and complete study of the space trilogy. Begins with a discussion of Lewis's life, showing how his values and Christian faith influenced these books.

Edwards, Bruce L. *C. S. Lewis: Life, Works, and Legacy.* 4 vols. Westport, Conn.: Praeger, 2007. Edwards assembled this multivolume collection of essays to provide wide-ranging views of Lewis's life and work. Volume 1 focuses on his life, while volumes 2 through 4 discuss Lewis as a "fantasist, mythmaker, and poet," as well as an apologist, theologian, philosopher, scholar, teacher, and public intellectual.

Hooper, Walter. *C. S. Lewis: A Complete Guide to His Life and Works.* 1996. New ed. San Francisco: HarperSanFrancisco, 2005. A useful volume containing a 120-page biography, chronology, summaries of major works, sample reviews, explanations of key ideas, and a lengthy bibliography of Lewis's works.

Howard, Thomas. *Narnia and Beyond: A Guide to the Fiction of C. S. Lewis.* 1987. New ed. San Francisco: Ignatius Press, 2006. Contains a lengthy chapter about *Out of the Silent Planet*, providing a highly personal and energetic discussion.

Lobdell, Jared. *The Scientifiction Novels of C. S. Lewis: Space and Time in the Ransom Stories.* Jefferson, N.C.: McFarland, 2004. In the 1940's and 1950's, the word "scientifiction" was sometimes used to describe a literary genre now defined as either science fiction or fantasy literature; Lewis's Ransom novels and short story are examples of scientifiction. Lobdell devotes a chapter to an analysis of each of these four works, including *Out of the Silent Planet*, and also draws some general conclusions about the nature of Lewis's "Arcadian" science fiction and its place within English literature.

Walsh, Chad. *The Literary Legacy of C. S. Lewis.* New York: Harcourt Brace Jovanovich, 1979. Evaluates the strengths and weaknesses of Lewis's works, concluding that Lewis's best work is his fiction. Praises Lewis's ability to combine great literary skill with a distinctly Christian worldview.

Wilson, A. N. *C. S. Lewis: A Biography.* Reprint. New York: W. W. Norton, 2002. Chronological biography interpreting Lewis's life and work from a Freudian perspective. Depicts him as neither a saint nor a full-time Christian apologist but as a writer of real passions and a contradictory nature unbefitting the cult following that developed after his death. Traces many of his preoccupations to the sometimes traumatic experiences of his early childhood and comes to some controversial conclusions regarding several of Lewis's relationships.

The Outsiders

Author: S. E. Hinton (1948-   )
First published: 1967
Type of work: Novel
Type of plot: Social realism
Time of plot: 1960's
Locale: Tulsa, Oklahoma

Principal characters:
PONYBOY CURTIS, a fourteen-year-old boy
SODAPOP "SODA" and DARRYL "DARRY," his brothers
JOHNNY CADE,
DALLAS "DALLY" WINSTON,
KEITH "TWO-BIT" MATHEWS, and
STEVE RANDLE, the Greasers, poor kids from the East Side
    of town who are friends of the Curtis brothers
BOB SHELDON,
RANDY ANDERSON, and
SHERRI "CHERRY" VALANCE, the Socs, rich kids from the
    West Side of town

The Story:

After his parents are killed in a car accident, Ponyboy Curtis becomes increasingly frustrated with the rules imposed on him by his oldest brother, Darry. Ponyboy thinks Darry hates him. He does not realize that Darry's rules are meant to keep Ponyboy and his other brother, Soda, out of trouble. Darry is worried that if his brothers get in trouble, the three will be split up and sent to a boys' home.

Ponyboy walks home from the movies alone. He is followed by a red Corvair full of Socs, the rich kids in town. Ponyboy notices the car and worries that the Socs might try to beat him up. His fears are not unfounded, since his friend Johnny Cade had recently been assaulted by such a group. The Socs get out of the car and threaten to cut off Ponyboy's long, greasy hair. The Socs pin Ponyboy to the ground, and he screams for help. Ponyboy's brothers and friends hear his cries for help and come to his aid. Ponyboy is shaken up but not seriously injured. Darry criticizes Ponyboy for his lack of common sense. He says that Ponyboy should know better than to walk home alone.

Later, Ponyboy goes to the drive-in with his friends Dally Winston and Johnny Cade. Dally starts talking dirty to two rich girls sitting near them. The redhead, Cherry Valance, tells Dally to leave them alone. Dally backs off and leaves. Cherry asks Ponyboy if he intends to pick up where Dally left off. Ponyboy says he does not. The girls strike up a conversation with Ponyboy despite the fact that he is from the wrong side of town.

Dally returns and starts taunting the girls again. Cherry throws her drink on him. Dally will not stop bothering the girls until Johnny intervenes on their behalf. When Johnny tells him to stop, Dally stalks off and does not come back.

Cherry tells Ponyboy that she and her friend, Marcia, left their boyfriends because the boys were drunk. The girls ask Ponyboy and Johnny to sit with them. Two-Bit arrives before the movie is over, sneaks up on the group, and frightens Johnny. Cherry is surprised by the strength of Johnny's reaction, until Ponyboy tells her that Johnny was jumped by a group of Socs a few months before.

After the movie, Two-Bit convinces the girls to let him give them a ride home. As they are walking to Two-Bit's car, a Mustang full of Socs pulls up. Bob Sheldon and Randy Anderson, Cherry and Marcia's boyfriends, plead with the girls to come with them and stop walking with "the bums." Two-Bit takes offense at the comment. Cherry and Marcia agree to go with Bob and Randy in order to prevent a fight. Before Cherry leaves, she tells Ponyboy not to take it personally if she does not talk to him at school on Monday. Ponyboy understands: They are not in the same social class, and they never will be. Cherry also tells Ponyboy that she hopes she never sees Dally again, because she will fall for him if she does.

Two-Bit leaves. Ponyboy and Johnny continue walking home but stop at a vacant lot down the street to talk about meeting the girls. They wish that they lived in a place not divided into Greasers and Socs, where everyone is just plain and ordinary. The boys fall asleep in the vacant lot. Johnny wakes Ponyboy and tells him that he is going to stay in the lot instead of going home. Ponyboy realizes he has missed his curfew and rushes home.

When Ponyboy gets home, Darry is still awake, worried and angry. Ponyboy tries to explain, but Darry is tired of his excuses. When Soda tries to stick up for Ponyboy, Darry yells at him. Ponyboy defends Soda. The argument comes to an abrupt end when Darry slaps Ponyboy in the face. It is the first time Darry has used physical violence against his brother, and, though he tries to apologize, Ponyboy bolts from the house. He returns to the vacant lot, wakes Johnny up, and tells him that they are running away.

After running for several blocks, Ponyboy tells Johnny about the fight with Darry. Ponyboy thinks it over and suggests that they walk to a nearby park and back. He hopes that may provide enough time for him to cool off and go back home. While at the park, the two boys are confronted by Bob, Randy, and a couple of their friends. Bob and Randy want to pick a fight over the girls. Johnny notices the rings on Bob's fingers and realizes Bob is the Soc who assaulted him. Bob and the other Socs grab Ponyboy and begin to drown him in a fountain. Johnny pulls out a switchblade and kills Bob to save Ponyboy.

When Ponyboy comes to, he and Johnny go to Dally for help. Dally tells them to hide out in an abandoned church in Windrixville. He gives them some money and a gun and tells them that he will visit as soon as it is safe. Ponyboy and Johnny disguise themselves by cutting their hair short and bleaching Ponyboy's blond. They pass their time in Windrixville by playing cards and reading Margaret Mitchell's *Gone with the Wind* (1936).

Dally arrives nearly a week later and reports that a rumble is being planned between the Greasers and the Socs. Cherry Valance is spying for the Greasers. She has told Dally that she will testify that the Socs were drunk and looking for a fight and that the boys must have fought back in self-defense. When Johnny hears Dally's news, he decides that he and Ponyboy should go back to Tulsa and turn themselves in. They cannot run forever, he reasons, and it is not fair to keep Darry and Soda worrying about Ponyboy. Dally tries to talk Johnny out of returning because he does not want Johnny to end up in jail and become hardened by it: Dally does not want Johnny to end up like him.

The three are heading back home, when they notice that the church is on fire. Ponyboy jumps out of Dally's car to investigate. A group of kids on a school picnic and their teachers are outside the church, waiting for firemen to arrive. One of the teachers realizes that some of the kids are missing. They hear faint screams coming from inside the church. Ponyboy runs into the burning building, followed by Johnny and Dally. Together, they manage to rescue the children trapped inside. Dally pulls Ponyboy out of the church just before the roof collapses. Ponyboy passes out. When he comes to, he learns that a large timber fell on Johnny and broke his back. Dally escaped with a severely burned arm but is other-

wise all right. Ponyboy also learns that they are being lauded as heroes, which strikes him as funny since he is used to being called a "punk" or a "hood."

Johnny dies before the rumble. Dally cannot cope with Johnny's death. While the rest of the gang fights the Socs and wins, Dally robs a grocery store. He pulls a gun on the police who are pursuing him and is shot to death while his friends look on. Ponyboy is traumatized by his experiences and suffers a break with reality. He thinks that he is the one who killed Bob and that Johnny is still alive.

At a court hearing, the judge acquits Ponyboy based on Randy and Cherry's testimony. Ponyboy returns to school but has a hard time readjusting to "normal" life. His grades drop. Ponyboy's English teacher knows he is capable of doing better and offers him a chance to improve his grade by writing an essay for extra credit. Ponyboy chooses to write an essay telling the Greasers' side of the story. He opens the essay with the first sentence of the novel, "When I stepped out into the bright sunlight from the darkness of the movie house, I had only two things on my mind: Paul Newman and a ride home." Ponyboy's essay is the novel, *The Outsiders*.

Critical Evaluation:

S. E. Hinton broke new ground in young adult fiction with the publication of *The Outsiders*. The novel's gritty, realist portrayal of teenage life was striking, as was the fact that it was written by a teenaged woman. Hinton has stated that she wrote *The Outsiders* because it was the kind of story that she wanted to read. Tired of books filled with clichés and obligatory happy endings, she longed to write stories about real people with real problems, hoping to earn the respect of her audience by giving them stories to which they could relate.

Hinton started a trend in young adult writing, which became a battleground for readers, parents, teachers, and librarians. Debate raged over whether *The Outsiders* and the books that followed in its footsteps were too realistic for their own good. Such books portrayed issues such as drug and alcohol abuse, teen pregnancy, death, and divorce. Parents, educators, and critics of realism worried that they could encourage bad behavior in their readers. These criticisms tended to be based on simplistic analyses of books' content, so that *The Outsiders* was seen as a story about teenage violence, rather than a story about the characters and how they dealt with such violence. Instead of focusing on what Ponyboy learned as a result of being both a victim and an aggressor, some critics deemed the book to be without merit for glorifying violence, missing Hinton's message entirely.

Hinton explores many themes over the course of the novel, such as bridging the gap between rich and poor, honor among the lawless, and the retention of innocence. In Ponyboy's first meeting with Cherry Valance, she tells him "Things are rough all over." Later in the story, Ponyboy asks her if she can see the sunset on the West Side of town. When she says yes, he tells her that he can see it on the East Side, too. When Ponyboy first meets Cherry, he thinks of her as just another Soc, wondering how a cheerleader who drives a Corvette could possibly have problems. By the end of the story, Ponyboy's question about the sunset is an acknowledgment that, while the worlds they live in are very different, there are still things in each that are the same and that provide common ground.

The Greasers are honorable, even though society at large might not see them that way. They stick up for one another and will stand together to defeat enemies or authority figures. Hinton's characters perform acts of honorable sacrifice. Dally takes the blame for a crime he did not commit instead of turning in his friend, Two-Bit. Johnny kills Bob in order to save Ponyboy. Ponyboy and Johnny go into a burning building to save children in peril. Dally goes in to save them. Their devotion and loyalty to one another is admirable.

Perhaps the most important of the themes Hinton explores is that of the retention of innocence. When Johnny explains to Ponyboy what Robert Frost's poem means by "staying gold," he is trying to tell Ponyboy not to give up his innocence and become jaded by the world, as Dally has. Johnny hopes that if Ponyboy passes this lesson on to Dally, it might help Dally recapture some of his lost innocence, too. The message comes too late for Dally, but it is not too late for readers.

Despite its critics, *The Outsiders* became a commercial success and won numerous awards. In 1967, it was named one of the best teen books by the *New York Herald Tribune* and was also a *Chicago Tribune Book World* Spring Book

Festival Honor Book. In 1983, a film adaptation directed by Francis Ford Coppola was released. With more than fourteen million copies in print, *The Outsiders* is among the best-selling young adult novels of all time.

Martel Sardina

Further Reading

Carratello, John, and Patty Carratello. *A Guide for Using "The Outsiders" in the Classroom.* Westminster, Calif.: Teacher Created Materials, 2001. Contains lesson plans, activities, and quizzes to facilitate teaching the novel to middle-grade students.

Daly, Jay. *Presenting S. E. Hinton.* Boston: Twayne, 1989. A comprehensive analysis of Hinton's works. Contains an author biography, individual chapters focused on each of her young adult novels, literary criticism, and supplemental information about the film adaptations of her works.

Hinton, S. E. Interview. In *The Outsiders.* New York: Speak/Penguin Putnam, 2003. The 2003 edition contains a bonus interview with Hinton in which she discusses writing the novel.

_____. *Some of Tim's Stories.* New York: Speak/Penguin Group, 2007. Contains further interviews with Hinton, discussing her young adult novels, their film adaptations, and her later works.

Howard, Todd. *Understanding "The Outsiders."* San Diego, Calif.: Lucent Books, 2001. A comprehensive look at the novel, including literary criticism.

Wilson, Antoine. *The Library of Author Biographies: S. E. Hinton.* New York: Rosen, 2003. Provides an overview of Hinton's works. Contains an author interview, selected book reviews, and a list of the awards each of her books has received.

The Overcoat

Author: Nikolai Gogol (1809-1852)
First published: "Shinel," 1842 (English translation, 1923)
Type of work: Short fiction
Type of plot: Social realism
Time of plot: Early nineteenth century
Locale: St. Petersburg, Russia

Principal characters:
AKAKII AKAKIIEVICH BASHMACHKIN, a government clerk
PETROVICH, a tailor
A PERSON OF CONSEQUENCE, a bureaucrat

The Story:

In one of the bureaus of the government, there works a clerk named Akakii Akakiievich Bashmachkin. He is a short, pockmarked man with dim, watery eyes and reddish hair beginning to show spots of baldness. His grade in the service is that of perpetual titular councilor, a resounding title for his humble clerkship. He had been in the bureau for so many years that no one remembered when he had entered it or who had appointed him to the post. Directors and other officials come and go, but Akakii Akakiievich is always seen in the same place, in the same position, doing the same work: copying documents. No one ever treats him with respect. His superiors regard him with disdain, and his fellow clerks make him the butt of their rude jokes and horseplay.

Akakii Akakiievich lives only for his work, without thought for pleasure or his dress. His frock coat is no longer the prescribed green but a faded rusty color. Usually it has sticking to it wisps of hay or thread or bits of litter someone had thrown into the street as he was passing by, for he walks to and from work in complete oblivion of his surroundings. Reaching home, he gulps his cabbage soup and perhaps a bit of beef, in a hurry to begin transcribing papers he brings home from the office. He goes to bed soon after his labors are finished. Such is the life of Akakii Akakiievich, satisfied with his pittance of four hundred rubles a year.

Even clerks on four hundred a year, however, must protect themselves against the harsh cold of northern winters. Akakii Akakiievich owns an overcoat so old and threadbare that over the back and shoulders one can see through the material to the torn lining beneath. At last he decides to take the overcoat to Petrovich, a tailor who does a large business repairing the garments of petty bureaucrats. Petrovich shakes his head over the worn overcoat and announces that it is beyond mending, fit only for footcloths. For one hundred and fifty rubles, he says, he will make Akakii Akakiievich a new overcoat, but he will not touch the old one.

When he leaves the tailor's shop, the clerk is in a sad predicament. He has no money for an overcoat and little prospect of raising so large a sum. Walking blindly down the street, he fails to notice the sooty chimney sweep who jostles him, blacking one shoulder, or the lime that falls on him from a building under construction. The next Sunday, he sees Petrovich again and begs the tailor to mend his old garment. The tailor surlily refuses. Then Akakii Akakiievich realizes that he must yield to the inevitable. He knows that Petrovich will do the work for eighty rubles. Half of that amount he could pay with money he saved, one kopeck at a time, over a period of years. Perhaps in another year he could put aside a

like amount by doing without tea and candles at night and by walking as carefully as possible to save his shoe leather. He begins that very day to go without the small comforts he had previously allowed himself.

In the next year, Akakii Akakiievich has some unexpected luck when he receives a holiday bonus of sixty rubles instead of the expected forty, which he had already budgeted for other necessities. With the extra twenty rubles and his meager savings, he and Petrovich buy the cloth for the new overcoat—good, durable stuff with calico for the lining and catskin for the collar. After some haggling, Petrovich agrees to twelve rubles for his labor.

At last the overcoat is finished. Petrovich delivers it early one morning, and opportunely, for the season of hard frosts has already begun. Akakii Akakiievich wears the garment triumphantly to work. Hearing of his new finery, the other clerks run to the vestibule to inspect it. Some suggest that the owner ought to give a party to celebrate the event. Akakii Akakiievich hesitates but is saved from embarrassment when a minor official invites the clerks, including Akakii, to drink tea with him after work.

Wrapped in his warm coat, Akakii Akakiievich starts off to the party. It had been years since he had walked out at night, and he enjoys the novelty of seeing the strollers on the streets and looking into lighted shop windows.

The hour is past midnight when he leaves the party; the streets are deserted. His way takes him into a desolate square, with only the flickering light of a police sentry box visible in the distance. Suddenly, two strangers confront him and with threats of violence snatch his overcoat. The clerk runs to the police officer's box to denounce the thieves. The police officer merely tells him to report the theft to the district inspector the next morning. Almost out of his mind with worry, Akakii Akakiievich runs all the way home.

Akakii Akakiievich's landlady advises him not to go to the police but to lay the matter before a justice of the peace whom she knows. That official gives him little satisfaction. The next day his fellow clerks take up a collection for him, but the amount is so small that they decide to give him advice instead. They tell him to go to the Person of Consequence, who, they believe, could speed up the efforts of the police. Finally, Akakii Akakiievich secures an interview, but the very important person is so outraged by the clerk's unimportance that he never gives the caller an opportunity to explain his errand. Akakii Akakiievich walks sadly home through a blizzard, which gives him a quinsy and puts him to bed. After several days of delirium, in which he babbles about his lost overcoat and the Person of Consequence, he dies. A few days later, another clerk sits in his place and does the same work at the bureau.

Before long, rumors begin to spread through the city that a dead government clerk seeking a stolen overcoat had been seen near Kalinkin Bridge. One night a clerk from the bureau sees him and almost dies of fright. After Akakii Akakiievich begins stripping overcoats from passersby, the police are ordered to capture the dead man. One night, the police come close to arresting him, but the ghost vanishes so miraculously that thereafter the police are afraid to lay hands on any malefactors, living or dead.

One night, after a sociable evening, the Person of Consequence is on his way to visit a lady friend about whom his wife knows nothing. As he relaxes comfortably in his sleigh, he feels a firm grip on his collar. Turning, he is eye to eye with Akakii Akakiievich. In his fright, he throws off his overcoat and orders his coachman to drive him home at once. The ghost of Akakii Akakiievich must have liked the important person's warm greatcoat. From that time on he never again molested passersby or snatched away their overcoats.

Critical Evaluation:

Nikolai Gogol's "The Overcoat" was the inspiration for many major nineteenth century Russian authors. The impact of this work was summarized by Fyodor Dostoevski in a now-famous statement: "We all come from under Gogol's 'Overcoat.'" Gogol's fiction, his life (particularly in his social origins), his orientation toward Russian society, and his literary aspirations anticipated experiences common to many of his literary followers.

Gogol's life was aristocratic to the core, containing at the same time many of the most venerable and lackluster elements of this dominant Russian social class. He was the son of a Ukrainian noble who enjoyed some prestige and little wealth. Gogol early abandoned any thought of leading a bucolic life. Instead, he moved to St. Petersburg, the capital of czarist Russia, and attended a school designed to prepare him for a profession in the department of justice. A career in the Russian civil service was entirely in keeping with one of the most esteemed values of the nobility, service to society. Gogol hoped to achieve this goal as a bureaucrat rather than as an agronomist.

After less than a year, however, Gogol became intolerant of the tedium of the bureaucratic life and began to write. He led a dissident and cavalier life, wrote an epic poem and, after borrowing money from his mother, published his own work. The poem was unsuccessful. Distraught, Gogol purchased all the copies he could locate and burned them. Ironically, he framed his literary life with the burning of his work. Shortly before his death, he spent an entire evening casually tossing a manuscript of the second part of *Myortvye dushi* (1842, 1855; *Dead Souls*, 1887) into a stove.

Disenchanted with St. Petersburg, with his literature, and with his career, Gogol again borrowed from his nearly penniless mother and left Russia for Western Europe. Like other Russian writers who followed, Gogol spent most of his productive life in Western Europe. He died in Russia in 1852. At the time of his death, he had become a religious fanatic, and his death was the result of a grotesque religious fast. Even in his death, he was a model for future writers, such as Dostoevski and Leo Tolstoy, both of whom became religious zealots in their later lives.

Gogol's published works are relatively few in number. He is best remembered for *Dead Souls* and for the comedic drama *Revizor* (pr., pb. 1836; *The Inspector General*, 1890). The latter was Gogol's most successful work to appear during his lifetime. Spoofing the Russian bureaucracy, it brought cascades of laughter from the otherwise sober Czar Nicholas I. Of his shorter works, "The Overcoat" is the best known. Although Gogol rejected a career as a Russian bureaucrat, he never deviated from his commitment to the aristocratic ideal of service to society. In fact, age intensified his desire to better Russia, and he became convinced that he was chosen to deliver a great message to his countryfolk.

In "The Overcoat," Gogol tailors a trenchant and unmistakable, and often repeated, statement. The Russian bureaucracy, once the agent and symbol of enlightenment and change in Russia, had become in Gogol's time the instrument of oppression and sterility for both those it purported to serve and those who functioned within it. Akakii Akakiievich, possessing neither an inclination toward agriculture nor an ability therein, is a model bureaucrat: loyal and conscientious. He is faceless, too; his days are spent as a copier of government documents, each day exactly like all the others. Underpaid and unpraised, Akakii Akakiievich is like all of his bureaucratic contemporaries, the foundation on which the nineteenth century Russian state stands. He rarely comes in contact with the public. His vapid, tedious, and impersonal professional existence eradicates his personal life. Akakii Akakiievich is virtually isolated from society and from his own humanity.

When Akakii Akakiievich's overcoat is stolen, he is forced into the role of Ivan Q. Public, confronting an irritated and disinterested police magistrate who scolds him for his lack of respect and sends him away and unaided. In the end, Akakii's death can be attributed as much to the newly acquired knowledge that the Russian bureaucracy is cold and unfeeling as to the loss of his coat.

It was precisely bureaucracy's icy inability to serve Russian society that forced Gogol to forsake a life as a civil servant. Yet, he could not divorce himself from his own, however poorly practiced, aristocratic ideal to serve society. Unable to serve from within the state, Gogol left Russia for Western Europe; unable to serve as a bureaucrat, Gogol left justice for literature. Service through literature was difficult, and Gogol knew it. This perhaps irreconcilable problem accounts for an aspect of Gogol's literature that is unique—his humor.

Gogol fashions in "The Overcoat" a literary pattern ideally suited to the needs of Russian writers. The unique Gogolian technique is a mix of scathing satire and gentle humor; such a combination was conspicuously missing in Russian literature. While *Dead Souls* remains the author's humorous magnum opus, "The Overcoat" contains ample evidence of Gogol's gift of satire. Dostoevski's dictum is correct—Russian literature did come from Gogol's "The Overcoat." No Russian writer ever duplicated Gogol's sense of humor. Maybe other Russian authors did not need to, but when Gogol lined his works with humor, he was shielding himself from what he considered to be the insanities and the difficulties of his literary mission.

The difficulty, or even the impossibility, of service to Russia is one message contained in "The Overcoat." Gogol, like all premier writers, identified a social problem the resolution of which became a mission for future Russian authors. After Gogol, writers did not hesitate to challenge the inadequacy of the Russian state and society even when, as was frequently the case, they were censored or incarcerated for doing so.

"Critical Evaluation" by John G. Tomlinson, Jr.

Further Reading

Alissandratos, Julia. "Filling in Some Holes in Gogol's Not Wholly Unholy 'Overcoat.'" *Slavonic and East European Review* 68, no. 1 (January, 1990): 22-40. Examines the patterns and allusions relating to religious texts in Gogol's story. Argues that Gogol parodies Russian religious tradition.

Bojanowska, Edyta M. *Nikolai Gogol: Between Ukrainian and Russian Nationalism.* Cambridge, Mass.: Harvard University Press, 2007. Bojanowska analyzes Gogol's life and works in terms of his conflicted national identity. Gogol was born in Ukraine when it was part of the Russian Empire; describes how he was engaged with questions of Ukrainian nationalism and how his works present a bleak and ironic portrayal of Russia and Russian themes.

Chizhevsky, Dmitry. "About Gogol's 'Overcoat.'" In *Gogol from the Twentieth Century*, compiled by Robert A. Maguire. Princeton, N.J.: Princeton University Press, 1976. An insightful essay that shows how Gogol's seemingly humorous story points to a serious moral vision: The devil ensnares humans into obsession not only with exalted things in life, but also with trivia.

Eichenbaum, Boris. "How Gogol's 'Overcoat' Is Made." In *Gogol from the Twentieth Century*, compiled by Robert A. Maguire. Princeton, N.J.: Princeton University Press, 1976. Analyzes Gogol's stylistic technique, highlighting the performative nature of the narrative by focusing on its puns, hyperbole, and abrupt shifts in tone.

Fanger, Donald. *The Creation of Nikolai Gogol.* Cambridge, Mass.: Belknap Press, 1979. Underscores the problematic nature of Gogol's text. Noting the presence of several thematic patterns, this analysis concludes that "The Overcoat" remains elusive, pointing always to movement rather than resolution.

Graffy, Julian. *Gogol's "The Overcoat": Critical Studies in Russian Literature.* London: Bristol Classical Press, 2000. Provides an analysis of the story, a survey of its critical reception, and a discussion of the numerous ways it has been adapted to other media. One in a series of books designed for students.

Maguire, Robert A. *Exploring Gogol.* Stanford, Calif.: Stanford University Press, 1994. One of the most comprehensive studies of Gogol's ideas and entire writing career available in English. Includes a chronology, detailed notes, and an extensive bibliography.

Nabokov, Vladimir. *Nikolai Gogol.* 1944. Reprint. New York: Oxford University Press, 1989. A dazzling evocation of the stylistic and verbal idiosyncrasies of Gogol's story. Nabokov's commentary identifies the salient features of Gogol's style and suggests what kind of worldview this stylistic display reveals.

The Ox-Bow Incident

Author: Walter Van Tilburg Clark (1909-1971)
First published: 1940
Type of work: Novel
Type of plot: Regional
Time of plot: 1885
Locale: Nevada

Principal characters:
GIL CARTER, a ranch hand
CROFT, his friend
CANBY, a saloon keeper
TETLEY, a rancher
GERALD, his son
DAVIES, an old storekeeper
MARTIN, a young rancher

The Story:

Gil Carter, a cowpuncher, and his friend, Croft, ride into the little frontier town of Bridger's Wells. At Canby's saloon, they rein in their horses. Canby is alone at the bar. He serves Gil and Croft with silent glumness and tells them that Rose Mapen, the girl Gil is looking for, has gone to San Francisco. He also tells the two cowboys that all the local cowhands and their employers are on the lookout for rustlers who have been raiding the ranches in the valley. More than six hundred head of cattle have been stolen, and the ranchers are regarding one another with suspicion. Gil and Croft feel suspicion leveled at them when a group of riders and townsmen come into the bar.

Gil begins to play poker and wins one hand after another. The stakes and the bad feeling grow higher and finally erupt in a rough confrontation between Gil and a man named Farnley. Gil downs his opponent but is knocked unconscious when Canby hits his head with a bottle.

A rider arrives at the saloon with word that rustlers have killed Kinkaid, Farnley's friend. Farnley does not want to wait for a posse to be formed, but cooler heads prevail, among them old Davies, a storekeeper, and Osgood, the Baptist minister. Everyone there joins in the argument for and against immediate action. Davies sends Croft and a young cowboy named Joyce to ask Judge Tyler to swear in a posse before a lawless manhunt begins. The judge is not eager to do so in the absence of Risley, the sheriff, but Mapes, a loud, swaggering, newly appointed deputy, demands that he be allowed to lead the posse.

Meanwhile, the temper of the crowd grows sullen. Ma Grier, who keeps a boardinghouse, joins the mob. When Judge Tyler arrives, his long-winded oration against a posse stirs the men up more than anything else could have done. Davies takes over again and almost convinces the men they should disband. At that moment, however, Tetley, a former Confederate officer and an important rancher, rides up with the news that his Mexican herder has seen the rustlers.

Mob spirit flares up once again. Mapes deputizes the men in spite of Judge Tyler's assertion that a deputy cannot deputize others. The mob rides off in the direction of Drew's ranch, where Kinkaid had been killed. There the riders find the first trace of their quarry. Tracks show that three riders are driving forty head of cattle toward a pass through the range. Along the way, Croft talks to Tetley's sullen son, Gerald, who is not cut out to be a rancher, a fact ignored by his stern, domineering father. Croft thinks the boy appears emotional and unmanly.

The stagecoach suddenly appears over a rise. In the darkness and confusion, the driver thinks that the riders are attempting a holdup. He fires, hitting Croft high in the chest. When he learns his mistake, he pulls up his horses and stops. One of the passengers is Rose Mapen, the girl Gil had hoped to find in Bridger's Wells. She introduces the man with her as her husband. Gil is furious.

Croft has his wound tended and continues with the posse. On a tip from the passengers, the posse heads now for the Ox-Bow, a small valley high up in the range. Snow is falling by the time the riders reach the Ox-Bow. Through the darkness, they see the flicker of a campfire and hear the sound of cattle. Surrounding the campfire, they surprise the three men sleeping there—an old man, a Mexican, and a young, dark-looking man—and tie them up.

The dark-looking young man insists that there is some mistake. He says that he is Donald Martin and that he had moved into Pike's Hole three days earlier. One of the members of the posse, however, a man from Pike's Hole, claims he does not know Martin or anything about him. Martin begins to grow desperate. He demands to be taken to Pike's Hole, where his wife and two children are. The members of the posse are contemptuous. Only Davies tries to defend Martin, but Mapes soon silences the old storekeeper. The cattle are proof enough. Besides, Martin has no bill of sale. He claims that Drew sold him the cattle and had promised to mail him a bill of sale.

The posse wants an immediate hanging. Tetley wants to force a confession, but most of the riders say it is no kindness to make the three wait to die. Martin tells them that the Mexican is only his rider and that he knows little about him because the man speaks no English. The old man is a simple-minded fellow who had agreed to work for Martin for very little pay. Martin is permitted to write a letter to his wife. Shortly afterward, when it is discovered that he possesses Kinkaid's gun, the Mexican begins to speak English, claiming that he had found the gun.

Tetley appoints three of the posse—his milksop son, Farnley, and Ma Grier—to lead the horses away from the men, whose necks would then be caught in the nooses of the ropes tied to the overhanging limb of a tree. Martin, despairing, makes Davies promise to look after his wife, and he gives Davies the letter he had written, and a ring.

A fine snow continues to fall as the three are executed. The Mexican and the old man die cleanly. Martin, whose horse has been started slowly by Gerald, has to be shot by Farnley. Tetley hits his son with the butt of his pistol for bungling the hanging. Then the posse rides away. As they ride out of the Ox-Bow, they meet Sheriff Risley, Judge Tyler, Drew, and Kinkaid, who was not dead after all. The judge shouts that every member of the posse will be tried for murder. The sheriff, however, says that he cannot arrest a single man present for the murders because identity is uncertain in the swirling snow. He asks for ten volunteers to continue the search for the real rustlers.

Only old Davies seems moved by the affair, more so after he learns that Martin's story is true and that the cattle had been bought from Drew without a bill of sale. Nearly maddened, he gives the ring and letter to Drew, who promises to look after Martin's widow. After Croft and Gil return to Canby's saloon, Davies begins to moan to Croft. Davies convinces himself that he himself caused the hanging of the three men. Gil gets drunk. Later that day, Gerald Tetley hangs himself, and a few hours later his father also commits suicide. The cowhands take up a collection for Martin's widow. In their room at Canby's, Gil and Croft can hear Rose laughing and talking in the bar. They decide to leave town.

Critical Evaluation:

The Ox-Bow Incident begins as a Western horse-opera with all the stage settings and characters of a cowboy thriller, but it ends as a saga of human misery. The novel has the action and pace of a classic drama. The mob assumes the nature of a Greek chorus, now on one side, now on the other. The story rises toward an inevitable climax and, as it does so, forcibly states the harsh truth: The law of survival is linked to the curse of relentless cruelty. Walter Van Tilburg Clark made the Western thriller a novel of art.

Although set against a Nevada landscape in 1885, the novel's portrayal of mob justice is timeless. The tragedy in the novel involves not only the theme of innocent people wrongly punished but also the theme that unjust and cruel acts can be carried out by intelligent, moral persons who allow their sense of social duty to corrupt their sense of justice.

Bridger's Wells, Nevada, the initial setting for the novel's development, offered its citizens recreational diversions limited to eating, sleeping, drinking, playing cards, and fighting. Into that frontier setting stepped Gil Carter and Croft, who learn that rustlers had provided the place with an exciting alternative, lynching. Osgood, the Baptist minister from the only "working church" in town, realized early on that hot mob temper could subdue individual reason and sense of justice. In times of despair, reason and justice seem less attractive than immediate action. Bartlett, a rancher who found rustling a particularly vile threat, argued that "justice" often proved ineffective and worked too slowly to guarantee that guilty men would pay the penalties for their crimes. He was able to persuade twenty townspeople to form an illegal posse, even though none of the men he exhorted owned any cattle and only a few of them even knew the allegedly murdered man. One man, physically weak and unsound, won over the rest by deriding those among his listeners who opposed his argument. Notwithstanding their thoughtfulness, the words of reason spoken by the storekeeper Davies proved unsuccessful, especially against the renewed harangues of the self-important Major Tetley.

Major Tetley's son Gerald, whom his father forced to take part in the posse, painfully realized the weakness of individuals who were afraid to challenge the mob and felt that to resist would be to admit weakness. "How many of us do you think are really here because there have been cattle stolen, or because Kinkaid was shot?" he asked. In the absence of Sheriff Risley, who as the legally constituted police authority might have stopped the lynching, the formation of the illegal posse, the manhunt, and the lynchings all proceed with the inevitability of a Shakespearean tragedy.

In the eleventh hour, no gesture suggesting innocence could spare the doomed men. When Davies, in an effort to save the life of a man he believed was innocent, wanted to communicate Martin's emotional letter to his wife to the posse, Martin himself objected. He used the incident to make another point, that even an initial promise to preserve the integrity of his letter would have proved futile among men in whom conscience had failed as a measure of just conduct. In a moment where bravery might understandably have failed among men about to be hanged, the Mexican removed a bullet from his own leg, washed the wound and dressed it with a fire-heated knife. He tossed the knife into the ground within an inch of where its owner's foot would have been had he not, in fear, drawn quickly away. The Mexican, who smiled often at the proceedings, did so again, seeing in the posse the absence of the very bravery they thought they all possessed. The sympathy that Martin's letter and the Mexican's courage might otherwise have elicited never materialized, because most of the posse either had simply made up their minds about the prisoners' fate or had believed that the rest had.

Davies, the one man who had had the least to do with the hangings, and perhaps did most to prevent them, was himself plagued with guilt, which he felt did not apply to those such as Tetley, for "a beast is not to blame." Davies' sense of guilt and justice make him realize, as no one else did, how little he had actually done to prevent the hangings from taking place. He faced the realization that he let the three men hang because he was afraid and lacked the "only thing Tetley had, guts, plain guts." The sensitive man, lacking the brute convictions of his opposite, was rendered impotent. Davies' final confession was accompanied by laughter in the background.

The Ox-Bow Incident has no hero yet cries out for one in a world where the lessons of the Ox-Bow may not be remembered, much less learned. Inasmuch as the novel was written in 1937 and 1938, while Nazism bullied a world into submission, the novel presented a theme in step with domestic as well as world developments. Clark once said of *The Ox-Bow Incident*, "What I wanted to say was 'It can happen here.' It has happened here, in minor but sufficiently indicative ways, a great many times."

"Critical Evaluation" by Frank Joseph Mazzi

Further Reading

Andersen, Kenneth. "Form in Walter Van Tilburg Clark's *The Ox-Bow Incident.*" *Western Review* 6 (Spring, 1969): 19-25. Discusses literary devices Clark uses to give *The Ox-Bow Incident* its "clean, ordered, classical" structure. Analyzes the novel's proportions, dramatic sequencing of events, unified tone, and use of irony, nature imagery, and contrasting sounds.

Bates, Barclay W. "Clark's Man for All Seasons: The Achievement of Wholeness in *The Ox-Bow Incident.*"

Western American Literature 3 (Spring, 1968): 37-49. Finds a serious flaw in every character in *The Ox-Bow Incident* except Swanson, Rose Mapen's husband, who alone is free, guiltless, rational, eloquent, and in control.

Benson, Jackson J. *The Ox-Bow Man: A Biography of Walter Van Tilburg Clark.* Reno: University of Nevada Press, 2004. The first full-length biography of Clark, focusing on his life as a writer and teacher and his significant role in transforming Western literature. Chapter 4 is devoted to an examination of *The Ox-Bow Incident* and the Western novel.

Kich, Martin. *Western American Novelists.* Vol. 1. New York: Garland, 1995. Provides a brief account of Clark's career and an extensive, annotated bibliography containing detailed commentary about the reviews of Clark's novels and short stories. Also includes an annotated list of reference works with entries on Clark and books with chapters on his fiction.

Laird, Charlton, ed. *Walter Van Tilburg Clark: Critiques.* Reno: University of Nevada Press, 1983. A collection of original material by Clark and evaluations of his work by several critics, most notably Wallace Stegner on "Clark's Frontier" and Robert B. Heilman on justice, male camaraderie, communities in opposition, and artistic techniques in *The Ox-Bow Incident.*

Lee, L. L. *Walter Van Tilburg Clark.* Boise, Idaho: Boise State College Press, 1973. Regards *The Ox-Bow Incident* as more than an anti-Western novel. Analyzes ambiguities and compares and contrasts major characters in the novel and their complex responses to physical and moral courage, the limits of nature as a force for good, and justice. A brief work.

Westbrook, Max. *Walter Van Tilburg Clark.* New York: Twayne, 1969. Analyzes *The Ox-Bow Incident* not as a novel against lynching but as a tragedy of those who willingly alienate themselves from the "grace of archetypal reality."

Yardley, Jonathan. "Broadening the Western's Horizons." *The Washington Post*, April 7, 2007. A review of *The Ox-Bow Incident*, in which Yardley provides biographical information about Clark and concludes that the novel is "proof that the story of the West can rise above cliche and become the material of literature."

P

The Painted Bird

Author: Jerzy Kosinski (Josek Lewinkopf, 1933-1991)
First published: 1965
Type of work: Novel
Type of plot: Social morality
Time of plot: 1939-1945
Locale: Eastern Europe

Principal characters:
THE YOUNG BOY, a war refugee
MARTA, an old woman with whom the boy first lives
OLGA, a wise old woman who saves the boy from death
LEKH, a peasant who traps and sells birds
GARBOS, a sadistic farmer who tries to kill the boy
EWKA, a young woman who introduces the boy to sex
GAVRILA, a Soviet army political officer who teaches the boy to read
MITKA, a Russian sniper who teaches the boy self-reliance
THE SILENT ONE, a resident of the orphanage where the boy is placed after the war

The Story:

In fear of Nazi reprisals, the parents of a six-year-old boy send the youngster to a distant village. The parents lose touch with the man who had placed the child in the village, and when the boy's foster mother dies, the young boy, left on his own, begins a series of travels from village to village. Considered to be either a Jew or a Roma (Gypsy) because of his dark hair and olive skin, the boy is treated horribly by the brutal and ignorant peasants he meets in his travels.

The young boy first lives in the hut of Marta, a disabled and superstitious old woman. When she dies of natural causes, the boy accidentally burns down her house. He is saved from villagers, who want to kill him, by Olga, a woman called "the Wise" for her knowledge of folk medicine. After being tossed into the river by the villagers and carried downstream on an inflated catfish bladder, the young boy lives with a miller and his wife, and witnesses a scene of unspeakable brutality. Jealous of a young farmhand's attraction to his wife, the miller gouges out his eyes with a spoon. The boy runs away and finds refuge with Lekh, who traps and sells birds, and who is in love with Ludmila. When villagers kill Ludmila, Lekh is heartbroken, and the young boy is forced to flee again.

The boy next stays with a carpenter and his wife who are afraid that the boy's black hair will attract lightning to their farm. Whenever there is as storm, the carpenter drags the boy out to a field and chains him to a heavy harness. When the carpenter threatens to kill him, the boy leads him to an abandoned bunker and pushes him into a sea of rats. Next, the young boy stays with a blacksmith who is helping the partisans; when the blacksmith is killed, the boy is turned over to German soldiers, but the one charged with his execution lets him escape into the woods. The young boy finds a horse with a broken leg and returns it to a farmer, who briefly shelters the boy, but he is forced to escape again when he witnesses a murder at a wedding celebration.

The terror is unrelenting. The boy is now staying with a giant farmer and first witnesses the trains carrying Jews to the death camps. A Jewish girl is found along the tracks. She is kept at the house next door, and the boy witnesses her gang rape and murder. When Germans search the village for more Jews, he flees, but is captured and given to an old priest, who delivers him to Garbos, a sadistic farmer with a huge and vicious dog named Judas. Garbos beats the boy daily and then hangs him from two hooks over Judas, hoping that he will fall and be killed by the dog. Garbos is afraid of killing the boy himself, for religious reasons. Meanwhile, the boy had been taking religious instruction from the old priest, but one day, as an acolyte, he trips and drops the missal during a service. The enraged congregation throws the boy into a large manure pit. At this point, the boy loses his voice.

The boy escapes again and lives with another cruel farmer named Makar and his family. The daughter, Ewka, initiates the boy into sex—what he thought was love. He witnesses Makar forcing the girl into sexual acts with her brother and a goat, and loses his love for Ewka. He escapes on skates he had made, but a gang of boys captures him and throws him into a hole in the frozen river. He is saved by a woman named Labina, but she dies. The eastern front of the war is pushing closer, and the boy witnesses another gruesome scene. A band of Kalmuks—mostly Soviet deserters aligned with the Germans—takes over a village and wantonly rapes and slaughters its inhabitants. The boy's first moment of stability comes when the advancing Soviet army captures and executes the Kalmuks and adopts the boy. He becomes a kind of mascot to Gavrila, the political officer of the regiment, and Mitka, a crack sniper. Gavrila teaches the boy to read and explains socialism to him, while Mitka teaches the boy revenge. When several Soviet soldiers are killed by drunken villagers, Mitka enacts his own vengeance with his high-powered rifle.

World War II ends, and the boy reluctantly leaves his Russian friends to be placed in an orphanage in the city from which he was first exiled. Six years pass; the boy is now twelve years old. The city has been damaged in the war, but not more severely than the children in the orphanages. The narrator befriends another orphan named the Silent One, and together they wander the city. When the Silent One sees the boy humiliated by a peasant merchant, he causes a terrible train wreck in a failed attempt to kill the man.

The boy is finally located by his parents, but he is not ready for the reconciliation, and he is still unable to speak. He is taken to the mountains for his health, and he learns to ski. He wakes up in a hospital room after a skiing accident, and picks up the phone and begins to speak. His speech convinces him that he is alive, and able to communicate.

Critical Evaluation:

The Painted Bird has emerged as one of the most powerful novels about World War II and about the Holocaust. Since it only obliquely deals with both events, the novel is a kind of allegory for the senseless cruelty and brutality of any war. Jerzy Kosinski claimed, falsely, that the novel was based on his own experiences. Kosinski was not averse to creating fiction in more than one realm; he was candid about this practice. The point of Kosinski's claim, it may be argued, is that the book's unspeakable brutalities are realistic—indeed, they are much less than what happened.

Characterization is notably thin in *The Painted Bird*, and even the narrator is two-dimensional. The scenes that he narrates are, however, often overwhelming, and the power of the novel comes in large part from its simple language and imagery. The point of view and sentence structure are remarkably simple. (Kosinski once claimed that he learned English writing the novel, which may explain some of its directness.) Such simple language only makes the horror greater: There is no complex linguistic shield that protects readers from the violence. What makes the events of the narrative even starker and more horrible is that there is no adult moral perspective to condemn the primitive or animalistic behavior of the characters. The narrator is a young boy with little understanding of what is happening to him, and Kosinski does not provide readers with an intermediary.

At one level, this short, episodic novel is an allegory. Kosinski has written that the novel is a fairy tale experienced by a child rather than told to him, and this is an apt description. Each incident in *The Painted Bird* can be considered as a stepping stone in an allegorical bildungsroman, or novel of education. In each encounter, the boy learns another lesson, only to discard it for a new lesson in the following chapter or incident—religion from the priest, politics from Gavrila, vengeance from Mitka and the Silent One, and so on. The final answer with which Kosinski leaves readers is ambiguous. At the end, the boy is losing the speechlessness that the horror of the world forced him into. There is evil in the world, surely, and, as the boy has seen, neither the religious nor the political solution negates it—in fact, they often exacerbate it. The only thing that is certain is the individual.

At another level the novel is about not merely an individual boy but also the Holocaust of World War II. *The Painted Bird* can be read as one of the most powerful indictments of the madness and terror of the Holocaust in literature. Although the horrors depicted in *The Painted Bird* are much less brutal than the actuality—no death camps or gas ovens are in the novel—they are horrible for their starkness and immediacy; they are the concrete and individual horrors of one alien child in a world gone mad.

The novel's major thematic question is the one at the center of the book of Job and other classic pieces of literature: What is one to make of the evil of the world? Kosinski has no clear answer—except that the novel, with all its horror, is its own answer. The boy begins to speak again; the novel is testimony to what he has witnessed—the powerful communication is that *The Painted Bird* is.

For all its realistic detail, the novel also has a symbolic meaning. A number of incidents in the novel have this symbolic quality—the story to which the title makes reference, for example. The painted bird is an apt symbol for the boy himself. Lekh captures a bird, paints it, and releases it. The bird's own flock, not recognizing it, pecks the bird to death. This bird also represents all of those who are marked as aliens and who thus are destroyed—including the millions in the death camps of World War II.

Animal imagery pervades the story. In chapter 1 alone, for example, there are stories of a pigeon among the chickens, a snake crawling out of its skin, and a squirrel set on fire by village boys. This imagery conveys the proximity of animal and human life. Kosinski's novel, in language and theme, forces readers to confront the potential horror of human behavior, without recourse to easy answers.

David Peck

Further Reading

Everman, Welch D. *Jerzy Kosinski: The Literature of Violation.* San Bernardino, Calif.: Borgo Press, 1991. Everman maintains that in *The Painted Bird*, Kosinski intends to show "that the boy's experience is not unique; what happened to him also happened to many others and could happen again to anyone."

Gladsky, Thomas. "Jerzy Kosinski: A Polish Immigrant." In *Living in Translation: Polish Writers in America*, edited by Halina Stephan. Atlanta: Rodopi, 2003. Focuses on Kosinski's acculturation to American culture and how his writing is influenced by having lived in two very different countries—the democratic United States and a totalitarian Poland.

Kosinski, Jerzy. *Notes of the Author on "The Painted Bird."* 3d ed. New York: Scientia-Factum, 1967. In this pamphlet, Kosinski explains the novel as made up of "fairy tales *experienced* by the child, rather than *told* to" the child.

Lavers, Norman. *Jerzy Kosinski.* Boston: Twayne, 1982. Lavers identifies the themes of freedom, revenge, and education, identifying *The Painted Bird* as a picaresque bildungsroman.

Lazar, Mary. *Through Kosinski's Lenses: Identity, Sex, and Violence.* Lanham, Md.: University Press of America, 2007. Lazar interviewed Kosinski scholars and friends to write this examination of the themes of identity, sex, and violence in Kosinski's work. The book includes excerpts from those interviews, as well as a bibliography and an index.

Lilly, Paul R. *Words in Search of Victims: The Achievement of Jerzy Kosinski.* Kent, Ohio: Kent State University Press, 1988. Lilly maintains that Kosinski's fiction "is about the art of writing fiction" and *The Painted Bird* is "primarily a book about language testing."

Lupack, Barbara Tepa, ed. *Critical Essays on Jerzy Kosinski.* New York: G. K. Hall, 1998. Collection of reviews of Kosinski's novels, including Elie Wiesel and Robert Coles's reviews of *The Painted Bird*, as well as essays analyzing this novel and Kosinski's other works.

Sherwin, Byron L. *Jerzy Kosinski: Literary Alarmclock.* Chicago: Cabala Press, 1981. Sherwin argues that "Kosinski prefers to convey the horror of the Holocaust by shocking us into feeling the terror of a single individual rather than by asking us to try abstractly to comprehend the pain, death and suffering of . . . millions."

Vice, Sue. "Autobiographical Fiction: Jerzy Kosinski *The Painted Bird*." In *Holocaust Fiction*. New York: Routledge, 2000. Vice examines *The Painted Bird* and other Holocaust novels that were both praised and deplored by critics and describes how these controversial receptions affected the ethics and practice of Holocaust literature.

Palace Walk

Author: Naguib Mahfouz (1911-2006)
First published: Bayn al-qaṣrayn, 1956 (English translation, 1990)
Type of work: Novel
Type of plot: Historical realism
Time of plot: 1917-1919
Locale: Cairo

Principal characters:
AL-SAYYID AHMAD ABD AL-JAWAD, a merchant-grocer
AMINA, his wife
FAHMY and KAMAL, their sons
AISHA and KHADIJA, their daughters
YASIN, Ahmad's son from a previous marriage
ZAYNAB, Yasin's wife

The Story:

Al-Sayyid Ahmad Abd al-Jawad is a middle-class merchant who hypocritically makes his family adhere to the strictest interpretations of the Qur'ān, keeping his wife and two daughters cloistered and his sons harshly disciplined. For his own delight, he partakes of the sexual, musical, and culinary pleasures of Cairo—singing, dancing, drinking, and cavorting with his friends until late at night.

Ahmad's son Yasin, from an embarrassing previous marriage, is physically and morally a replica of his father, a youth who had discovered his father's licentious behavior through a courtesan he visits. A younger son, Fahmy, is attracted to the neighbor's daughter, Maryam, whom he glimpses from their closely placed rooftops. At the same time, however, Fahmy is repulsed at the idea that she might be purposely and immodestly showing herself to him. In the meantime, Ahmad has been avidly courting Maryam's mother as she shops in his store.

Ahmad's wife, Amina, lives a life of solitude and austerity. She is representative of Muslim wives in Egypt in 1917, shut in behind household walls. Still, she manages to find some pleasure in her daily life: the morning baking of bread, the coffee-hour conversations with her children, the childish conflicts among the siblings as they joke and tease and share experiences, the unspoken but shared fears of Ahmad and his crushing righteousness, the boys' desire to escape outside the home, and the girls' longing for marriage.

Amina is a good wife and a good mother, yet her religious piety creates trouble in her life. One day, she leaves the house, convinced by her children to do so, after Ahmad travels on business to Port Said. She leaves the house without permission so that she can pray at the Sayyidna al-Husayn mosque, a holy place she has longed to see. Overcome by the experience and by fear, she faints in the heat and is hit by a car, fracturing her collarbone; she requires a doctor, so she cannot hide from Ahmad's wrath. His anger grows as he holds it in until her collarbone heals. Then, to the shock of the entire family, he sends her home to her mother, where she remains in limbo for weeks. She is told to come back to her family so that she can assist with the wedding of daughter Aisha.

Through the latticework of her home, Aisha had noticed the men passing in the street and dared to take a special interest in a young officer who had broken the rules by looking up at the women's quarter. Aisha received a marriage proposal from the young man, but her father had refused it because he had not chosen the prospective suitor himself. Later, however, a worthy suitor respectful of her father follows the rules and an engagement is arranged.

Amina's return home for the wedding heals the feuding between the quarrelsome sisters, embarrasses the hedonistic Ahmad because all the men know that the hired singer, Jalila, is a former lover of his (as she made publicly clear), and opens the innocent and idealistic Fahmy's eyes to the hypocrisy of his father. The same night, a lustful and drunk Yasin tries to rape the sleeping household servant, Umm Hanafi, whose screams alert an angry Ahmad. He expels her, not Yasin, from his home. Yasin is quickly married off to Zaynab, the pampered daughter of an old friend of Ahmad.

Once Yasin's lust has been sated, he begins to follow the ways of his father. Zaynab, accustomed to more freedom and more attention than Amina could ever imagine, leaves Yasin for good. Yasin has made contact with his mother, who is living with a lover. Kamal, the youngest of the family, upsets them all by becoming fascinated by Australian soldiers who set up camp along Palace Walk. The soldiers make it more and more difficult for the men of the neighborhood to spend as much time away from home as they are accustomed to. The women in the family, however, gain the approval of their husbands to visit each other, which means trips outside the home.

Fahmy, in contrast to Kamal, finds the occupation insulting, especially when the armistice ending World War I fails to end the British occupation. He participates in peaceful dissent by distributing anti-British pamphlets and marches in a rally that ends in violent action by the military. He is killed in the violence and becomes a martyr in the cause of nationalism and political independence.

Critical Evaluation:

Palace Walk provides a panoramic history of Egypt through the lives and fortunes of one family over three generations. The story illuminates Egyptian society as it changes from a feudal/medieval way of life to colonial life after the British invasion of World War I and to the political upheaval that leads to modern nationalism. The novel's Arabic title means "between two palaces," or "between the two palaces," phrases indicative of what happens to the family who follows its own fortunes: This family will be caught between a static, regional perspective and the changing national perspective; and between a culture basically untouched by modernity and the modern British colonial-administrative machine that challenges Egyptian assumptions.

Because the novel form had not existed in Arabic literature at the time Naguib Mahfouz wrote *Palace Walk*, the author prepared himself for the task by systematically reading the works of the major nineteenth century realistic novels of Fyodor Dostoevski, Charles Dickens, Honoré de Balzac, and Émile Zola. Though beginning with imitation of European novelistic forms, he adapted the form to a new culture, creating dialogue that captures the indirection of Egyptian discourse, which buries communication in ritual formulas of politeness, aphorisms, and quotations from the Qur'ān. In doing so he makes a foreign, unknown world gradually familiar.

The novel's slow, repetitive pace, although perfect for capturing the stasis of prenationalist Egypt, can be disturbing to modern readers; the action becomes exciting only as the children of the family gradually discover the hypocrisy of their father, the varieties of acceptable behavior outside the restrictive walls of Palace Walk, and nationalistic fervor. Male tyranny, hypocrisy, and the social and cultural changes wrought by British occupation are the dominant themes of the novel.

Mahfouz effectively and daringly portrays the damaging effects of medieval misogynist views (woman is the root of all evil) that determine the total dominance of husbands over their wives and of fathers over their daughters. Dominance over girls and women is assumed as an absolute right, sanctioned by the Qur'ān, and is enforceable by physical violence. Fahmy, the idealistic son, fears the potential evil of the women in his family without the strong dominance of his father. Fahmy's mother, Amina, is convinced that tyranny and manhood are equivalents.

Ahmad's goal at home is to make "his" women obedient and to inspire fear in his sons to the point that no one dares to look directly at his face. He hopes his sons will learn pride in the advantages they possess as young men, but he also insists that they obey him. The family hierarchy Mahfouz paints is medieval in its divisions, levels of power, and stasis, yet it promotes male self-indulgence as the norm. Men eat voraciously, drink and smoke until in a stupor, womanize and carouse half the night while telling dirty jokes with friends, sing romantic songs, and plot the seduction of widowed women. During the day they spy on neighboring women (despite rules against doing so) and plot accidental meetings, showing off their wealth with ostentatious displays of jewelry and attire. Ahmad's eldest son attempts rape twice, and Ahmad's fatherly solution is to quench his son's lustful violence with marriage. Mahfouz's males are not accustomed to introspection or self-analysis. They live in the moment, making statements such as the following: "Manners are better than learning."

Mahfouz also paints so clearly the intellectual and physical cloistering of wives and daughters, whose monotonous world is visible through a wooden latticework cage with tiny round openings that protect them from being seen on the street (an architectural version of the veil). Amina and her daughters can see a cistern, a school, and Palace Walk, and minarets in the distance. Amina is permitted trips outside the home only to visit her mother under her husband's supervision; as an alternative, Amina must depend on her youngest son to provide a view of the outside world, before he must move from the women's quarters. Obedience and subservience are Amina's fate. She and her daughters are uneducated and know almost nothing of the outside world (they think the earth stands on the back of an ox and assume the British are neighbors); only rudimentary news and knowledge can be gleaned from the light conversations of the boys and men of the family. Women are relegated to household duties: food preparation, cleaning, sewing, bearing and caring for infants and children. A daughter's marriage is at her father's discretion. Ahmad, in fact, asserts that no daughter of his will marry a man until he himself is satisfied that the suitor's primary motive for marrying her is a sincere desire to be related to Ahmad.

Having established this static, male-dominated world, Mahfouz relates the story of the British occupation and the nationalistic movement for an independent Egypt. Fahmy is virtually the only character in *Palace Walk* to speak for the modern world; when he embraces the concept of revolution or rebellion against English colonialism, he also is developing a global perspective. Egypt is not a collection of Islamic believers, as many of the other characters define their society, and certainly not simply an extended family, as his mother Amina sees it. Rather, Egypt is a modern nation-state, defined perhaps by Islamic and Arabic culture but sharing the human rights and liberties enjoyed by other nations. In the eyes of Fahmy and his cohort of student rebels, the globe's common political and social practices should guide Egypt's future, not provincial social and religious folkways. Aptly, in Shakespearean fashion, for Mahfouz, the disintegrating family parallels the disintegrating society.

Gina Macdonald and Andrew Macdonald

Further Reading

Dyer, Richard. "Timeless Rhythms of an Egyptian Family." *Boston Globe*, February 28, 1990, p. 43. A brief but insightful introduction to the novel, providing background on the author's preparation to produce the book, the difficulty of the translator to accurately render classical Arabic, and an overall view of the movement of the novel. Finds Mahfouz effectively capturing a society and a way of thinking.

El-Enany, Rasheed. Review of *Palace Walk*, by Naguib Mahfouz. *Third World Quarterly*, January, 1990. El-Enany contrasts the stilted, dated English of the translation of *Palace Walk* with the modern, spirited diction of the Arabic text.

Kilpatrick, Hilary. *The Modern Egyptian Novel: A Study in Social Criticism*. London: Ithaca Press, 1974. Examines Mahfouz's novels in the context of contemporary Egyptian fiction. Part of St. Antony's Middle East series.

Milson, Menahem. *Najib Mahfuz: The Novelist-Philosopher of Cairo*. New York: St. Martin's Press, 1998. A good introductory work for the beginning student of Mahfouz, offering insight into the author's work and life.

Moussa-Mahmoud, Fatma. "Depth of Vision: The Fiction of Naguib Mahfouz." *Third World Quarterly* 11 (April, 1989): 154-166. Presents a first-rate, comprehensive study of Mahfouz's life and work.

Najjar, Fauzi M. "Islamic Fundamentalism and the Intellectuals: The Case of Naguib Mahfouz." *British Journal of Middle Eastern Studies* 25 (May, 1998): 139-168. A discussion of the confusion in the Muslim world of literature and theology, a view that led to Mahfouz's stabbing. His novels, in contrast to this assumption, deal with questions of social justice, abuses of power, and the exploitation of the weak by the strong, all themes in *Palace Walk* as well.

Stock, Raymond. "Naguib Mahfouz Dreams—and Departs." *Southwest Review* 92, no. 2 (2007): 172-179. Traces how Mahfouz's dreams blend realism and surrealism as a storytelling technique.

Pale Fire

Author: Vladimir Nabokov (1899-1977)
First published: 1962
Type of work: Novel
Type of plot: Parody
Time of plot: Late 1950's and early 1960's
Locale: Northeastern United States and Zembla

Principal characters:
DR. CHARLES KINBOTE, a scholar
JOHN FRANCIS SHADE, a poet
SYBIL SHADE, John Shade's wife
GERALD EMERALD, a university instructor
JACK GREY or JACOB GRADUS, a madman and assassin

The Story:

Pale Fire purports to be a scholarly edition of the poem *Pale Fire* by the American poet John Shade. There is, as part of the novel, an editor's foreword, then the poem itself, followed by five times as many pages of editorial commentary as there are pages to the poem, and finally an index. The editor, Charles Kinbote, was a one-time colleague of Shade at Wordsmith University in New Wye, which is in Appalachia. Kinbote tells a story, or rather a number of stories, all by indirection—for there is no simple "and then" of events in the novel.

The primary story is realistic, introduced by Kinbote in the foreword and carried on in the rest of the editorial apparatus and in Shade's poem. In the poem, an autobiographical meditation written in loose, rhymed couplets, Shade recounts not only his own life and his love for his wife, Sybil, but his daughter's life and death. His daughter was an unattractive, intelligent girl, too sensitive for the world, who ended up, probably, killing herself. Kinbote may actually have been named V. Botkin—and he probably is quite mad. Newly arrived as a teacher at Wordsmith, he rents the house of Judge Goldsworth, next to Shade's house. Kinbote does not fit well into the academic world. Most of his colleagues, especially a young teacher named Gerald Emerald, make fun of his appearance and his manners. Moreover, Kinbote, who is gay, has a series of unfortunate love affairs. An admirer of Shade's work, Kinbote forces himself upon Shade and his wife, Sybil. Shade is working on his new poem; Kinbote believes that he has given Shade the major subject for the poem. He is to be cruelly disappointed.

Another madman, Jack Grey, once sentenced to prison by Judge Goldsworth but having escaped from an asylum for the criminally insane, arrives in New Wye, intent upon revenge. Grey mistakes Shade for the judge and shoots him. Kinbote believes, and Mrs. Shade accepts as truth, that Kinbote tried to save Shade. She gives Kinbote permission to edit the poem. Grey commits suicide in prison. Kinbote flees, going to the western United States, taking the poem with him. There he writes the notes and the index.

The most fascinating, fantastic, and perhaps "real" story in the novel is the one that Kinbote tells in his foreword, commentary, and index. This story is the subject that Kinbote thought Shade was writing about. Kinbote uses his scholarly apparatus (the foreword, commentary, and so on) to give his autobiography or, at least, what he believes is his autobiography. Disappointed to find that the great story he gave Shade is not the obvious matter of Shade's poem, Kinbote, as an artist-reader himself, "rewrites," or rather interprets, the poem to say what it should have said. Shade's poem is warped into something monstrous.

Gradually it is revealed that Kinbote is Charles Xavier the Beloved, deposed king of Zembla, a "distant northern land," somewhere in Europe. Zembla is a happy, romantic place, indeed a dream place, with a comfortably rigid social hierarchy, that is, a king, nobles, a small and efficient middle class, a happy peasantry, and the usual malcontents, the stirrers-up of trouble. Charles Xavier pretends to be merely an American academic to escape the far left, totalitarian revolutionaries who brought about the revolution in Zembla. They fear the king's return and are intent upon his assassination. Jack Grey, furthermore, is no madman but a man of many disguises and names, among them Jacob Gradus and de Grey, a committed believer in the revolution, an assassin sent by the revolutionaries and who accidentally kills Shade while trying to kill Charles.

Charles Xavier (or Charles Kinbote), telling about his life before he came to Wordsmith, asserts that he is truly beloved by most of his people but regretfully unsuccessful in his personal life, especially as a husband, because he is gay. Charles Xavier is a clever, attractive, learned man, but was harassed by continual palace intrigues. He was brought to marry in hopes of fathering an heir but could not consummate the marriage. The revolutionists, unsupported of course by the Zemblan people but backed by a giant neighboring state, dethroned and imprisoned the king.

The king, with the aid of friends and courtiers, escaped in a marvelous, operatic fashion, leaving everything behind, including his identity. After he arrived in America, other friends helped him to this new identity, that of Charles Kinbote, a scholarly authority on Zemblan literature. The Shadows, a secret group inside the Zemblan revolutionaries, sent Grey (Jacob Gradus), and the fate of Shade is intertwined with that of Charles Xavier. One of these Shadows, the one who gives Gradus the American address of Charles Xavier, is named Izumrudov, which is a Russian word for "emerald," linking Izumrudov with Gerald Emerald.

Critical Evaluation:

Many of the first critical studies of Vladimir Nabokov concentrated upon the form of his work, to the neglect of its human content. Nabokov himself contributed to this approach. His work seems to argue that art is a kind of magnificent play, denying that there was a "human interest" story to be found in good art. Nabokov personally was deeply caring about other human beings; his wife was of Jewish descent, and he was bitterly opposed to all racism, not just anti-Semitism. Politically, he was antifascist and, because he had been forced into exile and in a sense deprived of his beloved Russian language by the Communist revolution in Russia, anticommunist. Extremes of the political spectrum are what he regarded with distaste. They were, to Nabokov, not opposites but mirrors of each other, external controls over human beings.

Pale Fire is, at bottom, humanist and even realistic. Although ludic, it is more than mere form. The characters, despite their many qualities that call attention to the novel's satiric and ludic design, also exemplify differing points of view on the human condition. Nabokov also never denies the reality of the world. It exists and can be talked about. In his art there is no distinction between form and content; the way a story is told is necessarily a way of understanding and examining human existence. *Pale Fire* is a complex, experimental work and its messages are not simple. It can be read as a case study, as a parody of academic criticism—for example, of Nabokov's own editing of Alexander Pushkin's *Evgeny Onegin* (1825-1832, serial; 1833, book; *Eugene Onegin*, 1881), or of critical evaluations in general—or a prefiguring of modern deconstructionist criticism. All of these readings are correct, but they are also limiting.

The novel is constructive rather than deconstructive. Language and the structure find and create connections, uncovering and discovering reality and making order of that reality. At the same time, the novel shows that language cannot grasp all the complexities of existence. If Charles Kinbote is only a madman, the novel is merely a case study and says little about other human beings. Granted, the story Kinbote tells is too fantastic to be accepted as that of a sane person. *Pale Fire* is a madman's story, as far as the everyday world is concerned. It is not "story," however, with which Nabokov is concerned. The novel is a fiction: All of its stories are made up; it is through the imagination, which deals in fictions, that one understands. The book eschews nihilism and the absurd, despite its game-playing and craziness. Ultimately, it is about how the human imagination creates. For this reason, it is a humanistic novel.

Kinbote, in rewriting Shade's work, makes sense of

Kinbote's life. Nabokov, in turn, hints that he wrote the novel to make sense out of his own life. He and Kinbote both create their own fictive worlds. The name V. Botkin recalls the name Vladimir Nabokov. In a sense, Botkin (and so, Kinbote) is also Nabokov, Nabokov the European American, the exile. Nabokov is suggesting that everyone creates worlds out of the details of life. Everyone who imagines, tells stories, has fantasies, goes crazy, is an artist.

Pale Fire is about the order that the imagination tries to impose on reality. Some kind of personal order is absolutely necessary for people to live. *Pale Fire* is also about disorder, which is what the world is. A major theme of the novel is the interplay between order and disorder, between good and evil. Although there are absolutes of good and evil, the human world is gray rather than black or white. *Pale Fire* is, then, art making and commenting on reality. Art is controlled but not controlling. Art acknowledges multiple interpretations and multiple possibilities. In the novel, this is reflected in the variable nature of some of the characters' identities. Their names vary, their stories vary, the reader's reaction to the stories may vary. The implicit political comment of the novel is that externally imposed "reality," or authorized interpretations of reality, do not allow for doubt and for ambiguity. The novel implicitly supports the individual's right to find irony.

For instance, Shade's poem is in iambic pentameter couplets, loose ones perhaps, but they echo, in the twentieth century, the couplets of the eighteenth century English poets. Shade's choice of form recalls a time when intellectuals could believe that humanity might soon order the world through reason; art as order was a foremost value. In Nabokov's time, art was at best what Robert Frost (who is possibly the model for Shade) has said of the art of poetry—it is a momentary stay against confusion. This example shows how Nabokov weaves form (iambic pentameter) and content (the theme of reason and order versus madness and disorder) together. He does so, furthermore, in a playful way; play and serious work are also themes of the novel.

Another theme of the work is the pattern of two views of time, cyclic and linear. Kinbote's story is linear; he has moved through madness to a kind of death; his time will come to a stop. The time of art, however, is cyclic. The two stories echo each other, echo within themselves, and make connections. Gerald Emerald is Izumrudov, Izumrudov is Gerald Emerald, Grey is de Grey. Shade, perhaps, is half a Shadow. The characters and time repeat themselves, in a slightly different way each time. Time stops for the individual, but life and its forms continue.

L. L. Lee

Further Reading

Bader, Julia. *Crystal Land: Artifice in Nabokov's English Novels.* Berkeley: University of California Press, 1972. The discussion of *Pale Fire* is extensive and insightful, concentrating upon the novel as imaginative experience.

Boyd, Brian. *Nabokov's "Pale Fire": The Magic of Artistic Discovery.* Princeton, N.J.: Princeton University Press, 1999. Argues that the novel has two narrators—John Shade and Charles Kinbote—but maintains that Kinbote had some "strange and surprising help" in preparing his sections of the book.

_____. *Vladimir Nabokov: The Russian Years* and *Vladimir Nabokov: The American Years.* 2 vols. Princeton, N.J.: Princeton University Press, 1990-1991. Essential biography, not only for its information about Nabokov's life but also for its examination of his life's relation to his art.

Connolly, Julian W. *The Cambridge Companion to Nabokov.* New York: Cambridge University Press, 2005. Collection of essays offering a concise introduction to Nabokov's life and writings. Some of the essays discuss Nabokov as a storyteller, a Russian writer, a modernist, and a poet, while others analyze the major Russian novels and his transition to writing in English.

De la Durantaye, Leland. *Style Is Matter: The Moral Art of Vladimir Nabokov.* Ithaca, N.Y.: Cornell University Press, 2007. De la Durantaye focuses on *Lolita*, but also looks at Nabokov's other works, such as *Pale Fire*, to discuss the ethics of art in his fiction. Maintains that although some readers find Nabokov to be cruel, his works contain a moral message—albeit one that is skillfully hidden in his texts.

Dembo, L. S., ed. *Nabokov: The Man and His Work.* Madison: University of Wisconsin Press, 1967. This early collection of articles on Nabokov introduced many of the ideas that later critics would continue to discuss. Includes an excellent article by John O. Lyons on *Pale Fire*.

Grayson, Jane, Arnold B. McMillin, and Priscilla Meyer, eds. *Nabokov's World: The Shape of Nabokov's World.* New York: Palgrave Macmillan, 2002.

_____. *Nabokov's World: Reading Nabokov.* New York: Palgrave Macmillan, 2002. A two-volume collection of essays written by an international group of Nabokov scholars. Includes discussions of intertextuality in Nabokov's works, the literary reception of his writings, and analyses of individual books.

Rampton, David. *Vladimir Nabokov: A Critical Study of the Novels.* New York: Cambridge University Press, 1984. Although Rampton limits his discussion to a few novels, his concentration upon content is a good antidote to the many formal approaches to Nabokov. Based on Rampton's doctoral thesis.

Roth, Phyllis A., comp. *Critical Essays on Vladimir Nabokov*. Boston: G. K. Hall, 1984. Comprehensive, very helpful selection of articles on Nabokov. *Pale Fire* is treated in several of the essays.

Wood, Michael. *The Magician's Doubts: Nabokov and the Risks of Fiction*. Princeton, N.J.: Princeton University Press, 1995. Wood's close reading of Nabokov's texts shows the power and beauty of Nabokov's language and the subtlety of his art, and uncovers ethical and moral foundations in his work. Chapter 8 focuses on *Pale Fire*.

Pale Horse, Pale Rider
Three Short Novels

Author: Katherine Anne Porter (1890-1980)
First published: 1939; includes *Old Mortality* (1937); *Noon Wine* (1937); *Pale Horse, Pale Rider* (1938)
Type of work: Novellas
Type of plot: Psychological realism
Time of plot: Old Mortality, 1885-1912; *Noon Wine,* 1836-1905; *Pale Horse, Pale Rider,* 1918
Locale: New Orleans, Louisiana; Texas; Colorado

Principal characters:
MIRANDA
MARIA, her sister
GABRIEL, her uncle
ADAM BARCLAY, an officer whom Miranda loves
ROYAL EARLE THOMPSON, a farmer with a weak character
MRS. THOMPSON, his wife
OLAF HELTON, a strange farmhand who works for Mr. Thompson

The Story:

Old Mortality. Miranda and her sister Maria, age eight and twelve years, respectively, live after the death of their mother with their father and grandmother. Legends of the family's past surround them in the house, especially tales of their dead Aunt Amy, whose melancholy photograph hangs on the wall.

According to the story, Amy had toyed with the affections of her fiancé Gabriel by appearing scantily dressed at the Mardi Gras with another man. Harry, Amy's father, defended her honor by shooting the man. Amy and Gabriel married, and six weeks later, Amy died of consumption (tuberculosis). Although the two young sisters understand now that some details are untrue, they continue to believe the story.

Two years later, after their grandmother dies, the girls are sent to a convent school where, to relieve the sedate life, they read romantic novels. Except for Saturday afternoons, when their father sometimes appears, they are cut off from life. One Saturday, their father takes them to the racetrack, where their Uncle Gabriel's beautiful horse is entered in a race. Instead of the romantic figure of the family's legends, Miranda sees that Gabriel is an alcoholic who lives in a slum hotel with his second wife. The horse, rather than winning elegantly, ends the race trembling and bleeding at the nose.

Eight years later, Miranda, now married, returns to Texas to attend Gabriel's funeral. On the train, she meets her cousin, Eva, who tells her about Gabriel and Amy. Eva refutes every romantic family legend with realistic details of Amy's scandalous behavior and death from tuberculosis. When they arrive, Miranda finds herself distanced from her father. When Eva and he begin to speak of the past, Miranda vows she will face the truth and leave her fictions behind.

Noon Wine. As Royal Earle Thompson churns milk on the porch one day, a stranger arrives and, in an English unfamiliar to the Texas farmland, asks for work. Thinking the man will work cheaply and do all the nasty chores on the small dairy farm, Thompson hires him. Olaf Helton speaks almost not at all, even at dinner with Thompson, his wife, and two sons. All he reveals is that he is a Swede from North Dakota and that he knows how to make butter and cheese. He also plays the harmonica, the same tune over and over.

After a while, the farmhand's strangeness ceases to bother the Thompsons, especially Mr. Thompson, who sees his farm prosper with Helton's work. The cows and chickens are cared for, the yards are cleaned up, and the income from dairy products increases. He and his wife try repeatedly to make conversation with Helton, but it is no use. He remains silent, even when the two boys tease him. In the second year, an incident occurs that makes Mrs. Thompson uneasy. One day she comes upon Helton shaking her sons ferociously by the shoulders. When her husband questions Helton, he replies that the boys had entered his shack and damaged his harmonicas. Mr. Thompson threatens his sons with a beating if they ever do that again—the end of the incident.

Nine years pass, and Helton continues to work and play the harmonica. The boys grow into responsible young men, the farm makes a profit, and Mrs. Thompson's health gets no worse. One day another stranger appears in the hot, dusty yard and introduces himself as Mr. Homer T. Hatch. Hatch is looking for Helton, whom, he says, had escaped from a mental hospital in North Dakota, where he had been committed after killing his brother in a fight over a harmonica. Hearing the tune of the harmonica, Hatch realizes that Helton is on the farm and gets out a pair of handcuffs. In the scuffle that ensues, Mr. Thompson, thinking Hatch is going to harm his hired man, kills Hatch with an ax. Helton flees the farm but is caught by the sheriff's patrol and killed by a mob.

A jury acquits Mr. Thompson, but he keeps trying to explain to his neighbors exactly what had happened. Day after day, he makes the rounds of the small farms, telling his story. The boys take over the task of farming. One night, unable to sleep, and realizing that no one, not even his own family, believes him, he kills himself with his gun.

Pale Horse, Pale Rider. Miranda dreams of riding a horse with a stranger. When he beckons her to ride further with him, she demurs because she feels there will be another ride and another time. She wakes to face the world of World War I and the deadly influenza epidemic that is sweeping the country. Her job at a newspaper requires her to work late hours reviewing plays and vaudeville acts and putting up with complaining fellow employees. The war and its rumors take their toll. She makes the rounds of the veterans' hospital to bring flowers and cheer to wounded soldiers. They reject her offers. Professional patriots try to force her to buy bonds with money she does not have. Miranda finds peace and stability with Adam Barclay, a Texas-born officer who lives at the same rooming house as she. He accompanies her to the shows she has to review, and afterward they visit cafés and talk of their past lives and of the war.

Miranda is infected with the influenza virus, and as she gets sicker and sicker, affairs at work become too hard to handle. Other reporters deal with her reviews. Her dreams continue, now full of torturous images of childhood memories mixed with jungles and icy mountains. She gets more and more ill, but the hospitals are full. Adam appears at her bedside to care for her as the influenza progresses, and the two confess their love for each other. Soon afterward, Miranda dreams of singers who are swept away by death and, finally, that Adam had died. When at last she is taken to a hospital in a half-conscious state, she mistakes the doctor for a German murderer. Dreams continue to haunt her. On Armistice Day, she regains consciousness fully, only to learn that although the war had ended, Adam has died in the epidemic.

Gradually, with the help of friends, Miranda's health returns. She is able to read Adam's letters and cope with the fact that she has been the agent of his death. After a period of mourning, Miranda emerges as a stronger person.

"The Story" by Louise M. Stone

Critical Evaluation:

Pale Horse, Pale Rider is an important book in the literary career of Katherine Anne Porter. Following, as it did, her highly esteemed first collection of short stories, *Flowering Judas* (1930), this collection composed of three novellas marks an advance in technical interest and resources. It demonstrates clearly the artist's ability to handle the expansive complexity of forms larger than the conventional short story. The artistic success of the forms in *Pale Horse, Pale Rider* is complete; Porter is one of the few American masters of the short novel. She matches the weight and density of many fine conventional novels in her shorter form.

One should begin by acknowledging the real daring of *Pale Horse, Pale Rider*. When it was written, the short story of conventional length was difficult enough to place and publish, and a collection of short stories was, in fact, a rare thing. It was easier to publish a collection of poems than a book of stories. There were many reasons for that condition, some of them economic, others the whimsical rationale of publishers. In view of these facts, it is quite remarkable that *Pale Horse, Pale Rider* ever appeared. There could have been small encouragement for Porter to produce anything except a novel. Moreover, the short novel as a form was even more rare in the United States than a collection of short stories, for its difficulties began at the common marketplace. The magazines would from time to time publish a serious short story among their lighter and more conventional fiction, never willing to surrender the space necessary for the long story or short novel. The choice of the form, then, whether at the outset or as a result of the demands of the material in the process of making, represented a major decision on the part of the artist. In the face of such pressure and such an element of risk, it is a wonder and a triumph that Porter not only created exemplary models of the form but also managed to overcome all the odds so that these stories are now simply and beautifully a part of the American literary heritage.

From the beginning, Porter has been accepted and acknowledged as a master stylist. While this view may be true, it has certainly been misleading. Taxonomy, or classification, seems to be an essential part of human consciousness. It is a great strength that permits people to think and relate; yet it is also a dangerous weakness in that the rigid and unquestioning exercise of this power can quickly lead to nonthinking, to the comfortable, narcotic illusion that a label has a life of its own as valid as the thing that is so named and tagged. The arts are difficult enough to think about and have not been spared from this kind of danger. To call attention to Porter's style is a useful observation, but it is rather like describing an oak tree exclusively in terms of the shape and color of its leaves. Moreover, associatively, emphasis on style tends to imply virtuosity for its own sake and a certain absence of content, with the result that the critic need not come to terms with content at all. In the case of Porter, this habit or cliché of critics is particularly disappointing.

Porter writes very well indeed, sentence by sentence, but it is the supreme virtue of her style that it is designed not to call attention to itself but to fit hand-in-glove the matter and content of her stories, to carry the weight and to suggest the depth of complexity without once interrupting the magic spell that gives fiction its reality. All her virtuosity is at the service of her story and her characters. It is easy enough for a writer to divert the reader away from content and character by dazzling and intriguing verbal performance. Porter has never chosen that way. Her method has been the more difficult one; clearly, the reader is intended to weigh the story in a total and meaningful sense and not to stop short with admiration for its surface and decoration. What she has to say is important, and it is a critical mistake to ignore this fact.

The three novellas of *Pale Horse, Pale Rider* are arranged in a structure to make a larger, single statement and effect, and each demonstrates a different way of handling the short novel. The first, *Old Mortality*, is in three parts and is, in a sense, a smaller version of the whole book. It is superficially a romantic tale of America around the beginning of the twentieth century. Part 1 is set in the shifting, complex world of a large family, gossip and the tall tales of the past being its imitative form. The point of view is of the two young sisters, Maria and Miranda, and the thematic concern is the romance and tragedy of their beautiful Aunt Amy. A great deal, the whole substance of what might have been a romantic novel of the period, is packed into a few pages, filtered through the consciousness of the two sisters. Somehow it all seems leisurely, even digressive, as it should. Describing the way the family passed on its own history, Porter is able to give simultaneously a clue to her own method in this section and to indicate the flaw at the heart of her family's, and the reader's, history, a romantic commitment of the heart and the imagination to the past.

In part 2, Maria and Miranda are schoolgirls in a New Orleans convent. They are now characterized as quite different from the unquestioning girls they were. There is a single, central event—their meeting with Uncle Gabriel—the dashing figure of the tragic legend of Aunt Amy. The girls have a confrontation with the reality of the family story. Here, beautifully executing her chosen point of view, Porter avoids the easy way out—of letting this event have a shattering and instant impact on the two girls. The impact is implied. Readers see what the girls see and feel what the girls feel; however, readers are not invited, as they might be in the much more conventional story of youthful disillusionment, to greater and false intimacy. Nor is the romantic past neatly (and falsely) discredited. It is modified. In part 2, the center of consciousness is Miranda, a young woman now, going home to the funeral of Uncle Gabriel and sharing her train ride by coincidence with the practical and worldly Cousin Eva, who had always been the antithesis of Aunt Amy. Miranda is capable, up to a point, of judging and evaluating the events of the past and able to decide to break with it. However, the story, which has evolved and emerged as the story of Miranda growing up, is subtly and carefully shown to be incomplete. Porter, unlike many contemporary writers, is not willing to settle for the simplistic truth of young idealism. Miranda's resolution at the end changes nothing as finally as she imagines, yet is in itself an inevitable change.

In *Old Mortality*, certain basic conditions are firmly established that inform the character of the whole book. The subjects, the conflicts, are the past and the present, "romance" and "reality," a history of how the times and the world changed and became what they are. The larger theme is change and mutability. All these things are shown through character. Characters grow and change credibly and with ever-increasing dimension. The framework is within the terms of the conventional serious story, but these conventions will be given renewed vigor and life; for precisely at the point at which the conventional response or reaction could end the story and be a solution, the author will give the story an unexpected resonance. Her stories do not "end," then, but project a sense of life going on and echo afterward in the reader's mind, an effect that is artistically consistent with her theme and subject of change.

The second of the short novels, *Noon Wine*, stands in apparently sharp contrast to *Old Mortality*. In time, it parallels the first two parts of the other and, in fact, stands in relation to *Old Mortality* much as the second part of that story does to its first part. It is a rural tragedy, plain and harshly realistic, the other side of the coin, so to speak, of a family's romantic legends. There are two young people who grow up, too—

grubby, small, towheaded—but they are not involved in the consciousness of the story. Told from an omniscient point of view, the story settles into the tragedy of Mr. Thompson, as unlikely a tragic figure as can be imagined, one who for a large part of the story is tagged with characteristics that are conventionally unsympathetic in modern writing. In the end, he changes in the reader's view and estimation, his awful suicide becoming tragic, but not through the usual trick of the revelation of something new or unknown about his character. His character evolves, grows as things happen to him cumulatively, just as the character of Miranda grows and changes in *Old Mortality*, although in a rude and realistic setting and without the benefits of great intelligence or sensibility.

Taken together, the two short novels say: From these roots the living have grown to maturity. Both are part of the American heritage. The stories are related in such areas as theme, structure, and contrast, not in the areas of shared characters and plot. *Noon Wine*, like the other novellas, is about the mutability of understanding; what one sees is what one understands.

Pale Horse, Pale Rider combines elements of both the previous stories. There is a real, tragic romance, the love of Adam and Miranda, in many ways a parallel of the grand romance of Gabriel and Amy, in part a retelling of the Adam and Eve legend. There is the harsh reality of a country at war, in the closing days of World War I, and in the middle of the raging influenza epidemic that marked the end of that war. That sickness takes the life of Adam and almost kills Miranda as well. The story ends with the end of the war and Miranda leaving the hospital "cured." The final image projects a future, but now a strangely bleak and bitter one. All things have changed. Part of the subtlety of this story lies in the author's ability to use the war, conventionally, as the end of something of the old order and the loss of something indefinable from the American spirit, and yet to do this within the context of the home front. The raging epidemic, at first as seemingly remote as the bloody fields of France, gradually becomes part of the whole sickness that inflamed the world and destroyed so much. Miranda emerges as much a war casualty as any shell-shocked veteran.

The three short novels of *Pale Horse, Pale Rider* are related and designed to give a rich and complex social history. Porter is not often credited with being a social historian as well as a fine crafter of prose. Perhaps the reason is that she is only indirectly concerned with politics, and so those critics whose social vision is conditioned by their political views cannot grant the truth of her grand theme. Politics, however, is a two-dimensional enterprise, a game of "the image." Por-

ter's fictional art is based upon the flesh and spirit of character, and none of her characters remains an "image" for long.

The social history of *Ship of Fools* (1962) or *The Leaning Tower, and Other Stories* (1944), for example, is evident, and it is equally present in *Pale Horse, Pale Rider*; but in a larger sense, social history is, however complex, merely part of her design. Social history becomes, by the examples of recurring and parallel events, much more than chronology. It becomes a stage on which human beings act out their lives. The scenes change, but the human heart and all its mystery does not. Mutability is a fact of life, but it is not life. Her deepest concern is with people, with character, and in this compassionate and always honest concern, she joins the ranks of the very few great artists of fiction. *Pale Horse, Pale Rider*, her three short and related novels, would guarantee her that place among the few had she never written another line.

In Porter's rhetoric, there is great respect for the reader. She engages the reader's imagination and lets it work too. The result is a highly condensed fiction that does not seem so because of the richness of echo she has managed to suggest and evoke. There is nothing small about her work. Its aims are the grandest to which a writer can aspire. Its glory is the remarkable and daring achievement of those aims.

Further Reading

Bloom, Harold, ed. *Katherine Anne Porter*. New York: Chelsea House, 1986. Explains Porter's complex use of symbolism and irony. Asserts that the dream sequences of the Miranda stories reveal the unexpressed causes of her discontent.

DeMouy, Jane Krause. *Katherine Anne Porter's Women: The Eye of Her Fiction*. Austin: University of Texas Press, 1983. A feminist reading of Porter's fiction. DeMouy argues that Porter is a precursor of later feminism in her concentration on female characters trying to live independently in a world dominated by men.

Givner, Joan. *Katherine Anne Porter: A Life*. New York: Simon & Schuster, 1982. Explores key events that affected Porter's work. Explains the connection between Porter's near death experience and *Pale Horse, Pale Rider*.

Hendrick, George. *Katherine Anne Porter*. Boston: Twayne, 1965. Details Porter's life and works. Explores the theme of innocence and experience in the stories in which Miranda appears.

Lopez, Enrique Hank. *Conversations with Katherine Anne Porter: Refugee from Indian Creek*. Boston: Little, Brown, 1981. Stories about Porter's life as she told them to the man who was her companion during the last years of her life.

Stout, Janis. *Katherine Anne Porter: A Sense of the Times*. Charlottesville: University Press of Virginia, 1995. An intellectual biography containing chapters on Porter's background in Texas, her view of politics and art in the 1920's, her writing and life between the two world wars, and her relationship with the southern agrarians. Includes notes and bibliography.

Titus, Mary. *The Ambivalent Art of Katherine Anne Porter*. Athens: University of Georgia Press, 2005. A look at the ways in which Porter confronted issues of gender in her work and her life, including a study of some of her unpublished papers.

Unrue, Darlene Harbour. *Katherine Anne Porter: The Life of an Artist*. Jackson: University Press of Mississippi, 2005.

Comprehensive biography offering new insight into Porter's turbulent personal life and her writing.

_____. *Truth and Vision in Katherine Anne Porter's Fiction*. Athens: University of Georgia Press, 1985. Lists critical sources. Studies the themes of Porter's fiction, asserting that her works have a thematic unity built around Porter's understanding of truth.

Warren, Robert Penn, ed. *Katherine Anne Porter*. Englewood Cliffs, N.J.: Prentice-Hall, 1979. A collection of essays about Porter's work, by a variety of critics.

West, Ray. *Katherine Anne Porter*. Minneapolis: University of Minnesota Press, 1963. Sets the novellas in the context of Porter's southern background. Develops the idea that historic memory uses myths to portray truths.

The Palm-Wine Drinkard

Author: Amos Tutuola (1920-1997)
First published: 1952
Type of work: Novel
Type of plot: Folktale
Time of plot: Indeterminate
Locale: Nigeria

Principal characters:
THE NARRATOR, a young man
HIS WIFE
THE PALM-WINE TAPSTER
THE CURIOUS CREATURE, a skull in disguise
THE FAITHFUL MOTHER, helper of those in trouble
DANCE, the Red-Lady of Red-Town
THE RED-KING, her father
THE INVISIBLE PAWN, chief of all bush creatures

The Story:

The narrator lives contentedly as the son of a rich man who retains a palm-wine tapster for his son's exclusive use. Each day, the tapster draws enormous amounts of palm-wine for the narrator, who drinks it with his friends. One day, after the narrator's father has died, the tapster falls from a palm tree and is killed. The narrator misses his supply of palm-wine, and his friends no longer visit him, so he decides to go to Deads' Town to find his tapster.

The narrator's journey leads him from his town to various parts of the bush—that place outside civilization that is the habitation of all sorts of inhuman creatures. He has many adventures. For instance, he stays with a man who promises to give directions to Deads' Town if the narrator will find Death and bring him to the town. The narrator tricks Death into coming along to the town. After that, Death cannot return to his former home, and so Death enters the world. The narrator asks again for directions to Deads' Town, but his host says

that he must first rescue his daughter, who had been attracted to a handsome gentleman and followed him into the bush. The gentleman is really a curious creature of the bush. He had returned to the bush and, as he entered, given back each bodily part that he had rented from a human being, until he was nothing but a skull; he then held the young woman captive. The narrator searches for the host's daughter, finds her, and the two escape the bush.

The two marry and stay in her town until the day a child is born from her thumb, and is instantly able to speak, move, and eat and drink everything in sight. Driven from town because of this insatiable child, they wander into the bush, where they meet three persons named Drum, Dance, and Song. The child is so attracted by their music that he follows them. Released from their terrible companion, the narrator and his wife wander until they get to Wraith-Island. The beautiful creatures who live here have nothing to do but plant their magic seeds and then dance all day long. After an encounter with a huge creature that demands a sacrifice from the narrator for its field and an encounter with a tiny creature that can undo the work of all other creatures, the narrator and his wife leave Wraith-Island with some of the magic seeds.

In Unreturnable Heaven's Town, they encounter people who call themselves the enemies of God and who do everything exactly the opposite from the normal world. The narrator and his wife are beaten, stoned, scraped by rocks and broken bottles, and finally buried up to their necks. With the help of a friendly eagle, they escape from the town and, after a short recuperation, go on their way. As they pass a huge, white tree, two hands reach out of an opening in the tree and draw them inside. This is the land of the Faithful Mother, whose sole task is to solace and care for those who have experienced great difficulties in the world. As they enter this land they rent their fear and sell their death. When they leave, after staying the maximum allowable three months, they take back their fear, but can no longer be killed, because they had sold their death. This leads to the odd circumstance that they can feel fear in the face of danger, even though the danger cannot kill them.

In Red-Town, the narrator's wife speaks in riddles for the first time, and it develops that she has the gift of prophecy. Everything and everyone in this town is red-colored because of a mistake the Red-King had made years ago. By facing fearful creatures, the narrator frees them from their curse and settles down to use his magic seeds, soon becoming a rich man. While there, they meet the Red-Lady, daughter of the king and also the person who had been called Dance in an earlier adventure. She and her two companions play together in Red-Town until they play themselves right out of this world—only their names remain. When the narrator hires a farm laborer called the Invisible Pawn, who is really the chief of all bush-creatures, the Pawn's overenthusiastic completion of his labors angers the townspeople, so again they move on.

After passing through the town of the Wise-King, they reach Deads' Town and find the tapster, but cannot stay, because "alives" are not allowed to live with "deads." With a marvelous egg from the tapster, they return to the narrator's town, where they use the egg to feed people during a famine, until someone breaks the egg. Finally, the narrator ends a cosmic war between Heaven and Earth and the people prosper again.

Critical Evaluation:

Amos Tutuola's early life consisted of living as a servant away from his own family, attempting to advance his school-ing, and experiencing distant kindness from his master but cruelty from his master's cook. After leaving his master, he persisted in his studies and finally found an unsatisfactory job. Some of this determination in the face of life's vicissitudes appears in his narrators, who seem to undergo the most terrible trials without losing sight of their ultimate goals.

The effect of Tutuola's unsettled education is apparent in his use of English, which is not his native tongue. His style has been called naïve, but might also be called grotesque, fantastic, magical, or charming. Long run-on sentences, filled with unusual combinations and forms of words, paint pictures alien to the Western imagination yet are strangely compelling and familiar.

The titles of Tutuola's best-known works—the novels *The Palm-Wine Drinkard* and *My Life in the Bush of Ghosts* (1954)—are exemplary of one aspect of his style. "Drinkard" is not likely to appear in any dictionary of the English language, but the meaning is clear. The "ghosts" of the second title are not ghosts as that word is understood by the average American or European. Tutuola's English is eccentric—sometimes a word-for-word translation from Yoruba—but never inaccurate. If the narrator might be envious of a man, he says, "I would jealous him." If he means 2:00 A.M., he says, "two o'clock in the mid-night." The combination of flamboyance and uncomplicated innocence conveyed by his style is at first annoying, but eventually captivating, as his story unfolds.

In *The Palm-Wine Drinkard*, Tutuola's unusual style is the framework for motifs and figures from the folklore of his native Nigeria, strung together like the episodes in a picaresque novel, and connected by nothing more than the character of the narrator. Despite this literary form, Tutuola's novelistic writings (as remarked by the noted mythologist Geoffrey Parrinder in his foreword to *My Life in the Bush of Ghosts*) are truly African. That is, they reflect the tales Tutuola heard from childhood. They are distinguished from many recorded folktales by their descriptive technique. Folktales, as they have been collected in Africa and elsewhere, tend to describe briefly, using character types. The emphasis is on action and on confrontation, especially between human beings and creatures outside the human sphere.

Tutuola does for the African folktale, in a very different way, what Evangeline Walton does for Welsh mythology: He fleshes it out, offering a vivid description of actions that might have been taken for granted in a recorded tale. He makes use of what Robert P. Armstrong calls "precise hyperbole" and "visual hyperbole." The narrator's captivity in Unreturnable Heaven's Town would no doubt be disposed of in a standard, recorded tale with a few brief sentences. Tutuola spares no verb in describing the horrors that are visited upon him and his wife. The "barbing" of their hair by unsuitable implements like flat stones and broken bottles gains much of its effect from the typical Tutuolan technique of accretion—the repetition and variation of an activity until it overwhelms the reader with a descriptive barrage. It is quite possible that this aspect of Tutuola's style reflects the oral tradition directly, not in the same way as collected folktales.

As is shown in recorded performances, the oral tradition encourages drama, hyperbole, repetition, and what might be called joy in storytelling. Some of this spirit is evident in *The Palm-Wine Drinkard*. Some critics see Tutuola as a poet of the past, because he adapts folkloric material rather than pursuing the mythopoetic direction of some of his contemporaries, who are searching for a new African identity. Others, apparently unaware of the source of his material, have praised his Kafkaesque originality. The significance of Tutuola's work lies in combining these two characteristics: creating a narrative fabric in which old motifs and figures are juxtaposed to human beings in a new frame of reference. He begins with certain givens of folk belief: that the dead are not dead in a Western sense of the word but have gone somewhere to "live" with other "deads"; that the areas of forest or savannah lying outside the influence of town or city—called the bush—contain a variety of spirits and powers that may endanger or enrich the human being who ventures into them. To these assumptions, he adds another assumption that is also standard to many bush tales: Bush creatures may be dangerous and hostile but in the end their magic powers are no match for the cunning and determination of a human being.

The situations and figures in Tutuola's episodes range from those that seem to be peculiar to African folklore, like the Curious Creature who has rented his body parts to come to town and returns them on the way back into the bush, to universally recognizable motifs such as "how Death came into the world." Tutuola's narrator is a person of Tutuola's present, bringing with him the beliefs and thought patterns of the modern world. He is a Christian who may encounter the very enemies of God, but is never persuaded—or expected—to change his beliefs or his ideas. He enters a world in which time seems to change according to the situation, and yet, as one critic points out, he always notes the time in terms of a twenty-four-hour clock. He adapts to his surroundings, but does not yield to them. Because his vigorous, eccentric style and command of local lore newly validate both the form and the substance of an old genre, Tutuola has emerged as a significant figure in African literature.

James L. Hodge

Further Reading

Ajayi, Jare. *Amos Tutuola: Factotum as a Pioneer.* Ibadan, Nigeria: Creative Books, 2003. Ajayi, a Nigerian journalist, spent sixteen years researching and writing this first English-language biography of Tutuola. Provides information about his motivations for creative writing and his exploitation by publishers, among other subjects, and includes interpretations of his work.

Asagba, O. A. "The Folklore Structure in Amos Tutuola's *The Palm-Wine Drinkard*." *Lore and Language* 4, no. 1 (January, 1985): 31-39. Builds on earlier studies to analyze the novel's use of folklore motifs and to examine claims that it is a "quest" novel.

Coates, John. "The Inward Journey of the Palm-Wine Drinkard." In *African Literature Today*, compiled by Eldred D. Jones and edited by Eldred Durosimi Jones. New York: African Publishing, 1973. Examines the novel as a psychological development with allegorical overtones.

Collins, Harold R. *Amos Tutuola.* Boston: Twayne, 1969. Good treatment of Tutuola's writings, using his life and environment as background. Workmanlike survey of aspects and critiques of his work.

George, Olakunle. *Relocating Agency: Modernity and African Letters.* Albany: State University of New York Press, 2003. Examines works by Tutuola and three other Nigerian writers—D. O. Fagunwa, Wole Soyinka, and Chinua Achebe. Uses several modern critical theories, including poststructuralism and postcolonialism, to interpret these writers' works.

Gera, Anjali. *Three Great African Novelists: Chinua Achebe, Wole Soyinka, and Amos Tutuola.* New Delhi: Creative Books, 2001. Focuses on the use of the Yoruba and Igbo storytelling traditions in the works of Tutuola and two other Nigerian writers. Describes how the writers adapt these traditions to define themselves and their societies.

Irele, Abiola. "Tradition and the Yoruba Writer: Daniel O. Fagunwa, Amos Tutuola, and Wole Soyinka." In *Perspectives on Wole Soyinka: Freedom and Complexity*, edited by Biodun Jeyifo. Jackson: University Press of Mississippi, 2001. Compares Tutuola's work with the work of two other Yoruba writers.

Lindfors, Bernth, ed. *Critical Perspectives on Amos Tutuola.* Washington, D.C.: Three Continents Press, 1975. Reprint. London: Heinemann, 1980. Useful collection of critical comment on all of Tutuola's works, divided into early reactions, reappraisals, and later criticism.

Owomoyela, Oyekan. *Amos Tutuola Revisited.* New York: Twayne, 1999. An excellent introduction to Tutuola's life and works, written by a Yoruba writer and scholar. Argues that Tutuola symbolizes the African tradition from colonialism to postcolonialism. Includes notes, references, selected bibliography, and index.

Quayson, Ato. "Treasures of an Opulent Fancy: Amos Tutuola and the Folktale Narrative." In *Strategic Transformation in Nigerian Writing: Orality and History in the* *Work of Rev. Samuel Johnson, Amos Tutuola, Wole Soyinka, and Ben Okri*. Bloomington: Indiana University Press, 1997. A sound treatment of the element of orality in fiction by Tutuola and three other Nigerian writers. Focuses on Tuotola's novels *The Palm-Wine Drinkard* and *My Life in the Bush of Ghosts*.

Pamela
Or, Virtue Rewarded

Author: Samuel Richardson (1689-1761)
First published: 1740-1741
Type of work: Novel
Type of plot: Epistolary
Time of plot: Early eighteenth century
Locale: England

Principal characters:
PAMELA ANDREWS, a servant girl
MR. B——, her master
MRS. JERVIS, Mr. B——'s housekeeper
MRS. JEWKES, the caretaker of Mr. B——'s country home
LADY DAVERS, Mr. B——'s sister

The Story:

Pamela Andrews has been employed from a very young age as the servant girl of Lady B—— at her estate in Bedfordshire. She has grown very fond of her mistress, so the letter to her parents telling of her ladyship's death expresses her deep sorrow. Her own plans are uncertain, but it soon becomes clear that Lady B——'s son wants her to remain in his household. Taking her hand before all the other servants, he has said that he will be a good master to Pamela for his dear mother's sake if she continues faithful and diligent. Mrs. Jervis, the housekeeper, puts in a friendly word as well, and Pamela, not wishing to be a burden upon her poor parents, decides to remain in the service of Mr. B——. Shortly, however, she begins to doubt that his intentions toward her are honorable. When he kisses her one day, while she sits sewing in a summerhouse, she finds herself in a quandary as to what to do.

Once again, she discusses the situation with the good Mrs. Jervis and decides to stay if she can share the housekeeper's bed. Mr. B—— is extremely annoyed at this turn of affairs. He tries to persuade Mrs. Jervis that Pamela is a very designing creature who should be carefully watched. When he learns that she is writing long letters to her parents, telling them in great detail of his false proposals and repeating her determination to keep her virtue, he has as many of her letters intercepted as possible.

In a frightening interview with Mr. B——, Pamela, and Mrs. Jervis, he intimidates the housekeeper by his terrifying manner and tells Pamela to return to her former poverty. After talking the matter over with her friend, however, Pamela decides that Mr. B—— has given up his plan to ruin her and that there is no longer any reason for her to leave. Another interview with Mr. B——, however, convinces her that she should return to her parents upon the completion of some household duties entrusted to her. When Mr. B—— discovers that she is indeed planning to leave, a furious scene follows, in which he accuses her of pride beyond her station. That night he conceals himself in the closet of her room. When she discovers him, Pamela throws herself on the bed and falls into a fit. Pamela and Mrs. Jervis serve notice. Despite Mr. B——'s threats on the one hand and his cajoling on the other, Pamela remains firm in her decision to return home. The housekeeper is reinstated in her position, but Pamela sets out by herself in the coach Mr. B—— had ordered for her to return to her parents.

What she thinks is Mr. B——'s kindness is but designing trickery. Instead of arriving at her parents' humble home, Pamela becomes a prisoner at Mr. B——'s country estate, where the coachman has driven her. Mrs. Jewkes, the caretaker, has none of Mrs. Jervis's kindness of heart, and Pamela is cruelly confined. It is only by clever scheming that she is able to continue sending letters to her parents. She is aided by Mr. Williams, the village minister, who smuggles her mail out of the house. The young man soon confesses his love for Pamela and his desire to marry her. Pamela refuses his offer, but she devises a plan to escape with his help. Unfortunately, Mrs. Jewkes is too wily a jailer. When she suspects that the two are planning Pamela's escape, she writes to Mr. B——, who is still in London. Pamela's persecutor, aided by his agents, contrives to have Mr. Williams thrown into jail on a trumped-up charge.

Although her plot has been discovered, Pamela does not allow herself to be discouraged. That night, she drops from her window into the garden. When she tries to escape from the garden, however, she finds the gate padlocked. Mrs. Jewkes discovers her cringing in the woodshed. From that time on, her warder's vigilance and cruelty increase. At length, Mr. B—— arrives and frightens Pamela still further with his threats. With the help of Mrs. Jewkes, he attempts to force himself upon her, but opportunely Pamela is seized by fits. Mr. B—— expresses his remorse and promises never to attempt to molest her again. Pamela now suspects that her virtue will soon be rewarded, for Mr. B—— proposes marriage to her. Just as she is enjoying the thought of becoming Mrs. B——, an anonymous warning arrives, suggesting that she beware of a sham marriage. Pamela is greatly upset. At her request, a coach is called, and she sets out to visit her parents. On the way, however, letters arrive from Mr. B—— entreating her to return to him and offering an honorable proposal of marriage.

Pamela returns immediately to Mr. B——'s hall; despite all that has passed, she realizes that she is in love with Mr. B——. He, in turn, is delighted with her beauty and goodness. She and Mr. B—— are married by Mr. Williams before a few witnesses. Mr. Andrews, Pamela's father, is present. There is great rejoicing in the Andrews household when Mr. Andrews returns and is told of his daughter's virtue and of the happiness it brings her.

Pamela readily adapts herself to her new role as the wife of a gentleman. With typical virtue, she quickly forgives Mrs. Jewkes for her former ill treatment. The only flaw in her married state is that Lady Davers, Mr. B——'s sister, is angry with her brother because of his marriage to a servant girl. Pamela is alone when Lady Davers arrives. She insults Pamela, who flees to her husband for consolation. A terrible scene takes place between Mr. B—— and Lady Davers, but Pamela soon wins the love and respect of the good woman when she shows her the letters she wrote about her earlier sufferings.

One day, Mr. B—— tells Pamela of a previous love affair with Miss Sally Godfrey and takes her to see his daughter, who had been placed in a boarding school in the neighbor-hood. Pamela likes the little girl and asks to have the pretty child under her care at a future time. Mr. and Mrs. Andrews are pleased with Pamela's accounts of her happiness and of Mr. B——'s goodness to her. He gives the old people a substantial gift of money and thus enables them to set themselves up in a small but comfortable business.

Lady Davers's correspondence with Pamela continues at great length, and she increasingly expresses her approval of Pamela's virtue and her disgust with her brother's attempts to dishonor her. During a visit she pays the young couple, Mr. B—— expresses his regret for his earlier unmannerly conduct toward the one who has become his dearly beloved wife. Mr. B——'s uncle, Sir Jacob Swynford, visits his nephew; he is prepared to detest the inferior creature Mr. B—— has married. Pamela's charm, beauty, and virtue, however, win his heart completely, and the grumpy old man leaves full of praises for his lovely niece.

At last, Mr. B—— and Pamela decide to leave the country and return to London. Although her husband is still as attentive and thoughtful as ever, Pamela begins to suspect that he might be having an affair with another woman. She is particularly distressed that she cannot accompany him to the theater and other places of amusement, as she is about to have a child. The scene of the christening of their son is joyful; in addition to the family, tenants from the estate arrive to express their joy that Mr. B—— now has a son and heir.

Nevertheless, Pamela's suspicions after all are justified. An anonymous note informs her that the business trip Mr. B—— had taken was in reality a journey to a neighboring city with a countess with whom he is having an affair. Pamela controls her passions, and when Mr. B—— returns, he is so overcome by this further evidence of her kindness and understanding that he begs her forgiveness and promises to remain faithful to her from that day on. Pamela makes good use of the letters she had written to Lady Davers during this trying period by sending them to the countess, hoping that she might learn from them and turn away from the path of license.

True to her earlier wish, Pamela decides to take in Sally Godfrey's child and bring her up as a sister for her own son, Billy. Mr. B—— is faithful to his resolve to devote himself only to his wife, and he spends the remainder of his days admiring and praising her virtue.

Critical Evaluation:

Samuel Richardson has often been termed the founder of the English novel. Like most such titles, this one is an over-simplification of a complex issue and one that has been particularly disputed by students of Richardson's contemporary,

Daniel Defoe, who is also justly noted for his important contributions to the genre. The importance of Richardson's position in the tradition of the novel, however, is undeniable and is based on his redefinition of the form, through his success in *Pamela* in dealing with several of the major formal problems that Defoe and others had left unsolved.

The most significant of these problems was that of plot. Prior to the publication of *Pamela*, a novel was commonly defined as "a small tale, generally of love." Although this definition has more recently been applied to the novella, most of the sources in Richardson's era, notably Dr. Johnson's dictionary, construed it as referring to the novel. When *Pamela* appeared, it was considered a "dilated novel" because its subject matter was basically the single amorous episode that the short novels had previously emphasized. Nevertheless, its treatment was on a scale much closer to the romances of Defoe and Henry Fielding, two authors who did not confront the definition problem in most of their works, which tended to deal with many episodes within a larger context. Works such as Defoe's *Moll Flanders* (1722) and Fielding's *Tom Jones* (1749) fit more easily into the romance category (with the word "romance" understood to mean adventure more than love). Richardson combined the large scale of the romance and the intimate scope of the traditional novel to form the basis of the novel as readers have come to know it. Richardson's use of the epistolary style—a style of which he was perhaps literature's foremost practitioner—facilitated the birth of the new form, although it causes some problems for modern readers.

Pamela's plot structure was based on a radically new concept in the novel form. This innovative plot structure is the work's major strength and its major weakness. Viewed in context with later novels, it appears awkward, contrived, and lacking in realism. Indeed, a major criticism of Richardson's novel concerns the question of how the major characters found the time in the middle of all of their adventures to be writing lengthy letters to one another. In a purely technical sense, perhaps the worst defect in the plot is that it is too long for its essential purpose, causing it to be static in movement and lacking in tension; it reaches a climax and resolution midway through the book, thus leaving hundreds of pages of dull and uneventful narrative. The account of Pamela's married life, serving as it does only to confirm her virtue in the eyes of the world, could have been trimmed considerably, thus enhancing the overall effect of the novel. As it is, the falling action of the novel, consisting of Mr. B——'s adultery and Pamela's forgiveness as well as the growing appreciation on the part of Mr. B—— of his wife's virtue, is unconvincing and sentimental.

The strength of the plot structure lies in Richardson's epistolary form; notwithstanding its shortcomings, the author's form does convey a degree of realism. Letters are normally a means for the relation of one's doings, and they presuppose an actual writer and an actual reader. Preconceived notions concerning the normal functions of the mode make believable an actual maiden, an actual seducer, and an actual marriage. Richardson's manipulation of the machinery governing the epistles—the hidden pens and ink, the evasions and discoveries, and the secreting of letters in bosoms and undergarments—causes the effect to grow. The realism is further enhanced by the clustering and lingering effect that comes to surround each incident. An incident occurs and is reflected on, committed to paper, entrusted to a porter, and spied upon; it is either intercepted or received, reflected upon, and responded to. Although it slows down the action, the whole complex, repetitive effect lends great credibility to the original incident.

Richardson's epistolary form, after establishing the necessary suspension of disbelief in readers regarding a servant girl who can read and write, also logically excuses much of Pamela's smooth and affected rhetoric; since a letter is an editing of life rather than life itself, the writer has an editorial option to tailor and refurbish experience. By positing a servant girl with a certain flair for writing, Richardson can justify a further suspension of disbelief, although sometimes not as much as the circumstances demand.

The weakest part of the plot's structure in terms of realism is Richardson's handling of the sequence of incidents. While perhaps the incidents in *Pamela* do not disappoint the reader's preconceived notions of drawing-room and boudoir reality, they are little more than interesting fits of manners and rarely reveal any depth of character or morals. These incidents are little more than stylistically balanced situations; outrages in the summerhouse are followed by contrition and tearful farewells by triumphant reunions.

The same shallowness applies to some of Richardson's characters, who, being allegorical as demanded by the instructional premise of the novel, offer little depth of personality. The heroine herself, however, presents an interesting study: Pamela begins as the most fully allegorical figure and concludes by being the most fully human. Beginning in ignorance, she presents the prospect, particularly to readers used to the less sentimental Fielding, of becoming a satirical figure; yet she never does. Pamela is an incorruptibly good woman. What is interesting about her characterization is how the author converts readers to accept the reality of his protagonist and her maidenly dilemma. He manages this by placing her in a crisis that is inherently genuine and appropriate to her way of life. He supplies her with neatly counterpoised groups of friends and enemies and fleshes out her vulnerability with an impressive strength and a striking ability to cope—a believable middle-class trait. The implied spectacle of her parents nervously hanging on from letter to letter adds further believability to the picture.

Richardson also imbues Pamela with little vices which she realizes she has. Pamela, for example, knows that she is long-winded, prone to construe motives to her own advantage, and inclined to cling to praise and flattery. This realization of some of her own faults makes Pamela much more credible than a character who is merely symbolic and displays no insight into herself.

Despite Richardson's virtues and faults as a writer, it is his redefinition of the form of the novel that most makes him worth reading. *Pamela* was a radical departure from accepted concepts. While subsequent novelists learned from and modified Richardson's techniques, they for the most part drifted away from his epistolary form; while keeping his idea of treating a simple episode on a larger scale, they tended to follow the techniques developed by Fielding and Defoe. *Pamela* is thus as much of an anomaly in the twenty-first century as it was in the eighteenth century. Nevertheless, it is a vital part of literary tradition and was instrumental in creating the novel as it is now known.

"Critical Evaluation" by Patricia Ann King

Further Reading

Blewitt, David, ed. *Passion and Virtue: Essays on the Novels of Samuel Richardson*. Buffalo, N.Y.: University of Toronto Press, 2001. A collection of essays providing various interpretations of *Pamela* and Richardson's other novels. Includes discussions of *Pamela*'s textual authority and examines the politics of virtue and the structuring of social authority in this novel.

Flynn, Carol Houlihan. *Samuel Richardson: A Man of Letters*. Princeton, N.J.: Princeton University Press, 1982. Approximately one-third of this carefully researched, splendidly reasoned assessment of Richardson and his work is devoted to *Pamela*. Includes an index.

Keymer, Thomas. *Richardson's "Clarissa" and the Eighteenth Century Reader*. New York: Cambridge University Press, 1992. Although Keymer's major focus is on *Clarissa*, he makes cogent comparisons to *Pamela* and helps readers to understand the cultural milieu Richardson addressed.

Keymer, Thomas, and Peter Sabor. *Pamela in the Marketplace: Literary Controversy and Print Culture in Eighteenth-Century Britain and Ireland*. New York: Cambridge University Press, 2005. Recounts the cultural impact of *Pamela*, which after publication in 1740-1741 became the best-selling novel of its time and was the subject of numerous critiques, parodies, sequels, comedies, and operas.

Rivero, Albert J., ed. *New Essays on Samuel Richardson*. New York: Palgrave Macmillan, 1996. Contributors to this collection of scholarly essays approach Richardson's three novels, including *Pamela*, from a variety of theoretical perspectives. Includes an index.

Watt, Ian. *The Rise of the Novel: Studies in Defoe, Richardson, and Fielding*. 2d American ed. Berkeley: University of California Press, 2001. Contains an excellent chapter on *Pamela*, praising the psychological depth of the novel's characters. Analyzes Richardson's contribution to the development of English prose fiction and relates the novel to the social situation of its day.

Parable of the Sower *and* Parable of the Talents

Author: Octavia E. Butler (1947-2006)
First published: Parable of the Sower, 1993; *Parable of the Talents*, 1998
Type of work: Novels
Type of plot: Science fiction
Time of plot: 2024-2027 and 2032-2090
Locale: Robledo and Acorn, California

Principal characters:

LAUREN OLAMINA BANKOLE, the young, African American leader of the Earthseed religion

TAYLOR FRANKLIN BANKOLE, Lauren's husband

LARKIN OLAMINA BANKOLE/ASHA VERE, Lauren and Taylor's abducted daughter

MARCUS OLAMINA/MARCOS DURAN, Lauren's favorite brother

HARRY BALTER and ZAHRA MOSS BALTER, fellow refugees from Lauren's original neighborhood

ANDREW STEELE JARRET, newly elected president of the United States, who encourages violence against non-Christians

REVEREND OLAMINA, Lauren's father

CORY OLAMINA, Lauren's stepmother

KEITH OLAMINA,

BEN OLAMINA, and

GREG OLAMINA, Lauren's brothers

The Story:

In *Parable of the Sower*, Lauren Olamina is the only daughter of a Baptist minister who leads the family's walled community in California in the year 2024. The neighbors valiantly try to protect one another against the hordes of illiterate homeless people and thieves in the western United States, which is suffering from extreme poverty and climate change. Lauren's family scrapes out a living, but Lauren suspects that the community's walls offer only an illusion of safety, particularly because the police are both corrupt and ineffectual. Lauren learns what she can about survival tactics and struggles to articulate in her journals the principles of Earthseed, a religion that she believes she has discovered. Earthseed is based on the premise that God simply means the concept of inevitable change. Lauren also struggles to hide her hyperempathy, a delusional syndrome—caused by her birth mother's drug abuse—that causes her to experience the pain suffered by others.

As civilization continues to deteriorate, Lauren's brother Keith runs away and is murdered by drug dealers, and her father goes missing and is presumed dead. When Lauren is eighteen, her worst fears come true when a murderous group of drug addicts burns down her community. Lauren is briefly incapacitated but manages to grab the survival pack that she keeps prepared. While combing through the wreckage the next day for some sign of her family, she finds only two neighbors still alive: Harry Balter and Zahra Moss. Zahra

tells Lauren that she witnessed Lauren's stepmother and brothers being shot and burned. Zahra and Harry's own families have also been killed, so the three survivors form an alliance and decide to walk north in the hope of finding better lives in Oregon, Washington, or even Canada.

No longer sheltered, the trio must kill in self-defense for the first time, which is doubly traumatic for Lauren because of her hyperempathy. They witness rape, robbery, murder, wildfire, and even cannibalism. However, they manage to retain their own humanity and even assist others at the risk of their own safety. Lauren continues to write, refining her thoughts about Earthseed and her belief that, even in these dark times, humanity must not lose sight of the importance of traveling to other stars in order to ensure the long-term survival of the species.

During the trek north, Lauren meets Taylor Bankole, whom she calls by his surname. Bankole is a former doctor in his late fifties whose own community was also destroyed. In spite of their age difference, the couple falls in love and agrees to marry, and they ultimately lead their growing group to a parcel of land that Bankole purchased years earlier in an isolated area of Northern California. As the book closes, in 2027, the group establishes a community they call "Acorn," where they plan to grow their own food, establish a school for the children they hope to have, and protect one another until society regains some kind of order.

Parable of the Talents continues the narrative in 2032. Lauren, Bankole, and the other original inhabitants of Acorn have added to their community by finding other refugees and by having children of their own. Lauren has integrated her Earthseed beliefs into community life, holding a weekly gathering at which she preaches simple verses to remind her congregation that, while God as change is not to be worshiped, they must remember that they have the power to shape change and therefore God.

Although Acorn is isolated, Lauren keeps up with current events and is alarmed to learn that the newly elected President Jarret not only turns a blind eye to the violent persecution of non-Christians but also may actually be encouraging it. While looking for a community member's lost sister, Lauren is shocked to find her brother Marcus, whom she had believed to be dead. Marcus is living as a slave and wearing an electronic convict collar that can deliver excruciating pain or even kill at the push of a button. Lauren pays for her brother's release and welcomes him to Acorn, but tension soon develops. After recovering from the attack on their childhood home, Marcus has spent the intervening years as a Baptist preacher, and he is horrified by what he perceives as Lauren's blasphemous Earthseed teachings.

Shortly after Marcus leaves Acorn to pursue his own calling, Lauren and Bankole have their first and only child, a daughter named Larkin Olamina Bankole. However, when Larkin is two months old, Acorn is viciously attacked by a group of Jarrett's Christian America crusaders. The surviving adults are outfitted with slave collars, and Acorn is turned into a "rehabilitation" center called Camp Christian, while the young children are "rescued" and placed with Christian America foster families.

Lauren encourages her companions to watch for an eventual opportunity to escape, but the group endures seventeen agonizing months of hard physical labor, torture, rape, and despair over the loss of their children. When a landslide incapacitates the slave collars, the group kills their captors and scatters. Bankole has died of a heart attack caused by his slave collar, and Lauren desperately tries to track down information on her daughter. She appeals to Marcus for help. Now a rising Christian America minister named Marcos Duran, he insists that Lauren's captors were simply fringe fanatics, rather than prominent members of his own church.

Lauren is once again alone, but she soon attracts new companions, some of whom begin to share her vision of Earthseed. Finally horrified by the atrocities committed with President Jarrett's complicity, the people of the United States gradually begin to restore some order to society. However, in spite of her best efforts, Lauren is not reunited with her

daughter until years later, when the adult Larkin, renamed Asha Vere, realizes on her own that she may be related to this increasingly famous woman who now has a significant following. Lauren is overjoyed to find her daughter, but she is devastated to learn that Marcus has known of Larkin's whereabouts for years. Because Larkin was raised by her Christian America foster parents and developed a close relationship with her Uncle Marc, she is unable to muster any warmth or affection for her mother, and she is contemptuous of Earthseed. Deep down, she cannot help but feel that Lauren did not try hard enough to find her.

In spite of Lauren's grief over the permanent loss of her daughter, a last journal entry dated 2090 shows that Lauren achieves some degree of peace because she has helped humanity take its first step toward the stars. She has gone to witness the launch of shuttles that will take colonists, some of them descendents of her original Acorn community, to Earth's first starship, which is being assembled in orbit and on the moon.

Critical Evaluation:

Octavia E. Butler's *Parable of the Sower* and *Parable of the Talents* are grim yet beautifully written and uplifting works of literature. These books are science fiction in that they incorporate fictional future technology, such as the slave collars and the ship that will carry the first humans to the stars. More important, however, they are works of social science fiction, envisioning a future toward which Butler arguably felt the United States might be headed if it continued to ignore alarming environmental, economic, and social trends. The books examine the damage caused by violence in the name of religion, as well as the illusion of safety that many people take for granted. As is the case with much of Butler's work, these books also address the inhumanity of slavery, showing how previously moral people can become monsters when they hold complete power over others.

Much of these books' beautiful writing comes in the form of Lauren's Earthseed verses, which are sparse bits of poetry reminding readers that everything changes people and that people change everything they touch. Ostensibly excerpts from Lauren's eventually published volume titled *Earthseed: The Books of the Living*, these verses head the sections and individual chapters of both books. In *Parable of the Sower*, the chapters themselves consist entirely of Lauren's journal entries, written in the past tense but with effective immediacy. *Parable of the Talents* is framed by Larkin's retrospective observations of her mother's life, which Larkin has researched as an adult in an attempt to know herself. This technique is especially successful because readers can feel

Larkin's rage toward Lauren for abandoning her in favor of Earthseed, even though Larkin knows her feelings are somewhat irrational.

Larkin's narrative is interspersed with what little survived of Bankole's writings, titled *Memories of Other Worlds.* Bankole's work provides background history for Butler's narrative because he was old enough to remember the more civilized United States that existed before the "Pox," or the social apocalypse. The second novel also includes journal entries by Lauren, and there are even some sections from a book titled *Warrior,* written by Marcus after he became something of a celebrity preacher in the Christian America church. Essentially, then, the *Parable* volumes contain books within books, painting a multilayered picture of a grim future in which some manage to hold on to hope.

Over the course of the two books, Butler fully explores the implications of Lauren's hyperempathy. Lauren herself notes that she is a liability within a group, because she can quickly be incapacitated to the point where she cannot help others. As more "sharers" join Acorn, Lauren learns that the hyperempathic are particularly valued in the slave market because they can be easily controlled. However, Lauren knows that her hyperempathy actually saved her life when her walled neighborhood was destroyed; because she collapsed after seeing someone else shot, the rabid attackers did not notice her. Furthermore, while Lauren hates the danger her condition puts her in, she understands that if everyone had hyperempathy, torture would no longer exist. People might still kill one another when necessary, but they would try to do so quickly and painlessly to keep themselves from suffering too.

As is true of most of Butler's fiction, the *Parable* books also deal with racial issues. Lauren's home neighborhood includes families of several different races, but when Lauren, Zahra, and Henry are the only survivors, Lauren realizes that others will perceive Zahra and Harry as a biracial couple. To protect all three of them, Lauren, who has always been big and strong for her age, poses as a man, and she and Zahra pretend to be an African American couple traveling with a Caucasian friend. Lauren's journal entries also make clear that it is much easier for Caucasians to get the very few jobs that remain in American society. Interestingly, when the trio begins to add stragglers to their group, many of them are of extremely mixed heritage. Acorn, too, becomes a community with numerous ethnicities, perhaps to allow Butler to portray different racial groups getting along.

Finally, Lauren's role as a persecuted religious teacher parallels the story of Christ. In their writings, Larkin, Bankole, and Marcus bear witness to the effect that Lauren has on those around her, but readers can also infer Lauren's calm yet charismatic personality from her own journal entries. Once Lauren realizes her purpose and that of Earthseed, she never wavers, much as Christians are taught that Christ never wavered in his teachings.

The books' titles themselves come directly from the Bible, and the biblical parables of the sower and of the talents are played out within the novels. In the first book, Lauren literally carries seeds from her old neighborhood that she plants in Acorn, although she could also be said to be sowing a new purpose and sense of community in the people she meets. In *Parable of the Talents,* she uses her own talents and those of her community to work for something beyond immediate survival. By weaving all these rich elements into a compelling narrative, Butler has created works of literature likely to endure for many decades.

Amy Sisson

Further Reading

Agustí, Clara Escoda. "Butler's *Parable of the Sower.*" *Extrapolation* 46, no. 3 (Fall, 2005): 351-359. Examines the ways in which Lauren Olamina deals with the exploitation, rape, and enslavement of women in *Parable of the Sower.* Focuses in part on Lauren's relationships with her brother Keith and her stepmother Cory.

Butler, Octavia E. "'We Keep Playing the Same Record': A Conversation with Octavia E. Butler." Interview by Stephen W. Potts. *Science-Fiction Studies* 23, no. 70 (November, 1996). Transcribed interview in which Butler places *Parable of the Sower* in the context of her other work and discusses the then in-progress *Parable of the Talents.*

Jablon, Madelyn. *Black Metafiction: Self-Consciousness in African American Literature.* Iowa City: University of Iowa Press, 1997. The chapter titled "Metafiction as Genre" discusses how *Parable of the Sower* can be interpreted as a parable in itself; supported by extensive quotes from the work.

Lacey, Lauren J. "Octavia E. Butler on Coping with Power in *Parable of the Sower, Parable of the Talents,* and *Fledgling.*" *Critique* 49, no. 4 (Summer, 2008): 379-394. Compares Lauren's relationship to power with that of the heroine of Butler's final novel, *Fledgling* (2006). Discusses both the use of power by Butler's protagonists and the abuse of those protagonists by others with power.

Zaki, Hoda. "Future Tense." *Women's Review of Books* 11, no. 10 (July, 1994): 37-38. Summarizes *Parable of the Sower,* particularly noting its ties to the Christian Gospel and to African American slave narratives.

Parade's End

Author: Ford Madox Ford (1873-1939)
First published: 1950; includes *Some Do Not . . .* ,
    1924; *No More Parades*, 1925; *A Man Could Stand
    Up*, 1926; *The Last Post*, 1928
Type of work: Novels
Type of plot: Impressionism
Time of plot: World War I and after
Locale: England and France

Principal characters:
CHRISTOPHER TIETJENS, the "last English Tory"
SYLVIA TIETJENS, his wife
MARK, his brother
MACMASTER, his friend
GENERAL CAMPION, his godfather
VALENTINE WANNOP, his mistress

The Story:

Christopher Tietjens is probably the last real eighteenth century Tory in the England of pre-World War I. A thoroughly good man, he is so much a gentleman that he will not divorce his wife, Sylvia Tietjens, even though she is flagrantly unfaithful to him. It is even doubtful that the child she gave birth to is his, and she had earlier gone off for several weeks with another man; Christopher, however, holds that no gentleman should ever publicly disgrace a woman by divorcing her or even by admitting her infidelities. Sylvia hates her husband blindly because she could never break down his reserve, and all of her plots and meanness were for that purpose alone. She detested the various men she lived with, but she hated Christopher's virtue more.

Christopher's old-fashioned type of virtue grew out of his family background. His oldest brother, Mark, who had inherited the estate of Groby and its vast income, lives with a Frenchwoman whom he will probably never marry and who will certainly have no children, and the estate will one day belong to Christopher. The brothers fear that their father had committed suicide, for Sylvia had manipulated the old man into believing that Christopher lived off the earnings of immoral women and that he had sold her, his wife, to influential friends. Christopher thinks his father's suicide had been a sign that the family is weakening; consequently, he will not accept one penny of the estate for himself. Mark, therefore, had proposed to set Sylvia up at Groby, with arrangements for the estate to go to her son. Even if the boy were not Christopher's son, he must be treated as if he were a Tietjens. The plan suits Christopher, who has no interest in anything except protecting his wife's name and his son's future. Knowing that war is imminent, he wants to gather up the loose ends of his life before he leaves.

Christopher is one of the most brilliant men in the government service but, strangely, his brilliance coupled with his goodness makes everyone want to hurt him. His only real friend is Macmaster, a Scotsman and a Whig, who also is in the service. Perhaps their friendship is due primarily to the fact that Macmaster owes Christopher a great deal of money. Christopher has also loaned money to other men who, although they admire him, seem bent on ruining him.

Christopher often wishes to make Valentine Wannop his mistress. Valentine is a young suffragist, the daughter of his father's best friend, and a novelist whom Christopher admires greatly. Valentine is willing to accept Christopher as her lover, but they seem destined to have their plans obstructed by someone bent on hurting Christopher. Although no word of their desire is ever spoken between them, their feelings are obvious to others, who believe that Valentine already is Christopher's mistress. On the night before his departure for the army, Christopher asks Valentine to spend the night with him. She consents, but again they are kept apart. Later, they both agree that it had been for the best, as neither seemed suited for an affair.

In France, unjustified troubles continue to haunt Christopher. Sylvia is at the bottom of most of them. Because she seems to think he will soon be killed and out of her reach, she seems compelled to hurt him as much as possible while he still lives. Christopher's godfather, General Campion, is his highest ranking officer. The general, convinced by Sylvia that she is an abused wife, constantly berates Christopher for his brutality as a husband. He also berates him for getting dirty, mixing with his men, and helping them with their personal troubles; it is not fitting for an English officer to get into the dregs of war.

Christopher often thinks he is surrounded by people with troubles. One of his fellow officers, almost insane over an unfaithful wife, often has fits of madness that threaten to destroy company morale. The first in command is a drunken colonel whom Christopher tries to shield, thus getting himself into trouble with General Campion. Once, Christopher refuses leave to a Canadian because he knows his wife's lover would kill the man if he went home. When the Canadian is killed in battle later on, it preys on Christopher's mind that he had saved the soldier from one death only to lead him into another. Christopher's good intentions constantly bring him discredit.

To Christopher's distress, Sylvia travels to France to see him. Having accepted at last that no matter what she does, she cannot upset him emotionally, she remains true to her character in her determination to make him return to her in body. Her scheme fails. After she maneuvers him into her room, one of her former lovers and the drunken colonel open the door that she had left unlocked for them but that she had forgotten to lock when Christopher went in with her. Christopher is forced to throw out the two men to protect his wife's honor. Having decided it is Christopher's fault that his wife wants to entertain other men, General Campion again berates him.

It seems to Christopher that the whole war campaign is bogged down because of lack of effective communications between various parts of the army. To him, the failure is symbolic. Life, too, bogs down into beastly messes because of lack of communication between people. To him, the horror of the war is not his physical suffering and inconvenience but rather that the conflict is the end of everything that matters. Believing that England is not prepared either for victory or for defeat, that this is the end of everything good no matter who wins the battles, he finds it almost impossible to remember anything of his old creed or his way of life at home. With Valentine so far away, she, too, seems unreal to him. Like the others, General Campion admires and likes Christopher but cannot understand him and wants to make him suffer. Because Christopher had thrown the men out of Sylvia's bedroom, General Campion sends him to the front.

At the front, Christopher is placed second in command to hopelessly outnumbered troops under the leadership of the drunken colonel. Finally forced into assuming command, he tries to sustain the shattered morale of his troops. The only thing that keeps his mind in balance is a dream of standing on a hilltop in peace, serenity, and privacy. Privacy is what he desires above all else. The army gives a man no chance to be alone or to keep his life and thoughts to himself. Because of his reticent nature, the lack of privacy is the worst hardship for Christopher. When an exploding shell buries him and two of his men under a pile of dirt, he digs out one of the soldiers and carries the other to safety through enemy fire. On his return, General Campion sends for him and relieves him of his command because his uniform is not spotless and flawless and because he had been reported away from headquarters.

His heroism and disgrace mark the physical end of the war for Christopher.

Valentine receives a telephone call from Macmaster's wife, who says that Christopher is home and almost out of his mind. Ready to give up everything to live with him and care for him, Valentine goes to him at once. She does not know or care about the story of his mental deterioration. The fact that he had never written to her also is of no importance. She intends to become his mistress, although she realizes she might first have to be his nurse. Back home in Valentine's company on armistice night, Christopher is about to declare his love when they are interrupted by celebrating members of Christopher's old company. His mind fuzzy, he finds nothing sad in their being thwarted again or in the obvious hate he sees in the eyes of a wife whose husband's life he had saved in the trenches.

There are changes at Groby, too. Mark had married his Frenchwoman and made her Lady Tietjens, partly to spite Sylvia, who had leased the estate to an obnoxious rich American woman and her husband. It is said that Mark, having suffered a stroke just after the armistice, could not speak or move. The truth is that, partially paralyzed, he has simply withdrawn from the world. Like Christopher, he belongs to another era. Mark believes that the last of the Tietjens are misfits. Truth has given way to confusion and untruth, and the brothers are likely to be swallowed up in this mad new world to which neither belongs. Avoiding the rest of the world, he waits quietly for death. Christopher and Valentine now live in a cottage close by. Having refused to go back into government service or to accept help from his brother, Christopher becomes a dealer in antique furniture.

Sylvia finally decides to divorce Christopher so she can marry General Campion and go with him to India. Although she has given up all hope of getting Christopher to notice her again, she continues her petty attempts to make his life miserable. When she learns that Valentine is to have a baby, however, she becomes afraid that her attacks on Christopher and Valentine will harm the unborn child. She also begins to regret her last and cruelest act against Christopher and Mark: She had persuaded the American woman to cut down the Groby Great Tree, an immense cedar that had guarded the manor house for generations; for a time, she fears the wrath of the brothers because of her deed. Both feel, however, that the Groby Great Tree had symbolized the curse hanging over the family and that its removal might take away part of that curse. When they ignore her spite, she stops her vicious tricks and decides to let Christopher marry Valentine. Sylvia hates General Campion, too, but she wants to become a great official's wife and be resplendent in a tiara.

Dying, Mark rationalizes his father's death and knows that the old gentleman had not committed suicide but had died as a result of a hunting accident. He also realizes that the appearance and actions of Sylvia's son prove that Christopher is his father, and that the boy is the rightful heir to Groby. It seems to Mark that he can at last understand and love his brother, and he believes that the tales he had heard about Christopher are really lies told by people who cannot understand Christopher or him because the Tietjens do not belong to this century of deceit, confusion, and untruth. Before he dies, Mark speaks once more, assuring Valentine that Christopher is a good man and asking her to be kind to him.

Critical Evaluation:

During his long life, Ford Madox Ford published eighty-one books, of which thirty-two were novels, but of these only *The Good Soldier* (1915) and the tetralogy with the collective title *Parade's End* are generally regarded as having the status of major works. *Parade's End* is many things: a portrait of an English country gentleman before the cataclysm of World War I, an individual's experience of the hardships of that war, a vivid picture of a terrible marriage, and a romantic story with a happy ending.

Each of the four novels that form *Parade's End* makes use of impressionistic methods. Critical scenes carry most of the narrative burden, as the action moves with little transition from one scene to another, while the narrative moves backward and forward in time. An episode that concludes the sixth chapter of part 2 in the first novel, *Some Do Not . . .* , is, for example, not explained until part 1, chapter 3, of the second novel, *No More Parades*; the aftermath of that scene is not resolved until the final chapter of the third novel, *A Man Could Stand Up*. Jumps in time include that between the 1916 beginning of part 1 of *Some Do Not . . .* , when Tietjens, his memory shattered by his combat experiences, is preparing to return to the front from London, and the end of the same part four years earlier.

Ford's style in these novels also includes experiments with point of view, and the narrative voice switches from Tietjens to the object of his love, Valentine Wannop, to Sylvia, with brief stops along the way to the minds of other characters. In the final novel, *The Last Post*, Christopher Tietjens's older brother Mark becomes the central character, and most of that novel takes place in Mark's mind. Each of the main characters is portrayed not only by a third-person narrator but also through interior monologues in a stream-of-consciousness style. Contemporaries, including James Joyce and Virginia Woolf, were using similar techniques, but Ford created an idiosyncratic combination of narrative stream of consciousness and time shifts.

The four novels of *Parade's End* cover most of the adult life of Christopher. It is a life filled with frustration over the end of the world as he had known it, a world in which he seems to be the only person upholding moral standards. His wife, who both hates and loves him, treats him dreadfully. A classic shrew, she lies to Tietjens, lies to others to blacken his name, seduces anyone who catches her fancy, and fights to secure her son's rights as heir to the Tietjens's estates. Tietjens, in love with Valentine, refuses for years to consummate their love because of his marital vows. He endures much pain, not only from Sylvia but also from his experiences in the war and the sorrow he feels for the men under his command who are being slaughtered in the mire of trench warfare.

The first three novels paint a bitter picture of England's destruction. Only in *The Last Post*, in which Christopher does not appear at all but is reported to be happily engaged in the antique business while Valentine is pregnant, does the life of this character attain peace and happiness.

Parade's End is simultaneously a series of very funny novels and a bitterly accurate description of the destruction of a generation. Christopher and Sylvia are not only victims and victimizers, they are superbly drawn comic figures, and the attempts of both to get their own way provide a wealth of comic scenes. In one scene of *Some Do Not . . .* , Sylvia accuses her husband of adultery, reminds him that she has blackened his name with lies to his parents and his bank, and finally shies crockery at him in the attempt to break through his self-possession. Ford lightens even the bleak tone of the grimmest of the four novels, *No More Parades*, with a kind of French bedroom farce involving Sylvia and several officers in a French hotel. Valentine's protracted conversation with the headmistress of the school where she teaches introduces a new tone in the opening of *A Man Could Stand Up*, which shifts to the end of the war and provides the information that Christopher has survived the war. Finally, *The Last Post* includes a hilarious scene in which all the main characters except Christopher gather at Groby, the Tietjens's ancestral home, to fight over Christopher and the heritage of Groby.

Characterization is a major reason for the success of these novels, for all of the characters are sharply drawn. From Valentine and her novelist mother to General Campion, Mark Tietjens with his longtime French mistress, and Father Consett, who functions as whatever conscience Sylvia has, the characters who populate these novels are individualized and memorable.

It is beyond question that Christopher carries the heaviest

significance in *Parade's End*. It is clear that he is based on Ford's own character and experience and that his highly individual sense of values is very much Ford's own. The nostalgia for an earlier and more moral society is obviously an important element in the novels. Ford saw himself and his ideals clearly enough, however, to realize that they were anachronistic in the aftermath of World War I and to portray them as comic in the context of postwar society. *Parade's End* is a superb achievement.

"Critical Evaluation" by John M. Muste

Further Reading

Brown, Dennis, and Jenny Plastow, eds. *Ford Madox Ford and Englishness*. New York: Rodopi, 2006. Collection of essays that assess Ford's ideas about England and the concept of "Englishness. Considers him a key participant in Edwardian debates about these subjects. Many of Ford's works are analyzed in terms of their Englishness, including *Parade's End*.

Cassell, Richard A., ed. *Critical Essays on Ford Madox Ford*. Boston: G. K. Hall, 1987. An excellent collection of essays, most focusing on *The Good Soldier* but with significant attention paid to *Parade's End*.

Haslam, Sara. *Fragmenting Modernism: Ford Madox Ford, the Novel, and the Great War*. New York: Manchester University Press, 2002. Focuses on the modernist characteristics of Ford's works, such as their fragmentation, use of the personal narrative, and literary technique. Includes a bibliography and an index.

Kingsbury, Celia Malone. *The Peculiar Sanity of War: Hysteria in the Literature of World War I*. Lubbock: Texas Tech University Press, 2002. Examines the impact of World War I hysteria on standards of behavior and definitions of sanity as reflected in British novels, including *Parade's End*.

Mizener, Arthur. *The Saddest Story: A Biography of Ford Madox Ford*. 1971. Reprint. New York: Carroll & Graf, 1985. The definitive biography of Ford, a long and thorough study that includes an appendix with a separate discussion of *Parade's End*.

Sniton, Ann Barr. *Ford Madox Ford and the Voice of Uncertainty*. Baton Rouge: Louisiana State University Press, 1984. Studies Ford's style in detail, showing how its hesitancy and ambiguity reflect Ford's ambivalent attitude toward his times.

Wiesenfarth, Joseph, ed. *History and Representation in Ford Madox Ford's Writings*. New York: Rodopi, 2004. The book's essays analyze Ford's works of historical fiction and nonfiction, including *Parade's End*.

Paradise

Author: Toni Morrison (1931-   )
First published: 1998
Type of work: Novel
Type of plot: Historical
Time of plot: 1950's-1970's
Locale: Haven and Ruby, Oklahoma

Principal characters:
DEACON MORGAN and STEWARD MORGAN, twin brothers
ELDER MORGAN, their older brother
K. D. MORGAN, their nephew
SOANE MORGAN and DOVEY MORGAN, twin sisters, married to the Morgan twins
PATRICIA BEST CATO, a schoolteacher and unofficial town historian
CONNIE SOSA,
PALLAS TRUELOVE,
GRACE GIBSON,
MAVIS ALBRIGHT, and
SENECA, residents of the Convent
ARNETTE FLEETWOOD, K. D.'s girlfriend

The Story:

Nine men from the all-black town of Ruby, Oklahoma, are ready to launch a military-style assault against the five women living in a former nunnery called the Convent, located seventeen miles outside town. The women represent everything that, at minimum, two of the men, twin brothers Deacon (Deek) and Steward Morgan, have fought against all their lives: white people and "white blood," or light-skinned blacks. They enter the Convent and "shoot the white girl first. With the rest [of the women] they can take their time."

Ruby had been founded by the descendants of the original exiles from Louisiana and Alabama who, in 1889, traveled west toward the "free" territory of Oklahoma. Arriving there, they were turned away from town after town by Choctaws and poor whites. The most traumatic event, one the Morgans have never forgotten, was being turned away by citizens of the all-black town of Fairly, Oklahoma. Although the real reason for their "disallowing" was their lack of cash or capital, Deacon and Steward believe skin-color prejudice, and not economic discrimination, had kept them out of Fairly, a town of light-skinned blacks. So the "8-rock" blacks, so called for the blackness of the "deep deep level in the coal mines," founded the town of Haven and made it exclusive: No American Indians, whites, or light-skinned blacks were allowed to reside there. When the Great Depression took its toll on the town, the surviving people of Haven moved deeper into unpopulated Oklahoma Territory, avoided the major cities, and founded Ruby, named for the Morgan brothers' mother, who had died in transit.

The Morgan twins are married to twin sisters, Dovey and Soane. Steward and Dovey cannot have children, and Deacon and Soane had lost both of their sons in the Vietnam War. Sterility and death have led the four to other forms of compensation: Dovey has an imaginary friend, suggesting her withdrawal into childhood. Soane, who had an abortion (the result of an affair) shortly after she and Deacon were married, regularly takes a "tonic" (prepared by Connie Sosa) that prevents her from getting pregnant again; she also talks to birds, warning them to "watch out" for Deacon, who hunts quail. Deacon is having an affair with Connie, as had Steward, and both are losing their grip on power in Ruby.

A new minister, the Reverend Misner, has started a credit union, whose favorable interest rates threaten the Morgans' bank. The Morgans' nephew, K. D. Morgan, the son of their dead older brother, has insulted his pregnant girlfriend, Arnette Fleetwood, with a public slap in the face; now, her father, Arnold Fleetwood, wants justice. The Morgans are forced to promise to pay for her college education. K. D., who is having an affair with Grace "Gigi" Gibson, wants to end his relationship with Arnette, but because he is the only male left in the Morgan line, his uncles, Steward and Deacon, lay down the law: He will marry Arnette.

The Convent had been founded by a group of Catholic nuns who bought the place from an embezzler and pornographer who had been on the lam. One of the nuns had kidnapped Connie (then named Consolata) from the streets of Central America, brought her to the Convent, and converted her to Catholicism. However, Connie now practices Voodoo, which she learned from a girl who had been picked up by the settlers of Haven as they were heading west to found Ruby.

Mavis Albright is terrorized by her husband, Frank, and her three children. She accepts this abuse as punishment for having left her twin babies—the would-be siblings of the older children—in a car while shopping. Their death by suffocation had been the lead story on the local TV news. The female reporter had made it clear that Mavis is "the dumbest bitch in the world." One morning, Mavis steals Frank's mint-green Cadillac, takes some money, and goes to her mother for help. Her mother calls Frank, who pursues Mavis across several state lines before she escapes to the Convent.

Grace is involved with Mikey, a low-level thief who tells her about a place outside Tucson, Arizona, where there are two trees intertwined, like a couple making love forever. Grace waits for Mikey after he is released from prison, but he never shows up at the appointed meeting place. So she heads to Tucson, but no one there knows about the trees. She decides to head to Mexico and winds up prostituting to survive. She calls her grandfather, who tells her to come home. On the train back to the United States she meets a man named Dice, who tells her about a place where one can find the best rhubarb pie in the world—Ruby, Oklahoma. She accompanies Dice to Ruby, but once there, she is abandoned by him. Grace decides to leave and begins walking out of town. Roger Best, a funeral director and a widower, picks up Grace and drives her to the Convent.

A girl named Seneca is abandoned by Jean, her sister, and placed in foster care because the girls' mother is dead. After Seneca's release from care, she decides to take gifts to lonely men in prison. She becomes enamored of one prisoner, Eddie, who eventually talks Seneca into visiting his mother in Wichita, Kansas, to see if she will cash a savings bond for him. His mother refuses, shouting that Eddie will never be forgiven for running over a child. Shocked, Seneca flees to the bus station to leave town. A chauffeur offers her money to be the "plaything" of his employer, a married woman named Norma Fox, whose husband is on a business trip. Seneca stays with Fox for three weeks, suffering through sexual abuse before Fox's husband returns home. The chauffeur drops Seneca off at the bus station. At a loss for what to do, she takes a bus to Oklahoma and hitches a ride to the Convent.

Pallas Truelove is in high school when she meets Carlos, the school's maintenance man, and falls in love with him. He aspires to be an artist, so when Pallas mentions that her mother is a painter, Carlos gets Pallas to introduce him. Pallas's mother, Dee Dee (Divine), and Carlos begin an affair. Pallas is devastated and runs away. She runs into a gang of boys who rape her repeatedly until she eludes them by hiding in a lake. An American Indian woman drives her to Ruby, and then the daughter of schoolteacher Patricia Best Cato takes her to the Convent.

K. D. and Arnette are getting married, and before the reception can start, the Convent women crash the party and dance lewdly with each other, infuriating Deacon and Steward. With three other men, they head for the Convent and kill the women. The funeral director cannot find any bodies on the premises after the shooting, leading some to think that the slaughtered women found an alternate reality in which to thrive.

Critical Evaluation:

Paradise is one of Toni Morrison's most controversial novels, criticized for appearing to bracket racial injustice to concentrate on gender oppression, particularly the systematic exploitation and sexual abuse of girls and women. However, Morrison does not privilege gender; rather, she draws parallels between gender, race, and class.

It is true that except for Mavis, the one former housewife in the group, all the women at the Convent had suffered sexual abuse of one kind or another during their teenage years. Many of the women have internalized their abuse—for example, Mavis and Gigi have brutal, physical fights—just as the black men of Ruby have internalized the racism and skin-color prejudice that initially drove them into the nethermost regions of Oklahoma.

At the same time, for all its wonderful characterizations and explorations of American history, the novel's binary oppositions are contrived: not only is Ruby, a sanctuary for men, the polar opposite of the Convent, a sanctuary for women, Ruby's massive communal Oven, which symbolizes self-sufficiency and a kind of cultural nationalism, is opposed to the giant kitchen in the Convent where the women have a kind of "last supper" before the slaughter. Deacon and Steward, twin brothers, are married to Dovey and Soane, twin sisters. Reverend Misner, the progressive outsider, is opposed by another reverend who is a conservative insider.

That the novel succeeds in spite of these rather stock oppositions says a great deal about Morrison's ability to bring her characters to life. She teases out the repressed anger and frustration felt by women like Soane and Dovey and uncovers the ambivalence and complicity in their own oppression; the same could be said about Morrison's portrait of teacher and unofficial town historian Patricia Best Cato, who discovers the secret of the founders of Ruby—that skin-color prejudice trumps white racism. In the interest of protecting her precarious status in Ruby, Patricia burns all her notes and memos.

Morrison's portraits of Deacon and Steward are sympathetic to the burden of history that each must bear. Not only are they haunted by the heroic stature of their grandfather in his struggle against racism and prejudice, a struggle they can never emulate or measure up to, they also are haunted by their older brother's death in his tattered U.S. Army uniform. Elder Morgan, who had just returned from his tour of duty in World War I, had seen a black prostitute being jeered at by white sailors. Elder had joined in the heckling until the white men began to physically assault the woman. Elder had then rushed to her aid, tearing his uniform in the process. From that moment on, Elder had been haunted by his complicity with white men against a black woman, insisting to his wife that she bury him in his torn uniform as a form of punishment and atonement.

Significantly, when Deacon thinks of his brother's story, he sympathizes more with the white sailors than with his own brother, much less the prostitute. Deacon's adulterous relationship with Connie Sosa and his decision that he has to be the one to shoot her at the Convent add layers and layers of complexity to his character.

The multifaceted ironies underlying *Paradise* are perhaps best encapsulated in all the sick grandchildren of Arnold Fleetwood. Like the Morgan twins, Arnold, too, will not have a legacy beyond his troubled son, Jefferson. The first death recorded in Ruby had been the death of one of Arnold's sick children.

Tyrone Williams

Further Reading

Aguiar, Sarah Appleton. "'Passing on' Death: Stealing Life in Toni Morrison's *Paradise*." *African American Review* 38, no. 3 (Autumn, 2004): 513-519. Aguiar argues that death is a central leitmotif in *Paradise*, suggesting that the women at the Convent might have been dead when they arrived there. Also demonstrates how death permeates the values and ideas of the residents of Ruby.

Davidson, Rob. "Racial Stock and 8-Rocks: Communal Historiography in Toni Morrison's *Paradise*." *Twentieth Century Literature* 47, no. 3 (Autumn, 2001): 355-373. Examines the role that communal narratives play in *Paradise*. Emphasizes that since most of the narratives are controlled by the men of Ruby, Patricia Best Cato's "counternarrative" is crucial to uncovering the truth behind major town events, including its founding.

Omry, Keren. "Literary Free Jazz? *Mumbo Jumbo* and *Paradise*: Language and Meaning." *African American Review* 41, no. 1 (Spring, 2007): 127-141. Drawing upon cultural critic Theodor Adorno's analysis of jazz music, Omry argues that *Paradise* replicates the improvisational nature of jazz insofar as the Convent, a symbol of the present, exists in tension with the formal closure of Ruby, a town whose elders are desperate to hold on to the past.

Reames, Kelly Lynch. *Toni Morrison's "Paradise": A Reader's Guide*. New York: Continuum, 2001.

Schur, Richard L. "Locating Paradise in the Post-Civil Rights Era: Toni Morrison and Critical Race Theory." *Contemporary Literature* 45, no. 2 (Summer, 2004): 276-299. Schur argues that *Paradise*, like all of Morrison's novels, engages the legal and cultural contexts of their respective settings even when there are no direct references to historical events. Shows how *Paradise* interrogates the limitations and tunnel vision of the legal system via the relationship between Ruby and the Convent.

Stein, Karen F. *Reading, Learning, Teaching Toni Morrison*. New York: Peter Lang, 2009. An excellent primer for students just beginning their studies of Morrison and her works. Includes an introductory chapter about the background to Morrison's fiction.

Paradise Lost

Author: John Milton (1608-1674)
First published: 1667; revised, 1674
Type of work: Poetry
Type of plot: Epic
Time of plot: Creation of the world
Locale: Heaven, Hell, and Earth

Principal characters:
GOD THE FATHER
CHRIST THE SON
LUCIFER, later Satan
ADAM
EVE

The Poem:

In Heaven, Lucifer, unable to abide the supremacy of God, leads a revolt against divine authority. Defeated, he and his followers are cast into Hell, where they lie nine days on a burning lake. Lucifer, now called Satan, arises from the flaming pitch and vows that all is not lost, that he will have revenge for his downfall. Arousing his legions, he reviews them under the canopy of Hell and decides his purposes can be achieved by guile rather than by force.

Under the direction of Mulciber, the forces of evil build an elaborate palace, Pandemonium, in which Satan convenes a congress to decide on immediate action. At the meeting, Satan reasserts the unity of those fallen and opens the floor to debate regarding what measures should be taken. Moloch advises war. Belial recommends a slothful existence in Hell. Mammon proposes peacefully improving Hell so that it might rival Heaven in splendor. His motion is received with great favor until Beelzebub, second in command, rises and informs the conclave that God has created Earth, which he has peopled with good creatures called humans. It is Beelze-

bub's proposal to investigate this new creation, seize it, and seduce its inhabitants to the cause of the fallen angels.

Announcing that he will journey to Earth to learn for himself how matters are there, Satan flies to the gate of Hell. There he encounters his daughter, Sin, and his son, Death. They open the gate, and Satan wings his way toward Earth.

God, in his omniscience, has beheld the meeting in Hell, knows the intent of the evil angels, and sees Satan approaching Earth. Disguised as various beasts, Satan acquaints himself with Adam and Eve and with the Tree of Knowledge, the fruit of which God has forbidden to them.

Uriel, learning that an evil angel has broken through to Eden, warns Gabriel, who appoints two angels to hover about the bower of Adam and Eve. The guardian angels arrive too late, however, to prevent Satan, in the form of a toad, from beginning his evil work. He has influenced Eve's dreams.

Upon awaking, Eve tells Adam that in her strange dream she was tempted to taste of the fruit of the Tree of Knowledge. God, seeing that danger to Adam and Eve is imminent, sends the angel Raphael to the garden to warn them. At Adam's insistence, Raphael relates in detail the story of the great war between the good and the bad angels that led to the fall of the bad angels to eternal misery in Hell. At Adam's further inquiries, Raphael tells of the creation of the world: how Earth was created in six days, an angelic choir singing the praises of God on the seventh day. He cautions Adam not to be too curious, saying that there are many things done by God that are not for humans to understand or to attempt to understand. Adam then tells how he has been warned against the Tree of Knowledge of Good and Evil, how he asked God for fellowship in his loneliness, and how Eve was created from his rib.

After the departure of Raphael, Satan returns to the garden as a mist and enters the body of a sleeping serpent. In the morning, as Adam and Eve proceed to their day's occupation, Eve proposes that they work apart. Adam, remembering the warning of Raphael, opposes her wishes, but Eve prevails, and the two part. Alone, Eve is accosted by the serpent, which flatters her into tasting the fruit of the Tree of Knowledge. Eve, liking what she has tasted, takes the fruit to Adam, who is horrified when he sees what Eve has done. In his love for Eve, however, he also eats the fruit.

Having eaten, Adam and Eve know lust for the first time, and after their dalliance they know sickening shame. They also eat many apples, adding gluttony to their list, which they are rapidly completing, of the seven deadly sins. The guardian angels now desert the transgressors and return to God, who approves their efforts, saying they could not have prevented Satan from succeeding in his mission.

Christ descends to Earth to pass judgment. Before Adam and Eve, who had been reluctant, in their shame, to come out of their bower to face him, Christ sentences the serpent to be forever a hated enemy of humankind. He tells Eve that her sorrow will be multiplied by the bearing of children and that she will be the servant of Adam to the end of time. Adam, says Christ, will eat in sorrow; his ground will be cursed, and he will eat bread only by toiling and sweating.

Meanwhile, Death and Sin, having divined Satan's success, leave the gates of Hell to join their father on Earth. Within sight of Earth they meet Satan, who delegates Sin and Death as his ambassadors on Earth. Back in Hell, Satan proudly reports his accomplishments to his followers. He is acclaimed, however, by hisses as his cohorts become serpents, and Satan himself is transformed into a serpent before their reptilian eyes. Trees similar to the Tree of Knowledge appear in Hell, but when the evil angels taste the fruit, they find their mouths full of ashes.

God, angered at the disaffection of Adam and Eve, brings about great changes on Earth. He creates the seasons to replace eternal spring and creates the violence and misery of storms, winds, hail, ice, floods, and earthquakes. He causes all of Earth's creatures to prey upon one another. Adam and Eve argue bitterly (adding anger to their sins) until they realize they have to face their common plight together. Repenting their sins, they pray to God for relief. Although Christ intercedes for them, God sentences them to expulsion from Eden and sends the angel Michael to Earth to carry out the sentence. Adam and Eve, lamenting their misfortune, contemplate suicide, but Michael gives them new hope when he brings to Adam a vision of life and death; of the rise and fall of kingdoms and empires; of the activities of Adam and Eve's progeny through their evil days to the flood, when God will destroy all life except that preserved by Noah in the ark; and of the subsequent return to evil days and Christ's incarnation, death, resurrection, and ascension as the redeemer. Despite the violence, evil, and bloodshed in the vision, Adam and Eve are pacified when they see that their children will be saved. They walk hand in hand from the heights of Paradise to the barren plains below.

Critical Evaluation:

John Milton prepared himself for many years to create an epic poem in English that would rank with the epics of Homer and Vergil. *Paradise Lost* is nothing less than the Christian epic of humanity. One of Milton's models for *Paradise Lost* was the *Iliad* (c. 750 B.C.E.; English translation, 1611), an epic poem of the oral tradition that evolved as the composition of a number of poets but is commonly attributed to Homer. The *Iliad* celebrates heroes. A model of even greater influence was the *Aeneid* (c. 29-19 B.C.E.; English translation, 1553), an epic poem written by a single poet, Vergil, whose intent was to celebrate the national glory of Rome. Milton's original intent was to follow Vergil's lead and write a patriotic epic poem of England, but he changed his mind, espousing an even greater enterprise. In retelling the story of the Fall of Man, he attempts to do nothing less than "justify the ways of God to men."

To emphasize the importance of his subject matter, Vergil chose to write in a solemn tone using heightened language, and Milton adopted the same policy. Much of the difficulty of *Paradise Lost* for readers lies in the language. The poem uses uncommon words put together in long sentences containing multiple clauses constructed and ordered in peculiar ways. The convoluted syntax and unfamiliar language give the poem its distinctive cadences, its majestic rhythm, and its ceremonial atmosphere. The many classical, biblical, and geographical references add authority, pointing to the learning of the poet. In such ways, Milton brings grandeur to his poem.

The background to the poem is from the Bible and follows the teaching of Saint Augustine. Although Milton was involved in religious controversy in his life, this great poem, in its adherence to basic Christian doctrine, largely stands outside the issues of Milton's time. The cosmos as it is described in the poem conforms to the popular view of Milton's day. Chaos is bounded above by Heaven and beneath by Hell. Earth, at the center of a spherical "solar system," is suspended into chaos from the floor of Heaven. Above all is God, who is dazzling light. Hell, at the other extreme, is absolute lack of light. Within the cosmos, all beings exist in a hierarchy under God, and all beings owe obedience to their hierarchical superiors. The hierarchy, the Great Chain of Being, is of central importance, as is the doctrine of obedience. Satan and his followers rebel against the authority of God and are thrown out of Heaven, and Adam and Eve disobey God and are ejected from the Garden of Eden.

The characterizations of God and Satan are problematic, not the least because neither is human. Milton's readers, being human, however, understand character in anthropomorphic terms. God is invisible and can be defined by people only in terms of attributes, such as "Immortal" or "Almighty." God thus tends to seem abstract and distant rather than real. God is absolute authority. In addition, God is omniscient, knowing all that happens and all that will happen, but has given the lower orders free will. Consequently, God can be seen as tyrannical and cruel in not preventing evil. Easier to understand is the reflection of God, as seen in the Son of God, superior to all but the Creator: "Beyond compare the Son of God was seen/ Most glorious, in him all his Father shone/ Substantially expressed."

Satan, with his fallen nature, is easier to understand. Before his fall Satan was Lucifer, an archangel. In the early part of Milton's poem readers see his magnificent qualities and then follow the progress of his self-destruction, which is caused by pride and envy. The danger in the characterization of Satan is that readers tend to find him attractive; they sympathize with his resentment and admire his passionate determination. The strength of the characterization lies in these qualities. His gradual degeneration, however, is convincing; awareness of his sinfulness grows in readers' consciousness. At first Satan longs for good, but finally he embraces evil. Readers observe Satan metamorphose in a series of disguises, each a lower life-form than the one before—a continuum, recalling the Great Chain of Being, from archangel to serpent.

The problem of presenting Adam and Eve is that they must at first be innocent, free of sin, yet they must be intelligent and aware enough to be capable of choosing sin and strong enough to resist. Milton shows how the potential for their fall is present from the start. Satan is there in the Garden of Eden, observing, plotting, beginning to work at undermining Eve's integrity. Reaching her through a dream, he acquaints her with temptation. She ultimately succumbs to the temptation of surpassing her true place in the hierarchy, and the sin of pride accompanies her disobedience in eating the forbidden fruit. She tempts Adam to follow her into sin because she cannot bear to lose him, and Adam succumbs because he cannot bear to lose her. His sin also goes beyond disobedience. He violates the hierarchical order in putting Eve, who, the poem makes clear, is inferior to him, above himself and his power of reason, and therefore above God.

Adam and Eve and the world itself are incomparably diminished by the Fall, but it is also to be seen as the opportunity for a new hope and for the occasion of their later redemption. The Fall affords them the chance to develop for themselves virtues such as repentance, humility, and understanding.

Milton is considered the greatest poet after William Shakespeare, and *Paradise Lost* is his greatest poem. This huge work has not received universal acclaim, however. Some critics have objected to implications they see in the characterizations. It is hard to imagine that Milton could have better fit such a story into the form of an epic, but nevertheless critics have complained of what may be perceived as the work's depiction of God's tyranny and Satan's heroism. Milton's portrayal of Eve also has generated much criticism. In addition, some have voiced objections regarding the style of the poem, criticizing, for example, Milton's overuse of abstractions and his unnatural syntax. A great many critics, however, have found *Paradise Lost* fascinating and satisfying, one of the truly great and enduring works of literature of all time.

"Critical Evaluation" by Susan Henthorne

Further Reading

Broadbent, John Barclay. *Some Graver Subject: An Essay on "Paradise Lost."* New York: Barnes & Noble, 1960. Serves as an excellent introduction to *Paradise Lost*. Acknowledges the difficulties of reading the poem while systematically analyzing and explaining Milton's meanings.

Bryson, Michael. *The Tyranny of Heaven: Milton's Rejection of God as King.* Newark: University of Delaware

Press, 2004. Argues that the kinglike God of *Paradise Lost* is not Milton's admired model of divinity; instead, Milton favors the Son in *Paradise Regained*, who rejects kingship in favor of a form of spiritual self-government. Asserts that the two epics constitute a critique of the English people, who endorsed the government of kings by restoring Charles II to the throne.

Campbell, Gordon, and Thomas N. Corns. *John Milton: Life, Work, and Thought.* New York: Oxford University Press, 2008. Insightful and comprehensive biography is based in part on previously unavailable information about seventeenth century English history. Sheds light on Milton's ideas and the turbulent times in which he lived.

Duran, Angelica, ed. *A Concise Companion to Milton.* Malden, Mass.: Blackwell, 2007. Collection of essays offers analyses of Milton's works, discussions of his legacy, and a survey of more than three hundred years of Milton criticism. Essays examine Milton's work in relation to the Bible, religion, and spirituality and in relation to gender, sex, and marriage.

Kranidas, Thomas, ed. *New Essays on "Paradise Lost."* Berkeley: University of California Press, 1969. Essays by American scholars examine such topics as the poem's form, style, genre, and theme.

Lewis, C. S. *A Preface to "Paradise Lost."* New York: Oxford University Press, 1961. Classic work considers epic form in general and continues with a discussion of Milton's epic based on a specifically Christian interpretation. Rather dogmatic but nevertheless offers a lucid, enormously informative analysis of form and doctrinal issues.

Poole, William. *Milton and the Idea of the Fall.* New York: Cambridge University Press, 2005. Examines the origins and evolution of seventeenth century concepts of the biblical Fall of Man and how these concepts were expressed by seventeenth century English authors, including Milton. Describes how Milton adapted these ideas to create his own concept of the Fall and demonstrates how these ideas are reflected in *Paradise Lost.*

Rosenfeld, Nancy. *The Human Satan in Seventeenth-Century English Literature: From Milton to Rochester.* Burlington, Vt.: Ashgate, 2008. Analyzes works of seventeenth century literature, including *Paradise Lost* and *Paradise Regained,* to describe how Milton and other English authors presented a human depiction of Satan.

Paradise Regained

Author: John Milton (1608-1674)
First published: 1671
Type of work: Poetry
Type of plot: Epic
Time of plot: First century
Locale: Holy Land

Principal characters:
JESUS OF NAZARETH
SATAN

The Poem:

Jesus of Nazareth is baptized by John the Baptist. This rite is attended by Satan, the Adversary, cloaked in invisibility. Thunderstruck by the pronouncement from Heaven that Jesus is the beloved Son of God, Satan hastily assembles a council of his peers. They choose "their great Dictator" to attempt the overthrow of this new and terrible enemy. God, watching Satan set out on his evil mission, foretells the failure of the mission to the angel Gabriel. The angels sing a triumphant hymn.

Led by the Spirit, Jesus enters the desert and pursues holy meditations. In retrospect, he examines his life, considers his destiny, but does not wish for revelation of his future until God chooses to give it. For forty days he wanders unharmed through the perils of the desert; then for the first time he feels hunger. Just at that moment, he meets an aged man in rural clothing. The old man explains that he was present at the baptism, then expresses amazement at the lost and perilous situation of the wanderer. Jesus replies "Who brought me hither will bring me hence, no other Guide I seek." The old man then suggests that if Jesus were really the Son of God, he should command the stones to become bread. In his refusal, Jesus asks, "Why dost thou then suggest to me distrust, knowing who I am, as I know who thou art?" At this discovery, Satan abandons his disguise and enters a dispute attempting self-justification. Overcome in the argument, he vanishes as night falls. The other newly baptized people and Mary the mother of Jesus are distressed at his absence, but do not allow themselves to despair.

Satan calls a fresh council of war. He dismisses Belial's suggestion to "Set women in his eye and in his walk" and receives a vote of confidence for his own plan of using honor, glory, and popular praise combined with relief from the suffering of physical hunger.

Jesus dreams of the ravens who fed Elijah by Cherith's Brook and of the angel who fed him in the desert. Awakening, he looks for a cottage, a sheepcote, or a herd, but finds nothing. Suddenly, Satan appears again in a new form, but does not attempt to conceal his identity. He discloses a table loaded with delicious food and invites Jesus to eat. Jesus refuses the food, not because the food itself is unlawful but because it is the offering of Satan. Disgruntled, Satan causes the food to vanish and returns to the attack, offering wealth with which to buy power. When this is declined as an unworthy aim for life, Satan proposes the career of a glorious conqueror. Jesus retorts with references to Job and Socrates, as justly famous as the proudest conquerors, and he declares that desire for glory, which belongs to God, not humanity, is sacrilege. Satan then attempts to relate conquest to the freeing of the Jews from their Roman oppressors. Jesus replies that if his destiny is to free his people from bondage it will come about when God chooses. Satan asks another of his penetrating questions: Why did Satan hasten to overthrow himself by trying to found Christ's everlasting kingdom? This question tortures Satan internally, but he takes refuge in hypocritical assurances that he has lost hope of his own triumph.

Then, remarking that Jesus has seen little of the world, Satan takes him to the top of a mountain and shows him the terrestrial kingdoms, in particular the empires of Rome and Parthia, one of which he advises him to choose and to destroy the other with it. Jesus, however, refuses earthly empire. Then Satan tries a particularly Miltonic temptation. He offers the empire of the mind: philosophy, learning, poetry, particularly those of Greece and Rome. Against these, Jesus places the sacred literature of the Hebrews. Satan, baffled again, returns Jesus to the desert and pretends to depart. When Jesus sleeps again, Satan disturbs him with ugly dreams and raises a fearful storm. With morning and the return of calm weather, Satan appears for a last, desperate effort, no longer so much in hope of victory as in desire for revenge. He seizes Jesus, flies with him to Jerusalem, places him on the highest pinnacle of the Temple, and cries,

There stand, if thou wilt stand; to stand upright
Will ask thee skill. . . .
Now show thy Progeny; if not to stand,
Cast thyself down; safely if Son of God:
For it is written, He will give command
Concerning thee to his Angels, in their hands
They shall uplift thee, lest at any time
Thou chance to dash thy foot against a stone.
To whom thus Jesus. Also it is written,
Tempt not the Lord thy God; he said and stood.
But Satan smitten with amazement fell.

After Satan's second fall, a host of angels fly to the temple, take Jesus to a fertile valley, and spread before him a table of celestial food. After they sing another hymn of triumph, Jesus returns home to his mother's house.

Critical Evaluation:

Paradise Regained is composed of four books averaging about five hundred lines of blank verse each; the poem, therefore, contains more than two thousand lines. The Gospel of Luke, John Milton's principal source, is contained in seventeen verses spread over two chapters. Although Milton regarded this "brief epic" as his greatest masterpiece, that evaluation has not generally been shared by his critical or popular readership. Unlike his internationally acclaimed epic *Paradise Lost* (1667, 1674), *Paradise Regained* lacks both an intense conflict between worthy moral antagonists and the narrative action such conflicts afford. To many, the novel's Satan seems to have been pathetically reduced to an incompetent schemer who is no match for the stoical Jesus of Nazareth, who dominates the extended debates occupying most of the epic. Yet if Milton was not wholly wrong about his final work, in what does its greatness consist?

Although lacking some of the complexity of its forerunner, *Paradise Regained* can be breathtaking in its stark poetic simplicity and in its profound narrative expansion of Luke's brief account of Jesus' three temptations in the wilderness. To appreciate its narrative "action" is thus to understand how Milton uses a dialogical form of conflict drawn from the book of Job to illuminate and expand these three themes. Yet it is also to understand how Job-like this Jesus is, who is not merely an omniscient being who must "inevitably" triumph over Satan but a man undergoing extreme trial without assistance from friends or family, including his heavenly father. Confronted by the most powerful opponent he or any human will ever face, his success becomes a virtual summa of the virtues of the rational Christian, the person who diligently employs well-disciplined mental energies in conjunction with a well-grounded faith in divine providence. The temptations Jesus is required to face are lack of faith, hunger, desire for glory, desire to overthrow the enemies of his people by violence, and pride in being declared the beloved Son of God. Milton's anti-Trinitarianism allows him to present Jesus as the highest type of human being, the true Son of God whose example has something to teach all people, a being divine only in being fully and perfectly human. Like the rest of humankind, he can demonstrate his love of God only by maintaining his faith, hope, and integrity, which in turn empower his love of others and of self.

The contrast to this all-embracing love is the all-enslaving hate of Satan and his cohorts, who have by now become less like the mighty archangels of *Paradise Lost* and more like the spirits of worldly ambition, pride, and greed who deceive the faithful and the wicked alike. What they lack in epic splendor is compensated for in psychological realism, which portrays in them all the qualities of those who would achieve earthly glory only for the purposes of domination and exploitation. As he himself gradually realizes, Jesus is their moral opposite, the one who would subdue the world by first subduing himself and his passions, the egoistic cravings that would render his rule despotic rather than liberating. The more compassionate and less stoical aspect of Jesus' refusal to yield to any of Satan's temptations is dramatically highlighted by scenes that portray his devastated followers sadly "missing him thir joy so lately found," who they "began to doubt, and doubted many days." Even Mary begins to doubt, but as the maternal equivalent of her son, she "with thoughts/ Meekly compos'd awaited the fulfilling." This behavior was rewarded once Jesus "unobserv'd/ Home to his Mother's house private return'd." Such success depends upon a heroism neither military nor tragic but fundamentally individual and lyric—something available to anyone who sees personal ethics as the clue to social responsibility.

In a sense, then, Milton challenges the reader to reject mainstream heroic values in favor of the humble ethos with which Jesus conquered. Although primarily a Christian message, this epic trial of the worldly principles of leadership and learning can challenge anyone to examine how best to exercise them. Confronted with the imminent collapse of the great social programs inherited from the Enlightenment—confidence in the universal progress of knowledge, education, and democracy as solutions to all human ills—the postmodern reader can gain a rare opportunity to examine an earlier and ultimately quite different solution to the problems of the individual in society, a moral synthesis of classical and Christian values grounded in Milton's staunchly libertarian

belief in the inalienable freedoms of conscience and action. Just as his epic debates refuse to separate individual action from social consequences, they also refuse to privilege any single side of those debates. Both the "high Authority" of God's prophets and the "inspired Oracles" of Delphi can cause doubt, disbelief, or self-promotion in those who fail to understand them correctly. The alternative is to realize that "so much bounty is in God, such grace,/ That who advance his glory, not thir own,/ Them he himself to glory will advance."

However, what, ultimately, is divine glory? This goodness beyond thought is revealed in the fourth book, which, if read otherwise, appears anticlimactic. Here Jesus' temptation is not all the kingdoms and accomplishments of the world offered by Satan but his means of gaining them. Urging that ends justify means, he sees the successful leader as seizing any occasion to achieve his destiny. In reply, Jesus redefines that destiny as the individual's own ability to observe proper proportion, ignoring not only the "false portents" of success but any unearned or premature fame, which in the much earlier poem "Lycidas" (1645), Milton had described as "that last infirmity of Noble mind." By demonstrating the process whereby that last infirmity is overcome, *Paradise Regained* can be read as a worthy testament to a poet whose entire life was a struggle to balance the temptations of literary and political power.

"Critical Evaluation" by Catherine Gimelli Martin

Further Reading

Bryson, Michael. *The Tyranny of Heaven: Milton's Rejection of God as King.* Newark: University of Delaware Press, 2004. Bryson argues that the kinglike God of *Paradise Lost* is not Milton's admired model of divinity; instead, Milton favors the Son in *Paradise Regained*, who rejects kingship in favor of a form of spiritual self-government. Maintains that the two epics critique the English, who endorsed the government of kings by restoring Charles II to the throne.

Campbell, Gordon, and Thomas N. Corns. *John Milton: Life, Work, and Thought.* New York: Oxford University Press, 2008. Insightful and comprehensive biography written by the editors of the *Oxford Milton.* Based in part on new information about seventeenth century English history. Sheds light on Milton's ideas and the turbulent times in which he lived.

Duran, Angelica, ed. *A Concise Companion to Milton.* Malden, Mass.: Blackwell, 2007. Analyses of Milton's works. Includes discussions of his legacy, a survey of more than three hundred years of Milton criticism, and the essay "The Messianic Vision of *Paradise Regained*" by David Gay.

Fixler, Michael. *Milton and the Kingdoms of God.* Evanston, Ill.: Northwestern University Press, 1964. Examines *Paradise Regained* in the historical, religious, political, and literary contexts of Milton's life and works. Particularly valuable in exploring the Puritan dilemma.

Lewalski, Barbara K. *Milton's Brief Epic: The Genre, Meaning, and Art of "Paradise Regained."* Providence, R.I.: Brown University Press, 1966. Remains the single most comprehensive exploration of Milton's use of the literary and biblical traditions invoked in the poem, particularly the story of Job and its varying interpretations.

Mayer, Joseph G. *Between Two Pillars: The Hero's Plight in "Samson Agonistes" and "Paradise Regained."* Lanham, Md.: University Press of America, 2004. Describes the dilemmas facing the protagonists in both works. Jesus in *Paradise Regained* is caught between two opposing forces: his zeal to establish his kingdom and his ignorance about how to do so.

Rosenfeld, Nancy. *The Human Satan in Seventeenth-Century English Literature: From Milton to Rochester.* Burlington, Vt.: Ashgate, 2008. Analyzes works of seventeenth century literature, including *Paradise Lost* and *Paradise Regained*, to describe how Milton and other English authors present a human depiction of Satan.

Stein, Arnold. *Heroic Knowledge: An Interpretation of "Paradise Regained" and "Samson Agonistes."* 1957. Reprint. London: Frank Cass, 1966. A classic study of the dramatic aspects of *Paradise Regained*, especially in relation to the other major works of the mature Milton.

Paradox, King

Author: Pío Baroja (1872-1956)
First published: Paradox, rey, 1906 (English translation, 1931)
Type of work: Novel
Type of plot: Social satire
Time of plot: Early twentieth century
Locale: Spain; Tangier; Bu-Tata, Africa

Principal characters:
SILVESTRE PARADOX, a modern adventurer
AVELINO DIZ, his skeptical friend
ARTHUR SIPSOM, an English manufacturer
EICHTHAL THONELGEBEN, a scientist
HARDIBRÁS, a disabled soldier
UGÚ, a friendly black man
BAGÚ, a jealous medicine man
FUNANGUE, greedy prime minister of Bu-Tata

The Story:

After many adventures, Dr. Silvestre Paradox, a short, chubby man of about forty-five years, settles in a small Valencian town. Tiring at last of his quiet life, he announces one morning to his friend, Avelino Diz, his intention of taking a trip to Cananí, on the Gulf of Guinea. A British banker, Abraham Wolf, is setting out on his yacht *Cornucopia* with a party of scientists and explorers to establish a Jewish colony in Africa, and he has invited Paradox to go with him. Paradox suggests that Diz join the expedition.

In Tangier they meet several other members of the party, including General Pérez, his daughter Dora, and a disabled, scarred soldier named Hardibrás. They drink to the success of the venture with whiskey. When someone in the party feeds whiskey to a rooster, the fowl breaks into human speech and deplores what humans drink. Paradox declares that only nature is just and honorable. He is eager to go where people live naturally.

The group boards the yacht, Hardibrás swinging himself aboard by the hook he wears in place of his lost hand. There, Paradox and Diz meet others of the expedition: Mingote, a revolutionist who had tried to assassinate the king of Portugal; Pelayo, who had been Paradox's secretary until his employer fired him for crooked dealings; Sipsom, an English manufacturer; Miss Pich, a feminist writer and former ballet dancer; and The Cheese Kid, a former French cancan dancer. Wolf himself is not on board. He is conferring with Monsieur Chabouly, a French chocolate king who also is emperor of Western Nigritia, in an attempt to establish peaceful diplomatic relations between Chabouly's domain and the new state of Cananí.

The yacht heads out to sea. On the third day, stormy waves wash the captain overboard. The mate and the crew are drunk, so Paradox and two others are forced to take over the yacht. Paradox, alone at the wheel, converses with the wind and the sea, who tell him that they have wills of their own. Yock, his dog, admires his master's resolution and strength and declares that he is almost worthy of being a dog.

As the storm increases in fury, the mast breaks and crashes upon the deck. Paradox calls the passengers together and suggests that one of them, Goizueta, be appointed captain because of his maritime experience. Goizueta is elected. His first act, after saving one bottle of brandy for medicine, is to throw the rest of the alcohol overboard.

For a week they sail through heavy fog that never lifts to reveal their position. At last the ship's coal runs out, and they drift. One night some of the passengers and crew, Miss Pich, Mingote, and Pelayo among them, steal the only lifeboat and desert the ship.

When the fog lifts, the passengers see a beach not far away. The yacht strikes a rock, but all are able to save themselves on rafts that they load with supplies from the ship. The next morning the yacht breaks up, leaving the party marooned on an island. It is then proposed that Paradox be put in charge. After modestly protesting, he accepts and assigns jobs to all the survivors. Nevertheless, he fails to make provisions for their defense. The next night a band of islanders arrive in two canoes, surprise the sleepers, and take them bound to Bu-Tata.

The first demand made by Prime Minister Funangue is for rum. One of the party, Sipsom, explains that they can provide rum only if they are allowed to return to their base of supplies. In his greed, Funangue decides to ignore the advice of Bagú, the medicine man, who wants all the whites of the marooned yacht slain. A friendly islander, Ugú, is assigned to instruct the prisoners in tribal language and customs. From Ugú the captives learn Bagú's prejudices and superstitions. When the witch doctor later appears, Sipsom declares that one of the prisoners is a wizard fated to die on the same day as Bagú. If Bagú sides with them, however, the white magician will help the medicine man to marry Princess Mahu, King Kiri's daughter. Bagú accepts the proposal.

King Kiri, engaged in his favorite pastime of killing subjects whom he dislikes, pauses in his diversion long enough to receive the prisoners. After a conversation about vested interests, he orders that their lives be spared. Giving them permission to get supplies from their camp, he dispatches them under guard in two canoes. During the trip, the prisoners, having lulled the suspicions of the guards, are about to take their guns and free themselves, but Paradox objects. He says

that he has other plans. Diz scoffs at the way his friend puts on airs.

After damaging one canoe, the prisoners use the delay to impress the locals, who are black, with their white superiority by working magic tricks. A Frenchman in the party leads a discussion on the rights of individuals. The scheme works. After two weeks, the blacks agree to desert their king and accompany the whites to Fortunate Island, a defensible plateau suggested by Ugú. Although Paradox preaches the virtues of life out of doors, the others build Fortune House, a communal dwelling.

When King Kiri's army appears, Paradox's machine gun quickly repulses them, and a searchlight finally puts the blacks to flight. Peace has finally come to Fortune House. The blacks construct huts and spend their evenings at magic lantern shows. The *Fortune House Herald* begins publication.

Prime Minister Funangue and two attendants, appearing under a flag of truce, bring King Kiri's appeal for help. The Fulani are attacking Bu-Tata. Paradox and Thonelgeben, the engineer, return to the capital with the blacks. At Paradox's suggestion, the river is dynamited to turn Bu-Tata into an island. Bagú objects to such interference with nature and discusses the change with fish, serpents, and frogs. Only the bat refuses to voice an opinion.

One day, warriors from Bu-Tata appear at Fortune House with the head of King Kiri and beg one of the whites to become their ruler. At a meeting, all debate monarchial theories. When they fail to agree, Sipsom shows Paradox to the blacks and announces that he has been chosen by popular vote. The blacks then return to Bu-Tata for a coronation feast.

By this time, Paradox, who has reconciled to the advantages of civilization over life close to nature, becomes tired of Africa. At a session of Congress he argues against state support of art and criticizes formal education. Pelayo and Mingote, captured by Moors after the storm, arrive in Bu-Tata. Miss Pich had been raped by locals, and the others had been eaten.

Political life continues. Two white couples are married. Sipsom holds law court and gives judgment in complicated cases. Then the French capture Bu-Tata and burn it. The whites are released at the request of The Cheese Kid. Bagú is shot.

Three years later an epidemic fills the Bu-Tata Hospital. French doctors declare that the outbreak is the result of civilization, for one of the doctors had unknowingly taken smallpox to a local village while fighting another epidemic. Civilization has also driven Princess Mahu to dancing nude in a nightclub. As an enterprising journalist states regarding Bu-

Tata, the French army had brought civilization to that "backward" country.

Critical Evaluation:

The most prominent writer of the Generation of '98, Pío Baroja has been accused of pessimism, even misanthropy, for his scathing portraits of modern society. His satires are rendered with great detail in the dozens of novels he produced during the early decades of the twentieth century. Like other Spanish novelists of his time, Baroja reacted strongly against the social and political complacency he saw around him in Spain and the evils that those attitudes inflicted on the poor in the country, especially those in his native Basque region.

It is not surprising, therefore, to learn that *Paradox, King*, the third novel in a trilogy that Baroja titled "The Fantastic Life," has been called by one critic "a catalog of human flaws and life's pitfalls." The hero, a likable optimist who wants only to make life better for himself and his friends, continually stumbles into one depressing situation after another, and his efforts at remedying the ills of the people he encounters are met with only minimal success.

Fast paced and filled with action, *Paradox, King* holds readers' attention by moving quickly from scene to scene, highlighting the bumblings of the title character in his efforts to establish a perfect society in the outer regions of Africa. The presence of talking animals and supernatural events give the work a quality of fantasy similar to that found in travel literature dating to the Middle Ages. Loosely plotted and episodic in nature, the novel shares many qualities with the picaresque tradition, although Baroja's hero, Silvestre Paradox, is no rogue. The central motif of his journey to strange lands provides links with a number of important satires in the European canon, most notably François Rabelais's *Gargantua and Pantagruel* (1532-1564) and Jonathan Swift's *Gulliver's Travels* (1726). There are similarities, too, between the hero and his sidekick, Avelino Diz, and that more famous traveling duo from Miguel de Cervantes' *Don Quixote de la Mancha* (1605-1615).

The novel is a biting satire on the evils of modern society. Through his assemblage of an international cast of characters thrown together in the isolated African terrain, Baroja creates a microcosm of humanity, closed off from European society and able to start over in creating a political system based on different principles of human interaction. Through his portrait of Paradox and his companions' attempts to deal justly with the locals in Bu-Tata, the novelist offers a view of the decadence brought on by untethered reliance on authority, represented chiefly by the political leadership and by the clergy. The kingdom Paradox establishes among the locals is free from such authority and decidedly antiprogressive. The protagonist proclaims himself against art, science, or any authority. "Let us live the free life," he demands, "without restraints, without schools, without laws, without teachers." He commands that any schools established in the land be devoid of faculty, and that any training for the useful trades be voluntary. Naturally, the small successes he enjoys during his brief reign are quickly brought to an end when the French come to "civilize" the land; with them they bring disease and authoritarian rule, two components of "civilization" that Baroja singles out for special condemnation.

Perhaps the most stinging condemnation, however, is reserved for technology, the sign of progress for Baroja's contemporaries in the nineteenth and early twentieth centuries. A useful comparison may serve to highlight the Spanish novelist's aim in this respect. Readers familiar with American literature will see in *Paradox, King* parallels to another novel that highlights the evils of technology: Mark Twain's *A Connecticut Yankee in King Arthur's Court* (1889). Both novels rely on the motif of the journey—in Baroja's, a sojourn to a foreign land; in Twain's, a trip back in time. In both instances, the protagonists find themselves in a primitive civilization, and the possession of advanced technology gives them power. Both Paradox and Twain's Harry Morgan initially use their knowledge for good, establishing utopian societies in which people benefit from an increased standard of living, and in which communications are improved (both rely on the press as an agent for increasing people's awareness of and participation in social and political activities). Eventually, however, the possibility of consolidating power or overcoming enemies forces them to use the same technology for destructive purposes. While Paradox's decision to isolate his kingdom by dynamiting the river and forming an island may not be motivated by evil intent, the action is nevertheless futile. More telling yet is the hero's decision at the end of the work to return to civilization; even he becomes tired of the idyllic life, opting instead for the civilized cesspool he has tried so hard to escape.

The harshness of the novel's ending has led many critics to condemn Baroja as a nihilist. As with his other novels, *Paradox, King* offers little hope for the human race; instead, it seems to be only an angry cry against the evils the novelist sees around him. Like his forebears in the satiric tradition, he is able to bear the terrible burden of reality only by masking it in the face of comedy. Seen in this light, *Paradox, King* is a decided achievement in literary art.

"Critical Evaluation" by Laurence W. Mazzeno

Further Reading

Barrow, Leo L. *Negation in Baroja: A Key to His Novelistic Creativity.* Tucson: University of Arizona Press, 1971. Explores the novelist's technique of "creating by destroying," an approach he shares with other modern writers who rebel against conventional Western values. Discusses the style, dialogue, atmosphere, characterization, and landscape in *Paradox, King* and other novels to explain Baroja's philosophical, political, and social attitudes.

Landeira, Ricardo. *The Modern Spanish Novel, 1898-1936.* Boston: Twayne, 1985. A chapter on Baroja surveys the novelist's achievements and discusses *Paradox, King* and the other novels in the trilogy dealing with "The Fantastic Life." Calls the novel the bitterest of the three in attacking social ills.

Murphy, Katharine. *Re-Reading Pío Baroja and English Literature.* New York: Peter Lang, 2004. Murphy points out the many structural similarities between Baroja's early fiction and the novels of his contemporaries, most notably Joseph Conrad, Thomas Hardy, E. M. Forster, and James Joyce. Focuses on how Baroja treats human consciousness; the identity and role of the artist; European landscapes; and questions of form, genre, and representation.

Patt, Beatrice P. *Pío Baroja.* New York: Twayne, 1971. Excellent introduction to the writer and his works. Briefly discusses Baroja's attitudes toward the Church and state. Reviews Baroja's use of extended dialogue in *Paradox, King,* and points out how it permits him to introduce personal prejudices into a work he considered "half-fantasy, half-satirical poem."

Turner, Harriet, and Adelaida López de Martínez, eds. *The Cambridge Companion to the Spanish Novel: From 1600 to the Present.* New York: Cambridge University Press, 2003. This collection of essays tracing the development of the Spanish novel includes a discussion of Baroja and some of his works that situate him within the broader context of Spanish literature.

Parallel Lives

Author: Plutarch (c. 46-after 120 C.E.)
First transcribed: Bioi paralleloi, c. 105-115 C.E.
　　(English translation, 1579)
Type of work: Biography

Principal personages:
JULIUS CAESAR, Roman general and statesman
ALEXANDER THE GREAT, king of Macedon
MARC ANTONY, Roman statesman
DEMETRIUS, Macedonian king
MARCUS BRUTUS, Roman statesman
DION, statesman of Syracuse
DEMOSTHENES, Greek orator and statesman
CICERO, Roman orator and statesman
ALCIBIADES, Athenian general
CORIOLANUS, Roman leader
SOLON, Athenian lawgiver
POPLICOLA, Roman lawgiver
THESEUS, legendary Athenian hero
ROMULUS, legendary founder of Rome

The collection that is today known simply as Plutarch's *Lives* is derived from the *Parallel Lives,* a work in which Plutarch presented a large number of biographies (of which forty-six survive), alternating the lives of eminent Greeks with comparable lives of eminent Romans. A number of shorter essays compared the lives accorded biographical treatment. The collection as it survives includes some biographies written independent of the *Parallel Lives,* such as the biographies of Otho, Galba, Artaxerxes, and Aratus.

Plutarch considered the lives of famous men important for their moral implications, and his treatment shows his concern to apply the ethics of Aristotle to the judgment of those whose lives he reports. His treatment is more personal than political; like the biographer Suetonius, whose *De vita*

Caesarum (c. 120 C.E.; *History of the Twelve Caesars*, 1606) lacks the moral emphasis of Plutarch's work, Plutarch was interested in great figures as human beings liable to the errors and inevitable temptations that confront all human beings. Also, like Suetonius, Plutarch delights in anecdote and uses various tales concerning the Greeks and Romans partly for their intrinsic interest and partly to suit his moral intention.

Although there are inaccuracies in the *Lives*, the charm and liveliness of Plutarch's style give the biographies a convincing appeal that more than compensates for errors in fact. In any case, all history is the result of attempts to make intelligible statements about a past that must be reconstructed from the perspectives of the writers. If one says that in the *Lives* readers see the famous Greeks and Romans only as they appeared to Plutarch, then one must say of any history or biography that it is the past only as it appeared to the work's author. The conclusion might be that since biographies are sensible only relative to their authors, the character and the ability of the authors are of paramount importance. If the *Lives* are judged in this manner, then again Plutarch emerges as an excellent historian, for his work expresses the active concerns of a sensitive, conscientious, and educated Greek writer.

The comparisons that Plutarch makes between his Greeks and Romans have sometimes been dismissed as of minor historical importance. The error behind such judgment is that of regarding the comparisons as only biographical and historical. Plutarch's comparisons are attempts not only to recover the past but also to judge. In the comparisons a moralist is at work, and whatever the truth of the biographies, in the comparisons readers come close to the truth about the moral climate of Plutarch's day. Another way of putting this is to say that in his biographical essays Plutarch defines men of the past, but in the comparisons he defines himself and the men of his age.

Thus, in comparing Romulus, the legendary founder of Rome, with Theseus, the Athenian hero of Greek mythology, Plutarch first considers which of the two was the more valiant and the more aggressive for a worthy cause. The decision is given to Theseus, who voluntarily sought out the oppressors of Greece—Sciron, Sinnis, Procrustes, and Corynetes—and who offered himself as part of the tribute to Crete. Plutarch then finds both heroes wanting. "Both Theseus and Romulus were by nature meant for governors," he writes, "yet neither lived up to the true character of a king, but fell off, and ran, the one into popularity, the other into tyranny, falling both into the same fault out of different passions." Plutarch then goes on to criticize both men for unreasonable anger— Theseus against his son, Romulus against his brother. Fi-

nally, he severely takes Theseus to task for parricide and for the rapes he committed.

From even this brief comparison readers learn a great deal about Plutarch. Although he has an inclination to favor the Greeks, he gives the Romans their due, achieving a near balance of virtues and vices. He honors courageous action, provided it was motivated by a love of country and of humanity, and he approves the ancient morality that called for respect toward parents and faithfulness to friends and brothers.

Plutarch was aware of the difficulty and the dangers of the biographical tasks he undertook, and he gives the impression that the presence of the comparisons is intended both to unify and to justify the book as a whole. At the outset of his biographical survey of the adventures of Theseus he compares those biographies of men closer to his own time with biographies such as that of Theseus, in which he is forced to deal with fictions and fables. He writes, "Let us hope that Fable may, in what shall follow, so submit to the purifying processes of Reason as to take the character of exact history"; however, he recognizes the possibility that the purifying process might not occur and so begs the indulgence of the reader. He then compares Theseus and Romulus briefly, showing parallels of position and fortune in their lives, in order to justify his having decided to place their biographies side by side and to undertake a comparison of their moral characters.

Other comparisons that survive are those of Numa Pompilius, Romulus's successor as king of Rome and originator of Roman religious law, with Lycurgus, the Spartan lawgiver; of Poplicola, or Publius Valerius, the Roman ruler who converted a despotic command to a popular one, thus winning the name Poplicola (lover of the people), with Solon, the Athenian lawgiver; of Fabius, the Roman leader who was five times consul and then dictator, who harassed Hannibal with his delaying tactics, with Pericles, the Athenian soldier and statesman who brought Athens to the height of its power. There are also comparisons of Alcibiades, the Athenian general, with Coriolanus, the Roman leader; of Timoleon, the Corinthian, the opponent of Dionysius and other Sicilian tyrants, with Aemilius Paulus, the Roman who warred against the Macedonians; of Pelopidas, the Theban general who recovered Thebes from the Spartans, with Marcellus, the Roman consul who captured Syracuse; of Aristides, the Athenian general who fought at Marathon, Salamis, and Plataea, with Marcus Cato, the Roman statesman who disapproved of Carthage and destroyed the city in the Third Punic War. More comparisons include those of Philopoemen, the Greek commander of the Achaeans who defeated the Spartan tyrants Machanidas and Nabis, with Flamininus, the Roman general and consul who freed Greece from Philip V of Macedon;

of Lysander, the Spartan who defeated the Athenians and planned the government of Athens, with Sylla, the Roman general who defeated Mithridates VI, sacked Athens, and became tyrant of Rome; of Lucullus, who continued Sulla's (or Sylla's) campaign against Mithridates and pursued him into Armenia, with Cimon, the Greek who defeated the Persians on both land and sea at Pamphylia; of Crassus, one of the First Triumvirate with Pompey and Caesar, with Nicias, the Athenian who was captured by the Syracuse forces that repelled the Athenians; of Sertorius, a Roman general who fought in rebellion against Pompey in Spain, with Eumenes, the Greek general and statesman who was opposed by Antigoes; of Pompey, the Roman general who became Caesar's enemy after the formation of the First Triumvirate, with Agesilaus, the Spartan king who fought the Persians and the Thebans without preventing the downfall of Sparta. Finally, there are comparisons of Tiberius and Caius Gracchus, the Roman statesmen and brothers who fought and died for social reform in the effort to assist the poor landowners, with Agis and Cleomenes, the Spartan reformer kings; of Demosthenes, the Greek orator and statesman, with Cicero, the Roman orator and statesman; of Demetrius, the Macedonian who became king after numerous campaigns and after murdering Cassander's sons, with Antony, Caesar's defender and the lover of Cleopatra; and of Dion of Syracuse, who attempted to introduce Dionysius and his son to Plato, with Brutus, the slayer of Caesar.

Important biographies are those of Alexander the Great and Julius Caesar. Acknowledging the difficulty of his task, Plutarch declares his intention to write "the most celebrated parts," and he adds, "It must be borne in mind that my design is not to write histories, but lives. The most glorious exploits do not always furnish us with the clearest discoveries of virtue or vice in men; sometimes a matter of less moment, an expression or a jest, informs us better of their characters and inclinations."

Plutarch writes at the beginning of his biography of Timoleon that he has come to take a personal interest in his biographies, explaining that "the virtues of these great men" had come to serve him "as a sort of looking-glass, in which I may see how to adjust and adorn my own life." Over the centuries readers have responded with respect to Plutarch's moral seriousness, thus testifying to his power both as biographer and commentator.

Further Reading

Barrow, R. H. *Plutarch and His Times*. Bloomington: Indiana University Press, 1967. Comprehensive work provides a good introduction to Plutarch's life, times, and works. Contains two chapters on *Parallel Lives* in which the work is examined primarily in terms of its purpose, digressions, and historical sources.

Duff, Tim. *Plutarch's "Lives": Exploring Virtue and Vice*. New York: Oxford University Press, 1999. Examines the elements of moralism and the "soul of the Plutarchian hero" in the work. Provides a close reading of four pairs of parallel biographies.

Lamberton, Robert. *Plutarch*. New Haven, Conn.: Yale University Press, 2001. Places Plutarch's life and works in historical context and discusses him as a reader, writer, educator, thinker, and priest at Delphi. Provides background about and interpretation of *Parallel Lives*.

Plutarch. *Shakespeare's Plutarch*. Edited by T. J. B. Spencer. New York: Penguin Books, 1964. Reprints Thomas North's 1579 translation of the four lives from which William Shakespeare drew the plots of his Roman tragedies. Contains abundant quotations of parallel passages from the plays. Invaluable for an understanding of Shakespeare's literary debt to Plutarch.

Russell, D. A. *Plutarch*. 2d ed. Bristol, England: Bristol Classical, 2001. Offers an introduction to Plutarch's thought and writings from a literary perspective, aimed at the general reader. In the three chapters devoted to *Parallel Lives*, the life of Alcibiades receives the greatest emphasis.

Scardigli, Barbara, ed. *Essays on "Plutarch's Lives."* New York: Oxford University Press, 1995. Collection of essays includes analyses of some of the biographies as well as discussions of Plutarch as a biographer, his choice of heroes in *Parallel Lives*, and his adaptation of his source materials.

Wardman, Alan. *Plutarch's "Lives."* Berkeley: University of California Press, 1974. Sophisticated study ranges broadly throughout the fifty extant biographies, analyzing their form and nature. Also discusses Plutarch's concept of the ideal political leader, his means of depicting character, and the influence of philosophy and rhetoric on his biographical methods.

Parlement of Foules

Author: Geoffrey Chaucer (c. 1343-1400)
First published: c. 1380
Type of work: Poetry
Type of plot: Allegory
Time of plot: Fourteenth century
Locale: A dreamworld

Principal characters:
CHAUCER, the dreamer and narrator
SCIPIO AFRICANUS, his guide
DAME NATURE
THE FORMEL EAGLE
THREE TERCEL EAGLES, the highest-ranking birds

The Poem:

Parlement of Foules opens with comments on the hardships of love, which, the poet and narrator assures his reader, he knows only through his books; and books, he says, are the source of all people's new discoveries. The narrator, Chaucer, has read Cicero's *Somnium Scipionis*, one of the most popular stories during the Middle Ages. Chaucer tells the reader how, in this story, Scipio Africanus appears to the younger Scipio in a dream and shows him all the universe, pointing out how small the earth is in comparison with the rest. He advises the younger man to live virtuously and with knowledge that he is immortal, so that he might come swiftly to heaven after death.

Darkness forces the narrator to put his book aside; and, falling asleep, he dreams that the same Scipio Africanus comes to him and leads him to the gate of a beautiful garden. Over one-half of the gate is a message promising happiness to those who enter; above the other half is a warning of pain and sorrow. As the dreamer deliberates, his guide pushes him through the gates, explaining that neither motto applies to him because he is not a lover but adding that he might discover there something about which to write.

The two men arrive in a garden filled with every kind of tree and bird. Deer, squirrels, and other small animals are playing there. Music and fragrant breezes permeate the atmosphere. Around the garden are familiar personifications: Cupid, tempering his arrows, as well as Pleasure, Beauty, Youth, Jollity, Flattery, and many others. Nearby stands a temple of brass upon pillars of jasper. Women are dancing around it, and doves sit on the roof. Before the doors sits Dame Peace and Dame Patience "on a hill of sand." When he enters the temple, the dreamer sees the goddess Jealousy, the cause of the great sighing he hears around him; Venus and the youth Richess; Bacchus, god of wine; and Ceres, who relieves hunger. Along the walls are painted the stories of many unhappy lovers.

Returning to the garden, the dreamer notices Dame Nature, so fair that she surpasses all others as much as the sunlight does the stars. Around her are all the birds, ready to choose their mates, for it is St. Valentine's Day. Dame Nature decrees that the tercel eagle, the bird of highest rank, should have the first choice.

The tercel eagle asks for the lovely formel eagle who sits on Dame Nature's own hand, but immediately two other high-ranking fowls interrupt; they, too, love the formel eagle. A lengthy debate follows. One has loved her longest; another says that he has loved as deeply, if not as long. (This kind of discussion was popular in court circles in Chaucer's day.) The other birds, thought by scholars to represent different levels of English society, along with the clergy, peasants, and the bourgeoisie, soon weary of the debate, since they want to pick their own mates. They decide that each group should elect a spokesperson to give its opinion of the "cursed pleading."

The birds of prey choose the tercelet falcon, who suggests that the formel wed the worthiest knight, the bird of gentlest blood. The goose, speaking for the waterfowls, says simply, "If she won't love him, let him love another." The gentle turtledove dissents, and the seed fowls hold that a lover should serve his lady until he dies, whether or not she loves him in return.

The duck offers a saucy retort: "There are more stars, God wot, than a pair." The tercel chides him for having no idea of love. Then the cuckoo gives the verdict of the worm fowls: Give us our mates in peace, and let the eagles argue as long as they wish. Let them be single all their lives if they can reach no decision. One of the noble birds insults the cuckoo, calling him a murderer because of his usual diet, and Dame Nature has to intervene to keep peace.

Since none of the birds' opinions provides a solution, Dame Nature orders the formel eagle to choose the one she loves best. Although she advises the formel to wed the royal tercel, since he seems noblest, she says that the bird herself must make a choice. The formel pleads that she is still too young to marry; she wants to wait a year to decide. Dame Nature agrees, and at last all the birds are permitted to choose their own mates. Before they depart, they sing a charming roundel. The noise the birds make as they fly away awakens the poet, who immediately picks up other books, hoping that someday he will read something that will give him a dream to make him fare better.

Critical Evaluation:

The occasion of *Parlement of Foules* was the marriage of King Richard II of England to Anne of Bohemia. Since the convocation of the birds in the story takes place in the spring, it is possible that in selecting Valentine's Day—the day on which lovers traditionally choose mates—Geoffrey Chaucer was referring not to the customary date of February 14 but to May 3, the date of Richard and Anne's betrothal. This was also the feast day of Saint Valentine of Genoa. Although this saint was generally known only in the vicinity of his hometown, Chaucer had visited Genoa and may have heard his name. While the poem primarily celebrates the royal nuptials, it seems to serve a secondary function. Through the contention of the birds, Chaucer very subtly and gently questions the wisdom of certain practices and ideologies among the nobility.

In 1376, Chaucer, an emissary for the royal family, traveled to France to negotiate a marriage contract between King Richard (then ten years of age) and Marie, the five-year-old daughter of King Charles V of France. By means of this alliance, England hoped to end the Hundred Years' War that had raged between the two countries. Unfortunately, Marie died suddenly in 1377; nevertheless, England resumed negotiations the following year, proposing that Charles's younger daughter, Isabel, be the bride. When Isabel also died, a proposal was made for the hand of Catherine, Charles's one remaining daughter, who was then an infant. These negotiations were interrupted by political events, but, in 1380, Richard married Anne, the sister of Wenceslas, king of Bohemia. This alliance had been proposed and partly executed by the Vatican.

At the time of the wedding, Richard was fourteen years old, and his wife was about thirteen years of age. Although the young monarchs reputedly enjoyed a compatible marriage, it is doubtful that either of them had much, if any, power to make decisions regarding their union. Thus, when Chaucer has Dame Nature decree that the eagle's must "agre to his elecciou, whoso he be that shulde be hire feere," he may be implying that, even in noble families, individuals should be allowed some measure of control regarding marriage partners. Later, the formel eagle herself asks Nature for a year's respite in which to make her decision, even though she is under the goddess's "yerde," just as noble children are under the control of their parents, the state, and, in some cases, the Church.

Throughout the poem, Chaucer questions not only the es-tablishment of marriage contracts between nonconsenting children but also the principles of courtly love, a mystique of the noble class. In this context, it is important to note the symbolism of his personified birds. Chaucer draws on a long literary tradition of using animals to portray human attributes. His use of birds, in particular, stems from the influence of several French poets who associated them with various types of passion. The eagles, associated in nearly all ancient cultures with divinity, majesty, and power, represent gentlemen of the nobility. High-soaring birds, these suitors hold lofty ideals of pairing and love.

The falcon, or hawk, the spokesperson for the "noble" birds, was the breed most closely associated with the aristocracy, being both a pet and a medium of sport. Noblemen and noblewomen often carried falcons and engaged in frequent hawking expeditions. Moreover, elaborate rituals defined the steps in teaching a falcon to attack its prey. Since these birds were so closely bound to their noble masters, it is fitting that Chaucer's falcon should voice the sentiments of the aristocracy concerning the choice of a mate "Me wolde thynk how that the worthieste/ Of knyghthod, and lengest had used it,/ Most of estat, of blod the gentileste,/ Were sittyngest for hire, if that hir leste." Some of the "lower-class" birds, however, offer opinions that counter and challenge the romantic ideals of the nobles. When the turtledove, associated with lifelong fidelity even after the death of a mate, says on behalf of the seed fowl, or country gentry, that a gentleman should love his lady until his own demise, the duck retorts that this mandate is ridiculous. In this scenario, the duck may be seen in two lights. It is possible that Chaucer was drawing on the bird's usual medieval association with persons of low social standing. In this light, the tercel's reference to the duck as "cherl" is appropriate. Among the ancient Chinese, however, the mandarin duck was said to couple for life; the strength of its fidelity to a deceased mate supposedly surpassed even that of the medieval turtledove. If Chaucer was familiar with the alleged character of the mandarin, his duck may represent a member of the nobility who questions the social strictures of his own group.

The goose speaks on behalf of the waterfowl. According to some critics, these birds represent the merchant class; according to others, they represent the lowest segment of society. In either case, the goose is not an aristocrat. She therefore is bold enough to counter the courtly principle that women should hold their suitors in disdain in order that they might be "won over," by stating that a lover should not choose a partner who does not love in return. Rather than considering this a piece of practical wisdom, the sparrowhawk (a bird of the nobility) dismisses it as "a parfit resoun of a goose."

Through the lower birds' mundane views of love and the noble birds' rude rejoinders, Chaucer may have been warning his young monarch of a growing spirit of rebellion among the common people. Unfortunately, King Richard did not perceive the meaning of the avian allegory until it was too late. On June 12, an army of peasants and artisans invaded London, protesting their poverty, their high taxes, and their lack of economic autonomy—situations that had been ignored or dismissed by the nobility. Richard was able to quell the crowd's agitation with false promises, but the aura of their unrest remained.

On the surface, *Parlement of Foules* is a poem of light-hearted banter, written to celebrate a wedding. A close reading, however, reveals that it is also a work of social criticism and prophecy.

"Critical Evaluation" by Rebecca Stingley Hinton

Further Reading

Bennett, J. A. W. *"The Parlement of Foules": An Interpretation.* 1957. Reprint. Oxford, England: Clarendon Press, 1971. Compares Chaucer's style to the style of various poets in both antiquity and his own time. Contains several plates of illustrations, including a medieval representation of birds.

Boitani, Piero, and Ji Mann, eds. *The Cambridge Companion to Chaucer.* 2d ed. New York: Cambridge University Press, 2003. Collection of essays, including discussions of Chaucer's style, the literary structure of his works, the social and literary scene in England during his lifetime, and his French and Italian inheritances. Many of the essays analyze specific works, including *Parlement of Foules.*

Braddy, Haldeen. *Chaucer's "Parlement of Foules" in Its Relation to Contemporary Events.* New York: Octagon Books, 1969. Discusses the poem as a retrospective account of Chaucer's attempts to negotiate a marriage contract between the king of England and a princess of France. Also examines Chaucer's view of various social classes and his use of personified birds.

Howard, Donald R. *Chaucer: His Life, His Works, His World.* New York: Dutton, 1987. Discusses several of Chaucer's major poems, including *Parlement of Foules.* It also offers a glimpse into the milieu of fourteenth century England, with chapters on such topics as the Black Death, the peasants' revolt, and life in a royal court.

Lynch, Kathryn L. *Chaucer's Philosophical Visions.* Rochester, N.Y.: D. S. Brewer, 2000. Focuses on Chaucer's knowledge of and interest in late medieval English Scholasticism and other forms of philosophy, and how his works reflect his philosophical visions. Chapter 4 focuses on *Parlement of Foules.*

Rowland, Beryl. *Blind Beasts: Chaucer's Animal World.* Kent, Ohio: Kent State University Press, 1971. Discusses Chaucer's use of personified animals, including birds. Contains illustrated chapters on the medieval and ancient symbolic significance of the boar, hare, wolf, horse, sheep, and dog.

Parzival

Author: Wolfram von Eschenbach (c. 1170-c. 1217)
First published: c. 1200-1210 (English translation, 1894)
Type of work: Poetry
Type of plot: Arthurian romance
Time of plot: Age of chivalry
Locale: Western Europe

Principal characters:
GAMURET, prince of Anjou
PARZIVAL, Gamuret's son
GAWAIN, knight of King Arthur's court
KING ARTHUR
FEIREFIS, Parzival's half brother
LOHENGRIN, Parzival's son

The Poem:

Gamuret, younger son of King Gandein of Anjou, refuses to live as a vassal in the kingdom of his older brother, notwithstanding the brother's love for Gamuret. The young man, given gifts of gold by his king brother, as well as horses and equipment and men-at-arms, leaves Anjou to seek his fortune. Hoping to find for himself fame and love, Gamuret goes first to battle for Baruch at Alexandria; from there he goes to the aid of the Moorish queen Belakane. Belakane had been falsely accused of causing the death of her lover, Eisenhart, and was besieged in her castle by two armies under the command of Friedebrand, king of Scotland and Eisenhart's uncle.

Gamuret, after raising the siege, becomes the husband of Belakane, who gives birth to his son, Feirefis. Gamuret tires of being king of Assagog and Zassamank, and so he journeys abroad again in search of fame. Passing into Spain, Gamuret seeks King Kailet and finds him near Kanvoleis. The two enter a tournament sponsored by the queen of Waleis. Gamuret does valiant deeds and carries off all the honors of that tournament, thereby winning a great deal of fame as the victor. Two queens who had watched the lists during the tournament fall in love with Gamuret, but Queen Herzeleide wins his heart and marries him. They love each other greatly, but once again the call of honor becomes too great to let Gamuret remain a housed husband. Receiving a summons from Baruch, he leaves once more for Alexandria. In the fighting there he is treacherously killed and given a great tomb by Baruch. When news of his death reaches the land of Waleis, Queen Herzeleide sorrows greatly, but her sorrow is in part dissipated by the birth of a child by Gamuret. Herzeleide names the boy Parzival.

Parzival is reared by his mother with all tenderness and love. As he grows older he meets knights who fare through the world seeking honor. Parzival, stimulated by tales of their deeds, leaves his homeland in search of King Arthur of Britain. He hopes to become one of Arthur's knights and a member of the order of the Round Table. During his absence, his mother, Queen Herzeleide, dies. On his way to Arthur's court, Parzival takes a token from Jeschute and thus arouses the jealous anger of her husband, Orilus. Further along on his journey he meets a woman named Sigune and from her learns of his lineage and his kinship with the house of Anjou. Still later, Parzival meets the Red Knight and carries that knight's challenge with him to King Arthur. Having been knighted by the king, Parzival sets forth again in quest of knightly honor. Finding himself in the land of Graharz, he seeks out Gurnemanz, prince of the land, who teaches the young knight the courtesy and the ethics of knighthood.

From Graharz, Parzival journeys to Pelrapar, which he finds besieged by enemies. He raises the siege by overthrowing Kingron. After this adventure, Parzival falls in love with Queen Kondwiramur, and the two are married. Parzival, like his father before him, soon tires of the quiet life and parts from his home and queen to seek further adventures.

Parzival journeys to the land of the Fisher King and becomes the king's guest. In that land he first beholds the fabulous bleeding spear and all the marvels of the Holy Grail.

One morning he wakes to find the castle deserted. Parzival, mocked by a squire, rides away. Later he meets Orilus, who had vowed to battle the young knight for taking Jeschute's token. They fight, and Parzival is the victor, but he is able to reconcile Orilus to Jeschute once again and send the couple to find a welcome at the court of King Arthur.

Arthur, meanwhile, has gone in search of the Red Knight, whose challenge Parzival carries. Journeying in search of King Arthur, Parzival has the misfortune of falling into a love-trance, during which he overthrows Gagramor and takes vengeance on Sir Kay. He meets Gawain, who takes him back again to Arthur's court. There, Parzival is inducted into the company of the Round Table. At Arthur's court, both Gawain and Parzival are put to shame by two other knights. When in his anger and despair Parzival sets out to seek the Holy Grail, and Gawain rides off to Askalon, the whole company of the Round Table is dispersed.

While Parzival sought the Grail, Gawain had many adventures. He joined the knights of King Meljanz of Lys, who sought vengeance on Duke Lippaut. When the fighting is over, Gawain rode to Schamfanzon, where he is committed by the king to the care of his daughter Antikonie. Gawain wooed the maiden and thus aroused the wrath of the people of Schamfanzon. Gawain is aided, however, by the woman and by Kingrimursel. After Gawain swore to the king that he would ask Scherules to send back some kinsmen to him, Gawain left, also to search for the Holy Grail.

Parzival, meanwhile, travels for many days in doubt and despair. In the forest of Monsalvasch he fights with a knight of the Holy Grail and passes on. Then, on Good Friday, he meets a pilgrim knight who tells him he should not bear arms during the holy season. The knight tells him to seek out Trevrezent, a hermit who shows Parzival how he has sinned by being wrathful with God and indicates to Parzival that he is a nephew to Amfortas, one of the Grail kings. The two part in sorrow, and Parzival resumes his search for the Grail.

Gawain, continuing his adventures, has married Orgeluse. When Gawain decides to battle Gramoflanz, King Arthur and Queen Guinevere agree to ride to see the joust. Before the joust can take place Gawain and Parzival meet and do battle, each unknown to his opponent. Gawain is defeated and severely injured by Parzival, who is filled with grief when he learns with whom he has fought. Parzival vows to take Gawain's place in the combat with Gramoflanz, but the latter refuses to do battle with anyone but Gawain himself.

Parzival, released from his vow, longs to return once again to his wife. One morning before dawn he secretly leaves the camp of King Arthur. On his way back to his wife, Parzival meets a great pagan warrior who almost vanquishes him. After the battle he learns the pagan knight is Feirefis, Parzival's half brother, the son of Gamuret and Belakane. The two ride back to King Arthur's court, where both are made welcome by the king. In company, the half brothers win many honors. At a feast of the Round Table, Kondrie enters the great hall to announce Parzival's election to the Grail kingdom. Summoned to Monsalvasch, Parzival, his wife, and Lohengrin, Parzival's son, are guided there by Kondrie. Feirefis, although he fails to see the Grail, is baptized and married to Repanse de Schoie. With her he returns to his kingdom, which is held later by his son, Prester John.

"The Story" by Walter E. Meyers

Critical Evaluation:

Parzival is the masterpiece of Germany's greatest medieval poet. It is, moreover, the groundwork of the great body of Richard Wagner's operas on knightly themes. Despite its place in German literature and its influence on modern opera, *Parzival* is little known to readers of English. Wolfram von Eschenbach's influence on the legends of the Arthurian cycle is also important. The Arthurian legends had a relatively low moral tone prior to their treatment by this poet who, upholding the knightly virtues of fidelity to the plighted word, of charity, and of a true reverence toward God, lifted the moral tone of the Arthurian romances. Most interesting is the identity of the Grail in *Parzival*. Here it is not the chalice used at the Last Supper, as it is in other versions, but a precious stone of supernatural powers.

Written at the beginning of the thirteenth century, *Parzival* is the most famous German tribute to the Arthurian legends, a celebration of the high nobility of knighthood. This masterpiece is a panoramic vision of chivalric deeds, loosely centered on its hero, Sir Parzival, and the quest for the Holy Grail. It is a tale of magnificence and splendor, where the spectacle of one astonishing battle is soon eclipsed by another. There is little of the farce or sly comedy of the French or Celtic traditions. In sixteen books of verses, Wolfram introduces close to two hundred characters, with the birth of Parzival not coming until the close of book 2. The first two books are concerned with the exploits of Parzival's father, the gallant Gamuret, and many of the succeeding books relate the adventures of Sir Gawain, one of King Arthur's nephews.

In many respects *Parzival* is best seen against the tradition it represents and with which it is at odds. Its primary source is Chrétien de Troyes's *Perceval: Ou, Le Conte du Graal* (c. 1180; *Perceval: Or, The Story of the Grail*, 1844), but Wolfram also mentions a "master Kyot," whose identity re-

mains problematic to scholars. Wolfram's version is probably most familiar to contemporary audiences through Richard Wagner's opera *Parsifal* (1882).

The quest for the Holy Grail is one of the most ambitious adventures of the Arthurian court; American readers are probably most familiar with the tradition as it is recounted in T. H. White's popular novel, *The Once and Future King* (1939-1958). White's novel is based, in turn, on Sir Thomas Malory's *Le Morte d'Arthur* (1485). *Parzival* departs from Arthurian tradition in several significant respects, the most important being a general secularization of the legend. In Christian tradition, the Holy Grail is the vessel from which Christ drank during the Last Supper. In *Parzival*, it is something on the order of a magic rock, which furnishes each baptized beholder with whatever he desires in the way of food or drink. Another important deviation from Malory's account is that Percival is permitted to see the Grail only because he is sexually pure, whereas Wolfram's Parzival is not only happily married to Kondwiramur but is the father of the twins Kardeiz and Lohengrin.

What matters most in Wolfram's story is knightly honor, by which is understood one's repute in battle and the riches one displays. These riches include fine silken clothing; beautiful, gem-studded armor; lands; kingdoms; and women. In Wolfram's world, women offered themselves as prizes, to secure, not diminish, their honor. A woman's prestige was measured by the renown of her knight and protector, and her beauty was the means she had of enticing the ablest to her side. There was no taint of impropriety in such offerings; Herzeleide, Parzival's mother, and Orgeluse, Gawain's lady, offer themselves in this way.

Wealth was the visible proof of honor, since a knight's riches would frequently consist of things he had won by conquering other knights. Wolfram describes repeatedly the fabulous wealth (and corresponding generosity) of Feirefis, Parzival's half brother by a pagan queen. Since Parzival, the hero, must be the most honorable knight in this tale, it falls to his nearest kin to be the wealthiest. Since wealth is so nearly equivalent, however, with honor, Feirefis, although a pagan, is allowed to accompany Parzival to Monsalvasch, the Grail Castle, as his only companion.

While Feirefis can neither win the woman of his heart— Repanse de Schoie, the only one permitted to carry the Grail—nor even have the sight to see the Grail until he is baptized, this is not perceived as a serious obstacle. The baptismal ceremony is quickly performed, Feirefis showing no reluctance to renounce his religion to win Repanse de Schoie. Although it would be a mistake to read *Parzival* as a strictly secular tale, the energy that infuses it is not religious. The

Christian core is respected, but Wolfram is much more interested in the noble tradition of knighthood.

This kind of secularization makes for some disjunctions in the narrative. For example, when Parzival fails at first to ask the suffering Grail king, Anfortas, the question that would have healed him of his long-festering wound, he does so out of politeness. He was taught not to ask nosy questions. This leads, however, to his failure and shame, a burden that he carries for years. By one set of standards his behavior was impeccable, but, unbeknown to him, in this instance the rules changed on him. His return to grace and power is equally arbitrary, as he is given a second chance to return to Munsalvaesche to ask the question.

The religious element to this part of the story is at odds with the story's generally secular orientation. It is not because Parzival has expiated himself in any meaningful way that he is chosen to heal and later succeed Anfortas, but because he has been faithful to knightly conduct.

Unlike other Arthurian tales, in which knightly encounters are depicted frequently as contests between good and evil, *Parzival* reveals a world in which greatness tests greatness. There are none of the traditional villains of medieval romance: no evil knights, no ogres, no lecherous abductors. Everyone, to some degree, is noble, and all the battles seem to be fought to establish a hierarchy of nobility. In this context, the battles between Parzival and Gawain, and later Parzival and Feirefis (in which each knight is ignorant of the identity of his adversary), become emblematic of Wolfram's chivalric vision. Nobility strives with nobility, until it is finally reconciled in harmony. *Parzival* is a salute to that knightly ideal.

"Critical Evaluation" by Linda J. Turzynski

Further Reading

Barber, Richard. *The Holy Grail: Imagination and Belief.* New York: Allen Lane, 2004. Barber, an Arthurian expert, chronicles the history of legends about the Holy Grail from twelfth century romances to late twentieth century best sellers.

Blamires, David. *Characterization and Individuality in Wolfram's "Parzival."* New York: Cambridge University Press, 1966. Devotes a chapter to each of the nine major characters to explore the technique of individualization in Wolfram's romance, demonstrating that *Parzival* fits within the trend toward individuality in twelfth century literature.

Green, Dennis Howard. *The Art of Recognition in Wolfram's "Parzival."* New York: Cambridge University Press, 1982. Posits that much of the difficulty in reading *Parzival* lies in Wolfram's style of revealing while concealing. The audience is invited to cooperate in the process of recognition: "Penetrating the mysteries of the Grail thus becomes for the listeners what the attainment of Grail kingship is for Parzival."

Groos, Arthur. *Romancing the Grail: Genre, Science, and Quest in Wolfram's "Parzival."* Ithaca, N.Y.: Cornell University Press, 1995. Uses the theories of Mikhail Bakhtin to analyze several strands of narrative in *Parzival*, particularly the Arthurian legend and the search for the Holy Grail. Describes how Wolfram transformed Chrétien de Troyes's French tales about the Grail within the context of Germanic chivalric culture.

Hasty, Will, ed. *A Companion to Wolfram's "Parzival."* Columbia, S.C.: Camden House, 1999. Collection of essays providing various interpretations of *Parzival*, including discussions of its women characters, the significance of the Gawan story, its cultural contexts, tournaments and battles in the epic, and the book's modern reception.

Loomis, R. S. "Wolfram von Eschenbach's *Parzival*." In *The Development of Arthurian Romance.* New York: W. W. Norton, 1970. Introduction to the themes and origins of *Parzival*. Places the romance within the context of the growth of Arthurian literature from its beginnings to Sir Thomas Malory.

Murphy, G. Ronald. *Gemstone of Paradise: The Holy Grail in Wolfram's "Parzival."* New York: Oxford University Press, 2006. Examines Wolfram's depiction of the Holy Grail, analyzing why he represents the Grail as a translucent gemstone and an altar that is made portable by women only.

Poag, James F. *Wolfram von Eschenbach.* Boston: Twayne, 1972. Introductory overview with chapters on Wolfram's life, his literary outlook, *Parzival*, and his other works. Includes a bibliography.

Sivertson, Randal. *Loyalty and Riches in Wolfram's "Parzival."* New York: Peter Lang, 1999. Interprets the epic as a conflict between feudal loyalty and self-centered mercenary service. Argues that the epic heroically defends feudal values at a time when feudalism was on the decline.

A Passage to India

Author: E. M. Forster (1879-1970)
First published: 1924
Type of work: Novel
Type of plot: Social realism
Time of plot: c. 1920
Locale: India

Principal characters:
DR. AZIZ, a young Indian surgeon
MRS. MOORE, a visiting Englishwoman and Dr. Aziz's friend
RONALD HEASLOP, the city magistrate and Mrs. Moore's son
ADELA QUESTED, Ronald's fiancé, visiting India with Mrs. Moore
CECIL FIELDING, principal of the Government College and Dr. Aziz's friend

The Story:

Dr. Aziz is doubly snubbed this evening. He had been summoned to the civil surgeon's house while he was at supper, but when he arrived, he found that his superior had departed for his club without bothering to leave any message. In addition, two Englishwomen emerged from the house and took their departure in his hired tonga, or horse-drawn vehicle, without even thanking him.

The doctor starts back toward the city of Chandrapore afoot. Tired, he stops at a mosque to rest and is furiously angry when he sees an Englishwoman emerge from behind its pillars with, as he thinks, her shoes on. Mrs. Moore, however, had gone barefoot to the mosque, and in a surge of friendly feelings, Dr. Aziz engages her in conversation.

Mrs. Moore had recently arrived from England to visit her son, Ronald Heaslop, the city magistrate. Dr. Aziz finds they have common ground when he learns that she does not care for the civil surgeon's wife. Her disclosure prompts him to tell of the usurpation of his carriage. The doctor walks back to the club with her, although as an Indian, he himself cannot be admitted.

At the club, Adela Quested, Heaslop's prospective fiancé, declares she wants to see the real India, not the India seen through the rarified atmosphere of the British colony. To please the ladies, one of the members offers to hold what he whimsically terms a "bridge party" and invite some native guests. The bridge party is a miserable affair. The Indians retreat to one side of the lawn, and although the conspicuously reluctant group of Anglo-Indian ladies go over to visit them, an awkward tension prevails.

There is, however, one promising result of the party. The principal of the Government College, Mr. Fielding, a man who apparently feels neither rancor nor arrogance toward the Indians, invites Mrs. Moore and Adela to a tea at his house. Upon Adela's request, Mr. Fielding also invites Professor Godbole, a teacher at his school, and Dr. Aziz. At the tea, Dr. Aziz charms Fielding and the guests with the elegance and fine intensity of his manner. The gathering, however, breaks up on a discordant note when the priggish and suspicious Heaslop arrives to claim the ladies. Fielding has taken Mrs. Moore on a tour of his school, and Heaslop is furious at him for having left Dr. Aziz alone with his prospective fiancé.

Adela is irritated by Heaslop's callous priggishness during her visit and informs him that she does not wish to become his wife. Later that evening, during a drive into the countryside, a mysterious figure, perhaps an animal, looms out of the darkness and nearly upsets the car in which they are riding. Their mutual loneliness and a sense of the unknown draws them together, and Adela asks Heaslop to disregard her earlier rejection.

One extraordinary aspect of the city of Chandrapore is a natural formation known as the Marabar Caves, located several miles outside the city. Mrs. Moore and Adela accept Dr. Aziz's offer to escort them to the caves. The visit proves catastrophic for all. Entering one of the caves, Mrs. Moore realizes that no matter what was says, the walls return only a prolonged booming, hollow echo. Pondering that echo while she rests, and pondering the distance that separates her from Dr. Aziz, from Adela, and from her own children, Mrs. Moore sees that all her Christianity, all her ideas of moral good and bad, in short, all her ideas of life, amount only to what is made of them by the hollow, booming echo of the Marabar Caves. Adela enters one of the caves alone. A few minutes later she rushes out in a terrified state and claims she had been nearly attacked in the gloom. She also claims that Dr. Aziz was the attacker, and the doctor is arrested.

There always had been a clear division between the Indians and the Anglo-Indian community, but as the trial of Dr.

Aziz drew nearer, the division sharpens and each group demands strict loyalty from its members. When Mrs. Moore casually intimates to her son that she is perfectly certain Dr. Aziz is not capable of the alleged crime, he immediately ships her off to a coastal port of embarkation. After Fielding expresses the same opinion at the club, he is ostracized.

At the trial opening, a sensational incident occurs when one of Dr. Aziz's friends pushes into the courtroom and shouts that Heaslop has smuggled his mother out of the country because she would have testified to the doctor's innocence. Hearing the name of Mrs. Moore, the restless Indian spectators work it into a kind of chant as though Mrs. Moore was a deity. The English colony is not to learn until later that Mrs. Moore died aboard ship.

Adela's testimony concludes the trial. For her, the tense atmosphere of the courtroom, the reiteration of Mrs. Moore's name, and the buzzing sound in her own ears that persists since the time she left the caves, combines to produce upon her a trancelike effect. She relives the whole of the crucial day as she recollects its events under the interrogation of the prosecuting attorney. When she reaches the moment of her lingering in the cave, she falters, changes her mind, and withdraws all charges.

For several hours afterward, Chandrapore experiences a great bedlam. The Anglo-Indians sulk while the Indians exult. As far as the British are concerned, Adela had crossed the line. Heaslop carefully explains to her that he can no longer be associated with her. After accepting Fielding's hospitality for a few weeks, she returns home. Dr. Aziz's Anglophobia increases, but Fielding persuades him not to press for legal damages from Adela.

Two years later, the Muhammadan Dr. Aziz is court physician to an aged Hindu potentate who dies on the night of the Krishna festival. The feast is a frantic celebration, and the whole town is under its spell when Fielding arrives on an official visit. In the intervening time he had married again, and Dr. Aziz, assuming he had married Adela, tries to avoid his old friend. When he runs into him accidentally, however, he finds that it is Mrs. Moore's daughter, Stella, whom Fielding married. The doctor's shame at his mistake only causes him to become more distant.

Before they part for the last time, Dr. Aziz and Fielding go riding through the jungles. The misunderstanding between them has been resolved, but they have no social ground on which to meet. Fielding cast his lot with his countryfolk by marrying an Englishwoman. As the two men ride, rocks suddenly rear up before them, forcing their horses to pass in single file on either side. This event symbolizes the different paths they will travel from then on. The affection of two men,

however sincere, is not sufficient to bridge the vast gap between their races.

Critical Evaluation:

E. M. Forster was part of the intellectual Bloomsbury group, which flourished in London just before and after World War I. Educated at Cambridge, as were many of the group, Forster became one of England's leading novelists during the prewar Edwardian period. His Bloomsbury friends included biographer Lytton Strachey, novelist Virginia Woolf, art critic Clive Bell, painter Roger Fry, economist John Maynard Keynes, and philosopher G. E. Moore. The group rejected convention and authority and placed great faith in its own intellect and good taste.

Forster wrote several acclaimed novels between 1905 and 1910: *Where Angels Fear to Tread* (1905), *The Longest Journey* (1907), *A Room with a View* (1908), and *Howards End* (1910). After a hiatus of fourteen years came *A Passage to India*, the last work he published during his lifetime. (The early novel *Maurice* was published posthumously in 1970.) He once confessed that he did not understand post-World War I values and had nothing more to say. *A Passage to India*, however, belies this statement, as it remains relevant.

Forster took his title from the Walt Whitman poem by the same name, an odd choice, since Whitman's vision is of the total unity of all people while in Forster's novel the attempt to unite people fails at all levels. The book is divided into three sections: Mosque, Cave, and Temple. These divisions correspond to the three divisions of the Indian year: cool spring, hot summer, and wet monsoon. Each section is dominated by its concomitant weather. Each section also focuses on one of the three ethnic groups involved: Muslim, Anglo-Indian, and Hindu. The Cave could also have been called the Club. Just as the Mosque and the Temple are the Muslim and Hindu shrines, so is the Club the true Anglo-Indian shrine. Forster knew that religious-ethnic divisions control social modes of activity. The Muslims are said to be emotional; the British said to rely on intellect. Only the Hindus, in the person of Godbole, are said to have the capacity to love.

The novel, however, is much more than merely a social or political commentary. Forster belittles social forms on all sides of the conflict and favors neither the Indians nor the British. The bridge party, Fielding's tea party, and Aziz's cave party are all failures. More important than social forms are the relationships among individuals. The novel's theme is the search for love and friendship. Forster presents primarily relationships between men with the capacity for mutual understanding, and his male characters are the most clearly defined. The women—Mrs. Moore and Adela Quested—have no real possibility of finding friendship across ethnic lines. Mrs. Moore is too old, Adela too British. Both women want to see the "real" India, but they are unprepared for it when the experience comes. Mrs. Moore at the mosque and the first cave, and Adela at the cave and the courtroom, discover the real India, and both suffer an almost catatonic withdrawal.

The male characters are more complex. With his Muslim sensitivity, Aziz is determined to find humiliation no matter what the experience. He tries to be both physician and poet— healer of body and soul—but he is inept in both attempts. In the last section, readers see him abandoning both. Aziz needs love and friendship, but ultimately he is incapable of establishing a satisfying relationship among his own people, with the Hindus, or, more important, with Fielding. Muslim sensitivity prevents him from accepting friendship when it is offered.

Out of the multiple failures of the first two sections of the novel there is only the relationship between Aziz and Fielding that holds any promise of reconciliation. Muslim and Anglo-Indian, they meet in the final section in the Hindu province. Both men desire friendship and understanding, but in the final scene the very land seems to separate them. They are not in tune with nature, which is renewing itself in the monsoon downpour, and neither man has come to accept the irrational. They are not ready, in the Hindu sense of love, to accept things as they are. Only Godbole, a Hindu, can fully accept India and its people. The nothingness of the caves and the apparent chaos of the people do not disturb Hindus.

The most crucial scene in *A Passage to India* is the visit to the Marabar Caves. These caves puzzle and terrify both Muslims and Anglo-Indians and form the center of the novel. Only Godbole understands them. The Hindus had called India home before either the Muslims or the British. The caves are elemental; they have been there from the beginnings of the earth. They are not Hindu holy places, but Godbole can respect them without fear. Cave worship is the cult of the female principle, the sacred womb, mother earth. The Marabar Caves, both womb and grave, demand total effacing of ego. The individual loses identity; whatever is said returns as Ommm, the holy word.

The caves are terrifying and chaotic to those who rely on the intellect. The trip itself emphasizes the chaos that is India. Godbole can eat no meat; Aziz can eat no pork; the British must have their whisky and port. The confusion of the departure epitomizes the confusion that pervades the novel. Significantly, it is Godbole, the one person who might have helped, who is left out. Once in the caves, the party encounters the Nothingness that terrifies. Only Mrs. Moore seems to accept it on a limited scale, but the caves have reduced her

will to live. She retreats from the world of experience. She came to India seeking peace; she finds it in death.

The conclusion of the novel emphasizes the chaos of India, but it also hints at a pattern that the outsider, Muslim or British, cannot understand. Drenched in water and religion, the last chapters portray the rebirth of the god Shri Krishna. It is the recycling of the seasons, the rebirth and renewal of the earth that signals the renewal of the Hindu religious cycle. Godbole shows that humans may choose to accept and participate in the seeming chaos, or they can fight against it. They must, however, be in tune with the natural rhythms of the universe to receive true love and friendship. Neither Fielding nor Aziz, products of Western civilization, can accept the confusion without attempting to impose order. Although they move toward the irrational in the course of the novel, they do not move far enough.

"Critical Evaluation" by Michael S. Reynolds

Further Reading

Bloom, Harold, ed. *E. M. Forster's "A Passage to India."* Philadelphia: Chelsea House, 2004. Collection of old and new essays analyzing various aspects of the novel. Including essays by noted literary critics Lionel Trilling and Malcolm Bradbury.

Bradbury, Malcolm, ed. *E. M. Forster: "A Passage to India"—A Casebook*. 1970. New ed. Basingstoke, England: Macmillan, 1998. Essays examine the novel. Particularly interesting are an interview with Forster in which he discusses his writing of *A Passage to India* and a selection of early reviews and reactions to his novel.

Bradshaw, David, ed. *The Cambridge Companion to E. M. Forster.* New York: Cambridge University Press, 2007. Collection of essays analyzing various aspects of Forster's life and work, including discussions of Forster and the novel, women, and England; Forsterian sexuality; and postcolonial Forster. "*A Passage to India*" by Peter Childs focuses on this novel.

Child, Peter, ed. *A Routledge Literary Sourcebook on E. M. Forster's "A Passage to India."* New York: Routledge, 2002. Contains primary source documents about the British Empire; extracts from Forster's letters, books, and articles regarding the novel; an interview with Forster; a selection of early and modern reviews and analyses; and explication of key passages.

Das, G. K., and Christel R. Devadawson, eds. *Forster's "A Passage to India": An Anthology of Recent Criticism.* Delhi, India: Pencraft International, 2005. Examines the novel from postcolonial, feminist, and other twenty-first century perspectives. Includes discussions of the major characters, the myths and possibilities of cross-cultural friendships, and the irreconcilable differences between Islam and Hinduism.

Edwards, Mike. *E. M. Forster: The Novels*. Basingstoke, England: Palgrave, 2002. Edwards shows how readers can analyze four Forster novels—*A Passage to India, Howards End, A Room with a View*, and *The Longest Journey*—to understand the author's treatment of characters, locations, relationships, and other aspects of these works. Also discusses Forster's life, gives examples of how four literary critics approached Forster's writing, and provides suggestions for further analysis.

Godfrey, Denis. *E. M. Forster's Other Kingdom*. New York: Barnes & Noble, 1968. Focuses on the mystical themes in the novel. Shows how Mrs. Moore—a symbol of good—influences the other characters and the plot even after her death.

Herz, Judith Scherer. *"A Passage to India": Nation and Narration*. New York: Twayne, 1993. Overview of the novel with a section explaining the historical background of the British Raj. Detailed discussion of Forster's style and use of symbolism. Also addresses the problem of narrative voice.

Medalie, David. *E. M. Forster's Modernism*. New York: Palgrave, 2002. Medalie examines the relationship of Forster's writings to modernism, analyzing his works to demonstrate their modernist elements. Places Forster within the context of early twentieth century social, political, and aesthetic developments.

Passing

Author: Nella Larsen (1891-1964)
First published: 1929
Type of work: Novel
Type of plot: Social realism
Time of plot: Early twentieth century
Locale: New York

Principal characters:
IRENE REDFIELD, a black socialite
CLARE KENDRY, a black socialite who is passing as white
GERTRUDE MARTIN, a black socialite who is passing as white
BRIAN REDFIELD, Irene's husband
JOHN "JACK" BELLEW, Clare's husband

The Story:

Irene Redfield receives a letter from Clare Kendry that she considers dangerous, since she knows that Clare has been passing for white and that Clare's association with any black person is dangerous. Irene recalls that Clare has always been different, sneaky, and clever, as well as independent, selfish, and self-centered; she remembers Clare's poise as a teenager when her drunken father bellowed at her for disobeying him. When Clare's father was killed in a saloon fight, Clare was angry with him for abandoning her.

Irene reads the letter from Clare, who is in New York and wants to see her. Irene is determined not to see Clare, recalling the last time she had accidentally run into Clare. It is two summers earlier, and Irene is in Chicago, shopping for her sons, Brian, Jr., and Theodore. Feeling very warm and thirsty, she stops at the Drayton Hotel for tea. She notices a woman staring at her and thinks she is doing so because she is black. The woman approaches Irene and claims to know her, but Irene does not remember her, until she laughs; she then recognizes the laugh as belonging to Clare Kendry. There had been rumors about Clare's sudden disappearance from the black community twelve years earlier. Irene and Clare talk about what they had been doing over the years. Irene invites Clare to her house but immediately regrets it. Irene questions Clare about passing for white but Clare, noting that they were both drinking tea at the all-white Drayton Hotel, turns the question back. Irene gets angry and leaves, vowing to have nothing more to do with Clare.

A few days later, Clare repeatedly calls the Redfield residence, but Irene refuses to speak with her, letting her maid, Liza, answer the phone. Finally, exasperated by the constant ringing of the phone, she answers the phone and lets Clare badger her into visiting her. At Clare's home, Irene and another woman, Gertrude Martin, exchange cool greetings. Irene does not like Gertrude who, like Clare, is passing for white and is married to a white man. Irene's opinion of Gertrude does not improve when Gertrude tells her and Clare that she does not want to have any "dark" children. Irene's temper flares and she reminds Gertrude that her children—Brian, Jr., and Theodore—are "dark." At that moment, John "Jack" Bellew, Clare's husband, walks in and greets Clare with the nickname Nig. Amid tense silence, when Clare tells John to explain why he calls her that, John says that when he met Clare she was "white as a lily," but that she appeared to be getting darker. Nig was his affectionate way of telling her that one morning she would wake up a "nigger." Prompted by an angry but subdued Irene, John goes on to say that he hates black people. Suppressing both laughter and anger, Irene leaves, followed by Gertrude.

Just before she returns to New York, Irene receives a note from Clare, begging for understanding and forgiveness. Irene tears up the note and turns her thoughts to the situation at home. Her main concern is whether Brian, her husband, is still discontent and restless.

All this had occurred two years earlier in Chicago, and until that morning, Irene had not heard from Clare. Irene is suspicious of Clare's alleged love for her own people. She brings up the subject of Clare with Brian at breakfast. Brian expresses admiration of Clare's sense of adventure and talks of his desire to go to Brazil. Irene becomes angry, telling him that he had made the right decision when he set up his race philanthropy charities in New York. They part angrily from each other, and Irene feels uneasy about the security of her marriage.

Still upset over her fight with Brian, Irene tears up the letter from Clare and determines not to contact her. Days go by and Irene forgets about Clare. Instead, she continues to worry about Brian's restlessness and unhappiness. Several days later, Irene is shocked to answer her doorbell and find Clare standing there. To her own surprise, Irene is happy to see Clare, yet she warns Clare that it is not safe for them to be friends, given John Bellew's beliefs about blacks. Clare finds Irene's concern humorous and tells her that she wants to be invited to the Negro Welfare Dance that Brian organized. Irene gives in despite her own premonitions of disaster, but once Clare leaves she becomes angry with herself for giving in to Clare. Irene then gets angry with Clare, realizing that she is as selfish as she had always been.

Clare becomes a regular visitor to the Redfield household. Irene begins to notice how well Brian and Clare get along and gradually begins to suspect that Clare has designs on her husband. When Clare admits to Irene that she is bad and not to be trusted, Irene's suspicions flare into terror, especially since Brian seems even more distant and withdrawn. Irene begins to consider how she can rid herself of Clare, and she begins to wish horrible afflictions on Clare's family.

Meeting John on the street, she tells him she is black and is pleased to see his distress and hatred. For a moment, she considers destroying Clare, too, by revealing her race, but she cannot go through with it. As a black woman she feels loyalty to Clare even if only because of their gender and race.

Just before leaving for a party, Irene and Brian argue over how to raise their sons. Afterward, Irene admits to herself that the only thing she wants from Brian is security. She is shocked to realize that she has never loved Brian and never will. Yet she is determined to keep him, no matter what the cost. They go to the party with Clare. Shortly after they arrive, John rushes in after knocking loudly at the door, and he is demanding his wife. When he calls her a nigger, Clare begins to laugh. He seizes her arm, and Irene tries to stop—or help—him. In the next instant, Clare falls or jumps—or is pushed—out of the open window. Everyone except Irene rushes downstairs to the sidewalk. Irene is in shock, but she also is relieved that Clare is dead. A police officer comes upstairs and asks Irene if she is sure Clare had jumped. Brian had told the officer that John had pushed Clare, but Irene refutes her husband. The officer decides that Clare's death was probably an accident.

Critical Evaluation:

The publication of *An Intimation of Things Distant: The Collected Fiction of Nella Larsen* in 1992 furthered the resurrection of Nella Larsen's reputation as a significant figure of the Harlem Renaissance. Like her contemporary Jesse Redmon Fauset, Larsen was in the middle of the literary skirmishes between the champions of the Harlem Renaissance and those who saw the aestheticization of lower-class African American life as pandering to the Negrophilia of white Manhattanites.

Larsen's subject matter was the light-skinned, middle-class African American woman who was "afflicted" and endowed with means, taste, and ambition. Larsen's self-imposed limitations were decidedly unfashionable among the critics of the period, though popular with the general readership, but her works became anachronisms with the appearance of the works of Langston Hughes, Countée Cullen, and Claude McKay. Against the rough-hewn world depicted by these writers, Larsen's genteel angst fared badly, not least because her concerns seemed mostly those of middle-class African American women with too much time on their hands.

While some, like James Weldon Johnson, George Schuyler, and Jean Toomer, returned again and again to the peculiarly African American phenomenon of passing for white, only Larsen conflated the problem of racial and class boundaries with the problem of gender in asking what it meant to be a middle-class African American woman in the first half of the twentieth century. In *Passing*, Larsen simultaneously treats three seemingly intractable issues in a provocative, if melodramatic, narrative. For that reason alone, the book represents a significant landmark in the history of American literature. Beyond its important subject matter, however, *Passing* provides a concise, unelaborated story. Larsen's prose is sparse but effective. With a few deft strokes, characters become believable humans with vices and virtues. The plot moves swiftly, and the dialogue fleshes out characters and propels the narrative forward.

The principal theme of *Passing* is the social and cultural nexus in which light-skinned African American women find themselves. Though she never deals with it explicitly in her fiction, Larsen's work implies, even more ominously, that if African American women whose skin is so light they can pass for white cannot "make it" without discrimination, darker-skinned African American women have no chance at all. By "making it," Larsen means indirect but proximate access to economic, social, and cultural power. *Passing* takes for granted the hierarchies of race, class, and gender in American life. The three main female characters—Clare Kendry, Irene Redfield, and Gertrude Martin—understand that the best they can hope to do is to imitate white women. Both Clare and Gertrude have married white men, which is as close to real power—white male power—as they will ever get.

Irene, from whose point of view the story is told, disdains her female peers for their treason to their race, yet she too desires the proximity to power that Clare and Gertrude have by virtue of their marriages. This explains Irene's hostility to Gertrude, a mere acquaintance, and her ambivalence in her relations with Clare, her friend. Irene envies their passing even as she detests it. When Irene believes Clare to be a threat to her marriage, she wishes Clare were dead. Yet, loyal to her race, she refuses to betray Clare to her husband when she has the opportunity to do so, knowing that he hates "niggers," even though that same loyalty to race drives her to reveal her own race to him.

Passing also concerns the problem of class, which is at least as important to Irene as race, although the issue is raised explicitly only once when Irene thinks about Gertrude, who has married a white butcher. Marriage to this man has destroyed Gertrude's adolescent beauty and charm. Of the two light-skinned women married to white men, one is married to a rich bigot and forced to pass for white while the other is married to a man who accepts her for who she is but who is,the novel implies, only a butcher. The moral is clear: Only

a lower-class white man, "white trash," would knowingly marry an African American woman.

The irony of Irene's marriage to Brian Redfield is that he, though from the same middle class as she, would much prefer working with the poor in Brazil. Throughout the novel, Irene worries because Brian's dissatisfaction with sponsoring chic parties for the Negro Welfare League draws him further and further from her. By novel's end, Irene admits to herself that she has never loved Brian, though she remains desperate to save her marriage. She married him for his social and cultural connections, limited as they are by his being an African American. Small wonder that Irene feels superior to both Gertrude and Clare, for she married a man from a higher class than Gertrude's husband yet, unlike both Gertrude's and Clare's husbands, someone from her own race.

Tyrone Williams

Further Reading

Calloway, Licia Morrow. "Elite Rejection of Maternity in Nella Larsen's *Quicksand* and *Passing*." In *Black Family (Dys)function in Novels by Jessie Fauset, Nella Larsen, and Fannie Hurst*. New York: Peter Lang, 2003. Calloway's analysis of *Passing* focuses on Larsen's depiction of maternity and her handling of the class pressures upon upward-aspiring African Americans.

Carby, Hazel V. *Reconstructing Womanhood: The Emergence of the Afro-American Woman Novelist*. New York: Oxford University Press, 1987. In this study of the rise of black women novelists, Carby considers Larsen to be one of the most important novelists, female or male, to emerge from the Harlem Renaissance. Focuses on Larsen's aesthetics and her political and social critiques.

Davis, Arthur P. *From the Dark Tower: Afro-American Writers, 1900 to 1960*. Washington, D.C.: Howard University Press, 1982. Takes a historical perspective, focusing on Larsen's fiction and its place in the larger aesthetic ambience of black American writing of the twentieth century.

Davis, Thadious M. "Nella Larsen's Harlem Aesthetic." In *The Harlem Renaissance: Revaluations*, edited by Amritjit Singh, William S. Shiver, and Stanley Brodwin. New York: Garland, 1989. Argues that Larsen's aesthetic faithfully captures the spirit of her times. Emphasizes the tension Larsen evokes between the social and the personal. Part of the Critical Studies on Black Life and Culture series.

Hutchinson, George. *In Search of Nella Larsen: A Biography of the Color Line*. Cambridge, Mass.: Belknap Press, 2006. Examines Larsen's work, life, and place in social history, describing how she deals with personal issues of racial identity and fear of abandonment in her novels. Chapter 16 explores *Passing*.

Kramer, Victor A., ed. *The Harlem Renaissance Re-Examined*. New York: AMS Press, 1987. Especially important in this collection of contemporary background essays updating the critical views of Larsen and her literary associates is Lillie P. Howard's study of Larsen's use of the themes of crossing and of materialism.

Larsen, Nella. *Passing: Authoritative Text, Backgrounds and Contexts, Criticism*. Edited by Carla Kaplan. W. W. Norton, 2007. This edition of *Passing* includes a detailed introduction by Kaplan. The "Background and Contexts" section ties the novel to the historical events of the time the novel was written. Reprints fourteen contemporary reviews, including one by W. E. B. Du Bois, and includes discussions of race and passing by Larsen and Langston Hughes. The "Criticism" section contains fifteen interpretations of the novel.

McLendon, Jacquelyn Y. *The Politics of Color in the Fiction of Jessie Fauset and Nella Larsen*. Charlottesville: University of Virginia Press, 1995. A study of the theme of the "tragic mulatto" in the novels of Larsen and Jessie Redmon Fauset. Devotes a chapter to an analysis of *Passing*.

Ransom, Portia Boulware. *Black Love and the Harlem Renaissance (The Novels of Nella Larsen, Jessie Redmon Fauset, and Zora Neale Hurston): An Essay in African American Literary Criticism*. Lewiston, N.Y.: Edwin Mellen Press, 2005. Examines how Larsen, Jessie Fauset, and Zora Neale Hurston use their semibiographical fiction to focus on the tensions between black men and women who are trying to define themselves.

Wald, Gayle. *Crossing the Line: Racial Passing in Twentieth-Century U.S. Literature and Culture*. Durham, N.C.: Duke University Press, 2000. Examines the "passing narratives" of African American writers such as Larsen, James Weldon Johnson, and Jessie Redmon Fauset. Argues the literature uses the "passing plot" in an attempt to negotiate identity, agency, and freedom.

The Passion According to G. H.

Author: Clarice Lispector (1925-1977)
First published: A paixão segundo G. H., 1964 (English translation, 1988)
Type of work: Novel
Type of plot: Philosophical realism
Time of plot: 1960's
Locale: Rio de Janeiro

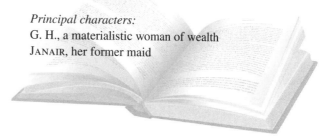

Principal characters:
G. H., a materialistic woman of wealth
JANAIR, her former maid

The Story:

A wealthy woman, G. H., finds herself alone without a maid, and without a lover. She is thinking about what had occurred the previous day, when she decided to clean out the small maid's quarters at the back of her Rio de Janeiro apartment. However, the room of her former maid, Janair, already was clean and was almost devoid of material possessions.

G. H. remembers the following: The only signs of previous occupancy in the quarters are simplistic black etchings on the white walls that represent a woman, a man, and a dog. G. H. believes these drawings represent the maid's disgust with her and her overindulgent lifestyle. G. H is resentful of this evaluation.

G. H. then opens a wardrobe and finds a cockroach scurrying out. Repulsed, she quickly slams the door of the wardrobe, cutting the insect in half in the process. She watches the viscera of the cockroach trickle out of its still-living body. Unable to look away, she starts a philosophical monologue that questions everything about her existence up to this moment. She says, in addressing her fear in life, that her

fear was not the fear of someone who was going toward madness and thus toward a truth—my fear was the fear of having a truth that I would come to despise, a defamatory truth that would make me get down and exist at the level of the cockroach.

Finished with her monologue, she puts the oozing innards of the cockroach into her mouth and consumes it.

Critical Evaluation:

Clarice Lispector's narrator in *The Passion According to G. H.* presents the reader with a woman who communicates in the first person and reveals a severely introspective adventure of self-discovery and deconstruction of life and reality. At times, this self-discovery reveals how nothingness can be more meaningful than reality. A seemingly trivial event, the killing of a cockroach, leads G. H. to a detailed self-examination not only of life, love, hope, and existence but also of how everything that humans are might be nothing more than linguistic justification of a nonreality. The narrative encounter delves into the possibility that much of what is assumed to be human might be nothing more than the linguistic antimatter of a nonentity.

The reader knows little about G. H., and even her name remains unknown: The initials G. H. are observed only on a piece of luggage. The relentless self-questioning leads to no meaningful answers, but rather an abundance of mystical vacuums in the woman's existence. One is aware of the woman's pretentious and arrogant life until the day of the novel, but one does not find solutions to what life and its events should represent tomorrow. *The Passion According to G. H.* is a work of questions that encourages the reader to further question life.

Structurally, the chapters are textually linked. Each chapter starts with the last sentence of the previous chapter. This work progressively takes the reader, chapter by chapter, into a vortex that descends from a pampered and protected life of wealth and privilege and eventually arrives in a place where nothing can be presupposed to be reality. G. H.'s well-defined world is reduced to the questions concerning the killing of a cockroach in her former maid's quarters, which represents the antithesis of G. H.

Although she is filled with overt fears of what her self-examination might reveal, G. H. is nevertheless driven by the fear of not confronting the truths that will be revealed. What remains of her self-evaluation is a secular reenactment of a spiritual rebirth, that is, the consumption of the martyred cockroach. This is the only clue that the reader is given that the woman has left her previous world of hyperconsumerism, mass consumption, to begin a new life, free from former restraints on reality.

Because the action in this work is almost nonexistent, critical evaluation must be based on the form and substance of the narrator's thoughts. Lispector's deconstruction of thought and of the linguistic representation of thought can be found in her idiosyncratic juxtaposition of the spoken word (or the logical textual meaning of it) and the philosophical or existential absurdity of the complete lack of true linguistic meaning. That is, G. H.'s self-interrogation leads her to discover the other side of everything linguistic: For example, what is ephemeral is also eternal. What is eternal in her manners and thoughts is actually only a momentary linguistic response to a circumstance.

Lispector employs a disjointed grammar and a continuous stream of narrative consciousness, repetition, and contradiction that forces the reader to continually verify the truth or lack of truth in the narrator's presentation of her life and values. The work at times swings wildly from simple concrete realities observed in a life of luxury to recognition that much of what exists might very well be nothing more than a reflection of another reality, one that is not so easily observed. G. H. muses on the possibility that life has no specific moments or locations, just a blurred continuum that is infinite. She thinks, for example, that

> Between two musical notes there exists another note, between two facts there exists another fact, between two grains of sand, no matter how close together they are, there exists an interval of space.

Eventually, the identity of the narrator becomes unstable. The reader becomes aware that the woman's existence and personality are in never-ending cycles of elimination and reconstruction. Lispector alludes to this "absence" of self by presenting G. H. as always becoming what is unseen, but existent, "As though I [G. H.] were also the other side of a cube, the side that you don't see because you are seeing the front side."

The Passion According to G. H. does use some standard literary techniques. For example, Lispector employs metaphor, especially during her descriptions of the apartment of her former maid. These sparse quarters are metaphorically described as representative of an ancient Egypt. The maid's room is transformed into a minaret, above the desert of the narrator's life. The closet becomes a sarcophagus for the cockroach and for the beliefs and history of the narrator's previous existence.

The interplay between the textual or spoken word and existential reality is often at the forefront of the work. The wealthy woman repeatedly ponders if linguistic expression (the spoken word) has value or is simply a pretext for ignoring a less accessible reality in this life. She states she has nothing to say, then says "But if I don't force myself to talk, silence will forever engulf me in waves." Doubt appears in the lack of confidence that the future can be understood by means of linguistic expression.

The world interdepended with me, and I am not understanding what I say, never! Never again shall I understand what I say. For how will I be able to speak without the word lying for me?

Eventually, the reader becomes aware of a convergence of the voices of the narrator, the novelist, and G. H. This fusion of self-consciousness leads to an acceptance of new possibilities in the mind of the reader, based upon the reconstructed realities of G. H. The killing of the cockroach becomes a moment of truth for the narrator. It is a pivotal point in time, where previous realities and present and future actualities merge. All time becomes relative to this space and time. All other reality disappears as G. H. focuses on the dying cockroach and its implications: "Before entering the room, what was I? I was what others had always seen me be, and that was the way I know myself." The previously arrogant and overtly proud woman of wealth is transformed within the small maid's quarters. She confronts her fears and realizes that, in witnessing the death of the least valued in a culture has led to her own reawakening and convergence to a new set of life values.

The narrator articulately expresses the very human trait of harboring a fear of confrontation to previously assumed realities in life. Indeed, in some ways it is a very frightening literary work, one that threatens to undo firm beliefs that are taken for granted. By reading and understanding what G. H. experiences, the reader also embarks upon a journey of undoing oneself. The trepidation of not being accepted or even of outright humiliation is at the core of G. H.'s hesitation to openly question previously held truths.

If I raised the alarm at being alive, voiceless and hard they would drag me away since they drag away those who depart the possible world, the exceptional being is dragged away, the screaming being.

This is a work that begins with overconfidence and ends with mere acceptance of the impossibility to completely understand the totality of human experience. The novel does not provide concrete answers to the meaning of life. It does, however, raise pertinent questions that one might use to evaluate one's own values and to evaluate how words and language are not always enough to reach a conclusive understanding of life. The narrator herself is fearful of what such self-examination might involve, stating

I don't know what to do with the horrifying freedom that can destroy me. But while I was held down, was I happy? Or was there—and there was—an uncanny restless something in my happy prison routine? Or was there—and there was—that throbbing something to which I was accustomed that I thought throbbing was the same as being a person? Isn't that it? Yes, that too.

Paul Siegrist

Further Reading

Cixous, Helene. *Reading with Clarice Lispector*. Minneapolis: University of Minnesota Press, 1994. Deals predominantly with literary theory, and applies that theory to analyze works by Lispector. Includes an index.

Fitz, Earl E. *Sexuality and Being in the Poststructuralist Universe of Clarice Lispector*. Austin: University of Texas Press, 2001. Detailed discussions concerning the style, sense of structure, characters, and themes in Lispector's writings, including *The Passion According to G. H.*

Moser, Benjamin. *Why This World: A Biography of Clarice Lispector*. New York: Oxford University Press, 2009. An extensive and well-researched work on this important Brazilian writer, one of Brazil's leading novelists. Includes an index and a bibliography.

Peixoto, Marta. *Passionate Fictions: Gender, Narrative and Violence in Clarice Lispector*. Minneapolis: University of Minnesota Press, 1994. Especially useful for readers who wish to expand their knowledge of gender issues in the works of Lispector. Also deals extensively with Lispector's unique usage of narration within text. Includes an index and a bibliography.

The Passion Flower

Author: Jacinto Benavente y Martínez (1866-1954)
First produced: La malquerida, 1913; first published, 1914
   (English translation, 1917)
Type of work: Drama
Type of plot: Tragedy
Time of plot: Early twentieth century
Locale: Castile, Spain

Principal characters:
ESTEBAN, a well-to-do Spanish peasant
RAIMUNDA, his second wife
ACACIA, her daughter
RUBIO and JULIANA, family servants
NORBERT, Acacia's former fiancé
FAUSTINO, Acacia's fiancé

The Story:

There is much excitement in the home of Esteban, a wealthy peasant living in an outlying section of a small town in Castile, Spain. The engagement of his stepdaughter Acacia to Faustino, son of Tio Eusebio, a friend of Esteban, has just been announced, and friends of Raimunda, Acacia's mother, are coming by to talk about the event. Acacia, after turning down several suitors, has finally consented to Faustino's suit. The women are wondering whether Acacia still thinks about Norbert, who some time before had broken off his engagement to her without explanation.

Fidelia, one of the callers, says that she saw Norbert leaving angrily with his gun after the engagement was announced that afternoon. Another, Engracia, shrewdly suspects that the young woman has accepted Faustino to get away from Esteban, against whom she has borne a grudge for marrying Raimunda so soon after the death of her first husband. Raimunda assures her friends that she has seen no signs of ill feeling toward Esteban from Acacia except in her unwillingness to call him "father." Certainly Esteban has been most generous to both of them.

Night is coming on. Faustino and his father, who live in the next village, will have no moonlight for their journey, and hungry husbands will soon be demanding suppers, so the party ends. Esteban offers to accompany his friends to the edge of the village.

Raimunda, still not certain how her daughter feels about the coming marriage, begins questioning her, and she is reassured by her daughter's replies. Only Juliana, a servant, strikes a sour note as she begins to tidy the house after the party, declaring that she wishes that Acacia's real father had lived to see this day. Milagros, a friend who has stayed to see Acacia's hope chest, also asks the young woman how she feels toward Norbert. When Milagros suggests that Acacia is still in love with him, Acacia's answer is to tear his last letter to her into bits and throw the pieces out the window into the darkness.

At that moment, a gunshot is heard outside, and Raimunda sends Juliana to investigate. The servant returns with villagers who are carrying the body of Faustino. No one saw the shot fired, but the women are sure Norbert was the assassin. When a trial is held, however, unbiased witnesses give Norbert an unbreakable alibi. Weeks later, the people of the village are still arguing about the incident. Esteban mopes about the house and talks so much about the killing that Acacia is almost frantic. Raimunda finally decides to send Juliana to find Norbert. She is sure that she can learn the truth from him.

The servant Rubio, who was becoming increasingly drunk and impudent, tries to keep Eusebio from calling on Esteban to discuss the murder. Eusebio's other sons, disgusted with what they regard as a miscarriage of justice, are threatening to shoot Norbert. Their father hints that even if the young man is innocent, rogues can be hired to assassinate him, or family servants may act through loyalty. Raimunda tells him that she prays every day that God will reveal and punish the murderer.

After Eusebio leaves, Juliana sneaks Norbert into the house. He assures Raimunda that he is completely innocent of the crime. Bernabe, another servant, arrives with accounts of Rubio's drunken boasting that he is now master in Esteban's house. The servant also repeats a song, heard in the tavern, that calls Acacia "the Passion Flower" because she inspires an unholy love in men. Norbert confesses that he broke off his engagement to Acacia because he had been threatened and had not been courageous enough to resist.

When Acacia appears, Raimunda, to test her suspicions, accuses her of being in love with her stepfather. The girl replies that her father is in the cemetery and that she hates the man who has taken his place. The arrival of Esteban brings further denunciation from Raimunda: Let him get Rubio's help to murder Acacia and her, if he wishes, but she will kill him if he approaches her daughter. Norbert, trying to leave the house in spite of Bernabe's warning, is shot by Eusebio's sons.

Norbert recovers from his wounds, but an atmosphere of hatred hangs over all because of the things that have been said and done. Raimunda and Juliana discuss the time when

Esteban came courting Raimunda; now they wonder whether he loved Acacia then. Juliana warns that great hatred such as Acacia's might contain the germ of great love.

Rubio, becoming insolent in his demands, proves that Esteban never actually told him to murder Faustino. Esteban had only spoken aloud his hope that no one would take Acacia from his house. There is still love between Esteban and Raimunda, however, and to preserve it they decide that they would be wise to send Acacia briefly to a convent and then try to find a husband for her. Acacia, who has been listening outside the door, bursts in with the announcement that she will not leave the house. Esteban acquiesces; since he has been the cause of all the trouble, he should be the one to go. At that Acacia breaks down, saying that Esteban must not go; she loves him.

Raimunda's screams denouncing him bring the neighbors to the scene. The trapped Esteban shoots Raimunda, who dies happy because Acacia has turned to her at the end as she lies dying, and not to Esteban. With her death, Raimunda has saved her daughter. Esteban will never have her now.

Critical Evaluation:

The Passion Flower is the rather cinematographic title given to the English-language version of Jacinto Benavente y Martínez's *La malquerida*, the drama on which Benavente's British and American reputation largely rests. Its production by Nance O'Neil in 1920 met with huge success and was in part responsible for the author's receiving the Nobel Prize in Literature in 1922.

Some critics have referred to the play as a classical drama, but scholars attempting to analyze the play according to Aristotelian principles would find it difficult to discover unity of action. The protagonist is at one juncture Raimunda, at another Esteban, and at yet another Acacia. It is impossible to designate any one of the three as the hero or heroine of the tragedy. Indeed, it would be more realistic to call the play's real protagonist the people and the chief theme of the drama the gradual awakening of public consciousness in this village of the Castilian uplands. In each successive act, public opinion in favor of punishing the guilty sinner increases in strength. Initially, the innocent Norbert is considered guilty, but after public opinion has sifted the evidence, he is led home in triumph by large crowds. Though the people of the village do not actually appear onstage, they function like an invisible chorus, constantly commenting on the tragic fatality of human beings.

More than any of the author's other works, *The Passion Flower* shows the strength of Benavente's female characters. Indeed, it is difficult to visualize the traditional character of the proud Castilian male in Esteban, who becomes a whimpering coward by the end of the play. Esteban, who can hardly face the glance of his wife, is far removed from the proud heroes of Spanish chivalry. In the early acts of the play, Esteban appears but little and never utters any but evasive words. After the murder has been committed, he crumbles and has not even the spirit to face his servant Rubio. In the great scene with Raimunda, her strength and courage contrast with his cowardice. He is the most inglorious antihero ever created by Benavente.

Acacia is, from the beginning, a rather strange character. Ever since her mother's marriage to Esteban she has shown a reserve toward her stepfather in spite of his kindness and obvious affection. By subtle touches that give an impression of gloomy sadness, Benavente instills increasing amounts of mystery into Acacia's characterization. One of these touches is the use of cleverly written dialogue that indicates either that a peculiar sexual hatred exists between Acacia and Esteban or that Acacia is an unbalanced neurotic. This mystery continues throughout the drama.

By contrast, Raimunda is a character who is essentially submissive in temperament. She has lived blandly unconscious of the tragedy near at hand. It takes a great shock to cause the scales to fall from her eyes and make her see her husband as he really is. When the crisis does come, she is torn by conflicting emotions: She still loves her husband passionately but wants him to suffer for his sin. Benavente develops this conflict by postponing the great scene of recrimination between husband and wife until the third act, by which time Raimunda's feelings of horror have softened, and pity for him has weakened her resolve. No scene in Benavente's works provides a better example of antithesis. Being both an honorable and a religious woman, Raimunda wishes Esteban to suffer to the fullest extent as an atonement to God for his sin—a spirit of justice characteristic of the Castilian mind—but the soft, womanly side of her character causes her to feel compassion for him when she sees him trapped on all sides like a wild beast.

The first performances of this play aroused a great deal of criticism. Some considered the tragedy too rough, the story that of too monstrous a sin; others speculated as to possible real models for the story of the love of a stepfather for his stepdaughter. Most of the criticism, however, gave way eventually to the public enthusiasm engendered by the play. *The Passion Flower* marked the summit of Benavente's literary career, and he became a leading influence for an entire generation of Spanish playwrights.

"Critical Evaluation" by Stephen Hanson

Further Reading

Goldberg, Isaac. *The Drama of Transition*. Cincinnati: Stewart Kidd, 1922. Provides a lengthy discussion of Benavente's achievement and offers insight into the critical reception of *The Passion Flower* both in Spain and throughout Europe. Also includes summaries of critical commentaries on Benavente by several early twentieth century scholars and artists.

Jameson, Storm. "The Drama of Italy and Spain." In *Modern Drama in Europe*. London: Collins, 1920. Places Benavente and his plays within the context of the dramatic works produced in twentieth century Spain, linking him with the earlier dramatist Lope de Vega Carpio as one of the country's major playwrights. Discusses formal qualities of Benavente's plays and provides insight into the dramatist's techniques.

Parker, Mary, ed. *Modern Spanish Dramatists: A Bio-bibliographical Sourcebook*. Westport, Conn.: Greenwood Press, 2002. Reference work includes an article about Benavente that contains a brief biography, discusses his dramaturgy and the themes of his plays, and provides an overview of the critical and scholarly responses to his work.

Peñuelas, Marcelino C. *Jacinto Benavente*. Translated by Kay Engler. New York: Twayne, 1968. Provides an introductory overview of the work of one of the most popular Spanish playwrights of the first half of the twentieth century. Establishes the relationship of *The Passion Flower* to the social and literary climate in which it was written.

Soufas, C. Christopher, Jr. "Benavente and the Spanish Discourse on Theater." *Hispanic Review* 68, no. 2 (Spring, 2000): 147-159. Examines why Benavente, once considered the leading twentieth century Spanish dramatist, later came to be seen as inferior to other Spanish playwrights. Discusses *The Passion Flower* and some of Benavente's other plays and describes the negative critical reception of his work.

Starkie, Walter. *Jacinto Benavente*. London: H. Milford, 1924. Includes commentary on *The Passion Flower* in a general discussion of Benavente's dialect plays. Analyzes character development and compares the work to similar dramas by other European playwrights.

Underhill, John Garrett. Introduction to *The Plays of Jacinto Benavente*. Vol. 1. New York: Charles Scribner's Sons, 1921. Discusses *The Passion Flower* as one of Benavente's "peasant dramas" in which the playwright dramatizes "the struggle of the individual conscience against the conscience of the masses."

Passions and Ancient Days

Author: Constantine P. Cavafy (1863-1933)
First published: English translation with original Greek, 1971
Type of work: Poetry

The works of Constantine P. Cavafy were not published during the poet's lifetime. At least, they cannot be said to have been published in the conventional sense. Frequently revising his early poems and suppressing those he thought were inferior, Cavafy shared much of his poetry with only his closest friends, often distributing his works in the form of privately printed broadsides, pamphlets, or small volumes. At the time of his death of cancer at the age of seventy, the poet left behind sixty-eight poems arranged thematically in two small books, a folder of sixty-nine additional poems printed on broadsides, and a large number of poetic drafts in various stages of completion. Two years after Cavafy's death, his literary executor, Alexander Singopoulos, issued a volume containing 153 of Cavafy's poems, all that the poet himself considered to be his finest work.

Passions and Ancient Days is an edition of twenty-one additional poems that the editors, Cavafy scholars Edmund Keeley and George Savidis, have judged to be of quality equal or superior to those appearing in Singopoulos's edition. At times, Cavafy seems to have suppressed these poems because they were dramatically different in tone and subject matter from his other work. (This seems to have been the case, for instance, with "King Claudius," Cavafy's only surviving poem on a Shakespearean theme.) At times, reading this book of rejected work, one thinks that the poet appears to have been excessively critical of his own work. In any case, the poems that Keeley and Savidis selected develop themes and images already introduced in the 153 canonical poems. For example, "Julian at the Mysteries" closely resembles six poems dealing with the historical figure of Julian the Apostate (c. 331-363 C.E.) such as "Julian in Nicomedia" (1924) and "On the Outskirts of Antioch" (1933). "The End of Antony" completes a cycle of earlier poems about the Roman politician and soldier Marc Antony (c. 83-30 B.C.E.), including "The Gods Abandon Antony" (1918) and "In a Township of Asia Minor" (1926). "September, 1903" and "December, 1903" are works that capture the erotic sensation of a single moment, similar to "Days of 1903" (1917) and "Days of 1896" (1927) among Cavafy's works in the Singopoulos edition.

The title *Passions and Ancient Days* is derived from a thematic structure that Cavafy once used for his poetry. In a commentary on his work, Cavafy said that all of his poems could be divided into three categories: the historical, the philosophical, and the erotic. In *Passions and Ancient Days*, "passions" refer to Cavafy's erotic poems and "ancient days" to his historical poems. Cavafy's philosophical poems are largely unrepresented among the twenty-one works included in this volume. *Passions and Ancient Days* reproduces each poem in the original Greek on the left-hand page, with an English translation by Keeley and Savidis on the right-hand page.

The erotic poems contain many of the same themes appearing in Cavafy's other work: passionate homosexuality; brief, often furtive, encounters with strangers; and the shame and secrecy imposed upon gays by an intolerant society. For example, "September, 1903" addresses the poet's own fears of admitting his feelings to others. He chides himself for his cowardice, wondering why he could not speak even the few words that may have ended his loneliness. He is grieved by the number of times he was near someone whom he could have loved if only he had had the courage to speak. Now, all he wants to do is to console himself by recalling the comforting illusion of what might have been.

Keeley and Savidis note that the conflict between illusion and reality is a repeated theme in all of Cavafy's erotic poems. For instance, in "December, 1903," a companion piece to "September, 1903," Cavafy observes that, while he can never speak of the love that he once felt, his lover's memory haunts him still. Imagining the sound of this person's voice adds a hidden level of meaning to each of the poet's thoughts and words. In both of Cavafy's "1903" poems—as well as in "Days of 1903" in the earlier collection—the lasting effects of a lost love or a chance encounter provide the incident that the author uses to develop the poem. Moments that may seem

insignificant to others, even to certain persons involved in them, can sometimes be of profound significance to someone in love. The cherished memory, replayed in one's mind or altered by fantasy, can provide a level of meaning far more satisfying than that derived from everyday life. For Cavafy, who was often reluctant to initiate encounters through fear of how others might respond to his sexuality, these moments give his erotic or romantic poems a wistful air of regret.

In "At the Theatre," the encounter itself is imaginary. While bored at a play, the poet glances around the audience and notices a young man whom other people were mentioning that very afternoon. The poet imagines the stranger (not as the poet sees him there, elegantly dressed and world-weary in one of the seats of the box circle) as he was described earlier—exciting, corrupt, and possessing a "strange beauty." The two of them never meet but Cavafy finds himself aroused far more than he ever has been before. In a nearly contemporary poem, "On the Stairs," he describes a brief encounter between himself and another patron at a house of prostitution. For a split second, their eyes meet, and the poet is aware—he is convinced that they are both aware—that these two men are capable of a love far more meaningful than the sheer physical pleasures of this "disgraceful house." In shame, however, the two of them avert their eyes. Their opportunity is lost, and they each rush away from the other, both of them still strangers.

The objects of Cavafy's passions are never named in the poems. (In their notes to the works, Keeley and Savidis do occasionally attempt to identify certain people from the poet's notes and unpublished prose.) Cavafy's lovers are faceless strangers whose brief appearance in the author's life leave an unexpected void. Little information is provided about these anonymous figures, so readers will find it easy to identify with the narrator of the poem. Even the gender of Cavafy's lover is often left unspecified, with the result that readers of all sexual orientations will find that they are able to relate to many of these works.

Unlike Cavafy's erotic poems, his historical poems are quite specific in both setting and focus. They usually derive from some incident that the author encountered in his wide reading of classical and Byzantine history. The themes explored by Cavafy's historical poems include the nature of Greek nationalism, the relationship between Christianity and paganism, and the author's surprising (and almost certainly ironic) interpretations of historical events. "Theophilos Palaiologos," for instance, deals with an incident that occurred during the conquest of Constantinople by the Ottoman Turks in 1453. The title character, a relative of the last Byzantine emperor, Constantine Palaiologos, is reported to have been in despair before the Turkish onslaught. His brief comment "Better to die than live" is quoted in a historical chronicle. Those five words, Cavafy says, are filled with all the weariness and sorrow of the Greek people, a nation that has been worn down by centuries of injustice and persecution. As in his erotic poems, where Cavafy finds meaning and deep passion in what appear to be insignificant moments, so does the poet in this work see the entire heritage of the Greek race reflected in a forgotten line of a forgotten work of history.

In "Return from Greece," Cavafy imagines a conversation between two Greek philosophers living in an unnamed eastern country sometime during the Hellenistic period (323-27 B.C.E.). One of them, named Hermippus, grows silent and nostalgic as a ship carries them farther and farther from Greece on their voyage home to the East. The other, the anonymous narrator of the poem, admonishes Hermippus that his hypocrisy is inappropriate to the Greek spirit. Hermippus should admit, the narrator continues, that they are relieved to be returning home. The two of them, he says, display a Hellenism that is tinged with the cultures of Asia, Arabia, and Persia; this fusion should be a cause of celebration. True Greeks do not try to conceal their origins but exult in their rich diversity.

"Poseidonians" explores the mixed heritage of modern Greeks from a slightly different perspective. Beginning with an incident described by the Alexandrian author Athenaeus (third century B.C.E.) in the *Deipnosophistai*, Cavafy portrays an ancient festival celebrated by the Greek inhabitants of Paestum, a city in southwestern Italy. Once a year, these citizens put on their Greek garments and engage in rituals that few of them understand, speaking a language that none of them still speaks. Then, lamenting the loss of their heritage, they drift away to their homes. Cut off from the society that once gave meaning to their lives, the Greek citizens of Paestum seem a people without a culture: No longer Greek, not yet Italian, they are forever lost.

Preserving his Greek heritage was of great importance to Cavafy, a Greek poet who lived and worked in the Egyptian city of Alexandria. Cavafy's historical poems explore the many threads—classical, Byzantine, Christian, Egyptian, Asiatic—that compose his culture. To Cavafy, Hellenism was a living tradition that absorbed much from the cultures with which it had come into contact, but which had also imbued those cultures with something of the Greek spirit. Through his poetry, Cavafy attempts to define both his culture and himself. The author's identity that emerges from *Passions and Ancient Days* is that of a poet, a Christian, a lover, a Greek living in a world that is not Greek, and a man whose regret for lost opportunities gives his works a melancholy flavor but also great meaning.

Jeffrey L. Buller

Further Reading

Anton, John P. *The Poetry and Poetics of Constantine P. Cavafy: Aesthetic Visions of Sensual Reality*. Chur, Switzerland: Harwood, 1995. Focuses on the early years of Cavafy's career, when he discovered his poetic self and created an authentic voice. Anton demonstrates Cavafy's aesthetic development by pointing out autobiographical elements in his poetry.

Bien, Peter. *Constantine Cavafy*. New York: Columbia University Press, 1964. A brief but informative introduction to Cavafy's life and poetry. Bien's essay is one of the best places for anyone who is unfamiliar with Cavafy's work to begin. The short bibliography provides suggestions for continued study.

Cavafy, Constantine P. *Collected Poems*. Translated, with introduction and commentary, by Daniel Mendelsohn. New York: Alfred A. Knopf, 2009.

_____. *The Unfinished Poems*. Translated, with introduction and commentary, by Daniel Mendelsohn. New York: Alfred A. Knopf, 2009. In these two volumes, Mendelsohn has compiled and translated all of Cavafy's poems into English, including works that the poet did not complete. These collections were well received by critics, who praised the accuracy of Mendelsohn's translations and the information contained in his commentary.

Chiasson, Dan. "Man with a Past: Cavafy Revisited." *The New Yorker*, March 23, 2009. This review of the two volumes of newly translated poems (above) provides an informed and accessible analysis of Cavafy's life, literary career, and poetry.

Jeffreys, Peter. *Eastern Questions: Hellenism and Orientalism in the Writings of E. M. Forster and C. P. Cavafy*. Greensboro, N.C.: ELT Press, 2005. Compares the work of the two writers, focusing on their shared interest in Hellenism and the East and the different ways in which they expressed this interest in their writing. Jeffreys also examines the writers' friendship.

Jusdanis, Gregory. *The Poetics of Cavafy: Textuality, Eroticism, History*. Princeton, N.J.: Princeton University Press, 1987. Contains a detailed thematic interpretation of Cavafy's poetry. Individual poems are explored in great depth, as are themes that appear repeatedly throughout the poet's work. Includes an introduction, index, and extensive bibliography.

Kapre-Karka, K. *Love and the Symbolic Journey in the Poetry of Cavafy, Eliot, and Seferis*. New York: Pella, 1982. A poem-by-poem analysis of Cavafy's erotic poetry, viewed alongside the works of T. S. Eliot and George Seferis. Examines the theme of the journey or of the pilgrimage in the poetry of all three writers.

Keeley, Edmund. *Cavafy's Alexandria: Study of a Myth in Progress*. Cambridge, Mass.: Harvard University Press, 1976. Reprint. Princeton, N.J.: Princeton University Press, 1996. Written by one of the editors and translators of *Passions and Ancient Days*, this work explores Cavafy's Hellenism and its relationship to the city of Alexandria, the setting for many of Cavafy's poems.

Liddell, Robert. *Cavafy: A Critical Biography*. With a new introduction and updated bibliography. London: Duckworth, 2000. The most readable biography of Cavafy available and a good introduction to his poetry. Liddell explores the relationship between Cavafy's poetry and his life, scholarship, and religious beliefs. Contains an index and a good general bibliography.

Pinchin, Jane Lagoudis. *Alexandria Still*. Princeton, N.J.: Princeton University Press, 1977. Relates Cavafy's poetry to the writing of E. M. Forster and Laurence Durrell as authors who explored the landscape and meaning of Alexandria. Provides a valuable insight into Cavafy's historical poems.

Past and Present

Author: Thomas Carlyle (1795-1881)
First published: 1843
Type of work: Essays

In *Past and Present*, Thomas Carlyle brings to the task of social commentary the same searching, tenacious, and idiosyncratic analysis that characterized his *Sartor Resartus* (1835). In the earlier work, Carlyle explores his crisis of faith; in *Past and Present*, however, he analyzes the problems of newly industrialized England both by invoking historical events and by dissecting contemporary issues. Carlyle offers his assessment in four books: "Proem," "The Ancient Monk," "The Modern Worker," and "Horoscope." While his method may at first appear haphazard, Carlyle weaves striking examples, blistering caricatures, and shrewd political analyses into a memorable pattern, closing with a stern warning about England's future.

Born into a family of resolute Scottish Calvinists, Carlyle was never shy about offering opinions, advice, criticism, and even insults in his essays. While he no longer accepted the tenets of the faith, Carlyle never shed its didactic approach. For this reason, some Victorian critics considered his style indecorous, even grotesque. Readers, however, will find his unpredictability and exaggeration surprisingly modern. Carlyle also inherited from his family an abiding respect for and insistence upon work. Throughout *Past and Present* he demands constructive efforts from all persons "each in their degree" and lambastes the idle gentry, whom he calls "enchanted dilettantes."

Despite his admiration for the worker and emphasis on solid, practical accomplishment, Carlyle remained scornful of the prevailing Victorian doctrine of utilitarianism. Expounded by Victorian optimists, including Jeremy Bentham and John Stuart Mill, utilitarianism sought to achieve "the greatest happiness of the greatest number." Its method required assessing every act, belief, or idea for its usefulness or "utility." Like the utilitarians, Carlyle had little use for existing religious and social institutions; however, he found their emphasis upon happiness infantile and their confidence in utility exaggerated and mechanic. To Carlyle, the utilitarians wasted energy in endlessly classifying and codifying human efforts. By contrast, he claimed that, given the appropriate conditions, a genuine "Aristocracy of Talent" would arise to lead society. Such "heroes" deserved to be worshiped; they possessed a vital energy capable of reinventing and ordering society. Later generations have deemed such views authoritarian, even fascistic, but Carlyle's defense of his position in *Past and Present* defies easy labeling.

In "Proem," Carlyle introduces most of the major themes of his work as well as his characteristic rhetorical strategies. In Carlyle's opinion, England in 1843 was burdened by a huge surplus of wealth and activity, improperly managed and frivolously expended. Able workingmen languished "enchanted" in poorhouses or were daily exploited by profiteering and callous employers. Early in the discussion, Carlyle takes a stand on one of the most controversial economic issues of his day: the infamous Corn Laws (repealed in 1846). These tariffs on imported grains were established to eliminate foreign competition and to keep the price of English farm products high; they also effectively robbed working people of their daily bread. Carlyle defends an early popular movement against the Corn Laws, the Manchester Insurrection of 1819, arguing that the agitators "put their huge inarticulate question, 'What do you mean to do with us?' in a manner audible to every reflective soul in this kingdom." Those who labor deserve to be responsibly and actively governed, rather than enduring the laissez-faire neglect of the political system. To achieve this organic, vital government, Carlyle urges his readers to "put away all Flunkyism, Baseness, Unveracity from us." Only a heroic nation of "faithful, discerning souls" will be capable of electing a heroic government, of discerning the Aristocracy of Talent crucial to England's future.

Also in "Proem," Carlyle creates the first of his imaginary characters, who appear periodically in the work to serve as "straw men," ludicrous proponents of the arguments he despises. Bobus Higgins, for example, typifies the fatuous, greedy middle classes, incapable both of self-rule and of choosing worthy leadership. In the following book, "The Ancient Monk," Carlyle turns to an actual historical figure to dramatize the diminished stature of profit-minded Victorians. The book presents a biography of Samson, abbot of the medieval monastery of St. Edmundsbury, whose deeds are recorded by his faithful biographer Jocelin of Brakelond. Given Carlyle's distaste for the social machine conceived by utilitarians, it is not surprising that he looked to an age of faith for his heroes. Throughout the essay, however, Carlyle emphasizes that it is Samson's works, rather than his faith alone, that make him heroic.

Abbot Samson, Jocelin assures the reader, made all "the Earth's business a kind of worship." The model for Carlyle's practical man, Samson "had a talent; he had learned to judge better than Lawyers, to manage better than bred Bailiffs." Medieval social vitality is expressed not only by Samson's stature but also by the monks' capacity to elect him without benefit of ballot box or bribery. Casting a critical eye on Victorian religious fads, Carlyle contrasts Abbot Samson's quiet efficiency with the "noisy theoretic demonstrations" of Tractarianism, or the Oxford Movement (beginning in 1833), which sought to enhance ceremony and ritual in the Church of England. He entreats his audience to dispose of "blockhead quacks" and acknowledge instead England's "real con-

querors, creators, and eternal proprietors," "those who ever cut a thistle, drained a puddle out of England, contrived a wise scheme in England, did or said a true and valiant thing in England."

Having offered both a definition and an exemplar of heroism, Carlyle's analysis continues in "The Modern Worker." In these chapters, Carlyle's language becomes the most militant and his arguments the most prescient. Lacking Samson's insight and distracted by the "Shows and Shams of things," Victorian society adheres only to the false gospels of "Mammonism" and "Dilettantism." Carlyle exposes what he terms "Social Gangrene" by citing some unforgettable cases, including the case of a poor Irish widow and mother of three whose appeals to various charitable institutions are repeatedly denied. Eventually, the widow contracts typhus and dies, but not before she spreads the contagion so that seventeen of her fellow laborers die with her. Carlyle asks, "with a heart too full for speaking, Would it not have been economy to help this poor Widow?" To Carlyle, society's studied neglect of the poorer classes is not only inhumane but also foolish. He remarks (with some irony) that, despite being rejected, the dying widow "proved her sisterhood" in the end; disease underscores the biological link between classes, the organic relationship of all humankind.

Though he defends honest labor, Carlyle repudiates profit as a motive for human endeavor. He foresees the rise and impact of advertising, impatiently dismissing the "Puffery" of an English hatter who "has not attempted to make better hats . . . but his whole industry is turned to persuade us that he has made such!" Things made only for profit are, to Carlyle, "no-things." Recalling his Calvinist roots, he insists that work must not be profaned by notions of economic gain; nor should it be trivialized by fantasies of happiness. Utilitarians such as Bentham and Mill degrade the dignity of labor, just as surely as do profiteers, by making happiness its goal. Both happiness and profit are ephemeral, irrelevant. Only work provides an index of human worth to Carlyle, a means of recognizing an Aristocracy of Talent. Society is not held together by cash payments or by supply and demand. In demanding "let us see thy work," Carlyle seeks a more organic social structure than economic class and a less arbitrary measure of success than a full purse.

In "The Modern Worker," Carlyle also makes it clear that democracy (at least as he defines it) does not represent the climax of political evolution. Liberty, he claims, "requires new definitions." He has little faith in the capacity of representative government to secure genuine liberty, nor can he tolerate that liberty which measures human relationships only in terms of cash flow. At its worst, democracy becomes the pursuit of economic liberty by hypocrites eager to enslave themselves anew by gratifying their most "brutal appetites." Carlyle expresses his belief that democracy is merely a transitional phase when he states,

> The Toiling Millions of Mankind, in most vital need and passionate instinctive desire of Guidance, shall cast away False Guidance; and hope, for an hour, that no-Guidance will suffice them: but it can be for an hour only.

Espousing his own brand of radicalism, Carlyle supports the people's right to topple inept or self-interested governments, but he does not extend to them the right to govern themselves. He sees genuine liberty only in an integrated society, one in which individuals perform appropriate work and coexist with inferiors, equals, and superiors. In closing, Carlyle returns to history for an example of such right governance, contrasting the talent of Oliver Cromwell with the empty platitudes of Sir Jabesh Windbag (another of Carlyle's symbolic characters).

In book 4, "Horoscope," Carlyle returns to the subject of true aristocracy, reiterating that it is "at once indispensable and not easily attained." He implores his readers to use the continuity between past and present to instruct the future. The nineteenth century has a new epic to write, "Tools and the Man" (in contrast to Vergil's "Arms and the Man"), which must address unprecedented social forces such as industry and democracy. Carlyle warns that the present parliamentary system, rife with corruption and ineptitude, is incapable of organizing labor and managing the working classes. Characteristically, he asserts that these problems can only be solved "by those who themselves work and preside over work," in other words, a "Chivalry of Labor." Carlyle's manifesto replaces a feudal aristocracy with an industrial aristocracy. He exhorts them to abandon an economics of supply and demand and to offer in its place "noble guidance" in return for "noble loyalty." He stresses that this must be a permanent bond. The freedom afforded by monthlong (versus lifelong) contracts is comparable to the liberty guaranteed by democracy; for Carlyle, it is a worthless commodity. While the bond between laborer and master is sacred to Carlyle, the worker is no mere serf. Carlyle raises the possibility of jointly owned ventures in which the worker's interests, as well as his efforts, are permanently represented.

The landed gentry remain relevant in Carlyle's scheme only to the extent that they exert themselves and use their accumulated resources on behalf of their fellow beings. Otherwise, they are scarcely human; they are "living statues" who are pampered, isolated, and absurd. Similarly, the "gifted"—

writers, artists, and thinkers—cannot be segregated from those who haul timber or dig ditches; their position in a "Chivalry of Labor" depends upon active contribution and is no more or less honorable than any other.

For Carlyle, these are the prerequisites for an epic future. Though he has been accused of fascism, Carlyle seeks, ultimately, to reawaken and to recover the connections between persons. (In this respect, his ideas heavily influenced Ralph Waldo Emerson and American Transcendentalism.) *Past and Present* closes with a memorable avowal of this human interdependence: "Men cannot live isolated: we are all bound together, for mutual good or else for mutual misery, as living nerves in the same body."

Sarah A. Boris

Further Reading

Calder, Grace J. *The Writing of "Past and Present": A Study of Carlyle's Manuscripts.* New Haven, Conn.: Yale University Press, 1949. Contains valuable information on Carlyle's writing process and stylistic eccentricities.

Carlyle, Thomas. *Past and Present.* Introduction and notes by Chris R. Vanden Bossche. Berkeley: University of California Press, 2005. In addition to the text, this volume contains an introduction that places the work in its historical context, as well as extensive textual annotations.

Fielding, K. J., and Roger L. Tarr, eds. *Carlyle Past and Present: A Collection of New Essays.* New York: Barnes & Noble, 1976. Presents a variety of approaches to the work and its author.

Holloway, John. *The Victorian Sage: Studies in Argument.* London: Macmillan, 1953. A landmark study of Carlyle's rhetorical strategies and persuasive tactics.

Levine, George. *The Boundaries of Fiction: Carlyle, Macauley, Newman.* Princeton, N.J.: Princeton University Press, 1968. A learned discussion of Carlyle's style in the larger context of Victorian prose.

Morrow, John. *Thomas Carlyle.* New York: Hambledon Continuum, 2006. Chronicles Carlyle's personal life and intellectual career and discusses his works.

Trela, D. J., and Rodger L. Tarr, eds. *The Critical Response to Thomas Carlyle's Major Works.* Westport, Conn.: Greenwood Press, 1997. Collection of reviews and essays about *Past and Present* and Carlyle's other major works that date from the initial publication of his works until the end of the twentieth century. The introduction discusses how Carlyle responded to his critics.

Ulrich, John McAllister. *Signs of Their Times: History, Labor, and the Body in Cobbett, Carlyle, and Disraeli.* Athens: Ohio University Press, 2002. Discusses how *Past and Present* and works by William Cobbett and Benjamin Disraeli were a response to the economic and cultural crises in England during the first half of the nineteenth century.

Waring, Walter. *Thomas Carlyle*. Boston: Twayne, 1978. An excellent introduction to Carlyle's ideas. Helps explain the philosophical tensions and social conditions of the early Victorian period.

Paterson

Author: William Carlos Williams (1883-1963)
First published: 1946-1958; includes book 1, 1946; book 2, 1948; book 3, 1949; book 4, 1951; book 5, 1958
Type of work: Poetry

A hasty reading of William Carlos Williams's *Paterson* may leave the reader at the end of the poem with a feeling not unlike that of a rural person on his or her first trip to a big city: There are so many different things to look at, in so many different shapes and sizes, and all the people seem to be rushing about so haphazardly that the uninitiated wind up their days bemused but happy. Such a reaction to *Paterson* is part of Williams's purpose. The poem interweaves the story of a city with the story of a man so that the two become interchangeable, and the jumbled kaleidoscope of city life turns and glitters like the conflicting ideas, dreams, loves, and hates that assail the minds of twentieth century human beings.

Looked at more closely, the poem can be seen to take on shape, like a city coming out from under a rolling fog or a person walking out of the shadows of trees in a park. Williams unifies his poem by letting the river that flows through the city serve as a symbol of life, both that of the city and that of the man. Life equated to a river flowing somewhere safe to sea is an image as old as poetry itself, but the ways in which Williams uses this image are so fresh and individual in style and presentation that it seems as if he had discovered the idea.

The poem is divided into four books, which correspond to four parts of the river: the portion above the falls; the falls themselves; the river below the falls; and the river's exit into the sea. Williams opens the first book, "The Delineaments of the Giants," with these lines:

Paterson lies in the valley under the Passaic Falls
its spent waters forming the outline of his back. He
lies on his right side, head near the thunder
of the water filling his dreams!

Having presented the blended image of city and man, the poet goes on to present symbols for women—a flower, a cliff, the falls—and to introduce one of the main concerns of *Paterson:* the search for a language by which human beings may "redeem" the tragedies of life. To counterbalance this somewhat abstract and nebulous idea, Williams intersperses his poem with many concrete passages, some in prose, which serve as an entrancing documentation of the backgrounds of the city and the man. In book 1, for instance, historical notes and newspaper clippings tell us of the finding of pearls in mussels taken from Notch Brook, near the city; of General Washington's encounter with "a monster in human form"; of the accidental drowning of a Mrs. Cumming at the falls; of the death there of a stuntman named Sam Patch; and of a great catch of eels made by the local people when a lake was drained. Paterson the man is represented by letters written to him, one from a misunderstood poet.

Williams rounds off book 1 with a quotation from John Addington Symonds's *Studies of the Greek Poets* (1873, 1876). Such diversity of material seems to call for a prestidigitator to make it all seem a part of the whole; Williams does it easily, for he is a master juggler who never quite lets his readers see all of the act that makes them fill in some of the parts from their own imagination.

Book 2, "Sunday in the Park," concerns itself chiefly with love, including the many kinds of lovemaking found in a city park, and with poetry, for *Paterson* is as much a tribute to language as it is to a city or a man. Fittingly, this section ends with another long passage from a letter written by the poet who is struggling to fit together her work, her life, and her friendship with the "dear doctor" to whom she writes.

Book 3, "The Library," continues to probe the inarticulateness of tragedy and death, searching for some way that language may assuage, even prevent those things we accept as a part of existence. Williams describes poetry in these lines: "The province of the poem is the world./ When the sun rises, it rises in the poem/ and when it sets darkness comes down/ and the poem is dark."

Book 3 also describes a great fire that sweeps the city and destroys the library. Williams continues to insert prose passages, one of which recounts the story of Merselis Van Giesen, whose wife was tormented by a witch that appeared to her nightly in the form of a black cat. In telling the story, Williams throws in several humorous comments. When the witch is revealed to be a Mrs. B., "who lived in the gorge in the hill beyond," he comments, "Happy souls! whose devils lived so near." Interspersing the tale with other witty remarks, the poet concludes with the husband shooting the cat with a silver bullet made from his cuff links. The shot is a difficult one because the cat is visible only to his wife, who must locate the target for him and direct his aim. He kills the cat, and, in the best tradition of witch stories, Mrs. B. suffers for some time with a sore on her leg.

The last book, "The Run to the Sea," opens with an idyll involving Corydon, Phyllis, and Paterson. This section also introduces the image of the bomb. The poem concludes when Paterson the man reaches the sea, but he, along with a dog found swimming there, is able to escape from this symbol of death and to head inland.

Paterson, which appeared in segments between 1946 and 1958, has been compared with Walt Whitman's *Leaves of Grass* (1855-1892), Archibald MacLeish's *Conquistador* (1932), and Hart Crane's *The Bridge* (1930). Admittedly the work lacks the eloquent brilliance of *Conquistador*, and to compare Williams with Whitman is to stretch the superlatives until they become tenuous. Whitman writes like a great wind, whereas Williams wafts with far gentler breezes.

Paterson is a poem filled with variety and surprises. There are times when Williams turns his kaleidoscope so quickly that the reader becomes dizzy and would like to quote back to the poet the line "Geeze, Doc, I guess it's all right but what the hell does it mean?" On the other hand, there are many passages of great lyrical beauty in *Paterson*, and a careful reading of the poem creates a feeling in the reader of having visited a typical American city and been taken on a tour of it by someone who tells its history as they walk along. More important, the reader becomes acquainted with Paterson himself, who is clever, witty, sensitive, wise, and deeply concerned with the people of his city and their problems. Thus does *Paterson* achieve its purpose and forge a bond between the reader of the poem and the poem's man and city.

Further Reading

Cappucci, Paul R. *William Carlos Williams' Poetic Response to the 1913 Paterson Silk Strike*. Lewiston. N.Y.: Edwin Mellen Press, 2002. Recounts the events in Williams's life and describes his poetry prior to 1913; shows how his life and work underwent significant changes in the year of the strike, when he sought inspiration in the work of Walt Whitman.

Copestake, Ian, ed. *The Legacy of William Carlos Williams: Points of Contact*. Newcastle, England: Cambridge Scholars, 2007. Essays provide numerous interpretations of Williams's work, including comparisons of his poetry to that of Robert Frost, Robert Lowell, and Robert Creeley and to the art of Jackson Pollock. Also includes an essay on *Paterson*.

_____. *Rigor of Beauty: Essays in Commemoration of William Carlos Williams*. New York: Peter Lang, 2004. The essays include two pieces about *Paterson*: "Getting the News from Poems: History, *In the American Grain*, and *Paterson*" and "Ideas as Forms of Beauty: Williams's *Paterson* and A. R. Ammons's *Tape for the Turn of the Year*."

Duffey, Bernard. *A Poetry of Presence: The Writing of William Carlos Williams*. Madison: University of Wisconsin Press, 1986. Considers Williams's epic as a lyrical dramatization of his descent into the ambiguities of his concept of himself as an American poet. Williams, who was a medical doctor, wanted to reenact the facts of human misery in a new and healing speech.

Mariani, Paul L. "Putting Paterson on the Map: 1946-1961." In *William Carlos Williams: The Poet and His Critics*. Chicago: American Library Association, 1975. Chronicles the struggle of critics and reviewers, including many notable poets, to understand the meaning and importance of a strangely structured but major new work.

Markos, Donald W. *Ideas in Things: The Poems of William Carlos Williams*. Rutherford, N.J.: Fairleigh Dickinson University Press, 1994. Interprets *Paterson* in the context of Williams's idealist belief in beauty as the emanation of a universal, ideal reality through the particular world of things. This Platonism links him to Ralph Waldo Emerson and Jonathan Edwards in the American tradition of individual perception and creative imagination.

O'Brien, Kevin J. *Saying Yes at Lightning: Threat and the Provisional Image in Post-Romantic Poetry*. New York: Peter Lang, 2002. Examines poems that were written in response to cataclysmic events. Chapters 5 and 6 focus on

Paterson, with the latter chapter providing a section-by-section reading of book 3 of the poem.

Sankey, Benjamin. *A Companion to William Carlos Williams's "Paterson."* Berkeley: University of California Press, 1971. Interpretive guide to the text, with pertinent information and comments by Williams. An introductory chapter presents Williams's philosophy, design, and methodology.

Schmidt, Peter. *William Carlos Williams, the Arts, and Literary Tradition.* Baton Rouge: Louisiana State University Press, 1988. Traces the relationship of Williams's poetry to precisionist, cubist, and Dadaist aesthetics and to the literary tradition that preceded modernism. Describes how Williams uses a variety of approaches to collage, while both critiquing and renewing epic form.

The Pathfinder
Or, The Inland Sea

Author: James Fenimore Cooper (1789-1851)
First published: 1840
Type of work: Novel
Type of plot: Adventure
Time of plot: 1758
Locale: Environs of Lake Ontario and the Oswego River, New York

Principal characters:
THOMAS DUNHAM, a U.S. Army garrison leader
MABEL DUNHAM, his daughter
CHARLES CAP, her uncle, a sailor
NATTY "PATHFINDER" BUMPPO, a frontier scout
JASPER WESTERN, his friend, a sailor
DAVY MUIR, the garrison quartermaster
ARROWHEAD, a Tuscarora chief
DEW OF JUNE, his wife
CHINGACHGOOK, Pathfinder's friend, a Mohican chief

The Story:

Mabel Dunham and Charles Cap, her seaman uncle, are on their way to the home of her father, Sergeant Thomas Dunham. They are accompanied by Arrowhead, a Tuscarora Indian, and his wife, Dew of June. When they reach the Oswego River, they are met by Jasper Western and Natty Bumppo, the wilderness scout known as Pathfinder among the English and as Hawkeye among the Mohicans. Pathfinder leads the party down the Oswego on the first step of the journey under his guidance.

Chingachgook, Pathfinder's Mohican friend, warns the party of the presence of hostile Indians in the neighborhood. They hide but are discovered and have a narrow escape. Arrowhead and Dew of June disappear, and Pathfinder's group fears they had been taken captive or else have betrayed the group. On the lookout for more hostile war parties, they continue their journey to the fort, which they reach thanks especially to Jasper's navigational skills on the river, and Mabel is joyfully welcomed by her father.

The sergeant tries to promote a romantic attachment between Mabel and Pathfinder, the sergeant's real purpose in having brought Mabel to the frontier. Actually, Mabel has already fallen in love with Jasper. When the commander of the post, Major Duncan, proposes Lieutenant Davy Muir as a possible mate for Mabel, at the lieutenant's request, the sergeant informs the major that Mabel is already betrothed to Pathfinder. Muir learns that he has been refused, but he apparently does not give up hope.

A contest of arms is proposed to test the shooting ability of the men at the post. Jasper scores a bull's-eye. Muir shoots from a strange position, and it is believed by all that he has missed, but he says he has hit Jasper's bullet, embedded in the target. Pathfinder uses Jasper's rifle and also strikes the bullet in the bull's-eye. The next test of marksmanship is to drive a nail into a tree with a bullet. Lieutenant Muir's shot barely touches the nail, Jasper almost drives the nail completely into the tree, and Pathfinder's shot completes the embedding of the nail. In the next test, shooting at a potato tossed into the air, Muir fails, but Jasper hits the potato in the center. A silken calash is one of the prizes, and Jasper desires it greatly as a present for Mabel. He mentions this to Pathfinder, who thereupon does no more than cut the skin of the potato. After he has lost the match, Pathfinder cannot resist killing two gulls with one bullet, which allows Mabel to understand how Jasper won the calash. In appreciation, she gives Pathfinder a silver brooch.

An expedition is planned to one of the Thousand Islands, to relieve the garrison there. The party is to leave in the *Scud*, a boat operated by Jasper. Before the party departs, however, Major Duncan receives a letter that causes him to suspect Jasper of being a French spy. Pathfinder refuses to believe the charge against his friend, but when the *Scud* sails under the command of Jasper, he is kept under strict surveillance by Sergeant Dunham and Cap. On the way, the *Scud* overtakes Arrowhead and his wife, who are taken aboard. After Pathfinder questions the Tuscarora chief, Arrowhead and his wife escape in a canoe that the *Scud* was towing astern. Becoming suspicious, Sergeant Dunham removes Jasper from his command and sends him below. Cap takes over the command of the boat, but Cap, being a saltwater sailor, is unfamiliar with freshwater navigation. When a storm comes up, it is necessary to call upon Jasper to save the ship from destruction in the breakers. The *Scud* escapes from *Le Montcalm*, a French ship, and Jasper brings the *Scud* safely to port at the isolated garrison in the Thousand Islands.

Pathfinder has fallen in love with Mabel, but when he proposes to her, she refuses him. Muir appears not to have given up his own suit, although he admits to Mabel that he has had three previous wives. Mabel detests him. Jasper also has fallen in love with Mabel, but he does not reveal it to anyone.

Sergeant Dunham decides to take some of his men to attack French supply boats, the outlying garrison's mandate. Starting out with his detachment, he leaves six men at the post, Muir among them, with orders to look after the two women. Soon after her father's departure, Mabel goes for a walk and meets Dew of June, who warns her of danger from Indians led by the French. Mabel, in turn, tells Muir, who seems unmoved by the information. Mabel then goes to Corporal M'Nab with her story, but he too fails to act on the warning. While they talk, a rifle cracks in the nearby forest, and M'Nab falls dead at Mabel's feet. She runs to the blockhouse, the most secure building in the garrison, to which Dew of June has told her to go. The attacking party comprises twenty Indians, led by the Tuscarora renegade Arrowhead. Mabel, Cap, and Muir survive the ambush—Mabel's survival with the help of Dew of June—but Cap and Muir are captured later. Mabel discovers Chingachgook, who has been spying around the garrison. She plans to acquaint him with the details of the situation, if he comes to the blockhouse, as she expects he will.

Instead, Pathfinder arrives secretly at the blockhouse. He has not been fooled by the dead bodies of the massacred peo-ple that the Indians have placed in lifelike poses around the garrison. Before Pathfinder can provide warning, the party of soldiers under Sergeant Dunham is ambushed, but the sergeant, although seriously wounded, manages to reach the blockhouse. Cap escapes from the Indians and also gains the protection of the blockhouse. The small group fights off the Indians during the night. Jasper arrives with men in the *Scud* in time to assist Pathfinder. Muir, however, still believing Jasper to be a spy, orders him bound. Frustrated at the failure of his ambush to destroy all of the whites, Arrowhead stabs Muir and disappears into the bushes, hotly pursued by Chingachgook, who later kills him. Muir dies, and Captain Sanglier, the French leader of the Indians, admits that the French spy had been Muir, not Jasper.

On his deathbed, Sergeant Dunham, thinking Jasper to be Pathfinder, takes Jasper's hand, places it in that of Mabel, and gives the two his blessing. He dies before the surprised witnesses can correct his error. Finally realizing that Mabel really loves Jasper and that Jasper loves her, Pathfinder relinquishes his claim to her. Pathfinder disappears into the wilderness with Chingachgook and is seen only once more by Jasper and Mabel. On several occasions over the years of her marriage to Jasper, Mabel receives valuable gifts of furs, but no name ever accompanies these gifts, although her feelings tell her from whom they came.

Critical Evaluation:

The Pathfinder is the fourth novel in James Fenimore Cooper's Leatherstocking series. In the chronology of hero Natty Bumppo's life, it is, however, the third tale. *The Pathfinder* resurrects Natty from the death described in *The Prairie*, which was written thirteen years earlier. *The Pathfinder* is distinguished by being the first and only Leatherstocking story in which the celibate and thoroughly independent frontier scout falls in love with a woman.

Cooper was an essentially romantic writer, in the romance tradition extending from Greek tales through Sir Thomas Malory's *Le Morte d'Arthur* (1485) and into the nineteenth century romances of American writers Nathaniel Hawthorne and Herman Melville and the twentieth century romances of Zane Grey. As a thorough and competent historian, Cooper could have backed up his fictional narrative with facts, but his primary purpose was to stir the reader's imagination through idealized portraits of frontier life. Cooper's most lasting appeal lies in his gift for storytelling. Working with even the simplest and least original plot, he was able to sustain the reader's interest by employing ambushes and chases, hairbreadth escapes, and harrowing violence, as well as sentiment, chivalry, and love relationships.

Linked inextricably with such a colorful and adventure-filled story line is the familiar Cooper setting; the primal beauty of forest and sea and the grandeur and rich abundance of unspoiled nature provide an appropriate backdrop for courageous deeds. The author was intimately familiar with the area around the mouth of the Oswego River in upstate New York, having spent the winter of 1808 there as a midshipman in the U.S. Navy, and both his knowledge and love of the land are apparent in the descriptive passages of *The Pathfinder.* Such love of nature is also consistent with the romance tradition, in which the world of nature, as God's greatest creation, is where God is most visible and accessible. Indeed, Pathfinder's refrain of feeling close to God in the forest reinforces this theme of virtually all romances and particularly of the Romantic period of literature, in which Cooper wrote, along with well-known poets such as John Keats, Percy Bysshe Shelley, William Wordsworth, and Samuel Taylor Coleridge, whose works echo the same view of nature.

Cooper's talents as a storyteller and descriptive writer, however, have obscured his merits as a serious artist whose works illustrate important social and religious concerns. One recurrent theme, for example, which is strongly apparent in *The Pathfinder,* is the idea that to achieve happiness and self-fulfillment, human beings must live according to their "gifts," or talents, be they great or limited. Cooper believed strongly in democracy, but in a conservative way. He felt that the American continent was the perfect environment in which people could develop fresh and individualistic forms of society, but he feared that some frontierspeople were moving too close to anarchy. The key to success was that all individuals recognize and accept their separate places within the scheme of things, places determined not by heredity but by natural talent that located each person in a "class."

Much of the interest in *The Pathfinder* stems from the question of Mabel Dunham's marriage, because it involves discoveries about talent and appropriate courses of action on the part of not only Mabel but also Natty, Lieutenant Muir, Jasper Western, and Sergeant Dunham. Indeed, the class/gifts theme in *The Pathfinder* is complex, with Cooper recognizing that "gentlemen" can be scoundrels, like the traitor Muir—who sells himself for wealth—and recognizing that commoners, like Pathfinder, can be honest, just, and heroic. Still, Pathfinder cannot win Mabel, at least partly because, although a commoner, she is unusually well-educated, while he is unlearned in a traditional academic sense, although a master of frontier and forest knowledge. Thus, the equalitarian scout and hero, who honors no distinctions of class or rank but only personal ability, loses Mabel to the better educated Jasper, who retreats to the city with Mabel and becomes a successful merchant.

Cooper's fundamental conservatism leads to the thematic implication that, although frontier life, circumstances, and strife may sometimes create completely heroic persons like Pathfinder, those persons will not carry the weight of American progress; instead they will ultimately be sterile and disappear, like Pathfinder and Chingachgook, the latter being the last of the Mohican tribe. Cooper suggests that real progress resides in people like Jasper and Mabel, who return to civilization, become successful in business, and build the future. In Cooper's ultimately conservative view, despite his interest in the ideals of the romantic tradition and of Romanticism, the unlearned and the natural do not inherit the earth.

In some sense, *The Pathfinder* is Cooper's last, or next to last, look at the American Dream of an equalitarian world of all races living together harmoniously in a beautiful natural world that, in turn, brings everyone closer to God. The story is a sentimental look back to when and where the dream was lost, to the time when American Indians and Europeans might have made a better, more harmonious world together but failed. What came instead was war, motivated by human greed, bigotry, ignorance, paranoia, envy, and other excesses.

Finally, though, Cooper can no longer believe in this dream; thus, merchant Jasper is the future of America, whereas Pathfinder retreats to his rapidly fading wilderness and watches from afar, unable or unwilling to continue contact with Jasper or Mabel. Pathfinder can only helplessly bemoan that "things they call improvements and betterments are undermining and defacing the land"; that "the glorious works of God" are "daily cut down and destroyed." Thus, as with frontiersman Daniel Boone, the most likely model for Pathfinder, the ideal of harmony with the Indians, of peaceful coexistence with a preserved and balanced natural world, is finally just a dream.

The American Civil War virtually eliminated American idealism and Romanticism, as the war's vast destruction put an end to any belief in depicting, or envisioning, humans behaving as they ideally and morally should. Instead, realism became prevalent among writers of fiction. Mark Twain, for example, lampoons Cooper's Leatherstocking tales in his "Fenimore Cooper's Literary Offenses" (1895). However, Twain failed to understand, or chose to ignore, that Cooper was writing romances, not novels. Thus, he unfairly criticizes Cooper's coincidences and exaggerations. Indeed, coincidences in romances, like Pathfinder's arrival at the blockhouse at just the moment when Mabel expects Chingachgook (then sending Dew of June upstairs so she cannot interfere with admitting him), reflect the moral emphasis of the genre, in the now seemingly antiquated belief that coincidences are God's providence, that God produces unlikely results to protect especially deserving people. Thus, Cooper's best novels, like *The Pathfinder*, endure despite the unjustifiably harsh attacks from realists such as Twain.

In addition to being aware of his true talents and calling and of his proper relationship to society, Natty Bumppo in *The Pathfinder* also has reached a high level of religious consciousness, another crucial Cooper theme. Through this self-sufficient hero, the author conveys his conviction, which grew stronger with age, that divine Providence is involved in human destiny. Natty's piety is natural, a faith taught to him by nature, which he calls "the temple of the Lord"; as he explains simply, "It is not easy to dwell always in the presence of God, and not feel the power of his goodness."

Related to this theme of religion are the elaborate biblical echoes in *The Pathfinder*. Early on, Cooper describes Pathfinder as "a sort of type of what Adam might have been supposed to be before the fall." Symbolically, Pathfinder's natural world is America as the new Eden or new Caanan, with endless possibilities for the new Adam and the new Eden/Caanan. By the end, Pathfinder/Adam has inappropriately fallen for Mabel/Eve, who is half his age; he then becomes a symbolic Jesus figure, because unlike Adam he sacrifices his own happiness, the sensual joy of life with Mabel, who has promised to marry him despite not loving him, to bring happiness to her and Jasper.

Much of the great emotional power of the story derives from these mythical, religious overtones, of the heroic leader who gives up his own happiness for the happiness of those he loves—Mabel and Jasper, the latter his true friend. Thus, in its religious themes, *The Pathfinder* reaches to the very essence of Christianity, to forgiveness of others and to self-sacrifice for the benefit of others. Therefore, despite some troublesome trappings of an admittedly antiquated genre—the romance—Cooper's novel profoundly and skillfully embodies themes that are fundamental to American life. Thus, it deserves its enduring place in American literature.

Revised by John L. Grigsby

Further Reading

Darnell, Donald. "Manners on a Frontier: *The Pioneers, The Pathfinder*, and *The Deerslayer*." In *James Fenimore Cooper: Novelist of Manners*. Newark: University of Delaware Press, 1993. Explores the role of social class on the frontier. The main characters in these three novels, Darnell claims, are fully aware and respectful of their own lower rank.

Franklin, Wayne. *James Fenimore Cooper: The Early Years*. New Haven, Conn.: Yale University Press, 2007. A biography of Cooper that covers his life and career from birth until he departed for Europe in 1826. His personal life and the writing and publishing history of his novels through and including *The Last of the Mohicans* are covered in this volume.

Kolodny, Annette. "Love and Sexuality in *The Pathfinder*." In *James Fenimore Cooper: A Collection of Critical Essays*, edited by Wayne Fields. Englewood Cliffs, N.J.: Prentice-Hall, 1979. Discusses Cooper's need to show the possibility of love for Natty Bumppo to make him a whole human being. Natty faces a choice between love of the forest and love of a woman.

Krauthammer, Anna. *The Representation of the Savage in James Fenimore Cooper and Herman Melville*. New York: Peter Lang, 2008. Focuses on Cooper's (and Herman Melville's) creation of American Indian, African American, and other non-European characters, including the character of Natty Bumppo in *The Pathfinder*. Discusses how these characters were perceived as "savages," both noble and ignoble, by American readers.

Motley, Warren. *The American Abraham: James Fenimore Cooper and the Frontier Patriarch*. New York: Cambridge University Press, 1987. Perceptive study of Cooper's fixation on the consequences of paternal failures, including those of Sergeant Dunham in *The Pathfinder*.

Newman, Russell T. *The Gentleman in the Garden: The Influential Landscape in the Works of James Fenimore Cooper*. Lanham, Md.: Rowman & Littlefield, 2003. Explores how Cooper's fiction redefines the concept of the gentleman through the influence of the natural world, including the water and the forest, on the positive male characters in the stories.

Person, Leland S., ed. *A Historical Guide to James Fenimore Cooper*. New York: Oxford University Press, 2007. Collection of essays, including a brief biography by Cooper biographer Wayne Franklin and a survey of Cooper scholarship and criticism. *The Pathfinder* is discussed in "Cooper's Leatherstocking Conversations: Identity, Friendship, and Democracy in the New Nation" by Dana D. Nelson. Features an illustrated chronology of Cooper's life and of important nineteenth century events.

Rans, Geoffrey. *Cooper's Leather-Stocking Novels: A Secular Reading*. Chapel Hill: University of North Carolina Press, 1991. Good introductory overview. The chapter "A Matter of Choice" shows how *The Pathfinder* focuses more on the mythical character of Natty Bumppo and less on the Indians and the wilderness than do the other Leatherstocking novels.

Rust, Richard D. "On the Trail of a Craftsman: The Art of *The Pathfinder.*" In *James Fenimore Cooper: New Historical and Literary Contexts*, edited by W. M. Verhoeven. Atlanta: Rodopi, 1993. Persuasive argument that *The Pathfinder* is the most carefully crafted, unified, and fully realized work of art by Cooper.

Wegener, Signe O. *James Fenimore Cooper Versus the Cult of Domesticity: Progressive Themes of Femininity and Family in the Novels.* Jefferson, N.C.: McFarland, 2005. Detailed study of the presentation of women in Cooper's fiction, arguing that Cooper created strong, varied female characters in defiance of the cult of domesticity of American society between 1820 and 1860.

Patience
Or, Bunthorne's Bride

Author: W. S. Gilbert (1836-1911)
First produced: 1881; first published, 1881
Type of work: Drama
Type of plot: Operetta
Time of plot: Nineteenth century
Locale: England

Principal characters:
REGINALD BUNTHORNE, a fleshly poet
ARCHIBALD GROSVENOR, an idyllic poet
THE LADY JANE, a rapturous maiden
PATIENCE, a dairymaid

The Story:

At Castle Bunthorne, twenty lovesick maidens pine and wilt for the love of Reginald Bunthorne, a fleshly poet. Reginald, however, loves only Patience, the village milkmaid. Patience does not know what love is and thus does not know that the utmost happiness comes from being miserable over unrequited love. The lovesick maidens set her straight, however, by showing her that to be in agony, weeping incessantly, is to be truly happy in love. Patience tries to remind them that just a year ago they had all been in love with dragoon guards, yet the maidens still scorn her for being so ignorant about real love. A year ago the maidens had not known Reginald.

The dragoon guards, billeted in the village, see Reginald approaching, followed by the lovesick maidens, singing and playing love songs directed to the fleshly poet. The maidens ignore their former loves, having eyes only for Reginald. Reginald himself has eyes only for Patience, the milkmaid. At the insistence of the maidens, he reads them his latest poem, into which he has poured his whole soul—as he does three times a day. The maidens swoon in ecstasy at the poetry, but Patience says it is just nonsense, which it is.

Later, alone, Reginald confesses that he is a sham, that he hates poetry and all other forms of aesthetic pleasure. When Patience comes upon him, he makes the same confession to her, telling her again that he loves only her, not poetry. However, Patience knows nothing of the love of which he speaks, for she has loved only her great-aunt, and that love does not count. After Reginald has left her, one of the maidens tells Patience that to love is to feel unselfish passion. Patience, ashamed that she has never been unselfish enough to love, promises that before she goes to bed that night she will fall head over heels in love with somebody. In fact, she remembers that when she was a little girl she had liked a little boy of five. Now she is sorry that she had not loved him. It is her duty to love someone. If necessary, she will love a stranger.

Archibald Grosvenor appears unexpectedly upon the scene. He is an idyllic poet who grieves because he is completely perfect. Since he has no rival on Earth in perfection, it is his lot to be loved madly by everyone who sees him. Recognizing Patience, he tells her that he is the little boy she had known when he was five. When he asks her to marry him, she refuses. He is perfect; therefore she will not be acting unselfishly in loving him. If he had only one small imperfection, she said, she could marry him in good conscience. Candor forces him to admit that such was not the case. Patience tells him, however, that he cannot love her even if she cannot return his love, for she has faults. Grosvenor agrees, and they sadly part.

Reginald Bunthorne prepares to raffle himself to the rapturous maidens, but before they can draw for him Patience enters and begs his forgiveness for not loving him sooner. Certainly to love such a creature would be unselfish; she would do her duty. As they leave together, the lovesick maidens turn back to the dragoon guards, preparing to fall in love with them once more.

Before their embraces end, Grosvenor enters, and the fickle maidens leave the guards to follow Grosvenor. They love him madly. All desert Reginald, all but Lady Jane, one of the unattractive older women. She hopes her faithfulness will be rewarded, but she knows her beauty is too far gone ever to lure Reginald away from Patience.

Grosvenor will not stop loving Patience to love the rapturous maidens. He pities them for not being able to receive his love and is annoyed by their attentions. They have followed him since Monday, with no half-holiday on Saturday. Then he reads them one of his poems. It tells of a little girl who put mice in the clock and vivisected her best doll and of a little boy who punched his little sisters' heads and put hot pennies down their backs. The maidens nearly swoon with admiration of his lyric beauty.

Patience continues to love Reginald, even though she finds the matter difficult. He has no good habits and is not attractive, but it is her duty to love him and she does, shunning the perfect Grosvenor who loves her. None of the rapturous maidens except plain Lady Jane still loves Reginald, the others having taken their allegiance to Grosvenor. Reginald, resentful because the other maidens have forsaken him, decides to change his character; he will now be as insipid as Grosvenor. Lady Jane promises her help.

The dragoon guards return to the maidens, dressed as foppishly as even Grosvenor could dress. They act insipidly and stupidly, and the lovesick maidens are impressed by this proof of their devotion. Reginald also becomes a changed man. He is mild and kind, even handsome. He tells Grosvenor that he must change, that he has too long had the devotion that once was Reginald's. On the threat of a curse from Reginald, Grosvenor changes his nature and becomes a cad, admitting that he has long wished for a reasonable pretext for getting rid of his perfection.

When Patience sees that Reginald is now perfect and Grosvenor is not, she is happy, for she can now unselfishly love Grosvenor. The lovesick maidens, seeing Grosvenor forsake aestheticism, know that since he is perfect he must be right. They, too, give up the arts and return to the dragoon guards. The duke of Dunstable, a dragoon officer, takes plain Lady Jane, leaving the now perfect Reginald quite alone, without a bride.

Critical Evaluation:

W. S. Gilbert collaborated with the composer Arthur Sullivan (1842-1900) on many highly successful comic operettas between 1875 and 1896, of which *Patience: Or, Bunthorne's Bride* is a major work. It satirizes both the mainstream and the avant-garde of British Victorian culture. These specific targets, however, are also manifestations of such universal human foibles as the desire to impress the opposite sex, jealousy of rivals in love and publicity, and the fickle nature of fame. *Patience* was one of the first literary works to recognize and satirize the cultural faddishness made possible by improved communication in the nineteenth century. *Patience* remains a favorite because of its essentially timeless conflicts and characters, and its highly polished lyrics matched with one of Sullivan's most accomplished scores.

Gilbert incorporates contemporary debates about art and artists in his libretto. By the 1870's, an artistic counterculture was challenging the established culture of Victorian England by emphasizing an otherworldly beauty at odds with everyday life. With its roots in the Oxford Movement to respiritualize the Anglican Church in the 1840's and in the Pre-Raphaelite movement among artists to separate themselves from realistic and popular art in the 1850's, this counterculture tried to reject everything modern, middle class, and commercial, in favor of whatever seemed ancient, aristocratic, and spiritual. Through newspapers and magazines such as the humorous *Punch*, these intellectual currents were made familiar to many people beyond the artistic and academic worlds of London and the universities. Medieval art, loose and flowing clothing, and an overly refined distaste for the crude ordinary world became popular among not only a few artists and students but also a wide range of people who wished to identify with the avant-garde.

Playing upon ordinary people's interest in these debates as well as their suspicion of artists in general and resentment of the counterculture's attacks on middle-class sensibilities, Gilbert's libretto parodies avant-garde ideas while ensuring that down-to-earth virtue ultimately triumphs. The central character, the outrageously dressed, hypersensitive artist Reginald Bunthorne, is a composite of several persons who were famous in the 1870's, including painter James A. McNeill Whistler, painter-poet Dante Gabriel Rossetti, poet Algernon Charles Swinburne, and the playwright and media star Oscar Wilde (whose lecture tour of the United States in 1882 was arranged by Gilbert and Sullivan's theater manager Richard D'Oyly Carte in part to educate American audiences about aestheticism so that they would attend *Patience*).

Within this specifically nineteenth century context, Gilbert's complex, farcical plot turns on the most traditional of themes: the many complications of love (requited and unrequited) and the rivalry between suitors of maidens and fame. In the first of the operetta's two acts, the major conflicts in love are neatly paralleled. On the female side, twenty lovesick maidens swooning for Bunthorne are set against the individual character Patience the milkmaid, who insists that she has no idea what love is. On the male side, the individual character Bunthorne, who loves only Patience (the one woman not infatuated with him), is set against the mainstream dragoon guards, stereotypical soldiers who expect that "every beauty will feel it her duty" to fall in love with a man in uniform. Bunthorne and the maidens are satirized for their artificial ultrapoetical pose, and Patience and the soldiers for their literal-minded inability to comprehend the pose.

In the second act, the conflicts focus the satire more directly on the masks the characters put on as they try to impress one another. Beneath the humorous surface lie not only tensions between appearance and reality, as Gilbert calls attention to the absurd traps the characters set for themselves, but also a need to disparage any commitment to anti-middle-class values as hypocritical. Thus, Bunthorne, who in his patter song directly admits "I'm an aesthetic sham," does not really admire the aesthetic women or believe in the values he pretends to personify, but maintains his pose to keep the fawning devotion of the female chorus. The lovesick maidens play a version of the same game, pretending to be aesthetic and, ironically, driving Bunthorne and Grosvenor away by their efforts to win them. Grosvenor feels oppressed by the devotion Bunthorne craves, but tolerates the lovesick maidens because of a misplaced sense of duty until he is given the chance to become commonplace. Even the soldiers, with equal insincerity and the funniest results of all, mimic Bunthorne's dress and manner in the hope of winning back the love of the maidens.

Only two characters, both women, are not hypocrites: Patience and Lady Jane. In satirizing Patience, Gilbert makes fun of her unsophisticated ignorance of the aesthetic fad and of her naïve willingness to accept at face value the other characters' overblown puffings about poetry, true love, and duty. In satirizing Lady Jane, however, Gilbert is less playful and shows a strain of mean-spiritedness. The audience is invited to laugh at Lady Jane for being a plain, middle-aged woman in love, and for maintaining her loyalty to Bunthorne and aestheticism when everyone else deserts them. Despite a poignant song in which she laments the inevitable depredations of aging, Jane is more ridiculed than sympathized with.

As is always the case in Gilbert's librettos, mainstream values triumph in the end. In *Patience*, that triumph involves Grosvenor's self-transformation into a perfect representative of the consuming middle class, "a steady and stolid-y, jolly Bank-holiday . . . matter-of-fact young man." All of the love-sick maidens except Lady Jane similarly reenter the middle class, declaring devotion to the exclusive department store Swears & Wells and pairing off with the soldiers. When the curtain falls with Bunthorne the only character not happily paired off, the cult of art and beauty has been tamed.

"Critical Evaluation" by Julia Whitsitt

Further Reading

Ainger, Michael. *Gilbert and Sullivan: A Dual Biography.* New York: Oxford University Press, 2002. Chronicles the lives and working partnership of Gilbert and his collaborator, describing how their different personalities spurred them to produce their best work.

Baily, Leslie. *Gilbert and Sullivan and Their World.* London: Thames & Hudson, 1973. Examines the original production of *Patience* and considers the play as a satire on Pre-Raphaelite poets and aesthetes, such as Dante Gabriel Rossetti and Oscar Wilde. Contains photographs and sketches of early productions of the opera.

Crowther, Andrew. *Contradiction Contradicted: The Plays of W. S. Gilbert.* Cranbury, N.J.: Associated University Presses, 2000. An examination of all of Gilbert's plays, including his collaborations with Sullivan. Crowther compares previous critiques of the plays with the plays themselves.

Dunn, George E. *A Gilbert and Sullivan Dictionary.* New York: Da Capo Press, 1971. Goes beyond the mere listing of characters to include allusions to Greek and Roman mythology; Latin, French, German, and Italian languages; mathematics; rhetoric; and other topics. Shows correlations between various Gilbert and Sullivan plays.

Godwin, A. H. *Gilbert and Sullivan: A Critical Appreciation of the Savoy Operas.* Port Washington, N.Y.: Kennikat Press, 1969. Includes a consideration of *Patience* as a satirical gust of common sense in the middle of the aesthetic movement. Describes the antecedents of the characters in the opera.

Jones, John Bush, ed. *W. S. Gilbert: A Century of Scholarship and Commentary.* New York: New York University Press, 1970. Includes a study of the sources Gilbert drew on in writing *Patience*, a consideration of the character of Archibald Grosvenor, and two pieces on the opera's place in the tradition of the Greek comic drama.

Moore, Frank Ledlie. *Handbook of Gilbert and Sullivan.* New York: Schocken Books, 1975. Gives a good overview and synopsis of *Patience* and examines its satire of the aesthetic movement. Considers the role of Richard D'Oyly Carte in the success of the play and in Gilbert and Sullivan's other work.

Wren, Gayden. *A Most Ingenious Paradox: The Art of Gilbert and Sullivan.* New York: Oxford University Press, 2001. An analysis of the operettas in which Wren explores the reasons for the continued popularity of these works. Chapter 8 is devoted to an examination of *Patience.*

Patience and Sarah

Author: Isabel Miller (1924-1996)
First published: 1969, as *A Place for Us*
Type of work: Novel
Type of plot: Love
Time of plot: Early 1880's
Locale: Connecticut and New York

Principal characters:
RACHEL DOWLING, a young woman
SARAH DOWLING, her elder sister
MA DOWLING and PA DOWLING, their parents
PARSON DANIEL PEEL, a bookseller who befriends Sarah
PATIENCE WHITE, a young woman who falls in love with Sarah
EDWARD WHITE, Patience's brother
MARTHA WHITE, his wife

The Story:

Patience White lives with her brother Edward, his wife, Martha, and their children. As Patience and Martha sit inhospitably doing some winter chores, Sarah Dowling delivers firewood to their home. Intrigued with this young woman, Patience invites her to dinner, later telling Sarah that she will go homesteading with her.

On the Sabbath, Patience skips a religious meeting to make plans with Sarah. Sarah confesses her feelings of love for Patience, and they kiss. Later, Sarah tells her sister Rachel that she has "found her mate" in Patience, so Rachel cannot go homesteading with her. This angers Rachel greatly.

The next day, Patience can barely suppress her happiness. Her mood changes, however, when Edward tells her that Pa Dowling had come to their house demanding that Patience be kept off his land. Meanwhile, Pa tells Sarah that Rachel has told him everything. For ten days, whenever Sarah tries to head for Patience's house, Pa beats her.

After Rachel tells Sarah to lie so that Pa will let her see Patience, Sarah and Pa go together to ask Patience if she wants to go away with Sarah. Patience says that she cannot. Back home, Sarah announces that she will leave as soon as possible. Being supportive, Ma tells Sarah that Patience was probably frightened. After cutting her hair so that she can "look like a boy," Sarah becomes Sam. In April, she leaves home with a few possessions in a bedroll; she stops by Patience's house, but Patience is not there.

Sarah/Sam heads north, doing chores in exchange for room and board as she travels. Everyone tries to detain her, thinking she is a runaway apprentice, until she meets Parson Daniel Peel in his wagon and he hires her to help with his bookselling. Traveling with Parson, Sarah/Sam learns to read and learns about the world. When she expresses her pleasure in his company, Parson makes advances, saying men have always loved one another; Sam replies that she is really Sarah. He begins treating her like a woman. As summer is ending, Parson heads to New York and Sarah starts for home.

Sarah wants to go directly to Patience but instead goes to her family. When Rachel speaks of Patience, Sarah pretends to have feelings for Parson. The next morning, as Sarah is at work bringing in corn, Patience comes to welcome her home.

On Sunday afternoon, Sarah goes to Patience's house, and Patience takes Sarah to bed for kisses. From then on, they are apart Monday through Saturday and together on Sunday afternoons. One Sunday, Patience shows Sarah that they can do more than kiss. Later, Patience again mentions homesteading. With Sarah reluctant, Patience compromises, insisting that Sarah see her every day for lessons. The first time, Sarah brings her mother, and the three enjoy playing cards.

The next day, during a storm, Sarah does not arrive at Patience's house, so Patience goes to her. After lessons, despite being urged to stay the night, Patience returns home. Every day after that, Sarah goes to her lessons with one of her sisters.

One Sunday, Martha finds Patience and Sarah kissing. They prepare to meet Edward, who decides to pray over the matter. Patience tells Sarah that he will probably ask her to leave, but it will not happen until Sarah is ready.

Martha points out to Patience the biblical passage of Saint Paul forbidding such behavior; the passage equally rebukes those who judge. Martha describes how she has thought life would be the three of them together and leaves. When Edward returns, he announces that his solution is that Patience must leave; he will buy her portion of the house and provide for her. She tells Sarah when she arrives with Ma Dowling, and, with Ma's support, Sarah agrees to go with Patience.

In March, Edward takes the women by sleigh to the coastal trader; to them, it feels like their wedding day. Edward arranges for their passage by ship to New York, then blesses them and hugs them both good-bye.

Sarah watches from the deck as the ship sets sail while Patience stays below. Going below, Sarah is grabbed by a man who releases her only when Patience appears. For the sake of safety, they begin training Sarah to behave like a lady.

When they arrive in New York, the ship's captain tells them where they can find safe lodgings; he admits that Edward asked him to look after them. They find a boarding-house, and after supper they are at last alone in their own room. Later, their fellow boarders warn the women that the area where they want to live, Genesee, is expensive—a problem echoed by Parson during a visit with his family and by a banker the women consult. Parson suggests that Sarah consider Greene County, but she does not tell Patience about the suggestion. The next morning, while Patience makes plans, Sarah lies to justify waiting, and the lie ruins her day. That night, Sarah wakes Patience and confesses. Patience forgives her, and they make love and then sleep contentedly.

They take a steamboat to Greene County, land in Hudson, and take a ferry to Kaatskill, where they begin their search. Sarah explores farms while Patience sews and paints. The other boarders speculate about the women, but they like Patience, and this admiration leads to her first sale of a painting.

In mid-May, Sarah and Patience find their farm and move. After the seller leaves, they hug and kiss in the open. That first night, they make a comfortable camp and begin work. A dog adopts them; they name him George. One night, he wakes them with his barking, warning them of a wolf. Sarah shoots the wolf, and the bounty she receives for it pays for their new roof.

A week later, Sarah and Patience move into their farm-house. While Patience bakes and paints, Sarah builds a bed. When the bed is finished, they attempt to initiate it, but they loosen its webbing. They work until late and then bed down on the floor, where love returns.

Critical Evaluation:

In 1969, when *Patience and Sarah* was first published as *A Place for Us*, few works of fiction had appeared that dealt positively with love between women. Isabel Miller wrote this work and three others—*The Love of Good Women* (1986), *Side by Side* (1990), and *A Dooryard Full of Flowers, and Other Short Pieces* (1993)—because she felt the world did not understand lesbianism. She made it her purpose to help educate the world, hoping to make being a lesbian easier for others. She set *Patience and Sarah* in the early 1880's (at a time before the word "lesbian" was used) to show that love between women was not new; it had a history. While the novel was originally designed to appeal to a broad audience (some suggest a younger audience), it has been a classic with all ages in the gay sector of the women's movement since its publication, partly because its publication coincided with the beginning of the gay liberation movement.

The story draws on the life of Mary Ann Willson, a painter, and Miss Brundidge, her companion; the couple lived on a farm in Greene County, New York, in the early nineteenth century. The voices telling the story alternate between Sarah's and Patience's; both have equal time, representing the equality of the relationship, and each speaks in the first person, drawing the reader into each woman's view of the relationship and the conflicts she experiences as she feels her way in this new world. Miller also uses this device to illustrate differences between the women, particularly in their styles of upbringing and their social classes. Patience's grammar and vocabulary follow a generally standardized dialect of English, peppered with biblical references. Sarah's word choices are associated more with working-class individuals or with those living in rural communities.

As Regina Minudri observed in an article for *Library Journal*, compared with other works available at the time the novel was published, *Patience and Sarah* provides a better introduction to lesbianism than either Radclyffe Hall's novel *The Well of Loneliness* (1928), with its speculation on the causes of lesbianism, or Lillian Hellman's play *The Children's Hour* (pr., pb. 1934), with its guilt-driven plot. In her examination of lesbian fiction published from 1969 to 1989, *The Safe Sea of Women*, Bonnie Zimmerman outlines characteristics that can be applied to *Patience and Sarah*. Lesbians are often cast as outsiders or as different and unique individuals given their time and place. In the early 1880's, Patience is educated, a painter, and financially independent; Sarah, the oldest of seven daughters, is physically strong and has been trained to be the boy in the family, so she wears men's clothes and does men's work. Neither is devout in the Puritan religion of the New England of their time. Their story raises the question whether they are lesbians because of these differences or whether their differences open them to nontraditional sexual expression.

Joy is the emotion exhibited by many characters in novels from this period. Sarah and Patience know that there are other women like them, because the Bible complains about them. Even though they have no living models, they are not confused in their love for each other; it is easy and natural. Their conflict arises in their attempts to find a safe environment in which to express their love and sexuality away from society's conventions and censure. Hence, they want to have their own farm.

Miller supplies her characters with the freedom they seek through pastoralism, an escape from the confining, civilized world into an idealistic, freeing frontier. Patience and Sarah move from the land of their families in Connecticut (referred to as "frosty" and lacking in passion, supposedly because of the Puritan religion) to Greene County, New York, where everyone seems open and friendly. There they establish a secluded farm and become amazingly self-sufficient. In this idyllic setting, the land cares for them, giving them gifts—first a dog becomes their protector, then a wolf gives his life to pay for their roof. Despite their happiness in their escape, Patience and Sarah yearn for community and role models. Sarah in particular wishes to meet others like them with whom to share their happiness.

Another theme of this novel is common to lesbian-feminist fiction: the general rejection of the religious definition of "homosexuality" as a sin beyond others. When Martha quotes Saint Paul to Patience, Patience notes that the passage equates the sin of engaging in homosexual activity with the sin of judging those who participate in such activity. It has also been suggested that lesbians in fiction often lack mothers or are unlikely to become mothers. Though Sarah's mother is very much present and supportive, Patience never mentions hers. Patience's brother believes the women can

succeed together because their union will produce no children. Overall, this work, an enduring classic of love between women, provides excellent material for the discussion of stereotypes about lesbians.

Su A. Cutler

Further Reading

D'Cruz, Doreen. "The Feminization of Female Homosexuality: Isabel Miller's *Patience and Sarah*." In *Loving Subjects: Narratives of Female Desire*. New York: Peter Lang, 2002. Focuses on Miller's depiction of lesbian sexuality and female desire in the novel.

Juhasz, Suzanne. *Reading from the Heart: Women, Literature, and the Search for True Love*. New York: Viking Press, 1994. Examines works by twentieth century women authors about the search for love and then presents focused discussion of works by Isabel Miller and Louisa May Alcott.

"Routsong, Alma." In *Gay and Lesbian Literature*, edited by Sharon Malinowski. Detroit, Mich.: St. James Press, 1994. Provides a biography of Miller, whose given name was Alma Routsong, as well as a list of critical sources and reviews of her works. Explores the ways in which particular works such as *Patience and Sarah* reflect Routsong's personal growth and change.

Wavle, Elizabeth M. "Isabel Miller." In *Contemporary Lesbian Writers of the U.S.: A Bio-bibliographical Critical Sourcebook*, edited by Sandra Pollack and Denise D. Knight. Westport, Conn.: Greenwood Press, 1993. Offers biographical information as well as discussion of Miller's major works, including *Patience and Sarah*, and their themes. Includes an informative section on the critical reception of Miller's works.

Zimmerman, Bonnie. *The Safe Sea of Women: Lesbian Fiction, 1969-1989*. Boston: Beacon Press, 1990. Does not provide in-depth analysis of *Patience and Sarah*, but uses the novel to illustrate general trends in lesbian fiction, such as the use of pastoralism, the depiction of a longing for home, and the lack of religious definitions of homosexuality as sin.

Peace

Author: Aristophanes (c. 450-c. 385 B.C.E.)
First produced: *Eirēnē*, 421 B.C.E. (English translation
   1837)
Type of work: Drama
Type of plot: Satire
Time of plot: Peloponnesian War
Locale: Athens

Principal characters:
TRYGAEUS, a citizen of Athens
HERMES
WAR
HIEROCLES, a soothsayer from Areus

The Story:

Being tired of the wars and hungry, Trygaeus, like most Athenian citizens, calls upon the gods for aid. Unlike the others, however, Trygaeus searches for a way to gain entrance to the heavens so that he might make a personal plea to Zeus and thus save himself, his family, and his country. He tried climbing ladders but succeeded only in falling and breaking his head. He decided to ride to heaven on the back of a dung beetle, in the manner of Bellerophon on Pegasus.

This attempt to make his way to heaven succeeds, but when Trygaeus arrives at the house of Zeus he finds that the gods moved to that point farthest away from Greece so that they need see no more of the fighting among those peoples and hear no more prayers from them. Affording the Greeks an opportunity for peace, which they ignore, the gods now abandon them and give the god War, aided by his slave Tumult, full power to do with them as he pleases.

Trygaeus soon finds out that War already begins to carry out his plans. He casts Peace into a deep pit and is now preparing to pound up all the cities of Greece in a mortar. Trygaeus watches him as he throws in leeks representing the Laconians, garlic for the Megarians, cheese for the Sicilians, and honey for the Athenians. Fortunately, this deed of destruction is momentarily postponed because War cannot find a pestle. After several unsuccessful attempts on the part of Tumult to find one for him, War himself has to leave the mortar and go make one.

His departure gives Trygaeus the chance he needs to save Peace, and immediately he calls on all the states of Greece to come to his aid. All come, but with noise enough to bring Zeus himself back from his retreat. Hermes, who was left in the house of Zeus, is aroused and angered by the noise and can be cajoled into allowing them to go on with their work only after many promises of future glorification.

Even at such a crucial moment the people refuse to work together. The Boeotians only pretend to work; Lamachus is in the way of everyone; the Argives laugh at the others but profit from their mistakes; the Megarians try hard but do not

have enough strength to do very much. The Laconians and the Athenians work earnestly and seriously, but it is primarily through the efforts of the farmers that Peace is finally freed. With her in the pit are Opora and Theoria. Everyone is now apparently happy, and to ensure the peace Opora is given to Trygaeus as a wife, and Theoria is sent to the Senate. All then descended to earth, where preparations for the wedding begin.

Before going on with the wedding, Trygaeus decides to make a sacrifice to Peace. During his preparations he is interrupted by Hierocles, a prophet from Areus. Trygaeus and his servant both try to ignore the prophet because they feel he is attracted only by the smell of cooking meat, but he is not to be put off so easily. When Hierocles learns to whom the sacrifice is being made, he begins to berate them and give them many oracles to show that this is not a lasting peace and that such cannot be achieved. When they are ready to eat the meat, however, he is prepared to agree with anything they say in order that he might satisfy his own hunger. Trygaeus, wishing to have nothing to do with the soothsayer, beats Hierocles and drives him away.

With peace newly restored to the country, the people of Athens seem to enjoy the feasting and mirth before the wedding. A sickle-maker approaches Trygaeus and praises him for bringing back peace and prosperity, but he is followed by an armorer and various other personages representing those trades that profit by the war. These people are unable to join in the festivities; theirs is not so happy a lot. Trygaeus, however, has no sympathy for them and offers only scorn. When they ask what they can do with their wares in order to regain at least the cost of manufacturing them, he mocks them. He offers to buy their crests and use them to dust the tables, and he offers to buy their breastplates for use as privies. He tells them to sell their helmets to the Egyptians who can use them for measuring laxatives, and he tells them to sell their spears as vine-props. When Opora appears, the whole party goes off to the wedding singing the *Hymen Hymenaeus*.

Critical Evaluation:

After a decade of fighting, Sparta and Athens were ready to make some kind of peace, and the peace of Nicias was nearly complete. In this play Aristophanes joyfully looks forward to a successful conclusion of the negotiations, although it was not to be achieved as quickly as he expected. In the play he anticipates some of the difficulties to be overcome within the various Greek states, and he shows that the farmers of the country will be most instrumental in bringing about the peace.

Peace is distinct from many of the plays of Aristophanes in representing not a bitter or frustrated complaint about contemporary politics but a kind of celebration in advance of an actual peace treaty, which was signed only ten days after the play was performed. Produced in 421 B.C.E., *Peace* was written with every expectation that the Peace of Nicias, which temporarily halted the conflict between Athens and Sparta, would soon become official and permanently put an end to the Peloponnesian War. Another cause for hope was that the Athenian general Cleon, one of the great obstacles to peace (at least in Aristophanes' opinion), had fallen during the previous summer in the same battle in which the leading Spartan general, Brasidas, had also been killed. Aristophanes' comic fantasy expresses an impatient longing for an end to the war, and one of its most remarkable features is an elaborate anticipatory celebration of the conclusion of actual negotiations.

The character Trygaeus reflects the play's topicality. Like many protagonists in the plays of Aristophanes, he is stubborn and self-assertive in achieving his goal. He flies up to heaven and finds out directly from Zeus himself what is preventing Peace, who is personified as a beautiful goddess, from returning as soon as possible to the earth. Trygaeus undertakes his fantastic mission not merely for himself or for the Athenians, but on behalf of all the Greeks. The play acknowledges that all of the Greeks are probably weary of the conflict, whatever private disputes they still may have. Although the identity of the chorus seems to change in the course of the play, at one point the play's Panhellenic aspect is emphasized by an indication that the chorus is composed of elements from all cities and all classes of Greece. Trygaeus's fantastic plan, or great idea as it is sometimes called, therefore seems nobler than the notions concocted by other Aristophanic protagonists. Moreover, Trygaeus, an elderly Athenian farmer, is rather pleasant and likable, despite the play's typical emphasis on obscenity, which was probably a traditional feature of the comic genre.

Mounted on his giant dung beetle, a grotesque comic parody of the winged horse Pegasus, Trygaeus ascends to heaven only to discover that most of the Olympian gods vacated Olympus in disgust with the bellicose ways of human beings. Their departure is an Aristophanic refutation of the traditional Greek concept of heroism, which asserts that the gods delight in the martial prowess of mortals. Trygaeus's beetle is also more than a comic prop. In Aesop's fable of the beetle and the eagle, which is mentioned in several of Aristophanes' plays, an avenging beetle who pursues an eagle right up to the throne of Zeus is a symbol of the righteous vengeance of the lowly on the mighty. This image is appropriate to the bold plan of an elderly Athenian peasant. The first half of the play depicts the determined hero's encounters with those few gods who remain: the Olympian Hermes and the personified abstractions War, Peace, Opora ("late harvest"), and Theoria ("sacred festival").

When Trygaeus discovers that an audience with Zeus on the matter of peace is impossible, he encounters only token resistance from Hermes to his new plan to bring Peace back to earth himself. As befits a play about peace, *Peace* contains no real contest in which the protagonist defends his or her plan against vigorous opponents and ultimately emerges the victor. As threatening as he seems, the god War is quickly dispatched. After Peace is retrieved from the place where she is buried—by a cooperative effort of the Greeks who form the chorus—and Trygaeus returns to earth, all that remains to do is celebrate and enjoy the benefits of peace. There is, again, only token resistance to the enjoyment of Trygaeus's success. Characters such as Hierocles, the arms-dealer, and the sons of Lamachus offer comic foils but no real challenge to Trygaeus, who busily prepares for the celebratory sacrifice and his marriage to Opora.

The wedding of the peasant Trygaeus and the goddess Opora, a literal marriage of heaven and earth, is symbolic of the new state of peace that is achieved. The extravagant enjoyment of food, wine, and love appears also in other plays of Aristophanes, especially when the protagonist overcomes all opposition to his or her plan. What makes *Peace* unusual is that the celebration is an event in which all Greeks are implicitly invited to participate, as spectators of a comic fantasy and in reality as the peace negotiations come to their conclusion. It should be noted that the celebratory mood of the play is also captured in some of the most beautiful and engaging lyrics of Aristophanes, choral songs that capture the essence of the longing for peace and the eager anticipation of its realization.

The celebration marked by *Peace*, which won second prize at the dramatic competition, was to be short-lived. The next few years were tense, and open hostilities broke out again between Athens and Sparta in 411 B.C.E. with part of Athenian territory occupied by a Spartan garrison. Aristophanes' message of peace and Panhellenism was lost in the renewed fighting of the Peloponnesian War.

"Critical Evaluation" by John M. Lawless

Further Reading

Aristophanes. *Acharnians*. Edited and translated by Alan H. Sommerstein. 2d corrected ed. Warminster, England: Aris & Phillips, 1984. Provides scholarly introduction, bibliography, Greek text, facing English translation, and commentary keyed to the translation. Sommerstein's translation supersedes most earlier versions.

Dover, Kenneth J. *Aristophanic Comedy*. Berkeley: University of California Press, 1972. Useful and authoritative study of the plays of Aristophanes. Chapter 10 gives a synopsis of the play, discusses problems in production, and comments on the play's themes of peace and Panhellenism. An essential starting point for study of the play.

Hall, Edith, and Amanda Wrigley, eds. *Aristophanes in Performance, 421 B.C.-A.D. 2007: Peace, Birds, and Frogs*. London: Legenda, 2007. A collection of papers originally delivered at a conference held in 2004. The papers discuss how Aristophanes' plays were staged at various times in England, South Africa, France, and Italy, and analyze specified performances of *Peace, The Birds*, and *The Frogs*.

Harriott, Rosemary M. *Aristophanes: Poet and Dramatist*. Baltimore: Johns Hopkins University Press, 1986. Harriott does not devote an individual chapter to each of Aristophanes' plays but instead discusses each play as it illustrates the central themes and techniques of the playwright's work.

Silk, M. S. *Aristophanes and the Definition of Comedy*. New York: Oxford University Press, 2002. Silk looks at Aristophanes not merely as an ancient Greek dramatist but as one of the world's great poets. He analyzes *Peace* and the other plays to examine their language, style, lyric poetry, character, and structure.

Spatz, Lois. *Aristophanes*. Boston: Twayne, 1978. A reliable introduction to the comedy of Aristophanes for the general reader. Chapter 2 summarizes the problems of the play and offers a good discussion of imagery.

Whitman, Cedric. *Aristophanes and the Comic Hero*. Cambridge, Mass.: Harvard University Press, 1964. A standard work on the characterization of the Aristophanic protagonist. Chapter 3, "City and Individual," contains an excellent discussion of themes and offers valuable comments on the special characteristics of the play.

The Peasants

Author: Władysław Reymont (1867-1925)
First published: Chłopi, 1904-1909 (English translation, 1924-1925)
Type of work: Novel
Type of plot: Social
Time of plot: Late nineteenth century
Locale: Poland

Principal characters:
MATTHIAS BORYNA, a well-to-do peasant
ANTEK, Matthias's son
DOMINIKOVA, a widow
YAGNA, her daughter
HANKA, Antek's wife

The Story:

It is autumn, and the peasants of Lipka village are hurrying to finish the harvest before winter. In Matthias Boryna's barnyard, the villagers gather to see a cow that had been chased from manor lands and is now dying of colic. Hanka, Matthias's daughter-in-law, takes the loss most to heart when old Kuba, the stableman, says that he can do nothing for the stricken cow.

That night, Matthias, charged with having fathered a servant girl's child, goes to visit the *voyt*, the headman of the village, to ask about his trial. The *voyt*, after assuring Matthias that he will get off easily in court, flatters Matthias and tells him he should marry again, now that his second wife is dead. Matthias pretends he is too old, but he is hopeful of marrying Yagna, the daughter of Dominikova. Yagna will some day inherit three acres of land. The next morning, the case against Matthias is dismissed. After the trial, Matthias meets Dominikova and tries to sound her out on her plans for her daughter.

On the day of the autumn sale, Matthias sells some hogs, and Hanka her geese. Old Matthias, pleased when Yagna accepts some bright ribbons, asks her hand in marriage. He does not know that his son, Antek, Hanka's husband, is secretly in love with Yagna. When Matthias settles six acres upon Yagna in return for the three she brought with her marriage portion, Antek and his father fight, and Matthias orders his son off the farm. Antek and Hanka move with their children into the miserable cabin of Hanka's father.

The wedding of Matthias and Yagna is a hilarious affair. In the middle of the merriment, Kuba, poaching on manor lands, is shot in the leg by a gamekeeper. Fearing the hospital, he cuts off his own leg and dies from loss of blood.

Winter comes swiftly, and wolves lurk near the peasants' stock barns. That winter, Hanka and Antek have to sell their cow so they can get food. Antek takes work with men building a new sawmill. Matthew, the foreman, is his enemy, for Matthew also loves Yagna. One day, Antek overhears Matthew bragging that he has been with Yagna in her bedroom. In a great fury, Antek strikes Matthew so hard that the carpenter breaks several ribs when he falls over the railing and into the river.

At Christmas, there is great rejoicing in Matthias's house, for Yagna is pregnant. At the midnight mass on Christmas Eve, Yagna and Antek see each other for a moment. Antek asks her to meet him behind the haystack. That winter, the peasants of the village come to Matthias to report that a part of the forest that the peasants use for gathering wood has been sold by the manor people. Unhappily, Matthias allows himself to be dragged into the dispute. While Matthias is away, Antek goes to his father's farm to see Yagna. Returning, Matthias nearly catches them together.

One night at the inn, Antek becomes drunk, ignores his wife, and asks Yagna to dance with him. Matthias arrives, seizes Yagna, and takes her away. On his way home, Antek finds his wife almost dead in the snow. From that time on, Matthias treats Yagna like a servant.

Antek loses his job, and Hanka is forced to go with the paupers seeking firewood in the forest. Walking home through the storm, Hanka is given a ride by Matthias. He insists that Hanka come back to his farm the next day. That night, Antek takes Yagna into the orchard. Coming upon them, Matthias lights up a straw stack to see them. Antek and the old man fight. Then Antek flees and the fire spreads, threatening the whole village. Yagna flees to her family. Everyone avoids Antek and refuses to speak to him.

At last, Matthias takes Yagna back, but only as a hired servant. Hanka is with him much of the time. When Yagna begins to see Antek again, the old man takes no notice.

Word comes that the squire is cutting timber on land the peasants claim. The next morning, a fight takes place in the forest as the villagers try to protect their trees. Antek thinks he might kill his own father in the confusion, but when he sees Matthias injured, he kills the woodcutter who wounded his father. Antek walks alongside as Matthias is carried home.

When spring comes, many of the villagers, Antek among them, are in jail after the fight in the forest. Fields go unplowed. Old Matthias lays insensible. Yagna has now begun to consort with the *voyt*. It seems as if the devil himself has possessed the village. Easter is a sad season, because the men are still in prison. Word goes around that the squire, who has been ordered to stop the sale of his land, is in desperate straits for money and vowing revenge upon the peasants. Shortly after Easter, Hanka gives birth to a boy, who is named Roch. Although gifts are given out in Antek's absence, the christening does not seem complete.

At last, the peasants are set free. Their homecoming is a happy occasion in every cabin but that of Matthias, for Antek has not been released. Yagna is also unhappy. Even Matthew, the carpenter who had once loved her, now ignores her for the younger Teresa. One night, Matthias arises from his stupor. For hours, he wanders the fields as if about to sow his land. In the morning, he falls over and dies.

Summer brings additional woes to the peasants. There are quarrels over Matthias's land. Some Germans arrive to occupy the squire's land, but the peasants threaten them, and they leave. The squire makes arrangements to parcel out the land to the peasants, and some of them buy new land for homesteading.

Old Dominikova and Simon, one of her sons, have quarreled, and Simon buys his own land from the squire. Simon and his wife, Nastka, receive many gifts from the villagers who want to spite old Dominikova. When the *voyt*'s accounts are found to be short, the villagers blame Yagna. Antek is released from prison and returns to work on the farm. He is still attracted to Yagna, but the duties of his farm and the possibility that he still might be sent to Siberia press even harder upon him. That summer, the organist's son, Yanek, comes home from school. In a short time, he and Yagna are seen together. At last, the peasants put Yagna on a manure cart and tell her never to return to the village.

The summer is dry and the harvest scanty. One day a wandering beggar stops at Nastka's house. He gives her some balm for Yagna, who has taken refuge there. As the sound of the Angelus rises through the evening air, he strides away. For the food Nastka has given him, he calls down God's blessing on her peasant home.

Critical Evaluation:

Although *The Peasants* was not translated into English until 1924, when its author was awarded the Nobel Prize in Literature, the Germans had already recognized its worth. It has been rumored that during the German occupation of Poland during World War I, German officers were required to read and study the novel as a text to enable them to understand the Polish customs and mores and, thus, have more success in controlling the stubborn and proud peasants than did the previous occupiers, the Russians.

The Peasants is epic in the sweep and significance of its story. The problems of Europe are contained in this novel: overpopulation, poor and overworked soil, ignorance, imperialism. The novel is at once a text on the subject of mass sociology and a human, heartwarming narrative. In keeping with the seasonal movement of its story, Władysław Reymont's masterpiece is divided into four volumes: *Autumn*, *Winter*, *Spring*, and *Summer*.

As an intimate, detailed picture of the Polish peasant, the book is magnificent. Using a naturalistic approach, Reymont gives an unbiased account of both the sordidness and the beauty of the peasants' lives. Between these extremes, there seems to be no middle ground. Life is filled either with animal joy and lustiness (as is shown in the elaborate details of the three-day celebration of Matthias and Yagna's wedding) or with intimate details of poverty, despair, and illness. Yet the peasants never surrender; they all accept their fate.

The novel is more than a sociological analysis of Polish life, however, for Reymont creates characters who are individual and vital. He explores in detail the universal struggles of society: the poor who produce against the rich who exploit; the young who struggle for what is legally theirs against the old who desperately try to hold on to their hard-earned land. He examines the eternal conflicts between women and men, between humans and nature, between religion and superstition, and the lonely struggle of one asserting and defending oneself in a harsh, unyielding, threatening world.

Reymont never allows himself to abandon the basic standard of naturalism: objectivity. Although the reader becomes more involved with some characters than others, the involvement is never caused by Reymont's intervention.

Yagna is perhaps the most interesting character in the novel. She is one of the few villagers not motivated by greed; true, she delightedly accepts a scarf and ribbons Matthias buys for her at the fair, but she is completely uninterested in the marriage settlement, which is handled by her greedy mother, Dominikova. The mother realizes the problems that may arise from the May-December marriage, but she is eager to obtain the six acres Matthias offers. The mother does not force Yagna to marry; Yagna is motivated solely by animal spirit and does not really care. Married to an old man, her health and vitality drive her into the younger arms of Antek and Matthew, but it is this same animalism that initially attracts Matthias to her. She lets her mother handle such things as marriage settlements; her own interests are more physical.

Yagna is driven by sexual passions she cannot begin to understand. She neither appears concerned about the quarrel she has caused between Antek and his father, nor does she worry about the rupture she has caused between Antek and Hanka. She sees only Antek's youth, and that is sufficient for her. She has the same intensity of sexual attraction for Matthew and is unable to control her passion. When he creeps into her darkened cottage before the wedding, she defends herself before her mother by pleading that she could not keep him off.

Yagna cannot transfer her passionate feelings to old Matthias Boryna, which he, a deeply proud man, resents. Although he has heard rumors about Yagna with Antek and Matthew, he ignores them until he sees her creeping into the warm protection of the straw stack with Antek. He then shows no mercy and blocks the entrance to the stack before he sets fire to the rick, hoping that both will be burned alive.

When Matthias takes Yagna back as a serving girl, the young woman accepts it stoically and does not beg for mercy. Like the true peasant, she accepts her lot with resignation and spends no time in self-recrimination. Her position is essentially tragic in the naturalistic sense. Young, attractive, and full of natural self-interest, she allows herself to be controlled by forces she cannot understand.

It is hard to visualize Antek as a sympathetic character, because all of his actions are motivated by jealousy or greed. He abuses Hanka, his wife, and defies both her and his father when he makes no secret of his affair with Yagna. After being expelled from his father's house, he finally gets a job at the mill but spends all of his wages at the tavern so that Hanka and her children are completely dependent upon Hanka's destitute, sick old father. During the harsh winter, when Hanka is nearly frozen while gathering forest wood in a raging snowstorm, it is old Boryna, not Antek, who comes to her aid. Yet, in spite of the hatred Antek bears his father, he instinctively kills the squire's woodcutter who attacks Matthias. Thus, through Antek, the author indicates that underneath the hardness and materialism of the villagers, a vestige of mutual concern remains. It is this element that keeps the book from depicting total despair. Despite the bitter environment, all the peasants retain a zest for life revealed in their delight in celebrations and in their love for food, drink, dance, and brightly colored clothes and ribbons. The dignity of humanity is described as the peasants stop their individual bickering to join forces against the squire and his men who attempt to overtake the ancestral forests of the peasants.

The book is an amazing portrait of common life in a Polish village. Reymont presents all details of daily life—sowing and harvesting the cabbage crops, house life, clothing, furniture, and food. The notes of the translator are invaluable, for without them, the reader might not understand the importance of certain ceremonies, traditions, and superstitions, which are so much a part of the Polish culture.

When the four-volume work appeared, many reviewers criticized it for redundancy, but, in a work more prose epic than novel, each detail enhances the rest. It becomes more than simply a narrative of Polish life; its universal aspect describes the emotions and impulses alive in the peasant everywhere. The work must be read as a whole, beginning with *Autumn* and ending with the harvest scenes of *Summer*, for then the reader may view a splendid picture of life in all aspects.

"Critical Evaluation" by Vina Nickels Oldach

Further Reading

Kridl, Manfred. *A Survey of Polish Literature and Culture.* Translated by Olga Sherer-Virski. 1956. New printing. New York: Columbia University Press, 1967. Claims *The Peasants* is universally acknowledged as "the richest and artistically the most perfect picture of peasant life in world literature." Excellent description of Reymont's ability to endow characters with individual traits while preserving the general impression of peasant life in Poland.

Krzyżanowski, Jerzy R. *Władysław Stanisław Reymont.* New York: Twayne, 1972. A chapter on *The Peasants* discusses Reymont's interest in rural peoples. Argues that it is inappropriate to consider the novel simply as a political tract; claims the novelist is adept at portraying the psychological dimensions of his characters.

Krzyżanowski, Julian. *A History of Polish Literature.* Translated by Doris Ronowicz. Warsaw: Polish Scientific, 1972. Places *The Peasants* in the context of a larger tradition of Polish novels depicting the life of rural folk. Highlights the struggle between traditional values and the changes wrought by the introduction of foreign elements into society.

Mikós, Michael J., ed. and trans. *Polish Literature from 1864 to 1918: Realism and Young Poland—An Anthology.* Bloomington, Ind.: Slavica, 2006. A comprehensive work, comparing two cultural movements—positivism and Young Poland—that place Reymont's naturalistic work *The Peasants* in its historical and literary contexts.

Miłosz, Czesław. *The History of Polish Literature.* 2d ed. Berkeley: University of California Press, 1983. Describes Reymont's plan to write the epic of the Polish peasantry. Explains how *The Peasants* presents traditional Polish values through a story that has more universal significance.

Pietrkiewicz, Jerzy. *Polish Prose and Verse.* London: Athlone Press, 1956. Insightful introduction, in English, about *The Peasants*, highlighting the use of the seasons as a unifying device and citing the psychological complexity Reymont achieves with both major and minor characters. Remaining text is in Polish.

Peder Victorious

Author: O. E. Rölvaag (1876-1931)
First published: Peder Seier, 1928 (English translation, 1929)
Type of work: Novel
Type of plot: Regional
Time of plot: Late nineteenth century
Locale: Dakota Territory

Principal characters:
BERET HOLM, a pioneer woman
PEDER VICTORIOUS, her youngest child
OLE,
STORE-HANS, and
ANNA MARIE, her other children
MR. GABRIELSEN, their minister
CHARLIE DOHENY, Peder's friend
SUSIE, Charlie's sister

The Story:

Peder Holm lives in three rooms. In one, he lives everything in English; here there is a magic touch. In the second, where he lives everything in Norwegian, things are more difficult. In the third room, only he and God are allowed. Before he was born, his mother had dedicated him to God, and God had become a very real person to the boy.

As Peder grows up, however, he is not always sure that God is the kind of being that his mother and the minister, Mr. Gabrielsen, talk about. Peder has been taught that God is love, and yet God is blamed for the death of Per Hansa, his father, the destruction of the crops, and the bleakness of the land. To Peder, such calamities cannot be reconciled with his God of love; he reads his Bible assiduously in an attempt to straighten out his thoughts.

Mr. Gabrielsen is sure that once Peder goes to seminary, he will be the right person to minister to the Norwegian settlement. The preacher expects English to supplant Norwegian as the common language there in the next twenty years, and Peder's English is fluent, though still tinged with an accent.

The whole community is in a fever of change. After a long argument in church about disciplining a girl whose shame has caused her to hang herself, one group breaks away and establishes a second church. There are two schools, one strictly Norwegian and one taught in English, to which the Irish come as well. An imminent community problem is the division of the territory before it enters the union. Such matters arouse the people nearly to fighting pitch, and the meetings in which they are discussed offer fine entertainment to all within riding distance.

Peder's mother, Beret, wants everything Norwegian kept intact; she tries to ensure that the children speak Norwegian to her at home, though this becomes hard after the children go to school. Most particularly, she wants Peder to enter the ministry. Often, though, she cannot understand him when he speaks English at school and church affairs. His voice is fine and loud, and he speaks often and enters into every kind of entertainment, which he finds right on the farm.

After a political meeting at the schoolhouse that Beret and her whole family attend and at which Peder recites Abraham Lincoln's Gettysburg address in English, his teacher speaks at length to Beret about letting him speak English all the time so that he can lose his Norwegian accent. Beret is so disturbed by this request that she speaks to her husband's picture that night. Although he seems to smile at her anxiety, she decides that Peder should go to the school that was attended only by Norwegians.

The change of schools does not help much. Beret asks a widowed friend about moving both their families back to Norway, but Sorine questions the wisdom of taking their children into a strange land. Beret cannot understand what Sorine could be talking about. Were not their children Norwegian? Sorine assures her that their children are American.

One thing helps Beret to keep her mind off her troubles. She can plan for the farm. Everyone in the settlement admits that she is prosperous. Soon she has a windmill and a fine big barn for both horses and cows. She never knows quite how she does that job; usually she feels overcome by her problems and tries a solution out of desperation, but her solutions tend to be the right ones.

Because her farm is going so well, Beret likes to give the minister donations for the missions. Her generosity gives her satisfaction until, just before Peder is to be confirmed, the preacher asks him at a meeting to read a part of the Bible in English. Beret objects, but she is even more incensed sometime later when he asks the blessing in English in her own house. She still wants Peder to be a minister, however.

Peder is beginning to have ideas of his own. In the first place, he begins to resent being kept at home, away from dances and parties. The Irish are great for parties, and Peder likes a great many of them, especially the Doheny family. He begins to go out at night without telling his mother where he is going. He cannot prevent her knowing that he is out, however, because she stays awake until he returns home. She begins to hear rumors about him, but he refuses to confide in her. When the minister hears that Peder is running around with girls, he begs Peder to go to the seminary immediately, but the young man refuses.

Instead, Peder begins to take part in rehearsals for a play, the first to be put on in the settlement. He has the role of the hero and Susie Doheny that of the heroine. To him, the lines in the play become real and Susie his true love. He is happier than he has ever been, and he sings all day and is tireless in his work. When the minister hears about the play, he begs Beret to remove Peder from that kind of temptation. Beret thinks it is up to the minister himself to restrain Peder. She is confused. Perhaps Peder is going astray, but lately he has been kinder than ever before. She questions him and is relieved when she hears that some of her old friends also are in the cast. Before the next rehearsal, Beret goes through the fields to the schoolhouse and peers in. There she sees Peder with Susie in his arms.

Beret hides in the shadows until the players leave. Her mind goes blank, then she begins to pick up small sticks that she piles close to the school. When a storm comes up and the heavy rain and wind prevent the sticks from burning, she creeps home. She is so tired that she merely looks at her husband's picture and falls on her bed. Hearing a noise, she looks around; there is her husband, Per Hansa, standing by her bed and telling her to let Peder have the girl he is so fond of. The next day, Peder feels that Beret is preoccupied. It is a shock and then a delight to him to hear her say they must hurry to the Dohenys' to arrange for his and Susie's wedding.

Critical Evaluation:

O. E. Rölvaag, perhaps the best-known Norwegian American author, interpreted the immigrant experience and depicted the human cost, as well as the material benefits, of becoming an American. Rölvaag himself immigrated from Norway in 1896 when he was twenty years old. In the United States, he was able to obtain the education he had always desired, but he experienced the pain of separation from home and family and he knew that immigrants continue to feel like outsiders in their new country while at the same time they become estranged from the old.

The myth of the American frontier as a second Eden where people could start a new, more prosperous life lured many immigrants to settle there. This myth included the necessity of being reborn as a new person, of cutting all ties with the past. Rölvaag believed that this results in rootlessness and spiritual disintegration. Rather than a melting-pot society of bland uniformity, he advocated the preservation of the Norwegian language and culture to provide a sense of continuity for the immigrants and their descendants. This philosophy is everywhere apparent in his fiction.

Peder Victorious is the second novel in Rölvaag's trilogy chronicling the Holm family. *Giants in the Earth* (1927), which covers events from 1873 to 1881, describes the struggles of Per and Beret Hansa, who are among the first to settle in Spring Creek in Dakota Territory. That novel concludes with Per's death in a snowstorm. *Peder Victorious* picks up the story in 1885 and takes it through 1895, covering Peder's childhood and youth. Peder is the youngest child of Per and Beret and the first child born in the Spring Creek settlement. By 1885, Spring Creek is no longer a frontier but an established community with churches and schools; more mundane cultural, social, and psychological conflicts have replaced the dramatic, mythical struggles of the first book. *Their Fathers' God* (1931), which follows Peder into young adulthood, continues these themes.

Polarity and division are recurring images in *Peder Victorious*. During the time of the novel, Dakota Territory is divided into the states of South Dakota and North Dakota. St. Luke's Lutheran Church is split and Bethel Congregation formed; the Holm family is separated when one son and his wife leave Spring Creek for Montana. The main emphasis, however, is on the internal conflicts of Peder and Beret, especially those resulting from the Americanization process. Much of the book is told from Peder's point of view, but Beret's is also considered; in fact, some critics contend that it is as much her story as his.

Beret has always been torn between sexuality and spirituality. She had felt a strong physical attraction for her husband and regrets not having taken advantage of the opportunities for a more active sexual relationship when he was alive. At the same time, she is devout and has never resolved her guilt about having become pregnant before they were married. Not only does she repress this part of her personality, but she is also extremely uncomfortable with Peder's developing sexuality.

Beret is well aware that she is caught between the Old World and the New and belongs to neither. For her, Norway represents civilization and established values, while the United States represents materialism and the potential loss of one's soul. She considers returning to Norway but realizes that her children would be strangers there and that even she would no longer fit in. Instead, she tries to pass her cultural values on to them. She is concerned with the preservation of the Norwegian language and is baffled when her children prefer to speak English. Unable to communicate intimately with her children, she becomes a stranger to them. Ironically, she achieves the American Dream of material prosperity: After Per's death, she becomes one of the most successful farmers in the area.

Peder thinks that Norway is all in the past; he considers himself an American and is clearly in rebellion against his mother and her values. The three rooms described in the beginning of the book symbolize the segmentation of his life into an English-speaking, a Norwegian-speaking, and a spiritual world. When he is young, he moves easily from one room to another, but as he grows older, he becomes increasingly comfortable only in the English-speaking world.

As a small child, Peder had felt a close, personal relationship with God. His father's tragic death, however, and the congregation's harsh treatment of an unmarried young woman who had become pregnant result in a distrust of God in general and Lutheranism in particular. The pastor thinks Peder should study for the ministry, but Peder rejects religion and concentrates on a secular life.

Although the Holm family speaks only Norwegian at home, once Peder starts school he is drawn to the English-speaking world. Everything interesting to him, everything that concerns the future, has to do with that world rather than with the Norwegian-speaking one, and he starts to speak English at home, too. Beret tries to teach him to read and write Norwegian, but he refuses to cooperate.

Peder, having revolted against Lutheranism, the Norwegian language and culture, and even his own family, considers himself to be completely Americanized, but there is evidence that his heart, too, is divided. When Pastor Gabrielsen, speaking English, urges him to enter the seminary, a prospect Peder does not welcome, Peder forgets himself and answers in Norwegian. Although he denies it, something deep inside is still identifiably Norwegian.

Peder dates two Norwegian girls, but it is Susie, the twin sister of his Irish friend, Charlie, who attracts him. Norwegian or Irish, Lutheran or Catholic, it does not matter—Peder believes in the great ideal of a mixed society where everyone is an American, and he wants to marry Susie. Beret feels it is morally wrong for them to marry, but she acquiesces. These conflicts are not, however, entirely resolved at the end of *Peder Victorious*. Peder gets his way and will marry Susie, but there is an ominous sense that his future will not be happy.

"Critical Evaluation" by Eunice Pedersen Johnston

Further Reading

Eddy, Sara. "'Wheat and Potatoes': Reconstructing Whiteness in O. E. Rölvaag's Immigrant Trilogy." *MELUS* 26, no. 1 (Spring, 2001): 129-149. Focuses on the complex relationship between Norwegian and Irish characters in *Peder Victorious* and the two other novels in the trilogy.

Haugen, Einar. *Ole Edvart Rölvaag*. Boston: Twayne, 1983. A detailed discussion of all Rölvaag's works from a Norwegian American perspective. Haugen, a former student of Rölvaag, is an expert on Norwegian American dialects, and he has studied Rölvaag's writing in the original Norwegian, as well as the English translations.

Haugtvedt, Erica. "Abandoned in America: Identity Dissonance and Ethnic Preservationism in *Giants in the Earth*." *MELUS* 33, no. 3 (Fall, 2008): 147-168. Explains how

Rölvaag is known for his advocacy of a culturally pluralistic America in which all ethnic groups would coexist. Examines how this philosophy applies to the depiction of ethnic identity in *Peder Victorious* and the other novels in the immigrant trilogy.

Moseley, Ann. *Ole Edvart Rölvaag*. Boise, Idaho: Boise State University Press, 1987. A brief, general introduction to Rölvaag's life and writings. Focuses on the importance of Rölvaag's work to the general student of American literature. Includes a useful bibliography.

Paulson, Kristoffer F. "Rölvaag as Prophet: The Tragedy of Americanization." In *Ole Rölvaag: Artist and Cultural Leader*, edited by Gerald Thorson. Northfield, Minn.: St. Olaf College Press, 1975. Discusses the physical and spiritual dangers that Rölvaag saw confronting immigrants.

Reigstad, Paul. *Rölvaag: His Life and Art*. Lincoln: University of Nebraska Press, 1972. An extensive discussion of Rölvaag's novels. Emphasizes the artistic merits of Rölvaag's work, rather than the social history aspects.

Simonson, Harold P. *Prairies Within: The Tragic Trilogy of Ole Rölvaag*. Seattle: University of Washington Press, 1987. Emphasizes Beret's role in all three novels of Rölvaag's immigrant trilogy. Argues that Beret is Rölvaag's most important character and the one who best represents his views.

Thaler, Peter. "Wheat and Potatoes: Ethnic and Religious Differences in O. E. Rolvaag's Immigrant Trilogy." In *Norwegian Minds, American Dreams: Ethnic Activism Among Norwegian-American Intellectuals*. Newark: University of Delaware Press, 1998. Focuses on the last two novels in the trilogy, *Peder Victorious* and *Den signede dag* (1931; *Their Fathers' God*, 1931), whose characters are the first generation of Norwegian Americans to be born and raised in the United States. Explains how Rölvaag wrote these novels when Norwegian life in the United States was on the decline; he tried to use his fiction to encourage the preservation of a distinct Norwegian American identity.

Pedro Páramo

Author: Juan Rulfo (1918-1986)
First published: 1955 (English translation, 1959)
Type of work: Novel
Type of plot: Psychological symbolism
Time of plot: Late nineteenth and early twentieth centuries
Locale: Comala, Jalisco, Mexico

Principal characters:
PEDRO PÁRAMO, a rural boss and landowner
JUAN PRECIADO, one of his many sons and the main narrator of the story
DOÑA EDUVIGES DYADA, a friend of Juan's dead mother
SUSANA SAN JUAN, Páramo's childhood sweetheart
FATHER RENTERÍA, the priest of Comala
ANA, Father Rentería's niece
ABUNDIO MARTÍNEZ, another of Páramo's sons, and his killer
MIGUEL PÁRAMO, the son whom Páramo acknowledges
DAMIANA CISNEROS, Páramo's housekeeper
FULGO SEDANO, Páramo's man of business
DOROTEA, an old procurer
DAMASIO (EL TILCUATE), a revolutionary in the hire of Páramo

The Story:

Juan Preciado, a peasant and Pedro Páramo's son, in fulfillment of the last will of his mother, arrives on foot to Comala looking for his father. During his journey, another man had joined him; the traveler turns out to be another of Páramo's sons. He tells Juan Preciado that their father was a "kindled rancor" and that he is dead. Preciado finds only one other person in Comala, Eduviges Dyada, an old friend of his mother, and she gives him shelter. The woman is dead, as is the companion of Preciado during the journey.

Pedro Páramo appears as a boy, dreaming of his childhood sweetheart, Susana San Juan, and doing some domestic chores. Susana is the only true, deep love of Páramo, in contrast to the many other women whom he has seduced, and raped. Eduviges Dyada tells Preciado that she should have been his mother, for on her nuptial night his true mother, advised by a soothsayer, asked Eduviges to take her place beside Páramo. Little by little, Páramo's moral profile is drawn by Eduviges. She continues to tell Preciado what kind of man his father is. She tells of Miguel Páramo—the only son whom Pedro acknowledges—a violent, sexual predator who died in an accident. Father Rentería, the local priest, enters the plot. His brother had been murdered and his niece raped by Miguel Páramo, but he nevertheless had to celebrate a funeral mass and perform the last Catholic rites for the soul of Miguel.

To add to this conflict of emotions, Father Rentería also believes he had betrayed his priestly state because he had not taken a firm stand against the abuses committed by wealthy people, Pedro Páramo in particular. The priest also had not given true hope and consolation to the poor. Once, when he went to confess to the parish priest of Contla, he was reprimanded and denied the absolution because he had allowed his parishioners to live lives of superstition and fear.

Pedro Páramo appears again, as an adult. He has grown, as Father Rentería says, as weeds do. He obtains all that he ever wanted—women, children, lands—by such unscrupulous means as unfulfilled promises, money, threats, violence, and death. His only redeeming trait is his love for Susana San Juan, who was previously married to Florencio and who, after becoming a widow, agreed to become Páramo's wife. She goes insane, and a change begins to transform Pedro's soul. He feels old, sad, and impotent, and his situation gets worse after Susana dies in his hacienda, Media Luna. On her deathbed, she believes herself to be with her dead husband. Páramo's life begins to disintegrate; he suspects that death will come soon. One morning a son, Abundio Martínez, grief stricken because of his wife's death, gets drunk and goes to his father to ask for money for the burial. Blinded by wine, Abundio stabs his father to death. Páramo falls as if he were a pile of stones.

Critical Evaluation:

In *Pedro Páramo*, Juan Rulfo delves, as no Mexican writer of fiction had done before, into the complex, atavistic, desolate, and fatalistic world of the Indians of Mexico. *Pedro Páramo* is a book of voices—voices of people, voices of nature, and voices of circumstance, morality, and passion. All of its characters are dead; they are only voices, murmurs, who live in a town, Comala, a village of echoes. All of these dead people, souls in pain, are presented as if they were living in another world, in a strange limbo of memory.

A mixture of fantasy and reality, *Pedro Páramo* contains thematic threads that express Rulfo's pessimistic vision of life. Each inhabitant of Comala relives a single moment of pain or guilt over and over again, but the experience never brings any increased self-awareness, any insight into the causes of behavior, or any suggestion of possible remedies for dilemmas. The characters are symbolic figures; they stand for the individual as a powerless victim of both external and internal forces. Rulfo's men and women are helpless in the face both of outside circumstances and of their own psychic problems. Comala is a microcosm in a state of irremediable chaos and inescapable disintegration. The despair of this situation is conveyed powerfully through the author's style, which is based on the basic rhythms of common speech.

Pedro Páramo stands as a landmark work in the evolution of the twentieth century Spanish American novel in that it represents, for many critics and other readers, the first example of the Spanish American New Novel. After the 1920's and 1930's, in which Spanish American fiction sought to paint realistic and detailed pictures of external Spanish American (and often national or even regional) realities, in which description often ruled over action, environment over character, types over the individual, and social message over artistic subtlety, and in which the understanding of the story required little attention on the part of the reader, the nature of Spanish American fiction began to change radically.

In the 1940's, as a result of internal and external influences (chiefly of Argentine short story writer Jorge Luis Borges and of American writer William Faulkner, respectively), Spanish American fiction developed a new narrative that, unlike its predecessor, treated the fictional world as just that—fiction. This new narrative presented various, and often alternative, versions of reality, entered the inner worlds of its characters, and expressed universal as well as regional and national themes. In doing so, it broke with tradition. The new Latin American narrative also was unafraid of unconventional modes of telling the story, of subtle presentation of theme, and of requiring the reader's participation at all levels of the narration. Though numerous Spanish American novels of the late 1940's and early 1950's possessed characteristics of Spanish America's new narrative, *Pedro Páramo* can be considered Spanish America's first New Novel.

The world the novel depicts, for example, is anything but the realistic world presented in the Spanish American novel of the 1920's and 1930's. The characters in the book are dead, and their stories come from voices from the grave. Juan Preciado, for example, the character whose narration opens the book, is dead as he narrates, and his narratee is not the reader, but the woman (Dorotea) with whom he shares his tomb. Likewise, the narration of other stories floats from the tombs of other characters, and the living, what few there are in the story's present, communicate freely with the dead; the dead themselves communicate with one another (as is the case with Preciado and Dorotea). Even beyond the specter of the dead, the story seems to be pervaded by an otherworldliness, all of which together places *Pedro Páramo* well outside the parameters of what anyone might consider realistic fiction.

Rulfo's novel paints a vivid realistic picture, however, of the relationship between the local despot (cacique) and those in his influence. The novel departs from tradition by not making this picture the novel's explicit moral message. Rather, the novel explores the inner workings of its characters, all of whom suffer from frustration, guilt, and obsessive desires. These misfortunes of the human condition are universal concerns and not at all limited to the Indians of the Jalisco region of Mexico.

While the novel's many departures from tradition help place *Pedro Páramo* within the rubric of the Spanish American New Novel, the aspect of Rulfo's work that most earns it classification as a New Novel and that which has inspired the most critical commentary and acclaim, as well as reader frustration, is the novel's unconventional presentation of its story. The relatively short novel is told in sixty-eight (or sixty-four, depending on the edition) sections that frequently shift in narrative voice and narrative focus. Different sections initiate, resume, and drop story lines and subplots with virtually no predictability. The sections present new characters with no introduction or context, and seem to be arranged in no logical order. So confusing is *Pedro Páramo* to first-time readers, and particularly to its first readers in 1955, that many might agree with one of the novel's first critics, who accused Rulfo of writing the novel in chronological order and then cutting it into pieces and rearranging it at random. A close reading of the text reveals, however, that Rulfo could not have first written the novel in chronological order. Even reconstructed into chronological order, the novel has numerous gaps in the story, and the story and its many subplots are like, in chronological order or not, snapshots taken over many years and many lives. Furthermore, the novel's structure is not nearly so chaotic as it may first appear. Rereading reveals its associative construction.

The unconventional presentation of the story in *Pedro Páramo*, therefore, characterizes the Spanish American New Novel. The New Novel demands an active, participatory reader, who not only must read the novel carefully but also must strive to make connections, work to identify changing narrative voices, seek to establish who is who, and attempt to assess the significance of the events, with little or no help from the author. That the reader may have to read and reread to understand what he or she is reading is a major and defining characteristic of the Spanish American New Novel in general and of *Pedro Páramo* in particular.

One final common characteristic of the New Novel, which is found in Rulfo's work, is that because the presentation of the story is so challenging, the presentation itself may overshadow the story, and the reader may be more concerned with how the story is told than with the story itself. The New Novel may actually be of more interest for how it tells what it tells than for what it actually tells.

The timing of Rulfo's novel made it a landmark novel in Spanish American literature. Its haunting story and its challenging presentation have won it enduring fame with its many readers. Few novels, in any literature, present the reader with so compelling a reading experience as that found in *Pedro Páramo*.

"Critical Evaluation" by Keith H. Brower

Further Reading

Beardsell, Peter. "Juan Rulfo: *Pedro Páramo*." In *Landmarks in Modern Latin American Fiction*, edited by Philip Swanson. New York: Routledge, 1990. Provides a detailed analysis of the novel and discusses its significance to the development of twentieth century Latin American literature.

Brotherston, Gordon. *The Emergence of the Latin American Novel*. New York: Cambridge University Press, 1977. Discusses the plot of *Pedro Páramo*; the nature of its narrative, themes, and atmosphere; and its place within the context of literature concerned with the Mexican Revolution. A good introduction to Rulfo's fictional world.

Detjens, Wilma Else. *Home as Creation: The Influence of Early Childhood Experience in the Literary Creation of Gabriel García Márquez, Agustín Yáñez, and Juan Rulfo.*

New York: Peter Lang, 1993. Describes how Rulfo's childhood home, the people he knew as a child, and events in Mexican history inspired the geographic setting and other elements of *Pedro Páramo*.

Dove, Patrick. "'Exígele lo nuestro': Transition and Restitution in Rulfo's *Pedro Páramo*." In *The Catastrophe of Modernity: Tragedy and the Nation in Latin American Literature*. Lewisburg, Pa.: Bucknell University Press, 2004. Analyzes the novel within the context of Mexican history and culture, describing how it reflects questions about national identity that arose after the Mexican Revolution.

Harss, Luis, and Barbara Dohmann. *Into the Mainstream: Conversations with Latin-American Writers*. New York: Harper & Row, 1967. Provides an interview-based overview of Rulfo and his works; the discussion of his writings is punctuated by comments from Rulfo himself. An excellent starting point for further study.

Leal, Luis. *Juan Rulfo*. Boston: Twayne, 1983. A solid study of Rulfo's life and career, with two chapters devoted to *Pedro Páramo*. Topics covered include the place of Rulfo's novel within the context of the novel of the Mexican Revolution, the novel's roots in Rulfo's short stories, its structure, initial critical reaction to the work, the work's multiple narrative threads, and the role of imagery.

McMurray, George R. *Spanish American Writing Since 1941: A Critical Survey*. New York: Frederick Ungar, 1987. Offers concise commentary on *Pedro Páramo* before discussing Rulfo's contribution to Spanish American fiction. Brief but good introduction.

Sommers, Joseph. *After the Storm: Landmarks of the Modern Mexican Novel*. Albuquerque: University of New Mexico Press, 1968. Discusses the narrative perspective of *Pedro Páramo*, its structure, its characters, and, as Sommers puts it, the work's "mythic underpinnings."

Wilson, Jason. "*Pedro Páramo* by Juan Rulfo." In *The Cambridge Companion to the Latin American Novel*, edited by Efraín Kristal. New York: Cambridge University Press, 2005. In addition to essays charting the development of the Latin American novel from the nineteenth century, this collection contains analyses of six of the most significant examples of the genre, including *Pedro Páramo*.

Pedro Sánchez

Author: José María de Pereda (1833-1906)
First published: 1883
Type of work: Novel
Type of plot: Picaresque
Time of plot: 1852-1879
Locale: Santander and Madrid, Spain

Principal characters:
PEDRO SÁNCHEZ, a provincial from the Cantabrian Mountains
AUGUSTO VALENZUELA, a politician from Madrid
CLARA, his daughter
SERAFÍN BALDUQUE, a former state employee
CARMEN, his daughter
MATA or MATICA, a student in Madrid
REDONDO, the editor of *El Clarín* of Madrid
BARRIENTOS, Governor Pedro Sánchez's secretary

The Story:

Pedro Sánchez, a young provincial proud of his descent from Sancho Abarco, a tenth century king of Navarre, had seen little of Spain when he left his father and three sisters to go to Madrid. Augusto Valenzuela, a visiting politician, has promised to look after Pedro's future in the capital. It is October, 1852, when Pedro takes the coach from Santander. Among the passengers are a down-at-heels bureaucrat, Serafín Balduque, and his attractive daughter, Carmen. From a student in the coach, Pedro learns of a cheap boardinghouse where he hopes to stay until he can contact Valenzuela.

The politician proves hard to find. After settling in his lodgings, Pedro calls at Valenzuela's house, where Pilita, his wife, and his daughter, Clara, give the young man a cool reception. The politician, finally tracked down after a dozen visits to his office, vaguely promises to keep Pedro in mind if anything should turn up. The boy, however, writes his father an optimistic letter in which he lies about his reception by the Valenzuela family.

Pedro's acquaintances at the boardinghouse are more helpful. Matica shows him around Madrid and, when Pedro's money gives out and he is about to return home, finds him a job on the antigovernment newspaper, *El Clarín*, at twenty-five *duros* a month. Pedro learns from the staff of the crookedness of Valenzuela. Occasionally Pedro sees Balduque. Mostly he spends his free time in efforts to become a writer.

In the autumn, when one of the *El Clarín* contributors enters government service, Pedro is advanced to writing reviews under his own name, which is announced as the pseudonym of a famous literary man. Redondo, the editor, hints that plays and novels by friends in the party are to get preferential treatment, while literary works by members of the opposition are to be severely criticized. One of Pedro's first tasks is to criticize *Clemencia*, by Pardo Bazán.

Pedro's success goes to his head. He abandons his old friends, even Matica. He sees Clara, and in spite of his disdain he finds himself falling in love with her. Valenzuela, however, does nothing to help the young man get ahead in Madrid. Since all *El Clarín* employees are revolution-minded, Pedro catches the fever and writes a fable attacking the government. Featured on the front page, it brings him much attention. Valenzuela sends for Pedro and offers him a meager job on a government publication, but he refuses it. Warned by Balduque that his refusal will put the police on his trail, Pedro takes refuge with Balduque and Carmen.

After the overthrow of the government in the revolution of July 17, 1854, there is no longer any reason for Pedro to stay in hiding. On his way from the Balduque house to the office of *El Clarín*, he sees a mob burning government buildings. When they begin shouting against Valenzuela, he diverts the rioters to the palace of Cristina, the queen mother, and rushes to save Clara. He is unwilling to admit, however, that he acted out of love for her.

Street fighting breaks out, with Pedro in command of a barricade. He is joined by Balduque, who is eager to get revenge for the wrongs committed against him. Balduque is killed, and Pedro and Matica are forced to break the news to Carmen. She refuses their offers of help.

Finally, Baldomero Fernández Espartero imposes peace on the troubled country. Valenzuela flees, and his family accepts an invitation to the country estate of the duchess of Pico. Pedro is rewarded with a provincial governorship. On his way to tell Clara good-bye, he finds himself proposing to her. A fall marriage is arranged. Through Pedro's efforts the government grants a pension to Carmen, but when he goes to tell her the news and to announce his approaching marriage, her lack of approval puzzles him. Matica is also unenthusiastic. Redondo is downright angry. The marriage is performed after Pedro had visited his father for the first time in three years.

Clara, her mother, her brother, and Barrientos, a secretary whom Pedro disliked from the first, accompanies him to the seat of his government. There everything goes wrong. Clara's family is extravagant and snobbish. Pedro's secretary sneers at him and so do the citizens. Finally, from a friendly editor, Pedro gets an explanation: His secretary is collecting bribes, and his wife is exploiting her husband's political position. Returning home unexpectedly, Pedro surprises Barrientos in his wife's bedroom. When Pedro and Barrientos meet in the street, they fight with sabers, and Pedro is wounded.

At last a change of government costs Pedro his governorship. Ashamed to return to Madrid, he gets Matica's promise to look after Carmen, and he gives up his political life. The passing years bring many changes in Pedro's affairs. Valenzuela soon dies, as does his wife. Barrientos is killed in a duel. Clara had several protectors and eventually dies, leaving Pedro free to return to Madrid and marry Carmen, but evil luck still plagues him. His new wife and their small son die during an epidemic. When he tries to squander his money, Pedro becomes rich. Homesick for the mountains, he sells his business and returns to Santander, but there he finds no happiness. His father is dead; the countryside and the people seem strange. Unhappy, Pedro writes his autobiography, ending it in true picaresque style, with the hope that the example of his disillusionment will serve as a warning to his readers.

Critical Evaluation:

Essentially a realist, José María de Pereda attempted to express his moral convictions through his novels, while portraying honestly the conditions of life in Spain as he saw them. *Pedro Sánchez* is one of his most successful explorations of the character of the Spanish people, despite its essentially pessimistic political message. By the time he wrote *Pedro Sánchez*, he had come to feel that the revolution was not working, and he also felt scorn for the newly rich who exploited liberalism for their personal ends. The novel shows the sincere disillusion of an enthusiast who left the provinces and plunged into the political life of the capital. Perhaps Pereda's didactic tendency injures his effects, and his grim satire occasionally degenerates into caricature, but Pereda understands character, and it is for this reason that *Pedro Sánchez* endures.

In treatment of subject matter and in composition, *Pedro Sánchez* is one of Pereda's most finished works. It is a mod-

ern picaresque novel, an autobiography satirizing all the phases of the protagonist's life as office seeker, journalist, political agitator, revolutionist, social lion, and governor. Pedro's opinions of life and politics in Madrid doubtless reflect those of the author, who had followed a somewhat similar career in the capital before he yielded to homesickness and returned disillusioned to his native region. There is nothing heroic about Pedro. He is an ordinary mortal with a weak moral sense, yet he arouses sympathy and pity when viewed in contrast to the snobbery and villainy of the people about him.

Pereda's keen sense of the ridiculous is everywhere evident in *Pedro Sánchez*; the novel displays a broad range of humor, from gentle irony to biting satire. Pereda excels in his ability to portray common people and to reproduce the popular vernacular with all of its lusty humor. In this regard, although the novel is essentially picaresque, *Pedro Sánchez* does advance realism in the Spanish novel. The characters in the book are real human beings, flawed and foolish, and intrinsically human. The author does not condescend to his characters; he understands them and portrays them with zest. Above all, he is never sentimental about his characters. Pedro is one of the great characters of Spanish literature, never idealized, but sympathetic and understandable. Women are relegated to secondary roles in the novel and in the author's view of society.

The narrative centers on the revolution of 1854, which Pereda witnessed as a student in Madrid. With great skill, the author moves Pedro through the stages of success, from journalist to revolutionary leader and official, always looking out for his own interests. Pedro, however, pays a price for his opportunism, the price of ultimate disillusionment. It is significant that he finally returns to his own native village, after his years of political intrigue. If the book has any message, it is that one should distrust the claims of would-be political saviors; a healthy skepticism should greet the birth of any new movement. Revolutions come and go, but the people endure.

Further Reading

Eoff, Sherman. "Pereda's Conception of Realism as Related to His Epoch." *Hispanic Review* 14 (1946): 281-303. A reassessment of both Pereda's contributions to Spain's literature and to his politics. Dated but still helpful.

_____. "Pereda's Realism: His Style." *Washington University Studies: New Series Language and Literature* 14 (1942): 131-157. Argues that Pereda's style is realistic and influenced by the author's own interpretations of realism and by other traditions in the Spanish novel. Dated but still helpful.

Klibbe, Lawrence Hadfield. *José María de Pereda*. Boston: Twayne, 1975. A good starting place for students and general readers interested in further study of Pereda and his work. Includes a bibliography.

Turner, Harriet, and Adelaida López de Martínez, eds. *The Cambridge Companion to the Spanish Novel: From 1600 to the Present*. New York: Cambridge University Press, 2003. Pereda's work is discussed in several of the essays in this companion to Spanish novels of the seventeenth century and later. References to the writer are listed in the index.

Valis, Noël Maureen. *Reading the Nineteenth-Century Spanish Novel: Selected Essays*. Newark, Del.: Juan de la Cuesta, 2005. Includes two essays, "Pereda's *Peñas arriba*: A Reexamination" and "Pereda and the Tourist Gaze," which examine Pereda's novels other than *Pedro Sánchez*.

Peer Gynt

Author: Henrik Ibsen (1828-1906)
First produced: 1876; first published, 1867 (English translation, 1892)
Type of work: Drama
Type of plot: Satire
Time of plot: Mid-nineteenth century
Locale: Norway

Principal characters:
PEER GYNT, a Norwegian farmer
ASE, his mother
SOLVEIG, a Norwegian woman whose love for Peer remains constant
THE GREAT BOYG, a troll monster
THE BUTTON MOULDER, threatens to melt Peer in his ladle

The Story:

Peer Gynt, a young Norwegian farmer with a penchant for laziness and bragging, idles away his hours in brawling and dreaming. Upbraided by his mother, Ase, for his willingness to waste his time, he answers that she is perfectly right. She ridicules him further by pointing out that had he been an honest farmer, Hegstad's daughter would have had him, and he would have been a happy bridegroom. He tells her that he intends to break the marriage of Hegstad's daughter, a wedding planned for that night. When his mother protests, he seizes her in his arms and sets her on the roof of their house, from where her unheeded cries follow him up the road to Hegstad's home.

At the wedding Peer is scorned by everyone present except Solveig, a girl unknown to him. Even she, however, avoids him as soon as she hears of his base reputation. Peer becomes drunk and begins to tell fantastic tales of adventure, stories that bridge an embarrassing gap in the marriage ceremony when the bride locks herself in the storeroom and refuses to come out. In desperation, the bridegroom appeals to Peer for help. As Peer leaves for the storeroom, his mother, who had been released from the roof, arrives. Suddenly the bridegroom cries out and points toward the hillside. Rushing to the door, the guests see Peer scrambling up the mountain with the bride over his shoulder.

Peer quickly abandons the bride and runs into the wilderness. Eluding the pursuit of Hegstad and his neighbors, he marries and then deserts the daughter of the elf-king of the mountains. He encounters the Great Boyg, the riddle of existence in the figure of a shapeless, grim, unconquerable monster. Peer tries repeatedly to force his way up the mountain, but the Boyg blocks his way. When Peer challenges the Boyg to a battle, the creature replies that though he conquers everyone, he does not fight.

Exhausted, Peer sinks to the ground. The sky is dark with carnivorous birds that are about to swoop down upon him. Suddenly he hears the sound of church bells and women's voices in the distance. The Boyg withdraws, admitting defeat because Peer has the support of women in his fight. An outlaw for having carried off Hegstad's daughter, Peer builds himself a hut in the forest, to which Solveig comes to keep him company. Their happiness is brief, however, for one day Peer meets the elf-king's daughter, whom he had deserted. With her is an ugly troll, Peer's son; unable to drive them off, he himself leaves after telling Solveig that she must wait for him a little while.

Before leaving the country, he pays a farewell visit to his dying mother. With his arms around her, Peer lulls her into her last sleep. Over her dead body he utters thanks for all his days, all his lullabies, all his beatings.

Peer goes adventuring around the world. In America he

sells slaves; in China, sacred idols. He has a thriving business in rum and Bibles. After being robbed of his earthly goods, he goes to the African desert and becomes a prophet. Prosperous once more, he sets himself up in Asian luxury. One day he rides into the desert with Anitra, a dancing girl. Stopping to rest, he cannot resist the urge to show off by proving to Anitra that he is still young in spirit and body. While he is performing, she steals his moneybag and horse and gallops away. Solveig has grown middle-aged while waiting for Peer's return. Peer, on the other hand, still struggles on with his planless life, still drifts around the all-consuming Boyg of life with no apparent purpose in mind.

On his way back to Norway at last, his ship is wrecked. Peer clings to a spar that can hold only one person. When the ship's cook attempts to grasp the spar also, Peer thrusts him into the ocean. He had saved his own life, but he doubted whether he had been successful in saving himself from his aimless existence.

On his return to Norway, Peer decides, however, that he is through with wandering, and he is willing to settle down to the staid life of a retired old man. One day on the heath he meets a Button Moulder, who refuses to let the aged Peer realize his dream of peace and contentment. Informed that he is to go into the Button Moulder's ladle to be melted, Peer becomes frantic. To lose his soul, his identity, is an end he had not divined for himself despite his aimless and self-centered life. He pleads with the Button Moulder to relent. He is at worst a bungler, he cries, never an exceptional sinner. The Button Moulder answers that Peer, not bad enough for hell nor good enough for heaven, is fit only for the ladle. Peer protests, but the Button Moulder remains adamant. Peer is to be melted into the ladle of nonentity unless he can prove himself a sinner worthy of hell. Hell being a more lenient punishment than nothingness, Peer desperately enlarges upon his sins. He tells the Button Moulder that he had trafficked in slaves, had cheated people and deceived them, and had saved his life at the expense of another. The Button Moulder ironically maintains that these iniquities are mere trifles.

While they argue, the Button Moulder and Peer come to a house where Solveig stands in the doorway ready for church, a psalmbook under her arm. Peer flings himself at her feet, begs her to cry out his sins and trespasses, but she answers that he is with her again, and that is all that matters. She is shocked when Peer asks her to cry out his crime to her; she says that it is he who makes life beautiful for her. Hearing her words, the Button Moulder disappears, prophesying that he and Peer will meet again. Peer buries his face in Solveig's lap, safe and secure with her arms to hold him and her heart to warm him. Solveig's own face is bathed in sunlight.

Critical Evaluation:

A satire on a person, one of those contradictory creatures with an upright body and groveling soul, *Peer Gynt* is an example of Henrik's Ibsen's symbolic treatment of the theme of individualism. This drama is a long episodic fantasy, with a picaresque, jaunty, boastful, yet lovable sinner. Ibsen combines folklore and satire with a symbolism that imparts a rich emotional impact to the drama. The unorthodox and untheatrical elements of the play, however, make stage presentation difficult. The play deals with the degeneration of the human soul, yet the triumphant note at the end regarding the redeeming power of love keeps the play from being tragic.

Peer Gynt was Ibsen's last verse play; his later dramas were written in prose, in keeping with his shift to more realistic themes. *Peer Gynt* is a masterpiece of fantasy and surreal effects, which, in combination with Ibsen's delicately graceful eloquence, makes the play difficult to stage, especially in a realistically oriented theater. In some ways, the play resembles a picaresque novel more than it does a play. It is episodic and involves a journey filled with disparate adventures. *Peer Gynt* has been faulted by some critics for being overloaded with "spectacle": too many rapid changes of exotic scene. It is just such qualities, however, that lend the play its greatest strength.

Such inspiration prompted Ibsen in 1874 to request that his famous contemporary, the Norwegian composer Edvard Grieg, compose incidental music for *Peer Gynt*. Grieg accepted the request with reluctance, having personal and artistic reservations about its feasibility. After two years of strenuous work, he completed the job, and in 1876, Ibsen's *Peer Gynt* was performed with Grieg's *Peer Gynt*, two orchestral suites of amazing beauty including "Anitra's Dance," "In the Hall of the Mountain King," and "Solveig's Song." To a large extent, this artistic collaboration proved fruitful because both Ibsen and Grieg intuitively agreed about the uniquely and distinctively Norwegian qualities of *Peer Gynt*. The protagonist, as drawn by the playwright, could have no other ethnic identity; the music, as composed by the musician, could have no other cultural origin, for Grieg was a master at absorbing and utilizing peasant and folkloric themes. Indeed, it has been somewhat acerbically observed that *Peer Gynt* will be remembered not as Ibsen's play but as Grieg's music.

The play describes the adventures of an egocentric but imaginative opportunist. To be sure, Peer is a lovable rogue, but a self-obsessed one. His preoccupation with himself—his own gratification—is his egocentricity; his upwardly mobile changes of locality and women constitute his opportunism; his exotic tastes suggest his imaginative approach toward coping with life. Still, his final return to native hearth and native woman—as he buries his head in Solveig's waiting lap—indicates the limits of adventuring.

Finally, it is this inevitable return to the home territory that makes *Peer Gynt* irrevocably, unavoidably, categorically a play about home, in this case Norway. Such a concept of territoriality is concisely expressed in a line from Mikhail Bulgakov's Russian play, *Dni Turbinykh* (pr. 1926, pb. 1955; *Days of the Turbins*, 1934), in which one character flatly asserts "Homeland is homeland," implying an influence of national identity that transcends egocentricity and opportunism as well as political affiliation and religious preference. Peer returns to the land of his origin in a denouement that shows his own as well as Ibsen's ultimate commitments, and those commitments lend the play its compelling force.

Further Reading

Bloom, Harold, ed. *Henrik Ibsen*. Philadelphia: Chelsea House, 1999. The interpretive essays of this biographical study include analyses of *Peer Gynt* and other plays by Ibsen.

Goldman, Michael. *Ibsen: The Dramaturgy of Fear*. New York: Columbia University Press, 1999. Analyzes dialogue, plot, and other elements of Ibsen's plays to demonstrate how he challenges his audience's opinions and expectations. Includes a discussion of *Peer Gynt*.

Groddeck, Georg. "*Peer Gynt*." In *Ibsen: A Collection of Critical Essays*, edited by Rolf Fjelde. Englewood Cliffs, N.J.: Prentice-Hall, 1965. A psychoanalytical exploration of *Peer Gynt*, emphasizing Peer's relationships with the women in his life.

Johnston, Brian. *To the Third Empire: Ibsen's Early Drama*. Minneapolis: University of Minnesota Press, 1980. A detailed and insightful survey of Ibsen's early dramatic production, this volume includes a major section devoted to *Peer Gynt*. Argues that the drama, which has a moral purpose, owes its appeal to the same playful strategies for dealing with reality that Ibsen argues against.

McFarlane, James. *Ibsen and Meaning: Studies, Essays, and Prefaces, 1953-87*. Norwich, England: Norvik Press, 1989. Compares and contrasts *Peer Gynt* with another Ibsen play, *Brand*. Unlike the protagonist of *Brand*, McFarlane argues, Peer Gynt lives entirely in his illusions.

_____, ed. *The Cambridge Companion to Ibsen*. New York: Cambridge University Press, 1994. Collection of essays, including discussions of Ibsen's dramatic apprenticeship, historical drama, comedy, realistic problem drama, and working methods. References to *Peer Gynt* are listed in the index.

Robinson, Michael, ed. *Turning the Century: Centennial Essays on Ibsen*. Norwich, England: Norvik Press, 2006. Collection of essays published in the journal *Scandinavica*, including discussions of Ibsen's style, language, and the reception of his plays in England.

Shapiro, Bruce G. *Divine Madness and the Absurd Paradox: Ibsen's "Peer Gynt" and the Philosophy of Kierkegaard*. Westview, Conn.: Greenwood Press, 1990. A discussion of the relationship between the character of Peer Gynt and Kierkegaardian philosophy, particularly the theory of the contrast between the aesthetic and the ethical spheres of existence.

Templeton, Joan. *Ibsen's Women*. New York: Cambridge University Press, 1997. Templeton examines the women characters in Ibsen's plays and their relationship to the women in the playwright's life and career. Chapter 4 includes an analysis of *Peer Gynt*.

Pelle the Conqueror

Author: Martin Andersen Nexø (1869-1954)
First published: Pelle erobreren, 1906-1910 (English translation, 1913-1916)
Type of work: Novel
Type of plot: Social realism
Time of plot: Late nineteenth century
Locale: Denmark

Principal characters:
PELLE KARLSSON, a young Swede
LASSE KARLSSON, his father
RUD PIHL, his playmate
ELLEN STOLPE, his wife
MASTER ANDRES, his master
MR. BRUN, his friend

The Story:

Among a shipload of migrant workers traveling from Sweden to the Danish island of Bornholm in the spring of 1877 are Lasse Karlsson, a Swedish farmhand who is old before his time, and his eight-year-old son, Pelle. Like other Swedes who travel to Bornholm, Lasse Karlsson is enticed from his homeland by the relatively high wages paid on the Danish island. Lasse and his son are hired to look after cattle on a large farm on the island. Their life there is neither pleasant nor unpleasant. The farm is a dreary one. The owner leaves the management of the place to a bailiff, drinks heavily, and seeks after women. Pelle's greatest happiness is going out to look after the cattle in the common pastures. After a time, he finds a playmate in Rud Pihl, the farmer's illegitimate son, who lives in a shack with his mother near the edge of the farm. For the elder Karlsson, life is not easy; he is old and weak, and the rest of the laborers make him the butt of jokes. Even so, the man and his son stay at Stone Farm for several years, since it is easier to remain there than to look for a new location.

The second winter finds Pelle in school, for the authorities insist that he attend. Though he is nine years old, he has never been formally educated. He is the only Swede among more than twenty Danish children. Gradually, however, Pelle makes a place for himself and even becomes a leader among his schoolmates.

After two years, Pelle is confirmed. Everyone now considers him capable of taking care of himself. Realizing that his father is content where he is, the boy decides to leave the farm by himself. Early one morning, he sets out toward the little town that is the chief city of the island. While trudging along the road, Pelle meets a farmer who has known him for some time and who gives him a ride into town. When Pelle confides to him that he is on his way to look for work, the farmer introduces him to a shoemaker who accepts Pelle as an apprentice.

Master Andres is an easy master but, even so, the six-year apprenticeship is not easy. The journeyman under whom Pelle works is a grouchy person who taunts Pelle for his rural upbringing. Pelle is not sure what he will do once his apprenticeship is over, for he sees that many shoemakers are out of work and that machine-made shoes are slowly taking the place of the handmade variety.

In the last year of Pelle's apprenticeship, Master Andres dies, and the business is sold. Rather than finish out his time with a new master, Pelle runs away from the shop. For several months, he simply drifts, picking up odd jobs. The only thing that saves him from becoming a ne'er-do-well is the friendship of Marie Nielsen, a dancer. She makes him look for

work, patches his clothes, and bolsters his self-esteem so that he does not become a mere tramp. Finally, a traveling shoemaker named Sort asks Pelle to join him for a time. The two travel about the country and are very successful. One day, they meet Pelle's father, who had just been evicted from the farm he had purchased during Pelle's apprenticeship. The sight of his father, broken and miserable, convinces Pelle that he ought to leave Bornholm for Copenhagen, where he hopes to make his fortune.

In Copenhagen, Pelle soon finds work, but the pay is slight. Finally he joins a newly organized trade union. He quickly becomes interested in the activity of the union and becomes a leader in the labor movement. He meets many people, among them Ellen Stolpe, the daughter of a leader in the stonemasons' union. The two fall in love and are married on the day Pelle becomes president of the shoemakers' union.

After his marriage, Pelle loses interest in the union; he spends as much time as possible with his wife and eventually with his two children. Then comes a very bad winter. All the workers were hard-pressed by lack of work. The hardship arouses Pelle once again to work with the union. His private life, too, has become miserable, for he discovers that his wife has become a prostitute to keep the family fed and sheltered. When he discovers this, Pelle leaves his wife.

The workers are successful in a general strike against their employers, but Pelle, who is recognized as a ringleader, is thrown into prison on charges of having been a counterfeiter; the police had discovered in his house a block of wood, a crude plate for a banknote. Pelle had made it just for something to do while unemployed. For six years, Pelle languishes in prison. When he is released, he reconciles with his wife. He also discovers that the lot of workers is considerably better than it was before his imprisonment, although in his own trade, machinery had taken the place of the shoemaker-craftsman. Pelle takes a job in a factory that specializes in metal fabrications, but he leaves the job when the management tries to use him as a strikebreaker.

Again, Pelle is out of work for quite a time. He picks up odd jobs wherever he can find them, and he spends a great deal of time in a public library reading about the labor movement and the ways of improving the lot of workers. He becomes a friend of the librarian, Mr. Brun, and the two of them start a cooperative shoe factory. Their experiment is successful, even though rival companies oppose them. Pelle and Mr. Brun prosper, allowing them to open their own leather factory and buy a large tract of land to build model homes for their employees.

Pelle is now convinced that by such peaceful measures, the lot of the working class can be improved. The former fire-brand addresses meetings, urging workers to take constitutional means to make their work conditions and wages better rather than to use the more combative and costlier means of the strike.

Critical Evaluation:

Pelle the Conqueror resembles successful radical and socialist literature in being basically autobiographical. Like Martin Andersen Nexø, who was born in one of the poorest slums of Copenhagen, Denmark, the central character of *Pelle the Conqueror* is a member of the working class. While he follows his own particular destiny, Pelle also represents choices for the working-class movement as a whole, and there can be no doubt that, beyond telling an interesting story, Nexø intended his book to help transform the life of working people. Lasse, Pelle, Kalle, and Erik are all meant to serve as social types and as indicators of working-class responses.

The background of *Pelle the Conqueror* is the struggle between workers and employers during the rise of the labor movement in Denmark in the last half of the nineteenth century. At no time, however, does social criticism overwhelm the narrative. The book indeed exposes the struggles of working people, but the maturing of a young man from direst poverty is always foremost. The author's love for common people and their daily concerns is perhaps best illustrated in the insight with which Nexø depicts small incidents of life. The many digressions from the main story to customs and experiences of other characters in whom Nexø was interested are anything but boring because of the sympathy and warm-heartedness with which they are presented.

Lasse, Pelle's father, is already an old widower when the novel opens; he is conservative, unwilling to rebel, and resigned to his fate. Pelle dreams of being like Erik, a fighter and rebel, but Erik's problem is that he is subject to rages; he is meant to suggest a certain type of rural worker who rebels blindly but without plans or organization. One day, goaded beyond endurance, Erik assaults the bailiff and is smashed on the head and severely injured, disabling him mentally. Kalle, at the other extreme, is willing to accept everything. Erik and Kalle represent opposite aspects of the rural working poor who, as a group, vacillate between blind rebellion and passive acceptance.

Pelle's youth, described in book 1 of the novel, represents the experience of the rural working class that, at the onset of industrialization, was attracted to the city and became the urban proletariat. The adolescence of the working class, corresponding to the stage of handicraft industry, is pictured in *Apprenticeship*, the second book, and Pelle's maturity as a workingman is portrayed in *The Great Struggle*, the third volume, which takes place during a time of trade union activity on a mass scale. The final book, *Daybreak*, contains Nexø's ideas for the future: profit sharing, communal living near nature, and human solidarity. Nexø rejects more radical solutions, such as revolutionary communism, and in the end Pelle is shown at rest.

Nexø's novel, which influenced proletarian, socialist, and communist writers around the world, stands as a monumental vision of class history and struggle summarized and dramatized in the life of a single, interesting man. *Pelle the Conqueror* is a competent novel that does an excellent job of dramatizing, individualizing, and organizing its vast subject.

Further Reading

Ingwersen, Faith, and Niels Ingwersen. *Quests for a Promised Land: The Works of Martin Andersen Nexø*. Westport, Conn.: Greenwood Press, 1984. The primary English-language reference on Nexø and his works. Discusses *Pelle the Conqueror* as a realistic work with a mythical dimension that tells an optimistic tale of a worker who is also a mythical liberator. Discusses the political, heroic, and ambiguous elements of the novel.

Lebowitz, Naomi. "Magic Socialism and the Ghost of *Pelle erobreren*." *Scandinavian Studies* 76, no. 3 (Fall, 2004): 341-368. Analyzes the relationship of Nexø and the main character in his novel, describing the autobiographical aspects of the work and discussing the criticism of its historical content.

Rossel, Sven H., ed. *A History of Danish Literature*. Lincoln: University of Nebraska Press, 1992. Includes a brief chapter examining *Pelle the Conqueror*'s symbolism and stark realism. Argues that the novel is a socialistic bildungsroman.

Slochower, Harry. "Socialist Humanism: Martin Andersen Nexø's *Pelle the Conqueror*." In *Three Ways of Modern Man*. 1937. Reprint. New York: Kraus, 1969. An excellent discussion of *Pelle the Conqueror* as the classic proletarian novel. Shows how the major characters and four parts reflect all facets of the rise of the workers' movement.

Pelléas and Mélisande

Author: Maurice Maeterlinck (1862-1949)
First produced: Pelléas et Mélisande, 1893; first published, 1892 (English translation, 1894)
Type of work: Drama
Type of plot: Symbolism
Time of plot: Middle Ages
Locale: Kingdom of Allemonde

Principal characters:
ARKËL, the king of Allemonde
GENEVIÈVE, the mother of Pelléas and Golaud
PELLÉAS and GOLAUD, Arkël's grandsons
MÉLISANDE, Golaud's wife
LITTLE YNIOLD, the son of Golaud by a former marriage

The Story:

Golaud, Arkël's grandson, gets lost while hunting, and as he wanders through the forest he comes upon Mélisande weeping beside a spring. She, too, is lost, her beautiful clothes torn by the briars and her golden crown fallen into the spring. She is like a little girl when she weeps. Golaud tries to comfort her. Although she will not let him touch her or reach for her crown, which he could have retrieved easily, she follows him out of the forest.

Afraid of Arkël, who wants his grandson to marry the daughter of an enemy to bring peace to the land, Golaud writes his half brother Pelléas that he has married Mélisande and wishes to bring her home if Arkël will forgive him. He will wait near the castle for Pelléas to signal that he and Mélisande could enter. Their mother, Geneviève, persuades Arkël, who is now too old to resist, to give his permission. Pelléas wants to visit a dying friend before Mélisande arrives, but Arkël persuades him to stay for the sake of his own sick father.

When Pelléas takes Mélisande to see Blind Man's Spring, a delightfully cool place on a stifling day, he realizes that Golaud had already found Mélisande beside a spring. As Pelléas asks her about that meeting, Mélisande, playing with her wedding ring, lets it fall into the water. As the ring falls, the clock in the castle grounds strikes twelve.

At this time as well, Golaud is hunting. When the clock strikes twelve, his horse bolts and runs into a tree, throwing Golaud. He is recovering from his accident when Mélisande comes to tell him that she wants to go away because the castle is too gloomy. He notices that her ring is gone. She says that she had lost it in the grotto by the sea while picking up shells for Little Yniold. Golaud sends her back immediately to find the ring before the tide comes in. Pelléas takes Mélisande to the grotto so that she can describe the place where she claims to have lost Golaud's wedding ring.

Whenever Golaud is away, Pelléas spends as much time as he can with Mélisande. Usually, Little Yniold is with them. Once, when the little boy was unable to sleep because he said Mélisande would go away, Pelléas takes him to the window to see the swans chasing the dogs. Little Yniold sees his father crossing the courtyard and runs downstairs to meet him. Returning to the room, Little Yniold notices that both Pelléas and Mélisande had been crying.

One night, Mélisande leans from a tower while she combs her beautiful long hair. Pelléas, coming into the courtyard below, entwines his hands in her hair and praises her beauty. When Golaud comes by shortly afterward, Pelléas cannot let go of Mélisande's hair. Golaud scolds them for playing at night like children.

On some days, the castle has a smell of death. Golaud, convinced that an underground lake in one of the crypts beneath the castle is responsible for the smell, leads Pelléas down into the crypts the next morning to see the lake and smell the overpowering scent of death there. Golaud swings the lantern around, which propels Pelléas toward the lake; Golaud, however, catches his arm and keeps him from falling into the water. When the half brothers come out on the terrace, Golaud tells Pelléas that Mélisande is young and impressionable and that she must be treated more circumspectly than Pelléas had treated her the night before, because she is with child.

Golaud tries to find out from Yniold how Pelléas and Mélisande act when the child is with them, what they say and what they do. When he cannot get the child to answer any of his questions satisfactorily, he lifts him so that the boy can look through the window of the room in which Pelléas and Mélisande are standing. Even then he does not learn from Yniold what Pelléas and Mélisande are doing.

A short time later, Pelléas's father is so much better that the prince decides to start on his delayed journey the next day. He asks Mélisande to meet him that night near Blind Man's Spring.

Arkël tells Mélisande that happiness ought to enter the castle now that Pelléas's father is recovered. He wonders why she had changed from the joyous creature she was when she entered the castle to the unhappy one she now seems to be. Although Mélisande disclaims being unhappy, Arkël senses her sadness. Golaud, coming to look for his sword, suddenly begins raging at Mélisande, and he drags her on her knees until Arkël intervenes.

That night, Mélisande meets Pelléas, and as they make love in the shadows, Pelléas feels that the stars are falling. When they move into the moonlight, their shadows stretch the length of the garden. Pelléas thinks Mélisande's beauty unearthly, as if she were about to die. As the gates clang shut, they realize that they are locked out of the castle for the night. Suddenly, Mélisande sees Golaud. Knowing they cannot flee from his sword, Mélisande and Pelléas kiss desperately. When Golaud strikes Pelléas at the brink of the fountain, Pelléas falls. Golaud pursues Mélisande into the darkness. An old servant finds Mélisande and Golaud at the gates early the next morning. Mélisande has a slight cut under her breast, not enough to harm a bird. She delivers a tiny, premature daughter. Golaud had tried without success to kill himself.

Golaud drags himself to Mélisande's room, where Arkël and the physician are attending her. The physician tries to convince Golaud that Mélisande is not dying of the sword wound, that she had been born without reason to die, and that she is dying without reason. Golaud cannot be convinced. He feels that he had killed both Pelléas and Mélisande without cause—that they are both children and had kissed simply as children do—but he is not sure.

When Mélisande wakes up, she seems to have forgotten her hurt and Golaud's pursuit, and she thinks her husband has grown old. Hoping to hear her confess to a forbidden love for Pelléas, Golaud asks the physician and Arkël to leave him alone with her for a moment. When he questions her, however, Mélisande innocently exclaims that she and Pelléas were never guilty. She asks for Pelléas. Because Golaud begs her to speak the truth at the moment of death, she asks who is to die. She cannot answer his questions any better than Little Yniold had done when Golaud lifted him to the window to spy for him.

Arkël shows Mélisande her tiny daughter. Mélisande pities the child because she looks sad. While Mélisande is looking at the baby, a group of women servants comes into the room. Mélisande stretches out her arms and then lays as if weeping in her sleep. Suddenly the servants kneel. The physician looks at Mélisande and sees that she is dead.

Critical Evaluation:

Maurice Maeterlinck wrote *Pelléas and Mélisande* and other symbolic plays as a reaction to the late nineteenth century positivistic belief in rationalistic solutions to all social and scientific problems. He felt that naturalistic, well-made plays that portrayed life realistically left little room in the

reader's or spectator's mind for imaginative, mystical responses. By setting his play in the distant Middle Ages in a mysterious kingdom called Allemonde, which literally means "all the world" (from the German *alle* and the French *monde*), he established a time and place very different from those used in the traditional drama of his era.

During the 1880's, Maeterlinck read medieval literature such as works by the Flemish mystic Jan van Ruysbroeck and many modern symbolical texts, including poems and stories by the French authors Phillipe-Auguste de Villiers de L'Isle-Adam, Stéphane Mallarmé, Charles Baudelaire, and Joris-Karl Huysmans. He also appreciated the writings of the German Romanticist writer Novalis and the American writer Edgar Allan Poe. William Shakespeare's plays and European fairy tales fascinated him. He wanted to express in his art a language that was purer and simpler than adult, scientific prose, one that would somehow suggest primitive peoples and deep emotions.

Born and raised in Ghent, Belgium, a city of canals and medieval buildings, Maeterlinck grew up surrounded by artifacts from the Middle Ages. He often felt haunted by death, and a foreboding atmosphere pervades most of his plays. An audience often feels as if something awful, but unknown, is about to strike and cause the death of one or more of the characters. To portray both this sense of dark oppression and the simplicity of primitive peoples, Maeterlinck's characters often repeat certain words or phrases, a practice he had noticed in Flemish peasants when they told stories. Maeterlinck's goal was not to evoke a rational understanding of the events that occur in his plays but rather to help the reader or spectator feel the emotions of suspense, anxiety, fear, and occasionally joy.

Pelléas and Mélisande, more mystical and emotional than rational, subsequently attracted several composers, among them Gabriel Fauré, Claude Debussy, Arnold Schoenberg, and Jean Sibelius, all of whom composed works based on the play in the first decade of the twentieth century. When it was staged in London in 1898, the play used sets designed from paintings by the Pre-Raphaelite artists Dante Gabriel Rossetti and Edward Burne-Jones, who portrayed slender, mysterious young women in medieval surroundings. The combination of the play's text with impressionistic music and beautiful art transported the spectators into the Allemonde of their and Maeterlinck's imaginations.

Allemonde is a place of degeneration, pending death, and fleeting hopes of happiness through love. Despite the political marriage arranged for him by his father, Golaud chooses to wed Mélisande, a fairylike creature without family relations, a lost soul he has found in a dark forest. Golaud hopes to find joy in his new relationship, and Mélisande does indeed seem to bring temporary happiness into the gloomy castle. Golaud, a widower, is renewed by her apparent love. His dying father, never named, temporarily recovers so that the family believes the physicians' optimistic reports. Pelléas thereupon resolves to leave Allemonde to visit Marcellus, his dying friend, and invites Mélisande to meet him by the Blind Man's Spring so that they may bid each other adieu. If they had not been discovered that night by the jealous Golaud, the tragedy of a murdered brother and fatally wounded wife would perhaps have been avoided. The brief, passionate moment between Pelléas and Mélisande is destroyed by Golaud's violence. The themes of passionate love and hovering death prevail throughout, and in the end death conquers in this very enclosed world.

In some ways, Allemonde resembles the realm of the legendary Fisher King. According to this myth, the king's wounds and sickness are reflected in the infertility of his realm. The fetid smells from beneath the palace in Allemonde suggest decay and the possible collapse of the structure and destruction of its inhabitants at any moment. In contrast to the Fisher King story, however, no Galahad arrives in Allemonde to free the king and restore fertility to his realm; instead, he remains ill, and his son, Golaud, kills his own brother, Pelléas, and wounds Mélisande.

Unlike an indestructible fairy, Mélisande, despite her mysterious past, is a mortal creature. She can survive neither her husband's attack nor giving birth to a premature daughter. She has no magical powers to prevent destruction and death. Although Maeterlinck wanted to escape the naturalistic style of his contemporaries, which realistically portrayed the dark moments of life, he succumbed to his own fascination with death by transforming into tragedy the optimistic medieval legends of a Fisher King who is healed and fairies who have power to grant wishes. The expectations aroused in the reader and spectator that magical events will occur in this strange, isolated, medieval setting are disappointed at the conclusion when death reigns. The wise grandfather Arkël's final words suggest that the tragedy will continue: "Come; the child must not stay here, in this room. . . . It must live now, in her stead. . . . The poor little one's turn has come."

The first production of *Pelléas and Mélisande* in Paris in 1893 accentuated the mystical tension between the opposing forces of love and death. It emphasized an unrealistic setting where emotions were more important than a concrete time and place. The set was extremely simple with overhead lighting casting shadows everywhere. The characters, who wore apparel similar to that of figures in paintings by the Pre-Raphaelite artists, performed behind a gauze curtain, sug-

gesting to the spectator a realm of mystery divorced from the real world. Both the drama and the set differed from the furnished sitting rooms of many contemporary naturalistic plays of the time.

Symbolism had been recognized as a poetic movement in reaction to more concrete types of poetry, but Maeterlinck was the first to introduce it so fully into the theater. He became honored internationally for his innovative works, and when he was awarded the Nobel Prize in Literature in 1911, he was commended for

> his diverse literary activity and especially his dramatic works . . . which sometimes in the dim form of the play of legend display a deep intimacy of feeling, and also in a mysterious way appeal to the reader's sentiment and sense of foreboding.

Maeterlinck wrote prolifically, including plays such as *L'Oiseau bleu* (pr. 1908, pb. 1909; *The Blue Bird*, 1909) and several books of essays on insects and parapsychology, but his popularity gradually waned. Maeterlinck is now most remembered and honored for innovative symbolist plays like *Pelléas and Mélisande*.

"Critical Evaluation" by Carole J. Lambert

Further Reading

Delevoy, Robert L. *Symbolists and Symbolism.* New York: Rizzoli, 1982. A beautifully illustrated chronicle of the Symbolist movement. Describes the cultural events of the era and the aesthetic theories of the Symbolist pictorial and literary artists. Includes an analysis of *Pelléas and Mélisande.*

Halls, W. D. *Maurice Maeterlinck: A Study of His Life and Thought.* Oxford, England: Clarendon Press, 1960. This brief biography is based on the author's research into Maeterlinck's letters and on interviews of his acquaintances. Includes concise critical summaries of each work. A good scholarly starting point for Maeterlinck studies.

Ingelbien, Raphael. "Symbolism at the Periphery: Yeats, Maeterlinck, and Cultural Nationalism." *Comparative Literature Studies* 42, no. 3 (2005): 183-204. Compares the works of Maeterlinck with those of William Butler Yeats, pointing out the similarities in the national, sociological, and linguistic contexts in which their work developed at the end of the nineteenth century.

Knapp, Bettina. *Maurice Maeterlinck.* Boston: Twayne, 1975. Discusses the writer's life and works with particular emphasis on his use of archetypes and symbols.

Lambert, Carole J. *The Empty Cross: Medieval Hopes, Modern Futility in the Theater of Maurice Maeterlinck, Paul Claudel, August Strindberg, and Georg Kaiser.* New York: Garland, 1990. The introduction and conclusion describe the cultural environment that stimulated Maeterlinck to write symbolic plays. Chapter 2 provides a detailed analysis of *Pelléas and Mélisande.* Includes an extensive bibliography.

McGuinness, Patrick. *Maurice Maeterlinck and the Making of Modern Theatre.* New York: Oxford University Press, 2000. Traces the development of Maeterlinck's vision of and theories about the theater, including his Symbolist plays and other dramas.

Maeterlinck, Maurice. "The Tragical in Daily Life." In *Theatre/Theory/Theatre: The Major Critical Texts from Aristotle and Zeami to Soyinka and Havel*, edited by Daniel Gerould. New York: Applause, 2000. This essay, written in 1896, expresses some of Maeterlinck's theories about the theater.

Mahony, Patrick. *Maurice Maeterlinck: Mystic and Dramatist.* 2d ed. Washington, D.C.: Institute for the Study of Man, 1984. The author, a friend of and editor for Maeterlinck during his travels in the United States, relates personal anecdotes and gives a summary of his life. Discusses some of the plays and prose works, as well as Maeterlinck's interest in psychic phenomena.

Penguin Island

Author: Anatole France (1844-1924)
First published: L'Île des pingouins, 1908 (English translation, 1914)
Type of work: Novel
Type of plot: Satire
Time of plot: Ancient to modern times
Locale: Alca

Principal characters:
MAËL, a missionary monk
KRAKEN, an opportunist penguin
ORBEROSIA, Kraken's mistress
TRINCO, a conqueror
PYROT, a scapegoat
MONSIEUR CERES, a cabinet minister
EVELINE, his wife
MONSIEUR VISIRE, prime minister of Penguinia

The Story:

In ancient times, Breton monk Maël is diligent in gathering converts to the Church. One day the devil causes Maël to be transported in a boat to the North Pole, where the priest lands on an island inhabited by penguins. Being somewhat snow-blind, he mistakes the birds for people, preaches to them, and, taking their silence as a sign of willingness, baptizes them into the Christian faith.

This error of the pious Maël causes great consternation in paradise. God calls all the saints together, and they argue whether the baptisms are valid. At last they decide that the only way out of the dilemma is to change the penguins into people. After this transformation, Maël tows the island back to the Breton coast so that he can keep an eye on his converts. Thus begins the history of Penguinia on the island of Alca.

At first, the penguins are without clothes, but before long the holy Maël puts clothes on the females. The novelty of covering excites the males, and sexual promiscuity increases enormously. The penguins begin to establish the rights of property by knocking one another over the head. Greatauk, the largest and strongest penguin, becomes the founder of power and wealth. A taxation system is established by which all penguins are taxed equally. This system is favored by the rich, who keep their money intended to benefit the poor.

Kraken, a clever penguin, withdraws to a lonely part of the island and lives alone in a cave. Finally, he takes as his mistress Orberosia, the most beautiful of penguin women. Kraken gains great wealth by dressing up as a dragon and carrying off the wealth of the peaceful penguins. When the citizens band together to protect their property, Kraken becomes frightened. It is predicted by Maël that a virgin will come to conquer the dragon. Kraken and Orberosia fashion an imitation monster. Orberosia appears to Maël and announces herself as the destined virgin. At an appointed time she reveals the imitation monster. Kraken springs from a hiding place and pretends to kill it. The people rejoice and thenceforth pay annual tribute to Kraken. His son, Draco, founds the first royal family of Penguinia. Thus begins the Middle Ages on the island of Alca.

Draco the Great, a descendant of the original Draco, has a monastery established in the cave of Kraken in honor of Orberosia, who is now a saint. There are great wars between the penguins and the porpoises at this time, but the Christian faith is preserved by the simple expedient of burning all heretics at the stake.

The history of the penguins in this far time had been chronicled by a learned monk named Johannes Talpa. Even though the battles raged about his ears, he was able to continue writing in his dry and simple style. Little record was left of the primitive paintings on the isle of Alca, but later historians believed that the painters were careful to represent nature as unlike nature as possible.

Marbodius, a literary monk, leaves a record of a descent into hell similar to the experience of Dante. Marbodius interviews Vergil and is told by the great poet that Dante had misrepresented him. Vergil is perfectly happy with his own mythology and wants nothing to do with the God of the Christians.

The next recorded part of Penguinian history treats modern times, when rationalistic philosophers begin to appear. In the succeeding generation their teachings take root. The king is put to death and nobility is abolished, leading to the founding of a republic. The shrine of Saint Orberosia is destroyed. The republic, however, does not last long. Trinco, a great soldier, takes command of the country; with his armies he conquers and loses all the known world. The penguins are left at last with nothing but their glory.

Then a new republic is established. It pretends to be ruled by the people, but the real rulers are the wealthy financiers. Another republic of a similar nature, New Atlantis, is growing up across the sea at the same time. It is even more advanced in the worship of wealth.

Father Agaric and Prince des Boscenos, as members of the clergy and nobility, are interested in restoring the kings of Alca to the throne. They decide to destroy the republic by taking advantage of the weakness of Chatillon, the admiral of the navy. Chatillon is seduced by the charms of the clever Viscountess Olive, who is able to control his actions for the benefit of the royalists. An immense and popular antirepublican movement begins, with Chatillon as its hero; the royalists hope to reinstate the king in the middle of the uproar. The revolution, however, is stopped in its infancy, and Chatillon flees the country.

Eveline, the beautiful daughter of Madame Clarence, rejects the love of Viscount Clena, after she learns that he has no fortune. She then accepts the attentions of Monsieur Ceres, a rising politician. After a short time they are married. Monsieur Ceres receives a portfolio in the cabinet of Mon-

sieur Visire, and Eveline becomes a favorite in the social gatherings of the politicians. Visire is attracted by her, and she becomes his mistress. Ceres learns of the affair, but he is afraid to say anything to Visire, the prime minister. Instead, he does his best to ruin Visire politically, but with little success at first. Finally, Visire is removed from office on the eve of a war with a neighboring empire. Eveline lives to a respectable old age and at her death leaves all of her property to the Charity of Saint Orberosia.

As Penguinia develops into an industrial civilization ruled by the wealthy class, the one purpose of life becomes the gathering of riches; art and all other nonprofit activities cease to be. Finally, the downtrodden workers revolt, and a wave of anarchy sweeps over the nation. All the great industries are demolished. Order is established at last, and the government reforms many of the social institutions, but the country continues to decline. Where before there had been great cities, wild animals now live.

Then hunters arrive, seeking the wild animals. Later shepherds appear, and after a time farming becomes the chief occupation. Great lords build castles. The people make roads, leading to new villages. The villages combine into large cities, and the cities grow rich. An industrial civilization develops, ruled by the wealthy class. History is beginning to repeat itself.

Critical Evaluation:

With its mixture of satire, burlesque, and fantasy, *Penguin Island* resembles Voltaire's *Candide: Ou, L'Optimisme* (1759; *Candide: Or, All for the Best*, 1759), 1947 and Thornton Wilder's play *The Skin of Our Teeth* (pr., pb. 1942). Like *Candide*, Anatole France's episodic novel is a reasoned attack upon unreason. Unlike Voltaire's work, which ridicules philosophical error for the most part, *Penguin Island* attacks the absurdities that have fastened onto human customs and institutions.

For its flights into fantasy and its ambitious attempt to explain the course of civilization in terms of a burlesque of history—past, present, and future—Penguin Island also may be compared to Wilder's *The Skin of Our Teeth*. Both works turn history into myth, comment with tolerance upon human follies, and suggest that a dim, ambiguous purpose ultimately controls human destiny. Wilder's comedy, however, is essentially optimistic and melioristic; in spite of natural and social disasters, his message is that the human animal will not only survive but also actually improve its lot in the universe. France is pessimistic. He believes that humanity's course is cyclical, not linear. By the conclusion of *Penguin Island*, the human race has reached the apex of its scientific and technological advances, after which point it retreats into barbarism. The future of Penguinia is not much brighter than its past; every movement forward is succeeded by a step backward, until the cycle is repeated endlessly. Whatever divine force operates in the universe, France seems to believe, its machinery—just as its intelligence—is beyond understanding. However, the author, always amiable, treats a doomed humankind with kindly tolerance instead of scorn. Although his satire occasionally has a cutting edge, he is more often the gentle ironist than the stern moralist. France exposes folly but does not castigate the foolish.

The two great subjects for his satire are the follies of human customs and institutions. The author analyzes the conventions of woman's role as opposed to her nature, as expressed throughout history—or through mythologized French history, France's particular field of investigation. Her "real" nature, France believes, is that of sexual temptress, concerned only, or mostly, with the satisfaction of her physical needs. The blessed Maël, for example, creator of the race of Alca, describes woman as a "cleverly constructed snare" by which a man is taken before he suspects the trap. Moreover, Maël opines that, for vulnerable man, the imagined sexual lure of a woman is more powerful than her real body. As proof of this idea, Orberosia is more attractive to the male pseudopenguins when she is clothed than when she is nude. An Eve figure, Orberosia is flagrantly promiscuous (among her many lovers is a hunchbacked neatherd, or herdsman) and is unfaithful to her husband, Kraken, yet she maintains the necessary social fiction of chastity. She even pretends to be the sole virgin among the Alcas.

Similarly, Queen Glamorgan tempts the pure monk Oddoul, who repulses her lascivious advances; for his chastity, he is disgraced; the "angel" Gudrune derides him as impotent; and a woman empties a chamber pot upon his head. So long as Glamorgan pretends to be chaste, she is socially accepted, no matter what may be her true morality. Other licentious women are safe from censure so long as they perform a role of conventional virtue. Examples include Queen Crucha, the fickle Viscountess Olive, and the adulterous Eveline Ceres. The appearance, not the fact, of virtue is important for women to maintain.

Just as France contrasts the pretended with the actual condition of women's chastity, so he contrasts ideal with real social institutions. Ideally, the state is intended to protect the weak, but it protects the powerful. To conceal abuses of power, social institutions employ fictions that make them appear benevolent. Even in heaven, among a council of the blessed, Saint Augustine argues that it is form, not substance, that matters. Saint Gal agrees that in the signs of religion and

the laws of salvation, "form necessarily prevails over essence." Among people, the national state, created by brute force, employs laws to formalize its power. The monk Bullock interprets the actions of a madman who bites the nose of his adversary as a sign of the creation of law; the murderer of a farmer, similarly, he condones as one who establishes the right of property. Taxes take money from the poor but never a proportionate share from the rich. The modern national state, according to France, is nothing more than an institution to consolidate wealth and, through warfare, to extend its influence.

Trinco (Napoleon) is the great hero of Penguinia because he creates an empire, no matter the cost. "Glory never costs too much," says a patriotic guide to young Djambi. Patriotism itself becomes formulaic. As Colonel Marchand observes, the armies of all nations are "the finest in the world"; so every nation must use its military force to test its strength. The Prince des Boscenos cynically argues that just causes, to triumph, need force. Thus, the national powers mobilize not to protect the weak but to support the mighty.

In the celebrated book 6, "The Affair of the Eighty Thousand Trusses of Hay," France shows how the Dreyfus case demonstrates in microcosm the abuses of institutional power. All the institutions of the state and of society—the government bureaucracy, the military, the Church—oppose Pyrot (Dreyfus). At first, only his Jewish relatives, seven hundred strong, dare to support his just cause. Later, the courageous writer Colomban (Émile Zola), along with liberals of different persuasions, join the battle as Pyrotists. They fight not only against falsehood (the count de Maubec has never delivered the eighty thousand trusses of hay, so Pyrot could not have stolen the lot), but also against prejudice and tradition. As Father Cornemuse puts the matter, Pyrot must be guilty, because he has been convicted; and the courts must be defended even if they are corrupt. Only after Justice Chaussepied examines the alleged evidence against the defendant—732 square yards of debris containing not a shred of proof, not a single word about the accused—does he declare the case a farce. Yet Justice Chaussepied's correct ruling results not so much from a recognition of the truth as from expediency; if he had allowed the folly to continue, the Pyrot case would have destroyed the political institutions of the state. Thus, the author once again drives home his point: People are slaves to customs and conventions. In *Penguin Island*, France shows how little headway reason, honesty, and justice make against these ancient stumbling blocks to progress.

"Critical Evaluation" by Leslie B. Mittleman

Further Reading

"Anatole France." *PMLA* 115, no. 5 (October, 2000). This overview describes the nature of France's works, compares him with other French writers, and assesses his literary influence and contributions to the history of French literature.

Auchincloss, Louis. "Anatole France." In *Writers and Personality*. Columbia: University of South Carolina Press, 2005. Novelist Auchincloss's observations about writers' personalities, including that of France. The chapter on France discusses how his personality and character are reflected in his fiction.

Bresky, Dushan. *The Art of Anatole France*. The Hague, the Netherlands: Mouton, 1969. A critical overview of France's work, with discussion of France's place within the French literary tradition. Includes sections on humor, utopianism, and questions of aesthetics.

Kennett, W. T. E. "The Theme of *Penguin Island*." *Romantic Review* 33, no. 3 (October, 1942): 275-289. Traces the theme of France's *Penguin Island*, an imaginary place populated by penguins, in the context of romantic European travelogue literature since the Renaissance.

May, James Lewis. *Anatole France: The Man and His Work: An Essay in Critical Biography*. 1924. Reprint. Port Washington, N.Y.: Kennikat Press, 1970. Profiles France's formative influences in the first half of the book, followed by critical discussions of France's works.

Stewart, Herbert Leslie. *Anatole France, the Parisian*. 1927. Reprint. Freeport, N.Y.: Books for Libraries Press, 1972. Correlates elements in France's works to specific personal, cultural, and philosophical influences. Emphasizes France's humanism and its effect on his work. Contains many anecdotes and pertinent quotations.

Virtanen, Reino. *Anatole France*. New York: Twayne, 1968. A chronologically arranged critical perspective on France's body of work. Traces the writer's debts to earlier satirists.

Wilson, Edmund. "Decline of the Revolutionary Tradition: Anatole France." In *To the Finland Station: A Study in the Writing and Acting of History*. 1940. Reprint. New York: New York Review of Books, 2003. Examines socialist, communist, and other revolutionary ideas advanced by writers, philosophers, and politicians from the French Revolution through the Russian Revolution. The chapter on France includes a discussion of his writing.

Penrod

Author: Booth Tarkington (1869-1946)
First published: 1914
Type of work: Novel
Type of plot: Comedy
Time of plot: Early twentieth century, before World War I
Locale: American Midwest, probably Indiana

Principal characters:
PENROD SCHOFIELD, an eleven-year-old boy
MRS. SCHOFIELD, his beleaguered and discouraged mother
MR. HENRY SCHOFIELD, his father
MARGARET SCHOFIELD, his nineteen-year-old sister
DUKE, his faithful old dog
SAM WILLIAMS, his best friend
MARJORIE JONES, his beautiful classmate and object of admiration
MAURICE LEVY, his well-behaved rival
HERMAN and VERMAN, his younger followers

The Story:

Penrod, who would rather hide in the haystall writing bloody adventure stories, is obligated to appear in a children's pageant as the Child Sir Lancelot. To further his humiliation, his mother and sister dress him for the performance in a silk bodice, stockings, and his father's flannel underwear. Ridiculed by fellow cast members Maurice and Marjorie, he appropriates and dons a pair of the janitor's capacious overalls, which brings down the house and ruins the pageant.

Penrod uses his Sunday School money to buy candy and attend a lurid cinematic melodrama about the evils of drink. Caught daydreaming in school, he attempts to excuse his inattention by describing the film's events as factual and pertaining to his visiting aunt and cousin. His mother hears about the story and demands that her husband suitably punish their son.

Before dancing class adjourns for the summer, a cotillion is planned for the children to demonstrate their manners and dancing skills. Penrod aspires to invite Marjorie to be his partner, but Maurice beats him to it. He is subsequently turned down by eleven other girls, leaving only an eight-year-old who sobs when he asks her. Penrod and his friend Sam plan revenge on Maurice by concocting a mixture of hair tonic, outdated smallpox medicine, and mouthwash and selling it to Maurice as "lickrish water." The potion makes Duke ill, but, inexplicably, Maurice enjoys the drink with no ill effects. Penrod then gets out of attending the dance by pretending to fall off the barn roof.

Two young African American brothers named Herman and Verman catch a raccoon and proudly sport deformities, such as having an amputated finger and being tongue-tied. Penrod and Sam stage a sideshow featuring these boys, the raccoon, some rats, and a dachshund. Posters and publicity bring several neighborhood children to the show, for which Penrod acts as ringleader. When attendance at subsequent shows lags and a rich boy sneers, Penrod adds this boy to the attractions, noting that his surname is the same as that of a currently infamous murderess. Featuring him as the murderess's nephew attracts many customers to the show, until the boy's snobbish mother, incensed and threatening lawsuits, closes down the attraction. Penrod and Sam's mothers insist that their fathers punish the boys, but each father secretly slips his son a quarter instead.

Penrod sings loudly while his sister Margaret and her guitar-playing boyfriend Bob are trying to "spark." Bob gives Penrod a dollar to leave, and Penrod buys himself an old accordion and some candy with which to serenade and treat Marjorie, who is babysitting her younger brother. Penrod bribes the little boy and enjoys Marjorie's company. Penrod's father secretly throws away his accordion, whereupon Penrod attends a local carnival, buying and consuming enough junk food to make him very ill for three days. Margaret is as enraged as her parents are at Bob for having made possible Penrod's eating spree. She breaks up with him. Marjorie likewise snubs Penrod because her own little brother has gotten sick from swallowing the money Penrod gave him.

An older boy from a tough neighborhood, Rupe Collins, starts to hang out with Penrod, who begins to imitate Rupe's bullying speech and actions. Penrod becomes intolerable to his family and friends, encouraging Rupe to abuse Sam, until Herman and Verman leap to Sam's defense by attacking Rupe with a rake, a lawn-mower, and a scythe. Rupe runs home, and Penrod resumes his normal behavior.

When the barber calls him a "little gentleman," he puts Penrod in an ugly mood. The boy finds a kettle of tar, and when his friends, including Marjorie and her little brother,

also call him "little gentleman," a tar-filled free-for-all erupts. Margaret's new beau, the Reverend Mr. Kinosling, is visiting and inadvertently applies the same epithet to Penrod, whereupon Penrod fills the reverend's hat with tar. Later, sipping tea with the local ladies, the cleric contrasts Penrod's failings with the beautiful manners of young Georgie Bassett. Their attention is then drawn by Georgie climbing a tree and shouting such taboo words as "hell," following Penrod's imitation of a revivalist preacher.

On Penrod's twelfth birthday, his great-aunt gives him his father's old slingshot. He meets a sophisticated and forward young lady named Fanchon, who elicits a promise that Penrod will dance with her at his birthday party. Marjorie also attends the party, where Fanchon teaches the children a scandalous new dance step. She becomes jealous of the attention Fanchon is commanding and slaps Penrod, removing him from the dance floor. All the other children are later punished for participating in the new dance, except for Penrod, whose parents are proud of his restraint. Penrod breaks a window with the slingshot but is pardoned by his father, who remembers his own boyhood. Penrod then finds a love note from Marjorie: "Your my Bow."

Critical Evaluation:

Penrod is an archetypal boy, resembling the earlier Tom Sawyer and the later Charlie Brown and Dennis the Menace, with his long-suffering dog, parents, friends, enemies, and an inability to avoid getting into trouble no matter what he attempts. Booth Tarkington writes ironically, but not without nostalgia and a certain amount of sentiment, about the unwritten code of conduct that sets boys at odds with all attempts to acculturate them into polite society.

Tarkington's technique of tongue-in-cheek understatement adds to the humor of Penrod's adventures, which are written to appeal to adults as well as children. While many of the situations and much of the dialogue (including the use of racial epithets) are dated, the central theme is timeless: boys yearning for excitement and accomplishment among their peers, while dodging their parents' and teachers' efforts to tame them. *Penrod* evokes small-town Americana in an age before electronic media and organized sports, when children spent most of their free time outdoors, using their imaginations to create their own entertainment. The children's blunt honesty frequently exposes the self-serving hypocrisy of the adults around them, as does their unwitting parody of adult behavior. Penrod is frequently punished for doing the same things, for the same reasons, that adults do, only with less subterfuge and finesse. Thus, the novel comments on the human tendency to think the best of oneself and one's actions, accord undeserved and sometimes begrudging respect to the rich and powerful at the expense of the hapless poor, and cover up mistakes by blaming others.

Some racial characterizations used in the chapters about Herman and Verman require comment. In Tarkington's time, many such terms were not overtly pejorative, as they are today, but descriptive, and they are used in the text without rancor, except by the bully Rupe Collins. The obvious poverty of these boys and their family, with their untreated physical deformities and imprisoned father, evokes sympathy from current readers but is treated matter-of-factly by Penrod, who shamelessly exploits the boys in his sideshow as "savages" and "wild animals." However, he considers them playmates and friends. It is not clear whether or not "Verman," as a homophone of "vermin," is intended to ridicule the ignorance of the boys' parents. Of more serious concern is the chapter "Coloured Troops in Action," in which Herman and Verman attack Rupe "in their simple, direct African way." Here, Tarkington describes the boys as "beings in . . . lower stages of evolution" as compared to Penrod and Sam, "two blanched, slightly higher products of evolution." This Darwinian justification for racial discrimination is an element of Tarkington's writing that, while mirroring the attitudes prevalent a century ago, is inconsistent with twenty-first century sensibilities.

Worthy of note is the neat parallelism in the chapters where Penrod plays both the role of the unwanted younger brother in the way of his sister's suitor and that of the suitor trying to get rid of his own girlfriend's younger brother. Penrod's singing is obnoxious to Bob, who gives him money to go away; Mitchy-Mitch's crying is obnoxious to Penrod, who likewise pays off the little boy to keep him quiet. Both younger brothers become sick as a result of this ploy, by inappropriate eating, which results in both young women rejecting their admirers. Besides humor, the result of this parallel construction is a tacit comment on the universality of the roles humans play and the stories they enact from generation to generation. This, along with other recognizable boyhood events and feelings, elevates *Penrod* from amusing storytelling to profundity and earns its place among other classics of American literature.

Sally B. Palmer

Further Reading

Anderson, David M. "The Boy's World of Booth Tarkington." *Society for the Study of Midwestern Literature Newsletter* 5 (1975): 35-42. Discussion of the settings of *Penrod* and Tarkington's other novels.

Macaigne, Bernard. "From Tom Sawyer to Penrod: The Child in American Popular Literature, 1870-1910." *Revue Française d'Etudes Americaines* 8, no. 17 (May, 1983): 319-331. Discussion of how children, especially boys, are represented in U.S. popular fiction of the late nineteenth and early twentieth century.

Sanders, Scott. Introduction to *Penrod*, by Booth Tarkington. Bloomington: Indiana University Press, 1985. Sheds light on the context in which the novel was written and published, as well as its place in literary history.

Sargent, Robert S., Jr. "Booth Tarkington and *Penrod*." *Enter Stage Right*, June 14, 2004. An article on the author and his character.

"Tarkington on *Penrod*." *The New York Times*, September 8, 1918. Contains Tarkington's comments on the setting and character of the novel.

Pensées

Author: Blaise Pascal (1623-1662)
First published: 1670 (English translation, 1688)
Type of work: Philosophy

Blaise Pascal, scientist and mathematician, became a member of the society of Port Royal after his conversion following a mystical experience in 1654. He was actively involved in the bitter debate between the Jansenists, with whom he allied himself, and the Jesuits; the series of polemical letters titled *Lettres provinciales* (1656-1657; *The Provincial Letters*; 1657) is the result of that great quarrel. Wanting to write a defense of Roman Catholic Christianity that would appeal to people of reason and sensibility, Pascal, about 1660, began to prepare his defense of the Catholic faith.

Like many other great thinkers whose concern was more with the subject of their compositions than with the external order and completeness of the presentation, he failed to complete a continuous and unified apology. When he died at the age of thirty-nine he left little more than his notes for the projected work, a series of philosophical fragments reflecting his religious meditations. These fragments form the *Pensées*. Despite its fragmentary character, the book is a classic of French literature, charming and effective in its style, powerful and sincere in its philosophic and religious protestations.

Philosophers distinguish themselves either by the insight of their claims or by the power of their justification. Paradoxically, Pascal distinguishes himself in his defense by the power of his claims. This quality is partly a matter of style and partly a matter of conviction. It was Pascal, in the *Pensées*, who wrote, "The heart has its reasons, which reason does not know," by which he meant not that emotion is superior to reason, but that in being compelled by a moving experience one submits to a superior kind of reason. Pascal also wrote that "All our reasoning reduces itself to yielding to feeling," but he admitted that it is sometimes difficult to distinguish between feeling and fancy. Pascal believed that the way to truth is through the heart and feeling, and that intuitive knowledge is the most important, not only because feeling or intuition is what leads the mind but also because it is essential to all reasoning, providing the first principles of thought. Much of the value of the *Pensées* results from the clarity with which Pascal presented his intuitive thoughts.

A considerable portion of the *Pensées* is taken up with a discussion of philosophical method, particularly in relation to religious reflection. The book begins with an analysis of the difference between mathematical and intuitive thinking and continues the discussion, in later sections, by considering the value of skepticism, of contradictions, of feeling, memory, and imagination. A number of passages remind the reader that a proposition that seems true from one perspective may seem false from another, but Pascal insists that "essential" truth is "altogether pure and altogether true." The power of skepticism and the use of contradictions in reasoning depend upon a conception of human thinking that ignores the importance of perspective in determining one's belief. Thus, from the skeptic's point of view nothing is known because people can be sure of nothing. The skeptic forgets, however, that "It is good to be tired and wearied by the vain search after the true good, that we may stretch out our arms to the Redeemer." Contradiction, according to Pascal, "is a bad sign of truth" since there are some certainties that have been contradicted and some false ideas that have not. Contradiction nevertheless has its use: "All these contradictions, which

seem most to keep me from the knowledge of religion, have led me most quickly to the true one."

Pascal had the gift of responding critically in a way that added value to both his own discourse and that of his opponent. Criticizing Michel Eyquem de Montaigne's skepticism, he came to recognize the truth—a partial truth, to be sure—of much that Montaigne wrote. His acknowledgment of this is grudging; he writes that "It is not in Montaigne, but in myself, that I find all that I see in him," and also "What good there is in Montaigne can only have been acquired with difficulty." As T. S. Eliot points out in an introduction to the *Pensées*, however, Pascal uses many of Montaigne's ideas, phrases, and terms.

Perhaps the most controversial part of the *Pensées* is Pascal's section on miracles. He quotes Saint Augustine as saying that he would not have been a Christian but for the miracles, and he argues that there are three marks of religion: perpetuity, a good life, and miracles. He writes, "If the cooling of love leaves the Church almost without believers, miracles will rouse them," and "Miracles are more important than you think. They have served for the foundation, and will serve for the continuation of the Church till Anti-christ, till the end." Although there are other passages that assert the importance of faith and that are in no way dependent upon miracles for their assertions (for example, "That we must love one God only is a thing so evident, that it does not require miracles to prove it"), Pascal seems unambiguously to assert that miracles are a way to faith. This idea is opposed by those who insist that belief in miracles presupposes a belief in God and the Gospel. Pascal had been profoundly affected by a miracle at Port Royal, but his defense of the importance of miracles goes beyond that immediate reference, using appeals to reason and authority as well as to feeling.

Pascal's "Proofs of Jesus Christ" is interesting not only because it pretends to offer demonstrations to appeal to unbelievers, but also because it uses persuasive references that throw light on the question of Jesus' historical status. He argues that it is because of the actions of unbelievers at the time of Christ that the faithful have witnesses to Him. If Jesus had made His nature so evident that none could mistake it, the proof of His nature and existence would not have been as convincing as it is when reported by unbelievers. Pascal emphasizes the function of the Jews as unbelievers when he writes,

The Jews, in slaying Him in order not to receive Him as the Messiah, have given Him the final proof of being the Messiah. And in continuing not to recognize Him, they made themselves irreproachable witnesses.

Pascal's famous wager is presented in the *Pensées*. He makes an appeal to "natural lights"—ordinary human intelligence and good sense. God either exists or He does not. How shall you decide? This is a game with infinitely serious consequences. You must wager, but how shall you wager? Reason is of no use here. Suppose you decide to wager that God exists. "If you gain, you gain all; if you lose, you lose nothing." Pascal concludes that there is everything to be said in favor of committing oneself to a belief in God and strong reasons against denying God. To the objection that one cannot come to believe simply by recognizing that one will be extremely fortunate if one is right and no worse off if one is wrong, Pascal replies by saying that if an unbeliever will act as if he (or she) believes, and if he wants to believe, belief will come to him.

This wager later inspired William James's *The Will to Believe, and Other Essays in Popular Philosophy* (1897), in which the American pragmatist argued that Pascal's method is essentially pragmatic. James's objection to Pascal's wager is that the wager alone presents no momentous issue; unless one can relate the particular issue being considered to a person's great concerns, the appeal of the wager is empty. If such proof would work for Pascal's God, it would work for any god whatsoever. James's use of the wager to justify passional decisions, however, is much like that of Pascal.

In a section titled "The Fundamentals of the Christian Religion," Pascal writes that the Christian religion teaches two truths: that there is a God whom people can know and that because of their corruption people are unworthy of Him. Pascal rejected cold conceptions of God that reduce Him to the author of mathematical truths or of the order of the elements. For Pascal, the God of salvation has to be conceived as He is known through Jesus Christ. The Christian God can be known, according to Pascal, but since people are corrupt they do not always know God. Nature assists God to hide Himself from corrupt people, although it also contains perfections to show that nature is the image of God.

In considering "The Philosophers," Pascal emphasizes thought as distinguishing people from brutes and making the greatness of humanity possible. "Man is neither angel nor brute," he writes, "and the unfortunate thing is that he who would act the angel acts the brute."

Pascal was on the one hand eager to defend the Christian faith and on the other hand determined to indicate the shortcomings of humanity. He is remorselessly critical in his attacks on skeptics, atheists, and other critics of the Church, not simply because they err, but because they do so without respect for the possibilities of human understanding or the values of religion. In regard to skepticism he wrote that his thoughts were intentionally without order to be true to the disorderly character of his subject.

It is not Pascal the bitter critic who prevails in the *Pensées*; it is, rather, the impassioned and inspired defender of the faith. Even those who do not share his convictions admire his style and the ingenuity of his thought, and much that is true of all humanity has never been better said than in the *Pensées*.

Further Reading

Adamson, Donald. *Blaise Pascal: Mathematician, Physicist, and Thinker About God*. New York: St. Martin's Press, 1995. Explores how Pascal dealt with the insights and conflicts produced by his mathematical, scientific, and religious experiences.

Hammond, Nicholas. *Playing with Truth: Language and the Human Condition in Pascal's "Pensées."* New York: Oxford University Press, 1994. Scholarly, readable discussion of the role that human language plays in argumentation, especially as it relates to the human condition as addressed by Pascal. Includes a thorough bibliography and an index.

_____, ed. *The Cambridge Companion to Pascal*. New York: Cambridge University Press, 2003. Fourteen essays provide an overview of Pascal's life and work, including discussions of grace and religious belief in his writings, *Pensées* and the "art of persuasion," and the reception of *Pensées* in the seventeenth and eighteenth centuries.

Jordan, Jeff, ed. *Gambling on God: Essays on Pascal's Wager*. Lanham, Md.: Rowman & Littlefield, 1994. Pascal scholars explain and evaluate the most controversial features of Pascal's philosophy of religion.

Kolakowski, Lezek. *God Owes Us Nothing: A Brief Remark on Pascal's Religion and on the Spirit of Jansenism*. Chicago: University of Chicago Press, 1995. An important philosopher of religion reflects on the main points of Pascal's views about faith and the relationship between God and humankind.

Loevlie, Elisabeth Marie. *Literary Silences in Pascal, Rousseau, and Beckett*. New York: Clarendon Press, 2003. Examines Pascal's *Pensées* and works by philosopher Jean-Jacques Rousseau and writer Samuel Beckett to describe how their texts use silence to "say the unsayable."

Marvin, Richard O'Connell. *Blaise Pascal: Reasons of the Heart*. Grand Rapids, Mich.: W. B. Eerdmans, 1997. A worthwhile discussion of Pascal's efforts to reconcile the demands of human rationality and the yearnings of feeling and hope, especially as the latter are expressed religiously.

Melzer, Sara E. *Discourses of the Fall: A Study of Pascal's "Pensées."* Berkeley: University of California Press, 1986. Critical discussion of the major dilemma in *Pensées*, that is, a strong claim for belief in a transcendent God (although limited by human language and understanding) set against an element of uncertainty.

Rogers, Ben. *Pascal.* New York: Routledge, 1999. An excellent biographical introduction to the thoughts of the phi-losopher, clearly presented and requiring no special background. Includes a bibliography.

Wetsel, David. *Pascal and Disbelief: Catechesis and Conversion in the "Pensees."* Washington, D.C.: Catholic University of America Press, 1994. A helpful discussion of Pascal's approach to an affirmative religious faith, which Pascal develops and defends in a context of skepticism.

The People, Yes

Author: Carl Sandburg (1878-1967)
First published: 1936
Type of work: Poetry

Although Carl Sandburg wrote *The People, Yes* during the Great Depression of the 1930's, his strong voice remained as cheerful and reassuring to later ages as it was in the time of bread lines and soup kitchens. However, in this work Sandburg does not raise his voice to shout down the pessimists, he does not sing hymns to America out of a sense of duty. His book arises from a genuine love of plain people who will somehow survive their blunders, somehow find the answers to where to? and what next?

Sandburg asks these questions in the opening in the voices of children of workers who come to build the Tower of Babel, and the questions are still unanswered at the end, when the poet looks forward to the "Family of Man" and the time when "brother may yet line up with brother." Between those two points, the poet pays his tribute to people, the American people in particular, as he presents the legends, sayings, slang, tall tales, and dreams of twentieth century America.

The best and most quoted sections of the work include the one that deals with Abraham Lincoln and the one about tall tales, beginning "They have yarns. . . ." Sandburg gained a solid reputation as an authority on Lincoln, having written a great biography and many poems, speeches, and articles about Lincoln, but nowhere is he more successful than in this short poem. Here, Sandburg presents the many talents of a great person by asking questions, such as "Lincoln? was he a poet?" and "Lincoln? was he a historian?" to which he supplies answers from speeches, letters, and conversations of the man himself. The tall-tales poem is an encyclopedia of laughs that range from the familiar "man who drove a swarm of bees across the Rocky Mountains and the Desert 'and didn't lose a bee'" to the less familiar story of a shipwrecked sailor who has caught hold of a stateroom door and floated in near the coast; when his would-be rescuers tell him he is off the coast of New Jersey, he takes a fresh hold on the door and calls back "half-wearily, 'I guess I'll float a little farther.'"

Much of *The People, Yes* is in this same lighthearted tone, for Sandburg loves the American language and the twists of its sayings. For irony, he quotes from a memorial stone: "We, near whose bones you stand, were Iroquois./ The wide land which is now yours, was ours./ Friendly hands have given us back enough for a tomb." He offers such homespun wisdom as "Sell the buffalo hide after you have killed the buffalo" and "The coat and the pants do the work but the vest gets the gravy." There are scores of other wisecracks and jokes, some new and some that wink at the reader like old friends from childhood.

Sandburg filled his book with American people—the real, the legendary, and the anonymous. Among the real ones are John Brown, "who was buried deep and didn't stay so"; Mr. Eastman, "the kodak king," who at the age of seventy-seven shot himself to avoid the childishness of senility; and the Wright brothers, who "wanted to fly for the sake of flying." The legends include Mike Fink, John Henry, and Paul Bunyan, to whom Sandburg devotes a whole section, explaining how the people created this Master Lumberjack, his Seven Axmen, and his Little Blue Ox. Of the anonymous, there are hundreds, and Sandburg pays tribute to them all, from the person who first said, "Wedlock is a padlock" to the one who first remarked, "No peace on earth with the women, no life anywhere without them."

By no means does Sandburg consistently handle the American people with kid gloves of gentleness and affection.

When he feels so inclined, he puts on the six-ounce gloves of a prizefighter (as he often did since his *Chicago Poems* first appeared in 1916) and flails away at what he hates: the liars who do not care what they do to their customers so long as they make a sale; the torturers and the wielders of the rubber hose; the cynics who shrug off the unemployed; the crooked lawyers; the judges who can be bought and the men who boast that they can buy them; and, most of all, the "misleaders," who spit out the word "peepul" as if it were scum hocked from their throats.

Of Sandburg's many books, both prose and poetry, *The People, Yes* comes closest to being his coda, the summing up of what he tried to say in a lifetime. As if to indicate as much, he includes echoes from earlier poems. There is the hyacinths-biscuits combination that appeared first in one of his most famous definitions of poetry; he mentions the Unknown Soldier, "the boy nobody knows the name of"; and he includes the refrain from his "Four Preludes on Playthings of the Wind": "We are the greatest city, the greatest people. Nothing like us ever was." Certainly the themes in this book are the same as those running through all of his poetry, his love of America and its democracy, the mystery of human beings and where they are going, the hope that people everywhere will someday blunder through the fogs of injustice, hypocrisy, and skulduggery into a bright world of peace. Sandburg put it all in *The People, Yes*, and expressed it there in the fluent style that is so very much his own. Not many American poets had a better ear for the right combination of words, and certainly not many could match his ability at writing dialogue, at putting on paper the way Americans really talk.

As in all books, there are caution signs for the reader to observe. No one should try to read *The People, Yes* at one sitting. It is not a narrative poem with suspense enough to carry the reader breathless to the end. Some sections are repetitious, and in places the Whitmanesque cataloging drones on monotonously. Instead, this is writing to be dipped into, savored for a time, put aside, and taken up again when one's sense of humor is drooping or faith in humanity needs restoring.

Further Reading

Arenstein, J. D. "Carl Sandburg's Biblical Roots." *ANQ* 16, no. 2 (Spring, 2003): 54-60. Examines the biblical roots of *The People, Yes*, describing how the story is Sandburg's retelling of the Tower of Babel tale from Genesis. Discusses Sandburg's concordance with Proverbs in his works.

Benét, William Rose. "Memoranda on Americans." *Saturday Review of Literature* 14, no. 17 (August 22, 1936). Written at the time of the publication of *The People, Yes*, this dated but helpful review discusses the work as a mélange and criticizes it for a lack of cohesiveness and depth. Provides a starting point for a comparison of the early criticisms of Sandburg's works with later discussions.

Beyers, Chris. "Carl Sandburg's Unnatural Relations." *Essays in Literature* 22, no. 1 (Spring, 1995): 97-112. Discusses the critical interpretations of Sandburg's literary works, describing critics' emphasis on the influence of Sandburg's public life on his poetry. Examines the literary techniques used in Sandburg's poems.

Crowder, Richard. "The People and the Union." In *Carl Sandburg*. New York: Twayne, 1964. Discusses Sandburg's skill as a writer, the development of the concept of *The People, Yes*, and how the work exemplifies the culmination of the poet's career. Focuses on the importance of the book to sociologists and historians as a handbook of folk literature.

Duffey, Bernard. "Carl Sandburg and the Undetermined Land." *Centennial Review* 23 (Summer, 1979): 295-303. A reevaluation of Sandburg as being more than merely a sentimental or populist poet. Discusses Sandburg's poetry as an authentic voice with a wholeness of perception rooted in identification with the American people.

Golden, Harry. *Carl Sandburg*. 1961. New ed. Urbana: University of Illinois Press, 1988. Examines Sandburg's personality and how it relates to his writing. Includes a discussion of *The People, Yes* as a poetic definition of the elemental forces of love, death, life, and work.

Murcia, Rebecca Thatcher. *Carl Sandburg*. Hockessin, Del.: Mitchell Lane, 2007. This biography, written for younger students, "profiles the revolutionary poet and author who lived as a hobo, served as a soldier, and worked as a political organizer." A compact and readable outline of Sandburg's life and times.

Reed, Brian M. "Carl Sandburg's *The People, Yes*, Thirties Modernism, and the Problem of Bad Political Poetry." *Texas Studies in Literature and Language* 46, no. 2 (Summer, 2004): 181-212. Argues that the poem fails to introduce an idea without belaboring it; maintains the poem lacks "the polish, complexity, variable tone, and layered ironies that typify most anthologized verse from the twentieth century."

Wooley, Lisa. "Carl Sandburg and Vachel Lindsay: Composite Voices of the Open Road." In *American Voices of the Chicago Renaissance*. DeKalb: Northern Illinois University Press, 2000. Describes how the two poets use language to convey simplicity, democracy, and Americanness—characteristics associated with Chicago's literary renaissance

Pepita Jiménez

Author: Juan Valera (1824-1905)
First published: Pepita Ximenez, 1874 (English
    translation, 1886)
Type of work: Novel
Type of plot: Psychological realism
Time of plot: c. 1870
Locale: Andalusia, Spain

Principal characters:
LUIS DE VARGAS, a student for the priesthood
DON PEDRO DE VARGAS, his father
PEPITA JIMÉNEZ, a young widow
ANTOÑONA, her housekeeper and duenna
COUNT DE GENAZAHAR, a designing nobleman

The Story:

On March 22, four days after returning to his home in
Andalusia, Luis de Vargas writes the first of his letters to his
uncle and favorite professor at the seminary. He reports that
his father intends to fatten him up during his vacation, to have
him ready to return in the fall to finish his training for the
priesthood. He mentions in passing that his father is courting
a twenty-year-old, attractive widow, Pepita Jiménez; his
father is fifty-five years old. Pepita had been married for
only a short time to an eighty-year-old moneylender named
Gumersindo. Luis is not eager to see his father marry again,
but he promises his uncle not to judge Pepita before he knows
her.

Luis' next letter, dated six days later, reports that he is already tired of the little town and anxious to get back to
school. In the meantime, he meets Pepita. Having decided
that she pays too much attention to the body and not enough
to the spirit, he cannot understand why the local vicar holds
so high an opinion of her. He hopes, however, that she will
have a good effect on his somewhat unsettled father.

In his next letter, Luis continues to criticize Pepita for her
coquetry toward his father. He tries to forgive her vanity
about her pretty hands by remarking that Saint Teresa had exhibited the same fault. In closing, he apologizes for not at
once fleeing the life that seems to be making a materialist of
him, but his father begged him to stay on a while longer.

In a letter dated April 14, Luis expresses concern over
Pepita's diabolic power, shown by the manner in which she
charms both his father and the vicar, and makes him write
more about her than about others in the town. Meanwhile, his
time is so occupied that it is May 4 before he writes again to
describe a picnic his father had given for Pepita. Luis had ridden a mule. While the others rode or played games, he stayed
behind to chat with the vicar and an old lady, an experience
more boring than he had believed possible. When he took a
walk and met Pepita alone, he could not understand his
strange excitement. She reproved him for being too serious
for his age and remarked that only very old people like the

vicar traveled by mule. That night, Luis tells his father that he
wants to learn to ride a horse.

In later letters Luis describes his embarrassment during
evening gatherings at Pepita's house, where he always feels
out of place. Nevertheless, he does enjoy his riding lessons
and the thrill of riding past her balcony on the day his father
decides he can ride well enough to do so. He later confesses
to his uncle that he is disturbed in his feelings over Pepita,
and as a result he has stopped going to her house. He thinks
that he would be wise to return to the seminary at once.

Luis is still more perplexed when Antoñona, Pepita's
housekeeper, scolds him for making her mistress unhappy.
When Luis calls to apologize and explain, the sight of tears in
Pepita's eyes upsets him, and before he knows it he kisses
her. Certain that he must leave as soon as possible, he tells his
father that he intends to depart on June 25, immediately after
the Midsummer Eve celebration. He ends his letter with assurances that his uncle will be seeing him within a week.

Five days after Luis' last letter, Pepita summons the vicar
to her house. She wants to confess that she no longer loves
Don Pedro because she has fallen in love with his son. Convinced that Luis loves her also without knowing it, she intends to keep him from carrying out his plans to become a
priest. The scandalized vicar orders her to remain engaged to
the father and lets Luis go away as he had planned. Pepita
promises. No one, however, could force Antoñona to keep
such a promise. She determines to take a hand in the situation.

In the Vargas household, meanwhile, Don Pedro worries
about his moping son and at last urges the boy's young
cousin, Currito, to engage Luis in some activity. Luis goes
with his cousin to the casino, where the Count de Genazahar
is among the gamblers. Having borrowed five thousand pese-
tas from Gumersindo, he had tried, after the old man's death,
to cancel the debt by marrying Pepita. Her curt refusal had
made him hate her. At the casino that night, Luis overhears
some of his slighting remarks about the young widow.

Antoñona visits Luis again and accuses him of behaving discourteously toward her mistress. Luis protests that he, too, is unhappy but that it is his duty to return to the seminary. Antoñona insists that he must first set things right with Pepita, so he promised to go to her house at ten o'clock that night. The streets would be full of Midsummer Eve revelers, and no one would notice him.

After Antoñona's departure, he regrets his promise, but he goes anyway. His talk with Pepita is long and difficult. Each make self-accusations. At last, sobbing, Pepita runs to her bedroom. Luis follows her. When he comes out, he is convinced that he is not among the men of whom priests are made. On his way home, seeing the Count de Genazahar in the casino, he stops. Declaring that he no longer wears his religious robe, he announces that he has beaten the count at cards.

During a long run of luck, he had won all the count's money. When the Count de Genazahar had wished to continue, Luis insultingly answered his promise to pay later by reminding him that he had failed to pay his debt to Gumersindo's widow. The count had challenged him to a duel and called for sabers. The fight was brief and bloody, and both men were wounded. Currito and a friend had taken Luis home to his worried father.

Alone with Don Pedro, Luis tries to confess that he is now his father's rival for Pepita's affections. Don Pedro merely laughs, and from his pocket he takes two letters. One from his brother in the seminary says that he feels Luis has no calling for the priesthood and would do better to remain at home. The other is Don Pedro's answer. Having realized that Pepita's affection had shifted to Luis, he would be happy in watching their happiness. He invites his brother to marry the young lovers.

The dean refuses the invitation, but a month later, after Luis' wounds have healed, the village vicar marries them. Don Pedro gives a splendid reception. Although it is local custom to serenade with cowbells anyone marrying a second time, the town thinks so highly of Luis and his bride that they are allowed to steal away without the embarrassing celebration.

Recovering after five months in bed, the count pays part of his debt and arranges to pay the remainder. After the birth of their son, Luis and Pepita take a trip abroad. For many years they and their farms prosper, and all goes well with them.

Critical Evaluation:

Naturalism and realism were the two literary currents in vogue when Juan Valera decided to write his first novel. Valera felt a profound antipathy for naturalism, with its emphasis on what he considered the gross and the vulgar, and he disliked realism for its lack of imagination. He believed that a good novel must be both inventive and amusing. Searching for an alternative to either naturalism or realism, he decided on a new form, the psychological novel. His work remains within the general framework of realism, but unlike his contemporaries, Valera describes an interior reality rather than the objective reality.

Valera, considered to be one of the three most important novelists of nineteenth century Spain (along with José María de Pereda and Benito Pérez Galdós), was also one of the major literary critics of that period. He was born into Spanish aristocracy, studied law and religion, was an elected deputy in congress, and had a long career as a diplomat, serving as an ambassador to Vienna and as a minister in Lisbon, Washington, D.C., and Brussels. Valera first received critical acclaim for his essays, which covered a wide array of subjects. An important literary contribution was his psychological analysis of his characters. Although Valera attempted earlier novels (some of which appeared in serial form in newspapers), *Pepita Jiménez* is his first completed novel, and is regarded as his best.

Valera was an elegant and refined author. He is acknowledged as the foremost stylist in his language of the nineteenth century. He was a keen observer who studied human passions and feelings, and a master of the understated emotion. In general he created well-developed characters, using balanced, artificial language to add depth to his novels and draw out the relationship between the characters. A writer who used a contemporary setting to address the problems existing in his society, he believed that a novel could be credible and true to life without portraying the vulgar things common in the works of naturalistic authors. He was an admirer of form and beauty and believed that the purpose of art was to inspire and create beauty. These views, along with his opposition to didactic literature, set him apart from his contemporaries, who followed the tenets of naturalism and realism. Unlike many of his contemporaries who wrote for a living and had to follow the established trends, Valera's wealth enabled him to formulate and try out his own literary theories.

One example of Valera's literary independence is his use of local color. In his novels, the description of the beautiful Andalusian landscape often enhances the story line, while allowing the author to focus his attention on the psyche and to explore the emotions of his characters. In *Pepita Jiménez*, Valera uses his favorite theme of love in his psychological analysis of the main character, seminary student Luis de Vargas. This novel, which is written in the form of a series of letters, reveals Luis' inner thoughts and feelings through his correspondence with his uncle, the dean of a cathedral.

Valera incorporates other perspectives into *Pepita Jiménez*, too. In the introduction to the novel, the author claims to have found this manuscript among the personal papers of the dean of an unnamed cathedral. This is followed by letters written by Luis, his uncle, and his father. Taken together, these letters provide an analysis of Luis' growing attraction to the young widowed Pepita Jiménez and his resulting internal conflict between physical love and spiritual duty. The combination of the different perspectives is particularly important since they provide a more complete picture by which an accurate evaluation of Luis' situation may be made when Luis is incapable of discerning the truth about himself. The frame of the preliminary letters underscores the contrast between true mysticism and the main character's perception of it.

Valera draws heavily upon his knowledge about sixteenth century ascetic and mystical literature to expose Luis' false mysticism and to criticize the preparation of candidates for service in the priesthood. To do this, Valera uses irony and parody of the mystical experience to show how Luis has misinterpreted his calling. The young seminary student rationalizes and employs mystical language to hide his true feelings, confusing religious devotion and human passion. Believing himself to be blessed by God (an error of pride) and uplifted to the mystical experience, he is unprepared for life outside the safety of the seminary walls. Instead of experiencing the truth and goodness of God and the absorption into God's love, Luis gradually abandons his soul to Pepita, whose beauty has captivated him. Torn between his growing love for Pepita and his vows to enter the priesthood, Luis is forced to evaluate his feelings and finally realizes that he has not, in truth, been called to the priesthood. At first, Luis intends to follow through with his original plans to take up his vows rather than to admit his mistake and marry Pepita. Eventually, however, Luis acknowledges his error and, enchanted by Pepita and the sensual happiness of the Andalusian landscape, renounces his vows to marry the woman he loves.

"Critical Evaluation" by Pamela Peek

Further Reading

Bianchini, Andreina. "*Pepita Jiménez*: Ideology and Realism." *Hispanofila* 33, no. 2 (January, 1990): 33-51. An examination of the novel's ideology and its place in the realm of realist literature. Also discusses the three-part structure of the novel.

DeCoster, Cyrus C. *Juan Valera*. New York: Twayne, 1974. A good beginning resource for the study of Valera's works. Contains an overview of his life and literary career and analyzes his literary characters and themes. One chapter is devoted to *Pepita Jiménez*.

Franz, Thomas R. *Valera in Dialogue = In Dialogue with Valera: A Novelist's Work in Conversation with That of His Contemporaries and Successors*. New York: Peter Lang, 2000. Chronicles the debate between Valera and his contemporaries and chief rivals, Benito Pérez Galdós and Leopoldo Alas, over the aesthetics of Spanish realist fiction. Describes how this debate influenced the later writing of Miguel de Unamuno y Jugo and Ramón María del Valle-Inclán.

Lott, Robert. *Language and Psychology in "Pepita Jiménez."* Champaign: University of Illinois Press, 1970. A well-regarded study of the language and psychology in *Pepita Jiménez*. The first part of the book offers an analysis of language, style, and rhetorical devices, while the second section is a psychological examination of the characters.

MacCurdy, G. Grant. "Mysticism, Love, and Illumination in *Pepita Jiménez*." *Revista de Estudios Hispanicos* 17, no. 3 (October, 1983): 323-334. An original approach to studying Valera's treatment of the themes of mysticism, love and romance, and spiritual illumination.

Taylor, Teresia Langford. *The Representation of Women in the Novels of Juan Valera: A Feminist Critique*. New York: Peter Lang, 1997. Interprets Valera's novels from a feminist perspective, focusing on his representation of women and the novel's underlying patriarchal ideology. Includes bibliographical references and an index.

Trimble, Robert. *Chaos Burning on My Brow: Don Juan Valera in His Novels*. San Bernardino, Calif.: Borgo Press, 1995. A critical study of Valera's novels. Includes an index and a bibliography.

Turner, Harriet, and Adelaida López de Martínez, eds. *The Cambridge Companion to the Spanish Novel: From 1600 to the Present*. New York: Cambridge University Press, 2003. There are numerous references to Valera in this historical survey of the Spanish novel, but the most extensive consideration of his work is found in two chapters: "The Regional Novel: Evolution and Consolation" by Alison Sinclair and "The Realist Novel" by Harriet Turner.

Valle, José del. "Historical Linguistics and Cultural History: The Polemic Between Rufino José Cuervo and Juan Valera." In *The Battle over Spanish Between 1800 and 2000: Language Ideologies and Hispanic Intellectuals*, edited by Valle and Luis Gabriel-Stheeman. New York: Routledge, 2002. Recounts the debate between Valera and Cuervo, a nineteenth century Colombian writer and linguist, over issues pertaining to the Spanish language. Their debates helped shape national identity and Hispanic culture.

Père Goriot

Author: Honoré de Balzac (1799-1850)
First published: 1834-1835 (English translation, 1860)
Type of work: Novel
Type of plot: Naturalism
Time of plot: c. 1819
Locale: Paris

Principal characters:
PÈRE GORIOT, a boarder at the Maison Vauquer
COUNTESS ANASTASIE DE RESTAUD and BARONESS
  DELPHINE DE NUCINGEN, Goriot's daughters
EUGÈNE DE RASTIGNAC, a young law student
MADAME DE BEAUSÉANT, Rastignac's cousin
MONSIEUR VAUTRIN and VICTORINE TAILLEFER,
  Rastignac's fellow boarders

The Story:

There are many conjectures at Madame Vauquer's boardinghouse about the mysterious Monsieur Goriot. He had taken the choice rooms on the first floor when he first retired from his vermicelli business, and for a time his landlady had eyed him as a prospective husband. When, at the end of his second year at the Maison Vauquer, he asked to move to a cheap room on the second floor, rumor had it that he was an unsuccessful speculator, a miser, and a moneylender. The mysterious young women who flitted up to his rooms from time to time were said to be his mistresses, although he protested that they were his two daughters. The other boarders called him Père Goriot. At the end of the third year, Goriot moved to a still cheaper room on the third floor. By that time, he was the common butt of jokes at the boardinghouse table, and his daughters visited him only rarely.

One evening, the impoverished law student, Eugène de Rastignac, comes home late from the ball that his wealthy cousin, Madame de Beauséant, has given. Peeking through the keyhole of Goriot's door, he sees the old man molding silver plate into ingots. The next day, he hears his fellow boarder, Monsieur Vautrin, say that early in the morning he had seen Père Goriot selling a piece of silver to an old moneylender. What Vautrin does not know is that the money thus obtained is intended for Goriot's daughter, Countess Anastasie de Restaud, whom Eugène had met at the dance the night before.

That afternoon, Eugène pays his respects to the countess. Père Goriot is leaving the drawing room when he arrives. The countess, her lover, and her husband receive Eugène graciously because of his connections with Madame de Beauséant, but when he mentions that they have the acquaintance of Père Goriot in common, he is quickly shown to the door, the count leaving word with his servant that he is not to be at home if Monsieur de Rastignac calls again.

After this rebuff, Eugène calls on Madame de Beauséant to ask her aid in unraveling the mystery. She explains that de Restaud's house will be barred to him because both of Goriot's daughters, having been given sizable dowries, are gradually severing all connection with their father and therefore will not tolerate anyone who has knowledge of Goriot's shabby circumstances. She suggests that Eugène send word through Goriot to his other daughter, Delphine de Nucingen, that Madame de Beauséant will receive her. She knows that Delphine will welcome the invitation and will become Eugène's sponsor out of gratitude.

Vautrin has another suggestion for the young man. Under Madame Vauquer's roof lives Victorine Taillefer, who has been disinherited by her wealthy father in favor of her brother. Eugène has already found favor in her eyes, and Vautrin suggests that for 200,000 francs he will have the brother murdered, so that Eugène might marry the heir. Vautrin gives him two weeks to consider the offer.

The next evening, Eugène escorts Madame de Beauséant to the theater, where he is presented to Delphine de Nucingen, who receives him graciously. The next day he receives an invitation to dine with the de Nucingens and to accompany them to the theater. Before dinner, he and Delphine drive to a gambling house where, at her request, he gambles and wins six thousand francs. She explains that her husband will give her no money, and she needs it to pay a debt she owes to an old lover.

Before long, Eugène learns that it costs money to keep the company of his new friends. Unable to press his own family for funds, he will not stoop to impose on Delphine. Finally, as Vautrin had foreseen, he is forced to take his fellow boarder's offer. The tempter has just finished explaining the duel between Victorine's brother and his confederate, which is to take place the following morning, when Père Goriot comes in with the news that he and Delphine have taken an apartment for Eugène.

Eugène wavers once more at the thought of the crime that is about to be committed in his name. He attempts to send a warning to the victim through Père Goriot, but Vautrin, suspicious of his accomplice, thwarts the plan and drugs their wine at supper so that both sleep soundly that night.

At breakfast, Eugène's fears are realized. A messenger bursts in with the news that Victorine's brother has been fatally wounded in a duel. After the girl hurries off to see him, another singular event occurs. After drinking his coffee, Vautrin falls to the ground as if he has suffered a stroke. When he is carried to his room and undressed, it becomes clear from marks on his back that he must be the famous criminal Trompe-la-Mort. One of the boarders, an old woman, has been acting as an agent for the police; she has drugged Vautrin's coffee so that his criminal brand could be exposed. Shortly afterward the police appear to claim their victim.

Eugène and Père Goriot prepare to move to their new quarters, for Goriot is to have a room over the young man's apartment. Delphine arrives to interrupt Goriot's packing. She is in distress. Père Goriot has arranged with his lawyer to force de Nucingen to make a settlement so that Delphine will have an independent income on which to draw; now she brings the news that her money has been so tied up by investments it will be impossible for her husband to withdraw any of it without bringing about his own ruin.

Delphine just finishes telling her father of her predicament when Anastasie de Restaud drives up. She has sold the de Restaud diamonds to help her lover pay off his debts, and she has been discovered by her husband. De Restaud buys them back, but as punishment, he demands control of her dowry.

Eugène cannot help overhearing the conversation through the thin partition between the rooms; when Anastasie says that she still needs twelve thousand francs for her lover, he forges one of Vautrin's drafts for that amount and takes it to Père Goriot's room. Anastasie's reaction is to berate him for eavesdropping.

The financial difficulties of his daughters and the hatred and jealousy they have shown prove too much for Père Goriot. At the dinner table, he looks as if he is about to have a stroke, and when Eugène returns from an afternoon spent with Delphine, the old man is in bed, too ill to be moved to his new home. He had gone out that morning to sell his last few possessions, so that Anastasie might pay her dressmaker for an evening gown.

In spite of their father's serious condition, both daughters attend Madame de Beauséant's ball that evening, and Eugène is too much under his mistress's influence to refuse to accompany her. The next day, Goriot feels worse. Eugène tries to summon the daughters, but Delphine is still in bed and refuses to be hurried. Anastasie arrives at Père Goriot's bedside only after he has lapsed into a coma and no longer recognizes her.

Père Goriot is buried in a pauper's grave the next day. Eugène tries to borrow burial money from the daughters, but each sends word that they are in deep grief over their loss and cannot be seen. He and a poor medical student from the boardinghouse are the only mourners at the funeral. Anastasie and Delphine send their empty carriages to follow the coffin, their final tribute to their indulgent father.

Critical Evaluation:

Honoré de Balzac's writing career spanned thirty years, from the decisive point in 1819 when he elected to abandon the study of law until his untimely death in 1850. His work until 1829 consisted of novels, stories, and sketches on a variety of philosophical and social themes. They are, on the whole, undistinguished; Balzac later averred that the decade from 1819 until he began work on *Les Chouans* in 1829 constituted his apprenticeship in the art of fiction. Certainly, the works of the last twenty years of his life show the benefits of that long period of development, in both stylistic and tonal precision and in general weight and narrative direction.

Many critics contend that the generative idea for the seventeen-volume *La Comédie humaine* (1829-1848; *The Human Comedy*, 1895-1896, 1911) came to Balzac as he was writing *Père Goriot*, in part because in the manuscript the name of the young student is Massiac, until, in the scene of the afternoon call at Madame de Beauséant's house, "Massiac" is abruptly scratched out and "Rastignac" inserted. The character Eugène de Rastignac had appeared in a minor role in *La Peau de chagrin* (1831; *The Wild Ass's Skin*, 1896), and the assumption is that the decision to reintroduce him at an earlier stage of his life in *Père Goriot* betokens a flash of inspiration that gave the author the idea of creating a cycle of interconnected novels depicting every aspect of society and having many characters in common. That the idea came to him quite so suddenly is doubtful since, as Henry Reed has pointed out, he had already decided to bring in Madame de Langeais and Madame de Beauséant and the moneylender Gobseck, all of whom had appeared in previous works. It is certain, however, that *Père Goriot* is the first work in which the device of repetition occurs and in which the uncertain fates of two main characters, Eugène and Vautrin, point so obviously to other stories.

The novel began as a short story about parental obsession and filial ingratitude. The title is most often translated into English as *Père Goriot* or *Father Goriot*, whereby the significance of the definite article is lost, which, because it is not grammatically necessary in French, is all the more pointed;

the sense is more truly rendered as Goriot the Father. The point is that the condition of fatherhood absorbs the whole life and personality of old Goriot. At one time a husband and a businessman, he has lost or given up these roles and now lives only in the paternal relation; at other times, he exists, in the boarders' neat phrase, as "an anthropomorphous mollusc." He seems at first glance horribly victimized, so betrayed and ill-repaid by his harpy daughters that his situation excites the silent sympathy of even such hard gems of the *haute monde* as the duchess of Langeais and Madame de Beauséant. His gratitude to his offspring for their least notice, ungraciously bestowed as it may be, and his joyful self-sacrifice and boundless self-delusion fill the reader with pity. Was there ever, Balzac seems to ask, a parent so ill-used?

Ultimately, Balzac leaves no doubt that Goriot reared the two girls in such a way as to ensure that they would be stupid, vain, idle, and grasping women. "The upbringing he gave his daughters was of course preposterous." As he lies dying, his outburst of impotent rage reminds one of Lear; their situations are similar in that each in the folly of his heart causes his own ruin. Lear's abasement leads to self-recognition and moral rebirth, but Goriot clings to his delusion with a mad tenacity to the end, demanding that reality conform to his dream of the rewards that are due to a devoted father. In fact, he is properly rewarded, for he has been the worst of fathers. Parenthood is both a privilege and a trust. Goriot has enjoyed the first and betrayed the latter, as he himself recognizes in a brief interval of lucidity: "The finest nature, the best soul on earth would have succumbed to the corruption of such weakness on a father's part." Indulging himself in the warmth of their goodwill, he has failed in his duty to their moral sense; as adults, they are mirror images of his own monumental selfishness, made, as it were, of the very stuff of it: "It was I who made them, they belong to me."

To this "obscure but dreadful Parisian tragedy" are added the separate tales of Rastignac and Vautrin, each quite self-contained and yet bound to the other tales by the most subtle bonds. One of these links is the recurrent reference to parenthood. At every turn, some facet of the parent-child relation is held up to the reader's notice: the wretchedness of the cast-off child Victorine Taillefer, for example, which so resembles Goriot's wretchedness; Madame de Langeais's disquisition on sons-in-law, later echoed by Goriot; the parental tone taken with Eugène both by Madame de Beauséant ("Why you poor simple child!") and, in a different way, by Vautrin ("You're a good little lad"), who give him wicked worldly advice in contrast to the good but dull counsel of his own mother; the filial relationship that develops between Eugène and Goriot; even Vautrin's enormously ironic nick-

names for his landlady (Mamma Vauquer) and the police (Father Cop).

Another element linking the *haute monde*, the Maison Vauquer, and the underworld is that they are all partners in crime. Goriot made his original fortune in criminal collusion with members of the de Langeais family. Vautrin neatly arranges the death of Mademoiselle Taillefer's brother for the benefit of the half-willing Rastignac. The Baron de Nucingen invests Delphine's dowry in an illegal building scheme. Vautrin, Goriot, and Anastasie all resort to Papa Gobseck the moneylender. The reader hears a precept uttered by Madame de Beauséant ("In Paris, success is everything, it's the key to power") enunciated a few pages later by Vautrin ("Succeed! . . . succeed at all costs"). The reader is clearly meant to see that whatever differences exist among the various levels of society, they are differences not of kind but of degree. Corruption is universal.

"Critical Evaluation" by Jan Kennedy Foster

Further Reading

Balzac, Honoré de. *Père Goriot: A New Translation.* Translated by Burton Raffel. Edited by Peter Brooks. New York: W. W. Norton, 1998. In addition to the text, this Norton Critical Edition features essays about Balzac written by his contemporaries and other novelists, such as Émile Zola, Henry James, and Marcel Proust, as well as interpretive pieces written by twentieth century scholars and critics.

Bellos, David. *Honoré de Balzac: "Old Goriot."* New York: Cambridge University Press, 1987. Provides a brief general overview of the relevant cultural contexts and major interpretive traditions of the work. Specifically intended as an introductory text for high school and college students.

Bloom, Harold, ed. *Honoré de Balzac.* Philadelphia: Chelsea House, 2003. Collection of essays on some of Balzac's individual novels, including "The Framed Image: The Chain of Metaphors in Balzac's *Le Père Goriot.*" Other essays discuss the creation of a fictional universe, use of narrative doubling, and allegories of energy in *The Human Comedy.*

Garval, Michael D. "Honoré de Balzac: Writing the Monument." In *"A Dream of Stone": Fame, Vision, and Monumentality in Nineteenth-Century French Literary Culture.* Newark: University of Delaware Press, 2004. Garval describes how France in the nineteenth century developed an ideal image of "great" writers, viewing these authors' work as immortal and portraying their literary successes in monumental terms. He traces the rise and fall of this literary development by focusing on Balzac, George Sand, and Victor Hugo.

Ginsburg, Michal Peled, ed. *Approaches to Teaching Balzac's "Old Goriot."* New York: Modern Language Association of America, 2000. Collection of essays by professors of English, French, and history. Contributors interpret the novel from diverse perspectives, including feminist and queer theories. Other essays discuss Balzac and the modern city, moral complexity, kinship, economics, and fathers and sons in the novel.

McCarthy, Mary Susan. *Balzac and His Reader: A Study of the Creation of Meaning in "La Comédie humaine."* Columbia: University of Missouri Press, 1982. Includes a long chapter on *Père Goriot*, in which McCarthy relies on reader-response theory to examine the ways in which Balzac uses his recurring characters to focus the reader's interpretation of the novel.

Madden, James. *Weaving Balzac's Web: Spinning Tales and Creating the Whole of "La Comédie humaine."* Birmingham, Ala.: Summa, 2003. Explores how Balzac structured his vast series of novels to create continuity both within and among the individual books. Madden examines internal narration, in which characters tell each other stories about other characters, and how this narration enables the recurring characters to provide layers of meaning that are evident throughout the series.

Maurois, André. *Prometheus: The Life of Balzac.* Translated by Norman Denny. Harmondsworth, England: Penguin Books, 1971. A thorough, generally objective, and highly readable account of Balzac's life. Provides detailed context for and some commentary on all of the major works, including *Père Goriot*.

Prendergast, Christopher. *Balzac: Fiction and Melodrama.* New York: Holmes & Meier, 1978. Argues for the importance of the stock conventions and devices of melodrama for the interpretation of Balzac's analyses of French society. Contains a detailed analysis of *Père Goriot* as well as an overview of previous critical work on the book.

Robb, Graham. *Balzac: A Life.* New York: W. W. Norton, 1994. A detailed biographical account of Balzac's life and work. Robb describes Balzac's philosophical perspectives and speculates on the psychological motivations underlying his writing.

Stowe, William W. *Balzac, James, and the Realistic Novel.* Princeton, N.J.: Princeton University Press, 1983. Discusses the solutions Balzac and Henry James adopted in solving various problems of realistic fictional representation. Includes a comparative study of issues of interpretation in *Père Goriot* and James's *The American*.

Pericles, Prince of Tyre

Author: William Shakespeare (1564-1616)
First produced: c. 1607-1608; first published, 1609
Type of work: Drama
Type of plot: Comedy
Time of plot: Hellenistic period
Locale: Eastern Mediterranean Sea and its littorals

Principal characters:
PERICLES, prince of Tyre
THAISA, his wife
MARINA, their daughter
CLEON, governor of Tarsus
DIONYZA, his wife
LYSIMACHUS, governor of Mytilene
ANTIOCHUS, king of Antioch

The Story:

In Syria, King Antiochus's wife died in giving birth to a daughter. By the time the child has grown to lovely womanhood, King Antiochus has conceived an unnatural passion for her. Her beauty attracts suitors to Antioch from far and wide, but King Antiochus, reluctant to give up his daughter, poses a riddle to each suitor. If the riddle goes unanswered, the suitor is executed. Many men, hoping to win the princess, lose their lives in this way.

Prince Pericles of Tyre arrives in Antioch to seek the hand of the beautiful princess. Having declared that he is willing to risk his life for the hand of the king's daughter, he reads the riddle posed to him, the solution to which discloses an incestuous relationship between King Antiochus and his daughter. Pericles understands but hesitates, prudently, to reveal his knowledge. Pressed by King Antiochus, he hints that he has fathomed the riddle. King Antiochus, unnerved and determined to kill Pericles, invites the young prince to stay at the court for forty days, in which time he can decide whether he will forthrightly give the solution to the riddle. Pericles, convinced that his life is in great danger, flees. King Antiochus sends agents after him with orders to kill the prince on sight.

Pericles, back in Tyre, is fearful that King Antiochus will ravage Tyre in an attempt to take Pericles' life. After consulting with his lords, he decides that he can save Tyre by going on a journey that lasts until King Antiochus has died. Thaliard, a Syrian lord who has come to Tyre to take Pericles' life, learns of Pericles' departure and returns to Antioch to report the prince's intention. Meanwhile, in the remote Greek province of Tarsus, Cleon, the governor, and his wife, Dionyza, grieve because there is famine in the land. As they despair, it is reported that a fleet of ships stands off the coast. Cleon is sure that Tarsus is about to be invaded, but actually the ships are those of Pericles, who has come to Tarsus with grain to succor the starving populace. Cleon welcomes the Tyrians, and his people invoke the Greek gods to protect their saviors from all harm.

Pericles receives word from Tyre that King Antiochus's agents are pursuing him relentlessly, and he is no longer safe in Tarsus. He thereupon takes leave of Cleon and sets sail. On the high seas the Tyrians meet disaster in a storm. The fleet is lost; Pericles is the only survivor. Washed ashore in Greece, he is helped by simple fishermen. Fortunately, the fishermen also retrieve Pericles' suit of armor from the sea.

With the help of the fishermen, Pericles travels to Pentapolis, the court of King Simonides, where a tournament is being held to honor the birthday of Thaisa, the king's lovely daughter. Among the gallant knights he meets, Pericles presents a wretched sight in his rusted armor. Even so, he defeats all antagonists and is crowned king of the tournament by Thaisa. At the banquet following the tournament, Pericles, reminded of his own father's splendid court, lapses into melancholy. Seeing his dejection, King Simonides drinks a toast to him and asks him who he is. He discloses that he is Pericles of Tyre, a castaway. His modesty and courteous deportment make an excellent impression on King Simonides and Thaisa.

Meanwhile, in Antioch, King Antiochus and his daughter, riding together in a chariot, are struck dead by a bolt of lightning. In Tyre, Pericles has been given up for dead, and the lords propose that Helicanus, Pericles' deputy, take the crown. The old lord, confident that his prince is still alive, directs them to spend a year in search of Pericles. In Pentapolis,

Thaisa, having lost her heart to Pericles, tricks her other suitors into leaving by reporting that she will remain a maiden for another year; she and Pericles are then married.

A short time before Thaisa is to give birth to a child, Pericles learns that King Antiochus is dead and that Helicanus has been importuned to take the crown of Tyre. Free to go home, Pericles, with Thaisa and Lychorida, a nurse, sails for Tyre. During the voyage the ship is overtaken by storms. Thaisa, seemingly dead after giving birth to a daughter, is placed in a watertight casket, and the casket is thrown into the raging sea. Pericles, fearful for the safety of his child, directs the seamen to take the ship into Tarsus, which is not far off. The casket containing Thaisa drifts ashore in Ephesus, and Thaisa's apparently dead body is taken to Cerimon, a skilled physician. Cerimon, suspecting that she is not really dead, discovers through his skill that Thaisa is actually quite alive.

Pericles, having reached Tarsus safely, remains there a year, at the end of which time he declares that Tyre has need of him. Placing little Marina, as he has named his daughter, in the care of Cleon and Dionyza, he sets out for Tyre. In the meantime Thaisa, believing that her husband and child have been lost at sea, takes the veil of a votaress to the goddess Diana.

Years pass, during which Pericles rules in Tyre. As Marina grows, it is clear that she is superior in every respect to her companion, the daughter of Cleon and Dionyza. When Marina's nurse Lychorida dies, Dionyza, jealous of the daughter of Pericles, plots against Marina, commissioning a servant to take the girl to a deserted place on the coast and kill her. As the servant threatens Marina, pirates arrive and frighten the servant away; they then take Marina aboard their ship. They transport her to Mytilene, where they sell her to a brothel owner.

In Tarsus, meanwhile, Dionyza persuades the horrified Cleon that for their own safety against the rage of Pericles they must mourn the loss of Marina and erect a monument in her memory. When Pericles, accompanied by old Helicanus, arrives in Tarsus to reclaim his daughter, his grief on seeing the monument is so great that he exchanges his royal robes for rags and vows never again to wash himself or to cut his hair. Pericles then leaves Tarsus.

In Mytilene, in the meantime, Marina confounds both the owners and the customers of the brothel by preaching the heavenly virtues instead of deporting herself wantonly. Lysimachus, the governor of Mytilene, goes in disguise to the brothel, and when Marina is brought to him he quickly discerns her gentle birth. He gives her gold and assures her that she will soon be freed from her vile bondage. Alarmed, the bawd places Marina in the hands of the doorkeeper. Marina shames him, gives him gold, and persuades him to place her as a teacher of the gentle arts. The money she then earns by teaching singing, dancing, and needlework she gives to her owner, the bawd.

When Pericles, now a distracted wanderer, comes to Mytilene, Lysimachus takes a barge out to the Tyrian ship, but he is told that Pericles, grieving the loss of both wife and daughter, will not speak to anyone. A Mytilene lord suggests that Marina, famous for her graciousness and charm, be brought to see Pericles. When Marina meets Pericles, she reveals to him that she knows a grief similar to his, for she has lost her father and mother. It soon becomes apparent to the bewildered Pericles that his daughter stands before him. Rejoicing, he puts aside his rags and dresses again in regal robes. The goddess Diana then puts him into a deep sleep, in which she directs him in a dream to go to the temple of Diana in Ephesus and there tell of the loss of his wife.

Pericles hastens to the temple, where he reveals his identity to the votaries in attendance. Thaisa, overhearing him, faints. Cerimon, who is also present, discloses to Pericles that the votaress who has fainted is his wife. Pericles and Thaisa are joyfully reunited. As Thaisa's father has died, Pericles proclaims that he and Thaisa will reign in Pentapolis and that Lysimachus and Marina, as husband and wife, will rule over Tyre. When the people of Tarsus learn of the evil done by Cleon and Dionyza, they burn the governor and his family alive in their palace.

Critical Evaluation:

By scholarly consensus, it appears that in the case of *Pericles, Prince of Tyre*, William Shakespeare finished a play that someone else had been commissioned to write. Recent scholarship indicates that Shakespeare revised the entire play of *Pericles, Prince of Tyre* from an earlier version by another playwright, probably Thomas Heywood. The play was tremendously popular in its day and was the basis of a prose version by George Wilkins. *Pericles, Prince of Tyre* is now considered to have been the first of the tragicomedies, or dark romances, that became so popular on the Jacobean stage. The play disregards considerations of time and place, delights in romantic improbabilities, and employs the obscure, compact style of Shakespeare's late plays. Probably it paved the way not only for *Cymbeline* (pr. c. 1609-1610, pb. 1623), *The Winter's Tale* (pr. c. 1610-1611, pb. 1623), and *The Tempest* (pr. 1611, pb. 1623) but also for the plays of Francis Beaumont and John Fletcher.

Although seldom performed, *Pericles, Prince of Tyre* possesses an interesting, romantic story and a certain sentimental beauty. It abounds in situations and surprises, although parts of its theme might be considered unpleasant. The similarities between it and Shakespeare's other late plays are striking. The likeness between Marina in *Pericles, Prince of Tyre* and Perdita in *The Winter's Tale* is clear. The meeting between father and daughter, long separated, is suggestive of *Cymbeline*, and the reunion of Pericles and Thaisa anticipates that of Leontes and Hermione. Pericles and Cerimon are wise and superior men in the manner of Prospero. The themes of reunion after long division, reconciliation, and forgiveness seem to recur in all of these late plays, beginning with *Pericles, Prince of Tyre*. Storms appear twice in the play, perhaps as a symbol of the storms of life; this resembles *The Tempest*. In Shakespeare's last plays, children are lost and found again, parents are divided and reunited, a wife is rejected and ill used and restored again. The recurring myth of royalty lost and recovered apparently had some special significance for Shakespeare and his audience.

The play is heavy with symbols and is particularly concerned with the concept of lost authority or control, without which life cannot properly be conducted. It is possible that some allusion to the late queen is intended, but the meaning may have been more personal to Shakespeare and may reflect a change or confusion in his life. The atmosphere, like that of *The Tempest*, is all sea and music. The brothel scenes are decidedly Shakespearean, with their joking references to disease. There is a hint of the attitudes of *Timon of Athens* (pr. c. 1607-1608, pb. 1623), namely, a certain anger and disgust with humanity in the midst of the poetry and music.

Up to the third act, Shakespeare's revisions apparently were mostly confined to style, but comparison to the prose story based on the earlier version of the play suggests that with the fourth act he began to make extensive revisions in the plot as well. Certainly, the later scenes are superior in quality to the earlier ones. There is a subtlety and delicacy in the handling of certain scenes—such as when Pericles strikes Marina when she reproves him for his stubborn grief—that mark them as clearly from the hand of Shakespeare. *Pericles, Prince of Tyre*, because of its uncertain place in the canon, has long been underrated as a play. Its importance, however, as the beginning of a new style for Shakespeare and other Jacobean playwrights cannot be overestimated.

Further Reading

Bergeron, David M. *Shakespeare's Romances and the Royal Family*. Lawrence: University Press of Kansas, 1985. Emphasizes the relationship of the masquelike elements of the play to the ceremonial forms predominant at the court of James I. One of the best historical analyses of *Pericles, Prince of Tyre*.

Fawkner, H. W. *Shakespeare's Miracle Plays*. Madison, N.J.: Fairleigh Dickinson University Press, 1992. Unlike many Shakespeare studies, this fascinating book does not condescend to *Pericles*. Instead, it considers the play as a mature, complex, and achieved work of art.

Frye, Northrop. *A Natural Perspective: The Development of Shakespearean Comedy and Romance*. New York: Columbia University Press, 1965. In this work and in his earlier *Anatomy of Criticism*, Frye establishes a critical model of the Hellenistic romance by which the reader may better understand the plot and genre of *Pericles*.

Jackson, MacD. P. *Defining Shakespeare: "Pericles" as Test Case*. New York: Oxford University Press, 2003. Argues that Shakespeare wrote *Pericles, Prince of Tyre* in collaboration with George Wilkins, a minor playwright who wrote the first two acts and portions of the brothel scenes in act 4 of the play. Discusses how identification of this play's authorship offers a methodology for investigating the coauthorship of other Shakespearean plays.

Knight, G. Wilson. *The Crown of Life*. New York: Oxford University Press, 1947. Discusses the play's verbal beauty, its adventure, and its spiritual richness. Knight was the first modern critic to take *Pericles, Prince of Tyre* seriously.

Lyne, Raphael. *Shakespeare's Late Work*. New York: Oxford University Press, 2007. Provides a detailed reading of *Pericles, Prince of Tyre* and other plays written at the end of Shakespeare's career, placing them within the context of his oeuvre. Argues that the late works have a distinct identity, defined as an ironic combination of belief and skepticism regarding faith in God, love of family, reverence for monarchs, and the theatrical depiction of truth.

Neely, Carol Thomas. *Broken Nuptials in Shakespeare's Plays*. New Haven, Conn.: Yale University Press, 1985. Presents an important feminist analysis of *Pericles*, arguing that the play affirms and subverts the conventional marriage plot of comedies.

Skeele, David, ed. *"Pericles": Critical Essays*. New York: Garland, 2000. Collection of essays from the late seventeenth century to the late twentieth century includes pieces by Ben Jonson and Algernon Charles Swinburne, providing a range of critical interpretations of the play. Also reprints reviews of productions of *Pericles* in England, the United States, and Japan dating from 1854 through the 1990's.

Vickers, Brian. *Shakespeare, Co-Author: A Historical Study of Five Collaborative Plays*. New York: Oxford University Press, 2002. Seeks to develop a coherent system for identifying Shakespeare's collaborative works. Discusses concepts of authorship in English Renaissance drama and describes methods used to determine authorship since the nineteenth century. Closely analyzes *Pericles, Prince of Tyre* and attributes the work to Shakespeare and George Wilkins.

The Persians

Author: Aeschylus (525/524-456/455 B.C.E.)
First transcribed: Persai, 472 B.C.E. (English translation, 1777)
Type of work: Drama
Type of plot: Tragedy
Time of plot: 480 B.C.E.
Locale: Susa, the capital of Persia

Principal characters:
XERXES, king of Persia
ATOSSA, his mother
PERSIAN ELDERS
GHOST OF DARIUS, Xerxes' father

The Story:

Xerxes, son of the late King Darius of Persia, is a man of overwhelming ambition who, eager to add more countries to his tremendous empire, leads a great army against the Greek states. During his absence, he leaves only the Persian elders to maintain authority in Susa, the capital. The old men wait apprehensively for some word of the invasion forces, and their fears grow as time passes and no message comes from Xerxes. They lament that the land has been emptied of the young men who marched valiantly to war, leaving their wives and mothers to wait anxiously for their return.

Atossa, widow of Darius and mother of Xerxes, is also filled with vague fears. One night she sees in a dream two tall, beautiful women, one in Persian dress and the other in Greek robes. When the women begin to quarrel, King Xerxes appears and yokes them to his chariot. The woman in Asian costume submits meekly enough, but the other breaks the reins and overturns the chariot, throwing young Xerxes to the ground. Then, in Atossa's dream, Darius comes and, seeing his son on the ground, tears his robes with grief. Upon awakening, Atossa goes to pray for her son's safety. While she is making a sacrifice before the altar, she sees an eagle pursued and plucked by a hawk. To her these visions seem to portend catastrophe for the Persians.

The elders, after hearing her story, advise Atossa to pray to the gods and to beg great Darius to intercede, from the realm of the dead, to bring success to the Persian expedition. Atossa, her thoughts far across the sea with her son, asks the elders where Athens is. The elders tell her that it is in Attica, in Greece, and that the citizens of Athens are a free people who derive great strength from their freedom. Their words do little to reassure the troubled mother.

A messenger arrives and announces the defeat of the Persian host in a great battle fought at Salamis; Atossa is relieved to learn that Xerxes, however, has been spared. The news throws the elders into sad confusion, but Atossa tells them that men must learn to bear the sorrows put upon them by the gods. Quieted, the elders listen while the messenger relates the story of the defeat. At Salamis, more than 1,200 Persian ships had been arrayed against 310 vessels of the Greeks. The defenders, however, proved themselves craftier than their enemies. Deceitfully, a Greek from the Athenian fleet informed Xerxes that at nightfall the far-outnumbered Greek ships would leave their battle stations and fly, under cover of darkness, to escape the impending sea fight. Xerxes immediately gave orders for his fleet to close in around the bay of Salamis and to be on the alert that night to prevent the escape of the Athenian vessels. The wily Greeks kept their places in the bay, and when morning came, the light showed the Persian ships crowded so closely into the outlet of the bay that they were unable to maneuver. The Greeks thereupon moved against the Persians and destroyed them.

Meanwhile, the messenger continues, Xerxes had sent troops to the island of Salamis, where he planned to cut off all Greeks who sought refuge on land. The Greeks, having destroyed the Persian fleet, put their own soldiers ashore. In the fierce fighting that followed, the Persians, unable to escape by water, were slain. Seeing his great army scattered and killed, Xerxes ordered the survivors to retreat. As the Persians, now without ships, marched overland through hostile Greek territory, many of them perished of hardships or were slain by enraged men of the lands through which they traveled.

The elders of Susa bewail the terrible misfortune brought upon Persia by the king's desire to avenge his father, who was defeated years before by the Greeks at Marathon. Having heard the story of her son's defeat, Atossa retires to make offerings to the gods and to pray for the warriors who have lost their lives in the war with Athens. In mourning, she invokes the spirit of Darius, for whom she and the old men have great need at this most depressing time. The shade of Darius appears and asks what dire event has occurred in Persia to make necessary his summons from the lower regions. The elders are struck speechless with fear and respect by his august appearance, but Atossa bravely confronts the ghost of her dead husband and tells him that Persia has met disaster not by plague or by internal strife but by defeat at the hands of the Athenians.

Darius is shocked to hear of the losses Xerxes has suffered and to learn of the ambitious scope of his enterprise. He laments his son's god-offending pride in bridging the sacred Hellespont and in gambling all the power and wealth of Persia on the success of his ill-fated expedition. Atossa tries to defend Xerxes by saying that he was influenced by evil advisers. Darius reminds his listeners that he and his forebears never jeopardized the welfare of the country to such an extent.

In despair, the old men ask Darius how Persia can redeem its great defeat. The dead king replies that the Persians must never again attack Greece, for the gods unquestionably favor those free people. He urges the elders to teach the young people of Persia to restrain all god-provoking pride, and he advises Atossa to welcome Xerxes and to comfort him on his return. With these words, the shade of Darius disappears into his tomb.

When Xerxes returns, he is filled with sorrow that he did not perish on the field of battle and with remorse for the catastrophe he has brought upon his people. He blames only himself for his defeat. The old men sing a dirge, asking what befell various of the great Persian warriors who fought with Xerxes. Xerxes replies that some drowned in the sea battle and others were slaughtered on the beach. Many, he says, were killed and buried without final rites. In the deepest despair, Xerxes joins the elders in their grief. Even though his greatest ambition has been dashed, he praises the bravery and virtues of the Greeks, whom he tried in vain to conquer.

Critical Evaluation:

The Persians is the only surviving example of a Greek drama based entirely on an actual historical event. Although other extant Greek tragedies allude to contemporary Greek history, they transfer the action of the plays to mythical times or faraway places. In a sense, *The Persians* also moves the locale of its action to the exotic court of the Persians; however, the poet was interested in portraying the specific aftermath of the Battle of Salamis, a naval battle in which the Persians were decisively defeated. The play is therefore to be understood in part as an extraordinary celebration of this astonishing victory of Greek over barbarian.

The Persians is also unique as the only extant example of a monodrama, that is, a play that was complete in itself and not presented as part of a dramatic trilogy. All elements of the story are explored by the end of the play, and none is left to be explored in a sequel. On the dramatic level, however, the only real event in the course of the play is the arrival of news of the Persian defeat, which is followed by the effect that this announcement has on the court of Xerxes. Scene after scene explores the unfolding of horror at the calamity that has already taken place.

The appearance of the ghost of Darius, who acts as a semidivine interpreter, adds a new moral and even theological dimension to this work. Aeschylus incorporates this element to emphasize that the defeat of the Persians was no ordinary victory of one political entity over another. The stunning defeat was the work of Zeus, the supreme god of the Greeks, and a punishment for the excessive arrogance of the Persians.

Other Greek plays that are now lost took their subjects from contemporary history, but as the only surviving example of such historical tragedy, *The Persians* occupies a special place in literary history. Instead of presenting a myth and exploring its moral implications for his audience, Aeschylus struggled with the considerable challenge of making a living person (Xerxes died in 465 B.C.E.) the tragic hero of a drama. Virtually everyone in Aeschylus's audience had had firsthand experience of the Persian threat, and it is believed that Aeschylus was himself an eyewitness to the Battle of Salamis, which he describes in the exciting speech of the play's messenger. This account of the battle constitutes the only version by an eyewitness of any event from the Persian wars. Beyond this historical connection, the play may have had some role in contemporary politics as political propaganda glorifying the recent victory over the Persians. Implied praise of Themistocles' grand naval strategy, by which the Persians were defeated, may have been intended to influence contemporary debates about the extension and development of Athenian naval power.

The Persians is, after all, a dramatic work. Aeschylus focuses entirely on the arrival of a messenger announcing the defeat at Salamis and the reaction of the Persians who are attached to the royal court. In this depiction, history gives way to fantasy about an exotic people whose private habits and characters were known to the Greeks, if at all, only through hearsay. Catalogs of fallen Persians are recited, many of whose names were clearly concocted by the dramatist, and the entire Persian court turns to mourning. Although, in its broad outline, the story of the Persian defeat is one of a fall from prosperity to adversity, the play itself concentrates almost entirely on the effects of defeat. Elaborate and moving passages of ritual lamentation are a central feature. It is interesting that among the ancient dramatists, Aeschylus was famous for his elaborate use of spectacle. Certainly, production of *The Persians* permitted Aeschylus to give full expression to dramatic display and fantasy as exotically dressed members of the Persian royal court lament the disaster that has befallen them.

Aeschylus is careful to express no open contempt for the defeated Persians. The fear and grief of Queen Atossa are as moving as the despair of any heroine from Greek tragedy. Even Xerxes, whose arrogant acts are depicted as the obvious cause of the calamity, is not singled out for condemnation. Instead, the disaster of Salamis is represented as a disaster for all of Persia, and the entire people share in the blame. At the crucial moment, as the Persians seek to understand the ultimate causes of their downfall, the ghost of Darius appears. Darius, with whose name the growth of Persian power and the prosperity of the empire were synonymous, acts as an interpreter for all that has happened. In his extraordinary commentary, one detects Aeschylus's search for the ultimate nature of guilt and punishment, which reaches well beyond the immediate circumstances of the defeated Persians. Darius makes it clear that Xerxes is indeed guilty but that a calamity of this magnitude must exceed the limits of individual responsibility. Beyond the specific crimes of Xerxes or of other Persians, the dramatist explores the implications of an age-old law of fate: Ultimately, disaster strikes anything that has grown too great.

As a dramatist deeply interested in ideas, Aeschylus especially wanted to communicate the moral implications of his stories. The probable first reaction of his audience was satisfaction at this representation of the humiliation of barbarian might by Greek courage and ingenuity, but the drama of the Persian defeat also engaged the minds and even the sympathies of the viewers. Poised on the verge of developing their own empire, the Athenians were invited to consider the fate of the Persians as a warning for their own future. Seen in its broadest context, *The Persians* is a model for the human condition and what appears to be the inevitable cycle of prosperity and adversity.

"Critical Evaluation" by John M. Lawless

Further Reading

Aeschylus. *The Persians*. Translated by Janet Lembke and C. J. Herington. New York: Oxford University Press, 1981. This edition represents a happy collaboration between a practicing poet and a classical scholar. Lembke's translation captures lyric qualities of the seemingly prosaic play, while Herington's informative introduction provides an excellent orientation for the reader new to the drama of Aeschylus.

Gagarin, Michael. *Aeschylean Drama*. Berkeley: University of California Press, 1976. Chapter 2 offers a detailed analysis of *The Persians* that shows that the presentation of political propaganda is not inconsistent with tragic practice. Also explores the moral theme of calamity brought on by excessive pride.

Harrison, Thomas. *The Emptiness of Asia: Aeschylus' "Persians" and the History of the Fifth Century*. London: Duckworth, 2000. Examines how Aeschylus's drama reflects ancient Athenian ideas about empire. Analyzes the play's representation of Persia, the Athenian self-image, and fifth century Athenian politics.

Podlecki, Anthony J. *The Political Background of Aeschylean Tragedy*. Ann Arbor: University of Michigan Press, 1966. Chapter 2 presents a succinct introduction to the historical and political background of *The Persians*. Podlecki displays an excellent understanding of Themistocles, the Athenian general whose plan to encounter the Persians at Salamis saved the Greeks.

Rosenbloom, David Scott. *Aeschylus: "Persians."* London: Duckworth, 2006. This companion to the play discusses historical context, themes, and performance history and interprets other aspects of the drama. Includes chronology, bibliography, and glossary.

Spatz, Lois. *Aeschylus*. Boston: Twayne, 1982. Chapter 2 presents a detailed analysis of the historical and political significance of *The Persians*. Offers a particularly good discussion of the play as simultaneously alien to Greek audiences and paradigmatic of the human condition.

Winnington-Ingram, R. P. *Studies in Aeschylus*. New York: Cambridge University Press, 1983. Chapter 1 offers an excellent discussion of the theological aspects of *The Persians*, concentrating on the figure of Zeus. Though not actually present in the play, Zeus is mentioned repeatedly as the cause of the Persian disaster.

Personae
The Collected Poems of Ezra Pound

Author: Ezra Pound (1885-1972)
First published: 1926
Type of work: Poetry

From the beginning, Ezra Pound's problem was how to re-create what he found meaningful in the past in a way that would yet sound new to his contemporaries. He solved the problem partially in *Hugh Selwyn Mauberley* (1920) and completely in *Cantos* (1948). That he did solve it is attested by the enormous influence of his poetry and criticism on the poetic idiom, an influence felt even by those who find it difficult to understand his works. The solution to what was essentially a problem of form meant, inevitably, any number of false starts that the later Pound sought, quite humanly, to ignore.

In *Personae*, his 1926 collection of shorter poems, Pound notes that the collection includes all of his poems up to that date except for the unfinished *Cantos*. The statement is misleading, however. The volume contains a relatively small selection of the very early Pound, the poet who, with no difficulty, had two of his poems published in *The Oxford Book of Victorian Verse* ("Ballad for Gloom" and "The Portrait," neither reprinted in *Personae*), and the Pound who bears such clear resemblance to the Pre-Raphaelites, Algernon Charles Swinburne, the poetry of the 1890's, William Butler Yeats, and Robert Browning. Of the 145 poems printed in Pound's first volumes—*A Lume Spento* (1908), *A Quinzaine for This Yule* (1908), *Personae, Exultations* (1909), and *Canzoni* (1911)—only 42 survive in the *Personae* volume of 1926. Basically, this is the Pound concerned with medieval themes, Provençal forms, and the tradition of the aesthetes generally.

In both imagery and idea, "Grace Before Song," from *A Lume Spento*, bespeaks the aesthetic ideal of the 1890's. Concern with fleeting moods, lack of concern with society—

these attitudes describe at least one aspect of that era's decadence. In line with the English decadence, Pound, too, drew heavily on Swinburne and the Pre-Raphaelites. The medieval atmosphere of the Pre-Raphaelite ballad is also to be found in his "Ballad Rosalind."

The Pre-Raphaelite ideal of feminine beauty is never absent from these early poems; indeed, it never quite seems to have left Pound. As for the impact of Swinburne, it is defined by Pound himself in the reverential "Salve O Pontifex—for Swinburne; an hemi-chaunt." Of the early Yeats, Pound was almost a disciple. One critic has pointed out that "The Tree" is a compendium of Yeatsian influences. Pound clearly echoes Yeats's opening lines from "He Thinks of His Past Greatness When a Part of the Constellations of Heaven," with their references to the hazel tree and grief for all things known.

The central fact of these early volumes is the tremendous variety of influences and modes they reveal. Pound shows himself to be a seeker who is willing to try anything at least once. These early volumes also reflect Pound's concern with translation as a means of providing techniques for the developing poet and insight into earlier states of mind. At this time, Pound's translations, mainly from Provençal and early Italian, were unfortunately colored by Pre-Raphaelite diction and turns of phrase. Thus he not only failed to "make it new," to quote a favorite phrase of Pound, but also produced obfuscated translations.

Ripostes, published in 1912, is generally taken to mark a turning point in his poetry, but there is still a good deal of the old preciosity in "A Virginal" and "Silet." The best poems (and some of the worst) in this volume are translations and adaptations. As always, Pound is concerned not with literal translation but with a revival of the spirit of the poet and his time; ultimately, the translation is as much Pound's work as it is that of the original poet. *Ripostes* contains Pound's famous version of "The Seafarer," for it was inevitable that Pound should attempt at least one example of Anglo-Saxon form. (He repeated it later in "Canto I.") The volume also contains "The Return," modeled on a poem by Henri de Régnier. The poem deals with the return of the Greek gods, who, to Pound, represent eternally recurrent states of mind that he later defines again in *Cantos*. It stands as a metaphor of Pound's efforts to make what is still alive in the past speak to and help salvage the present. It also suggests a shift in allegiance away from the poets of the English decadence to the French Symbolists.

By the time he published *Ripostes*, Pound had begun to teach others, becoming a propagandist for the Imagist movement, with its stress on compactness and concreteness. In 1914, he edited the anthology *Des Imagistes*, and in the following year he published what was essentially a set of variations on the Imagist mode in *Cathay*, a book of translations from the Chinese based on notes left by the expert on Japanese art Ernest Fenollosa. Inaccurate as they are, these translations are still considered the best introduction to Chinese poetry available to Westerners. Pound knew not a word of Chinese; clearly, his ability to work with Fenollosa's notes was the result of a deeply felt affinity with the nature of Chinese poetry, its avoidance of abstract statement, and its reliance on concrete imagery to suggest mood and idea. In the famous "River-Merchant's Wife: A Letter," the wife's sense of loss and desire for her absent husband are suggested not by direct assertions but by indirect description.

In 1916, again working from Fenollosa's notes, Pound, who knew no more Japanese than he did Chinese, published *"Noh" or Accomplishment*. Again inaccurate in many ways, the work made Japanese drama available to the Western mind. In the same year, Pound published *Lustra*, which presented the work of Pound's Imagist period, a Pound free of clutter. Certainly Pound seemed to think so, as can be noted in "Salutation the Second."

The sardonic attitude toward his audience is repeated in a number of poems: "Tenzone," "The Condolence," "Salutation," "Causa," "Commission," "Further Instructions," and "Salvationists." The satiric muse has taken possession of Pound, and it is employed to pillory many of the states of mind later satirized in *Cantos* as useless, confused, uncreative. Among these satiric poems are "The Garden," "Les Millwin," "The Bellaires," and "Our Contemporaries." Seeking hardness and directness, Pound had turned to the Latin and Greek epigrammatists, and a number of the poems reflect this study. Though scarcely Imagistic, the epigrams— "The New Cake of Soap," "Epitaph," "Arides," "The Bath Tub," and a number of others—are concentrated and in this way reflect one of the major concerns of the Imagistic movement. The translations, too, have shed their Pre-Raphaelite haze, a fact exhibited in the translation from the Provençal of Bertrans de Born. Imagist poems proper, as well as adaptations from the Chinese, appear, including what has become the archetype of the Imagist poem, "In a Station of the Metro."

The relatively bald statements of the satires, the sharp pictures of the Imagist poems, are mingled with poems that show the astonishing qualities of Pound's ear in such lyrics as "The Spring," an adaptation of Ibycus, and "Dance Figure," which is apparently based on the mood of "The Song of Songs."

Lustra gives the impression of an author testing his technical skills in preparation for a major work. That work came in 1920 with *Hugh Selwyn Mauberley*, which a number of critics consider Pound's "breakthrough," the poem in which he became, finally, modern. Other long poems of the period are the culminations of earlier developments: Translations as a means of re-creating an earlier poetic mood may be seen in "Homage to Sextus Propertius," satire in "Moeurs Contemporaines" and "Villanelle: The Psychological Hour." A sequence rather than a single poem, *Hugh Selwyn Mauberley* was new in its tight juxtaposition of disparate moods and images, in its containment of a complex of attitudes and experiences, and in its careful, often ironic, control of tone. The poem maintains a duality and a deliberate ambivalence that can be confusing. It mocks, at the same time that it bids farewell to, the aesthete in Pound.

If the aesthete is out of step with his time, the time itself was not much to be proud of, and several poems deal with its pervasive tawdriness. World War I, the ultimate shock to the aesthete, raised the question of the relevance of art and culture in a period of confusion and change. Neither the Pre-Raphaelites nor the aesthetes seemed to have very much to say in such a time because they failed to reflect the mood of the decade. Such successful writers as the pseudonymous "Mr. Nixon" (who probably represents Arnold Bennett) were seen to be as tawdry as their age. In the tenth poem of Pound's sequence he states that in an age of cheapness and insincerity that is impatient of craftsmanship or indifferent to the heroic example of the artist, the stylist has sought shelter from the world. In the second part of *Hugh Selwyn Mauberley*, the poet drifts toward death, unable to create what "the age demanded" and also unable to provide what the age needed, poetry that would relate his private passions to the society around him. The ultimate confrontation of poet and society took place in *Cantos*, the long, major poem on which Pound was already then at work.

Further Reading

Bloom, Harold, ed. *Ezra Pound*. New York: Chelsea House, 1987. Collection of essays by major Pound scholars addresses the politics, prejudices, and obscurity of language in Pound's poetry. In his essay, Louis L. Martz declares that *Personae* is Pound's definitive collection of poetry. An essay by Max Nänny deals with such aspects of Pound's use of language as context, contiguity, contact, and tropes.

Durent, Alan. *Ezra Pound, Identity in Crisis: A Fundamental Reassessment of the Poet and His Work*. Totowa, N.J.: Barnes & Noble, 1981. Addresses Pound's representation of the American experience as one that does not please Americans but must be acknowledged.

Kenner, Hugh. *The Poetry of Ezra Pound*. 1951. Reprint. Lincoln: University of Nebraska Press, 1985. Overview of Pound's work by the world's leading Pound scholar. Discusses how Pound helped shape the poetry of his contemporaries.

Knapp, James F. *Ezra Pound*. Boston: Twayne, 1979. Provides an informative general introduction to Pound's work and life. Offers readings of the poet's often obscure use of language.

Nadel, Ira Bruce. *The Cambridge Introduction to Ezra Pound*. New York: Cambridge University Press, 2007. Introductory overview contains information about Pound's life, poetry, and prose as well as the contexts and critical reception of his work. Includes discussion of *Personae*.

_____, ed. *The Cambridge Companion to Ezra Pound*. New York: Cambridge University Press, 1999. Collection of essays presents discussions of such topics as Pound and the making of modernism, Pound's influence on American poetry, his politics, and his depiction of women and gender.

Pratt, William. *Ezra Pound and the Making of Modernism*. New York: AMS Press, 2007. Describes Pound as the "mastermind" of modernism, tracing his involvement and impact in the literary movement. Describes Pound's evolution as a poet and his significant influence on twentieth century American poetry.

Persuasion

Author: Jane Austen (1775-1817)
First published: 1818
Type of work: Novel
Type of plot: Domestic realism
Time of plot: Early nineteenth century
Locale: Somersetshire and Bath, England

Principal characters:
SIR WALTER ELLIOT, the owner of Kellynch Hall
ELIZABETH ELLIOT, his oldest daughter
ANNE ELLIOT, his second daughter
MARY MUSGROVE, his youngest daughter
CHARLES MUSGROVE, her husband
HENRIETTA and LOUISA, Charles Musgrove's sisters
CAPTAIN FREDERICK WENTWORTH, a naval officer
MRS. CLAY, Elizabeth Elliot's friend
WILLIAM ELLIOT, Sir Walter's cousin and heir to Kellynch Hall

The Story:

Sir Walter Elliot is a conceited man, vain of both his good looks and his title. He lives at his country seat, Kellynch Hall, with two of his daughters, Elizabeth and Anne. Elizabeth, handsome and much like her father, is the oldest and her father's favorite. Anne, sweet, self-effacing, and quietly intelligent, is ignored and underrated by both. Mary, the youngest daughter, is married to an agreeable young man named Charles Musgrove; they live in an untidy house at Uppercross, three miles from Kellynch Hall.

Living beyond his means had brought financial disaster to Sir Walter. On the advice of his solicitor and of a family friend, Lady Russell, he is persuaded to rent Kellynch Hall and take a smaller house in Bath. Anne would have preferred to take a modest house near home, but as usual, her father and sister have their way in the matter.

Reluctantly, Sir Walter lets his beloved country seat to Admiral Croft and his wife, who is the sister of a former suitor of Anne, Captain Frederick Wentworth. Anne and Captain Wentworth had fallen in love when they were both very young, but the match had been discouraged. Anne's father felt that the young man's family was not good enough for his own, and Lady Russell considered the engagement unwise because Captain Wentworth had no financial means beyond his navy pay. Anne had followed their advice and broken the engagement, but Wentworth had advanced and became rich in the navy, just as he had said he would. Anne, now twenty-seven years old, has not forgotten her love at age nineteen, and no one else has taken Captain Wentworth's place in her affection.

With all arrangements completed for the renting of Kellynch Hall, Sir Walter, Elizabeth, and her friend, Mrs. Clay, are off to Bath. Before they depart, Anne warns Elizabeth that Mrs. Clay's is not a disinterested friendship and that she is scheming to marry Sir Walter if she can. Elizabeth will

not believe such an idea, nor will she agree to dismiss Mrs. Clay.

Anne is to divide her time between her married sister, Mary Musgrove, and Lady Russell until Christmas. Mary and her family also live near her husband's father and mother and their two daughters, Henrietta and Louisa. During her visit to the Musgroves, Anne meets Captain Wentworth again while he is staying with his sister at Kellynch Hall. She finds him little changed in eight years.

Because the Musgroves take the Crofts and Captain Wentworth into their circle immediately, the captain and Anne meet frequently. He is coldly polite to Anne, but his attentions to the Musgrove sisters lead Mary to begin matchmaking. She cannot decide, however, whether he prefers Henrietta or Louisa. When Louisa encourages Henrietta to resume a former romance with a cousin, Charles Hayter, it seems plain that Louisa is destined for Captain Wentworth.

Further events increase the likelihood of such a match. During a visit to friends of Captain Wentworth at Lyme Regis, Louisa suffers an injury while the captain is assisting her in jumping down a steep flight of steps. The accident is not his fault, for he had cautioned Louisa against jumping, but he blames himself for not refusing her firmly. Louisa is taken to the home of Captain Wentworth's friends, Captain and Mrs. Harville and Captain Benwick. Quiet, practical, and capable during the emergency, Anne has the pleasure of knowing that Captain Wentworth relies on her strength and good judgment, but she feels that a match between him and the slowly recovering Louisa is certain.

Anne reluctantly joins her family and the designing Mrs. Clay at Bath. She is surprised to find that they are glad to see her. After showing her the house, they tell her the news—mainly how much in demand they are and about the presence of a cousin, Mr. William Elliot, who suddenly appeared to make his peace with the family. Mr. Elliot is the heir to Sir Walter's title and estate, but he had become estranged from the family years before because he did not marry Elizabeth, as Sir Walter and Elizabeth felt he should have. Also, he had affronted Sir Walter's pride by speaking disrespectfully of his Kellynch connections.

Now, however, these matters are explained away, and both Sir Walter and Elizabeth are charmed with him. Anne, who had seen Mr. Elliot at Lyme Regis, wonders why he chose to renew a relationship so long neglected. She thinks it might be that he is thinking of marrying Elizabeth, now that his first wife is dead; Lady Russell thinks Anne is the attraction.

News shortly arrives of Louisa Musgrove's engagement to Captain Benwick. Joy, surprise, and a hope that Captain Wentworth has lost his partiality for Louisa are mingled in Anne's first reaction. Shortly after Anne hears the news, Captain Wentworth arrives in Bath. After a few meetings, Anne knows that he has not forgotten her. She also knows that he is jealous of Mr. Elliot, although his jealousy is groundless.

Even if Anne feels any inclination to become Lady Elliot, the ambition is short-lived, for Mr. Elliot's true character now comes to light. Anne learns from a former schoolmate, who had been friendly with Mr. Elliot before he basely ruined her husband, that his first design in renewing acquaintance with Sir Walter's family was to prevent Sir Walter from marrying Mrs. Clay and thus having a son who would inherit the title and estate. Later, when he met Anne, he had been genuinely attracted to her. This information is not news to Anne, since Mr. Elliot had proposed to her at a concert the night before. She gives him no encouragement.

Convinced that Anne still loves him as he does her, Captain Wentworth pours out his heart to her in a letter. Soon all is settled happily between them. Both Musgrove girls are also married shortly afterward, but, much to Mary's satisfaction, neither of their husbands is as rich as Wentworth. Mrs. Clay, sacrificing ambition for love, leaves Bath with Mr. William Elliot and lives under his protection in London. Perhaps she hopes some day to be Lady Elliot, though as the wife of a different baronet.

Critical Evaluation:

Completed a year before Jane Austen's death but published posthumously in 1818, *Persuasion* is the novelist's last long work. The novel completes her study of English country families begun in *Sense and Sensibility* (1811) and *Pride and Prejudice* (1813). The story begins with a description of Sir Walter Elliot of Kellynch Hall in Somersetshire, who, be-

cause he is egotistical, improvident, and idle, has managed to fritter away much of his patrimony. When his extravagance necessitates the letting of Kellynch Hall and the renting of a smaller house in Bath, his capable daughter, Anne Elliot, must make most of the provisions, while her father pouts like a spoiled child. Austen uses Sir Walter as well as his deceitful and scheming cousin and heir William Elliot to criticize the indolent, debilitated gentry of her era.

Like Austen's earlier novels, *Persuasion* articulates and criticizes late eighteenth century English views of courtship and marriage. While in the novel marriage is clearly the greatest good achievable by a young woman, the path to this achievement is not a smooth one for Anne. She must defy her family to marry the man she loves. Austen shows the reader that she leaves very little behind when she does marry. Prior to marriage, Anne had cared for her selfish father and older sister, as well as aiding her hypochondriac younger sister and her children. Since Anne had no status in her family, becoming Mrs. Wentworth would in any case have been a distinct improvement.

Because Anne has previously rejected Captain Wentworth, the normal slow pace of courtship slows to a snail's pace. As in all of Austen's novels, much time is given over to reading and interpreting the sentiments of others. The reader is allowed greater knowledge of Anne's views than of the views of Wentworth. The courtship proceeds to some extent by negation, for whereas initially Anne dreads seeing Captain Wentworth again, later she is convinced he loves Louisa rather than herself. Eighteenth century politeness leads to this false conclusion, since Wentworth must be gracious to all but effusive toward none, especially not toward Anne, who had previously rejected him.

Other courtship rituals in *Persuasion* are instructive as well. The Reverend Charles Haytor is initially thought unsuitable for Henrietta Musgrove because he is a simple curate, but once he secures a better living he becomes the perfect match. William Elliot renews his acquaintance with his cousin, Sir Walter, when he hears that the latter is courting Mrs. Clay; he is afraid Sir Walter will have a male heir, thus cutting him out of his inheritance. Money is at the root of these courtship considerations, not love. Even Captain Wentworth is more palatable to Sir Walter and Elizabeth and more defensible as a lover for Anne because he has risen in the world in the intervening eight years.

Austen employs several interesting new devices in *Persuasion*. Although she describes Sir Walter and a number of other characters, Anne's appearance and demeanor are never described directly but allowed to be gleaned from the reactions of other characters. At the beginning of the novel, her whole family thinks she is drab, and even Wentworth opines that she has altered for the worse in eight years. As the book progresses, Anne comes to be considered more attractive by the other characters, and in the end both William Elliot and Wentworth judge her to be a beauty. Certainly Mrs. Musgrove and Lady Russell have commented on her excellent character throughout the story, but love and appreciation apparently cause Anne's appearance to improve and blossom.

Austen achieves another interesting effect in the denouement of the story when Wentworth writes a letter in the same room in which Anne is talking to Captain Harville about his dead sister Fanny, who was engaged to Captain Benwick, who has since then become engaged to Louisa Musgrove. Harville is not critical of Benwick but wonders why he was not eternally loyal to his dead sister. A conversation ensues between Anne and Harville about men and women and which gender is the most steadfast in love. Anne defends her gender, while Harville defends his. The conversation is just barely audible to Wentworth, and Anne is not speaking to be heard by him, yet the exchange could easily be between Anne and Wentworth. As Wentworth writes his letter pouring out his love for her, he hears her defending the constancy of women in love and can deduce from what she says that she will accept him. Several previous small instances of indirect discourse between Anne and Wentworth culminate in this final exchange that seals their love for each other.

As in all of her work, Austen in her final novel, *Persuasion*, continues to examine courtship, marriage, the family, and the gentry. She also continues her studies of the first impressions, last impressions, pride, prejudice, and persuasion that go into changing those central aspects of life.

"Critical Evaluation" by Isabel B. Stanley

Further Reading

Bloom, Harold, ed. *Jane Austen's "Persuasion."* Philadelphia: Chelsea House, 2004. Collection of essays providing various interpretations of *Persuasion*, including discussions of the character Anne Elliott and the "radical pessimism," satire, sensibility, and innovation in the novel.

Copeland, Edward, and Juliet McMaster, eds. *The Cambridge Companion to Jane Austen.* New York: Cambridge University Press, 1997. One essay in this excellent overview focuses on an analysis of *Persuasion*, *Emma*, and *Mansfield Park*, while other essays deal with broad issues, such as class consciousness, religion, and domestic economy in Austen's works. Includes a chronology and an assessment of late twentieth century developments in Austen scholarship.

Dwyer, June. *Jane Austen.* New York: Continuum, 1989. Dwyer offers readings of each of Austen's major novels, including *Persuasion*, and in separate chapters discusses the writer's life and her literary techniques and concerns.

Gard, Robert. *Jane Austen's Novels: The Art of Clarity.* New Haven, Conn.: Yale University Press, 1992. Gard writes what he calls a corrective to criticism that has moved readers too far from the texts of Austen's novels into theoretical concerns. His chapter on *Persuasion* discusses Austen's mature abilities as a novelist.

Harris, Jocelyn. *A Revolution Almost Beyond Expression: Jane Austen's "Persuasion."* Newark: University of Delaware Press, 2007. Harris analyzes the novel within its political, historical, satiric, and sexual contexts, concluding that Austen was "outward-looking, intertextually aware, self-conscious, [and] even revolutionary."

Kirkham, Margaret. *Jane Austen, Feminism, and Fiction.* Totowa, N.J.: Barnes & Noble, 1983. Kirkham places Austen's work within the feminist tradition, arguing that the writer's concerns are those of her feminist contemporaries. She includes a chapter on eighteenth century feminism. The chapter on *Persuasion* demonstrates how Austen uses the novel as a feminist critique of society.

Lambdin, Laura Cooner, and Robert Thomas Lambdin, eds. *A Companion to Jane Austen Studies.* New York: Greenwood Press, 2000. Twenty-two essays interpret Austen's works, including *Persuasion*: "*Persuasion*'s Box of Contradictions" by Claudia Stein and "Degrees of Maturity: The Bibliographic History of Jane Austen's *Persuasion*" by Laura Cooner Lambdin and Robert Thomas Lambdin.

Paris, Bernard J. *Character and Conflict in Jane Austen's Novels: A Psychological Approach.* Detroit, Mich.: Wayne State University Press, 1978. Analyzes the characters Anne and Wentworth, and makes a case for *Persuasion* as Austen's most romantic novel. Evaluates the roles played in the novel by such secondary characters as Lady Russell, Mrs. Musgrove, and Mrs. Croft.

Scott, P. J. M. *Jane Austen: A Reassessment.* Totowa, N.J.: Barnes & Noble, 1982. Contains a full assessment of *Persuasion*, which the author considers the culmination of Austen's work. Examines the egotism and idleness of the entire Elliot family, except Anne.

Thompson, James. *Between Self and World: The Novels of Jane Austen.* University Park: Pennsylvania State University Press, 1988. Considers late eighteenth century views of courtship and marriage in Austen's novels. Shows *Persuasion*'s place in the Austen canon that, as a whole, revolves around reading or interpreting the sentiments of others.

Peter Ibbetson

Author: George du Maurier (1834-1896)
First published: 1891
Type of work: Novel
Type of plot: Historical
Time of plot: Mid-nineteenth century
Locale: France and England

Principal characters:
PETER IBBETSON
COLONEL IBBETSON, his guardian
MIMSY SERASKIER, his dearest friend and later the duchess
  of Towers
MR. LINTOT, his employer
MRS. DEANE, a widow

The Story:

Peter Pasquier moves from England to Paris, where he is called Pierre, at the age of five years. His father is a dreamy-eyed inventor, his mother a soft-spoken woman devoted to her family. Peter has many childhood friends, but the dearest are Mimsy Seraskier and her beautiful mother, who live nearby. Mimsy is a delicate, shy child. She and Peter are inseparable friends, making up their own code language so that no one can intrude on their secret talks.

Now twelve years old, Peter faces the death of his father, who had been killed in an explosion, and less than one week later his mother dies giving birth to a stillborn fetus. His mother's cousin, Colonel Ibbetson, arrives from England to take Peter home with him. Peter weeps when he is forced to leave his friends, and Mimsy is so ill from her grief that she cannot even tell him good-bye. Colonel Ibbetson gives Peter his name, and he becomes Peter Ibbetson. The colonel sends him to school, where he spends six years. Events at the school touch him very little, and he spends most of his time dreaming of his old life in Paris.

When he leaves school, Peter spends some time with Colonel Ibbetson. The colonel's only request is that Peter become a gentleman, but Peter begins to doubt that the colonel himself fits the description, for he has a very poor reputation among his acquaintances. His most recent victim is Mrs. Deane, a woman he had ruined with malicious lies. The colonel seems to derive great pleasure from telling scandalous tales about everyone he knows, and Peter grows to hate him for this habit. After a time, he runs away to London and joins the cavalry for a year. Following his term in the army, he is apprenticed to Mr. Lintot, an architect he had met through Colonel Ibbetson. He takes rooms in Pentonville and begins a new chapter in his life there.

Peter works industriously for Mr. Lintot and achieves some success, but his outer life is lonely and dull. The only real joy he finds is in music, which moves him deeply. He saves money carefully to attend a concert occasionally. His

nightly dreams are still of his childhood in Paris and of Mimsy, but these dreams are becoming blurred.

Peter views the belief in a creator and life after death with skepticism, believing instead that humans would have to work back to the very beginning of time before they could understand anything about a deity. He believes it is possible to go back, if only he knows the way. His ideas on sin are unorthodox; to Peter, the only real sin is cruelty to the mind or body of any living thing. During this period of his life, his only acquaintances are the friends of Mr. and Mrs. Lintot, for Peter is a shy young man, too much concerned with his speculations and dreams for social gaiety. At one party, however, he sees a great lady who is to be his guiding star for the rest of his life. He is told she is the duchess of Towers, and although he is not introduced to her, he notices her look at him in a strange manner, almost as if she finds his face to be familiar.

Sometime after his first sight of the duchess of Towers, Peter revisits Paris, where he finds his old home and those of his friends replaced with modern bungalows. The only news he has of his old friends is that Madame Seraskier had died and that Mimsy and her father had left Paris many years ago. He returns to his hotel, emotionally exhausted from the disappointments of the day.

Peter's real and true inner life begins that night, for he learns how to dream true. When he falls asleep, the events of the day pass before him in distorted fashion. He finds himself surrounded by demon dwarfs. As he tries to escape them, he looks up and sees the duchess of Towers standing before him. She takes his hand and tells him he is not dreaming true, and then he is transported back to the happy days of his childhood and sees himself as he was then. At the same time, he retains his adult identity. He exists as two people at the same time, his adult self looking at his child self. The duchess tells him he can transport himself into any scene he has already experienced, but only if he dreams true. To do this, he must lie on his back with his arms over his head, and as he goes to sleep, he must think ceaselessly of the place he wants to be in his dreams. He must, however, never forget in his dream who and where he is when awake; in this way, his dream will be tied to reality. The duchess had learned the trick from her father.

When Peter wakes up, he realizes that at last one of his greatest desires has come true; he had looked into the mind of the duchess. Nevertheless, the matter puzzles him, for he had always thought such a fusion is possible only between two people who know and love each other. The duchess is a stranger to him.

Peter returns to Pentonville and outwardly resumes his normal life. His inner self, however, becomes his real life, and he masters the art of dreaming true and reliving any experience he wishes. He visits with his mother and Mimsy frequently in his dreams, and his life is no longer bleak and lonely. One day, he again meets the duchess of Towers in his outer life. Then he discovers why she had been in his true dream. She is Mimsy, grown now and married to a famous duke. She had had the same dream as he when she had rescued him from the dwarfs, and she, too, had been unable to understand why a stranger had invaded her dreams.

Although he does not meet again the grown Mimsy in his dreams, Peter sees the child Mimsy almost every night. His life continues without interruption until he meets Mrs. Gregory, formerly Mrs. Deane, whom Colonel Ibbetson had tried to ruin with slander. She tells him that Colonel Ibbetson had told her and many others that he is Peter's real father. The recorded marriage and birth dates prove he is lying; the story is another product of the colonel's cruel mind. Peter is so enraged that he goes to the colonel's house to force an apology. The two men fight; in his fury, Peter strikes at Colonel Ibbetson and kills him.

Peter is tried and sentenced to be hanged for the murder of his uncle. While he is in prison, the grown Mimsy appears in his dream again and tells him his sentence has been changed to life imprisonment because of the circumstances under which the murder had been committed. She promises Peter that she will continue to come to him in his dreams, allowing them to spend the rest of their lives together.

In his prison cell, Peter is the happiest man in England. Attendants are kind to him during the day, and he is with Mimsy at night. At last, they learn that they are distant cousins, and then they discover that they can project themselves into the past through the character of any of their direct ancestors. Either of them, not both at once, can become any ancestor he or she chooses, and thus they relive scenes in history that had occurred hundreds of years before. They go

back to the days when monsters roam the earth and might have gone back to the beginning of time, but Mimsy dies.

Mimsy returns to Peter seven times, urging him to continue his search for the beginning of time. She can come to him now only because he is the other half of her soul. She asks him to write down his method and to urge others to follow him, and she gives him some books in their secret code, telling him of things she learned. Before he begins to write the secrets, he dies in his cell. His cousin, Madge Plunket, who later arranges for the publication of the manuscript, feels that she will remember until her own death the look of happiness and peace upon his face.

Critical Evaluation:

After a long and successful career as an artist and illustrator, George du Maurier, at the age of fifty-five and with the urging of his friend, Henry James, began to write his first novel, *Peter Ibbetson*. In this work, he wrote about subjects and themes that obsessed him—his childhood in France, the fantasies of youth, the power of dreams, and the transcendent nature of romantic love. The work is structured in two parts. In part 1, du Maurier gives a loving autobiographical account of his childhood in Passy, which he tells with precise detail. He describes that time as one of remote innocence. He then abandons the illusion of reality established there and in part 2 develops the theme of psychic phenomenon, or "dreaming true," as he calls it.

The duality of the plot is consistent with other dualities in the novel. Peter Ibbetson embodies the two cultures of his parents. His emotional life is centered in Passy. As he matures, however, he exhibits the traits of a cultivated Englishman, admires the British aristocracy, enters into manly sports such as boxing and swimming, adopts a snobbish persona, and proclaims a conventional morality.

The duality extends to Peter's name as well. Born Pierre Pasquier de la Mariere, he is reborn, so to speak, in England as Master Peter Ibbetson. Colonel Ibbetson, who gives Peter his new name, becomes his surrogate father. Although dead, Peter's actual father, le beau Pasquier, continues to live in Peter's dreamworld. Colonel Ibbetson, on the other hand, plays no part in Peter's inner life but determines his external existence. The colonel's villainous role leads to Peter's imprisonment, where all of his dreaming begins. The splitting of the father figure into two distinct roles—one hated, the other admired—is an attractive fantasy. The ambiguous attitude that a child may have toward his or her father is dealt with by a screening process that simplifies the ambiguity by dividing the parent into two personalities, one threatening and the other loving.

The theme of duality also involves the central women of the novel, Madame Seraskier, Madame Pasquier, and the duchess of Towers. Both the descriptions and illustrations (done by du Maurier himself) reveal them to be nearly identical in beauty and stature. Madame Seraskier is presented with an idealized beauty that is associated with Peter's mother. Like his mother, she possesses warmth, kindness, simplicity, grace, naturalness, courtesy, sympathy, and joy. It is not surprising, therefore, that they both die about the same time. What appears to be involved here is the Oedipal wish to possess the mother without guilt by splitting he mother figure into the virginal and the sexual object. With the deaths of the idealized mother and the "divine" Madame Seraskier, Peter is free to fall in love with the duchess of Towers. The duchess is thus a composite figure: She is an allowable sexual object because she is sufficiently distanced from the mother, and yet her character includes all of the desirable traits of Peter's mother.

Finally, an important duality is that of Peter's mind itself, as he conducts his life for about thirty years on two levels, that of everyday consciousness and that of dreams. As the novel moves toward its conclusion, du Maurier goes beyond the theme of reality versus dreaming to imply that dreaming may actually be the most compelling reality. The duality is more aesthetic than moral. Associated with Peter's dreams are childhood, unspoiled nature, songs, beautiful people, works of art and literature, freedom, and timelessness. In his waking life, on the other hand, there are ugly people (Colonel Ibbetson, Pentonville schoolmates, and prison inmates), ugly scenes (in Pentonville), spoiled nature (the stump of his childhood apple tree and the general destruction wrought by "progress" on Passy), and imprisonment.

A progression of styles in *Peter Ibbetson* reinforces that theme of lost innocence and joy. In the last chapter of the novel the spirit of the duchess of Towers returns to Peter to inform him what life is like beyond death. No matter how intensely or for how long she proclaims the joys of the afterlife (an amazing twenty pages), her style betrays her and her language reflects the loss of the childhood life. As the novel moves Peter further and further from his childhood, the language and tone reflect his loss. It is starkly philosophical in the Pentonville section, fragmented and anxious in the prison scenes, and lyrical but abstract and hollow toward his death. The powerful imagery, the charming simplicity, and the quickened joyful tone of the early chapters stand for the reader and for the hero as a potent memory of a lost paradise.

The most notable feature of *Peter Ibbetson* that marks it as romantic fiction is that it is filled with the author's own personality made larger than life. Du Maurier's personal dreams and conflicts are visible on every page. Although it is an intensely personal novel, it still embodies a universal theme. In the words of Deems Taylor, who turned the novel into an opera in 1931, du Maurier's tale is

the Freudian wish expressed in terms of romance, our rebellious human hope of a world more enjoyable than the one we live in, our flight into dreams, wherein we can find sanctuary from a waking life that is, on the whole, a disappointment.

Du Maurier had the unusual advantage of being able to illustrate his own novels. *Peter Ibbetson* includes eighty-four drawings with depictions of all the major characters, the dreamy scenes of Passy, and the dark and threatening world of Pentonville and, later, of prison. The female characters all bear a striking resemblance to one another in their tall, elegant, genteel figures. The theme of lost innocence and youth is visually reinforced in the last few illustrations. Peter is drawn as a gaunt, wrinkled figure in a shabby, wrinkled suit, but the duchess of Towers retains her elegance, though her hair has become white.

"Critical Evaluation" by Richard Kelly

Further Reading

Auerbach, Nina. *Daphne du Maurier, Haunted Heiress*. Philadelphia: University of Pennsylvania Press, 2000. This biography of George du Maurier's granddaughter, novelist Daphne du Maurier, includes discussion of her grandfather and other strong men in her life, characters reflected in her fiction. Also examines *Peter Ibbetson*.

James, Henry. "George du Maurier." *Harper's Weekly Magazine*, April 14, 1894, 341-342. A dated but perceptive discussion of *Peter Ibbetson*. As a personal friend of George du Maurier and as a great novelist himself, James offers highly instructive commentary on du Maurier's fiction.

Kelly, Richard Michael. *The Art of George du Maurier*. Brookfield, Vt.: Ashgate, 1996. Examines the connections between du Maurier the artist-illustrator and du Maurier the writer of fiction.

_____. *George du Maurier*. Boston: Twayne, 1983. A comprehensive discussion and analysis of du Maurier's life, art, and written work. Contains a lengthy analysis of *Peter Ibbetson* that explores the psychodynamics of the novel.

Ormond, Leonée. *George du Maurier*. Pittsburgh, Pa.: University of Pittsburgh Press, 1969. The definitive biography of du Maurier, profusely illustrated. Ormond relates many elements of du Maurier's life directly to the subjects and themes of *Peter Ibbetson*.

Stevenson, Lionel. "George du Maurier and the Romantic Novel." In *Essays by Divers Hands, Being the Transactions of the Royal Society of Literature*, edited by N. Hardy Wallis. London: Oxford University Press, 1960.

Argues persuasively that du Maurier's three novels are "masterpieces of romantic fiction."

Wood, T. Martin. *George du Maurier, the Satirist of the Victorians: A Review of His Art and Personality*. London: Chatto & Windus, 1913. This dated but still useful book contains an appreciative commentary on *Peter Ibbetson*, concluding, "It is by this book I like to think du Maurier will be remembered as a writer."

Peter Pan
Or, The Boy Who Wouldn't Grow Up

Author: Sir James Barrie (1860-1937)
First produced: 1904; first published, as a play, 1928; as prose, "Peter Pan in Kensington Garden," in *The Little White Bird*, 1902; revised as *Peter and Wendy*, 1911
Type of work: Drama
Type of plot: Fantasy
Time of plot: Late nineteenth century
Locale: London and Neverland

Principal characters:
PETER PAN, the boy who would not grow up
WENDY, his friend
TINKER BELL, Peter's fairy
CAPTAIN JAMES HOOK, a pirate captain
NURSE NANA, a dog

The Story:

In the nursery of the Darling home, a dog is the nurse, or nanny. Perhaps that is one reason there is so much joy there. Nurse Nana bathes the three children and gives them their suppers and in all ways watches over them. One night, Mrs. Darling, on Nana's night off, sits with the children as they sleep. Drowsing, she is awakened by a slight draft from the window, and, looking around, she sees a strange boy in the room. She screams, and Nana, who has just returned home, lunges for the intruder, but the boy leaps out the window, leaving only his shadow behind. He had been accompanied also by a ball of light, but it too has escaped. Mrs. Darling rolls up the boy's shadow and puts it in a drawer, thinking that the boy will come back for it sometime soon and thus may be caught.

When Mr. Darling is told of the incident he considers it a little silly; at present he is more concerned with finding a different nurse for the children. Believing that the dog, Nana, is getting too much authority in the household, Mr. Darling drags her out of the house and locks her up.

Mr. and Mrs. Darling go out the following night, leaving only a maid to look in on the children occasionally. After the lights are out and the children are asleep, the intruder returns. The boy, whose name is Peter Pan, is accompanied by Tinker Bell, a fairy who appears as a ball of light. Peter finds his

shadow after searching in all the drawers in the nursery, but in his excitement he shuts Tinker Bell in one of the drawers.

As Peter tries to get his shadow to stick to him again, he makes enough noise to awaken Wendy, the daughter of the household. Peter tells Wendy that he ran away the day he was born because he heard his parents talking about all the things he would do when he was a man; he went to live with the fairies so that he would never have to grow up. Suddenly he remembers Tinker Bell, and he looks for her until he finds her in one of the nursery dressers. Tinker Bell, a ball of light no bigger than a fist, is so small that Wendy can hardly see her. She is not a very polite fairy—she calls Wendy horrible names.

Peter tells Wendy, the only girl of the three Darling children and instantly his favorite, that he and Tinker Bell live in Neverland with the lost boys, boys who had fallen out of their baby carriages and were never found again. He had come to Wendy's house to listen to her mother tell stories to the others. Peter, begging Wendy and her brothers to go back to Neverland with him, promises to teach them to fly. The idea is too much for the children to resist. After a little practice they all fly out the window, barely escaping their parents and Nana, who has broken her chain to warn Mr. and Mrs. Darling of the danger to the children.

In Neverland, the Indians, with their chief and their princess, help to protect the lost boys against a group of mean pirates led by Captain Hook, who has a hook where one of his hands used to be. It is Hook's greatest desire to capture Peter Pan, for Peter is the one who tore off Hook's arm and fed it to a crocodile. The crocodile so liked the taste of the arm that he now follows Hook everywhere, waiting for a chance to eat the rest of him. The crocodile has, unhappily, also swallowed a clock, and its ticking warns Hook whenever the crocodile approaches.

To this strange land Wendy and her brothers fly with Peter Pan. The lost boys, seeing Wendy first in the sky when they arrive, think that she is a giant bird, and one of them shoots her with a bow and arrow. The jealous Tinker Bell had suggested the deed. Peter arrives and, after finding that Wendy is only stunned, banishes Tinker Bell for a week to punish her for provoking the attack. He then tells the others that he has brought Wendy to them. They promptly build her a house and ask her to be their mother. Wendy thinks that taking care of so many children is a great responsibility, but she quickly assumes her duties by telling them stories and putting them to bed.

Jealous, the pirates plan to steal Wendy and make her their mother; they intend to force the other children to walk the plank. Peter overhears them plotting, however, and he saves the children and Wendy. He himself escapes by sailing out to sea in a bird's nest.

Wendy and her brothers begin to worry about their parents, and they decide that they should return home. The lost boys, delighted at the thought of having a real grown-up mother, eagerly accept Wendy's invitation to come live with her and her brothers and parents. Peter refuses to go, because he wants always to be a little boy and have fun. He lets the others go, however, and asks Tinker Bell to show them the way.

The pirates have learned of the children's journey, and as Tinker Bell and the children begin to fly from Neverland, Hook and his men seize them. When Peter finds out that Hook has captured all his friends, he vows to get revenge on the pirate once and for all.

On the pirate ship, the children are being prepared to walk the plank. They are all paraded before Wendy, who is tied to the mast. Unknown to the pirates, however, Peter is also on board, and by using tricks and false voices he leads first one pirate and then another to his death. These strange happenings are too much for Hook. When he knocks the seat out from under Peter and the boy remains in place, calmly sitting on air, the pirate throws himself overboard, into the waiting jaws of the patient crocodile.

Meanwhile, at the Darling home, Mrs. Darling and Nana wait, with little hope, for the children to return. They have left the nursery window open constantly, so that their loved ones might enter easily should they ever come home, but Peter and Tinker Bell fly ahead of the others and close the window so that Wendy and the others will think they are not wanted. Peter, however, does not know how to get out of a room through the door, and thus he is forced to fly out the window again, leaving it open behind him. Wendy and her brothers fly in and slip into their beds, and Mrs. Darling and Nana are overcome with joy when they find the children safe again.

The Darlings adopt the lost boys, who have great fun romping with Mr. Darling. Peter returns and tries to get Wendy to fly away with him, but she refuses to leave her parents again. She does go once each year to clean his house for him, but each time they meet she sees him a little less clearly. Once or twice she tries to get him to see her as something more than a mother, but Peter does not know what she means. Then comes the day when Wendy can no longer fly without a broomstick to help her. Peter, watching her, sadly wishes he could understand all that she says. He picks up his pipes and plays softly, perhaps too softly to awaken humans in a grown-up world.

Critical Evaluation:

Loved by adults as much as by children, *Peter Pan* portrays the joys of perpetual childhood. Even in a realistic age, few can resist the mischievous Peter and his followers, for through them adults can live again those carefree childhood days filled with dreams and play. The special magic of Sir James Barrie's writing is in its ability to make dreams seem real, and for that reason this charming, whimsical play marks a high point of pure fantasy in the modern theater.

Barrie insisted that he did not recall having written *Peter Pan*, his most famous work and probably the greatest of all children's plays. In fact, the final stage version grew over a number of years in a haphazard fashion. It began as a six-chapter segment in a novel for adults, *The Little White Bird* (1902), then became, in turn, a three-act stage play (1904); a novel based on the earlier prose version (1906); a longer novel, titled *Peter and Wendy* (1911), taken from the play and with an extra chapter, "When Wendy Grew Up"; and finally the well-known stage version in 1928. In spite of all these versions and revisions, Barrie may have been right in saying that he was not the primary author of *Peter Pan*. As he explains in his dedication, the real genesis of *Peter Pan* was a series of stories he made up and told to five young brothers, the sons of close friends, in the late 1890's and the summer of

1901: "I made Peter by rubbing the five of you violently together, as savages with two sticks produce a fire. That is all he is, the spark I got from you."

One of the primary reasons for the popularity of *Peter Pan* is that in this work Barrie, one of the shrewdest judges of public taste ever to write drama, takes the two most basic elements of popular children's literature—the fairy tale and the adventure tale—and synthesizes them. Utilizing an extraordinary theatrical sense, he compresses an enormous amount of vivid detail into the temporal and spatial limitations of the stage. Nearly as much happens in the play as in the full-length novel *Peter and Wendy*. Almost every fantasy adventure imaginable is presented in *Peter Pan*—including encounters with Indians, pirates, and wild beasts—and each scene climaxes with a cliff-hanger: Wendy is accidentally shot with an arrow, Peter is abandoned on a rock surrounded by rising water, the children are captured by pirates, Tinker Bell is poisoned and near death (to be rescued by the audience), and Captain Hook threatens the boys with walking the plank.

At the same time, the play offers the safety of an ideal children's dream. The beasts look ferocious but are easily tamed (the boys foil the wild animals by looking between their legs at them). Benevolent magic pervades the atmosphere and is always available when needed (to save Wendy from the arrow and Peter from the rock), and for all of his demoniac appearance, Captain Hook is no match for Peter, who, in fact, toys with the pirate leader in their final clash.

In addition to providing excitement on the level of plot, *Peter Pan* evokes basic emotional and psychological responses. The primary struggle in the play is over possession of Wendy—as a mother. The play thus explores the ambivalent attitudes of children toward parents and, by extension, the human conflict of the desire for freedom versus the need to be part of a family or a society. The authoritarian father figure, Captain Hook, is villainous (traditionally, the same actor plays both Hook and Mr. Darling), but the "mother," Wendy, is idealized. While all the children are having adventures, they play at being siblings in a family, and, when offered adoption into a real family, they desert Neverland to join the Darling household.

Only Peter refuses to grow up, and even his rejection is based on disappointment at having been abandoned. (Once, in his absence from home, his mother had forgotten about him, and when he returned, there was another boy sleeping in his bed.) So only Peter remains in Neverland. At the end of the play, he has forgotten most of the adventures he had with Wendy and the others. For Peter there can be neither past nor future, only the joyous immediate moment. It is a state of being that all, children and adults alike, can enjoy for a few delightful hours in the theater—before returning to the real world, where children grow up and parents grow older.

Further Reading

Birkin, Andrew. *J. M. Barrie and the Lost Boys: The Love Story That Gave Birth to Peter Pan*. New York: Clarkson N. Potter, 1979. Collective biography of Barrie and the Davies family draws heavily on documentary evidence. Explores in considerable detail how Barrie's love for the Davies boys and their mother led to the writing of *Peter Pan*.

Chaney, Lisa. *Hide-and-Seek with Angels: A Life of J. M. Barrie*. New York: St. Martin's Press, 2006. Biography focuses on Barrie's inner life, from the time of his childhood in Scotland to his experiences as an internationally successful author. Traces the origins and evolution of *Peter Pan*.

Dudgeon, Piers. *Captivated: J. M. Barrie, the du Mauriers, and the Dark Side of Neverland*. London: Chatto & Windus, 2008. Recounts how Barrie developed an intense interest in writer George du Maurier and his family, eventually becoming "Uncle Jim" to du Maurier's eight grandchildren. Maintains that four of those children were the models for the "lost boys" in *Peter Pan*.

Geduld, Harry M. *Sir James Barrie*. Boston: Twayne, 1971. Provides a clear account of the development of the Peter Pan story from Peter's first appearance. Offers a Freudian interpretation of the womb imagery in the play and of the relationship between Mr. Darling and Wendy.

Hanson, Bruce K. *The Peter Pan Chronicles: The Nearly One Hundred Year History of "The Boy Who Wouldn't Grow Up."* Secaucus, N.J.: Carol, 1993. Presents a performance history of the play, with detailed discussions of the most famous productions. Organized around the performers who have played Peter in various productions.

Rose, Jacqueline. *The Case of Peter Pan: Or, The Impossibility of Children's Fiction*. Philadelphia: University of Pennsylvania Press, 1993. Heavily theoretical analysis questions how the play constructs a child audience for the benefit of adult illusions about childhood.

White, Donna R., and C. Anita Tarr, eds. *J. M. Barrie's "Peter Pan" in and out of Time: A Children's Classic at One Hundred*. Lanham, Md.: Scarecrow Press, 2006. Collection of scholarly essays traces the influence of Barrie's play on children's literature and popular culture and analyzes the play from feminist, postcolonial, and pop-cultural perspectives. Some of the essayists discuss *Peter Pan* within the context of the "decadent" 1890's and examine androgyny, female sexuality, and power in the play.

Peyton Place

Author: Grace Metalious (1924-1964)
First published: 1956
Type of work: Novel
Type of plot: Domestic realism
Time of plot: Late 1930's to mid-1940's
Locale: New Hampshire

Principal characters:
ALLISON MACKENZIE, a teenager and aspiring writer
CONSTANCE MACKENZIE, her mother
SELENA CROSS, Allison's friend
NELLIE CROSS, Selena's mother
LUCAS CROSS, Selena's stepfather
TOMAS MAKRIS, Allison's principal and Constance's suitor
DR. MATTHEW SWAIN, Selena's doctor
SETH BUSWELL, a newspaper editor
TED CARTER, Selena's boyfriend
NORMAN PAGE, Allison's boyfriend
RODNEY HARRINGTON, the son of mill owner Leslie
    Harrington
BETTY ANDERSON, Rodney's girlfriend

The Story:

Allison MacKenzie and her friend Selena Cross are eighth graders in Peyton Place, an isolated New England town that thrives on gossip and scandal. Allison is the illegitimate daughter of Constance MacKenzie and a married man from New York, with whom Constance had an affair. Selena's family lives on the wrong side of the tracks, and her stepfather Lucas makes sexual advances toward her. She develops a romantic relationship with classmate Ted Carter, while Allison experiences her first kiss with Rodney Harrington and embarks on a friendship with Kathy Ellsworth, a newcomer to Peyton Place. The school principal (another newcomer named Tomas Makris) is attracted to Constance.

Two years later, Constance and Tom are dating. Allison writes stories for the local newspaper, and her friendship with Norman Page becomes romantic. Selena is pregnant and convinces Dr. Swain to terminate the pregnancy because Lucas is the father. Rodney gets Betty pregnant; his father gives her money to have an abortion as well, but she leaves town, presumably still pregnant. Allison's innocence is also shattered. Nellie Cross, who works as the MacKenzies' housekeeper, is guilt-ridden after she discovers that her husband impregnated her daughter and commits suicide. The same day, Constance, consumed with fear that Allison will fall prey to the same fate that she herself has, tells Allison the truth about her father. Devastated, Allison runs to her room, only to discover Nellie's body hanging in her closet. Yet another tragedy occurs when Allison's friend Kathy loses her arm in a carnival ride accident.

The advent of World War II transforms the town of Peyton Place. Allison leaves to pursue her writing career in New York, while Constance and Tom get married. Rodney, whose

father kept him out of the war, is killed in a car accident, while Norman returns as a war hero. Selena and her younger brother Joey live comfortably, but Lucas returns to menace them. Selena kills him and buries his body in Joey's sheep pen. Eventually, she confesses and goes on trial for murder. Allison, whose heart has been broken by her first love affair, returns to Peyton Place in time for the sensational trial, which ends with Dr. Swain's revelation that Selena had once been pregnant with Lucas's child. The jury acquits her, while Allison and her mother reconcile. The novel closes with Allison returning to Road's End, one of her old haunts, and musing about the town that she once feared but still loves.

Critical Evaluation:

Peyton Place generated controversy about its sexual themes, controversy that one would have expected in the staid 1950's. A number of New England communities banned the novel after its publication in 1956, and while many small-town newspapers condemned its content, such critiques may have been less in reaction to the salacious content of the novel than motivated by fear about the dialogue its revelations might provoke. The publicity helped the novel sell sixty thousand copies in ten days, a record at the time, and it topped *The New York Times* best-seller list for over a year. A popular film adaptation, directed by Mark Robson and starring Lana Turner, was released in 1957. A hastily written sequel, *Return to Peyton Place* (1957), was followed by a film adaptation of its own in 1961. A nighttime television serial loosely based on the novel's characters was broadcast from 1964 to 1969.

Grace Metalious approached six publishing houses before Julian Messner's wife, Kitty, helped convince him to publish the novel. Kitty Messner also helped edit the novel, excising passages she felt were too romantic and insisting that Metalious make Lucas Cross a stepfather, not a father, to Selena. Metalious was angered by that change in particular, believing it diminished Selena's tragedy.

Emily Toth, author of a Metalious biography, believes that most of Kitty's recommendations improved the novel's style but diminished the emphasis on Allison as a writer. Perhaps Messner wished to forestall the inevitable parallels between Metalious and her heroine that emerged after the novel's publication. While Metalious always insisted that the novel was fiction, not autobiography, a number of its plots were rooted in reality. Most famously, Selena's murder of Lucas is likely based upon an actual patricide in Gilmanton, New Hampshire. As speculation about Metalious's source material swirled and more libraries banned the novel for its sensational content, sales exploded.

Despite the condemnation and censorship, the novel earned the praise of a number of literary critics, particularly for its efforts to undermine assumptions about propriety. In *The New York Times Book Review*, Carlos Baker compared Metalious to Sinclair Lewis, a fellow rebel against small-town hypocrisy. Other critics discussed the ways in which the author's passionate opening description of Indian summer offered a subversion of the rather stolid portrayals of New England that dominated American conceptions of the region, a holdover from the Puritan era. More important, though, the novel's opening imagery invokes feminine power, both sexual and psychological, and intimates the tenuous nature of the control held by patriarchal institutions in Peyton Place.

While defenders and detractors vigorously debated the value of *Peyton Place* in the years immediately after its publication, the novel has long suffered from neglect. A year after Metalious's untimely death, her husband and June O'Shea published *The Girl from Peyton Place* (1965), which remained the only biography of the author until Toth published *Inside Peyton Place: The Life of Grace Metalious* in 1981. Two literary critics, Madonne Miner and Ruth Pirsig Wood, have analyzed the novel along with other examples of best-selling women's fiction, but aside from Toth's biography, no book-length evaluations of the author's four novels have been written.

The 1999 republication of the novel by Northeastern University Press and, more particular, Ardis Cameron's introduction to the edition provided a timely reminder about the significance of the novel's primary theme, society's need to define appropriate notions of womanhood and to condemn

women who do not conform to the ideal. The novel's dissection of perversions and repressions offers insight into two crucial issues about American womanhood in the 1950's: the impact of Sigmund Freud's theories of motherhood and sexual deviance on women struggling to find an identity for themselves in a culture that cherished normalcy, and postwar anxieties about the return of women to the domestic sphere after a period of public independence. The novel's engagement with issues such as incest, spousal abuse, and women's sexual desires helped pave the way for Betty Friedan's groundbreaking feminist critique of patriarchal culture in *The Feminine Mystique* (1963).

A telling indication of the growing interest in Freudian psychoanalysis in the United States and the fears about bad mothering that it created is the prevalence of psychoanalytic discourse in the popular culture of the 1940's. Numerous novels and films directed at a female audience, such as the films *Now, Voyager* (1942) and *Mildred Pierce* (1945), explored maternal conflicts within a psychoanalytic framework. Metalious entered this debate after ideas about womanhood were reshaped by popular psychological writings about feminine neuroses that emerged at the start of World War II. During and after the war, rhetoric about motherhood took a decided turn for the worse.

Perhaps the influence of Freud, the growing literature on female sexual behavior, the fears about women who entered the workforce while men fought, or a general malaise imposed by the horrors of the war affected the language of writers such as Philip Wylie, whose antimother rhetoric in *Generation of Vipers* (1942) sounded the keynote for the era. In 1947, Ferdinand Lundberg and Marynia F. Farnham's *Modern Woman: The Lost Sex* picked up where had Wylie left off, and David Levy's psychological case studies in *Maternal Overprotection* (1943) were remarkably similar to the portraits of obsessive motherhood found in the era's popular films. These three books influenced the emerging portraits of the obsessive mother and frigid woman that Metalious revisited in her novel.

Ruth Pirsig Wood argues that the fates of Selena and Allison assure readers that they will be rewarded if they play by society's rules. However, Metalious may be suggesting otherwise. Despite the fact that many literary critics still perceive popular fiction as the upholder of regressive ideologies, Metalious effectively used the framework of popular fiction to confront stereotypes about women and motherhood and contributed to the debate about women's dissatisfactions that culminated in second-wave feminism.

The characters of *Peyton Place* reflect the ways in which popular psychological and sexual theories construct an idea of motherhood that often intersects with deviance, putting women into impossible positions. Instead of indicting her female characters who struggle, often unsuccessfully, to conform to society's rigid rules, Metalious instead indicts a community that refuses to see these women and their ambitions and needs sympathetically. The representative of concerned paternalism, the ever-watchful Dr. Swain, is not capable of single-handedly saving Peyton Place from those bent on destroying the women who do not conform. Portraying the types of women accused of poor mothering by 1940's popular psychologists, Metalious demonstrates that it is constraints of gender and class, as well as the repression of sexual desire, that create the hellish America painted by those such as Wylie, not female ambition or the avoidance of acceptable feminine roles.

Stephanie Lewis Thompson

Further Reading

Callahan, Michael. "Peyton Place's Real Victim." *Vanity Fair*, March, 2006, 32. Provides an overview of Metalious's life and describes the novel's evolution.

Cameron, Ardis. Introduction to *Peyton Place*, by Grace Metalious. Boston: Northeastern University Press, 1999. Cameron encouraged Northeastern University Press to reprint the long-neglected novel for its fiftieth anniversary. Her introduction praises Metalious's detailed examination of a small town, arguing that it offers surprising insights into the nature of postwar American culture and the regulation of women's lives.

Gumbel, Andrew. "The Original Desperate Housewife: America Remembers Grace Metalious." *The Independent* (London), February 20, 2006. Explores the possible resurgence of interest in the novel with its fiftieth anniversary; mentions that actress Sandra Bullock has acquired the film rights to Toth's biography of Metalious.

Metalious, George, and June O'Shea. *The Girl from Peyton Place*. New York: Dell, 1965. Published the year after the author's death, this biography was cowritten by her former husband.

Miner, Madonne M. *Insatiable Appetites: Twentieth-Century American Women's Bestsellers*. Westport, Conn.: Greenwood Press, 1984. Examines five best sellers, including *Peyton Place*. Focuses on the use of fairy-tale motifs in the novel, such as the splitting and doubling of characters and the distribution of reward and punishment.

Sova, Dawn B. *Banned Books: Literature Suppressed on Sexual Grounds*. New York: Facts On File, 1998. Reviews the initial reaction to the novel and its history of censorship.

Toth, Emily. *Inside Peyton Place: The Life of Grace Metalious*. Rev. ed. Jackson: University Press of Mississippi, 2000. Sympathetic portrait of the author. Describes the parallels between Metalious's life and those of her characters, as well as the controversy surrounding the novel.

Wood, Ruth Pirsig. *Lolita in Peyton Place: Highbrow, Middlebrow, and Lowbrow Novels of the 1950's*. New York: Garland, 1995. Discusses the novel as an example of 1950's middlebrow fiction, which assured female readers that they would be rewarded for following society's rules and punished for subverting them.

Phaedra

Author: Jean Racine (1639-1699)
First produced: Phèdre, 1677; first published, 1677 (English translation, 1701)
Type of work: Drama
Type of plot: Tragedy
Time of plot: Antiquity
Locale: Troezen, ancient Greece

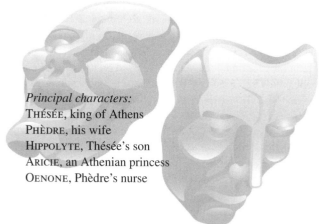

Principal characters:
THÉSÉE, king of Athens
PHÈDRE, his wife
HIPPOLYTE, Thésée's son
ARICIE, an Athenian princess
OENONE, Phèdre's nurse

The Story:

After the death of his Amazon queen, Thésée marries Phèdre, the young daughter of the king of Crete. Phèdre, seeing in her stepson, Hippolyte, all the bravery and virtue of his heroic father, but in more youthful guise, falls in love with him. In an attempt to conceal her passion for the son of Thésée, slayer of the Minotaur, she treats him in an aloof and spiteful manner until at last Hippolyte decides to leave Troezen and search for his father, who is absent from the kingdom. To his tutor, Théramène, he confides his desire to avoid both his stepmother and Aricie, an Athenian princess who is the daughter of a family that opposes Thésée. Phèdre confesses to Oenone, her nurse, her guilty passion for Hippolyte, saying that she merely pretends unkindness to him to hide her real feelings.

Word comes to Troezen that Thésée is dead. Oenone talks to Phèdre in an attempt to convince the queen that her own son, not Hippolyte, should be chosen as the new king of Athens. Aricie hopes that she will be chosen to rule. Hippolyte, a fair-minded young man, tells Aricie that he will support her for the rule of Athens. He feels that Phèdre's son should inherit Crete and that he himself should remain master of Troezen. He also admits his love for Aricie, but says that he fears the gods will never allow it to be brought to completion. When he tries to explain his intentions to his stepmother, she in turn drops her pretense of hatred and distrust and ends by betraying her love for Hippolyte. Shocked, he repulses her, and she threatens to take her own life.

The people of Athens, however, choose Phèdre's son to rule over them, to the disappointment of Aricie. There are also rumors that Thésée still lives. Hippolyte gives orders that a search be made for his father. Phèdre, embarrassed by all she had told Hippolyte, broods over the injury she now feels, and wishes that she had never revealed her love. Phèdre is proud, and now her pride is hurt beyond recovery. Unable to overcome her passion, however, she decides to offer the kingdom to Hippolyte so that she might keep him near her. Then news comes that Thésée is returning to his home. Oenone warns Phèdre that now she must hide her true feeling for Hippolyte. She even suggests to the queen that Thésée be made to believe that Hippolyte had tempted Phèdre to adultery.

When Thésée returns, Phèdre greets him with reluctance, saying that she is no longer fit to be his wife. Hippolyte makes the situation no better by requesting permission to leave Troezen at once. Thésée is greatly chagrined at his homecoming. When scheming Oenone tells the king that Hippolyte had attempted to dishonor his stepmother, Thésée flies into a terrific rage. Hippolyte, knowing nothing of the plot, is at first astonished by his father's anger and threats. When accused, he denies the charges, but Thésée refuses to listen to him and banishes his son from the kingdom forever. When Hippolyte claims he is really in love with Aricie, Thésée, more incensed than ever, invokes the vengeance of Neptune upon his son.

Aricie tries to convince Hippolyte that he must prove his innocence, but Hippolyte refuses because he knows that the revelation of Phèdre's passion will be too painful for his father to bear. The two agree to escape together. Before Aricie can leave the palace, however, Thésée questions her. Becoming suspicious, he sends for Oenone to demand the truth. Fearing that her plot has been uncovered, Oenone commits suicide.

Meanwhile, as Hippolyte drives his chariot near the seashore, Neptune sends a horrible monster, part bull and part dragon, which destroys the son of Thésée. When news of his death reaches the palace, Phèdre confesses her guilt and drinks poison. Thésée, glad to see his guilty queen die, wishes that the memory of her life might perish with her. Sorrowfully, he seeks the grief-stricken Aricie to comfort her.

Critical Evaluation:

The issue of free will, predestination, and grace that interested Jean Racine in the seventeenth century was a restatement, in theological terms, of a problem of universal concern. To what extent is one free to create one's own existence and to be responsible for one's actions? Are the terms of human existence within the arena of human control, or are the terms established by some external force? Can human suffering be justified as the result of one's actions, or is suffering the imposition of a capricious deity?

The specific manner in which these questions are answered depends upon one's view of human nature and human potential. When one chooses between predestination and free will, one is either asserting or denying a belief in one's ability to make wise and ethically sound decisions. Emphasis on the dignity of humanity and on the potential for choice often coincides with an optimism regarding human behavior. Conversely, a belief in humanity as depraved and irresponsible will be found in conjunction with a distrust of humanity's ability to act in a positive and meaningful way. This view of the human condition is presented in *Phaedra* by Racine and presents humankind as predetermined or predestined.

Racine was reared by the Jansenists at Port-Royal in France and he returned to Port-Royal after completing *Phaedra*. The Jansenists held ideas on the problem of free will and predestination in opposition to the dominant position of the Catholic Church as set forth by the Jesuits. The Jesuits attempted to bring salvation within the grasp of all humanity, whereas the Jansenists emphasized a rigid determinism. They rejected the Jesuit doctrine that people could attain salvation through good works and insisted that humans were predestined to salvation or damnation. This denial of free will was based on the conviction that humankind was left completely corrupt and devoid of rational control after the fall from God's grace suffered by Adam and Eve. Humanity was incapable of participating in the process of regeneration because Original Sin had deprived it of its will. The passions had gained control, and they could only lead to evil. Human passion was considered capable of leading to falsehood, crime, suicide, and general destruction. It is inevitable that the Jansenists would regard with alarm any doctrine that allowed for the activity of human free will. Only God's gift of mercy could save humanity, and that mercy was reserved for those who had been elected to salvation.

The basic ideas in *Phaedra* present a similar distrust of the passions, a similar curtailment of free will, and a consequent emphasis upon humanity's lack of control. Human passion is depicted as controlling reason. The area of human choice and responsibility is severely limited. Phèdre is pursued by an overwhelming sense of fatality.

In the preface to *Phaedra*, however, Racine suggests the possibility of free will. He states that Phèdre is

neither completely guilty nor completely innocent. She is involved, by her destiny and by the anger of the gods, in an illicit passion of which she is the first to be horrified. She makes every effort to overcome it.

Does Phèdre actually make the effort Racine attributes to her? To what extent is she free to make a choice? To what extent is this merely the illusion of free will? Racine continues to state in the preface that "her crime is more a punishment of the gods than an act of her will."

Phèdre's genealogy would seem to support the argument of fatality. She is initially referred to not by name, but as the "daughter of Minos and Pasiphae." Throughout the play, she gives the appearance of being overwhelmed by a cruel destiny that is linked to her past. She exhibits perfect lucidity regarding the full implications of her situation, yet she seems incapable of resolving her dilemma. All of her actions are performed "in spite of myself."

Phèdre's fall precedes the opening of the play and is the result of passion overwhelming reason. One learns that Phèdre made numerous but ineffective attempts to overcome her love for Hippolyte. She built a temple to Venus, sacrificed innumerable victims, and attempted to surmount her passion through prayer. As the play opens, Phèdre resorts to her final effort—suicide. Ironically, her attempted suicide will only serve to add physical weakness to her already weakened emotional condition and prevent her from overcoming the temptations with which she will be confronted.

The first temptation is offered by Phèdre's nurse, Oenone. By implying that her suicide would constitute betrayal of the gods, her husband, and her children, Oenone attempts to persuade Phèdre to turn back on death and reveal her love for Hippolyte. The news of Thésée's apparent death further tempts Phèdre by removing the crime of potential adultery. In addition, Phèdre is tempted to offer the crown to Hippolyte to protect her children and to appeal to his political aspirations.

Phèdre's interview with Hippolyte, however, turns into a confession of love that unfolds without a semblance of rational control. Although she expresses shame at her declaration, her passion is presented as part of the destiny of her entire race. At the moment following the confession to Hippolyte, Phèdre prays to Venus, not as in the past to free her from passion, but to inflame Hippolyte with a comparable passion. Whereas Phèdre had previously implored Oenone to aid her in overcoming her love, she now beseeches her assistance in furthering it.

Thésée's return presents Phèdre with a choice of either revealing or denying her love for Hippolyte. She, however, allows Oenone to deceive Thésée by accusing Hippolyte of fostering the illicit passion. Yet is this actually a moment of choice, assuming that choice involves a rational action? On the contrary, Phèdre's statement to her nurse at the end of act 3, scene 3, implies complete lack of control.

The final temptation to which Phèdre succumbs is her refusal to reverse the course of events by confessing her lies to Thésée. Once again, Phèdre is prevented from acting in a rational manner, for upon learning of Hippolyte's love for Aricie, she is overwhelmed by a blinding jealousy and even goes so far as to wish for the destruction of Aricie.

Despite Racine's enigmatic remarks in the preface, the pattern of temptation and defeat developed in the play eliminates entirely the possibility of free will. Although Phèdre wishes to overcome her passion, all of her efforts are in vain. The series of temptations presented to Phèdre serves to emphasize her lack of control and conspires to bring about her ruin. From the possibility of an early death with honor, Phèdre is led, through a series of defeats, to a guilty and dishonorable death. The play concludes on a note of pessimism. There is no possibility of salvation for those afflicted with passion. Racine presents humanity's fate as predestined and not subject to human control.

"Critical Evaluation" by Phyllis Mael

Further Reading

Abraham, Claude. "*Phèdre*." In *Jean Racine*. Boston: Twayne, 1977. Focuses on Racine's radical alterations of the characterizations from his sources, Euripides and

Seneca. Emphasizes the musicality of Racine's language and his emphasis on the importance of the human eye.

Campbell, John. *Questioning Racinian Tragedy.* Chapel Hill: University of North Carolina Press, 2005. Analyzes individual tragedies, including *Phaedra*, and questions if Racine's plays have common themes and techniques that constitute a unified concept of "Racinian tragedy."

Clark, A. F. B. "*Phèdre.*" In *Jean Racine.* 1939. Reprint. New York: Octagon Books, 1969. An overview of Racine's work that includes chapters on the age of Racine, classical tragedy before Racine, Racine's life, and each of his plays. Clark demonstrates that *Phaedra* marks Racine's transition from secular to sacred plays, as the protagonist is a "Greek woman with a Jansenist conscience," with full awareness of her sin.

Desnain, Véronique. *Hidden Tragedies: The Social Construction of Gender in Racine.* New Orleans, La.: University Press of the South, 2002. Analyzes *Phaedra* and four other plays from a feminist perspective. Argues that the strength of Racine's plays is not their universality but their emphasis on gender differences, with different standards imposed on men and women.

Mourgues, Odette de. *Racine: Or, The Triumph of Relevance.* New York: Cambridge University Press, 1967. Focuses on the patterns created by the interdependence and function of Racine's tragic components. Mourgues praises Racine's poetic depth and asserts that, in his tragedies, language reigns supreme.

Racevskis, Roland. *Tragic Passages: Jean Racine's Art of the Threshold.* Lewisburg, Pa.: Bucknell University Press, 2008. Examines *Phaedra* and Racine's other secular tragedies, demonstrating how these works construct space, time, and identity. Argues that the characters in these plays are in various stages of limbo, suspended between the self and the other, onstage and offstage, or life and death.

Weinberg, Bernard. "*Phèdre.*" In *The Art of Jean Racine.* Chicago: University of Chicago Press, 1969. Contains one chapter for each of Racine's plays. Declares *Phaedra* to be the author's most complete dramatic achievement because of the play's originality, unity, and characterization.

Yarrow, Philip John. "From *Mithridate* to *Phèdre.*" In *Racine.* Totowa, N.J.: Rowman & Littlefield, 1978. In this chapter of his exhaustive study of Racine's oeuvre, Yarrow examines Racine's motivations for writing *Phaedra*, explores Racine's debt to Euripides and Seneca, and proclaims that the play is the culmination of Racine's work.

Pharsalia

Author: Lucan (39-65 C.E.)

First transcribed: Bellum civile, 60-65 C.E. (English translation, 1614)

Type of work: Poetry

Type of plot: Epic

Time of plot: 70-47 B.C.E.

Locale: Rome, Spain, Northern Africa, Greece, and Asia Minor

Principal characters:

CAESAR, emperor of Rome

POMPEY, an enemy of Caesar

CRASSUS, a triumvir

JULIA, a daughter of Pompey, wife of Caesar

GAIUS TREBONIUS, one of Caesar's generals

KING JUBA, the Libyan ruler

SCAEVA, a hero in Caesar's army

CATO, an enemy of Caesar

BRUTUS, an enemy of Caesar

The Poem:

The First Triumvirate dissolves after the deaths of Crassus and Julia, who was Caesar's wife and the daughter of Pompey. After his conquest of Gaul, Caesar advances to the Rubicon, then stops to consider his next move. Public morality in Rome is being corrupted by the wealth acquired from plundering its conquests, and public officials are dishonest. When Caesar decides to march on Rome, news of his decision terrifies the Romans. The senate flees, and Pompey hurries to the Adriatic port of Brindisi. Realizing he has lost the allegiance of Rome, and that crossing the Alps to reach his allies in Spain is impractical, Pompey sends for help from Eastern cities. Although Rome is ready to fall, Caesar decides to seize the area under Pompey and block the seaport controlling the Adriatic, but Pompey abandons Brindisi to Caesar.

Pompey decides to seek help from Sicily and Sardinia, while Caesar marches on Rome. In Rome, Caesar is greeted with silence except from a defiant Metellus, and he loots the treasury. Meanwhile, Pompey finds support from Greece and Asia Minor, so Caesar hurries back to Gaul. There he finds Marseilles pleading neutrality, and Caesar prepares an assault against it. Leaving Gaius Trebonius in charge, Caesar moves on to Spain, where he attacks the Pompeians. At first they successfully resist him, but they finally surrender.

Caesar has less success elsewhere. At Curicta, the Pompeians string underwater cables across the straits and wreck Caesar's ships. Curio, Caesar's lieutenant in Sicily, sails to Libya, where in a battle with King Juba, he and his men are massacred. There is now a stalemate. The Roman senators, in exile, meet in Epirus and appoint Pompey dictator.

Caesar hurries to Rome to declare himself dictator before joining his fleet at Brindisi and sailing across the Adriatic to Illyria, where Pompey is encamped. The two armies face each other. Pompey tries to breach Caesar's defenses under cover of a wood. Pompey would have won a victory had not one of Caesar's men, Scaeva, rallied his comrades and slaughtered the Pompeians. Scaeva is killed, and Pompey traps Caesar, but Pompey restrains his troops, having scruples against killing his son-in-law.

Caesar now quits this region and leads his army into Thessaly. Pompey is urged by councillors to reoccupy Rome but decides he should pursue Caesar until he has a peace and can disband his army. Despite a witch's predictions of disaster and ominous portents, Pompey's men are eager for battle, and Pompey reluctantly assents. The armies clash at Pharsalus with great enthusiasm: one to establish tyranny, the other to resist it. The slaughter is great, and Pompey is defeated.

Caesar surveys the scene and gloats. Pompey rides off without waiting for the final scene. He rides from city to city, greeted by weeping citizens, his fame undimmed by the defeat. He now looks to his former allies among the Eastern princes, focusing on Parthia. His associates insist that he approach Ptolemy, the boy king of Egypt, and Libya instead, so Pompey sails to Egypt. Ptolemy is persuaded by his councillors to murder Pompey and keep the Romans out of their country. Pompey is decoyed ashore, stabbed to death, and decapitated. His trunk is rescued from the ocean by one of his servants, cremated on a pyre, and buried in a mound.

Pompey's ghost now swoops down for vengeance, first in Cato's heart and then in the heart of the noble Brutus. Cato assumes the role of protector of Rome, rearming the partisans of liberty and rescuing the survivors of Pharsalia. The

dead Pompey sends his son, Sextus, back to Egypt to take orders from Cato. Gnaeus, his other son, in Libya, sets out to rescue his father's body and ravage Egypt's sacred pyramids, but he is dissuaded by Cato. The Pompeians are inspired again by Cato to fight tyranny and renew the war. They cross the desert sands of Africa and reach the Oracle of Jupiter Ammon. There they meet emissaries from the Eastern powers who want to consult the Oracle, but Cato proceeds.

In the meantime, Caesar pursues the Pompeian survivors of Pharsalia as far as the Hellespont, where he stops to identify himself as a descendant of Aeneas. He then goes to Alexandria and takes Ptolemy hostage. Ptolemy's sister, Cleopatra, seduces Caesar. Pothinus, who had engineered the assassination of Pompey, now conspires the death of Caesar but postpones the deed to keep from endangering Ptolemy. The attack on Caesar fails, and Caesar sets fire to the ships and the city and seizes the Pharos, capturing Pothinus and putting him to death. Cleopatra's younger sister now takes command of the Egyptian army. She orders the execution of Ptolemy as a sacrifice and the assassination of Caesar, but Caesar successfully beats off the attack.

Critical Evaluation:

In *Pharsalia*, Lucan is more rhetorical than poetic, often epigrammatic, and often invective, although there are passages of real brilliance. Lucan, who completed his education in Athens, was a Stoic, influenced partly by his uncle, Seneca, and partly by his studies under the Stoic philosopher Cornutius in Athens. Lucan also was a republican, and this poem reflects his philosophical views. It was written over the last five years of his life; the first three books were completed only before the last year, and the poem was broken off at the tenth book when Lucan was executed for conspiring against Nero. Evidence within the poem indicates Lucan intended two more books in which Caesar would return to Rome and defeat Scipio and Cato, leaders of the Pompeians; Pompey's ghost would reappear; and Caesar would be assassinated. Lucan's views, which included a hatred of the Caesarean dynasty, were affected by the events in those years: his estrangement from Nero, involvement in a plot to assassinate Nero, and final trial.

As Lucan indicates in his opening lines, the theme of the poem is the civil war between Pompey and Caesar. This involved not only fellow citizens but also fratricide between relatives (Caesar and his father-in-law, Pompey) and affected not only Rome but also the Western world. In the early manuscripts, *Pharsalia* was titled "Bellum civile" (concerning the civil war). Throughout the epic, Lucan introduces passages that reinforce this theme: In book 1, as Caesar approaches

Rome, Lucan points out that there is panic similar to that in Thebes when two powerful brothers turned on each other. In book 2, the feud between Sulla and Marius, with its brutal slaughter, is recalled. As the poem progresses, it is clear that Lucan is also lamenting the tragic destruction of the Roman Republic and the demise of liberty.

The theme enables Lucan to indulge his predilection for violent realism and his taste for the macabre to present the horror of civil war. He depicts bizarre incidents in the sea battle off Marseilles, where a body is torn in half, the top half falling into the sea to vainly struggle against drowning, and two fathers fight over a headless body, each claiming it is that of his respective son. In the bloody battle of Pharsalia, brother despoils brother, son mutilates father, and a victorious Caesar is served breakfast in a place where he can survey the mounds of corpses settling into corruption and the streams running red. Packs of wild animals and huge flocks of birds feast on the corpses, dropping fragments of gore and flesh as they take flight after gorging themselves.

Although the poem is a lament for the losses of the civil war, the greatest casualty, from Lucan's point of view, was the destruction of the Republic, and with it, republican liberty, at the hands of the Caesarian dynasty. Liberty is the key image, and republican Cato, the third and last of the major characters, is the nearest to being the hero of the poem. Lucan set out to offset or undercut Vergil's glorification of the founders of Rome, the reputed ancestors of the Caesars. In so doing, he embarks upon innovations in epic poetry, the most obvious being discarding the role of gods and goddesses, setting a precedent for a new fusion of history and poetry, mingling both pleasing and revolting details.

There is a progression of events in which first Pompey, then Caesar, and finally Cato dominate. Caesar is depicted as a ferocious and treacherous ogre, tireless and ruthless, the antihero who destroyed the republic. One cannot help but relate Lucan's hatred of Caesar to his own feud with Nero, Caesar's descendant and successor. Pompey is identified with the republican cause, but his motives and intentions are suspect, and he is unable, sometimes reluctant, to defend himself or his cause against an energetic and ruthless Caesar. He is an eminently respectable person, but not an engaging one. He is neither a successful general nor a successful leader, and he has outlived his reputation, although he continues to have a large following. Cato is the moral hero, a superhuman figure near to the Stoic ideal of a perfect man. He is the only one of the protagonists to emerge from the catastrophic civil war with his luster undimmed, the embodiment of liberty. Although the unfinished epic ends with a victorious Caesar in Alexandria, allied to Cleopatra, his life is still in danger because of a plot for his assassination. Hints within the poem indicate that Cato will emerge at the end as the hero, with his suicide on behalf of the republican cause, and that Caesar will be assassinated in the senate.

Lucan has been described as the classic exponent of the Stoicism of the age of Nero, showing confrontations between the forces of destiny and fortunes and individuals with strong moral virtues. When omens appear, as when Caesar crosses the Rubicon, and before the battle at Pharsalia; when allies want to consult the Delphic Oracle about the future of Rome; when Sextus Pompey disgraces his father by insisting on consulting the witch Erichtho—the noble characters defy that future.

Lucan's treatment of some women characters—the vignettes of Marcia, Cato's wife, and Cornelia, wife of Pompey—may reflect the strong affection between Lucan and his wife, Polla Argentaria. After Lucan's death, his widow celebrated his birthday every year with a gathering of his friends. According to tradition, she also assisted him in the writing of *Pharsalia*.

Poet Robert Graves labeled Lucan the "father" of the costume film. *Pharsalia*, he said, "consists of carefully chosen, cunningly varied, brutally sensational scenes, linked by . . . historical probability and alternated with soft interludes in which deathless courage, supreme self-sacrifice, memorable piety, Stoic virtue, and wifely devotion" appeal to popular taste.

Thomas Amherst Perry

Further Reading

Bartsch, Shadi. "Lucan." In *A Companion to Ancient Epic*, edited by John Miles Foley. Malden, Mass.: Blackwell, 2005. An analysis of *Pharsalia*, including discussion of its contents, language, narrator's voice, reception, stoicism, and depiction of Vergil.

Clark, John. "The Later Roman Epic." In *A History of Epic Poetry: Post-Virgilian*. New York: Haskell House, 1964. Summarizes the epic, book by book, and finds its strength in its exalted style and earnest dedication. Considers Lucan the foremost writer of the Latin literature of decadence.

D'Alessandro Behr, Francesca. *Feeling History: Lucan, Stoicism, and the Poetics of Passion*. Columbus: Ohio State University Press, 2007. Examination of *Pharsalia* focusing on Lucan's use of apostrophe—the rhetorical device in which the narrator talks directly to his or her characters. Describes the ethical and moral stance that the poet-narrator takes toward his characters and his audience.

Graves, Robert. Introduction to *Lucan, "Pharsalia": Dramatic Episodes of the Civil Wars*. London: Cassell, 1961. Argues that this epic is a historical phenomenon anticipating many twentieth century literary genres.

O'Hara, James J. "Postscript: Lucan's *Bellum civile* and the Inconsistent Roman Epic." In *Inconsistency in Roman Epic: Studies in Catullus, Lucretius, Vergil, Ovid, and Lucan*. New York: Cambridge University Press, 2007. Examines contradictory passages in *Pharsalia*, describing how these inconsistencies shed light on the major problems in Lucan's epic.

Sullivan, J. P. "The Stoic Opposition? Seneca and Lucan." In *Literature and Politics in the Age of Nero*. Ithaca, N.Y.: Cornell University Press, 1985. Argues that this epic is written from the standpoint of an emotional republican who believes that Caesar and the later heads of the Roman state held power illegally and that power must be restored to the senate.

The Phenomenology of Spirit

Author: Georg Wilhelm Friedrich Hegel (1770-1831)
First published: Die Phänomenologie des Geistes, 1807
    (English translation, 1868; also known as *The Phenomenology of Mind*, 1910)
Type of work: Philosophy

The Phenomenology of Spirit is one of the most significant philosophical treatises of the nineteenth century. It laid the foundation for the many philosophical and psychological investigations and controversies of that century and continues to be an essential text. Though it is often critiqued, qualified, and even violently rejected, no serious thinker has ever been able to ignore *The Phenomenology of Spirit*'s central claim of the dialectical progress of consciousness toward an absolute understanding of the world. Georg Wilhelm Friedrich Hegel's landmark study of the history and progress of human consciousness, toward what he calls spirit, developed and brought into common usage ideas such as phenomenology, the dialectic, and the master/slave relation.

Phenomenology is the study of the human mind's ability to perceive and bring meaning to an object or the world, and not the study of an object itself or of the world itself. To quote Hegel, phenomenology "is the science of knowing in the sphere of appearance." Like his immediate predecessor, Immanuel Kant, Hegel was an idealist who believed that the mind creates the vast system of meanings and relationships that constitute the human world. What sets *The Phenomenology of Spirit* apart from Kant and the work of other idealists is that these thinkers did not discuss the lessons of history, while Hegel argued that the circular progress of history brings humanity to a full realization of its knowledge of the world. Where Kant asserted that there are nonchanging and nonhistorical rules and categories, called a priori, which help guide individuals to give meaning to the world, Hegel taught that the progressive unfolding of history develops what constitutes human understanding of the world. He refers to this hard-won and progressively created gallery of images, past customs, cultural laws, and feelings as spirit.

In Hegel's study of the human ability to see the world, the human spirit has mutated and developed through time in a dialectical process. For Hegel, there is no such thing as progress without an opposition between two parties, peoples, or ideas. He writes that there must always be a thesis, or dominant force, and an antithesis, an opposing and subordinate force to the thesis. These two opposites, far from simply ignoring or destroying each other, engage in a conversation, or dialogue (hence the word "dialectic") that results in what Hegel calls a synthesis. This synthesis is often a combination of the two previously opposing ideas, but it can also be an entirely new notion created by the dialogue between the two. *The Phenomenology of Spirit* does not simply show that any concept or knowledge is developed out of two opposing ideas. No single synthesis is ever the culmination or the end in Hegel. *The Phenomenology of Spirit* teaches that with the passage of time, any new synthesis becomes itself a thesis, which through time inevitably becomes opposed to an antithesis, resulting in another dialectic that in turn creates another new synthesis. Hegel defined this continuing process, the "long process of culture toward genuine philosophy," as the progress of human history.

The Phenomenology of Spirit has three major divisions: the preface, the introduction, and the body of the text. The preface, essential reading for understanding Hegel's phenomenological system, is one of the most quoted passages of Hegel's philosophy. It contains a synopsis of Hegel's notion of the dialectic, his study of the progress of consciousness to absolute spirit, and a discussion of the importance of the study of consciousness, or phenomenology. Hegel wrote this preface in 1807 after he had finished writing the rest of the book, and it provides a lucid interpretation of *The Phenomenology of Spirit*. Hegel's introduction is useful for providing fairly clear definitions of many of the terms used in the rest of the book.

The bulk of the text consists of eight chapters, which Hegel organized into six major discussions respectively entitled "Consciousness," "Self-Consciousness," "Reason," "Spirit," "Religion," and finally, "Absolute Knowing." Each of the six division titles represents major shifts and mutations in the shape of human consciousness, or spirit, toward the goal of absolute knowing.

The first discussion describes early forms of consciousness that provide only a realization of the world as an object (sense-certainty), of a set of chaotic particulars (perception), and finally of a crude unity where the conscious mind is nevertheless still unaware of itself in its surroundings (appearance). The subsequent step, self-consciousness, occurs when the mind becomes aware that it in large part helps create the world, and that the very ability to perceive is also an object in the world. This self-awareness can become self-indulgent. The next dialectical mutation of spirit, which Hegel calls reason, turns away from self-indulgence but still keeps the positive elements of self-awareness. Reason then begins to posit laws that focus consciousness on the structure of the world and thereby end the possibly fatal fascination with the self. Eventually, reason becomes so sure of its ability to understand the world, that this mode of perception appears, to the person who is watching the world, as actual truth.

This leap or transformation of spirit (which Hegel rather confusingly calls spirit, whereby he does not mean the same spirit as the complete spirit that develops through the dialectic of history) is of great importance, for it is the first time that humanity "is conscious of itself as its own world, and of the world as itself." In other words, humanity is beginning to understand its relation with itself and with all of the facts, images, and objects that have come to constitute the human perception of the world through time. The next step, religion, is taken when spirit takes a new shape in seeking for some-

thing that transcends human spirituality. This shape tends to see the world as an expression of a supreme God, which Hegel believes is actually humanity's spirit become externalized. For Hegel, religion is largely humanity's temporary need for a reality larger than itself. He believed that God is a dialectically created form of consciousness that fulfills this need.

The final mutation—which Hegel insists is not an ending but another starting point where "Spirit starts afresh and apparently from its own resources to bring itself to maturity"—is absolute knowing. This is where a person or whole society can attain "the goal, Absolute Knowing, or Spirit . . . as they are in themselves and as they accomplish the organization of their realm." The perceiving self is able to see the world in a new way and also able to become aware of its own relationship with itself and thus embark on another journey of phenomenological self-discovery:

> In the immediacy of this new existence, the spirit has to start afresh to bring itself to maturity as if, for it, all that preceded were lost and it had learned nothing from the experience of the earlier spirits.

Hegel discusses the shapes of consciousness created by the dialectic of history. He provides these different states to show how human understanding of the world is historically developed or mediated rather than being simply the result of whimsical ideas, God's laws, or some abstract eternal forces such as Kant's a priori. Below is a summary of the more important modes. It is important to understand that these specific modes of consciousness further develop the previous categories.

In chapters 1 through 3 (the "Consciousness" section), Hegel describes sensory, perceptual, and understanding consciousness. These describe the movement from simple object-perception to a mode of impulsive categorization of everything and from then to the first steps toward an overall unifying mode of consciousness. Chapter 4 discusses how, during the struggles of different cultures and individuals, master and slave consciousnesses develop. The master is ruler of his (or her) own realm, but as ruler the master is not interested in progress and only maintains the boundaries of his domain. Progress depends upon the slave consciousness, which develops new forms of consciousness to provide for the master. These are, respectively, the stoic (which teaches self-denial), the skeptical (where happiness is found in a cynical rejection of authority), the unhappy (resulting in a strong will), and the idealistic consciousness (which can help to change mere ideas into reality).

Chapter 5 catalogs the rational, empirical, and ethical shapes of reason. These are to show that reason exists solely within the subject, then solely in the perceived object. Finally, reason creates the ethical consciousness, which tries to reconcile these two opposing perspectives. The result of these dialectical developments is that the "real world" becomes known as an extension of both the individual mind and the ever-developing spirit. This means that spirit expresses itself within the human mind and then within the world, but also that material objects and cultural institutions begin to express the same spirit. Chapter 6 further catalogs how spirit exists and develops within physical and cultural objects and laws by its discussion of the legal and spiritual consciousness, culminating in the tragic and alienation consciousness. This unhappy collection of states of mind leads, however, to what Hegel calls the beautiful soul, which forgives and comes to terms with its alienation.

Chapter 7 includes discussions of the natural religious consciousness, where what was once a mental idea of spirit becomes externalized and worshiped in the forms of animals or celestial objects. One of the more fascinating and important forms of consciousness Hegel discusses is the artistic consciousness, which describes how art can itself express the shape of the spirit of the age in which the object was created. This passage alone has inspired volumes of art and literary criticism. This shape of consciousness leads to what Hegel calls the revealed religion (consciousness), which he feels is one of the ultimate expressions of spirit in the world. Of the New Testament of the Bible, Hegel writes that it captures some of the best revelations of spirit to be found.

The final chapter discusses the absolute consciousness. This is what enabled the writing of *The Phenomenology of Spirit* itself, and it is a moment where spirit is able to go beyond the subject/object dichotomy and become both the subject and object of individual perception. The idea that subject and object can be thus intermingled may seem confusing, but this is part of the beauty—and frustration—of *The Phenomenology of Spirit*. While it may seem that Hegel runs in circles, his definition of the truly absolute way of seeing the world is to be able to become part of "a circle that returns into itself, that presupposes its beginning, and reaches its beginning only in its end."

James Aaron Stanger

Further Reading

Hegel, George Wilhelm Friedrich. *The Phenomenology of Spirit*. Translated by A. V. Miller. New York: Oxford University Press, 1977. Still the authoritative translation of Hegel's major work. Contains an insightful summary and analyses of the text by J. N. Findlay.

Kainz, Howard P. *G. W. Hegel*. New York: Twayne, 1996. An excellent overview of Hegel's philosophical system that is readable and attempts to define terms as Hegel used them. Includes an autobiographical sketch written by Hegel at the age of thirty-four and a brief chronology of his life. Discusses philosophical influences on Hegel as a student.

Kaufmann, Walter. *Hegel: Reinterpretation, Texts, and Commentary*. Garden City, N.Y.: Doubleday, 1965. Contains a useful translation of Hegel's seminal preface to *The Phenomenology of Spirit*, as well as Kaufmann's scholarly yet clearly written insights. Dated but recommended.

Kojève, Alexandre. *Introduction to the Reading of Hegel: Lectures on Phenomenology*. Translated by James H. Nichols, Jr., edited by Allan Bloom. Ithaca, N.Y.: Cornell University Press, 1989. Kojève was instrumental in reviving Hegel's philosophy, especially *The Phenomenology of Spirit*. Clearly written, and appropriate for beginning students on Hegel. Originally published in 1947.

Krasnoff, Larry. *Hegel's "Phenomenology of Spirit": An Introduction*. New York: Cambridge University Press, 2008. Accessible overview, in which Krasnoff explains the central thesis of the work: Humankind attains its freedom through "retrospective self-understanding." Includes a brief biography of Hegel.

Moyar, Dean, and Michael Quante, eds. *Hegel's "Phenomenology of Spirit": A Critical Guide*. New York: Cambridge University Press, 2008. Twelve essays providing various interpretations of the work, including discussions of its justification of science, its conception of ethics and morality, and its ideas about religion.

Pinkard, Terry. *Hegel: A Biography*. New York: Cambridge University Press, 2000. A detailed account of Hegel's life that gives a clear sense of what kind of person he was. Provides a series of lucid analyses of Hegel's academic career and his writings.

Plant, Raymond. *Hegel*. New York: Routledge, 1999. An excellent biographical introduction to the thoughts of the philosopher, clearly presented and requiring no special background. Includes a bibliography.

Rosen, Michael. *Hegel's Dialectic and Its Criticism*. New York: Cambridge University Press, 1984. Emphasizes Hegel's dialectic method of seeking truth. Discusses the difficulty in understanding many of Hegel's ambiguous phrases.

Singer, Peter. *Hegel: A Very Short Introduction*. New ed. New York: Oxford University Press, 2001. Broad, clearly written overview of Hegel's ideas and major works. Part of the Past Masters series.

Stern, Robert. *Routledge Philosophy Guidebook to Hegel and "The Phenomenology of Spirit."* New York: Routledge, 2002. Introductory overview explaining the philosophical concepts of Hegel's work and placing the book within the context of Hegel's life and other works.

Westphal, Kenneth R., ed. *The Blackwell Guide to Hegel's "Phenomenology of Spirit."* Malden, Mass.: Wiley-Blackwell, 2009. A comprehensive resource on Hegel's book, with select chapters by noted scholars. For advanced readers and students. Part of the Blackwell Guides to Great Works series.

The Phenomenon of Man

Author: Pierre Teilhard de Chardin (1881-1955)
First published: Le Phénomène humain, 1955 (English translation, 1959)
Type of work: Philosophy

When *The Phenomenon of Man* appeared in France in December, 1955, it was hailed as a major publishing event. The English translation, which appeared in 1959, appeared to be an event of equal interest and significance among English-speaking readers. Pierre Teilhard de Chardin, born in Auvergne, France, in 1881, was an ordained member of the Society of Jesus. Early in his student days at a Jesuit college, he became interested in geology and mineralogy. He then began to study philosophy, followed by an interval of teaching physics and chemistry, and then began the study of theology. During his teaching years and theological studies, he acquired a competence in paleontology, and it was as a paleontologist that he was to become best known to the world.

Teilhard de Chardin's interests gradually centered on the general facts and theories of the evolutionary process and finally were pinpointed on what was to become his life's work: the evolution of the human race. Professionally, he was a geologist and paleontologist; as a thinker, he felt impelled to formulate a philosophy of evolution that would take into account human history, human personality, and the future possibilities for humanity on Earth. It is this formulation of concepts that constitutes Teilhard de Chardin's *The Phenomenon of Man*. Sir Julian Huxley, in an illuminating introduction, remarks that Teilhard de Chardin was a visualizer of power who saw the whole sweep of the natural history of the world, from the alpha of the origins of things to the omega of collective reflection and the fulfillment of personality. Teilhard de Chardin saw these matters with the eyes of the poet and mystic, but always with an imagination and faith supported by rational inquiry and scientific knowledge. His thoughts and conclusions are bold and visionary, but the vision is always disciplined by the demands of reality.

The Phenomenon of Man admittedly presents many difficulties for the general reader, and possibly for the professional, but Teilhard de Chardin tells the story of the evolutionary process in a style at once so finished and so engaging that the reader will find it well worth the time and concentration it will require. Much of the pleasure is a result of the excellence of the translation by Bernard Wall, who is quick to say that the writer's style is completely and undisputedly his own.

Teilhard de Chardin's basic hypothesis of the interiority of all created things may be presented in his own interpretation: Things possess both an exterior and an interior aspect that are coextensively related. A person who looked closely would find an interior even in his or her own depths. Once this fact has been realized, it may also be ascertained, in one manner or another, that the interior is present everywhere in nature since the beginning of time. When speaking of the "within" of the earth, for example, Teilhard de Chardin means not its depth in matter but the "psychic" part of the stuff of the universe that has been enclosed since the first appearance of Earth. In every portion of sidereal matter, throughout the cosmos, the interior world lines all points of the exterior one.

From this hypothesis, Teilhard de Chardin develops a law of complexity and consciousness, according to which a consciousness becomes more perfected as it forms the interior lining of a more complicated structure, so that the more developed the consciousness, the fuller and more organized the structure. Spiritual perfection and material complexity are only dual aspects of the same phenomenon. *The Phenomenon of Man* is the story of the application of this law, which is dealt with on three levels of the evolutionary spiral: prelife, life, and thought.

In physical perspective, life presupposes and supports the theory of a prelife. In the beginning, apparently through some fantastic accident, a fragment of particularly stable atoms detached itself from the sun, took its place in the cosmos, folded in on itself, and assumed the spherical shape that Teilhard de Chardin regards as of utmost importance in the evolution of matter and the emergence of consciousness. The fundamental composition of this Earth seems to have established itself from the beginning in a series of complex substances arranged in layers that form what are known as the barysphere, lithosphere, hydrosphere, atmosphere, and stratosphere, and demonstrating the powers of synthesis inherent in the universe. On the small, spherical surface of the new planet, the powers of synthesis had ideal conditions under which to operate. Teilhard de Chardin explicates the process of cosmogenesis in the life-before-life of early Earth—the genesis of ever more elaborate structures and organizations shown in the passage from subatomic units to atoms, from atoms to inorganic molecules, and later to organic molecules.

Prelife, dormant because of its diffusion in outer space, had no sooner entered the nascent sphere of the new Earth than its activities were awakened and set in motion, along with the awakening of the powers of synthesis enclosed in matter. During the millions of years of prelife, the "complexification" of matter, the energies of synthesis were causing ever greater tensions within the earth. Something tremendous was about to happen: the advent of life in the world and the formation of another envelope over the planet, the biosphere.

Teilhard de Chardin regards the appearance of life on the globe as a point of coming to maturity in the process of terrestrial evolution, a forward step of magnitude, the start of a new order in the evolutionary process. The fact that life had a beginning at one point in the natural history of the earth in no way denies the basic condition of human knowledge that each thing has its roots in the cosmos, but to accept the theory that every being has had a cosmic embryogenesis does not contradict or disprove its beginning at some definite moment in history, a change in aspect or nature. Teilhard de Chardin describes a time before the threshold of life was passed—a terrestrial era of megamolecules out of which there originated the cell, the natural granule of life with its increase in consciousness in accordance with the law of complexi-

fication. Life had no sooner started than it swarmed over the face of the earth, ramifying as it expanded.

To illustrate this process of expansion and ramification, Teilhard de Chardin uses the picture of the Tree of Life, with its roots lost in the unknowable world of primordial matter and its trunk branching out into an unbelievable multitude of types. In the course of the millions of years of its growth, the Tree of Life pushed through the fish, the amphibia, the reptiles, the birds, the mammals, the placentals, and on to the primates. These last had reached such a degree of complexification—of cephalization and cerebralization—that they became the leading shoot of the tree. Psychic tension was increasing on Earth, presaging a new order of things for the world; the active lines of descent became warm with consciousness as they achieved their most complex structure. In the mammals—the most highly developed of creatures in structure and consciousness—after millennia, the brain began to function and thought was born at some localized point of development.

When humans first come into the reader's view, they are already a crowd spread all over the Old World, from the Cape of Good Hope to Peking. Their infancy or "hominization" lasted thousands of years. As to what the nature of this leap from primate to human is, Teilhard de Chardin believes that hominization was more than simply the rise of a new species. Hominization brought a new quality into the world and has added a new (and final) envelope to the earth. That which makes humans different from all other species and places them at the summit of the evolutionary process is the phenomenon of reflection, the power acquired by consciousness to turn in upon itself, to regard and know itself, to know and to know it knows. This power of reflection makes humans not only different but also quite "other," separating humanity from the rest of creation by an abyss that no other species can cross.

Has evolution stopped after its long process leading to humankind, which apparently has undergone no significant physical change since its first appearance on the planet? In answer to this question, Teilhard de Chardin launches out on bold speculations that are not easy to follow. He asserts that humanity spread over an earth whose sphericity caused it to turn in on itself rather than to become diffuse and separated as it would have done on an unlimited surface. Through migration and intermarriage, humankind has formed an almost solid mass of hominized substance, and the process continues. As a result of recent inventions, humans are found over earth and sea, in every part of the world. From the first spark of conscious reflection, there came a glow that, in ever-widening circles, has covered the earth with a new layer that has spread over and above the biosphere. This is the "thinking" layer that Teilhard de Chardin has called the noosphere.

It would appear that evolution is an ascent to consciousness. Therefore, the further complexification of the noosphere should be expected to culminate in a supreme consciousness, which Teilhard de Chardin calls the Omega point, where the noosphere will be intensely unified and will have achieved a hyperpersonal organization. The Omega point may well be reached outside time and space, but since, for Teilhard de Chardin, the supreme importance of the human personality is a matter of faith, Omega must be in some way loving and lovable at this very moment. To satisfy the requirements of humanity's reflective activity, Omega must be independent of the collapse of the forces with which evolution is interwoven. Its four attributes are autonomy, actuality, irreversibility, and transcendence. Teilhard de Chardin suggests that it is humanity's task to organize this global layer of thought (the noosphere) more adequately so that humans might better understand the process of evolution on the earth and direct it more fully toward the fulfillment of human personality.

It is possible that the reader will find it extremely difficult—perhaps impossible—to follow Teilhard de Chardin's theories in their line of development to the point of convergence and realization he or she visualizes. There are, however, paths along which the reader can follow with the immense pleasure and profit attendant on being in the presence of a unique mind and a rare spirit. Teilhard de Chardin has the gifts to bring into full play humanity's matchless endowment, its power of reflection.

Further Reading

Birx, H. James. *Pierre Teilhard de Chardin's Philosophy of Evolution*. Springfield, Ill.: Charles C Thomas, 1972. Provides a philosophical perspective of Teilhard de Chardin's attempt to synthesize science and religion. Discusses his emphasis on evolutionary theory addressed primarily in *The Phenomenon of Man*.

Faricy, Robert L. *Teilhard de Chardin's Theology of the Christian in the World*. New York: Sheed and Ward, 1967. Synthesizes the central theme in Teilhard de Chardin's writings—the relationship between human endeavor and Christian revelation. Describes his attempt to address evolution, anxiety, death, and the finite nature of humanity, while dealing with supernatural revelation, the Second Coming, and other topics.

Grau, Joseph A. *Morality and the Human Future in the Thought of Teilhard de Chardin*. Cranbury, N.J.: Associated University Presses, 1976. Discusses ethical considerations in the philosophy of Christian humanism presented in *The Phenomenon of Man* and other works, including thoughts on love, education, politics, and freedom.

Grumett, David. *Teilhard de Chardin: Theology, Humanity, and Cosmos*. Dudley, Mass.: Peeters, 2005. A reexamination of Teilhard de Chardin's theology, focusing on his roots as a French Catholic theologian. Describes how he develops his theology by using biblical and other religious motifs to analyze his experiences of war, exile, and scientific endeavor.

Lubac, Henri de. *Teilhard de Chardin: The Man and His Meaning*. Translated by René Hague. New York: Hawthorn Books, 1966. A theological perspective on Teilhard de Chardin's writings interspersed with his personal letters and notes. Divided into two periods: his spiritual development and his defense of Christianity.

Medawar, Peter. *"The Phenomenon of Man."* In *The Strange Case of the Spotted Mice, and Other Classic Essays on Science*. New York: Oxford University Press, 1996. Medawar, a Noble Prize-winning immunologist, maintains *The Phenomenon of Man* is "nonsense" and is "tricked out with a variety of metaphysical conceits" that demonstrate how Teilhard de Chardin deceives both himself and his readers.

Meynard, Thierry, ed. *Teilhard and the Future of Humanity*. New York: Fordham University Press, 2006. Scholarly essays examine the relevance of Teilhard de Chardin's philosophy in the modern globalized world. Includes discussions of the idea of God and the person, spiritual resources for the future, politics, and economics.

Philaster
Or, Love Lies A-Bleeding

Authors: Francis Beaumont (c. 1584-1616) and John
    Fletcher (1579-1625)
First produced: c. 1609; first published, 1620
Type of work: Drama
Type of plot: Tragicomedy
Time of plot: The past
Locale: Sicily

Principal characters:
PHILASTER, the heir to the crown of Sicily
KING OF SICILY, a usurper
ARETHUSA, his daughter
PHARAMOND, a pompous Spanish prince
DION, a Sicilian lord
EUPHRASIA, his daughter, disguised as Bellario the page

The Story:

The king of Calabria has usurped the crown of Sicily from Prince Philaster's father, now dead. Because the Sicilian people love their young prince, however, the king does not dare imprison him or harm him in any way, but he does plan to marry his daughter, Arethusa, to Pharamond, a Spanish prince, who would thereby become heir to both thrones. Pharamond proves to be pompous and conceited. When Philaster, who is quite free and outspoken in his manners, tells Pharamond that only over his dead body could he marry Arethusa, the king admonishes Philaster to restrain himself. Philaster declares that he will restrain himself only when he is better treated; he believes that he is suddenly possessed by the spirit of his late father. Philaster is promised aid by the loyal Lord Dion and by two noble gentlemen, Cleremont and Thrasilene.

At an audience with Princess Arethusa, Philaster is taken aback when he hears Arethusa tell him that she loves him deeply, and he declares his love for her in return. To avoid detection under the suspicious eyes of the court, he promises to send his servant to Arethusa as their messenger. When Pharamond enters Arethusa's apartment, Philaster departs with words of scorn for the boastful Spanish prince. Later, he has difficulty in persuading his servant, Bellario—who is actually Lord Dion's daughter, Euphrasia, in disguise—to enter Arethusa's service.

At court, meanwhile, Pharamond attempts the virtue of Galathea, a court lady who leads him on but refuses all his base suggestions. Later, he makes an assignation with Megra, a court lady of easy virtue. Galathea, having overheard the conversation between Pharamond and Megra, reports the prince's dissolute ways to Arethusa.

That night the king discovers Megra in the prince's apartment. Pharamond is in disgrace. Megra, however, manages to extricate herself to some extent by insinuating that Arethusa is as wicked as she and that Bellario is more than a mere servant to Arethusa. The princess makes much of

Bellario because the page is a gift from Philaster. The king, who has not even heard of Bellario's existence, is confounded by Megra's suggestions.

Megra's story convinces even Philaster's friends that Arethusa is unfaithful to the prince, but when they tell Philaster what has happened he refuses to believe them. Nevertheless, his trust in Arethusa is shaken. When Bellario delivers a letter from Arethusa to Philaster, who is still in doubt, the disguised girl innocently damns herself by speaking in praise of Arethusa and by describing Arethusa's virtuous affection for the page. Philaster accuses Bellario of perfidy and, overcome with the passion of jealousy, threatens to take the page's life. Only because of Bellario's sincere protestations of innocence does Philaster, although still not convinced, spare his servant.

The king orders Arethusa to discharge her young page. When Philaster finds Arethusa depressed over Bellario's dismissal, he reveals his suspicions and declares that he will give up his claim to the throne and become a hermit. The wretched Arethusa, knowing that she is guiltless, can do nothing to prevent Philaster's departure.

Philaster goes to a nearby forest and wanders about disconsolately. At the same time the king and the court enter the forest to hunt. During the chase, Arethusa disappears. The hunters find her riderless horse but no trace of the princess. Bellario, having been banished from court, also went into the forest. When he encounters Philaster, the page is brusquely ordered away. In another part of the forest, Arethusa, stunned by recent events and without direction in her wandering, sits down to rest and suddenly faints. Bellario appears in time to revive her, only to be told by Arethusa that efforts to help her in her distress are wasted; the princess is prepared to die.

Philaster comes upon the pair. Thinking that their meeting was planned, and that Bellario and Arethusa are lovers, he tells Bellario to take his wretched life. When Bellario disregards his order, Philaster angrily dismisses the page and then, assuming the role of an agent of justice, attempts to kill Arethusa. He only wounds her, however. A peasant comes upon the scene of violence. In the fight that follows, Philaster is seriously wounded, but he flees when he hears horsemen approaching.

When Pharamond, Lord Dion, and others of the hunting party arrive to find Arethusa wounded, they immediately begin their search for her attacker. In his flight, Philaster, who was hurt and is now bleeding, comes upon Bellario asleep. Distractedly, Philaster wounds the page before collapsing from loss of blood. Faithful Bellario administers gently to Philaster and convinces the prince that he had made a mistake in his belief that Arethusa had been unfaithful to him. Hearing Philaster's pursuers, they flee. Bellario is captured, but not before the page had led them away from the prince. To further protect the fugitive, Bellario confesses to the attack on Arethusa. When Philaster overhears this confession, he comes out of hiding to defend Bellario. The king orders that both be imprisoned, but Arethusa, somewhat recovered from her injuries, prevails upon her father to give her the custody over the prince and the page.

In prison, Philaster, about to be executed, and Arethusa, his guard, pledge their troth. The king disavows his daughter when he learns of the marriage. The people of Sicily, aroused by Philaster's imprisonment and impending execution, seize Pharamond and threaten total revolt. The king, fearful for his safety and at last repentant for his usurpation of the throne, promises to restore the crown of Sicily and to approve Arethusa's marriage to Philaster, if the prince will only calm the enraged citizens. The people return quietly to their homes when Philaster assures them that he is now quite free and that he is their new ruler.

The king, still not satisfied with the relationship between Arethusa and Bellario, commands that Bellario be tortured in order that he might learn the truth. Philaster protests vehemently against the order. As the king's servants prepare to strip Bellario for the ordeal, the page reveals that she is, in reality, Euphrasia, daughter of Lord Dion. Having loved Philaster from childhood and despairing, because of a difference in rank, of ever marrying him, she had allowed everyone to think that she had gone overseas on a pilgrimage. Instead, she had disguised herself as a boy and taken service with Philaster to be near him. Philaster and Arethusa, moved by Euphrasia's devotion, make her a lady-in-waiting to the queen.

Critical Evaluation:

Philaster is the first tragicomedy on which Francis Beaumont and John Fletcher collaborated for London's King's

Men company between approximately 1608 and 1613. Beaumont probably wrote most of the play, but it was likely Fletcher who made it a tragicomedy, following the pattern he had introduced in his first play, *The Faithful Shepherdess* (c. 1608). In that play's preface, Fletcher explains,

A tragi-comedy is not so called in respect of mirth and killing, but in respect it wants deaths, which is enough to make it no tragedy, yet brings some near it, which is enough to make it no comedy, which must be a representation of familiar people, with such kind of trouble as no life be questioned.

Closely related to the sixteenth century Italian pastoral romance, *Philaster* and other tragicomedies also are distinguished by distant and exotic settings, plots that move quickly and often unrealistically, shallow and stereotypical characters, sudden character reversals for which an audience is unprepared, and contrasts between love and lust, and honor and deceit. Whereas uncertainty about the fate of the heroes assures some degree of tension in tragicomedy, happy conclusions are the norm, although they usually follow from surprises or sudden revelations.

Philaster shares traits with comedies and tragedies by William Shakespeare. In Shakespeare's *As You Like It* (pr. c. 1599-1600, pb. 1623), for example, a usurper rules, young women don male disguises, and there is a pastoral element. In *Twelfth Night: Or, What You Will* (pr. c. 1600-1602, pb. 1623), which also has an exotic setting, a young woman disguises herself as a man and becomes part of a love triangle. *Hamlet, Prince of Denmark* (pr. c. 1600-1601, pb. 1603), like *Philaster*, opens with a young prince suffering the indignities of disenfranchisement in his usurper's court. In *Othello, the Moor of Venice* (pr. 1604, pb. 1622), a father denounces his daughter for marrying without his advice and consent.

Despite its improbable plot and its rapid succession of short scenes, *Philaster* has dramatic integrity, which is largely attributable to the unifying presence of its title character, whose fate is the focal point. Widely admired and loved, Philaster initially is portrayed as honorable, loyal, and stoic, an icon of perfection. Later, however, his easy embrace of the false story of Arethusa and Bellario's deception and his inexplicable wounding of Arethusa somewhat diminish him while also making him more human—a good person, although flawed.

From the beginning, the playwrights develop a clear contrast between Philaster and Pharamond, a prince of Spain who comes to Sicily as official suitor to claim a bride and thus eventually gain control of the kingdom. Pharamond, who is boorish and sexually promiscuous, is marrying Arethusa solely for dynastic reasons. The courtier Dion says that Pharamond is prince only by accident of birth and just as easily could have been born a slave. In other words, there is nothing inherently princely about him. His quick liaison with the lascivious Megra not only heightens the contrast between him and the regal Philaster, setting the stage for inevitable conflict, but also ironically victimizes the unlawful king. At the end, however, the monarch benevolently pardons Pharamond and Megra and blesses the forthcoming marriage of his daughter to Philaster, who will inherit the throne.

The king is a peripheral figure in the play despite his office, an ineffectual villain with only minor bouts of conscience. His failure to gain the citizenry's acceptance of his usurpation, his impotence during the uprising crisis, and his inability to orchestrate a political marriage for Arethusa dramatize the public and private consequences of his earlier illegal actions. These details may be oblique allusions by Beaumont and Fletcher to intemperate behavior in the court of King James I. Indeed, the prominence of the three courtiers, led by Dion, keeps politics in the forefront. Functioning as chorus, they are superficially loyal to the present monarch while retaining a reservoir of affection and respect for Philaster. Dion hopes to encourage Philaster to lead an insurrection, but one erupts without Philaster's leadership and ironically he ends it.

The king's acceptance of the marriage between Arethusa and Philaster initially seems incredible because his daughter, in an affront to traditional parental responsibility, not only has wed secretly but also has made a match with her father's blood rival. In fact, the king has no choice, for he is informed only after the marriage has taken place, and his preferred suitor proved to be totally unacceptable. Importantly, Philaster, the putative rival, saves the king's crown by putting down the rebellion, thus demonstrating not only loyalty and usefulness but also worthiness as a future ruler.

Although Beaumont and Fletcher do not develop Arethusa in any depth, the princess is an important figure in the action and comes across as strong-willed and independent, in the tradition of such Shakespearean comic heroines as Beatrice, Rosalind, and Viola; in her willful disregard in the conflict with her father she outdoes Desdemona. Arethusa also has other forebears. When in trouble, she flees to the country, like the heroines of Sir Philip Sidney's *Arcadia* (1590, as *The Countess of Pembroke's Arcadia*) and other sixteenth century pastoral romances. The page who serves her, supposedly the male Bellario but actually Dion's daughter, Euphrasia, is also a stock character of the pastoral.

Emerging from both the love and political plots, the play's primary theme is a Renaissance commonplace: Virtue is rewarded. Beaumont and Fletcher use their characters to dramatize various manifestations of love: Philaster and Arethusa exemplify romantic love that culminates in marriage; the behavior of Pharamond and Megra illustrates lust and base sexuality; and Bellario (Euphrasia) represents the ideal of platonic love and selfless, disinterested friendship.

Successful when it was initially performed at the public Globe theater and the private Blackfriars theater, *Philaster* continued to be popular both on stage and in print throughout the seventeenth century. Its lasting appeal can be attributed in part to its being a forerunner of Restoration heroic drama, tragic epic plays in which love and honor are presented in an exaggerated and improbable manner, usually in the context of political or military conflict. In 1695, Elkanah Settle wrote an opera based on the play, and an adaptation (attributed to the duke of Buckingham) was presented in 1714: *The Restauration: Or, Right Will Take Place*.

"Critical Evaluation" by Gerald H. Strauss

Further Reading

Appleton, William W. *Beaumont and Fletcher: A Critical Study*. London: George Allen & Unwin, 1956. This standard critical study of the playwrights' collaborative work favorably compares *Philaster* to their earlier and later tragicomedies, discusses Shakespearean influences (tragic and comic), and shows how Beaumont and Fletcher modified traditional pastoralism.

Ashe, Dora Jean. Introduction to *Philaster*. Lincoln: University of Nebraska Press, 1974. The introduction to this authoritative text, edited by Ashe, analyzes the play and examines such matters as genre, plot, characterization, the pastoral tradition, and political satire.

Braunmuller, A. R., and Michael Hattaway, eds. *The Cambridge Companion to English Renaissance Drama*. 2d ed. New York: Cambridge University Press, 2003. This collection of essays discussing various aspects of English Renaissance drama includes numerous references to Beaumont and Fletcher and information about *Philaster*.

Clark, Sandra. *Renaissance Drama*. Malden, Mass.: Polity Press, 2007. This accessible overview of Renaissance drama places the plays of Beaumont and Fletcher, including *Philaster*, within their broader literary context.

Finkelpearl, Philip J. *Court and Country Politics in the Plays of Beaumont and Fletcher*. Princeton, N.J.: Princeton University Press, 1990. Finkelpearl claims that the playwrights dramatized the amorality of their age through political criticism of the monarch and court. He groups

Philaster with *The Maid's Tragedy* and *A King and No King* as a trilogy about the consequences of a ruler's intemperance.

Leech, Clifford. *The John Fletcher Plays.* London: Chatto & Windus, 1962. Wide-ranging study asserting that

Philaster is notable for its variety, for how the playwrights deal with pretense, and for the importance of comedy in a largely serious play. Points out that Fletcher places stereotypical characters in atypical situations that provide novelty for audiences.

The Philippics

Author: Demosthenes (384-322 B.C.E.)

First transcribed: Philippicae, 351-341 B.C.E. (English translation, 1852)

Type of work: Essays

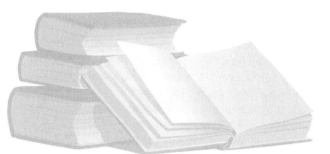

Occasionally in history, genius and a crisis in human affairs unite to produce a person whose name rings down through the ages long after the particular events have faded into the dimness of antiquity. Such a person was Demosthenes. Almost every educated person has heard of him and knows that he was a famous Greek orator. The events and the crisis in ancient Greece that helped make him famous, however, are unknown except to students of ancient history.

As an Athenian lawyer and orator, Demosthenes might have won little fame had it not been for Philip of Macedon, whose ambition was to conquer and rule as much of the world as he could. When the danger to Athens became great, Demosthenes did all he could to arouse his fellow Athenians to the defense of their city-state. Such crises have recurred in various forms throughout history. On one hand was Philip of Macedon, a tyrant who sought control of many lands and peoples; on the other was Demosthenes, a believer in democracy and local sovereignty who did all that one person could to arouse his contemporaries to fight against Philip and, later, Philip's son, Alexander the Great. In this conflict between democracy and tyranny there is no doubt of Demosthenes' sincerity; it rings out from his orations almost as clearly today as it must have more than two thousand years ago.

By common consent of his contemporaries and later generations, Demosthenes was the greatest of the Greek orators, in a culture that produced a great many with ability in rhetoric and oratory. Scholars of all periods have praised his speeches, and the number of manuscripts found in Egypt containing fragments of his speeches has been second only to papyri containing fragments of the Homeric epics. In modern times it is difficult to appreciate the greatness of the speeches from the standpoint of formal rhetoric as the an-

cient Greeks knew and used it. What Cicero praised in the orations is now to be found only by the serious student of Greek language and culture.

Modern readers, however, may find in the speeches what Demosthenes' admirers in the ancient world seem to have overlooked or ignored. Readers can see that Demosthenes was an able and sincere statesman laboring for democratic ideals at a time when his fellow citizens in Athens were inclined to do little to oppose the forces of tyranny led by Philip of Macedon. Demosthenes knew human nature as he knew his art, and he employed his knowledge of both to speak out forcefully for what he believed in. He spoke out not for the sake of his rhetoric but for the sake of Athens; he spoke not to a select group, to no aristocracy, but to all Athenians. He wished to persuade them to rise to the defense of their city and the way of life and government that it represented. There is little flamboyance in the orations, at least as they are translated. Demosthenes spoke plainly and sincerely; his art was like all great art, hiding beneath the cloak of apparent simplicity, reflecting great care and preparation. Demosthenes' tone is serious, befitting his topic.

As in the case of so many ancient authors, the authenticity of work supposedly done by Demosthenes is open to question. More than sixty orations, as well as some letters and poems, have been attributed to him. Scholars currently accept only about forty of the speeches as authentic. Many of the orations accepted as his are nonpolitical, having been composed for delivery in cases at law. These orations furnish much material about Greek culture. Demosthenes' true fame rests on the speeches called *The Philippics*. These were not the only orations on political subjects that he made, nor were they the only speeches he gave that had to do with the threat of Philip to Athens. Quite a number of his other orations, such as the *Olunthiakos* (349-348 B.C.E.; *Olynthiacs*, 1570), deal with Philip's depredations in the Greek peninsula and other portions of the eastern Mediterranean world.

The first *Philippic* was delivered in 351 B.C.E. At that time Philip, stopped at Thermopylae, had sent his armies into Thrace, dispatched a fleet to attack the islands of Lemnos and Imbrus, and interfered with the commerce of Athens by attacking shipping. Demosthenes said that the Athenians might be made aware of the danger and should take steps to defend themselves. The orator obviously felt that Athens in 351 B.C.E. had more to fear from the Macedonian king than from its traditional enemy, Thebes, or from a combination of other unfriendly city-states. It was not as an alarmist that Demosthenes spoke; he spoke, rather, to awaken his fellow Athenians to an awareness of the need for watchfulness and preparedness. In this first *Philippic* he encouraged his city to meet the danger, pointing out its advantages and strengths. In practical fashion, he suggested ways in which the city could economically take steps to meet the danger, which at that time was not as great as it would become in passing years.

It was not enough, as Demosthenes knew, merely to hope that Philip had died, as rumor had it. Demosthenes realized that failure to provide for defense through inaction sets up circumstances that are an invitation to strong-arm tyranny. Later history has shown that leaders have often failed to realize this truism of politics. Demosthenes realized, as leaders sometimes have failed to do, that free people do not have a choice between action and inaction. To oppose Philip, to warn him that Athens was prepared to defend itself, the orator suggested a military force of moderate size, with good officers to lead it. He recommended that at least 25 percent of the personnel be Athenians, the rest mercenaries. Knowing that to equip, pay, and keep in the field a large force was beyond the economic power of the city, he urged the establishment of a small but efficient military force. The answer to the problem, he said, lay in making the best use of what could be afforded, not in hitting blindly only at places here Philip had already struck.

The Athenians did nothing. In 344 B.C.E., seven years later, Demosthenes again spoke pointedly in the second *Philippic*. By that time Philip, allied with the Messenians, had become a more powerful threat to Athens. Demosthenes himself had headed an embassy to Messene and Argos to warn those cities against the oppressor, to no avail. Philip, in turn, had sent an emissary to Athens to complain about Demosthenes' charges and to vindicate his own conduct. Demosthenes spoke to explain carefully what Philip was do-

ing and what the pro-Macedonian group in Athens was doing to endanger the city. He ended by pointing out that Philip's conduct now made the Athenians' problem one of defending their city and homes, not merely of looking after claims and interests abroad. Philip's benevolence was shown to be double-edged.

In the third of the *Philippics*, delivered in 341 B.C.E., Demosthenes cried out that Athenians had to learn that a state of war existed, even though Philip talked of peace. Philip aimed at the Chersonese, which controlled the route of grain ships between Athens and the Euxine. Demosthenes urged that the Chersonese be protected as a means of protecting Athens. He was right in his predictions: Philip attacked the Propontine cities in the following year. The Athenians, to their credit and Demosthenes', played their part in resisting the tyrant.

The fourth and last of the *Philippics* was also delivered in 341 B.C.E., just before Philip laid siege to the Propontine cities. In this oration, as he had in the third *Philippic*, Demosthenes urged resistance, even advocating an alliance with Persia. Although the fourth *Philippic* is generally accepted as authentic, some scholars have viewed it with suspicion, claiming for several reasons that it is spurious and not really a product of Demosthenes' own hand.

Further Reading

Bury, J. B., and Russell Meiggs. "Rise of Macedonia." In *A History of Greece to the Death of Alexander the Great*. 4th ed. New York: St. Martin's Press, 1975. Includes discussion of *The Philippics* within an account of the conflict between Athens and Philip II of Macedonia. The account is favorable to Philip at Demosthenes' expense but offers a good historical introduction.

Gibson, Craig A. *Interpreting a Classic: Demosthenes and His Ancient Commentators*. Berkeley: University of California Press, 2002. Gibson has translated the commentaries of a group of ancient scholars who interpreted Demosthenes' works. He describes the source of these ancient writings and how they were transmitted through successive generations.

Jaeger, Werner. "Demosthenes." In *Paideia: The Ideals of Greek Culture*. Translated by Gilbert Highet. 2d ed. 3 vols. New York: Oxford University Press, 1986. Provides an excellent short introduction to Demosthenes' political orations, including *The Philippics*, within the context of a cultural history of Greece.

_____. *Demosthenes: The Origin and Growth of His Policy*. Translated by Edward S. Robinson. 1963. Reprint. New York: Octagon Books, 1977. Presents an investigation of Demosthenes' orations for the purpose of promoting understanding of his political thought. Includes ample discussion of the speeches opposing Philip.

Pickard-Cambridge, A. W. *Demosthenes and the Last Days of Greek Freedom: 384-322 B.C.* 1914. Reprint. Piscataway, N.J.: Giorgias Press, 2002. Clear and concise summaries, with translations of key passages, of the speeches against Philip are worked into a detailed history of Demosthenes' times.

Wooten, Cecil W. *A Commentary on Demosthenes' "Philippic" I: With Rhetorical Analyses of "Philippics" II and III.* New York: Oxford University Press, 2008. Provides the first substantive commentary on the first *Philippic* published since 1907, analyzing the work's rhetorical and stylistic techniques, placing it within its historical con-

text, and pointing out its grammatical problems. Also describes how the second and third *Philippics* differ from the first.

_____. "Style and Argumentation in the Speeches of Demosthenes." In *Cicero's "Philippics" and Their Demosthenic Model.* Chapel Hill: University of North Carolina Press, 1983. Offers a good description of the basic feature of Demosthenes' oratorical style. Useful for readers with little prior knowledge of Demosthenes.

Worthington, Ian, ed. *Demosthenes: Statesman and Orator.* New York: Routledge, 2000. Collection of essays addresses such topics as how views of Demosthenes have changed over time, Demosthenes' inactivity during the reign of Alexander the Great, and his public speeches. Includes discussion of *The Philippics.*

Philoctetes

Author: Sophocles (c. 496-406 B.C.E.)
First produced: Philoktētēs, 409 B.C.E. (English translation, 1729)
Type of work: Drama
Type of plot: Tragedy
Time of plot: Antiquity
Locale: Island of Lemnos

Principal characters:
PHILOCTETES, an abandoned Greek warrior
NEOPTOLEMUS, Achilles' son
ODYSSEUS, the king of Ithaca
A SAILOR, disguised as a trader
HERAKLES, a Greek immortal
CHORUS OF SAILORS, under the command of Neoptolemus

The Story:

Odysseus abandons Philoctetes on the barren island of Lemnos after the warrior is bitten on the foot by a snake while preparing to make a sacrifice at the shrine on the island of Chrysa. The wound never heals, and the smell that comes from it and the groans of suffering of Philoctetes are the reasons Odysseus gives for making him an outcast. Philoctetes, however, with his invincible bow, once the property of Herakles, becomes indispensable to the Greeks in their war against Troy. Landing for the second time on Lemnos, Odysseus describes the cave in which Philoctetes lives. Neoptolemus identifies it by the stained bandages drying in the sun, the leaf-stuffed mattress, and the crude wooden cup he finds.

Instructed by Odysseus, Neoptolemus is to lure Philoctetes on board with his bow by declaring that he, too, hates Odysseus because the king deprived him of the weapons of his father, Achilles. Neoptolemus is disgusted by this decep-

tion, but wily Odysseus pleads necessity and promises him honor and glory. When Neoptolemus agrees to obey, Odysseus leaves him.

The chorus of sailors reports that they hear the painful approach of Philoctetes. He asks who they are and whether they, too, are Greeks. Imploring their pity, he tells them not to fear him, although he became a savage through solitude and great suffering. Neoptolemus answers Philoctetes, who asks Neoptolemus who he is and why he comes. The young warrior says that he is the son of Achilles and that he does not know Philoctetes, who replies that he must indeed be vile if no word of him reached the Greeks. His wound grew worse and because he is alone on the island he has to use all his energy to remain alive. He shoots birds with his great bow, and, in order that he might drink in winter, he is forced to build a fire to melt the ice. He curses the Atreidae and Odysseus, who abandoned him, and wishes that they might suffer his agony. Neoptolemus, answering as he was instructed, says that he, too, curses Odysseus, who deprived him of his rights and robbed him of his father's arms. He asserts that he intends to sail for home.

Philoctetes, declaring that their grief is equal, wonders also why Ajax allows these injustices. He is told that Ajax is also dead. Philoctetes is certain that Odysseus is alive, and this fact Neoptolemus confirms. After hearing of the death of other friends, Philoctetes agrees with Neoptolemus that war inevitably kills the good men but only occasionally and by chance kills the bad. Neoptolemus stresses his determination never to return to Troy. He then says good-bye to Philoctetes, who implores them not to abandon him and to suffer for one day the inconvenience of having him on board the ship on which Neoptolemus is sailing. When he begs on his knees not to be left alone again, the chorus expresses their willingness to take him with them. After Neoptolemus agrees, Philoctetes praises the day that brings them together and declares himself bound in friendship to the young warrior for all time.

As Odysseus planned, a sailor disguised as a trader comes to help Neoptolemus in tricking Philoctetes. He says, hoping to persuade Philoctetes to go quickly on board, that Odysseus is pursuing him in order to compel him to rejoin the Greek army, for Helenus, Priam's son, prophesied that Philoctetes is the one man who will defeat Troy. Philoctetes swears that he will never go with his most hated enemy, and the disguised trader returns to his ship.

Neoptolemus asks permission to hold the mighty bow while Philoctetes prepares to leave the island. Suddenly the wound in Philoctetes' foot begins to pain him beyond endurance. He hands the bow to Neoptolemus and writhes on the ground until the abscess bursts and the blood flows. The sailors advise Neoptolemus to leave with the bow while the exhausted man sleeps. Neoptolemus refuses, for the bow is useless without Philoctetes.

When Philoctetes awakens, Neoptolemus reveals to him that he came to take the warrior to fight against Troy. Philoctetes refuses to go. When Neoptolemus insists on keeping the bow, Philoctetes, enraged and despairing, curses such treachery and declares that he will starve without his weapon. Neoptolemus's loyalties are divided between duty and compassion, but before he decides on the course to pursue, Odysseus arrives and demands that Philoctetes accompany them. When he remains adamant, Odysseus and Neoptolemus leave, taking with them the bow.

The chorus of sailors assures Philoctetes that it would be best to fight on the side of the Greeks, but, out of pride, he is determined not to fight alongside the men who made him an outcast. He begs for a sword to kill himself. Then Neoptolemus returns, followed by Odysseus; he decides to redress the wrong he did Philoctetes and to return the bow. Odysseus, unable to change the young warrior's decision, goes to tell the other Greeks of this act of treachery. Meanwhile, Neoptolemus again tries to persuade Philoctetes to join them. When Philoctetes again refuses, Neoptolemus, in spite of the return of Odysseus, gives back the bow. He is then forced to keep Philoctetes from killing Odysseus.

When Odysseus again leaves them, Neoptolemus reveals the whole of Helenus's prophecy, which foretold that the wound would be cured when Philoctetes returns and that, together with Neoptolemus, he will conquer Troy. Philoctetes, declaring Odysseus was faithless once and will be so again, implores Neoptolemus to take him home, as he first promised. Neoptolemus, however, is afraid that the Greeks will attack his country in retaliation. Philoctetes swears that he will defend the country with his bow.

Before they can leave, Herakles, from whom Philoctetes inherited the bow, appears on the rocks above the cave. He informs Philoctetes that Zeus made a decision. Philoctetes should return to the Greek army where he will be healed. Also, with Neoptolemus, he will kill Paris and take Troy. Philoctetes, heeding the voice of the immortal, willingly leaves Lemnos to fulfill his destiny.

Critical Evaluation:

Scholars consider Sophocles in many ways the greatest and most modern of the Greek tragedians. Sophocles' innovations include increasing the number of actors from two to three and diminishing the role of the chorus, thus making room for greater character depth, psychological complexity, and intricate plots. Greek myth still provides the background, yet each of Sophocles' plays focuses on unique moral dilemmas in human terms.

One of Sophocles' main themes, seen in *Oidipous Tyrannos* (c. 429 B.C.E.; *Oedipus Tyrannus*, 1715) and *Antigonē* (441 B.C.E.; *Antigone*, 1729) as well as in *Philoctetes*, is the suffering of the individual caused when a strong-willed person contradicts the will of the gods or the rational solution to a problem. Sophocles does not reveal the will of the gods until the end of *Philoctetes*, when the Greek sailor disguised as a trader explains that Helenus, a prophet and son of the Trojan king Priam, was captured by Odysseus. Helenus prophesies before the warriors that the Greeks will never take Troy until they persuade Philoctetes to leave his island and come with them. This puts the burden of responsibility upon Odysseus, since it was his idea to maroon Philoctetes, and now Philoctetes is needed to win the war.

In Homer's epic *Iliad* (c. 750 B.C.E.; English translation, 1611), the poet reviews the Greek troops gathering to begin the assault upon Troy to retrieve Helen, wife of commander Menelaus. Homer says that seven ships were led by Philoctetes, the master archer "superbly skilled with bow in lethal combat." Homer explains that after the battle, Philoctetes lay in agony upon the shores of the island of Lemnos. From this threadbare legend, Sophocles develops his three primary characters—Philoctetes, Odysseus, and Neoptolemus—in a profound statement about the meaning of suffering and personal integrity.

Sophocles' drama explores the idea that people learn the meaning of life only through suffering. Often in Greek stories, misery and torment are caused by the arbitrary workings of the universe. Knowledge and virtue are attained through coping with difficult circumstances such as the ten years of Philoctetes' abandonment or the twelve "impossible" labors of Herakles.

Philoctetes and Herakles, the most famous of Greek heroes, share similar stories. Herakles suffers because of the wrath of Hera, queen of the universe; Philoctetes suffers because of the help he gave to Herakles. According to some Greek authorities, Hera sent the snake to injure Philoctetes. When the dying Herakles lies upon a funeral pyre on Mount Oeta, none of his followers will light the fire. Herakles offers Philoctetes his bow in exchange for lighting the fire, thus helping Herakles to be transposed to Olympus. Both Herakles and Philoctetes experience restoration. Herakles becomes an immortal after his labors; physicians heal Philoctetes' incurable wound after his bow brings about the fall of Troy.

Philoctetes' identity is linked to enduring pain. According to one myth, Philoctetes is wounded accidentally while in the act of sacrificing to Apollo on the island of Chrysa. The snake that bites him may have been either the guardian of an unmarked shrine or a punishment sent by Hera for helping Herakles. Philoctetes' pain is so great that he cries out, uttering oaths and curses, becoming a nuisance to Odysseus and his men. Odysseus regards the festering wound as a bad omen that terrifies the warriors. Philoctetes tells Odysseus that "You have joy to be alive, and I have sorrow/ because my very life is linked to this pain."

Nevertheless, while isolated on Lemnos, Philoctetes builds his skills and attempts to restore his confidence. His arrows never miss the birds and wild animals that are his food during his isolation. When Herakles rescues him at the end of the play, Philoctetes' restoration is complete.

In *Philoctetes*, Sophocles compares a multidimensional hero (Odysseus) to a static, one-dimensional sufferer (Philoctetes). Philoctetes' unhealed wound is a symbolic blemish upon his psyche, a sign that he is not yet initiated into complete understanding of himself and the gods. Odysseus is himself wounded in a boar hunt, according to Homer's *Odyssey*. Odysseus is also nearly killed by a host of other monsters such as the Cyclopes, Circe, and Scylla, but he always overcomes the physical challenge with knowledge and craft. Odysseus's and Philoctetes' wounds are important signs of contact with the transcendent, divine world. Odysseus overcomes his wounds, earning his glory through cunning, and Philoctetes must also rise to the occasion.

Odysseus's advice to Neoptolemus to lie to Philoctetes when they go to Lemnos shows his willingness to abandon absolutes. However, Odysseus is in error by telling Neoptolemus that only Philoctetes' bow is needed for the Greeks to have victory. In fact, the prophet Helenus specifically stated that both Philoctetes and his weapon needed to be transported to Troy. Philoctetes needs to rise above the limitations and challenges imposed upon him in order to obey the command of the gods and salvage his place in history. However, Philoctetes waits until he sees the *deus ex machina* appearance of Herakles in order to make his decision to leave the island.

Neoptolemus's name means "young warrior," and he is just that—pure and strong but gullible and naïve. When Odysseus brings Neoptolemus with him to Lemnos, Sophocles presents the problem of two very different people with the same desire: to win the Trojan War. Neoptolemus is Achilles' son, who may feel sublimated hatred against Odysseus because of the fact that Odysseus received his father's armor after his death. Neoptolemus feels ashamed of his part in tricking the innocent Philoctetes, and he gives him his word that he will take Philoctetes back to Greece—directly countering Odysseus's desire to get the bow.

A sympathetic brotherhood emerges between Neoptolemus and Philoctetes as the full extent of his pain and suffering becomes apparent. Neoptolemus is too honest to fully comply with Odysseus's trickery, changing his mind once he gets to know Philoctetes' story. Sophocles raises the question of whether the greater end (winning the Trojan War) justifies the smaller means (telling lies to Neoptolemus and Philoctetes). Sophocles shows the value of personal integrity and honesty over scheming and conniving to achieve a desired result. Neoptolemus willingly goes with Odysseus to retrieve Philoctetes, but then he feels sympathetic toward the abandoned man and guilty that he uses trickery to get the bow. In the end, the honor goes to the one who endured suffering with grace, Philoctetes.

"Critical Evaluation" by Jonathan Thorndike

Further Reading

Beer, Josh. *Sophocles and the Tragedy of Athenian Democracy.* Westport, Conn.: Praeger, 2004. Analyzes Sophocles' plays within the context of Athenian democracy in the fifth century B.C.E., focusing on the political issues in the dramas. Examines Sophocles' dramatic techniques and how they "revolutionized the concept of dramatic space." Chapter 9 discusses *Philoctetes*.

Gardiner, Cynthia P. *The Sophoclean Chorus: A Study of Character and Function.* Iowa City: University of Iowa Press, 1987. Uses *Philoctetes* to reexamine the undervalued role of the chorus in Greek drama and how Sophocles skillfully uses choral odes for dramatic irony. Discusses the extent to which the chorus participates in the plot of deception.

Garvie, A. F. *The Plays of Sophocles.* Bristol, England: Bristol Classical, 2005. Concise analysis of Sophocles' plays, with a chapter devoted to *Philoctetes*. Focuses on Sophocles' tragic thinking, the concept of the Sophoclean hero, and the structure of his plays.

Kitto, H. D. F. *Greek Tragedy: A Literary Study.* London: Methuen, 1939. Reprint. New York: Routledge, 2002. An excellent study of Sophocles' innovations, such as his emphasis on character development, especially of Neoptolemus in *Philoctetes*, which Kitto claims has a wider range than any other character in Greek tragedy.

Kitzinger, Margaret Rachel. *The Choruses of Sophokles' "Antigone" and "Philoktetes": A Dance of Words.* Boston: Brill, 2008. Analyzes the function of the chorus in the play. Argues that the chorus views the action from the perspective of the dancers and the singers; the chorus has a particular way of communicating on humankind's place in the larger order defined by how the singers and dancers reflect that order.

Morwood, James. *The Tragedies of Sophocles.* Exeter, England: Bristol Phoenix Press, 2008. Analyzes each of Sophocles' seven extant plays, with chapter 7 devoted to *Philoctetes*. Discusses several modern productions and adaptations of the tragedies.

Ringer, Mark. *"Electra" and the Empty Urn: Metatheater and Role Playing in Sophocles.* Chapel Hill: University of North Carolina Press, 1998. Focuses on elements of metatheater, or "theater within theater," and the ironic self-awareness in Sophocles' plays. Analyzes plays-within-plays, characters who are in rivalry with the playwright, and characters who assume roles in order to deceive one another. *Philoctetes* is discussed in chapter 6.

Roisman, Hanna M. *Sophocles: Philoctetes.* London: Duckworth, 2005. A companion to the play, discussing its initial performances, characters, reception over time, and the mythology on which it is based. Places the play within the context of ancient Greek theater and the historical events of its time.

Segal, Charles. *Tragedy and Civilization: An Interpretation of Sophocles.* Cambridge, Mass.: Harvard University Press, 1982. Develops the idea of the civilizing power of tragedy and the importance of society, language, and friendship. Discusses the difference between heroic and civilized values and how Sophocles juxtaposes them.

Philosopher or Dog?

Author: Joaquim Maria Machado de Assis (1839-1908)
First published: Quincas Borba, 1891 (English translation, 1954)
Type of work: Novel
Type of plot: Psychological
Time of plot: 1869-1872
Locale: Rio de Janiero and Barbacena, Brazil

Principal characters:
RUBIÃO (PEDRO RUBIÃO DE ALVARENGA), the protagonist
CHRISTIANO DE ALMEIDA E PALHA, an entrepreneur
SOPHIA, Christiano's wife
MARIA BENEDICTA, her cousin
CARLOS MARIA, an arrogant young man
DR. JOÃO DE SOUZA CAMACHO, a lawyer and publisher
DOÑA TONICA, an unmarried, middle-aged woman
QUINCAS BORBA, a dog named for his late owner
DOÑA FERNANDA, a kind woman

The Story:

Quincas Borba (Joaquim Borba dos Santos), a wealthy man and a self-proclaimed philosopher, dies and leaves his large estate to his friend, Rubião, a teacher. The only condition of the bequest is that Rubião care for Quincas Borba's dog, also named Quincas Borba, as if the dog were human. Rubião travels from the provincial town of Barbacena to the city of Rio de Janiero to establish himself with his newly inherited wealth. On the train, he meets Christiano Palha and Palha's wife, Sophia. Rubião soon becomes infatuated with Sophia.

In Rio, Palha borrows money from Rubião to invest in business, and the two men become partners. Rubião also meets Carlos Maria, an arrogant young man, and Freitas, an unsuccessful middle-aged man, who exploit Rubião for his wealth and innocence. Major Siqueira and his thirty-nine-year-old daughter, Doña Tonica, attach themselves to Rubião, hoping that Rubião will marry Doña Tonica, who meanwhile becomes jealous of Sophia.

Rubião misinterprets as a love offering a box of strawberries Sophia had sent him. At the Palhas's house in Santa Thereza, he clutches her hand and makes his affection clear to her. Distressed by Rubião's advances, Sophia suggests to her husband that they end their relationship with Rubião. Having borrowed money from Rubião, however, Palha is reluctant to break with him.

Guilt-ridden about his infatuation with Sophia, Rubião begins to worry that the deceased Quincas Borba has somehow transmigrated into his dog's body. This anxiety is one of the first signs of Rubaio's impending madness.

Rubião becomes friends with Dr. Camacho, a lawyer and the editor of a politically oriented newspaper called *Atalaia*. On his way to meet Dr. Camacho, Rubião rescues a small child, Deolindo, in danger of being run over by a carriage and horses. Rubião then goes on to Dr. Camacho's office, where he subscribes generously to the capital fund for *Atalaia*. Dr. Camacho flatters Rubião by publishing an account of Rubião's heroism in saving Deolindo. Although Rubião is at first modest and dismissive about his heroism, as he reads Camacho's account he becomes increasingly self-important.

Maria Benedicta, Sophia's young cousin, is another potential wife for Rubião, but Rubião is too infatuated with Sophia to be interested in Maria Benedicta. After the incident at Santa Thereza, Rubião appears more cosmopolitan and confident. He spends his inherited money freely, often in support of others in addition to Palha and Dr. Camacho. When his impoverished friend, Freitas, falls ill, Rubião generously gives Freitas's mother a substantial sum of money. Later, he pays Freitas's funeral expenses.

Rubião tries to stay away from Sophia, but he finds an envelope addressed in Sophia's handwriting to Carlos Maria. When he confronts her with the envelope, she tells him to open it. He refuses and leaves. Although Carlos Maria had flirted with Sophia, the envelope contains only a circular about a charitable committee on which Sophia serves.

Palha's business flourishes as Rubião's wealth begins to dwindle. Rubião becomes subject to fits of madness, believing that he is Napoleon III of France. When Rubião gets into a carriage alone with Sophia, she thinks he is still attracted to her. She panics and orders him to get out. Thinking he is Napoleon III, Rubião treats Sophia as if she were the emperor's mistress, but eventually he leaves the carriage.

After Carlos Maria's flirtation with Sophia, Doña Fernanda acts as a matchmaker and brings Carlos Maria and Maria Benedicta together. Although Maria Benedicta is not beautiful, Carlos Maria marries her because she adores him. Following their marriage, they travel to Europe, returning to Rio de Janiero after Maria Benedicta becomes pregnant.

For a time, Rubião's friends accept his madness as he continues to provide meals and entertainment for them. Eventually, however, Rubião's house falls into disrepair as his belief in himself as the emperor becomes constant. Doña Tonica becomes engaged to a man who dies before the wedding. Children on the street, including Deolindo, whose life Rubião had saved, make fun of him as a madman. Prodded by Doña Fernanda, a woman who barely knows Rubião, Sophia convinces Palha to set Rubião up in a little rented house on Principe Street. No one visits Rubião in his new humble residence. His former "friends" miss the luxury of Rubião's wealthy surroundings in the house in Botafogo.

Rubião continues to believe he is Napoleon III, but Doña Fernanda thinks he can be cured. She manages to get him to enter an asylum. She also rescues Quincas Borba and sends the dog to the sanatorium to be with Rubião. After a short time, appearing to be regaining his sanity, Rubião escapes the asylum and returns to Barbacena with Quincas Borba, his only friend. Rubião dies there, and within three days, Quincas Borba dies there as well.

Critical Evaluation:

Considered by many to be Brazil's greatest novelist, Joaquim Maria Machado de Assis was the son of a mulatto (mixed race) house painter and a Portuguese woman. Little is known of his early life, but, by the time he was seventeen years old, he was working as an apprentice printer and had already published his first poems. *Philosopher or Dog?*, which serves as a sequel to *Memórias Póstumas de Brás Cubas*

(1881; *The Posthumous Memoirs of Brás Cubas*, 1951; better known as *Epitaph of a Small Winner*, 1952), is one of the masterpieces with which his long career culminated.

Philosopher or Dog? does not pretend to be realistic. Rather, it presents a world rich in metaphor and illusion, a world like the one that exists but also more orderly and more harrowing. One of the novel's themes is summed up in the philosopher Quincas Borba's apparently comical moral to an eccentric story he tells Rubião: "To the victor the potatoes." Though Quincas Borba thinks the story is about the triumph of humanity, it instead describes the amorality of the human struggle for survival.

The main subject of the novel is self-love, whose antidote is love. Self-deception and self-justification support the self-love of almost all the characters. Palha and Sophia both love themselves and care about Rubião only for what they can get from him. Carlos Maria is a blatant narcissist. Dr. Camacho is a self-involved manipulator who appeals to Rubião's vanity by printing in his newspaper the story of Rubião's rescue of Deolindo. Doña Tonica and Maria Benedicta blindly seek husbands to assure them of their own identities and worth. Only Doña Fernanda and Quincas Borba, the dog, love selflessly and faithfully. Although he begins as a naïve innocent, Rubião gradually succumbs to the conflicting egos of those around him and escapes into a madness in which he imagines himself to be a powerful emperor. Machado de Assis does not offer stereotypical heroes and villains. Rather, he portrays his characters with insight and compassion.

Early in the novel, Rubião withholds the fact that philosopher Quincas Borba has sent him a letter that suggests his own insanity. Rubião is afraid that, on the basis of the philosopher's madness, Quincas Borba's will might be nullified. Rubião would therefore receive no inheritance. Rubião, however, is not a bad man. The good are beguiled by selfish and vain thoughts, and the selfish and vain are capable of acts of kindness and charity. One may expect Palha to cheat Rubião, but the results both reward and frustrate that expectation. Palha appears to be a conniving spendthrift more interested in Rubião's money than in Rubião himself.

Palha nevertheless proves to be a successful businessman and, in the end, he assumes at least minimal responsibility for Rubião's care by renting the little house for him. He also visits Rubião in the asylum and unhesitatingly gives him a small amount of money, enabling Rubião to escape. It is clear, however, that Palha's generosity is not proportional to the generosity Rubião had shown him. In his portrayal of Palha, Machado de Assis is mocking the illusions that self-interest may create. He is also showing that if self-interest were the only criterion for villainy, all people could be considered villains.

Philosopher or Dog? is carefully built out of metaphorical details that can help one understand the author's intentions. *Palha* means "straw" in Portuguese, and the word *rubião* refers to an "ear" of a particular type of red corn. Thus, by his name, Rubião is identified as a product of the country. Palha, the character, represents a sophisticated city man in contrast with the country man Rubião. He is also a man of straw rather than a man of real substance. *Sophia* is the Greek word for "wisdom." Rubião is infatuated with Sophia, the woman, but cannot possess her. He also is attracted to the idea of wisdom and, even before his madness, cannot possess it either. Sophia herself is only ironically wise. A self-centered social climber, she exhibits little wisdom.

The stars in the constellation called the Southern Cross also provide Machado de Assis with a metaphor that frames the action of the story. Viewing things from the stars' point of view is a way of gaining perspective on human foibles. The author's understanding of the stars' perspective is also ironic. Early in the novel, the remote stars "seemed to be laughing at the inextricable situation" of Rubião's infatuation with Sophia. The reader also sees their relationship as gently comical. Rubião tells Sophia her eyes are more beautiful than the stars, because the closer one gets to the stars the less beautiful they seem, while the reverse is true of Sophia's eyes. Knowing of Rubião's infatuation, however, one suspects that a careful examination of Sophia's eyes would reveal her shallow vanity.

Rubião also asks Sophia to look at the Southern Cross every night, wherever she is. He tells her that he, too, wherever he is, will stare at the stars, "and their thoughts would join them in intimacy between God and men." The very last words of the novel reveal that "The Southern Cross, which the beautiful Sophia would not gaze upon as Rubião begged her to do, is too high in the heavens to distinguish between man's laughter and tears."

The humor in *Philosopher or Dog?* similarly evokes laughter and tears. Though often comical, Rubião is as good a man as exists in the world of the novel. Nevertheless, he suffers a sad fate because of causes and effects beyond his control. God, like the stars, is too far away to see details clearly, and selfish humans are left to make the best they can of their lives. Though undeniably pessimistic, *Philosopher or Dog?* reminds readers that selfless love, such as is exhibited by the dog Quincas Borba and the kindly Doña Fernanda, is our only hope of salvaging human decency in an indifferent universe.

Thomas Lisk

Further Reading

Caldwell, Helen. *Machado de Assis: The Brazilian Master and His Novels.* Berkeley: University of California Press, 1970. Caldwell was one of the first to translate Machado de Assis's work into English. Her chapter on *Philosopher or Dog?* provides a succinct and helpful overview of the major themes and unities of the novel, which she calls "a subtle web of allusion and symbol."

Duarte, Eduardo de Assis. "Machado de Assis's African Descent." *Research in African Literatures* 38, no. 1 (Spring, 2007): 134-151. Focuses on how Machado de Assis's work expresses his African ancestry in regard to slavery and interracial relations in nineteenth century Brazil.

Fitz, Earl. *Machado de Assis.* Boston: Twayne, 1989. A good introduction to Machado de Assis's work. Contains chapters on the major themes, analysis of style and technique in his work, including *Philosopher or Dog?*, and an annotated bibliography.

Graham, Richard, ed. *Machado de Assis: Reflections on a Brazilian Master Writer.* Austin: University of Texas Press, 1999. Essays by noted scholars address, among other topics, the question of the realism or antirealism of Machado de Assis's novels, which "are full of subtle irony, relentless psychological insights, and brilliant literary innovations."

Kristal, Efraín, and José Luiz Passos. "Machado de Assis and the Question of Brazilian National Identity." In *Brazil in the Making: Facets of National Identity*, edited by Carmen Nava and Ludwig Lauerhass, Jr. Lanham, Md.: Rowman & Littlefield, 2006. This essay discussing Machado de Assis's impact on Brazilian identity is included in a collection examining the character of the country and its citizens.

Nuñes, Maria Luisa. *The Craft of an Absolute Winner: Characterization and Narratology in the Novels of Machado de Assis.* Westport, Conn.: Greenwood Press, 1983. Gives a detailed analysis of Machado de Assis's handling of characterization and narrative technique in his novels, including *Philosopher or Dog?*

Philosophical Investigations

Author: Ludwig Wittgenstein (1889-1951)
First published: Philosophische Untersuchungen/ Philosophical Investigations, 1953
Type of work: Philosophy

Philosophical Investigations is the work of one of the most creative and controversial philosophers of the twentieth century. In it, Ludwig Wittgenstein presents his ideas concerning the nature of mind and language, often focusing on the relation between language and states of consciousness. The book is composed of numbered sections of various lengths that were compiled from notes that the author kept but never published. Unlike Wittgenstein's earlier work the *Tractatus Logico-Philosophicus* (1921; English-German bilingual edition, 1922), composed of meticulously numbered aphorisms in the form of a mathematical proof, the *Philosophical Investigations* gives the impression of an informal discussion covering a wide range of the author's concerns.

Born in Vienna in 1899 to a wealthy Austrian family, Wittgenstein studied engineering but soon shifted his interest to the more theoretical areas of mathematics and philosophy. Wittgenstein studied at Cambridge with philosophers Bertrand Russell and G. E. Moore. It was at Cambridge where Wittgenstein's unusual capacity for philosophical inquiry first came to the attention of the academic world. It was also there that Wittgenstein began to develop the philosophy that was to make him famous in the following years.

Continuing Wittgenstein's lifelong interest in language and mind, *Philosophical Investigations* introduces the concept of the "language-game," which Wittgenstein uses to explain the functioning of language in a variety of contexts. It has been pointed out that while many of the arguments in the *Philosophical Investigations* can be viewed as attempts to correct errors in philosophy as a whole, a number of Wittgenstein's discussions are seemingly attempts to correct or refute positions that he set out in the earlier *Tractatus Logico-Philosophicus.* A large portion of the *Philosophical Investigations* is concerned with setting out a philosophy that is at considerable variance with the work he had done in the early years of the twentieth century.

The construction of the *Philosophical Investigations* is

such that the reader is called upon to unify the various themes treated by Wittgenstein. While Wittgenstein might have objected that the work was not properly finished, and so cannot be assumed to have the coherence of a well-polished treatise, it nevertheless returns repeatedly to a number of issues, in particular those of language-games and the possibility of private languages. Wittgenstein begins with a passage from Saint Augustine's *Confessiones* (397-400; *Confessions*, 1620) meant to illustrate a common but, according to Wittgenstein, limited view of how language works. Wittgenstein admits that Augustine's conception of how he learned the proper names and significance of objects by ostensive definition (uttering an object's name and pointing to it) has some relevance. Wittgenstein argues that although Augustine describes a system of communication, "not everything that we call language is this system." Language, for Wittgenstein, is much richer and more complex than the simple naming and recognition described by Augustine. Wittgenstein argues for a much more expansive and flexible view of language as an intricate yet integrated system in which each part acquires meaning by virtue of its relationship to other elements in the system. Language allows words to perform a wide variety of functions, even though, as he points out, they all look alike (they are all words in a language).

While the earlier *Tractatus Logico-Philosophicus* is exceptionally difficult to understand because of its compactness and abstract language, Wittgenstein's expression in the *Philosophical Investigations* tends toward concrete examples to illustrate particular points. He frequently draws from mechanics and relies heavily on metaphor to help the reader grasp his arguments. In section 11, Wittgenstein suggests that just as tools in a toolbox have many diverse functions, so do words, though people are often slow to recognize this. In one of Wittgenstein's most powerful metaphors, in section 12 he compares language to looking into the cabin of a locomotive. There, one sees handles all more or less alike, but one should not think they are all simply handles (though they are indeed handles). As Wittgenstein tells us, each performs a singularly different function, such as opening a valve, starting a pump, or braking. Just as turning the wrong handle in the cabin of a locomotive might have dire consequences, so the misuse of language (confusing the uniform appearance of words with their diverse functions), for Wittgenstein, is the main cause of error and nonsense in philosophy.

Wittgenstein calls the many processes and activities of language learning and use language-games. He calls the whole, "consisting of language and the actions into which it is woven," the language-game, and it is the operation of this game, its rules as it were, that he wishes to explain.

Wittgenstein is not concerned with showing how to play the language-game. Most people are already capable and experienced at playing the language-game in a vast array of situations, although, oddly enough, few can do much to explain the rules of the game. Most people, Wittgenstein implies, express themselves without knowing how or why they make themselves understood. In a pivotal passage of the *Philosophical Investigations*, section 23, Wittgenstein insists that the term "language-game" itself is meant "to bring into prominence the fact that the *speaking* of a language is part of an activity, or a form of life." Such activities as giving orders and obeying them, giving descriptions, playacting, guessing riddles, telling jokes, and solving arithmetic problems are all typical of the many ways language can be used.

Just as words, phrases, and sentences are part of the web of the language-game, each obtaining meaning through relationship to the other parts of the system, so too, according to Wittgenstein, there is no one aspect common to all that we call language. Instead, all language is made up of language-games that are related to one another in multiple, diverse ways. Sections 65 to 67 deal explicitly with the concept of "family resemblances," a metaphor Wittgenstein uses to illustrate how the many activities of language are linked to one another. Wittgenstein concedes that it might be objected that he has not provided the "essence" of a language-game and thus the core of language. He argues that upon careful examination, no such essence may be found to exist. There is no atom of language. In section 66, Wittgenstein provides the example of games ("board games, card-games, Olympic Games, and so on"), insisting that people "*look and see*," not think, but simply look carefully at how such games function. The result is that "we see a complicated network of similarities overlapping and crisscrossing: sometimes overall similarities, sometimes similarities of detail," but no one thing common to all. Such similarities are like the various resemblances between members of a family—build, feature, color of eyes, gait, temperament, and others—that interlace and overlap.

Wittgenstein's aim in the *Philosophical Investigations* is to end, once and for all, the notion that there can be one and only one fundamental aspect of language that governs meaning. It is in this assertion, in particular, that the reader sees the philosopher arguing against the efforts of himself, Russell, and others to locate and describe the basic, or atomic, components of language. The result of misconceptions about the way language functions, according to Wittgenstein, has been a confusing and mostly fruitless approach to solving philosophical problems. Rather than break phrases or sentences down into their "atomic" components in order to see what they mean, people must instead carefully investigate the contexts of phrases or sentences. It is through context and relationship that meaning is revealed. The activity of philosophy thus is one of untying knots, dissolving confusion, or, as Wittgenstein puts it in section 109, "a battle against the bewitchment of our intelligence by means of language." Thus philosophy in the *Philosophical Investigations* takes on a therapeutic aspect, as the focus shifts from solving problems to uncovering pieces of nonsense and confusion that have cropped up in human understanding.

Concerned about the misuse of philosophy, Wittgenstein sees the shifting of its aims as clearly beneficial to its conduct. From an admission of human ignorance of the nature of a philosophical problem, Wittgenstein envisions working, through understanding the connections between the parts of language, to lay everything out in front of oneself in a clear fashion. Philosophy, he stresses, "neither explains nor deduces anything," since "everything lies open to view." Philosophy, then, consists in the revealing of the hidden aspects of things whose importance is veiled because of their simplicity and familiarity. One might say it is like putting on a pair of glasses when one's vision is blurred, or discovering that a hammer one has been searching for has been in one's hand all along.

Wittgenstein's belief in the communal nature of language and experience is seen also in his arguments against the possibility of private language, a language whose words refer exclusively to the private sensations of an individual and that can be known only by that person. Wittgenstein wishes to refute certain empiricist philosophers who assert that knowledge of language and even of one's own experiences depends on a private inner slate on which words are affixed to particular experiences. Wittgenstein does not deny the possible existence of private experiences; he argues that any reference to them is meaningless because such private experiences are unverifiable. Wittgenstein's focus is on correcting errors that have caused philosophy to go awry as well as on avoiding a skepticism that would undermine the fundamentally shared experience of language and meaning.

The remainder of section 1 and the entirety of section 2 deal with a number of issues, including Wittgenstein's further thoughts on the nature of language and mind, problems in philosophy, the foundations of mathematics, intentionality, verification, understanding, anticipation, perception, and meaning. In addition, some of Wittgenstein's concerns in the *Philosophical Investigations*, especially those having to do with the connection between perception and knowing, look forward to what would be his final philosophical exercises on the nature of certainty in the year and a half before

his death. *Philosophical Investigations*, as Wittgenstein notes in the preface to the work, is a journey over a wide range of "landscapes," involving many and varied approaches to a number of philosophical concerns. Its modest purpose, he stresses, is only to stimulate others to think, not to present a single or even fully consistent vision of the world. In this, most agree he succeeded.

Howard Giskin

Further Reading

Baker, Gordon P., and P. M. S. Hacker. *Wittgenstein: Understanding and Meaning.* Vol. 1 in *An Analytical Commentary on the "Philosophical Investigations."* 2d rev. ed. by P. M. S. Hacker. Malden, Mass.: Blackwell, 2004. Hacker, a noted Wittgenstein scholar, has undertaken revision of Baker's four-volume work *An Analytical Commentary on the "Philosophical Investigations"* (1980-1996). This first volume of the revised edition consists of two parts: a collection of essays on the *Philosophical Investigations* and an exegesis of sections 1-184 of the work.

Grayling, A. C. *Wittgenstein.* New York: Oxford University Press, 1988. Provides an introduction to Wittgenstein's philosophy, outlining the main tenets of his thought. Discusses the place of Wittgenstein's work in twentieth century analytical philosophy.

Hacker, P. M. S. *Wittgenstein.* New York: Routledge, 1999. Offers an excellent biographical introduction to the thoughts of the philosopher, clearly presented for the general reader.

_____. *Wittgenstein's Place in Twentieth-Century Analytic Philosophy.* Malden, Mass.: Blackwell, 1996. Monumental work by a leading authority on Wittgenstein thoroughly examines philosophical history before, during, and after Wittgenstein's time.

Kenny, Anthony. *Wittgenstein.* Rev. ed. Malden, Mass.: Blackwell, 2006. Presents a readable introductory account of the range of Wittgenstein's thought, focusing on his philosophy of language and mind. Chapters 9 and 10 deal with language-games and private languages, respectively.

McGinn, Marie. *Wittgenstein and the "Philosophical Investigations."* New York: Routledge, 1997. Well-written guide provides a capable introduction to the work for students.

Malcolm, Norman. *Ludwig Wittgenstein: A Memoir.* 2d ed. New York: Oxford University Press, 1984. Excellent work written by Wittgenstein's most prominent American philosophical student allows the reader to see the force of Wittgenstein's personality as well as his particular way of practicing philosophy. Includes numerous letters that Wittgenstein wrote to Malcolm.

Monk, Ray. *Ludwig Wittgenstein: The Duty of Genius*. New York: Free Press, 1990. Thorough and detailed work is the definitive biography of Wittgenstein. Examines his private life as well as his work in philosophy.

Travis, Charles. *Thought's Footing: A Theme in Wittgenstein's "Philosophical Investigations."* New York: Oxford University Press, 2006. Delineates several key themes in the *Philosophical Investigations*. Describes

Wittgenstein's ideas about the way things are versus the way people think and talk about things. Analyzes *Philosophical Investigations* as a response to the ideas of Gottlob Frege.

Williams, Meredith, ed. *Wittgenstein's "Philosophical Investigations": Critical Essays*. Lanham, Md.: Rowman & Littlefield, 2007. Collection of essays focuses on the major themes in the work. Includes discussions of language-games in Wittgenstein's later thought, his ideas about obedience to rules and private language, and his philosophy of the mind.

Philosophy of Art

Author: Hippolyte Taine (1828-1893)
First published: Philosophie de l'art: Leçons professées à l'École des Beaux-Arts, 1865 (English translation, 1865)
Type of work: Art history and philosophy

Hippolyte Taine combines a historical interest in his subjects with an interest that is philosophical. Two of his wide-ranging works are *Histoire de la littérature anglaise* (1863-1864, 4 vols.; *The History of English Literature*, 1871) and *Les Origines de la France contemporaine* (1876-1894, 6 vols.; *The Origins of Contemporary France*, 1876-1894). In his studies, he regarded history and philosophy as sciences; he believed that a study of the nature of art and of art production could proceed, in the manner of any scientific study, by attention to the observable facts and by the framing of inductive generalizations. Consequently, his *Philosophy of Art* is to some extent a description of some predominant art periods and to some extent an attempt to generalize philosophically from the data of his historical inquiries. Taine's studies include those of the art of Greece, the Netherlands, and Italy.

Taine's working assumption is that no work of art is isolated, and that the only way to understand a particular work of art or the nature of art in general is by attending to the conditions that lead to a work of art. According to this theory, the character of a work of art is determined by the artist, but that artist is shaped by a number of inescapable cultural influences. Taine believes that works of art present, in perceptible form, the essential character of the time and place in which the artist works. In his words, "The work of art is determined

by an aggregate which is the general state of the mind and surrounding manners." Taine points out, for example, that the nude statues of Greek art reflect the Grecian preoccupation with war and athletics and with the development of the healthy human animal; that the art of the Middle Ages reflects the moral crisis resulting from feudal oppression; that the art of the seventeenth century reflects the values of courtly life; and that the art of industrial democracy expresses the restless aspirations of human beings in an age of science.

The work of art itself is conditioned by the wholes of which it is a part and a product. In the first place, according to Taine, the work of art exhibits the artist's style, that prevailing mode of aesthetic treatment that runs through all the works of an artist, giving them an underlying resemblance to one another. Second, the work of art reflects the prevailing manner of the school of artists to which the individual artist belongs. Finally, it expresses the times and the social milieu of taste, conviction, and manners within which the artist is working and by which he or she must be affected. Taine summarizes his belief when he writes that "to comprehend a work of art, an artist or a group of artists, we must clearly comprehend the general social and intellectual condition of the times to which they belong."

In addition to the influence of taste and style, Taine also believes in considering "moral temperature," the spiritual milieu, whether mystic or pagan or something foreign to both, that infects the artist and, consequently, his or her work. The philosophy of art, as Taine understands it, is the attempt to study the art of various countries and ages to discover the conditions under which the art of a particular place and time is created and, finally, the conditions in general for any art whatsoever. A report of those general conditions would be a philosophy of art.

In examining individual works of art, the first step in aesthetics, Taine finds that imitation is an important feature in most of them, particularly in works of poetry, sculpture, and painting. Taine is interested in arriving by inductive means at a theory of the nature of art. He speculates whether exact imitation is perhaps the ultimate goal of art, but he concludes that it is not because exact imitation does not produce the finest works of art. Photography, for example, is useful as a means of making accurate reproductions of scenes, but he does not believe that it can be ranked with such fine arts as painting and sculpture. Another reason for concluding that works of art are not essentially concerned with exact imitation is that many works of art are intentionally inexact.

There is a kind of imitation, however, that is essential to art, according to Taine, and that is the imitation of what he calls "the relationships and mutual dependence of parts." Just as a painter, even when reproducing a human figure, does not represent every feature of the body—its exact size, color, and weight—but rather what might be called the logic of the body, so artists in general, in creating works of art, do not aim at deception through exact representation but, rather, at presenting the essential character of an object. Because the essential character of an object is simply the predominant feature of the object as affected by the place and time of its existence, the artist's objective, according to Taine's analysis, is to put that principal feature of the object into perceptible form. In painting a lion, for example, the important thing is to represent him as carnivorous; in painting the Low Countries the artist must imitate their alluvial character.

Taine knows that the artist is often doing something quite different from making the dominant feature of nature the predominant feature of the work of art, but he believes that all art can be explained as the imitation of essential quality. What the artist presents may be not the essential character of some physical scene or object; it may be the prevailing temper of the times. This view is made clear in part 2 of *Philosophy of Art*, in which Taine considers artistic production. The first part, on the nature of art, concludes with the summary statement that

The end of a work of art is to manifest some essential or salient character, consequently some important idea, clearer and more completely than is attainable from real objects. Art accomplishes this end by employing a group of connected parts, the relationships of which it systematically modifies.

The law of art production—that a work of art is determined by the general state of mind and surrounding circumstances—Taine defends in two ways. He refers to experience to argue that the law of production applies to all works of art; he then analyzes the effects of "a general state of mind and surrounding circumstances" to claim that the law reveals a necessary connection. As an example, Taine considers the effect of melancholy as a state of mind, with the circumstances that make melancholy characteristic of an age. He argues that in a melancholy age the artist is inevitably melancholy. As a result, the artist portrays all objects as being predominantly melancholy, painting "things in much darker colors." During a renaissance, when there is "a general condition of cheerfulness," the works of art will express a joyful condition. Whatever the combination of moods in an age, the art of that age will reflect the combination. It could not be otherwise, Taine argues, because artists cannot isolate themselves from their age. As historical examples, he refers to the Greek period, the feudal age, the seventeenth century, and the nineteenth century.

A "general situation" resulting from a condition of wealth or poverty, or of servitude or liberty, or from a prevailing religious faith, or from some other feature of the society, has an effect on individual artists, affecting their aptitudes and emotions.

In Greece we see physical perfection and a balance of faculties which no manual or cerebral excess of life deranges; in the Middle Ages, the intemperance of over-excited imaginations and the delicacy of feminine sensibility; in the seventeenth century, the polish and good breeding of society and the dignity of aristocratic salons; and in modern times, the grandeur of unchained ambitions and the morbidity of unsatisfied yearnings.

According to Taine, the four terms of a causal series by reference to which the production of art can be explained are the general situation, the tendencies and special faculties provoked by that situation, the individual who represents and embodies the tendencies and faculties, and the material—such as sounds, forms, colors, or language—by the use of which the character is given sensuous form. Taine argues that artists imitate the prevailing quality of their age because they cannot escape being a part of their age, because nothing else would be accepted, and because they work for acceptance and applause.

Philosophy of Art is a clear and sensible defense of the idea that art reflects the Zeitgeist, or the spirit of the times. Opposing his position are those theories that emphasize the role of extraordinary individuals, those eccentrics who by their genius transcend the perspectives and sentiments of their age. The attempt to reconcile these two basic philosophical perspectives only hides the truth that resides in each. The moral seems to be to read Taine for an appreciation of the influence of the social milieu, and to read someone else, say Friedrich Nietzsche, for an aesthetics in which the artist is shown as an individual rebel who falsifies nature.

Further Reading

Dewald, Jonathan. *Lost Worlds: The Emergence of French Social History, 1815-1970*. University Park: Pennsylvania State University Press, 2006. Assesses the role of Taine and other nineteenth and twentieth century French intellectuals in creating an interest in social history and private life, among other topics.

Eustis, Alvin. *Hippolyte Taine and the Classical Genius*. 1951. Reprint. Berkeley: University of California Press, 1981. A short work that focuses on Taine's assessment of classical society and its artists, noting the importance the critic places on social conditions and on the production of high-quality art.

Gullace, Giovanni. "The Concept of Art in Taine and Brunetière." In *Taine and Brunetière on Criticism*. Lawrence, Kans.: Coronado Press, 1982. Excellent analysis of Taine's ideas about art in his *Philosophy of Art*. Extracts salient comments from this work, and provides a summary of the critic's principal beliefs about the objective qualities of all great art.

Kahn, Sholom J. *Science and Aesthetic Judgment: A Study in Taine's Critical Method*. 1953. Reprint. Westport, Conn.: Greenwood Press, 1970. A scholarly examination of Taine's writings on art, exploring how he is able to balance the need for objective analysis with the more elusive art of judgment, especially value judgment. Emphasizes the importance of the historical dimensions of art criticism.

Murray, Chris., ed. "Hippolyte Taine (1828-93)." In *Key Writers on Art: From Antiquity to the Nineteenth Century*. New York: Routledge, 2003. A brief but comprehensive entry on the cultural significance of Taine's theories of art and art production. The volume includes an index.

Weinstein, Leo. *Hippolyte Taine*. New York: Twayne, 1972. General biographical study of Taine. Discusses his analysis of the nature of art and the conditions necessary for its production. Examines his judgments on the art of Europe, his notion of the ideal, and the emphasis he places on personal and national character in creating great art.

Phineas Finn, the Irish Member

Author: Anthony Trollope (1815-1882)
First published: 1867-1869, serial; 1869, book
Type of work: Novel
Type of plot: Political realism
Time of plot: Mid-nineteenth century
Locale: British Isles

Principal characters:
PHINEAS FINN, a personable young Irishman
LORD BRENTFORD, an important Whig
LORD CHILTERN, his profligate son
LADY LAURA STANDISH, Brentford's beautiful daughter
MR. KENNEDY, a very wealthy member of Parliament
VIOLET EFFINGHAM, a charming girl with a large fortune
MADAME MARIE MAX GOESLER, a pretty, wealthy young widow
MARY FLOOD JONES, a pretty young Irishwoman

The Story:

Young Phineas Finn, just admitted to the bar, is tempted to postpone his career as a barrister by an offer to run for election as a member of Parliament from the Irish borough of Loughshane. Phineas's father, a hardworking doctor, reluctantly agrees to support Phineas, as a member of Parliament receives no salary and can only hope that once his party is in power he will be rewarded with a lucrative office.

Phineas is elected. Among those to whom he says goodbye before leaving for London is pretty Mary Flood Jones, a girl devoted to Phineas but no richer than he. Phineas's well-wishers in London include Lady Laura Standish, the daughter of Lord Brentford, an influential Whig. Phineas begins to fall in love with Laura and sees a rival in the aloof and unprepossessing but rich Mr. Kennedy, who is also a Whig and a member of Parliament. Laura tries to encourage a friendship between Phineas and her brother, Lord Chiltern, a violent young man who has quarreled with their father. Lord Brentford has made it clear that he will reconcile with his son if Chiltern marries rich, lovely, and witty Violet Effingham, a friend from childhood. Chiltern loves her deeply and has proposed repeatedly, but Violet is levelheaded and, although she is fond of Chiltern, does not intend to ruin herself deliberately.

At Laura's recommendation, Phineas accepts an invitation to visit Loughlinter, the Kennedy estate in Scotland. Phineas makes friends there with several Whig leaders and becomes the special disciple of Mr. Monk, a cabinet minister with independent views. Phineas proposes to Laura, who tells him she is engaged to marry Kennedy. She explains that, against her father's wishes, she has exhausted her personal fortune by paying her brother's debts; she is consequently obliged to marry someone with money.

Last-minute fright prevents Phineas from carrying out his elaborate plans for his first speech in Parliament. Laura has been married for several months when she begins to find life with her strict, demanding husband oppressive. Chiltern, having once again unsuccessfully proposed to Violet, invites Phineas to hunt with him. During the hunt, Chiltern suffers an injury and Phineas takes cares of him; the two become close friends. Although he has no hopes for being successful with Violet, the young nobleman confides to Phineas that he will fight any other aspirant for her hand.

In the voting on the Reform Bill, the question of the ballot divides Parliament, and the government is dissolved. The capriciousness of Lord Tulla, who had ensured Phineas's original success, prevents Phineas from running again for the Loughshane parliamentary seat. Lord Brentford, however, who has the English borough of Loughton "in his pocket," offers that seat to Phineas, who is easily elected.

Phineas, who had rescued Kennedy from two attackers late one night, visits at Loughlinter again. Gradually, he has transferred his affections from Laura to Violet, but his plan to confide in Laura is prevented by her confession to him that life with her husband has grown intolerable. Phineas, despairing of an opportunity to see Violet, finds his excuse in a letter from Chiltern that contains a conciliatory message for his father. Phineas takes the letter to Lord Brentford, at whose house Violet is staying. Lord Brentford agrees to forgive his son if Chiltern resumes his courtship of Violet.

Phineas sends this message to Chiltern; to avoid duplicity, he adds that he himself hopes to win Violet's hand. He later finds the opportunity to propose to Violet. Although she rejects him, he feels that her negative answer is not conclusive.

Because Phineas refuses to give up his courtship of Violet, Chiltern challenges him to a duel. They fight secretly in Belgium, but word of the duel leaks out afterward, partly because of Phineas's injury; he had been wounded before he could fire. At last, Phineas confides in Laura, who becomes angry—as much because of her own affection for him as because of her brother's claims on Violet.

Phineas meets the beautiful and charming widow Madame Goesler, who becomes interested in him. Phineas had been left a legacy of three thousand pounds and soon receives an even more substantial income upon being appointed to an office that pays one thousand pounds annually. Laura feels that she has wronged Phineas and takes it upon herself to urge his suit with Violet. Violet, however, knows that Phineas originally courted Laura, and she dislikes being in second place. She refuses when Phineas proposes to her again.

Parliament passes the English Reform Bill, which redistributes parliamentary representation to conform to actual population. The seat for the borough of Loughton is among those voted out of existence. Because Phineas has proven an able and loyal Whig, he has been promoted to a higher office that pays two thousand pounds a year. Having no borough to run for, he despairs of keeping the office after the next election. Loughshane, however, is made available again by the caprice of Lord Tulla, and Phineas is assured of success.

Chiltern proposes to Violet once more and is finally accepted, and he and his father are at last reconciled. Miserable over Violet's engagement, Phineas confides in Madame Goesler. He also tells Laura of his heartbreak, but she chides him, saying he will soon forget Violet just as he has forgotten her.

Lord Brentford finally learns of the duel between his son and Phineas, whom he accuses of treachery. Phineas discovers the real cause of Lord Brentford's anger: Chiltern and Violet, quarreling over Chiltern's unwillingness to work, have broken their engagement.

Madame Goesler has made a conquest of the elderly and widely respected duke of Omnium. Although tempted to accept, she finally refuses his proposal of marriage. Not the least of her motives is her attachment to Phineas. When Laura's husband accuses her of having Phineas as a lover, Laura decides to leave him. Phineas again asks Violet to marry him, and she tells him that, although she and Chiltern have quarreled, she cannot love anyone else.

Phineas causes a great sensation at home by bringing Mr.

Monk to Ireland with him. Caught up with Mr. Monk in political fervor, Phineas pledges himself to support Irish tenant rights in Parliament. Mr. Monk has warned him against such promises; he predicts that Phineas will be forced to resign his office if he votes in opposition to his party. Without means of support, he then will have to give up his promising career. Phineas confides in Mary Flood Jones about this danger and about his unsuccessful love for Violet. Phineas and Mary become engaged.

After Laura has taken up residence with her father, Kennedy seeks legal aid to force her to return to him. To escape persecution, she decides to live abroad. She confesses to Phineas that she has always loved him and worked for him, although she was heartbroken when he told her of his love for Violet. Laura urges him to ensure his career by marrying Madame Goesler for her money. Phineas does not mention his engagement to Mary. When Madame Goesler offers her hand and money to Phineas, he can only refuse. His first feeling is one of bitter disappointment.

Chiltern and Violet reconcile. The Irish Reform Bill is passed, abolishing Phineas's seat for the borough of Loughshane—his career in Parliament is over. The intervention of friends in the government, however, results in Phineas receiving a permanent appointment as poor-law inspector in Ireland. It pays a yearly salary of one thousand pounds, enabling Phineas and Mary to plan an immediate wedding.

Critical Evaluation:

Anthony Trollope's *Phineas Finn, the Irish Member*, an example of literature of political reform, has been grouped with George Eliot's *Felix Holt, the Radical* (1866), Walter Bagehot's *The English Constitution* (1867), Thomas Carlyle's *Shooting Niagara: And After* (1867), and Matthew Arnold's *Culture and Anarchy* (1869). A portrait of the British government in the early nineteenth century, *Phineas Finn* has a straightforward plot in which the protagonist during his six years in Parliament eventually acquires the wisdom and courage to act on his convictions. His own character and the particular conflict contribute to his development, in the course of which Trollope is able to make the point that the government is far more dedicated to the status quo than to significant reform.

By novel's end, the change Phineas has undergone is revealed when he supports legislation proposed by his friend Joshua Monk that will help his native Ireland but simultaneously threaten the political establishment. By doing so, Finn learns that those who act on their convictions and attempt to initiate social change endanger their political careers. Thus, after voting for Monk's Irish bill, which grants

tenants in Ireland specific rights, Phineas loses his seat in Parliament.

Finn's acquisition of wisdom may be seen as a partial response to those among his acquaintances who seem to hold few personal political beliefs. Barrington Earle, for instance, is opposed to change and despises conviction. It is Earle who encourages Phineas to enter politics in the first place, but when Phineas reveals that he plans to use his vote to serve Ireland and not necessarily the Liberal Party, Earle feels only disgust for him, for he realizes that Finn cannot be immediately useful to him. Earle's sentiments are echoed by Finn's countryman and fellow politician Lawrence Fitzgibbon: "I never knew a government yet that wanted to do anything." For doing nothing, Fitzgibbon is eventually awarded with a secretaryship.

The character who most influences Phineas is Joshua Monk, a member of the cabinet. Monk maintains that individuals should enter politics only as a means of implementing personal convictions. Toward the end of the novel, Monk tells Finn, whose job as an undersecretary has shifted his attention away from Ireland toward North America, that "most probably you know nothing of the modes of thought of the man who lives next door to you." Monk criticizes his peers for their insensitivity to their constituents. He himself, before proposing before Parliament his Irish reform legislation, accompanies Finn to Ireland and acquaints himself with the conditions of that country.

Other minor characters also serve as Phineas's mentors. Phineas's London landlord Jacob Bunce reminds Finn that Parliament has never yet improved the lot of the common people, and this notion justifies Bunce's taking his views to the streets and finding himself arrested and jailed for standing too near Minister Turnbull's carriage. Mr. Low, Phineas's legal mentor, believes that Finn entered politics for the wrong reasons and that he should have first established himself in the legal profession, as Low did before he ran for office. According to Low, Finn does not have a sufficient grasp of the laws of the land to serve his country. Somewhat like Monk, Low asserts that Phineas is out of touch with elements vital to true political effectiveness. Indeed, Trollope's characterization of Finn as a pleasant young man who knows how to make himself useful in Parliament and who seeks reelection twice because he loves the social life of a politician confirms Low's observations.

The wisdom that Phineas gradually acquires is also born out of his own conflict between expediency and conscience, between doing what is useful for his party and acting upon what is right. Trollope uses several other characters to illustrate the poles of Phineas's conflict. Lawrence Fitzgibbon and Barrington Earle clearly stand in opposition to Joshua Monk, who, in contrast to Earle and Fitzgibbon, is a man of conviction. The conflict is also represented by Sir Robert Kennedy and Lord Chiltern. Kennedy, who is married to Laura Standish, is a middle-aged member of Parliament whose reticence reveals not the wisdom acquired through years of political involvement but the total absence of any personal convictions that would endanger his career or party. By contrast, Laura's brother, Lord Chiltern, a social outcast, is ruled almost entirely by passion and conviction. A "wild" man who has reputedly killed a man with his bare hands, Chiltern refuses to obey his father on almost every issue. He stays out of politics and refuses to give up the blood sports that associate him with the old English nobility and which, to Trollope, seems to be more representative of true masculinity than do the politicians with whom Phineas associates. Phineas develops a lasting contempt for Kennedy, but he respects and befriends Lord Chiltern. This friendship is significant in the development of Phineas's character, especially considering that Phineas and Chiltern at one point duel over Violet Effingham, but Trollope implies that this act demonstrates conviction, courage, and manhood in both of them.

Trollope also suggests the intensity of Phineas's conflict through his female characters. Laura Standish, for example, makes a marriage of convenience to Robert Kennedy, who proves to be a tyrant and whom she eventually leaves. Violet Effingham, on the other hand, follows her heart in finally agreeing to marry Lord Chiltern, whom she has loved since childhood. Drawn to the dangerous though masculine side of Chiltern, she refuses a marriage of convenience and seems headed toward a happy life with him. Trollope also contrasts Madame Max Goesler and Mary Flood. Marriage to Madame Max, as she is called, would ensure Phineas access to the most prestigious political circles in London. Eventually, however, Finn follows his heart, rejects Madame Max, and marries his first love, Mary Flood, the most sincere and steadfast female character in the novel.

Phineas Finn, the Irish Member is a satirical, somewhat cynical novel about British politics. In his analysis, Trollope shows that those who wish to retain their political offices must vote with their parties; thus, presumably, they often must vote against their own hearts or convictions. Those who wish to advance socially and politically had best choose marriages of convenience. Finally, those who wish to maintain the unsullied reputations necessary for staying in office might be wise to follow in Sir Robert Kennedy's footsteps by holding few convictions and saying nothing.

"Critical Evaluation" by Richard Logsdon

Further Reading

Berthoud, Jacques. Introduction to *Phineas Finn, the Irish Member*, by Anthony Trollope. New York: Oxford University Press, 1999. Informative essay elucidates the novel's political and cultural background.

Bury, Laurent. *Seductive Strategies in the Novels of Anthony Trollope, 1815-1882*. Lewiston, N.Y.: Edwin Mellen Press, 2004. Focuses on scenes of seduction in all of Trollope's novels, arguing that seduction was a survival skill for both men and women in the Victorian era. Examines how Trollope depicted the era's sexual politics.

Felber, Lynette. *Gender and Genre in Novels Without End: The British Roman-Fleuve*. Gainesville: University Press of Florida, 1995. Study of multivolume novels written during three periods of history includes examination of *Phineas Finn, the Irish Member* and the other novels in Trollope's Palliser series. Argues that these novels inherently have "narrative features designated feminine."

Halperin, John. *Trollope and Politics: A Study of the Pallisers and Others*. London: Macmillan, 1977. Discussion of Trollope's political novels approaches them as direct reflections of the political activities of his time.

Markwick, Margaret. *New Men in Trollope's Novels: Rewriting the Victorian Male*. Burlington, Vt.: Ashgate, 2007. Examines Trollope's novels, tracing the development of his ideas about masculinity. Argues that Trollope's male characters are not the conventional Victorian patriarchs and demonstrates how his works promoted a "startlingly modern model of manhood."

_____. *Trollope and Women*. London: Hambledon Press, 1997. Discusses how Trollope could simultaneously accept the conventional Victorian ideas about women while also sympathizing with women's difficult situations. Demonstrates the individuality of his female characters and addresses his depiction of both happy and unhappy marriages, male-female relationships, bigamy, and scandal.

Mullen, Richard, and James Munson. *The Penguin Companion to Trollope*. New York: Penguin Books, 1996. Comprehensive guide describes all of Trollope's novels, short stories, travel books, and other works, providing discussion of plot, characters, background, tone, allusions, and contemporary references that place the works in their historical context.

Sadleir, Michael. *Trollope: A Commentary*. Reprint. New York: Octagon Books, 1975. Biography focuses on the events of the author's life and political career as reflected in his novels.

Phineas Redux

Author: Anthony Trollope (1815-1882)
First published: 1873-1874, serial; 1874, book
Type of work: Novel
Type of plot: Political
Time of plot: Mid-nineteenth century
Locale: England

Principal characters:
PHINEAS FINN, an Irish politician and a widower
MADAME MARIE MAX GOESLER, a wealthy and pretty widow
LADY LAURA KENNEDY, Phineas's beloved
MR. KENNEDY, her estranged husband
LORD CHILTERN, Laura's brother
VIOLET CHILTERN, his wife
LADY GLENCORA, the duchess of Omnium
MR. BONTEEN, a conniving politician

The Story:

The conservatives have been in control of the government for more than a year. The liberals, in planning a return to power, want to get every good man they can muster. Thirty years of age, Phineas Finn had retired from politics two years earlier to marry his childhood sweetheart and settle down in a modest but permanent position in Ireland. He is invited back to resume his political career. His wife had died in the interval, and he had saved enough to permit him to live two or three years without being given an office. The urging of his friends seems to imply that he will not have to wait long for an office, so he agrees to give up his security for the more exciting life of a member of Parliament. He is to run for the borough of Tankerville, which is held by a corrupt conservative named Browborough.

While awaiting the election, Phineas visits Lord Chiltern and Violet, who are happily married. Chiltern has at last found the occupation perfectly suited to his temperament and enthusiasm for hunting—master of the Brake Hounds. Also visiting the Chilterns are Adelaid Palliser and Mr. Maule, a gloomy and idle but rather pleasing young man, who is devoted to and loved by Adelaid.

In the Tankerville election, Phineas campaigns for separation of church and state. Although Browborough wins by seven votes, the seat is to be contested on evidence that Browborough bought votes. In a desperate effort to keep his party in power, the conservative leader also advocates separation of church and state.

On his way to visit Lady Laura Kennedy and her father in Dresden, Phineas is summoned by her estranged husband to his estate. Kennedy's mind has become deranged; his one purpose in life is to get his wife back. He forbids Phineas from visiting her and accuses him of adultery. Although he knows he is not guilty, Phineas cannot reason with Kennedy. Later, in Dresden, Laura confides that her love for Phineas is

the real reason behind the failure of her marriage; Phineas, however, has long felt nothing but friendship for Laura.

On his next visit to the Chilterns, Phineas sees Madame Marie Max Goesler. The first meeting is awkward because of their earlier relationship, but soon they are friends again. She tells Phineas that she has been acting as unofficial companion and nurse to the old duke of Omnium, now on his deathbed. Lady Glencora, the duke's niece, has become her intimate friend.

Adelaid's good breeding attracts the uncouth squire and fox hunter Spooner. Unaware of the subtleties of social behavior, Spooner feels he is more eligible than Maule, whose income is small. Spooner's proposal of marriage is refused with horror, and Maule's proposal is accepted. Maule and Adelaid feel that they can marry if his father will let them live in the abandoned Maule Abbey. The father, however, is opposed to his son's marriage to a woman without a fortune. Angry at the implied reminder that the property will be his son's after his death, he refuses the request.

Quintus Slide, representative of all that is bad in journalism, gives Phineas a letter written to his newspaper by Kennedy. The letter is a madman's accusation, implying that Phineas and Laura are guilty of adultery. Slide intends to print the letter and enjoys the feeling of power its possession gives him; believing that Phineas is interested only in upholding the institution of marriage, he offers to give Phineas a day to persuade Laura to return to Kennedy. Instead, Phineas goes to Kennedy's hotel to urge him to retract the letter. Kennedy shoots at Phineas but misses. Despite efforts to keep the affair hushed up, the news leaks out later. When Phineas obtains an injunction against Slide forbidding him from printing the letter, the journalist becomes enraged and writes an editorial in which he refers to the letter, although he does not quote it. He makes the story seem even worse than it is, and the whole affair begins to damage Phineas's career.

Long disliked by and jealous of Phineas, Mr. Bonteen achieved advancement through party loyalty. After the death of the old duke of Omnium, the new duke has given up his former office of Chancellor of the Exchequer, a post that Bonteen is now expected to fill as soon as the liberals return to power. Bonteen is using his influence against Phineas, who despairs of getting an office, so Madame Goesler and her friend, Lady Glencora, now duchess of Omnium, resolve on a counterintrigue. Although the duchess prevents Bonteen from acquiring the position of chancellor, she is unable to secure an office for Phineas.

Normally, the liberal party supports separation of church and state, but they decide officially to oppose it, knowing that the conservatives are using the issue only to keep control of the government. Although with some misgivings at first, Phineas goes along with his party. The conservatives are defeated.

Bonteen and his wife befriend a woman victimized by a fortune hunter turned preacher named, variously, Emilius or Mealyus. Mealyus hopes to get half of his wife's fortune as a settlement, but Bonteen is working to prove a rumor that Mealyus is a bigamist. One night, after Phineas had been publicly insulted by Bonteen in their club, Bonteen is murdered. Phineas and Mealyus are both arrested, but the latter is released when he proves he could not have left his rooming house that night. Circumstances look dark for Phineas. Laura, Madame Goesler, the duchess of Omnium, Phineas's landlady, and the Chilterns are the only ones convinced of his innocence.

Kennedy dies and leaves everything to Laura; she dreams that she might be happy with Phineas at last, although she senses at the same time that her hope is impossible. On the trail of evidence to help Phineas by destroying Mealyus's alibi, Madame Goesler goes to Prague; she suspects Mealyus of having another rooming house key made there during a recent trip. Then Mealyus's first wife is discovered, and Mealyus is arrested for bigamy. At Phineas's trial, the circumstantial evidence against him breaks down when Madame Goesler wires from Prague that she has found proof of Mealyus's duplicate key. Laura realizes that Madame Goesler has saved Phineas, and now she hates her as a rival.

The late duke of Omnium had willed a handsome fortune to Madame Goesler. She did not need the money and is now afraid of suspicion that she had been the duke's mistress, so she refuses to accept it. The duchess takes up the cause of Maule and Adelaid; they are too poor to marry, and it is out of the question to expect Maule to work. Adelaid is a niece of the old duke, and the duchess persuades Madame Goesler to let Adelaid have the fortune she herself will not accept. Adelaid and Maule are able to marry, and Maule's father is so pleased with her fortune that he turns Maule Abbey over to them after all. Spooner, who has clung to his hope of marrying Adelaid, is so miserable that he gives up fox hunting for a time. Quintus Slide, who has consistently denounced Phineas and Laura in his newspaper, is sued for libel by Chiltern. Chiltern wins the suit, and Slide is forced to leave the paper.

Phineas is the hero of the day—overwhelmingly re-elected in Tankerville, sought by the ladies, acclaimed everywhere—but the knowledge that he is suspected by friends as well as by strangers makes him miserable and bitter. Gradually, as his spirits improve, he is able to meet people and to resume his seat in Parliament. He also is offered the same office he had filled so well in his earlier parliamentary career. Although he is almost at the end of his funds and needs the position, the knowledge that the offer is made simply because he had not committed murder prompts him to refuse.

While visiting Laura at her request, Phineas feels it only honorable to tell her that he plans to propose to Madame Goesler. At first, Laura is violent in her denunciation of Madame Goesler, but she is at last calmed. Hers is the unhappiness of knowing that she had brought all of her misery on herself by marrying one man while loving another. Now deeply in love with Madame Goesler, Phineas proposes marriage and is joyfully accepted. No longer a poor man, Phineas will be able to continue his career in Parliament without being the slave of his party.

Critical Evaluation:

The fourth novel of Anthony Trollope's famous Palliser series, *Phineas Redux* extends the story of one of the author's favorite heroes while offering a sobering portrait of political life in the nineteenth century. Inspired in part by Trollope's own unsuccessful bid for political office, the novel exposes the backroom dealings that brought people to power and led to alliances more often aimed at keeping incumbents in office than doing what was right for the country.

At the center of the novel is the young Irish politician whose name graces two titles in the Palliser series. In the first, *Phineas Finn, the Irish Member* (1869), the hero is introduced to political life when he becomes the darling of high-ranking members of the Liberal party, including one destined to be prime minister, Plantagenet Palliser. At the end of that novel, Phineas leaves London for his homeland to marry his childhood sweetheart. When the action of *Phineas Redux* opens, he is back in London, a widower and political aspirant once more. Through him, Trollope gives readers a look at the machinations involved in bringing political issues before Parliament and the British people; he also gives a realistic look at campaigning techniques and the efforts of the press to influence political decisions.

Throughout the novel, the author's focus is on character as well as action. In the course of running for a seat in Parliament, debating key issues such as church disestablishment, and defending himself against a murder charge, Phineas Finn emerges as a man of high moral fiber, willing to stand up for unpopular ideas even at the expense of losing favor with his own party. Trollope also portrays the human side of his hero, as he agonizes over his feelings for Laura Kennedy, once his beloved but now married to a man whose extreme jealousy leads to near catastrophe for the hero. Phineas engages in social situations with a number of other figures, notably Lady Glencora Palliser, Plantagenet's wife; Madame Marie Max Goesler, a rich widow who assists in a number of ways to further his career; and the Chilterns, a family whose domestic bliss offers readers a portrait of the idyllic life prized by Trollope and many of his contemporaries.

A number of memorable villains also populate the novel, several of whom rise above the stereotypes normally associated with the popular fiction of the period. Phineas's political nemesis, Mr. Bonteen, is filled with a hatred brought on by the snubs and jostlings that occur in the world of elective and appointive officeholding; after readers have come to despise him, however, he is murdered, and Phineas is accused of the crime. The twist permits Trollope to humanize both villain and hero, as readers' sympathies go out to the man slain unjustly and to the accused, who cannot be guilty. Similarly, Trollope manages to evoke both contempt and pity for Kennedy. A recluse whose dabbling into politics has brought him nothing but trouble, Kennedy becomes fixated on his hatred for Phineas; Trollope is careful to paint him as a character whose actions stem from a dementia that makes him deserving of treatment rather than incarceration.

The journalist Quintus Slide does not fare so well, however; through him, Trollope strikes out at the muckraking press, that insidious creation of the nineteenth century that preyed on people like Phineas. Slide makes his living by appealing to the prurient interests of readers more interested in salacious gossip than the truth. His pursuit of the lurid details of Phineas's relationship to Laura Kennedy—many of them invented—is the spur for much of the hero's misfortune, and Trollope offers no excuse to compensate for Slide's despicable behavior.

Perhaps the greatest triumph in the novel, however, is Trollope's depiction of his female characters. Three women dominate the novel: Laura Kennedy, Lady Glencora Palliser, and Madame Goesler. Each plays a significant role in Phineas's growth toward mature self-awareness. Laura's sad tale, a life married to the wrong man, is presented sensitively, without undue sentiment; readers feel genuine sympathy for her when Phineas finally recognizes that he cannot rekindle his old passion after Kennedy is out of the way. Although he has no amorous interest in Lady Glencora, nor she in him, their genuine friendship is the source of her patronage of him; her insistent pursuit of appointments for Phineas permits him to rise—and fall—in the political arena, getting a taste of the sordidness of the profession as well as its rewards. Similarly, the patronage of Madame Goesler plays a key role in the hero's rise to prominence in his party; however, the two become more than friends, and in Madame Goesler, Phineas finds a fit partner for life.

Through Phineas's relationships with these women, Trollope demonstrates his strong belief in the role of women as men's equals in society. Whereas Laura Kennedy is treated as an object to be possessed by her husband, both Lady Glencora and Madame Goesler are seen as partners with the men they love, helping them achieve greatness in their fields without becoming mere helpmates in the more traditional sense. It is not surprising that Trollope's novels became favorites among twentieth century feminist critics for studying the question of male-female relationships in the nineteenth century.

Establishing the place of *Phineas Redux* in the Trollope canon is not easy. Just as he uses the Barsetshire series of novels to depict country life with all its joys and all its faults, Trollope uses *Phineas Redux* and the other novels in the Palliser series as a means of exploring London life and national politics. Each of the novels in the series contributes in some way to filling in that portrait. Although *Phineas Redux* has connections to other novels in the series, and to others by Trollope, it can stand alone as a complex, sensitive, and, at times, chilling portrait of Victorian society.

"Critical Evaluation" by Laurence W. Mazzeno

Further Reading

Bury, Laurent. *Seductive Strategies in the Novels of Anthony Trollope, 1815-1882.* Lewiston, N.Y.: Edwin Mellen Press, 2004. A study of seduction in Trollope's novels. Argues that seduction was a survival skill for both men and women in the Victorian era. Demonstrates how Trollope depicted the era's sexual politics.

Felber, Lynette. *Gender and Genre in Novels Without End: The British Roman-Fleuve.* Gainesville: University Press of Florida, 1995. A study of multivolume novels written during three periods of history, including *Phineas Redux* and the other novels in Trollope's Palliser series. Argues that the narratives of these novels inherently have "narrative features designated feminine."

Hall, N. John. *Trollope: A Biography.* New York: Oxford University Press, 1991. A critical biography of the novelist. Reviews the publication history of *Phineas Redux* and analyzes the novel's political background. Demonstrates how Trollope allows his characters to grow as the story progresses.

Markwick, Margaret. *New Men in Trollope's Novels: Rewriting the Victorian Male.* Burlington, Vt.: Ashgate, 2007. Examines Trollope's novels, tracing the development of his ideas about masculinity. Argues that Trollope's male characters are not the conventional Victorian patriarchs and demonstrates how his works promoted a "startlingly modern model of manhood."

_____. *Trollope and Women.* London: Hambledon Press, 1997. Examines how Trollope could simultaneously accept the conventional Victorian ideas about women while also sympathizing with women's difficult situations. Demonstrates the individuality of his female characters. Discusses his depiction of both happy and unhappy marriages, male-female relationships, bigamy, and scandal.

Morse, Deborah Denenholz. *Women in Trollope's Palliser Novels.* Ann Arbor: UMI Research Press, 1987. Examines Trollope's ambivalent attitude toward women in the Palliser series. A chapter on *Phineas Finn* and *Phineas Redux* analyzes portraits of the three Englishwomen whom Phineas loves, all of whom are strong and articulate.

Mullen, Richard, and James Munson. *The Penguin Companion to Trollope.* New York: Penguin Books, 1996. A comprehensive guide, describing all of Trollope's novels, short stories, travel books, and other works; discusses plot, characters, background, tone, allusions, and contemporary references; and places the works in their historical context.

Super, R. H. *The Chronicler of Barsetshire: A Life of Anthony Trollope.* Ann Arbor: University of Michigan Press, 1988. Critical biography by a distinguished scholar. Praises *Phineas Redux*, of all his novels, as the most "firmly embedded in contemporary British politics." Notes the confusion caused by Trollope's introduction of the murder and trial, which distract readers from political issues.

Walton, Priscilla L. *Patriarchal Desire and Victorian Discourse: A Lacanian Reading of Anthony Trollope's Palliser Novels.* Buffalo, N.Y.: University of Toronto Press, 1995. Although somewhat specialized in its approach, a chapter on *Phineas Redux* illuminates Trollope's attitudes toward feminist issues.

The Phoenician Women

Author: Euripides (c. 485-406 B.C.E.)
First produced: Phoinissai, 409 B.C.E. (English translation, 1781)
Type of work: Drama
Type of plot: Tragedy
Time of plot: Antiquity
Locale: Thebes

Principal characters:
JOCASTA, Oedipus's wife
ANTIGONE, Oedipus's daughter
POLYNICES, Oedipus's exiled son
ETEOCLES, Polynices' brother and the king of Thebes
CREON, Jocasta's brother
MENOECEUS, Creon's son
TIRESIAS, the blind prophet
OEDIPUS, the deposed king of Thebes
CHORUS OF PHOENICIAN MAIDENS

The Story:

Before the royal palace of Thebes, Jocasta, the mother of King Eteocles, prays to the sun god for aid in reconciling her two sons and avoiding fratricidal war over the kingdom of Thebes. In her supplication she recalls that her family has already suffered unbearable horrors; her husband, Oedipus, plucked out his eyes upon discovering that in marrying her he had married his own mother and had conceived two sons and two daughters by her. At first the sons had confined their father in the palace in order to hide the family shame and had decided to rule the kingdom between them in alternate years. However, Eteocles has refused to yield the throne to Polynices, who, after marrying the daughter of Adrastus, king of

Argos, has raised a host from seven city-states and is already at the gates of Thebes to win his rightful place by force of arms.

Antigone, viewing the besieging armies from the palace tower, recognizes the justice of Polynices' claim but prays that Thebes will never fall. In desperate fear, Jocasta cuts off her hair and dresses in mourning. Then, in the hope that war can be averted, she arranges a meeting under a truce between her two sons. Eteocles is willing to receive Polynices back in Thebes, but not as an equal to share the throne; Polynices, unable to endure exile and equally unable to accept such ignoble terms, remains bent on war.

Eteocles then sends for his uncle Creon to work out battle strategy. The two, agreeing that the situation is grave, finally decide not to attempt any counterattack with their vastly outnumbered troops; instead, they will post men at the seven gates of the city in a defensive action. Creon also sends his son Menoeceus to summon the blind prophet Tiresias for further advice. The prophet, after warning Creon that the means for saving Thebes will be something he will be unwilling to accept, announces that Menoeceus must be sacrificed. Horrified, Creon refuses and urges his son to flee at once. Menoeceus pretends to agree, but shortly after his departure a messenger hurries to Creon with the news that his son plunged a sword into his own throat at the very moment that the Argives launched their first fruitless assault against the gates of the city.

Jocasta, upon hearing that her two sons have decided to determine the fate of Thebes by a single combat apart from their armies, rushes off with Antigone to the battlefield to stop them if she can. As she departs, Creon arrives carrying his son's corpse; he has come to seek Jocasta's aid in preparing for Menoeceus's funeral. A second messenger brings him word that Jocasta has gone outside the walls of Thebes and there found her two sons dying, each the other's victim. Eteocles, unable to speak, bade his mother farewell with his eyes, and Polynices with his dying breath begged his mother to bury him in Theban soil. Then the grief-stricken Jocasta seized a sword and thrust it through her own throat. Upon that stroke, the Theban warriors fell upon the surprised Argives and drove them from the field. Menoeceus's sacrifice has not been in vain.

Antigone, returning with servants bearing the bodies of her mother and her two brothers, is met by blind King Oedipus, who has emerged from his confinement in the palace and who begins to express his grief in groans and lamentations. Creon, resolutely taking over the rule bequeathed to him by Eteocles, commands Oedipus to cease and to prepare for exile. Determined to restore order in the tragic city, Creon

is compelled to put aside personal feelings in submitting to the prophecies of Tiresias. Antigone, the new king insists, must prepare to marry his son Haemon; furthermore, while the body of Eteocles is to be given burial fit for a king, Polynices' corpse must be left to rot as a warning to all who might contemplate taking up arms against the city. Oedipus, refusing to beg, prepares to leave at once, but Antigone flouts Creon's commands. Rather than marry Haemon, she is determined to accompany her father into exile and to bury the body of Polynices with proper religious rites. As father and daughter set out from Thebes, Oedipus laments the sad history of his life but courageously submits to the fate that the gods have decreed for him.

Critical Evaluation:

Euripides was the youngest of the three great dramatic playwrights of Greek antiquity. An outspoken social critic and artistic innovator, he wrote plays that were considerably less popular with Athenian audiences of the fifth century B.C.E. than those of Aeschylus and Sophocles, his older theatrical peers. His disenchantment with official Athenian policy led him to forsake his native city late in life, and he spent his last years as a voluntary exile in the court of King Archelaus of Macedonia. Succeeding generations, however, found Euripides' unique blend of intense emotion, psychological realism, and lush poetic dialogue more congenial than the relatively austere dramas of his rivals, and his plays were frequently revived and produced in late Hellenic and Hellenistic times. The fact that nineteen complete plays by Euripides exist while only seven each by Sophocles and Aeschylus survive is evidence of Euripides' preeminence as dramatic poet in later antiquity.

Written late in his career, *The Phoenician Women* is remarkable in several respects. It is the longest of Euripides' surviving plays, and it boasts the largest cast of characters in any Greek drama. Moreover, it is the most innovative and original retelling of the story of the royal house of Thebes, a tale that had already served as the basis for some of the earlier dramas of Euripides' peers. The broad mythic resonance, exceptional range of emotional and melodramatic material, and linguistic richness of *The Phoenician Women* made it a favorite with actors, audiences, and scholars, and it became one of the most widely read, performed, and studied of the great Greek dramas for nearly one thousand years after its first performance. Knowledge of Greek language and literature, however, died out in Western Europe in the years following the collapse of the Roman Empire, and when it was revived during the Renaissance the prevailing taste for more tightly constructed dramas, such as Sophocles' *Antigonē*

(441 B.C.E.; *Antigone*, 1729), caused *The Phoenician Women* to suffer a loss of reputation and popularity from which it has not yet fully emerged.

Verbally ornate, artistically ambitious, simultaneously intellectual and emotional, and bitingly ironic, *The Phoenician Women* is a brilliant product of Euripides' late style. Despite the absence of a main character to provide dramatic focus, the logic of its thematic development and the powerful coherence of its imagery transcend the work's limitations to create a superbly crafted poetic drama.

The ostensible theme of the play is war; however, the treatment of this theme is so complex that in the end warfare becomes a metaphor for the tragic vicissitudes of the human condition. No single character dominates the play's action, but as the members of the Theban royal family—Jocasta, Antigone, Creon, Polynices, Eteocles, Creon, and Oedipus—interact with one another in various ways, their encounters bring different facets of family life, politics, and statecraft into conjunction with the problem of war. Interlinked images of blood and bloodshed permeate the language of the text, providing a constant reminder that the blood ties that bind the family (and the state) together cannot prevent—indeed all too frequently cause—the shedding of blood.

Looming over the entire action of the play is the changeable, and finally inimical, presence of the gods. This presence makes itself felt not through the actual presence or appearance of a divine character but rather through a complex pattern of shifting references to the gods, which takes on life in the language of the play. In the play's closing moments the remorseless operation of divine compulsion in human affairs is recapitulated in Oedipus's final speech. He recalls that his victory over the Sphinx was divinely ordained and that it has led him not to glory but to incest, dishonor, and exile. Euripides' pessimistic view of the human condition echoes in the defeated resignation of the last words Oedipus speaks: "The constraint the gods lay on us we mortals must bear."

This complex theme is developed through an equally complex structure. Intricate patterns of linked opposites are integrated into an edifice of balanced paradox. For example, Dionysus, ordinarily regarded as a beneficial deity, is called "gentle and terrible," and the dancing of his maenads is compared to the "dance of death"; the salvation of the city of Thebes requires that all surviving branches of the royal house of Thebes must be destroyed. The dramatic structure reflects the same principle of balance: Jocasta's prologue speech matches Oedipus's entering speech later in the play; her monody matches Antigone's; the entrance of blind Tiresias led by his daughter as he returns to Thebes from Athens at the end of the play. Within this carefully balanced structure Euripides plays out his pessimistic theme: Neither human intellect, attempted negotiation, nor noble self-sacrifice can prevent the divinely ordained destruction of the Theban royal family.

The high order of artistry with which Euripides develops his tragic theme allows it to transcend his own time and speak across the centuries. For the original Athenian audience there was one final interlocking piece to his design: Thebes unmistakably parallels Athens, and the war between Argos and Thebes thus mirrors the great war between Sparta and Athens that was drawing to a close outside the city walls. As Thebes is besieged in the play, so was Athens besieged at the time of the play's first production. The city's resources drastically depleted, no salvation was possible for Athens, which faced inevitable defeat at the hands of its bitterest enemy, Sparta. Feeling, like Oedipus, the "constraint" of the gods, that first Athenian audience heard the chorus close the play with a deeply ironic and finally hopeless response to his last speech: "Great Victory, continually crown my life."

"Critical Evaluation" by R. A. Martin

Further Reading

Collard, Christopher. *Euripides*. New York: Oxford University Press, 1981. Provides a short overview of textual and critical scholarship of Euripides' work, with the emphasis on directing attention to bibliographical resources in each area. Written for high school students.

Euripides. *The Phoenician Women*. Edited with translation and commentary by Elizabeth Craik. Warminster, Wiltshire, England: Aris & Phillips, 1988. This edition of the play contains the Greek text with literal English translation on facing pages, more than one hundred pages of detailed textual commentary, and an excellent introductory essay.

Luschnig, C. A. E. *The Gorgon's Severed Head: Studies in "Alcestis," "Electra," and "Phoenissae."* New York: Brill, 1995. Examines three plays from various periods in Euripides' career and concludes that all three demonstrate his use of innovative dramatic techniques and traditional stories, his depiction of characters who create themselves and each other, and his treatment of gender issues. The chapters on *The Phoenician Women* focus on the elements of space and time in the play.

Melchinger, Siegfried. *Euripides*. Translated by Samuel R. Rosebaum. New York: Frederick Ungar, 1973. Offers a clearly written introduction to Euripides' work. Includes brief summaries and interpretations of all the extant plays.

Morwood, James. *The Plays of Euripides*. Bristol, England: Bristol Classical, 2002. Presents concise overviews of all of Euripides' plays, devoting a separate chapter to each. Demonstrates how Euripides was constantly reinventing himself in his work.

Papadopoulou, Thalia. *Euripides: "Phoenician Women."* London: Duckworth, 2008. Companion to the play discusses Euripides' dramatic technique, use of rhetoric, and characterization as well as the function of the chorus. Explains aspects of the play's performance and traces its critical reception over the years.

Vellacott, Philip. *Ironic Drama: A Study of Euripides' Method and Meaning*. New York: Cambridge University Press, 1975. Important study of Euripidean drama as veiled social criticism deals with all the extant plays and offers interpretations of them in the context of Athenian civic and military history from approximately 438 B.C.E. to the posthumous production of *Bakchai* (*The Bacchae*, 1781) in 405 B.C.E.

Webster, T. B. L. *The Tragedies of Euripides*. New York: Methuen, 1967. Discusses the development of Euripides' career as an artist through detailed examination of the complete plays and the existing fragments. Provides summaries and interpretations of all pieces of Euripidean text that have survived; one of the most complete works of its kind.

Phormio

Author: Terence (c. 190-159 B.C.E.)
First produced: 161 B.C.E. (English translation, 1598)
Type of work: Drama
Type of plot: Comedy
Time of plot: Second century B.C.E.
Locale: Athens

Principal characters:
CHREMES, a rich gentleman of Athens
DEMIPHO, Chremes's miserly brother
ANTIPHO, Demipho's son
PHAEDRIA, Chremes's son
GETA, a slave
PHORMIO, a parasite
NAUSISTRATA, Chremes's wife

The Story:

Demipho and Chremes, two wealthy Athenian brothers, leave the city on journeys and entrust the welfare of their two sons to Geta, a slave belonging to Demipho. For a time, the two young men, Antipho and Phaedria, who are both of exemplary habits, give the slave little trouble. When both fall in love, however, before their fathers return, Geta's troubles begin. His sympathy for Antipho and Phaedria causes him to help both of them, but he realizes only too well that both fathers will be angry when they learn what has happened.

Phaedria, the son of Chremes, has fallen in love with a lovely young harp player owned by a trader named Dorio, who refuses to part with the girl for less than thirty minae. Unable to raise the money, Phaedria is at his wits' end. His cousin Antipho has fallen in love with a young Athenian girl of a good but penniless family.

Antipho has already married the girl, even though he knows that his father, who is something of a miser, will be furious to learn that his son has married a girl who brings no dower. Geta, in an effort to smooth out the problem, has contacted a parasitical lawyer named Phormio, who brings suit against Antipho under an Athenian law that makes it mandatory for an unprovided-for girl to be married to her nearest relative. Antipho does not contest the suit, and so he has the excuse that he was forced by the court to marry the young woman.

Shortly after the wedding, the two older men return. As soon as he learns what had happened, Demipho orders his son to give up his wife, whereupon Antipho and Geta again call on Phormio for assistance. Phormio warns the old man that he will be unable to avoid keeping the girl, even though Demipho claims that the girl is not actually a relative. Phormio contends that the girl is indeed a relative, the daughter of Demipho's kinsman, Stilpo, who has lived in Lemnos. Demipho declares he never had a relative by that name.

During this time, Phaedria is trying desperately to raise the thirty minae to purchase his beloved harpist from Dorio, who has given him three days to find the money. Then Phaedria learns from a slave that a sea captain, about to sail, wants to purchase the girl and that Dorio, anxious to make a sale, has promised to sell the girl to him. Phaedria appeals to Dorio, but he promises only to hold off the sale of the slave girl until the following morning.

After seeing Phormio, Demipho goes to his brother Chremes and talks over the situation with him. They finally agree that the only answer to the problem of Antipho's wife is to send her away with a sum of money. Chremes agrees to have his wife, Nausistrata, tell the girl that she is to be separated from her husband. While they are planning, Geta visits Phormio once again.

Phormio hatches a plan to satisfy everyone and make some money for himself. He offers to marry Antipho's cast-off wife if he is given a large sum of money. With part of that money he expects to have a good time, and with the rest, which he is to turn over to Phaedria, that young man is to purchase his beloved harpist. Geta presents the first part of Phormio's plan to the brothers, who readily acquiesce, even though Demipho hates to see Phormio receive payment for marrying the girl.

After the arrangements are made, Chremes is horrified to learn that the girl he is advising his brother to cast off is his own daughter by a second wife whom he had married in Lemnos. Even worse is that his Athenian wife, Nausistrata, does not know of the other marriage. Chremes takes his brother into his confidence and tells him what has happened. They both agree to let the marriage stand, and Chremes offers to add a dower to the girl.

The only difficulty, as the old men see it, is how to redeem their money from Phormio, who no longer needs to marry the girl. Phormio, having given part of the money to Phaedria, is unwilling to return that part of the money that was to have been his for his trouble.

While the old men are hunting for Phormio, he is in conversation with Antipho. Geta goes to them with the news that Antipho's uncle is also his father-in-law and that Antipho's troubles are at an end. Asked where he had learned this fact, Geta replies that he had overheard a conversation between Chremes and a servant. The information makes both Antipho and Phormio happy, Antipho because he will be able to keep his wife, and Phormio because he now has information to use in keeping the money he received from Chremes and Demipho.

When Chremes and Demipho confront Phormio, he refuses to give back the money, and in answer to their threats he replies that if they try to bring a suit against him he will tell Nausistrata about Chremes's affair in Lemnos and the true identity of Antipho's wife. During the argument the brothers lay hands on the lawyer. Phormio, infuriated by their treat-

ment of him, calls out to Nausistrata. When she comes out of the house, Phormio tells her about Chremes's other wife. She is somewhat mollified, however, when she realizes that the other woman is dead and that she will have something to hold over her husband's head.

Seeing that Nausistrata has been converted to his side, Phormio tells them also that he has given thirty minae to Phaedria so that he might purchase the harpist from Dorio. Chremes begins to protest, but Nausistrata silences him with the statement that it is no worse for the son to have such a mistress than for the father to have two wives. Nausistrata, pleased at the turn of events—for her son now has his beloved and her rival is dead—asks Phormio if there is anything she can do for him. Fun-loving Phormio says that he would be vastly pleased, and her husband much exasperated, if she would ask the lawyer to dinner. Nausistrata, proud of her newly found power over her husband, agrees.

Critical Evaluation:

Unlike much of Terence's other work, *Phormio* is highly amusing. In addition to presenting one of the most engaging rascals in the history of the theater, the play is fast-paced, brilliantly constructed, suspenseful, and rich in irony. Terence's ability in characterization is evident, but *Phormio* tends to be more farcical than his other comedies, though it is also more vigorous. This may be because the playwright did not adapt it from Menander, as was usually the case in Terence, but from Apollodorus of Carystus, a contemporary of Menander. Because the original source has not survived, it is difficult to judge how much of *Phormio* is derived from its source. Certain features are distinctly Terentian, such as the dual romance, the excellent use of plot, the smooth colloquial dialogue, and the polished maxims. Others are attributable to the Greek New Comedy, among them the stock character types, the concentration on domestic problems, and the prominence of a love story. The most likely scenario is that Terence took his material from Apollodorus in this play and reworked it according to his own formula, in the same way that Molière borrowed from *Phormio* in writing *The Cheats of Scapin* (1671).

When *Phormio* was first performed at the Roman games in 161 B.C.E., Terence was in his late twenties and had established a reputation as a successful dramatist. Of low birth and originally a slave, he had enjoyed a meteoric rise in his fortunes, becoming a member of the Scipionic coterie, a group of Roman aristocrats interested in the importation of Greek culture. His success as a dramatist can be indirectly gauged from his prologues, in which he self-confidently answers the attacks of the elderly playwright Luscius Lanuvinus. One year after *Phormio* was presented, however, Terence took a trip to Greece from which he never returned. It is thought that his ship sank as he was returning to Rome in 159 B.C.E.

In *Phormio*, Terence shows an unusual detachment from the plight of the two adolescent young men, Antipho and Phaedria, presenting them as rather silly, impulsive, and feckless youths who are helpless before their fathers. Instead of differentiating them, which is his normal practice, Terence emphasizes their similarity. Moreover, he pokes fun at their superficiality and self-absorption. It seems clear that Terence was growing beyond the stage of taking youthful romances seriously. He does not even present the young women whom Antipho and Phaedria love: They are incidental to the plot except as prizes.

What does interest Terence is the character of Phormio: self-possessed where the two youths are cowardly, roguish where the two youths wish to appear respectable, clever where the two youths are witless, and determined where the two youths are fickle. Phormio is mature and confident of his powers, the ideal hero of many young men. It is he alone who outwits the two formidable fathers to award Phaedria his harp player; and it is he who enabled Antipho to marry in the first place through a ruse that, surprisingly enough, turns out to be true. Terence, having outgrown his interest in adolescent lovers, apparently needed a more vital character to command the stage, and he found one in the adventurer Phormio.

Instead of giving Antipho and Phaedria contrasting qualities, Terence chooses to give them different problems. Antipho's difficulty is to keep the wife he already has in the face of his father's opposition. Phaedria's trouble is that he cannot raise the money to purchase the mistress he loves from her pimp, who is presented as a practical businessman. Phormio undertakes to solve both problems, not so much for his own gain but to demonstrate his gift for intrigue. He wants to show off his virtuosity before the admiring slave Geta and the two young men. He is shown thinking on his feet, as it were, outfacing Demipho and his three toady lawyers, discarding a useless alibi, obtaining a large sum from Chremes under false pretenses, and adapting quickly to a dangerous situation in which Demipho is intent on regaining the money. In all of this, through chance and his quick wit, he is master of the situation.

Demipho and Chremes after all deserve to be swindled, as tightfisted and authoritarian old men, and their sons, being the shallow, erotic boys they are, deserve a hard time before their problems are settled. The complex but clearly developed plot provides opportunities to witness the chagrin of all four in an amusing light. The most amusing scenes, however,

are the climactic ones in which Chremes tries his hardest to keep the secret of his bigamous marriage from his wife, while Demipho's concern over money forces Phormio to reveal it, thereby ensuring that Chremes will be at his wife's behest for the rest of his life.

In the end, once the plot has been unraveled and the characters have received their proper rewards and punishments, the Terentian comedy seems rather trivial and commonplace, requiring no great effort of thought. If it is amiable and technically skilled, the assumptions behind it are those of middle-class audiences everywhere: that young love should be fulfilled, that the old should make allowances for the fancies of youth, and that parental authority should be respected by youth. These premises make Terence, along with Plautus, the forerunner of bourgeois comedy from William Shakespeare to Neil Simon.

"Critical Evaluation" by James Weigel, Jr.

Further Reading

Barsby, John. "The Stage Action of Terence, *Phormio*." *Classical Quarterly* 43, no. 1 (1993): 329-335. Discusses how productions of *Phormio* are staged. Helpful, especially, for readers concerned with dramatic technique.

Duff, J. Wight. *A Literary History of Rome: From the Origins to the Close of the Golden Age*. 3d ed. Edited by A. M. Duff. New York: Barnes & Noble, 1967. Gives a plot line and places *Phormio* in the context of Terence's other plays. Discusses other playwrights' influence on *Phormio* and examines the chronology of Terence's plays in relation to the prologues. Claims that discrepancies exist in play presentation that could confuse the interpretation of prologues.

Dutsch, Dorota M. *Feminine Discourse in Roman Comedy: On Echoes and Voices*. New York: Oxford University Press, 2008. Analyzes the dialogue of female characters in Terence's plays, noting its use of endearments, softness of speech, and emphasis on small problems. Questions whether or not Roman women actually spoke as depicted.

Flickinger, Roy C. "A Study of Terence's Prologues." *Philological Quarterly* 9 (1940): 81-93. Examines the prologues and explains that Terence used them as a defense of his works; in *Phormio*, for example, Terence refers to himself as "the old playwright" and says his aim in writing this play is "to answer, not provoke." Argues that the study of prologues is important in understanding Terence.

Leigh, Matthew. *Comedy and the Rise of Rome*. New York: Oxford University Press, 2004. Analyzes the comedies of Terence and Plautus, placing them within the context of political and economic conditions in Rome during the third and second centuries B.C.E. Discusses how audiences of that time responded to these comedies.

Rose, H. J. *A Handbook of Latin Literature from the Earliest Times to the Death of St. Augustine.* 1967. Reprint. Wauconda, Ill.: Bolchazy-Carducci, 1996. Covers Terence's major works in chronological order. Summarizes

Phormio, then discusses its critical reception. Maintains that *Phormio* is one of Terence's better plays.

Segal, Erich, ed. *Oxford Readings in Menander, Plautus, and Terence.* New York: Oxford University Press, 2001. Includes essays on the originality of Terence and his Greek models and on the dramatic methods of characterization in *Phormio*.

The Piano Lesson

Author: August Wilson (1945-2005)
First produced: 1987; first published, 1990
Type of work: Drama
Type of plot: Magical Realism
Time of plot: 1936
Locale: Pittsburgh, Pennsylvania

Principal characters:
BERNIECE, a widow living in Pittsburgh with her uncle and daughter
BOY WILLIE, Berniece's brother
LYMON, Boy Willie's friend
MARETHA, Berniece's daughter
DOAKER, Berniece and Boy Willie's uncle
WINING BOY, Doaker's brother
AVERY, a minister

The Story:

Boy Willie Charles and his friend Lymon arrive at the Pittsburgh home of Berniece, Boy Willie's widowed sister. The two men have driven to Pittsburgh from Mississippi in a truck full of ripe watermelons. When he arrives at his sister's home, Boy Willie announces to Berniece an ambitious plan that will require her cooperation: He wants to buy a parcel of land in Mississippi on which the Charles family's ancestors served as slaves and sharecroppers. Boy Willie has saved some of the money he will need to make the purchase, and he intends to sell the watermelons in his truck to raise more. For Boy Willie to acquire enough cash to make the purchase, however, Berniece must agree to sell the old piano sitting in her living room and split the proceeds with her brother. Although the piano has been in Berniece's possession since she moved to Pittsburgh, Boy Willie claims half ownership of the instrument.

Berniece strongly opposes the sale of the piano, which is imbued with symbolic value. Doaker and Wining Boy, Berniece and Boy Willie's uncles, detail the complicated history of the instrument. The piano was originally acquired in 1856 by Robert Sutter, the man who owned members of the Charles family. The piano was an anniversary gift from Sutter to his wife, Ophelia. Lacking cash for the purchase, Sutter acquired the instrument by trading two Charles family slaves, Mama

Berniece and her nine-year-old son Walter. Papa Boy Willie, Mama Berniece's husband, wished to memorialize Mama Berniece and Walter. An expert wood sculptor, he obtained Ophelia's permission to carve their portraits and other memorable Charles family scenes into the wood of the piano.

The piano remained with the Sutters after the emancipation of the slaves, but on July 4, 1911, members of the Charles family stole the piano from the Sutters' home. The group included Doaker, Wining Boy, Berniece and Boy Willie's father, and Boy Charles, the grandson of the woodcarver and Mama Berniece. Boy Charles maintained that as long as the Sutter family had possession of the piano, the Charles family was still spiritually enslaved; by stealing the instrument, Boy Charles believed he would finally liberate his family from the Sutters. After the theft, Boy Charles hid from Sutter and the police in a yellow train boxcar. When Robert Sutter's son discovered the theft and Boy Charles's whereabouts, he burned the boxcar where Boy Charles was hiding, killing him. Sutter never recovered his stolen piano; it remained in the Charles family, and Berniece took the instrument to Pittsburgh when she moved there in 1933.

Berniece is unwilling to part with the piano because she considers it a sacred relic that holds the Charles family's history through slavery, emancipation, and Reconstruction.

Hearing that his sister will not agree to sell the piano, Boy Willie offers a King Solomon solution to their dispute: cut the piano in half and let Berniece retain her part while he sells his half. To Boy Willie, the instrument holds only sentimental value: Since his sister is neither playing the piano nor giving lessons to earn a profit from it, it is, in his view, a useless family heirloom. By contrast, the land that Boy Willie wishes to acquire from the sale of the piano would give him standing and even a degree of equality with whites in the Jim Crow South. Berniece, however, believes that the piano embodies the Charles family's history. She points out to Boy Willie that their father gave his life to wrestle the piano from the Sutter family. Indeed, Berniece tells her brother that their mother, Mama Ola, polished the piano with her tears and prayed for her husband's soul over the instrument. In Berniece's view, selling the instrument would dishonor her father's sacrifice and her parents' memory.

According to Doaker, another party is laying claim to Berniece's piano. Doaker maintains that the ghost of the recently deceased James Sutter, Ophelia's grandson, is restlessly searching for his family's missing piano. According to Doaker, the ghost periodically visits Berniece's home at night and plays the piano. Doaker reports hearing piano music late at night. When he goes into the living room to find out who is playing, he sees the piano keys moving without a human being nearby. Charles family ghosts are also reportedly creating mischief. According to local legend, several Sutter family members, including James, have died by the hand of the ghost of the Yellow Dog railroad, by being pushed into wells—revenge for the killing of Boy Charles.

Despite his sister's protest, Boy Willie makes arrangements to sell the piano to a used musical instrument dealer in Pittsburgh. When he and Lymon try to move the piano, however, they cannot budge the instrument. As Boy Willie and Lymon consider how to move the piano, the Reverend Avery, a minister in Pittsburgh, arrives to exorcise Sutter's ghost from Berniece's home. While Avery exhorts the ghost to depart the premises, Berniece begins to play the piano, invoking the names of her family's slave ancestors as she plays. Boy Willie, suddenly sensing Sutter's presence, rushes upstairs to grapple with Sutter's ghost. After a struggle, Boy Willie is able to eject Sutter's ghost from the premises. Convinced by the ordeal that the piano is more than a sentimental family heirloom, Boy Willie relinquishes his claim on the instrument and returns with Lymon to Mississippi.

Critical Evaluation:

The compelling debate between Berniece and Boy Willie at the heart of August Wilson's *The Piano Lesson* is a debate over how African Americans should view their ancestors' tragic experience of slavery. Boy Willie would like to erase the past and focus on the present; he wishes to get rid of the family piano that is so problematically entangled with his family's embarrassing history of enslavement. He wants to buy land, farm it, and earn his own living; he craves an economic independence enjoyed by few African Americans in the South during the first half of the twentieth century. Moreover, by purchasing the parcel of land on which his ancestors were held as slaves and on which they worked as sharecroppers, Boy Willie believes he will symbolically negate the legacy of slavery: He will own the tract of land on which his ancestors were bound as human property.

The acquisition of land was an important first step for many former slaves and their descendants in their quest to become economically free from the legacy of slavery and to achieve economic and social equality with white Americans. Soon after the Civil War, some American lawmakers proposed various plans to compensate former slaves for their unrequited labor by offering them forty acres of land to farm and a mule to plow it. Such plans were never realized, and millions of slaves and their descendants, like Berniece, moved North toward economic opportunity and away from overt racial repression in the South. Those African Americans who remained in the South often labored for white employers for low wages, never attaining economic empowerment. By acquiring land, Boy Willie believes he can achieve a version of the American Dream.

To Berniece, however, the piano symbolizes her family's noble endurance through slavery and Reconstruction. By stealing the piano from the Sutter family, the descendants of their former owners, Boy Charles and his brothers attempted to free themselves from slavery's legacy. They would own the instrument that was used to break up their family during antebellum days; in a sense, they would thereby negate the sale of their enslaved ancestors. The images carved into the piano remind the contemporary Charles family of their ancestors' experience during slavery—and their endurance through that national nightmare. In Berniece's view, the Charles family's past, though painful and humiliating, must remain alive, carried forward by her mother, her uncles, and herself to her daughter Maretha and generations of African Americans removed from slavery by the passage of time.

Both Boy Willie and Berniece offer compelling arguments. In a sense, the siblings in Wilson's play articulate a variation of the debate between Booker T. Washington and W. E. B. Du Bois at the turn of the twentieth century. In his famous Atlanta Exposition Address of 1895 and elsewhere, Washington advised African Americans to move beyond the humiliating legacy of slavery and to focus their efforts on learning trades and developing economic opportunities rather than on agitating for civil and social rights. In *The Souls of Black Folk: Essays and Sketches* (1903) and his many other writings, Du Bois articulated his belief that economic opportunities would come only after African Americans had achieved social and political rights. He also believed in keeping the African American culture and its past alive, though it might be painful and tragic. In his play, Wilson resolves the debate between Berniece and Boy Willie by giving Berniece the victory. Her brother learns that living with dignity in the present and achieving selfhood require acknowledging the past by keeping alive its symbols and, if necessary, by wrestling with its ghosts. That is the piano lesson at the heart of Wilson's play.

The Piano Lesson, which won the Pulitzer Prize in drama and the New York Drama Critics Circle Award in 1990, is part of Wilson's ten-play cycle about African American life during the twentieth century. Wilson devoted more than twenty years to this ambitious project, in which each play is set in a different decade of the twentieth century and articulates issues and themes that confronted African Americans during that decade. Other plays in the cycle include the Pulitzer Prize-winning *Fences* (pr., pb. 1985), *Joe Turner's Come and Gone* (pr. 1986, pb. 1988), and *Ma Rainey's Black Bottom* (pr. 1984, pb. 1985). Wilson completed the final play in the cycle, *Radio Golf* (pr. 2005, pb. 2007), shortly before his death in 2005.

James Tackach

Further Reading

Bogumil, Mary L. *Understanding August Wilson*. Columbia: University of South Carolina Press, 1999. Contains critical analyses of *The Piano Lesson* and other Wilson dramas.

Elkins, Marilyn, *August Wilson: A Casebook*. New York: Garland, 1994. A collection of essays and interviews on Wilson's plays.

Nadel, Alan, ed. *May All Your Fences Have Gates: Essays on the Drama of August Wilson*. Iowa City: University of Iowa Press, 1994. A collection of critical essays on Wilson's plays, including *The Piano Lesson*. Essays discuss the plays individually, as well as addressing Wilson's (then unfinished) cycle of plays as a whole.

Pereira, Kim. *August Wilson and the African American Odyssey*. Urbana: University of Illinois Press, 1995. Provides a persuasive defense of Boy Willie's argument for selling his sister's piano.

Rothstein, Mervyn. "Round Five for a Theatrical Heavyweight." *The New York Times*, April 15, 1990, sec. 2, p. 1. A contemporary review of *The Piano Lesson*, published shortly after its debut.

Shannon, Sandra G. *The Dramatic Vision of August Wilson*. Washington, D.C.: Howard University Press, 1995. Contains an analysis of *The Piano Lesson*, including a discussion of how Wilson, with the assistance of director Lloyd Richards, revised early drafts of the play to create the finished product.

Tackach, James, and Emilie Benoit. "August Wilson's *The Piano Lesson* and the Limits of Law." *Law, Culture, and the Humanities* 4, no. 2 (2008): 280-291. A discussion of the legal issues in Wilson's play.

Wilson, August. *Conversations with August Wilson*. Edited by Jackson R. Bryer and Mary C. Hartig. Jackson: University Press of Mississippi, 2006. A collection of interviews with the playwright, in which he discusses individual plays, his cycle of plays, his influences, and issues facing African American dramatists.

Wolfe, Peter. *August Wilson*. New York: Twayne, 1999. An excellent introductory overview of Wilson's dramatic world and concise discussions of his individual plays.

The Piano Teacher

Author: Elfriede Jelinek (1946-   )
First published: Die Klavierspielerin, 1983 (English
    translation, 1988)
Type of work: Novel
Type of plot: Psychological realism
Time of plot: 1970's-1980's
Locale: Vienna

Principal characters:
ERIKA KOHUT, a piano teacher
ERIKA'S MOTHER, her controlling mother
WALTER KLEMMER, a music student

The Story:

Erika Kohut is a pianist who lives with her mother and teaches at a music conservatory. Erika's consciousness is filled with an angry, absurdist, flow of impressions, evoking strong memories and emotions. The thirty-eight-year-old Erika is still a very compliant daughter to her overbearing mother, a controlling bully who manages every aspect of her daughter's life.

Erika's mother had anticipated that her daughter's talent would enable her to realize her own ambitions for greater wealth and social status. Because Erika's father is absent, taken away long ago in an agitated state to a mental institution, Erika's mother places all her hopes on her daughter, imagining her as a famous musician, envied and idolized by everyone. Despite all her mother's scheming and dreaming, however, Erika has not become a brilliant pianist. Years ago, for her debut, she chose to play a piece so esoteric that she alienated the judges, leading her away from performing and into teaching instead.

While doing everything possible to encourage Erika's musical accomplishments, Erika's mother warns her against boyfriends, whom she thinks would destroy all of Erika's achievements. To discourage her daughter's interest in men, her mother forbids her from wearing makeup and buying pretty things for herself, and she even threatens to harm Erika if she has anything to do with a man. Erika defies her mother's control and her thrifty domestic regime by splurging on frivolous dresses that she has no intention of wearing. This leads to one of their bitterest quarrels. Erika then smothers her mother with apologetic kisses, but a suggestion of aggression and animosity remains against the woman she considers her jailer and tormentor.

Despite their disagreements, however, Erika is in many ways her mother's daughter—as she makes her way home through the crowded streets of Vienna, she comports herself as a haughty queen subject to plebeian inconveniences. She is also competitive and envious; in high school she had re-

ported to the authorities a girl whose activities as a prostitute enabled her to buy the pretty clothes denied Erika.

At the same time, there are many signs of Erika's own true dissent. Buying the frilly dresses is one sign, but her rebelliousness takes a twisted and dangerous form when she begins to secretly visit the peep shows in the red-light district of the city. While Erika's visits to these shows and to sadomasochistic pornographic movies suggest that in one way she is assuming the power of the male voyeur, this underworld is nevertheless devoted to male sexuality and masculine preferences that encourage Erika to take them as guidelines for the construction of a submissive female sexual identity. Additionally, these sex shows and porn films provide nothing for Erika in the way of erotic pleasure—she so lacks an emotional or sensual life that at one point she cuts her genitalia to feel some sort of sensation.

Although in one part of her life she seeks some kind of libidinous life in the red-light district, Erika's work persona is, like her home life, bereft of the erotic. One day, she finds that she is attracted to a young music student, Walter Klemmer. So obsessed is she that at one point she punishes a young woman flutist who is flirting with him by slipping a smashed glass into the woman's pocket.

Erika's first sexual experience with Klemmer is in a lavatory of the conservatory; the second is in the cleaning staff's closet. Both episodes are joyless and unromantic—the second time, Erika is so repelled that she vomits into a pail afterward. Klemmer, on the other hand, is aggressive and forces her submission. She responds to her encounters with him by composing a list of demands. Erika has gained the upper hand by dictating to him how he may abuse her. At the same time, Erika, on one level, hopes he will take the initiative and abjure violence and reject her demands; she desperately hopes he will initiate a gentle and loving relationship.

Even as Erika seems to be entering into a submissive relationship with Klemmer, she also criticizes his musical abilities to the director of the school, preventing him from performing as a soloist in the upcoming recital. Enraged by her control over him as a teacher and repelled by her list of demands, Klemmer barges into her apartment, shuts her shaken and frightened mother away, and brutally rapes Erika. Having felt he has taught her a lesson, Klemmer regains his serenity.

Later, Erika procures a knife from her kitchen and puts on one of her old-fashioned pretty dresses. She then leaves to find Klemmer. When she confronts him, she does not exercise vengeance by attacking him as expected; instead, she requires him to bear witness as she stabs herself in the shoulder. Having finished with the brutal Klemmer on terms that suggest both sadistic power and masochistic submission, she returns home to the very mother who is responsible for the pathologies of her love life.

Critical Evaluation:

Elfriede Jelinek's *The Piano Teacher* is both a psychological study and social critique. On a psychological level, the novel explores the way in which the mother-daughter relationship will determine the nature of the daughter's relationship with men in her adult life. Erika's mother asks her to sacrifice her own normal psychological development to rescue the family by means of her special musical gifts. Her hard-driving mother keeps her daughter in a regressed, dependent position, yet she also makes her the "man" of the house.

The power relation between the two women is a complex one. Despite her mother's domineering ways, Erika is not simply compliant and docile; she also dissents and resists through her infuriated emotional life. Instead of gaining independence, however, she is drawn into power struggles with her mother, which she sometimes wins. Erika is able to find ways to control and manipulate her often-baffled mother. Love and hate are difficult to distinguish in the intense bond between the women. Similarly, when Erika embarks on a relationship with Walter Klemmer, she appears as the masochistic partner but remains in subtle control.

Jelinek's depiction of romantic love is one that is largely shaped by motives of power, humiliation, and sexuality that quickly shades into violence. Both comic and tragic, the romance of Klemmer and Erika is utterly sabotaged by each partner's unloving impulses. Erika presents herself as a victim, or as an object available for punishment and ridicule. However, as in her relationship with her mother, she is both powerless and mysteriously powerful. Erika's masochistic desires begin to tyrannize Klemmer, whose need to keep the upper hand is subverted by Erika's need to herself gain power and freedom from the victim status that has been so hurtful to

her. Her imperious list of masochistic demands and the wound she inflicts upon herself demonstrate the way in which Erika has made herself her own victim even as she attempts to free herself from this status by exerting control over her twisted sexuality. To further complicate the situation, even as Erika triggers a streak of sadism and violence in Klemmer, her relationship to him is complicated by a deep but largely buried wish for genuine care and love; beneath her perverse sexual conduct is a more basic longing for a trusting bond that will allow her to love and be loved.

Erika has been so psychologically damaged by her possessive and controlling mother that she has no idea who she is or what she feels. Shaped by her ambitious mother to be a perfectionist and a high achiever, her personality has been falsified to such a degree that there is a void where her identity should be. A classic textbook example of a narcissistic personality disorder is Erika's fury and anguish, which allow her to feel that she exists as a real person; it is her suffering that suggests there is an autonomous individual struggling to break free of the shallow and artificial grandiose identity her mother has imposed on her. Groomed for success, Erika's failures—in her career and in love—nonetheless point to the existence of a more authentic personality. When Erika cuts herself on her shoulder in front of Klemmer and then returns home to her mother, she is suggesting she is aware she has collaborated with both her mother and Klemmer as they aggressively imposed their wills on her. Having never had the freedom to develop her own identity or her own sexuality, her task now is to dismantle the false self that has made her a yielding masochist. The task of self-destruction, while wreaking havoc on her life, is the only way in which she can ever free herself from her role as victim of both her mother and her lover.

A sense of authenticity, while depicting a self in the process of undermining its own false premises, emerges in the flow of the language assigned to Erika. This musical flow of voices constitutes a rich linguistic form of dissent from social convention and social pressure and is considered one of Jelinek's major achievements. The language of the novel conveys a dark, enraged, and anguished emotional texture that constitutes a form of emancipation from the repressive and controlling environment overwhelming Erika's instincts and intuitions. It is this dissonant, often hysterical, but nevertheless highly musical deployment of language as inventive resistance that the Nobel committee especially noted when awarding Jelinek the Nobel Prize in Literature in 2004.

Although Erika must change her situation from within, it is clear that her upbringing is responsible for her dilemma, an upbringing not unlike the fascist authoritarianism associated with Austria in the Nazi era. Another important subject in this novel is the way in which fascism remains a part of contemporary Austrian society. While on the surface Erika represents the crowning achievement of a distinguished musical culture, she has become the acquiescent servant of a culture industry that serves to distract from other, more pathological social and psychological problems. The Austrian world of high musical art is here peeled back to expose perverse sadomasochistic images of power and domination; both Klemmer and Erika's mother can be seen as instances of the dark side of a culture that continues to produce fascistic personalities who, through a process of cultural amnesia, go unrecognized.

Jelinek's exposure of the continuing fascism of her society was accompanied by attacks by the right-wing Austrian political leader Jorg Haider, only proving her thesis of historical denial and the failure to examine the fascistic structures that still permeate family and male-female relationships. For women, especially, these structures inhibit the construction of the integral self.

Margaret Boe Birns

Further Reading

Barthofer, Alfred. "Vanishing in the Text: Elfriede Jelinek's Art of Self-Effacement in *The Piano Teacher* and *Children of the Dead*." In *The Fiction of the I: Contemporary Austrian Writers and Autobiography*, edited by Nicholas Meyerhofer. Riverside, Calif.: Ariadne Press, 1999. Suggests that Jelinek dismantles a mythical self constructed by the social ideology, causing her fictional "I" to vanish into the flow of linguistic dissidence.

Fiddler, Allyson. *Rewriting Reality: An Introduction to Elfriede Jelinek*. Oxford, England: Berg, 1994. An excellent introduction to Jelinek, suitable for undergraduates. Surveys her major work and provides close readings and the historical, feminist, and literary contexts of her fiction.

Johns, Jorun B., and Katherine Arens. *Elfriede Jelinek: Framed by Language*. Riverside, Calif.: Ariadne Press, 1994. Essays on Jelinek examine her modernist prose style, her postmodern reinvention of genre, and her feminist and antifascist themes.

Konzett, Matthias. *The Rhetoric of National Dissent in Thomas Bernhard, Peter Handke, and Elfriede Jelinek*. New York: Camden House, 2000. Analyzes how Jelinek and two other Austrian writers created new literary strategies to expose and dismantle conventional ideas that impede the development of multicultural awareness and identity.

Maltzan, Carlotta von. "Voyeurism and Film in Elfriede Jelinek's *The Piano Teacher*." In *Literature, Film, and the Culture Industry in Contemporary Austria*, edited by Margarete Lamb-Faffelberger and Franz-Peter Greisner. New York: Peter Lang, 2002. Examines voyeurism as a source of self-estrangement in *The Piano Teacher*. Part of a larger study linking literature and film in Austria.

Meyer, Imke. "The Trouble with Elfriede Jelinek and Autobiography." In *The Fiction of the I: Contemporary Austrian Writers and Autobiography*, edited by Nicholas Meyerhofer. Riverside, Calif.: Ariadne Press, 1999. Explores the limitations and pitfalls of choosing a biographical reading of Jelinek's work, including *The Piano Teacher*.

Morgan, Ben. "Elfriede Jelinek." In *Landmarks in German Women's Writing*, edited by Hilary Brown. New York: Peter Lang, 2007. Article on Jelinek is part of a larger study of twelve women writers from the Middle Ages to the twenty-first century who have made major contributions to German-language literature.

Piccolruaz Konzett, Matthias, and Margarete Lamb-Faffelberger, eds. *Elfriede Jelinek: Writing Woman, Nation, and Identity*. Madison, N.J.: Fairleigh Dickinson University Press, 2007. Features essays on Jelinek's contributions to world literature and about her influence on German and European literature. Also examines her relationship to sociopolitical issues, especially the legacy of fascism.

Pickwick Papers

Author: Charles Dickens (1812-1870)
First published: 1836-1837, serial; 1837, book
Type of work: Novel
Type of plot: Social realism
Time of plot: 1827-1828
Locale: England

Principal characters:
MR. SAMUEL PICKWICK, the founder of the Pickwick Club
MR. AUGUSTUS SNODGRASS,
MR. TRACY TUPMAN, and
MR. NATHANIEL WINKLE, other members of the club
MR. WARDLE, the owner of Manor Farm
RACHAEL WARDLE, his sister
EMILY WARDLE, his daughter
MRS. BARDELL, Mr. Pickwick's housekeeper
MR. PERKER, a lawyer
SAM WELLER, Mr. Pickwick's servant
ARABELLA ALLEN, Mr. Winkle's beloved
MR. ALFRED JINGLE, a rascal

The Story:

Samuel Pickwick, Esq., is the founder and perpetual president of the justly famous Pickwick Club. To extend his own researches into the quaint and curious phenomena of life, he suggests that he and three other Pickwickians should make journeys to places remote from London and report on their findings to the stay-at-home members of the club. The first destination decided upon is Rochester. As Mr. Pickwick, Mr. Tracy Tupman, Mr. Nathaniel Winkle, and Mr. Augustus Snodgrass go to their coach, they are waylaid by a rough gang of cab drivers. Fortunately, the men are rescued by a stranger who is poorly dressed but of the friendliest nature. The stranger, who introduces himself as Alfred Jingle, also appears to be going to Rochester, and the party mounts the coach together.

After they arrive at their destination, Mr. Jingle arouses Mr. Tupman's curiosity by telling him that there is to be a ball at the inn that evening and that many lovely young ladies will be present. Because, says Mr. Jingle, his luggage has gone astray, he has no evening clothes, and so it will be impossible for him to attend the affair. This is a regrettable circumstance because he had hoped to introduce Mr. Tupman to the many young ladies of wealth and fashion who will be present. Eager to meet these young ladies, Mr. Tupman borrows Mr. Winkle's suit for the stranger. At the ball, Mr. Jingle, observing a middle-aged lady being assiduously attended by a doctor, goes up to her and starts dancing with her, much to the doctor's anger. Introducing himself as Dr. Slammer, the angry gentleman challenges Mr. Jingle to a duel, but Mr. Jingle refuses to give his name.

The next morning, a servant identifies Mr. Winkle as the gentleman wearing the suit as described by the doctor and tells Mr. Winkle that Dr. Slammer is awaiting his appearance to fight a duel. Mr. Winkle had been drunk the night before, and he decides he is being called out because he had conducted himself in an unseemly manner that he can no longer remember. With Mr. Snodgrass as his second, a trembling Mr. Winkle approaches the battlefield. Much to his relief, Dr. Slammer roars that he is the wrong man. After much misunderstanding, the situation is satisfactorily explained, and no blood is shed.

During the afternoon, the travelers attend a parade, where they meet Mr. Wardle in a coach with his two daughters and his sister, Miss Rachael Wardle. Mr. Tupman is impressed by the elder Miss Wardle and accepts for his friends and himself Mr. Wardle's invitation to visit his estate, Manor Farm. The next day, the four Pickwickians depart for the farm, which is a distance of about ten miles from the inn where they are staying. They encounter difficulties with their horses and arrive at Manor Farm in a disheveled state, but they are soon washed and mended under the kind assistance of Mr. Wardle's daughters. In the evening, they play a hearty game of whist, and Mr. Tupman squeezes Miss Wardle's hand under the table.

The next day, Mr. Wardle takes his guests rook hunting. Mr. Winkle, who will not admit himself unable to cope with any situation, is given the gun to try his skill. He proves it by accidentally shooting Mr. Tupman in the arm. Miss Wardle offers her aid to the stricken man. Observing that their friend is in good hands, the others travel to a neighboring town to watch the cricket matches. Here, Mr. Pickwick unexpectedly encounters Mr. Jingle, and Mr. Wardle invites him to return to Manor Farm with his party.

Convinced that Miss Wardle has a great deal of money, Mr. Jingle misrepresents Mr. Tupman's intentions to Miss Wardle and persuades her to elope with him. Mr. Wardle and Mr. Pickwick pursue the couple to London. Here, with the help of Mr. Wardle's lawyer, Mr. Perker, they go from one inn to another in an attempt to find the elopers. Finally, through a sharp-featured young man cleaning boots in the yard of the White Hart Inn, they are able to identify Mr. Jingle. They indignantly confront him as he is displaying a marriage license. After a heated argument, Mr. Jingle resigns his matrimonial plans for the sum of £120. Miss Wardle tearfully returns to Manor Farm. The Pickwickians returns to London, where Mr. Pickwick engages as his servant Sam Weller, the sharp, shrewd young bootblack of the White Hart Inn.

When Mrs. Leo Hunter invites Mr. Pickwick and his friends to a party, they spy Mr. Jingle. He, seeing his former acquaintance, disappears into the crowd. Mrs. Hunter tells Mr. Pickwick that Mr. Jingle lives at Bury St. Edmonds. Mr. Pickwick sets out in pursuit in company with Sam Weller, for the old gentleman is determined to deter the scoundrel from any fresh deceptions he might be planning. At the inn where Mr. Jingle is reported to be staying, Mr. Pickwick learns that the rascal is planning to elope with a rich young lady who stays at a boarding school nearby. Mr. Pickwick agrees with the suggestion that to rescue the young lady he should hide in the garden from which Mr. Jingle is planning to steal her. When Mr. Pickwick sneaks into the garden, he finds nothing suspicious; he had been deceived, and the blackguard had escaped.

Mr. Pickwick's housekeeper is Mrs. Bardell, a widow. Mr. Pickwick, when trying to tell her about having hired Sam Weller, beats about the bush in such a manner that she mistakes his words for a proposal of marriage. One day, Mr. Pickwick is resting in his room when he receives notice from the legal firm of Dodgson and Fogg that Mrs. Bardell is suing him for breach of promise. The summons is distressing; but first, Mr. Pickwick has more important business to occupy his time. After securing the services of Mr. Perker to defend him, he goes to Ipswich, having learned that Mr. Jingle had been seen in that vicinity. The trip to Ipswich is successful. The Pickwickians are able to catch Mr. Jingle in his latest scheme of deception and to expose him before he has carried out his plot.

At the trial for the breach-of-promise suit brought by Mrs. Bardell, lawyers Dodgson and Fogg argue so eloquently against Mr. Pickwick that the jury fines him £750. When the trial is over, Mr. Pickwick tells Dodgson and Fogg that even if they put him in prison he will never pay one cent of the damages, since he knows as well as they that there had been no grounds for suit.

Shortly afterward, the Pickwickians go to Bath, where fresh adventures await Mr. Pickwick and his friends. On that occasion, Mr. Winkle's weakness for women involves the friends in difficulties. In Bath, the Pickwickians meet two young medical students, Mr. Allen and Mr. Bob Sawyer. Mr. Allen hopes to marry his sister, Arabella, to his friend, Mr. Sawyer, but Miss Allen professes extreme dislike for her brother's choice. When Mr. Winkle learns that Arabella had refused Mr. Sawyer because another man had won her heart, he feels that he must be the fortunate man, because she had displayed an interest in him when they had met earlier at Manor Farm. Mr. Pickwick kindly arranges to have Mr. Winkle meet Arabella in a garden, where the distraught lover can plead his suit.

Mr. Pickwick's plans to further his friend's romance are interrupted, however, by a subpoena delivered because he had refused to pay Mrs. Bardell. Mr. Pickwick is taken back to London and placed in the Fleet Street prison. With the help of Sam Weller, Mr. Pickwick arranges his prison quarters as comfortably as possible and remains deaf to the entreaties of Sam Weller and Mr. Perker, who think that he should pay his debt and regain his freedom. Dodgson and Fogg prove to be of lower caliber than even Mr. Pickwick had suspected. They had taken Mrs. Bardell's case without fee, gambling on Mr. Pickwick's payment to cover the costs of the case. When they saw no payment forthcoming, they had Mrs. Bardell arrested as well and sent to the Fleet Street prison.

While Mr. Pickwick is trying to decide what to do, Mr. Winkle and his new wife, Arabella, come to the prison and ask Mr. Pickwick to pay his debts so that he can visit Mr. Allen with the news of Mr. Winkle's marriage to Arabella. Arabella feels that Mr. Pickwick is the only person who can arrange a proper reconciliation between her brother and her new husband. Kindness prevails; Mr. Pickwick pays the damages to Mrs. Bardell so that he will be free to help his friends in distress.

Winning Mr. Allen's approval of the match is not difficult for Mr. Pickwick, but when he approaches the elder Mr. Winkle, the bridegroom's father objects to the marriage and threatens to cut off his son without a cent. To add to Mr. Pickwick's problems, Mr. Wardle comes to London to tell him that his daughter, Emily, is in love with Mr. Snodgrass and to ask Mr. Pickwick's advice. Mr. Wardle brought Emily to London with him.

The entire party comes together in Arabella's apartment. All misunderstandings end happily for the two lovers, and a jolly party follows. The elder Mr. Winkle pays a call on his new daughter-in-law. Upon seeing what a charming and lovely girl she is, he relents, and the family is reconciled.

After Mr. Snodgrass marries Emily Wardle, Mr. Pickwick dissolves the Pickwick Club and retires to a home in the country with his faithful servant, Sam Weller. Several times, Mr. Pickwick is called upon to be a godfather to little Winkles and Snodgrasses; for the most part, however, he leads a quiet life, respected by his neighbors and loved by all of his friends.

Critical Evaluation:

Mr. Pickwick, the lovable, generous old gentleman of one of Charles Dickens's most popular novels, is one of the best-known characters of fiction. Mr. Pickwick benignly reigns over all activities of the Pickwick Club; under every circumstance, he is satisfied that he has helped his fellow creatures by his well-meaning efforts. The height of this Dickensian comedy is reached, however, with the creation of servant Sam Weller and his father. Sam's imperturbable presence of mind and his ready wit are indispensable to the Pickwickians. *Pickwick Papers* has importance beyond its humorous incidents and characterization. It is the first novel of a literary movement to present the life and manners of lower- and middle-class life.

At the time a publisher in 1836 proposed that Dickens write the text for a series of pictures by the sporting artist Robert Seymour, Dickens was experiencing the first thrill of fame as the author of *Sketches by Boz* (1836). He was twenty-four years old and had been for some years a court reporter and freelance journalist; *Sketches by Boz* was his first literary effort of any length. The work the publisher proposed was of a similar kind: short, primarily humorous descriptions of cosmopolitan life, sometimes illustrated, and to be published monthly. Although Dickens already had the plan of a novel in mind, he was in need of cash and accepted the offer as a stop-gap. He made one stipulation: that he, and not Seymour, have the choice of scenes to be treated. He did this because he himself was no sportsman and had little knowledge of country life beyond what his journalistic travels had shown him. It is evident from the digressive character of the first few chapters that he viewed the enterprise as an expedient.

For *Pickwick Papers*, Dickens was able to disguise his ignorance of country life by a canny selection of scenes and topics. Actual sporting scenes are kept to a minimum and treated with broad humor and slight detail. On the other hand, he knew country elections, magistrates, and newspapers well, and the chapters describing the Eatanswill election and those dealing with Mr. Nupkins, the mayor of Ipswich, and Mr. Pott, the editor of the Eatanswill *Gazette*, abound in

atmosphere and choice observation. Most useful of all was his intimate knowledge of stagecoach travel, of life on the road, and of the inhabitants and manners of inns great and small. The device of a journey by coach unifies the first part of the novel, and a large portion of the action, including several key scenes, takes place in inns and public houses: Mr. Pickwick meets Sam Weller at the White Hart Inn, Mrs. Bardell is apprehended at the Spaniards, Sam is reunited with his father at the Marquis of Granby, and the Wellers plot Stiggins's discomfiture at the Blue Boar.

A theme that Dickens developed in later works appears in embryo here: the quicksand quality of litigation. Readers note that every figure connected with the law is portrayed as venal if not downright criminal, except Mr. Perker, who is merely a remarkably cold fish. Another feature of later works is the awkward treatment of women. The author's attitude toward women is extremely ambiguous. Two of the women in the novel are unqualifiedly good. Sam's Mary is described perennially as "the pretty housemaid," and the fact that Sam loves her appears to complete the list of her virtues in Dickens's view. As a character, she has neither depth nor ethical range; no more has Arabella Allen, the dark-eyed girl with the "very nice little pair of boots." She is distinguished at first by flirtatious archness and later by a rather servile docility. The daughters of old Wardle first come to the reader's attention in the act of spiting their unmarried aunt and never redeem this impression. Other female characters are rather poorly developed. None has, as do some of the male figures such as Jingle and Trotter, a human dimension.

The author's sentiments about the institution of marriage are also curious. Mr. Winkle makes a runaway match, Mr. Snodgrass is forestalled from doing so only by a lack of parental opposition, and Mr. Tupman escapes after a ludicrously close call. Mr. Pickwick, the great advocate of heart over head, however, is not and never has been married, and in fact, he shows his greatest strength as a character in his struggle for justice in a breach-of-promise suit; Mr. Weller, the other beneficent father figure of the work, makes no bones about his aversion to the connubial state: "'vether it's worth while goin' through so much, to learn so little . . . is a matter o' taste. I rayther think it isn't'."

Angus Wilson, among others, contends that *Pickwick Papers*, like most first novels, is autobiographical. There is evidence for this position in the fact that Dickens's estimation of the women in his life also tended to extremes of adulation and contempt. More pertinent to the main thrust of the novel, which is the development of Mr. Pickwick from buffoon to "angel in tights," and the concurrent development of Sam, is the author's relationship to his father, whom he adored. The elder Dickens's imprisonment for debt in 1824 was the great trauma of the author's childhood; it was made the more galling because the author, the eldest son, was put to work at a blacking factory and able to join the family circle in the prison only on Sundays. Scarcely more than a child, he felt unable either to aid or to comfort his father in his distress; at the same time, he felt that his father had abandoned him to a harsh world.

As a young man, Dickens wrote into his first novel an account of those times as he would have wished them to be. Mr. Pickwick is the epitome of those qualities of Dickens senior that so endeared him to his son, which included unsinkable good spirits and kindness that did not count the cost. To these, Pickwick adds financial sense, ethical sense, and a sensitivity to the best feelings of his spiritual son, Sam Weller. Sam, in turn, bends all of his cockney keenness of eye and wit, courage, and steadfastness, to the service not only of this ideal father unjustly imprisoned but also of his immensely endearing shadow-father Tony Weller. Clearly, this material has its roots in Dickens's life, but it is just as clear that his genius tapped a universal longing of sons to see their fathers as heroes and themselves as heroic helpers.

"Critical Evaluation" by Jan Kennedy Foster

Further Reading

Dexter, Walter. *Pickwick's Pilgrimages*. New York: Haskell House, 1992. A study of the actual places Mr. Pickwick visits in Dickens's novel. The conditions Pickwick and his companions would have encountered illuminate the story. Includes particularly good descriptions of Rochester, Ipswich, Bath, Bristol, and Tewkesbury.

Dexter, Walter, and J. W. T. Ley. *The Origin of Pickwick*. Folcroft, Pa.: Folcroft Library Editions, 1974. A study of some of Dickens's sketches that were used in *Pickwick Papers*. Examines the publishing history of the early numbers of *Pickwick Papers* and Dickens's early illustrations.

Fitzgerald, Percy. *Bozland: Dickens' Places and People*. Ann Arbor, Mich.: Gryphon Books, 1971. A consideration of people and places in Dickens, with emphasis on Pick-

wickian inns and actual towns and locales depicted in *Pickwick Papers*. Examines Mr. Pickwick's relationship to lawyers in the light of actual legal practice during Dickens's time.

Hardy, Barbara. *Dickens and Creativity*. London: Continuum, 2008. Focuses on the workings of Dickens's creativity and imagination, which Hardy argues is at the heart of his self-awareness, subject matter, and narrative. *Pickwick Papers* is discussed in chapter 3, "The Awareness of Art in *Sketches by Boz, Pickwick Papers, Oliver Twist, Barnaby Rudge, The Old Curiosity Shop, A Christmas Carol*, and *The Chimes*," and in chapter 5.

Jordan, John O., ed. *The Cambridge Companion to Charles Dickens*. New York: Cambridge University Press, 2001. Collection of essays examines Dickens's life and times, analyzes his novels, and discusses Dickens and language, gender, family, domestic ideology, the form of the novel, illustration, theater, and film.

Lockwood, Frank. *The Law and Lawyers of Pickwick*. New York: Haskell House, 1972. A late Victorian study of the legal mores depicted in *Pickwick Papers*. Mr. Pickwick's trial took place in 1827, a time before the legal reforms of 1843, which the author examines in relationship to the novel.

Noyes, Alfred, et al. *A Pickwick Portrait Gallery*. Port Washington, N.Y.: Kennikat Press, 1970. A series of insightful character analyses of various members of the Pickwick Club by outstanding writers and critics of the first half of the twentieth century. Particularly good for Samuel Pickwick, Sam Weller, and Mrs. Bardell.

Parker, David. *The Doughty Street Novels: "Pickwick Papers," "Oliver Twist," "Nicholas Nickleby," "Barnaby Rudge."* New York: AMS Press, 2002. Parker, a longtime curator of the Dickens House, traces Dickens's work on four early novels during the period when the writer lived on Doughty Street in London.

Paroissien, David, ed. *A Companion to Charles Dickens*. Malden, Mass.: Blackwell, 2008. Collection of essays discussing Dickens as a reformer, Christian, and journalist. Also examines Dickens and the topics gender, technology, the United States, and the uses of history. Includes the essay "The *Pickwick Papers*" by David Parker.

Picture Bride

Author: Cathy Song (1955-   )
First published: 1983
Type of work: Poetry

Cathy Song, born in Hawaii to Asian American parents, published *Picture Bride*, her first book of poetry, in 1983. The collection, which won for the author the 1982 Yale Younger Poets Prize, encompasses many of Song's most noted works. Themes of womanhood, motherhood, childhood, and family relationships appear throughout *Picture Bride*, artfully woven in poems that invoke quietude and fluidity. Song's voice flows through her poems, carrying the reader from one image to another. Skillfully designed themes and literary devices craft her work's settings, backdrops, and scenes.

Song approaches her subjects with a certain delicacy, a certain lightness: "Rinsing through his eyes/ and dissolving all around him/ is sunlight on water" ("Untouched Photograph of Passenger"). She appeals to the senses: "I turn bolts of cloth into wedding dresses/ like chiffon cakes in the summer" ("The Seamstress"). She often enchants and delights the reader with color: "The same blue tint/ of the hydrangea in glass,/ here on the table,/ now as I write" ("Hotel Geneve"). Weaving color, delicacy, and lightness together, she produces memorable images: "The light at each window/ becoming dimmer like a pulse/ beneath the thickening/ walls of ice, blue and iridescent" ("January"). Interlacing images, the poet creates poignant scenes.

In "The Youngest Daughter," a young girl acts as caretaker for her aging mother. The caretaking is reciprocal in that the mother lovingly massages her daughter's face, spotlighting Song's clever use of metonymy (the use of the name of one thing for that of another thing): "My skin, aspirin colored,/ tingles with migraine. Mother/ has been massaging the left side of my face." Rather than flatly stating the she feels pain, the narrator offers a closely associated word: "migraine." The descriptive word "migraine" instantly connects the reader to a particular type of pain. This produces a description charged with the power to evoke specific emotions in the reader.

By arranging the collection into five sections, each named for a flower, Song is sharing with her reader her appreciation of art. These flowers represent paintings by Georgia O'Keeffe and constitute one aspect of the visual imagery, alluring use of color, and sensual appeal that pervade Song's work.

Evidence of Song's identification with O'Keeffe is heavily illustrated in two poems: "From the White Place," which employs sensual imagery, and "Blue and White Lines After O'Keeffe," which is delivered from the painter's perspective. Lines from each of these poems indicate Song's understanding of the artist's fascination with the barrenness of the deserts of the American Southwest: "I climb the stairs/ in this skull hotel./ Voices beat at the walls,/ railings/ fan out like fish bones ("Blue and White Lines After O'Keeffe"). Also, "When she came out west,/ her frail fields/ collapsed into tumbleweed ("From the White Place").

Song also favors the work of Japanese printmaker Kitagawa Utamaro, finding in his work the elements of femininity, beauty, and sadness. She often portrays these elements in her own writing and dedicates to him her poem "Beauty and Sadness," which describes the women whose likenesses he captures: "Crouching like cats,/ they purred amid the layers of kimono/ swirling around them/ as though they were bathing/ in a mountain pool with irises/ growing in the silken sunlit water."

"Beauty and Sadness" also illustrates Song's frequent use of the scenes and elements of nature. Additionally, in "Leaving," she utilizes organic imagery and provides another example of metonymy: "We feasted/ on those pictures of the world,/ while the mud oozed/ past the windows/ knocking over the drab green leaves/ of palm fronds/ as we ate our spinach." The poem describes children's activities when confined indoors due to inclement weather. The reader is not intended to believe that the children always ate spinach on rainy days, but spinach stands in for the idea of food and mealtime. Synchronization of the images of "drab green leaves," "palm fronds," and "spinach" evoke a "green-ness" that is juxtaposed against the rain and mud.

Song expands the reader's experience with her use of metonymy to convey the entire subject matter of her title poem, "Picture Bride." She depicts the tale of her grandmother, who had traveled from Korea to the United States to marry a man who had seen her only in a photograph. In the poem, the man accepts the photograph as a substitute for the real woman. Everything that defines her—physical appearance, personality, mannerisms, personal history—is placed on hold until they meet. In the meantime, the photograph stands in for the woman.

[A] man waited,
turning her photograph
to the light when the lanterns
in the camp outside
Waialua Sugar Mill were lit
and the inside of his room
grew luminous
from the wings of moths
migrating out of the cane stalks?

In "The White Porch," Song uses a closely associated device known as a synecdoche (the use of a part for the whole or the whole for a part), in which the narrator secretly invites a lover into her bedroom using sheets tied into a rope to give him discreet access through an upper-floor window: "cloth, hair and hands/ smuggling you in." Synecdochically, the cloth represents the braided sheets, and the hair and the hands represent the narrator.

The narrator in "The White Porch" reflects upon the earlier days of her youth. Youth, a common theme found among the poems in *Picture Bride*, is sometimes juxtaposed against images of aging. "The Violin Teacher" speaks of a young music student tutored by an aged teacher.

Upon arriving, he would nod to her
from the corner where he stood
preparing a medicinal drink,
the color and texture of ox blood.
The room reeked of eucalyptus and menthol,
like a forest she would often think.
He sometimes rubbed his hands in ointment.

The personas in many of the poems recall memories of childhood and speak of grandparents, relatives, former homes, and ties to the old world of China: "You find you need China:/ your one fragile identification" ("Lost Sister"). Other personas speak of longing and escapism, including the narrator in "The Youngest Daughter," who longs for her personal independence, and the narrator in "Lost Sister," who has escaped to a new home across an ocean. Similarly, a young man has his picture taken upon his "passage out/ of the deteriorating village" ("Untouched Photograph of Passenger").

Central to all the poems in the book is Song herself. She infuses herself into each piece, making her presence known in subtle but sure fashion. Paradoxically, she often appears distanced through the instrument of time. She writes with honesty without the need for uncharacteristic boldness or starkness, and she writes about important pieces of her own being, illustrating memories, experiences, ancestry, femininity, and so forth.

As Song sketches a narrator with hands and hair, so does she portray herself with the parts that stand for her whole being. A reading of *Picture Bride* brings about familiarity with the poet's world. Through stirring imagery and figurative renderings, the reader becomes versed in Song.

Glenda Griffin

Further Reading

Chen, Fu-jen. "Body and Female Subjectivity in Cathy Song's *Picture Bride*." *Women's Studies* 33, no. 5 (July, 2004): 577-612. Asserts that the image of the body is dominant in Song's poetry and that all her work radiates from that centrality.

Haley, Elsie Galbreath. "Cathy Song." In *Critical Survey of Poetry*, edited by Philip K. Jason. 2d rev. ed. Vol. 6. Pasadena, Calif.: Salem Press, 2003. An encyclopedic essay that provides biographical information about Song and analyses of her poetry. Part of a multivolume set that surveys poetry from around the world. A good place to start for students who are new to Song's work.

Kyhan, Lee. "Korean-American Literature: The Next Generation." *Korean Journal* 34, no. 1 (Spring, 1994): 20-35. Kyhan reviews the history of Korean American literature and devotes the third section to Song. Shows how Song focuses on identity and the self in relation to her ethnic identity, her interest in the stories of her parents and grandparents, and her status as a woman examining the identity of ethnic women.

McFarland, Ron, Laura Mitchell, and C. L. Chua. "Cathy Song." In *American Ethnic Writers*. Rev. ed. Vol. 3. Pasadena, Calif.: Salem Press, 2009. An encyclopedic entry covering Song's biography and criticism and analyses of her works. Part of a multivolume set that explores American ethnic writers.

Wallace, Patricia. "Divided Loyalties: Literal and Literary in the Poetry of Lorna Dee Cervantes, Cathy Song, and Rita Dove." *MELUS* 18, no. 3 (Fall, 1993): 3-19. Wallace strives to distinguish between the "literal" and "literary" in the work of three poets, including Song. Considers Song as a poet who can "transform what seems simple or ordinary—including words themselves—by lifting things out of their ordinary settings."

The Picture of Dorian Gray

Author: Oscar Wilde (1854-1900)
First published: 1890, serial; 1891, book
Type of work: Novel
Type of plot: Fantasy
Time of plot: Late nineteenth century
Locale: England

Principal characters:
DORIAN GRAY, a young man
LORD HENRY WOTTON, his tempter
BASIL HALLWARD, an artist
SIBYL VANE, an actor
JAMES VANE, her brother
LADY AGATHA, Lord Henry's philanthropic aunt
HETTY MERTON, a country girl who loves Dorian

The Story:

One day in his London studio, painter Basil Hallward is putting a few finishing touches on a portrait of his handsome young friend, Dorian Gray. Lord Henry Wotton, a caller, indolently watches the painter at work. When his friend admires the subject of the painting, the artist explains that Dorian is his ideal of youth and that he hopes Lord Henry will never meet him because the older man's influence will be absolute and evil.

While Hallward and Lord Henry are talking, Dorian arrives at the studio and Hallward, much against his will, is forced to introduce the young man to Lord Henry. Hallward signs the portrait and announces that it is finished. When Lord Henry offers to buy the picture, the painter says it is not his property and that it belongs to Dorian, to whom he is presenting it. After listening to Lord Henry's witty conversation, Dorian looks at his portrait and grows sad. He will become old and wrinkled, he says, while the picture will remain the same. Instead, he wishes that the portrait may grow old while he remains forever young. He says he would give his soul to keep his youth. There is, however, no overt Faustian bargain struck with Satan. Rather, Dorian's powerful narcissism is sufficient to magically draw the portrait's perpetual youth and beauty into himself.

Dorian and Lord Henry become close friends. One of the gifts Lord Henry gives the young man is a book about another young man who attempts to realize in his brief lifetime all the passions of human history. Dorian makes the book a pattern for his own life. In a third-rate theater, he sees a young actor named Sibyl Vane playing the role of Juliet with such sincerity and charm that he falls in love with her on the spot. After he has met her in person, Dorian dreams of taking her away from the cheap theatrical troupe and making her a great actor who will thrill the world.

One night, Dorian takes Lord Henry to watch Sybil's performance. Tonight, however, she is listless and wooden; she is so uninspired in her acting that the audience hisses at her.

Dorian goes to her dressing room after the final curtain. Sibyl explains to him that before meeting him she thought acting her only reality. Now, she says, Dorian's love has taught her what reality actually is, and she can no longer act. Dorian coldly tells her she has killed his love and that he never intends to see her again.

Later, when Dorian returns to his home, he notices something in his portrait that he has never before seen, a faint line of cruelty about the mouth. Looking at his own features in a mirror, he finds no such line on his own lips. Dorian is disturbed, and he resolves to reform, to see no more of Lord Henry, and to ask Sibyl to forgive him and then marry her. This very night, he writes her a passionate letter, but before he can post the letter, Lord Henry visits in the morning and brings the news that Sibyl had killed herself in her dressing room last night.

After his friend leaves, Dorian decides there is no point to his good resolutions. The portrait will have to bear the burden of his shame. In the evening, he attends the opera with Lord Henry. The following day, when Hallward attempts to reason with him over scandalous reports that are beginning to circulate about his behavior, Dorian expresses no emotion over Sibyl's suicide. His part in her tragic story will never be revealed, for she knew him only as a Prince Charming. When Hallward asks to see his painting of Dorian, the young man refuses, and in a sudden rage shouts that he never wishes to see the painter again. Later, he hangs the portrait in an old schoolroom upstairs, locks the door, and hides the key where only he can find it.

Rumors about Dorian continue, and the young man becomes suspected of strange vices. Gentlemen walk out of their club rooms when he enters, hosts of balls and parties at country houses invite him less and less, and many of his former friends refuse to acknowledge him when they meet. It is reported that he has been seen in low dives with drunken sailors and thieves. Dorian's looks do not change, however; only the portrait reflects his life of crime and debauchery. Like the hero of the book that Lord Henry gave him, Dorian spends his life pursuing fresh experiences and new sensations. One interest succeeds the next, and he immerses himself in turn in the study of religious rituals, perfumes, music, and jewels. He frequents opium dens and has sordid affairs with women.

On the eve of Dorian's thirty-eighth birthday, Hallward visits him again. Although the two have been estranged for years, Hallward comes in a last attempt to persuade Dorian to change his dissolute ways. He is still unable to believe many of the stories he has heard about Dorian. With a bitter laugh, Dorian says that Hallward should see what he has truly become. He takes Hallward to the schoolroom and unveils the portrait. The artist is horrified, for only by the signature can he identify his own handiwork. Dorian, in anger that he has betrayed his true self to his former friend, seizes a knife that lies nearby and stabs Hallward in the neck and back, killing him.

Dorian locks the door behind him and goes down to the drawing room. Because Hallward had intended to leave for Paris tonight, Dorian knows the painter will not be missed for some time. He decides that removing the body is not enough. He wants it completely destroyed. Suddenly, he thinks of Alan Campbell, a young chemist who once was his close friend. By threatening the young scientist with exposure of a crime only he knows about, Dorian forces Campbell to destroy Hallward's body with fire and chemicals. From this night forward, the hands of the portrait show smears of blood.

Late one night, commonly dressed, Dorian leaves an opium den. A drunken woman addresses him as Prince Charming. A sailor who overhears her follows Dorian out. The sailor is James Vane, Sibyl's brother, who has sworn revenge on the man who betrayed his sister, the man he knows only by the cognomen—Prince Charming—that Sybil gave him. He would have killed Dorian then and there had Dorian not looked so unspoiled and young. Sibyl had committed suicide eighteen years ago, yet the man before James seems no more than twenty years old. When Vane returns to the opium den, the woman tells him that Dorian had ruined her many years ago as well, and that he has not changed in appearance since then.

Some time later, at his country home, Dorian sees James watching him outside a window. Subsequently, during a hunt on the estate, James is shot and killed. His death is believed to be an accident, but Dorian feels his own evil presence is the true cause of the incident. Campbell had committed suicide as well some time earlier under strange circumstances, and Hallward's disappearance is being investigated. Dorian decides to reform. His first virtuous act is to spare rather than corrupt Hetty Merton, a local girl who is infatuated with him.

Back in London, Dorian goes to the old schoolroom. He examines his painting, hoping that his one good act has mitigated to some degree the horror of the portrait. It has not. He decides to destroy the picture that stands as the awful record of his guilt. Now, the portrait also has an appearance of cunning and triumph. Using the knife with which he had murdered Hallward, Dorian stabs the frightful portrait. The servants in the house hear a horrible cry of agony. When they force open the locked door of the room, they find, hanging on the wall, a fine portrait of their young master. On the floor is a dead body, withered and wrinkled and with a knife in its breast. Only by the rings on his hands do they recognize Dorian, who had killed himself in a desperate attempt to kill his conscience.

Critical Evaluation:

The critical writings of Oscar Wilde and the writings of his contemporaries Joris-Karl Huysmans (1848-1907) and Walter Pater (1839-1894) all emphasize the relationship of art to sensuality and suggest that life imitates art—not that art imitates life. These influences are evident in Wilde's *The Picture of Dorian Gray*, his only novel. The initial appearance of the work in serial form in the July, 1890, issue of *Lippincott's Monthly Magazine* had elicited savage attacks by critics in the *St. James's Gazette*, the *Daily Chronicle*, and the *Scots Observer*, who branded the story as immoral and an incitement to vice. Pater, however, and critic Julian H. Hawthorne (1846-1934), had written favorable reviews.

Over the years, *The Picture of Dorian Gray* has been viewed as gothic entertainment, a cautionary tale, and even a philosophical treatise using the medium of fiction. The novel may be any or all of these things, but its unity derives from the motif of the mirror image, the opposite, the contrast— Dorian Gray and his portrait furnish the first and most obvious example of this motif. Other examples are Basil Hallward and Lord Henry Wotton, both of whom are vying for influence over Dorian. Hallward is virtuous, sincere, and idealistic. Lord Henry is clever, insouciant, and amoral (at least in his witty conversation). He plays the role of the tempter.

In chapter 2, Hallward is shocked by Dorian's reaction to the portrait. He picks up a palette-knife with the intention of destroying the painting, but Dorian prevents him, saying it would be an act of murder. In chapter 13, after Hallward has seen the loathsome picture, Dorian seizes a knife previously used to cut a piece of cord and murders his friend with it. In chapter 20, Dorian takes up that same knife and, in his attempt to destroy his portrait, kills himself.

Early in the novel, Lord Henry's aunt, Lady Agatha, wishes Dorian to play the piano for the residents of Whitechapel, as part of her effort to raise the cultural level of the poor. Instead, Dorian is prowling the East End with quite different experiences in mind. He casts Sybil Vane aside, ruining her life and prompting her suicide. The wretched woman in the opium den who identifies Dorian as Prince Charming tells James Vane that almost eighteen years earlier Dorian had made her what she has become. Near the end of the novel, Dorian tells Lord Henry that he has spared Hetty Merton. The contrast is made specific when Dorian says Hetty reminds him of Sybil. Dorian's renunciation, however, is not morally superior to his rejection of Sybil, because both women are the products of his vanity.

The most interesting relationship in the novel is that of Dorian and Lord Henry. The latter has often been identified with the author—understandably so, since Wilde, like his fictional character, filled every conversation with brilliant epigrams and delighted in shocking Victorian sensibilities. This identification has tempted some, therefore, to identify Dorian with Lord Alfred Douglas, the young man whose friendship with Wilde would eventually bring about the writer's ruin. However, the men did not become acquainted until 1891, so Douglas could scarcely have been Wilde's model in the initial publication one year earlier. In 1895, Lord Douglas's father, the marquess of Queensberry, publicly called Wilde a sodomite, a charge that led to three trials and culminated in Wilde's conviction for homosexuality and his sentence of two years in prison. The first trial, occasioned by Wilde's unwise suit against Queensberry for libel, is of literary interest because of the way *The Picture of Dorian Gray* importantly and ironically figures in the testimony.

Queensberry's defense attorney, Edward Carson, used *The Picture of Dorian Gray* extensively in his cross-examination of Wilde. He forced Wilde to admit that the book Dorian receives in one passage is Huysmans's novel *À rebours* (1884; *Against the Grain*, 1922), considered by many at the time to be scandalous. Interestingly, the name of the Mephistophelean character who gives Dorian the book, Lord Henry, had not been raised in the questioning. Instead, Carson had read aloud three long passages from the text, all spoken by Hallward. The first describes Dorian to Lord Henry before the young man makes his first appearance in the story. The other two are long speeches: In the first, Hallward tells Dorian that he worships him with romance of feeling and, in the second, Hallward warns that people are speaking of Dorian's behavior as vile and degraded.

Carson's approach was probably a wise one. After all, he was a barrister, not a literary critic, and his task was to prove his client justified in labeling the "despoiler" of his son a sodomite. He chose passages that would most readily strike the court as lurid and reflective of the story's homosexual subtext. Wilde also blurred his direct association with any of the characters in an 1894 letter to Ralph Payne. He writes that Hallward is who Wilde himself thinks he is, Lord Henry is who the world thinks Wilde is, and Dorian is who Wilde himself would like to be—in other ages perhaps.

A number of critics writing since the end of the Victorian era have denied, despite the protagonist's ultimate destruction, that *The Picture of Dorian Gray* is a moral tale. They assert that it is among the earliest postmodern novels. If the universe is mindless, if there is no moral code sanctioned by a deity, if morality is no more than a series of decisions society has made over time, then Dorian is contemporary. He is neither all good nor all bad, but divided—alienated and plagued by verities in which he no longer believes, but from which he cannot free himself.

Wilde could have chosen "The Portrait of Dorian Gray" as his title, but the choice of the word "picture" instead of "portrait" indicates a look into Dorian's character well beyond what his portrait, no matter how skillfully rendered, could reveal. On the other hand, Wilde had been received into the Roman Catholic Church shortly before his death in 1900. It is reasonable to assume that on that occasion, at least, Wilde had accepted the concept of sin.

Wilde's novel is aptly suited for dramatization. Since 1945, it has been adapted several times into film, opera, and stage, musical, and teleplays.

"Critical Evaluation" by Patrick Adcock

Further Reading

Beckson, Karl E. *The Oscar Wilde Encyclopedia.* New York: AMS Press, 1998. A comprehensive compendium of useful information on Wilde and his times. One of the entries is a lengthy and thorough analysis of *The Picture of Dorian Gray*.

Gillespie, Michael Patrick. *"The Picture of Dorian Gray": "What the World Thinks Me."* New York: Twayne, 1995. A study of the novel, which Gillespie maintains is a fictional model of the moral contradictions in late Victorian society. Includes information about the historical and literary contexts in which the novel was written and about the book's critical reception.

Joyce, Simon. "Sexual Politics and the Aesthetics of Crime: Oscar Wilde in the Nineties." *ELH* 69, no. 2 (Summer, 2002): 501-523. Discusses the Victorian fascination with the gentleman (or aristocrat) criminal, especially if his crimes are deviant. Dorian Gray is a titillating example.

Kileen, Jarlath. *The Faiths of Oscar Wilde: Catholicism, Folklore, and Ireland*. New York: Palgrave Macmillan, 2005. Examination of Wilde's work, focusing on his lifelong attraction to Catholicism. Explores the influence of his Protestant background, and his antagonism toward it, on his work. The chapter entitled "Body and Soul: Nature, the Host, and Folklore in *The Picture of Dorian Gray*," provides an analysis of this novel.

McCormack, Jerusha Hull. *The Man Who Was Dorian Gray*. New York: St. Martin's Press, 2000. John Gray, the supposed model for Wilde's most famous character, is profiled in this examination of the life of a decadent poet turned priest. This work reveals much about early twentieth century literary society and an emerging gay culture.

McKenna, Neil. *The Secret Life of Oscar Wilde*. London: Century, 2003. A controversial and groundbreaking biography focusing on the influence of Wilde's sexuality, and of homosexuality in the Victorian era, on his life and work. Includes illustrations, a bibliography, and an index.

Nunokawa, Jeff. *Oscar Wilde*. New York: Chelsea House, 1995. Includes an extensive discussion of *The Picture of Dorian Gray* as a love story, emphasizing the relationships between Gray and the two other major male characters in the book, Lord Henry Wotton and Basil Hallward.

O'Connor, Maureen. "*The Picture of Dorian Gray* as Irish National Tale." In *Irishness in Nineteenth-Century British Culture*, edited by Neil McCraw. Burlington, Vt.: Ashgate, 2004. Examines the role of the expatriate Irish writer in England and the gothic Irish tale, which the English associate with their exotic neighbors.

Sammells, Neil. "Theory into Practice: *Dorian Gray* and *Salome*." In *Wilde Style: The Plays and Prose of Oscar Wilde*. New York: Longman, 2000. Argues that the primary aesthetic of Wilde's work is not art but style. Analyzes the element of style in *The Picture of Dorian Gray*.

Sedgwick, Eve Kosofky. *Epistemology of the Closet*. Updated ed. Berkeley: University of California Press, 2008. A classic study of homosexuality in literature. In her treatment of *The Picture of Dorian Gray*, Sedgwick emphasizes sentimental love rather than sex. Includes a discussion of the narcissistic qualities of the title character. For advanced readers.

Wilde, Oscar. *The Picture of Dorian Gray: Authoritative Texts, Backgrounds, Reviews and Reactions, Criticism*. Edited by Michael Patrick Gillespie. New York: W. W. Norton, 2007. Contains the 1890 serial and 1891 book, as well as essays providing historical and social context, contemporary reviews, and later essays providing various interpretations of the work.

Pierre
Or, The Ambiguities

Author: Herman Melville (1819-1891)
First published: 1852
Type of work: Novel
Type of plot: Philosophical
Time of plot: Early nineteenth century
Locale: New York

Principal characters:
PIERRE GLENDINNING, a wealthy, cultivated young man
MRS. GLENDINNING, his mother
LUCY TARTAN, his fiancé
ISABEL, his illegitimate half sister and later wife
GLEN STANLY, his cousin
DELLY ULVER, a farm woman

The Story:

Pierre Glendinning is a young man who lives amid luxury and ease, the heir to vast estates that form the larger portion of two counties in New York State. His time is taken up with outdoor recreation, reading, and the courting of beautiful and well-to-do Lucy Tartan, a woman of whom Pierre's mother approves completely. Mrs. Glendinning, who is jealous of

her influence over her son, sees nothing to fear in quiet, nonaggressive Lucy Tartan.

One evening, however, a strange incident occurs when Mrs. Glendinning and Pierre visit a sewing bee in a nearby home. One of the women there shrieks and faints when she sees Pierre. The incident bothers the young man, but he is totally unprepared for a note he receives from the young woman a short time later. In the note, she requests that Pierre visit her in the evening at the farm where she is employed. Pierre, disturbed by the mystery involved, goes to the farm and discovers that the woman, Isabel, is his half sister, the illegitimate child of his father and a Frenchwoman. Pierre resolves immediately to acknowledge Isabel as his sister, but the question of how to accomplish the acknowledgment is a weighty one.

At first, Pierre intends to tell his mother of his discovery, but his mother's attitude toward Delly Ulver, a farm woman who had been born an illegitimate child, warns Pierre that he can expect no sympathetic understanding from Mrs. Glendinning. He next thinks of approaching his minister for help with his problem, but the minister follows his mother's opinion, which causes Pierre to fall back on his own thinking. He also realizes that his mother cannot bear to have her husband proven to be an adulterer, nor can he bring himself to dishonor his father's name. The only road that seems open to Pierre is to acknowledge Isabel by making her his wife rather than his sister.

When Pierre tells his mother that he has been married secretly, she orders him to leave the house immediately. Disowned and cast forth from his mother's affections, he also tells Lucy Tartan that he has married another woman. His story throws Lucy into an almost fatal illness.

Having been disowned by his family, Pierre takes Isabel from her home at the farm and goes to New York City. They are accompanied by Delly Ulver, whom Pierre has decided to help. Although he announced that he and Isabel had been married, Pierre and his half sister entered into no such union; the announcement is only a means to permit them to live together. In New York City, they find life barren and difficult, for Pierre has only a small supply of money. He had hoped to find a haven for himself and the two women with his wealthy cousin, Glen Stanly, but the cousin refuses to recognize Pierre and throws him out of his home.

Forced to rely upon his own resources, Pierre resolves to become an author. He has, he believes, acquired quite a reputation by publishing some short poems and some essays in various periodicals. He also thinks he has great talent, sufficient, at least, to enable him to write a philosophical work. After much difficulty, he manages to find a publisher who agrees to take his unwritten novel and to advance him enough money to live. For months Pierre, struggling to write his great work, lives in three miserable, unheated rooms in a vast tenement, along with Isabel and Delly Ulver, who acts in the capacity of servant to them both.

One day, word comes to Pierre that his mother had died just a few weeks after he had left for New York City; her heir is Pierre's cousin, Glen Stanly. The news makes Pierre very bitter, particularly when he discovers that his cousin is a suitor for the hand of Lucy Tartan, whom Pierre still loves dearly. Despite the feeling of utter helplessness that the news creates in his mind, Pierre keeps working on his book. Pierre is unable to keep Isabel from realizing that she is not alone in his affections, and the woman becomes jealous and dislikes the fact that another woman could claim his attentions and love. Her attachment for Pierre goes much deeper than ordinary love for a brother by a sister.

Sometime later, Pierre receives a letter from Lucy. She had rebuffed Glen Stanly's suit, and she writes to tell Pierre that he alone has her affections. She tells Pierre that, even though he is married, she wishes to travel to New York City to live near him. Pierre cannot prevent her from joining his household, although he lies to Isabel and tells her that Lucy is his cousin. Lucy arrives the next day. As she enters the tenement where Pierre lives, her brother and Glen Stanly try to take her away by force. Pierre interferes on her behalf, and the two men have to leave without her.

Lucy, listening only to the prompting of her heart, refuses to leave Pierre, even though she is told by Pierre that Isabel is his wife. Having brought along her painting materials, she intends to support herself as a painter of portraits. Isabel dislikes the idea of a third woman in the home, but she is powerless to turn Lucy out. The two women live in a state of distrustful and watchful truce.

Glen Stanly and Lucy's brother, not wishing to see Lucy remain near Pierre, send him a letter of premeditated insults in hopes of provoking him. Angered by their message, Pierre finds two pistols in the apartment of a friend and sets out to find Stanly and Lucy's brother. He encounters them on a crowded street. When they meet, Stanly lashes at Pierre with a whip, whereupon Pierre draws his pistols and kills his cousin. The police immediately seize Pierre and arrest him.

In prison, Pierre has no hope of life. Nor does he care to live, for he feels that fate has been too cruel to him. One evening, Isabel and Lucy are allowed to visit him for a few hours. When Isabel reveals that she is Pierre's sister, the shock of her announcement kills Lucy immediately. Pierre, driven mad by her death, seizes a vial of poison Isabel carried in her bosom. He drinks a portion of the poison, and Isabel empties the vial of the remainder.

A short time later, Lucy's brother is looking for her, still hoping to rescue her from Pierre's influence. When the turnkey opens the cell door, Pierre is already dead, lying close to Lucy. Isabel still has sufficient life to say that no one knew the real Pierre. She then dies as well, completing the tragedy of their ambiguous relationship.

Critical Evaluation:

Pierre is the most controversial of Herman Melville's novels. The work was condemned by contemporary reviewers, and readers since then have had difficulty in understanding the book and in determining Melville's intent. Critics still differ widely, with some regarding *Pierre* as a failure and others praising it as Melville's masterpiece.

Travel books about a world that was still being explored and discovered fascinated mid-nineteenth century readers, and Melville pleased this audience with his first two books about travels in the South Seas, *Typee* (1846) and *Omoo* (1847). The erudite and brilliant Melville could not restrain his intellect and imagination, however, and his third novel, *Mardi* (1849), was, in the guise of a travel book, really a philosophical satire. This effort confused readers and reviewers, and the book was a failure. Melville returned to relatively simple accounts of sea voyages in his next two books, *Redburn* (1849) and *White-Jacket* (1850), but in *Moby Dick* (1851), his interest in psychological and philosophical issues burst forth again.

Pierre was Melville's next work, and in it he initially appears to give his readers what they want. Melville's account of the idyllic life lived by Pierre Glendinning and his mother on their country estate is similar in tone and style to the sentimental romances that were then popular, particularly among female readers. Although the first third of the novel is filled with purple passages, and a reader might suspect a leg pull, Melville's style and story are no different from many nineteenth century novels that present such scenes without irony. Nevertheless, there are some unsettling touches, such as Pierre and his mother calling each other brother and sister. This rhetorical attempt to increase the closeness between mother and son is a foreshadowing of the darker forces that destroy the lives of both.

That Melville does intend the book as a satire becomes clear when Pierre meets his supposed sister, Isabel. It is never established without doubt that Isabel is, indeed, Pierre's sister—some critics have maintained that Pierre's interest in Isabel is primarily sexual and therefore incestuous, and that he accepts the "sister" hypothesis to be near her, but also because this arrangement prevents him from acting on a physical urge that frightens and confuses him. Readers of romances expected complications before the obligatory happy ending, but plot changes with such sordid overtones were not welcome.

The middle portion of the novel switches the satire to the gothic novel, another type of fiction popular in the nineteenth century. The mystery surrounding Isabel's parentage, the dark forest in which she lives, Pierre's internal struggle when faced with the evidence of his father's portrait, and his taunting stay under the balanced rock are elements and scenes that suggest the standard plot devices of the gothic novel with its delight in weird plot twists and touches of the supernatural. Before Melville shifts the direction of *Pierre* again, he has toyed with the excesses of this literary form.

Pierre's acceptance of Isabel as his sister, which he considers a noble gesture, has disastrous effects for him and everyone he knows. His fiancé, Lucy Tartan, who has also been like a sister because she and Pierre grew up together, is momentarily cast aside for a stranger. The idea that two people who have known each other since childhood and are as close as brother and sister are the best candidates for marriage is another plot device familiar in nineteenth century novels, and, like Pierre's relationship with Isabel, again raises the issue of incest. Instead of explaining to his mother what he takes to be the truth about Isabel's parentage, Pierre chooses to spare his father's reputation (which, if he is correct, he no longer has any reason to respect) by concocting the fiction that Isabel is his wife, a lie that eventually kills his mother, grievously wounds Lucy, and causes the loss of his inheritance. Here the satire of the first part of the novel bears fruit; Melville may be suggesting that people nurtured in sentimental fantasies are so ill-equipped to deal with reality that when they must do so, the result is yet another sentimental fantasy. Incestuous wishes, familiar in literature since the Greeks, are symbolic of human self-absorption.

The last part of the novel has still another orientation occasioned by the philosophical theories of Plotinus, which appear in a pamphlet Pierre finds. Plotinus asserts that there are two measures of time: the chronometrical, or celestial measure, which does not change with changing circumstances (like a clock set to Greenwich time); and the horological, which is a measure set to a specific locality. Plinlimmon argues that although chronometrical time may be more correct in an absolute sense, to attempt to live one's life according to it at all times (to go to bed at noon in China, for example, because it is nighttime by Greenwich time) is to invite difficulties that will make life impossible. Humans live in a horological world, flawed by all sorts of local customs, and to attempt to live chronometrically is to invite disaster. Pierre fails to understand the meaning of this warning, and in the last part of the novel he is trying and failing to write a chronometrical book. He becomes enraged when Glen Stanly receives what he takes to be his inheritance, and he shoots his cousin. Then, Pierre and Isabel commit suicide, in another attempt to live up to a code of honor only they understand.

In Pierre, Melville gives readers a main character with whom they at first identify, then whose motives and actions they suspect, and finally, from whom they recoil. Although Pierre tries to base his actions (such as his relationship with Isabel) on what he thinks are firm moral principles, his shooting of Stanly and his suicide demonstrate that he is, in fact, thrown by the winds of emotion. The entire novel is riddled with contradictions and puzzles, so it is well to remember its subtitle—*The Ambiguities*—which might well have been its only designation.

"Critical Evaluation" by Jim Baird

Further Reading

Bloom, Harold, ed. *Herman Melville*. New ed. New York: Bloom's Literary Criticism, 2008. Collection of critical essays analyzing Melville's works. Includes the essay "We Are Family: Melville's *Pierre*."

Delbanco, Andrew. *Melville: His World and Work*. New York: Knopf, 2005. Delbanco's critically acclaimed biography places Melville in his time, with discussion about the debate over slavery and details of life in 1840's New York. Delbanco also discusses the significance of Melville's works at the time they were published and their reception into the twenty-first century.

Dillingham, William B. *Melville's Later Novels*. Athens: University of Georgia Press, 1986. In two essays—"The Wonderful Work on Physiognomy: *Pierre*" and "Convenient Lies and Duty-Subterfuges: *Pierre; or the Deceptions*"—Dillingham discusses Melville's satirical treatment of Pierre as a victim of several strange nineteenth century theories, including physiognomy, or reading character through facial expression.

Dimock, Wai-Chee. "*Pierre*: Domestic Confidence Game and the Drama of Knowledge." *Studies in the Novel* 16, no. 4 (Winter, 1984): 396-409. Considers *Pierre* a battleground for Melville's investigations of theories of epistemology and psychology, with no clear conclusions being reached about either field in the novel.

Duban, James. "Subjective Transcendentalism: *Pierre*." In *Melville's Major Fiction: Politics, Theology, and Imagination*. DeKalb: Northern Illinois University Press, 1983. Regards *Pierre* as Melville's comment on the disastrous consequences of what the Transcendentalists proposed, using intuition as a guide to action. The notes contain an excellent review of criticism.

Higgins, Brian, and Hershel Parker. *Reading Melville's "Pierre: Or, The Ambiguities."* Baton Rouge: Louisiana State University Press, 2006. Chronicles the disappointing publishing history of *Pierre*. Publishers, concerned with the treatment of incest and other controversial subjects, offered to pay him only half of the normal royalties. Melville amended the manuscript, adding passages denouncing the publishing industry and reflecting his sense of despair about his literary career. Higgins and Parker try to reconstruct the original version of the novel to analyze the book and demonstrate how the additions marred the original.

_____, comps. *Critical Essays on Herman Melville's "Pierre: Or, The Ambiguities."* Boston: G. K. Hall, 1983. A collection of critical essays about the novel. Contains a dated, but still useful, bibliography of other works on *Pierre*.

Kelley, Wyn, ed. *A Companion to Herman Melville*. Malden, Mass.: Blackwell, 2006. Collection of thirty-five original essays aimed at twenty-first century readers of Melville's works. Includes discussions of his travels; Melville and religion, slavery, and gender; and the Melville revival. Includes the chapter "Artist at Work: *Redburn, White-Jacket, Moby-Dick*, and *Pierre*."

Spanos, William V. "Pierre's Extraordinary Emergency: Melville and the 'Voice of Silence.'" In *Herman Melville and the American Calling: Fiction After "Moby-Dick," 1851-1857*. Albany: State University of New York Press, 2008. Analyzes Melville's major works after *Moby Dick*. Argues that these works share the metaphor of the orphanage: a place that represents both estrangement from a symbolic fatherland and the myth of American exceptionalism.

Piers Plowman

Author: William Langland (c. 1332-c. 1400)

First published: c. 1362-c. 1393, as *The Vision of William, Concerning Piers the Plowman* (A Text, c. 1362; B Text, c. 1377; C Text, c. 1393)

Type of work: Poetry

Type of plot: Religious

Time of plot: Fourteenth century

Locale: England

Principal characters:

THE POET, also known as Will

PIERS THE PLOWMAN, an English plowman who becomes an allegorical figure of Christ incarnate

LADY MEDE, an allegorical figure representing both just reward and bribery

CONSCIENCE,

REASON,

THOUGHT,

WIT,

STUDY,

CLERGY,

SCRIPTURE,

FAITH,

HOPE, and

CHARITY, allegorical figures

The Poem:

The narrator, generally referred to as Will and presented as the author of the poem, wanders the world dressed as a hermit, until one May morning, near Malvern Hills, he falls asleep and dreams. In the vision, he sees a field full of folk of all social classes, including beggars, members of religious orders, knights, kings, and plowmen, going about the various activities of life, with a tower at one end and a dungeon located in a hollow beneath. At this point, a group of mice and rats assemble to determine what action to take against a cat at court who has been terrorizing them for some time. They agree that the best plan will be to put a bell around the cat's neck, but then they realize they do not have the courage to attempt it. One sensible mouse suggests that they are better off with the cat than with a different cat or on their own.

A woman named Holy Church explains to Will that the castle is the home of Truth, or God, and that the dungeon is the home of Wrong, or Satan. She advises Will that to save his soul he needs to follow Truth. The poet then witnesses the making of arrangements to marry Lady Mede (Reward) to False; dispute over the marriage is eventually brought to London to be adjudicated before the king. The king proposes instead that she marry Conscience, who refuses the marriage, precipitating a series of debates on the nature of meed, or reward. The vision ends hopefully, with the king resolving to rule with the help of Reason and Conscience.

In a second dream vision, the poet hears a sermon calling for the repentance of society delivered to the field of folk by Reason, followed by the public confessions of representatives of each of the seven deadly sins. Society decides to search for Truth, and the farmer Piers Plowman, a long time follower of Truth, offers to show the people the way if they will help him plow his half-acre field. The attempt at plowing together eventually fails, despite the efforts of Hunger to help Piers motivate the workers. Before they leave to seek Truth, Piers is offered a pardon by Truth, telling him only to "Do-Well." Piers then tears the pardon to pieces, vowing to seek Truth himself. After waking, the dreamer spends a long time pondering the meaning of this vision and again becomes a wanderer.

The poet continues to seek Do-Well, and, after a waking dispute with two Franciscan friars on the nature of Do-Well and Do-Evil, falls into a third dream. In this vision, Thought advises him to progressively explore key stages called Do-Well, Do-Better, and Do-Best. In his exploration he meets such characters as Wit and his wife, Dame Study, who directs him to her cousin, Clergy, and his wife, Scripture. Failing to understand their explanations of Do-Well, Do-Better, and Do-Best, the frustrated dreamer falls asleep in his dream, and is snatched up in this dream-within-a-dream by Fortune, accompanied by such followers as Lust and Recklessness, whom the poet in turn follows throughout his life. Scripture and the Emperor Trajan, who has been a virtuous man although a pagan, shows him the error of his ways before he has a vision of the natural universe as guided by Reason before waking back into the "outer" dream. Then he meets Imaginative, with whom he engages in a series of discussions about the nature of learning and religion.

After spending several years as a wandering beggar, Will

falls into a fourth vision, in which he continues his investigation of religious ideas at a dinner at the house of Conscience with such characters as Clergy, Patience, and Scripture. After hearing some dubious advice from a doctor of divinity, Conscience and Will go traveling with Patience and meet Hawkin the Active Man, who wears a badly soiled coat of Christendom. Hawkin undergoes a religious conversion himself, recognizing his sinfulness and his dependence upon grace as a result of their discussions.

During the fifth vision, Will listens to Anima's discourse on the ideals of spiritual development and the nature of charity. In an inner dream within this dream, he meets Piers Plowman again, who shows him the Tree of Charity that grows in people's bodies. The narrator then meets the characters of Faith (Abraham), Hope (Moses), and the Good Samaritan (Charity and Christ). The Samaritan explains the nature of the Trinity and the need for repentance.

After another long period of travel, the poet sleeps again and, in a sixth vision, witnesses the Crucifixion; a debate by Mercy, Truth, Righteousness, and Peace on the ethical issues of the Redemption; and the Harrowing of Hell.

In another waking section, Will writes down the dreams to this point and then attends Easter Mass with his family before falling into the seventh dream, in which he sees Piers, now identified with Jesus Christ, beginning the building of the Christian Church, a house called Unity. The church community is attacked by Pride and his host of vices, and takes refuge in Unity with Conscience leading the resistance.

In the next waking section, the poet meets Need, then falls asleep and, in the eighth dream vision, sees the Antichrist and the massed powers of sin attack Unity. After the dreamer is smitten by Old Age, he enters Unity to find it under attack by Hypocrisy. After some discussion, in which Conscience argues that only Piers Plowman is needed to help them, Good Manners persuades Peace to let Friar Flatterer into Unity to see to the sick, but once in, he weakens Contrition and opens the way for the entry of Sloth and Pride. Conscience calls for Clergy to help defend Unity, but he has been put into a daze by the Friar. The dream ends with Conscience resolved to set off on a pilgrimage in search of Piers Plowman, at which point the dreamer wakes up.

"The Story" by William Nelles

Critical Evaluation:

Like Geoffrey Chaucer's *Canterbury Tales* (1387-1400), William Langland's *Piers Plowman* is one of the great vernacular works of the fourteenth century. Unlike Chaucer's poetry, however, Langland's work is apparently of and for the people, rather than the court. That the poem was popular can be seen in the meter in which it was written and by the existence of more than fifty manuscripts. Within the manuscripts are three different texts, the second and third being revisions containing additions to the first and earliest. The three texts, or versions, have been dated respectively by scholars at about 1362, 1377, and 1393.

Langland's poem is in part a work of social protest, written from the viewpoint of the common person. The last half of the fourteenth century was a period of disaster and social unrest, the time of severe visitations of the plague (with accompanying moral, social, and economic upheavals), of the Peasant Revolt of 1381, and of John Wycliffe's Lollard movement. Langland often inserted, on behalf of the common folk, protests against unfair dealings by the Crown, the courts, the clergy, and even the tradesmen. Being of the common folk himself, the poet recognized the trouble visited upon them, and he cried out bitterly against the cheating of the poor by the butcher, the baker, the miller, and others.

Most authorities now grant that the poem was probably written by one person, although some doubt has been expressed in the past on this point. Internal evidence indicates the author to be Langland, a recipient of minor orders in the Church and a married man living in London. Despite allusions and references to himself and to happenings of the times, however, the author has retained the anonymity typical of the medieval author. The alliterative verse, much like the metrical structure used in *Beowulf* (c. 1000) and other Anglo-Saxon poems, was the native style of versification lost when the conventions of the metrical system were popularized by court poetry. In the hands of medieval writers, including Langland, the Old English alliterative verse had not the subtlety and power it once had in the ninth and tenth centuries. As used by Langland, the measure consisted of lines of any number of syllables, divided into half-lines. Each half-line was given two heavy beats in important words, with the heavy beats accentuated by alliteration, as in such a line as "And wo in winter-tyme—with wakynge a nyghtes."

To emphasize the social or metrical aspects of *Piers Plowman* seems unfair to the poem, for it is essentially a religious work, filled with the religious doctrines, dogma, views, and sentiments of medieval Catholicism. In the poem, the poet has a series of visions that he relates to the reader, each vision concerned with humanity's relationships to God, relationships that concerned every aspect of life, according to medieval thought.

In the first vision, which is probably the best known, the poet dreams of a vast field of people going about all the tasks and activities of the poet's world. The vision is explained to him by a lady named Holy Church, who informs him that the castle at one end of the field is the home of Truth, or God, and that in the dungeon in the valley dwells the Father of Falsehood, or Satan. When asked by the poet how he might save his soul, the lady replies that he should learn to accept Truth, along with love and pity for his fellow humans. The poet then envisions a long, involved sequence in which appears Lady Mede, representing just reward and bribery simultaneously. A king proposes to marry Lady Mede to Conscience, after her rescue from False, but Conscience proclaims against her and refuses. Bribery, it is implied, cannot be reconciled with conscience. Reason, sent for by the king, promises to serve him, too, if Conscience would be another counselor. One interesting part of this sequence of the poem is Conscience's explanation of Latin grammar, with its declensions and agreement of noun and adjective, as a symbolic representation of the relationship between humanity and God. The king in the vision demands a full explanation because, as he points out, English, the only language he knows, had no such grammatical relationships.

In another vision, the poet views the seven deadly sins. After a sermon by Conscience, Piers Plowman offers to show the company the way to Holy Truth, but only after he had plowed a half-acre field. Mentioned in this section are Piers's wife and children: Dame Work-while-I-am-Able, Daughter Do-this-or-thy-Dame-shall-beat-thee, and Son Suffer-thy-Sovereigns-to-have-their-Wishes-Dare-not-Judge-them-for-if-thou-Dost-thou-shalt-Dearly-Abide-it. At the end of this vision Piers is granted a pardon for himself and his heirs forever.

In the next sequence the poet takes up Piers's quest for Truth. This quest is divided somewhat ambiguously into three parts, searches for Do-Well, Do-Better, and Do-Best. To achieve the state of Do-Well, the poet learns, one must fear God, be honest, be obedient, and love one's fellow human; this seems to be the task of the ordinary person. Do-Better, apparently the lot of the priest, represents the teaching of the gospel and helping everyone. Do-Best, the seeming lot of the bishop, involves everything in the first two categories, as well as the wise administration of the Church to save all souls.

Piers appears again and again in the poem, each time being more clearly an incarnation of the Christ. Seen at first as a hardworking, sincere, and honest plowman, Piers later shows up in the poem as the figure who can explain to the poet the Tree of Charity and the nature of the Trinity of God. He appears also as the Good Samaritan and, later, as the builder of the Church and the one who will joust in God's armor against Satan. These appearances serve to hold the poem

together; without them the work would be a loosely coupled series of episodes and digressions.

The poem presents much biblical lore, from both the Old and New Testaments. The events in Eden, Job's trials, the perfidy of Judas, Jesus' suffering and crucifixion, along with many other familiar and traditional Christian elements, are recorded in the poem. There are digressions on sin and virtue, on the nature and value of learning, and on the activities of laity and clergy, some good and some bad. These individual portions of the poem are beautifully executed and deeply moving. They are probably of more worth when considered by themselves insofar as a modern reader is concerned. To read *Piers Plowman* in its entirety is tedious, largely because of its rambling qualities, and few general readers will have the patience to do so nowadays, even with the help of a translation into modern English.

Further Reading

Alford, John A., ed. *A Companion to "Piers Plowman."* Berkeley: University of California Press, 1988. Eleven original essays, each followed by a selective bibliography, provide beginning and advanced students with essential information on every major aspect of Langland's poem. Includes an introduction surveying the six hundred years of the poem's critical history.

Baldwin, Anna P. *A Guidebook to "Piers Plowman."* New York: Palgrave Macmillan, 2007. Student guide to the text, including information on Langland's sources; the religious, political, and social issues raised by the poem; and Langland's historical, theological, and psychological assumptions in writing the poem.

Blanch, Robert J., ed. *Style and Symbolism in "Piers Plowman": A Modern Critical Anthology.* Knoxville: University of Tennessee Press, 1969. Reprints thirteen essays from a number of scholarly journals, many of them unavailable in smaller libraries. Designed to orient the beginning student to the major issues in the study of *Piers Plowman*.

Hewett-Smith, Kathleen M., ed. *William Langland's "Piers Plowman": A Book of Essays.* New York: Routledge, 2001. Collection of interpretative essays, including discussions of the poem's historical context, Langland and Geoffrey Chaucer as religious writers, gender issues, and the use of allegory in the work.

Hussey, S. S., ed. *"Piers Plowman": Critical Approaches.* London: Methuen, 1969. Twelve original essays on the poem. Hussey's introduction to the collection surveys the basic information about Langland and *Piers Plowman* for beginning students.

Kasten, Madeleine. *In Search of "Kynde Knowynge": "Piers Plowman" and the Origin of Allegory*. New York: Rodopi, 2007. Kasten applies literary and cultural critic Walter Benjamin's theories about German baroque allegory to this analysis of the narrative allegory in *Piers Plowman*.

Kelen, Sarah A. *Langland's Early Modern Identities*. New York: Palgrave Macmillan, 2007. Traces the reception of *Piers Plowman* from the sixteenth through the nineteenth centuries, examining how readers in these years interpreted the poem to fit their own ideas of the Middle Ages.

Scott, Anne M. *"Piers Plowman" and the Poor*. Dublin: Four Courts, 2004. A scholarly examination of the poem within a deeper investigation of medieval ideas about poverty and the poor. For advanced students. Includes a bibliography and an index.

Simpson, James. *"Piers Plowman": An Introduction to the B Text*. 2d rev. ed. Exeter, England: University of Exeter Press, 2007. A detailed overview of the B version of the poem, which is the most frequently encountered form of the work. Summarizes the range of critical opinion on key issues and includes comparisons to similar material found in the *Canterbury Tales*, a contemporary work by Geoffrey Chaucer.

Zeeman, Nicolette. *"Piers Plowman" and the Medieval Discourse of Desire*. New York: Cambridge University Press, 2006. A scholarly treatment of how *Piers Plowman* and other medieval literature explores the nature of intellectual and spiritual desire.

Pilgrim at Tinker Creek

Author: Annie Dillard (1945-   )
First published: 1974
Type of work: Nature writing

Annie Dillard is no mere "nature writer," and *Pilgrim at Tinker Creek*, winner of the 1975 Pulitzer Prize in nonfiction, is more than a book about simply "walking around the woods." *Pilgrim at Tinker Creek* blends spirituality, environmentalism, awe, and wonder with narrative, research, questions, and answers. Although the work is set at Tinker Creek in Virginia's Roanoke Valley, it could be a story about any natural place, experienced anew by any person journeying through, like a pilgrim.

Pilgrim at Tinker Creek is organized into fifteen chapters, each with simple titles such as "Seeing" or "The Present." The chapters move chronologically through the seasons, starting with winter in January. No chapter, however, is limited to what is happening at Tinker Creek in a given month. Rather, the chapters are thematic, as indicated by their titles. There is a larger theme of spirituality, as the book explores the two routes to God in the tradition of neoplatonic Christianity. The first half of the book shows the positive route, *via positiva* (celebrating a creator's glory, reveling in balance and existence, knowing that a god exists and is good); the second half shows the negative route, *via negativa* (acknowledging God's unknowability, as well as the bizarre fecundity and voraciousness of the natural world, where eventually everything will die and nothing can ever really be known).

The book starts with what is perhaps its best-known scene: Dillard's old tomcat returns from a night of prowling and traverses her body and bed, leaving bloody footprints across her chest that look like roses. She showers away the scarlet marks, musing on what it means to wake to beauty and violence from unknown adventures. The scene sets the tone for the rest of the book, which treads a tightrope between opposites.

Dillard says that a partial inspiration for the book comes from writer Henry David Thoreau, who, in composing *Walden: Or, Life in the Woods* (1854), wanted to find a way to keep a journal of mind; Dillard, like Thoreau, is certainly a Transcendentalist. However, before the first chapter ends, Dillard has turned *Walden* on its head and redefined "nature writing." In the course of a basic description of Tinker Creek and the surrounding landscape, she slips in paragraphs written in second person, references an obscure story about a canary, tells readers about the habits of giant water bugs, quotes Albert Einstein and Blaise Pascal, and grapples with the concepts of grace, death, spirituality, and wonder.

Dillard maintains this whirlwind style throughout the book. She is a storyteller, and she realizes the story of the land is more than just the recollections of daily walks through the land—it includes all the writing and research that has come before, from folklore to religion to small-town news. She often refers to what she is reading or has read or wants to read, leading to chapters that form encyclopedias of the sublime. For example, in "Seeing," she uses an anecdote to tell about her childhood ability to see insects at a distance, tying sight to the following topics: drawing, brain circuitry, perception, amoebas in river water, cataracts, internal monologues, and various medical triumphs related to surgery for the blind. Her prose moves effortlessly and with exuberance, as if she is encountering all these ideas the same way she encounters critters and plants on her walks along the creek.

By the middle of the book, Dillard starts to link new observations to metaphors and philosophies from the beginning of the book. She has already established that the creek represents mystery. An earlier chapter examines sight, while a later chapter muses on shadows. In "The Fixed," she combines the two ideas: She is startled by a strange bird's shadow on the frozen river—she looks up and sees a magnificent woodpecker. Mystery solved. The river, the mystery, and the shadow merge in one moment, leading to clarity, and Dillard is spiritually charged by the sudden understanding.

Dillard also wants to show her readers her conception of spiritual glory as it relates to nature, and this desire takes the form of many anecdotes, biological facts, passages from religious texts (including the Qur'ān), and simple questions. Ultimately, by chapter 8, "Intricacy," she has pared down her quest, to two questions: Should humans concern themselves with the question of who created the planet? Should humans be concerned with why the planet was created? Her mood takes a darker turn as she quips about how amazing it is that there can exist in nature anything beautiful at all.

The delights of mystery and understanding cannot last uninterrupted. Chapter 9, "The Flood," is the bridge between the *via positiva* and *via negativa*. Readers notice an immediate tonal shift as Dillard watches the swollen river and remembers the catastrophic flooding from tropical storm Agnes in 1972. Recollecting how the meager creek soon topped a bridge and threatened her neighbors' homes, she imagines drowning. She describes horrific things caught in the flood water, like dead horses. She recounts a fantastic urban legend about how one electric light bulb still worked at the governor's house, and how electricians could not figure out why it still worked. At the end of the chapter, in quintessential Dillard style, she convinces herself that a flooded neighbor's house is now sprouting amazing edible mushrooms in its living room, including on its bookshelves, and even on the kitchen table.

From any flood comes fecundity, the title of chapter 10. Staying with her cynical view of nature, Dillard creates a litany of instances where growth is astonishing and scary and seemingly illogical. She touches on her usual odd cases—the tenacity of cockroaches, the horrors of parasitic wasps, the peculiar barnacle. She also includes her fascination with the number of miles of roots one plant produces; how lacewings eat their own eggs, even as they lay them; and how planarians feast upon their discarded tails. She refers to all these life cycles as ordained yet infused with the luck of survival.

The book next examines stalking, which is clearly an analogy to meditation. To stalk a muskrat, Dillard has to wait in one place for the animal to come to her. She invokes Heisenberg's principle of indeterminacy, which states that humans cannot know a particle's position and velocity at the same time. No matter how much is known, Dillard is saying, there forever remains the unknown—the essence of *via negativa*.

The next few chapters cover copperhead snakes, leeches, snapping turtles, and parasites, all things that Dillard has encountered and feels compelled to discuss with the same wonder she applied to muskrats, water bugs, and woodpeckers from the first half of the book. This wonder, however, is tinged with revulsion and, in the case of the copperhead, an awareness of danger. Dillard asserts that a marvelous creator must have dreamed up these things, even if the result is tattered butterflies, maimed spiders, and scarred turtles.

The final two chapters, "Northing" and "The Waters of Separation," document the fall and the coming winter, the restlessness of migration, and offerings. She brings back the image of her tomcat's roselike paw prints when she tells a story about how starving people can get rosy splotches on their skin. Circling back to a metaphor to extend this story, she talks about avoiding starvation; she cites Ezekiel, who told people to explore the gaps—the little places, the lowdown crevices, the cracks too easily ignored. Dillard implores readers to stalk these gaps, as she has done in this book.

Dillard's writing in *Pilgrim at Tinker Creek* is a stunning example of how to make intellectual connections and delight readers with lyrical language. Also, her writing is environmental writing of a different breed. Unlike environmentalists Bill McKibben, Rachel Carson, and Edward Abbey, for example, Dillard is not a polemicist. Her focus is not on industrialization, pollution, or rampant progress, nor is it a defense of one endangered species or place. There is no doubt, however, that she is concerned about the environment and knows the dangers of modern consumption. She has chosen, however, to engage readers with the sheer mystery, beauty, terror, and even humor of one creek in one state. That this book won the Pulitzer Prize shows how desperately readers needed, and continue to need, her viewpoint.

Jen Hirt

Further Reading

Dillard, Annie. *An American Childhood.* New York: Harper & Row, 1987. Memoir of Dillard's childhood in Pittsburgh, Pennsylvania. Includes discussion of the origins of some ideas explored in *Pilgrim at Tinker Creek.*

Johnson, Sandra Humble. *The Space Between: Literary Epiphany in the Work of Annie Dillard.* Kent, Ohio: Kent State University Press, 1992. Scholarly work that focuses on the epiphanies inherent in Dillard's works. Also examines the particular influence of Romantic poet William Wordsmith on Dillard.

McClintock, James. *Nature's Kindred Spirits: Aldo Leopold, Joseph Wood Krutch, Edward Abbey, Annie Dillard, and Gary Snyder.* Madison: University of Wisconsin Press, 1994. Illustrates how a variety of writers, including Dillard, had interacted with nature and come away changed, deeply influencing their writing.

Parrish, Nancy C. *Lee Smith, Annie Dillard, and the Hollins Group: A Genesis of Writers.* Baton Rouge: Louisiana State University Press, 1999. A volume of the Southern Literary Studies series, this work examines the Hollins Group, made up of women, including Dillard, who graduated from Hollins College in 1967 and achieved literary fame.

Smith, Linda. *Annie Dillard.* Boston: Twayne, 2002. Part of the Twayne American Authors series, this work includes scholarly essays and biographical material on Dillard.

The Pilgrim Hawk
A Love Story

Author: Glenway Wescott (1901-1987)
First published: 1940
Type of work: Novel
Type of plot: Psychological realism
Time of plot: An afternoon in May, 1929
Locale: Chancellet, France

Principal characters:
ALWYN TOWER, a young American novelist
MADELEINE CULLEN, a wealthy, middle-aged, attractive Irishwoman
LARRY CULLEN, her husband and an Irish aristocrat
ALEXANDRA HENRY, Tower's friend, a wealthy young American

The Story:

In the late 1920's, a time when Americans lived in romantic self-exile in Europe, Alwyn Tower's friend, Alexandra Henry, renovates a stable in Chancellet, a town in France. The interior is ultramodern, with a gigantic picture window looking out on a wild English-type garden in the back. Unexpectedly, Madeleine Cullen, en route to Budapest in a sleek, dark Daimler, stops off to see her friend, Alexandra. A handsome woman with Irish eyes and a London voice, she emerges from the car in fine French clothes and on spectacularly high heels. On her wrist, encased in a blood-stained gauntlet, perches a leashed hawk wearing a plumed Dutch hood. Ricketts, a dapper young Cockney chauffeur, and the stout, slightly inebriated Mr. Cullen help her over the cobblestones. Lucy, the hawk, is an exemplary bird, a symbol of love and lust.

Tower, Alexandra, and the two guests gather in the living room, where Mr. Cullen talks volubly about falcons and falconry. Later, the four take a walk in the formal garden of a nearby chateau. The Cullens, after leaving their two wild boys at Cullen Hall in Ireland, travel constantly; they have been involved with Irish revolutionaries and gone on pigsticking hunts in Tangier and lion hunts in the jungle. In these activities, Mrs. Cullen is the initiator; Mr. Cullen merely follows where she leads.

After the ritual feeding of Lucy in the living room, the bird is placed on a bench in the wild garden, while Mrs. Cullen and Alexandra rest before dinner. At the chromium bar on the balcony, the drunken Mr. Cullen talks to Tower as he would have to a bartender. He tells Tower that he almost killed an Irish poet out of jealousy (not really justified, as his wife allowed him his own infidelities). Comparing himself with his superlative wife, he mentions that he is a bad horseman, marksman, and sportsman, loathed travel, and above all, despises Lucy because the bird is constantly perched on Madeleine's wrist, preventing him from getting close to his wife. As Mr. Cullen continues to talk, Tower's malice (the scorn of a captive hawk by a potentially captive hawk) increases.

Finally, the very drunken Mr. Cullen creeps up on Lucy, removes her hood, and cuts her leash. Mrs. Cullen thereupon kicks off her high heels and recaptures the bird. Then, just as the Cullens are about to resume their journey to Budapest, Mr. Cullen himself tries to get free by pulling a gun. It is unclear whether he intends to shoot the chauffeur (whom he suspects of coveting his wife), Mrs. Cullen, Lucy, or himself, but Mrs. Cullen, with the bird on her wrist flapping madly in the attempt to hold on, rushes back into the house and out to the garden to throw the revolver into the pond.

Critical Evaluation:

Glenway Wescott's *The Pilgrim Hawk* is a tapestry woven of five layers: the hawk's intrinsic or obvious resemblance to the characters; the extrinsic significance imposed by Alwyn Tower as a young man observing the relationship between the Cullens and the hawk; Tower's interpretations ten years later as the middle-aged narrator; the actual intentions of the author (who is very close to Tower); and the reader's opportunities to see symbolic meaning in the hawk. With complete control, Wescott conducts the reader in and out of this labyrinth of symbols.

Wescott differentiates his characters partly by the degree of awareness with which each plucks the bird of its symbolic resemblances to human nature. Tower and Alexandra (who is normally not curious) are eager to see such correspondences. Sitting erect in a straight kitchen chair, Mrs. Cullen makes swift transitions from hawk to human until she sees that her husband, sunk into a soft easy chair, senses certain comparisons to himself.

Tower and his ambiguous responses are almost as interesting and crucial to the story as the exotic characters whose behavior he witnesses. One of the experiences Wescott creates is the reader's puzzled effort to sift and separate the narrator's reflections and judgments in 1929 from those he makes in 1940 as he reflects. Wescott cunningly keeps Tower's voice out of the dialogue until the end, when he converses with Alexandra; the effect is that readers hear his mature voice at some distance, contemplating, musing, shifting back and forth in time and attitude. His tone fluctuates between intense curiosity, intellectual excitement, emotional

reserve, repulsion, fascination, sadness, amusement, wit, and irony. Tower constantly sees symbols, and he seizes any pretext to express insights on love, marriage, drunkenness, the aristocracy, animals as compared with people, sports, and numerous other subjects. Out of all this, his character is distilled.

Tower's interest in the Cullens is an extension of his interest in himself. Outdoors people, the Cullens are self-centered, nonintrospective, self-indulgent, strenuous, and emotionally idle. Tower feels a cool affinity first with Mrs. Cullen (who signals her desire for his understanding), because, like an artist, she is in control of an artificial but satisfying situation that may at any moment revert to the chaos of nature. Then, reluctantly, Tower's sympathy shifts to Cullen, for Tower, too, is a lover, and he understands the predicament of a drunken, weak, vain, jealous, dull, mediocre, irritable, boring, conceited, childish fool who is in love with his wife.

Tower sees that Madeleine Cullen tries to create situations that will give full rein to her husband's masculinity while at the same time she restrains his wildness. He is a passionate man with streaks of animal ferocity and a desire for the liberty of the wilderness; like the falconer in William Butler Yeats's "The Second Coming" (1920), Mrs. Cullen strives to control his gyrings, but she is wild herself. She has always wanted to possess and herself train a real haggard, or trained falcon; now she has two. She needs to feel on her pulse an avatar of wildness: Controlling the falcon, she controls herself. When she persuades Tower to take Lucy on his wrist, Mrs. Cullen becomes electric with restlessness.

Like most falcons, Lucy makes frequent, though hopeless escape attempts. As a species, birds are free; only individuals are captive. All human beings are captives, however, and all must attempt to free themselves individually. Exceptional is the bird that loves captivity; exceptional is the human being who truly loves freedom. In captivity, both birds and people require a falconer. The human paradox is seen in the Cullens's relationship: He needs freedom, but she needs a captive; at the same time, he fears freedom, and she is loath to be a captor. Thus, Lucy both humiliates and sublimates Cullen: He frees Lucy both to be rid of her and to make a symbolic gesture of escape; he attempts his own actual release when he pulls the gun.

Wescott shows Mrs. Cullen's falconry to be expert when she recaptures first the hawk, then the husband. Drink, food, and philandering are to Cullen what a hood, a pigeon, and Mrs. Cullen's stroking fingers are to Lucy: a tranquilization of the instinct to wildness. Blind to what she is doing to her husband, Mrs. Cullen, too, is hooded. Both the gun and the hawk are new in the Cullens's life, because in middle age they have exhausted love and become dependent on such semblances of love as distractions, deceptions, and disguises.

Tower predicts that, having been given the Cullens as examples, Alexandra will never marry. Alexandra returns to the United States, however, where she meets and marries Tower's brother; it is Tower who does not marry. Married or not, every man becomes a haggard and must spend most of his life on some perch. Having surrendered to domestication, hawks become scornful of each other; they never breed in captivity. Even wild hawks rarely die of disease, but death by starvation is common. Madeleine has seen people in the Dublin insane asylum whose eyes had an expression similar to that of a starving hawk. Like the lover and the artist, hawks that lose their technique enter a hopeless spiral of deterioration. The hawk in the sky looks down on his prey; Tower the writer looks down from his tower on human behavior, as when he devours Cullen's story, with the conscious intention of remembering every word and image of that afternoon. Although he occasionally turns his scrutinizing eye upon himself, Tower employs diversionary tactics to avoid the truth. Told the details of the aging hawk's life, he has an intuition of growing old as an artist and a lover; he was failing in 1929; in 1940, he is bitter, nervous, apathetic, full of false pride, bereft of inspiration, and bored.

The concept of vision is one of Wescott's most effective motifs. He describes the hawk's eyes, their function in the hunt, the purpose of the hood; then in various ways, he compares the hawk's eyes with those of the other characters. Tower mentions his long-sightedness, expresses fear of going blind, and his immediate fear (which he shares with Cullen) that the hawk may attack his eyes. Tower's testimony, with its ambiguous tone and compulsive philosophizing, is a failed artist's and lover's means of trying to see while remaining purblind to the meaning of that bizarre afternoon. At the same time, however, the reader's vision comes into focus. Wescott's use here of the Jamesian point of view is one of the most successful in American literature.

Further Reading

Cunningham, Michael. "Michael Cunningham on *The Pilgrim Hawk* by Glenway Wescott." In *Unknown Masterpieces: Writers Rediscover Literature's Hidden Classics*, edited by Edwin Frank. New York: New York Review of Books, 2003. A collection of essays by prominent writers who discuss little-known but much admired works by other authors. Novelist Michael Cunningham explains why *The Pilgrim Hawk* may be the finest short novel in twentieth century American literature.

Johnson, Ira. *Glenway Wescott: The Paradox of Voice*. Port Washington, N.Y.: Kennikat Press, 1971. A chapter on *The Pilgrim Hawk* provides a comprehensive analysis of the novel that focuses on its composition, characterization, use of symbols, treatment of the theme of love, and Wescott's integration of autobiographical elements.

Rosco, Jerry. *Glenway Wescott Personally: A Biography*. Madison: University of Wisconsin Press, 2002. Biography focusing on how Wescott came to terms with his gayness. Recounts Wescott's early fame and later struggles to write, his relationship with museum curator Monroe Wheeler, his work on homosexuality with sex researcher Alfred Kinsey, and his friendships with other artists and writers.

Rueckert, William H. *Glenway Wescott*. New York: Twayne, 1965. General study of the writer's literary achievements. Places *The Pilgrim Hawk* in the context of Wescott's career, seeing it as part of a trilogy that includes *The Grandmothers* (1927) and *The Apple of the Eye* (1924); together these form a "symbolic autobiography" of the novelist.

Schorer, C. E. "The Maturing of Glenway Wescott." In *Twentieth-Century American Literature*, edited by Harold Bloom. New York: Chelsea House, 1988. Discusses *The Pilgrim Hawk* as an international novel and links Wescott with other American authors of the 1920's and 1930's. Reviews the novel's organization, and comments on Wescott's style.

Stout, Janis. P. "'Practically Dead with Fine Rivalry': The Leaning Towers of Katherine Anne Porter and Glenway Wescott." *Studies in the Novel* 33, no. 4 (Winter, 2001): 444. Compares *The Pilgrim Hawk* with Katherine Anne Porter's *The Leaning Tower*. Argues that the novels should be read together as a conversation between the two writers, who had discussed their work on the books. Cites similarities in the novels and discusses how they were influenced by the rise of Nazism and Adolf Hitler.

Wescott, Glenway. *Continual Lessons: The Journals of Glenway Wescott, 1937-1955*. Edited by Robert Phelps, with Jerry Rosco. New York: Farrar, Straus & Giroux, 1990. Excellent source for determining Wescott's ideas about the value of *The Pilgrim Hawk*. Includes comments on the novel's composition and publication history, as well as Wescott's brief remarks about thematic issues.

Pilgrimage

Author: Dorothy Richardson (1873-1957)
First published: 1915-1967; includes *Pointed Roofs*,
    1915; *Backwater*, 1916; *Honeycomb*, 1917; *The*
    Tunnel, 1919; *Interim*, 1919; *Deadlock*, 1921;
    Revolving Lights, 1923; *The Trap*, 1925; *Oberland*,
    1927; *Dawn's Left Hand*, 1931; *Clear Horizon*,
    1935; *Dimple Hill*, 1938; *March Moonlight*, 1967
Type of work: Novels
Type of plot: Bildungsroman
Time of plot: Late nineteenth and early twentieth centuries
Locale: England

Principal characters:
MIRIAM HENDERSON, an Englishwoman
MICHAEL SHATOV, a Russian émigré
HYPO WILSON, an admirer of Miriam
AMABEL, a female admirer

The Story:

Miriam climbs the staircase and looks down from the bedroom of the second floor to the garden below, aware of the sense that she is leaving behind everything familiar to her. She thinks back over her days of quiet, sun-filled mornings. She remembers the afternoons she spent reading books, and the moments when she played duets on the piano with her sister, Harriet. Her packed trunk stands in the hallway downstairs, ready for the trip to Hanover, Germany the next morning. A governess position at a girls' boarding school awaits Miriam.

Miriam crosses the English Channel and takes a train to Germany. She already regrets her decision to become a governess. As night falls, the train rushes her across the countryside toward Germany, and Miriam doubts her ability to teach English to young girls. She is leaving the house of her family because her father is bankrupt. There is no looking back. Miriam knows that she has to take her place in the world. Nervous but expectant, she feels freedom might await her.

After several months at her position in the boarding school, Miriam is confronted by Fräulein Pfaff, headmistress of the school. They stand in the central room of the school, along with the other teaching staff. While Fräulein Pfaff chastises the teachers for talking about men in front of the schoolgirls, Miriam grows angry. She realizes that the Fräulein is talking about her. She vows not to bow to Fräulein Pfaff's spiteful attitude but sees that she might be asked to resign her teaching post with the girls. Meanwhile, back in England, one of Miriam's sisters becomes engaged to be married. Miriam announces to Fräulein Pfaff that she will go home to England. Once again, she boards a train. This time, when it pulls out from the bright platform in the night, it is to return to England. Miriam disembarks at the English station with her first year of work behind her.

Upon her return to England, Miriam is asked by her mother to assume a teaching position with young children. At her eighteenth birthday, Miriam puts up her hair and goes to work as a resident governess in a school for the daughters of gentlemen. By the end of the teaching year, she goes on a seaside holiday in Brighton and visits the Crystal Palace.

Dispirited by her year of teaching at the boarding school, Miriam accepts another position as governess. She travels to the home of a wealthy English family. She watches the Corrie family, occupants of a large house, with their evening gowns and decorum. Miriam puzzles over her own position as worker in the home. She recalls that her own father is bankrupt and that she cannot give up the necessary income from her governess work, regardless of her feelings about her position. In addition, she quizzes the father of the family on the fact that she, Miriam, must instruct the children in religion. How can she do this, she wants to know, while she herself is a nonbeliever?

Lacking other occupational options, despite her wide reading and knowledge of music, the young Miriam continues to chafe at her position as governess. She leaves to take a job as a dental assistant, and she takes up residence in the London boardinghouse of Mrs. Bailey.

While she boards at Mrs. Bailey's, Miriam meets Michael Shatov, a Russian Jew. She tutors him in English and becomes engaged to him. The two discuss philosophy, Zionism, and feminism. Through their conversations, Miriam realizes that she is caught. Their differences are too much. Miriam grows frustrated. She knows that she does not want to marry Michael. When Michael approaches her physically, Miriam cannot respond. Unable to respond to Michael's physical advances, and at odds with him on other points, Miriam knows that she will leave England and Michael.

Troubled, Miriam embarks on a long tour of Switzerland. She returns to England, only to return to Michael. After a long conversation, Michael again asks Miriam to accept his proposal of marriage. Miriam tries to impress upon him the value that she assigns to friendship. She is pursued, also, by Hypo Wilson, a persistent lover. In addition, a female friend named Amabel grows increasingly attached to Miriam. Startled, Miriam realizes that Amabel wanted to consume Miriam's life in the same way her other attachments do. Miriam realizes that she has the temperament of both the male and the female. Increasingly, however, she wants close contact with neither.

Ensconced in Mrs. Bailey's boardinghouse, Miriam decides to break free of all of her attachments except one. She leaves her lover, Hypo. In a further effort to free herself from attachments, she introduces Michael to Amabel with the hopes that they will become interested in each other. They do. Quietly, Miriam rejoices. Not long afterward, Michael and Amabel marry. Miriam leaves again for Switzerland after a sojourn on a Quaker farm.

Amabel and Michael, married and settled in London, are unhappy. Miriam spends a weekend with them when she returns to London, and she claims little responsibility for their unhappiness in life. Alone in a different room in London, Miriam looks out the window and surveys her life. After the long years of her journey, Miriam claims that writing will be the central act of her life.

Critical Evaluation:

Considered by many critics to be an innovator in form, Dorothy Richardson completed all the novels of *Pilgrimage* during a lifetime of clerical jobs and a writing career that included book reviews, columns, and the extended novel form. Richardson's formal education was brief, but she read widely in the literature and science of her day. Upon settling in London in 1895, to work as a dental assistant, she met the writer H. G. Wells; through her extended liaison with Wells, Richardson was introduced to the world of writers, feminism, and social criticism. This environment was the foundation of her adult life as well as of her most important work, *Pilgrimage*.

In *Pilgrimage*, Richardson located herself as an innovator in the novel form and as a social critic. *Pilgrimage* marks an attempt to create a new language for writing, a language modernism reveled in. Richardson's deliberate record of details, conversations, actions, and thoughts reflected her idea that all phenomena were important.

More particularly, Richardson's experiments in sentence structure support her view of a "female" writing style. As she wrote, "Feminine prose, as Charles Dickens and James Joyce

have delightfully shown themselves to be aware, should properly be unpunctuated, moving from point to point without formal obstructions." Richardson's complicated and innovative experiments with syntax also mirror the effect that life had on Miriam Henderson, the protagonist of Richardson's work. In Miriam's quest for a life both examined and independent, she cannot move, free and unobstructed, as Richardson's sentences do. One might say that Miriam's life experience is the very opposite of Richardson's stylistic effects. The "feminine sentence" runs unfettered and free, but the feminine life, as seen by Richardson, runs into obstacles and problems from young adulthood onward. Miriam, as she embarks on her pilgrimage out of her family home and into the world, demonstrates the complexity of a woman's existence.

The theme of *Pilgrimage* may be broadly stated as the coming-into-being of a woman writer after a long journey. Miriam states in the last volume of *Pilgrimage*, "While I write, everything vanishes but what I contemplate." *Pilgrimage* holds at its center the duality of internal and external life. Richardson validates each moment of her heroine's life by laying claim to it in print; even so, her heroine proclaims the joy of obliterating all experience but one: the act of writing. In this sense, one can argue that the narrator and author are fused, which is a demonstration of the theme of *Pilgrimage*.

The novel begins with Miriam leaving the family home for Germany, and the entire nine volumes are told through Miriam's point of view. Seen originally as a novel without a plot, the work has since been understood as a bildungsroman. In an interesting twist on the novel of education, Richardson begins with her subject as an adult rather than with the more usual story of a child approaching the end of youth. In each advancing section, a new dimension to Miriam's journey unfolds in a haphazard fashion. As Miriam moves from youth to womanhood, issues of female identity, romance, and work are raised. Richardson asks the reader to share in the examination of these issues. Upon receiving Michael Shatov's proposal of marriage, Miriam meditates on marriage as a prison in which a woman has no place for herself. Since there is no narrator adding comments or analysis, the reader must go along with Miriam on her quest, finding answers as the journey proceeds.

Richardson achieves her highest artistic success in her fusion of protagonist and narrator; as Miriam proceeds through her pilgrimage, no particular outcome is assured. The reader becomes as much a participant in the journey as the protagonist. Miriam critiques the nature of male and female existence as she reaches for a way of being that will encompass reality in all of its forms. The form of *Pilgrimage*, in its fractured passages, reminiscences, and dialogue, makes ample room for all these forms.

Further Reading

Bluemel, Kristin. *Experimenting on the Borders of Modernism: Dorothy Richardson's "Pilgrimage."* Athens: University of Georgia Press, 1997. The first chapter assesses Richardson's work and previous studies of her. Subsequent chapters explore Richardson's handling of gender, problems of the body, and science in *Pilgrimage*, and the author's quest for an ending to this long work. Includes notes and bibliography

Fromm, Gloria G. *Dorothy Richardson: A Biography.* Champaign: University of Illinois Press, 1977. An excellent introduction to Richardson's life and work. Offers an interesting analysis of *Pilgrimage*, highlighting the relationship between Richardson's life and her art.

Gregory, Horace. *Dorothy Richardson: An Adventure in Self-Discovery.* New York: Holt, Rinehart and Winston, 1967. A compelling study of the events of Richardson's life. An important work for the reader interested in the autobiographical nature of *Pilgrimage*.

Hanscombe, Gillian E. *The Art of Life: Dorothy Richardson and the Development of Feminist Consciousness.* London: Peter Owen, 1982. Offers textual examination of *Pilgrimage*. Includes an interesting assessment of Richardson's attempt to develop a feminine writing style. Comprehensive index provides access to important sections.

Parsons, Deborah L. *Theorists of the Modernist Novel: James Joyce, Dorothy Richardson, Virginia Woolf.* New York: Routledge, 2007. A study of the aesthetic theories of Richardson and two other modernist writers, James Joyce and Virginia Woolf. Examines the forms of realism, characterization, gender representation, and other elements of Richardson's work.

Radford, Jean. *Dorothy Richardson.* Bloomington: Indiana University Press, 1991. Analyzes structure, characters, and themes in *Pilgrimage*. Contains a useful section on reading and readership in Richardson's novel.

Staley, Thomas F. *Dorothy Richardson.* Boston: Twayne, 1976. A lucid examination of Richardson's life and work. A good place to start a study of Richardson.

Thomson, George H. *A Reader's Guide to Dorothy Richardson's "Pilgrimage."* Greensboro, N.C.: ELT Press, 1996. Provides a time scheme for the novel's narrative, a chronology of events, a discussion of the relationships among the principal characters, and an alphabetical directory listing and describing the characters.

Winning, Joanne. *The Pilgrimage of Dorothy Richardson.* Madison: University of Wisconsin Press, 2000. Winning argues that Richardson's thirteen-volume novel contains a subtext of lesbian desire and sexuality, and she compares this novel to works by other lesbian modernist writers.

The Pilgrimage of Charlemagne

Author: Unknown
First transcribed: Voyage de Charlemagne à Jérusalem et à Constantinople, c. 1100 (English translation, 1927)
Type of work: Poetry
Type of plot: Folklore
Time of plot: c. 800
Locale: Paris, Jerusalem, and Constantinople

Principal characters:
CHARLEMAGNE, the Frankish king and emperor of the West
HUGO, the emperor of Greece and of Constantinople
ROLAND,
OLIVER,
WILLIAM OF ORANGE,
NAIMES,
OGIER OF DENMARK,
GERIN,
BERENGER,
TURPIN THE ARCHBISHOP,
ERNAUT,
AYMER,
BERNARD OF BRUSBAN, and
BERTRAM, Charlemagne's twelve peers

The Poem:

Emperor Charlemagne, accompanied by his queen, the twelve peers, and many others, goes to the Abbey of St. Denis. Charlemagne is elegantly garbed and wears his fine sword as well as his splendid crown. Proud of his prepossessing mien, he boasts of his power and majestic appearance, confidently asking the queen if she had ever seen another as impressive as he. Impatient with this vanity, the queen chides Charlemagne for his inordinately high opinion of himself and suggests that there is a king handsomer than he.

The emperor, angry over this public humiliation, commands the queen to name the rival king so that their respective courts could meet and decide which of the two is handsomer, threatening the queen with decapitation if it is determined that she has spoken falsely about the other king's superior appearance. Frightened, the queen tearfully pleads for mercy, pretends forgetfulness, and then amends her claim to say that, although richer, the other king is not nearly so brave as Charlemagne. Still unsatisfied, Charlemagne demands to know the identity of the other king, again threatening to cut off the queen's head immediately if she does not acquiesce. The queen then admits that it is Hugo, the emperor of Greece and Constantinople and ruler of vast lands in Persia.

When Charlemagne and his entourage return to the palace in Paris, the emperor declares to the assembled peers and knights of France that, attended by his imperial retinue, he will go on a pilgrimage to the Holy Land to pray in Jerusalem at the Holy Sepulchre, to make the Stations of the Cross, and then to continue on to Constantinople to visit Emperor Hugo. For the journey, with the blessings of Archbishop Turpin, all twelve peers—Roland, Oliver, William of Orange, Naimes, Ogier of Denmark, Gerin, Berenger, Ernaut, Aymer, Bernard of Brusban, Bertram the Strong, as well as Turpin—the rest of the imperial retainers, and Charlemagne himself, are outfitted as pilgrims. Equipped with pilgrims' scrip, they carry no weapons, only sharp oaken staves, but they are accompanied by many beasts of burden, laden with riches. With blessings from the Abbey of St. Denis, the imperial troupe, including Turpin, sets off. Along the way, Charlemagne draws Bertram aside to call his attention to the eighty-thousand-man pilgrimage and to boast once more of the power and the might of the leader of such a group.

Arriving in Jerusalem, the emperor and his fellows visit the shrine of the Last Supper, where the bearded Charlemagne and his twelve peers audaciously sit in the chairs allegedly once occupied by Christ and his twelve disciples. A passing Jew observes this charade and forthwith informs the patriarch of Jerusalem, who instantly collects a procession of priests and acolytes to investigate the phenomenon.

The patriarch of Jerusalem respectfully greets Charlemagne, who identifies himself as Charles of France, mighty conqueror of twelve kings in search of a thirteenth conquest, and as a devout Christian pilgrim. The patriarch declares that he who occupies Christ's seat must be Charles the Great—Charles Magnus or Charlemagne—above all other crowned heads. The patriarch generously accedes to Charlemagne's request for sacred relics, giving him St. Simon's armlet; Lazarus's shroud; a vial of St. Stephen's blood; a piece of the Holy Shroud; one of the nails from the Cross; the crown of thorns; the chalice, the silver bowl, and Christ's own dinner knife from the Last Supper; clippings from the whiskers and the hair of St. Peter; a vial of the Virgin's milk; and a piece of the Virgin's robe. As Charlemagne accepts these relics, a disabled person is cured of his afflictions, attesting the divine power of the relics. A magnificent gold and silver chest is made for transporting these holy treasures, and the collection is consigned to the keeping of Archbishop Turpin.

Charlemagne and his men stay four months in Jerusalem. Then, with pledges of Christian fealty and defense of the faith, they leave for Constantinople, where Charlemagne's thoughts have lately turned again to Emperor Hugo. Arriving a few miracles later, the travelers are stunned by the beauty and opulence of Constantinople. Emperor Hugo, however, is not there to greet them. Inquiry discloses that he is plowing, under a silken-canopied chariot with a gold plow and golden-yoked oxen, making furrows as straight as a taut bowstring. When Charlemagne seeks out Hugo, the two emperors greet each other cordially, each noting the other's comely physique. Hugo, having earlier been apprised of Charlemagne's noble bearing, welcomes the French peers and knights graciously, promising lavish gifts and warm hospitality if they will remain for an extended visit. Remembering the queen's words, Charlemagne and his company are astonished by the richness of Hugo's palace and courtiers.

Suddenly, however, the palace is struck by a strong wind. The entire building seems to spin, and the Frenchmen become dizzy and cannot stand up. Just as suddenly the wind dies down, and the Frenchmen regain their balance. Then dinner is served, a fine feast in which no gustatory request or desire is not met. Spiced claret flows freely. Oliver is smitten with love for Hugo's beautiful blonde daughter. Minstrels sing to musical accompaniment, and great entertainment ensues.

After the feast is over, Hugo leads Charlemagne and his twelve peers to a luxuriously appointed apartment where they are to spend the night. More wine is brought, and the Frenchmen begin to make themselves comfortable. The wily Hugo, however, unbeknownst to his guests, posts a spy in a nearby stairwell to report on the visitors' postprandial conversation. Filled with wine and unaware that they are being overheard, Charlemagne and his twelve companions wax jolly and daring. They begin to brag, as is their late-evening custom following much wine. At first, they merely note the vulnerability of Hugo's rich estates to their superior military power, but then each one, in turn, begins making a derogatory boast about individually overpowering Hugo's might. In this way, *les gabs* (a typical epic-formula device) are played out—the bragging, boasting, half-serious, and half-joking vaunts of Charlemagne and his twelve peers.

As was fitting, Charlemagne begins the boasting. He scoffs that, were Hugo to array his best knight in two suits of armor, he, Charlemagne, would wield Hugo's own sword to penetrate that armor and pin the knight into the earth to a long spear's depth. Charlemagne's nephew, Roland, boasts that he would take Hugo's ivory horn and, with a single blast, level Constantinople as well as singe Hugo's very beard. At Roland's urging, Oliver speaks next. He says that if Hugo would but loan him his daughter for a night, Oliver would demonstrate his sexual prowess by possessing her one hundred times before the morrow. Archbishop Turpin is invited to make the next contribution. Befitting his calling, Turpin proposes a harmless physical feat involving the juggling of apples while vaulting two galloping horses to mount a third. William of Orange thereupon proposes to use a large, decorative gold-and-silver ball in that very room to demolish more than 160 cubits of wall around Hugo's palace, and Ogier of Denmark jeers that he would play Samson and dislodge a palace pillar to bring the entire structure down.

The aged Naimes boasts that, clad in Hugo's own chain-mail tunic, he would jump from the battlements of the palace and back so quickly that Hugo would not even notice and then destroy the hauberk with a mere quiver. Berenger brags that he would jump from the highest tower in the palace onto the upturned blades of the swords of all of Hugo's knights without suffering a scratch. Bernard then claims he would divert a river, cause a flood, and force Hugo to beg from a high tower for surcease. Ernaut boasts that he would sit in a vat of molten lead until it hardened and then shake himself loose from it. In like manner, Aymer boasts that he would banquet at Hugo's table, then don a cap to make himself invisible and deliver Hugo a beard-shattering blow. Bertram offers to beat two shields together so loudly that the sound would deafen or disperse all wildlife in the area. Finally, Gerin brags that he would stack two coins upon a post, stand at a league's distance, and, with his spear, topple one coin without disturbing the other, then run the league's distance to catch the falling coin before it hit the ground.

Hugo's spy promptly reports these mocking, derisive taunts to Hugo, which both spy and emperor construe literally. Hugo, outraged at such an affront to his hospitality, gathers his knights and confronts Charlemagne the next morning. Somewhat taken aback, Charlemagne tries to soothe Hugo's ire by explaining the influence of the claret and the French custom of *les gabs*, but Hugo will have none of it. Hugo demands that the boasts be fulfilled or he will order Charlemagne and his twelve peers beheaded. In desperation, Charlemagne prays over his trove of relics. Then an angel appears to him, reassuring him that no peer will fail to execute his boast—yet another miracle to rescue the French—but warning him to foreswear such mockery and bragging in the future.

Charlemagne calls together his peers and offers Hugo the choice as to which boast should be attempted first. William of Orange is given the initial challenge. With divine assistance, he heaves the gold-and-silver ball through more than 160 cubits of wall and the palace as well, causing massive destruction. Next, Bernard, with God's aid, creates a mighty flood, which God abates in his own good time. So impressed is Hugo that he requires no further demonstrations of Frankish power and immediately becomes Charlemagne's vassal.

The occasion is celebrated with great feasting, and the two emperors display themselves regally before their assembled knights and attendants. The combined courts judge Charlemagne the fairest of the two kings. Then the French depart for their journey back to Paris. Buoyed by this bloodless conquest, Charlemagne is in such a good mood that he forgives the queen and does not have her beheaded.

Critical Evaluation:

Some twentieth century scholars have claimed that medieval writers were deficient in imagination and thus unable to create plots, depending instead on historical events to provide their stories. Charlemagne's journey to Jerusalem, a complete fabrication, is a literary work that clearly demonstrates that heroic legends when embodied in medieval romances did not, and did not need to, rely on historical events. Charlemagne never went to Jerusalem. In fact, the closest he came to Jerusalem was when the patriarch of Jerusalem sent him the keys to the city and to the Holy Sepulchre as a reward for his generous support of Christian churches in the Holy Land. In Charlemagne's fictional pilgrimage to Jerusalem, medieval writers combined real persons with fantasized events to create original literature of a kind that will later be compared to a historical novel.

The source of this tale is alleged to have been the Abbey

of St. Denis, which claimed to possess a number of holy relics brought back by Charlemagne from the Holy Land. The best known of these putative relics was the crown of thorns. However, skeptical twentieth century scholarship also credits missionary zeal, possibly venality, with the creation of this tale of Charlemagne's pilgrimage.

As for the vanity, arrogance, and braggadocio of Charlemagne's spurious exploits, such actions undoubtedly create a reasonable counterbalance for the more respectful histories and legends that depict Charlemagne as a pious, noble, and high-minded leader. When Charlemagne is described as feeling threatened by the possibility that Emperor Hugo might be more handsome than he is, Charlemagne becomes less imperial and more human. Although such impertinent questions were certainly never raised in Charlemagne's authoritarian times, the freer atmosphere of the High Middle Ages—sometimes characterized as the Renaissance of the twelfth century, during which time this poem appears to have been written—must have tolerated such irreverence. Thus the earthy tale of Charlemagne's imagined trip to Jerusalem suggests but another facet of Charlemagne's undoubtedly multifaceted personality, however fanciful the depiction may be.

Further Reading

Cobby, Anne Elizabeth. *Ambivalent Conventions: Formula and Parody in Old French.* New York: Rodopi, 1995. Cobby's study of parody in the fabliaux devotes almost eighty pages to an analysis of *The Pilgrimage of Charlemagne.* She demonstrates how the work subverts the conventions of medieval French epics and romances to create a complex and nuanced parody.

Cobby, Anne Elizabeth, and Glyn S. Burgess, eds. Introduction to *The Pilgrimage of Charlemagne* and *Aucassin and Nicollette,* translated by Glyn S. Burgess. New York: Garland, 1988. In this introduction, Cobby discusses the aesthetic qualities of *The Pilgrimage of Charlemagne,* provides information on textual matters, and comments on possible sources of inspiration for its writing.

Grigsby, John L. *The Gab as a Latent Genre in Medieval French Literature: Drinking and Boasting in the Middle Ages.* Cambridge, Mass.: Medieval Academy of America, 2000. The medieval gab was a literary genre featuring characters who were idle braggarts. Grigsby examines this genre, focusing his discussion on *The Pilgrimage of Charlemagne.*

Muir, Lynette. *Literature and Society in Medieval France: The Mirror and the Image, 1100-1500.* New York: St. Martin's Press, 1985. Muir traces the composition history of the poem, noting how the work differs from other *chansons de geste* in its extensive use of humor and fantastic detail.

Polak, Lucie. "Charlemagne and the Marvels of Constantinople." In *The Medieval Alexander Legend and Romance Epic,* edited by Peter Noble et al. Millwood, N.Y.: Kraus International, 1982. Polak examines the technological marvels described as part of the hero's visit to Constantinople, suggesting possible historical inspirations for those imagined marvels.

The Pilgrim's Progress

Author: John Bunyan (1628-1688)
First published: part 1, 1678; part 2, 1684
Type of work: Novel
Type of plot: Allegory
Time of plot: Any time since Christ
Locale: Unnamed

Principal characters:
CHRISTIAN
FAITHFUL
HOPEFUL
MR. WORLDLY WISEMAN
EVANGELIST
DESPAIR
IGNORANCE
APOLLYON, a giant devil

The Story:

John Bunyan lays down in a den to sleep. In his sleep, he dreams that he sees a man, named Christian, standing in a field and crying out in pain and sorrow because he and his whole family, as well as the town in which they live, are to be destroyed. Christian knows of this catastrophe because he had read about it in the book—the Bible—that he holds in his hands.

Evangelist, the preacher of Christianity, soon comes up to

Christian and presents him with a roll of paper on which it is written that he should flee from the wrath of God and make his way from the City of Destruction to the City of Zion. Running home with this hope of salvation, Christian tries to get his neighbors and family to go away with him, but they do not listen and think he is either sick or mad. Finally, he shuts his ears to his family's entreaties to stay with them and runs off toward the light in the distance. Under the light, he knows he will find the wicket gate that opens into Heaven.

On his way, Christian meets Pliant and Obstinate; Christian is so distracted by them that he falls in a bog called the Slough of Despond. He cannot get out because of the bundle of sins on his back. Finally, Help comes along and helps Christian out of the sticky mire. Going on his way, he soon falls in with Mr. Worldly Wiseman, who tries to convince Christian that he could lead a happier life if he gives up his trip toward the light and settles down to the comforts of a burdenless town life. Fearing that Christian is about to be led astray, Evangelist comes up to the two men and quickly shows the errors in Mr. Worldly Wiseman's arguments.

Soon, Christian arrives at a closed gate where he meets Good-Will, who tells him that if he knocks, the gate will be opened to him. Christian does so. He is invited into the gate-keeper's house by the Interpreter and learns from him the meaning of many of the Christian mysteries. He is shown pictures of Christ and Passion and Patience; Despair in a cage of iron bars; and a vision of the Day of Judgment, when evil people will be sent to the bottomless pit and good people will be carried up to Heaven. Christian is filled with both hope and fear after having seen these things. Continuing on his journey, he comes to the Holy Cross and the Sepulchre of Christ. There his burden of sins falls off, and he is able to take to the road with renewed vigor.

Soon he meets Sloth, Simple, Presumption, Formalism, and Hypocrisy, but he keeps to his way and they keep to theirs. Later, Christian lies down to sleep for a while. When he continues on again, he forgets to pick up the roll of paper Evangelist had given him. Remembering it later, he runs back to find it. Running to make up the time lost, he suddenly finds himself confronted by two lions. He is afraid to pass by them until the porter of the house by the side of the road tells him that the lions are chained and that he has nothing to fear. The porter then asks Christian to come into the house. There he is well treated and shown some of the relics of biblical antiquity by four virgins: Discretion, Prudence, Piety, and Charity. They give him good advice and send him on his journey, armed with the sword and shield of Christian faith.

In the Valley of Humiliation, Christian is forced to fight the giant devil, Apollyon, whose body is covered with the shiny scales of pride. Christian is wounded in this battle, but after he has chased away the devil, he heals his wounds with leaves from the Tree of Life that grew nearby. After the Valley of Humiliation comes the Valley of the Shadow of Death, in which Christian has to pass one of the gates to Hell. To save himself from the devils who issue out of the terrible hole, he recites some of the verses from the Psalms.

After passing through this danger, he has to go by the caves of the old giants, Pope and Pagan; when he has done so, he catches up with a fellow traveler, Faithful. As the two companions go along, they meet Evangelist, who warns them of the dangers in the town of Vanity Fair.

Vanity Fair is a town of ancient foundation that, since the beginning of time, has tried to lure travelers away from the path to Heaven. Here all the vanities of the world are sold, and the people who dwell there are cruel and stupid and have no love for travelers such as Christian and Faithful. After having learned these things, the two companions promise to be careful and continue into the town. There they are arrested and tried because they would buy none of the town's goods. Faithful is sentenced to be burned alive, and Christian is put in prison. When Faithful dies in the fire, a chariot comes down from Heaven and takes him up to God. Christian escapes from the prison. Accompanied by a young man named Hopeful, who had been impressed by Faithful's reward, he sets off once more.

They pass through the Valley of Ease, where they are tempted to dig in a silver mine free to all. As they leave the valley, they see the pillar of salt that had once been Lot's wife. They become lost and are captured by a giant, Despair, who lives in Doubting Castle; there they are locked in the vaults beneath the castle walls and lie there until Christian remembers he has a key called Promise in his pocket; with this, they escape from the prison.

They meet the four shepherds—Knowledge, Experience, Watchful, and Sincere—who show them the Celestial Gate and warn them of the paths to Hell. Then the two pilgrims pass by the Valley of Conceit, where they are met by Ignorance and others who had not kept to the straight-and-narrow path. They pass on to the country of Beulah. Far off, they see the gates of the city of Heaven glistening with pearls and precious stones. Thinking that all their troubles are behind them, they lie down to rest.

When they go toward the city, they come to the River of Death. They enter the river and begin to wade through the water. Soon, Christian becomes afraid, and the more afraid he gets, the deeper the waters roll. Hopeful shouts to him to have hope and faith. Cheered by these words, Christian gains confidence, the water becomes less deep, and finally, with

Hopeful, crosses the river safely. They run up the hill toward Heaven, and shining angels lead them through the gates.

Critical Evaluation:

The seventeenth century's literary greatness began with such dramatic works as William Shakespeare's *Hamlet, Prince of Denmark* (pr. c. 1600-1601, pb. 1603) and *The Tempest* (pr. 1611, pb. 1623). To the seventeenth century belongs the height of Jacobean drama, the flowering of the sonnet, and the achievements of Renaissance lyric poetry. Such works may all be considered literary products of a Humanistic century—they are the high-water mark of Humanistic philosophy with its belief in the importance of humanity and of human interests. In the middle of Humanism's great artistic accomplishment appeared John Bunyan's *The Pilgrim's Progress*. The full title of the work published in 1678 is *The Pilgrim's Progress from This World to That Which Is Come*. In 1684, Bunyan published *The Pilgrim's Progress from This World to That Which Is Come the Second Part*.

The Pilgrim's Progress reaches back to medieval literature for its dream-vision form; Bunyan's narrator goes to sleep and dreams his fable of the Christian religion. Bunyan's "novel" is a classic example of the multifaceted nature of a literary century, reflecting as it does the popularity of the conversion story during the time. What is more significant, the work shows with much skill one of the most attractive qualities of the age, for Bunyan draws on his Humanist contemporaries and their techniques to make his tale of the salvation of a soul one of the unique masterpieces of English literature.

The Pilgrim's Progress is usually classified as a novel, but according to traditional definitions of the novel genre, *The Pilgrim's Progress* is decidedly too predestined in the outcome of its plot to make it engaging, as a novel should be. The work is also so allegorical that one may decide that it is not a novel, since novels generally are somewhat realistic. It is Bunyan's literary genius that endowed the book with classic appeal. The success of *The Pilgrim's Progress*, as distinguished from the countless other stories of personal salvation that were written at about the same time, is its ability to show the Christian experience through the character Christian's eyes. By making all the pitfalls, the specters of doubt and fear, and the religious terror that Christian experiences real to this believable, impressionable narrator, Bunyan makes them just as real to his reader. Therefore, the reader of the book is really not any more sure than Christian that his salvation is assured. Bunyan has struck a true and profound element of Christianity through his use of the Humanistic technique of viewing events through the eyes of his narrator.

Christian is a gullible, hence believable, character. He understands, perhaps too well for his own soul's well-being, the doubts and terrors that plague the would-be good Christian. Christian understands how one may lose faith under dire and trying conditions. Christian himself suffers through his commitment to his faith. His journey is a test of endurance; the straight-and-narrow path is not necessarily filled with rejoicing, as Bunyan shows.

For example, Christian and his companion traveler, Hopeful, find a meadow paralleling their way and an inviting stile to help them cross the fence. So they choose the easier path. After a while, it becomes pitch dark, and they lose their way. To make matters worse, a traveler ahead of them falls into a pit and is "dashed in pieces with his fall." Christian and Hopeful rush to the pit and hear only groans. The two of them repent and muster courage to return to the river. By now, the waters have risen greatly, adding to their dangers. "Yet they adventured to go back, but it is so dark, and the flood is so high, that in their going back they had like to have been drowned nine or ten times." These are the perils and dangers of trying to be a Christian in the world. With a stroke of genius, Bunyan turns what could be a dry, pessimistic sermon into high adventure.

Bunyan seemed most productive in his own life when under duress. *The Pilgrim's Progress* was begun and largely written during prison terms that Bunyan served for preaching without a license. A Baptist minister, he was a religious outlaw after the Restoration restored the Church of England, but he refused to stop preaching. Originally arrested in 1660 and sentenced to three months, he eventually served twelve years because he continued to preach. During these years, he wrote his autobiography, *Grace Abounding to the Chief of Sinners* (1666).

In *Grace Abounding to the Chief of Sinners*, Bunyan considers himself to be a chief sinner, and he relates the experiences of his dissolute youth and of his reckless membership in the parliamentary army for three years beginning when he was sixteen years old. Therefore, readers assume that Christian's trials in *The Pilgrim's Progress* originated in real life with a man who knew temptation.

The Pilgrim's Progress has been translated into more than one hundred languages over the centuries, and the simple story's appeal continues. It combines biblical language and the subject of simple folk in a combination that has brought it popularity. Bunyan's ability to draw pictures with words has no doubt aided the novel's classic success. One critic has noted that Bunyan seems to have thought in pictures. Bunyan heightens the dramatic effect of his story, for example, with the picture of Christian opening the book at the beginning of the dream, reading, weeping, and asking, "What shall I do?"

Bunyan was apparently a simple man, or at any rate, he had a keen sense of priorities about his life. In his autobiography, he does not name his father or mother, and he hardly mentions such ordinary points in time as his birthplace or home. Such lack of detail indicates a literary intention: Bunyan aims, in his autobiography, to universalize his experience. *Grace Abounding to the Chief of Sinners* tends to emphasize Bunyan's own personal conflicts, while playing down other people in his life. Bunyan understood well what was real to him, and it is this sense of realism that has made *The Pilgrim's Progress* a classic. *The Pilgrim's Progress* is thoroughly convincing in describing the momentousness of Christian's experiences. Bunyan's ability to convey this significance endows the novel with the enduring quality of universality.

"Critical Evaluation" by Jean G. Marlowe

Further Reading

Brown, John. *John Bunyan, 1628-1688: His Life, Times, and Work*. 1885. New ed. Eugene, Oreg.: Wipf & Stock, 2007. Generally considered the definitive biography of Bunyan. Brown devotes two chapters to *The Pilgrim's Progress*, including an assessment of its literary reputation. Contains several appendixes, including a list of editions, versions, illustrations, and imitations of *The Pilgrim's Progress*.

Davies, Michael. *Graceful Reading: Theology and Narrative in the Works of John Bunyan*. New York: Oxford University Press, 2002. Davies interprets *The Pilgrim's Progress* and other works, assessing their narrative style within the context of postmodernism and examining Bunyan's theology within the context of seventeenth century Calvinism.

Dunan-Page, Anne. *Grace Overwhelming: John Bunyan, "The Pilgrim's Progress" and the Extremes of the Baptist Mind*. New York: Peter Lang, 2006. Analyzes the book from the perspective of seventeenth century religious dissent. Dunan-Page examines how Bunyan's spiritual experiences, particularly his suffering, are reflected in his work.

Furlong, Monica. *Puritan's Progress*. New York: Coward, McCann & Geoghegan, 1975. Although dated, this is an excellent starting point for research, containing a solid introduction to Bunyan and the life of the Puritans. Includes a good summarized discussion of parts 1 and 2 of *Pilgrim's Progress* and an excellent bibliography.

Hill, Christopher. *A Tinker and a Poor Man: John Bunyan and His Church, 1628-1688*. New York: Alfred A. Knopf, 1988. Examines Bunyan, his writings, his life, and the turbulent times in which he lived. Gives an extensive list of publication dates of all of Bunyan's work.

Luxon, Thomas, H. *Literal Figures: Puritan Allegory and the Reformation Crisis in Representation*. Chicago: University of Chicago Press, 1995. Discusses allegory, specifically in relation to Puritanism, and offers a solid starting point for study. Provides a modern interpretation of Bunyan and his work.

Mullett, Michael. *John Bunyan in Context*. Pittsburgh, Pa.: Duquesne University Press, 1997. Mullett's reevaluation of Bunyan's career contradicts previous biographies by depicting his subject as being less revolutionary and more opportunistic. Includes separate chapters analyzing each of Bunyan's major works. Also includes bibliographical references and an index.

Newey, Vincent, ed. *"The Pilgrim's Progress": Critical and Historical Views*. New York: Barnes & Noble, 1980. Collection of concise essays covering Bunyan, symbolism, and theology in relation to *Pilgrim's Progress*.

Owens, W. R., and Stuart Sim, eds. *Reception, Appropriation, Recollection: Bunyan's "Pilgrim's Progress."* New York: Peter Lang, 2007. Essays explore how *The Pilgrim's Progress* has been translated, adapted, illustrated, and interpreted in different cultures since its first publication. Includes discussions of the book's reception in the Romantic period and its influence on the Victorian novel and the novels of Samuel Beckett.

Sadler, Lynn Veach. *John Bunyan*. Boston: Twayne, 1979. Good summation of Bunyan's life with excellent explanations of *Pilgrim's Progress*. Includes an extensive bibliography and a chronology of Bunyan's life.

The Pillars of Society

Author: Henrik Ibsen (1828-1906)
First produced: Samfundets støtter, 1877; first published,
    1880 (English translation, 1880)
Type of work: Drama
Type of plot: Psychological realism
Time of plot: Nineteenth century
Locale: A Norwegian seaport

Principal characters:
CONSUL BERNICK, a businessman and the leader of the
    town
MRS. BERNICK, his wife
OLAF, their son
MARTHA, the consul's sister
JOHAN TONNESEN, Mrs. Bernick's brother
LONA HESSEL, Mrs. Bernick's half sister
DOCTOR RORLUND, a schoolmaster
DINA DORF, Bernick's charge
AUNE, a foreman shipbuilder

The Story:

Consul Bernick is the unquestioned leader of the town, with his wealth and influence extending into every enterprise. He owns the large shipyard that is the source of most of the townspeople's income, and he has successfully fought the project of building a seacoast railway. He also introduced machines into the yards, leading Aune, his foreman, to stir up the workers because the machines mean the loss of jobs. Bernick, not wishing to have his authority questioned, threatens Aune with loss of his job if he does not stop his speaking and writing against the machines.

There is only one breath of scandal about Consul Bernick, and that concerns his wife's family, a tale from many years before. Johan Tonnesen, Mrs. Bernick's brother, is seen leaving the rear window of the house of Mrs. Dorf, a married woman. Later, Johan leaves town and goes to America. It is said that before he left, he stole the strongbox containing Bernick's mother's fortune. What makes the matter worse is that Mrs. Bernick's half sister, Lona Hessel, follows her younger half brother to America and is like a mother to him. Only Bernick's standing in the town prevents his ruin, and he made it clear to his wife that her family is a disgrace to him.

Mrs. Dorf's husband deserts her and their daughter. When Mrs. Dorf dies soon afterward, Bernick's sister, Martha, takes the child into their home. The girl, Dina, is a constant annoyance to Bernick. Not only does she have a disgraceful background, but she talks constantly about exercising her own free will and acting independently of his desires. Doctor Rorlund, the schoolmaster, loves Dina, but he will not marry her or let anyone know of his attachment because he is afraid of the town's feelings about her. His beautiful words about goodness and kindness conceal his moral cowardice. He promises that they will be married when he can improve her position.

In the meantime, Bernick changes his mind about allowing a railroad to come to the community. Formerly, the proposed road would have competed with his shipping. Now he realizes that a spur line through the town will bring timber and minerals to his shipyard. The railroad will be a good thing for the town because it will be a good thing for Bernick. A pillar of society, he is aiding the town.

There remains constant trouble at the shipyard. The American owners of a ship Bernick is repairing had sent a cable, instructing him to get the ship under way immediately, although it is so rotted that it will require several weeks to make it safe. Bernick is torn between the profits to be gained by getting the ship afloat at once and the conscience that keeps him from sending its crew to certain death.

He grows even more disturbed because Lona and Johan have returned from America and the town has revived the old gossip. Many try to ignore the pair, but Lona refuses to be ignored. She feels no disgrace, nor does Johan. Johan and Dina are at once drawn to each other, and she begs him to take her back to America so that she can be free and independent.

Bernick and his wife will not hear of this plan, but for quite different reasons. Mrs. Bernick still feels her brother's disgrace. Bernick, however, knows that Johan is blameless. It had been Bernick, not Johan, who was forced to flee the married woman's house. Johan took the blame because he had no great reputation to save and was anxious to leave the town and strike out for himself. What he did not know was that Bernick had spread the story about the theft of his mother's money.

Johan, thinking that the town will soon have forgotten a boyish escapade with another man's wife, renews his promise not to tell that it was Bernick who had been involved. He tells Bernick that Lona knows the true story but that she will not reveal the secret. Johan is grateful to Martha, Bernick's sister, for caring for Dina. Martha had refused several offers of marriage to care for the younger girl who was so disgracefully orphaned.

Johan learns also that Martha has not married because she has always loved him and has waited for him to return. Martha tells Johan that her brother's strict moral principles make him condemn Johan and also try to turn her against him. Johan is puzzled, for he thinks Bernick has been grateful to him for assuming Bernick's own guilt. Johan cannot understand his brother-in-law's attitude.

Lona, too, forgives Bernick for his past acts, even his jilting of her in favor of her rich half sister. Bernick tells her why he had acted as he did. His mother's business had been in great danger, and he needed money to avoid bankruptcy. For that reason he had renounced Lona, whom he loves, for her wealthier relative. For the same reason, he spread the story that Johan had taken old Mrs. Bernick's money. In reality, there was no money; had the town learned the truth, it would have meant ruin for Bernick. Bernick completely justifies himself by saying that as the pillar of the town, he was forced to act deceitfully and maliciously.

Lona begs him to tell the truth at last, to keep his life from being built on a lie. Bernick says that the cost is too great; he cannot lose his money and his position. In addition, the railway project, which stands to make Bernick a millionaire, would fail with any whisper of a scandal. While he struggles with his conscience over this problem, he is still faced with the repair of the American ship. He forces Aune to get the ship ready to sail in two days—even though its unseaworthiness means death for its crew—and lays plans to pretend that Aune was the one who failed to take proper time and precautions to make the vessel safe. Bernick then plans to stop the sailing and take credit for losing his profit rather than risk the lives of the sailors. He needs public acclaim, for soon the town will learn that he had bought up all the land through which the railroad will run. It will be hard to convince the townspeople that they will benefit from his wealth.

To make matters worse, Johan becomes difficult. He had not known about the story of the theft, but he would forgive the lie if Bernick would now tell the truth. Johan wants to marry Dina, but his name must first be cleared. Bernick refuses the pleas of both Johan and Lona, lest he be ruined. He will not release Johan from his promise of secrecy. Lona will not tell the true story because she still loves Bernick. Besides, she thinks he himself should tell the truth so that he could be whole again. When Johan, planning to leave on the American ship, vows to return in two months and to tell the truth at that time, Bernick decides to allow the ship to sail. If it sinks, he will be free of Johan forever.

On the night of the sailing, Bernick arranges for a celebration in his honor for the purpose of getting the citizens into the proper frame of mind before they learn that he had bought property along the railroad route. Shortly before the celebration, he learns that his son, Olaf, had stowed away on the unseaworthy ship. He tries to call it back, but it is already out to sea. Then he is told that Johan took Dina with him to America, but that they had sailed on a different ship. He would lose his son and gain nothing.

Bernick is overjoyed when he learns that his wife had found the boy on board and brought him home before the ship sailed. Word comes also that Aune stopped the sailing of the ship and brought it back to the harbor. Bernick, saved from the evil of his deeds, stands up before the townspeople and confesses that he, and not Johan, was the guilty man. He promises also that he will share the profits from the railroad. Lona is happy. She tells Bernick that at last he has found the real pillars of society—truth and freedom. Only on them can society build a firm foundation.

Critical Evaluation:

Measured against such Henrik Ibsen masterpieces of social realism as *Et dukkehjem* (pr., pb. 1879; *A Doll's House*, 1880), *Gengangere* (pb. 1881, pr. 1882; *Ghosts*, 1885), and *Vildanden* (pb. 1884, pr. 1885; *The Wild Duck*, 1891), *The Pillars of Society* is considered an inferior work. It was, however, the drama in which Ibsen first committed himself to the realistic form and is, therefore, crucial to an understanding and appreciation of Ibsen's theater. *The Pillars of Society* contains in embryo most of the major subjects, themes, and character types that were to dominate Ibsen's plays over the succeeding dozen years. Three concerns in *The Pillars of Society* became central to his realistic dramas: the nature and powers of society, the relationship between exceptional persons and that society, and the manner in which suppressed corruption in the past inevitably surfaces to destroy present success.

Nineteenth century middle-class Norwegian society was, to Ibsen, hypocritical, materialistic, stifling, and essentially corrupt. The alliance between narrow religious moralism (with its emphasis on sin, guilt, and rigidly controlled behavior) and selfish business interests (with their respectable facade that concealed the greedy exploitation of the many by the few) led to a society that corrupted or stifled all evidence of creativity or imagination.

The exceptional individual has one of two choices: involvement or rejection. If the exceptional person accepts the community's mores and practices, the person will inevitably be corrupted; if the person rejects them, social ostracism and condemnation are the necessary consequences. Consul Bernick accepted the values and exploited them in his drive for money, power, and respectability. For the nonconformist, social isolation is the only option—if the individual is strong enough to make the break. Lona Hessel has the requisite determination and imparts enough of it to Johan Tonnesen to enable them both to flee the country. However, the price of such a divorce from their roots is great, and the impulse to return and find some sort of compromise, with all its dangers of contamination, is very strong.

In addition to presenting the pervasive atmosphere of inhibition and hypocrisy, Ibsen usually structures his realistic social plays on specific examples of concealed corruption. Bernick has based his public image, his business success, and his marriage on a lie when, as a young man, he enticed his fiancé's brother, Johan Tonnesen, into taking the blame for his illicit love affair, then later blamed him for the "theft" of the "Bernick family fortune." In Ibsen's view, however, nothing can be successfully founded on a lie. Bernick's affair with Mrs. Dorf and the subsequent voluntary disgrace of Johan necessarily tempt Bernick to expand the lie to cover his company's financial insolvency, to abandon the woman he really loves in favor of a financially advantageous match, to commit conscious fraud, and, finally, to attempt murder. In *The Pillars of Society*, as in other plays, it is a figure out of the past, Lona, who crystalizes these pressures and forces the revelation of the truth.

In spite of the complexities and ambiguities that Ibsen explores in *The Pillars of Society*, he supplies a conventional "happy ending." This final victory of optimism over dramatic logic is one of the signs that this play stands at the beginning of Ibsen's mature career. If the story is more contrived, the characters more manipulated, and the themes more boldly stated than in Ibsen's subsequent masterpieces, all of the ingredients are present in *The Pillars of Society* to make it the essential play in Ibsen's transition from an impressive, but traditional, nineteenth century playwright to his historical role as the founder of modern drama.

Further Reading

Haugen, Einar. *Ibsen's Drama: Author to Audience*. Minneapolis: University of Minnesota Press, 1979. Written by a superb teacher and scholar, this volume is a masterful introduction to Ibsen's works and their place in European cultural history. Comments on *The Pillars of Society* are found throughout the book.

Johnston, Brian. *The Ibsen Cycle: The Design of the Plays from "Pillars of Society" to "When We Dead Awaken."* Boston: Twayne, 1975. With emphasis on the philosophical content of Ibsen's later plays, this volume discusses *The Pillars of Society* in the context of nineteenth century capitalist society.

McFarlane, James. *Ibsen and Meaning: Studies, Essays, and Prefaces, 1953-87*. Norwich, England: Norvik Press, 1989. In a major contribution to Ibsen criticism, McFarlane discusses *The Pillars of Society* in the context of *A Doll's House* and *Ghosts*, concluding that Ibsen's portrait of Bernick, the male protagonist, is marked by a great deal of irony.

_____, ed. *The Cambridge Companion to Ibsen*. New York: Cambridge University Press, 1994. Collection of essays, including discussions of Ibsen's dramatic apprenticeship, historical drama, comedy, realistic problem drama, and working methods. References to *The Pillars of Society* are indexed.

Meyer, Michael. *Ibsen: A Biography*. Garden City, N.Y.: Doubleday, 1971. A standard biography of Ibsen. Contains a good discussion of *The Pillars of Society* and its place in Ibsen's oeuvre. Meyer regards this play primarily as an indictment of the universal pettiness of small-town life, but also gives a helpful summary of the play's historical background.

Moi, Toril. *Henrik Ibsen and the Birth of Modernism: Art, Theater, Philosophy*. New York: Oxford University Press, 2006. A reevaluation of Ibsen, in which literary scholar Moi refutes the traditional definition of Ibsen as a realistic and naturalistic playwright and describes him as an early modernist. References to *The Pillars of Society* are indexed.

Robinson, Michael, ed. *Turning the Century: Centennial Essays on Ibsen*. Norwich, England: Norvik Press, 2006. Collection of the essays published in the journal *Scandinavica* since the 1970's, including discussions of Ibsen's style, language, and the reception of his plays in England.

Weigand, Herman J. *The Modern Ibsen: A Reconsideration*. New York: Holt, 1925. Reprint. Salem, N.H.: Ayer, 1984. An excellent introduction to Ibsen's later plays, this volume contains a good essay on *The Pillars of Society*. Weigand finds the play interesting although it not representative of Ibsen's best work.

The Pilot
A Tale of the Sea

Author: James Fenimore Cooper (1789-1851)
First published: 1823
Type of work: Novel
Type of plot: Historical
Time of plot: Late eighteenth century
Locale: Northeastern coast of England

Principal characters:
LIEUTENANT RICHARD BARNSTABLE, the commander of the *Ariel*
MR. EDWARD GRIFFITH, an officer aboard an American frigate
LONG TOM COFFIN, the coxswain of the *Ariel*
MR. MERRY, a midshipman
MR. GRAY, the pilot, in reality John Paul Jones
COLONEL HOWARD, a Tory
KATHERINE PLOWDEN, his niece
CECILIA HOWARD, another niece of Colonel Howard
CAPTAIN MANUAL, an officer of the marine corps
CAPTAIN BORROUGHCLIFFE, a British officer
CHRISTOPHER DILLON, a kinsman of Colonel Howard
ALICE DUNSCOMBE, a friend of Katherine and Cecilia

The Story:

Toward the close of a bleak wintry day during the American Revolution, a small schooner and a frigate sail through shoal waters off the northeastern coast of England and anchor in a small bay beneath some towering cliffs. As darkness settles, a whaleboat is put ashore from the schooner *Ariel*. The boat is in the charge of the *Ariel*'s commander, Lieutenant Richard Barnstable, who has been ordered to make a landing near the cliffs and retrieve a pilot known only as Mr. Gray.

With the aid of a weather-beaten old Nantucket whaler, Long Tom Coffin, Barnstable climbs the cliff and there meets his mysterious passenger, a man of middle height and sparing speech. Before he completes his mission, however, he also encounters Katherine Plowden, his fiancé, who gives him a letter and a signal book. The woman is staying temporarily at the St. Ruth's Abbey manor house, the home of her uncle, Colonel Howard, a wealthy South Carolina Tory who had fled from America at the outbreak of the war. From her, Barnstable learns that another niece, Cecilia Howard, and her friend, Alice Dunscombe, also guests at the abbey as well. Cecilia Howard is in love with Lieutenant Edward Griffith, first officer aboard the frigate. Alice Dunscombe is reported to be in love with the mysterious pilot, but she refuses to marry him because she is completely Loyalist in her sympathies.

Darkness had fallen by the time the pilot was brought to the deck of the frigate, and a storm is now rising. Only Captain Munson of the frigate knows the pilot's identity, a secret concealed from everyone else aboard the ship and its escort, the *Ariel*. Captain Munson, seeing the pilot by the light of the battle lanterns on deck, thinks him greatly changed in appearance since their last meeting.

As the storm rises, the pilot guides the frigate safely through dangerous, wind-lashed shoal waters and out to open sea. At sunrise, the frigate signals the *Ariel* and orders Barnstable to go aboard the larger ship for a council of war. There, plans are made to harass the English by sending landing parties ashore to raid the mansions and estates of the gentry in the neighborhood.

Barnstable wants these expeditions to serve another purpose, for he hopes to rescue Katherine Plowden and Cecilia Howard from the abbey, where they live unhappily with Colonel Howard, their uncle and guardian.

Meanwhile, at the abbey, Colonel Howard is holding a conference with Christopher Dillon, a kinsman, and Captain Borroughcliffe, a British officer in charge of a small detachment of troops stationed at the abbey. Dillon, an impoverished gentleman, hopes to marry, with the colonel's approval, one of his wealthy cousins. The three men discuss the progress of the American Revolution, other political questions, and the piracies of John Paul Jones. They agree that extra precautions should be taken, for there are rumors that Jones himself has been seen in the neighborhood.

That night, Griffith and the pilot, accompanied by a marine corps officer, Captain Manual, go ashore on a scouting expedition. As a result of Griffith's imprudent conduct, they are seen and seized. When a sentry reports the arrest of strange seamen lurking in the neighborhood, Captain Borroughcliffe orders them brought to the abbey for examination.

On their arrival at the abbey, the prisoners say only that they are seamen out of employment, a suspicious circumstance in itself. When the seamen offer no further information of any consequence, they are imprisoned to await Borroughcliffe's pleasure. Katherine and Cecilia bribe the sentry on duty and obtain permission to visit the prisoners. They recognize Griffith in disguise. Alice Dunscombe also visits the pilot, whom she recognizes. After drinking too much wine at dinner, Borroughcliffe begins to interview the men and, in his intoxicated condition, unwittingly helps them escape.

Believing that the men had come from a ship lying offshore, Dillon mounts a horse and rides to a neighboring bay, where the war cutter *Alacrity* lays at anchor. Alarmed at the possible presence of an American ship in the area, the cutter puts out to sea, with Dillon among its volunteer crew. Barnstable and Long Tom Coffin, waiting in the *Ariel*'s whaleboat, engage the cutter in a furious battle that ends when Coffin pins the captain of the cutter to the mast with his whaler's harpoon. Dillon is among the prisoners taken. Frightened, he offers to return to the abbey and, in return for his own freedom, secure the release of the Americans held there.

After their escape, the pilot leaves Griffith and Manual, who rejoin a party of marines who had remained in hiding while their captain was with Griffith and the pilot, reconnoitering the abbey. Attacked by Borroughcliffe and his troops, the marines are surrounded. Griffith is recaptured, and Manual is forced to surrender.

Trusting Dillon's word of honor, Barnstable sends Long Tom Coffin with Dillon to the abbey to arrange for the transfer of prisoners. Dillon, however, dishonoring his parole, has Coffin held prisoner while he and Borroughcliffe plan to trap Barnstable and his men. When Borroughcliffe boasts of his intentions, Coffin makes a surprise attack upon him and seizes and binds the British officer. He then follows Dillon to the apartments of Katherine and Cecilia and there take Dillon prisoner. He succeeds in getting Dillon aboard the *Ariel*, as a British battery on the shore opens fire on the schooner. A lucky shot wrecks the mainmast as the schooner puts out to sea, where a heavy storm completes the *Ariel*'s destruction.

Barnstable, a true captain, decides to go down with his ship, and he orders Mr. Merry, a midshipman, to take charge of the crew and lower the boats. Coffin throws Barnstable overboard, saving his commander's life. The ship goes down with Coffin and Dillon aboard. When Dillon's body is later washed up by the sea, Barnstable orders his burial. Shortly afterward, Mr. Merry appears at the abbey in the disguise of a peddler. Barnstable signals by means of flags to Katherine, using signals from the code book which she had given him. Later, they meet secretly and lay plans for surprising the abbey and the soldiers who guard it. Borroughcliffe hears of the plot, however, and Barnstable walks into Borroughcliffe's ambush. At this juncture, however, the pilot arrives with a party of marines from the frigate and makes prisoners of the Tories and the British.

Later, Griffith releases Borroughcliffe and his soldiers because Borroughcliffe had behaved in an honorable manner toward his prisoners. There is a final interview between Alice Dunscombe and the pilot. During their talk, she addresses him as John and says that if she should speak his real name, the whole countryside would ring with it. The pilot insists that he will continue his activities for the cause of patriotism, regardless of the unsavory reputation it might gain for him in England. Colonel Howard and his two nieces are taken aboard the frigate for the return voyage to America.

The American ship is not yet out of danger. The next morning, a man-of-war breaks through the morning mists, its decks cleared for action. There is tremendous activity aboard the frigate in preparation for the battle, and the women are taken below for safety as the English ship of the line blazes a three-tiered broadside at the American vessel. One shot strikes Captain Munson and cuts him down. Griffith, who now knows the pilot's identity, begs for permission to reveal it to the crew, to encourage them in the fight, but the pilot refuses. Meanwhile, the British ship has been reinforced by two others, but the Americans are lucky enough to disable the smallest of their attackers. Then, as the other ships close in upon the battered American ship, the pilot takes the wheel and daringly guides the vessel through the shoal waters that only he knows well. Outmaneuvered, the pursuing British ships drop behind.

Colonel Howard, wounded during the engagement, lives long enough to see his nieces married by the ship's chaplain to their lovers. He dies insisting that he is too old to change his politics, and he blesses the king.

The frigate sails to Holland, where the pilot is put ashore. To all but Griffith, among those who watch his small boat dwindling to a speck against the horizon, his identity remains a mystery.

Critical Evaluation:

The Pilot is a novel that combines military adventure, a certain romantic interest, and a political analysis within the confines of a particular historical era. The mixture is not always successful, but aspects of *The Pilot* remain interesting as both literature and political argument.

James Fenimore Cooper said that *The Pilot* was originally conceived as a sea novel, one that would be accurate in its details of naval life and strategy. One way that Cooper demonstrates his expertise is in the multitude and variety of the technical terms he uses. This terminology is so pervasive in *The Pilot* that much of the action, especially during sea battles, is nearly incomprehensible. On the other hand, this mystification (resembling the "wood lore" of the Leatherstocking series) does work to make the pilot himself, the hero of the novel, appear superhuman. The reader, to whom much of the terminology remains inaccessible, can only marvel at the skill and knowledge of Cooper's hero, who not only defeats the enemy in several battles but stands above the other officers (such as Griffith) in seafaring skill.

In *The Pilot*, Cooper claims to have drawn his characters according to "palpable nature," without reference to unknown or metaphysical qualities. This intention, though undoubtedly sincere (and a reaction against the excesses of romantic fiction), is not carried out in practice in regard to the pilot himself who, the reader is meant to understand, embodies the ideal qualities of a leader. For example, the pilot is calm even under the most severe stress. Cooper opens the novel with Mr. Gray extricating the ship from a severe storm. Everyone else is terrified, and with good reason, it appears, but the pilot is completely steady and absolutely unafraid.

Furthermore, when the pilot gives an order, the crew obeys as if he were the commander. Cooper describes this obedience in almost mystical terms. The pilot is able to impose discipline when no one else can. So Cooper's intention to describe his characters only according to palpable nature is subordinated to the need he felt for portraying an authentic leader, hero, and warrior. This need flows from the political intent of the work. *The Pilot* raises a political question that was important in Cooper's own life and, more significantly, was critical during the Revolutionary War. The issue was one of loyalty.

The Pilot is a novel centered on characters torn between conflicting loyalties. When the American War of Independence began, men and women in the colonies were faced with a clear choice. Those Americans who remained loyal to England were disloyal to the emerging nation. Those who fought on the side of the revolution were accused of treason. This accusation is, for example, repeated frequently by Colonel Howard and his supporters against the rebels.

To answer this charge, it was necessary for Cooper to show both that a noble conception of loyalty was maintained by the Americans and that there were leaders among the rebels—wise, cool-headed, and selfless—who could inspire genuine loyalty. It was to fill this requirement that Gray is described by Cooper as an authentic leader and hero and, most of all, is defended against the charge of treason. (John Paul Jones, born in Scotland, served in the English merchant marine before emigrating to America.) Treason and loyalty, then, cease being absolute terms, as Colonel Howard argues, and become politically relative.

It is in the romantic threads of the novel that Cooper attempts to show the divisions of loyalty, and the relative nature of the term, in its sharpest and most dramatic form. Alice Dunscombe is an old friend and sweetheart of Gray, but she was born in England and, unlike Gray, has remained passionately loyal to the land of her birth. The two are united in the friendship of the past and, indeed, in their current feelings for each other. At the same time, they are divided by conflicting political loyalties. Thus, the reader is asked to judge the political beliefs and feelings of characters, not in absolute terms but in historical terms. Cooper wants these characters understood as they understand themselves; so, although readers may tend to sympathize with the views of one rather than the other, they are still able to feel sympathy for each as a person.

The villain in *The Pilot* is Christopher Dillon; Dillon's villainy lies not in his loyalty to England and to Colonel Howard, but in his cowardice and opportunism. Mr. Gray, or John Paul Jones, has not committed treason, precisely because he is loyal to his own beliefs; he is honest and not a coward—because he openly defends what he believes. The content of these beliefs is another matter. As characters such as Alice Dunscombe and Colonel Howard debate with the Americans, two distinct political positions emerge. On the one hand, the colonel supports a notion of loyalty based on birth and on the established social and political order. Disruption of that order, he argues, leads to nothing but misery and bloodshed. The Americans answer that loyalty can only be freely and consciously given. Theirs is a romantic view, derived from the theory of social contract, a theory that states that political society is based only upon the agreement of each of its members to participate. Hence the Americans argue that they are loyal only to liberty and, furthermore, that liberty is a necessary condition for genuine loyalty. Cooper does capture the political arguments raging during the Revolutionary War. He not only expresses these arguments in terms of conflicting loyalties, but he also penetrates the political assumptions behind the labels.

The Pilot, however, suffers from a weakness common to many novels that attempt to explore the political reality within a historical conflict. This weakness is especially evident in Cooper's big scenes (those scenes, for example, between Alice Dunscombe and John Paul Jones), in which there is a tendency for characters to make speeches to the reader rather than to talk with one another. In other words, the ideas are expressed verbally rather than through dramatic action.

In *The Pilot*, Cooper faced the double necessity of creating a hero—which he could accomplish through action at sea—and, at the same time, of exploring the historical and political motives of that hero. The shape of *The Pilot*, and its strengths and weaknesses as a novel, flow from Cooper's attempt to resolve this difficulty.

Howard Lee Hertz

Further Reading

Darnell, Donald. "Manners in a Revolution: *The Spy*, *The Pilot*, and *Lionel Lincoln*." In *James Fenimore Cooper: Novelist of Manners*. Newark: University of Delaware Press, 1993. Discusses Cooper's ambivalence toward his hero, John Paul Jones, a strong leader of questionable ethics. Darnell believes Cooper's criticism of Jones stems from Jones's humble birth, which makes him unfit for true heroism.

Franklin, Wayne. *James Fenimore Cooper: The Early Years*. New Haven, Conn.: Yale University Press, 2007. Part one of a biography of Cooper covering his life from birth until he departed for Europe in 1826. This volume describes the creation and publication of *The Pilot*. The many references to the novel are listed in the index, with much of the relevant material contained in chapter 13, "Old Tales and New."

House, Kay Seymour. "The Unstable Element." In *James Fenimore Cooper: A Collection of Critical Essays*, edited by Wayne Fields. Englewood Cliffs, N.J.: Prentice-Hall, 1979. Describes how the sea functions for Cooper's seamen much as the forest does for his frontiersmen. Long Tom Coffin shares many traits with Natty Bumppo, and both show what can happen to the common person when challenged by the elements.

Person, Leland S., ed. *A Historical Guide to James Fenimore Cooper*. New York: Oxford University Press, 2007. Collection of essays, including a brief biography by Cooper and a survey of Cooper scholarship and criticism. *The Pilot* is discussed in the chapter "'More than a Woman's Enterprise': Cooper's Revolutionary Heroines and the Compromise of Domesticity." Features an illustrated chronology of Cooper's life and important nineteenth century historical events.

Philbrick, Thomas. *James Fenimore Cooper and the Development of American Sea Fiction*. Cambridge, Mass.: Harvard University Press, 1961. Claims Cooper created the genre of the American sea novel. Shows how Cooper drew from history and from British writers to compose *The Pilot*.

Ringe, Donald A. *James Fenimore Cooper*. New York: Twayne, 1962. Remains one of the best book-length introductions to Cooper. The brief section on *The Pilot* describes the novel's themes and influences, and shows the importance of the physical environment to this work.

Walker, Warren S. "The Gull's Way." In *James Fenimore Cooper: An Introduction and Interpretation*. New York: Holt, Rinehart and Winston, 1962. Describes how *The Pilot* established the genre of the sea novel in the United States, and traces the influences of earlier British sea novels. Includes a chronology and a bibliography.

Pincher Martin

Author: William Golding (1911-1993)
First published: 1956
Type of work: Novel
Type of plot: Psychological realism
Time of plot: World War II
Locale: Mid-Atlantic Ocean

Principal characters:
CHRISTOPHER MARTIN, British navy crewman
NATHANIEL, his shipmate and friend
MARY, Nathaniel's fiancé
MR. CAMPBELL and MR. DAVIDSON, searchers in the rescue

The Story:

Christopher Martin is a crew member of the English destroyer *The Wildebeest*, which was just sunk by a German torpedo in the Mid-Atlantic. Martin does not make it into the safety boats that others manage to get aboard. He has his life-belt on, however, and after the ship sinks, he works to inflate the belt. He succeeds in this, and then, in his own imagination, he manages to kick off his seaboots. Martin begins his struggle to survive in the Mid-Atlantic.

Martin is trying to keep mind and body together. At times, he transcends his physical situation and sees himself as pure mind. He has an enormous will to survive, and it is this struggle of will that readers encounter in the novel; Martin insists, "I will not die!"

After believing himself to have successfully removed his seaboots, Martin begins the impossible task of orienting himself in a reality in which the horizon is the same, no matter which way he looks. The first order of business is to get through the night. Without the aid of a compass, Martin has to wait until dawn to get a sense of where he is. He focuses on a "bright patch" against the sky; he decides that he is not far from the coast of North Africa.

The physical suffering that Martin endures is detailed in the opening seventy-five pages of the novel. Not only does Martin have to survive the blistering rays of the sun glinting off the ocean, but he also has to fight fatigue and the harsh effects of the saltwater. During this time, Martin's mind flashes back to his memories of his friend and shipmate, Nathaniel. Nathaniel had seemed the least likely to survive, but, in Martin's imagination, Nathaniel had made it into a lifeboat. Martin, who had been in the crow's nest when the destroyer was hit, had called for Nathaniel's help but received no immediate response. Martin now spends much of his psychic energy worrying that he did not give the correct call regarding the ship's position and the position of the destroyer that had launched the fatal torpedo. He finally decides that he made the right call, and those thoughts no longer torment him.

Miraculously, Martin is washed up on a large cluster of rocks that surface seemingly out of nowhere. On this rocky surface, Martin clings to life, fighting off not only despair and fatigue but also the life-threatening presence of the limpets that feed off the waters surrounding the rock. For some time, Martin fights his way through the limpets; he finally gains supremacy—tentatively—of the rocky surface.

As Martin gets more desperate, he realizes that he must fight not only the elements but also the threat of madness. Physical survival is difficult, but Martin finds fresh rainwater in small pools across the rock, and he protects himself from the tempests and the scorch of the sun by wedging himself into a crevice. Crablike, he retreats to this crevice when danger gets intolerable.

At one point, Martin questions his sanity when he sees a red lobster feeding from the rock just below the water's surface. He questions his sanity at this point because lobsters are not red when they are alive; they only turn that color as they are being boiled to death.

Martin begins to see pictures, and as Martin's chances for survival become less and less, the pictures get brighter and more real. These pictures include scenes in which he tries to seduce Mary, the woman whom Nathaniel had intended to marry. Martin recalls Mary struggling to remove herself from his presence. She fights him off by pushing down her skirt and telling him that she wants nothing to do with him. Martin recalls the shock and the sense of betrayal that he felt when Nathaniel told him that he wanted to wed Mary.

Many times during his ordeal, Martin wishes that he had saved his seaboots because the cold and the harshness of the ocean are causing him great pain. At the same time, it is getting difficult to concentrate on his survival and do what he can to aid in a rescue. At one point, Martin imagines that he has affixed a piece of tinfoil to the highest part of the rock. He hopes that this piece of foil will give off reflections that rescue ships in the area will pick up.

Throughout his ordeal on the rock, Martin's mind wanders to memories of his friends and of women he tried to love. The pictures of these memories alternately cause him anguish and hope. He repeats to himself that his mind and his body have not yet completely separated, and his ability to recall the pictures is proof that he is still alive. Finally, however, the elements are too much for Martin to withstand. At this point, the novel shifts to the perspective of Mr. Campbell and Mr. Davidson, who are searchers in the rescue effort. As they pull Martin's lifeless body out of the water, Mr. Davidson curses the lifebelt, for it gives hope in hopeless circumstances. Mr. Campbell wonders if Martin had suffered a great deal. Mr. Davidson tells him not to worry; after all, Martin is still wearing his seaboots—he had not even had time to kick them off.

Critical Evaluation:

Published in 1956, William Golding's *Pincher Martin* is one of the strongest literary links between the age of British high modernism and the postmodern novel. The novel has been overlooked for many years, but it has begun to receive the attention that it deserves. In many ways, *Pincher Martin* is a literary achievement on the scale of James Joyce's *Ulysses* (1922) and Virginia Woolf's *Mrs. Dalloway* (1925). Although *Pincher Martin* lacks the symbolic scope of these earlier novels, it is, just as they were, concerned with the mental processes of a main character observed over a relatively short span of time. In *Pincher Martin*'s case, this time span is the life that can be lived and fought for in the very brief minutes before death.

Joyce and Woolf focused on the extension of the modern novel and used both realism and symbolism, but Golding was much more concerned with the allegorical relationship between seen reality and hidden reality. The medieval allegorist took as the starting point of meaning the intersection between the physical and spiritual worlds, but Golding worked his allegory in the intersection between the physical world and the world of the subconscious.

As the American title, *The Two Deaths of Christopher Martin*, implies, the story concerns Christopher Martin's struggle to survive both physical and metaphysical death. The novel is one of psychological realism, but the main focus of the work is on one person's ontology, or being, in the world.

The first focus of Martin's ontological status after the shipwreck is his determination to lighten himself, thus increasing his chances for survival, by removing his seaboots. He believes that he has accomplished this feat, and he begins to hope for survival. His lifebelt, an allegorical symbol for the reality of hope, becomes his next focus. He relies on his lifebelt to hold him above the waters, but as the novel demonstrates, he still takes in enormous amounts of water—amounts that will drown him, though his will to live survives.

It is the focus on this will to live that forms the major drama of the first half of the novel. Martin continues to insist, long after the physical point of death, that he will not die. At first, this will to live engages readers in a sympathetic struggle for survival along with Martin. Readers are enthralled by the drama and can hope, along with Martin, that this will to live will, indeed, save him.

Rescue remains a virtual impossibility through Martin's psychological survival on the rock. It becomes clear that Martin is obsessed with a fear of death, rather than with being saved by a will to live. This will to live parallels the "will to power" that has influenced questions of the role will plays in the determination of not only life and death but also people's everyday negotiations with the world.

As important as this struggle of will is for Martin, Golding also makes the point that for the "will to survive" to have any meaning, there must be a point of reference for people to refer to to center their being. This point of reference is at first completely lacking in Martin's struggle. Shipwrecked at night, with no reference point by which to orient himself, Martin is allegorically cast from and into an amniotic life where external references are lacking. In this opening section of the book, Martin struggles by focusing completely on himself. He becomes his own center to his own universe. His lifebelt—a symbol, as Mr. Davidson says at the end of the novel, of false hope—along with his struggle to remove his seaboots, become the reference points on which Martin must focus.

This struggle to find reference points for hope and a meaning in life is allegorized by Golding in the references to the Christian faith. First, Martin's own first name, Christopher, recalls the legend of the man who bore the Christ child across dangerous waters and who was then given his name, meaning "Christ-bearer." Martin's failure causes readers to question the simplicity of an understanding of life that merely floats along the surface of experience. The rock that Martin imagines himself as having reached is symbolic of the "rock," or St. Peter, upon which Christ founded his church. Again, the rock, as readers learn at the end of the novel, is a figment of Martin's imagination and permits the questioning of the foundations of faith.

Finally, Martin's recollections of his seemingly inferior partner, Nathaniel, reinforce the Christian symbolism of the novel. Nathaniel, it is to be remembered, was a disciple of Christ and was, in fact, that disciple in which Christ found no guile. In the novel, the Nathaniel of Martin's imagination is also a figure of guilelessness, his innocence underscored by his pledge to marry Mary, a woman whose name extends the symbolism of the Christian story allegorized in Martin's struggle for survival.

Finally, Golding's novel displays the many ways in which psychology has come to figure in people's lives. There is much imagery of the subconscious, with perhaps the lobster, a scuttling creature whose presence invokes a reference to T. S. Eliot's Prufrock. The lobster represents the unnatural circumstance of Martin's "two deaths"—the death of the body and the death of consciousness. The novel lends itself to interpretations along psychological, symbolic, allegorical, and archetypal lines.

Susan M. Rochette-Crawley

Further Reading

Babb, Howard S. *The Novels of William Golding*. Athens: Ohio State University Press, 1970. In his chapter on *Pincher Martin*, Babb sees the novel as Golding's most "problematic." Babb focuses on the difficulty of reading the novel and character Christopher Martin's extreme rationality.

Dick, Bernard F. *William Golding*. Boston: Twayne, 1987. In the Twayne series tradition, this book serves as an excellent starting point. Contains a chronology and, in the section on *Pincher Martin*, focuses upon the existential aspects of the novel.

Kinkead-Weekes, Martin, and Ian Gregor. *William Golding: A Critical Study*. 3d rev. ed. London: Faber, 2002. An updated edition of one of the standard critical accounts of Golding that features a biographical sketch by Golding's daughter, Judy Carver. In the section on *Pincher Martin*,

Kinkead-Weekes and Gregor struggle with the question of realism that the novel poses.

McCarron, Kevin. *William Golding.* 2d rev. ed. Tavistock, England: Northcote House/British Council, 2006. An introductory overview of Golding's life and works. Includes a bibliography and an index. Good as an updated resource.

Tiger, Virginia. *William Golding: The Unmoved Target.* New York: Marion Boyars, 2003. An examination of Golding's novels in which Tiger draws upon her conversations and correspondence with the author to describe how these books explore themes of human destiny and vision. Devotes a chapter to an analysis of *Pincher Martin.*

The Pioneers
Or, The Sources of the Susquehanna

Author: James Fenimore Cooper (1789-1851)
First published: 1823
Type of work: Novel
Type of plot: Historical
Time of plot: 1793
Locale: New York State

Principal characters:
JUDGE TEMPLE, a frontier landowner
ELIZABETH TEMPLE, his daughter
NATTY BUMPPO, an old hunter, also known as Leatherstocking
OLIVER EDWARDS, Natty's young friend
INDIAN JOHN, Natty's American Indian companion
HIRAM DOOLITTLE, a local magistrate

The Story:

On a cold December day in 1793, Judge Temple and his daughter, Elizabeth, are traveling by sleigh through a snow-covered tract of wilderness near the settlement of Templeton. Elizabeth, who has been away from her home attending a female seminary, is now returning to preside over her father's household in the community in which he had been a pioneer settler after the Revolutionary War. Hearing the baying of hounds, the judge decides that Leatherstocking, an old hunter, has startled game in the hills, and he orders his coachman to stop the sleigh so he can have a shot at the deer if it comes in his direction. A few minutes later, as a great buck leaps onto the road, the judge fires both barrels of his fowling piece at the animal, apparently without effect. Then a third report and a fourth are heard, and the buck drops dead in a snowbank.

At the same time, Natty Bumppo, the old hunter, and a young companion appear from the woodland. The judge insists that he shot the buck, but Leatherstocking, by accounting for all the shots fired, proves that the judge could not have killed the animal. The argument ends when the young stranger reveals that he had been wounded by one of the shots fired by the judge. Elizabeth and her father then insist that he accompany them into the village in their sleigh, so he could have his wound dressed as soon as possible.

The young man gets into the sleigh with obvious reluctance and says little during the drive. In a short time, the party arrives at the Temple mansion, where his wound is treated. In answer to the judge's questions, he gives his name as Oliver Edwards. His manner remains distant and reserved. After he departs, a servant in the Temple home reports that Edwards had appeared three weeks before in the company of old Leatherstocking and that he lives in a nearby cabin with the hunter and an American Indian known as Indian John.

Judge Temple, wishing to make amends for having accidentally wounded Edwards, offers him a position as his secretary. When Elizabeth adds her own entreaties to those of her father, Edwards finally accepts the judge's offer, with the understanding that he will be free to terminate his employment at any time. For a while, he attends faithfully and earnestly to his duties in Judge Temple's mansion during the day, but his nights are spent in Leatherstocking's cabin. So much secrecy surrounds his comings and goings, and the reserve of Leatherstocking and his Indian friend, that Richard Jones, the sheriff and a kinsman of the judge, gets suspicious. Among other things, he wonders why Natty always keeps his cabin closed and never allows anyone except the Indian and Edwards to enter it. Jones and some others decide that Natty had discovered a mine and is now working it.

Jones also suspects that Edwards is part Indian, his father a Delaware chief.

Hiram Doolittle, the local magistrate, prowls around the shack and sets the dogs guarding it free. In the meantime, Elizabeth and Louisa Grant, the minister's daughter, go for a walk in the woods. There they are attacked by a savage panther and are saved only by the timely arrival of Leatherstocking, who shoots the animal. Natty, however, had also shot a deer, in defiance of Judge Temple's strict game laws. With the charge that the old hunter had killed a deer out of season as his pretext, Doolittle persuades Judge Temple to sign a warrant so that the magistrate can gain entrance into the cabin and search it. Jones is more convinced than ever that Leatherstocking is secretly smelting ore from a mine.

Doolittle, now at the cabin, is refused entrance by Leatherstocking, who has a rifle in hand. Then the magistrate attempts to force his way over the threshold, but the old hunter seizes him and throws him twenty feet down an embankment. As the result of his mistreatment of an officer, Leatherstocking is arrested. Found guilty, he is given a month's jail sentence and a fine, and is placed in the stocks for a few hours. When Elizabeth attempts to see what assistance she can give the humiliated old woodsman, she learns that he is planning to escape. Edwards, who had given up his position with the judge, is planning to flee with his old friend; he provided a cart in which to carry the old hunter to safety. Elizabeth promises to meet Leatherstocking the following day on the top of a nearby mountain and to bring with her a can of gunpowder.

The next day, Elizabeth and her friend, Louisa, start out on their expedition to meet Leatherstocking. On the way, Louisa changes her mind and turns back, declaring that she dare not walk unprotected through the woods where they had lately been menaced by a panther. Elizabeth continues on alone until she comes to a clearing in which she finds old Indian John, now dressed in the war costume and feathers of a great Mohican chief. When she stops to speak to Indian John, she suddenly becomes aware of dense clouds of smoke drifting across the clearing and discovers that the whole mountainside is ablaze. At that moment, Edwards appears, followed by Leatherstocking, who leads them to a cave in the side of the mountain. There the old Indian dies of exhaustion, and Elizabeth learns that he had been in earlier days Chingachgook, a great and noble warrior of the Mohican tribe. When danger of the fire passes, Edwards conducts Elizabeth down the mountainside until she is within hearing of a party of men who are looking for her. Before they part, Edwards promises he will soon reveal his true identity.

The next day, the sheriff leads a posse up the mountain in search of Leatherstocking and those who aided him in his escape from jail. Leatherstocking is again prepared to defend the cave to which he had taken Elizabeth the day before with his rifle, but Edwards declares that the time has now come to let the truth be known. He and Natty bring from the depths of the cave an old man seated in a chair. The stranger's face is grave and dignified, but his vacant eyes show that his mind is gone. Edwards announces that the old man is really the owner of the property on which they stand. Judge Temple interrupts with a shout of surprise and greets the old man as Major Effingham.

The young man tells his story. His name, he says, is Edward Oliver Effingham, and he is the grandson of the old man who sits before them. His own father had been, before the revolutionary war, a close friend of Judge Temple. They had gone into business together, but the outbreak of the war found them on opposite sides during the struggle. Judge Temple had some money entrusted to him by his friend, money that actually belongs to his friend's father, but when he received no reply to letters he wrote to the Effinghams, he at last decided that all the family had been lost in a shipwreck off Nova Scotia. He invested the money in his own enterprises.

The judge had never met Major Effingham; he would not have recognized him if he had seen the helpless old man who had for years been hidden in the cabin on the outskirts of Templeton. During those years, he was nursed faithfully by Leatherstocking and his Indian friend; by Leatherstocking because he had served with the major on the frontier years before, by Indian John because the major was an adopted member of the Mohican tribe.

Judge Temple orders that the old man be carried to the Temple mansion at once, where he will receive the best of care. Old Major Effingham thinks himself back home once more, and his eyes gleam with joy. He dies, happy and well cared for, soon afterward.

Edward Effingham also explains his belief that Judge Temple had stolen his father's property and the money left in trust years before. In his resentment, he came to Templeton to assist his grandfather and to regain in some manner the property that he believed Judge Temple had unrightfully possessed. Now the judge is happy to return that part of the property that belongs to the Effinghams, and there is a reconciliation between the two men. As it turns out, however, the property stays in the family, for Elizabeth and Edward Effingham are married within a short time.

Elizabeth and Edward want to build a new cabin for Leatherstocking, but the old hunter refuses their offer. He intends to go off into the woods to hunt and trap in the free wilderness until he dies. Settlements and towns are not for him.

He does not listen to their pleas and sets out on his long journey, pausing only long enough to view the stone tablet on Indian John's grave, a monument that Edward Effingham had erected. Then he trudges off toward the woods, his long rifle over his shoulder. Elizabeth and her husband watch him go. Tears are in their eyes as they wave a last farewell to the old hunter just before he disappears into the forest.

Critical Evaluation:

At the time that *The Pioneers* was written, authors in the United States were working on establishing a definitive American fiction, one that drew from the rich literary tradition of Europe but still reflected the newly emerging character of the young country. Hailed as the American Sir Walter Scott, James Fenimoore Cooper appeared to be the writer who would spearhead the development of a characteristically American literature. Cooper's novels had the stirring adventure, moral concerns, elevated sentiment, and sense of historical significance that Scott's works possessed. The Leatherstocking tales, as a series of Cooper's novels came to be called, also portrayed a distinctively American scene, focusing on characters and issues unique to the American experience. Like the other Leatherstocking novels, *The Pioneers* deals with many issues important to the new America: the vanishing frontier, the making of law, property rights, the role of class in a new democracy, and the treatment of Native Americans.

Although skinny old Natty Bumppo hardly seems a nineteenth century romantic hero (his handsome young friend Oliver Edwards was intended to fulfill that type), his popularity led Cooper to write four more novels tracing the hunter's adventures as a youth to his death as an old man: *The Last of the Mohicans* (1826), *The Prairie* (1827), *The Pathfinder* (1840), and *The Deerslayer* (1841). Cooper's series first established the frontier hero as an American legend who would continue to grace novels, film, and television. Leatherstocking is a mythic figure, possessing almost superhuman abilities even as an old man. He has the skill to shoot through a turkey's head from one hundred yards away and the strength to save the character Benjamin from drowning by lifting him out of the water with a fishing spear. He seems to run through walls of fire when he saves Elizabeth, Judge Temple's daughter, on the burning mountain. Natty represents the "natural man," akin to French philosopher Jean-Jacques Rousseau's "noble savage," an uncompromising individualist living outside social and institutional boundaries.

The novel's opening scene, in which Natty and Judge Temple both lay claim to the slain deer, embodies the novel's central theme. In the conflict between Natty and Temple, the interest in preserving the wilderness encounters civilization's desire to domesticate it. Natty witnesses the rapid encroachment of civilization on his beloved wilderness. Living peacefully in nature, altering it only slightly to fulfill his limited needs, Natty laments the changes wrought by the growing town of Templeton. He abhors the "wasty ways" of the townspeople, who shoot hundreds of pigeons at one time using cannons, trap thousands of fish in their large nets, and chop down huge numbers of trees for their fireplaces. Temple, with an Anglo-European education and a middle-class background, represents the civilized man. He values the environment not for its own sake, like Natty, but for its usefulness to society. He also represents an American ideal. Like Cooper's father (founder of Cooperstown, New York), Temple is a loyal American; having supported the revolutionary cause, he is now helping to build the country by establishing a small town in the middle of the wilderness.

Law and land are pervasive themes. Temple believes in written law, while Natty follows the natural law. Natty had been living upon the land years before it became the town of Templeton. The game laws and property rights established by the newly emerging institutions seem ridiculous to him. A person should be allowed to shoot a deer at anytime and at any place, Natty believes. He hunts responsibly and sparingly in contrast to the wasteful methods of the townspeople; he clearly adheres to the spirit of the law. Ironically, however, he is caught by the letter of the law.

Charged with violating the game laws and assaulting Hiram Doolittle, a deceitful and blundering fool, Natty stands trial. The trial and his imprisonment are a cruelly pathetic display. This harmless frontiersman is painfully out of place in the institutional arena of written law. Cooper complicates the notion of law, showing that it is rarely black and white and often administered inequitably. Natty is thrown in prison for shooting a deer, but Judge Temple suffers no consequences for wounding Oliver. Temple is faced with passing judgment on a man who has saved his daughter's life, a man he knows does not deserve punishment. For the sake of preserving the image of the law, Temple tries to have it both ways, convicting Natty but offering to pay his fine. Cooper asks the reader to consider the fine distinctions between law and justice, to consider carefully how the law should be designed and administered.

The notion of property also leads to complicated conflicts in the novel. Temple believes in property rights. Natty, like his Indian friend Chincachgook (Indian John), is suspicious of anyone's right to own what should be shared by everyone. The novel seems to emphasize the concept of property by tracing a complex trail of land ownership; the land in question first belonged to the Mohican tribe, then to Major Effingham, then to Judge Temple, who wills it to his daughter, Elizabeth, and then finally to Effingham's grandson, Oliver. The source of animosity among Natty and Oliver and Temple is their belief that Temple stole the land from Effingham. The concepts of land ownership and property rights are obscured by the presence of Chincachgook, a constant reminder that the new country is being established on the backs and with the blood of American Indians. On two occasions, at the turkey shoot and on Mount Vision, Chincachgook speaks of the demise of his people and of the lies of white people. By defending Effingham's property rights, Natty and Chincachgook take part in their own demise. The interests of property, the foundation of the new civilization, isolate and eventually ruin the natural man.

Neither Natty nor Temple is completely sainted or vilified, for Cooper understands the complex issues facing the country. Cooper seems to cherish the frontiersman as an American icon, but recognizes that the frontiersman must be sacrificed for the sake of the emerging America. Natty Bumppo is a symbol of the country's lost innocence.

"Critical Evaluation" by Heidi Kelchner

Further Reading

Clark, Robert, ed. *James Fenimore Cooper: New Critical Essays*. London: Vision, 1985. Includes three essays on *The Pioneers*, addressing Cooper's representation of American Indian languages as elements of the frontier, the importance of game laws in defining American democracy, and issues of ownership and property. Somewhat dense, but illuminating.

Darnell, Donald. "Manners on a Frontier: *The Pioneers, The Pathfinder*, and *The Deerslayer*." In *James Fenimore Cooper: Novelist of Manners*. Newark: University of Delaware Press, 1993. Describes the variety of social classes presented in the novel and how the classes coexist without overt conflict. Against this backdrop, it is natural that the "gentleman" Oliver Edwards should emerge as leader.

Franklin, Wayne. *The New World of James Fenimore Cooper*. Chicago: University of Chicago Press, 1982. Proposes Cooper as a major and undervalued artist who used striking imaginative energy to address important issues. Examines Cooper's comment that *The Pioneers* was written to contradict the idea that American society was unpolished.

Krauthammer, Anna. *The Representation of the Savage in James Fenimore Cooper and Herman Melville*. New York: Peter Lang, 2008. Focuses on Cooper's and Melville's creation of American Indian, African American, and other non-European characters, including the character of Natty Bumppo in *The Pioneers*. Discusses how these characters are perceived as "savages," both noble and ignoble, by American readers.

Person, Leland S., ed. *A Historical Guide to James Fenimore Cooper*. New York: Oxford University Press, 2007. Collection of essays, including a brief biography by Cooper and a survey of Cooper scholarship and criticism. *The Pioneers* is discussed in the chapter "Cooper's Leatherstocking Conversations: Identity, Friendship, and Democracy in the New Nation." Features an illustrated chronology of Cooper's life and important nineteenth century historical events.

Philbrick, Thomas. "Cooper's *The Pioneers*: Origins and Structure." In *James Fenimore Cooper: A Collection of Critical Essays*, edited by Wayne Fields. Englewood Cliffs, N.J.: Prentice-Hall, 1979. Demonstrates how Cooper was inspired by descriptive poetry, specifically by James Thomson's *The Seasons* (1730, 1744, 1746). This influence leads to Cooper's images of natural change and to the corresponding themes of social change.

Rans, Geoffrey. *Cooper's Leather-Stocking Novels: A Secular Reading*. Chapel Hill: University of North Carolina Press, 1991. The introduction examines the lasting interest in Cooper's works. The chapter "Interrupted Prelude" explores the ideologized landscape and the characterization important to an understanding of the Leatherstocking tales.

Tawil, Ezra F. *The Making of Racial Sentiment: Slavery and the Birth of the Frontier Romance*. New York: Cambridge University Press, 2006. Examines the frontier romance, a popular genre of nineteenth century American fiction, focusing on the way novels by Cooper and Harriet Beecher Stowe redefined the concept of race. Pages 80 to 91 provide a detailed analysis of *The Pioneers*.

Taylor, Alan. *William Cooper's Town: Power and Persuasion on the Frontier of the Early American Republic*. New York: Vintage Books, 1995. This Pulitzer Prize-winning book recounts the lives and relationship of father and son. Cooper's father, William, founded Cooperstown, New York, in 1876, and became a successful businessperson, judge, and U.S. representative. His political power and prestige eventually declined, leading James Fenimore to write *The Pioneers*, in part to justify his father's career.

The Pirates of Penzance
Or, The Slave of Duty

Author: W. S. Gilbert (1836-1911)
First produced: 1879; first published, 1880
Type of work: Drama
Type of plot: Operetta
Time of plot: Nineteenth century
Locale: England

Principal characters:
MAJOR GENERAL STANLEY, of the British army
RICHARD, the pirate king
FREDERIC, the pirate apprentice
MABEL,
EDITH,
KATE, and
ISABEL, General Stanley's daughters
RUTH, a pirate maid of all work

The Story:

Frederic, the pirate apprentice, has reached his twenty-first birthday, and at midnight he will be free of his indenture. The pirate king announces that Frederic will then become a full-fledged member of the band. Frederic says that he served them only because he was a slave to duty; now he is going to leave the pirates. Astounded, the king asks for reasons. Frederic will not tell, but Ruth, the pirate maid of all work, confesses that she had been Frederic's nurse when he was a baby. She had been told to apprentice him to a pilot, but being hard of hearing, she had thought the word was "pirate." Afraid to reveal her mistake, she, too, had joined the pirates to look after her charge.

Frederic also announces that when he leaves the pirates he is going to do his best to exterminate the whole band. Individually, he loves them all, but as a crew of pirates they must be done away with. The pirates agree that they are such unsuccessful pirates, and that they can not blame him for leaving. Frederic tells them he knows why they are such poor pirates. When they remind him that he is still one of them until midnight, he feels that it is his duty to give them the benefit of his knowledge. The trouble is that they are too kindly. They never attack a weaker party and are always beaten by a stronger one. Then, too, if any captive says he is an orphan, he is set free; the pirates themselves had all been orphans. Word about the soft-hearted pirates spreads, and now everyone who is captured declares himself an orphan. The pirates know that Frederic is right, but they hate to be grim and merciless.

Asked what Ruth will do when he leaves their band, Frederic says he will take her with him. He wonders if she is attractive. Ruth declares that she is, but since he had had no opportunity to see another female face, Frederic cannot be sure. The king assures him that she is still a fine-appearing woman, but when Frederic tries to give her to the king, he will not have her.

Ruth has him almost convinced that she is a fair woman when Frederic sees a bevy of beautiful maidens approaching. Ruth, realizing that her cause is lost, admits that she has deceived him; she is forty-seven years of age. Frederic casts her aside.

Frederic hides as the girls approach, but he feels that he ought to reveal himself again as the women, believing themselves alone, prepare for a swim. When they hear his story, they are filled with pity for his plight and admiration for his handsome figure. From a sense of duty, one of the sisters, Mabel, accepts his affection. Her sisters—Kate, Edith, and Isabel—wonder whether her sense of duty would have been so strong had Frederic been less handsome.

Frederic warns the women about the pirates. Before they could escape, however, the band, led by their king, appears and seizes them. At the same time, their father, Major General Stanley, appears in search of his daughters. He brags of his great knowledge—he knows about everything but military skill. As soon as he learns something of military tactics, he will be the greatest general ever. When the pirates tell him they are going to marry his daughters, the general, much to their sorrow, begs them not to take his lovely daughters from him because he is an orphan. Unhappily, the pirates give up; they cannot harm an orphan.

Later, at his home, a ruin that he had purchased complete with ancestors, the general grieves because he had lied to the pirates. He knows that his falsehood about being an orphan will haunt him and his newly purchased ancestors. Frederic consoles him by telling him that the lie was justified to save his daughters from the pirates. At midnight, Frederic will lead the police to the outlaw band for capture. He must wait until then, because he is still one of them.

When the police enter, the women praise them for going so nobly to their deaths. The police, not cheered by the praise, agree that theirs will be a noble death. At midnight, Frederic prepares to lead them to the pirate hideout. At that moment, the pirate king and Ruth appear, laughing at a joke they had just discovered. Frederic had been born on February 29 in a leap year. Thus, he is not twenty-one years old, but only five years old. His apprenticeship will not be up until 1940. Frederic, thinking that he looks more than five years old, also laughs at that paradox.

Because Frederic is again one of the pirate band, he feels it his duty to tell the pirates that Major General Stanley is not an orphan, that he had lied. The pirates leave at once to capture the villain and to torture him for his falsehood. A struggle ensues between the pirates and the police. The pirates win, but when the police challenge them to surrender in the name of Queen Victoria, the pirates yield, for they love their queen. Before the police can take them away, Ruth enters and tells all assembled that the pirates are really noblemen gone wrong. Then the general forgives them their youthful fling and sends them back to their ranks, giving them his daughters for their brides.

Critical Evaluation:

W. S. Gilbert collaborated with the composer Arthur Sullivan (1842-1900) on eleven highly successful comic operettas between 1875 and 1889, of which *The Pirates of Penzance* is the fourth major work. Like the others, *The Pirates of Penzance* combines topical satire and parody with essentially conservative themes. Penzance, in the rugged coastal area of Cornwall (traditionally known for smuggling) provides a picturesque backdrop for a work that has remained a favorite because of its whimsical plot devices; good-humored satire of the army, the police, and the institution of marriage; and sparkling songs and dialogue.

In his libretto, Gilbert shapes the timeless tale of cruel pirates falling upon innocent maidens into a mock-heroic romp, in which virtue ultimately triumphs, but not before extremes of duty have led to absurdly funny situations. In the world of Victorian England, duty reigned as a supreme virtue, but by 1879, even the most earnest Victorians were ready to laugh at themselves as long as their basic values were ultimately affirmed. Gilbert bases his work on the premise that anything, even commitment to doing one's duty, can become silly if carried beyond reasonable limits. Frederic, the hero, desires nothing more than to be an honest man, but he takes the notion of duty so seriously that he regards breaking the

terms of his apprenticeship to the pirates as worse than actually being a pirate. He accepts, in all seriousness, the extension of his commitment to the pirates because of a paradox in reckoning dates. Major General Stanley, having lied to the pirates to save himself and his adopted daughters, feels overwhelming guilt for this betrayal of his duty to be honest. Ruth, whose incredible mistake in apprenticing Frederic to a pirate instead of a pilot sets the entire plot into motion, has joined the pirate band herself rather than abandon her duty to her charge. The pirates are so softhearted that they never actually hurt anyone, and they finally give up without a struggle when reminded of their duty to Queen Victoria.

While the absurd extensions of duty provide a universal satiric theme, Gilbert also satirizes specific Victorian institutions. Gilbert deftly exploits the humorous possibilities in the ways that newly professionalized police as well as military officers changed during the nineteenth century. The first modern urban police forces had been introduced in London in 1829, and the police jokes in *The Pirates of Penzance* show some ambivalence about the place of the police in society. Like many citizens, Gilbert demonstrates a good-natured affection for police officers, whose "lot is not a happy one" because they are torn between their duty to arrest wrongdoers and their natural sympathies with criminals' "capacity for innocent enjoyment." At the same time, the police are ridiculed both for their false bravado before the confrontation with the pirates and for their bumbling inability to overcome and arrest the pirates.

The Victorian era saw not only the novelty of professionalized law enforcement but also pressure for changes in the tradition-bound military. Three laws reforming the army were passed in the early 1870's, but officers at the time of *The Pirates of Penzance* were still more likely to be gentlemen whose military knowledge, like that of Major General Stanley, had "only been brought down to the beginning of the century." Officers usually purchased their commissions and had been educated in British public schools (privately run, all-male, boarding academies) at which they learned much more about classical languages and playing sports than about modern science, technology, or warfare. Gilbert satirizes the major general from the middle-class perspective, portraying him as a pompous product of moneyed, behind-the-times aristocracy and over-education in the totally useless knowledge required on the entrance examinations for the two service academies.

The women in the operetta personify the stereotypical Victorian maiden, whose goal it is to hold out for the best marriage possible, and the stereotypical Victorian spinster, whose goal it is to marry anyone at all. The pirates desire to marry the maidens "with impunity," circumventing the women's calculations and avoiding the tedious negotiations with fathers that were common at the time. The young women refuse until the finale, when the pirates' true identities as noblemen are revealed. This patently silly turn of events parodies the harsh reality that, in an age of limited opportunities for women to be independent and of nearly impossible divorce, a young woman's husband was her destiny. One of the maidens, Mabel, seems to have the best of all possible situations when she and Frederic fall in love, because she is both doing her duty by redeeming him from a life of crime and winning a handsome husband. When Frederic and Mabel promise, in their duet, to be faithful to each other "till we are wed, and even after," Gilbert makes even these starry-eyed lovers express the typical Victorian combination of romantic idealism and hardheaded realism about marriage. Ruth's hopeless love for Frederic even more poignantly demonstrates the woman's position: Devoid of youth, beauty, and wealth, she can only watch sadly as the young, beautiful, and rich Mabel wins his heart in an instant. Even as the curtain falls at the end of the operetta, she is alone, with no sympathy from the other characters.

Despite the subversive possibilities in satirizing the concept of duty, the uniformed authorities, and the institution of marriage, *The Pirates of Penzance* concludes with the accepted Victorian order of things restored. The outlaws give up when the police invoke the queen's name; Major General Stanley not only gives his daughters in betrothal to the formerly pirate noblemen but also orders them to "resume [their] ranks and legislative duties," thus bringing full circle the theme of duty. By scrupulously doing one's duty, the finale asserts, one brings about the best possible results for the greatest number of people. These good results include, for the men, assuming their rightfully high places in the social structure, and for the women, marrying well.

"Critical Evaluation" by Julia Whitsitt

Further Reading

Ainger, Michael. *Gilbert and Sullivan: A Dual Biography.* New York: Oxford University Press, 2002. Chronicles the lives and working partnership of Gilbert and his collaborator, Arthur Sullivan, examining how their different personalities spurred them to produce their best work.

Benford, Harry. *The Gilbert and Sullivan Lexicon in Which Is Gilded the Philosophic Pill.* New York: Richard Rosen Press, 1978. Explains jokes, allusions, institutions, and slang terms used by Gilbert and Sullivan in their plays.

Crowther, Andrew. *Contradiction Contradicted: The Plays of W. S. Gilbert.* Cranbury, N.J.: Associated University Presses, 2000. An examination of Gilbert's plays, including his collaborations with Sullivan. Crowther compares previous critiques of the plays with the plays themselves.

Geis, Darlene. *The Gilbert and Sullivan Operas.* New York: Harry N. Abrams, 1983. Supplies a history and synopsis of *The Pirates of Penzance.* Contains photographs from a television series of Gilbert and Sullivan operas.

Mander, Raymond, and Joe Mitchenson. *A Picture History of Gilbert and Sullivan.* London: Vista Books, 1962. Contains a foreword by Bridgette D'Oyly Carte, whose family is famous for its production of the original versions of Gilbert and Sullivan operas. Includes photographs of historic performances and notes that give the reader special insight into the style of production.

Williamson, Audrey. *Gilbert and Sullivan Opera.* London: Marion Boyars, 1953. Contains a chapter on *The Pirates of Penzance.* Explains the development of some of the play's ideas and the relation of *The Pirates of Penzance* to other Gilbert and Sullivan operas.

Wren, Gayden. *A Most Ingenious Paradox: The Art of Gilbert and Sullivan.* New York: Oxford University Press, 2001. An analysis of the operettas in which Wren explores the reasons for their continued popularity. Chapter 6 is devoted to an examination of *The Pirates of Penzance.*

The Pit
A Story of Chicago

Author: Frank Norris (1870-1902)
First published: 1903
Type of work: Novel
Type of plot: Naturalism
Time of plot: 1890's
Locale: Chicago

Principal characters:
CURTIS JADWIN, a speculator in wheat
LAURA DEARBORN, later his wife
SHELDON CORTHELL, an artist in love with Laura
MR. CRESSLER and MRS. CRESSLER, friends of the Jadwins
GRETRY, Jadwin's broker

The Story:

From the first evening that Laura Dearborn meets Curtis Jadwin, she knows that she interests him. She attends the opera with her sister, Page, and her Aunt Wess as the guests of their longtime friends, the Cresslers. Jadwin also is a guest that evening, and the marked attention he pays her is so flattering to her that she listens only absently to avowals of love from her old and devoted suitor, Sheldon Corthell. Corthell is an artist. The life of the capitalist Jadwin who makes and breaks fortunes and human lives from the floor of the Board of Trade seems to Laura more romantic than painting.

The next day, Mrs. Cressler tells Laura part of Jadwin's story. He had been born into a poor family and had worked to educate himself. When he gained possession of some land in Chicago in default of a loan, he sold it, bought more real estate, and by shrewd dealings eventually owned a portion of one of the wealthiest sections of real estate in Chicago. He also speculated in the wheat market, and he is now a familiar figure on the floor of the Board of Trade.

Stopping by the Board of Trade one morning in answer to the summons of Gretry, his broker, Jadwin pauses in the Pit—the huge room downstairs in which all the bidding takes place—to watch the frenzied excitement of bidders and sellers. Gretry has received information that in a few days the French government will introduce a bill placing heavy import duties on all foreign goods. When this news becomes more widely known, the price of wheat will drop considerably. Gretry urges Jadwin to sell his shares at once, and Jadwin agrees.

The deal is a tremendous success. Jadwin pockets a large profit. The Cresslers try to persuade Jadwin to stop his speculating. Mr. Cressler had almost ruined himself at one time through his gambling with wheat, and he fears that the same might eventually happen to his friend. Jadwin, however, is too much interested in Laura to pay attention to the warning or even to hear the words of his friends. One evening at the Cresslers, he asks Laura to marry him. Laura, in a capricious

mood, says that, although she loves no one as yet, she might some day come to love him. She had given Sheldon Corthell the same encouragement. That night, ashamed of her coquetry, she writes to both men to tell them that she does not love either of them and that they must never speak of love to her again if they are to continue as friends. Corthell accepts her refusal and leaves for Europe. Jadwin calls on Laura while she is out and refuses to leave until he has spoken to her. He is eloquent in pleading his suit, and they are married in July.

The early years of their marriage are completely happy. Their home is a mansion, exquisitely furnished and with beautiful grounds. At first, Laura has a difficult time adjusting to her luxurious surroundings, but as time passes, she finds great pleasure in satisfying her interests in art, decorating her home, and entertaining her friends.

Jadwin, caught up in the excitement of the Pit, invests all his money in successful speculative enterprises. For some time, he aligns himself with the bears in the wheat market. As he sees the country becoming more prosperous and the wheat crops increasing, he decides to change to the side of the bulls. He resolves to buy as much wheat as he can and, if possible, to corner the market. Luck is with him. One year, when European crops are very poor, Jadwin buys a tremendous amount of wheat at a low price, determined to hold it until he can ask his own price. Laura is worried by his constant attendance at the Board of Trade, and he promises to give up speculating as soon as he concludes an important deal.

One evening, Laura has dinner with Corthell, who had returned from Europe. Late that night, Jadwin comes home with the announcement that the deal had concluded and that he cleared half a million dollars. He keeps his promise to give up speculating in the Pit, but within a short time, he grows restless. He begins again to try his luck in the wheat market.

Because Jadwin keeps his activities hidden from the public, he is spoken of as the unknown bull. After he purchases as much wheat as he can, it suddenly becomes evident that he is in a position to corner the world's wheat and name his own price. Cressler, meantime, has been drawn into speculation by the group of bears who are certain that they could break the unknown bull. Cressler has no idea that the bull is his own friend, Jadwin.

Weeks go by while Laura sees her husband only at breakfast. He spends his days and many of his nights at the board. Laura, lonely and unhappy, begins to see more and more of Corthell. Corthell is still in love with Laura and finally declares his feelings for her. Laura, who still loves her husband, is kind in her dismissal.

In cornering the market, Jadwin now rides on a wave of power and prosperity, but he begins to have strange, irritating headaches. He attempts to ignore them, just as he disregards his moods of loneliness and depression.

Mrs. Cressler confides that her own husband is not well. She invites Laura to call on her one afternoon. Laura arrives, but Mrs. Cressler is not yet home. She wanders into the library and sees Mr. Cressler seated in a chair. He had shot himself through the temple.

Jadwin is horrified when he realizes that Cressler had lost all of his money in speculation with the bears, and he feels that he is responsible for his friend's death. Jadwin himself is in a tight spot, for now that he has forced the price of wheat to a new high, he needs to corner a bumper crop in addition to the millions of bushels he already owns. His enemies are waiting for the time when the unknown bull can buy no more wheat. At that moment, the price would drop considerably. Jadwin puts every penny he owns into his attempt to keep wheat cornered, but he is defeated by the wheat itself. The grain flows in, millions of bushels at a time. Almost out of his mind, he buys and buys, and still the wheat harvest continues. He no longer controls the market. He is ruined.

Jadwin walks into his home one night a broken man. Laura nurses him through days and nights of illness. When he is well enough, the two set out for the West to begin life again. Although they have lost their money, the Jadwins are much happier than they had been for many years.

Critical Evaluation:

Scientific theories and economic realities have often influenced a writer's assumptions and style. The biological and economic determinism popular in the late nineteenth century shaped the literary theory of naturalism that Émile Zola popularized in Europe. Stephen Crane, the first American proponent of this genre, introduced readers to the forms of naturalism during the early 1890's and was soon followed by Jack London, Theodore Dreiser, Frank Norris, and others. Authors who drew on naturalism dealt with four implicitly antagonistic elements—frankness, objectivity, determinism, and fatalism. As with a scientific theory in the hands and heads of subjective human observers, naturalism often succumbed to a not-so-subtle moralism.

Norris, one of the most promising American followers of Zola, died young. His fame as a novelist had been secured by the publication of *McTeague* in 1899, and the brilliance of his career grew more intense with the appearance of *The Octopus* in 1901. The latter title was the first volume of Norris's intended Epic of the Wheat trilogy. *The Octopus* deals with the production of wheat, while *The Pit* describes the marketing of the grain; the final, unwritten volume, "The Wolf," was to have covered the consumption of wheat.

Like his mentor Zola, Norris depicts large, dramatic scenes, such as the vast expanses of the San Joaquin Valley in California or the tumult on the floor of the Chicago grain exchange. These vivid scenes testify to the nation's fertile soil, a hard-working populace, the technological imagination of inventors, and the organizational flair of entrepreneurs. Considering the menacing determinism in the titles of Norris's books, it becomes evident that the human and social potential of the growing nation is countered by the fatalism of the life-cycle analogy, and the realities of the victors-and-the-vanquished syndrome.

Henry James and William Dean Howells were abandoned; Norris and his colleagues became the literary spokespersons of the populists, and the vanguard of the muckrakers. Norris sensed the passing of the old America of warmth, community, and lasting personal relationships. He was eager to humanize the new emerging society that was altered by the impersonal forces of urbanization and controlled by unsavory business tactics. To others, the decline of the genteel tradition signaled the passing of the great race and the entrance of mass culture. To Norris, both the individual and the masses were at the mercy of society and its fixed patterns. Norris's voice was the voice of a generation, like many before, bewildered and adrift. He opposed the basic premise of a society without a core, a society in which the acquisition of money had become a sanctified goal. The ideal of objectivity would have been difficult to achieve.

Zola bequeathed objectivity to naturalism, and Norris wrestled with its thin edge. *The Pit*, like its predecessor, *The Octopus*, is a propaganda novel but by no means a cheap diatribe. Norris, an ethical person, could not detach himself from the unethical values and practices of his society, but he could condemn them. He was candid in his descriptions of the undesirable changes that had taken place. A deterministic universe works out its inexorable process through the activities on the floor of the Chicago grain exchange. As if the occupants of that great building were a nationwide audience viewing a play in its bowels, the pit, the Jadwins of the world rise and fall, just as they had throughout recorded history. Norris's characters are the microcosm of larger society.

Furthermore, there was some destruction of character in the principal personages of *The Pit*, but their demise represents something much larger than the individual. The acquisition of fortunes had its shortcomings. The new leisure class, the Curtis and Laura Jadwins of America, often discovered too late that wealth did not always improve the quality of life.

Chicago had been an ideal location for the story. In Chicago, one could find almost everything that money could buy. The city had become the clearinghouse for western America, a mecca for would-be financiers, meat-packing tycoons, and grain gamblers. This was the raw yet dynamic city that would later inspire poet Carl Sandburg. At one time, Jadwin gives up his speculating, but his addiction is too strong; eventually it nearly kills him. Such is the charisma of the city, of its seemingly infinite potential for success. Many perished before Jadwin; tragedy is timeless and inevitable.

In the opening pages, the reader is presented with the inside story about the Pit. Anxiously waiting for the opening act of an opera, and the prestigious patrons, Laura hears of a man's failure to dominate the corn market. Even before being introduced to Curtis Jadwin, Laura becomes acquainted with disaster and with the cruelties of the market. Yet she is drawn to the men who speculate. She admires their social position and envies their luxury-filled lives. Laura looks to the future as if nothing inopportune could possibly happen. She would not always face life with such naïveté.

When Jadwin's friend, Cressler, is lured back into wheat speculation, he loses everything. Jadwin's efforts to corner the market could have been successful, but fate steps in and, through nature, destroys his plans. He had tested luck once too often and overnight is ruined financially and broken in health and spirit. In nursing her husband back to health, Laura asserts her own strength and demonstrates her love for Curtis.

While the novel's conclusion is to some extent tragic, it is not without an optimistic note. The Jadwins lose everything they think life has to offer, but they regain their future. They have each other's love for the first time in years. In possession of one of life's most simple sources of strength and happiness, marriage, Curtis and Laura leave Chicago and move to the West, probably to California. Norris himself lived in California, and there naturalism had most productively taken root. There, as he had proclaimed in *The Octopus*, the endless struggle of the individual against economic forces had been well under way.

"Critical Evaluation" by Eric H. Christianson

Further Reading

Graham, Don. *The Fiction of Frank Norris: The Aesthetic Context*. Columbia: University of Missouri Press, 1978. The chapter on *The Pit* discusses differences between this novel and Norris's other fiction. *The Pit* contains many musical and literary allusions and, most significant, it reflects Norris's preoccupation with drama. Like a drama, the novel has few main characters and is staged in confined settings. In addition, *The Pit* includes a professional opera and plays.

_____, comp. *Critical Essays on Frank Norris*. Boston: G. K. Hall, 1980. Includes the anonymous contemporary review "*The Pit*: A Dispassionate Examination of Frank Norris' Posthumous Novel," Warren French's "It's When You Are Quiet That You Are at Your Best," and Joseph Katz's "Eroticism in *The Pit*."

Hochman, Barbara. *The Art of Frank Norris: Storyteller*. Columbia: University of Missouri Press, 1988. This study of recurrent motifs shows Norris as a more complex writer than do traditional assessments of his work. The chapter "Coming of Age in *The Pit*" uses the symbolic wheat pit to discuss the novel.

Hussman, Lawrence E. *Harbingers of a Century: The Novels of Frank Norris*. New York: Peter Lang, 1999. A reevaluation of Norris's novels, in which Hussman demonstrates how these books "rehearsed" many of the themes that appeared in later twentieth century American fiction. Chapter 6 analyzes *The Pit*, focusing on its theme of "subsuming the self."

McElrath, Joseph R., Jr. *Frank Norris Revisited*. New York: Twayne, 1992. Critical biography offering a thorough discussion of *The Pit*, which McElrath calls "a novel of complications" because of its "sustained alternating portraits of [Laura's and Jadwin's] worsening psychological condition."

McElrath, Joseph R., Jr., and Jessie S. Crisler. *Frank Norris: A Life*. Urbana: University of Illinois Press, 2006. Comprehensive biography providing an admiring portrait of Norris. McElrath and Crisler maintain that Norris remains relevant to and deserves to be read by twenty-first century audiences.

Pizer, Donald. *The Novels of Frank Norris*. 1966. Reprint. New York: Haskell House, 1973. A comprehensive and systematic examination of Norris's novels, with particular attention paid to the author's intellectual background and philosophical influences. Discusses Norris's rationale in writing *The Pit*, as well as the influence on Norris of French naturalists Joseph LeConte and Émile Zola.

West, Lon. *Deconstructing Frank Norris's Fiction: The Male-Female Dialectic.* New York: Peter Lang, 1998. West contradicts many critics by arguing that Norris was less of a naturalist and more of a Romantic. He focuses on Norris's representation of the "natural man" and of refined women characters in his fiction, finding connections between Norris's characters and Carl Jung's archetypes of the "great and terrible mother" and the "punishing superego-like father."

The Plague

Author: Albert Camus (1913-1960)
First published: La Peste, 1947 (English translation, 1948)
Type of work: Novel
Type of plot: Impressionistic realism
Time of plot: 1940's
Locale: Oran, Algeria

Principal characters:
DR. BERNARD R. RIEUX, a young physician
JEAN TARROU, a traveler
COTTARD, a fugitive
JOSEPH GRAND, a clerk
RAYMOND RAMBERT, a journalist
FATHER PANELOUX, a priest

The Story:

At first, Dr. Bernard R. Rieux gives little thought to the strange behavior of the rats in Oran. One morning, he finds three on his landing, each animal lying inert with a rosette of fresh blood spreading from its nostrils. The concierge grumbles at having to clean up the rats, but Rieux is a busy doctor and just then he has personal cares. Madame Rieux is leaving Oran. She suffers from a lingering illness, and Rieux thinks that a sanatorium in a different town might do her good. His mother is to keep house for him while his wife is absent.

The doctor is also being bothered by Raymond Rambert, a persistent journalist, who wants to do a story for his metropolitan paper on living conditions among the workers in Oran. Rieux refuses to help him, for he knows that an honest report will be censored.

Day by day the number of dead rats increases in the city. After a time, trucks come by each morning to carry them away. People step on the furry dead bodies when they walk in the dark. Rieux's first case of fever involves his concierge, who has a high temperature and painful swellings. Rieux is apprehensive. By making telephone inquiries, he learns that his colleagues are getting similar cases.

The prefect is averse to taking any action because he does not want to alarm the population. Only one doctor is convinced that the sickness is bubonic plague; the others reserve judgment. When the deaths rise to thirty a day, however, even the town officials get worried. When a telegram instructs the prefect to take drastic measures, the news spreads like wild fire: Oran is in the grip of the plague.

Rieux is called to the apartment of someone named Cottard, who has tried to hang himself. Joseph Grand, a clerk and Rieux's former patient, cut the man down just in time to save him, but he can give no satisfactory reason for his attempt to kill himself. Rieux is interested in Cottard, who seems rather an eccentric person.

Grand, too, is a strange man. For many years, he has been a temporary clerk, overlooked in his minor post, whom a succession of bureaucrats keep on without investigating his status. Grand has been too timid to call attention to the injustice of his position. In the evenings he works hard on a novel he is writing, from which he seems to derive much solace. Rieux is surprised when he sees the work. In all of those years, Grand has only the first sentence of his novel finished, and he is still revising it. He has once been married to Jeanne, but she had left him.

Jean Tarrou is an engaging fellow, a political agitator concerned with governmental upheavals over the whole continent. He keeps a meticulous diary of the ravages and sorrows of the plague. Tarrou had left home at an early age because he disliked his father's profession as prosecutor; the thought of the wretched criminals condemned to death because of his father's zeal horrified him. After having been an agitator for years, he finally realizes that the workings of politics often result in similar executions. He had fled to Oran just before the plague started. Here he finds an answer to his problem in organizing and directing sanitary workers.

One of Tarrou's neighbors is an old man who each morning calls the neighborhood cats to him and shreds paper for them to play with. Once all the cats are around him, he will spit on them with great accuracy. After the plague grows worse, the city authorities kill all cats and dogs to check possible agents of infection. The old man, deprived of his targets, stays indoors, disconsolate.

As the blazing summer sun dries the town, a film of dust settles over everything. The papers are meticulous in reporting the weekly total of deaths, but once the number passes the nine hundred mark, the press reports only daily tolls. Armed sentinels are posted to permit no one to enter or leave the town. Letters are forbidden. Since the telephone lines cannot accommodate the increased traffic, the only communication with the outside is by telegraph. Occasionally, Rieux receives an unsatisfactory wire from his wife.

The disposal of the dead bodies presents a problem. The little cemetery is soon filled, but the authorities make more room by cremating the remains in the older graves. At last two pits are dug in an adjoining field, one for men and one for women. When those pits are filled, a greater pit is dug, and no further effort is made to separate the bodies of men and women. The corpses are simply dropped in and covered with quicklime and a thin layer of earth. Discarded streetcars are used to transport the dead to the cemetery.

Rieux is in charge of one of the new wards at the infirmary. There is little he can do, however, for the serum from Paris is not effective. He observes what precautions he can, and to ease pain he lances the distended buboes. Most of the patients die. Castel, an older physician, is working on a new serum.

Father Paneloux preaches a sermon on the plague in which he calls Oran's pestilence a retribution. Monsieur Othon, the judge, has a son under Rieux's care by the time Castel's new serum is ready. The serum does the boy little good; although he does show unexpected resistance to the disease, he dies a painful death. Father Paneloux, who has been watching as a lay helper, knows the boy is not evil; he can no longer think of the plague as a retribution. His next sermon is confused. He seems to be saying that human beings must submit to God's will in all things. For the priest, this view means rejecting medical aid. When he himself catches the fever, he submits to Rieux's treatment only when forced to do so. Father Paneloux dies a bewildered man.

Rambert, who is not a citizen of Oran, tries his best to escape. Convinced that there is no way to legally leave the city, he plans to leave with some illicit smugglers. Then the spirit of the town affects him, and he chooses to stay to help Rieux

and the sanitation teams. He has realized that only in fighting a common evil can he find spiritual comfort.

Cottard seems content with plague conditions. Wanted for an old crime, he feels safe from pursuit during the quarantine. When the plague eases a little, two officers come for him, but he escapes. He is recaptured in a street gunfight. Grand catches the fever but miraculously recovers to work again on his manuscript. Tarrou, also infected, dies in Rieux's house. The plague ends as the colder weather of January arrives. Rieux hears by telegram that his wife has died.

The streets are crowded again as lovers, husbands, and wives are reunited. Rieux dispassionately observes the masses of humanity. He has learned that human contact is important for everyone. For himself, he is content to help fight disease and pain.

Critical Evaluation:

In the decade and a half after the end of World War II, as the West strove to repair the physical, psychic, and spiritual damage, the voice of Albert Camus was one of the major artistic, philosophical, and moral sources of strength and direction. Camus offered reasoned yet passionate affirmation of human dignity in the face of an "absurd" universe, an absurdity that had been made evident to all by the Nazi horrors.

The Plague is the most thorough fictional presentation of Camus's mature thinking. In earlier works—notably the play *Caligula* (pb. 1944; English translation, 1948), the novel *L'Étranger* (1942; *The Stranger*, 1946), and the essay *Le Mythe de Sisyphe* (1942; *The Myth of Sisyphus*, 1955)—Camus articulated his concept of the "absurd." Human beings are absurd because they have neither metaphysical justification nor essential connection to the universe. They are not part of any divine scheme and, being mortal, all of their actions, individual and collective, eventually come to nothing. The only question, then, is how to deal with their absurdity.

Camus's answer lies in his concept of "revolt." Human beings revolt against their condition first by understanding it and then, in the face of their cosmic meaninglessness, creating their own human meanings. In his earlier works, Camus explored that problem in terms of the individual; in *The Plague*, Camus extends his moral and philosophical analysis to the question of human beings as social creatures. What, Camus asks, in the face of an absurd universe, is one person's relationship to, and responsibility for, another?

The paradox that lies at the center of Camus's revolt concept is that of heroic futility. People struggle in spite of—even because of—the fact that, ultimately, they must lose. While the idea of the absurd denies a cosmic meaning to human beings, it does affirm their common bond. Since all people must die, all are brothers and sisters. Mutual cooperation, not self-indulgence, is the logical ethic that Camus derives from his perspective of the absurd. Camus chooses a plague as an appropriate metaphor for the human condition, since it intensifies this awareness of human mortality and makes the common bond especially clear.

Camus carefully divides the novel into five parts that correspond to the progression of the pestilence. Parts 1 and 5 show life before the plague's onslaught and after its subsidence. Parts 2 and 4 concentrate on the details of communal and personal suffering and, in particular, on the activities and reactions of the main characters as they battle the disease. Part 3, the climax of the book, shows the epidemic at its height and the community reduced to a single collective entity, where time has stopped, personal distinctions are lost, and suffering and despair have become routine.

The story is narrated by Dr. Bernard R. Rieux, who waits until almost the end of the novel to identify himself, in a factual, impersonal, almost documentary style. His account is occasionally supplemented by extracts from the journal of Jean Tarrou, but these intrusions, while more subjective and colorful, are characterized by an irony that also keeps the reader at a distance. Both narratives are juxtaposed against vivid, emotionally charged scenes. This continual alternation between narrative austerity and dramatic immediacy, and from lucid analysis to emotional conflict, gives *The Plague* much of its depth and impact.

Three of the principal characters—Rieux, Tarrou, and Joseph Grand—accept their obligation to battle the epidemic as soon as it is identified. Rieux is probably the character who comes closest to speaking for Camus. Since Rieux is a medical doctor who has devoted his life to the losing battle with disease and death, the plague is simply an intensification of his normal life. From the outset, he accepts the plague as a fact and fights against it with all the skill, endurance, and energy he can muster. He finds his only certitude in his daily round. There is no heroism involved, only the logic of the situation. Even after the plague has retreated, Rieux has no conviction that his actions had anything to do with its defeat. Yet Rieux learns much from his experience and, as the narrator, his is Camus's final word on the meaning of the ordeal.

Unlike Rieux, whose ideas are the practical consequence of his professional experience, Tarrou first experiences the philosophical revelation, then shapes his life to it. Seeing his father, a prosecuting attorney, condemn a man to death, Tarrou becomes enraged with the inhumanity of his society and turns to revolutionary politics. That, too, he comes to realize, inevitably involves him in condemning others to death. Thus, long before coming to Oran, he has felt infected with

the "plague"—defined as whatever destroys human life—which has reduced him to a purposeless life colored only by the ironical observations he jots down in his journal. When the plague arrives, he quickly and eagerly organizes the sanitation squads; the crisis gives him the opportunity to side with the victims of life's absurdity without fearing that his actions will inadvertently add to their misery. Such obvious, total commitments, however, are not available under normal conditions, and so Tarrou appropriately dies as one of the plague's last victims.

Both Rieux and Tarrou are too personally inhuman—Rieux with his abstract view of humanity, Tarrou with his desire for secular sainthood—to qualify as heroic; the most admirable person in the book is Grand, who accepts his role in the plague automatically, needing neither professional nor philosophical justifications, simply because "people must help each other." His greater humanity is further demonstrated by the fact that, while carrying out his commitment to the victims of the plague, he continues to show active grief over the loss of his wife and tenaciously revolts in his artistic attempt to write the perfect novel (even though he cannot manage the perfect first sentence).

Among the other principal characters, the journalist Raymond Rambert opts for "personal happiness," Father Paneloux presents the Christian reaction to the pestilence, and Cottard acts out the role of the criminal. Caught in Oran by accident when the plague breaks out, Rambert turns his energies to escape, exhausting every means, legal and otherwise, to rejoin his wife. It is in him that the issue of exile or separation from loved ones is most vividly presented. For most of the novel he rejects the view that the plague imposes a social obligation on all, insisting that individual survival and personal happiness are primary. Although Rieux is the book's principal advocate of collective responsibility, he admits to Rambert that happiness is as valid an option as service. Even when Rambert finally decides to remain voluntarily and continue the fight, the issue remains ambiguous. At the end, as Rambert embraces his wife, he still wonders if he made the right moral choice.

If Rieux accepts Rambert's happiness as a decent option, he does not extend that tolerance to Father Paneloux's Christian view of the epidemic. *The Plague* has been called the most anti-Christian of Camus's books and that is probably correct, although it could be argued that the ethical values advocated are essentially Christian ones. As a system of beliefs, however, it is clear that Christianity—at least as understood by Paneloux—is tested by the pestilence and found wanting. If the priest's beliefs are inadequate, however, his actions are heroic, and it is this incongruity between his theological convictions and his existential behavior that gives his character and fate a special poignancy.

Near the beginning of the epidemic, Paneloux preaches a sermon in which he proclaims that the plague is a manifestation of divine justice. Later in the book, after he has become one of the most active fighters against the plague and a witness to the suffering and death of many innocent people, Paneloux's simple vision of sin and punishment is shaken. He preaches a second sermon in which he advocates a blind, total acceptance of a God who seems, from the human vantage point, to be indifferent, arbitrary, even, perhaps, evil. Driven to this extreme, Paneloux finally dies of the plague. Significantly, he is the only victim whose body is unmarked by the disease; he has been destroyed emotionally and spiritually because his religious vision is inadequate to the challenge and because he cannot live without that theological justification.

The most ambiguous character of all is Cottard. A criminal, he has lived in a constant state of fear and exile. Unable to endure such separation, he attempts to commit suicide near the beginning of the book. Once the plague sets in and all are subjected to that same sense of fear and solitude, Cottard rejoins humanity and flourishes; the plague is his natural element. Once it dissipates and he is again faced with isolation, Cottard goes berserk.

Thus, Camus describes the various human reactions to the plague—acceptance, defiance, detachment, solitary rejection, social commitment, criminality. The only value of the epidemic, Rieux admits, is educational, but the price paid for the knowledge is high. Nevertheless, even in the middle of the ordeal, there are moments of supreme pleasure and meaningful human connection. Shortly before the plague's last onslaught that takes Tarrou's life, he and Rieux defy regulations and go for a short swim. For a few brief moments, they are at one with the elements and in natural instinctive harmony with each other. The interlude is brief, of course, and both men return to the struggle—Tarrou to die, Rieux to chronicle its passing. He finally concludes that the only victory won from the plague amounts to "knowledge and memories" and the conviction that human beings are, on the whole, admirable.

"Critical Evaluation" by Keith Neilson

Further Reading

Carroll, David. *Albert Camus, the Algerian: Colonialism, Terrorism, Justice.* New York: Columbia University Press, 2007. Analyzes Camus's novels, short stories, and political essays within the context of the author's complicated relationship with his Algerian background. Carroll concludes that Camus's work reflects his understanding of both the injustice of colonialism and the tragic nature of Algeria's struggle for independence. Includes a bibliography and an index.

Fitch, Brian T. *The Narcissistic Text: A Reading of Camus's Fiction.* Buffalo, N.Y.: University of Toronto Press, 1982. A sophisticated study of Camus as a writer of metafiction. The chapter on *The Plague* examines how, through the use of several writer figures and by calling attention to its own narrative design, the novel makes its own artifice overt.

Hughes, Edward J., ed. *The Cambridge Companion to Camus.* New York: Cambridge University Press, 2007. Collection of essays interpreting Camus's work, including "Layers of Meaning in *La Peste*" by Margaret E. Gray. Other essays discuss his life and times, formative influences, and relationship with Jean-Paul Sartre, as well as Camus and the theater and social justice, violence, and ethics in his work.

Kellman, Steven G. *"The Plague": Fiction and Resistance.* New York: Twayne, 1993. A general overview, including a chronology and a bibliography, of Camus's novel. Discusses the historical, philosophical, and biographical contexts of the work and provides analyses of its style, structure, characters, and themes.

_____, ed. *Approaches to Teaching Camus's "The Plague."* New York: Modern Language Association, 1985. A collection of essays primarily concerned with pedagogical strategies for the college-level study of Camus's novel. Provides a bibliographical survey and thirteen individual essays that situate the novel within the contexts of French literature, philosophy, medicine, and history.

Longstaffe, Moya. *The Fiction of Albert Camus: A Complex Simplicity.* New York: Peter Lang, 2007. Examines Camus's novels and short stories, discussing the coherent themes and philosophy expressed in these works. Longstaffe also discusses the origins of Camus's philosophy and the narrative techniques of his fiction.

Tarrow, Susan. *Exile from the Kingdom: A Political Rereading of Albert Camus.* Tuscaloosa: University of Alabama Press, 1985. A rereading, in chronological order, of Camus's journalism and fiction as works that are linked to historical events and as embodiments of his ambivalence about political issues. Includes one chapter on *The Plague*, entitled "A Totalitarian Universe."

Todd, Olivier. *Albert Camus: A Life.* Translated by Benjamin Ivry. New York: Alfred A. Knopf, 1997. Making use of material such as unpublished letters made available after the death of Camus's widow, this detailed biography reveals much about Camus's love affairs and his many important friendships.

The Plain-Dealer

Author: William Wycherley (1641?-1715)
First produced: 1676; first published, 1677
Type of work: Drama
Type of plot: Comedy of manners
Time of plot: Seventeenth century
Locale: London

Principal characters:
CAPTAIN MANLY, a misanthropic gentleman in the king's service
FREEMAN, Manly's lieutenant
OLIVIA, Manly's mistress
VERNISH, Manly's trusted friend
WIDOW BLACKACRE, a rich widow deceived by Freeman
FIDELIA, Manly's page, an heir in disguise

The Story:

The plain-dealer, Captain Manly, returns to London after his ship had been sunk in a battle with the Dutch. He is looking for another ship because he dislikes the hypocrisy of the age and wishes to be away from the sycophancy of court and social life. Among the acquaintances who call at his quarters in London is Lord Plausible, who attempts to persuade the captain to seek his ship through influential people instead of waiting for an assignment. Manly demonstrates his love of plain dealing by showing Lord Plausible the door.

After Lord Plausible's departure, Manly instructs the two sailors who serve him not to admit anyone to his lodgings except his ship's lieutenant, Freeman. When Freeman arrives, he and Manly discuss the relative merits of plain dealing and hypocrisy. Freeman holds that no one can have a successful career without being hypocritical, but he cannot convince Manly that such a policy is better than telling the truth at all costs.

While they talk, Widow Blackacre forces her way past the sailors and enters Manly's rooms. Manly makes her welcome because she is a cousin of his fiancé, Olivia. The widow, who is extremely litigious, wants Manly to appear on her behalf at a court hearing the following day. She threatens to have him subpoenaed if he does not appear. Freeman, well aware that the widow has a great deal of money, starts to court her. The widow, who has a son, Jerry, who is almost as old as Freeman, ridicules the idea because she wants to manage her own affairs and would not be able to do so if she were married.

Manly tries to find information about Olivia, whom he has entrusted with most of his fortune while he was at sea. Olivia hears of Manly's arrival in London, but she is none too anxious to see him because she used his fortune as her own and had married Vernish, the only man Manly trusts and calls his friend. Olivia pretends to be a plain-dealer like Manly. When visited by her cousin Eliza, Lord Plausible, and others, she belabors them for their hypocrisy, saying they speak only ill of people in their absence but praise them to their faces. Her cousin reminds her that her comments about people are much worse and that she is not invited out enough in company to have an opportunity to say anything good about people to their faces.

Olivia, going on to speak plainly about Captain Manly, reveals that she does not love him and wishes to be rid of his attentions. No one present knows as yet of her secret marriage to Vernish. Manly enters her apartment unnoticed, and after the others leave, he and Olivia have words. Freeman and Manly's page remind him to recover his money and jewels from Olivia, so Manly goes back to request them. Olivia announces to all three that she is married, though she does not say to whom, and that she cannot return the money because her husband has it.

Olivia, noticing Manly's page, becomes infatuated and tells Manly to send the young page as messenger if they are to have any further dealings. As Manly leaves, Widow Blackacre, accompanied by her son, enter, and Freeman once more begins his suit for her hand. When she repulses him, he decides to use law instead of ordinary courtship to gain his ends.

The following morning, Manly, Freeman, and the page appear at Westminster Hall as witnesses in Widow Blackacre's lawsuit. While away from Freeman for a time, Manly instructs his page to go to Olivia and arrange an assignation for him, for Manly has decided to get revenge by making her unknown husband a cuckold. This is a bitter errand for the page, who is actually a young woman in disguise. She had some time before fallen in love with Manly and had disguised herself as a boy to be near him.

At the court session, Freeman finds Widow Blackacre's son and befriends him by giving him some money. The boy tells Freeman that his mother refuses to let him have any money until he comes of age. Learning that the boy has not yet appointed a guardian for himself, Freeman persuades the boy to name him as guardian, an act that transfers Widow Blackacre's money from her hands into his. Freeman also has the boy turn over to him all the widow's legal documents.

When Manly returns to his lodgings, his page informs him that she has succeeded in setting up an assignation with Olivia; Manly can substitute himself for the page in the darkness. When Manly hears the comments Olivia has made about him, he becomes even more furious and eager to have revenge. A little later, Widow Blackacre arrives, hoping to find Freeman and her son. When she confronts them, they tell her that she is helpless, since they have her documents and Freeman has been appointed the boy's guardian. The widow threatens to prove that her son is illegitimate and so cannot inherit her husband's estate.

That evening, the page goes to Olivia's home. When Vernish appears, the page escapes without being discovered, only to return later with Manly after Olivia had sent her husband away. Manly refuses to seduce Olivia and leaves. The page is trapped when Vernish returns unexpectedly, but she escapes by disclosing herself to Vernish as a woman, incapable of cuckolding him. Vernish's attempt to rape her is foiled by the entrance of his wife.

The page escapes through a window and returns to Manly. Later, Manly and Vernish meet. Manly is not yet aware that Vernish is Olivia's husband, and Vernish is unaware that Manly is trying to seduce Olivia. Because they still trust each other as the best of friends, Manly tells Vernish he has been intimate with Olivia before her marriage, a fact that makes Vernish all the more certain she has cuckolded him after marriage. The page, entering during the conversation, takes Manly aside and tells him another assignation with Olivia has been set for that evening. When they part, Vernish tells himself that he will pretend to leave town and thus trap the unknown man who is seducing Olivia.

In the meantime, Freeman and several bailiffs overhear Widow Blackacre plan to use court hangers-on to prove that her son was born out of wedlock. Rather than marry Freeman and lose control of her estate, the widow finally grants an allowance to the boy and an annuity to Freeman. The lieutenant is satisfied, as the money is all he wants.

That evening, Manly and the page go to Olivia's apartment. There, Manly overcomes Vernish in a duel. Olivia, in shame, tries to escape with the jewels and money, but Manly takes them from her. In the scuffle, the page's wig comes off, disclosing her as a woman. Manly, impressed by her faithfulness and beauty, immediately asks her to marry him. She tells Manly she is Fidelia, heir to a large fortune. They plan to begin a new life in the West Indies.

Critical Evaluation:

William Wycherley's final play, *The Plain-Dealer*, signaled a change in late-Restoration comedy. Unlike the sophisticated, witty comedies of Sir George Etherege and his own early mannered plays, *The Plain-Dealer* is a sharp, mordant satire upon false wit. Wycherley's railing, bitter, misanthropic tone greatly influenced the exaggerated style of such writers as John Crowne, Nathaniel Lee, and Thomas Otway.

Nineteenth century critics, most notably Thomas Macaulay, considered Wycherley a libertine playwright whose indecent morality, as represented by Manly's conduct, rendered his drama repugnant for serious investigation. Among early twentieth century critics of Restoration comedy, Montague Summers regarded *The Plain-Dealer* as a moral satire and Manly as Wycherley's representative, and he noted how the hero's invective is directed at the prime evils of the age: hypocrisy, materialism, vice. The judgment of later scholars, who carefully studied seventeenth century social conventions, tended to reject Summers's view of the comedy as a moral satire, just as it rejected the stuffy Victorian prejudices concerning the play's supposed immorality.

For Wycherley, as for his contemporaries, the touchstone of wit was not mere cleverness, although spontaneity, freshness, and pungency were, to be sure, important signs of wit; rather, sound judgment was the practical test that separated a would-be wit from a true one, a coxcomb from a gallant. To this convention, Wycherley insists on adding the virtue of naturalness—truth to reality—as a necessary part of wit. In *The Plain-Dealer*, Manly is the major test for the author's theory of wit, but he is not, as some critics have asserted, either the mouthpiece for the author or the perfect model for his type of wit. Until the conclusion of the play, Manly is deficient in judgment. He has mistaken the pretense of loving for real love, the affectation of friendship for truth. Olivia, his faithless lover, is quite correct in her cynical view of him: "He that distrusts most the world, trusts most to himself, and is but the more easily deceived, because he thinks he can't be deceived." Olivia puts her finger on the chief flaw in Manly—his vanity. Because he rebukes so heartily the evils of the world, he cannot believe that he himself can be guilty of the same evils. Yet Olivia is right when she says, "I knew he loved his own singular moroseness so well, as to dote upon any copy of it." By imitating the image of moroseness in Manly, Olivia and Vernish easily deceive him.

In his satire on false wit, however, Wycherley makes the point that at least some people in the world possess integrity, even though they neglect to rail, as Manly does, against society. Fidelia is true to Manly, even though he mistreats her when she is disguised as a man. She is a stock theatrical figure, quite wooden and lacking in human responses, except when Vernish threatens to rape her. A more convincing character is Freeman, a "complier with the age," who is nevertheless a friend to Manly, outspoken but not candid to the extent of injuring his own fortunes or humiliating fools. Although he cheats the Widow Blackacre out of three hundred pounds a year, he shows her some slight generosity when he has power over her in settling for money instead of marriage. For a widow with property, as she says, "Matrimony . . . is worse than excommunication, in depriving her of the benefit of the laws." Freeman is not perfect, as Manly wishes to be, and prefers to live with people, despite their faults, rather than condemn them as rascals.

The chief model for tempered wit in the play is Eliza, a minor character so far as the action is concerned yet always an example of good judgment. Eliza is cozened neither by Olivia's fine speeches nor by her actions: She judges clearly, with wit, honesty, and amused detachment. A good test of her mettle is her conversation with Olivia concerning *The Country Wife* (1675), a cuckolding comedy and Wycherley's third and most vigorous play. To Olivia, the play is a "hideous obscenity," although she remembers perfectly its ribald scenes. To Eliza, however, the play is not obscene but amusing; with admirable tact, she says that she can "think of a goat, a bull, or satyr, without any hurt." In another scene of the play, she expresses her contempt for the ill-tempered conventions of the age: "railing now is so common, that 'tis no more malice, but the fashion"; Eliza's integrity is secure, so she responds to life naturally and rejects the artificial fashions that mark the failure of wit.

Some characters of the play lack wit and are satirized as fools, coxcombs, and mean-spirited materialists. The "petulant" Widow Blackacre belongs to the last group. She is by no means a fool, but because her energy is expended in litigation she is an object of censure. The subplot involving the widow, Freeman, and Major Oldfox, an old fop who imagines himself a poet, is coarse but not offensive. With sharp realism, Wycherley satirizes the creatures of the law courts, schemers, and cheats. Yet his satire cuts more at the form than the substance of their corruption. Similarly, the author reduces to a single facile dimension the coxcombs who surround Olivia. Novel, as his name suggests, pretends to be a wit by copying the latest fashions of decorum, but he lacks originality. Lord Plausible, a "ceremonious," flattering coxcomb, employs the old-fashioned courtesies of the previous age; he, too, is unoriginal. As for Jerry, the widow's son, and with the sailors from Manly's ship and assorted minor characters, they are all blockheads too simple even to imitate the manners of their betters or to understand the spirit of wit.

Manly understands most of the conventions governing true wit, although he exaggerates railing as necessary for plain dealing. Yet the coxcomb Novel disproves the need for railing when he says, "railing is satire, you know; and roaring and making a noise, humor." Novel is wrong; so is Manly, whose misanthropy drives him to excess. Unlike Novel, Manly is, however, capable of reformation, and Wycherley's point is precisely that the imperfect hero may improve himself by learning the truth about his nature. From Fidelia, Manly learns that not all women are treacherous; from Freeman, he learns to be tolerant of the imperfections of others; from his own experiences, he learns the most valuable lessons—that revenge is mean-spirited and that true wit must come from true judgment. By the end of the play, having learned both wit and judgment, Manly is able to satirize his previous folly: "I will believe there are now in the world/ Good-natured friends, who are not prostitutes,/ And handsome women worth to be friends."

"Critical Evaluation" by Leslie B. Mittleman

Further Reading

Holland, Norman. *The First Modern Comedies: The Significance of Etherege, Wycherley, and Congreve.* 1959. New ed. Bloomington: Indiana University Press, 1967. The chapter on *The Plain-Dealer* focuses on the play as the dramatization of the question, Can an idealist live in the real world? Discusses the play's focus on the conflict between appearance and nature. Suggests that the title character is both innately good and a deviant from his society.

Hughes, Leo, ed. Introduction to *The Plain-Dealer*, by William Wycherley. Lincoln: University of Nebraska Press, 1967. A useful general introduction to Wycherley's play. Includes information on definitive texts and variants, stage history, and social and theatrical contexts. Compares Wycherley's drama with that of Ben Jonson and John Dryden; briefly discusses the play's origins in Molière's *The Misanthrope* (1666).

Kachur, Barbara A. *Etherege and Wycherley.* New York: Palgrave Macmillan, 2004. Discusses the plays of Wycherley and Sir George Etherege within the context of culture and history in the early years of Charles II's reign. Examines Wycherley's place within the Carolean theater, and devotes a chapter to an analysis of honor, courage, and heroism in *The Plain-Dealer.*

Rogers, Katharine M. *William Wycherley.* New York: Twayne, 1972. A good basic introduction. Chapter on *The Plain-Dealer* discusses Wycherley's adaptation of Molière's *The Misanthrope* to the English stage. Suggests that in *The Plain-Dealer*, the moral zeal nearly overbalances the comedy, resulting in a main character who is almost tragic. Argues the play has incompatible moral viewpoints and conflicting levels of reality.

Thompson, James. *Language in Wycherley's Plays*. Tuscaloosa: University of Alabama Press, 1984. Focuses on the role of language in exposing characters' inner psychological realities. Suggests that the sense of extremes in *The Plain-Dealer* is created by linguistic contrasts. Describes the play as Wycherley's most chaotic and discordant work.

Vance, John A. *William Wycherley and the Comedy of Fear*. Newark: University of Delaware Press, 2000. Detailed examination of four of Wycherley's plays, including *The Plain-Dealer*. Argues that Wycherley was not particularly concerned with broad political, social, and moral issues in his plays, but focused instead on the actions and motivations of his insecure and fallible characters.

Young, Douglas M. *The Feminist Voices in Restoration Comedy: The Virtuous Women in the Play-Worlds of Etherege, Wycherley, and Congreve*. Lanham, Md.: University Press of America, 1997. Analyzes *The Plain-Dealer* and three other plays by Wycherley in which a female character demands independence from and equality with her male partner as a condition of marriage or courtship.

Planet of the Apes

Author: Pierre Boulle (1912-1994)
First published: La Planète des singes, 1963 (English translation, 1963)
Type of work: Novel
Type of plot: Science fiction
Time of plot: 2500 to at least 3200 C.E.
Locale: Outer space, France, and a planet orbiting Betelgeuse

Principal characters:
JINN and PHYLLIS, a young couple space-surfing on holiday
ULYSSE MÉROU, an obscure journalist
PROFESSOR ANTELLE, a wealthy scientist and inventor
ARTHUR LEVAIN, a brilliant young physicist, assistant to Antelle
NOVA, a beautiful, naked young woman who is part of a band of wild humans
ZIRA, a female chimpanzee scientist performing experiments on humans
ZAIUS, the pompous orangutan in charge of experiments on humans
CORNELIUS, Zira's fiance, a brilliant chimpanzee archaeologist
SIRIUS, the precocious child of Nova and Ulysse

The Story:

Some time after 3200 C.E., Jinn and Phyllis are on a recreational ride in their specially designed spacecraft when they notice a bottle drifting near them. Inside it they find a long message written in "the language of the Earth." They are startled to find that it repeatedly refers to humans as intelligent beings. Ulysse Mérou, a young French journalist, wrote the message, which relates the story of his experiences.

In 2500, Ulysse accompanies the wealthy Professor Antelle and Levain on a privately funded expedition to a planet of the star Betelguese. The passengers on Antelle's spaceship will experience the round-trip journey as taking two years in each direction. However—because of the relativistic effects of stopping at the destination planet and turning around to come home—when they return, about seven hundred years will have passed on Earth.

The travelers reach their destination safely. The atmosphere seems breathable. Exiting their craft, the men soon see a small human footprint on the shore of a lake. A gorgeous, naked young woman appears and dives into the water. The explorers name her Nova. She fears the men until they remove their clothes. Then, she frolics near them but seems unable to speak, and she kills their pet chimpanzee.

A band of wild humans peers furtively from the underbrush. Finding the earthmen's clothes on the bank, they tear them into shreds and damage the explorers' landing craft beyond repair. The savages do not harm the explorers themselves, but soon a hunting party of clothed, talking, civilized apes appears. The apes wantonly shoot many of the humans and capture others, including the explorers. The survivors are taken to zoos or to research labs.

Ulysse is placed in the same cage as Nova and eventually mates with her. He displays such intelligence that the lab director Zira is platonically drawn to him. They gradually learn each other's language, and Zira comes to believe his claim to have arrived from another planet. On her planet, humans are bestial. Zaius, however, insists that Ulysse's apparent cleverness derives from tricks learned by rote during an earlier period of captivity. When Ulysse addresses Zaius and Zira by name, Zaius insists that Ulysse is merely parroting what he hears.

Ulysse learns that each of the three advanced species on the Planet of the Apes has separate talents and functions. The orangutans rule "official science" as figureheads. They are pedantic, stuffy, narrow-minded, and obsessed with honors and distinctions. The chimpanzees are brilliant, sensitive, and creative. The gorillas perform jobs requiring brute strength, such as being hunters and guards, but they also serve as organizers, office managers, and businessmen.

Zira obtains permission to take Ulysse out into the city, but he must go naked and wear a muzzle, leash, and chain. He is impatient to be free, but Zira warns him that Zaius is extremely powerful and wishes to send Ulysse to the brain lab, where experimental operations would transform him into a cripple or a vegetable. Ulysse's only hope is to unmask his rational nature in a formal speech, in ape language, when the national biological congress meets in a month. Members of the public and many journalists will attend, and the power of public opinion alone can defeat Zaius.

Zira helps Ulysse prepare by slipping him a flashlight and several books in ape language, which he conceals in his cage. On a trip to the zoo, Ulysse encounters Antelle, who has been reduced to a subhuman state by his captivity and is unable to speak or recognize his former friend. At the congress, Ulysse delivers a humble, impassioned, persuasive appeal for interspecies cooperation. Afterward, he faints from the strain but is freed, clothed, and accepted into the ape community.

Now a lab assistant, Ulysse tries in vain to teach captive wild humans to talk. Cornelius takes him to an archaeological excavation, which shows evidence that a civilization as advanced as the ape's own once existed there more than ten thousand years earlier. A doll in human form, which is clothed and which talks, suggests that the ancient civilization may have been human.

Ulysse learns that Nova has become pregnant. If the baby seems to have intelligence superior to that of an animal, it and Ulysse will be seen by the apes as highly dangerous: Such intelligence in his offspring would be an indication that it is possible for Ulysse to breed a human super-race to challenge ape supremacy. Father and child would surely be killed. Meanwhile, Ulysse is taken to see gruesome experiments in the brain surgery lab. One female subject, however, has recovered ancestral memories. She recites them in a trance, telling how humans gradually degenerated until their ape slaves took over and the humans fled into the jungle.

Nova gives birth. Because all humans look alike to the other apes, Zira and Cornelius arrange to save Ulysse and his family by secretly substituting them for other human experimental subjects who are to be sent aloft in a space shuttle. Cornelius's friends have detected the location of Ulysse's mother ship and programmed the shuttle to rendezvous with it. Zira is strongly moved at Ulysse's departure, but cannot bring herself to kiss him good-bye because she finds him so unattractive.

The escape succeeds. On the voyage home, Nova learns to talk, and her child Sirius displays extraordinary intelligence. However, when the family reaches Paris and lands at Orly airport, the officer who meets their craft is a gorilla. Evidently, humans on Earth have degenerated also, as they did on the Planet of the Apes, and Ulysse must again flee into outer space.

Jinn and Phyllis finish reading Ulysse's narrative. Jinn persuades Phyllis that the idea of intelligent humans is too absurd to take seriously. As the couple returns to their home planet, Phyllis takes out her compact and powders "her dear little chimpanzee muzzle." Capable only of imitating human inventions on the Planet of the Apes at the time of Ulysse's visit there, the chimpanzees have now become capable of creating inventions of their own, and apes may have conquered the entire galaxy.

Critical Evaluation:

Pierre Boulle published *Planet of the Apes* in 1963, at a time when the French colonial empire was coming to an end. In 1954, the country suffered a humiliating military defeat, losing its Southeast Asian colonies in Vietnam, Laos, and Cambodia. In much of Africa, it granted independence peacefully—to Tunisia and Morocco in 1956, to Guinea in

1958, and to its remaining West African holdings in 1960. The French withdrawal from Algeria in 1962, however, was especially traumatic. Not only did the former colonizers lose possession of the vast reserves of oil recently discovered beneath the Sahara Desert, but a million French settlers, many from families that had lived in Algeria for three generations, had to abandon everything they owned and flee the country. A powerful French conservative faction insisted on holding Algeria at all costs; when they learned that President Charles de Gaulle had decided to abandon the country, many high-ranking military officers formed the O.A.S. (Organization of the Secret Army), tried to foment a civil war in France, and at least twice attempted to assassinate de Gaulle with bombs.

Boulle's fantasy reenacts France's worst nightmare of being defeated by the "dark-skinned," "inferior" beings who had originally been invaded and colonized by the mother country (*la mère patrie*). His description of ape society satirizes racism by schematically depicting black-furred gorillas (equivalent to African Blacks), orange-furred orangutans (equivalent to Arabs), and brown-furred chimpanzees (equivalent to Asians), who combine to overwhelm pale-skinned caucasians. It simultaneously dramatizes the absurd view that racial others are bestial.

Boulle does not depict a historically accurate conflict between the colonized—whose main weapons were political assassinations, sabotage, and terrorism—and the colonizers—who denied free elections, resorted to torture in interrogations, and accepted the death of many noncombatants as "collateral damage." Instead, he imagines a dominant species that becomes so soft and self-indulgent that it loses its will to resist rebellion. Boulle's other major novel, *Le Pont de la Rivière Kwai*, (1952; *The Bridge over the River Kwai*, 1954) also tells a story of captive caucasians—the British in Burma during World War II—dominated by captors of a darker-skinned "race," the Japanese.

It is probably inaccurate to dismiss Boulle himself simply as a racist, however. Although the British captives in *The Bridge over the River Kwai* call their Japanese jailors "monkeys" (six times), "gorillas" (twice), "barbarous," "savage," or "primitive" (seven times), and "children" or "brutes" (sixteen times), the three members of the British secret service demolition team, planning to destroy the bridge that their compatriots are forced to build, use no such language. These secret service agents are not frustrated or enraged because they are not helpless. Moreover, in Boulle's memoir, *Aux Sources de la Rivière Kwai* (1966; *The Source of the River Kwai*, 1967), the author judges even his Nazi and Asian enemies dispassionately, and his footnotes more than once confess former racial prejudices that he has later overcome. He

takes advantage of the historical moment in France, however, to give great emotional resonance to his fable.

Instead of self-righteously preaching proper moral behavior, Boulle adopts the Enlightenment satiric strategy of wry detachment that one finds in Voltaire's *Candide: Ou, L'Optimisme* (1759; *Candide: Or, All for the Best*, 1759; also as *Candide: Or, The Optimist*, 1762; also as *Candide: Or, Optimism*, 1947): The sophisticated implied author remains hidden, while the naïve protagonist and the readers must witness scenes of outrageous cruelty in exotic places. These spectators may eventually recognize that similar cruelty exists in their own supposedly superior society, where they have done nothing to end it. Thus, Boulle argues indirectly for animal rights and against "speciesism" (the belief that humans have the right to do anything they want to lesser forms of life) by turning the tables against humans. In *Planet of the Apes*, wild humans are not only sacrificed to ensure that experimental space vehicles will be safe for apes but also hunted, wantonly shot for sport, imprisoned in zoos and laboratories, and crippled or killed by gratuitous experiments with brain surgery in order to satisfy ape scientists' idle curiosity.

The blatant sexism in *Planet of the Apes* may also be satirical, judging by the circumstances in which it appears. In the framing narrative, the two chimpanzees on vacation illustrate a caricatural gender opposition. Phyllis, the female, is impulsive, sensitive, emotional, and not as educated as her mate. Jinn, the male, is competent and rational but somewhat dogmatic and close-minded. At the conclusion of the main narrative, the hero enjoys the devotion of an ideally beautiful woman, whom he trains to be human—a classic version of the Pygmalion myth—but the couple has no place to go in the real world. As at the conclusion of Kurt Vonnegut's *Slaughterhouse-Five: Or, The Children's Crusade, a Duty-Dance with Death* (1969), the phallocratic love nest in *Planet of the Apes* is frankly revealed as a self-mocking fantasy.

Laurence M. Porter

Further Reading

Greene, Eric. *"Planet of the Apes" as American Myth: Race, Politics, and Popular Culture*. Middletown, Conn.: Wesleyan University Press, 1999. Analyzes the American film adaptation of Boulle's novel, as well as the film's four sequels, television spin-offs, and further episodes published in *Adventure Comics*. Compares these various American texts to the original French novel.

Haraway, Donna. *Primate Visions: Gender, Race, and Nature in the World of Modern Science*. New York: Routledge, 1989. Written by a leading theorist of the construction of the human/nonhuman dichotomy. Chapter 7, "Apes in Eden, Apes in Space: Mothering as a Scientist for National Geographic," and Chapter 16 "Reprise," discuss interspecies communication; the issues it raises concerning human sexual, gender, and racial identity; and animal rights.

McHugh, Susan Bridget. "Horses in Blackface: Visualizing Race as Species Difference in *Planet of the Apes*." *South Atlantic Review* 65, no. 2 (Spring, 2000): 40-72. An alert, broadly based cultural critique, focused on how the American film version problematizes and blurs the boundaries between genders, species, and races.

Porter, Laurence M. "Text of Anxiety, Text of Desire: Boulle's *Planète des singes* as Popular Culture," *The French Review* 68, no. 4 (March, 1995): 704-714. Focuses on the French novel, while contrasting it with the American film, and emphasizes how Boulle, without being himself a racist, exploits France's anxiety over losing its colonies in Africa and Southeast Asia between 1954 and 1962 by surreptitiously representing people of color as various species of apes.

Plantation Boy

Author: José Lins do Rego (1901-1957)
First published: Menino de engenho, 1932; *Doidinho*, 1933; *Bangüê*, 1934 (English translation, 1966)
Type of work: Novels
Type of plot: Regional
Time of plot: Early twentieth century
Locale: Northeastern coast of Brazil

Principal characters:
CARLOS DE MELLO, the narrator
COLONEL JOSÉ PAULINO CAZUZA, his grandfather and the owner of Santa Rosa plantation
UNCLE JUCA, Colonel José Paulino's son
AUNT MARIA, Colonel José Paulino's daughter
MR. MACIEL, a schoolmaster
COELHO, Carlos's schoolmate
MARIA ALICE, a married cousin of Carlos
COUSIN JORGE, the owner of the Gameleira plantation
MARREIRA, a tenant farmer on the Santa Rosa plantation

The Story:

Menino de engenho. At the age of four, Carlos de Mello sees the bloody body of his dead mother shortly after his father killed her in an insane rage. The boy is taken from his city home in Recife to live with his maternal grandfather and aunts and uncles at the family sugar plantation, Santa Rosa. His father is confined to an asylum for the insane, where he dies, completely paralyzed, ten years later; Carlos never sees him again.

At Santa Rosa, Carlos begins a new life, the life of a plantation boy. Aunt Maria becomes his mother. On his first morning at the plantation, he is initiated into country life by learning to drink milk warm from the cow's udder and to bathe in a pool by a waterfall. A few days later his cousins, two boys and a girl, arrive. The boys teach him wild country ways, such as how to ride bareback and how to go on secret swims. His cousin Lili, who is quiet, fair, and fragile, soon dies of a childhood illness.

One day, the famous bandit Antonio Silvino comes to Santa Rosa. Everyone fears what he will do, but he has come only to visit the colonel and pay his respects. Another time, the family has to abandon the plantation mansion and move to higher ground because the annual rains have turned into a flood that threatens the sugar mill and the house itself. The rains also leave behind rich soil that will mean a superior crop of sugar cane the next year. When a fire threatens the cane crop, all the plantation workers and neighboring owners come together to cut a swath between the fire and the rest of the fields to prevent the fire from spreading further.

Carlos always goes with his grandfather, Colonel José Paulino, on his inspection tours of the plantation. The colonel has expanded the original Santa Rosa plantation by buying neighboring properties, and now the plantation measures nine miles from end to end. The colonel has more than four thousand people under his protection, including former slaves who stayed on after the abolition of slavery in 1888 and still do the same work they did before. There are also tenant farmers who work the plantation in exchange for living on and farming their patches of land. On his inspection tours the colonel threatens shirkers, rewards the trustworthy, gathers news, offers food to the hungry and medicine to the ill—he is "the lord of the manor" visiting his lands and his "serfs." The colonel is also judge and jury for his workers. Carlos sees him put a man in stocks for "compromising" a young girl, but the man continues to deny his guilt. Finally, the girl confesses that it is Uncle Juca who has made her pregnant.

Carlos's country education includes the alphabet and reading lessons, but he learns much beyond his years from the plantation workers. As Zé Guedes walks Carlos to his lessons, he teaches the boy the lessons of life, introducing him to the prostitute Zefa Cajá, who provides the twelve-year-old Carlos with his first experience with sex—and syphilis. He learns country tales and superstitions as well. He comes to believe that a werewolf lives in the forest and that there are *zumbis* and *caiporas* (the spirits of dead cattle and dead goats) on the plantation.

When Aunt Maria gets married, Carlos feels abandoned; he feels that he has lost a mother for the second time. Soon after, however, at the age of twelve, he is sent away to a secondary school. On the train to the city with Uncle Juca he watches the beloved fields and forests of Santa Rosa plantation recede in the distance.

Doidinho. An anxious Carlos arrives with Uncle Juca at the Institute of Our Lady of Mount Carmel, a boys' school dominated by a rigid Jewish master, Mr. Maciel, who relies on discipline and is completely lacking in knowledge of child psychology. Although Carlos makes painful academic progress, his social adjustment is impossible from the outset. His extreme sensitivity sets him apart from his peers and leads him into flights of imagination that manifest themselves in exaggerated stories that he tells his schoolmates. Withdrawn, restless, and unable to endure his failure in military exercises, Carlos runs away from school and heads home to Santa Rosa plantation. As he approaches the plantation, however, he feels as alone and frightened as he did upon leaving it.

Bangüê. Nine years after his flight from the institute, Carlos, at the age of twenty-four, has graduated from law school and returned to Santa Rosa. He describes himself as a neurotic young man, unsure of his place and purpose in life. He has become an ambivalent daydreamer, one moment on top of the world with imagined plans for Santa Rosa and for himself as the powerful lord, the next moment in the depths of disillusionment and despair. For one entire year, Carlos does nothing but lie in his room reading newspapers and swatting flies.

A beautiful married cousin, Maria Alice, brings warm love into Carlos's life. When she arrives at Santa Rosa he is at last aroused from his indolence, and for a time he seems to live through her, believing that she will help him to become the great lord of his dreams. During their affair he becomes a new person, riding over the plantation, shouting orders, settling quarrels, and taking an interest in the work of the plantation for the first time since childhood. Eventually, however, Maria Alice returns to her husband, and for the third time Carlos loses a woman he has idolized. His despair becomes greater than ever, and he returns to his room, his newspaper, and his flies. Alternately filled with hate and desolate self-pity, he wishes Maria dead one day and dreams of marrying her the next.

When old José Paulino dies, it is found that Carlos has inherited the Santa Rosa plantation. Once again he becomes energetic, full of plans and dreams of restoring the estate to its former glory. The situation at Santa Rosa becomes increasingly hopeless, however. Crops fail, and workers desert in search of higher wages. Worst of all, Carlos becomes convinced that Uncle Juca, bitter at not having inherited the plantation, is conspiring with a black tenant farmer named Marreira to kill Carlos and take over the plantation. Instead of caring for the declining land, Carlos becomes preoccupied with fearfully watching Marreira, whose success is representative of the rise of the working class in Brazil. Carlos eventually gathers enough courage to ask Marreira to leave, but when he finally turns from his imagined enemy he finds that his real enemy has defeated him. The factory that has long ground the plantation's cane and refined the sugar refuses to extend credit any longer. Faced with the prospect of disposing of the plantation at public auction, Carlos instead sells it to Uncle Juca. Carlos then leaves Santa Rosa, having learned nothing of value from his experience. As the train speeds away with him, Carlos glimpses Marreira's prosperous mansion, symbol of the new social environment in which he has been unable to compete.

Critical Evaluation:

José Lins do Rego's *Plantation Boy* is the title given in English translation to three of the six novels known as the Sugar Cane Cycle. The trilogy *Menino de engenho* (plantation boy), *Doidinho* (literally, "daffy boy"), and *Bangüê* (old plantation) was followed by *O moleque Ricardo* (1935; black boy Richard), *Usina* (1936; the sugar refinery), and *Fogo Morto* (1943; dead fires), none of which has been translated into English. *Menino de engenho* views the plantation through the eyes of Carlos from the age of four to twelve; *Doidinho* describes Carlos's early schooling under the tough discipline of a parochial school; and *Bangüê*, which picks up after a lapse of time in which Carlos has finished law school, traces his inability to follow in his grandfather's footsteps. Lins do Rego wrote thirteen novels and published several collections of essays, but he remains best known for the Sugar Cane Cycle.

Menino de engenho is somewhat autobiographical, for the author's mother died a few months after his birth, and he was raised by his aunts and grandfather on his father's plantation. The novel is divided into forty chapters that are more like vignettes, or related tales, than chapters of a sustained narrative. Indeed, the narrative seems modeled on a collection of personal observations or memories. Characters are developed by accretion, their appearance in various vignettes gradually producing more rounded images. Uncle Juca, for example, who at first appears merely as the man responsible for bringing the four-year-old boy from Recife to Santa Rosa, gradually emerges as a hardworking and competent plantation boss who satisfies his sexual urges with whatever worker's daughter, sister, or even wife is at hand and unattended. The grandfather's character is similarly sketched in brief, seemingly unconnected observations that coalesce across the work to create the gruff but actually beneficent plantation owner whom all admire.

No less important than the characters is the setting, which also emerges gradually and provides the historical backdrop of a Brazilian plantation early in the twentieth century. The setting is what one critic has called "the debris of a vanishing order." Evidence of the previous order is visible everywhere, particularly in the relationship between Carlos's grandfather and his workers. Once slaves and now free, they go on with their lives much as they had before the abolition of slavery. The colonel is shown to be a kind, just patriarch who rules over them, but they depend on him for everything—their land, their food, their livelihood, and the settlement of their disputes.

Carlos's observations re-create the world of plantation life and the local customs, religious festivals, superstitions, and folklore. Carlos describes bandits, storytellers, mystics, and idiosyncratic characters such as the curmudgeonly Aunt Sinhàzinha, who terrifies everyone, young and old. The content and structure of the chapter-tales are reminiscent of the popular folktales of northeastern Brazil known as *literatura de cordel*, or stories on a string, so called because crudely published pamphlets containing these stories were literally strung along strings to catch the eyes of prospective buyers.

An important influence on the novels is Gilberto Freyre's sociohistorical work. Freyre's most famous work, *Masters and Slaves* (1933), is recalled in the narrator's admittedly precocious comments on "the Big House and the slave quarters," a literal translation of Freyre's original-language title, *Casa Grande e Sanzala*. Lins do Rego was involved in the region-tradition movement founded by Freyre, who is considered to be Lins do Rego's most profound intellectual influence. The result in *Plantation Boy* is a regionalism that fuses a lively view of local life and history with a submerged critique of the patriarchal plantation system. Carlos loves and admires his grandfather, but he also notices the poverty in which the workers live. He observes the shacks in which the families live and the many children clothed in tatters or even naked, some with the big bellies of constant hunger. He notes the difference between his childhood and that of the little plantation boys with whom he plays. Woven among all these reminiscences is Carlos's longing for maternal love, his morbid fear of death and disease, and his ever-present pessimism.

Lins do Rego's creation of a decadent postslavery Brazilian Northeast has been compared to William Faulkner's decadent rural American South. Certainly both writers are regionalists who describe crumbling plantation societies based on single-crop economies that are ruled by formerly slaveholding aristocracies. *Plantation Boy* is enjoyable reading, but its major strength lies in its vivid documentation of a time and place long since gone.

Linda Ledford-Miller

Further Reading

Chamberlin, Bobby J. "José Lins do Rêgo." In *Latin American Writers*, edited by Carlos A. Solé and Maria Isabel Abreu. New York: Charles Scribner's Sons, 1989. Provides a fine introduction for the beginning reader of the author's fiction. Notes the autobiographical elements of his work along with its regional and folkloric influences.

Ellison, Fred P. *Brazil's New Novel: Four Northeastern Masters.* 1954. Reprint. Westport, Conn.: Greenwood Press, 1979. Classic work in the field provides an excellent introduction to the new Brazilian regionalism of the 1930's and 1940's. One chapter is devoted to an examination of Lins do Rego's works.

Hulet, Claude L. "José Lins do Rêgo." In *Brazilian Literature 3, 1920-1960: Modernism.* Washington, D.C.: Georgetown University Press, 1975. Chapter on Lins do Rego is part of an anthology of Brazilian literature in Portuguese with introductions in English. Includes a short biography of the author followed by critical commentary and discussion of his style and techniques.

"José Lins do Rêgo (Cavalcânti)." In *World Authors, 1950-1970,* edited by John Wakeman. New York: H. W. Wilson, 1975. Gives an overview of the author's life and summarizes each of the novels of the Sugar Cane Cycle. Includes a brief discussion of Lins do Rego's detailed naturalism and simple, direct style.

Omotoso, Ebenezer. "The Myth of Black Female Sexuality in José Lins do Rego's Sugar-Cane Cycle Novels." In *Gender Perceptions and Development in Africa,* edited by Mary E. Modupe Kolawole. Lagos, Nigeria: Arrabon Academic, 1998. Presents a feminist examination of Lins do Rego's depiction of women and sexuality in his novel cycle.

Swarthout, Kelley. "Gendered Memories of Plantation Life: Teresa de la Parra's *Las Memorias de Mama Blanca* and José Lins do Rego's *Menino de engenho.*" *Latin American Literary Review* 35, no. 69 (January-June, 2007): 46-66. Examines the novels' depictions of childhoods spent on the sugar plantations of Venezuela and Brazil, describing how these works document the decline of a patriarchal rural life.

Vincent, Jon. "José Lins do Rêgo." In *Dictionary of Brazilian Literature,* edited by Irwin Stein. New York: Greenwood Press, 1988. Provides an overview of Lins do Rego's life and work and discusses his involvement in the region-tradition school of thought and writing founded by the Brazilian sociologist Gilberto Freyre.

Platero and I
An Andalusian Elegy

Author: Juan Ramón Jiménez (1881-1958)
First published: Platero y yo, 1914 (English translation, 1956)
Type of work: Poetry

Juan Ramón Jiménez was awarded the Nobel Prize in Literature in 1956. Though he is most famous for his poetry, his contributions to the development of Spanish prose are considered equally important. He began writing poetry at the age of fourteen, and he began experimenting with prose poetry at seventeen. His first prose poem, "Andén" ("The Railway Platform"), shows a strong influence of Spanish Romanticism in its imagery, structure, and vocabulary. It tells of a woman afflicted with a mental disorder that causes her to wait forever on the platform for a train to bring her the child that she never had. The Spanish romantic poet Gustavo Adolfo Bécquer and the Nicaraguan modernist Rubén Darío, along with the Germans Johann Wolfgang von Goethe and Heinrich Heine and the French Charles Baudelaire and Stéphane Mallarmé, were clearly influential in his early prose poems. Jiménez went on from there to set new standards for prose poetry in a series of highly original works that started in 1917 with *Platero and I,* one of the best examples of prose poetry in Spanish literature.

Platero and I, written between 1907 and 1912, is based on material Jiménez gathered in his hometown of Moguer (in the province of Andalusia) while recuperating from the severe depression caused by his father's sudden death in 1900. At a time when many of his contemporaries—the writers of the literary Generation of '98—were focusing on Castile, a province long dominant in the history of Spain, Jiménez turned for inspiration to his native Andalusia. *Platero and I* draws on many of the area's resources and characteristics, including the country towns, the ringing bells, the sounds of children, the animals, the small houses, and the golden moon. The work also draws on the traditionally impressionistic style of the region. The elegiac tone of *Platero and I,* however, is markedly different from Jiménez's other poetry of that time. The tone here expresses grief and real suffering.

The first publication of *Platero and I,* in 1914, was an abbreviated version of the poem, written for a collection of children's literature, that contained only 73 of the 135 prose poems that were composed over a number of years and make up the complete edition of 1917. During his lifetime, Jiménez wrote 250 prose poems that he ultimately hoped to publish in a collection titled "Versos para ciegos" (verses for the blind). This title reveals that Jiménez thought poetry to be distinguished from prose based only on the presence in poetry of assonant or consonant rhyme. Once an author eliminates rhyme, the verses become like poetry read to a blind person. Unable to see the physical disposition of the text on the printed page and unguided by the familiar presence of rhyme, the blind person would not be able to distinguish between poetry and prose. The poetic element of *Platero and I* is Jiménez's masterful use of the natural rhythm of the Spanish language to generate melodic sentences that are flexible in syntax and in the use of clause structures—sentences that produce the almost cinematographic effects of slow motion and close-up and wide-angle views. He frequently suppresses cause-and-effect relationships and logical connections in an impressionistic style of writing that values the poetic image above all else.

"Platero" is the name generally given to a type of silver-colored donkey (*plata* is the Spanish word for silver). In these prose poems, the donkey is Jiménez's companion, the one to whom the author makes his observations and in whom he confides. Although it may be tempting to look for parallels between Platero and Juan Ramón and Miguel de Cervantes' Sancho Panza and Don Quixote, Platero, unlike Sancho, neither speaks nor participates actively in the work. On the contrary, Platero is the ideal listener and, though not "blind," perhaps also the ideal reader.

The events in *Platero and I* take place in one year, starting in one spring and ending in the next. Platero is actually a synthesis of the many silver donkeys the author knew during the years of his recuperation in Moguer. The symbolism in Platero's year of life is important for Jiménez, for it represents the natural cycle of birth to rebirth. As if to underline the importance of rebirth, Jiménez associates a second, traditional symbol with Platero's death: the butterfly, whose evolution from larva to winged creature has for centuries symbolized the transformation and renewal of life. In the last chapter of *Platero and I*, Jiménez, accompanied by children from the area, visits Platero's grave. As if responding to the poet's question, "Do you still remember me?" a butterfly appears and flies "like a soul" from lily to lily. These symbols anticipate a new beginning for Jiménez, who, only a few years before, was so fearful of death that he had to have a doctor with him at all times.

Jiménez uses the first person and the third person to alternate between subjective and objective narrative perspectives. The perspectives also vary between a child's view and that of an adult. What the views have in common is a firm grounding in reality; in this work, Jiménez first introduces death, violence, abuse, cruelty, deformity, racism, the ugly side of so-cial reality, human suffering, and human abuse of other human beings. Jiménez's descriptions of nature and its beauty, of the joys of being a child and of being with children, counterbalance the work's sometimes overwhelming accumulation of harsh realism.

Death has many manifestations in *Platero and I*. It is part of a larger process of growth and transformation such as that of Platero. It is sad and lonely like that of Pinito (poem 94), the loner whom the townspeople have dehumanized to being the epitome of stupidity, and it can be tender and sorrowful like that of the young girl who dies of tuberculosis (poem 46) or that of the little girl who so loves to play with Platero (poem 81).

Violence, abuse, and cruelty to animals appear frequently in the poems. In "The Mangy Dog" (poem 27), the vineyard guard kills a dog with his shotgun for no reason other than that the animal is physically unattractive. "The Old Donkey" (poem 113) shows what can happen to animals that grow old and are of no further use to their human owners. A dog saves itself once from death in the boneyard only to have its life ended by the winter's cold wind. The animal in "The White Mare" (poem 108) must cope not only with old age, like the old donkey, but also with being beaten by its master with a stick and a sickle. As the mare lies dying, people gather to curse it and poke fun at it, and the children throw stones at it. Jiménez tells Platero that in the darkness of the street, the mare's cadaver attains a cloudlike whiteness and light that the cold evening sky complements with small pink clouds. In Jiménez's works, whiteness, like that of the lilies at Platero's grave, consistently symbolizes purity and transcendence.

Deformity appears in "The Half-Wit Child" (poem 17), which describes a mute who, while not worthy of the attention of others, was all that his mother had in life. Jiménez looks back, remembering him, and, after his death, he looks ahead to envision him enjoying his eternal reward.

"Sarito" (poem 74) presents the problem of racism. A former black servant of a friend in Seville is now a traveling bullfighter who has stopped to visit. Most people eye him with suspicion, and one resident starts a fight with him. Jiménez receives him openly and affectionately. Nevertheless, the black Sarito knows to keep his distance, as he must, even from a friend.

Poem 95, "The River," chronicles the decline that pollution from the copper mines upstream has brought to an area. In retrospect, Jiménez looks back on the lively hustle and bustle of the fishermen, wine merchants, and others who once sailed the waters; when he looks at the now lifeless stream, the color of rust, he compares it to the trickle of blood from a cadaver.

Nature has many manifestations in *Platero and I*. In "The Eclipse" (poem 4), nature is a source of humor as the gradual darkening of the sun fools the hens into returning to their roost early, as if it were night. An unexpected warm spell, a rather cruel joke, tricks the swallows (poem 13) into returning, only to have them suffer when it turns cold again. Thunderstorms pound the area, keeping all in fear and suspense (poem 71) and sometimes killing people (poem 18).

Jiménez is at his impressionist best when describing nature. A sunset becomes a "Scarlet Landscape" (poem 19), wounded by its own crystals and dressed in a bleeding purple. Its light turns small plants and flowers transparent. Employing a synesthesia that combines the senses of touch, sight, and smell, Jiménez describes the light as embalming the moment with a moist, luminous, and pungent perfume. This technique frequently appears elsewhere in *Platero and I*, as in "The Pomegranate" (poem 96), where the poet describes the bitter, dry taste of the outer skin, then the first taste of sweetness—a "dawn made briefly into a ruby"—and finally the center of the fruit, "edible amethysts." He extends this poetic image to the limits of language: silence. The poet confesses that he can no longer talk, caught up as he is in a taste as sweet as what the eye sees when lost in the multiple colors of a kaleidoscope.

Children come and go constantly through the poems of *Platero and I*. Jiménez had a special place in his heart for children, whether rich or poor, whether from Moguer or from Argentina, where he visited in 1948, or from Puerto Rico, where he lived and finally died. "The Magi" (poem 122) is typical. Jiménez's description of the day in January when Spanish children normally receive their Christmas gifts combines the excitement of a child with an adult's love of children. Once the children have finally gone to bed, the poet plans with Platero how they and other adults will dress up in sheets, quilts, and old hats and parade at midnight beneath the window of the children's room, leaving the children astonished, trembling, and marveling at the magi who have come to leave them gifts.

Joseph A. Feustle, Jr.

Further Reading

Cardwell, Richard A. "'The Universal Andalusian,' 'The Zealous Andalusian,' and the 'Andalusian Elegy.'" *Studies in Twentieth Century Literature* 7, no. 2 (Spring, 1983): 201-224. Explores the influence that Francisco Giner de los Ríos and the philosophy of Krausism had on Jiménez. Discusses how the intellectual atmosphere of the time influenced Jiménez's contemporaries, including Antonio Machado, José Ortega y Gasset, and Miguel de Unamuno y Jugo, all well-known members of the literary Generation of '98.

Fogelquist, Donald. *Juan Ramón Jiménez*. Boston: Twayne, 1976. This solid overview of the poet's life and works provides a good introduction for students and general readers.

Jiménez, Juan Ramón. *Platero and I*. Translated by Antonio T. de Nicoläs. Boulder, Colo.: Shambhala, 1978. Complete, excellent translation attempts to keep the lyricism, rhythm, and beauty of the original text intact, although in reality this is a linguistic impossibility.

Kluback, William. *Encounters with Juan Ramón Jiménez*. New York: Peter Lang, 1995. Analyzes Jiménez's writing through the device of imagining a conversation with Jiménez and following Jiménez and Platero on an adventure to confront the foibles and opinions of humankind.

Olson, Paul R. *Circle of Paradox: Time and Essence in the Poetry of Juan Ramón Jiménez*. Baltimore: Johns Hopkins University Press, 1967. Essential study examines the major symbols in Jiménez's poetry.

Skyrme, Raymond. "Divining the Distant: The Poetics of *Platero y yo*." *Romance Quarterly* 47, no. 4 (Fall, 2000): 195-204. Presents analysis of *Platero and I*, examining the language, imagery, and vision in the collection's poems.

Wilcox, John C. *Self and Image in Juan Ramón Jiménez: Modern and Post-modern Readings*. Champaign: University of Illinois Press, 1987. Reveals the art of Jiménez's early poetry by focusing on the relationship between the author and the reader. Many of the poems examined have parallels in *Platero and I*.

The Playboy of the Western World

Author: John Millington Synge (1871-1909)
First produced: 1907; first published, 1907
Type of work: Drama
Type of plot: Comic realism
Time of plot: Early twentieth century
Locale: County Mayo, Ireland

Principal characters:
CHRISTOPHER MAHON, a braggart
OLD MAHON, his father
MARGARET "PEGEEN" FLAHERTY, his sweetheart
WIDOW QUIN, a villager

The Story:

One evening a young man arrives at a small inn on the wild Mayo coast of Ireland and announces that he has run away from home. He says that his name is Christopher Mahon and that he ran away because he had killed his father during a fight. The farmers who are passing the time in the inn are very much pleased by his exhibition of courage. Christopher is especially admired by Margaret "Pegeen" Flaherty, the pretty young daughter of Michael Flaherty, the innkeeper. She and the others press the young man to tell his story again and again.

At home, Christopher had been a meek and obedient son, controlled by his domineering father. He accepted the insults of his parent until the latter tried to force him into marrying a rich old woman. At last, in desperation, he hit his father over the head. Seeing the old man fall, Christopher presumed that he was dead.

The experience at the inn is something new for Christopher, who for the first time in his life is regarded as a hero. When the news of his story spreads among the villagers, they flock to look at this paragon of bravery. The young women are particularly interested in him—and the not-so-young as well. Dame Quin, a thirty-year-old widow, is much taken with the young taproom hero. Christopher, however, is attracted to pretty Pegeen. He is flattered by her admiration and, in an attempt to live up to her opinion of him, he begins to adopt an attitude of bravado. Before long, he himself believes that he had done a courageous deed.

Each year the village holds a festival in which the men compete with each other in various sports. Christopher is naturally expected to take part. His early timidity having long since disappeared, he makes every effort to appear a hero in the eyes of Pegeen, to whom he is now openly betrothed. She had broken her engagement with a young farmer, Shawn Keogh, soon after Christopher arrived on the scene.

While her Playboy, as Pegeen calls him, is taking part in the sports activities, an old man comes to the inn. He is looking for a young man whose description fits Christopher's appearance. Dame Quin, who still has designs on the boy, deliberately misdirects the stranger. When the man returns from his wild goose chase, he arrives in time to see Christopher hailed as a hero because he had just won the mule race. Old Mahon, not dead from Christopher's blow, recognizes his son and flies into a rage. He insists that Christopher go home with him, and, through his angry tirade, he humiliates his son in front of the spectators.

The Playboy, however, had enjoyed too long the thrill of being a hero. He does not give in timidly as he would have done at an earlier time. Much to his father's astonishment, he again strikes the old man over the head. Once again it appears that old Mahon is dead. The reaction of the people, however, is not at all what Christopher might have expected. Killing one's father some miles away is one thing, but killing him in front of a number of spectators who might be involved in the affair is another. The people mutter angrily among themselves, and even Pegeen joins with them in denouncing the murderer.

Deciding at last that the only thing to do is to hang Christopher for his crime, they tie up the struggling young man and prepare to lead him away. Old Mahon, however, had proved himself a tough fellow once before, and he does so again. The first blow from Christopher had only stunned him, so that, soon after the boy had run away, his father was able to follow him to the village. This second blow had merely knocked him unconscious for a short time. As Christopher struggles and the noose is slipped over his head, Mahon crawls through the door on his hands and knees.

While the villagers stand around dumbfounded, Mahon walks over to his son and quickly unties him. Far from being angry with Christopher for hitting him, he is pleased to discover that his son is not the timid weakling he had thought him to be. The two leave the inn, arm in arm, deaf to the pleas of Pegeen, both of them jeering at the foolishness of the people on the Mayo coast.

Critical Evaluation:

The Playboy of the Western World, John Millington Synge's last completed work, is the author's greatest play, and in many ways his most difficult to interpret. The play may be viewed as a satire of Western myths and conventions, beginning with the age-old habit in the West of cheerfully, even eagerly, extending a welcome to criminals and fugitives seeking shelter. In the romantic sphere, the play uses a comic reversal of the traditional situation of man as the sexual aggressor, instead having Christopher hotly pursued and competed for by Pegeen and her rivals. Greek myths are also satirized, beginning with the obvious parallel between Christopher and Oedipus as having committed patricide. In the same vein, Christopher becomes a mock-heroic counterpart to Odysseus as he wanders into the Mayo village seeking refuge, and eventually crowns his conquests there by winning a mule race.

On another level, *The Playboy of the Western World* is a deeply symbolic play; its meaning revolves around the emotional and moral growth of the hero through a series of ritual "murders" of his father. The first "murder" is a spontaneous, unconscious, almost accidental act; Christopher's blow is a reflex reaction to his father's incessant taunting and ridiculing of the young man's physical and sexual abilities. It is crucial to examine the reactions of the Irish peasants to Christopher's deed. Steeped in mythical, preintellectual concepts, they view the patricide as a necessary and admirable act. Because the violence occurred far away and reaches them only by the report of an intriguing visitor, it exists for them only as a fantasy, not as a down-to-earth, bloody deed; the murder is like another folktale in which the hero gloriously kills all obstacles in his path. Thus they lionize Christopher, who as a result blossoms from a sniveling, terrified boy to a confident braggart and ladies' man.

Unfortunately, Christopher's new stature is based on a lie, as becomes known when Old Mahon appears in the village and humiliates his son, thus necessitating the second "murder." This second act of violence, however, is essentially different from the first; faced with a threat to his self-image, reputation, and independence, Christopher now makes a conscious—and therefore moral—decision to kill his father. The qualitative difference in the two acts is immediately reflected in the villagers' reaction to this second "murder." They are horrified and drag the hero off to hang him; he has grown, through this rational and very real action, past the comprehension of their primitive unconsciousness and must be punished.

Christopher's growth is completed and his triumph as hero complete, however, only with the third "murder." This time the act is purely verbal and symbolic, and consists of Christopher's discovery that he can order his father to do his will. Thus, Christopher at the end of the play has transcended the primitive stage of physical murder; he has asserted his power by throwing off the domination of a tyrannical father, thus reaching the full status of hero.

Further Reading

Bloom, Harold, ed. *Modern Critical Interpretations: John Millington Synge's "The Playboy of the Western World."* New York: Chelsea House, 1988. Eight representative essays consider the character Christopher's self-transformation and parallels with Christ; the realistic and fantastic aspects of the play; the play's complexity and ambiguity; and the play's irony, wit, and poetry.

Castle, Gregory. *Modernism and the Celtic Revival.* New York: Cambridge University Press, 2001. Analyzes how Synge and other Irish Revivalists employed techniques of anthropology to translate, reassemble, and edit material from Irish folk culture, to combat British imperialism. Chapter 4 analyzes *The Playboy of the Western World*.

Frazier, Adrian, ed. *Playboys of the Western World: Production Histories.* Dublin: Carysfort Press, 2004. A history of the play's production, from its initial staging to later twentieth century performances in Ireland, the United Kingdom, Northern Ireland, and the United States. The second part of the book focuses on a 2004 production, providing details about the play's staging and discussing its relevance for modern audiences.

Gonzalez, Alexander G., ed. *Assessing the Achievement of J. M. Synge.* Westport, Conn.: Greenwood Press, 1996. Collection of fourteen original essays interpreting Synge's drama, including three essays focusing on *The Playboy of the Western World*: "Resentment, Relevance, and the Production History of *The Playboy of the Western World*," "The Playboy, Critics, and the Enduring Problem of the Audience," and "A Young Man's Ghost."

Greene, David, and Edward M. Stephens. *J. M. Synge: 1871-1909.* Rev. ed. New York: Macmillan, 1989. The standard, authorized biography based on Synge's diaries, letters, and manuscripts. Provides the basic accounts of the composition of *The Playboy of the Western World* and its riotous reception in 1907.

Kopper, Edward A., Jr., ed. *A. J. M. Synge Literary Companion.* Westport, Conn.: Greenwood Press, 1988. A valuable collection of sixteen essays by leading scholars, covering all aspects of Synge's life and work. An excellent introduction to the critical literature that includes good bibliographies.

McDonald, Ronan. *Tragedy and Irish Literature: Synge, O'Casey, Beckett*. New York: Palgrave, 2002. Examines the work of Synge and two other Irish playwrights, describing how the culture of suffering, loss, and guilt shapes their ideas of tragedy. Defines a peculiarly Irish form of tragedy by locating common themes and techniques in the playwrights' works.

Owens, Cóilîn, and Joan Radner, eds. *Irish Drama: 1900-1980*. Washington, D.C.: Catholic University of America Press, 1990. Places the play in the general context of the Irish dramatic movement. Includes a concise introduction, map, and one of the best detailed annotations to the text of the play.

Ritschel, Nelson O'Ceallaigh. *Synge and Irish Nationalism: The Precursor to Revolution*. Westport, Conn.: Greenwood Press, 2002. Argues that Synge's plays are deeply rooted in ancient Irish literature, describing how his use of this material reflects his nationalist agenda.

The Plough and the Stars

Author: Sean O'Casey (1880-1964)
First produced: 1926; first published, 1926
Type of work: Drama
Type of plot: Social realism
Time of plot: 1916
Locale: Dublin, Ireland

Principal characters:
FLUTHER GOOD,
PETER FLYNN,
MRS. GOGAN,
MOLLSER GOGAN,
BESSIE BURGESS,
THE COVEY,
NORA CLITHEROE, and
JACK CLITHEROE, neighbors in a Dublin tenement house
CAPTAIN BRENNAN, of the Irish Citizen Army
CORPORAL STODDART and SERGEANT TINLEY, of the Wiltshires

The Story:

Fluther Good has put a new lock on the door of the Clitheroes, and Mrs. Gogan brings in a hatbox, just delivered for Nora Clitheroe. Mrs. Gogan is convinced that Nora is putting on airs and buying too many new clothes to hold on to her husband. Nora's uncle, Peter Flynn, drifts in and out, readying his uniform of the Irish National Foresters. Peter has a chip on his shoulder that all the tenement dwellers take turns knocking off. He is an ineffectual man and he knows it.

When the Covey, Nora's cousin, comes in, telling them that he has been laid off from work because the boys have mobilized for a demonstration for independence, he arouses both Peter and Fluther. The Covey is less inclined to follow the flag of the Plough and the Stars than to go ahead with his work. Peter and the Covey are arguing away when Nora comes home and quiets them, declaring that there is small hope of ever making them respectable. She is pleased with the way Fluther had put on the lock, but Bessie Burgess, a vigorous but rather coarse woman, scornfully berates Nora for treating her neighbors shamefully, not trusting them. As Fluther breaks up the women's wrangling, Jack Clitheroe comes home and sends Bessie away. He tells Nora that he will speak to Bessie when she is sober again.

Jack is despondent because the Citizen Army is to meet tonight. He had lost the rank of captain to Ned Brennan and, sulking, refuses to attend meetings. Wanting to be a leader, he does not have strength of leadership. Nora tries to get his mind off the meeting by making love to him. They are interrupted by Captain Brennan with a dispatch from the general telling Jack where to report. Jack does not understand why he is to report until Brennan tells him that the boys have given him the title of commandant, word of which is in a letter Nora had never delivered. Disturbed because Nora had withheld the letter, Jack goes to the meeting with Brennan.

Mollser Gogan, a child in the last stages of tuberculosis, asks Nora if she might stay with her, since everyone else has gone to the demonstration. Fluther and Peter, overwhelmed by the oratory of the speakers at the demonstration, go to a bar to pour in more courage. Even in the public house, the voice of the speaker follows them, urging bloodshed and war. Bessie and Mrs. Gogan are engaged in a verbal battle when they enter. Bessie, drunk, is ready for a hair-pulling, but the barman sends both women away. Peter is left holding Mrs. Gogan's baby, as Mrs. Gogan forgets the child as she is piloted out of the bar. He hurries out to find her.

Fluther, though he had intended to give up drinking before the meeting, decides the time has come for all the liquor he can hold, and he is generous enough to stand treat, even to the Covey and Rosie, a prostitute. Fluther and the Covey get into an argument on the labor movement, and the barman has to separate them. Rosie and Fluther leave when Jack, Brennan, and other officers, their eyes shining with excitement, come in for a drink before moving off with the Citizen Army.

The next day, Mollser is so weak that Mrs. Gogan puts her out in the sun in front of the house; they can hear shooting in the distance. Looking for Jack, Nora and Fluther had spent the night going to all the barricades without finding him. When they come back to the house, Nora is leaning heavily on Fluther. Bessie shouts down curses from her window. The Covey sighs that the fight will do the poor people no good.

Bessie gives Mollser a mug of milk when she comes downstairs. The men begin to gamble to keep their minds off the shooting, but they stop when Bessie reappears, laden down with booty, to say that looting had begun in the shops. Fluther and the Covey leave immediately. The guns scare Mollser so much that Bessie takes her into the house. Even timid Peter starts to follow Bessie and Mrs. Gogan when they set out with a baby carriage to hold their loot, but the sound of the big guns again stops him. He is envious, however, when he sees the Covey, then Bessie and Mrs. Gogan, return with piles of loot.

Brennan and Jack stop at the steps to let a wounded comrade rest. It is with difficulty that Jack gets away from Nora, who had run down to him when she heard his voice. When the two officers finally take their man away, Nora is ready to faint.

Fluther comes back with a jug of whiskey. Roaring drunk, he is too fuddled to go out for a doctor for Mollser, who is suddenly very sick. Bessie, praying when she hears the guns, goes off toward the shooting to find a doctor.

A few days later the rebellion is still going on. Mollser has died, and Nora had a stillborn baby. Both bodies are in the same coffin in Bessie's room, the only room in the tenement that seems safe from the shooting. Fluther, the Covey, and Peter, having taken refuge there, play cards to while away the time.

Nora is on the verge of insanity. Bessie has stayed up with her for three nights and is herself almost dead for sleep. Each

time Bessie sits in the chair in front of the fireplace for a nap, Nora wakes up. Once, when Nora gets up, Brennan, in civilian clothes, is in the room telling the men how Jack had died. Nora does not recognize him. Brennan wants to stay with the others; he says there is nowhere to go any more. Corporal Stoddart, an English soldier, comes in to escort the coffin out of the house. Mrs. Gogan is the only one allowed to go with the coffin. As she is thanking Fluther for making the funeral arrangements, the soldier hears a sniper shoot another English soldier. The English, trying to find the sniper, are rounding up all the men in the district, and so Fluther, the Covey, Peter, and Brennan are forced to go with the corporal to spend the night in the Protestant church.

Bessie has again fallen asleep. Nora gets up to prepare tea for Jack. As she stands at the window looking for him, the soldiers below shout for her to go away. Bessie, awakened, tries to pull her back, but Nora struggles so hard that Bessie falls back against the window frame as she pushes Nora. Two shots, fired quickly, strike Bessie. She is dead before Mrs. Gogan comes home. Two English soldiers, investigating the room for snipers, find the mistake they had made in killing Bessie. They calmly pour themselves cups of tea while Mrs. Gogan takes Nora downstairs to put her into Mollser's bed.

Critical Evaluation:

Sean O'Casey's bitter childhood and early adulthood help account for his adherence to the Marxist idea of class war. He believed that the Irish would have to reckon with the problem of Irish poverty before they could ever hope to win independence. It is with this problem of some poor people caught in the middle of the famous Easter Rebellion of 1916 that O'Casey deals in *The Plough and the Stars*. In the play, the desperate situation of a group of tenement dwellers overshadows the dream of national independence. The Covey seems always to give O'Casey's own views on humanity versus nationality. The play was the cause of a patriotic riot when it was first produced by the Abbey Theatre in Dublin.

The Plough and the Stars is the last of O'Casey's realistic plays about the Irish Civil War and, along with *Juno and the Paycock* (1924), represents the high point of his artistic achievement. Although it may lack the depth of characterization present in *Juno and the Paycock*, it probably has a greater theatrical impact. Juxtaposing scenes of the most intense pain and violence against moments of earthy, vital humor, O'Casey succeeds in capturing and dramatizing both the folly and the heroism of this Irish national tragedy.

The play is set during the Easter Uprising of 1916, when extremists proclaimed an Irish Republic and seized the Dublin General Post Office. A short, bloody struggle ensued and ravaged most of the city for several days before the nationalists surrendered. *The Plough and the Stars* describes the impact of these events on the inhabitants of a single tenement dwelling, which, because of O'Casey's careful selection of characters and conflicts, becomes a microcosm of Dublin at war.

The play's title points to many of its themes. On one level the title refers to the flag of the Citizen Army, a leftist labor movement that was one of the two groups sponsoring the uprising. Thus, O'Casey specifically identifies himself with the radical workers rather than with the ardent nationalists. On a more symbolic level, however, the flag suggests a conflict— the "plough" versus "the stars"; that is, the practical realities of poverty and human relationships versus the abstract ideal of pure nationalism. While O'Casey admired the courage and dedication of the rebels, he felt that their fanatical actions at best attacked only superficial evils and at worst are suicidal, unleashing forces that destroyed not only the insurrectionists but also large numbers of innocent people caught up in the resulting violence. The ways in which impersonal, abstract ideals can destroy human relationships, a major theme in O'Casey's previous plays, reaches its fullest statement in *The Plough and the Stars*.

This theme is illustrated in the play's first act in the dispute between newlyweds Jack and Nora Clitheroe. In spite of her social and cultural pretensions, Nora is the embodiment of domesticity, valuing only her husband, her home, and her family to be. She can understand neither Jack's devotion to a political cause nor his apparent taste for the military style; she fears only his injury or death and is willing to deceive him to keep him out of combat. For his part, Jack seems deeply, if sentimentally, in love with Nora, and at times he is tempted to accede to her desires, but his commitment is too strong. He and his comrades are caught up in the fervor of the times.

O'Casey makes the audience wonder, however, how much of that commitment is dedication, how much is ego, and, when the fighting becomes intense, how much is fear of being thought a coward. The outcome of the domestic conflict is predictable: Jack is killed in combat and Nora, too delicate to stand the pressure, goes insane. Others are not so weak. If O'Casey's vision does not spare those who bring havoc on themselves and their loved ones, he also pays homage to those victims who are forced by circumstance to assume the burdens. Frequently, those who seem the least promising become, under pressure, the most heroic.

Fluther Good behaves like an amiable drunk during most of the play and is quick to loot liquor stores when given the opportunity. When Mollser Gogan dies and Nora has her breakdown, however, Fluther braves bullets and arrest to bring aid and comfort. Bessie Burgess, the lone English partisan in the tenement, seems ill-tempered and bigoted in the early parts of the play, deriding Nora and fighting constantly with Mrs. Gogan, another querulous woman. Yet, in the last act, it is Bessie who ministers to the dying Mollser and the mad Nora, finally sacrificing her life trying to shield the girl from sniper fire. Her rival, Mrs. Gogan, assumes the burdens after Bessie dies.

Bessie and Mrs. Gogan, like Juno in the earlier play, represent the strength of an Ireland torn to pieces by civil war. They do what they can—and must—to keep the continuity of life intact while the men, with their abstract notions of nationalism, heroism, and manhood, destroy. While the fighting rages, young Mollser dies of tuberculosis because there is no one available to help her. Mollser is O'Casey's symbol for the real Irish situation: poverty and neglect are the real evils, and until they are dealt with, the question of nationalism is largely irrelevant. As long as the Jack Clitheroes and the Brennans can be stirred up to violence by the demagogic appeals of the "Voice," these problems will continue to be ignored. However, as long as Ireland is capable of producing people like Bessie Burgess, Mrs. Gogan, and Fluther Good, O'Casey suggests that there is hope.

Further Reading

Ayling, Ronald. *Sean O'Casey: Modern Judgments*. Nashville, Tenn.: Aurora Press, 1970. Includes valuable comments on *The Plough and the Stars*. Considers O'Casey's poetic gifts, his use of symbols, his socialism, and his place in Irish drama and literature.

Hogan, Robert. *The Experiments of Sean O'Casey*. New York: St. Martin's Press, 1960. A synthesis of dramatic theory and theatrical practice. Argues that in his Dublin trilogy, O'Casey is expanding his technical capacities, and that *The Plough and the Stars* is a stage in his continuing experimentation.

Kilroy, Thomas, ed. *Sean O'Casey: A Collection of Essays*. Englewood Cliffs, N.J.: Prentice-Hall, 1975. An excellent selection from leading Irish, British, and American critics who discuss O'Casey's politics, dramatic technique, and development. The critics offer differing assessments of his achievement as a political dramatist.

Krause, David. *Sean O'Casey: The Man and His Work*. New York: Macmillan, 1975. One of the best studies of O'Casey's dramatic work. Describes the economic, political, and religious tensions in the Dublin of his time.

McDonald, Ronan. *Tragedy and Irish Literature: Synge, O'Casey, Beckett*. New York: Palgrave, 2002. Compares the work of three Irish playwrights, including O'Casey, analyzing how the themes of suffering, loss, and guilt are reflected in their respective dramas.

Murray, Christopher. *Sean O'Casey: "The Shadow of a Gunman," "Juno and the Paycock," "The Plough and the Stars."* London: Faber, 2000. An analysis of the plays in O'Casey's Dublin trilogy, placing these works within the context of Irish society and theater in the 1920's.

_____. *Sean O'Casey: Writer at Work—A Biography.* Dublin: Gill & Macmillan, 2004. A biography focusing on O'Casey's literary career, tracing the development of his writing from his early nationalist work to his later socialist writings.

Sean O'Casey Review 3 (Spring, 1976). Special issue on *The Plough and the Stars*. Contains valuable essays on the first production, O'Casey's realism and pacifism and socialism, the historical background to the drama, and Bessie Burgess as Cathleen Ni Houlihan.

Stewart, Victoria. *About O'Casey: The Playwright and the Work*. London: Faber & Faber, 2003. Describes the political and social conditions in Ireland that led to O'Casey's association with the Abbey Theatre in Dublin, as well as his subsequent literary career. Includes interviews with O'Casey and those who worked with him.

The Plumed Serpent

Author: D. H. Lawrence (1885-1930)
First published: 1926
Type of work: Novel
Type of plot: Psychological realism
Time of plot: Twentieth century
Locale: Mexico

Principal characters:
KATE LESLIE, an Irishwoman
DON RAMÓN CARRASCO, a Mexican Indian scholar and the reincarnated Quetzalcoatl
GENERAL CIPRIANO VIEDMA, the reincarnated Huitzilopochtli, god of war
DOÑA CARLOTA, Don Ramón's first wife
TERESA, his second wife
OWEN RHYS, Kate Leslie's cousin

The Story:

Kate Leslie is the widow of an Irish patriot. Restless after her husband's death, she moves to Mexico with Owen Rhys, her American cousin. Mexico, however, oppresses Kate. Dark and secretive, the arid land weighs upon her spirit like a sense of doom. She sees it as a country of poverty, brutality, and bloodshed.

Owen and one of his friends take her to a bullfight. It is a distressing experience, for to her the ritual of death is like modern Mexico, vulgar and cruel, without muster or passion. She is unable to endure the spectacle and the reek of warm blood and announces that she is returning alone to the hotel. A downpour of rain begins as she is leaving the arena, and she is forced to wait in the exit tunnel with a crowd whose speech and gestures fill her with alarm. She is rescued from her predicament by a small, authoritative man in uniform who introduces himself as General Cipriano Viedma. A Mexican Indian, he is impassive and withdrawn yet vitally alert. They talk while waiting for the automobile he had summoned to take Kate to her hotel, and she feels unaccountably drawn to him.

Mrs. Norris, the widow of a former English ambassador, invites Kate and Owen to her house for tea the next day. The general and his friend, Don Ramón Carrasco, are among the guests. Don Ramón is a landowner and a distinguished scholar. There are reports of a strange happening near his estate at Sayula. A naked man is supposed to have risen from the Lake of Sayula and tell the villagers that Quetzalcoatl and the old gods of Mexico are soon to return to Earth. Don Ramón promised an investigation. The story appeals to Kate's Celtic imagination; she wants to go to Sayula to see the lake from which the Aztec gods are to be reborn.

Kate and Owen dine with Ramón before his return to Sayula. The guests talk about Mexican politics and the happening at the lake. One impassioned young man declares that only a great miracle, like the return of Quetzalcoatl, could save Mexico. Cipriano seldom speaks but sits, his eyes black and unfathomable, looking from Kate to his host. After dinner, he and Kate walk in the garden. In the darkness, she feels that he is a man of strange, almost primitive potency and impulses.

When Owen returns to the United States, Kate decides to go to Sayula for a time. There she finds an old Spanish house that pleases her. With the house comes a servant, Juana, and her two sons and two daughters. Kate likes the house and its surroundings, and she rents it for an indefinite stay.

The people of Sayula are restless and filled with a spirit Kate has not seen elsewhere in Mexico. One night, she hears drums beating in the village plaza. Men naked to the waist are distributing leaflets printed with a hymn to Quetzalcoatl. Later, the peons begin to dance to the savage and insistent rhythms of the drums. In the torchlight, the dance looks like a ritual out of old, almost forgotten times, a ritual people remember in their blood rather than in their minds. Some people say that Don Ramón is behind the new cult of Quetzalcoatl that is springing up.

Several weeks after Kate arrives in Sayula, Don Ramón and his wife, Doña Carlota, come to call. Doña Carlota is devoutly pious and eager to be friendly. When Kate visits Jamiltepec, Don Ramón's hacienda, she finds soldiers guarding the gates. A drum is beating in the patio. Doña Carlota hates the sound and tells Kate that she is afraid because her husband is involved in the business of Quetzalcoatl. She confides that he wishes to become a god, the reincarnation of the Plumed Serpent that the Aztecs had worshiped. Cipriano arrives at the hacienda for supper. That night there is a dance in the patio. Don Ramón promises that the reborn gods will bring new life to the country. The rains begin, ending the hot, dry season.

Refusing to witness her husband's heresies, as she calls them, Doña Carlota returns to Mexico City. Meanwhile, the work of the men of Quetzalcoatl continues. During one of his visits, Cipriano asks Kate to marry him, but she puts him off. Don Ramón continues to write and publish his hymns to Quetzalcoatl. Cipriano's soldiers distribute them. After he is denounced by the clergy, Don Ramón has the holy images removed from the church at Sayula and burned.

One day a group of Don Ramón's political and religious enemies, disguised as bandits, attacks Jamiltepec and tries to assassinate Don Ramón. Kate happens to be at the hacienda when the raiders appear; she kills one of the attackers and saves Don Ramón's life after he had been seriously wounded. Afterward, she stays much to herself, afraid of her own disturbed emotions; but she is being drawn slowly toward the dark, powerful forces of primitive awareness and power that she finds in Don Ramón and Cipriano. The general believes himself to be the living Huitzilopochtli, god of war. Fascinated and repelled, Kate yields to his masculine dominance.

Don Ramón marries them with pagan rites, and Kate becomes Malintzi, bride of the red-knifed god of battles.

When Don Ramón reopens the church, which he had converted into a sanctuary of the old Aztec gods, Doña Carlota protests against his blasphemy. Overcome by hysteria and fear of his implacable will, she suffers a stroke and dies a short time later. Meanwhile, Cipriano has been spreading the new doctrines among his soldiers. On an appointed night, he is declared the living Huitzilopochtli, god of the knife. In the rites of his assumption, he sacrifices three of the prisoners captured after the attack on Don Ramón some weeks before.

Don Ramón marries again. His bride is Teresa, daughter of a dead landowner of Jalisco. Watching Teresa's passive, female submission to her husband, Kate begins to fear the dark potency, the upsurge of blood with which Don Ramón and Cipriano are arousing all Mexico. Men wearing the white-and-blue serapes of Quetzalcoatl and the red-and-black serapes of Huitzilopochtli are seen everywhere. When the Church excommunicates the leaders, revolt breaks out. The president of Mexico declares the Church outlawed, and the faith of Quetzalcoatl becomes the official religion of the republic. Kate views these happenings with a sense of horror. The pride and strength of the old gods seems to menace her spirit and her womanhood. She decides to return to Ireland.

In the end, however, Kate cannot leave. Cipriano's attraction is stronger than her European sensibility and her will. Afraid of his violence but awed by the strength of a spirit stronger than her own, she feels wanted but not needed. The need, she realizes, is her own, not Cipriano's. He has revealed to her the deep, dark, hot life of the senses and the blood, and she is trapped in his primitive world. She can never escape.

Critical Evaluation:

The Plumed Serpent provides a stage for the talents of the modernist period's least understood novelist. In this tale of revolution and romance, D. H. Lawrence combines many of the striking aspects of his better-known works of fiction. The novel is set in Mexico, a country that represents a frightening and intriguing exoticism to Lawrence's English-speaking characters. Lawrence chose Mexico not only because of his personal fascination for the country but also the turbulent political climate he describes with hope and fear. *The Plumed Serpent* is an attempt by Lawrence to work out the conflict within himself concerning issues of social class and political power. Bound up in the interweaving of fear and hope, Lawrence's political philosophies found a topical context in a fictional Mexico. For contemporary readers, the novel may be read as a discussion on the relationship between the individual and society.

In the consciousness of an individual, Kate Leslie, *The Plumed Serpent*'s heroine, the novel does its finest work. The narrative displays Lawrence's unique ability to construct characters whose physical, spiritual, and psychological characteristics impress readers as the kind of truth about the human condition that only good fiction can tell. The relationship between Irish Kate and the Mexico and Mexicans she encounters engenders the thematic and artistic accomplishments that should give readers of Lawrence good reason to reappraise *The Plumed Serpent*.

Mexico's role in the novel serves many artistic purposes for Lawrence, and must be understood by *The Plumed Serpent*'s readers as a complex entity that is setting and symbol. Lawrence was drawn to and made a study of Mexico and New Mexico. *The Plumed Serpent* can be compared to E. M. Forster's *A Passage to India* (1924); the non-English settings of both works are wrought with painstaking authenticity. The literary critic F. R. Leavis thought that the long passages of the novel describing indigenous rituals and costume must have entertained Lawrence but were likely to bore readers. This sentiment was not shared by the novelist Katherine Anne Porter, who praised Lawrence's evocation of the spirit and detail of Lawrence's portrayal of Mexico in an early review of *The Plumed Serpent*. Of course, Lawrence's Mexico represents more than the country itself.

As a politically unstable nation, and as a society that is characterized by a profound gulf between its classes, Mexico functions as an analogy for any climate in which revolution might be fomented. This logic is most clear in Kate's initial attempts to understand Mexico in terms of her own national identity. The Irish, like the Mexicans, bear the psychic scars of oppression and grapple with the impulse to revolt. Mexico, Kate is warned early in the novel, is another Ireland. Mexico in the novel represents any modern nation in which political institutions, be they fascist, democratic, or socialist, fail those who subscribe to them. Furthermore, both Mexico and Ireland are nations in which the Catholic Church exerts great influence. Lawrence's disillusionment with both politics and Christianity as modes of social order yields another role for Mexico to fulfill in *The Plumed Serpent*. It is Mexico's ancient rhythms, its gone but not forgotten pantheon of pagan deities that become, for Lawrence, metaphors for the kind of reinvention that one might submit to in pursuit of new power and perspective.

Although the cult of Quetzalcoatl is a part of Mexico's history and therefore a return to old ways for its practitioners, for Kate, the central figure of the novel, the mystical religion represents a new language, new customs, and new beliefs. Lawrence seems to hope that the resurgent religion might serve the expansion of human consciousness. Kate, after all, has come to Mexico with an expatriate's desire to escape the problems of her native land. Although contemporary Mexico, much to Kate's dismay, shares Ireland's sense of turmoil, it also proposes, at least in Lawrence's fiction, solutions.

The shock of Quetzalcoatl, with its visceral imagery and violent rituals, jars Kate into a self-examination that makes the novel as much of a psychic examination as it is a physical adventure. Don Ramón and Cipriano exploit the frustrations of downtrodden peasants, and Kate is forced to question her own assumption that she is born to a ruling class, that she is separate from the rabble that initially frightens her. She must question, too, the importance of the individual in relation to the masses and the structure that governs them. Lawrence refuses to offer his reader the kind of simple solution to the problem of social inequity that he has, in the form of contemporary politics and religion, already derided.

Critics have complained that Kate's submission to Cipriano and the new order represent a subjugation of the individual will to the elite few who are strong enough to hold culture's reigns. Kate's submission, one may argue, underscores the importance of the individual as the receiver of political as well as artistic information. Kate is not brainwashed into marrying Cipriano and staying in Mexico; she searches her own soul for clues to the proper course of action. By making Kate responsible for authorizing the ascension of Quetzalcoatl, Lawrence reminds his readers of their ultimate responsibility for the meaning of the novel he offers them. This is a role new readers of Lawrence may relish.

"Critical Evaluation" by Nick David Smart

Further Reading

Burack, Charles Michael. *D. H. Lawrence's Language of Sacred Experience: The Transfiguration of the Reader.* New York: Palgrave Macmillan, 2005. Burack maintains that Lawrence structured *The Plumed Serpent*, *Lady Chatterley's Lover*, *The Rainbow*, and *Women in Love* as if they were religious initiation rites intended to evoke new spiritual experiences for readers.

Clark, L. D. *Dark Night of the Body: D. H. Lawrence's "The Plumed Serpent."* Austin: University of Texas Press, 1964. Noteworthy especially for its strong focus on Kate. Includes biographical and bibliographic materials.

Cushman, Keith, and Earl G. Ingersoll, eds. *D. H. Lawrence: New Worlds.* Madison, N.J.: Fairleigh Dickinson University Press, 2003. Collection of essays that reinterpret Lawrence's work. Includes discussions of his influence on British fiction and debates over his English identity.

Also includes the chapter "'Demonish Maturity': Identity, Consumption, and the Discourse of Species in *The Plumed Serpent*."

Draper, R. P., ed. *D. H. Lawrence: The Critical Heritage.* 1970. Reprint. New York: Routledge, 2001. Reflects the mixture of criticism and praise with which Lawrence's contemporaries reacted to his work. Includes critiques of *The Plumed Serpent* by William Butler Yeats, Virginia Woolf, and T. S. Eliot.

Fernihough, Anne, ed. *The Cambridge Companion to D. H. Lawrence.* New York: Cambridge University Press, 2001. Collection of essays interpreting Lawrence's work from various perspectives—including discussions of Lawrence and modernism, psychoanalysis, and sexual politics—and an assessment of Lawrence's critical and cultural legacy.

Leavis, F. R. *D. H. Lawrence: Novelist.* 1955. Reprint. New York: Penguin Books, 1994. Leavis's appraisal of the art-ist, although dated, is a must-read. Leavis, however, is highly critical of *The Plumed Serpent.*

Parmenter, Ross. *Lawrence in Oaxaca: A Quest for the Novelist in Mexico.* Salt Lake City, Utah: Peregrine Smith Books, 1984. Reveals the depth of Lawrence's fascination with Mexico. Contains an extensive chapter on how Lawrence's time in Oaxaca affected the composition of *The Plumed Serpent.*

Worthen, John. *D. H. Lawrence: The Life of an Outsider.* New York: Counterpoint, 2005. Written by a distinguished Lawrence scholar, this compelling and readable biography is accompanied by several photographs.

Wright, T. R. *D. H. Lawrence and the Bible.* New York: Cambridge University Press, 2000. Wright maintains that the Bible played a significant role in almost all of Lawrence's works, and he analyzes Lawrence's use of biblical allusions and themes. *The Plumed Serpent* is discussed in chapter 11.

Plutus

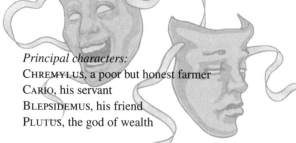

Author: Aristophanes (c. 450-c. 385 B.C.E.)
First produced: *Ploutos*, 388 B.C.E. (English translation, 1651)
Type of work: Drama
Type of plot: Satire
Time of plot: Fifth century B.C.E.
Locale: Athens

Principal characters:
CHREMYLUS, a poor but honest farmer
CARIO, his servant
BLEPSIDEMUS, his friend
PLUTUS, the god of wealth

The Story:

Chremylus, a Greek farmer, goes to the temple of Apollo in Athens and asks the oracle there how his son might attain affluence without having to resort to knavery. The oracle directs Chremylus to follow the first man he encounters as he emerges from the temple and to take the stranger home with him. The first man Chremylus sees is a blind beggar, whom he follows impatiently. At first the beggar refuses to reveal his identity to Chremylus, but when Cario, Chremylus's servant, threatens to push the blind man over a cliff, he fearfully reveals that he is Plutus, the god of riches, blinded by Zeus for telling the god that he will favor only good men. Zeus does not want Plutus to discriminate among men. The unhappy Plutus declares to Chremylus that if he had his sight back again he would favor only the good and shun the wicked.

When Chremylus offers to restore his sight to him, Plutus expresses fear of the wrath of Zeus. Chremylus declares that if Plutus were to get his sight back, even for a moment, Zeus would be superseded, because the dispensation of all wealth, upon which Zeus is dependent for his authority, would be in the power of Plutus; money, after all, pays even for sacrifices offered up to Zeus. It would then be Plutus, according to Chremylus, not Zeus, who would be all things to all men. Plutus is delighted to hear these words.

Chremylus, after sending Cario to summon the neighboring farmers, ushers Plutus into his house. When Cario tells the farmers that Plutus is at Chremylus's house and that he will lift them out of their poverty, they are delirious with joy. Chremylus, welcoming them, notices that his friend Blepsidemus is skeptical of Cario's report; Blepsidemus suspects that Chremylus has stolen a treasure. Chremylus declares that Plutus is truly in his house and that all good and deserving people will soon be rich. Even Blepsidemus becomes convinced, and he agrees that it is essential to restore Plutus's eyesight.

As Chremylus prepares to take Plutus to the temple of Asclepius to have his sight restored, the goddess of poverty, a hideous old woman, appears and objects to the prospect of being cast out of Chremylus's house after having lived with him for many years. Blepsidemus and Chremylus are terrified at the sight of the goddess, but Chremylus quickly regains his composure and engages her in a debate over which deity, the god of riches or the goddess of poverty, is more beneficial to humanity. Chremylus declares that with Plutus once again able to see, those who deserve it will receive money; thus society will be benefited. The goddess of poverty answers that progress will come to a halt because Plutus will distribute wealth equally. The two then argue the difference between beggary and poverty, with the goddess maintaining that men who entertain her are brave, alert, and strong, whereas those who entertain Plutus are soft, fat, and cowardly. She declares that men are virtuous when she is their guest but are corrupted when Plutus is their guest.

Chremylus is not convinced by her arguments, and the goddess, having been defeated, departs in sorrow and anger. Chremylus now takes Plutus to the temple of Asclepius, the god of healing. He observes every detail of the required ritual and lays Plutus on a couch. A priest tells them to sleep. Plutus's eyes are wiped with a cloth, and then a purple mantle is placed over his head. At a signal from Asclepius, two serpents come forth from the sanctuary and slither under the mantle. In a short time, Plutus, his sight restored, arises from the couch.

Now those people who have acquired their wealth by unfair means look with fear upon Plutus, but the poor rejoice in their new good fortune. Plutus is happy, and he vows to correct all of the mistakes he made when he was blind. Chremylus is rewarded with great wealth for his service to the god.

Later, while Plutus is a guest in the house of Chremylus, a just man comes to petition the god. In the past he helped his friends when they were in need, but they did not respond in kind when he himself became indigent. The man becomes wealthy again through the power of Plutus. He offers an old cloak and a worn-out pair of sandals as tribute to the god.

Soon afterward, an informer comes to the house and complains that he has been ruined by the change wrought in Plutus. Cario strips the informer of his fine coat and bedecks him in the just man's threadbare cloak. An old woman, presuming to be a young one, comes to see the god. She is distressed because her young lover, who previously had flattered her in order to get money from her, has deserted her now that Plutus has made him independent. The youth appears with a wreath to give to Plutus in appreciation.

Hermes, the messenger of the gods, appears and reports that Zeus and the other gods are furious because human beings no longer make oblations to them. He declares that he himself is actually starving, as he is receiving no offerings in the form of cakes or figs or honey, and he urges Cario to succor him. Cario condescends to retain Hermes to preside at the games that Plutus surely will sponsor. A priest of Zeus also arrives and complains of hunger; when everyone is rich, there are no more offerings to the gods. Chremylus, calling attention to the fact that Plutus has now taken the place of Zeus in human fortunes, hints that the priest of Zeus would do well to become the priest of Plutus. Zeus having been deposed, Plutus is installed as the supreme god.

Critical Evaluation:

If *Plutus* had not survived, a vital link in the history of Greek comedy would have been lost. So different is this play from the other surviving works of Aristophanes, one might suppose it to be an aberration or to have been written by a different author. In fact, evidence suggests that Aristophanes wrote other works similar to *Plutus*, which was presented in 388 B.C.E. The unusual features of this play are also not explained away by the fact that the work was written when Aristophanes was approximately sixty. The poet went on to write two more plays, now lost. *Plutus* may be regarded as the sole surviving example of the new comic genre referred to as Middle Comedy. The term distinguishes this play from the other surviving plays of Aristophanes, all of which are representative of the style and concerns of Old Attic Comedy. On the other hand, *Plutus* is not to be classed with New Comedy, which is best represented by Menander (c. 342-291 B.C.E.).

What distinguishes *Plutus*—and thus the genre of Middle Comedy—from other plays of Aristophanes is a general retreat from direct political or personal satire, an absence of crude obscenity, and a curtailing or complete omission of some of the traditional elements of Old Comedy, such as choral lyrics. The beginnings of some of these changes are apparent in *Ekklesiazousai* (392 B.C.E.?; *Ecclesiazusae*, 1837). Other features of *Plutus* are not so common in Aristophanes' earlier work, such as the use of moral allegory with personified abstractions (the Greek word *ploutos* means "wealth"), the focus on social interaction that suggests the comedy of manners, which would develop later, and passionate, unapologetic idealism. Also different from Aristophanes' earlier plays is the lack of topical controversy in *Plutus*: Virtually no person could object to the central concept of *Plutus*, that Wealth is a blind god and therefore may favor scoundrels and abandon good people to the misery of poverty.

Plutus is not devoid of humor. Although verbal jesting is reduced in the play in comparison to earlier works, it contains some of the irrelevancy and situational humor of the earlier plays. For example, the antics that Cario reports from the temple of Asclepius, where Plutus's sight is restored, are mildly amusing as a parody of ancient techniques of healing. Cario's wife is interesting as a comic character who happens to be female. Her reception of her husband's news adds significantly to the humor of the scene. When the god Hermes comes seeking employment, there is some amusement in the fact that despite his varied skills a suitable position for him is discovered only with considerable difficulty: Finally it is decided that he is to take charge of games that Plutus will soon celebrate.

The reader will detect some of the typical structure of Aristophanic comedy in *Plutus*, especially observable in the contest between Plutus and Penia (poverty) and in the series of episodes that follow the restoration of Plutus's sight. The various individuals who appear before him serve to underscore the consequences of his regaining his sight. In form, at least, this design is paralleled in earlier plays of Aristophanes in which the protagonist realizes a plan and then contemplates the positive and negative results.

A diminished role for the chorus is the most outstanding characteristic of *Plutus*. Despite some traces of lost choral lyrics, in most of the text the presence of the chorus is indicated merely by the Greek word *chorou*. It is doubtful that the chorus sang a composition relevant to the action of the play. More likely, the notation indicates some kind of interlude during which the chorus danced and played music before the next scene took place.

Many of the characteristics of *Plutus* prefigure developments in later Greek and Roman comedy. The reduction of the role of the chorus, for example, has the effect of placing more emphasis on the episodes that were originally seen as insertions between choral songs. The consequent development of a play in five acts, which is typical of New Comedy and becomes the established pattern for all later drama, is already seen in this play.

The move away from topicality—that is, specific references to actual individuals and events—naturally results in a preference for types who exemplify common human traits. Cario, for example, is a prototype of the wily slave who will have a role to play in nearly every subsequent Greco-Roman comedy. Misers, shrewish wives, young men in love, and other types common to European drama may have their origins in the works of Greek Middle Comedy, of which *Plutus* is the one surviving example. The play's turning away from politics and toward larger aspects of the human condition must have acted to release comedy from the close link to the city of Athens and to the worship of Dionysus, the god of drama. The gradual freeing of drama from the context of Athenian political life and the specific sacred festivals gave birth to a wide range of new dramatic plots and characters.

Some political satire at the expense of specific individuals is still to be found in *Plutus*, and the reduced economic circumstances of Athens in the fourth century leave a direct mark on the play, because economic conditions may no longer have permitted the provision and training of an expensive chorus. The play is much more concerned, however, with the moral metaphysical aspects of wealth and poverty than with specific economic, social, or political conditions that created the distribution of wealth.

Some of the features of Old Comedy that *Plutus* lacks worked to ensure its survival in later times. The play is virtually free of topical references that need explanation to all but ancient Athenians and offers an edifying moral message, so *Plutus* became the most popular work of Aristophanes in later centuries, especially during the Byzantine period.

"Critical Evaluation" by John M. Lawless

Further Reading

Dover, K. J. *Aristophanic Comedy*. Berkeley: University of California Press, 1972. Authoritative study is an essential starting point for students of Aristophanes' work. Chapter 16 gives a synopsis of *Plutus*, discusses the role of slaves in this new genre of comedy, and comments on the connection between wealth and morality that is made in the play.

Harriott, Rosemary M. *Aristophanes: Poet and Dramatist*. Baltimore: Johns Hopkins University Press, 1986. Examination of the works of Aristophanes focuses on the central themes of the works and the techniques of the author. Includes discussion of *Plutus*.

McLeish, Kenneth. *The Theatre of Aristophanes*. New York: Taplinger, 1980. Provides an overview of the dramatic technique of Aristophanes. Useful for understanding the magnitude of the change from Old to Middle Comedy.

Murray, Gilbert. *Aristophanes: A Study*. Oxford, England: Clarendon Press, 1933. Classic work offers valuable insights into all the plays of Aristophanes. Chapter 10 presents an excellent discussion of *Plutus*.

Silk, M. S. *Aristophanes and the Definition of Comedy*. New York: Oxford University Press, 2002. Looks at Aristophanes as one of the world's great poets as well as an important dramatist. Analyzes *Plutus* and other plays to examine their language, style, lyric poetry, character, and structure.

Spatz, Lois. *Aristophanes*. Boston: Twayne, 1978. Provides a reliable introduction to the comedy of Aristophanes for the general reader. Chapter 9 discusses the themes of *Plutus* and emphasizes its differences from earlier Aristophanic comedy.

Pnin

Author: Vladimir Nabokov (1899-1977)
First published: 1957
Type of work: Novel
Type of plot: Narrative
Time of plot: 1950's
Locale: New York and New England

Principal characters:
TIMOFEY PNIN, an instructor of Russian at Waindell College
LIZA WIND, Pnin's former wife
ERIC WIND, Liza's second husband
VICTOR WIND, Liza's son
JOAN CLEMENTS, Pnin's landlady
LAURENCE CLEMENTS, her husband, a professor of philosophy at Waindell College
HERMAN HAGEN, the head of the German Department at Waindell College
JACK COCKERELL, the head of the English Department at Waindell College
LEONARD BLORENGE, the head of the French Department at Waindell College
MARGARET THAYER, a librarian at Waindell College
MIRA BELOCHKIN, the love of Pnin's youth
THE NARRATOR, an Anglo-American writer

The Story:

Timofey Pnin, an instructor of Russian at Waindell College, is taking a train to give a lecture to the Cremona Women's Club. Sadly, he is on the wrong train. The discovery of his mistake and his subsequent attempts to get to Cremona in time for the lecture cause him to undergo a sinking spell: He plunges into a recollection of a time in his childhood when he suffered from a fever and struggled in vain to find the key to the recurring pattern of foliage on his wallpaper. The spell passes, but when he is about to begin his lecture he has a fleeting sense that some of the beloved people from his past, including his parents, are in the audience.

Pnin moves into a room rented to him by Joan and Laurence Clements. The room has been vacated by the Clements' daughter Isabel, who has married and moved away. Pnin learns that his former wife, Liza Wind, wants to

visit him. Pnin's marriage to Liza ended when she abandoned him for Eric Wind. When Liza arrives, she tells Pnin that she would like him to send some money in her name to her son Victor at boarding school. After her departure, Pnin is devastated with sorrow, and he resists all attempts by Joan Clements to cheer him up.

Pnin continues his routine at Waindell College, teaching classes and conducting research on the history of Russian culture. The librarian indicates to Pnin that Isabel's marriage is in trouble and that he might have to relocate, but he does not pay full attention to her words. In the evening, Pnin watches a Soviet propaganda film and imagines himself back in the Russia of his youth. As he falls asleep that night, he is awakened by the noisy return of Isabel, who is about to burst into her old room until she is stopped by her mother.

Lisa's son Victor visits Pnin in Waindell. Victor has a recurring dream in which his father is a king who is forced into exile by a revolution in his country. Victor has an extraordinary IQ and is a talented artist. During his correspondence with Pnin, he begins to develop a fondness for this man who, in Victor's eyes, has an exotic background. On the night of his arrival, Victor, who usually suffers from insomnia, falls asleep instantly, while Pnin seems to step into Victor's dream, as he sees himself fleeing from a castle and pacing a deserted shore while awaiting the arrival of a boat to take him to safety.

Pnin visits a summer retreat in the woods of New England, where he finds a collection of Russian émigrés much like himself. Immersed in the culture and companionship of his fellow intelligentsia, Pnin seems fully relaxed. One woman staying at the summer house mentions Mira Belochkin, the woman Pnin had loved in his youth, and this causes Pnin to reflect upon his old romance. However, he is also reminded of Mira's terrible death in a Nazi concentration camp.

Pnin moves into a house he has rented on his own, and he throws a housewarming party to celebrate the event. One of his guests is his protector at Waindell, Dr. Hagen, who will soon be leaving the college to move to a more prestigious institution. With Hagen's departure, Pnin will be out of a job, and when Hagen learns that Pnin is thinking of buying his rented house, Hagen informs Pnin of his bleak prospects. Pnin is troubled by the news, and when he washes dishes later that night, he absentmindedly drops a nutcracker into the soapy water, and he hears the sound of breaking glass. He fears that the broken object is a wonderful punch bowl given to him by Victor but learns to his relief that it was only a wine glass. The marvelous bowl is intact.

In the final chapter of the novel, the narrator, who has remained in the background until now, comes to the fore and begins to describe his own memories of Pnin. The narrator had an affair with Liza before she married Pnin (and it was apparently her suicidal despair over the outcome of the affair that led her to accept Pnin's proposal). The narrator has accepted a job at Waindell College, and he has offered a position to Pnin as well, but Pnin refuses to work under his old acquaintance. As the novel ends, the narrator arrives in Waindell and catches a glimpse of Pnin driving out of town, leaving the narrator behind in his stead.

Critical Evaluation:

Vladimir Nabokov is best known for his novel *Lolita* (1955), which he was just completing when he began work on *Pnin*. The two books could hardly be more different in their subject matter, however. Whereas *Lolita* tackles the difficult topic of an adult man's affair with a young girl, *Pnin* offers a warmly humorous portrait of the travails and triumphs of a Russian émigré professor at a small American college. Parts of the novel appeared as individual stories in *The New Yorker* magazine, but the full complexity of the work only became apparent when Nabokov published it in its entirety in 1957. It was nominated for a National Book Award, marking the first of five such nominations for Nabokov.

At the center of the work stands Timofey Pnin. To many at Waindell College, Pnin seems to be something of a joke—a bumbling fool who has major difficulties with the English language. To those who take the time to get to know him better (and to readers as well), Pnin emerges as a kind and noble individual who strives mightily to find peace and harmony in a difficult world. While one may laugh at such traits as his fascination with gadgets (which leads him to put his canvas shoes into his landlady's front-loading washing machine just to see what will happen), his innate kindness—whether to his former wife's son or to a stray dog—is truly touching. When his memories of the past touch on the dreadful fate of his first love, Mira Belochkin, a victim of Nazi atrocities, the true pathos of Pnin's experience comes into clear focus.

Memory itself is one of Nabokov's favorite themes, and in this novel, as in many of his other works, one becomes aware of the importance of memory as a way of preserving and reviving the past. This task carries special significance to those, like Pnin, who have been forced to leave their homelands and experience the difficult dislocation and loss that emigration entails. The novel also exposes the limitations of memory, however, and the fact that one's memories may be unreliable or false. In fact, certain things that Pnin says about his past do not jibe with the narrator's account, forcing readers to determine for themselves which account is accurate. The novel thus confronts questions of the nature of truth and the motives of Pnin or his narrator for distorting that truth.

This problem becomes especially acute in the final chapter, when the narrator suddenly focuses the story on himself and his own experiences. Nabokov's handling of this narrator and of his relation to Pnin stands out as one of the most intriguing aspects of the work. The narrator claims to be Pnin's friend, yet he often describes Pnin in terms that are condescending or tinged with mockery. When readers learn that the narrator had an affair with Pnin's wife just before she married Pnin, they may conclude that this is the reason Pnin refuses to work under him at Waindell. It is also possible that Pnin distrusts the narrator's very attitude toward Pnin, and in his suspicion of the way the narrator talks about Pnin's past, Pnin may be expressing the anxiety any literary character might have about the control exerted over him by his creator, the author. According to clues scattered in the novel, the narrator is an urbane Anglo-American writer named Vladimir Vladimirovich, and he is an expert on butterflies. These are the very traits of Nabokov himself: His full name was Vladimir Vladimirovich Nabokov, he wrote both in English and Russian, and he was a specialist in Lepidoptera.

The narrator is not, in fact, the real Vladimir Nabokov. Any figure depicted in a work of fiction, even a first-person narrator, is a fictional creation, just as much subject to the control of the real author as any other character in the work. At the end of the novel, it appears that the long-suffering Pnin is allowed his freedom from the control of the narrator and escapes the bounds of the text, whereas the unsympathetic narrator becomes trapped in Pnin's former position, both at Waindell and within the text itself.

Thus, although the world created in *Pnin* looks very much like a plausible academic setting with a plausible set of people inhabiting it, Nabokov salts the text with several reminders of the overall artificiality of the work. These include sets of characters with similar names such as Christopher and Louise Starr, Louis and Christina Stern, and Chris and Lew, the pair of Englishmen who prevent Liza's suicide. A second set includes Bob Horn in the United States and Robert Karlovich Horn in Russia. This doubling and tripling of names could be a sign of the narrator's laziness when it comes to inventing such names, but it is surely a sign of Nabokov's presence as designer and creator. Another indication of the fictionality of the work is the role given to recurring images of squirrels in the text. While some readers have seen the squirrel as suggestive of the survival of Mira Belochkin's spirit after death (*belka* in Russian means "squirrel"), others have simply viewed it as a marker of the author's penchant for patterning. Nabokov's *Pnin* offers ample evidence of the power of fiction to capture the poignant and fleeting experiences of life and to mold them into shimmering and timeless works of art.

Julian W. Connolly

Further Reading

Barabtarlo, Gennady. *Phantom of Fact: A Guide to Nabokov's "Pnin."* Ann Arbor, Mich.: Ardis, 1989. A detailed study of *Pnin* that both addresses the broad thematic and structural designs of the novel and provides commentary on many specific passages in the work.

Boyd, Brian. *Vladimir Nabokov: The American Years.* Princeton, N.J.: Princeton University Press, 1991. This definitive biography of Nabokov contains an excellent discussion of the main themes and devices of *Pnin*, as well as its place in Nabokov's career.

Connolly, Julian. "*Pnin:* The Wonder of Recurrence and Transformation." In *Nabokov's Fifth Arc: Nabokov and Others on His Life's Work*, edited by J. E. Rivers and Charles Nicol. Austin: University of Texas Press, 1982. A close examination of the spiral structure of *Pnin*, with commentary on the special significance of Victor Wind in Pnin's life.

De Vries, Gerard, Donald B Johnson, and Liana Ashenden. *Vladimir Nabokov and the Art of Painting.* Amsterdam: Amsterdam University Press, 2006. Includes a chapter of the representation and use of art history in *Pnin*.

Diment, Galya. *Pniniad: Vladimir Nabokov and Marc Szeftel.* Seattle: University of Washington Press, 1997. In this fascinating study of a real-life model for Nabokov's character Pnin (Marc Szeftel, Nabokov's colleague at Cornell), Diment delves into the relationship between Nabokov the author and Pnin and Vladimir Vladimirovich, his created characters.

Gordon, Ambrose, Jr. "The Double Pnin." In *Nabokov: The Man and His Work*, edited by L. S. Dembo. Madison: University of Wisconsin Press, 1967. Gordon sees the character of Pnin as containing contrasting aspects of the émigré experience that he calls the "Alien" and the "Exile," and he compares Pnin's story to that depicted in James Joyce's *Ulysses*.

Smith, Zadie. "Pnin and Reality." In *Changing My Mind: Occasional Essays*. New York: Penguin Press, 2009. Examines the relationship between the world represented by the novel and the real world inhabited by its writer and readers.

Poem of the Cid

Author: Unknown
First published: Cantar de mío Cid, early thirteenth
  century (English translation, 1808)
Type of work: Poetry
Type of plot: Epic
Time of plot: c. 1075
Locale: Fief of Bivar, north of Burgos, Spain

Principal characters:
RUY DÍAZ, called My Cid, Lord of Bivar
ALFONSO, the king of León, by whom the Cid was exiled
DOÑA XIMENA, the Cid's wife
MARTÍN ANTOLINEZ, one of the Cid's chief lieutenants
DOÑA ELVIRA and DOÑA SOL, the Cid's daughters
MINAYA ALVAR FÁÑEZ, the Cid's chief lieutenant and
  companion
FÉLIX MUÑOZ, the Cid's nephew and rescuer of his
  daughters
GARCÍA ORDOÑEZ, lord of Grañón, the Cid's enemy
DIEGO and FERNANDO GONZÁLEZ, the princes of Carrión,
  suitors and husbands to the Cid's daughters, two
  villains
GONZALO ANSÚREZ, the count of Carrión, father of Diego
  and Fernando González

The Poem:

By royal edict, the Cid is banished from Christian Spain by King Alfonso VI of Castile. The royal edict allows him nine days in which to leave the kingdom but forbids him from taking with him any of his wealth and goods. Any man in the kingdom who offers aid to the Cid will forfeit his estate. Nevertheless, the Cid enlists the aid of Martín Antolinez in swindling two moneylenders, Raquel and Vidas, in exchange for two large sealed coffers, supposedly loaded with the Cid's riches but containing only sand. The Cid and a small force of vassals then ride away and make a secret camp. On the morning of the Cid's actual departure from the country, with a fair-sized group of loyal vassals, Mass is said for all at the abbey where Doña Ximena, the Cid's wife, and his two infant daughters, Doña Elvira and Doña Sol, have been ordered to remain.

Becoming a soldier of fortune, the knight leads his host in conquest of one Moorish territory after another, each time generously sharing the spoils and booty among his knights and vassals, even the lowliest. Thus he builds up a larger and stronger force with every foray, and after each victory Mass is said in thanksgiving. The Cid fights his way to the eastern side of the peninsula, where he fights his most crucial battle and wins his greatest victory when he takes as his prisoner Count Ramón of Barcelona. After Count Ramón has been humbled and forced to give up all his property, he is granted his liberty.

Although Minaya Alvar Fáñez returns to King Alfonso with gifts and a glowing report of the Cid's successes, the king does not revoke his decree of banishment. Minaya's estates are restored, however, and he was granted freedom to come and go without fear of attack. The Cid continues his campaigns against the Moorish territories in order to increase his favor with King Alfonso. After he has conquered the provinces of Valencia and Seville, however, his men grow tired of fighting, and many wish to return to Castile. The Cid, although still generous and understanding, proves himself master by threatening all deserters with death.

Again the Cid sends Minaya to King Alfonso, this time with a gift of one hundred horses and a request that Doña Ximena and her daughters be permitted to join him in Valencia. Visibly softened by the Cid's growing power, King Alfonso grants this request. In addition, he returns to the Cid's men their former estates.

Shortly after a triumphant reunion with his family in Valencia, the Cid overcomes the king of Morocco. As a gesture of victory, he sends the Moroccan's tent to King Alfonso. This dramatic gift earns the Cid's pardon as well as the king's request that the Cid give his daughters in marriage to Diego and Fernando, the princes of Carrión. At the victory feast, many marvel at the great length and abundance of the Cid's beard, for he had sworn at the time of his banishment that his beard would never again be cut. The fullness of his beard has now taken on a mystical significance related to the Cid's power and success.

The Cid has reservations about giving his daughters to the princes of Carrión. His daughters are, he thinks, too young for marriage. Also, he distrusts the two men. However, with a great show of humbleness and subservience, he returns Doña Elvira and Doña Sol to the king with word that Alfonso will honor the Cid by disposing of his daughters' future as the monarch sees fit.

After the weddings, the elaborate wedding feast, to which all the Cid's vassals as well as those of the territory of Carrión have been invited, lasts for more than two weeks. The Cid expresses some satisfaction in having his family united with noblemen as rich as Prince Diego and his brother Fernando.

Two years of happiness follow, then, one day, one of the Cid's pet lions escapes. Far from showing valor in the emergency, Diego hides from the lion under the bench on which the Cid is asleep, and Fernando flees into the garden and hides behind a winepress. After the Cid's vassals easily subdue the lion, the favored princes become the butt of much crude humor and scorn. The Cid, however, choosing to ignore the evident cowardice of his daughters' husbands, makes excuses for them.

Once again the Cid is forced to war with the Moroccans, this time against the mighty King Bucar. After a great battle, Bucar is killed and his vassals are subdued. The Cid is jubilant. As the spoils are divided, he rejoices that at last his sons-in-law have become seasoned warriors. His vassals are half amused and half disgusted at this, because it is common knowledge among them that neither Diego nor Fernando showed the slightest bravery in the conflict, and at one point the Cid's standard-bearer had been forced to risk his life to cover for Fernando's shocking cowardice.

Diego and Fernando are richly rewarded for their supposed valor, but their greed is not satisfied. Resentful and injured by the insults and scorn heaped on them by the Cid's vassals, they begin a scheme for revenge by telling the Cid that, proud of their marriages and their wealth, they would like to make a journey to Carrión to show off their wives and to sing the Cid's praises. In secret, they plan not to return from this journey. The noble and generous Cid, always ready to think the best of anyone, grants their request without question. He adds further to the princes' treasure and sends them off with a suitable company of his own vassals as an escort of honor. Then, belatedly concerned for the safety of his daughters, he also sends with them his nephew, Félix Muñoz, after charging the young nobleman with the care of Doña Elvira and Doña Sol.

When they are safely away from Valencia, the princes send the company on ahead and take their wives into the woods. There, with viciousness, they strip the women of their rich garments and their jewels, whip them, and leave them, wounded and bleeding, to die. Félix Muñoz, whose suspicion has been aroused by the princes' desire to separate their wives from the rest of the party, follows the princes' tracks and finds the women. He nurses them back to consciousness and returns them to the Cid.

The princes' scheme of revenge rebounds to their further disgrace. Word of their wicked and dishonest acts spreads quickly, and King Alfonso, in his great displeasure with the Carrións, swears to try them in Toledo. The Cid swears to avenge the treatment his daughters have received by marrying Doña Elvira and Doña Sol to the richest men in the land.

At the trial, the princes are first ordered to return the Cid's valued swords, which he had given them as tokens of his high regard. Then they are ordered to return his gold; because they have squandered it all, they are forced to give him equal value in horses and property. In the meantime, ambassadors from Aragón and Navarre have arrived to ask for the Cid's daughters as queens for their kings. The Cid is jubilant, but still he demands that the princes of Carrión pay in full measure for their brutality: trial by combat with two of the Cid's chosen knights. King Alfonso charges the princes that if they injure their opponents in the least, they will forfeit their lives. Proved craven in the fight, the princes are stripped of all honor and wealth. The Cid rejoices that, once banished, he can now count two kings of Spain among his kinsmen. He dies, Lord of Valencia, on the Day of Pentecost.

Critical Evaluation:

In this national epic of eleventh century Spain, 3,735 lines of uneven length in three cantos relate the major events in the Cid's life. The poem is based on historical fact. Such a man lived; he died in 1099. His character and exploits have been, as one might expect, embroidered, amplified, and distorted to suit the purpose of making him a heroic figure in Spanish history and legend. Of all the epics of the Cid, *Poem of the Cid* is unique in its qualities of realism, verity, and poetic excellence. The Cid is drawn as a typical Spanish warrior, proud, ruthless, realistic, and calculating. At the same time, he shrewdly doles out praise and favors to his vassals and is generous to a fault. In victory, he is quick to do honor—even to overdo it—to his loyal lieutenants. Although exiled by King Alfonso VI, he continued to hold the position of the king, if not the man himself, in high regard.

Poem of the Cid, while based in part on historical characters and actual events, has its origins as literature in ancient folklore and in early European epic. The traditional plot of *Poem of the Cid* may first be found in *The Story of Si-Nuhe*, an ancient Egyptian legend that dates to the Twelfth Dynasty (c. 1950 B.C.E.) and recounts events remarkably similar to those of the later Spanish poem. In the Egyptian legend, Si-

Nuhe, a governmental official under Amenemhet I, is forced to flee Egypt when the pharaoh dies and his son, Sesotris I, comes to the throne. Si-Nuhe's wanderings take him as far as Retenu (Syria and Israel), where he marries the king's eldest daughter and rules over a pastoral paradise known as Yaa. Despite all these achievements, however, Si-Nuhe wishes only to return home. Word of Si-Nuhe's victories repeatedly reaches Sesotris, who forgives Si-Nuhe, permitting him to reenter Egypt. Si-Nuhe leaves Yaa in the care of his son and arrives in Egypt, where he finds himself greeted as a great hero.

This story pattern, that of the nobleman who accomplishes great deeds in exile until he is restored to his lands by a monarch, is common throughout world literature. What the author of *Poem of the Cid* has done is to associate this traditional tale with a specific historical figure, Ruy Díaz of Bivar (or Vivar), who was also known as the Cid Campeador. "Cid" is a Spanish corruption of the Arabic title *seid*, which means "lord," and *campeador* is a term of uncertain origin that appears to mean "victor." (This is a common title for epic heroes; for example, the German word for "victor," *Siegfried*, is the name of the hero in the *Nibelungenlied*, c.1200.)

The poem's author has also adopted an ancient literary style that may be traced to the early European epics *Iliad* (c. 750 B.C.E.; English translation, 1611) and *Odyssey* (c. 725 B.C.E.; English translation, 1614). This style uses formulaic phrases, stylized battle scenes, and frequently repeated epithets. Because such a style is commonly associated with oral poetry, it is believed that *Poem of the Cid* either existed as an oral poem before it was written down or was intentionally written in an archaic style so that it would appear to have been an oral poem.

Most scholars believe that the origins of *Poem of the Cid* may be found among the *juglares*, wandering storytellers who preserved and embellished traditional tales. It has been argued, however, that *Poem of the Cid* was a specific literary creation, the work of an individual unknown author. Complete agreement on this issue is unlikely to occur. Nevertheless, whether the product of a single author or a long-standing oral tradition, *Poem of the Cid* contains themes and elements of plot that may be observed elsewhere in European folklore.

One central motif that appears throughout *Poem of the Cid* is the importance of loyalty. The ill treatment that the Cid receives from King Alfonso might have caused the Cid to resent the king, but the hero continues to remain loyal, and he is ultimately rewarded for his allegiance. In turn, the Cid demonstrates that he is the sort of figure who is owed loyalty by others. He is generous and forgiving, ready to honor the deeds of his followers. He is also ready to demand loyalty from vacillating vassals. Through these qualities, the Cid is contrasted sharply to the worthless characters of the poem, Diego and Fernando, who take advantage of the Cid's generosity. Genuine nobility, the poem suggests, is not found in aristocratic birth as much as it is in persons who have learned compassion and refinement. While a true gentleman may be proud, he is never haughty; while he may take pride in his possessions, he is never greedy. Many of the same values later described by Baldassare Castiglione in *Il libro del cortegiano* (1528; *The Book of the Courtier*, 1561) trace their origin to medieval epics such as *Poem of the Cid*.

Somewhat incongruous with the Cid's character as straightforward, guileless, and trusting is that he occasionally takes on the aspect of a folkloric trickster. The Cid is capable of outright deceit if it proves necessary to remove himself from difficulty; for example, he originates the plan that cheats Raquel and Vidas, the two moneylenders, out of six hundred marks in return for two coffers of sand. The Cid makes it clear, however, that he does this only "because I must and have no other choice."

Side by side with all that is mythic in *Poem of the Cid* is a keen attention to the details of Spanish history and the Spanish countryside. The poem is filled with the names of towns, rivers, and historical figures. Far more realistic than other medieval Spanish epics, *Poem of the Cid* includes recognizable settings rather than idealized and magical kingdoms. In its description of actual places and realistic events, *Poem of the Cid* stands at the beginning of a tradition that would lead to gritty novels such as *Lazarillo de Tormes* (1554), *Guzmán de Alfarache* (1599), *The Life of the Swindler* (1626), and even *Don Quixote de la Mancha* (1605, 1615). *Poem of the Cid* should be viewed, therefore, as a combination of a folkloric plot, courtly values, and realistic geographic and historical details. Its influence extended to the later Spanish novel.

"Critical Evaluation" by Jeffrey L. Buller

Further Reading

Chasca, Edmund de. *The Poem of the Cid*. Boston: Twayne, 1976. Offers an excellent place to begin for a general literary and historical account of the poem. Includes discussion of medieval epic poetry and the historicity of *Poem of the Cid* as well as examination of the use of humor and epic formulas in the work and speculation on its authorship.

Cowell, Andrew. "Taking an Identity: *The Poem of the Cid*." In *The Medieval Warrior Aristocracy: Gifts, Violence,*

Performance, and the Sacred. Rochester, N.Y.: D. S. Brewer, 2007. Examination of *Poem of the Cid* is part of a larger work that focuses on how medieval epic heroes, like the Cid, reflected society's concerns about the nature of the warrior elite.

Fletcher, Richard A. *The Quest for the Cid*. New York: Random House, 1990. Presents a historical account of the period 711-1516, providing a valuable discussion of the cultural background of *Poem of the Cid*. Includes extensive bibliography.

Matulka, Barbara. *The Cid as a Courtly Hero*. New York: Institute of French Studies, Columbia University, 1928. Explores the figure of the Cid from his appearance in medieval epics through Pierre Corneille's treatment in *Le Cid* (pr., pb. 1637; *The Cid*, 1637). Provides a short, informative account of such literary motifs as the love-test, voluntary death, and the Cid's sword.

Menéndez Pidal, Ramón. *The Cid and His Spain*. Translated by Harold Sunderland. London: John Murray, 1934. De-tailed discussion of *El Cid* and its background by the author of the poem's most influential critical edition. Includes attention to the struggle for Valencia, the invasion (and subsequent repulsion) of the Almoravides, the court of the Cid, and the process by which the historical figure of the Cid was transformed into a legend.

Montgomery, Thomas. *Medieval Spanish Epic: Mythic Roots and Ritual Language*. University Park: Pennsylvania State University Press, 1998. Examines *Poem of the Cid* and other medieval Spanish epics, describing how they originated in ancient myths about the initiation of young warriors. Places these epics within their cultural and social contexts and analyzes their poetic language.

Smith, Colin. *The Making of the "Poema de mio Cid."* New York: Cambridge University Press, 1983. Claims that *Poem of the Cid* was an experimental work, the first epic to be composed in Castilian, and that Per Abad, the figure who is usually regarded as the poem's copyist, was actually its author.

Poems

Author: Sidney Lanier (1842-1881)
First published: 1877/1884; includes *Poems*, 1877;
    Poems of Sidney Lanier, 1884
Type of work: Poetry

The poetic fame of Sidney Lanier, after Edgar Allan Poe one of the most important nineteenth century poets of the southern United States, rests on a small body of poetry found in the posthumous volume *Poems*. This contains the verse Lanier included in his earlier *Poems*, along with a number of pieces that had received only magazine publication before the poet's death in 1881, plus a group of unrevised early poems that his wife felt were worthy of publication.

Lanier was a poet of both theory and practice. His theory of technique was influenced by his great love for music. Precociously musical, he became a brilliant flutist who played with symphony orchestras in Dallas and Baltimore. His moralistic theory of poetic content was possibly influenced by his early training in a devoutly Christian family as well as by his own fundamentally religious nature. This shows itself in some of his nature poems as a passionate love for God's plants and creatures that approaches the fervor of Saint Francis of Assisi.

Lanier's theory of prosody is expounded principally in his work *The Science of English Verse* (1880), in which he develops in extensive detail and with copious illustration the thesis that the same laws govern both versification and music. Three brief quotations illustrate this thesis:

When we hear verse, we *hear* a set of relations between sounds; when we silently read verse, we *see* that which brings to us a set of relations between sounds; when we imagine verse, we *imagine* a set of relations between sounds.

When those exact co-ordinations which the ear perceives as rhythm, tune, and tone-color, are suggested to the ear by a series of *musical sounds*, the result is . . . MUSIC.

When those exact co-ordinations which the ear perceives as rhythm, tune, and tone-color, are suggested to the ear by a series of *spoken words*, the result is . . . VERSE.

There is absolutely no difference between the sound-relations used in music and those used in verse.

Lanier's application of his prosodic theory may be studied in many of his poems, but it may be seen easily in such poems as "The Symphony," "The Marshes of Glynn," and "Song of the Chattahoochee." In "The Symphony," Lanier attempted the difficult task of composing a poem somewhat as a musician would. Such instruments as the violin, flute, clarinet, horn, and hautboy (oboe) are personified and used to develop the theme of love, the enemy of trade (materialism), which pervades the poem. Nowhere is Lanier's belief in the essential identity of sound relations in music and in verse better illustrated than in the four lines that introduce the horn passage in the poem: "There thrust the bold straightforward horn/ To battle for that lady lorn./ With hearthsome voice of mellow scorn,/ Like any knight in knighthood's morn."

It has been objected that Lanier tried the impossible in "The Symphony" and that his achievement, though notable, is successful only in part. Perhaps his theory is better illustrated in "Sunrise" and "The Marshes of Glynn." In "Sunrise," the sibilance of the forest can be heard: "Ye lispers, whisperers, singers in storms,/ Ye consciences murmuring faiths under forms,/ Ye ministers meet for each passion that grieves,/ Friendly, sisterly, sweetheart leaves." In "The Marshes of Glynn," the sounds and even the silence of the great marshes near Brunswick, Georgia, may be heard and felt by the reader. A passage near the close of the poem describes in this fashion the coming of the high tide of evening:

> The creeks overflow: a thousand rivulets run
> 'Twixt the roots of the sod; the blades of the
>   marsh-grass stir;
> Passeth a hurrying sound of wings that
>   westward whirr;
> Passeth, and all is still; and the currents cease
>   to run;
> And the sea and the marsh are one.

In these lines the sounds of the moving waters and grasses and of the whirring wings are followed by a silence that is palpable.

Because of Lanier's repeated use of onomatopoeia in his verse he has often been compared with Poe, but Lanier's theory of poetic content is quite different. Poe, in "The Philosophy of Composition," concedes that "passion, or even truth, may . . . be introduced, and even profitably introduced, into a poem"; however, he asserts, "Beauty is the sole legitimate province of the poem." In another essay, "The Poetic Princi-

ple," Poe attacks what he calls "the heresy of the didactic." "Every poem, it is said, should inculcate a moral," he declares, "and by this moral is the poetical merit of the work to be adjudged." He goes on:

> Would we but permit ourselves to look into our own souls, we should immediately there discover that under the sun there neither exists nor *can* exist any work more thoroughly dignified—more supremely noble than this very poem—this poem *per se*—this poem which is a poem and nothing more—this poem written solely for the poem's sake.

Lanier loved art as much as Poe did, but Lanier was on the side of the moralists. In his series of lectures posthumously published as *The English Novel and the Principle of Its Development* (1883), he leaves no doubt as to his position when he states:

> We may say that he who has not yet perceived how artistic beauty and moral beauty are convergent lines which run back into a common ideal origin, and who therefore is not afire with moral beauty just as with artistic beauty—that he, in short, who has not come to that stage of quiet and eternal frenzy in which the beauty of holiness and the holiness of beauty mean one thing, burn as one fire, shine as one light within him; he is not yet the great artist.

Although Lanier wrote occasional poems such as his verse narrative "The Revenge of Hamish," in which the moral element is not a major one, most of his poetry is charged with moral purpose or shines with "the beauty of holiness." "The Symphony" bitterly indicts the cruel, greedy practices of trade and sings the gospel of brotherly love. In "The Marshes of Glynn," he writes, "As the marsh-hen secretly builds on the watery sod,/ Behold I will build me a nest on the greatness of God." Even a dialect poem such as "Thar's More in the Man than Thar Is in the Land" contains a moral lesson, as the title itself suggests. Occasionally his moral earnestness dims Lanier's artistic sight, however, as in "Song of the Chattahoochee," in which the river is made to say, "I am fain for to water the plain./ Downward the voices of Duty call—." This is a flagrant example of what John Ruskin called the pathetic fallacy. People may act with moral purpose; when the Chattahoochee River flows downward, however, it is not because it knows that "The dry fields burn, and the mills are to turn,/ And a myriad flowers mortally yearn," but because, as Lanier himself very well knew, the law of gravity is a part of the earthly scheme of things.

Though Lanier is not primarily a regional poet, many of his lines sing eloquently of his southern origin. He is in love with the beautiful marshes of Glynn, with their "moss-bearded live-oaks." He mourns that "Bright drops of tune, from oceans infinite/ Of Melody" were ended when a pet mockingbird "died of a cat, May, 1878." He grieves in "Corn" that the rich soil of his native state is being washed away because of the greed of cotton farmers who lay the surface bare and then leave their erosion-ruined areas and head for Texas to repeat their folly. In "A Florida Sunday," he holds "in my being" rich-scented orange trees, pea-green parakeets, "pranked woodpeckers that ne'er gossip out," palmettos, pines, and mangroves. In such poems, Lanier is as clearly a southern poet as Robert Frost is a New England one when he describes his New Hampshire countryside.

A fault that many readers have found with Lanier is that, as a poet, he too often lets his heart overflow and his whole being "quiver with the passionate thrill." At times a noble emotion may descend into sentimentality and at others the poet's feeling may blur the expression of "the great thought." The lush music of Lanier's lines may also create the lulling mental effect that one finds in Algernon Charles Swinburne. Part of Lanier's trouble seems to be that he is striving too hard to attain the right combination of "rhythm, tune, and tone-color." He sometimes forces his comparisons so that they become too-obvious poetic conceits, as in "Marsh Song—at Sunset," with its metaphors drawn from William Shakespeare's *The Tempest* (pr. 1611, pb. 1623). Some of his sentences, such as the thirty-six-line one that opens "The Marshes of Glynn," lack clarity because of their great length and intricate structure.

In spite of the undisciplined emotionalism, hazy thought, and strained effects of his lesser poems, Lanier seems well assured of a permanent place in American literature. The melody of his best lines; the love of God, human beings, and nature found in poems such as "The Marshes of Glynn" and "The Symphony"; the simple beauty of "A Ballad of Trees and the Master"; the stoic acceptance of "The Stirrup-Cup," in which the consumptive poet says uncomplainingly to Death, "Hand me the cup whene'er thou wilt"—for these Lanier will continue to be loved.

Further Reading

De Bellis, Jack. *Sidney Lanier.* New York: Twayne, 1972. Provides an excellent critical overview of Lanier's life and works. Includes careful readings of the major poems, a discussion of Lanier's fiction, and a biographical chronology.

_____. *Sidney Lanier: Poet of the Marshes.* Atlanta: Georgia Humanities Council, 1988. Brief but fine introduction to Lanier's major works includes careful readings of selected poems. Focuses on the poetry's relationship to nature and music.

Gabin, Jane S. *A Living Minstrelsy: The Poetry and Music of Sidney Lanier.* Macon, Ga.: Mercer University Press, 1985. Provides an informative account of Lanier's life and artistic career. Includes sensitive readings of the poems and is particularly enlightening on the subject of the relationship of the poetry to music.

Kerkering, Jack. "'Of Me and of Mine': The Music of Racial Identity in Whitman and Lanier, Dvořák and Du Bois." *American Literature* 73, no. 1 (March, 2001): 147-184. Analyzes the issue of racial identity in the poetry of Lanier and Walt Whitman, the music of Antonín Dvořák, and *The Souls of Black Folk* (1903) by W. E. B. Du Bois. Compares visions of American unity in Lanier's "Centennial Cantata" (1875) with Whitman's *Leaves of Grass* (1855).

Parks, Edd Winfield. *Sidney Lanier: The Man, the Poet, the Critic.* Athens: University of Georgia Press, 1968. Examines Lanier's complete artistic life, tracing his development as a poet and a thinker. Discusses his own writings as well as his commentaries on and concerns with the works of others. Considers why Lanier never became a major poet.

Starke, Aubrey Harrison. *Sidney Lanier: A Biographical and Critical Study.* New York: Russell & Russell, 1964. Presents a full, critical exploration of Lanier's poetry and creative nature.

Poems

Author: Sir Walter Ralegh (c. 1552-1618)
First published: 1813, as *The Poems of Sir Walter Raleigh Now First Collected, with a Biographical and Critical Introduction*
Type of work: Poetry

Sir Walter Ralegh, like so many other Renaissance courtiers, considered the writing of poetry one of the polite arts, to be practiced in one's leisure moments for the pleasure of friends. In his busy political, military, and adventuring career, his poetic efforts apparently carried little weight, and he never seems to have encouraged their publication, although he was much interested in presenting to the public his *History of the World* (1614) and his treatises on his expeditions to the new world. As a result of this carelessness, on his part and on the part of publishers who did publish his work and who sometimes published work that was not his under his name, over the years countless verses have been attributed to him, and no one can be sure how many of them he actually wrote. The small body of work that is unquestionably his, however, shows him to be a poet of high ability.

Ralegh was perhaps second only to Edmund Spenser and Sir Philip Sidney as poets in the court of Elizabeth I. He shunned the opulence of the typical poetry of his time for a sparse, dignified style that has many echoes of his predecessors, Sir Thomas Wyatt and Henry Howard, earl of Surrey. The melancholy quality that pervades much of Ralegh's work is close to that of almost all of Wyatt's poems and to the last lyrics of Surrey, written while he was in the Tower awaiting trial and execution. Ralegh himself spent more than ten years in the Tower, hoping against hope for release, and a sense of the constant closeness of death runs through his later work. Life is precarious, "beauty, fleeting," and death near at hand for all. Ralegh's answer to Christopher Marlowe's famous pastoral lyric "Come Live with Me and Be My Love" (1600) is filled with this sense of the transience of all things:

> Time drives the flocks from field to fold,
> When rivers rage and rocks grow cold,
> And Philomel becometh dumb;
> The rest complains of cares to come.
> The flowers do fade, and wanton fields
> To wayward winter reckoning yields;
> A honey tongue, a heart of gall,
> Is fancy's spring, but sorrow's fall.

Ralegh protests against the actions of time in another lyric, "Nature that washt her hands in milke," in which he describes the creation of the perfect woman by Nature, at the request of Love. This paragon no sooner exists than Time, "being made of steel and rust,/ Turns snow, and silk and milk to dust." The final stanza is the eternal human lament:

> Oh, cruel time! Which takes in trust
> Our youth, our joys and all we have,
> And pays us but with age and dust,
> Who in the dark and silent grave
> When we have wandered all our ways
> Shuts up the story of our days.

While Wyatt's laments are most often those of the Petrarchan lover, scorned by the lady to whom he offers devotion, Ralegh's melancholy seems to derive from a more general vision of the human condition. Even in those sonnets in which he takes the conventional stance of the rejected lover, he seems conscious of a larger world. One of these concludes, "And at my gate despair shall linger still,/ To let in death when love and fortune will."

Ralegh's sense of the destructive powers of time has particular force in his elegy on Sir Philip Sidney, an excellent poem in which the writer pays tribute to a fellow courtier-soldier-poet. There is in the "Epitaph" a touch of envy of Sidney, who died with an unblemished reputation and was freed from the threats of time and evil men:

> What hath he lost, that such great grace hath won?
> Young years for endless years, and hope unsure,
> Of fortune's gifts, for wealth that still shall dure,
> Oh, happy race, with so great praises run!

Like many other writers of his century, Ralegh uses his poetry to chastise the court for its hypocrisy, its vice, and its folly. Few men, indeed, suffered more from the false appearances of monarchs and their ministers. The brief stanzas of "The Lie" move over the whole spectrum of society:

Say to the court it glows,
And shines like rotten wood;
Say to the church, it shows
What's good, and doth no good:
If church and court reply,
Then give them both the lie.

The tone of Ralegh's poetry is not unmitigated gloom; few men were more vibrantly alive than this courtier-adventurer, and he could compose sprightly, witty lyrics with the best of his contemporaries, following out a pseudological argument in the manner of John Donne, singing lyrically about the beauty of the moon or defining love in the ordinary vocabulary of his day:

Yet what is love? I pray thee sain.
It is a sunshine mixed with rain;
It is a tooth-ache, or like pain;
It is a game where none doth gain;
The lass saith no, and would full fain:
And this is Love, as I hear sain.

There is much of the medieval heritage in Ralegh's work. Folk wisdom, proverbs, and the haunting quality of many of the early ballads lurk under the surface of several of his poems, notably one addressed to his son. The poem begins quietly and continues in a matter-of-fact way that reinforces its horror. Three things, "the wood, the weed, and the wag," prosper separately, but, together they bring destruction:

The wood is that, that makes the gallows tree,
The weed is that, that strings the hangman's bag;
The wag, my pretty knave betokens thee.
Now mark, dear boy: while these assemble not,
Green springs the tree, hemp grows, the wag is wild;
But when they meet, it makes the timber rot,
It frets the halter, and it chokes the child.

Medieval in a different sense is one of Ralegh's last and best poems, "The Passionate Man's Pilgrimage." Its Christian allegory is that of a traveler's journey to salvation:

Give me my scallop-shell of quiet,
My staff of faith to walk upon,
My scrip of joy, immortal diet,
My bottle of salvation,
My gown of glory, hope's true gage,
And thus I'll take my pilgrimage.

Ralegh's irregular metrical pattern is admirably suited to his subject; the simplicity of his acceptance of redemption in the second section is mirrored in the short rhymed lines, the clarity of the language, and the images of silver, nectar, milk, and crystal. The fourth section, with its theme of judgment, is harsher in both rhythm and vocabulary, as Ralegh speaks of Christ as the advocate, pleading the cause of sinful man in a court where bribery and forgery have no place, a compelling allusion to the trial in which Sir Edward Coke, not Christ, was the King's Counsel, and the verdict was, in the minds of most, a travesty of justice. The concluding stanza has a macabre quality. Ralegh is said to have written these last lines on the night before his execution: "Just at the stroke when my veins start and spread/ Set on my soul an everlasting head./ Then am I ready like a palmer fit,/ To tread those blest paths which before I writ."

Ralegh's longest extant poem is a fragment of a still more extensive work called "Ocean's Love to Cynthia." The original version, so far as scholars have been able to deduce, was addressed to Queen Elizabeth about 1587, when Robert Devereux, earl of Essex, seemed to be replacing Ralegh in her esteem. In its first form the poem evidently served its purpose, for Ralegh was reinstated in Her Majesty's favor until his indiscreet affair and hasty marriage with one of her maids of honor in 1592. It has been suggested that the surviving fragment of the poem was written from the Tower, where Ralegh had been imprisoned with his bride, in an attempt to mollify Elizabeth's resentment.

The quatrains of the extant text are presented as the outpourings of a disillusioned lover of the queen. There is no real narrative link; the whole poem is essentially the exposition of a state of mind. It is written in four-line stanzas with alternate rhymes, a compact form that lends itself to the development of a slightly different point in each quatrain. The extant manuscript is evidently an unfinished version of the poem, for occasionally Ralegh left two, three, or five lines as a separate unit to be revised later. However, even if the poem as it exists is unfinished, it demonstrates forcefully Ralegh's power to convey his deep and intense disillusionment. Toward the end of the fragment the poet, speaking as a shepherd, ponders the paradox of his state of mind. His mistress may treat him well or ill, but she is with him forever: "She is gone, she is lost, she is found, she is ever fair." He can only take life as it comes, let his flocks wander at will, and live with his despair: "Thus home I draw, as death's long night draws on;/ Yet every foot, old thoughts turn back mine eyes;/ Constraint me guides as old age draws a stone/ Against the hill, which over-weighty lies." He must, in the last analysis, trust in the mercies of God.

Ralegh never entirely fulfilled his promise as a poet. His intense interest in colonizing projects, his career at court, and his later political misfortunes probably combined to prevent his devoting his energies to poetry, and his gigantic project, the history of the world, left far from complete at his death, occupied his last years in the Tower. The works he did leave, however, are among the best of the Elizabethan age. The virtues of his poems are their quiet strength and the melancholy tone that was the almost inevitable result of his skeptical, inquiring mind.

Further Reading

Bates, Catherine. *Masculinity, Gender, and Identity in the English Renaissance Lyric.* New York: Cambridge University Press, 2007. Analyzes the depiction of masculine identity in works by Ralegh and other English Renaissance poets. Argues that these poets create alternative models of masculinity, often portraying men as broken and abject instead of as powerful and in control.

Hammond, Gerald, ed. Introduction to *Selected Writings*, by Sir Walter Ralegh. Manchester, England: Carcanet, 1984. Hammond's introduction to this collection gives substantial attention to Ralegh's poetry, addressing its themes and styles as well as the influence of others on Ralegh's work.

May, Steven W. *The Elizabethan Courtier Poets: The Poems and Their Contexts.* Columbia: University of Missouri Press, 1991. Includes a discussion of Ralegh's career. Examines Ralegh's genres and looks closely at the relationship between Ralegh's poetry and his position as courtier to Elizabeth I

_____. *Sir Walter Ralegh.* Boston: Twayne, 1989. Provides a solid general introduction to the life and the major works of the writer.

Oram, William A. "Raleigh, the Queen, and Elizabethan Court Poetry." In *Early Modern English Poetry: A Critical Companion*, edited by Patrick Cheney, Andrew Hadfield, and Garrett A. Sullivan, Jr. New York: Oxford University Press, 2007. An analysis of Ralegh's poetry in the context of his relationship with Elizabeth I and the court politics of his day.

Trevelyan, Raleigh. *Sir Walter Raleigh.* London: Allen Lane, 2002. Exhaustive biography written by a direct descendant of Ralegh. Draws from Ralegh's poems and prose to recount his life.

Ure, Peter. "The Poetry of Sir Walter Ralegh." In *Elizabethan and Jacobean Drama: Critical Essays*, edited by J. C. Maxwell. Liverpool, England: Liverpool University Press, 1974. Ure examines Ralegh's friendship with Edmund Spenser and its effects on Ralegh's poetry. Notes particularly the dark quality of Ralegh's writing from the Jacobean period.

Poems and Ballads

Author: Algernon Charles Swinburne (1837-1909)
First published: 1866, First Series; 1878, Second
    Series; 1889, Third Series
Type of work: Poetry

Poems and Ballads, published in three series, contains the major part of Algernon Charles Swinburne's great lyric poetry. Whether the first series of these remarkable poems brought him fame or notoriety is a debatable question. One critic called him the most immoral of all English poets and has pointed to *Poems and Ballads: First Series* as the most obscene book of poetry in the English language. Other critics, like George Meredith and John Ruskin, were fascinated by Swinburne's rich melodies and technical virtuosity. These two opinions of Swinburne reflect the most striking qualities of *Poems and Ballads*: The poems are an open revolt against Victorian prudery, and they are among the most technically perfect poems in English. To the reader of 1866, they were unlike anything published in England; while the critics loudly and indignantly denounced the volume, the public avidly bought it.

Swinburne's major themes in the 1866 volume are sex, freedom, sadism, masochism, and the beauty of evil and of things corrupt or decaying. Influenced by the growing interest in the Marquis de Sade and Charles Baudelaire, Swinburne presents his themes without equivocation. Few poems before 1866 celebrated the pleasures of physical love with the straightforwardness of "Les Noyades," in which sex is public and intensified by impending death, or "Fragoletta," in which sex is given overtones of psychological maladjustment. Such sexual deviations are used by Swinburne for their ability to shock the prudish reader. In the 1866 volume, sexual deviations include homosexuality, in the group of poems called "Hermaphroditus" and in "Sappho"; incest, in "Phaedra"; and sexual flagellation, in such poems as "A Match." The reasons for this focus, however, may be far greater than merely the desire to shock. Swinburne is celebrating the human body itself, the sexual pleasure that alone remains after the soul is eliminated. In this sense, his use of the shocking is both a way to jar the apathetic public and to point toward a new religion.

This paganism is especially evident in "Laus Veneris," Swinburne's rehandling of the Tannhäuser legend. In this poem, the tragedy is that the knight who has renounced Christ believes in him and the lover who has embraced Venus does not believe in her. Another poem that glorifies this pagan outlook is "Hymn to Proserpine," in which the speaker, a pagan of 313 C.E., when Christianity was proclaimed to be the state religion, bitterly laments the passing of pagan sensuality and predicts an eventual collapse of Christianity.

The glorification of sensuality, however, leads Swinburne into another characteristic theme: If sexual ecstasy is truly to be the height of human existence, humans must be free from all restraints. In the bitter "St. Dorothy," the chaste virgin and her lover die horrible deaths because they are trapped by the restraints of Christianity; in "The Masque of Queen Barsabe" (a miracle play about David, Bathsheba, and Nathan), the prophet is forced to admit that the adulterous queen is right.

Related to this desire for sexual freedom is Swinburne's adoration of the prostitute. In "Dolores," the peak of Swinburne's masochistic eroticism, the prostitute is "Our Lady of Pain," a semigoddess who gives the worshiper an excessive pleasure of suffering. "Faustine," addressed to another prostitute, revels in the pleasure of damnation, a pleasure that only a masochist could enjoy. Sadistic love is the theme of "Satia Te Sanguine" ("Satiate thyself with blood"), and "The Leper," in which the lover has the sadistic pleasure of coldly watching his beloved while she is slowly consumed by a fatal disease.

Sensuality, however, would lack much of its charm to Swinburne if it were a permanent state; thus, he places it within a world that is characterized above all by the passing of time. "Ilicet" ("Let us go") is a lament for this passing of time, and "The Triumph of Time," as its title implies, laments the mutability of human existence and the inevitable ending

to love. "Before Parting" and "Before Dawn" are further laments for the ending of love. Related to these poems are the two eulogies, "In Memory of Walter Savage Landor" and "To Victor Hugo," both of which rather sentimentally note the transience of human life.

In contrast to the sentimentality of these eulogies are the two grotesque ballads "After Death" and "The Bloody Son," which present realistic pictures of death. This view is the exception in Swinburne's poetry; the poems that display a yearning to die far outnumber the realistic ones. In "The Garden of Proserpine," the weariness of life is contrasted with the peaceful rest of death, and in "Hendecasyllabics" the speaker seeks rest from "the long decline of roses."

Poems and Ballads: Second Series marks a change in Swinburne's thought. No longer is he the outspoken rebel against Victorian conventionality. His tone has changed from nervous ranting and naughty excitement to a calm, sad strain, almost of lamentation. During the twelve years between the two series, Swinburne's friends—Dante Gabriel Rossetti, George Meredith, and Benjamin Jowett—had brought his attention to Elizabethan drama, and in the 1878 volume, Swinburne published the lyrics that this study had produced.

Instead of the eroticism of 1866, the second series is obsessed with death, so much so that more than one-half of the fifty-five poems are either eulogies or laments. The theme of death can be divided into three parts, each of which Swinburne describes: the death of famous men, the death of youth, and the death of nature. Some of the most remarkable poems in this volume are on the deaths of famous persons: Barry Cornwall, Baudelaire, Théophile Gautier (one of Swinburne's favorite contemporaries), and Hugo (the leading exponent of French Romanticism). In these poems, Swinburne's concern is twofold: In each, he laments the passing of a great poet, to him the crown of existence, and the defeat of a struggling, vivacious man by a force over which he has no control. This last concern partly relates him to the then-growing movement of naturalism, especially as interpreted by Émile Zola, as well as to his own sense of futility, which had already appeared in the 1866 volume.

A second aspect of the theme of death deals with the death of nature. This is the theme of "A Forsaken Garden," the poem many consider to be the best in the volume. Here, Swinburne laments the mutability of life and the decay that characterizes nature. Other poems related to this theme are "At a Month's End," "The Year of the Rose," and "Four Songs of Four Seasons"; in each, the poet observes the decay and death that are part of nature.

Finally, there is a group of lyrics in which Swinburne laments the death or the passing of youth and, with youth, the passing of love. "A Wasted Vigil" and "Age and Song," for example, show the inevitable decay of youth itself that, being caught up in the world of nature, must die even as nature dies.

The second series also reveals Swinburne's increased dependence upon and appreciation for Continental poetry, especially the mature poetry of Baudelaire and Gautier. More and more, Swinburne concentrates on the sharply defined image or symbol as developed by these poets and takes his emphasis from the melodious line. It is in *Poems and Ballads: Third Series*, published in 1889, that Swinburne most shows the fruits of this influence. During 1879, he was so near death that his friends thought there was no hope for him, but Theodore Watts-Dunton rescued him and, by caring for him with almost parental control, nursed him back to health. The third series reflects this encounter with death and the reconciliation of the rebel to the middle class.

By far the least remarkable of the three volumes, the 1889 *Poems and Ballads* introduces a thread of patriotism hardly noticeable in Swinburne's work before this time. "The Commonweal," for example, extols the jubilee of Queen Victoria, an attitude that would have been inconceivable in the young Swinburne, and "The Armada" is an almost Tennysonian exaltation of English sea power. This volume shows a more obvious attempt to rely on literary experiences rather than on his own experiences for the source of his poetry. Especially striking are the echoes of Robert Browning's "Caliban upon Setebos" (1864) in "Caliban on Ariel," for example.

The most interesting poems in this volume are those lyrics capturing, through fleeting but precise symbols, moments that are as ephemeral but profound as those captured in words by Paul Verlaine and Stéphane Mallarmé. In poems such as "In Time of Mourning," "The Interpreters," "The Recall," and "By Twilight," Swinburne grasps the poetic vision that was fundamental to the French Symbolists and would be of utmost importance in twentieth century lyrical poetry.

In the three series of *Poems and Ballads*, Swinburne shows a profundity of thought expressed in a depth of emotion, a combination that easily accounts for his widespread influence on the poets who followed him. There are few forms of versification, however difficult, that do not appear in these pages. In his translations of François Villon and in his re-creations of the early English ballad, Swinburne shows that translation and the meager ballad could be the vehicles of great art. In the sestinas and sonnets, he shows that he has mastered the most difficult rhyme patterns. In fact, he shows a mastery in technical matters that is perhaps unmatched in English poetry. All in all, Swinburne's *Poems and Ballads* is

one of the most unusual and most outstanding works of nineteenth century poetry, a publication that mocked its contemporaries with such art that it became a seminal work in the formation of the poetic theory of the following age.

Further Reading

Hyder, Clyde K., ed. *Algernon Swinburne: The Critical Heritage*. New York: Routledge, 1995. A compilation of contemporary reviews and later criticism, tracing the critical reception of Swinburne's work. Includes an introductory essay providing an overview of his life and writings.

Louis, Margot K. *Swinburne and His Gods: The Roots and Growth of an Agnostic Poetry*. Buffalo, N.Y.: McGill-Queen's University Press, 1990. Divided into two sections, "Sacred Elements" and "The New Gods," this ambitious work explores the mythological overtones of demons and angels, violence and harmony, and the individual and God in Swinburne's poems.

McGann, Jerome J. *Swinburne: An Experiment in Criticism*. Chicago: University of Chicago Press, 1972. Emphasizes New Criticism, which looks beyond a given text to the author's life and environment for interpretation. Provocative and comprehensive discussions of Swinburne's use of language, the social context of *Poems and Ballads*, and autobiographical ambiguity.

Maxwell, Catherine. "Beneath the Woman's and the Water's Kiss: Swinburne's Metamorphoses." In *The Female Sublime from Milton to Swinburne: Bearing Blindness*. New York: Manchester University Press, 2001. Traces John Milton's influence on Swinburne and other Victorian poets. Argues that these poets attain vision at the cost of "symbolic blindness and feminization."

_____. *Swinburne*. Tavistock, England: Northcote House/British Council, 2004. An introduction to Swinburne's best-known works, including *Poems and Ballads*, providing close readings of selected poems. Describes how Swinburne's work challenges readers to explore new perspectives and ideas.

Rooksby, Rikky, and Nicholas Shrimpton, eds. *The Whole Music of Passion: New Essays on Swinburne*. Brookfield, Vt.: Ashgate, 1993. Interprets Swinburne's poetry through studies of Swinburne and Romantic authority, dramatic monologue, and the 1890's, and through comparisons of his work with that of George Eliot and Percy Bysshe Shelley. One essay uses John Ruskin's social criticism to explore Swinburne's poetry as an expression of a fallen age, devoid of family values, discipline, and order.

Poems, Chiefly in the Scottish Dialect

Author: Robert Burns (1759-1796)
First published: 1786
Type of work: Poetry

Since the first publication of Robert Burns's verse in the famous Kilmarnock edition entitled *Poems, Chiefly in the Scottish Dialect*, the poet's fame has increased and spread. Other editions of his work, containing later poems, only enhanced his reputation. Unlike many writers who achieve early fame only to see it fade, Burns is still widely read and appreciated.

At least part of the reason for this continuing appreciation is that Burns was essentially a transitional figure between the eighteenth century neoclassicists and the Romantics who were soon to follow. Possessing some of the qualities of each school, he exhibits few of the excesses of either. He occasionally used the couplet that had been made a skillful tool by Alexander Pope and his followers, but his spirit was closer to the Romantics in his attitude toward life and his art.

Although Burns occasionally displayed a mild conservatism, as in the early "The Cotter's Saturday Night," he was fundamentally a rebel, and rebellion is a basic trait of the Romantics. It would have been hard for Burns to be a true neoclassicist because his background, which figures constantly in his poems, simply did not suit him for this role. He had a hard early life and a close acquaintanceship with the common people and the common circumstances of life. He was certainly not the uneducated, "natural" genius that he is sometimes pictured as—having had good instruction from his father and a tutor and having done considerable reading on his own—but he lacked the classical education that earlier poets thought necessary for the writing of true poetry.

Like the neoclassicists, however, Burns was skillful in taking the ideas and forms of earlier poets—in Burns's case, the Scottish poets Allan Ramsay and Robert Fergusson, as well as the anonymous composers of ballads and folk songs—and treating them in his own individual way. Thus, his verse has a wide variety of stanza forms and styles. Despite the variety of his techniques, his basic outlook in his poems is remarkably consistent. This outlook also may have a great deal to do with his popularity. Perhaps more than any other poet since Geoffrey Chaucer, Burns possessed the genial personal insight and the instinct for human feelings that can make a poem speak to everyone. Burns always saw the human aspect of things. His nature poetry, for instance, marks a departure from the intellectualizing of the eigh-

teenth century poets; Burns's lines about nature treat it primarily as a setting in which people live.

The warmth of Burns's verse arises from this humane attitude combined with the experience he had of being in close personal contact with the people about whom he wrote. His writing never deals with subjects that he did not know intimately. Burns loved several women and claimed that they each served as great poetic inspiration. The reader may well believe this statement when he or she encounters the simple and lucidly sincere poems "Highland Mary," "Mary Morison," and the well-known song "Sweet Afton." It was this quality of sincerity that another great Scot, Thomas Carlyle, found to be Burns's greatest poetic value.

Burns was not an original thinker, but he had a few strong convictions about religion, human freedom, and morality. His condemnation of Calvinism and the hypocrisy it bred is accomplished with humor and yet with sharpness in two of his best poems, "The Holy Fair" and the posthumously published "Holy Willie's Prayer." In these and several other poems, Burns pokes occasionally none-too-gentle fun at the professional religionists of his time. Burns's intensely personal viewpoint saved him from preaching, as was the style of earlier versifiers. It is to be expected that the few poems that contain examples of his rare attempts to be lofty are unsuccessful.

Having grown up in a humble environment, Burns was especially sensitive to social relations and the value of human freedom and equality. On this subject, too, he is never didactic, but few readers have remained unmoved by the lines of probably his most famous poem, "A Man's a Man for A' That," in defense of the lower classes:

> Is there, for honest poverty
> That hings his head, an' a' that?
> The coward slave, we pass him by—
> We dare be poor for a' that!
> For a' that and a' that,
> Our toil's obscure and a' that;
> The rank is but the guinea's stamp,
> The man's the gowd for a' that.
>
> . . . .
>
> Then let us pray that come it may,

As come it will for a' that,
That sense and worth, o'er a' the earth,
Shall bear the gree, an' a' that.
For a' that, an' a' that,
It's coming yet for a' that,
That man to man, the warld o'er,
Shall brithers be for a' that.

It was this powerful feeling for democracy that led Burns, in his later years, to a tactless advocacy of the principles of the French Revolution, a crusade that did his career as a minor government official no good. It is questionable whether Burns's heated protest against Calvinism and the strict morality it proclaimed was simply a rationalization of his own loose behavior. However many the romances he had, and however many the illegitimate children he fathered, there can be little doubt of Burns's sincere devotion, at least at the time, to the woman of his choice. In a larger sense, too, the poet's warm sympathy for others is evidence of a sort of ethical pattern in his life and work that is quite laudable.

The poetic techniques in Burns's poems are unquestionably a chief reason for his popularity. Few poets have so well suited the style to the subject, and his use of earlier stanza forms and several kinds of poetic diction has a sureness and an authority that are certain to charm even the learned student of poetry. There are three types of diction in his poetry: Scottish dialect, pure English, and a combination of the two. In "Tam O' Shanter," a later work that is perhaps his masterpiece, Burns uses dialect to tell an old legend of the supernatural with great effect. The modern reader who takes the trouble to master the dialectal terminology will be highly rewarded. In this, as in most of Burns's poems, the pace and rhythm of the lines are admirably well suited to the subject.

Burns's use of the English idiom, as in "The Vision," was seldom so successful. Usually Burns wrote in standard English when he had some lofty purpose in mind, and with the exception of "The Cotter's Saturday Night," this combination was often fatal to the poetic quality of these poems. For the general reader, probably the most enjoyable and rewarding reading consists of the poems and songs that Burns did in English, with occasional Scottish touches here and there in the lines. Most happy is this joining of language and dialect in such a poem as the famous little love lyric, "A Red, Red Rose." These three kinds of poetic diction can be found side by side in one of Burns's best poems, the highly patriotic "The Jolly Beggars," which gives as fine a picture of the Scottish lower classes as can be found anywhere.

Naturally, Burns was most at home when he wrote in his native dialect; and, since one of the most striking characteristics of his verse is the effortless flow of conversational rhythms, it is not surprising that his better poems developed as natural effusions in his most familiar diction.

The total achievement of Burns is obviously great, but it should not be misunderstood. Burns lacked the precision and clarity of his predecessors in the eighteenth century, and he never reached the exalted heights of poetic expression attained by Percy Bysshe Shelley and John Keats not long after him. For vigor and the little touches that breathe life into lines of poetry, however, he was unexcelled by earlier or later poets.

The claim that Burns wrote careless verse has been perhaps too much emphasized. His poems and songs are surely not carefully carved jewels, but neither are they haphazard groupings of images and rhymes. The verses seem unlabored, but Burns worked patiently at them, and with considerable effort. That they seem to have been casual utterances is only further tribute to his ability. It may be that the highest praise of all was paid to Burns, both as man and poet, by Keats, who said that one can see in Burns's poems his whole life; and, though the life reflected was not an altogether happy one, the poet's love of freedom, of people, and of life itself appears in nearly every line.

Further Reading

Burns, Robert. *The Canongate Burns*. 2 vols. Edited by Andrew Noble and Patrick Scott Hogg. Edinburgh: Canongate Books, 2001. This two-volume collection contains all of Burns's poetry, including previously unpublished works and poems newly attributed to him. The annotations include translations for the Scottish dialect terms, as well as background on Burns's life, poetry, and political beliefs.

Carruthers, Gerard. *Robert Burns*. Tavistock, England: Northcote House/British Council, 2006. Comprehensive overview of Burns's poetic career, treating his works in their chronological order of publication. Discusses Burns's social and religious satires, the political commentary in his work, and his representation of love and gender.

Crawford, Robert. *The Bard: Robert Burns—A Biography*. Princeton, N.J.: Princeton University Press, 2009. A sympathetic biography of Burns, depicting him as a rebel and radical who imagined himself a poet to become one.

McGuirk, Carol. *Robert Burns and the Sentimental Era*. Athens: University of Georgia Press, 1985. Critical look at Burns's sentimental approach to poetry, including his passion for his nation.

_____, ed. *Critical Essays on Robert Burns*. New York:

G. K. Hall, 1998. Collection of essays about Burns's life and work, including a comparison of his poetry to that of William Wordsworth, his lyrical and satirical verse, his use of Scottish diction, and Burns and the "imagined community" of Scotland.

McIlvanney, Liam. *Burns the Radical: Poetry and Politics in Late Eighteenth-Century Scotland*. East Linton, Scotland: Tuckwell, 2002. Depicts Burns as a sophisticated political poet whose work was influenced by Scottish

Presbyterian ideology, the political theory of the Scottish Enlightenment, and English and Irish political traditions.

McIntyre, Ian. *Dirt and Deity: A Life of Robert Burns*. London: HarperCollins, 1995. Comprehensive biography that recounts the events of Burns's life and offers an extensive evaluation of his songs and poetry. The final chapter examines the legendary reputation that Burns acquired after his death—a legend that bears little resemblance to the reality of his life.

Poetic Edda

Author: Unknown
First transcribed: Edda Sæmundar, ninth to twelfth century (English translation, 1923)
Type of work: Poetry
Type of plot: Saga
Time of plot: Mythical times
Locale: Early Scandinavia and Asgard, home of the northern gods

The Poem:

Voluspo. Odin, chief of the gods, calls an ancient wise woman to prophesy for him. She tells first of the creation of the earth from the body of the giant Ymir and catalogs the dwarfs who live beneath the earth. She then describes Yggdrasil, the great ash tree that supports the universe. Its roots reach clear to the underworld, and it is guarded by the three Norns—Past, Present, and Future—who control the destinies of human beings. She also tells briefly how Loki tricked the giant who built Asgard, the home of the gods, and how Loki himself was punished when he killed Odin's much-loved son Balder. He was bound to a rock so that the venom of a serpent dripped onto his face. The prophet last foretells a great battle. Odin and the other gods will confront the forces of evil, such as the wolf Fenrir, one of Loki's children, who is fated to kill Odin himself. In conclusion, the wise woman foretells the emergence of a new world that will rise out of the destruction of the old one.

The Ballad of Grimnir. Odin makes a wager with his wife, Frigg, about the relative virtues of two men they have saved from being lost at sea. Frigg accuses King Geirröth, the man Odin has saved, of miserliness and lack of hospitality. Odin goes to Geirröth disguised as Grimnir and is taken prisoner and tortured. The king's son, Agnar, befriends the prisoner,

Principal characters:
ODIN, chief of the gods
FRIGG, Odin's wife
BALDER, the beloved, Odin's son
THOR, the thunder god, Odin's son
LOKI, a mischief maker, son of a giant
FREYJA, the goddess of love, who carries off half the slain from the battlefield

however, and is rewarded with the mythological lore that makes up most of the poem.

The Lay of Hymir. Thor seeks a kettle big enough to brew ale for a feast of all the gods. He and the god Tyr go to the home of the giant Hymir, where they escape the wrath of Hymir's nine-hundred-headed grandmother. Hymir then provides a feast for them at which Thor eats two oxen. Finally, they join in a fishing contest in which Thor demonstrates his prowess by hooking Mithgarthsorm, the great serpent that surrounds the earth. Thor and Tyr steal the kettle and carry it home.

The Lay of Thrym. Loki manages to recover Thor's hammer when the giant Thrym steals it and holds it hostage, demanding Freyja for his wife. Thor goes to Thrym, disguised as Freyja in bridal dress, and takes Loki, disguised as his serving woman, with him. After Thor and Loki have some difficulties in accounting for their huge appetites and masculine looks, Thor is given the precious hammer as a wedding gift, whereupon he slays Thrym and the two return to Asgard.

Balder's Dream. Acting on an ominous dream his son Balder has had, Odin rides into the underworld, where a wise woman tells him that the blind god Hoth, guided by Loki, will throw the dart of mistletoe that will kill the otherwise im-pervious Balder. The murder will later be avenged by Vali, whom Odin conceives for that purpose.

Lay of Völund. Völund is a hero who, along with his brothers, captures and lives with the swan maidens, Valky-ries who live on earth disguised as swans. When the swan maidens leave, the brothers seek them. In doing so, Völund is captured by a Swedish king, Nithuth, who accuses him of stealing his treasure. While making his escape, Völund kills Nithuth's sons and sends their skulls, set in silver, to their fa-ther. He then makes good his escape by flying away on wings he has made for himself.

The Lay of Helgi the Son of Hjorvarth. Helgi is befriended by a Valkyrie who sends him a sword that allows him to do great deeds. Together with Atli, he subdues the ferocious daughter of a giant. Later, as a king in his own right, he mar-ries Svava, the Valkyrie who aided him. He dies in a duel with King Alf.

The First Lay of Helgi Hundingsbane. At an early age, Helgi, a son of Sigmund, begins to do valorous deeds. Urged on by the Valkyrie Sigrun, he later engages another king, Granmar, in a sea battle in order to release Sigrun from her obligation to marry Granmar's son Hothbrodd.

Of Sinfjotli's Death. Helgi's brother Sinfjotli is killed by his stepmother, Borghild, in revenge for his murder of her brother. She kills him by making him drink poisoned ale.

Gripir's Prophecy. Sigurth, another of Sigmund's sons, receives a prophecy about his life. Gripir tells him that he will avenge his father's death and fight a terrible dragon named Fafnir. Then Gripir tells him how he will be sent to court Brynhild for King Gunnar, whose form he will take on. As Gunnar, he rides through a ring of fire and wins Brynhild. When she learns of his deception, however, she goads her brother-in-law to kill him.

The Ballad of Regin. Regin tells Sigurth how Loki has killed Regin's brother Otr, having mistaken him for an actual otter. Otr's father, Hreithmar, demands payment in gold as recompense. When Hreithmar refuses to share the "man-money" with his sons Fafnir and Regin, Fafnir kills him and takes all the treasure. Once Sigurth comes of age, Regin urges him to fight with Fafnir.

The Ballad of Fafnir. In Sigurth's battle with the dragon Fafnir, the hero tastes blood from the dragon's heart and im-mediately discovers that he can understand the speech of birds. When he learns from the birds that Regin plans to kill him, he kills Regin as well as the dragon.

The First Lay of Guthrun. In Guthrun's lament for her dead husband, Sigurth, she tells of his being killed as the re-sult of Brynhild's fury at his deception when he courted her

disguised as Gunnar. Brynhild blames the murder on her brother Atli, who forced her to marry Gunnar.

The Short Lay of Sigurth. Brynhild describes her rage at having to marry Gunnar. In the end she kills herself.

The Greenland Lay of Atli. When Guthrun's brothers visit her at her husband Atli's court, Atli kills them. In revenge, Guthrun kills Atli's sons and feeds their hearts to her hus-band; then she stabs him and burns the court to the ground.

Critical Evaluation:

The two parts of the complex group of poems known as the *Poetic Edda* have rather different characteristics. The first part is composed of stories about the gods of the peoples of ancient Scandinavia. These stories deal with the creation of the earth and its peoples and with the lore that relates to the gods and their histories. Taken as a group, these poems depict a world of cold and danger in which even gods such as Balder could become the victims of evil and treachery.

Some themes in these stories are familiar ones and bear close similarities with the creation stories of other peoples. They include the figure of a trickster god, here named Loki, and journeys into the underworld, such as Odin's journey for information and Balder's mother's effort to recover her dead son. Other typical subjects involve riddle telling and in-sult contests; the recounting of lore about the gods, giants, dwarfs, and other supernatural beings; and proverbs intended to instruct people in how to live.

Always in the background of these poems there is a sense of doom, which distinguishes them in tone from the Greek myths with which they are often contrasted. The afterlife de-picted in the *Poetic Edda* is a shadowy land; only those who die heroically in battle can expect to be carried to Valhalla, where they will be feasted by the gods. Indeed, even that re-ward is temporary, for they wait in Valhalla for the final battle against evil, at which time they must aid the gods in their fight.

The poems of the second half of the *Poetic Edda* deal mostly with the legends of human heroes from Norse tradi-tion. Because few of these poems are strictly narrative and many are incomplete, the stories they tell often seem frag-mented, repetitious, and even contradictory. Nevertheless, they represent the main thread of a story that is retold in two other important heroic poems of early Scandinavian and Germanic literature, the *Völsunga Saga* (c. 1200-1300) and the *Nibelungenlied* (c. 1200; English translation, 1848). The latter poem was composer Richard Wagner's source for the plot of his great *Ring* cycle of operas.

In the *Poetic Edda*, as in much early Northern literature, a prominent theme is the need for a family or tribe to get revenge for the death of one of its own, a social imperative in a world without law enforcement. This created endless feuding among tribal groups, as one killing led inevitably to the next. If a family failed to avenge a murder, either with another murder or by demanding a monetary payment, that family faced unbearable shame.

A common theme of this literature is a tribe's attempt to mend a feud through intermarriage, for murder of a family member, even a member by marriage, was taboo. Attempts to establish peace in this way often failed, however. Such attempts provide the motives behind much of the action of the story of Sigurth and Brynhild, and they are visible even in the lyric fragments that make up the *Poetic Edda*.

Ann D. Garbett

Further Reading

Acker, Paul, and Carolyn Larrington, eds. *The "Poetic Edda": Essays on Old Norse Mythology*. New York: Routledge, 2002. Collection of essays presents analyses of the major poems in the work from feminist, structuralist, poststructuralist, and other modern standpoints. Includes introductions that provide an overview of the *Poetic Edda*'s critical history.

Bellows, Henry Adams, ed. and trans. *The Poetic Edda*. New York: American-Scandinavian Foundation, 1957. Includes a general introduction that gives an excellent overview of the poems, their origins, manuscript texts, and verse forms.

Kellogg, Robert. "Literacy and Orality in the *Poetic Edda*." In *Vox Intexta: Orality and Textuality in the Middle Ages*, edited by A. N. Doane and Carol Braun Pasternack. Madison: University of Wisconsin Press, 1991. Discusses the *Poetic Edda* as a collaboration between the oral and the literate worlds. Examines evidence of the oral origins of the poems that make up the work.

MacCulloch, John A. *Eddic [Mythology]*. Vol. 2 in *The Mythology of All Races*. New York: Cooper Square, 1964. Retells the stories told in the *Poetic Edda*, analyzing and ordering them by subject and discussing their relationships to the mythologies of other peoples.

Ólason, Vésteinn. "The Middle Ages: Old Icelandic Poetry." In *A History of Icelandic Literature*, edited by Daisy Neijmann. Lincoln: University of Nebraska Press, 2006. Offers a discussion of the *Poetic Edda* within its historical context.

Ross, Margaret Clunies. *A History of Old Norse Poetry and Poetics*. Rochester, N.Y.: D. S. Brewer, 2005. Guide to the literature of early Scandinavia places the *Poetic Edda* within its social context. Describes both eddic and skaldic poetic genres and the various styles and subjects of Old Norse poetry.

Tucker, John, ed. *Sagas of the Icelanders*. New York: Garland, 1989. Collection of essays covers subjects of general interest in early Icelandic literature, including the figure of the heroine, the poets' rhetorical modes, and the figure of the poet. Some essays discuss individual characters from the stories, including some of the gods.

Poetical Meditations

Author: Alphonse de Lamartine (1790-1869)
First published: Méditations poétiques, 1820 (English translation, 1839)
Type of work: Poetry

When his volume of *Poetical Meditations* appeared in 1820, Alphonse de Lamartine brought French poetry into the Romantic mode that had already become an established poetic form in England and Germany. Even in this work, however, Romanticism is slow to emerge. The number of poems in different editions of *Poetical Meditations* varies between two dozen and three dozen, but only a few poems fully exhibit the Romantic style.

Most of the poems are composed in Alexandrines, the basic verse form of French neoclassicism, and the subjects are often drawn from philosophical meditations of the previous century. Still, much is new. The detailed descriptions of external nature evoke emotions appropriate to the poems in a way the more analytical descriptions of, for example, Jean-Jacques Rousseau's *Les Rêveries du promeneur solitaire* (1782; *The Reveries of the Solitary Walker*, 1783) do not. The autobiographical elements are also distinctly Romantic.

An analysis of the first ten poems included in the first edition of *Poetical Meditations* will define Lamartine's style, clearly Romantic but with debts to previous literary traditions. The opening poem, "L'Isolement," finds Lamartine, its first-person narrator, alone on a mountain from which he can contemplate the panorama of the landscape before him. Rousseau had exploited just such a panorama in his *Émile: Ou, De l'éducation* (1762; *Émile: Or, Education*, 1911), in which his Savoyard vicar used the view of nature to persuade his young pupil of the existence of God. For Lamartine, the purpose of nature is evocative rather than pedagogical.

The first quatrain of "L'Isolement" sets a mood of quiet melancholy: Lamartine sits sadly under an old oak tree at sunset. The references to age and the end of the day imply a basis for his emotion. The landscape, rather than Lamartine, performs the action of the poem while he remains a spectator of this "changing tableau unrolling at my feet." The active waters of the river draw his eyes to the calm lake and finally to the rising evening star. The sequence of objects, progressing ever farther from the narrator, suggests vast contemplation.

The description of nature retains neoclassical elements. Lamartine calls the rising Moon "the misty chariot of the queen of shadows," a periphrasis of the very sort William Wordsworth had hoped to avoid when he advocated that Romantic poetry use "the real language of men." However, the contrast of the "somber woods" with the moon "whitening" the horizon reflects the dark/light color scheme to which the early Romantics were drawn.

The "gothic steeple" of a nearby church provides an additional Romantic motif, but then, switching to an impersonal invocation of "the traveler" who might observe this scene, Lamartine rejects the tableau because, in his mood of despair, it has no appeal to him. Finally, he turns toward death as his only hope. For the sun of the earthly landscape he will substitute the "true sun" of an idealized afterlife.

In the final quatrains, both neoclassical and Romantic images return. Lamartine hopes to be carried away on the "chariot of Dawn," a traditional personification. However, he then imagines the similar rising motion of an autumn leaf blown on the evening wind. Emotionally he cries out, "I am like the withered leaf" and appeals to the "stormy wind" to carry him away. The poet's identification of himself with the leaf and attribution of his own emotional agitation to the wind reflects the Romantic pathetic fallacy through which nature was united with human feelings.

In his second poem, "L'Homme," dedicated to Lord Byron, Lamartine extols the poetic vision of his Romantic pre-

decessor. While Byron was only two years older than Lamartine, he had already published *Childe Harold* (1812) and had impressed Lamartine with the "savage harmony" of his verse. Lamartine's characterization of Byron in the opening section of "L'Homme" uses many Romantic devices. He compares the sound of Byron's poetry with lightning and wind "mixed by the storm with the voice of waterfalls," combining many of the sublime elements of nature the Romantics favored. He further portrays Byron as an eagle, dominating the landscape and deriving "voluptuous enjoyment from the cries of his prey." The important use of natural elements, the linking of the poet to nature using the image of the bird, and the savagery of the predator adding a gothic element combine to create an intensely Romantic passage.

After this preliminary description, however, Lamartine's tone changes. The balance of the rather long poem retreats from nature imagery to examine philosophically the role of the poet in relationship to the will of God. Lamartine traces the Fall of Man and his own personal evolution as a poet but never returns to the descriptive mode of his first lines.

With "Le Soir," Lamartine returns to the first-person meditation in a natural setting that he had used in "L'Isolement" with the substitution of more fluid eight-syllable lines for the Alexandrine. As in the earlier poem, however, the moon still appears as the neoclassical "chariot of the night." The principal action of the poem occurs when the rising Moon casts its light upon Lamartine and causes him to ask whether the moonlight presages philosophical enlightenment. The experience inspires deep emotions. Lamartine says that the moon has "enflamed my heart" and caused "unknown emotions." The tone of the poem, however—marked as it is by a long series of questions as to the moon's intent—remains one of philosophical hesitancy.

Only after an abstract consideration of death in "L'Immortalité" does Lamartine return, in "Le Vallon," to his important use of nature imagery. The world-weary narrator seeks out the valley of his youth to await death. Such emotion coming from a poet who was not yet thirty years old reflects a Romantic despair. The poet then surrounds himself with elements of nature. At first, the "obscure valley" seems mysterious, but then two brooks "joining their waters and their murmuring" flow off into anonymity. Lamartine sees them as an emblem of his own life but notes that his soul is more troubled than their calm waters.

In "Le Vallon," Lamartine again progresses to a meditation on his life. This time, however, he never leaves the landscape. He calls on it to become for him a "place of forgetfulness" like the river Lethe, a refuge from trouble, and finally a place to hear the voice of God. Despite occasional classical allusions, the continued presence of nature and its close relationship to the speaker make this one of Lamartine's most Romantic poems.

In "Le Désespoir" and "La Providence à l'homme," general meditations on God and humankind displace the personal tone and nature imagery. However, in "Souvenir," the personal element returns as Lamartine recalls a lost love. Still seeing himself as old as an oak tree that is dropping its leaves, he remembers "your young, brilliant image/ Embellished by regret." The breeze reminds him of his beloved at their last meeting, when its "loving breath" caressed her hair. The linking of the love experience to nature gives a new meaning to this imagery.

The theme of lost love introduced in "Souvenir" was surely a reference to Julie Charles, whom Lamartine called Elvire in his poetry. Although Julie was married, Lamartine had fallen in love with her during the summer of 1816. He hoped to see her again the following summer but did not because she died from tuberculosis. Lamartine had already included a reference to her in the last line of "L'Immortalité," in which he called on Elvire to answer him. In the ninth edition of *Poetical Meditations* he would also insert the poem "À Elvire" in the third position in the volume. An important evocation of Julie Charles occurs in the tenth poem of the first edition, "Le Lac," which would become the piece for which Lamartine is best known.

Before "Le Lac" in the first edition, the Romantic elements are again restrained in "L'Enthousiasme." While enthusiasm appears as an eagle bearing inspiration to Lamartine, the dominant focus of the poem is not on the natural elements. In "Le Lac," however, nature dominates. Lamartine begins with a plea that it might be possible to stop advancing time if it leads inevitably to the death of a beloved. This appears, however, as dropping an anchor while crossing an ocean surrounded by "eternal night" that isolates humans from both past and future. The image of the ocean yields to that of a lake, emblematic of a shorter period of life, near which Lamartine waits in vain for Julie.

In the first section of the poem, Lamartine addresses the lake as if it were his friend and witness to his joy with his beloved. Not only has the lake "seen" Julie sitting beside it, it has seemed to speak through the murmuring of its waters. Thus, Lamartine asks the lake directly, "Do you remember?" as he recalls words Julie had spoken on its bank.

Julie's speech forms the central portion of "Le Lac," set off from the rest by a distinct verse structure. Elsewhere Lamartine varies the Alexandrine quatrains by reducing the fourth line to six syllables. As Julie speaks, the second line is also reduced, emphasizing how quickly her utterance will pass. The sense of her speech reinforces the desirability of halting time for those who are happy in the present. If a new dawn must come, however, lovers should seize the "fugitive hour" of their joy.

While Julie implores passing time to have pity on lovers, Lamartine sees it as jealous of them. In the final section of the poem, returning to his own voice and distinctive verse form, he groups together "eternity, nothingness, and past time" as "dark abysses" swallowing human life. Faced with this prospect, he finds hope for immortality only in nature. Thus he calls on the lake, rocks, and surrounding forest, a scene he had already endowed with human sensitivity, to retain the memory of his love for Julie.

The lengthy enumeration of objects in nature coupled with the intensity of emotion in this final passage exemplifies the fusion of feeling with landscape that typifies Romanticism. The contrast of "black fir trees" with the silver moon reflects the extremes of Romantic nature description, and the lyricism reinforces the meaning of the lives.

The remaining poems in *Poetical Meditations* incorporate the same varied tendencies seen in the early texts. In "Le Lac," however, Lamartine has established Romantic lyricism as a component of French poetry.

Dorothy M. Betz

Further Reading

Birkett, Mary Ellen. *Lamartine and the Poetics of Landscape.* Lexington, Ky.: French Forum, 1982. Places Lamartine's poetry in the tradition of landscape description, focusing on his descriptive techniques. There is no specific section devoted to *Poetical Meditations*, but material from the collection is quoted extensively throughout the work.

Boutin, Aimeé. *Maternal Echoes: The Poetry of Marceline Desbordes-Valmore and Alphonse de Lamartine.* Newark: University of Delaware Press, 2001. Feminist and psychoanalytical critique of maternal imagery in the two poets' works. Argues that both poets found their own voices by echoing their mothers' voices.

George, Albert Joseph. *Lamartine and Romantic Unanimism.* New York: Columbia University Press, 1940. Analyzes Lamartine's work in terms of his ideas concerning philosophy and his views on politics and history. An extensive index directs the reader to comments on the *Poetical Meditations.*

Lamartine, Alphonse de. *The "Méditations poétiques."* Edited by David Hillery. Durham, England: University of Durham Press, 1993. An introduction to a selection from the poems, this volume includes brief essays on the social, political, literary, and technical background to the poems, as well as the themes of love and death, religion, and nature.

Lombard, Charles M. *Lamartine*. New York: Twayne, 1973. This volume presents a standard approach to Lamartine's life and work accompanied by a useful chronology of his life and a selected bibliography. Chapter 2 introduces,

summarizes, and comments on the importance of *Poetical Meditations*.

Scott, Clive. *The Poetics of French Verse: Studies in Reading*. New York: Oxford University Press, 1998. Discusses the use of rhyme, accent, syllable, and other "expressive resources" of French verse. Provides interpretive readings of several French poems, including selected poems of Lamartine.

Poetics

Author: Aristotle (384-322 B.C.E.)
First transcribed: Peri poētikēs, c. 334-323 B.C.E.
   (English translation, 1705)
Type of work: Literary criticism

The significance of the *Poetics* cannot be overemphasized. In format, content, and methodology, Aristotle's analysis of the literature of Greece is the origin of Western literary criticism. His examination of the components and aims of comedy, epic, and tragedy evolved into what is probably the first, and certainly the most influential, formalist analysis of literature in the Western tradition.

At the center of Aristotle's analysis lies his explanation of the concept of mimesis, the process of representing reality in works of literature. Mimesis does not imply mimicry of the everyday world, however; Aristotle is careful to stress that the job of "the poet" (which later critics have expanded to mean the author of any form of imaginative literature) is to present portraits of humankind as a means of helping audiences learn something about themselves. Far from being lies, as Plato calls the works of poets, good poems and dramas are useful to society because readers and audiences can learn from the experiences of fictional characters without having to experience for themselves the traumas and heartbreaks they can see in tragedy or the foibles and humiliations they can experience through comedy.

Unfortunately, during the later Renaissance and neoclassical periods, the process of description employed by Aristotle in examining the drama and poetry of classical Greece became a prescription for producing and evaluating similar works. French and English dramatists of the seventeenth and eighteenth centuries endeavored to produce plays that adhered slavishly to the unities of time, place, and action they found set down by Aristotle. Although later generations

abandoned the criteria set forth in the *Poetics* for determining the value of specific genres, Aristotle's method of analysis became the basis for the method of literary analysis known as genre criticism. The idea of judging the worth of a particular poem, play, story, or novel by comparing it to designated criteria that characterize other, similar productions has become a staple of literary criticism.

Although his reputation as one of the greatest philosophers of all time rests principally on his work in metaphysics, Aristotle nowhere shows himself more the master of illuminating analysis and style than in the *Poetics*. The conception of tragedy that Aristotle developed in this work has perpetuated the Greek ideal of drama through the ages.

Aristotle begins his essay with an exposition of the Greek idea that all poetry, or art, is representative of life. For the Greeks, the idea of poetry as imitative or representational was a natural one because a great deal of Grecian art was representational in content. By "representation" was meant not a literal copying of physical objects, although it was sometimes that, but a new use of the material presented by sense.

Aristotle's intention in the *Poetics* is to analyze the essence of poetry and to distinguish its various species. Among the arts that Aristotle mentions are epic poetry, tragedy, comedy, dithyrambic poetry, flute playing, and lyre playing. These arts, all of which a poet in Aristotle's time may have been expected to practice, are regarded as representative of life, but they are distinguished from one another by their means and their objects. The means include rhythm, language, and tune, but not all the arts involve all three, nor are these means used in the same way. For example, flute playing involves the use of rhythm and tune, but dancing involves rhythm alone.

When living persons are represented, Aristotle writes, they are represented as being better than, worse than, or the same as the average. Tragedy presents people who are somewhat better than average, while comedy presents people who are somewhat worse. This point alone offers strong evidence against a narrow interpretation of Aristotle's conception of art, for if people can be altered by the poet, made better or worse than in actual life, then poetry is not merely an uncreative copying of nature. A comment later in the *Poetics* indicates that the poet, in representing life, represents things as they are, as they seem to be, or as they should be. This concept certainly allows the artist a great deal more freedom than is suggested by the word "imitation."

Aristotle explains the origin of poetry as the natural consequence of humanity's love of imitation, tune, and rhythm. People enjoy looking at accurate copies of things, he says, even when the things are themselves repulsive, such as the lowest animals and corpses. The philosopher accounts for this enjoyment by claiming that it is the result of people's love of learning; in seeing accurate copies, one learns better what things are. This view is in opposition to Plato's idea that art corrupts the mind because it presents copies of copies of reality (physical objects being considered mere copies of the universal idea or kind). Aristotle believed that universals, or characteristics, are to be found only in things, while Plato thought that the universals had some sort of separate existence.

Comedy represents inferior persons in that they are a laughable species of the ugly. The comic character makes mistakes or is in some way ugly, but not so seriously as to awaken pity or fear.

Epic poetry differs from tragedy in that it has a single meter and is narrative in form. A further difference results from the Greek convention that a tragedy encompass events taking place within a single day, while the time span of the epic poem is unlimited.

Aristotle defines tragedy as a representation of a heroic action by means of language and spectacle so as to arouse pity and fear and thus bring about a catharsis of those emotions. The relief, or catharsis, of the emotions of pity and fear is the most characteristic feature of the Aristotelian conception of tragedy. According to Aristotle, tragedy arouses the emotions by bringing a person who is somewhat better than average into a reversal of fortune for which he or she is responsible; then, through the downfall of the hero and the res-

olution of the conflicts resulting from the hero's tragic flaw, the tragedy achieves a purging of the audience's emotions. The audience feels pity in observing the tragic hero's misadventures because the character is a vulnerable human being suffering from unrecognized faults. Fear then results from the realization of the audience that they, like the hero, can err and suffer.

Aristotle defines plot as the arrangement of the events that make up the play, character as that which determines the nature of the agents, and thought as what is expressed in the speeches of the agents. Diction is the manner of that expression. The plot is an important element in the tragedy (the others being character, diction, thought, spectacle, and song) because a tragedy is a representation of action. The characters exist for the sake of the action, not the action for the sake of the characters.

The two most important elements of the tragedy and of its plot are peripeteia and discovery. By "peripeteia" is meant a change of a situation into its opposite state of fortune—in tragedy, a change from a good state of affairs to a bad one. A discovery is a revelation of a matter previously unknown. The most effective tragedy, according to Aristotle, results from a plot that combines peripety and discovery in a single action.

To modern readers, Aristotle's definitions of the beginning, middle, and end of a tragedy may seem either amusing or trivial, but they contain important dramatic truths. The philosopher defines the beginning as that which does not necessarily follow anything else but does necessarily give rise to further action. The end necessarily follows from what has gone before but does not necessarily lead to further events. The middle follows the beginning and gives rise to the end.

Aristotle's definitions make sense when one realizes that the important thing about the beginning of a play is not that it is the start but that, relative to the audience's interest and curiosity, no earlier event is needed and further events are demanded. Similarly, for the ending, the closing events of a play should not be merely the last events presented; they should appear necessary as a result of what has already happened, and they should not give rise to new problems that must be solved if the audience is to be satisfied.

Aristotle writes that anything that is beautiful not only must have orderly arranged parts but also must have parts of a large enough, but not too large, size. An animal a thousand miles long or something too small to be seen cannot be beautiful. A play should be as long as possible, allowing a change of fortune in a sequence of events ordered in some apparently inevitable way, provided the play can be understood as a whole. In his conception of unity, Aristotle emphasizes a point that continues to be useful to all who compose or criticize works of art: If the presence of a part makes no difference, it has no place in the work.

A good tragedy should not show worthy persons passing from good fortune to bad, for that is neither fearful nor pitiful but shocking. Even worse is to show bad people acquiring good fortune, for such a situation causes irritation without arousing pity and fear. The tragic hero, consequently, should be one who is better than the audience but not perfect; the hero should suffer from a flaw that shows itself in some mistaken judgment or act resulting in the hero's downfall. There has been considerable discussion about the kind of flaw Aristotle means, but it seems clear from the examples he gives that the flaw should be such that a character who has it must inevitably be defeated in action. It is not inevitable that all human beings have that flaw, but all are liable to it. Hence the tragic hero arouses fear in all those who see the resemblance between the hero's situation and their own. The hero arouses pity because a human being cannot be perfect like the gods; a human's end is bound to be tragic.

Aristotle concludes the *Poetics* with careful discussion of diction and thought, and of epic poetry. Among his sensible conclusions is that what is believable although not possible is better in a play than an event that is possible but not believable.

Throughout the *Poetics*, Aristotle offers remarkably clear analyses of what Greek tragedy actually is and of what he thinks it ought to be. He shows not only an adroit analytical intellect but also an understanding of the practical problems of the art of poetry; he is sophisticated enough to realize that most questions as to the value, length, beauty, and other features of a work of art are settled relative to the kind of audience the judge prefers.

Further Reading

Aristotle. *Poetics*. Translated by Richard Janko. Indianapolis: Hackett, 1987. First-rate translation of the *Poetics* is accompanied by thorough, extensive notes that aid the reader's understanding.

Barnes, Jonathan. *Aristotle: A Very Short Introduction*. Rev. ed. New York: Oxford University Press, 2000. Provides an accessible overview of all aspects of Aristotle's philosophy. Chapter 19, "The Arts," focuses on the ideas in the *Poetics*.

_____. "*Rhetoric* and *Poetics*." In *The Cambridge Companion to Aristotle*, edited by Jonathan Barnes. New York: Cambridge University Press, 1995. Informative essay discusses the ideas contained in the *Poetics* and in Aristotle's *Rhetoric*.

Edel, Abraham. *Aristotle and His Philosophy*. New Brunswick, N.J.: Transaction Books, 1996. A veteran interpreter of Western thought presents a careful study of Aristotle's writings, including the *Poetics*.

Else, Gerald F. *Plato and Aristotle on Poetry*. Edited by Peter Burian. Chapel Hill: University of North Carolina Press, 1986. Posthumous edition of the work of an outstanding Aristotelian scholar and translator devotes eleven chapters to discussion of the *Poetics*.

Halliwell, Stephen. *Aristotle's "Poetics."* Chapel Hill: University of North Carolina Press, 1986. Provides thorough and extensive commentary on *Poetics*. Includes Halliwell's own translation and a helpful bibliography.

Husain, Martha. *Ontology and the Art of Tragedy: An Approach to Aristotle's "Poetics."* Albany: State University of New York Press, 2001. Examines the *Poetics* using Aristotle's *Metaphysics* as a touchstone. Demonstrates the relationship between the works and how the latter illuminates the former.

McLeisch, Kenneth. *Aristotle*. New York: Routledge, 1999. Provides a concise but complete explication of the *Poetics* that is clearly written and accessible to the general reader.

Olson, Elder, ed. *Aristotle's "Poetics" and English Literature: A Collection of Critical Essays*. Chicago: University of Chicago Press, 1965. Collection presents discussion of the *Poetics* and its history as well as essays that demonstrate the Aristotelian method of literary analysis. An informative editor's introduction offers an excellent place to begin study of the *Poetics*.

Robinson, Timothy A. *Aristotle in Outline*. Indianapolis: Hackett, 1995. Clearly written survey covers Aristotle's full range of thought in a manner accessible to beginning students.

Strathern, Paul. *Aristotle in Ninety Minutes*. Chicago: Ivan Dee, 1996. Brief volume provides an easily understood introductory overview of Aristotle's philosophy.